Core Kanji

A Catalogue of
2,088 Essential Kanji

For Use with
Learn to Read in Japanese,
Volumes I – IV

With Memorable Kanji Descriptions,
Retrieval Cues for Kanji Readings,
Comparisons Among Similar Characters,
an Index to 4,300 Kanji Pronunciations,

and Kanji ID,
a Powerful Tool for
Identifying Kanji

by
Roger Lake and Noriko Ura

Copyright © 2022 and 2024 by Roger Lake
All rights reserved

Core Kanji

A Catalogue of
2,088 Essential Kanji

Contents

Efficient Kanji Study	vii
How to Use this Book	ix
How to Use Kanji ID	xi
Kanji Memorization Drills	xiv
How We Selected the Kanji for this Book	xvi
How to Read the Kanji Listings	xviii
Core Kanji Catalogue	1
Hiragana Chart	412
Katakana Chart	412
Kanji Table	413
Kanji Group Index	425
Kanji Trait Index	434
Rendaku	454
Kanji Pronunciation Index	455
Books in the *Learn to Read in Japanese* Series	494

Efficient Kanji Study

If you would like to learn to read in Japanese, we have developed a method that can simplify the process. In our four *Learn to Read in Japanese* books, we usually introduce 8-10 new Japanese kanji in each chapter, and then we use each of those characters in at least three Japanese sentences that are formatted to facilitate reading practice.

In total, the four Japanese Readers contain more than **8,300 practice sentences** that use only kanji that students have learned or are currently studying, and those sentences are accompanied by readily accessible romaji equivalents, as well as English translations, making it easy for students to check their accuracy as they read.

This *Core Kanji* book is designed to serve as your primary kanji reference while you read the four Readers. It contains essential information about 2,088 kanji, consisting of:

   1) their usual **pronunciations**,
   2) their **meanings**,
   3) **sample Japanese words** that illustrate each of their usual pronunciations,
   4) memorable **descriptions** to help you to recognize them more easily in the future,
   5) brief sentences that contain **retrieval cues** (or mnemonics) for the character's usual pronunciations,
   6) kanji **groups** in which kanji with similar traits are assembled, and
   7) for some characters, additional **comparisons** to other kanji.

In addition to an abundance of sentences, the four Readers contain many **vocabulary terms** that are formatted for reading practice, together with mnemonics to aid in their recall. For still more practice, the second and third Japanese Readers direct you to online resources that contain another 3,000 sentences that are appropriate to your skill level and are accompanied by hiragana/katakana or romaji equivalents and English translations. Altogether, we provide or point you to more than **11,300**

sentences and **6,500 vocabulary terms**, presented in a format that facilitates reading practice.

After you have read this material several times, you will be ready to move beyond selected text and start reading unselected Japanese sentences, such as those found in books and newspapers. As you do so, you will inevitably encounter characters that aren't immediately familiar, and you will need to look for a new way to identify kanji, since you will no longer have the advantage of knowing their pronunciations.

To address this problem, we've devised **Kanji ID**, an innovative method for looking up kanji. This technique allows you to identify any of the 2,088 kanji taught in this book by recognizing one of its distinctive characteristics and then searching for that trait in the Kanji Trait Index starting on page 434. In the Trait Index, you will find a corresponding group number that leads directly to the desired kanji. For further information about Kanji ID, please refer to the discussion on page xi.

How to Use this Book

This book is an efficient tool for memorizing and recalling kanji. If you use it in combination with our four Japanese Readers, you will be able to acquire a solid knowledge of the core kanji characters.

In each chapter of the Readers, we begin by asking you to turn to the *Core Kanji* catalogue and to review the entries for the 8-10 "New Kanji" that are listed on the chapter's opening page. The first three Readers include abbreviated versions of the catalogue, but the fourth book, due to space limitations, does not. Therefore, readers of the fourth book are asked to use this stand-alone *Core Kanji* catalogue for kanji reference.

After you have studied the kanji that are introduced in each chapter, we suggest that you take a "pre-test" by turning back to the chapter's New Kanji list and trying to vocalize the pronunciations associated with each character. You may verify that your answers are correct by checking the "Kanji Pronunciations" table on the same page. When you feel confident in your ability to vocalize all of the pronunciations for each kanji in the New Kanji list, you may start reading, taking care to conceal the romaji and English "answers" on the right side of each page until you have made a good-faith effort to read the Japanese text on the left side.

That's basically all you need to do. Just keep reading. You will naturally make some mistakes as you proceed, but please don't allow yourself to think that there must be something wrong with you if you can't read the Japanese text perfectly. Trial and error are essential elements of the "Active Recall" teaching method that we use in our Readers. Congratulate yourself for all of the parts that you did get right and keep on reading – perhaps after taking a short break.

Don't hesitate to return to this *Core Kanji* catalogue as many times as necessary in order to review the DESCRIPTIONS, PRONUNCIATIONS and CUES for any kanji that you find troublesome. As you gain more experience, you will often find it helpful to review the GROUP and COMPARE sections in individual kanji entries, where the character that you are studying is compared to other kanji. Be prepared to re-read the

Japanese Readers several times. After a while, you will start to recognize the kanji as old friends.

The Kanji Pronunciation Index at the back of this book contains 4,300 pronunciations (or "readings") that make it possible for you to look up kanji based on their pronunciations, which you can determine by referring to their romaji equivalents printed in the Readers.

In order to make your study of vocabulary easier, you may want to get a copy of our Glossary which contains definitions for more than 9,700 Japanese words and phrases, supplemented by mnemonics and comparisons to other terms.

When you are ready to engage in serious reading practice, you may want to consider purchasing the **PDF versions** of our books and reading them on a laptop or a desktop computer. I often read these materials on a 14-inch Windows touchscreen laptop with six open windows. The windows contain two copies of one of our Japanese Readers (one copy displaying Japanese text, and the other its romaji equivalents and English translations), two copies of this *Core Kanji* catalogue (allowing me to compare different kanji side by side), the Glossary and the Pronunciation Index. In addition, you will need the PDF version of this *Core Kanji* catalogue if you plan to use Kanji ID with an iPhone – see the discussion of Kanji ID on the next page.

Please visit JapaneseAudioLessons.com and click on the "Efficient Japanese Reading Practice on a Computer" tab for more information about how to practice reading Japanese on a computer.

We wish you tremendous success in your kanji studies.

Roger Lake

San Jose, California
February 26, 2024

How to Use Kanji ID

Kanji ID is a powerful tool for identifying kanji. We recommend it primarily for students who have read all four of our Japanese Readers and become familiar with the 2,088 kanji that they teach.

If you haven't progressed that far in your Japanese studies, it's reasonable to put off learning Kanji ID while you continue your reading practice. When you need to identify unfamiliar kanji that you encounter, you will find it convenient to refer to the **Kanji Pronunciation Index** located at the back of this book.

However, at some point in your studies, you will see the need for a method that doesn't require you to know a kanji's pronunciation in order to identify it. At that time, you will probably want to learn the Kanji ID method.

Here's how Kanji ID works: when you encounter a kanji character that isn't immediately recognizable, please begin by noticing its salient traits. For example, if the character is 買, you may see that this kanji contains two searchable traits: *three eyes* at the top and *money chest* at the bottom. If you then search for one of those traits, *three eyes*, in the **Kanji Trait Index** (page 434), you will find seven possible trait descriptions, from which you should select "Three eyes at top 署 – 1324." Next you should turn to entry 1324 in the *Core Kanji* catalogue and examine the GROUP section of the entry, where you will see a group of characters that are consistent with this description, including the desired kanji, which is "買(う) kau = to buy, # 89."

If you decide to try to identify 買 by searching the Kanji Trait Index for *money chest* instead, you will find ten possible trait descriptions, from which you should select "Money chest below one item, other 費 – 0656." If you then turn to reference 0656 in the catalogue, you will find a GROUP of kanji that also contains "買(う) kau = to buy, # 89."

Please be aware that **underlined numbers** in the catalogue are used to denote **kanji groups**. To illustrate this, return to entry 1324 (署) in the catalogue and observe that its reference number, 1324, is underlined, indicating that this number is associated with a kanji group, whose members are shown in the GROUP section of the entry. In addition, in the COMPARE section of this entry, you will see the number 1088, also underlined, indicating that kanji 1324 belongs to the group 1088, in addition to its own group. If you want to know the **traits** that define those two groups, you may search for "1088" and "1324" in the **Kanji Group Index** (page 425).

Note that the Group Index includes 27 **kanji groups of one**, i.e., "groups" that only contain one kanji. For example, the group *sun (day)*, # 0032, contains only the kanji 日. Although we use "sun" with modifiers to describe a number of kanji groups (e.g., *sun under bell*, # 0266), the character 日, when used alone, occupies a solitary space. Although it may seem illogical to define a group of one, we have done this in order to link every character in our *Core Kanji* catalogue to at least one distinctive trait.

Before using Kanji ID in the real world, we suggest that you practice by identifying the kanji listed in the Kanji Table (page 413). For example, you might begin with 回 (character 0004). Look closely at this kanji, note its salient traits, and then search for one or more of those traits in the **Kanji Trait Index** (page 434).

If you are unable to identify the character 回 on the first try, you can determine its identity by turning to reference number 0004 in the *Core Kanji* catalogue, where you can infer from the kanji's DESCRIPTION that its traits are *kite* and *concentric boxes*. You may observe that this reference number is underlined (0004), informing you that 0004 denotes a kanji **group**, as well as a character. The underlined number 1360 that appears in the COMPARE section of this reference tells you that 回 is a member of a second kanji group, # 1360, in addition to its own group, # 0004.

If you look up group 0004 in the Kanji Group Index, you will see that, as expected, 回 is associated with the traits *kite* and *concentric boxes*. It's possible to use either of these terms (or alternatively, *boxes, concentric*) to search for 回 in the Kanji Trait Index. In addition, if you return to the Group Index and look up #1360, the other group associated with 回, you will see that *box, closed, other* is another trait that could be used to search for 回.

It's important to keep in mind that the kanji in this book are printed in a **standard kaisho** style which differs somewhat from kaisho characters that are written by hand or printed in a **calligraphic** font. You can see examples of calligraphic kaisho characters in the book *Kanji & Kana: A Guide to the Japanese Writing System*, by Wolfgang Hadamitzky and Mark Spahn (revised in 1997), which contains a table listing 1,945 kanji printed in "brush form," accompanied by pronunciations and sample Japanese words.

To see how hand-written or calligraphic characters can affect the appearance of kanji, please look at the table below which contains eight sets of characters, each consisting of two kanji. In each set, the *numbers* on the left are our kanji reference numbers, the *kanji* on the left are the characters we use in this catalogue, and the kanji on the *right* are the equivalent characters used by Hadamitzky & Spahn.

Please note that the kanji on the right contain some traits that may be difficult to recognize at first glance. (This may be easier to see if you first cover the more familiar kanji on the left with a pen or your finger.) These traits include *tire stop above X* in #25, *net* in #202, *skeet shooter* in #221, *tree* in #383, *eat* and *oil derrick* in #399, *cage* in #583, *three eyes* in #1030, and *skeet shooter* again in #1072.

25. 文文 202. 集集 221. 紙紙 383. 親親

399. 飲飲 583. 無無 1030. 薦薦 1072. 孫孫

Please continue your Kanji ID practice by examining the other kanji that are listed in the Kanji Table starting on page 413. You should be able to identify them all, using only the tools found in this book.

When looking up kanji characters in public places like restaurants and subways where this book might be too bulky to carry, you can use PDF versions of the Kanji Trait Index and the *Core Kanji* catalogue with an **iPhone**. Please visit JapaneseAudioLessons.com and click on the Kanji ID tab for detailed instructions.

Kanji Memorization Drills

Kanji memorization drills are useful tools for reinforcing your knowledge of kanji shapes and pronunciations. We provide four versions to accompany the four Japanese Readers in this series. They are titled *Kanji Memorization Drills* Versions One, Two, Three and Four. These books teach 608, 1,208, 1,528 and 2,088 kanji respectively.

The volumes are formatted in three columns. In the **first column**, there are kanji characters followed by small numbers that denote the number of pronunciations you should try to learn for the individual characters. In the **second column,** you will find the kanji's unique listing numbers taken from the Kanji Catalogue, plus mnemonics (which we also call CUES in the Catalogue) that approximate the Japanese pronunciations and help students to remember them. In the **third column**, there are sample Japanese words that contain the actual kanji readings.

Where feasible, I have sorted the kanji into informal groups of similar characters and arranged those characters so that they fit within the confines of a single page, to make it easier for students to compare them as they study.

In order to employ the memorization drills effectively, I suggest that you use **three tools**: 1) an index card, roughly 3 x 5 inches in size, 2) a pen with a fine point and 3) an eraser tool. The purpose of the index card is to conceal the second and third columns while you test yourself on the pronunciations of the kanji in the first column. The purpose of the pen is to make small erasable dots in the margin to the left of any characters whose pronunciations you cannot readily recall. The purpose of the eraser tool is to erase those dots after you have successfully re-tested yourself on the missed kanji.

Like the other books in the *Learn to Read in Japanese* series, the memorization drills are also available in **PDF format** from our PDF store at JapaneseAudioLessons.com. Although I don't generally suggest conducting the kanji drills on a computer screen, since I have not been able to find a way for students to insert removable marks next to kanji in PDF documents during computer-based study, I have found the PDF versions of the drills to be very helpful when I encounter a challenging kanji character and want to perform a quick review of the differences between it and similar kanji. This is due to the fact that, unlike the printed versions of the drills, the PDF versions are searchable, and a search for a given kanji or its reference number typically takes me to a page which contains multiple other kanji that closely resemble the one that is challenging me.

You may be tempted to purchase only the fourth version of the drills, since it teaches all 2,088 of the kanji, and it is true that this might be the only version you will need if you only intend to use the document to review the differences between similar kanji, as just described. However, please keep in mind that the drills are already quite challenging in the 608-kanji version, and if you plan to use them for comprehensive drilling and begin with the fourth version, you may find them overwhelming. To avoid cognitive overload during intensive drilling, it's probably best to start with the first version of the drills and then complete the other three versions in successive order. Of course, once you have worked your way up to the fourth version of the drills, you should no longer need to return to the first three versions, since all of the kanji drills from the earlier versions are repeated in the fourth one.

I hope that the Kanji Memorization Drills will help you to achieve Japanese reading fluency.

How We Selected the Kanji for this Book

The kanji that we have chosen to teach in this book are "core" in the sense that they are the ones most often used by Japanese people. When selecting them, we were primarily guided by the list of 2,136 常用漢字 (Jouyou Kanji), or "Kanji for Daily Use," which was issued by the Japanese government in 2010 and includes 1,026 characters taught in primary school, plus 1,110 more taught in secondary school. However, we discovered that even native Japanese people may find it difficult to read some of the characters on the Jouyou list. The kanji that it contains are certainly taught in the Japanese educational curriculum, but some of them are rarely used in everyday Japanese writing, and people's memories of seldom-used characters tend to fade with time.

Noriko, who is a Japanese citizen and a prolific reader of Japanese books, examined each kanji in the Jouyou list in order to determine whether we should teach it, and she sometimes questioned the need to include a specific character, saying things like, "I can't read it," or "I can recognize it, but I don't know how to say it," or "We write (this Japanese word) using hiragana instead of with (this kanji)."

Even after Noriko had questioned a kanji character in this way, we made a good-faith effort to find three high-quality reading practice sentences that contained it, as we did for all of the other kanji that we introduced in our four books. In order to locate such sentences, we searched a variety of sources, including the "Japanese" dictionary by Renzo Inc. and websites such as Tatoeba.org, Reverso.net, Linguee.com and Yourei.jp. If those searches did not provide us with useful sentences, we sometimes resorted to general internet searches, using words that included the character in question.

For most kanji, it was fairly easy to locate three good reading practice sentences, and for others it was more challenging. However, when we searched the above sources for three suitable sentences containing the Jouyou kanji that Noriko had identified as questionable, we were unsuccessful, and this reinforced our inclination to omit those kanji from our core kanji list, reasoning that we couldn't ask students to learn characters that are so rarely used.

The Jouyou kanji list does *not* include some of the characters that are used to spell the names of some Japanese prefectures, wards and large cities. For example, it doesn't contain 幌 poro, which is used to write 札幌 Sapporo, a city of about two million people. To address this issue, we added to our core kanji list all of the characters that are used to spell the names of *Japanese prefectures*, the *wards of Tokyo* and the *largest cities of Japan*. By subtracting and adding kanji in this way, we effectively modified the Jouyou list and arrived at the set of 2,088 characters taught in this book.

How to Read the Listings in the *Core Kanji* Catalogue

The listing for 飲 (to drink) is reproduced in the left column as an example. The column on the right contains explanations of the information found in the different sections of the listing.

---

399. 飲

PRONUNCIATIONS: in, no

MEANINGS: to drink or swallow

EXAMPLES: 飲食 inshoku = drinking and eating; 飲む nomu = to drink or swallow

DESCRIPTION: on the left, 食(べる) taberu (to eat, # 398); on the right, 欠 kaku (to lack, # 1238) which can be seen as, at the top, an h-shaped chair that is leaning to the right and, at the bottom, 人 hito (person, # 13); taken together these two radicals resemble an oil derrick

CUES: the oil **In**dustry in **No**rway uses 欠 (oil derricks) like this to make money so that its employees can 食 (eat) and 飲む **no**mu (drink)

COMPARE: other similar kanji at # **536** and # **1974**

PRONUNCIATIONS: Please note that, in some cases, a pronunciation is italicized, indicating that it is "exceptional." See the discussion of exceptional pronunciations on page 455.

MEANINGS: These are not intended to suggest that the kanji can necessarily be used by itself in Japanese writing. Many kanji, including this one, must be used in combination with other characters.

EXAMPLES: These are words that illustrate the use of this kanji, with their pronunciations and meanings.

DESCRIPTION: In this section, we describe the kanji as an image. 飲 contains two radicals. The radical on the left is 食, which is a kanji in its own right (# 398). Although 食 means "to eat," it isn't used as a word by itself, so we show it as part of the word 食(べる). The reason that we enclose べる in parentheses is to indicate that it isn't really important here. The emphasis is on 食 as a component of 飲.

The radical on the right, 欠, resembles an oil derrick, in our opinion.

CUES: "Cues" are verbal retrieval cues, or homophones, that match the pronunciations of the kanji. You will find two Cues in this sentence: "**In**dustry" and "**No**rway." Please compare these Cues to the pronunciations shown in the first section. Note that the primary Cues "**In**" and "**No**," which match the pronunciations of the kanji, are shown in bold capitalized text.

The **CUES** section also demonstrates the use of at least one word that contains the kanji under discussion. In this example, that word is "飲む **no**mu." The pronunciation of the kanji is shown in bold underlined text.

COMPARE: In this section we call attention to other kanji that are similar to this kanji. Underlined numbers denote the two kanji groups to which this kanji (# 399) has been assigned.

xviii

Core Kanji Catalogue
Kanji for Volume One

Simple Shapes

0001[1]. 一 PRONUNCIATIONS: hito, ichi, itsu, *tsui, o* MEANING: one EXAMPLES: 一人 hitori = one person; 一つ hitotsu = one item; 一 ichi = one; 一日 ichinichi = one day; 唯一の yuiitsu no = only, exclusive; 一日 tsuitachi = 1st of the month; 一昨日 ototoi = the day before yesterday CUES: I met 一人 **hito**ri (one person), and **He To**ld me that, when he is **Itchy**, he **Eats Tsui**te (sweet) **O**ranges GROUP: 一 ichi = one, # 1; 二 ni = two, # 2; 三 san = three, # 3

0002. 二 PRONUNCIATIONS: ni, futa, *futsu*, ha MEANING: two EXAMPLES: 二 ni = two; 二つ futatsu = two items; 二人 futari = two people; 二日 futsuka = the 2nd of the month, two days; 二十日 hatsuka = the 20th of the month; 二十歳 hatachi = 20 years old CUES: when my **Nie**ce squeezed into a **Fu**ll **Ta**xi, she injured her 二つの **futa**tsu no (two) **Foo**ts (feet) and smashed her **Ha**t COMPARE: similar kanji at # **1**[1] and # **1496**[1]

0003. 三 PRONUNCIATIONS: mitsu, san, mi, *sha* MEANING: three EXAMPLES: 三越 Mitsukoshi = name of a department store; 三 san = three; 三つ mittsu = three items; 三日 mikka = the 3rd of the month; 三味線 shamisen = three-stringed Japanese lute CUES: when my family **Mee**ts **San**ta, we feed him a **Mea**l, and he gives us 三つ **mi**ttsu no (three) presents to **Sha**re COMPARE: similar kanji at # **1**[1]

0004[1]. 回 PRONUNCIATIONS: kai, mawa MEANINGS: times, to rotate EXAMPLES: 三回 sankai = three times; 回る mawaru = to turn, intransitive; 回す mawasu = to turn, transitive DESCRIPTION: concentric boxes; this looks like a square kite CUES: I wash this **K**ite in **Ma**donna's **Wa**shing machine and watch it 回る **mawa**ru (rotate) many 回 **kai** (times) GROUP: 回(る) mawaru = to turn, # 4; 壇 dan = stage, # 679; (輪)廻 rinne = samsara, # 692 COMPARE: similar kanji at # **1360**[1]

0005. 品 PRONUNCIATIONS: pin, shina, hin MEANINGS: goods, grade, class EXAMPLES: 返品 henpin = returned goods; 品物 shinamono = merchandise; 品質 hinshitsu = quality DESCRIPTION: three boxes CUES: these three **Pin**k boxes contain **Shin**y **A**rtistic 品物 **shina**mono (goods) for **Hin**dus COMPARE: similar kanji at # **1034**[1]

0006. 四 PRONUNCIATIONS: yon, yo, shi MEANING: four EXAMPLES: 四 yon = four; 四つ yottsu = four items; 四日 yokka = 4th of the month; 四季 shiki = four seasons DESCRIPTION: this looks like the floor plan of a house; it has four sides but is divided into three spaces CUES: over **Yo**nder, there are 四件の **yon**ken no (four) houses with four sides and three interior spaces like this, occupied by **Yo**delers and **Sh**eep GROUP: this is a group of one COMPARE: similar kanji at # **1360**

---

[1] Underlined numbers denote kanji groups. When such numbers appear in the COMPARE section of the entry for a given kanji, they inform us that the kanji is *a member* of the underlined group.

0007. 呂 **PRONUNCIATION: ro**
MEANINGS: spine, backbone **EXAMPLE:** 風呂 furo = bath, bathhouse, bathtub
DESCRIPTION: this resembles two stacked vertebrae **CUES:** when I **R**ow, these stacked vertebrae stick out; afterwards I put on my **R**obe and walk to the 風呂 fu**ro** (bath)
COMPARE: similar kanji at #**1079**

0008. 中 **PRONUNCIATIONS: chuu, naka, juu MEANINGS:** inside, middle
EXAMPLES: 散歩中 sanpo chuu = in the middle of a walk; 真ん中 mannaka = middle; 中村 Nakamura = a family name; 一日中 ichinichijuu = all day long
DESCRIPTION: this resembles a piece of chicken on a skewer, i.e., yakitori (chicken on a stick) **CUES:** 中村さん **Naka**mura-san (Mr. Nakamura) **C**hews on this yakitori 中 **naka** (inside) his car parked outside the **N**ational **C**athedral and drinks **J**uice **COMPARE:** 申(す) mousu = to humbly say, # 10; other similar kanji at #**657**

0009. 虫 **PRONUNCIATIONS: mushi, chuu MEANING:** insect **EXAMPLES:** 虫 mushi = worm, insect, bug; 害虫 gaichuu = harmful insects **DESCRIPTION:** compared to 中 naka (inside, # 8), this adds an insect on the ground below **CUES:** I heard a **M**ushy story about a 虫 **mushi** (insect) that lies on the ground like this and goes 中 (inside) a house to **C**hew up the furniture **COMPARE:** other similar kanji at #**657** and #**1754**

0010. 申 **PRONUNCIATIONS: mou, moushi, shin MEANING:** to humbly say
EXAMPLES: 申す mousu = to humbly speak; 申込書 moushikomisho = application form; 申請する shinsei suru = to apply or request
DESCRIPTION: two lips stitched together; this also resembles a 田(んぼ) tanbo (rice paddy, # 68) on a stick, or a 車 kuruma (car, # 283) without its wheels **CUES: M**oses 申す **mou**su (speaks humbly) after these lips are stitched together with thread on a **M**ormon **S**hip by a **Shin**to priest
COMPARE: 中 naka = inside, middle, # 8; other similar kanji at #**1157**

0011. 立 **PRONUNCIATIONS: ta, da, tachi, dachi, date, ri, ryuu, ritsu MEANING:** to stand **EXAMPLES:** 立つ tatsu = to stand; 目立つ medatsu = to stand out; 立場 tachiba = position; 夕立 yuudachi = evening rain shower; 天橋立 amanohashidate = a sandbar in Kyoto Prefecture; 立派 rippa = splendid; 建立 konryuu = the act of building (a temple or monument); 起立する kiritsu suru = to stand up
DESCRIPTION: at the top, a tire stop, as seen in 対(する) tai suru (to confront, # 674); at the bottom, two shaky legs standing on a platform; taken together, these resemble a tax collector on shaky legs **CUES:** this **T**ax collector, who acts **D**affy and is at**T**aching **D**amp **C**heese to his head, carries a **D**amp **T**eddy bear as he 立つ **ta**tsu (stands) on these shaky legs and faces his critics, who **R**idicule him for wearing **R**eused **R**itzy clothes **GROUP:** 立(つ) tatsu = to stand, # 11; 泣(く) naku = to cry, # 12; 位 kurai = rank, # 270; 端 hashi = edge, # 730; 粒 tsubu = drops, # 1135; 笠 kasa = lamp shade, # 1311; 翌(日) yokujitsu = the next day, # 1457; 拉(ぐ) hishigu = to crush, # 1767

0012. 泣 **PRONUNCIATIONS: na, kyuu**
MEANING: to cry **EXAMPLES:** 泣く naku = to cry; 号泣 goukyuu = lamentations, wailing
DESCRIPTION: on the left, a water radical, which reminds us of tears; on the right, 立(つ) tatsu (to stand, # 11) **CUES:** when I **N**ag my children, they 立 (stand) and 泣く **na**ku (cry) tears like this, and they look **C**ute **ALSO COMPARE:** other similar kanji at #**11**

0013. 人 PRONUNCIATIONS: hito, bito[22], to, nin, jin, ri, *na* MEANING: person EXAMPLES: 人 hito = person; 恋人 koibito = lover; 玄人 kurouto = expert, professional; 素人 shirouto = amateur; 人間 ningen = human being; 日本人 nihonjin = Japanese person; 一人 hitori = 1 person; 大人 otona = adult DESCRIPTION: a symmetrical person with two long legs CUES: I met a 人 **hito** (person) with long legs like these, and **H**e **T**old me that he smoked **T**obacco with **N**injas and wore **J**eans when he wanted to look **R**eally **N**atural GROUP: 人 hito = person, # 13; 入(る) hairu = to enter, # 14; 八 hachi = eight, # 15; (永)久(に) eikyuu ni = forever, # 30; 大(きい) ookii = big, # 188; 火 hi = fire, # 443; 欠(く) kaku = to lack, # 1238 COMPARE: other similar kanji at # 397 and # **1926**

0014. 入 PRONUNCIATIONS: hai, nyuu, i, iri MEANINGS: to enter, to put into EXAMPLES: 入る hairu = to enter; 入学 nyuugaku = entering a school; 入れる ireru = to put into; 気に入る ki ni iru = to like; 入口 iriguchi = entrance DESCRIPTION: compared to 人 hito (person, # 13), 入 adds a line at the top extending to the left, suggesting wind-swept hair CUES: this 人 (person) with this wind-swept hair 入る **hai**ru (enters) **H**eidi's house to give her some fruit from **N**yu**u**yooku (New York) that was **I**rradiated to kill germs, but Heidi is **I**rritated by this GROUP: 入(る) hairu = to enter, # 14; 込(む) komu = to get crowded, # 357; 比(喩) hiyu = simile, # 2021 ALSO COMPARE: other similar kanji at # **13**

0015. 八 PRONUNCIATIONS: hachi, you, ya, ha MEANING: eight EXAMPLES: 八 hachi = eight; 八日 youka = the 8th of the month, eight days; 八つ yattsu = eight items; 八百 happyaku = eight hundred DESCRIPTION: 八 resembles the Eiffel tower, which begins with "ei," like the word "eight" CUES: at the time we were leaving to see this Eiffel tower, 八 **hachi** (eight) chicks were **H**atching from **Y**olks on our **Y**acht in the **H**arbor COMPARE: other similar kanji at # **13** and # **105**

0016. 公 PRONUNCIATIONS: ku, kou, ooyake MEANING: public EXAMPLES: 公家 kuge = the Imperial court; 公園 kouen = park; 公 ooyake = public DESCRIPTION: at the top, 八 hachi (eight, # 15); at the bottom, the katakana character ム mu (the sound made by a cow) CUES: in a 公園 **kou**en (park) in **Ku**wait, there are 八 (eight) ム (cows), some **C**olts, and several **O**ld **Y**ak **E**tchings, for 公の **ooyake** no (public) enjoyment ALSO COMPARE: other similar kanji at # **1546**

0017. 六 PRONUNCIATIONS: *ro, roku, mu, mui* MEANING: six EXAMPLES: 六本木 Roppongi = a district in Tokyo; 六人 rokunin = six people; 六つ muttsu = six objects; 六日 muika = the 6th of the month, six days DESCRIPTION: at the top, a tire stop, as seen in 対(する) tai suru = to confront, # 674; at the bottom, 八 hachi (eight, # 15), which resembles a wide skirt that might belong to a mother hen CUES: after tripping over this tire stop while **R**oaming along a **R**oad in **Ku**wait, this mother hen gathers 六 **roku** (six) chicks under this 八 (skirt) to keep them away from **M**oonies and **M**oody **E**agles ALSO COMPARE: other similar kanji at # **105** and # **1860**

---

[2] "Bito" follows the rules of rendaku (see p. 454). The superscript [2] indicates that we do not provide a separate retrieval cue for it.

0018. 十　PRONUNCIATIONS: *ta, too, juu, ju, ji, tsu*　MEANINGS: ten, full　EXAMPLES: 二十歳 hatachi = 20 years old ; 十 too = 10; 十日 tooka = 10 days, the 10th of the month; 十 juu = 10; 十分 juubun = enough; 十分 juppun (10 minutes), which can also be pronounced jippun; 二十日 hatsuka = the 20th of the month; **Note:** 十分 juubun (enough) and 十分 juppun (10 minutes) can also be pronounced jippun　DESCRIPTION: this looks like a "t" which is the first letter of the word "ten" in English and the word "too" in romaji　CUES: we have 十 **juu** (ten) **T**all cans of **T**omato **J**uice for the **J**ury in the **J**eep, in a **T**suitcase (suitcase)　COMPARE: similar kanji at # **1828**

0019. 高　PRONUNCIATIONS: *taka, kou, daka*　MEANINGS: high, tall, expensive　EXAMPLES: 高い takai = high, tall, expensive; 高校 koukou = high school; 円高 endaka = rise in the yen's value　DESCRIPTION: at the top, a tire stop, as seen in 対(する) tai suru (to confront, # 674); below that, two 口 (boxes) separated by the roof of a two-sided lean-to; these can be seen as two cans; the lower box inside the two-sided lean-to is *not* covered by a napkin, unlike the box in 同 (じ) onaji (the same, # 339)　CUES: these two **T**all **C**ans have been stacked to help create this 高い **taka**i (tall) **C**ourthouse in **D**akha, with this tire stop at the top　GROUP: 高(い) takai = high, # 19; 橋 hashi = bridge, # 139; (草)稿 soukou = a manuscript, # 1467　ALSO COMPARE: other similar kanji at # **1467** and # **1474**

0020. 七　PRONUNCIATIONS: *nana, shichi, nano*　MEANING: seven　EXAMPLES: 七つ nanatsu = seven items; 七時 shichiji = 7:00; 七日 nanoka = 7th of the month, seven days　DESCRIPTION: this is an upside-down **7** (seven)　CUES: **N**ancy's **N**anny gave her 七 **nana** (seven) bites of **S**heep **C**heese for taking a **N**ap with **N**orma　GROUP: 七 nana = seven, # 20; 切(る) kiru = to cut, # 103; 窃(盗) settou = theft, # 2062

0021. 宅　PRONUNCIATION: *taku*　MEANINGS: house, home　EXAMPLES: お宅 otaku = your honorable home; 帰宅 kitaku = the return home　DESCRIPTION: at the top, a bad haircut, which resembles a roof; at the bottom, 七 shichi (seven, # 20), wearing a slanted hat　CUE: in this 宅 **taku** (home), 七 (seven) **T**all people are **C**ooped up under this roof, and they all wear slanted hats like this　GROUP: (お)宅 otaku = your honorable home, # 21; 託(する) taku suru = to entrust, # 1367 (identical pronunciation)

0022. 千　PRONUNCIATIONS: *sen, chi, zen*　MEANING: thousand　EXAMPLES: 千 sen = 1,000; 千葉 Chiba = name of a prefecture in Japan; 三千 sanzen = 3,000　DESCRIPTION: this resembles the katakana character チ chi (identical pronunciation), which could stand for cheese　CUES: a **Sen**ator keeps 千 **sen** (1,000) blocks of チ (**Ch**eese) like this at the **Z**en center　GROUP: 千 sen = 1,000, # 22; 飛(ぶ) tobu = to fly, # 574; (上)昇 joushou = rising, # 1363; 挿 (絵) sashie = an illustration, # 1769; 升 masu = a measuring box, # 2049　ALSO COMPARE: other similar kanji at # 629 and # 1363

0023. 手 **PRONUNCIATIONS: te, de², shu, ta, zu, *ma* MEANING:** hand **EXAMPLES:** 右手 migi te = right hand; 派手 hade = flashy, colorful; 運転手 untenshu = driver; 下手 heta = unskillful; 上手 jouzu = skillful; 上手い umai = delicious, skillful (usually written うまい) **DESCRIPTION:** a hand belonging to Ted Cruz, with six fingers at the top and a wrist curving to the left at the bottom **CUES:** when **T**ed **Shoo**ed away a **T**arantula at the **Z**oo, his **Ma** (mother) noticed that this 手 **te** (hand) has six fingers **COMPARE:** 毛 ke = hair, # 688; other similar kanji at # **1554**

0024. 又 **PRONUNCIATION: mata MEANING:** again **EXAMPLES:** 又 mata = again **DESCRIPTION:** a simple table belonging to a matador **CUE:** a **Mata**dor liked this table so much that he bought it 又 **mata** (again) **GROUP:** 又 mata = again, # 24; 支(社) shisha = branch office, # 26; 最(近) saikin = recently, # 42; 取(る) toru = to take, # 58; 寝(る) neru = to sleep, # 372; (今)度 kondo = this time, # 498; 渡(る) wataru = to cross, # 499; 受(ける) ukeru = to receive, # 577; 授(業) jugyou = class, # 578; (南)極 nankyoku = the antarctic, # 610; 趣(味) shumi = hobby, # 715; 緊(張) kinchou = tension, # 732; 浸(す) hitasu = to soak, # 797; 暇 hima = free time, # 803; 騒(ぐ) sawagu = to make noise, # 826; 寂(しい) sabishii = lonely, # 864; 収(入) shuunyuu = income, # 1113; 賢(い) kashikoi = intelligent, # 1290; (監)督 kantoku = director, # 1421; 奴(隷) dorei = a slave, # 1582; 侵(す) okasu = to invade, # 1591; 双(子) futago = twins, # 1596; 淑(女) shukujo = a lady, # 1684; 腎(臓) jinzou = a kidney, # 1991; (自)叙(伝) jijoden = an autobiography, # 2004

0025. 文 **PRONUNCIATIONS: mon, *mo*, bun, bumi MEANINGS:** sentence, script, culture **EXAMPLES:** 文句 monku = complaint; 文字 moji = letter, character; 文 bun = sentence; 文化 bunka = culture; 恋文 koibumi = love letter **DESCRIPTION:** at the top, a tire stop, as seen in 対(する) tai suru (to confront, # 674); at the bottom, crossed legs, which can also be seen as an X **CUES:** some **Mon**ks told **Mo**ses that Daniel **B**oone's business is **B**oo**mi**ng, but Daniel sits on this tire stop all day with these X (legs crossed) and expresses 文句 monku (complaints) about the world **COMPARE:** similar kanji at # **259**

0026. 支 **PRONUNCIATIONS: shi, sasa, tsuka MEANINGS:** to support; a branch **EXAMPLES:** 支社 shisha = branch office; 支える sasaeru = to support; 差し支え sashitsukae = hindrance, inconvenience, trouble **DESCRIPTION:** a combination of 十 shi (man, warrior, # 66) (identical pronunciation), and 又 mata ("again," # 24); together they resemble a man standing on a table **CUES:** this 十 (man) has spread a **Sh**eet on this 又 (table) at our 支社 **shi**sha (branch office), and he stands on it all day, trying to sell **S**alty **S**andwiches, ever since we sent him a **Tsu**itcase (suitcase) of **Ca**ffeine **ALSO COMPARE:** similar kanji at # **24** and # **1121**

0027. 卒 **PRONUNCIATIONS: sotsu, so, tozo MEANINGS:** to end, sudden **EXAMPLES:** 卒業 sotsugyou = graduation; 卒倒する sottou suru = to faint or swoon; 何卒 nanitozo = I beg you, kindly, by all means **DESCRIPTION:** at the top, a tire stop, as seen in 対(する) tai suru (to confront, # 674); below that, two 人 hito (people, # 13); at the bottom, 十 too (ten, # 18); taken together, these resemble a double-breasted kimono on a hanger, but they can also be seen as a brush, with handles at the top and bottom **CUES: Sot**tish **Su**perman wore this double-breasted kimono to his 卒業 **sotsu**gyou (graduation), where he sang a **So**lo and **To**asted **Zo**oey **GROUP:** 卒(業) sotsugyou = graduation, # 27; (軽)率 keisotsu = thoughtless, # 1408 (identical pronunciation) **ALSO COMPARE:** other similar kanji at # <u>1658</u>, # <u>1860</u> and # <u>1926</u>

0028. 卵 **PRONUNCIATIONS: tamago, ran MEANING:** egg **EXAMPLES:** 卵 tamago = egg; ゆで卵 yudetamago = boiled egg; 卵黄 ran'ou = egg yolk **DESCRIPTION:** two eggs containing yolks; the radical on the right resembles a signature seal, as seen in 印 shirushi (sign, # 1046), with a yolk inside **CUES:** I will eat these two 卵 **tamago** (eggs) with **Tama**les and **Go**at cheese on my **Ran**ch **COMPARE:** similar kanji at # <u>1046</u> and # <u>1535</u>

0029. 点 **PRONUNCIATIONS: ta, tsu, ten MEANINGS:** spot, dot **EXAMPLES:** 点てる tateru = to perform the tea ceremony; 点く tsuku = to turn on, intransitive; 点ける tsukeru = to turn on, transitive; 点 ten = score; 百点 hyakuten = 100 points **DESCRIPTION:** at the top, a cannon (this can also be seen as a taser); in the middle, a 口 (box) which resembles a tsuitcase (suitcase); at the bottom, a hot fire **CUES: Tar**zan removes this cannon from this **Tsu**itcase (suitcase) and uses this hot fire to 点ける **tsu**keru (ignite) it to signal the start of a **Ten**nis match **COMPARE:** similar kanji at # <u>611</u> and # <u>1542</u>

0030. 久 **PRONUNCIATIONS: kyuu, hisa, ku MEANINGS:** long time, lasting **EXAMPLES:** 永久に eikyuu ni = forever, permanently; 久しぶり hisashiburi = after a long time; 屋久島 Yakushima = an island south of Kyushu **DESCRIPTION:** a cute dancer with a ponytail, slightly different from the dancer seen in 放(送) housou (broadcasting, # 117) and other kanji; compared to such dancers, this one has no face **CUES:** this **C**ute dancer asked for a man's salad, but she waited until after **H**is **Sa**lad had been left outside the **C**ooler 久しぶり **hisa**shiburi (for a long time) **GROUP:** this is a group of one **ALSO COMPARE:** 欠(席) kesseki = absence, # 1238, which we describe as an oil derrick in this catalogue; other similar kanji at # <u>13</u>

0031. 当 **PRONUNCIATIONS: tou, ata, a MEANINGS:** just, right **EXAMPLES:** 本当 hontou = truth; 当然 touzen = naturally; 当り atari = per, apiece, used as a suffix (this can also be written 当たり); 当たり前の atarimae no = right, reasonable, natural; 手当て teate = medical treatment; 突き当たり tsukiatari = T-intersection **DESCRIPTION:** at the top, a switch with three prongs; at the bottom, a tool with three toes for dividing objects (this can also be seen as three hairs flowing to the left) **CUES:** this is a tool with a three-pronged switch and three **To**es which will 当然 **tou**zen (naturally) divide objects in an 当たり前の **a**tarimae no (reasonable) way, and it can also be used to **At**tach **A**rt to a bulletin board **COMPARE:** similar kanji at # <u>1165</u> and # <u>1625</u>

Sun

0032. 日 **PRONUNCIATIONS: ka, bi, hi, jitsu, nichi, ni, nou, tachi, ta, te, toi, su, you MEANINGS:** day, sun **EXAMPLES:** 二日 futsuka = the 2nd day of the month, 2 days; 誕生日 tanjoubi = birthday; 日にち hinichi = date; 平日 heijitsu = weekday; 一日 ichinichi = one day; 日光 Nikkou = a town in Japan, sunshine; 昨日 kinou = yesterday; 一日 tsuitachi = the first day of the month; 明日 ashita = tomorrow; 明後日 asatte = the day after tomorrow, usually written あさって; 一昨日 ototoi = the day before yesterday, usually written おととい; 明日 asu = tomorrow; 今日 kyou = today

Note: ichinichi and tsuitachi are both written 一日; asu and ashita are both written 明日
DESCRIPTION: a rectangle divided into two halves, resembling a window with two panes
CUES: 日光 **ni**kkou (sunshine) flows through this window of a **Ca**bin on the **Be**ach, bringing **He**at to the **Ji**ttery **Su**perstar **Nie**tzche, who rubs his **Kn**ees and **No**se while **Ta**nned **Chi**ldren shoot at **Ta**rgets, watch **Te**levision, play with **To**ys, drink **Sou**p and eat **Yo**gurt
GROUP: this is a group of one

0033. 昔 PRONUNCIATIONS: mukashi, seki, jaku MEANINGS: old days, ancient times
EXAMPLES: 昔 mukashi = olden times; 昔日 sekijitsu = old times; 今昔 konjaku = past and present DESCRIPTION: at the top, a plant radical (see # 43) on a platform; at the bottom, 日 hi (sun, # 32) CUES: nowadays old people fund **Mu**seums with **Ca**sh, but in 昔 **mukashi** (the olden days), all they had was this 日 (sun), these plants, and a **Se**lfish **Ki**ng named **Ja**ck
GROUP: 昔 mukashi = olden times, # 33; 借(り る) kariru = to borrow, # 485; 葛(藤) kattou = conflict, # 1531; (国)籍 kokuseki = nationality, # 1604; 惜(しい) oshii = unfortunate, # 1708; 措(置) sochi = an action, # 1709; (倒)錯 tousaku = perversion, # 1771
ALSO COMPARE: kanji containing plants above sun and big (PSB) at # 1353

0034. 早 PRONUNCIATIONS: haya, baya², sou, sa, wa MEANING: early
EXAMPLES: 早い hayai = early; 素早い subayai = speedy, nimble; 早退 soutai = leaving early; 早速 sassoku = immediately, sudden; 早稲田 Waseda = a university in Shinjuku
DESCRIPTION: a 日 hi (sun, # 32) on 十 juu (ten, # 18); this resembles a spinning top
CUES: **Pr**ince **Ha**rry's **Y**acht features this spinning top that was **So**ld in **Sa**pporo and spins 早い **haya**i (early) in the morning when no one is **Wa**tching
COMPARE: 速(い) hayai = fast, # 359; other similar kanji at # **1365**

0035. 晩 PRONUNCIATION: ban
MEANING: evening EXAMPLE: 今晩 konban = this evening DESCRIPTION: on the left, 日 hi (sun, # 32); on the right, a fish-head guy (see # 80) with glasses and lopsided legs CUE: this fish-head guy with glasses and lopsided legs wants to go to the **Ba**nk while this 日 (sun) is still shining, since it will be closed 今晩 kon**ban** (this evening)
COMPARE: 映(画) eiga = movie, # 36; other similar kanji at # **1140** and # **1314**

0036. 映 PRONUNCIATIONS: utsu, ei, ha MEANINGS: to be imaged, to be reflected
EXAMPLES: 映す utsusu = to project on a screen, or to be reflected; 映画 eiga = movie; 映える haeru = to shine or look attractive
DESCRIPTION: on the left, 日 hi (sun, # 32); on the right, 大(きい) ookii (big, # 188), wearing glasses; this resembles a movie screen on a stand, but it can also be seen as two eyes on a stand
CUES: by **U**tilizing this 日 (**Sun**) on the left, we can 映す **utsu**su (project) 映画 **ei**ga (movies) about **Ap**es in **Ha**waii onto this screen on the right
ALSO COMPARE: 晩 ban = evening, # 35; other similar kanji at # **43** and # **1314**

0037. 晴 **PRONUNCIATIONS:** ha, ba, sei, *har* **MEANING:** to clear up **EXAMPLES:** 晴れる hareru = to clear up, to be sunny, to refresh (spirits), to be cleared (of a suspicion); 素晴らしい subarashii = wonderful; 晴天 seiten = fair weather; 晴海通り Harumi Doori = name of a street in Tokyo
DESCRIPTION: on the left, 日 hi (sun, # 32); on the right, 青(い) aoi (blue, # 155), which resembles an owl's perch on a 月 (moon)
CUES: in Hawaii, when the weather 晴れる **ha**reru (clears up), we see this 日 (sun) next to a 青 (blue) sky, and we can sit in a **Ba**r and watch **Sa**ils moving out in the **Har**bor
ALSO COMPARE: similar kanji at # **154** and # **1112**

0038. 暖 **PRONUNCIATIONS:** atata, dan **MEANING:** warm (atmosphere) **EXAMPLES:** 暖かい atatakai = warm (atmosphere); 暖める atatameru = to warm up the atmosphere, transitive; 暖房 danbou = heating, heater
DESCRIPTION: on the left, 日 hi (sun, # 32); at the upper right, five lines which could represent a barbecue grate; on the lower right, 友(達) tomodachi (friend, # 459)
CUES: Ataturk with a **Tan** is this 友 (friend) who **Dan**ces in this 日 (sun) until it gets 暖かい **atata**kai (warm), after which he turns his attention to this barbecue grate
ALSO COMPARE: 温(かい) atatakai = warm (objects), # 257; 温(める) atatameru = to warm up an object, such as water, # 257; 曖(昧な) aimai na = vague, # 1940, which substitutes 心 (heart) and an ice dancer for the 友 (friend) at the lower right; other similar kanji at # **459** and # **1177**

0039. 円 **PRONUNCIATIONS:** en, maru, maro **MEANINGS:** yen, round, circle **EXAMPLES:** 千円 sen'en = 1,000 yen; 円い marui = round; 円やか maroyaka = round, mild taste, mellow **DESCRIPTION:** 日 hi (sun, # 32) on its side, with legs **CUES:** 千円 sen'**en** (1,000-yen) coins are 円い **maru**i (round) like this reclining 日 (sun), and since they have legs like these, they are able to dance and **En**tertain people who are **Maro**oned in **Mars O**rbit **GROUP:** this is a group of one
ALSO COMPARE: 丸(い) marui = round, # 866, which is the kanji that is usually used to spell marui (round); other similar kanji at # **1314**

0040. 声 **PRONUNCIATIONS:** koe, goe², sei **MEANING:** voice **EXAMPLES:** 声 koe = voice; 歌声 utagoe = a singing voice; 声援 seien = cheering, support **DESCRIPTION:** at the top, 士 shi (man, warrior, # 66); below that, 日 hi (day, or sun, # 32) on its side, with a handle on the left, resembling a co-ed holding a mask, with openings for two eyes **CUES:** this 士 (man)'s girlfriend is a **Co-Ed** who wears this mask when they go **S**ai**ling**; the mask doesn't block these two eyes or her mouth, nor does it affect her 声 **koe** (voice)
COMPARE: 眉(毛) mayuge = eyebrow, # 1645; other similar kanji at # **1314** and # **1468**

0041. 昨 **PRONUNCIATIONS:** ki, to, saku **MEANINGS:** yesterday, previous **EXAMPLES:** 昨日 kinou = yesterday; 一昨日 ototoi = the day before yesterday, usually written おととい; 昨晩 sakuban = last night
DESCRIPTION: on the left, 日 hi (sun, # 32); on the right, this is a serrated axe, reportedly, but it can also be seen as a ladder or stairs
CUES: 昨日 **ki**nou (yesterday) someone used this serrated axe to **Ki**ll a **To**rtoise and then left its body in a **Sack** out in this 日 (sun) **GROUP:** 昨(日) kinou = yesterday, # 41; 作(文) sakubun = written composition, # 482 (identical pronunciation); (階)段 kaidan = stairs, # 559; 興(味) kyoumi = interest, # 693; 暇 hima = free time, # 803; 印 shirushi = symbol, # 1046; 酢 su = vinegar, # 1373; 臼 usu = a mortar, # 1735; 潟 kata = a lagoon,

1736; 鍛(える) kitaeru = to train, # 1813; 詐(欺) sagi = a fraud, # 1858; 搾(取) sakushu = exploitation, # 2038

0042. 最 PRONUNCIATIONS: sai, mo, motto MEANING: the most
EXAMPLES: 最近 saikin = recently; 最初 saisho = the first; 最高 saikou = the best; 最上 saijou = the best; 最悪 saiaku = the worst; 最後 saigo = the last; 最寄の moyori no = nearest, neighboring; 最早 mohaya = by now, no longer; 最も mottomo = the most
DESCRIPTION: at the top, 日 hi (day, or sun, # 32), which looks like a large sign, on a platform; at the lower left, 耳 mimi (ear); at the lower right, 又 mata ("again"), but this resembles a simple table
CUES: 最近 **sai**kin (recently), when this **S**ign is turned on, I **s**it at this 又 (table), and this 耳 (ear) can hear a lawn **M**ower from behind the sign and also the traffic on the **M**otorway ALSO COMPARE: other similar kanji at # **24** and # **1713**

0043. 英 PRONUNCIATION: ei
MEANINGS: English, excellent
EXAMPLES: 英語 eigo = the English language; 英雄 eiyuu = hero DESCRIPTION: compared to 映(画) eiga (movie, # 36) (identical pronunciation), this kanji omits the 日 (sun) on the left and adds a double plant radical, consisting of a horizontal line intersected by two short verticals, at the top; it retains the movie screen on a stand which can also be seen as two eyes on a stand CUE: this movie screen shows an 英語の **ei**go no (English language) 映 (movie) about **A**pes, and the plant radical above it reminds us of the plants they eat
GROUP: 映(画) eiga = movie, # 36; 英(語) eigo = the English language, # 43; (中)央 chuu'ou = center, # 1063
ALSO COMPARE: other similar kanji at # **1314**

0044. 白 PRONUNCIATIONS: shiro, shira, haku, paku² MEANING: white
EXAMPLES: 白い shiroi = white; 白髪 shiraga = grey or white hair; 白髪 hakuhatsu = grey or white hair; 潔白 keppaku = innocence;
Note: hakuhatsu and shiraga are both written 白髪
DESCRIPTION: 日 hi (sun, # 32) with a ray of light emerging from the top
CUES: this ray of light from this 日 (sun) shines on 白い **shiro**i (white) **S**heep that **R**oam at a **S**heep **R**anch near the **H**arbor in **K**uwait
ALSO COMPARE: 百 hyaku = one hundred, # 47; 自(分) jibun = one's self, # 55; other similar kanji at # **2014**

0045. 的 PRONUNCIATIONS: teki, mato
MEANINGS: target, having characteristics of
EXAMPLES: 目的 mokuteki = purpose; 日本的 nihonteki = having the characteristics of Japan; 自動的な jidouteki na = automatic; 的 mato = target, center of attention
DESCRIPTION: on the left, 白(い) shiroi (white, # 44); on the right, a giant hook containing a tear drop CUES: this giant hook attaches to a 白 (white) **T**echie with the 目的 moku**teki** (purpose) of dragging him offstage for having stepped on his **Ma**'s (**M**other's) **T**oes, causing her to shed this tear
ALSO COMPARE: similar kanji at # **988** and # **2014**

0046. 泊 PRONUNCIATIONS: haku, paku², to MEANING: to stay overnight
EXAMPLES: 二泊 nihaku = a two-night stay; 三泊 sanpaku = a three-night stay; 泊まる tomaru = to stay overnight
DESCRIPTION: compared to 白(い) shiroi (white, # 44), or 白(髪) hakuhatsu (white hair, # 44) (identical pronunciation), this adds a water radical (see # 12) on the left; it retains the 日 (sun) with a ray of light at the top
CUES: I 泊まった **to**matta (spent the night) in a 白 (white) hotel by this water near the **H**arbor in **K**uwait and listened to the croaking of the **T**oads
ALSO COMPARE: other similar kanji at # **2014**

0047. 百 **PRONUNCIATIONS: hyaku, byaku², pyaku², o,** *hya* **MEANING:** hundred **EXAMPLES:** 百 hyaku = 100; 三百 sanbyaku = 300; 八百 happyaku = 800; 八百長 ya'ochou = a rigged affair; 八百屋 ya'oya = green grocer; 百科 hyakka = many objects **DESCRIPTION:** at the top, this looks like a limousine antenna; at the bottom, 日 hi (sun, # 32), which could be the body of the limousine **CUES: H**imalayan **Y**ak owners traveled in 百 **hyaku** (100) **O**range limousines like this as they ate **H**ealing **Y**ams **COMPARE:** other similar kanji at # **491**

0048. 星 **PRONUNCIATIONS: hoshi, sei** **MEANING:** star **EXAMPLES:** 星 hoshi = star; 星座 seiza = constellation **DESCRIPTION:** at the top, 日 hi (sun, # 32); at the bottom, 生(きる) ikiru (to live, # 208), or (先)生 sensei (teacher, # 208) (identical pronunciation) **CUES:** this 日 (sun) that 生 (lives) is a 星 **hoshi** (star), admired by **H**orses and **S**heep as they eat **S**age grass **ALSO COMPARE:** other similar kanji at # **1918**

0049. 昼 **PRONUNCIATIONS: hiru,** *piru²*, **chuu** **MEANINGS:** daytime, noon **EXAMPLES:** 昼 hiru = noon; 昼間 hiruma = daytime; 真っ昼間 mappiruma = broad daylight; 昼食 chuushoku = lunch **DESCRIPTION:** at the upper left, a lean-to with a double roof; under the lean-to, 日 hi (sun, # 32) on a platform, with a projection over its right shoulder that resembles a hose [the upper part of this kanji can also be seen as 尺(度) shakudo (criterion, # 1484)]; taken together, these resemble a gas pump on a plaform under a double roof **CUES:** since it gets so hot at 昼 **hiru** (noon), the **H**eat has **R**uined this gas pump on a platform under this double roof, where I **C**hew my 昼食 **chuu**shoku (lunch) **ALSO COMPARE:** other similar kanji at # **668**, # **1484** and # **1899**

0050. 母 **PRONUNCIATIONS: haha, bo,** *kaa,* **ba,** *omo* **MEANING:** mother **EXAMPLES:** 母 haha = mother; 祖母 sobo = grandmother; お母さん okaasan = honorable mother; 乳母 uba = wet nurse; 伯母さん obasan = aunt, middle-aged woman; 母屋 omoya = main building or main room; お祖母さん obaasan = grandmother; **Note:** it isn't practical to divide the baa in obaasan into two component pronunciations, so this word must be learned as a combination of the two kanji **DESCRIPTION:** a modified 日 hi (day, or sun, # 32), this is said to have originally represented a mother's breasts **CUES:** this is a 母 **haha** (mother) who frequently says "**Ha Ha**" and comes from a **B**oring town in California with only one **Ba**r and an **O**ld **M**or**o**n **GROUP:** this is a group of one

Eye

0051. 目 **PRONUNCIATIONS: me, moku, boku** **MEANING:** eye **EXAMPLES:** 目 me = eye; 目上 meue = one's superior; 目的 mokuteki = purpose; 注目 chuumoku = attention; 面目ない menbokunai = ashamed **DESCRIPTION:** compared to 日 hi (day, # 32), this adds an additional horizontal line and resembles a refrigerator **CUES:** among **Me**chanics with big 目 **me** (eyes) who work on refrigerators like this, the one who came to our house is the **Mo**st **Coo**l, and he takes his annual **Bo**nus as **Koo**l-Aid **GROUP:** 目 me = eye, # 51; 見(る) miru = to see, # 53; 自(分) jibun = by oneself, # 55; 首 kubi = neck, # 56; 耳 mimi = ear, # 57

0052. 着 **PRONUNCIATIONS: ki, gi, tsu, chaku** **MEANINGS:** to arrive, to put clothes on **EXAMPLES:** 着る kiru = to wear clothes; 着物 kimono; 水着 mizugi = swimsuit; 着く tsuku = to arrive; 着ける tsukeru = to wear (accessories); 着席 chakuseki = taking a seat **DESCRIPTION:** at the top, 王 ou (king, # 1077), wearing rabbit ears, which may represent a king in a jolly mood [this part of the kanji can also be seen as a truncated 羊 hitsuji (sheep, # 1223), missing its tail]; at the bottom, 目 me (eye, # 51) with a line above its left shoulder and extending down to the left, suggesting a trailing gown **CUES:** this 目 (eye) belonging to a 王 (king) is full of fun when he 着く **tsu**ku (arrives) at his palace in **Ki**ev with some **Ge**ese while 着ている **ki**te iru (wearing) this trailing gown and these rabbit ears, while carrying his **Tsu**itcase (suitcase), after drinking a lot of **Cha**mpagne and **Koo**l-Aid **ALSO COMPARE:** (時)差 jisa = time difference, # 631; other similar kanji at # **1893** and # **2002**

0053. 見 **PRONUNCIATIONS: mi, ken**
MEANINGS: to see, to look
EXAMPLES: 見る miru = to look at or see; 拝見する haiken suru = to humbly look at or see
DESCRIPTION: compared to 目 me (eye, # 51), this adds two lopsided legs at the bottom **CUES:** this 目 (eye) on lopsided legs 見る **mi**ru (looks) in a **Mi**rror and 見る **mi**ru (sees) **Ken** and Barbie **ALSO COMPARE:** other similar kanji at # **51** and # **1341**

0054. 覚 **PRONUNCIATIONS: obo, sa, za², zama, kaku MEANINGS:** to memorize, realize, wake up **EXAMPLES:** 覚える oboeru = to memorize; 目が覚める me ga sameru = to wake up; 目覚める mezameru = to wake up; 目覚しい mezamashii = outstanding, striking, spectacular; 覚悟する kakugo suru = to be prepared for something unwelcome
DESCRIPTION: compared to 見(る) miru (to look, # 53), this adds three old boys on a roof at the top **CUES:** these three **O**ld **Bo**ys on a roof 覚える **obo**eru (memorize) lines for a play; if you 見 (look) up, you can see a **Sa**murai, his **Za**mbian friend **Ma**x, and **Ka**rl the **Koo**l-Aid vendor **ALSO COMPARE:** similar kanji at # **991** and # **1341**

0055. 自 **PRONUNCIATIONS: ji, shi, mizuka, ono MEANING:** self **EXAMPLES:** 自分 jibun = by oneself, on one's own; 自然 shizen = nature; 自ら mizukara = personally, on one's own initiative; 自ずから onozukara = naturally **DESCRIPTION:** compared to 目 me (eye, # 51), this adds a tiny ray, which can be seen as a "self," at the top
CUES: this 目 (eye) belonging to this tiny self is good, so I can drive my **Jee**p 自分で **ji**bun de (by myself) to transport some **Shi**eep, after giving **Mizu** (water) to the **Ca**t with the **O**range **No**se **ALSO COMPARE:** 白(い) shiroi = white, # 44; other similar kanji at # **51** and # **1381**

0056. 首 **PRONUNCIATIONS: kubi, shu**
MEANINGS: neck, chief, top
EXAMPLES: 首 kubi = neck; 首相 shushou = prime minister **DESCRIPTION:** in this kanji, 目 me (eye, # 51) can be viewed as a person's body; above the body is a narrow neck; above the neck is a compressed head with two antennae on a platform **CUES:** this head with antennae, supported by a narrow 首 **kubi** (neck) above this 目 (body), peers over the wall of its **Cu**bi**c**le and **Shoo**s co-workers away **ALSO COMPARE:** other similar kanji at # **51** and # **349**

0057. 耳 **PRONUNCIATIONS: mimi, ji**
MEANING: ear **EXAMPLES:** 耳 mimi = ear; 耳鼻科 jibika = ENT specialist
DESCRIPTION: compared to 目 me (eye, # 51), this adds with five projections at the corners, one of which could be an ear lobe **CUES: Mi**mi sits in her **Jee**p, showing off this 耳 **mimi** (ear) which **Mi**mics, or resembles, an 目 (eye)
ALSO COMPARE: other similar kanji at # **51** and # **1713**

0058. 取 **PRONUNCIATIONS:** to, do², shu, tori **MEANING:** to take **EXAMPLES:** 取る toru = to take or get; 受け取る uketoru = to receive; 気取る kidoru = to put on airs; 取得する shutoku suru = to acquire; 取引 torihiki = business deal **DESCRIPTION:** on the left, 耳 mimi (ear, # 57); on the right 又 mata (again, # 24), which resembles a simple table **CUES:** someone 取った **to**tta (took) a **T**orpedo from this 又 (table) and used it to **Sh**oot a **T**ory in this 耳 (ear) **ALSO COMPARE:** other similar kanji at # **24** and # **1713**

Soil

0059. 土 **PRONUNCIATIONS:** tsuchi, to, mi, do **MEANING:** soil **EXAMPLES:** 土田 Tsuchida = family name; 土地 tochi = land; お土産 omiyage = souvenir; 土曜日 doyoubi = Saturday **DESCRIPTION:** this resembles a mound of soil; compared to (兵)士 heishi (soldier, # 66), 土 has shorter arms **CUES:** this kanji points up to the moon, where **Ts**uki **Chee**se (moon cheese) is as common as 土 **ts**uchi (soil), and **To**ads conduct **Mee**tings under **Do**mes **GROUP:** this is a group of one

0060. 塩 **PRONUNCIATIONS:** shio, en **MEANING:** salt **EXAMPLES:** 塩 shio = salt; 塩分 enbun = salt content **DESCRIPTION:** on the left, 土(地) tsuchi (soil, # 59); at the upper right, a short crutch suspended over a block of salt; at the lower right, 皿 sara (bowl, # 567) **CUES:** a **Sh**iite **O**rphan who lives in this 土 (soil) helps us to break this 口 (block) of 塩 **shio** (salt) with this crutch, and after it trickles into this 皿 (bowl), we **En**joy eating it **ALSO COMPARE:** other similar kanji at # **1407** and # **2080**

0061. 増 **PRONUNCIATIONS:** fu, zou, ma **MEANING:** to increase **EXAMPLES:** 増える fueru = to increase; 倍増する baizou suru = to double; 増す masu = to increase or grow **DESCRIPTION:** on the left, 土 tsuchi (soil, # 59); at the upper right, 田(んぼ) tanbo (rice paddy, # 68), with two units of rice at the top, which can also be seen as rabbit ears [**Notice** how this radical on the right differs from the radical on the right in 猫 neko (cat, # 72)]; at the lower right, 日 hi (sun, # 32) **CUES:** this 田 (rice paddy) grows **F**ood in an agricultural **Z**one and produces these two units of rice annually, thanks to this 日 (sun) and this 土 (soil); after new **Ma**chines were introduced, its production 増えた **fu**eta (increased) further **GROUP:** 増(える) fueru = to increase, # 61; 贈(る) okuru = to give a present, # 84; (断)層 dansou = fault, # 1250; 僧 sou = monk, # 1522; 憎(む) nikumu = to detest, # 1651

0062. 室 **PRONUNCIATIONS:** shitsu, shi, muro **MEANINGS:** room, cellar **EXAMPLES:** 室内 shitsunai = indoors; 至福 shifuku = supreme bliss; 室町 Muromachi = Japanese era ending in 1573 **DESCRIPTION:** at the top, a bad haircut; in the middle, 一 ichi (one, # 1) above the katakana ム mu, which is the sound made by a cow; at the bottom 土 tsuchi (soil, # 59) **CUES:** I keep this 一 (one) ム (cow) with my **Sh**eets and a **Sh**eep in this 室 **shitsu** (room), which features a floor of 土 (soil) like this and **Mu**rderous **Ro**gues with bad haircuts like this for roommates **GROUP:** this is a group of one **COMPARE:** other similar kanji at # **63**

0063. 屋 PRONUNCIATIONS: ya, oku
MEANINGS: house, store EXAMPLES:
本屋 honya = bookstore; 部屋 heya = room;
小屋 koya = cabin; 屋根 yane = roof; 屋上 okujou = rooftop DESCRIPTION: compared to 室 shitsu (room, # 62), this omits the bad haircut at the top and adds a lean-to with a double roof at the upper left; it retains the 一 (one) ム (cow) on 土 (soil) CUES: since I live in a land of falling yams, the addition of this heavy **Y**am-proof 屋根 **ya**ne (roof) and an **O**ak lean-to has allowed me to convert this simple 室 (room) into a more durable (小)屋 ko**ya** (cabin) GROUP: 室 shitsu = room, # 62; (部)屋 heya = room, # 63; 倒(れる) taoreru = to fall down, # 563; 至(る) itaru = to lead to, # 609; 到(着する) touchaku suru = to arrive, # 612; 握(る) nigiru = to grasp, # 1372; 致(す) itasu = to do, # 1463; 窒(素) chisso = nitrogen, # 2024
ALSO COMPARE: other similar kanji at # **1899**

0064. 堂 PRONUNCIATION: dou
MEANINGS: hall, grand building EXAMPLE:
食堂 shokudou = dining hall DESCRIPTION: at the top, a roof holding three old boys, as seen in 覚(える) oboeru (to memorize, # 54); in the middle, kuchi 口 (mouth, # 426), which resembles a hall; at the bottom, 土 tsuchi (soil, # 59), suggesting a mound of soil CUE: this 口 (hall), which is a 食堂 shoku**dou** (dining hall), is built on this mound of 土 (soil), and these three old boys stand on its roof eating **Dou**ghnuts GROUP: this is a group of one COMPARE: similar kanji at # **991**

0065. 熱 PRONUNCIATIONS: atsu, netsu, ne MEANINGS: hot objects, fever
EXAMPLES: 熱い atsui = hot (objects); 熱 netsu = fever; 熱心に nesshin ni = enthusiastically DESCRIPTION: in the upper left, 土 tsuchi (soil, # 59) appears twice, separated by some lopsided legs, as though soil were walking on soil; this suggests items that grow in soil, like vegetables; on the upper right, 九 kyuu (nine, # 111), with a slash across its left leg; at the bottom, a hot fire CUES: 九 (nine) vegetables which were slashed after being grown in this 土 (soil) walking on 土 (soil) are being cooked by this fire At **Su**perman's house and are 熱い **atsu**i (hot); they will **N**et **Su**perman a profit when he sells them **N**ext door
COMPARE: 暑(い) atsui = hot atmosphere, # 278; 厚(い) atsui = thick, # 185; other similar kanji at # **611**, # **1737** and # **1989**

Warrior
0066. 士 PRONUNCIATIONS: shi, ji², se
MEANINGS: man, warrior EXAMPLES:
武士 bushi = samurai, warrior; 兵士 heishi = soldier; 紳士 shinshi = gentleman; 富士山 fujisan = Mt. Fuji; 博士 hakase = a Ph.D.
DESCRIPTION: compared to 土 tsuchi (soil, # 59), 士 has a longer horizontal line at the top and resembles a person CUES: this 兵士 hei**shi** (soldier) needs these long arms in order to catch **Sh**eep for Settlers
ALSO COMPARE: other similar kanji at # **1468**

0067. 仕 PRONUNCIATIONS: shi, tsuka, ji MEANINGS: work, service
EXAMPLES: 仕事 shigoto = work; 仕様 shiyou = means, method; 仕える tsukaeru = to serve; 給仕 kyuuji = service, waiter/waitress
DESCRIPTION: compared to 士 shi (man, warrior, # 66) (identical pronunciation), this kanji adds a man with a slanted hat on the left
CUES: this man on the left tilts his hat back in order to gaze at this 士 (man) on the right, for whom he does 仕事 **shi**goto (work), carrying an extra **Sh**eet in a **T**suitcase (suitcase) in his Car, which is a **J**eep GROUP: this is a group of one
ALSO COMPARE: 使(用) shiyou = use (noun), # 480, or 使(う) tsukau = to use, # 480, both of which also help us to pronounce this; other similar kanji at # **1468**

Rice Paddy

0068. 田 **PRONUNCIATIONS: ta, den, da, ina MEANINGS:** rice paddies, field **EXAMPLES:** 田中 Tanaka = family name; 田んぼ tanbo = rice paddy; 田園 den'en = pastoral, rural; 上田 Ueda = family name; 田舎 inaka = countryside, home town **DESCRIPTION:** a square rice paddy divided into four sections **CUES:** **T**arzan and his **Den**tist went to this 田んぼ **tan**bo (rice paddy) on a **D**ark night, but this was considered **In**appropriate behavior **COMPARE:** other similar kanji at # **220**

0069. 界 **PRONUNCIATION: kai MEANING:** world **EXAMPLE:** 世界 sekai = the world **DESCRIPTION:** at the top, 田 (rice paddy, # 68), which resembles a square kite; at the bottom, an arrow pointing up **CUE:** we shoot **K**ites like this up into the sky, where they will be seen by 世界 se**kai** (the world) **GROUP:** (世)界 sekai = the world, # 69; (紹)介 shoukai = introduction, # 659; 堺 Sakai = a city in Osaka Prefecture, # 2083; two of these are pronounced "kai" **ALSO COMPARE:** other similar kanji at # **220**

0070. 町 **PRONUNCIATIONS: machi, chou MEANING:** town **EXAMPLES:** 町 machi = town; 町名 choumei = town name or street name **DESCRIPTION:** on the left, 田 (rice paddy, # 68); on the right, this J-shaped radical is said to be a nail **CUES:** this 田 (rice paddy) and this nail can be seen near a rice-producing 町 **machi** (town), where workers wear **Match**ing outfits and buy nails like this from Margaret **Cho** **COMPARE:** other similar kanji at # **220** and # **702**

0071. 留 **PRONUNCIATIONS: ryuu, to, todo, ru MEANING:** absence **EXAMPLES:** 留学 ryuugaku = foreign study; 留める tomeru = to fasten, button or attach; 留まる todomaru = to stay; 留守 rusu = absence from home **DESCRIPTION:** at the upper left, a backpack; at the upper right, 刀 katana (sword, # 102); at the bottom, 田 (rice paddy, # 68) **CUES:** this backpack and this 刀 (sword) were **Re**united at this 田 (rice paddy) in **To**kyo where **To**ads **Do**ze after their owner, a local **Ru**ler who had been 留守 **ru**su (absent from home) with the backpack, came back **GROUP:** 留(守) rusu = absence, # 71; 貿(易) boueki = trade, # 85 **ALSO COMPARE:** other similar kanji at # **220**

0072. 猫 **PRONUNCIATION: neko MEANING:** cat **EXAMPLES:** 猫 neko = cat **DESCRIPTION:** on the left, a woman contorting her body [**Note** how this woman differs from the kneeling guy seen in 持(つ) motsu (to hold, # 216); in addition to the curvature seen in its long vertical stroke, the two horizontal strokes in the radical on the left in 猫 are written from right to left (or top to bottom)]; on the right, a plant radical (see # 43) above 田 (rice paddy, # 68) **CUE:** this woman on the left came to this 田 (rice paddy) to look for her 猫 **neko** (cat) among these plants, and she recoiled like this when she discovered a **N**est of **Co**bras **ALSO COMPARE:** other similar kanji at # **948** and # **1740**

0073. 由 **PRONUNCIATIONS: yu, yuu, yui MEANING:** reason **EXAMPLES:** 経由で keiyu de = via, by way of; 理由 riyuu = reason; 由緒 yuisho = a history or lineage **DESCRIPTION:** compared to 田(んぼ) tanbo (rice paddy, # 68), this adds a unit of rice, possibly a metric ton, at the top; it can also be seen as a rice paddy on a stick **CUES:** there is a **U**nit of rice at the top of this 田 (rice paddy), and the 理由 ri**yuu** (reason) is that a **You**th will be taking the rice to some **Yu**kon Eagles **ALSO COMPARE:** 曲 kyoku = song, # 82; other similar kanji at # **942** and # **1157**

0074. 届

PRONUNCIATIONS: todo, todoke **MEANINGS:** to reach, to deliver **EXAMPLES:** 届ける todokeru = to deliver, transitive; 届 todoke = registration, notification **DESCRIPTION:** compared to (理)由 riyuu (reason, # 73), which consists of one unit above a rice paddy (or a rice paddy on a stick), this adds a lean-to with a double roof, which could be part of the Tokyo Dome, at the upper left **CUES:** the 由 (reason) that I can't 届ける **todo**keru (deliver) this unit is that the **To**kyo **Do**me collapsed on me, I'm stuck under this double roof, and I'm drinking water from a **To**kyo **Do**me **Ke**ttle **COMPARE:** other similar kanji at # **942**, # **1157** and # **1899**

0075. 戻

PRONUNCIATION: modo **MEANINGS:** to return, revert **EXAMPLE:** 戻る modoru = to return to a place **DESCRIPTION:** on the upper left, a lean-to with a double roof, and a layer of snow on top; under the roof, 大(きい) ookii (big, # 188), which could represent a 大 (big) modest doorman **CUE:** this 大 (big) **Mo**dest **Do**orman wants to 戻る **modo**ru (return) to his duties, but he's stuck under this double roof with a layer of snow on top **COMPARE:** similar kanji at # **1134**

0076. 黒

PRONUNCIATIONS: kuro, guro², koku **MEANING:** black **EXAMPLES:** 黒い kuroi = black; 目黒 Meguro = a ward in Tokyo; 黒板 kokuban = blackboard **DESCRIPTION:** at the top, a 田 (rice paddy, # 68) on 土 tsuchi (soil, # 59), but this resembles a sincere guy wearing bifocals; at the bottom, a fire **CUES:** this fire started under this sincere guy wearing bifocals, and he was about to turn 黒い **kuro**i (black), but **Ko**oky **Ro**y Rogers put out the flames with a can of **Co**ke **COMPARE:** other similar kanji at # **545** and # **611**

0077. 画

PRONUNCIATIONS: ga, kaku **MEANINGS:** drawing, painting **EXAMPLES:** 映画 eiga = movie; 漫画 manga = comics; 計画 keikaku = plan **DESCRIPTION:** this is a model of a 田 (rice paddy, # 68) which is connected to a handle and carried in a box **CUES:** a **Ga**mbler is making an 映画 ei**ga** (movie) which is set in a rice paddy, and when he shows us this model of this 田 (paddy) with this handle, which he keeps in this box, he **Ca**ckles about his 計画 kei**kaku** (plans) **GROUP:** (映)画 eiga = movie, # 77; 横 yoko = side, # 135; 演(奏) ensou = musical performance, # 756; 黄(金) ougon = gold, # 976; 再(三) saisan = many times, # 1032 **ALSO COMPARE:** other similar kanji at # **1794**

0078. 理

PRONUNCIATION: ri **MEANINGS:** reason, rational **EXAMPLES:** 理由 riyuu = reason; 料理 ryouri = cooking **DESCRIPTION:** on the left, 王 ou (king, # 1077); on the right, 里 (a sincere guy) wearing bifocals, as seen in 黒(い) kuroi (black, # 76) **CUE:** this 王 (king) and this 里 (sincere guy) are **Rea**sonable and have their 理由 **ri**yuu (reasons) for their actions **COMPARE:** 現(在) genzai = present time, # 739; other similar kanji at # **545** and # **1772**

0079. 隅

PRONUNCIATION: sumi **MEANING:** inside corner **EXAMPLE:** 引き出しの隅 hikidashi no sumi = inside corner of a drawer **DESCRIPTION:** on the left, β beta from the Greek alphabet, suggesting a Greek citizen named Sumisu (Smith); on the right, 田 (rice paddy, # 68) growing from a pot, with roots below **CUES:** the roots of this 田 (rice paddy) are growing more vigorously in the right upper 隅 **sumi** (inside corner) of this pot, since they are trying to avoid this β (Greek) observer **Sumi**su-san (Mr. Smith) on the left **COMPARE:** other similar kanji at # **1120** and # **2030**

0080. 魚 **PRONUNCIATIONS:** sakana, zakana², uo, gyo **MEANING:** fish **EXAMPLES:** 魚 sakana = fish; 小魚 kozakana = small fish; 魚 uo = fish; 金魚 kingyo = goldfish **DESCRIPTION:** at the top, an h-shaped chair leaning to the right, which resembles a fish head; in the middle, 田 (rice paddy, # 68), which looks like scales on a fish; at the bottom, four legs **CUES:** we have a **S**ack of **Ca**nadian 魚 **saka**na (fish) like this that we caught in the **U**ber **O**cean; they are covered with scales like these, each of them has four legs like these, and we will use them to make fish **Gyo**za **ALSO COMPARE:** other kanji with fish heads at # 87, # **618**, # 936 and # 1140; other similar kanji at # **220** and # **611**

0081. 角 **PRONUNCIATIONS:** kado, kaku, tsuno **MEANING:** outside corner **EXAMPLES:** 角 kado = outside corner; 四角い shikakui = square, rectangular; 角 tsuno = horn, antler, feeler **DESCRIPTION:** at the top, a fish head above 田 (rice paddy), as seen in 魚 sakana (fish, # 80); at the bottom, a pair of ordinary legs, different from the lopsided legs seen on the fish-head guy with glasses seen in 晩 ban (evening, # 35); let's call this a fish-head guy with *bifocals* and *straight legs* **CUES:** this fish-head guy with bifocals and straight legs got caught in a **Ca**r **D**oor at a 角 **kado** (corner) near a **Ca**ctus farm, where he kept a **Tsu**itcase (suitcase) full of **No**tebooks **ALSO COMPARE:** other similar kanji at # **618** and # **1032**

0082. 曲 **PRONUNCIATIONS:** ma, kyoku, gyoku² **MEANINGS:** to bend, musical tune **EXAMPLES:** 曲がる magaru = to bend or turn; 曲 kyoku = song, musical composition; 音曲 ongyoku = songs with samisen accompaniment **DESCRIPTION:** a six-section coop with two wires at the top, resembling a stringed musical instrument **CUES:** this **Ma**chine is a six-section coop with two wires at the top that I can 曲がる **ma**garu (turn) in order to play various 曲 **kyoku** (songs) for the **Kyo**to **Ko**ol-Aid Club **COMPARE:** (理)由 riyuu = reason, # 73; other similar kanji at # **1321**

Money Chest
0083. 貝 **PRONUNCIATION:** kai **MEANINGS:** shell, shellfish **EXAMPLE:** 貝 kai = shell **DESCRIPTION:** 目 me (eye, # 51), supported by two legs, but this can be seen as a three-drawer money chest **CUE:** the **Kai**ser keeps his 貝 **kai** (shells) in this three-drawer money chest with these two legs **COMPARE:** (道)具 dougu = tool, # 100, which is a three-drawer cabinet on a *table* supported by two legs; other similar kanji at # **1870**, # **2002** and # **2058**

0084. 贈 **PRONUNCIATIONS:** oku, zou **MEANING:** to give a present **EXAMPLES:** 贈る okuru = to give a present; 贈り物 okurimono = a present; 贈呈 zoutei = a presentation (of a gift, etc.) **DESCRIPTION:** compared to (倍)増(する) baizou suru = to double, # 61 (identical pronunciation), this substitutes 貝 kai (money chest, # 83) for 土 (soil) on the left; it retains the 田 (rice paddy) above the 日 (sun) in an agricultural zone that produces two units of rice **CUES:** I will take money from this **O**ak 貝 (money chest) on the left and take it to the agricultural **Z**one where this 田 (rice paddy) above this 日 (sun) produces these two units of rice in order to 贈る **oku**ru (give) a bonus to the workers **ALSO COMPARE:** 送(る) okuru = to send out, # 348; other similar kanji at # **61** and # **2058**

0085. 貿 PRONUNCIATION: bou
MEANING: to trade EXAMPLE: 貿易 boueki = trade DESCRIPTION: compared to 留(守) rusu (absence from home, # 71), this substitutes 貝 kai (money chest, # 83) for the 田 (rice paddy) at the bottom; it retains the backpack and the 刀 (sword) CUE: I have this backpack and this 刀 (sword) on top of this three-drawer 貝 (money chest), and I would like to 貿易する **bou**eki suru (trade) them for a **Bow**ling ball
COMPARE: other similar kanji at # **71** and # **707**

0086. 質 PRONUNCIATIONS: shitsu, shichi MEANINGS: contents, quality, to inquire EXAMPLES: 質問 shitsumon = question; 品質 hinshitsu = product quality; 質屋 shichiya = pawnshop
DESCRIPTION: compared to 貝 kai (money chest, # 83), this adds two pairs of pliers on the top CUES: I bought these two pairs of pliers with money from this three-drawer 貝 (money chest) and was told that they have 品質 hin**shitsu** (product quality), but my 質問 **shitsu**mon (question) is, will you give me some **Sh**eets of paper that I can wrap them in, in exchange for some **Sh**eep **Ch**eese?
COMPARE: other similar kanji at # **352**, # **707** and # **892**

0087. 負 PRONUNCIATIONS: fu, o, ma
MEANINGS: to lose, to owe, to bear, to be wounded EXAMPLES: 負債 fusai = debt; 負う ou = to be indebted to, or to bear responsibility, to be injured; 負ける makeru = to lose; 負かす makasu = to defeat
DESCRIPTION: compared to 貝 kai (shell, money chest, # 83), this adds an old fish head (see # 80), which has no value, on the top
CUES: a **Fo**olish guy keeps this **O**ld fish head, which he plans to give to his **Ma** (mother), on this 貝 (money chest), after he accepted it as payment for a 負債 **fu**sai (debt), on which he 負けた **ma**keta (lost) money

GROUP: 負(ける) makeru = to lose, # 87; 急(ぐ) isogu = to hurry, # 312; 色 iro = color, # 473; 危(ない) abunai = dangerous, # 547; (交)換(する) koukan suru = to exchange, # 554; 絶(対に) zettai ni = absolutely, # 673; 象 zou = elephant, # 906; (想)像 souzou = imagination, # 907; (欠)陥 kekkan = a flaw, # 1660; 喚(く) wameku = to yell, # 1885 ALSO COMPARE: other similar kanji # **656**

0088. 員 PRONUNCIATION: in
MEANINGS: member of group, official
EXAMPLE: 社員 shain = company employee
DESCRIPTION: at the top, 口 kuchi (mouth, # 426); at the bottom, 貝 kai (money chest, # 83); taken together, these resemble a person wearing a hat CUE: 員 **in** (members) are **In**siders, who have access to three-drawer 貝 (money chests) like this and wear hats like this
GROUP: 社員 shain = company employee, # 88; (受)賞(する) jushou suru = to win an award, # 991; (佐)賀(県) sagaken = Saga Prefecture, # 994; 損(害) songai = harm, # 1258; (補)償 hoshou = compensation, # 1662; 韻(文) inbun = verse, # 2036

0089. 買 PRONUNCIATIONS: ka, kai, bai MEANING: to buy EXAMPLES: 買う kau = to buy; 買い手 kaite = buyer; 買取 kaitori = a purchase or sale; 売買 baibai = buying and selling DESCRIPTION: at the top, three eyes, suggesting an ability to see the future; at the bottom, 貝 kai (money chest, # 83) (identical pronunciation)
CUES: this three-drawer 貝 (money chest) has these three eyes and can see the future, which allows me to 買う **ka**u (buy) **C**ars, **K**ayaks and **B**ikes at bargain prices
COMPARE: other similar kanji at # **656** and # **1324**

0090. 貸 PRONUNCIATIONS: ka, tai

MEANING: to lend **EXAMPLES:** 貸す kasu = to lend; 賃貸 chintai = lease, rental **DESCRIPTION:** at the upper left, a man with a slanted hat who is about to fall off this 貝 kai (money chest, # 83); at the upper right, a leaning woman with a ball over her right shoulder **CUES:** this leaning woman with a ball above her right shoulder is trying to **C**atch this man with a slanted hat before he falls off this 貝 (money chest), after which she plans to ask him to 貸す **ka**su (lend) her money to buy food for her **T**iger **COMPARE:** 借(りる) kariru = to borrow, # 485; other similar kanji at # 249 and # 707

0091. 資 PRONUNCIATION: shi

MEANINGS: resources, capital **EXAMPLES:** 資料 shiryou = literature, documents; 資金 shikin = funds, capital **DESCRIPTION:** at the top, 次(第に) shidai ni (gradually, # 536) (identical pronunciation), or 次(に) tsugi ni (next, # 536), which resembles a water radical next to an oil derrick (see # 399) used to pump water for sheep; at the bottom, 貝 kai (shell, money chest, # 83), which suggests investment capital **CUE:** I save 資金 **shi**kin (funds) in this three-drawer 貝 (money chest), and 欠 (next) I intend to buy some **S**heep **ALSO COMPARE:** other similar kanji at # 536 and # 707

0092. 慣 PRONUNCIATIONS: na, kan

MEANING: to get used to **EXAMPLES:** 慣れる nareru = to get used to; 習慣 shuukan = customs, habits **DESCRIPTION:** on the left, a man standing erect; on the upper right, 田 (rice paddy, # 68) with a horizontal line drawn through it, which is said to represent a string of coins; on the lower right, 貝 kai (shell, money chest, # 83) **CUES:** when we asked about this string of coins on this 貝 (money chest), this man on the left was **N**asty, pulling himself up to his full height and saying that it was his 習慣 shuu**kan** (custom) to keep them there until he uses them to buy **Can**dy **ALSO COMPARE:** other similar kanji at # 135, # 336, # 656 and # 2063

0093. 頭 PRONUNCIATIONS: atama, zu, tou, kashira

MEANINGS: head, top, counter for a large animal **EXAMPLES:** 頭 atama = head; 頭痛 zutsuu = headache; 牛五頭 ushi gotou = five cows; 頭文字 kashira moji = first character of a word **DESCRIPTION:** on the left, 豆(腐) toufu (bean curd, # 721) (identical pronunciation), which resembles a TV set resting on toes, with a cloth over it, but this could also represent a square head on a stand, covered by a cloth; on the right, 貝 kai (shell, money chest, # 83) with a platform mounted on top, where the head could fit **CUES:** this 口 (square) on the left represents an 頭 **a**tama (head) that was removed from this platform on the right for repair after he was **At**tacked by his **Ma** (mother) at the **Zoo**, for stepping on her **T**oes while she was **C**ashing a check for a **R**abbi, and he is resting on this stand on the left, covered by this napkin **ALSO COMPARE:** other similar kanji at # 721; # 1126 and # 2070

0094. 願 PRONUNCIATIONS: nega, gan

MEANINGS: to wish, a prayer **EXAMPLES:** 願う negau = to wish or beg; 願望 ganbou = wish, longing **DESCRIPTION:** on the left, a one-sided lean-to; inside the lean-to, 白(い) shiroi (white, # 44) at the top, and 小(さい) chiisai (small, # 253) at the bottom; this can be seen as a small white guy, or as a sun above small (ignoring the ray above the sun), in a lean-to; on the right, 貝 kai (shell, money chest, # 83) with a platform where a head belongs, but the head is missing, as seen in 頭 atama (head, # 93) **CUES:** losing his head has had a **Nega**tive effect on this 小 (small) 白 (white) guy in this lean-to, and he 願う **nega**u (begs) **Gan**dalf to find it **GROUP:** 願(う) negau = to wish, # 94; 隙(間) sukima = gap, # 879; 原(因) gen'in = cause, # 888; (治)療 chiryou = medical treatment, # 1069, (起)源 kigen = origin, # 1267; 寮 ryou = a dormitory, # 1501; (官)僚 kanryou = a bureaucrat, # 1592; (明)瞭な meiryou na = obvious, # 2002 **ALSO COMPARE:** other similar kanji at # 888 and # 1126

0095. 顔 **PRONUNCIATIONS:** kao, gao², gan **MEANING:** face
EXAMPLES: 顔 kao = face; 笑顔 egao = smiling face; 洗顔 sengan = face washing
DESCRIPTION: at the upper left, a cow bell; at the lower left, a one-sided lean-to containing three cords, or maybe a rocker bottom shoe, but these can also be seen as scratches, suggesting the face of a beat-up cow; on the right, 貝 kai (money chest, # 83) with a platform on top where a face could fit, as seen in 頭 atama (head, # 93)
CUES: these scratches at the lower left belong to the 顔 **kao** (face) of a **C**ow wearing this cow bell; **Gan**dalf hopes to restore the face **to** its head, which is missing from this platform on top of this 貝 (money chest) **COMPARE:** similar kanji at # **406**, # **1126** and # **1569**

0096. 頃 **PRONUNCIATIONS:** koro, goro **MEANINGS:** about (referring to time)
EXAMPLE: 頃 koro = approximate time, often pronounced goro **DESCRIPTION:** on the left, the katakana character ヒ hi, which reminds us of a hero; on the right, 貝 kai (shell, money chest, # 83) under a platform where a head belongs, but the head is missing, as seen in 頭 atama (head, # 93), suggesting the need for a coroner
CUES: this ヒ (hero) on the left, who is a **Coroner**, is examining this headless guy on the right, who was found near a merry-**Go**-**Ro**und, because he has to conduct an autopsy
ALSO COMPARE: similar kanji at # **1126** and # **2048**

0097. 類 **PRONUNCIATION:** rui
MEANINGS: sort, variety **EXAMPLES:** 書類 shorui = documents; 衣類 irui = clothes; 種類 shurui = variety **DESCRIPTION:** at the upper left, 米 kome (uncooked rice, # 326); at the lower left, 大(きい) ookii (big, # 188); taken together, these two radicals imply a big rice harvest; on the right, 貝 kai (shell, money chest, # 83) with a platform on top, which reminds us of a person without his head, as seen in 頭 atama (head, # 93)
CUE: a 大 (big) harvest of this 米 (rice) came in, and we want King **Lou**is to look at some 書類 sho**rui** (documents) about the harvest, but his head is missing from this platform **ALSO COMPARE:** similar kanji at # **1126** and # **1387**

0098. 頼 **PRONUNCIATIONS:** tano, tayo, rai **MEANINGS:** trust, request
EXAMPLES: 頼む tanomu = to request, beg, ask, entrust to; 頼る tayoru = to rely on, depend on; 依頼 irai = request, commission
DESCRIPTION: compared to 頭 atama (head, # 93), this substitutes (約)束 yakusoku (promise, # 99), which can be seen as a bundle or as a 木 (tree) wearing glasses, for the 豆 (bean curd) on the left; it retains the platform above a 貝 (money chest) on the right **CUES:** in response to an 依頼 i**rai** (request), a **Ta**ll **No**rwegian makes this 束 (promise) to a **Ta**ll **Yo**rkshire man to retrieve the head that is missing from this platform on the right, but first he wants to finish his **Ri**ce **ALSO COMPARE:** similar kanji at # **1126** and # **1806**

0099. 束 **PRONUNCIATIONS:** taba, soku, *tsuka* **MEANINGS:** bundle, sheaf
EXAMPLES: 花束 hanataba = a bouquet; 約束 yakusoku = promise, appointment; 束の間 tsuka no ma = moment
DESCRIPTION: a 木 ki (tree, # 118) wearing glasses, which can also be seen as two eyes; this represents a bundle **CUES:** this 木 (tree) is surrounded by **T**an**B**ark, which sometimes gets **S**oaked by sprinklers, and it was given these glasses and a 花束 hana**taba** (bouquet) as a reward for producing a **Ts**ui**t**case (suitcase) full of **Ca**shew nuts
COMPARE: other similar kanji at # **1806**

Table Cabinet

0100. 具 **PRONUNCIATION: gu**
MEANINGS: to equip, tool **EXAMPLES:** 道具 dougu = tool; 具体的に gutaiteki ni = concretely; 具合 guai = condition
DESCRIPTION: like 貝 kai (shell, money chest, # 83) and other similar kanji, this contains 目 me (eye, # 51), which can also be seen as a three-drawer cabinet, at the top, but it contains a *table* supported by two legs at the bottom **CUE:** I keep 道具 dou**gu** (tools) in this cabinet on this table, together with the **Goo** that I use to grease them
GROUP: 具(合) guai = condition, # 100; 真 makoto = truth, # 101; 慎(重) shinchou = prudent, # 632; 鎮(める) shizumeru = to alleviate, # 1722

0101. 真 **PRONUNCIATIONS: makoto, ma, shin** **MEANINGS:** truth, genuine
EXAMPLES: 真 makoto = truth, sincerity; 真面目な majime na = sincere; 真ん中 mannaka = middle; 真っ直ぐ massugu = straight; 写真 shashin = photograph; 真実 shinjitsu = truth; 真理 shinri = truth
DESCRIPTION: compared to (道)具 dougu (tool, # 100), which resembles a simple table cabinet, this kanji adds a machine with a shiny antenna to the top of 目 me (eye, # 51); this can also be described as 十 (ten) above 目 (eye) on legs **CUES:** this cabinet on this table contains strings for **Ma**'s (Mother's) **Ko**to (Japanese harp), and it has a **Ma**chine with this **Shi**ny antenna at the top, which delivers 真実の **shin**jitsu no (true) news
GROUP: 真 makoto = truth, # 101; 慎(重) shinchou = prudent, # 632 (identical pronunciation); 鎮(める) shizumeru = alleviate, # 1722 **ALSO COMPARE:** other similar kanji at # **100**

Sword

0102. 刀 **PRONUNCIATIONS: katana, tou, chi** **MEANINGS:** sword, knife
EXAMPLES: 刀 katana = sword; 短刀 tantou = dagger; 太刀 tachi = long sword
DESCRIPTION: compared to 力 chikara (force, # 107), 刀 is missing a handle at the top, suggesting a blade without a handle **CUES:** I bought this 刀 **kata**na (sword) from a **Ca**talogue store in **Na**rnia in order to cut my **To**enails; it was **Ch**eap, but it's missing its handle **GROUP:** five "blade" kanji: 刀 katana = sword, # 102; 力 chikara = force, # 107; 九 kyuu = nine, # 111, 万 man = ten thousand, # 113; 方 kata = honorable person, # 114
ALSO COMPARE: the katakana カ ka; kanji containing 刀 at # **2062**

0103. 切 **PRONUNCIATIONS: setsu, ki, gi², sai** **MEANINGS:** to cut, serious, earnest
EXAMPLES: 親切 shinsetsu = kind; 大切 taisetsu = important; 切る kiru = to cut; 横切る yokogiru = to cut across; 一切 issai = everything in affirmative sentences, nothing or never in negative sentences **DESCRIPTION:** on the left, 七 shichi (seven, # 20); on the right, a 刀 katana (sword, # 102) **CUES:** it takes 七 (seven) people to 切る **ki**ru (cut) with this big 刀 (sword); if you want to buy one, a friend **Set**s yo**U** up, but it's very 大切 tai**set**su (important) to wear a **Ki**mono and **Si**gn a contract **ALSO COMPARE:** other similar kanji at # **20** and # **2062**

0104. 初 **PRONUNCIATIONS: haji, sho, hatsu** **MEANINGS:** for the first time, to begin
EXAMPLES: 初めて hajimete = for the first time; 最初 saisho = the beginning; 初恋 hatsukoi = first love **DESCRIPTION:** on the left, a happy man named Jimmy Carter who, unlike the Shah, as seen in (会)社 kaisha (company, # 271), has two lips; on the right 刀 katana (sword, # 102) **CUES:** this **H**appy **J**immy, who has a pointy hat and these two lips, kisses this 刀 (sword) before his 初めての **haji**mete no (first) battle and **Sh**ows it to his admirers, after which all of the people remove their **Hat**s **COMPARE:** 始(める) hajimeru = to

begin, # 540; other similar kanji at # **1615** and # **2062**

0105. 分　PRONUNCIATIONS: bun, pun, bu, *ita*, fun, wa　MEANINGS: to divide, to understand, minute　EXAMPLES: 十分 juubun = enough (this can also be read as juppun, or jippun, = 10 minutes); 五分 gobu = half; 大分 ooita = Oita, a prefecture in Kyushu; 五分 gofun = 5 minutes; 分かる wakaru = to understand; 分かれる wakareru = to separate or branch off　DESCRIPTION: at the top, 八 hachi (eight, # 15); at the bottom, a 刀 katana (sword, # 102) belonging to Daniel Boone　CUES: when Daniel **Boo**ne lived in the **Pun**jab, after drinking **Boo**ze, he tried to 分かる **wa**karu (understand) an **Ita**lian magnet, using this 刀 (sword) to cut it into 八 (eight) parts, which then 分かれた **wa**kareta (separated) from one another; this was **Fun** to **Wa**tch　GROUP: 八 hachi = eight, # 15; 六 roku = six, # 17; 分(かる) wakaru = to understand, # 105; 穴 ana = hole, # 964　ALSO COMPARE: other similar kanji at # **2062** and # **2076**

0106. 召　PRONUNCIATIONS: shou, me　MEANING: to eat　EXAMPLE: 召喚する shoukan suru = to summon; 召し上がる meshiagaru = to honorably eat　DESCRIPTION: at the top, 刀 katana (sword, # 102); at the bottom, 口 kuchi (mouth, # 426), which resembles a box　CUES: a **Shou**gun is **Me**rry as he 召し上がる **me**shiagaru (honorably eats) with this 口 (mouth), after cutting his food with this 刀 (sword)　ALSO COMPARE: other similar kanji at # **560**

0107. 力　PRONUNCIATIONS: chikara, riki, ryoku　MEANINGS: strength, power, force　EXAMPLES: 力 chikara = force; 力作 rikisaku = masterpiece; 努力 doryoku = effort　DESCRIPTION: compared to 九 kyuu (nine, # 111), 力 leans to the right; compared to 刀 katana (sword, # 102), 力 has a handle for control　CUES: in **Chi**cago **Ra**mbo, who leans a little to the right like this, controlled his motorcycle's 力 **chi**kara (force) with this handle attached to this 刀 (sword), before **Ri**cky and Pope **Leo** Cut him off with a popemobile　ALSO COMPARE: the katakana 力 ka; other similar kanji at # **102** and # **1846**

0108. 助　PRONUNCIATIONS: tasu, jo, suke　MEANING: to help　EXAMPLES: 助ける tasukeru = to help; 助手 joshu = assistant; 飲み助 nomisuke = heavy drinker　DESCRIPTION: on the left, a tall solar panel, as seen in 祖(父) sofu (grandfather, # 272); on the right, an even taller 力 chikara (force, # 107)　CUES: a **Ta**ll **Su**perintendent of schools, whose name is **Jo**nah, uses the electricity from this tall solar panel to maximize this 力 (force), and he is able to 助ける **tasu**keru (help) people obtain **S**uperior **Ke**ttles　COMPARE: other similar kanji at # **752** and # **1846**

0109. 男　PRONUNCIATIONS: otoko, dan, nan, o　MEANING: male　EXAMPLES: 男の子 otoko no ko = boy; 男性 dansei = man; 長男 chounan = first-born son; 正男 Masao = a boy's given name　DESCRIPTION: at the top, 田 (rice paddy, # 68); at the bottom, 力 chikara (force, # 107)　CUES: this 男性 **dan**sei (man), who is wearing an **O**ttoman-era **Co**at, exercises this 力 (force) by **Dan**cing in this 田 (rice paddy) with **Nan**cy Pelosi, who is **O**ld　GROUP: 男 otoko = male # 109; 湧(く) waku = to gush out, # 903; 虜 toriko = captive, # 1107; 勇(気) yuuki = courage, # 1282　ALSO COMPARE: other similar kanji at # **220** and # **1746**

0110. 勢 PRONUNCIATIONS: **ze**i, **se**i, *se*, ikio MEANINGS: vigor, power EXAMPLES: 大勢 oozei = many people; 勢力 seiryoku = power, influence; 伊勢崎 isesaki = a city in Japan; 勢い ikioi = power, energy DESCRIPTION: compared to 熱(い) atsui (hot, # 65), this substitutes 力 chikara (force, # 107), for the hot fire at the bottom; it retains 土 (soil) using lopsided legs to walk on 土 (soil) at the upper left and 九 (nine) with a slash across its left leg CUES: this 土 (soil) at the upper left walks on these lopsided legs across more 土 (soil) towards a **Z**any guy who uses a **S**aber to slash 九 (nine) kinds of vegetables with 力 (force) before **Se**lling them to 大勢の oo**ze**i no (many) **I**cky **O**gres ALSO COMPARE: other similar kanji at # **1737**, # **1746** and # **1989**

0111. 九 PRONUNCIATIONS: **kyu**u, **ku**, kokono MEANING: nine EXAMPLES: 九 kyuu = nine; 九月 kugatsu = September; 九つ kokonotsu = nine objects DESCRIPTION: compared to 力 chikara (force, # 107), 九 kyuu, like Cuba, doesn't lean right CUES: this **C**uban guy with 九 **kyu**u (nine) **K**ooky kids eats **C**oconuts with **N**omads and, compared to 力 (force), doesn't lean right ALSO COMPARE: other similar kanji at # **102**, # **827** and # 1737

0112. 究 PRONUNCIATION: **kyu**u MEANING: to investigate thoroughly EXAMPLES: 研究 kenkyuu = research or study DESCRIPTION at the top, a bad haircut, as seen in 宅 taku (home, # 21), supported by two lopsided legs; taken together, these remind us of soaring bird from Cuba [**N**otice how this differs from the hen with four legs seen in 変 hen (strange, # 553)]; at the bottom, 九 kyuu (nine, # 111) (identical pronunciation) CUES: when their 研究 ken**kyu**u (research) on this soaring **C**uban bird was done, the spirits of these 九 **K**yuu (nine) 研究者 ken**kyu**usha (researchers) soared with it GROUP: (研)究 kenkyuu = research, # 112; 空 sora = sky, # 248; 窓 mado = window, # 311; 突(然) totsuzen = abrupt, # 868; 控(除) koujo = a deduction, # 1637; 窮(地) kyuuchi = plight, adversity, # 1805 (identical pronunciation); 窯 kama = an oven, # 1893; (洞)窟 doukutsu = a cave, # 1920; 窒(素) chisso = nitrogen, # 2024; 搾(取) sakushu = exploitation, # 2038; 窃(盗) settou = theft, # 2062 COMPARE: kanji containing hens with four legs at # 695; other similar kanji at # **827**

0113. 万 PRONUNCIATIONS: **ba**n, **ma**n MEANING: ten thousand EXAMPLES: 万事 banji = everything; 二万 niman = 20,000 DESCRIPTION: compared to 力 chikara (force, # 107), 万 has a flat top; compared to 刀 katana (sword, # 102), 万 has a neck, allowing its flat top to swivel CUES: **Ba**nkers in **Ma**nila use this swiveling flat top on 万 **ma**n to count 一万円 ichi**ma**n'en (10,000 yen) bills GROUP: 万 man = 10,000, # 113; (激)励 gekirei = encouragement, # 1338; 栃(木県) tochigi ken = Tochigi Prefecture, # 2085 ALSO COMPARE: other similar kanji at # **102**

0114. 方 (sometimes written 方) PRONUNCIATIONS: *kue,* **ka**ta, **ga**ta², hou, pou² MEANINGS: honorable person, direction, method EXAMPLES: 行方 yukue = whereabouts; 方 kata = honorable person; 読み方 yomikata = reading method; 夕方 yuugata = evening; 方がいい hou ga ii = it would be better; 一方 ippou = one side DESCRIPTION: compared to 万 man (ten thousand, # 113), which wears a flat hat on its head, 方 kata wears a nicer hat with this feather in it (the radicals at the top can also be seen as a tire stop) CUES: this nice feather hat that this 方 **ka**ta (honorable person) is wearing is his 方 **ka**ta (method) of impressing people; during a **Q**uest, if there is a **Ca**tastrophe you can count on him to

Hold you tightly   **ALSO COMPARE:** other similar kanji at # **102** and # **920**

0115. 族   PRONUNCIATION: zoku

MEANINGS: family, tribe   **EXAMPLE:** 家族 kazoku = family   **DESCRIPTION:** on the left, a 方 kata (honorable person, # 114) named Zooey; on the right, a crutch held up by her father, a Native American chief, who is wearing a war bonnet   **CUE:** this 家族 ka**zoku** (family) of these disabled Native American 方 (honorable people) drinks mostly beer, but **Zoo**ey drinks **Kool**-Aid   **COMPARE:** similar kanji at # **324**, # **920** and # **2080**

0116. 旅   PRONUNCIATIONS: ryo, tabi

MEANINGS: trip, to travel   **EXAMPLES:** 旅行する ryokou suru = to travel; 旅 tabi = trip, travel   **DESCRIPTION:** compared to (家)族 kazoku (family, # 115), this replaces the Native American chief at the lower right with a man wearing a slanted hat who has a long Y-shaped leg extending forward; he appears to be stepping out on a journey; it retains the 方 (honorable person) on the left and the crutch at the upper right   **CUES:** this 方 (honorable person) named Pope **Leo** and this companion who carries this crutch will 旅行する **ryo**kou suru (travel) and are taking this first step on their 旅 **tabi** (trip) with their **Tab**by cat   **GROUP:** 旅(行する) ryokou suru = to travel, # 116; 派(手) hade = gaudy, # 764; 脈 myaku = pulse, # 770   **ALSO COMPARE:** other similar kanji at # **920** and # **2080**

0117. 放   PRONUNCIATIONS: hou, pou², hana, pana²   MEANINGS: to emit, release

EXAMPLES: 放送 housou = broadcasting; 奔放 honpou = wild; 放す hanasu = to release; 開けっ放し akeppanashi = left open   **DESCRIPTION:** on the left, a 方 kata (honorable person, # 114) named Hopeful Hannah; the bottom half of 方 resembles an h, which helps us to pronounce her name; on the right, a dancer with a ponytail, which can also be seen as a crutch above X   **CUES:** this **Hop**eful 方 (honorable person) named **Hann**ah wants to 放送する **hou**sou suru (broadcast) information to dancers like this, and she will also work to 放す **hana**su (release) dancers from jail   **COMPARE:** similar kanji at # **2016**

Tree

0118. 木   PRONUNCIATIONS: gi, ki, moku, boku, ko, mo   MEANINGS: wood, tree

EXAMPLES: 六本木 roppongi = district in Tokyo; 木の実 kinomi = nut, fruit, berry; 木曜日 mokuyoubi = Thursday; 土木 doboku = public works, civil engineering; 木の葉 konoha = leaf; 木綿 momen = cotton   **DESCRIPTION:** a tree with a central trunk and four branches; when used as a kanji component, the trunk may curl left at the bottom, and the two lower branches may not touch the trunk [for example, see the radical at the lower left in shin 新 (# 383) which can be written 新]   **CUES:** when you return with your **Gui**tar and take out your house **Key**, this 木 **ki** (tree) in the front yard reminds you to buy **Mo**re **Ko**ol-Aid, but not the **Bo**ring **Ko**ol-Aid, since that's no better than **Co**la, and to **Mo**w the lawn   **GROUP:** 木 ki = tree, # 118; 末 matsu = end, # 119; 本 hon = book, # 123

0119. 末   PRONUNCIATIONS: sue, matsu, ma   MEANING: end   EXAMPLES: 末

っ子 suekko = youngest child; 週末 shuumatsu = weekend; 末期 makki = the hour of death   **DESCRIPTION:** compared to 木 ki (tree, # 118), this adds another pair of branches; the longer branches are at the top   **CUES:** people on **Sue**de **Mat**s sit around this tree with two pairs of branches, which are longer at the top because it's **Magic** and can reach for the sky on 週末 shuu**matsu** (weekends)   **COMPARE:** 未(来) mirai (future, # 672), in which the longer branches are at the bottom; other similar kanji at # **118** and # **672**

0120. 案 **PRONUNCIATION: an MEANINGS:** plan, idea **EXAMPLES:** 案内する annai suru = to show around; 案 an = proposal, idea **DESCRIPTION:** at the top, a bad haircut; in the middle, 女 onna (female, # 275); at the bottom, 木 ki (tree, # 118) **CUE:** Queen **An**ne is a 女 (female) with this bad haircut, and she will 案内する **an**nai suru (show us around) and demonstrate her 案 **an** (proposal) for living in 木 (trees) like this one **GROUP:** 案 an = proposal, # 120; 安(心) anshin = relief, # 236 (identical pronunciation); 宴(会) enkai = party, # 1391

0121. 菜 **PRONUNCIATIONS: sai, na MEANINGS:** vegetable, side dish **EXAMPLES:** 野菜 yasai = vegetable; 菜っ葉 nappa = green leafy vegetables **DESCRIPTION:** at the top, a plant radical (see # 43), suggesting vegetables; in the middle, four lines which could represent a barbecue grate; at the bottom, 木 ki (tree, # 118) **CUES:** during the Vietnam war, people installed barbecue grates like this in 木 (trees) like this in **Sai**gon and cooked **Na**tural 野菜 ya**sai** (vegetables), represented by this plant radical at the top **COMPARE:** similar kanji at # **1935**

0122. 休 **PRONUNCIATIONS: kyuu, yasu MEANING:** rest **EXAMPLES:** 休暇 kyuuka = vacation; 休む yasumu = to rest **DESCRIPTION:** compared to 木 ki (tree, # 118), this adds a man with a slanted hat on the left **CUES:** this man tilts his hat back so that he can use it as a pillow when he 休む **yasu**mu (rests) against this **Cu**ban 木 (tree), but first he plans to drink some **Ya**k **Su**up **GROUP:** 休(む) yasumu = to rest, # 122; 体 karada = body, # 124; 褒(める) homeru = to praise, # 829; 保 tamotsu = to maintain, # 1216; 傑(作) kessaku = a masterpiece, # 1808

0123. 本 **PRONUNCIATIONS: hon, moto, pon, bon MEANINGS:** book, a counter for long thin objects, main, true, real **EXAMPLES:** 本屋 honya = bookstore; 四本 yonhon = four bottles; 山本 Yamamoto = a family name; 一本 ippon = one bottle; 何本 nanbon = how many bottles **DESCRIPTION:** a 木 ki (tree, # 118) in Honduras, with a horizontal line across the lower trunk, which could represent an open book **CUES:** this 本 **hon** (book) near the bottom of this 木 (tree) in **Hon**duras tells the story of a **Mo**torcycle that ran into a **Po**ny and broke its **Bon**es **GROUP:** 本 hon = book, # 123; 体 karada = body, # 124; 鉢 hachi = bowl, # 1277 **ALSO COMPARE:** other similar kanji at # **118**

0124. 体 **PRONUNCIATIONS: karada, tai, tei MEANING:** body **EXAMPLES:** 体 karada = body; 身体 shintai = the human body; 体裁 teisai = appearance, looks **DESCRIPTION:** compared to 本 hon (book, # 123), this adds a man with a slanted hat on the left **CUES:** this man on the left was on a plane, and he tilted his hat back to examine this 本 (book) about **Ca**racas' **Da**rk underworld, but his 体 **karada** (body) got **T**ired, and he fell asleep during **T**ake-off **ALSO COMPARE:** 休(む) yasumu = to rest, # 122; other similar kanji at # **122** and # **123**

0125. 林 **PRONUNCIATIONS: hayashi, bayashi², rin MEANING:** grove **EXAMPLES:** 林 hayashi = grove; 小林 Kobayashi = a family name; 森林 shinrin = forest **DESCRIPTION:** two 木 ki (trees, # 118) **CUES: Hay** is growing in **Ash**land near this 林 **hayashi** (grove) of 木 (trees) with **Wrin**kled bark **COMPARE:** 森 mori = forest, # 127; other similar kanji at # **943**

0126. 磨 **PRONUNCIATIONS:** su, miga, ma **MEANINGS:** grind, polish, scour, brush **EXAMPLES:** 磨る suru = to grind; 磨く migaku = to brush; 研磨 kenma = grinding, abrading, polishing **DESCRIPTION:** at the upper left, a lean-to with a chimney; inside the lean-to, a 林 hayashi (grove, # 125); under this grove, 石 ishi (stone, # 458) **CUES:** Superman will **M**eet the **Ga**mbler who installed this 林 (grove) and this 石 (stone) inside this lean-to, and his **Ma** (mother) told him to 磨く **miga**ku (brush) his shoes before entering **ALSO COMPARE:** similar kanji at # **1475** and # **1775**

0127. 森 **PRONUNCIATIONS:** mori, shin **MEANING:** forest **EXAMPLES:** 森 mori = forest; 森林 shinrin = forest **DESCRIPTION:** three 木 ki (trees, # 118) **CUES:** **M**au**ree**n likes to visit these three 木 (trees) in this 森 **mori** (forest) and worship the **Shin**tou spirits there **COMPARE:** other similar kanji at # **943**

0128. 枝 **PRONUNCIATIONS:** eda, ji **MEANING:** branch **EXAMPLES:** 枝 eda = branch; 爪楊枝 tsumayouji = toothpick **DESCRIPTION:** on the left, 木 ki (tree, # 118); on the right, 支(店) shiten (branch store, # 26), which can be seen as 士 shi (man, # 66)) on 又 mata (table, # 24) **CUES:** this 士 (man) had an **E**xcellent **D**aughter who cut an 枝 **eda** (branch) from this 木 (tree), carried it home in a **J**eep and used it to make this 又 (table) **GROUP:** 枝 eda = branch, # 128; (二)枚 nimai = two sheets, # 129; (学)校 gakkou = school, # 130; 村 mura = village, # 131; (機)械 kikai = machine, # 138; 技(術) gijutsu = techno-logy, # 1133; (病)棟 byoutou = hospital ward, # 1271; 株 kabu = stock, # 1302; 材(料) zairyou = material, # 1378; 枕 makura = a pillow, # 1770; 枯(れる) kareru = to wither, # 1834; 柿 kaki = a persimmon, # 1947; 桟(橋) sanbashi = a wharf, # 1977; 抹(殺) massatsu = erasure, # 2017 **ALSO COMPARE:** other similar kanji at # **1121**

0129. 枚 **PRONUNCIATION:** mai **MEANING:** counter for flat thin objects **EXAMPLE:** 紙二枚 kami nimai = two sheets of paper **DESCRIPTION:** on the left, a 木 ki (tree, # 118); on the right, a dancer with a ponytail **CUE:** this dancer is a **Mi**ser who might give you some of the paper that she makes from this 木 (tree); if you ask for some, she says, "何枚 nan**mai** (how many sheets) do you need?" **GROUP:** (二)枚 nimai = two sheets, # 129; (性)格 seikaku = personality, # 762; 条(件) jouken = condition, # 1352 **ALSO COMPARE:** other similar kanji at # **128**

0130. 校 **PRONUNCIATION:** kou **MEANING:** school **EXAMPLE:** 学校 gakkou = school **DESCRIPTION:** on the left, 木 ki (tree, # 118); at the upper right, 六 roku (six, # 17; at the lower right, crossed roads; the radical on the right can also be seen as a tire stop above 父 chichi (father, # 143) **CUE:** a 学校 gak**kou** (school) is near this 交 (crossing) of 六 (six) roads, and it's usually **C**old because it's shaded by this 木 (tree) **ALSO COMPARE:** other similar kanji at # **128** and # **1139**

0131. 村 **PRONUNCIATIONS:** son, mura **MEANING:** village **EXAMPLES:** 村長 sonchou = village mayor; 村 mura = village **DESCRIPTION:** this is a mural showing, on the left, 木 ki (tree, # 118) and, on the right, 寸(前) sunzen (on the verge, # 1369), which resembles a kneeling sunny guy who has dropped a piece of gum on the ground **CUES:** my **S**on painted a **Mura**l which depicts a 村 **mura** (village), with this 木 (tree) on the left and this kneeling sunny guy on the right; the sunny guy has dropped this piece of gum on the ground **GROUP:** 村 mura = village, # 131;

将(来) shourai = the future, # 374; (絶)対(に) zettai ni = absolutely, # 674; 団(体) dantai = group, # 686; 得 toku = profit, # 706; (奮)闘 funtou = hard struggle, # 728; (注)射 chuusha = injection, # 932; 樹(木) jumoku = trees, # 1089; (焼)酎 shouchuu = shochu, # 1099; 尊(敬す る) sonkei suru = to respect, # 1208; (指)導 shidou = guidance, # 1261; 謝(る) ayamaru = to apologize, # 1283; 寸(前) sunzen = on the verge, # 1369; (忍)耐 nintai = patience, # 1434; (検) 討 kentou = examination, # 1493; 尋(ねる) tazuneru = to ask, # 1512; 奪(う) ubau = to rob, # 1568; 爵(位) shaku'i = peerage, # 1603; 封 (筒) fuutou = an envelope, # 1619; 冠 kanmuri = a crown, # 1786; (屈)辱 kutsujoku = humiliation, # 1799; 奨(励) shourei = encouragement, # 1906; 肘 hiji = an elbow, # 1954 ALSO COMPARE: other similar kanji at # **128**

0132. 付 PRONUNCIATIONS: **pu, fu, zu, tsuke, tsu** MEANINGS: to adhere, to issue EXAMPLES: 貼付 tenpu = pasting; 寄付 kifu = donation; 事付け kotozuke = message; 植付 uetsuke = planting; 付く tsuku = to adhere, intransitive DESCRIPTION: on the left, a man with a slanted hat; on the right, 寸(前) sunzen (on the verge, # 1369), which resembles a kneeling sunny guy who has dropped a piece of gum on the ground CUES: this man on the left, whose name is **Pu**tin, tilts his hat back to speak to this **Foo**lish kneeling sunny guy who accompanied him to the **Zoo**, where this piece of gum 付(いた) **tsu**ita (adhered), first to their **Tsuit**Ke**i**s (suitcase) and later to their **Tsu**its (suits) ALSO COMPARE: other similar kanji at # **1004**

0133. 符 PRONUNCIATIONS: **pu, fu** MEANING: tag EXAMPLES: 切符 kippu = ticket; 護符 gofu = talisman, charm DESCRIPTION: compared to 付(く) tsuku (to adhere, # 132), or (寄)付 kifu (donation, # 132) (identical pronunciation), this kanji adds a short 竹 take (bamboo, # 134), which looks like two clamps, at the top; it retains the man with a slanted hat and the sunny kneeling guy who has dropped some gum CUES: this man with a slanted hat, whose name is **Pu**tin, **Foo**lishly clamped some 切符 kip**pu** (tickets) together using these 竹 (bamboo) clamps and this gum, and now they 付 (adhere) to each other ALSO COMPARE: similar kanji at # **1004** and # **2074**

0134. 竹 PRONUNCIATIONS: **take, chiku** MEANING: bamboo EXAMPLES: 竹の子 takenoko = bamboo shoot; 竹林 chikurin = bamboo grove DESCRIPTION: on the left, a crutch, with a vertical line below; on the right, this is said to be the same radical as the one on the left although the vertical line on the right curves under at the bottom; when this is written as a bamboo radical [e.g., in (切)符 kippu (ticket, # 133)], the vertical lines are much shorter CUES: these two cowboys, viewed from the side, each with his hat pushed back on his head, are **Ta**ll **Ke**nnedys admiring some 竹 **take** (bamboo); the cowboy in front is kneeling, and they are both drinking **Ch**eap **K**ool-Aid ALSO COMPARE: other similar kanji at # **2074**

0135. 横 PRONUNCIATIONS: **yoko, ou** MEANINGS: sideways, crooked EXAMPLES: 横 yoko = side or width; 横断する oudan suru = to cross (a street, etc.) DESCRIPTION: at the left, 木 ki (tree, # 118); on the right, 黄(色) kiiro (yellow, # 976), which consists of a plant radical (see # 43) above a model of a rice paddy with a handle, as seen in (映)画 eiga (movie, # 77), with the addition of two slanted legs extending below CUES: **Yo**ko **O**no keeps this 黄 (yellow) model of a rice paddy with a handle, with plants above it and slanted legs below, 横 **yoko** (beside) this 木 (tree) in **O**hio GROUP: (習)慣 shuukan = customs, # 92; 横 yoko = side, # 135; 演(じる) enjiru = to perform, # 756; 黄(色) kiiro = yellow, # 976; 貫(く) tsuranuku = to penetrate, # 1621 ALSO COMPARE: other similar kanji at # **77** and # **1740**

0136. 様 **PRONUNCIATIONS: you, sama**
MEANINGS: appearance, honorific form of address
EXAMPLES: 様子 yousu = condition, state; お客様 okyakusama = very honorable customer
DESCRIPTION: on the left, a 木 ki (tree, # 118); on the upper right, 王 ou (king, # 1077), wearing rabbit ears [this part of the kanji can also be seen as a truncated 羊 hitsuji (sheep, # 1223), missing its tail]; on the lower right, 水 mizu (water, # 251)
CUES: a **Y**ogurt seller named **Y**olanda 様 **sama** (very honorable Yolanda) will jump down from this 木 (tree) to rescue this 王 (king) wearing rabbit ears who is drowning in this 水 (water) because she is a good **Sama**ritan **ALSO COMPARE:** other similar kanji at # **1529** and # **1893**

0137. 機 **PRONUNCIATIONS: hata, ki**
MEANING: machine **EXAMPLES:** 機織り hataori = weaving, weaver; 機械 kikai = machine; 飛行機 hikouki = airplane
DESCRIPTION: on the left, 木 ki (tree, # 118) (identical pronunciation); at the upper right, the upper halves of two 糸 (skeet shooters, # 219), each consisting of two flexed elbows; at the lower right, a platform transected by a halberd (combination lance and axe) on the right and supported by 人 hito (person, # 13) on the left
CUES: we made this 機械 **ki**kai (machine) from four components: this 木 (tree), these two truncated 糸 (skeet shooters), this **H**alberd sent by **T**arzan, and this 人 (person) under a platform, who operates it using a **K**ey **COMPARE:** other similar kanji at # **1862**, # **1908** and # **1926**

0138. 械 **PRONUNCIATION: kai**
MEANINGS: machine, gadget **EXAMPLE:** 機械 kikai = machine **DESCRIPTION:** on the left, 木 ki (wood, # 118); on the right, a halberd (combination lance and axe); compared to the leaning woman with a ball seen 式 shiki (ceremony, # 249), this adds a long left leg; in the center, a person with a welcoming stance as seen in 葬(る) houmuru (to bury, # 1273), but it can also be seen as two hands tied together by a set of handcuffs **CUE:** the **Kai**ser owned a 機械 ki**kai** (machine) made from this 木 (wood), and it included these handcuffs and this halberd to deal with criminals **COMPARE:** other similar kanji at # **128**, # **1862** and # **1924**

0139. 橋 **PRONUNCIATIONS: hashi, bashi², kyou** **MEANING:** bridge **EXAMPLES:** 橋 hashi = bridge; 新橋 Shinbashi = district in Tokyo; 歩道橋 hodoukyou = pedestrian bridge
DESCRIPTION: on the left, 木 ki (wood, # 118); at the top right, 天 ten (sky, # 189); at the lower right, the lower portion of 高(い) takai (tall, # 19), which contains a two boxes, including one without a napkin inside a two-sided lean-to
CUES: we built a 橋 **hashi** (bridge) using **H**ashi (chopsticks) made of 木 (wood) like this in **Kyou**to, and it was so 高 (tall) that it reached this 天 (sky)
GROUP: 橋 hashi = bridge, # 139; 矯(正) kyousei = correction, # 2061 (identical pronunciation) **ALSO COMPARE:** other similar kanji at # **19** and # **1467**

0140. 机 **PRONUNCIATIONS: ki, tsukue**
MEANING: desk **EXAMPLES:** 机上 kijou = on the desk, theoretical, academic; 机 tsukue = desk
DESCRIPTION: on the left, 木 ki (wood, # 118) (identical pronunciation); on the right, a finished desk, which is so tall that a tsuitcase (suitcase) can fit below it **CUES:** if we put a tsuitcase (suitcase) containing **K**eys under this 机 **tsukue** (desk) made from this 木 (wood), the desk will be **Ts**uit**C**ase no **U**e (above the suitcase)
COMPARE: similar kanji at # **1462** and # 1511

0141. 構 PRONUNCIATIONS: **kou, kama, gama** MEANINGS: fine, to mind EXAMPLES: 結構 kekkou = fine, splendid, considerably; 構う kamau = to mind or care about; 心構え kokorogamae = a mental attitude DESCRIPTION: on the left, 木 ki (wood, # 118); at the upper right, 井(戸) ido (well, # 983); at the lower right, 再(三) saisan (many times, # 1032), which resembles a model of a 田 (rice paddy) with a vertical handle, standing on the legs of 円 (yen) CUES: people used this 木 (wood) when they built this 結**kou**な kek**kou** na (fine) **C**ourthouse with this 井 (**w**ell) and this 再 (model of a rice paddy with a handle) in the lobby; since they 構う **kama**u (care about) quality, they consulted the **Kama** Sutra, spent a lot of 円 (yen), and strengthened the building so that it would provide protection from **Gamma** rays COMPARE: other similar kanji at # **1032** and # **1825**

0142. 箱 PRONUNCIATIONS: **hako, bako²** MEANING: box EXAMPLES: 箱 hako = box; 靴箱 kutsubako = shoe box DESCRIPTION: at the top, shortened 竹 take (bamboo, # 134); on the lower left, 木 ki (tree, # 118); on the lower right, 目 me (eye, # 51) CUE: I have my 目 (eye) on this 木 (tree) and this 竹 (bamboo), which I will use to make 箱 **hako** (boxes) for storing my **H**at and my **C**oat COMPARE: other similar kanji at # **787** and # **2074**

Crossing

0143. 父 PRONUNCIATIONS: **tou, fu, chichi, bu, ji** MEANING: father EXAMPLES: お父さん otousan = honorable father; 祖父 sofu = grandfather; 父 chichi = father; 秩父 Chichibu = a city in Saitama Prefecture; 伯父さん ojisan = uncle; お祖父さん ojiisan = grandfather; **Note:** we can't divide the 祖父 jii in the word ojiisan into two component pronunciations, so please learn this word as a combination of the two kanji DESCRIPTION: a father with thick eyebrows, sitting with crossed legs (which can also be described as an X) CUES: this 父 **chichi** (father) has these thick eyebrows, sits with these crossed legs exposing his **T**oes, cooks good **F**ood, drinks **B**ooze, eats **C**heap **C**heese and drives a **J**eep GROUP: 父 chichi = father, # 143; 釜 kama = a pot, # 1896

0144. 交 PRONUNCIATIONS: **kou, maji, ma, ka** MEANINGS: crossing, mingling EXAMPLES: 交通 koutsuu = traffic; 交差点 kousaten = traffic intersection; 交わる majiwaru = to keep company with; 交ぜる mazeru = to mix (this can also be spelled 混ぜる mazeru, # 1294); 交わす kawasu = to exchange DESCRIPTION: compared to (学)校 gakkou (school, # 130) (identical pronunciation), this kanji omits the 木 (tree) on the left; it retains the crossed roads under 六 (six); this can also be seen as a tire stop above 父 chichi (father, # 143) CUES: this 交差点 **kou**saten (traffic intersection) of 六 (six) roads outside a **C**ourthouse has **M**agic traffic signals with **M**agnets that keep **C**ars from colliding COMPARE: other similar kanji at # **1139**

0145. 郊 PRONUNCIATION: **kou** MEANING: suburb EXAMPLE: 郊外 kougai = suburbs DESCRIPTION: on the left, 交 kou (crossing, # 144) (identical pronunciation); on the right, ß beta from the Greek alphabet CUE: this ß (Greek) guy lives near this 交 (crossing) in the 郊外 **kou**gai (suburbs) of Athens, and he's **C**old, since his house is unheated ALSO COMPARE: similar kanji at # **1139** and # **1843**

Mountain

0146. 山 PRONUNCIATIONS: **yama, san, zan** MEANING: mountain EXAMPLES: 山登り yamanobori = mountain climbing; 富士山 fujisan = Mt. Fuji; 火山 kazan = volcano DESCRIPTION: this resembles a mountain, with a peak in the center

CUES: a **Y**ak with **M**agic friends, like **S**an**t**a Claus, lives on this 山 **yama** (mountain) in **Z**anzibar COMPARE: similar kanji at # **1385**, # **1942** and # **2079**

0147. 出 PRONUNCIATIONS: **shutsu, da, sui, de, shu** MEANINGS: to leave, to put out EXAMPLES: 外出する gaishutsu suru = to go out; 出す dasu = to put out; 出納 suitou = accounts; 出る deru = to leave or go out; 出席 shusseki = attendance; 出張 shucchou = business trip DESCRIPTION: two 山 yama (mountains, # 146), suggesting two volcanoes CUES: these two volcanoes 出す **d**asu (put out) lava, which 出る **d**eru (emerges), **S**hoots up into the air, **D**ashes down the slopes and burns a **S**weet **D**ebutante's **S**hoes COMPARE: similar kanji at # **927**

Moon

0148. 月 PRONUNCIATIONS: **tsuki, ge, getsu, gatsu** MEANING: moon EXAMPLES: 毎月 maitsuki = every month; 月給 gekkyuu = monthly salary; 月曜日 getsuyoubi = Monday; 二月 nigatsu = February DESCRIPTION: compared to 日 hi (day, or sun, # 32), this adds two legs CUES: this 日 (sun) with two legs runs to pack a **Ts**uitcase (suitcase) of **Q**uiche for a **G**ue**s**t, who will take it to the 月 **tsuki** (moon), where he hopes to **G**et **S**uper rich by **G**athering **S**oot from moon volcanoes GROUP: this is a group of one

0149. 勝 PRONUNCIATIONS: **shou, ka, masa** MEANINGS: to win, victory EXAMPLES: 優勝 yuushou = victory, championship; 勝つ katsu = to win; 勝る masaru = to outclass, to outdo DESCRIPTION: on the left, 月 tsuki (moon, # 148); at the upper right, 人 hito (person, # 13), with the number 二 (two) inscribed on it, and flames rising above each shoulder; taken together, these resemble a bonfire; at the lower right, 力 chikara (force, # 107)

CUES: in order to achieve a 優勝 yuu**shou** (victory), this 月 (moon) **Sh**one its light with this 力 (force) to ignite this bonfire, and it 勝った **ka**tta (won) a **Ca**lendar and a **Ma**ssa**g**e COMPARE: other similar kanji at # **1305** and # **1746**

0150. 服 PRONUNCIATIONS: **fuku, puku²** MEANING: clothes EXAMPLES: 洋服 youfuku = Western clothes; 屈服する kuppuku suru = to surrender DESCRIPTION: on the left, 月 tsuki (moon, # 148); on the right, a dressing room, with a hook for hanging clothes; inside the dressing room, 又 mata ("again," # 24), but this resembles a simple dressing table CUE: I will try on some 洋服 you**fuku** (Western clothes) by the light of this 月 (moon) in **Fuku**oka, near this 又 (table), in this dressing room with this clothes hook GROUP: (洋)服 youfuku = Western clothes, # 150; 報(告) houkoku = report, # 386

0151. 育 PRONUNCIATIONS: **soda, iku, haguku** MEANING: to bring up or raise a child EXAMPLES: 育てる sodateru = to raise; 教育 kyouiku = education; 育む hagukumu = to nourish, nurture DESCRIPTION: at the top, a tire stop, as seen in 対(して) taishite (against, # 674); in the middle, the katakana ム mu, which is the sound made by a cow; at the bottom, 月 tsuki (moon, # 148) CUES: this ム (cow) under a tire stop sits on this 月 (moon), thinking that giving **S**oda is bad when one 育てる **soda**teru (raises) a child, and that a child's 教育 kyou**iku** (education) should be mostly about **E**ar **C**ooties and how to **H**atch a **G**oose in a **C**oop ALSO COMPARE: other similar kanji at # **616** and # **1125**

0152. 背 **PRONUNCIATIONS: hai, se, sei, somu MEANINGS:** back, height **EXAMPLES:** 背景 haikei = background, setting; 背が高い se ga takai = the height is tall; 背中 senaka = the back of the body; 背 sei = height; 背く somuku = to rebel against, disobey **DESCRIPTION:** at the top, 北 kita (north, # 373), which can be seen as a vertical bench next to a ヒ (hero), but 北 can also be seen as two people sitting back-to-back, comparing their sitting heights; at the bottom 月 tsuki (moon, # 148) **CUES:** in a **H**igh place on the 北 (north) side of this 月 (moon), these two **S**ecretaries sit back-to-back, and they are the **S**ame 背 **sei** (height) which they find **S**o **M**oving **ALSO COMPARE:** other similar kanji at # **1991** and # **2048**

0153. 胃 **PRONUNCIATION: i**

MEANING: stomach **EXAMPLES:** 胃 i = stomach; 胃癌 igan = stomach cancer **DESCRIPTION:** at the top, 田 (rice paddy, # 68); at the bottom, 月 tsuki (moon, # 148) **CUE:** during the **E**vening, a man in this 田 (rice paddy) rubs his 胃 **i** (stomach) while gazing at this 月 (moon) **COMPARE:** other similar kanji at # **220** and # **2087**

0154. 明 **PRONUNCIATIONS: aka, *ashi*, aki, ake, a, mei, min, myou MEANINGS:** bright, obvious, tomorrow **EXAMPLES:** 明るい akarui = bright, cheerful; 明日 ashita = tomorrow; 明らかな akiraka na = obvious; 有明 ariake = dawn; 明日 asu = tomorrow; 明後日 asatte = the day after tomorrow, usually written あさって; 明ける akeru = to end or expire, or to start; 説明 setsumei = explanation; 鮮明 senmei = bright, vivid, clear; 明朝体 minchoutai = Ming dynasty, or Ming-style font; 明日 myounichi = tomorrow; 明後日 myougonichi = the day after tomorrow; **Note:** ashita, asu and myounichi are all written 明日, and they all have the same meaning; *also*, asatte and myougonichi are both written 明後日 and have the same meaning **DESCRIPTION:** on the left, 日 hi (day, or sun, # 32); on the right, 月 tsuki (moon, # 148) **CUES:** when this 日 (sun) and this 月 (moon) shine together, the sky is 明るい **aka**rui (bright), and we can expect someone to come to the **Aca**demy 明日 **ashi**ta (tomorrow) and give an **A**shy ashtray, **A K**ey, **A K**ettle and some **A**nchovies to **M**ay, our **M**ean cat, who will **M**eow in response **GROUP:** 晴(れる) hareru = to clear up, # 37; 明(るい) akarui = bright, # 154; 朝 asa = morning, # 291; 腸 chou = intestine, # 1497; (同)盟 doumei = an alliance, # 1513 (identical pronunciation); 萌(える) moeru = to sprout, # 2087

0155. 青 **PRONUNCIATIONS: ao, sei, *sao* MEANINGS:** blue, fresh **EXAMPLES:** 青い aoi = blue; 青年 seinen = young man; 真っ青な massao na = deep blue, ghastly pale **DESCRIPTION:** at the top, compared to 土 tsuchi (soil, # 59), this radical has an extra horizontal line, where an owl might perch, so let's call this an owl's perch; at the bottom, 月 tsuki (moon, # 148) **CUES:** an **O**wl sitting on this perch on top of this 月 (moon) sees an 青い **ao**i (blue) sky and feels **S**afe but still makes a **S**our face **COMPARE:** other similar kanji at # **1112**

0156. 情 **PRONUNCIATIONS: nasa, jou MEANINGS:** emotion, feelings **EXAMPLES:** 情けない nasakenai = disappointing, regrettable; 愛情 aijou = love **DESCRIPTION:** compared to 青(い) aoi (blue, # 155), this kanji adds an erect person on the left; it retains the owl's perch on the 月 (moon) **CUES: NASA** sent **Joan**, this astronaut on the left, some 情けない **nasa**kenai (regrettable) instructions, ordering her to repair this owl's perch on this 月 (moon), but she

drew herself up to her full height like this and refused
COMPARE: similar kanji at # **1112** and # **2063**

0157. 前 PRONUNCIATIONS: mae, zen
MEANINGS: front, before **EXAMPLES:** 二年前 ninen mae = two years ago; 駅前 eki mae = in front of the station; 午前九時 gozen kuji = 9:00 a.m. **DESCRIPTION:** on the top, an upside-down bench, with its legs sticking up; on the lower left, 月 tsuki (moon, # 148); on the lower right, the katakana character リ Ri, who is a maestro **CUES:** this 月 (moon) and this リ Ri, who is a **Mae**stro, are carrying this bench to a **Zen** temple, but the 月 is standing 前 **mae** (in front of) リ and will get to the temple 前 **mae** (before) リ **GROUP:** 前 mae = before, # 157; 揃(う) sorou = to assemble, # 644; 煎(じる) senjiru = to boil, # 650 **ALSO COMPARE:** other similar kanji at # **1236**

0158. 消 PRONUNCIATIONS: ke, ki, shou
MEANINGS: to disappear, to erase **EXAMPLES:** 消す kesu = to erase, turn off, extinguish, wipe out; 消える kieru = to go out (referring to, e.g., a fire); 消化 shouka = digestion (food and information); 消防署 shoubousho = firehouse **DESCRIPTION:** on the left, a water radical (see # 12); at the upper right, a three-pronged switch (not on a roof); at the lower right, 月 tsuki (moon, # 148) **CUES: Ke**vin Costner lives on this 月 (moon), where there is this three-pronged switch that can 消し **ke**su (turn off) the flow of this water to his enemies, who live in **Ki**ev, where they have good **Shou**s **COMPARE:** other similar kanji at # **1625** and # **1991**

0159. 散 PRONUNCIATIONS: chi, san
MEANING: to disperse **EXAMPLES:** 散る chiru = to disperse or scatter; 散歩 sanpo = a walk **DESCRIPTION:** at the upper left, a plant radical (see # 43); at the lower left, 月 tsuki (moon, # 148); on the right, a dancer with a ponytail **CUES:** as this **Ch**eerful dancer takes a 散歩 **san**po (walk) in the **San**d, she imagines growing these plants on this 月 (moon)
COMPARE: 落ちる ochiru = to fall, # 526; other similar kanji at # **526** and # **2087**

Evening

0160. 夕 PRONUNCIATION: yuu
MEANING: evening **EXAMPLES:** 夕方 yuugata = evening; 夕べ yuube = last night **DESCRIPTION:** this is a half 月 tsuki (moon, # 148) shining in the Yukon **CUE:** this 夕 (half moon) shines above the **Yu**kon during the 夕方 **yuu**gata (evening) **ALSO COMPARE:** the katakana 夕 ta; other similar kanji at # **801**

0161. 多 PRONUNCIATIONS: oo, ta
MEANING: many **EXAMPLES:** 多い ooi = a lot; 多分 tabun = probably **DESCRIPTION:** two 夕 yuu (half moons, # 160) **CUES:** 多い **oo**i (many) 夕 (half moons) like these are **O**rbiting Jupiter, and I saw them on my **T**ablet computer
ALSO COMPARE: other similar kanji at # **801** and # **352**

0162. 名 PRONUNCIATIONS: na, mei, myou
MEANING: name **EXAMPLES:** 名前 namae = name; 有名 yuumei = famous; 名字 myouji = family name **DESCRIPTION:** on the upper left, 夕 yuu (half moon, # 160); on the lower right, kuchi (mouth, # 426), which resembles a card with names written on it
CUES: Napoleon's **Ma**id went into a **Mee**ting in **Yo**semite, wrote her 名前 **na**mae (name) on this 口 (card) and hung it from this 有名 yuu**mei** (famous) 夕 (half moon) **GROUP:** (有)名 yuumei = famous, # 162; (感)銘 kanmei = a deep impression, # 1666 (identical pronunciation)

0163. 外 PRONUNCIATIONS: **so**to, **ho**ka, **ha**zu, **ga**i, **ge** MEANING: outside EXAMPLES: 外 soto = outside; 外に hoka ni = besides, in addition; 外す hazusu = to remove; 外人 gaijin = foreigner; 外科 geka = surgery (medical specialty) Note: both soto and hoka are written 外 DESCRIPTION: on the left, 夕 yuu (evening, # 160); on the right, a radical that resembles the katakana character ト to, which reminds us of tomatoes CUES: in order to get these ト (tomatoes) during this 夕 (evening), Justice **So**tomayor has to go 外 **so**to (outside) the **H**ockey **A**rena near the **Ha**waiian **Zo**o and find a **Gu**ide, who keeps a **Ge**cko ALSO COMPARE: 他(の) hoka no = another (undefined) object, # 505; other similar kanji at # __801__ and # __1826__

0164. 死 PRONUNCIATIONS: **shi**, **ji** MEANINGS: to die, death EXAMPLES: 死ぬ shinu = to die; 死亡 shibou = death; 早死に hayajini = early death, dying young DESCRIPTION: at the top, a horizontal line which could be a sheet; on the left, 夕 yuu (evening, # 160); on the right, the katakana character ヒ hi, which reminds us of a hero CUES: if this ヒ (hero) 死ぬ **shi**nu (dies) during this 夕 (evening), they will put his body under this **Sh**eet and carry it off in a **Je**ep GROUP: 死(ぬ) shinu = to die, # 164; 残(念) zannen = regrettable, # 605; 列 retsu = line, # 1124; 葬(式) soushiki = funeral, # 1273; 例 rei = example, # 1317; (繁)殖 hanshoku = proliferation, # 1396; (分)裂 bunretsu = division, # 1465; (猛)烈 mouretsu = fierce, # 1610; (特)殊 tokushu = unique, # 1675 ALSO COMPARE: other similar kanji at # __2048__

0165. 夢 PRONUNCIATIONS: **yu**me, **mu** MEANING: dream EXAMPLES: 夢 yume = dream; 悪夢 akumu = nightmare DESCRIPTION: at the top, a plant radical (see # 43); in the middle, three eyes on a platform; at the bottom, 夕 yuu (evening, # 160), which resembles a half 月 (moon) CUES: in my 夢 **yu**me (dreams), I have three eyes on a platform like this, and **You**thful **M**ermaids eat plants like this in the light of this 夕 (half **M**oon) COMPARE: other similar kanji at # __801__ and # __1603__

Master

0166. 主 PRONUNCIATIONS: **shu**, **omo**, **nushi**, **zu** MEANINGS: lord, master, proprietor, main EXAMPLES: 主人 shujin = husband, master, landlord, landlady, proprietor, host or hostess; 主婦 shufu = housewife; 主な omo na = main, chief; 地主 jinushi = land owner; 坊主 bouzu = Buddhist monk DESCRIPTION: compared to 王 ou (king, # 1077), this adds a tiny cap at the top CUES: since this 主人 **shu**jin (master) is not a 王 (king), he wears this tiny cap instead of a crown, but he has good **Sh**oes, he uses an **O**ld **Mo**bile phone, and he likes to visit **N**ew **Sh**eep at the **Zo**o GROUP: 主(人) shujin = husband, # 166; 住(む) sumu = to reside, # 167; 注(ぐ) sosogu = to pour, # 168; 駐(車する) chuusha suru = to park, # 381; 電柱 denchuu = telephone pole, # 1225; 往(来) ourai = traffic, # 1416 ALSO COMPARE: other similar kanji at # __1077__ and # __1876__

0167. 住 PRONUNCIATIONS: **juu**, **su** MEANING: to reside EXAMPLES: 住所 juusho = address; 住む sumu = to reside DESCRIPTION: compared to 主(人) shujin (master, # 166), this adds a man with a slanted hat on the left CUES: this man on the left, who drinks a lot of **Ju**ice and graduated **Su**mma cum laude, tilts his hat back to gaze at this 主 (master) outside a house where they both 住む **su**mu (reside) ALSO COMPARE: (主)任 shunin = foreman, # 483; other similar kanji at # __166__

0168. 注 **PRONUNCIATIONS:** chuu, soso **MEANINGS:** to pour carefully, to pay attention **EXAMPLES:** 注文する chuumon suru = to order; 注意する chuui suru = to warn; 注ぐ sosogu = to pour **DESCRIPTION:** compared to 主 shu (master, # 166), this add a water radical (see # 12) on the left **CUES:** while **Chew**ing gum, this 主 (master) 注ぐ **soso**gu (pours) this water and often spills it, which is why the carpet's condition is only **So-So**, and therefore 注意してください **chuu**i shite kudasai (please be careful) **ALSO COMPARE:** other similar kanji at # **166**

0169. 玉 **PRONUNCIATIONS:** dama, tama, gyoku **MEANINGS:** a round object, a jewel **EXAMPLES:** 10円玉 juuen dama = ten-yen coin; 玉 tama = ball, jewel; 玉ねぎ tamanegi = onion; 玉座 gyokuza = throne **DESCRIPTION:** compared to 王 ou (king, # 1077), this adds an object on the lower right, which may represent a tamale, or perhaps a ball **CUES:** 王 (kings) like this one from **Dama**scus who like **Tama**les like this one on the lower right sometimes pay for them with 玉 **tama** (jewels), but other Syrians prefer to eat **Gyo**za with **Ko**ol-Aid **ALSO COMPARE:** other similar kanji at # **170** and # **1077**

0170. 国 **PRONUNCIATIONS:** kuni, koku, goku, ko **MEANING:** country **EXAMPLES:** 国 kuni = country; 韓国 kankoku = South Korea; 中国 chuugoku = China; 国会 kokkai = Diet **DESCRIPTION:** a 玉 tama (jewel or ball, # 169), which resembles a ball next to a 王 (king), inside a box **CUES:** my 国 **kuni** (country) is like this 玉 (jewel) in a box, and it's full of **Cun**ning people who drink a lot of **Co**ke and **Go**ld **Ko**ol-Aid, and dig up a lot of **Co**al **GROUP:** 玉 tama = ball, # 169; 国 kuni = country, # 170; 宝 takara = treasure, # 1292; (完)璧(な) kanpeki na = perfect, # 1933 **ALSO COMPARE:** other similar kanji at # **1360**

Above & Below

0171. 上 **PRONUNCIATIONS:** a, kami, jou, nobo, u, ue, uwa **MEANINGS:** up, above, to raise, to give **EXAMPLES:** 上げる ageru = to give, or to raise something up; 川上 kawakami = upriver; 上手 jouzu = skillful; 上る noboru = to go up; 上手い umai = skillful, delicious (usually written うまい); 上 ue = up; 上着 uwagi = outer garment **DESCRIPTION:** compared to 土 tsuchi (soil, # 59), 上 is asymmetrical and looks like a stick planted in the ground; it also resembles a taser, as seen in (予)定 yotei (plan, # 455) **CUES:** when we saw that this stick 上っていた **nobo**tte ita (was rising) asymmetrically from the surface, we **A**sked some **Commie**s (communists) if **Jo**an of Arc might have inserted it in the ground, but **Nobo**dy thought so, since she is just an **U**gandan **Ueitaa** (waiter) who lives in an **U**ber **Wag**on **ALSO COMPARE:** 登(る) noboru = to climb, # 297; 下 shita = below, # 172; 止(める) tomeru = to stop, transitive, # 173; other similar kanji at # **172** and # **1673**

0172. 下 **PRONUNCIATIONS: ka, kuda, ge, *he*, moto, o, sa, shimo, shita**
MEANINGS: down, below, to hang down, to lower
EXAMPLES: 地下鉄 chikatetsu = subway; 下る kudaru = to descend; 下さる kudasaru = to give to me; 下品な gehin na = vulgar; 下手 heta = unskillful; 足下 ashimoto = underfoot; 下ろす orosu = to withdraw money; 下がる sagaru = to hang (intransitive), to step back, or go down; 下げる sageru = to lower or to hang down (transitive); 川下 kawashimo = downstream; 下着 shitagi = undergarment
DESCRIPTION: compared to 不 fu (negation, # 176), 下 descends into the ground asymetrically
CUES: this tool for digging **C**abbages from the ground 下 **shita** (below) was designed by a **C**ool **D**ad who works at the **G**etty **M**useum, flies a **H**elicopter, rides a **M**otorcycle, swims in the **O**cean, plays the **S**axophone, eats **S**heets of **M**olasses and is good at **S**heep **T**alk
GROUP: 上 ue = above, # 171; 下 shita = below, # 172; 不(便) fuben = inconvenient, # 176; (一)杯 ippai = one cup, # 848; (安)否 anpi = safety, # 1329; 峠 touge = a mountain pass, # 1802

0173. 止 **PRONUNCIATIONS: to, ya, shi, do MEANING:** to stop **EXAMPLES:** 止まる tomaru = to stop, intransitive; 止める tomeru = to stop, transitive; 止める yameru = to stop doing something, to give up; 中止する chuushi suru = to cancel; 通行止め tsuukoudome = road closed; **Note:** tomeru and yameru are both written 止める **DESCRIPTION:** this resembles a barrier built to keep traffic out of a farm; it can be seen as containing a taser, as seen in 点(く) tsuku (to ignite, # 29) **CUES:** we put up this barrier so that cars will 止まる **to**maru (stop) before they run into our **T**omato and **Y**am farm, but **S**heep can enter through the side **D**oor
GROUP: 止(める) tomeru = to stop, # 173; 正

(しい) tadashii = correct,# 174 **ALSO COMPARE:** other similar kanji at # **1929**

0174. 正 **PRONUNCIATIONS: tada, shou, sei, masa MEANING:** correct
EXAMPLES: 正しい tadashii = correct; 正直な shoujiki na = honest; 正確 seikaku = precise, accurate; 正夢 masayume = a dream come true
DESCRIPTION: 止(まる) tomaru (to stop, # 173), with a cap added at the top **CUES:** if a car 止 (stops) and everything is 正しい **tada**shii (correct), a **T**axi **D**arts up, and the driver places this cap on top of this 止 (barrier), **Show**ing that it is **S**afe for the car to proceed to the **M**assage parlor **ALSO COMPARE:** other similar kanji at # **1150**

0175. 政 **PRONUNCIATION: sei**
MEANINGS: politics, government
EXAMPLES: 政治 seiji = politics, government; 政治家 seijika = politician **DESCRIPTION:** on the left, 正(しい) tadashii (correct, # 174); on the right, a dancer with a ponytail
CUE: 政治家 **sei**jika (politicans) should pass 正 (correct) laws to ensure that dancers like this can find **S**afe places to practice
GROUP: 政(治) seiji = politics, # 175; 整(う) totonou = to be ready, # 1247
ALSO COMPARE: other similar kanji at # **1150**

0176. 不 **PRONUNCIATIONS: bu, fu**
MEANING: negation **EXAMPLES:** 運動不足 undoubusoku = not enough exercise; 不便 fuben = inconvenient; 不足 fusoku = insufficiency **DESCRIPTION:** at the top, a horizontal line; below that, three descending lines; compared to 下 shita (below, # 172), 不 descends into the ground symmetrically, like a carrot divided into three parts **CUES:** digging in soil with my **B**oot, I encounter this symmetrical three-part carrot, but it's 不足 **fu**soku (insufficient) as a **F**ood source
GROUP: 不(便) fuben = inconvenient, # 176; (一)杯 ippai = one cup, # 848; (安)否 anpi = safety, # 1329 **ALSO COMPARE:** other similar kanji at # **172**

Knee

0177. 年 **PRONUNCIATIONS: nen, toshi**
MEANING: year **EXAMPLES:** 三年 sannen = three years; 今年 kotoshi = this year
DESCRIPTION: at the top, a crutch; below that, a vertical pole, attached to a knee that is protruding to the left **CUES:** my **N**egative **N**ephew has been sitting here, with this knee protruding to the left, for a 年 **nen** (year), holding this crutch, playing with his **Toy Sh**eep and waiting for help
ALSO COMPARE: 午(後) gogo = afternoon, # 207; other similar kanji at # **1808** and # **2080**

0178. 降 **PRONUNCIATIONS: o, fu, kou, bu** **MEANINGS:** to precipitate, to step down
EXAMPLES: 降りる oriru = to get off a train, etc.; 降る furu = to rain or snow; 下降 kakou = descent; 小降り koburi = light rain
DESCRIPTION: on the left, ß beta, a character from the Greek alphabet; on the upper right, a dancer with a ponytail; on the lower right, a character similar to 年 nen (year, # 177), sitting facing left, with a knee protruding **CUES:** after a trip across the **O**cean, this ß (Greek) guy and this dancer with a ponytail rush to 降りる **o**riru (get off) their ship, such that she leaps over this knee belonging to a seated person on the dock; they both buy **F**ood, the dancer buys some **C**ola, and the Greek guy buys **Boo**ze
ALSO COMPARE: other similar kanji at # **1808** and # **2030**

0179. 五 **PRONUNCIATIONS: go, itsu**
MEANING: five **EXAMPLES:** 五人 gonin = five people; 五つ itsutsu = five items
DESCRIPTION: unlike 年 nen (year, # 177) and 降(る) furu (to precipitate, # 178), the knee in 五 faces to the right; 五 contains five straight lines; it resembles a golfer staring down a fairway
CUES: 五 **go** (five) **G**olfers **E**at **Su**shi as they stare like this down a fairway
GROUP: 五 go = five, # 179; (英)語 eigo = English, # 435 (identical pronunciation); 互(い に) tagai ni = mutually, # 1207; (覚)悟 kakugo = preparedness, # 1526 (also identical pronunciation); 瓦 kawara = a roof tile, # 1710; 瓶 bin = a bottle, # 1711 **ALSO COMPARE:** other kanji containing radicals resembling 五 at # 1174

0180. 決 **PRONUNCIATIONS: ki, ketsu, ke** **MEANINGS:** to decide, to do decisively
EXAMPLES: 決める kimeru = to decide or arrange; 決まる kimaru = to be decided or arranged; 解決 kaiketsu = settlement, resolution, solution; 決して kesshite = never
DESCRIPTION: on the left, a water radical (see # 12); on the right, compared to the left-facing knees in 年 nen (year, # 177) and 降(る) furu (to precipitate, # 178), this knee is facing right and is mounted on a stand, resembling a tiller for steering a boat, but compared to (中)央 chuu'ou (center, # 1063), it has damage to its left eye and can be seen as a single eye on a stand **CUES:** a pilot moves this tiller when he 決める **ki**meru (decides) to turn his boat in this water and, while eating **Qui**che, he pours tea from a **Ke**ttle into his **S**oup, spilling some onto his **K**eds (a brand of shoes)
GROUP: 決(める) kimeru = to decide, # 180; 快(い) kokoroyoi = pleasant, # 734 **ALSO COMPARE:** other similar kanji at # **1808**

0181. 片 **PRONUNCIATIONS: kata, pen, hen** **MEANINGS:** one side, piece **EXAMPLES:** 片方 katahou = one side, the other side, one of a pair; 片付ける katazukeru = to put in order; 一片 ippen = a slice or piece; 破片 hahen = shard, fragment **DESCRIPTION:** a person kneeling, holding a tray with an object on it **CUES:** this person, who is kneeling on one knee, holds out this tray with this **Cat**alogue of **Pen**s on it, but a **Hen** that is watching can only see 片方 **kata**hou (one side) of it **GROUP:** (一)片 ippen = a slice, # 181; (出)版 shuppan = publication, # 1086

Child

0182. 子 PRONUNCIATIONS: su, ko, go², shi, ji MEANING: child EXAMPLES: 様子 yousu = condition; 子供 kodomo = child; 迷子 maigo = a lost person; 男子 danshi = boy; 王子 ouji = prince DESCRIPTION: a modified katakana マ ma (which reminds us of mother) above a thin child with arms CUES: this thin 子 **ko** (child) from **Su**dan loves this マ (mother), and when he gets **C**old at night, he sleeps under a **S**heepskin in a **J**eep COMPARE: 字 ji = character, # 183 (identical pronunciation); 了(承) ryoushou = understanding, # 760; other similar kanji at # **2078**

0183. 字 PRONUNCIATION: ji MEANING: character EXAMPLE: 漢字 kanji = kanji DESCRIPTION: compared to (王)子 ouji (prince, # 182) (identical pronunciation), this kanji adds a bad haircut at the top CUE: this 子 (child) has this bad haircut, but he writes excellent 字 **ji**i (characters), and we are giving him a **J**eep ALSO COMPARE: other similar kanji at # **2078**

0184. 学 PRONUNCIATIONS: ga, mana, gaku MEANINGS: study, learning, science EXAMPLES: 学校 gakkou = school; 学ぶ manabu = to learn; 学のある人 gaku no aru hito = a learned person DESCRIPTION: compared to 覚(える) oboeru (to memorize, # 54), this substitutes 子 ko (child, # 182) for 見 (to look) at the bottom; it retains the three old boys on a roof CUES: this 子 (child) attends a 学校 **ga**k**k**ou (school) with a **G**arden, and these three old boys on this roof **Ma**nage his education, allotting him a **G**allon of **K**ool-Aid every week ALSO COMPARE: 字 ji = character, # 183; other similar kanji at # **991** and # **2078**

0185. 厚 PRONUNCIATIONS: atsu, kou MEANING: thick EXAMPLES: 厚い atsui = thick; 濃厚 noukou = density, concentration DESCRIPTION: on the left, a one-sided lean-to belonging to Superman; under the lean-to, 日 hi (sun, # 32), which looks like a heavy weight resting on 子 ko (child, # 182) CUES: this poor 子 (child) is getting crushed under this heavy 日 (weight) in this lean-to At **Su**perman's house, and he will likely become somewhat 厚い **atsu**i (thick, i.e., wide) as a result, but he will just have to **C**ope with that COMPARE: other similar kanji at # **2078**

0186. 乳 PRONUNCIATIONS: nyuu, chichi, u, chi MEANING: milk EXAMPLES: 牛乳 gyuunyuu = cow's milk; 乳 chichi = milk; 乳母 uba = wet nurse; 乳首 chikubi = nipple DESCRIPTION: on the upper left, a barbecue grate; on the lower left, a 子 ko (child, # 182); on the right, an L, which resembles a breast CUES: this 子 (child) at this mother's breast is staying warm near this barbecue grate and drinking 乳 **chichi** (milk) in **Nyuu**yooku (New York), while **Chichi** (my father) looks on and eats **U**ber crackers and **Ch**eese COMPARE: other similar kanji at # **671** and **735**

0187. 教 PRONUNCIATIONS: oshi, kyou, oso MEANING: to teach EXAMPLES: 教える oshieru = to teach; 教室 kyoushitsu = classroom; 教わる osowaru = to be taught DESCRIPTION: this is a situation that concerns OSHA (the Occupational Safety and Health Administration): on the upper left, 土 tsuchi (soil, # 59); below that, a pair of scissors; below the scissors, 子 ko (child, # 182); on the right, a dancer with a ponytail CUES: OSHA Informs and 教える **oshi**eru (teaches) this 子 (child) and this dancer in **Kyou**to that they should stay out of this 土 (soil), not play with these scisssors and not eat **O**ld **So**y sauce GROUP: this is a group of one COMPARE: other similar kanji at # **1471**

Big

0188. 大 PRONUNCIATIONS: tai, oo, dai, *oto, yama* MEANING: big EXAMPLES: 大変 taihen = terrible; 大きい ookii = big; 大学 daigaku = university; 大人 otona = adult; 大和 yamato = ancient Japan DESCRIPTION: compared to 人 hito (person, # 13), this kanji has arms and appears to be expanding in all directions CUES: this 大きい **oo**kii (big) 人 (person) is **T**ired and **O**verweight, and he lives on a **D**iet of **O**rganic **T**omatoes near a **Y**ama (mountain) GROUP: 大(きい) ookii = big, # 188; 天 ten = sky, # 189; 犬 inu = dog, # 190; 太る futoru = to get fat, # 191; 夫 otto = husband, # 614 **ALSO COMPARE**: other similar kanji at # 13

0189. 天 PRONUNCIATIONS: ama, ten MEANINGS: sky, heavens EXAMPLES: 天の川 ama no gawa = Milky Way; 天国 tengoku = heaven; 天気 tenki = weather DESCRIPTION: compared to 大(きい) ookii (big, # 188), this has a horizontal line above it, which reminds us of a tent CUES: in the Am**a**zon, the 天 **ama** (sky) is like this **T**ent over a 大 (big) forest ALSO COMPARE: other similar kanji at # **188**, # **614** and # **1811**

0190. 犬 PRONUNCIATIONS: inu, ken MEANING: dog EXAMPLES: 犬 inu = dog; 番犬 banken = watchdog DESCRIPTION: compared to 大(きい) ookii (big, # 188), this adds a ball above the kanji's right arm CUES: this 犬 **inu** (dog), which is 大 (big) and belongs to the **In**uit tribe, chases this ball that **Ken** threw to Barbie ALSO COMPARE: other similar kanji at # **188** and # **945**

0191. 太 PRONUNCIATIONS: futo, buto², tai, ta MEANINGS: to get fat, big, thick EXAMPLES: 太る futoru = to get fat; 小太り kobutori = plump; 太陽 taiyou = the sun; 太郎 tarou = a boy's given name DESCRIPTION: compared to 大(きい) ookii (big, # 188), this adds a ball near the kanji's left leg CUES: this 大 (big) person 太る **futo**ru (gets fat) to the point that he has to sleep on a **F**uton, he can only chase balls like this near the floor, he **T**ires easily, and he worries about the **Tar** in his cigarettes GROUP: 太(る) futoru = to get fat, # 191; (無)駄 muda = useless, wasteful, # 628; (ご無沙)汰 gobusata = a long silence, # 1613 (identical pronunciation) ALSO COMPARE: other similar kanji at # **188**

0192. 喫 PRONUNCIATIONS: ki, kitsu MEANING: to consume or smoke EXAMPLES: 喫茶店 kissaten = coffee house; 喫煙 kitsuen = smoking DESCRIPTION: at the top left, 口 kuchi (mouth, # 426), suggesting smoking; in the upper center, an owl's perch, as seen in 青(い) aoi (blue, # 155); on the upper right, 刀 katana (sword, # 102); at the bottom, 大(きい) ookii (big, # 188) CUES: this 大 (big) guy juggles this owl's perch and this 刀 (sword) while using this 口 (mouth) to smoke cigarettes that he made in **Ki**ev, using a **Kit** that he got from **S**uperman, and he often smokes them at a 喫茶店 **ki**ssaten (coffee shop) ALSO COMPARE: other similar kanji at # **1103**, # **2062** and # **2073**

0193. 咲 PRONUNCIATIONS: za, sa MEANING: to blossom or bloom EXAMPLES: 早咲き hayazaki = early blooming; 咲く saku = to blossom DESCRIPTION: on the left, 口 kuchi (mouth, # 426); on the right, an occultist, as seen in 送(る) okuru (to send, # 348), who wears a hat with two antennae CUES: this occultist, who wears this hat with two antennae, uses this 口 (mouth) to ask **Za**chory to harvest some flowers that have 咲いた **sa**ita (blossomed) and put them in our **S**alads ALSO COMPARE: similar kanji at # **348**, # **1811** and # **2073**

0194. 狭 **PRONUNCIATIONS: sema, kyou, seba MEANING:** narrow **EXAMPLES:** 狭い semai = narrow, cramped; 狭小 kyoushou = cramped, narrow, confined; 狭める sebameru = to narrow or reduce **DESCRIPTION:** on the left, a woman contorting her body; on the right, an 夫 otto (husband, # 614), who is a 人 hito (person, # 13) with two pairs of arms; in addition, flames are shooting out from between those arms on both sides **CUES:** inside a 狭い **sema**i (narrow) aisle in a **Se**cluded **Ma**rket in **Kyou**to, this lady on the left contorts her body to squeeze past this 夫 (husband) on the right, who **Se**lls **Bar**bed wire and is surrounded by these flames **GROUP:** 狭(い) semai = narrow, # 194; 頬 hoo = cheek, # 890; 挟(む) hasamu = to pinch, # 1009; 峡(谷) kyoukoku = a canyon, # 1818 (identical pronunciation) **ALSO COMPARE:** 券 ken (ticket, # 1305), where the flames in the bonfire at the top are *above* the two pairs of arms on a 人 (person); other similar kanji at # **948**

0195. 実 **PRONUNCIATIONS: jitsu, ji, mi, mino MEANINGS:** real, fruit **EXAMPLES:** 実は jitsu wa = as a matter of fact; 実行 jikkou = practice, action, deed, implementation; 木の実 kinomi = nut, fruit, berry; 実る minoru = to bear fruit or ripen **DESCRIPTION:** at the top, a bad haircut; at the bottom, 夫 otto (husband, # 614), plus an extra pair of arms, for a total of three pairs **CUES:** this 夫 (husband) with an extra pair of arms is a **Ji**ttery **S**uperstar with this bad haircut and a **Jee**p who raises 実の **jitsu** no (real) 木の実 kino**mi** (nuts) and has **M**eals with **Mino**taurs **ALSO COMPARE:** other similar kanji at # **333**

0196. 険 **PRONUNCIATIONS: kewa, ken MEANINGS:** steep, danger **EXAMPLES:** 険しい kewashii = steep; 危険 kiken = danger **DESCRIPTION:** on the left, ß from the Greek alphabet; at the top right, a steep roof; under the roof, 人 hito (person, # 13), which resembles a washing machine, intersected by a horizontal keg, with a handle at the top (this can also be seen as two eyes on a person with a flat cap) **CUES:** this horizontally-placed **K**eg is stuck in **W**ater inside this washing machine, and this roof is too 険しい **kewa**shii (steep) to allow this ß (Greek) guy named **Ken** to climb up, grab this handle and fix it **COMPARE:** similar kanji at # **1432** and # **2030**

0197. 漢 **PRONUNCIATION: kan MEANING:** Chinese **EXAMPLE:** 漢字 kanji = Chinese character **DESCRIPTION:** on the left, a water radical (see # 12); at the upper right, a plant radical (see # 43); at the middle right, a pair of reading glasses, which can also be seen as two eyes; at the bottom right, 夫 otto (husband, # 614), who is 大 (big) and has two pairs of arms **CUE:** Chinese 夫 (husbands) come from across this water, they are fond of these plants, they often wear glasses like these, they have 大 (big) ideas, and they print 漢字 **kan**ji (Chinese characters) on their **Can**dy wrappers **GROUP:** 漢(字) kanji = Chinese character, # 197; 難(しい) muzukashii = difficult, # 198; 嘆(く) nageku = to grieve, # 792 **ALSO COMPARE:** other similar kanji at # **258** and # 1915

0198. 難 **PRONUNCIATIONS: nan, muzuka, gato, gata, niku MEANING:** difficulty **EXAMPLES:** 困難 konnan = difficulty; 難しい muzukashii = difficult; 有難う arigatou = thank you; 有難い arigatai = grateful, usually written ありがたい; 難い nikui = difficult, used as a suffix, usually written にくい **DESCRIPTION:** compared to 漢 kan (Chinese, # 197), this omits the water radical on the left and adds a net, which can be seen as a man with a slanted hat next to a 主 (master) with three pairs of arms (see # 203); it retains the 夫 (husband) wearing glasses, who is fond of plants **CUES:** **N**ancy Pelosi's 夫 (husband is this 漢 (Chinese) person wearing these glasses who wants to assist some cats in this net, which is 難しい **muzuka**shii (difficult) to penetrate; he wants to **Muzz**le **Zu**ckerberg's **Cat**, which is inside the net, and help another **Gato** (male cat, in Spanish), a **Gata** (female cat, in Spanish), and his **Ni**ece from **Ku**wait **ALSO COMPARE:** other similar kanji at # **197** and # **2046**

0199. 笑 **PRONUNCIATIONS: wa**ra, **e**, **shou MEANINGS:** to smile or laugh **EXAMPLES:** 笑う warau = to laugh; 笑顔 egao = smiling face; 爆笑 bakushou = burst of laughter **DESCRIPTION:** at the top, compressed 竹 take (bamboo, # 134) which resemble clamps; at the bottom, 天 ten (sky, # 189) **CUES:** there was a **Warr**ant for my arrest, but I went out under this 天 (sky) and watched this 竹 (bamboo) blow in the wind, and it made such an **E**xcellent **Sh**ow that I had to 笑う **wara**u (laugh) **COMPARE:** similar kanji at # **1811** and # **2074**

Net
0200. 曜 **PRONUNCIATION: you**
MEANING: day of the week **EXAMPLE:** 日曜日 nichiyoubi = Sunday **DESCRIPTION:** on the left, a 日 hi (sun, # 32) shining in Yosemite; on the upper right, the katakana ヨ yo, repeated, suggesting feathers, which reminds us of a bird; on the lower right, a net, which can be seen as a man with a slanted hat next to a 主 (master) with three pairs of arms (see # 203) **CUE:** every 曜日 **you**bi (day of the week) in **Y**osemite, this 日 (sun) shines on this bird in this net **GROUP:** (火)曜(日) kayoubi = Friday, # 200; (洗)濯 sentaku = laundry, # 201; (活)躍 katsuyaku = activity, # 992
ALSO COMPARE: other similar kanji at # **352**; kanji with different kinds of feathers at # 1457

0201. 濯 **PRONUNCIATION: taku**
MEANINGS: laundry, wash **EXAMPLE:** 洗濯 sentaku = laundry **DESCRIPTION:** compared to 曜 you (day of the week, # 200), this substitutes a water radical (see # 12) for 日 (sun) on the left; it retains the feathers, suggesting a bird, and the net, which can be seen as a man with a slanted hat next to a 主 (master) with three pairs of arms (see # 203) **CUE:** using this **T**ap water and **Ko**ol-**A**id, we wash this bird in this net whenever we do the 洗濯

sen**tak**u (laundry) **ALSO COMPARE:** other similar kanji at # **200** and # **352**

0202. 集 **PRONUNCIATIONS: a**tsu, **shuu, tsudo MEANINGS:** to collect, gather, congregate **EXAMPLES:** 集まる atsumaru = to congregate, intransitive; 集合 shuugou = an assembly; 集う tsudou = to gather or meet **DESCRIPTION:** at the top, a net, which can be seen as a man with a slanted hat next to a 主 (master) with three pairs of arms (see # 203); at the bottom, 木 ki (tree, # 118) **CUES:** this net has been placed in this 木 (tree) to 集める **a**tsu**me**ru (collect) **A**tsui (hot) flying travelers, who travel without **Sh**oes and carry **Ts**uitcases (suitcases) full of **Do**ugh (money) **ALSO COMPARE:** other similar kanji at # **1352** and # **2046**

0203. 進 **PRONUNCIATIONS: su**su, susumu, shin, jin² **MEANING:** to move forward **EXAMPLES:** 進む susumu = to advance; 進 Susumu = a boy's given name; 進出する shinshutsu suru = to advance or expand; 精進料理 shoujinryouri = vegetarian cuisine, as eaten by Buddhist monks **DESCRIPTION:** at the lower left, a snail; at the upper right, riding on the snail, a net, which can also be seen as a man with a slanted hat standing to the left of a 主(人) shujin (master, # 166) with an extra pair of arms **CUES:** this net on this snail 進む **susu**mu (advances) slowly and collects **S**uperior **S**ouvenirs to benefit **S**uperman's **S**ummer **M**usic program at a **Shin**tou shrine **COMPARE:** 勧(める) susumeru = to advise, # 698; other similar kanji at # **2046**

0204. 準 **PRONUNCIATION: jun**
MEANINGS: standard, preparation **EXAMPLE:** 準備 junbi = preparation **DESCRIPTION:** at the upper left, a water radical (see # 12); at the upper right, a net, which can be seen as a man with a slanted hat next to a 主 (master) with an extra pair of arms (see # 203) and which resembles a fish trap; at the bottom 十 juu (ten, # 18) **CUE:** 十 (ten) fishermen are placing this fish trap in this water as 準備 **jun**bi (preparation) for **Jun**gle fishing **COMPARE:** similar kanji at # **1658** and # **2046**

Cow

0205. 牛 **PRONUNCIATIONS:** gyuu, ushi **MEANING:** cow **EXAMPLES:** 牛肉 gyuuniku = beef; 牛 ushi = cow **DESCRIPTION:** this is the front half of a cow, seen from above; at the top, the head; below that, the horns, with a bigger horn on the left; below them, the front legs and the anterior trunk of the body **CUES:** a **G**uatemalan **You**th, who is an **Us**her at an **I**ndian theatre, owns this 牛 <u>ushi</u> (cow) with one horn that is bigger than the other **GROUP:** 牛 ushi = cow, # 205; 午(後) gogo = afternoon, # 207; (先)生 sensei = teacher, # 208 **ALSO COMPARE:** kanji containing 牛 at # <u>304</u> and # <u>1765</u>

0206. 失 **PRONUNCIATIONS:** ushina, u, shitsu, shi **MEANINGS:** to lose; to slip away **EXAMPLES:** 失う ushinau = to lose; 失せる useru = to disappear; 失礼 shitsurei = discourtesy; 失業者 shitsugyousha = unemployed people; 失敗する shippai suru = to fail **DESCRIPTION:** a fusion between 牛 ushi (cow, # 205) and 大(きい) ookii (big, # 188) **CUES:** this 大 (big) 牛 (cow) is an **Us**hi (cow) from **N**arnia, and she is **u**ber in some ways, but she steps on our **Sh**eets, and she is 失礼 <u>shitsu</u>rei (rude) to our **Sh**eep **ALSO COMPARE:** other similar kanji at # <u>304</u> and # <u>614</u>

0207. 午 **PRONUNCIATION:** go **MEANING:** noon **EXAMPLES:** 午前 gozen = in the morning; 午後 gogo = in the afternoon **DESCRIPTION:** compared to 牛 ushi (cow, # 205), this cow is missing her head [or this can be seen as a crutch resting on 十 juu (ten, # 18)] **CUE:** this 牛 (cow) hides her head in the 午後 go**go** (afternoon), when the **G**olden sun shines brightest **GROUP:** 午 go = noon, # 207; 許(可) kyoka = permission, # 1141; 陶(器) touki = chinaware, # 1741; 鬱(病) utsubyou = depression, # 1783; 缶 kan = a tin can, # 1832 **ALSO COMPARE:** 年 nen = year, # 177; other similar kanji at # <u>205</u>, # <u>1658</u> and # <u>2080</u>

0208. 生 **PRONUNCIATIONS:** i, fu, ha, ba², ki, jou, nama, na, o, sei, shou, u, yoi **MEANINGS:** to be born, to live **EXAMPLES:** 生きる ikiru = to live; 芝生 shibafu = lawn; 生える haeru = to grow or sprout; 芽生え mebae = budding; 生地 kiji = material, cloth, texture; 誕生日 tanjoubi = birthday; 生 nama = raw; 生る naru = to bear fruit; 生い茂る oishigeru = to grow thickly; 先生 sensei = teacher; 一生 isshou = a lifetime; 生まれる umareru = to be born; 弥生時代 yayoi jidai = the Yayoi era **DESCRIPTION:** at the top, 牛 ushi (cow, # 205); at the bottom, a platform; compared to the owl's perch seen in 青(い) aoi (blue, # 155), this adds a cow's horn at the upper left **CUES:** after this 牛 (cow) 生まれる <u>u</u>mareru (is born), it stands on this platform and watches out for **E**agles and **F**oolish **H**ackers who might want to **K**ill it, including **J**oe **Nama**th, who is **N**asty and **O**ld, but they play it **S**afe when they go to **Sh**ows by taking **U**ber and sharing expenses with **Y**ogis from **I**ndia **ALSO COMPARE:** similar kanji at # 205 and # <u>1918</u>

0209. 性 **PRONUNCIATIONS:** saga, sei, shou **MEANINGS:** innate nature, sex, gender **EXAMPLES:** 性 saga = one's nature, or custom; 性 sei = gender; 男性 dansei = man, male; 女性 josei = woman, female; 相性 aishou = affinity, compatibility **DESCRIPTION:** compared to (先)生 sensei (teacher, # 208) (identical pronunciation), this kanji adds an erect radical, which could be a chromosome, on the left; it retains the 牛 (cow) standing on a platform **CUES: Saga**cious researchers stand straight and tall like this as they confidently **Say** that chromosomes like this one on the left determine the 性 <u>sei</u> (gender) of this 牛 (cow) on this platform, and they can **Sh**ow us these chromosomes under a microscope **ALSO COMPARE:** similar kanji at # <u>1918</u> and # <u>2063</u>

0210. 産 **PRONUNCIATIONS: san, u, ubu,** *yage* **MEANINGS:** to give birth, to produce **EXAMPLES:** 産業 sangyou = industry; 産む umu = to give birth, produce, lay an egg; 産着 ubugi = baby clothes; お土産 omiyage = souvenir **DESCRIPTION:** at the top, a bell resting on a one-sided lean-to, which is a sanitarium; inside the lean-to, 生(きる) ikiru (to live, # 208), which resembles a cow standing on a platform **CUES: San**ta keeps has this bell on the roof of this lean-to, which rings to announce that 牛 (cows) on platforms like this 生 (live) inside, and he supports a 産業 **sang**you (industry) that creates treatments for **O**ozing wounds caused by poorly fitting **U**gandan **B**oots, including **Y**am and **G**ekko-based ointments **ALSO COMPARE:** other similar kanji at # **1569** and # **1918**

Plants

0211. 花 **PRONUNCIATIONS: hana, bana², ka MEANING:** flower **EXAMPLES:** お花見 ohanami = honorable flower viewing; 生け花 ikebana = Japanese flower arrangement; 花粉 kafun = pollen **DESCRIPTION:** at the top, a plant radical (see # 43); at the bottom, 化(学) kagaku (chemistry, # 487) (identical pronunciation), which consists of a man with a slanted hat and the katakana ヒ hi and reminds us of a hero who packs things into cartons and his friend who watches **CUES:** this man at the lower left tilts his hat back to examine this ヒ (hero) who is packing **H**annah's 花 **hana** (flowers), which come from plants like these, into **C**artons **ALSO COMPARE:** other similar kanji at # **1413**

0212. 茶 **PRONUNCIATIONS: cha, sa MEANING:** tea **EXAMPLES:** お茶 ocha = honorable tea; 喫茶店 kissaten = cafe **DESCRIPTION:** at the top, a plant radical (see # 43); in the middle, a peaked roof; at the bottom, 十 juu (ten, # 18), flanked by diagonal lines; taken together, these resemble a symmetrical bush, growing in a small house **CUES: K**ing **C**harles' 茶 **cha** (tea) bushes grow in small houses like this and are symmetrical, since he **Sa**ws them back every year **COMPARE:** other similar kanji at # **1382** and # **1658**

Temple

0213. 寺 **PRONUNCIATIONS: tera, dera², ji MEANING:** temple **EXAMPLES:** 寺 tera = temple; 清水寺 Kiyomizudera = a temple in Kyoto; 寺院 jiin = temple **DESCRIPTION:** at the top, 土 tsuchi (soil, # 59); at the bottom, 寸(前) sunzen (on the verge, # 1369), which resembles a sunny kneeling guy who has dropped a piece of gum, but this resembles an asymmetrical structure with a terrace at the top, like a building that has been built into the side of a hill **CUES:** this 寺 **tera** (temple), which is built into the side of a hill, features a **Ter**race and a **Jee**p, but it is covered in this 土 (soil) **COMPARE:** 守(る) mamoru = to protect, # 214; other similar kanji at # **215**

0214. 守 **PRONUNCIATIONS: su, mori, mamo, shu MEANINGS:** to protect, guard or defend **EXAMPLES:** 留守 rusu = absence from a house; 子守 komori = nanny, baby sitter; 守る mamoru = to protect; 守備 shubi = defense, garrisoning **DESCRIPTION:** compared to 寺 tera (temple, # 213), this substitutes a bad haircut, which can also be seen as a roof, for the soil at the top; it retains 寸 (the building built into the side of a hill) which can also be seen as a sunny guy who has dropped his gum – see # 132 **CUES:** while the monks were 留守 r**usu** (absent), **S**uperman and **M**aureen removed the 土 (soil) from this 寺 (temple), added this roof which resembles a bad haircut, in order to 守る **mamo**ru (protect) it from falling **M**ammoths, and tied it down with **Sh**oelaces **GROUP:** 守(る) mamoru = to protect, # 214; 狩(り) kari = hunting, # 923

0215. 時 **PRONUNCIATIONS:** *to, ji, toki, doki*² **MEANING:** time **EXAMPLES:** 時計 tokei = clock, or watch; 時間 jikan = time; 時 toki = time; 開花時 kaikadoki = blossoming time **DESCRIPTION:** compared to 寺 tera (temple, # 213), this adds 日 hi (sun, # 32) on the left; it retains the soil on a temple with a terrace, built into the side of a hill [but this also resembles 寸 (a kneeling sunny guy, # 1369)] **CUES:** this 日 (sun) shines on this 寺 (temple), and the temple's sundial says the 時 **toki** (time) is 一時 ichi**ji** (1:00), when **To**lstoy comes in his **Jee**p and we go eat **To**mato Quiche **GROUP:** 寺 tera = temple, # 213; 時 toki = time, # 215; 持(つ) motsu = to hold, # 216; 待(つ) matsu = to wait, # 217; 特 (に) toku ni = especially, # 218; 侍 samurai, # 1118; (平)等 byoudou = equal, # 1132; 詩 shi = poem, # 1301

0216. 持 **PRONUNCIATIONS:** mo, ji **MEANINGS:** to hold or possess **EXAMPLES:** 持つ motsu = to hold or have; 支持する shiji suru = to support **DESCRIPTION:** compared to 寺 tera (temple, # 213), this adds a kneeling guy on the left [**Note**: this kneeling guy differs from the contorted woman seen in 猫 neko (cat, # 72); in addition to the relatively straight line characterizing the long vertical stroke in the radical on the left in 持, its two horizontal strokes are written from left to right] **CUES:** this guy on the left crawls up to this 寺 (temple) in the **Mo**rning, since his feet hurt from walking all night, asking whether they 持つ **mo**tsu (have) a **Jee**p that he can use **ALSO COMPARE:** other similar kanji at # **215**

0217. 待 **PRONUNCIATIONS:** ma, tai **MEANINGS:** to wait or handle **EXAMPLES:** 待つ matsu = to wait; 招待 shoutai = invitation **DESCRIPTION:** compared to 寺 tera (temple, # 213), this adds a man with two hats on the left **CUES:** this man with two hats 待 **ma**tsu (waits) at this 寺 (temple) and says that he just bought his second hat at the **Ma**ll and is **T**ired of shopping **ALSO COMPARE:** similar kanji at # **215**

0218. 特 **PRONUNCIATIONS:** to, toku **MEANINGS:** special, notable **EXAMPLES:** 特急 tokkyuu = limited express train; 特別な **toku**betsu na = special **DESCRIPTION:** compared to 寺 tera (temple, # 213), this adds 牛 ushi (cow, # 205) on the left **CUES:** this 特別な **toku**betsu na (special) 牛 (cow) on the left was given to this 寺 (temple) by **To**lstoy, and it is **To**tally **C**ool **ALSO COMPARE:** other similar kanji at # **215** and # **1765**

Skeet Shooter

0219. 糸 **PRONUNCIATIONS:** ito, shi **MEANING:** thread **EXAMPLES:** 糸 ito = thread, yarn; 糸目 itome = stitches; 金糸 kinshi = golden thread **DESCRIPTION:** at the top, two flexed elbows open to the right; the lower arm of the lower elbow has a shield at its right extreme tip; at the bottom, three legs; taken together, these resemble a gun mounted on platform with legs and remind us of a skeet shooter, also known as a skeet thrower, a machine that launches clay targets into the air for target practice (**Note**: the three legs that support 糸 are sometimes written as short parallel lines, or sometimes as a spinning nail – see the examples on page xiii) **CUES:** this skeet shooter with three legs has been repaired with 糸 **ito** (thread), and we use it to fire at the mosqu**I**tos that sting our **S**heep **GROUP:** this is a group of one

0220. 細 **PRONUNCIATIONS:** hoso, boso, koma, sai **MEANINGS:** slender, detail **EXAMPLES:** 細い hosoi = thin; 心細い kokorobosoi = downhearted; 細かい komakai = minute, small; 詳細 shousai = details **DESCRIPTION:** on the left, 糸 (skeet shooter, # 219), consisting of two flexed elbows above three legs; on the right, 田(んぼ) tanbo (rice paddy, # 68) **CUES:** a **Ho**me-schooled **S**oldier, who is just a **B**oy **S**oldier, and who is in a **Co**ma, is **S**ilent as this 糸 (skeet shooter) shoots at this 細い **hoso**i

(narrow) 田 (rice paddy) where he is hiding, leaving trails of smoke which are 細い **koma**kai (small)
GROUP: 田(んぼ) tanbo = rice paddy, # 68; (世)界 sekai = the world, # 70; 町 machi = town, # 70; 留(守) rusu = absence, # 71; 魚 sakana = fish, # 80; 男 otoko = male, # 109; 胃 i = stomach, # 153; 細(い) hosoi = thin, # 220; 思(う) omou = to think, # 308; 番(号) bangou = number, # 328; (興)奮 koufun = excitement, # 727; 鼻 hana = nose, # 795; 畳 tatami = a mat, # 876; 畑 hatake = field, # 889; 翼 tsubasa = a wing, # 912; 異(なる) kotonaru = to differ, # 970; 翻(訳) hon'yaku = translation, # 1087; (待)遇 taiguu = treatment, # 1120; 略 ryaku = abbreviation, # 1272; 審(議) shingi = scrutiny, # 1368; 藩(士) hanshi = a warrior, # 1537; 雷 kaminari = thunder, # 1723; 獣 kemono = an animal, # 1733; 畜(生) chikushou = a beast, # 1773; (貯)蓄 chochiku = savings, # 1774; (皮)膚 hifu = skin, # 1777; 塁 rui = a base, # 1853; (均)衡 kinkou = balance, # 1875; (湖)畔 kohan = a lakeshore, # 1988; 畏(敬) ikei = awe, # 1998; 累(積) ruiseki = an accumulation, # 2006; 堺 Sakai = a city, # 2083 **ALSO COMPARE:** other similar kanji at # **2006**

0221. 紙 PRONUNCIATIONS: kami, gami², shi MEANING: paper EXAMPLES: 紙 kami = paper; 折り紙 origami = Japanese paper-folding craft; 紙幣 shihei = paper money
DESCRIPTION: on the left, 糸 (skeet shooter, # 219); on the right, 氏 shi (mister, # 709) (identical pronunciation), which can also be seen as a pavilion with a flat roof, or as a leaning woman under a lean-to **CUES:** this 糸 (skeet shooter) is firing skeets onto the flat 紙 **kami** (paper) roof of this pavilion, since it is occupied by **Comm**ies (Communists) who are using **Shi**elds for protection **ALSO COMPARE:** other similar kanji at # **1195**

0222. 低 PRONUNCIATIONS: hiku, tei
MEANINGS: low, short in stature
EXAMPLES: 低い hikui = low; 最低 saitei = the worst **DESCRIPTION:** compared to 紙 kami (paper, # 221), this substitutes a guy with a slanted hat for the 糸 (skeet shooter) on the left; it retains the 氏 shi (mister, # 709) which can also be seen as a leaning woman under a lean-to and which we have described as a paper pavilion with a flat roof, but this pavilion is elevated on a flat rock
CUES: this guy on the left has **Hic**cups that are knocking his hat off kilter, and he is too 低い **hiku**i (low) to see over this 紙 (paper) pavilion which has been **Ta**ped to this flat rock
ALSO COMPARE: other similar kanji at # **1195**

0223. 絵 PRONUNCIATIONS: kai, e
MEANINGS: picture, drawing, painting
EXAMPLES: 絵画 kaiga = painting; 絵本 ehon = picture book **DESCRIPTION:** on the left, 糸 (skeet shooter, # 219); on the right, 会(議) kaigi (meeting, # 293) (identical pronunciation)
CUES: this 糸 (skeet shooter) will attend this 会 (meeting) to shoot paint at a 絵画 **kai**ga (painting) of the **Kai**ser, and he hopes to produce an **E**xcellent 絵 **e** (picture) **ALSO COMPARE:** 給(料) kyuuryou = salary, # 997; other similar kanji at # **1056** and # **1382**

0224. 経 PRONUNCIATIONS: kyou, ta, kei, he MEANING: to pass through
EXAMPLES: 経文 kyoumon = sutras, scriptures; 経つ tatsu = to elapse or pass, referring to time; 経験 keiken = experience; 経る heru = to pass (time), to go through or by way of
DESCRIPTION: on the left, 糸 (skeet shooter, # 219); on the upper right, 又 mata ("again," # 24), which resembles a dog groomer's table; on the lower right, 土 tsuchi (soil, # 59) **CUES:** this 糸 (skeet shooter) gets some 経験 **kei**ken (experience) by shooting toward this dog groomer's 又 (table) on this 土 (soil) in **Kyou**to, where the dogs wear dog **Ta**gs, sit in **C**ages, and **He**lp themselves to dog food
ALSO COMPARE: other similar kanji at # **1894**

0225. 約 **PRONUNCIATION: yaku**
MEANINGS: approximately, to promise, to shorten
EXAMPLES: 予約 yoyaku = reservation; 約束 yakusoku = promise; 契約 keiyaku = contract; 約一年 yaku ichinen = approximately one year **DESCRIPTION:** compared to (目)的 mokuteki (purpose, # 45), this substitutes a 糸 (skeet shooter, # 219) for 白 (white) on the left; it retains the giant hook containing a tear drop **CUE:** this giant hook, made from a **Yak** horn, grabs this 糸 (skeet shooter) and binds him to his 契約 kei**yaku** (contract), causing him to shed this tear
ALSO COMPARE: other similar kanji at # 988

0226. 続 **PRONUNCIATIONS: zoku, tsuzu MEANING:** to continue **EXAMPLES:** 接続 setsuzoku = connection; 続く tsuzuku = to continue, intransitive **DESCRIPTION:** on the left, 糸 (skeet shooter, # 219); on the right, 売(る) uru (to sell, # 425), which includes 士 shi (man, or warrior, # 66) on a roof with lopsided legs **CUES: Z**ombies in **Ku**wait 売 (sell) skeets to this 糸 (skeet shooter), who stores them in his **Tsui**tcase (suitcase) at the **Zoo** and 続く **tsuzu**ku (continues) to fire them at this 士 (man) on this roof with lopsided legs **ALSO COMPARE:** 結(果) kekka = result, # 231; other similar kanji at # **425**

0227. 緑 **PRONUNCIATIONS: midori, ryoku MEANING:** green **EXAMPLES:** 緑 midori = green; 緑茶 ryokucha = green tea
DESCRIPTION: on the left, 糸 (skeet shooter, # 219); on the upper right, a green flag, which can also be seen as hair streaming left, on a platform; on the lower right, 水 mizu (water, # 251) **CUES:** this 糸 (skeet shooter) fires at this 緑 **midori** (green) flag which is flying from a **Mi**niature **Dory** floating in this 水 (water), while Pope **Leo** drinks **Koo**l-Aid and 緑茶 **ryoku**cha (green tea)
GROUP: 緑 midori = green, # 227; 線 sen = line, # 228 **ALSO COMPARE:** other similar kanji at # **999** and # **1529**

0228. 線 **PRONUNCIATION: sen**
MEANING: line **EXAMPLES:** 線 sen = line; 二番線 nibansen = Track Number Two
DESCRIPTION: compared to 緑 midori (green, # 227), this substitutes 白(い) shiroi (white) for the green flag at the upper right; it retains the 糸 (skeet shooter) on the left, and 水 (water) at the lower right **CUE:** this **Sen**ator 白 (White) is drowning in this 水 (water), and this 糸 (skeet shooter) shoots a 線 **sen** (line) to save him
GROUP: 線 sen = line, # 228; 泉 izumi = spring, # 252; 腺 sen = a gland, # 2020
ALSO COMPARE: 綿 men = cotton, # 1189; other similar kanji at # **227** and # **1529**

0229. 練 **PRONUNCIATIONS: ren, ne**
MEANINGS: to practice or train
EXAMPLES: 練習する renshuu suru = to practice; 練る neru = to knead or plan carefully
DESCRIPTION: on the left, 糸 (skeet shooter, # 219); on the right, 東 higashi (east, # 508), which can also be seen as a tree wearing bifocals
CUES: this 糸 (skeet shooter) in Wyoming 練習 **ren**shuu suru (practices) shooting 東 (east), since that's where its enemy the **Rent** collector lives in Nebraska
COMPARE: other similar kanji at # **1271**

0230. 絡 **PRONUNCIATIONS: raku, kara MEANING:** to get entangled with
EXAMPLES: 連絡する renraku suru = to contact; 絡まる karamaru = to become entangled in **DESCRIPTION:** on the left, 糸 (skeet shooter, # 219), consisting of two flexed elbows above three legs; on the right, a dancer with a ponytail leaping over a box **CUES:** this 糸 (skeet shooter) shoots at this dancer as a way to 連絡する ren**raku** suru (contact) her about the approach of a **Rac**coon with a bad **Chara**cter, and she leaps over this box to escape

the beast **GROUP:** (連)絡 renraku = contact, # 230; 終(わる) owaru = to finish, # 233; 後(で) ato de = later, # 335 **ALSO COMPARE:** other similar kanji at # **1033**

0231. 結 **PRONUNCIATIONS: ke, ketsu, musu, yu MEANINGS:** to tie, bind, organize, fasten **EXAMPLES:** 結果 kekka = result; 結婚 kekkon = marriage; 団結 danketsu = unity, combination; 結ぶ musubu = bind, connect, conclude, organize, e.g., 手を結ぶ te wo musubu = to join hands; 髪を結う kami wo yuu = to put up the hair **DESCRIPTION:** compared to 続(く) tsuzuku (to continue, # 226), this substitutes 口 kuchi (mouth, # 426), which resembles a box, for the platform with lopsided legs at the lower right; it retains 糸 (skeet shooter) and 士 (man) **CUES:** this 糸 (skeet shooter) will 結婚する **ke**kkon suru (marry) this 士 (man) standing on this 口 (box) of wedding clothes, who wears **Ke**ds (a brand of shoes), likes to put **Ke**tchup in his **S**oup, sells **M**ovie **S**ouvenirs and lives in the **Yu**kon **ALSO COMPARE:** other similar kanji at # **1453**

0232. 緒 **PRONUNCIATIONS: o, cho, sho MEANINGS:** rope, beginning **EXAMPLES:** 鼻緒 hanao = straps of geta (wooden clogs); 情緒 joucho = emotion; 一緒に issho ni = together **DESCRIPTION:** on the left, 糸 (skeet shooter, # 219); on the right, 者 mono (person, # 276) **CUES:** this 糸 (skeet shooter) fires skeets toward this **O**lder 者 (person) whom he has **Ch**osen, and she **Sh**ows up, and they are 一緒に is**sho** ni (together) at last **ALSO COMPARE:** other similar kanji at # **1088**

0233. 終 **PRONUNCIATIONS: owa, o, shuu MEANINGS:** to end or finish **EXAMPLES:** 終る owaru = to finish, intransitive (this can also be spelled 終わる); 終える oeru = to finish, transitive; 最終電車 saishuu densha = last train **DESCRIPTION:** on the left, a 糸 (skeet shooter, # 219); on the right, 冬 fuyu (winter, # 234), which consists of a dancer above icy reflections **CUES:** this 糸 (skeet shooter)'s contract 終わる **o**waru (finishes) when this 冬 (winter arrives), and he remembers his **O**ld **Wa**rs and goes back to **O**hio and starts **Sh**ooting **GROUP:** 終(る) owaru = to finish, # 233; 冬 fuyu = winter, # 234 **COMPARE:** (連)絡 renraku = contact, # **230**; other similar kanji at # **234**

0234. 冬 **PRONUNCIATIONS: tou, fuyu MEANING:** winter **EXAMPLES:** 冬期 touki = winter; 冬 fuyu = winter **DESCRIPTION:** a dancer with a ponytail jumps over two reflections on a patch of ice **CUES:** this dancer with a ponytail escapes from **T**olstoy by taking a big leap over these two reflections on a patch of ice in 冬 **fuyu** (winter); "I **F**ooled **Y**ou," she cries **GROUP:** 終(わる) owaru = to finish, # 233; 冬 fuyu = winter, # 234; 寒(い) samui = cold, # 507; 尽(くす) tsukusu = to use up, # 1507

Female

0235. 女 **PRONUNCIATIONS: onna, jo, o, me, nyou, ma MEANING:** female **EXAMPLES:** 女の人 onna no hito = woman; 女性 josei = woman; 女将 okami = mistress, landlady, hostess; 乙女 otome = maiden; 女房 nyoubou = one's wife; 海女 ama = fisherwoman **DESCRIPTION:** at the top, a horizontal cross; at the bottom, an X-shaped figure carrying the cross; compared to the dancer seen in 冬 fuyu (winter, # 234), this kanji has a bent arm on the left, overlapping a second bent arm on the right, whereas the dancer has a ponytail extending to the left **CUES:** an **O**ld **N**asty taskmaster is forcing some 女の人 **onna** no hito (women) named **J**osephine and **O**prah to carry this cross to **M**exico, but they will **N**eed **Y**ogurt if they are going to make it to the **M**all **COMPARE:** other similar at # **2039**

0236. 安 **PRONUNCIATIONS: an, *a*, yasu MEANINGS:** inexpensive, secure, peaceful **EXAMPLES:** 安心する anshin suru = to feel relieved; 安部 Abe = a surname; 安い yasui = cheap **DESCRIPTION:** compared to 案 an (plan, idea, # 120) (identical pronunciation), this kanji omits the 木 (tree) at the bottom; it retains the bad haircut above a 女 (female) named Anne **CUES:** Queen **An**ne is this 女 (female) with this bad haircut who gives us 安心 **an**shin (relief) by showing us the **A**rt of cooking 安い **yasu**i (cheap) **Y**ak **S**oup **ALSO COMPARE:** other similar kanji at # **120** and # **2039**

0237. 妻 **PRONUNCIATIONS: tsuma, zuma², sai MEANING:** wife **EXAMPLES:** 妻 tsuma = wife; 稲妻 inazuma = lightning; 夫妻 fusai = married couple **DESCRIPTION:** at the top, a cross with a trident intersecting it, but this trident can be seen as a comb; at the bottom, 女 onna (female, # 235) **CUES:** my 妻 **tsuma** (wife) is this 女 (female) and a **T**super (**su**per) **Ma** (**ma**ther) who is a **S**cientist, and she wears this cross and this comb in her hair **COMPARE:** other similar kanji at # **877**, # **2039** and # **2086**

0238. 要 **PRONUNCIATIONS: kaname, you, i MEANING:** important **EXAMPLES:** 肝心要 kanjin kaname = the main point; 要するに you suru ni = in short; 必要 hitsuyou = necessary; 要る iru = to need **DESCRIPTION:** at the top, three eyes suspended from a platform; at the bottom, 女 onna (female, # 235) **CUES:** because she has three eyes like these, this 女 (female) **Ca**nadian **Mer**maid knows all of the 必要 hits**uyou** (necessary) things that her family 要る **i**ru (needs) to eat, such as **Y**ogurt and **E**els **COMPARE:** other similar kanji at # **1415**, # **2039** and # **2086**

0239. 好 **PRONUNCIATIONS: su, zu², kono, kou MEANING:** to like **EXAMPLES:** 好きです suki desu = I like it; 好き zuki = enthusiast, used as a suffix, e.g., ryokouzuki = travel lover; 好む konomu = to like or favor; 好物 koubutsu = favorite food **DESCRIPTION:** on the left, 女 onna (female, # 235); on the right, 子 ko (child, # 182) **CUES: Su**perman 好き **su**ki (likes) the way that this 女 (female) and this 子 (child) hide their **C**old **N**oses in their **C**oats **ALSO COMPARE:** other kanji containing 女 on the left at # **2039**; other similar kanji at # **2078**

0240. 婚 **PRONUNCIATION: kon MEANING:** marriage **EXAMPLE:** 結婚 kekkon = marriage **DESCRIPTION:** on the left, 女 onna (female, # 235); at the upper right, 氏 shi (mister, # 709), which described as a paper pavilion in 紙 kami (paper, # 221); on the lower right, 日 hi (sun, # 32) shining in the **Con**go **CUE:** this 女 (female) from the **Con**go will 結婚する kek**kon** suru (marry) this 氏 (mister), and she is writing wedding invitations in this 日 (sun) **GROUP:** (結)婚 kekkon = marriage, # 240; 昏(睡) konsui = stupor, # 1074 (identical pronunciation) **ALSO COMPARE:** other kanji containing 女 on the left at # **2039**; other similar kanji at # **1195**

0241. 姉 **PRONUNCIATIONS: ane, nee, shi MEANING:** older sister **EXAMPLES:** 姉 ane = older sister; お姉さん oneesan = honorable older sister; 姉妹 shimai = sisters **DESCRIPTION:** on the left, 女 onna (female, # 235); on the right, 市 shi (city, # 242) (identical pronunciation), which looks like a spinning lady with wide hips **CUES:** compared to 妹 (little sister, # 244), this 姉 **ane** (big sister) has wider hips like these, tells more **An**ecdotes, eats more **Ne**ctarines, and is more **Chi**c, since she lives in this 市 (city)

COMPARE: other kanji containing 女 on the left at # **2039**; other similar kanji at # **242**

0242. 市 **PRONUNCIATIONS: shi, ichi**
MEANINGS: market, city, municipal
EXAMPLES: 都市 toshi = city; 市長 shichou = mayor; 市場 ichiba = (physical) market; **Note:** 市場 can also be pronounced "shijou" = (abstract) market **DESCRIPTION:** compared to 巾 (Bo Peep), as seen in 帽(子) boushi (hat, # 243), this adds a hat at the top, with a point in the middle; it retains the spinning lady with wide hips (this kanji can also be seen as Bo Peep under a tire stop) **CUES:** this lady with these wide hips and this pointy hat spins around the 都市 to**shi** (city) looking for her **Sh**eep who are **Itch**ing to see her **GROUP:** 姉 ane = older sister, # 241; (都)市 toshi = city, # 242; 製(品) seihin = finished product, # 580; 制(服) seifuku = a uniform, # 1155; 肺 hai = lung, # 1508; 柿 kaki = a persimmon, # 1947 **ALSO COMPARE:** other kanji containing Bo Peep at # 1768

0243. 帽 **PRONUNCIATION: bou**
MEANINGS: cap, headgear **EXAMPLE:** 帽子 boushi = hat **DESCRIPTION:** on the left, 巾 (Bo Peep), a spinning lady with wide hips; on the upper right, 日 hi (sun, # 32); on the lower right, 目 me (eye, # 51); 日 and 目 resemble two tall hats **CUES:** this 巾 (Bo Peep) is trying to decide between these two **Bo**dacious 帽子 **bou**shi (hats) **GROUP:** 帽(子) boushi = hat, # 243; 冒(す) okasu = to risk, # 812; 眼(鏡) megane = eyeglasses, # 1423; (明)瞭(な) meiryou na = obvious, # 2002 **ALSO COMPARE:** other similar kanji at # **1768** and # **2002**

0244. 妹 **PRONUNCIATIONS: imouto, mai** MEANING: younger sister **EXAMPLES:** 妹 imouto = younger sister; 姉妹 shimai = sisters **DESCRIPTION:** on the left, 女 onna (female, # 235); on the right, 未(来) mirai (future, # 672), which resembles a 木 (tree) with two pairs of branches, with the longer branches at the bottom **CUES:** compared to 姉 (big sister, # 241), 妹 **imouto** (little sister) has these narrow hips, she has **Immo**bile **Toe**s, she plays with **M**ice, and she is a woman of the 未 (future)
ALSO COMPARE: other kanji containing 女 on the left at # **2039**; other similar kanji at # **672**

0245. 味 **PRONUNCIATIONS: mi, aji, i**
MEANING: taste **EXAMPLES:** 意味 imi = meaning; 趣味 shumi = hobby; 地味な jimi na = subdued, inconspicuous, unattractive; 味 aji = taste; 美味しい oishii = delicious (usually written おいしい) **DESCRIPTION:** compared to 未(来) mirai (future, # 672) (identical pronunciation), this adds 口 kuchi (mouth, # 426), which resembles a mirror or a box, on the left; it retains the 木 (tree) with two pairs of branches, the lower branches being longer **CUES:** as I look into this 口 (**M**irror) and contemplate the 未 (future), I see that I am **A**ging, but I still have good 味 **aji** (taste) when choosing **E**aster clothes **ALSO COMPARE:** (曖)昧(な) aimai na = vague, # 1941; other similar kanji at # **672** and # **2073**

Crafted Object

0246. 工 **PRONUNCIATIONS: kou, ku**
MEANING: crafted object or craft **EXAMPLES:** 工場 koujou = factory, 大工 daiku = carpenter **DESCRIPTION:** this resembles an I-beam, seen on end **CUES:** this 工 **kou** (crafted object) resembles an I-beam, seen on end, which is used inside **Co**al mines and in **Co**oling towers **COMPARE:** the katakana character エ e; similar kanji at # **247**

0247. 紅 **PRONUNCIATIONS:** kou, *momi*, beni **MEANINGS:** scarlet, red **EXAMPLES:** 紅茶 koucha = black tea; 紅葉 momiji = Japanese maple, autumn colors; 紅 beni = red, rouge, lipstick; 口紅 kuchibeni = lipstick **DESCRIPTION:** on the left, 糸 skeet shooter (# 219); on the right, 工 kou (crafted object, # 246) (identical pronunciation) **CUES:** this 糸 (skeet shooter) shoots 紅茶 koucha (black tea) at this 工 (crafted object), which is a tube of 口紅 kuchibeni (lipstick), but its owner, who works in a **Co**al mine, just cleans her **Mo**torcycle **Mi**rrors and leaves for **Beni**hana (a chain of teppanyaki restaurants) **GROUP:** 工 kou = crafted object, # 246; 紅(茶) koucha = black tea, # 247; 空 sora = sky, # 248; 式 shiki = ceremony, # 249; 試(験) shiken = examination, # 436; (時)差 jisa = time difference, # 631; (成)功 seikou = success, # 634; 恐(れ) osore = fear, # 869; 江(戸) edo = old name for Tokyo, # 1026; 拭(く) fuku = to wipe, # 1114; (建)築 kenchiku = architecture, # 1219; 攻(撃) kougeki = criticism, # 1395; 尋(ねる) tazuneru = to ask, # 1512; (要)項 youkou = outline, # 1573; 貢(献) kouken = a contribution, # 1617; 控(える) hikaeru = to refrain, # 1637; (技)巧 gikou = technique, # 1727; 虹 niji = a rainbow, # 2018; **Note** that several of these kanji can be pronounced "kou" **ALSO COMPARE:** other kanji containing 工 at # 456

0248. 空 **PRONUNCIATIONS:** su, a, muna, kuu, kara, sora, zora² **MEANINGS:** sky, empty **EXAMPLES:** 空く suku = to become empty; 空く aku = to become vacant; 空き地 akichi = vacant lot; 空しい munashii = empty, fruitless; 空港 kuukou = airport; 空車 kuusha = free taxi; 空 kara = empty; 空 sora = sky; 夜空 yozora = night sky; **Note:** suku and aku are both written 空く; in addition, kara and sora are both written 空 **DESCRIPTION:** at the top, a soaring bird from Cuba, as seen in (研)究 kenkyuu (research, # 112), which is a super-sized albatross with two lopsided legs; at the bottom, 工 kou (crafted object, # 246), which could be part of a vacant cooling tower **CUES:** this **Su**per-sized **A**lbatross with two lopsided legs, whose **Mo**od is **Na**sty, rebounds from this 空いている aite iru (vacant) 工 (crafted object) **Coo**ling tower near the 空港 **kuu**kou (airport) in **Cara**cas and **Soar**s into the 空 **sora** (sky) **ALSO COMPARE:** other similar kanji at # 112 and # 247

0249. 式 **PRONUNCIATION:** shiki **MEANINGS:** ceremony, formula **EXAMPLE:** 結婚式 kekkon shiki = wedding ceremony **DESCRIPTION:** a woman with a ball above her right shoulder leans over a 工 kou (crafted object, # 246); compared to the halberd seen in (機)械 kikai (machine, # 138), she is mssing her left leg **CUE:** this woman with a ball above her shoulder, who is participating in a 式 **shiki** (ceremony), leans over this 工 (crafted object), and she sees that it is a **Shift Key** **GROUP:** 貸(す) kasu = to borrow, # 90; 式 shiki = ceremony, # 249; 試(験) shiken = examination, # 436; (時)代 jidai = era, # 552; 袋 fukuro = bag, # 581; 拭(く) fuku = to wipe, # 1114; 武(器) buki = weapon, # 1418; (月)賦 geppu = a monthly payment, # 2058 **COMPARE:** similar kanji at # 247, # 376 and # 1195

Water

0250. 川 **PRONUNCIATIONS:** kawa, sen, gawa **MEANING:** river **EXAMPLES:** 川 kawa = river; 河川 kasen = river; 小川 ogawa = brook **DESCRIPTION:** a flowing river **CUES:** this 川 **kawa** (river) supplies water for a **Ca**r **Wa**sh in the **Cen**ter of a town, where there is a **Gas War** **COMPARE:** 小(さい) chiisai = small, # 253; (九)州 kyuushuu = Kyushu island, # 1071; other similar kanji at # 253 and # 1090

0251. 水 PRONUNCIATIONS: mizu, sui, zui² MEANING: water EXAMPLES: 水 mizu = water; 水曜日 suiyoubi = Wednesday; 洪水 kouzui = flood DESCRIPTION: a waterfall flowing between two cliffs at a miniature zoo CUES: outside the cafeteria at a **Mi**niature **Zoo**, 水 **mizu** (water) was flowing between these two cliffs, and we ordered **Sw**eet drinks ALSO COMPARE: kanji resembling 水 at # **814**; other similar kanji at # **253**

0252. 泉 PRONUNCIATIONS: sen, izumi MEANING: fountain EXAMPLES: 温泉 onsen = hot spring; 泉 izumi = spring (of water) DESCRIPTION: compared to 線 sen (line, # 228) (identical pronunciation), this kanji omits the skeet shooter on the left; it retains 白 (white) and 水 (water) CUES: this **Sen**ator 白 (**W**hite) bathed in an 温泉 on**sen** (hot spring) which was supplied by this 水 (water) from a natural 泉 **izumi** (spring), where **Ea**gles are **Zoom**ing ALSO COMPARE: other similar kanji at # **228** and # **1529**

0253. 小 PRONUNCIATIONS: chii, shou, ko, o, a MEANING: small EXAMPLES: 小さい chiisai = small; 小学校 shougakkou = elementary school; 小鳥 kotori = little bird; 小川 ogawa = brook; 小豆 azuki = red bean DESCRIPTION: like 水 mizu (water, # 251), 小 contains a central line with a curve at the bottom, but the secondary lines surrounding this middle line are smaller and straighter in 小, which resembles a chimpanzee wearng a coat CUES: a 小さい **chii**sai (small) **Chi**mpanzee registered and then **Sho**wed up wearing a **C**oat at a 小学校 **shou**gakkou (elementary school) in **O**saka, where it majored in **A**rt GROUP: 川 kawa = river, # 250; 水 mizu = water, # 251; 小(さい) chiisai = small, # 253; 少(々) shoushou = a little, # 254 (identical pronunciation) ALSO COMPARE: other similar kanji at # **814** and # **1010**

0254. 少 PRONUNCIATIONS: suku, suko, shou MEANING: small amount EXAMPLES: 少ない sukunai = a little; 少し sukoshi = a little; 少々 shoushou = a little DESCRIPTION: compared to 小(さい) chiisai (small, # 253), or 小(学校) shougakkou (elementary school, # 253) (identical pronunciation), this kanji adds the katakana ノ no, suggesting that no one is satisfied with a 小 (small) amount CUES: our **Suc**culent plants are 少ない **suku**nai (few), and **S**uperman and his **C**o-workers got 少し **suko**shi (a little) pleasure from them at our 小 (small) plant **Sho**w, but ノ (**no**) one was satisfied COMPARE: other similar kanji at # **253** and # **1010**

0255. 泳 PRONUNCIATIONS: oyo, ei MEANING: to swim EXAMPLES: 泳ぐ oyogu = to swim; 水泳 suiei = swimming DESCRIPTION: on the left, a water radical (see # 12), suggesting swimming; on the right, 水 mizu (water, # 251), with two small lines added above it, which could represent two feathers in a hat CUES: **O**prah eats **Yo**gurt and drinks this water on the left, and honest **A**be drinks this 水 (water) on the right while wearing a hat with these two feathers, before they 泳ぐ **oyo**gu (swim) ALSO COMPARE: other similar kanji at # **814**

0256. 浴 PRONUNCIATIONS: yu, a, yoku MEANING: to bathe EXAMPLES: 浴衣 yukata = summer kimono; 浴びる abiru = to bathe; 浴室 yokushitsu = bathroom DESCRIPTION: on the left, a water radical (see # 12); on the right, a bathroom containing a bathtub, with water vapor rising from the top CUES: this bathroom in the **Yu**kon near the **A**rctic with water vapor rising from the roof and this spring of water outside is a good place to 浴びる **a**biru (bathe), after which one can put on a 浴衣 **yu**kata (summer robe) and eat **Yo**gurt and **C**ookies COMPARE: 沿(う) sou = to run along, # 1414; other similar kanji at # **660**

0257. 温 PRONUNCIATIONS: atata, on, nuku MEANING: warm objects EXAMPLES: 温かい atatakai = warm (water, etc.); 温める atatameru = to heat up water, etc., transitive; 温度 ondo = temperature; 温泉 onsen = hot spring; 温もり nukumori = warmth
DESCRIPTION: on the left, a water radical (see # 12), which reminds us of water vapor; on the upper right, 日 hi (sun, # 32); on the lower right, 皿 sara (bowl, # 567)
CUES: **Ata**turk with a **Tan** is the **Own**er of this 皿 (bowl) of **N**utritious **K**ool-Aid which is getting 温かい **atata**kai (warm) under this 日 (sun) and emitting this water vapor
ALSO COMPARE: 暖(かい) atatakai = warm atmosphere, # 38; other similar kanji at # **1407**

0258. 薄 PRONUNCIATIONS: usu, haku MEANINGS: dilute, thin, weak EXAMPLES: 薄い usui = pale, thin, light, watery, dilute, weak (taste); 薄情 hakujou = cruel, heartless, uncaring
DESCRIPTION: on the left, a water radical (see # 12); at the top, a plant radical (see # 43); at the middle right, the upper portion of 犬 inu (dog, # 190) which includes a tiny ball; below that, 田 (んぼ) tanbo (rice paddy, # 68); at the lower right, a sunny kneeling guy who has dropped his gum, as seen on the right in 村 mura (village, # 131)
CUES: combining this water with this plant material from this 田 (rice paddy), this 寸 (sunny guy) and this truncated 犬 (dog) are producing 薄い **usu**i (thin) rice tea appropriate for **U**surers and **H**ackers from **Ku**wait
GROUP: 漢(字) kanji = Chinese character, # 197; 薄い usui = pale, # 258; 落(ちる) ochiru = to fall, # 526; 茨(城県) Ibaraki ken = Ibaraki prefecture, # 1007; 満(足) manzoku = satisfaction, # 1153; 藩(士) hanshi = a feudal retainer, # 1537; (海)藻 kaisou = seaweed, # 2008
ALSO COMPARE: other similar kanji at # **865**, # **1721** and # **1740**

0259. 済 PRONUNCIATIONS: sai, su, zai MEANING: to finish EXAMPLES: 救済 kyuusai = help, rescue, relief; 済む sumu = to end (intransitive), to manage, to do without; 済ます sumasu = to finish, transitive; 経済 keizai = economy
DESCRIPTION: on the left, a water radical (see # 12), which suggests an ocean; at the upper right, 文(化) bunka (culture, # 25), which contains a tire stop above a crossing (which can also be described as an X); at the lower right, a truncated 月 tsuki (moon, # 148)
CUES: a **Sc**ientist known for her 文 (culture), who graduated **Su**mma cum laude, is still trying to 済ます **su**masu (finish) her dissertation on 月 (moon) phenomena, and she is happy to discover this truncated moon shining near this ocean in **Za**ire (the former name of the Congo)
GROUP: 文(化) bunka = culture, # 25; (経)済 keizai = economy, # 259; 対(して) taishite = against, # 674; (一)斉(に) issei ni = all together, # 952; (書)斎 shosai = a home library, # 1560 (identical pronunciation); (洗)剤 senzai = detergent, # 1601 (also identical pronunciation); (指)紋 shimon = a fingerprint, # 1676; 蚊 ka = a mosquito, # 2009 ALSO COMPARE: other similar kanji at # **1601**

0260. 活 PRONUNCIATIONS: ka, katsu MEANINGS: life, lively, activity EXAMPLES: 活気 kakki = liveliness; 生活 seikatsu = life, livelihood; 活躍 katsuyaku = great effort
DESCRIPTION: on the left, a water radical (see # 12); on the right, 舌 shita (tongue, # 1213)
CUES: in **Ca**lifornia, I watch my **Ca**ts using 舌 (tongues) like this to drink water like this, and I enjoy their 活気 **ka**kki (liveliness)
COMPARE: similar kanji at # **1213**

Rain

0261. 雨 **PRONUNCIATIONS: ame, ama, same, u,** *yu* **MEANING:** rain **EXAMPLES:** 大雨 ooame = heavy rain; 雨傘 amagasa = Japanese umbrella; 小雨 kosame = light rain or drizzle; 雨量 uryou = amount of rain; 梅雨 tsuyu = rainy season **DESCRIPTION:** this resembles rain drops on two window panes hanging from a platform **CUES:** in Am**e**rica, the amount of 雨 **ame** (rain) that is seen on window panes like these varies depending on the location, and the same is true in the **Ama**zon, over the **Sa**lt **m**ines of **Me**xico, and in **U**ganda and the **Yu**kon **COMPARE:** similar kanji at # **262**

0262. 雪 **PRONUNCIATIONS: setsu, yuki,** *buki* **MEANING:** snow **EXAMPLES:** 新雪 shinsetsu = new snow; 雪 yuki = snow; 吹雪 fubuki = snowstorm **DESCRIPTION:** at the top, 雨 ame (rain, # 261); at the bottom, this resembles hair streaming to the left, as seen in 急(ぐ) isogu (to hurry, # 312), but it can also be seen as three layers of ice **CUES:** since there are these three layers of ice on the ground, this 雨 (rain) must be 雪 **yuki** (snow), which some of our **Set**tlement's **Su**per pioneers say is **Yuck**y, and that's why they are **Book**ing vacations in Florida **GROUP:** 雨 ame = rain, # 261; 雪 yuki = snow, # 262; 電(気) denki = electricity, # 263; 雲 kumo = cloud, # 264; (地)震 jishin = earthquake, # 265; 漏(水) rousui = water leak, # 740; 雰(囲気) fu'inki = ambience, # 1201; 露 tsuyu = dew, # 1390; 霊 rei = ghost, # 1575; 霧 kiri = fog, # 1696; 需(給) jukyuu = supply and demand, # 1699; 雷 kaminari = thunder, # 1723; 儒(教) jukyou = Confucianism, # 1909; 曇(る) kumoru = to become cloudy, # 1911; 零 rei = zero, # 1946; 霜 shimo = frost, # 2032 **ALSO COMPARE:** other similar kanji at # **1165**

0263. 電 **PRONUNCIATION: den** **MEANING:** electricity **EXAMPLE:** 電気 denki = electricity **DESCRIPTION:** at the top, 雨 ame (rain, # 261); at the bottom, 田 (rice paddy, # 68), with a wire emerging from it, suggesting an electrical transformer **CUE:** this wire is emerging from this 田 (transformer) under this 雨 (rain), suggesting that 電気 **den**ki (electricity) is being generated from lightning strikes in **Den**mark **ALSO COMPARE:** other similar kanji at # **262** and # **1003**

0264. 雲 **PRONUNCIATIONS: kumo, gumo²,** **un** **MEANING:** cloud **EXAMPLES:** 雲 kumo = cloud; 雨雲 amagumo = rain cloud; 雲海 unkai = sea of clouds **DESCRIPTION:** at the top, 雨 ame (rain, # 261); in the middle, 二 ni (two, # 2); at the bottom, the katakana ム mu, which is the sound made by a cow **CUES:** these 二 (two) ム (cows) belong to Governor **Cuomo**, and the 雲 **kumo** (clouds) suggest that this 雨 (rain) is coming, so **U**ndoubtedly he should put them back in the barn **ALSO COMPARE:** 曇(り) kumori = cloudy, # 1911, which adds a small 日 hi (sun) to the top of 雲; other similar kanji at # **262** and # **1056**

0265. 震 **PRONUNCIATIONS: shin, furu** **MEANINGS:** to tremble or shake **EXAMPLES:** 地震 jishin = earthquake; 震える furueru = to tremble **DESCRIPTION:** at the top, 雨 ame (rain, # 261); at the bottom, a Shinto shrine which is a one-sided lean-to containing an arrow, supported by the letter L and the letter Y **CUES:** this 雨 (rain) is falling during a 地震 ji**shin** (earthquake), and since only this L and Y are supporting this lean-to and arrow that make up this **Shin**to shrine, it will 震える **furu**eru (tremble) and collapse into **Fu**ll-blown **Ru**in **ALSO COMPARE:** other similar kanji at # **262** and # **1105**

Sound

0266. 音 PRONUNCIATIONS: oto, on, in, ne MEANING: sound EXAMPLES: 音 oto = sound; 音楽 ongaku = music; 母音 boin = vowel; 音色 ne'iro = timbre

DESCRIPTION: at the top, 立(つ) tatsu (to stand, # 11), but this resembles an Ottoman-era bell; at the bottom, 日 hi (day, # 32), which resembles a two-drawer cabinet
CUES: during the **Ott**oman era, people discovered that this 立 (bell) on this two-drawer 日 (cabinet) full of **On**ions makes an **In**credible 音 **oto** (sound) which annoys the people **N**ext door
GROUP: 音 oto = sound, # 266; 暗(い) kurai = dark, # 268; 意(味) imi = meaning, # 317; 億 oku = 100 million, # 318; 職(業) shokugyou = occupation, # 696; (環)境 kankyou = environment, # 719; 織(る) oru = to weave, # 753; 響(く) hibiku = to resound, # 840; 闇 yami = darkness, # 950; (知)識 chishiki = knowledge, # 1335; 鏡 kagami = mirror, # 1355; 章 shou = chapter, # 1365; 障(害) shougai = an obstacle, # 1495; (記)憶(する) kioku suru = to remember, # 1540; (表)彰 hyoushou = commendation, # 1807; 臆(病な) okubyou na = timid, # 1973; 韻(文) inbun = verse, # 2036 (identical pronunciation) **ALSO COMPARE:** kanji containing a 立 (bell) on a 口 (box) at # 269

0267. 部 PRONUNCIATIONS: he, be, bu
MEANINGS: part, section, counter for books or magazines **EXAMPLES:** 部屋 heya = room; 子供部屋 kodomobeya = child's room; 全部 zenbu = entirely; 部長 buchou = division manager **DESCRIPTION:** on the left, compared to 音 oto (sound, # 266), this bell is on a 口 (box) instead of a 日 (cabinet); on the right, ẞ from the Greek alphabet, suggesting that Helen, a right-wing Greek citizen, owns the bell; **Note:** this is a reversal of 陪(審) baishin (jury, # 2030), in which a left-wing ẞ (Greek) guy is on the *left* **CUES:** **He**len is a right-wing ẞ (Greek) 部長 **bu**chou (division manager) who keeps this 立 (**Be**ll) on this 口 (box) in her 部屋 **he**ya (room) for **B**uddhist ceremonies **ALSO COMPARE:** other similar kanji at # 269 and # 1843

0268. 暗 PRONUNCIATIONS: kura, an
MEANING: dark **EXAMPLES:** 暗い kurai = dark; 暗示 anji = hint
DESCRIPTION: on the left, 日 hi (sun, # 32); on the right, 音 oto (sound, # 266), which depicts a bell on a cabinet, where curry ramen is stored
CUES: even when this 日 (sun) shines on this 立 (bell), there are 暗い **kura**i (dark) places in this 日 (cabinet) below it, where we keep **C**urry **Ra**men, but **An**ts are getting into them **ALSO COMPARE:** other similar kanji at # **266**

0269. 倍 PRONUNCIATION: bai
MEANINGS: to double or multiply
EXAMPLES: 三倍の sanbai no = three times as much; 倍増する baizou suru = to double
DESCRIPTION: compared to 部(屋) heya (room, # 267), this omits ẞ on the right and adds a man with a slanted hat on the left; it retains the 立 (bell) on the 口 (box) **CUE:** this man is tilting his hat in order to examine this 立 (bell) on this 口 (box) which he wants to **B**uy and then resell it for 倍増 **bai**zou (double) the price **GROUP:** 部(屋) heya = room, # 267; 倍(増する) baizou suru = to double, # 269; 競(技) kyougi = competition, # 935; (栽)培 saibai = cultivation, # 1234; 賠(償) baishou = compen-sation, # 1661; (解)剖 kaibou = anatomy, # 1985; 陪(審) baishin = a jury, # 2030; **Note** that four of these kanji can be pronounced "bai" **ALSO COMPARE:** kanji containing a 立 (bell) on a 日 (two-drawer cabinet) at # 266

0270. 位 **PRONUNCIATIONS: i, kurai, gurai**² **MEANINGS:** rank, place, approximately **EXAMPLES:** 第一位 dai ichi i = first place; 位 kurai = rank; どれ位 doregurai = how far (or long, many, much) **DESCRIPTION:** compared to 倍(増する) baizou suru (to double, # 269), this omits the 口 (box) on the lower right; it retains the man with a slanted hat and 立 (to stand), which resembles an Easter bell **CUES:** this man tilts this hat back in order to examine this 立 (**E**aster bell), and he uses it to win 第一位 dai ichi **i** (first place) in a bell-ringing competition, for which he receives a prize of **Ku**waiti **R**ice and a high 位 **kurai** (rank) **ALSO COMPARE:** other similar kanji at # **11**

Shah

0271. 社 **PRONUNCIATIONS: sha, ja, yashiro MEANINGS:** shrine, company of people **EXAMPLES:** 会社 kaisha = company; 神社 jinja = a Shinto shrine; 社 yashiro = a Shinto shrine **DESCRIPTION:** on the left, the Shah, who lacks the protruding upper lip displayed by Happy Jimmy, as seen in 初(めて) hajimete (the first time, # 104); on the right, 土 tsuchi (soil, # 59) **CUES:** this **Sh**ah and a **Ja**panese partner are looking at this 土 (soil), on which **Y**aks and **Sh**eep **R**oam, where they plan to build a 会社 ka**isha** (company) **COMPARE:** other similar kanji at # **1160**

0272. 祖 **PRONUNCIATIONS: jii, baa, so, zo**² **MEANING:** ancestral **EXAMPLES:** お祖父さん ojiisan = grandfather; お祖母さん obaasan = grandmother; 祖父 sofu = grandfather; 祖母 sobo = grandmother; 祖先 sosen = ancestor; 先祖 senzo = ancestor; **Note:** the 祖父 jii in ojiisan and the 祖母 baa in obaasan are actually combinations of two kanji **DESCRIPTION:** on the left, the Shah (see # 271); on the right, 目 me (eye, # 51) on a base, resembling a solar panel **CUES:** this **Sh**ah, who uses a **J**eep to bring hay to his sheep, which say **B**aa, is praying at the tomb of his 祖父 **so**fu (grandfather), which resembles this 目 (**S**olar panel) **ALSO COMPARE:** other similar kanji at # **752** and # **1160**

0273. 神 **PRONUNCIATIONS: kou, shin, jin, kami, gami**², **kan, ka, mi MEANINGS:** gods, mind, soul **EXAMPLES:** 神戸 Koube = a city in Japan; 神道 Shintou = a Japanese religion; 神社 jinja = Shintou shrine; 神 kami = god; 女神 megami = goddess; 神田 Kanda = an area in Tokyo; 神奈川 Kanagawa = a prefecture in Japan; お神酒 omiki = sake offered to the gods **DESCRIPTION:** compared to 申(す) mousu (to humbly speak, # 10), this adds the Shah (see # 271), wearing skinny jeans, on the left **CUES:** this **Sh**ah, who is feeling **C**old, 申 (speaks humbly) as he stands on a roof **Sh**ingle in his skinny **J**eans praying to the 神道 **shin**tou (a Japanese religion) 神 **kami** (gods), but a **Commi**e (Communist) from **Kan**sas is waiting to **Ca**ll him to a **M**eeting **ALSO COMPARE:** other similar kanji at # **1157** and # **1160**

0274. 祝 **PRONUNCIATIONS: iwa, shuku, shuu MEANING:** to celebrate **EXAMPLES:** 祝う iwau = to celebrate; 祝日 shukujitsu = national holiday; 祝儀 shuugi = celebration, wedding, gratuity **DESCRIPTION:** on the left, the Shah (see # 271); on the right, 兄 ani (big brother, # 420) **CUES:** this **Sh**ah **iwau** 祝う (celebrates) with this 兄 (big brother); they are happy that eels are on the menu and say "**E**els are **W**acky!" as they **Sh**uck corn for the feast and **Sh**oot off fireworks **ALSO COMPARE:** similar kanji at # **420** and # **1160**

0275. 礼 PRONUNCIATION: **rei**
MEANINGS: to bow; propriety; a gift in token of gratitude EXAMPLES: お礼 orei = gratitude, thanks DESCRIPTION: on the left, the Shah (see # 271); on the right, the letter L, which reminds us of a Lady but could also represent a breast, as seen in 乳 chichi (milk, # 186) CUE: this Shah feels お礼 orei (gratitude) to this Lady, who helped him after he was 失礼 shitsurei (rude) to her COMPARE: other similar kanji at # 735 and # 1160

Person

0276. 者 PRONUNCIATIONS: **mono, sha, ja²** MEANING: person EXAMPLES: 悪者 warumono = villain; 学者 gakusha = scholar; 金の亡者 kane no mouja = a money-grubbing person DESCRIPTION: at the top, 土 tsuchi (soil, # 59); in the middle, a pair of scissors; at the bottom, 日 hi (sun, # 32), which resembles a two-drawer cabinet CUES: this 者 mono (person) is playing a Monotonous game with this 土 (soil) and these Sharp scissors that he keeps in this 日 (cabinet) COMPARE: similar kanji at # 1088

0277. 都 PRONUNCIATIONS: **tsu, to, miyako** MEANING: capital EXAMPLES: 都合 tsugou = circumstances, convenience; 都市 toshi = city; 京都 Kyouto = city in Japan; 都 miyako = capital DESCRIPTION: on the left, 者 mono (person, # 276); on the right, β beta, from the Greek alphabet, suggesting that this is a Greek 者 (person) CUES: this β (Greek) 者 (person) carries a Tsuitcase (suitcase) of Tomatoes to a 都市 toshi (city) known as Athens, where 都合がいい tsugou ga ii (it will be convenient) to Meet Yak Owners ALSO COMPARE: other similar kanji at # 1088 and # 1843

0278. 暑 PRONUNCIATIONS: **atsu, sho**
MEANING: hot atmosphere EXAMPLES: 暑い日 atsui hi = hot day; 暑中 shochuu = mid-summer, hot season DESCRIPTION: at the top, 日 hi (sun, # 32); at the bottom, a 者 mono (person, # 276) CUES: this 者 (person) stands under this 日 (sun) At Superman's house, feels too 暑い atsui (hot), and decides to go to the Shore ALSO COMPARE: 熱(い) atsui = hot objects, # 65; 厚(い) atsui = thick, # 185; other similar kanji at # 1088

Closed Boxes

0279. 園 PRONUNCIATIONS: **en, zono, sono** MEANINGS: park, spacious garden EXAMPLES: 公園 kouen = a park; 花園 hanazono = a flower garden; 竹の園 takenosono = a bamboo garden DESCRIPTION: on the perimeter, a fence, which reminds us of a park; inside the fence, at the top, 土 tsuchi (soil, # 59) above a 口 (box) and, at the bottom, a machine on a pole, with a handle on the left and two lips extending to the right, which could be a megaphone CUES: an Engineer is using this megaphone with two lips to tell children playing in this 土 (soil) above this 口 (box) in this enclosed 公園 kouen (park) to enter the Zone to the North, and have Sonograms done COMPARE: other similar kanji at # 351, # 718 and # 1360

0280. 困 PRONUNCIATIONS: **koma, kon** MEANING: in trouble EXAMPLES: 困る komaru = to be troubled, inconvenienced; 困難 konnan = difficult DESCRIPTION: a 木 ki (tree, # 118) stuck in a box CUES: while this 木 (tree) was in a Coma, someone built this box around it, so that it 困っている komatte iru (is in trouble), and some Coneheads say that this is a 困難な konnan na (difficult) situation COMPARE: other similar kanji at # 1360

0281. 図 PRONUNCIATIONS: **zu, to, haka** MEANINGS: drawing, to plan EXAMPLES: 図 zu = drawing; 地図 chizu = map; 図書館 toshokan = library; 図る hakaru = to plot or attempt DESCRIPTION: a framed drawing of two people riding on a giraffe, which can also be seen as an X **CUES:** this is a framed 図 **zu** (drawing) of these two people riding on this giraffe, returning from the **Zoo,** where they saw some **Toa**ds, and heading to the 図書館 **to**shokan (library), where there is going to be a **Hac**kathon **COMPARE:** other similar kanji at # **601**, # **1360** and # **1953**

0282. 面 **PRONUNCIATIONS: omo, ji, men, *noo*, tsura** **MEANINGS:** mask, face, features **EXAMPLES:** 面白い omoshiroi = interesting; 真面目な majime na = sincere; 面倒 mendou = annoyance; 地面 jimen = the surface of the earth, the ground; 箕面市 Minooshi = a city near Osaka; 面 tsura = a face **DESCRIPTION:** this resembles an old limousine with an antenna, seen from the back, with 目 me (eye, # 51) imprinted on it **CUES:** this **O**ld **Mo**torcar is a **J**eep with this antenna, and this working 目 (eye) on its back panel is an 面白い **omo**shiroi (interesting) innovation that protects it from 面倒な **men**dou na (annoying) **Men** from the **N**orth who might want to **Tsue** (sue) the **R**appers who ride in it **COMPARE:** similar kanji at # **522** and # **2002**

Car

0283. 車 **PRONUNCIATIONS: kuruma, sha** **MEANINGS:** car or cart **EXAMPLES:** 車 kuruma = car, wheel; 自転車 jitensha = bicycle **DESCRIPTION:** a two-wheeled car seen from the top, with a wheel above and below **CUES:** this **C**urvy, **R**oomy, **M**agnificent 車 **kuruma** (car) belongs to the **Sh**ah **COMPARE:** 重(い) omoi = heavy, # 284; other similar kanji at # **1966** and # **2075**

0284. 重 **PRONUNCIATIONS: omo, kasa, chou, juu, e** **MEANINGS:** heavy, layer **EXAMPLES:** 重い omoi = heavy; 重ねる kasaneru = to pile up; 慎重な shinchou na = cautious, prudent; 体重 taijuu = a person's weight; 紙一重 kamihito'e = paper-thin (difference) **DESCRIPTION:** a 車 kuruma (car, # 283), with an extra hubcap added to each wheel **CUES:** this 車 (car) is 重い **omo**i (heavy) because **O**ld **M**oses added these extra hubcaps to each wheel, and **Ca**sanova and Margaret **Cho** 重ねた **kasa**neta (piled up) even more weight by adding **Ju**ice and **E**ggs to the trunk **GROUP:** 重(い) omoi = heavy, # 284; 動(く) ugoku = to move, # 286; 働(く) hataraku = to labor, # 287; 種(類) shurui = variety, # 1098; 衝(撃) shougeki = impact, # 1561; 腫(瘍) shuyou = a tumor, # 1701; 勲(章) kunshou = a medal, # 1938; 薫(製) kunsei = smoked food, # 1951

0285. 転 **PRONUNCIATIONS: koro, ten** **MEANING:** to roll **EXAMPLES:** 転ぶ korobu = to fall; 自転車 jitensha = bicycle **DESCRIPTION:** on the left, 車 sha (vehicle, # 283); on the upper right, 二 ni (two, # 2); on the lower right, the katakana ム mu, which is the sound made by a cow **CUES:** these 二 (two) ム (cows) were struck by this 車 (vehicle), which is a 自転車 ji**ten**sha (bicycle), after its rider had a **C**oronary (heart attack) in **Ten**nessee **ALSO COMPARE:** other similar kanji at # **1056** and # **1966**

0286. 動 **PRONUNCIATIONS: dou, ugo** **MEANING:** to move **EXAMPLES:** 自動車 jidousha = car; 動く ugoku = to move, intransitive; 動かす ugokasu = to move, transitive **DESCRIPTION:** on the left, 重(い) omoi (heavy, # 284); on the right, 力 chikara (force, # 107) **CUES:** a 重 (heavy) 自動車 ji**dou**sha (car) which 動く **ugo**ku (moves) under its own 力 (force) can escape **Do**berman dogs and **U**ber **Go**phers **ALSO COMPARE:** (自)転(車) jitensha = bicycle, # 285; other similar kanji at # **284** and # **1846**

0287. 働 PRONUNCIATIONS: **hatara, dou** MEANINGS: to work, operate EXAMPLES: 働く hataraku = to labor; 労働者 roudousha = laborer DESCRIPTION: compared to 動(く) ugoku (to move, # 286), or (自)動(車) jidousha (car, # 286) (identical pronunciation), this kanji adds a man with a slanted hat on the left; it retains 重 (heavy) and 力 (force) CUES: this man with a slanted hat 働く **hatara**ku (labors) making **Hat**s for **Ara**bs, using this 力 (force) to 動 (move) 重 (heavy) hats from one place to another, and he gets paid good **Dough** (money) for doing so ALSO COMPARE: other similar kanji at # **284** and # **1846**

0288. 輸 PRONUNCIATION: **yu** MEANING: to transport EXAMPLES: 輸入する yu'nyuu suru = to import; 輸出する yushutsu suru = to export DESCRIPTION: on the left, 車 kuruma (car, # 283); on the right, compared to 前 mae (before, # 157), the upside-down bench at the top has been replaced by a roof, so this resembles a house CUE: 前 (before) I moved to this house in the **Yu**kon, I 輸入した **yu**nyuu shita (imported) 車 (cars) like this one ALSO COMPARE: 輪 wa = a round shape, # 690; other similar kanji at # **733** and # **1966**

0289. 軽 PRONUNCIATIONS: **karu, garu², karo, kei** MEANING: light weight EXAMPLES: 軽い karui = light; 尻軽な shirigaru na = frivolous, of loose morals; 軽やか karoyaka = light, easy, minor; 軽自動車 keijidousha = a lightweight car DESCRIPTION: compared to 経(験) keiken (experience, # 224) (identical pronunciation), this kanji substitutes 車 kuruma (car, # 283) for the skeet shooter on the left; it retains 又 (table) above 土 (soil) CUES: a **C**at on the **R**oof of this 車 (car) watches as I sit at this 又 (table) on this 土 (soil) and eat **C**arrots and **C**ake; after I finish, my body still feels 軽い **karu**i (light) ALSO COMPARE: other similar kanji at # **1894** and # **1966**

0290. 乾 PRONUNCIATIONS: **kawa, kan** MEANING: to get dry EXAMPLES: 乾く kawaku = to get dry; 乾電池 kandenchi = dry cell battery DESCRIPTION: the radical on the left is not the same as 車 kuruma (car, # 283), since the axle doesn't travel all the way through, so let's call this a California wagon; at the upper right, a crutch; at the lower right, the letter Z, which reminds us of zebras CUES: this zebra with this crutch is lurking outside this **C**alifornia **Wa**gon, so let's stay inside, where 乾いている **kawa**ite iru (it's dry), and we can eat from **Can**s COMPARE: 渇(く) kawaku = to get thirsty, # 1928; other similar kanji at # **1308**, # **1835** and # **2080**

0291. 朝 PRONUNCIATIONS: **sa, chou, asa** MEANING: morning EXAMPLES: 今朝 kesa = this morning; 朝食 choushoku = breakfast; 朝 asa = morning DESCRIPTION: compared to 乾(く) kawaku (to get dry, # 290), this substitutes 月 tsuki (moon, # 148) for the zebra with the crutch on the right; it retains the California wagon on the left CUES: I'm sitting in this California wagon in the early 朝 **asa** (morning), watching this 月 (moon) fade away, feeling **Sa**d that I was **Cho**sen for early morning watch duty, and hoping that the day will get warm **ASA**P (as soon as possible) ALSO COMPARE: 明(日) ashita = tomorrow, # **154**; other similar kanji at # **1308**

Now

0292. 今 PRONUNCIATIONS: **ima, kon, k, ko, ke** MEANING: now EXAMPLES: 今 ima = now; 今度 kondo = this time, next time; 今日 kyou = today; 今年 kotoshi = this year; 今朝 kesa = this morning DESCRIPTION: at the top, a roof, with a ceiling under it; at the bottom, the number 7 CUES: **I**magine that 今 **ima** (now) it is 7 o'clock, and it's time for the **Con**ductor to step under this roof, turn the **K**ey, start the **C**ommuter train and settle back to drink a **K**eg of beer **COMPARE:** other similar kanji at # **1491**

0293. 会 PRONUNCIATIONS: kai, gai, e, a MEANING: to meet (people) EXAMPLES:
会社 kaisha = company; 会議 kaigi = meeting; 運送会社 unsougaisha = moving company; 会得する etoku suru = to grasp, understand, master; 会う au = to meet someone **DESCRIPTION:** at the top, a peaked roof; in the middle, 二 ni (two, # 2); at the bottom, the katakana ム mu, which is the sound made by a cow **CUES:** the **Kai**ser wants to buy these 二 (two) ム (cows) under this peaked roof, but first he will 会う **a**u (meet) a **Gu**ide who is an **E**xpert on cows and who will take him to a 会議 **kai**gi (meeting) with the seller in **A**frica **COMPARE:** other similar kanji at # **1056** and # **1382**

0294. 合 PRONUNCIATIONS: ai, gou, a, ga MEANING: to match or harmonize, to come together EXAMPLES: 具合 guai = condition, state; 都合 tsugou = circumstances, convenience; 合う au = to come together, to match or suit; 合わせる awaseru = to put together, combine or harmonize; 合戦 gassen = battle **DESCRIPTION:** at the top, a peaked roof; at the bottom, a napkin above a 口 (box) **CUES:** this napkin fits neatly on this 口 (box) under this roof, suggesting that our plans to market **I**ce-cold **G**oat milk will 合う **a**u (come together) in **A**frica, if 都合がいい tsu**gou** ga ii (circumstances are good), and if we can buy **Ga**s for our milk trucks **COMPARE:** other similar kanji at # **1251**

0295. 答 PRONUNCIATIONS: kota, tou MEANING: to answer a question EXAMPLES:
答える kotaeru = to reply; 回答 kaitou = answer, response **DESCRIPTION:** at the top, two shortened 竹 take (bamboo, # 134), which could represent a question on the left and a corresponding answer on the right; at the bottom, 合(う) au (to match or suit, # 294), which resembles a peaked roof above a napkin covering a box **CUES:** when I met with my **C**olorado **T**ax attorney in this little house and asked about my **T**obacco investments, her 答え **kota**e (answer), which 合 (matched) my needs, was to invest in this 竹 (bamboo) instead **ALSO COMPARE:** other similar kanji at # **1251** and # **2074**

0296. 容 PRONUNCIATION: you
MEANINGS: content, to let in **EXAMPLE:** 内容 naiyou = content **DESCRIPTION:** at the top, a bad haircut; at the bottom, a bathroom with water vapor rising from it, as seen in 浴(びる) abiru (to bathe, # 256) **CUE:** after receiving this bad haircut, I fled to **Y**osemite, explored its 内容 nai**you** (contents) and bathed in this bathroom **GROUP:** (内)容 naiyou = content, # 296; 溶(岩) yougan = lava, # 815 **COMPARE:** other similar kanji at # **660**

Bench Hats
0297. 登 PRONUNCIATIONS: tou, to, nobo MEANING: to climb EXAMPLES:
登録 touroku = registration; 登頂する touchou suru = to reach the summit; 登山 tozan = mountain climbing; 登る noboru = to climb **DESCRIPTION:** at the top left and top right, two radicals that resemble upside-down benches; let's call them bench hats; in the middle, 口 kuchi (mouth, # 426), which resembles a TV set, under a napkin, supported by toes resting on a base; this radical at the bottom can also be seen as an upside-down bench **CUES:** this **T**V set, which is covered by this napkin and these two bench hats, and is supported by these **T**oes, is displaying a **T**ortoise that can 登る **nobo**ru (climb) like **Nobo**dy else **GROUP:** 登(る) noboru = to climb, # 297; (出)発 shuppatsu = departure, # 298; 祭 matsuri = festival, # 377; (国)際 kokusai = international, # 379; (警)察 keisatsu = police, # 896; 廃(れ)る sutareru = to decline, # 1221; 擦(る) kosuru = to rub, # 1429; 澄(む) sumu = to become clear, # 1674 **ALSO COMPARE:** other similar kanji at # **721** and # **2070**

0298. 発 **PRONUNCIATIONS: ha, hatsu, patsu², ho MEANINGS:** departure, to disclose **EXAMPLES:** 発表 happyou = presentation; 発明 hatsumei = invention; 東京発 toukyou hatsu = departing from Tokyo; 出発する shuppatsu suru = to depart; 発作 hossa = attack or fit, e.g., 心臓発作 shinzou hossa = heart attack **DESCRIPTION:** at the top left and top right, two radicals that resemble upside-down benches; let's call them bench hats; at the bottom, a happy expansive guy with lopsided legs, including a long right leg and a protruding toe on his right foot **CUES:** this **Ha**waiian guy with these lopsided legs who is wearing these two bench **H**ats gives a 発表 **ha**ppyou (presentation) with this right leg extended, but the sock on this right foot has a **H**ole in it **COMPARE:** 登(る) noboru = to climb, # 297; other similar kanji at # **297** and # **1221**

Peaked Roof

0299. 冷 (sometimes written 冷)
PRONUNCIATIONS: rei, tsume, hi, sa MEANING: cold object (not cold atmosphere) **EXAMPLES:** 冷蔵庫 reizouko = refrigerator; 冷たい tsumetai = cold object; 冷やす hiyasu = to chill; 冷める sameru = to cool off **DESCRIPTION:** on the left, a water radical (see # 12) which suggests rain; on the right, a house with a peaked roof, which we rent from Melvin, and a wobbly table under a napkin (the **alternative** kanji shown above also contains a peaked roof on the right, above another drop of rain and マ ma) **CUES:** this table in Melvin's house is wobbly because one of its legs is too long, and when it **R**ains, the floors are 冷たい **tsume**tai (cold), so we will **Tsue** (sue) **M**elvin to get him to **H**eat the house, and use a **Sa**w to shorten this table leg [**alternatively**, when it **R**ains, drops like this penetrate this roof, and the floors are 冷たい **tsume**tai (cold), so this マ **ma** (mother) will **Tsue** (sue) **M**elvin to get him to **H**eat the house, and use **Sa**p to plug the leaks] **COMPARE:** similar kanji at # **962** and # **1946** (alternative font)

0300. 全 **PRONUNCIATIONS: matta, sube, zen MEANINGS:** all, entire **EXAMPLES:** 全く mattaku = entirely; 全て subete = all, everything; 全部 zenbu = all, everything **DESCRIPTION:** at the top, a Zen temple with a peaked roof; under the roof, 王 ou (king, # 1077); compared to 金 kane (money, # 301), 全 is missing two short slanting lines at the bottom **CUES:** a **Mat**ador and a **Sub**editor come to this **Zen** temple to talk about 全部 **zen**bu (everything) with this 王 (king) **ALSO COMPARE:** other similar kanji at # **1077**, # **1382** and # **2026**

0301. 金 **PRONUNCIATIONS: kin, gin, kon, gon, kane, kana MEANINGS:** money, gold, metal **EXAMPLES:** 金曜日 kinyoubi = Friday; 金属 kinzoku = metal; 賃金 chingin = wages; 金剛力 kongouriki = superhuman strength; 黄金 ougon = gold; お金 okane = money; 金物 kanamono = hardware **DESCRIPTION:** compared to 全 zen (everything, # 300), this adds two slanting lines on the ground floor, which may represent money; altogether, this resembles a symmetrical house that could be a kindergarten **CUES:** my teacher at this **Kin**dergarten drinks **Gin**, she knows 全 (everything) about the **Con**go, she uses a **Gong** to tell us when recess is finished, and she gave me these two pieces of お金 o**kane** (money) that are lying on the ground floor to buy some **Can**adian **E**ggs and **Can**aries **ALSO COMPARE:** other similar kanji at # **2010**

0302. 銀 **PRONUNCIATION: gin MEANING:** silver **EXAMPLES:** 銀 gin = silver; 銀行 ginkou = bank **DESCRIPTION:** on the left, 金 kane (money, # 301); on the right, 良 (い) yoi (good, # 303), with L and Y at its base but without its pointy hat **CUE:** I went to the 銀行 **gin**kou (bank) to get this 金 (money) for some 良 (good) **Gin ALSO COMPARE:** other similar kanji at # **805** and # **2010**

0303. 良 **PRONUNCIATIONS: ryou, i, yo, ra MEANING:** good **EXAMPLES:** 良好 ryoukou = favorable, satisfactory; 不良 furyou = delinquent, poor condition; 良い ii = good, usually written いい; 良い yoi = good; 良かった yokatta = it was good; 奈良 Nara = a city in Japan; 野良犬 nora inu = stray dog; **Note:** yoi and ii are both written 良い **DESCRIPTION:** compared to 食(べる) taberu (to eat, # 398), this removes the roof from the tavern; it retains 白(い) shiroi (white, # 44) and the letters L & Y, which remind us of light years **CUES:** Pope Leo wears 白 (white) suits at Easter, he is Light Years ahead of his peers, and he's a 良い **yoi** (good) person who feeds **Y**ogurt to his **R**abbits **ALSO COMPARE:** other similar kanji at # 398 and # **805**

0304. 鉄 **PRONUNCIATIONS: te, de², tetsu MEANING:** iron **EXAMPLES:** 鉄砲 teppou = gun; 豆鉄砲 mamedeppou = peashooter; 地下鉄 chikatetsu = subway **DESCRIPTION:** on the left, (お)金 okane (money, # 301); on the right, 失(礼) shitsurei (discourtesy, # 206) which is a fusion of 牛 ushi (cow, # 205) and 大きい ookii (big, # 188) **CUES:** I paid this 金 (money) for this 大 (big) 牛 (cow) in **T**exas, and it needed a **T**etanus shot which **S**uperman gave it via a 鉄 **tetsu** (iron) needle **GROUP:** 牛 ushi = cow, # 205; 失(礼) shitsurei = discourtesy, # 206; 鉄(砲) teppou = gun, # 304; 秩(序) chitsujo = order, # 1482 **ALSO COMPARE:** kanji that combine 牛 (cow) with 木 (tree) at # 1675; other similar kanji at # **2010**

0305. 館 **PRONUNCIATIONS: kan, yakata, date MEANING:** large building **EXAMPLES:** 旅館 ryokan = Japanese inn; 図書館 toshokan = library; 館 yakata = mansion, palace; 田舎館 Inakadate = a village in Aomori **DESCRIPTION:** on the left, 食(事) shokuji (meal, # 398); at the upper right, a bad haircut; at the lower right, bunk beds **CUES:** this is a 旅館 ryo**kan** (Japanese inn), where these 食 (meals) are prepared on the left, and these bunk beds on the right, under a roof that looks like this bad haircut, are lighted by **Can**dles to discourage **Y**ak **Att**a**c**ks during the night when the **D**arkness is **T**errifying **ALSO COMPARE:** similar kanji at # **880** and # **1974**

Heart

0306. 心 **PRONUNCIATIONS: kokoro, shin, jin², koko, goko MEANINGS:** heart, mind **EXAMPLES:** 心 kokoro = heart; 心配する shinpai suru = to worry; 肝心 kanjin = essential; 心地 kokochi = feeling, sensation, mood; 居心地 igokochi = the way one feels in a particular ambience **DESCRIPTION:** the small line on the left represents one ventricle of a heart, the large curved line represents the other ventricle, and the two lines at the upper right represent shingles, protecting the heart of a man named Roy Rogers **CUES:** don't throw **C**oconuts at **R**oy's **S**hingles, since you may damage his 心 **kokoro** (heart); instead eat your **C**oconuts over on the **G**old **C**oast **GROUP:** this is a group of one

0307. 必 **PRONUNCIATIONS: kanara, hitsu, hi MEANINGS:** without fail, necessary **EXAMPLES:** 必ず kanarazu = without fail; 必要 hitsuyou = necessary; 必死に hisshi = desperate, frantic **DESCRIPTION:** a 心 kokoro (heart, # 306) belonging to a Canadian rat, sliced in half **CUES:** if you want the **Ca**nadian **R**at to expire 必ず **kanara**zu (without fail), it is 必要 **hitsu**you (necessary) that you slice this 心 (heart) in two, before it **Hit**s yo**U** with its tail and bruises your **Hee**l **ALSO COMPARE:** other similar kanji at # **1297**

0308. 思 **PRONUNCIATIONS: omo, shi**
MEANINGS: to think, thought **EXAMPLES:** 思う omou = to think/feel; 思想 shisou = thought, idea **DESCRIPTION:** at the top, 田(んぼ) tanbo (rice paddy, # 68); at the bottom, 心 kokoro (heart, # 306) **CUES:** **O**saka **M**osquitoes breed in this 田 (rice paddy), and we 思う **omo**u (think) that they sting our **S**heep, which have 心 (hearts) like this **GROUP:** 思(う) omou = to think, # 308; (知)恵 chie = wisdom, # 720; (遠)慮 enryo = reserve, # 1194

0309. 恥 **PRONUNCIATIONS: ha, haji**
MEANINGS: shame, dishonor **EXAMPLES:** 恥ずかしい hazukashii = embarrassed, shy; 恥 haji = shame, dishonor **DESCRIPTION:** on the left, 耳 mimi (ear, # 57); on the right, 心 kokoro (heart, # 306) **CUES:** when Prince **Ha**rry heard the beating of this 心 (heart) in this 耳 (ear), he felt 恥ずかしい **ha**zukashii (embarrassed) and consulted a **Ha**rvard Genius **ALSO COMPARE:** other similar kanji at # **1713**

0310. 忘 **PRONUNCIATIONS: wasu, bou**
MEANING: to forget **EXAMPLES:** 忘れる wasureru = to forget; 忘年会 bounenkai = end-of-year party **DESCRIPTION:** at the top, a shaky table, as seen in 亡(くなる) nakunaru (to die, # 585); at the bottom, 心 kokoro (heart, # 306) **CUES:** during a **Wa**r in the **Su**ez Canal, I was sitting at this 亡 (shaky table) on my patrol **B**oat studying a map, and I 忘れた **wasu**reta (forgot) to take medication for this 心 (heart)
ALSO COMPARE: other similar kanji at # **585**

0311. 窓 **PRONUNCIATIONS: mado, sou**
MEANING: window **EXAMPLES:** 窓 mado = window; 同窓会 dousoukai = reunion of graduates **DESCRIPTION:** at the top, a bird from Cuba with two lopsided legs, as seen in (研)究 kenkyuu (research, # 112), soaring above ム mu (the sound made by a cow) which, together, remind us of a Cuban cowbird; at the bottom, 心 kokoro (heart, # 306) **CUES:** when I was living in a **Ma**rs **Do**me, I sat on a **So**fa, looked through a 窓 **mado** (window) and saw this ム (cow) bird with these two lopsided legs and this big 心 (heart) **ALSO COMPARE:** other similar kanji at # **112** and # **1678**

0312. 急 **PRONUNCIATIONS: kyuu, iso**
MEANING: to hurry or rush
EXAMPLES: 急に kyuu ni = suddenly; 急ぐ isogu = to hurry **DESCRIPTION:** at the top, a cute fish head (see # 80) that seems isolated; in the middle, long hair streaming to the left, suggesting speed; at the bottom, 心 kokoro (heart, # 306) **CUES:** this **C**ute fish is **Iso**lated from the others, but he has a lot of 心 (heart), and 急に **kyuu** ni (suddenly) he can 急ぐ **iso**gu (hurry) **ALSO COMPARE:** other similar kanji # **87** and # **1165**

0313. 悪 **PRONUNCIATIONS: waru, aku, a, o** **MEANING:** bad **EXAMPLES:** 悪い warui = bad; 悪 aku = evil; 悪しからず ashikarazu = don't take it badly; 嫌悪 ken'o = hatred, disgust **DESCRIPTION:** at the top, 亜 (the Red Cross logo, sandwiched between two platforms); this can also be seen as three eyes hanging from a platform; at the bottom, 心 kokoro (heart, # 306) **CUES:** **Wa**r **Ru**ined the health of this 心 (heart), and it was feeling 悪い **waru**i (bad), but it got help from this 亜 (Red Cross) and also some **A**cupuncture treatments from its **A**unt in **O**saka **GROUP:** 悪 aku = evil, # 313; 壷 tsubo = jar, # 1274; 亜(鉛) aen = zinc, # 1589 **ALSO COMPARE:** other kanji with three eyes hanging from a platform at # **1415**

0314. 念 **PRONUNCIATION: nen**
MEANINGS: thought, to ponder **EXAMPLES:** 残念 zannen = too bad **DESCRIPTION:** at the top, 今 ima (now, # 292), which contains a 7 under a ceiling under a peaked roof; at the bottom, 心

kokoro (heart, # 306); together these two radicals look like something moving to the right **CUE:** 今 (now), this 心 (heart) belonging to my **N**egative **N**ephew is driving him to the right of the political spectrum, and that's 残念 zan**nen** (too bad) **COMPARE:** other similar kanji at # **1491**

0315. 息 **PRONUNCIATIONS:** *musu, i, iki, soku* **MEANINGS:** son, breath, respiration **EXAMPLES:** 息子 musuko = son; 息吹 ibuki = breath; 息吹く ibuku = to breathe; 息 iki = breath, respiration; 休息 kyuusoku = rest, relief, relaxation **DESCRIPTION:** compared to 思(う) omou (to think, # 308), this substitutes 自 ji (self, # 55) for the 田 (rice paddy) at the top; it retains 心 (heart) **CUES:** a person close to this 自 (self)'s 心 (heart) is my 息子 **musu**ko (son), who is a **M**usical **U**ber driver with big **E**ars and **I**cky 息 **iki** (breath), and who is always **S**oaked with sweat **ALSO COMPARE:** other similar kanji at # **1381**

0316. 娘 **PRONUNCIATION:** *musume* **MEANINGS:** daughter, young woman **EXAMPLE:** 娘 musume = daughter **DESCRIPTION:** on the left, 女 onna (female, # 235); on the right, 良(い) yoi (good, # 303), which contains **L** & **Y** at its base **CUE:** our 娘 **musume** (daughter) is this 良 (good) 女 (female) who worked at the **M**useum during the **S**ummer **COMPARE:** other kanji containing 女 on the left at # **2039**; other similar kanji at # **805**

0317. 意 **PRONUNCIATION:** *i* **MEANINGS:** meaning, intention, mind **EXAMPLES:** 意味 imi = meaning; 意見 iken = opinion **DESCRIPTION:** compared to 音 oto (sound, # 266), this adds 心 kokoro (heart, # 306) at the bottom **CUE:** this 音 (sound) in this 心 (heart) sounds **E**erie and must have some kind of 意味 **i**mi (meaning) **ALSO COMPARE:** other similar kanji at # **266**

0318. 億 **PRONUNCIATION:** *oku* **MEANING:** one hundred million **EXAMPLE:** 五億 go oku = 500 million **DESCRIPTION:** on the left, a man with a slanted hat; on the right, 意(味) imi (meaning, # 317), which includes a bell at the top **CUE:** this man tilts his hat back in order to examine this bell which can play 一億の ichi**oku** no (100 million) **O**ld **K**ool-Aid jingles that have 意 (meaning) for people **ALSO COMPARE:** other similar kanji at # **266**

0319. 怒 **PRONUNCIATIONS:** *oko, do, ika* **MEANING:** angry **EXAMPLES:** 怒る okoru = to get angry; 激怒 gekido = fury, outrage; 怒り ikari = anger, fury **DESCRIPTION:** at the upper left, 女 onna (female, # 235); at the upper right, 又 mata ("again," # 24), which resembles a simple table; at the bottom, 心 kokoro (heart, # 306) **CUES:** this 女 (female) with this fiery 心 (heart) is an **O**ld **C**oder, and she 怒った **oko**tta (got angry) when some **D**oughnuts and some **E**aster **C**andy disappeared from this 又 (table) **GROUP:** 怒(る) okoru = to get angry, # 319; 努力 doryoku = effort, # 519 (identical pronunciation); 奴(隷) dorei = a slave, # 1582 (also identical pronunciation) **ALSO COMPARE:** other kanji containing 女 on the left at # **2039**

X's

0320. 区 **PRONUNCIATION:** *ku* **MEANINGS:** ward, section **EXAMPLES:** 区役所 kuyakusho = ward office; 区別する kubetsu suru = to distinguish or differentiate **DESCRIPTION:** a building in Kuwait that is open on one side, resembling a storefront, containing an X **CUE:** this 区役所 **ku**yakusho (ward office) in **K**uwait is a storefront, and this X marks the spot where citizens from the ward are served **GROUP:** 区(役所) kuyakusho = ward office, # 320; 医(者) isha = doctor, # 325; 駆(ける) kakeru = to run, # 776; (一)匹 ippiki = one small

animal, # 818; 欧(州) oushuu = Europe, # 1334; 匠 takumi = an artisan, # 1653; 殴(る) naguru = to beat up, # 1748; (中)枢 chuusuu = center, # 1953. 匿(名) tokumei = anonymity, # 1962
ALSO COMPARE: other kanji containing X at # <u>1953</u>

0321. 気 **PRONUNCIATIONS: ki, gi, ke, ge, ku** **MEANINGS:** spirit, air **EXAMPLES:** 天気 tenki = weather; 気持ち kimochi = feeling; 風邪気味 kazegimi = a bit of a cold (upper respiratory infection); 寒気 samuke = a chill; 何気ない nanigenai = casual; 意気地 ikuji = self-respect **DESCRIPTION:** at the top right, a lean-to with a triple roof; at the bottom, an X **CUES:** when I stayed at this spot marked with an X in this lean-to in **Ki**ev, I played with **Ge**ese, I wore **Ke**ds (a brand of shoes) like the other **Gu**ests, I drank **Ko**ol-Aid, and the 天気 ten**ki** (weather) was good
GROUP: (天)気 tenki = weather, # 321; 倉(庫) souko = warehouse, # 1170; 創(造) souzou = creation, # 1171; 汽(車) kisha = steam-powered train, # 1431 (identical pronunciation)
ALSO COMPARE: other similar kanji at # <u>1953</u>

0322. 歳 **PRONUNCIATIONS: sai, zai², sei, chi** **MEANINGS:** age, year **EXAMPLES:** 十六歳 juurokusai = 16 years old; 万歳 banzai = "10,000 years," i.e., "long live!"; お歳暮 oseibo = year-end gift; 二十歳 hatachi = 20 years old **DESCRIPTION:** at the top, 止(まる) tomaru (to stop, # 173); below 止, a two-sided lean-to supported by a long halberd (combination lance and axe); on the lower left, a nail flanked by diagonal slashes; this kanji resembles a math problem in division, as seen in constructions like 3 |̄12x̄ = 4x **CUES:** 歳 **sai** (age) is a number, and it is divisible like this, but I remain **Si**lent about my age and 止 (stop) before I **Sa**y it, lest people **Ch**eat me ALSO COMPARE: other similar kanji at # <u>702</u>, # <u>915</u> and # <u>1929</u>

Native American Chief

0323. 知 **PRONUNCIATIONS: chi, ji, shi** **MEANINGS:** to know; knowledge **EXAMPLES:** 知識 chishiki = knowledge; 知人 chijin = acquaintance; ご存知 gozonji = to honorably know; 知る shiru = to know; 知らせる shiraseru = to inform; 知り合い shiriai = acquaintance
DESCRIPTION: on the left, a Native American chief, wearing a war bonnet; on the right, the 口 kuchi (mouth, # 426) of a sheep, which resembles a box **CUES:** this Native American **Ch**ief is a veterinary dentist with a **J**eep who specializes in **Sh**eep, and he 知る **shi**ru (knows) a lot about 口 (mouths) like this
GROUP: 知(る) shiru = to know, # 323; 口 kuchi = mouth, # 426; (温)和 onwa = calm, # 513; (参)加 sanka = participation, # 714; 程 hodo = extent, # 954; 聖(人) seijin = a saint, # 1500; 如(才ない) josainai = clever, # 1578; (愚)痴 guchi = complaint, # 1581 ALSO COMPARE: kanji with 口 (box) on the *left* side at # 2073; other similar kanji at # <u>324</u>

0324. 短 **PRONUNCIATIONS: mijika, tan** **MEANING:** short **EXAMPLES:** 短い mijikai = short (object); 長短 choutan = length **DESCRIPTION:** on the left, a midget Native American chief, wearing a war bonnet; on the right, a TV set with a napkin above it, resting on toes on a platform (which can also be seen as an upside-down bench), as seen in 豆(腐) toufu (bean curd, # 721) **CUES:** this Native American chief is a **Mi**dget with a **J**eep **Ca**r; he has a good **Ta**n, but he is too 短い **mijika**i (short) to see over this TV set
GROUP: (家)族 kazoku = family, # 115; 知(る) shiru = to know, # 323; 短(い) mijikai = short, # 324; 医者 isha = medical doctor, # 325; 喉 nodo = throat, # 794; 疑(う) utagau = to doubt, # 978; (気)候 kikou = climate, # 996; 矢 ya = arrow, # 1045; (愚)痴 guchi = complaint, # 1581; 挨(拶) aisatsu = a greeting, # 1649; 凝

(る) koru = to grow stiff, # 1680; 疾(風) shippu = a gale, # 1734; 嫉(妬) shitto = jealousy, # 1890; (模)擬 mogi = imitation, # 2003; 矯(正) kyousei = correction, # 2061 **ALSO COMPARE:** other similar kanji at # **721** and # **2070**

0325. 医   PRONUNCIATION: i

MEANING: medicine   **EXAMPLE:** 医者 isha = medical doctor   **DESCRIPTION:** an Native American chief, wearing a war bonnet, in a building that is open on one side

CUE: this Native American chief is an 医者 **i**sha (doctor) with **E**agle eyes, staring out of this storefront clinic, which is open on one side   **COMPARE:** other similar kanji at # **320** and # **324**

Uncooked Rice

0326. 米   PRONUNCIATIONS: yone, kome, gome², bei, mai   MEANINGS: rice, America

EXAMPLES: 米酢 yonezu = rice vinegar; 米 kome = uncooked rice; 餅米 mochigome = glutinous rice; 米国 beikoku = U.S.A.; 白米 hakumai = white rice   **DESCRIPTION:** this resembles a comet with eight projections   **CUES:** a **Y**ogi in the **Ne**therlands can arrange these 米 **kome** (uncooked rice) grains into an eight-sided **Com**et like this, **Ba**ke them in an oven and feed them to **Mi**ce   **COMPARE:** other similar kanji at # **1387**

0327. 来   PRONUNCIATIONS: ko, ki, ku, rai   MEANINGS: to come, next

EXAMPLES: 来ない konai = will not come; 来ます kimasu = will come; 来る kuru = will come; 来年 rainen = next year; 来日する rainichi suru = to visit Japan   **DESCRIPTION:** compared to 米 kome (rice, # 326), this adds a tire stop, as seen in 対(する) tai suru (to confront, # 674) at the top   **CUES:** the **Co**ders who 来る **ku**ru (come) for dinner 来週 **rai**shuu (next week) will get **Qui**che, **Koo**l-Aid and this 米 (**Ri**ce), and they can park their cars against tire stops like this   **ALSO COMPARE:** other similar kanji at # **1387** and # **1860**

0328. 番   PRONUNCIATION: ban

MEANINGS: watch, turn, order   **EXAMPLES:** 一番 ichiban = number one; 番 ban = turn; 番号 bangou = number   **DESCRIPTION:** at the top, 米 kome (rice, # 326), with a slash drawn over it; at the bottom, a 田 (rice paddy, # 68   **CUE:** someone has drawn a slash over the 米 (rice) at the top, suggesting that it is the 番 **ban** (turn) of this 田 (paddy) in **Ban**gladesh to supply rice   **ALSO COMPARE:** other similar kanji at # **220** and # **1368**

0329. 隣   PRONUNCIATIONS: rin, tonari   MEANINGS: neighbor, next door

EXAMPLES: 隣人 rinjin = neighbor; 隣 tonari = next door   **DESCRIPTION:** on the left, ß beta from the Greek alphabet; at the top right, 米 kome (rice, # 326); at the bottom left, 夕(方) yuugata (evening, # 160); at the bottom right, a left-facing knee, as seen in 降(る) furu (to rain, # 178), suggesting a sitting person   **CUES:** this **Wri**nkled ß (Greek) named **To**bias of **Na**rita lives 学校の隣 gakkou no **tonari** (next door to a school) and sits with this bent knee in the 夕 (evenings), sorting through this 米 (rice)   **ALSO COMPARE:** other similar kanji at # **801**, # **1387**, # **1808** and # **2030**

Sheep

0330. 洋   PRONUNCIATION: you

MEANINGS: ocean, abroad

EXAMPLES: 西洋 seiyou = the western part of the world; 洋服 youfuku = Western clothes; 東洋 touyou = the eastern part of the world

DESCRIPTION: compared to 羊 hitsuji (sheep, # 1223), this adds a water radical (see # 12) on the left; it retains the animal with two horns, two ears which can also be seen as antennae, four legs and a tail, and it includes the upper portion of a Y at the top, which reminds us of yogurt

CUE: 西洋 sei**you** (the western part of the world) is across this water, where a lot of people keep 羊 (sheep) like this and eat **Yo**gurt

ALSO COMPARE: other similar kanji at # **1223**

0331. 半 **PRONUNCIATIONS: han, naka**
MEANINGS: half, middle **EXAMPLES:** 一時半 ichijihan = half past 1:00; 半分 hanbun = half, or a ½ share; 半ば nakaba = half, the middle **DESCRIPTION:** compared to 羊 hitsuji (sheep, # 1223), which contains three horizontal lines, this kanji has two, and it adds a nose at the top; this can also be seen as a telephone pole on fire **CUES: Han**sel noticed that this 羊 (sheep) painting at the National Cathedral only depicts 半分 **han**bun (half) of the animal and adds this nose to its head **ALSO COMPARE:** similar kanji at # **1054**

0332. 業 **PRONUNCIATIONS: waza, gyou, gou MEANINGS:** business, vocation **EXAMPLES:** 仕業 shiwaza = deeds, acts; 卒業 sotsugyou = graduation; 工業 kougyou = industry; 授業 jugyou = class; 自業自得 jigoujitoku = paying for one's mistakes **DESCRIPTION:** at the bottom, 木 ki (tree, # 118); above this tree are several extra branches, capped by a tray carrying four lights, resembling a Christmas tree **CUES:** when I went to **W**atch **Z**achary teach a 授業 ju**gyou** (class), he had decorated the room with this Christmas tree, and he served the students **G**yoza made with **G**oat meat **GROUP:** (卒)業 sotsugyou = graduation, # 332; 僕 boku = I, # 333; (打)撲(傷) dabokushou = a bruise, # 1375 **ALSO COMPARE:** kanji with extra branches on *husband* rather than on *tree* at # 333

0333. 僕 **PRONUNCIATIONS: boku, shimobe MEANING:** I (male) **EXAMPLES:** 僕 boku = I (male); 僕 shimobe = manservant, menial **DESCRIPTION:** on the left, a man with a slanted hat, who is bony; on the right, compared to (工)業 kougyou (industry, # 332), which we have described as a Christmas tree, this radical substitutes 夫 otto (husband, # 614), plus an extra pair of branches, for the tree trunk at the lower center **CUES:** 僕 **boku** (I) am this **B**ony **K**ool-Aid salesman on the left, and ever since I cut the central trunk from this 業 (Christmas tree), making it resemble a husband with an extra pair of arms who is decorated with lights, I stay in bed, tilting my hat back like this to watch TV and wishing that my **Sh**eets had **M**ore **B**ells on them **GROUP:** 実(行) jikkou = implementation, # 195; 僕 boku = I, # 333; (打)撲(傷) dabokushou = a bruise, # 1375 (identical pronunciation) **ALSO COMPARE:** other similar kanji at # **332**

Man with a Double Hat

0334. 行 **PRONUNCIATIONS: i, okona, kou, gyou, yu, ya MEANINGS:** to go, carry out, conduct a business **EXAMPLES:** 行く iku = to go; 行う okonau = to conduct; 銀行 ginkou = bank; 行事 gyouji = event; 東京行き toukyou yuki = bound for Tokyo; 流行る hayaru = to become popular or successful (usually spelled はやる) **DESCRIPTION:** on the left, a man from Italy with a double hat; on the right, a nail, as seen in 丁(寧) teinei (courteous, # 702), with a line above it which could represent a hammer **CUES:** this man with two hats works with this hammer and nail, and then he likes to **E**at, and he 行く **i**ku (goes) to see an **O**ld **C**oder who is his **N**anny and trades one of his two hats for some **C**orn to put in **G**yoza for the **Yu**le celebration to be held in his **Y**ard **COMPARE:** similar kanji at # **625**

0335. 後 **PRONUNCIATIONS: ushi, ato, kou, go, sa, nochi MEANINGS:** behind, later, rear **EXAMPLES:** 後ろ ushiro = behind; 後で ato de = later; 後悔 koukai = regret; 午後 gogo = afternoon; 明後日 asatte = the day after tomorrow, usually written あさって; 後ほど nochihodo = afterward, later **DESCRIPTION:** on the left, a man with a double hat; on the right, a dancer with a ponytail who is an usher, pointing a truncated 糸 (skeet shooter, # 219), which consists of two flexed elbows and resembles a gun, above her head to the right, or rear **CUES:** this dancer guards her **U**ber **Sh**eep with this gun that she is pointing towards the 後ろ **ushi**ro (rear), but the man on the left offers to take them in exchange for an **A**tomic clock, some **C**ola, some **G**old, some g**N**occhi, a **S**axophone, and one of his hats **COMPARE:** other similar kanji at # **230**

Every

0336. 毎 PRONUNCIATIONS: mai, goto MEANING: every EXAMPLES: 毎週 maishuu = every week; 三日毎に mikka goto ni = every three days DESCRIPTION: at the top, a crutch; at the bottom, 田 (rice paddy, # 68), with several extended lines CUES: 毎日 **mai**nichi (every day), **M**ichael Jackson grabs this crutch, loads the **G**oats into the **T**oyota, and goes out to this 田 (rice paddy) GROUP: 慣(れる) nareru = to get used to, # 92; 毎(週) maishuu = every week, # 336; 海 umi = ocean, # 337; (後)悔 koukai = regret, # 675; (頻)繁 hinpan = frequent, # 1266; 梅 ume = plum, # 1299; 毒(物) dokubutsu = poison, # 1349; 敏(感) binkan = sensitive, # 1608; (一)貫 ikkan = consistency, # 1621; 侮(辱) bujoku = insult, # 1963 ALSO COMPARE: other similar kanji at # **2080**

0337. 海 PRONUNCIATIONS: umi, kai, a, una MEANINGS: ocean, sea, beach EXAMPLES: 海 umi = ocean; 海外 kaigai = overseas; 海女 ama = fisherwoman, female pearl diver; 海原 unabara = ocean DESCRIPTION: compared to 毎 mai (every, # 336), this adds a water radical (see # 12), suggesting the ocean, on the left CUES: 毎 (every) year I go to the 海 **umi** (ocean) to watch **U**ber **M**ilitary exercises with the **K**aiser near this water, but the show seems **A**rtificial, and I am **U**naffected by it ALSO COMPARE: other similar kanji at # **336** and # **2080**

What

0338. 何 PRONUNCIATIONS: nan, nani, ka, ga MEANING: what EXAMPLES: 何人 nannin = how many people; 何 nani = what; 幾何学 kikagaku = geometry; 如何 ikaga = how? (deferential) DESCRIPTION: compared to 可(愛い) kawaii (cute, # 615) (identical pronunciation), this kanji adds a man with a slanted hat on the left; it retains a carton inside a one-sided lean-to, which is used as a garage CUES: **N**ancy and her **N**anny see this **C**arton in the **G**arden, and ask this man, who tilts his hat back so that they can see his face, 何ですか **nan** desu ka (what is it?) COMPARE: 伺(う) ukagau = to ask humbly, # 341; other similar kanji at # **1176**

0339. 同 PRONUNCIATIONS: ona, dou MEANINGS: the same, the said EXAMPLES: 同じ onaji = the same; 同情 doujou = sympathy, pity DESCRIPTION: compared to 何 nani (what, # 338), this kanji is 同じ **ona**ji (the same) on both the right and the left, and there is a line above the box, representing a napkin CUES: this line above this box in this two-sided lean-to, which is 同じ **ona**ji (the same) on the left and on the right, represents an **O**ld **N**apkin that was used to wrap a **D**oughnut ALSO COMPARE: other similar kanji at # **1620**

0340. 向 PRONUNCIATIONS: mu, kou, nata MEANINGS: to face, opposite side EXAMPLES: 向く muku = to face toward; 向こう mukou = the other side; 方向 houkou = direction; 日向 hinata = sunny place, in the sun DESCRIPTION: compared to 同(じ) onaji (the same, # 339), the old napkin above this box has moved to the opposite side of the roof of this two-sided lean-to CUES: the **M**oor is **C**old on the 向こう **mu**kou (opposite) side of this roof, where the **N**ational **T**alent contest is held ALSO COMPARE: other similar kanji at # **1467**

0341. 伺 **PRONUNCIATION: ukaga**
MEANINGS: to pay respects, visit, inquire
EXAMPLE: 伺う ukagau = to ask humbly, to visit humbly **DESCRIPTION:** compared to 何 nani (what, # 338), there is an old napkin above the box inside this one-sided lean-to, as seen in 同 (じ) onaji (the same, # 339) **CUE:** this man on the left, who is an **U**ber **Ca**lifornia **G**ambler, 伺う **ukaga**u (humbly visits) this lean-to and tilts his hat back in order to examine the napkin covering this box, and he 伺う **ukaga**u (humbly inquires) about the contents of the box before betting on them **GROUP:** 伺(う) ukagau = to ask humbly, # 341; (上)司 joushi = one's superior, # 608; 飼(う) kau = to keep a pet, # 830; 覗(く) nozoku = to snoop, # 982; (名)詞 meishi = a noun, # 1320

0342. 荷 **PRONUNCIATIONS: ni, ka, ri**
MEANINGS: to carry, luggage **EXAMPLES:** 荷物 nimotsu = luggage; 出荷する shukka suru = to ship or send; お稲荷さん o'inarisan = the god of harvests, wealth, etc. **DESCRIPTION:** compared to 何 nani (what, # 338), this adds a plant radical (see # 43) at the top **CUES: C**ustoms officer: "何 (what) is this plant material that your **Nie**ce is carrying in her 荷物 **ni**motsu (luggage)?" Answer: "It's a **Ca**rton of **C**hristmas **Wr**eaths."
ALSO COMPARE: other similar kanji at # **1176**

Mu

0343. 去 **PRONUNCIATIONS: sa, kyo, ko** **MEANINGS:** to leave, past **EXAMPLES:** 去る saru = to leave; 去年 kyonen = last year; 過去 kako = the past **DESCRIPTION:** at the top, 土 tsuchi (soil, # 59); at the bottom, the katakana ム mu, which is the sound made by a cow **CUES:** a **Sa**laryman purchased this ム (cow) in **Ky**oto 去年 **kyo**nen (last year), but now it's covered in this 土 (soil), so he's sending it down to **Ko**be
GROUP: (過)去 kako = the past, # 343; 法(律)

houritsu = law, # 344; (返)却(する) henkyaku suru = to return something, # 1562; 脚(本) kyaku-hon = a script, # 1563; 蓋 futa = a cover, # 1793

0344. 法 **PRONUNCIATIONS: hou, pou, ho MEANING:** law **EXAMPLES:** 法律 houritsu = law; 方法 houhou = method; 文法 bunpou = grammar, syntax; 法華経 hokekyou = the Lotus Sutra **DESCRIPTION:** compared to 去(る) saru (to leave, # 343), which reminds us of a samurai and his ム (cow) covered with 土 (soil), this adds a water radical (see # 12) on the left **CUES:** this 土 (**so**iled) ム (cow) 去 (**l**eaves), but since there's a **H**ole in the bridge, it falls into this water, and we decide to pass a 法律 **hou**ritsu (law) telling the **P**olice to prohibit cows on the bridge, which we **H**ope will solve the problem
ALSO COMPARE: other similar kanji at # **343**

0345. 伝 **PRONUNCIATIONS: den, tsuta, tsuda MEANINGS:** to convey, transmit, hand down **EXAMPLES:** 伝言 dengon = message; 伝える tsutaeru = to convey or hand down; 手伝う tetsudau = to help **DESCRIPTION:** on the left, a man with a slanted hat; at the upper right, 二 ni (two, # 2); at the lower right, the katakana ム mu, which is the sound made by a cow **CUES:** these 二 (two) ム (cows) collided with this man, even though he had tilted his hat back to improve his vision, and he sustained a **D**ental injury, his **Tsui**t (suit) was **T**attered, and his **Tsui**tcase (suitcase) was **D**amaged, but he delivered his 伝言 **den**gon (message) anyway
COMPARE: 仏(教) bukkyou = Buddhism, # 678; other similar kanji at # **1056**

Snail

0346. 週 PRONUNCIATION: shuu
MEANING: week EXAMPLE: 来週 raishuu = next week DESCRIPTION: on the lower left, a snail; the snail carries a tent containing 土 tsuchi (soil, # 59) near the top and a box containing shoes at the bottom, hidden under the soil CUE: our **Sho**es arrive 毎週 mai**shuu** (every week) in this box hidden under this 土 (soil), carried in this tent on this snail GROUP: (来)週 raishuu = next week, # 346; 調(子) choushi = condition, # 441; (一)周 isshuu = round tour, # 630 (identical pronunciation); 彫(る) horu = to carve, # 1698

0347. 達 PRONUNCIATIONS: tachi, dachi, ta, tatsu MEANINGS: arrive, attain, reach EXAMPLES: 人達 hitotachi = people; 友達 tomodachi = friend; 達成 tassei = achievement; 速達 sokutatsu = express mail DESCRIPTION: on the lower left, a snail; on the snail, at the top, 土 tsuchi (soil, # 59); below that, 羊 hitsuji (sheep, # 1223); this radical on the right also resembles a needle, as seen in 幸(せ) shiawase (happiness, # 385) CUES: this snail carries this 羊 (sheep) which is covered by this 土 (soil), and it attracts many 人達 hito**tachi** (people), who are at**Tach**ing signs with **Da**rk **Chee**se and **Ta**ffy to this snail, complaining about the sheep's condition; this is titsu for **Tatsu**, since the sheep's owner is attaching his signs as well GROUP: this is a group of one ALSO COMPARE: other similar kanji at # **383**, # **384**, # **802** and # **1803**

0348. 送 PRONUNCIATIONS: oku, sou
MEANING: to send EXAMPLES: 送る okuru = to send, or to drop off; 放送 housou = broadcast DESCRIPTION: on the lower left, a snail; on the snail, 天 ten (sky, # 189), with two lines added at the top, suggesting a person wearing a flat hat with antennae CUES: this person wearing this hat with two antennae is an **Occu**ltist who rides on this snail while she 送る **oku**ru (sends out) **Sor**did electronic messages GROUP: 咲(く) saku = to blossom, # 193; 送(る) okuru = to send, # 348; 関(係) kankei = relationship, # 701

0349. 道 PRONUNCIATIONS: dou, tou, michi MEANINGS: road, street, direction EXAMPLES: 道路 douro = road; 神道 shintou = a Japanese religion; 道 michi = street DESCRIPTION: on the lower left, a snail from Michigan; on the snail, 首 kubi (neck, # 56), which includes antennae CUES: this snail is carrying this 首 (neck) to its **Dor**mitory, which is infested with **To**ads, but there is a bottle-首 (neck) in this 道 **michi** (street) in **Michi**gan GROUP: 首 kubi = neck, # 56, 道 michi = street, # 349; (指)導 shidou = guidance, # 1261 (identical pronunciation) ALSO COMPARE: other similar kanji at # **2002**

0350. 遅 PRONUNCIATIONS: oso, oku, chi MEANINGS: slow, late EXAMPLES: 遅い osoi = late, slow; 遅れる okureru = to be delayed; 遅刻する chikoku suru = to be tardy DESCRIPTION: on the lower left, a snail, which is carrying a lean-to with a double roof; under the lean-to, 羊 hitsuji (sheep, # 1223), an animal with two horns, two ears, four legs and a tail CUES: this snail carries this **O**ld **So**malian 羊 (sheep) under this double roof, but the snail moves slowly, and it appears that the sheep will be 遅い **oso**i (late) to lunch, he will 遅れる **oku**reru (be delayed) to the **Occu**lt museum, and he will 遅刻する **chi**koku suru (be tardy) on his trip to the **Chee**se factory ALSO COMPARE: other similar kanji at # **802**, # **1223** and # **1899**

0351. 遠 **PRONUNCIATIONS: en, too, doo MEANING:** distant, far **EXAMPLES:** 遠慮 enryo = reserve; 遠い tooi = far; 待ち遠しい machidooshii = long for, look forward to **DESCRIPTION:** compared to (公)園 kouen (park, # 279) (identical pronunciation), this kanji omits the fence on the perimeter and adds a snail on the lower left; it retains the 土 (soil) above a box and the pole with a handle on the left and two lips on on the right, which resembles a megaphone **CUES:** this snail carries an **E**ngineer who designed this megaphone with two lips which is hidden under this 土 (soil), and although it scares **Toa**ds and **Do**es, he uses it to speak to 遠い **too**i (distant) people **GROUP:** (公)園 kouen = a park, # 279; 遠(い) tooi = far, # 351; 猿 saru = monkey, # 1055 **ALSO COMPARE:** other similar kanji at # **718**

0352. 選 **PRONUNCIATIONS: sen, era MEANING:** to choose **EXAMPLES:** 選挙 senkyo = election; 選ぶ erabu = to choose **DESCRIPTION:** on the lower left, a snail; on the snail's back, at the top, two 己 (backward S's), which can be seen as snakes but which may also represent two backward people running for senator in the era of Bush; these are supported by 共(に) tomo ni (together, # 969), which reminds us of a hill in Kyoto **CUES:** this snail is a 選挙 **sen**kyo (election) van, carrying these two 己 (backward candidates) for the **Sen**ate, who are campaigning 共 (together), from which one had to 選ぶ **era**bu (choose) during an **E**ra of turmoil **GROUP:** 質(問) shitsumon = question, # 86; 多(い) ooi = a lot, # 161; (日)曜(日) nichiyoubi = Sunday, # 200; (洗)濯 sentaku = laundry, # 201; 選(ぶ) erabu = to choose, # 352; 座(る) suwaru = to sit, # 497; 歌(う) utau = to sing, # 534; 替(える) kaeru = to replace, # 551; 飛(ぶ) tobu = to fly, # 574; (肺)炎 haien = pneumonia, # 788; (相)談 soudan = consultation, # 790; 爽(快) soukai = refreshing, # 798; 移(る) utsuru = to move, # 801; 競(技) kyougi = competition, # 935; (火)災 kasai = fire, # 1019; (本)州 honshuu = Honshu island, # 1071; 賛(成) sansei = agreement, # 1115; (合)唱 gasshou = chorus, # 1152; 晶 shou = crystal, # 1231; 翌(日) yokujitsu = the next day, # 1457; 潜(水) sensui = diving, # 1586; 麗(しい) uruwashii = beautiful, # 1627; 淡(い) awai = thin, # 1654; 琴 koto = a Japanese harp, # 1712; 傘 kasa = an umbrella, # 1743; 脊(椎) sekitsui = the spine, # 1867; 挫(ける) kujikeru = to lose heart, # 1976; (便)箋 binsen = writing paper, # 2051; 櫻 sakura = cherry, # 2086 **ALSO COMPARE:** other similar kanji at # **486** and # **1078**

0353. 連 **PRONUNCIATIONS: ren, tsu, tsura MEANINGS:** linking, accompanying **EXAMPLES:** 連絡する renraku suru = to contact; 連れて行く tsurete iku = to bring a person along; 連なる tsuranaru = to stand in a row **DESCRIPTION:** on the lower left, a snail; above the snail, a rental 車 kuruma (car, # 283) **CUES:** this **R**ental 車 (car) broke down, and after I 連絡した **ren**raku shita (contacted) the agency, they sent this snail to pick up the car, after which they 連れて行った **tsu**rete itta (took me along) to my destination, but I left my **Tsu**it (suit) and my **Tsu**itcase (suitcase) of **R**amen in the trunk **COMPARE:** similar kanji at # **2075**

0354. 運 **PRONUNCIATIONS: hako, un MEANINGS:** to transport, luck **EXAMPLES:** 運ぶ hakobu = to carry or transport; 運動 undou = exercise, 運 un = luck, fortune **DESCRIPTION:** compared to 連(絡) renraku (contact, # 353), this substitutes 軍(人) gunjin (soldier, # 725), who appears to be wearing a hat, for the 車 (car) on the upper right; it retains the snail at the lower left **CUES:** this snail 運ぶ **hako**bu

(carries) this 軍 (soldier), and the soldier 運ぶ hakobu (carries) a **H**at on **C**old days; **U**ndoubtedly the hat helps to keep him warm
ALSO COMPARE: other similar kanji at # **2075**

0355. 違 **PRONUNCIATIONS: chiga, i, taga** **MEANINGS:** to differ, wrong **EXAMPLES:** 違う chigau = different; 違反 ihan = violation, offense; 仲違い nakatagai = disagreement **DESCRIPTION:** on the lower left, a snail, carrying a radical resembling 五 go (five, # 179) that looks the same whether it is right side up or upside down; this represents two feet facing in opposite directions, separated by a 口 (box) **CUES:** these two feet are 違う **chiga**u (different) in that they face in opposite directions, and both feet have been been bitten up by the **Ch**iggers and **A**nts that live in this 口 (box), so that it isn't **E**asy for them to **T**ag **A**long when this snail goes to the store **COMPARE:** similar kanji at # **1174**

0356. 返 **PRONUNCIATIONS: kae, gae², hen** **MEANING:** to return something **EXAMPLES:** 返す kaesu = to return an item; 寝返る negaeru = to betray; 返事 henji = reply **DESCRIPTION:** on the lower left, a snail; on the right, an F over an X; this can also be seen as a 又 (table) under a lean-to **CUES:** when I got this F on my paper and had it marked with this X, I put it on this snail and 返した **kae**shita (returned it) to the teacher, but the teacher **C**alled **E**sther, my mother, and sent the paper back to us on a **H**en **COMPARE:** similar kanji at # **1166**

0357. 込 **PRONUNCIATIONS: ko, komi** **MEANING:** to get crowded **EXAMPLES:** 込む komu = to get crowded; 申込書 moushikomisho = application form **DESCRIPTION:** on the lower left, a commuter snail; on the right, 入(る) hairu (to enter, # 14) **CUES:** many people 入 (enter) this snail bus in order to **C**ommute to work, but it 込む **ko**mu (gets crowded), often **C**omically so; **Note:** Japanese people often use another spelling, 混む, # 1294, for komu when it appears alone and means "to get crowded"; they use 込む in compound words, like 飛び込む tobikomu = to dive **COMPARE:** similar kanji at # **14**

0358. 迎 **PRONUNCIATIONS: muka, gei** **MEANING:** to welcome **EXAMPLES:** 迎える mukaeru = to greet/welcome; 歓迎する kangei suru = to welcome **DESCRIPTION:** on the lower left, a snail; on the snail, two standing figures who could be Moonies **CUES:** these two **M**oonies **C**all out to potential donors as they ride on this snail to the station, where they will 迎える **muka**eru (greet and welcome) a colleague **G**aily **COMPARE:** similar kanji at #**1046** and # **1535**

0359. 速 **PRONUNCIATIONS: haya, soku, sumi** **MEANING:** fast **EXAMPLES:** 速い hayai = fast; 速達 sokutatsu = express mail; 早速 sassoku = immediately; 速やかな sumiyaka na = swift **DESCRIPTION:** compared to 束 soku (bundle, # 99) (identical pronunciation), this kanji adds a snail at the lower left; it retains the 木 (tree) wearing glasses that sometimes gets soaked **CUES:** this 束 (bundle), which resembles a 木 (tree) wearing glasses, is 速い **haya**i (fast), in spite of riding on a snail, since his glasses allow him to see far ahead and avoid obstacles; he is heading to Prince **H**arry's **Y**acht, where he will **S**oak in the tub with **Sumi**su-san (Mr. Smith) **ALSO COMPARE:** 早(い) hayai = early, # **34**; other similar kanji at # **1806**

0360. 遊 **PRONUNCIATIONS: aso, yuu** **MEANINGS:** to play, have fun **EXAMPLES:** 遊ぶ asobu = to play; 遊園地 yuuenchi = playground **DESCRIPTION:** on the lower left, a snail; above the snail, 方 kata (honorable person, # 114), a crutch, and 子 ko (child, # 182) **CUES:** this 方 (honorable person) on the left is an **As**sociate salesman from the **Yu**kon who 遊ぶ **aso**bu (plays) on this snail with this 子 (child) who uses this crutch **ALSO COMPARE:** other similar kanji at # **920**, # **2078** and # **2080**

0361. 過 **PRONUNCIATIONS: su, ka, ayama, sugo** **MEANINGS:** to pass through, excessively **EXAMPLES:** 食べ過ぎる tabesugiru = to overeat; 過ぎる sugiru = to exceed; 過去 kako = the past; 過ち ayamachi = fault, error; 過す sugosu = to spend or to pass time (this can also be spelled 過ごす) **DESCRIPTION:** on the lower left, a snail; on the right, two boxes each containing a carton; in the upper box, the carton has slipped out of place **CUES: Su**perman placed these two **Ca**rtons into the center of these larger boxes for transport on this snail, but he やり過ぎた yari**sugi**ta (overdid it), such that this carton in the center of the upper box slipped out of place, and the **Aya**tollah got **Ma**d, but later he gave Superman some **Su**perior **Go**lf clubs **GROUP:** 過(去) kako = the past, # 361; 鍋 nabe = pot, # 1374; (戦)渦 senka = the turmoil of war, # 1871, and (戦)禍 senka = war damages, # 2042, three of which can be pronounced "ka" **ALSO COMPARE:** other similar kanji at # 832

0362. 辺 **PRONUNCIATIONS: hen, ata, be, nabe** **MEANINGS:** area, around, peripheral, edge **EXAMPLES:** この辺 kono hen = around here; その辺り sono atari = around there; 水辺 mizube = waterside; 田辺 Tanabe = a family name **DESCRIPTION:** on the lower left, a snail; on the right, a 刀 katana (sword, # 102) used to guard hens **CUES:** I keep this 刀 (sword) on the back of this snail when guarding the **Hen**s in this **hen** 辺 (area) from **At**tack; **Be**tty is my favorite, and then there is **Na**sty **Be**cky **ALSO COMPARE:** other similar kanji at # **2062**

0363. 建 **PRONUNCIATIONS: ta, da², tate, kon, ken** **MEANING:** to erect a building **EXAMPLES:** 建てる tateru = to build; 建て date = story or floor (of a building); 建物 tatemono = building; 建立 konryuu = act of building a temple or monument, etc.; 建築 kenchiku = architecture **DESCRIPTION:** the radical seen at the lower left of this kanji is different from the snail radical seen earlier in this section; we call it a "3x snail," since it consists of a 3 intersected at the bottom to form an X; on the right, a three-fingered hand across the top of a telephone pole with two horizontal crossbars, which is similar to the three-fingered hand in 書く kaku (to write, # 415) **CUES:** before they 建てる **ta**teru (erect) a **T**axi garage for a **T**all **T**echie who is a **Con**ehead, **Ken** and Barbie must review their plans 3x and 書 (write) them down **COMPARE:** other similar kanji at # **692**, # **820** and # **877**

Fence

0364. 用 **PRONUNCIATIONS: you, mochi** **MEANINGS:** errand, to use **EXAMPLES:** 用事 youji = errand; 利用する riyou suru = to use; 用いる mochiiru = to use **DESCRIPTION:** a two-sided lean-to containing a telephone pole with two arms; this resembles a Japanese fence, made from pieces of bamboo and tied together with rope **CUES:** we will 利用する ri**you** suru (use) this fence to enclose a cow, so that we can make our own **Yo**gurt and stop **Mooch**ing from the neighbors **COMPARE:** similar kanji at # **367**

0365. 通 **PRONUNCIATIONS: too, tsuu, doo, kayo** **MEANING:** to pass through **EXAMPLES:** 通る tooru = to pass through; 通り toori = street, way; 通学する tsuugaku suru = to commute to school; 通り doori = in accordance with, avenue; 通う kayou = to commute **DESCRIPTION:** on the lower left, a snail; at the upper right, the katakana character マ ma, which represents a mammoth; at the lower right, 用 you (errand, # 364) which resembles a fence (see # 364) **CUES:** this マ (mammoth) on this 用 (fence) 通う **kayo**u (commutes) on this snail to its job at a lakeside hotel, where other マ (mammoths) 通る **too**ru (pass through) the lobby **To**wing **Ts**u**i**tcases (suitcases), **D**olphins swim by, and the staff **C**all **Yo**gis to teach yoga **ALSO COMPARE:** 道(路) douro = road, # 349, spelled with "ou" rather than "oo"; other similar kanji at # **1143**

0366. 踊 **PRONUNCIATIONS: you, odo**
MEANINGS: to dance or skip **EXAMPLES:** 舞踊 buyou = dancing; 踊る odoru = to dance
DESCRIPTION: on the left, a square top on 止 (める) tomeru (to stop, # 173), suggesting a hesitant squarehead; on the right, the katakana character マ ma, which represents a mammoth, above 用 you (errand, # 364) (identical pronunciation), which resembles a fence
CUES: this 止 (hesitant) squarehead goes behind this 用 (fence), removes the **Y**oke from this マ (mammoth) and 踊る **odo**ru (dances) with it, which leaves a distinctive **Od**or of mammoth on the squarehead **ALSO COMPARE:** other similar kanji at # **1143** and # **1534**

0367. 備 **PRONUNCIATIONS: sona, bi**
MEANINGS: to be prepared or equipped with
EXAMPLES: 備える sonaeru = to prepare, have, equip with; 準備 junbi = preparation; 設備 setsubi = equipment, facility
DESCRIPTION: on the left, a man with a slanted hat; at the top right, a plant radical (see # 43) above a one-sided lean-to; at the bottom right, 用 you (errand, # 364), which resembles a fence
CUES: this man on the left tilts his hat back to examine the **Son**ar equipment that he uses to monitor the **B**eer that is kept in a 設備 setsu**bi** (facility), which is this lean-to under this roof garden, with this 用 (fence) protecting it
GROUP: 用 you = errand, # 364; (準)備 junbi = preparation, # 367; (狩)猟 shuryou = hunting, # 1397; (凡)庸 bon'you = mediocre, # 2035

Vertical Bed
0368. 痛 **PRONUNCIATIONS: tsuu, ita**
MEANING: pain **EXAMPLES:** 頭痛 zutsuu = headache; 痛い itai = painful
DESCRIPTION: compared to 通(学) tsuugaku (to commute to school, # 365) (identical pronunciation), this omits the snail on the lower left and adds a sick bed, as seen in 病(気) byouki (illness, # 369) at the upper left; it retains the マ (mammoth) on a 用 (fence) **CUES:** since this マ (mammoth) damaged my **T**suit (suit) from **It**aly, I'm making it sleep on this 用 (fence) pressed against the headboard of this sick bed, which 痛い **ita**i (hurts) **ALSO COMPARE:** other similar kanji at # **369** and # **1143**

0369. 病 **PRONUNCIATIONS: ya, yamai, byou** **MEANINGS:** illness, disease, sick
EXAMPLES: 病む yamu = to fall sick; 病 yamai = illness; 病気 byouki = illness
DESCRIPTION: on the upper left, a sick bed shown vertically, with legs pointing to the left and a headboard at the top; inside the bed, 内 uchi (within, # 396), suspended from a horizontal beam, resembling a chest x-ray of a Yankee, with ribs superimposed on lungs [this also resembles a 人 (person) emerging from a two-sided lean-to]
CUES: this 内 (chest x-ray) of a **Y**ankee in this sick bed suggests a 病気 **byou**ki (illness) which could be a disorder in the **Y**ankee's **M**ind, or maybe it's **B.O.** (bacterial overgrowth)
GROUP: 痛(い) itai = painful, # 368; 病(気) byouki = illness, # 369; 疲(れる) tsukareru = to get tired, # 370; (治)療 chiryou = medical treatment, # 1069; 症(状) shoujou = symptoms, # 1085; 疫(病) ekibyou = plague, # 1142; 癖 kuse = habit, # 1215; 癒(す) iyasu = to cure, # 1293; (愚)痴 guchi = complaint, # 1581; (腫)瘍 shuyou = a tumor, # 1702; 疾(風) shippu = a gale, # 1734; 痕(跡) konseki = traces, # 1857; 嫉(妬) shitto = jealousy, # 1890; (下)痢 geri = diarrhea, # 2055; (天然)痘 tennentou = smallpox, # 2070; 癌 gan = cancer, # 2079 **ALSO COMPARE:** other similar kanji at # **397**

0370. 疲 PRONUNCIATIONS: hi, tsuka
MEANINGS: to get tired, fatigue EXAMPLES:
疲労 hirou = fatigue, weariness; 疲れる
tsukareru = to get tired DESCRIPTION: on the upper left, a sick bed shown vertically, with legs pointing to the left and a headboard at the top; inside the bed, at the top, an arrow pointing to the right, intersected by a vertical line, representing a guy named Straight Arrow, who has a long cape that trails down to the end of the bed on the left (this can also be seen as a chimney perforating the top of a lean-to); at the bottom, 又 mata ("again," # 24), which can be seen as a table, but this looks like Straight Arrow's springy legs
CUES: this Straight Arrow 疲れた **tsuka**reta (got tired) from working in the **H**eat and is sleeping in this sick bed, and he left his **Tsu**it (suit) in the **Car**
COMPARE: similar kanji at # **369** and # **833**

0371. 彼 PRONUNCIATIONS: kare, kano MEANINGS: he, she
EXAMPLES: 彼 kare = he; 彼女 kanojo = she
DESCRIPTION: on the left, a man with a double hat; at the upper right, an arrow pointing to the right, intersected by a vertical line, representing a guy named Straight Arrow, who has a long cape on the left that trails down to the floor (this can also be seen as a periscope perforating the top of a lean-to); at the lower right, 又 mata ("again," # 24), which can be seen as a table, but this looks like Straight Arrow's springy legs CUES: this man on the left works at a **Ca**lifornia **Re**staurant where he wears these two hats, as a cook, cooking with **Can**ola oil, and as a waiter, serving this Straight Arrow whom he refers to as 彼 **kare** (he) COMPARE: (津)波 tsunami = tidal wave, # 878; other similar kanji at # **833**

0372. 寝 PRONUNCIATIONS: shin, ne
MEANINGS: to sleep or lie down EXAMPLES:
寝室 shinshitsu = bedroom; 寝る neru = to go to bed, to sleep DESCRIPTION: on the left, a bench shown vertically; at the top, a bad haircut; on the right, long hair streaming to the left above a cloth that is resting on 又 mata ("again," # 24), which resembles a simple table CUES: this person with this bad haircut **ne**ru 寝る (sleeps) on this bench, but first she sits at this cloth-covered 又 (table), says her **Shin**to prayers and arranges this long hair to the left so that it won't get tangled in her **N**ecklace

COMPARE: 眠(る) nemuru = to sleep, # 376; similar kanji at # **24**, # **998** and # **1165**

0373. 北 PRONUNCIATIONS: kita, ho, hoku, boku² MEANING: north
EXAMPLES: 北 kita = north; 北海道 hokkaidou = Hokkaido; 北方 hoppou = northward; 北部 hokubu = the northern part; 敗北 haiboku = defeat DESCRIPTION: on the left, a bench, shown vertically; on the right, the katakana character ヒ hi, which resembles a king next to this bench and reminds us of a hero; together, these two radicals seem to point north
CUES: this ヒ (hero) next to this bench is a **K**ing checking his **T**ax code, with his head pointing 北 **kita** (north), where he keeps a **H**ome at the North Pole, and the **H**ome is **C**ool even during the summer
COMPARE: other similar kanji at # **998** and # **2048**

0374. 将 PRONUNCIATIONS: *kami*, *shou* MEANINGS: future, army general
EXAMPLES: 女将 okami = mistress, landlady, hostess, proprietress; 将来 shourai = the future DESCRIPTION: on the left, a bench shown vertically; at the upper right, several lines that suggest a barbecue grate; at the lower right, 寸(前) sunzen (on the verge, # 1369), which resembles a kneeling sunny guy who has dropped a piece of gum on the ground CUES: this 寸 (kneeling sunny guy) is a **Comm**ie (Communist), and after he picks up this gum, he wants to **Sh**ow us life as it will be in the 将来 **shou**rai (future), after the Revolution, when all workers will have benches and barbecue grates like these COMPARE: other similar kanji at # **131**, # **998** and # **1177**

Citizen

0375. 民 PRONUNCIATIONS: min, tami
MEANING: people EXAMPLES: 市民 shimin = citizen; 民 tami = the people, a nation
DESCRIPTION: on the upper left, a lean-to with a double roof; at the lower right, a leaning woman trying to squeeze into it
CUES: this leaning woman, who is a 市民 shi**min** (citizen), is squeezed into this lean-to with a double roof, which is why she is **M**ean and complains about

Taxi Meters
COMPARE: 眠(る) nemuru = to sleep, # 376; (彼)氏 kareshi = boyfriend, # 709, which has a *single* roof; other similar kanji at # **376** and # **1899**

0376. 眠 PRONUNCIATIONS: nemu, min MEANING: to sleep EXAMPLES: 眠る nemuru = to sleep; 睡眠を取る suimin wo toru = to get some sleep DESCRIPTION: compared to (市)民 shimin (citizen, # 375) (identical pronunciation), this kanji adds 目 me (eye, # 51) on the left; it retains the mean citizen squeezed into a lean-to with a double roof CUES: this 目 (eye) of this 民 (citizen) is wide open, and she can't 眠る **nemu**ru (sleep), because her **N**eighbors' **Mu**sic affects her rest, and this makes her **Mean** GROUP: (市)民 shimin = citizen, # 375; 眠(る) nemuru = to sleep, # 376 ALSO COMPARE: other similar kanji at # 249, # 1195, # **1899** and # **2002**

Festival
0377. 祭 PRONUNCIATIONS: sai, matsu, matsuri MEANINGS: festival, to worship EXAMPLES: 祭日 saijitsu = holiday; 祭る matsuru = to worship; 祭 matsuri = festival DESCRIPTION: at the top, a peaked roof carrying a three-legged rocker bottom bench on the left and a slice of pizza on the right; the bench on the left can be called a bench hat; at the bottom, 丁 tei (a counter for tools, # 702), which resembles a nail, with projections on the sides that suggest spinning, and a flying carpet above it; these lower radicals can also be seen as 二 (two) above 小 (small) CUES: as they admired this spinning nail under this flying carpet and this peaked roof, which is decorated for a **S**cientific 祭 **matsuri** (festival), a **Ma**tador and **Su**perman sat on a **Ma**t that **Su**perman had **Re**paired and enjoyed seeing this three-legged bench and this pizza slice on the roof GROUP: 祭 matsuri = festival, # 377; (国)際 kokusai = international, # 379 (identical pronunciation); (自)然 shizen = nature, # 611; 燃(える) moeru = to burn, # 1240 ALSO COMPARE: other similar kanji at # **297** and # **1347**

0378. 途 PRONUNCIATIONS: to, *zu* MEANINGS: route, way EXAMPLES: 途中 tochuu = on the way; 一途に ichizu ni = wholeheartedly DESCRIPTION: on the lower left, a snail; on the right, 丁 tei (a counter for tools, # 702), which resembles a nail, with projections on the sides that suggest spinning, with a stool above it, under a peaked roof; unlike 祭 matsuri (festival, # 377), this roof carries no decorations and isn't associated with a flying carpet CUES: under this peaked roof and this stool, this spinning 丁 (nail) carried by this snail revolves like a **To**rnado 途中 **to**chuu (on the way) to the **Zo**o ALSO COMPARE: similar kanji at # **637**

0379. 際 PRONUNCIATIONS: sai, giwa, kiwa MEANINGS: contact, edge of an area EXAMPLES: 国際 kokusai = international; 手際 tegiwa = skill; 際立つ kiwadatsu = to stand out or be conspicuous DESCRIPTION: compared to 祭 matsuri (festival, # 377), or 祭(日) saijitsu (holiday, # 377) (identical pronunciation), this kanji adds ß from the Greek alphabet on the left; it retains the peaked roof with a bench hat on the left, and the spinning nail under a flying carpet, which can also be seen as 二 (two) above 小 (small) CUES: this 祭 (festival) has a 国際 koku**sai** (international) flavor, with exhibits on ß (**G**reek) **S**cience and **G**eeky **W**arriors, and it is **K**eenly **W**atched by the world ALSO COMPARE: similar kanji at # **297**, # **377**, # **1347** and # **2030**

Horse
0380. 駅 PRONUNCIATION: eki MEANING: train station EXAMPLE: 駅 eki = station DESCRIPTION: on the left, 馬 uma (horse, # 958), which includes a mane flowing to the right, four legs and a tail; on the right, a square mounted high above the ground which reportedly represents a "wakeful eye" CUE: this reminds us of the old custom of changing 馬 (horses) like this at the royal 駅 **eki** (station) under this 尺 (wakeful eye) belonging to **E**dward the **K**ing ALSO COMPARE: other similar kanji at # **826** and # **1484**

0381. 駐 **PRONUNCIATION: chuu**
MEANING: to park a vehicle
EXAMPLE: 駐車する chuusha suru = to park a vehicle **DESCRIPTION:** compared to 駅 eki (station, # 380), this substitutes 主(人) shujin (master, # 166) for the wakeful eye on the right; it retains 馬 (horse) **CUE:** this 主 (master) 駐車する **chuu**sha suru (parks) this 馬 (horse), while the horse **Chew**s hay **ALSO COMPARE:** other similar kanji at # **166** and # **826**

0382. 験 **PRONUNCIATION: ken**
MEANING: to examine
EXAMPLES: 試験 shiken = examination; 経験 keiken = experience
DESCRIPTION: compared to (危)険 kiken (danger, # 196) (identical pronunciation), this kanji substitutes 馬 uma (horse, # 958) for β on the left; it retains the laundromat with a peaked roof, containing a keg stuck sideways in a washing machine **CUES: Ken** and this 馬 (horse) have arrived from the **Ken**tucky Derby to visit Barbie, and he will 経験する kei**ken** suru (experience) this stuck-keg problem when he does his laundry **ALSO COMPARE:** other similar kanji at # **826** and # **1432**

Needle
0383. 親 **PRONUNCIATIONS: oya, shin, shita** **MEANINGS:** parent, intimate
EXAMPLES: 親 oya = parent; 両親 ryoushin = parents; 親しい shitashii = intimate, close
DESCRIPTION: at the upper left, 立(つ) tatsu (to stand, # 11); at the lower left, 木 ki (tree, # 118); taken together, these resemble a 立 (bell) at the top, which can be seen as a syringe, and a needle at the bottom, which contains an eye; on the right, 見(る) miru (to look, # 53) **CUES:** when 親 **oya** (parents) say **Oya**suminasai (good night) to their kids, they should 見 (look) at their beds and check for **Shin**y needles like this and for **Shi**ite **Ta**ffy
GROUP: (人)達 hitotachi = people, # 347; 親 oya = parent, # 383; 辛(い) karai = spicy, # 384;

幸(せ) shiawase = happiness, # 385; 報(告) houkoku = report, # 386; 辞(める) yameru = to resign, # 387; 新(聞) shinbun = newspaper, # 389 (identical pronunciation); (固)執(する) koshitsu suru = to be persistent, # 1553; (主)宰 shusai = sponsorship, # 1803; 薪 maki = firewood, # 1965 **ALSO COMPARE:** other similar kanji at # **384**, # **389** and # **1341**

0384. 辛 **PRONUNCIATIONS: kara, shin, tsura** **MEANINGS:** spicy, bitter, hot, salty
EXAMPLES: 辛い karai = spicy, hot; 香辛料 koushinryou = spices; 辛い tsurai = painful, tormenting (karai and tsurai are both written 辛い)
DESCRIPTION: at the top, 立(つ) tatsu (to stand, # 11), which resembles a bell; at the bottom, 十 juu (ten, # 18); taken together, these resemble a syringe and a needle; they can also be seen as a tower with three levels **CUES:** while singing **Kara**oke and eating 辛い **kara**i (spicy) food on a **Shin**gle at a dude ranch, I found this needle in the food, so I **Tsu**ed (sued) the **Ran**ch **GROUP:** (友)達 tomodachi = friend, # 347, which has five levels; 親 oya = parent, # 383, in which the needle has three levels and is based on a 木 (tree); 辛(い) karai = spicy, # 384, which has three levels; 幸(せ) shiawase = happiness, # 385, which has four levels **ALSO COMPARE:** other similar kanji at # **383** and # **1803**

0385. 幸 **PRONUNCIATIONS: shiawa, sachi, saiwa, kou** **MEANINGS:** happiness, good luck **EXAMPLES:** 幸せ shiawase = happiness; 幸子 Sachiko = a girl's given name; 幸い saiwai = lucky, happy; 幸福 koufuku = happiness
DESCRIPTION: compared to 辛(い) karai (spicy, # 384), which can be seen as a 立 (bell) above 十 (ten), this adds another 十 (ten) at the top and resembles a tower with four levels
CUES: I live in this four-level tower in a **Shia** country torn by **War**, and there are some **Sad Children** here, and a lot of 辛 (spicy) food, but if I

can take **Silent Walks** and fight off **Colds**, that means 幸せ <u>shiawa</u>se (happiness) for me

ALSO COMPARE: 達 tachi (plural, # 347), where the tower has five levels; other similar kanji at # <u>383</u>, # <u>384</u> and # <u>1803</u>

0386. 報 **PRONUNCIATIONS: hou, muku MEANINGS:** report, news **EXAMPLES:** 報告 houkoku = report; 予報 yohou = forecast; 報いる mukuiru = to reward or repay

DESCRIPTION: on the left, 幸(せ) shiawase (happiness, # 385), containing 十 (ten) above a 立 (bell) above 十 (ten) and resembling a syringe with a needle; on the right, a dressing room, with a hook at the top for hanging clothes and a table at the bottom **CUES:** we received a 報告 <u>hou</u>koku (report) about a **Hornet** with this 幸 (needle)-like stinger near this hook in this dressing room, but a **Moonie** drinking too much **Kool**-Aid had reported it **ALSO COMPARE:** 服 fuku = clothes, # <u>150</u>; other similar kanji at # <u>383</u> and # <u>1803</u>

0387. 辞 **PRONUNCIATIONS: ji, ya MEANINGS:** word, to resign **EXAMPLES:** 辞書 jisho = dictionary; 辞める yameru = to resign a position **DESCRIPTION:** on the left, 舌 shita (tongue, # 1213); on the right, 辛(い) karai (spicy, # 384), which consists of a 立 (bell) above 十 (ten) and resembles a needle

CUES: **J**immy **C**arter showed us this 舌 (tongue), and he also brought out this 辛 (needle), to illustrate the sharp taste of the **Y**am dishes that he was tasting at work, saying that therefore he will 辞める <u>ya</u>meru (resign) from his job **ALSO COMPARE:** 止(める) yameru = to stop doing something, to give up, # 173; other similar kanji at # <u>383</u>, # <u>1213</u> and # <u>1803</u>

0388. 南 **PRONUNCIATIONS: minami, nan MEANING:** south **EXAMPLES:** 南 minami = south; 南米 nanbei = South America **DESCRIPTION:** this two-sided lean-to is a weather station, with 十 juu (ten, # 18) at the top, resembling an antenna; inside the weather station, a compass needle pointing south **CUES:** in this weather station with this antenna, which is located near the **M**inaret of **M**ickey's mosque, this compass needle points 南 <u>minami</u> (south), rather than north, according to his **N**anny **GROUP:** 南 minami = south, # 388; (貢)献 kouken = a contribution, # 1618 **ALSO COMPARE:** other kanji with 十 at # <u>1828</u>

Pliers

0389. 新 **PRONUNCIATIONS: nii, shin, ara, atara MEANINGS:** new, fresh **EXAMPLES:** 新潟 Niigata = a city on Honshu Island; 新聞 shinbun = newspaper; 新たな arata na = new, fresh; 新しい atarashii = new, fresh **DESCRIPTION:** compared to (両)親 ryoushin (parents, # 383) (identical pronunciation), this kanji substitutes a pair of pliers for 見 (to look) on the right; it retains the 立 (bell) at the top, which can be seen as a syringe, and the 木 (tree) at the bottom, which resembles a needle **CUES:** I use this 新しい <u>atara</u>shii (new) **N**eedle, which is **S**hiny, and this pair of **A**rabian pliers to **A**ttack **R**ats **GROUP:** 親 oya = parent, # 383; 新(聞) shinbun = newspaper, # 389; 薪 maki = firewood, # 1965 **ALSO COMPARE:** other similar kanji at # <u>383</u> and # <u>892</u>

0390. 近 **PRONUNCIATIONS: chika, jika², kin MEANINGS:** near, close **EXAMPLES:** 近い chikai = close; 身近 mijika = close at hand, closely related; 近所 kinjo = neighborhood; 最近 saikin = recently **DESCRIPTION:** on the lower left, a snail; on the snail, a pair of pliers **CUES:** this snail is an electrician with a **C**heap **C**ar who carries this pair of pliers that he uses on wires that are 近い <u>chika</u>i (near) the **K**indergarten where he works **COMPARE:** 丘 oka = hill, # 1473; other similar kanji at # <u>892</u>

0391. 所 **PRONUNCIATIONS:** tokoro, dokoro², jo, sho **MEANING:** place **EXAMPLES:** 所 tokoro = place; 台所 daidokoro = kitchen; 近所 kinjo = neighborhood; 場所 basho = place **DESCRIPTION:** on the left, a snow-covered lean-to under a double roof, but this can also be seen as a P under a roof, which could stand for a "Place" belonging to **T**olstoy; on the right, a pair of pliers **CUES:** after **T**olstoy had a **Cor**onary (heart attack), **J**onah used these pliers to fix up his 所 **tokoro** (Place) for a **Show** **COMPARE:** similar kanji at # **892** and # **1134**

Old

0392. 古 **PRONUNCIATIONS:** furu, go, ko **MEANINGS:** old, referring to things **EXAMPLES:** 古い furui = old; 名古屋 Nagoya = city in Japan; 古代 kodai = ancient times **DESCRIPTION:** a 口 (box) under a cross [which can also be seen as 十 juu (ten, # 18)], resembling a tomb **CUES:** a **Foo**lish **Roo**ster often sits on this **G**old cross above this 古い **furui** (old) tomb, where my **Co**ach was buried **COMPARE:** 舌 shita = tongue, # 1213; other similar kanji at # **394**

0393. 苦 **PRONUNCIATIONS:** niga, ku, kuru, guru² **MEANINGS:** bitter, painful **EXAMPLES:** 苦い nigai = bitter; 苦手 nigate = weak point; 苦労 kurou = hardship; 苦しい kurushii = hard, painful; 見苦し migurushi = unsightly **DESCRIPTION:** compared to 古(い) furui (old, # 392), this adds a plant radical (see # 43) at the top; it retains the tomb under a cross [which can also be seen as 十 juu (ten, # 18)] **CUES:** my **Nie**ce **Ga**thers flowers in a cemetery in **Ku**wait, and it's 苦い **niga**i (bitter) for her to see these 古 (old) tombs overgrown with plants like these, with **Ku**waiti **Roo**sters perched on them **ALSO COMPARE:** other similar kanji at # **394**

0394. 故 **PRONUNCIATIONS:** *furu*, ko, yue **MEANINGS:** past, to cause **EXAMPLES:** 故郷 furusato = hometown (usually written ふるさと); 事故 jiko = accident; 故障 koshou = breakdown; 故に yue ni = therefore **DESCRIPTION:** compared to 古(い) furui (old, # 392) (identical pronunciation), this kanji adds a dancer with a ponytail on the right; it retains the box under a cross [which can also be seen as 十 juu (ten, # 18)] **CUES:** due to a **Foo**lish **Roo**ster, this 古 (old) dancer from **Co**lombia was involved in a 事故 ji**ko** (accident), and now she has to fly home by **U.A.** (United Airlines) **GROUP:** 古(い) furui = old, # 392; 苦(い) nigai = painful, # 393; (事)故 jiko = accident, # 394; 湖 mizuumi = lake, # 716; (住)居 juukyo = dwelling, # 809; 克(明な) kokumei na = detailed, # 1718; 据(える) sueru = to set up, # 1719; 裾 suso = a hem, # 1796; 枯(れる) kareru = to wither, # 1834

0395. 個 **PRONUNCIATION:** ko **MEANINGS:** individual, counter for eggs, etc. **EXAMPLES:** 卵三個 tamago sanko = three eggs; 個人 kojin = individual **DESCRIPTION:** on the left, a man with a slanted hat; on the right, 古(い) furui (old, # 392, which resembles a box under a cross [which can also be seen as 十 juu (ten, # 18)], inside a cold box **CUE:** this man on the left is a 個人 **ko**jin (individual), and he tilts his hat back to examine this box where he keeps 古 (old) food **C**old **GROUP:** 個(人) kojin = individual, # 395; 固(体) kotai = solid, # 731 (identical pronunciation); 箇(所) kasho = place, # 1881

Inside

0396. 内
PRONUNCIATIONS: nai, uchi, dai **MEANING:** inside **EXAMPLES:** 国内 kokunai = inside the country; 家内 kanai = my wife; その内に sono uchi ni = before long; 境内 keidai = grounds (of a temple)

DESCRIPTION: a 人 hito (person, # 13) extending her head through a hole in the roof of a two-sided lean-to

CUES: this 家内 ka**nai** (wife) with a **K**nife and some **U**ber **Chee**se, who is 内 **uchi** (inside) a dwelling, puts her head through a hole in the roof of this two-sided lean-to and complains about her **D**iet **COMPARE:** other similar kanji at # **397**

0397. 肉
PRONUNCIATION: niku

MEANING: meat **EXAMPLE:** 肉 niku = meat

DESCRIPTION: two 人 hito (people, # 13) emerging from a two-sided lean-to, but these look like ribs on an chest x-ray, surrounded by meat

CUE: this is an x-ray of some 肉 **niku** (meat) that was sent to us by my **Nie**ce in **Ku**wait

GROUP: 病(気) byouki = illness, # 369; 内 uchi = within, # 396; 肉 niku = meat, # 397; 納(得する) nattoku suru = to agree, # 705; (豆)腐 toufu = bean curd, # 722; (人)柄 hitogara = personality, # 1533

Eat

0398. 食
PRONUNCIATIONS: ta, sho, ku, shoku, jiki **MEANING:** to eat

EXAMPLES: 食べる taberu = to eat; 食感 shokkan = texture of food; 食う kuu = to eat (rough speech); 食事 shokuji = meal; 餌食 ejiki = victim, prey **DESCRIPTION:** compared to 良(い) yoi (good, # 303), this adds a peaked roof, suggesting a tavern; it retains 白 (white) and the letters L & Y, which remind us of Light Years

CUES: I went to this 白 (white) **T**avern by the **S**hore, where I 食べた **ta**beta (ate) 良 (good) food and drank **K**ool-Aid, after which they **Sh**owed **C**ookies for dessert, but I lost my appetite after I realized I had dropped my **J**eep **K**ey**s** **L**ight **Y**ears away

GROUP: 食(べる) taberu = to eat, # 398; (出)張 shucchou = business trip, # 477; 長(い) nagai = long, # 502; (手)帳 techou = pocket notebook, # 1244; (栄)養 eiyou = nutrition, # 1264; (発)展 hatten = development, # 1346; 喪(失) soushitsu = a loss, # 1828; 畏(敬) ikei = awe, # 1998 **ALSO COMPARE:** other kanji containing 食, usually in modified forms so that the L&Y may not be clearly visible, at # **1974**; other kanji containing L&Y at # **805** and # **1105**

0399. 飲
PRONUNCIATIONS: in, no
MEANINGS: to drink or swallow
EXAMPLES: 飲食 inshoku = drinking and eating; 飲む nomu = to drink or swallow

DESCRIPTION: on the left, 食(べる) taberu (to eat, # 398); on the right, 欠(く) kaku (to lack, # 1238) which can be seen as, at the top, an h-shaped chair that is leaning to the right and, at the bottom, 人 hito (person, # 13); taken together, these two radicals resemble an oil derrick

CUES: the oil **I**ndustry in **N**orway uses 欠 (oil derricks) like this to make money so that its employees can 食 (eat) and 飲む **no**mu (drink) **ALSO COMPARE:** other similar kanji at # **536** and # **1974**

0400. 飯
PRONUNCIATIONS: han, pan², meshi **MEANING:** a meal **EXAMPLES:** ご飯 gohan = meal, cooked rice; 残飯 zanpan = leftover food; 冷や飯 hiyameshi = cold rice

DESCRIPTION: on the left, 食(事) shokuji (meal, # 398); on the right, an F over an X, which can also be seen as a 又 (table) under a lean-to

CUES: Hansel cooked this 食 (meal), including ご飯 go**han** (cooked rice), but it's **M**essy, and it gets an F; we're also marking it with this X **ALSO COMPARE:** other similar kanji at # **1166** and # **1974**

Various

0401. 物　**PRONUNCIATIONS: motsu, butsu, bu, mono**　**MEANINGS:** stuff, tangible things　**EXAMPLES:** 荷物 nimotsu = luggage; 動物 doubutsu = animal; 物価 bukka = price of goods; 物 mono = tangible thing
DESCRIPTION: on the left, 牛 ushi (cow, # 205); on the right, this radical reportedly represents a variety of streamers, or "assorted things," which may produce a monotonous sound when the wind blows
CUES: when we sit by the castle **M**oats, this 牛 (cow), old **B**oots, empty **B**ooze bottles and other assorted 物 **mono** (things) like these streamers make **Mono**tonous noise in the wind
GROUP: this is a group of one
ALSO COMPARE: 事 koto = intangible thing, # 416; other kanji containing streamers at # 1702; other similar kanji at **1765**

0402. 易　**PRONUNCIATIONS: yasa, eki, i**　**MEANINGS:** easy, fortune telling
EXAMPLES: 易しい yasashii = easy; 貿易 boueki = trade; 安易な an'i na = easy
DESCRIPTION: at the top, 日 hi (sun, # 32); at the bottom, a variety of streamers, as seen in 物 mono (tangible thing, # 401), which reportedly represent simple, various things, implying that things under the sun are simple and easy　**CUES:** a **Y**ankee **Sa**w these streamers under this 日 (sun) and told **E**dward the **K**ing that life is 易しい **yasa**shii (**E**asy)　**ALSO COMPARE:** kanji resembling 豚 buta (pig) at # 1504; other similar kanji at # **1702**

0403. 場　**PRONUNCIATIONS: jou, ba**　**MEANING:** place　**EXAMPLES:** 会場 kaijou = site of an event; 場所 basho = place
DESCRIPTION: compared to 易(しい) yasashii (easy, # 402), this adds 土 tsuchi (soil, # 59) on the left; it retains the 日 (sun) and a modified version of the streamers
CUES: Joan of **A**rc has a **B**ar on this patch of 土 (soil) which is a nice 場所 **ba**sho (place), and her life is 易 (easy)
ALSO COMPARE: other similar kanji at # **1702**

0404. 湯　**PRONUNCIATIONS: yu, tou**　**MEANINGS:** hot water, hot bath　**EXAMPLES:** お湯 oyu = honorable hot water; 熱湯 nettou = boiling water　**DESCRIPTION:** compared to 易(しい) yasashii (easy, # 402), this adds a water radical (see # 12) on the left; it retains the 日 (sun) and a modified version of the streamers
CUES: in the **Yu**kon, **To**ads love this cool water and have 易 (easy) lives, but they don't like 湯 **yu** (hot water)
ALSO COMPARE: similar kanji at # **1702**

0405. 家　**PRONUNCIATIONS: ie, ka, uchi, ke, ge², ya**　**MEANINGS:** house, person　**EXAMPLES:** 家 ie = house; 家族 kazoku = family; 家内 kanai = my wife; 家 uchi = home, but Japanese people usually spell this うち, to avoid confusion with ie (house); 田中家 tanakake = the Tanaka family; 公家 kuge= the Imperial Court; 家主 yanushi = landlord
DESCRIPTION: at the top, a bad haircut which resembles a roof with a chimney; at the bottom, this radical is also found in 豚 buta (pig, # 1504); it can be seen as a vertical pig with a flat head at the top and some limbs extending to the left; it is not the same as the radicals seen in 物 mono (thing, # 401) and in 易(しい) yasashii (easy, # 402), although they are similar　**CUES:** this **Y**ellow 豚 (pig) lives in this 家 **ie** (house), which is only a **Ca**bin, where people make **U**ber **Ch**eese, drink from **K**egs and grow **Y**ams
ALSO COMPARE: other similar kanji at # **1504**

Rocker-bottom

0406. 参 **PRONUNCIATIONS:** mai, san **MEANINGS:** to humbly come or go, to visit a temple or shrine **EXAMPLES:** 参る mairu = to humbly come or go; 参加 sanka = participation **DESCRIPTION:** at the top, the katakana character ム mu (the sound made by a cow); in the middle, a wide 大 (big, # 188); at the bottom, three cords which resemble a rocker-bottom shoe **CUES:** wobbling on this rocker-bottom shoe, this ム (cow) travels many **M**iles as she 参ります **mai**rimasu (humbly goes) to **San** Francisco **GROUP:** 顔 kao = face, # 95; 参(加) sanka = participation, # 406; 珍(しい) mezurashii = unusual, rare, # 407; 修(理) shuuri = repairs, # 1049; 診(察) shinsatsu = a medical exam, # 1242; (悲)惨(な) hisan na = miserable, # 1678 (identical pronunciation); 鬱(病) utsubyou = depression, # 1783 **ALSO COMPARE:** other similar kanji at # **1678**

0407. 珍 **PRONUNCIATIONS:** mezura, chin **MEANINGS:** rare, strange **EXAMPLES:** 珍しい mezurashii = unusual, rare; 珍味 chinmi = delicacy, dainties **DESCRIPTION:** on the left, 王 ou (king, # 1077); on the right, a rocker-bottom shoe **CUES:** when this 王 (king) visited a 珍しい **mezura**shii (unusual) **M**exican **Z**oo to see a **R**am, he wore this rocker-bottom shoe, but he fell and hurt his **Chin** **ALSO COMPARE:** other similar kanji at # **406**, # **1382** and # **1772**

0408. 歩 **PRONUNCIATIONS:** aru, ayu, po, ho **MEANINGS:** to walk, step **EXAMPLES:** 歩く aruku = to walk; 歩み ayumi = walking, step, history, record; 散歩する sanpo suru = to walk; 歩道 hodou = sidewalk **DESCRIPTION:** at the top, 止(める) tomeru (to stop, # 173); at the bottom, 少(し) sukoshi (a little, # 254); together these resemble a rounded sole with an ankle above it **CUES:** wearing shoes with rounded soles like this in **A**ru**b**a, I will 歩く **aru**ku (walk) for the Clean Air Trust fundraiser, together with **A Y**ou**t**h I know, in order to help 止 (stop) **P**ollution 少 (a little), near my **H**ome **ALSO COMPARE:** other similar kanji at # **1010** and # **1929**

Gate

0409. 門 **PRONUNCIATIONS:** mon, kado **MEANINGS:** gate, doors **EXAMPLES:** 門 mon = gate; 門出 kadode = leaving one's home, starting in life **DESCRIPTION:** two swinging doors that form a gate **CUES:** a **M**onk watches this 門 **mon** (gate), through which he can see a **C**athedral **D**ome **COMPARE:** other similar kanji at # **1755**

0410. 問 **PRONUNCIATIONS:** ton, mon, to **MEANINGS:** to question or inquire **EXAMPLES:** 問屋 tonya = wholesaler; 問題 mondai = a problem; 質問 shitsumon = a question; 問う tou = to ask, question, inquire, to charge (with a crime) **DESCRIPTION:** compared to 門 mon (gate, # 409) (identical pronunciation), this adds 口 kuchi (mouth, # 426), in the gate, but 口 could represent a painting **CUES: To**ny Blair hung this **Mon**et 口 (painting) in this 門 (gate) and charged people a **T**oll to walk past it, but this created some 問題 **mon**dai (problems) **ALSO COMPARE:** other similar kanji at # **1755**

0411. 間 **PRONUNCIATIONS:** ken, ma, aida, gen, kan **MEANINGS:** duration of time, between **EXAMPLES:** 世間 seken = society, other people; 間違える machigaeru = to make a mistake; 間もなく mamonaku = before long; 間 aida = duration, between; 人間 ningen = human being; 時間 jikan = time, hour **DESCRIPTION:** compared to 門 mon (gate, # 409), this adds 日 hi (day, or sun, # 32) inside the gate, suggesting time **CUES:** standing near this 門 (gate), **K**en, his **M**a (mother), Barbie's friend **I**da, and **G**enghis **K**han measure the 間 **ai**da (duration) of time by watching the shadows that this 日 (sun) casts on the ground **ALSO COMPARE:** other similar kanji at # **1755**

0412. 聞 **PRONUNCIATIONS:** bun, ki, gi **MEANINGS:** to listen, hear, ask **EXAMPLES:** 新聞 shinbun = newspaper; 聞く kiku = to hear or ask; 人聞き hitogiki = reputation **DESCRIPTION:** compared to 門 mon (gate, # 409), this adds 耳 mimi (ears, # 57) inside the gate **CUES:** Daniel **Boo**ne had big 耳 (ears) like this, and he used to sit in this 門 (gate) reading a 新聞 shin**bun** (newspaper) while wearing a **Ki**mono and feeding **Ge**ese, while he 聞いた **ki**ita (listened) to gossip **ALSO COMPARE:** other similar kanji at # **1713** and # **1755**

0413. 開 **PRONUNCIATIONS:** a, kai, hira **MEANINGS:** to open, to begin **EXAMPLES:** 開ける akeru = to open, transitive; 開く aku = to open, intransitive; 開発 kaihatsu = development; 開く hiraku = to open or unfold, transitive; **Note:** both aku and hiraku are written 開く **DESCRIPTION:** compared to 門 mon (gate, # 409), 開 adds a figure in the gate, who resembles a tower that supports a catapult and has a welcoming or open stance **CUES:** my **A**unt stands in this 門 (gate) with this welcoming stance, signaling that she will 開ける **a**keru (open) the gate so that people may bring their **Ki**tes inside, where they can **H**ear **Ra**p music **ALSO COMPARE:** similar kanji at # **573** and # **1755**

0414. 閉 **PRONUNCIATIONS:** to, shi, hei **MEANING:** to close **EXAMPLES:** 閉じる tojiru = to close; 閉める shimeru = to close, transitive; 閉鎖する heisa suru = to close down **DESCRIPTION:** compared to 門 mon (gate, # 409), this adds Tolstoy standing in the gate, who is extending his left hip in a forbidding stance **CUES:** **T**olstoy stands in this 門 (gate) and extends this left hip to create a **Shi**eld to block passage, signifying that the gate 閉まっている **shi**matte iru (is closed) to people who want to harvest **H**ay **ALSO COMPARE:** other similar kanji at # **1417** and # **1755**

Trident

0415. 書 **PRONUNCIATIONS:** ka, sho **MEANING:** to write **EXAMPLES:** 書く kaku = to write; 辞書 jisho = dictionary **DESCRIPTION:** at the top, a three-fingered hand resembling a trident is grasping a vertical line which can be seen as a brush, or perhaps as an extension of the axis of 土 tsuchi (soil, # 59); at the bottom 日 hi (sun, # 32) resembles a two-drawer cabinet **CUES:** I'm grasping this brush with this three-fingered hand to 書く **ka**ku (write) a story in this 土 (soil) on this 日 (cabinet) about a **C**arpenter who starred in a Broadway **Sh**ow **COMPARE:** similar kanji at # **877**

0416. 事 **PRONUNCIATIONS:** koto, goto, ji **MEANINGS:** an intangible thing or matter **EXAMPLES:** 事 koto = intangible thing, matter; 仕事 shigoto = work; 用事 youji = errand **DESCRIPTION:** this vertical line with a curve at the bottom is a brush; it is intersected by a horizontal line and a rectangle near the top, representing a test sheet (which also forms two eyes along the shaft) and an answer book, and by a three-fingered hand holding it near the bottom **CUES:** this test sheet, this rectangular answer book and this brush being held by this three-fingered hand will be used for a test covering 事 koto (intangible things), such as Koto (Japanese harp) music, **Gho**st **To**es and **Ji**had **COMPARE:** 物 mono = tangible thing, # 401; other similar kanji at # **877** and # **1314**

0417. 律 PRONUNCIATIONS: richi, ritsu MEANING: law EXAMPLES: 律儀な richigi na = conscientious; 法律 houritsu = law
DESCRIPTION: on the left, a man with a double hat; on the right, the three-fingered hand seen in 建(てる) tateru (to build, # 363), holding a rod (which can also be seen as a telephone pole) with twin horizontal lines representing sheets of paper near the bottom
CUES: this man on the left doesn't pay his taxes, and the **Rea**son he **Chea**ts is that he thinks that the tax 法律 hou**ritsu** (laws) written on these two sheets of paper, impaled on this rod being held by this three-fingered hand, are just **Writ**ten **Sugg**estions, but if he is caught, he will have to forfeit one of his two hats
COMPARE: similar kanji at # **820** and # **877**

0418. 静 PRONUNCIATIONS: shizu, jou, sei MEANINGS: quiet, serene
EXAMPLES: 静か shizuka = quiet, serene; 静脈 joumyaku = vein; 安静 ansei = rest
DESCRIPTION: compared to 青(い) aoi (blue, # 155), this adds a monster with a fish head (see # 80), which someone has stabbed with a trident, on the right; it retains the owl's perch on a 月 (moon)
CUES: the sky is 青 (blue), and it's 静か **shizu**ka (quiet), now that a **Sh**eep herder from **Zu**rich has stabbed this fish monster with this trident, and **Jo**an of Arc is **Sa**fe **ALSO COMPARE:** other similar kanji at # **936** and # **1112**

0419. 君 PRONUNCIATIONS: kun, kimi
MEANING: suffix for (usually) male names of younger people EXAMPLES: 石田君 ishida kun = young man Ishida; 君 kimi = you (informal male speech) **DESCRIPTION:** at the top, someone named Kimmy has been stabbed in the face with a trident; at the bottom, 口 kuchi (mouth, # 426)
CUES: "Hey 君 **kimi** (you)! A **Cu**nning person has stabbed **Kimm**y with this trident, and this 口 (mouth) is wide open."

GROUP: 君 kimi = you, # 419; 群(れ) mure = herd, # 929; 郡 gun = a county, # 1230; 伊(勢神宮) ise jinguu = the Ise Grand Shrine, # 2081

Lopsided Legs
0420. 兄 PRONUNCIATIONS: ani, *nii*, kyou, kei MEANINGS: older brother, male elder
EXAMPLES: 兄 ani = my older brother; お兄さん oniisan = your older brother; 兄弟 kyoudai = siblings; 父兄 fukei = parents, guardians **DESCRIPTION:** a square head on lopsided legs which could belong to an animal
CUES: 兄 **ani** (older brother) has this square 口 (head) and these lopsided legs, and he ate like an **A**nimal when he visited his **Ni**ece in **Kyou**to, where she offered him some **Ca**ke
GROUP: 祝(う) iwau = to celebrate, # 274; 兄 ani = older brother, # 420; 競(技) kyougi = competition, # 935, and (状)況 joukyou = circumstances, # 1249, both of which can also be pronounced "kyou"; (政)党 seitou = political party, # 1399; 克(明な) kokumei na = detailed, # 1718; 呪(い) noroi = a curse, # 1844

0421. 元 PRONUNCIATIONS: moto, gen, gan MEANINGS: base, origin, source
EXAMPLES: 元 moto = base, origin, source; 元気 genki = cheerful, healthy; 元日 ganjitsu = January 1 **DESCRIPTION:** 二 (two, # 2) on lopsided legs **CUES:** a **Mo**torcycle gang led by these 二 (two) leaders, **Gen**ghis and **Gan**dalf, rests on lopsided legs like these and has a solid 元 **moto** (base) for a 元気な **gen**ki na (healthy) lifestyle
GROUP: 元 moto = base, # 421; (病)院 byouin = hospital, # 424; 頑(張る) ganbaru = to do one's best, # 622; 完(全な) kanzen na = perfect, # 759; 冠 kanmuri = a crown, # 1786
ALSO COMPARE: other similar kanji at # 1496

0422. 先 **PRONUNCIATIONS: sen, ma, saki MEANINGS:** previous, before **EXAMPLES:** 先生 sensei = teacher; 先ず mazu = first of all; 先 saki = tip, point, first, future; 先に saki ni = ahead, formerly, beyond; 先ほど sakihodo = a while ago **DESCRIPTION:** a senator, standing on a platform consisting of 一 (one) above lopsided legs, holding a shield on the left **CUES:** this **Sen**ator, who used to be a 先生 **sen**sei (teacher), is standing on this platform with these lopsided legs at the **Ma**ll and holding this shield, which he keeps in a **Sack** that he bought in **I**ndia, to shield himself from accusations about things that happened 先ほど **saki**hodo (a while ago) **ALSO COMPARE:** other similar kanji at # **423**, # **429** and # **1855**

0423. 洗 **PRONUNCIATIONS: sen, ara MEANING:** to wash with water **EXAMPLES:** 洗濯 sentaku = laundry; 洗う arau = to wash **DESCRIPTION:** compared to 先 sen (previous, # 422) (identical pronunciation), this kanji adds a water radical on the left; it retains the senator standing on a platform and holding a shield **CUES:** this **Sen**ator, who returned from Saudi **Ara**bia 先 (previously), where there is a water shortage, stands on this platform with these lopsided legs, holds this shield out to this water on the left and 洗う **ara**u (washes) it **GROUP:** 先(生) sensei = teacher, # 422; 洗う arau = to wash, # 423 **ALSO COMPARE:** other similar kanji at # **429** and # **1855**

0424. 院 **PRONUNCIATION: in MEANING:** institution **EXAMPLE:** 病院 byouin = hospital **DESCRIPTION:** on the left, β beta from the Greek alphabet; at the upper right, a bad haircut; at the lower right, 元 moto (base, # 421) **CUE:** a β (Greek) doctor with a bad haircut like this built a 病院 byou**in** (hospital) on this 元 (base) with lopsided legs for people with **In**fections **ALSO COMPARE:** other similar kanji at # **421** and # **2030**

0425. 売 **PRONUNCIATIONS: u, bai, uri MEANING:** to sell **EXAMPLES:** 売る uru = to sell; 販売 hanbai = sales; 読売 Yomiuri = name of a newspaper **DESCRIPTION:** at the top, a statue of a (兵)士 heishi (soldier, # 66) made in Uganda; at the bottom, a roof above lopsided legs **CUES:** we 売る **u**ru (sell) this **U**gandan 士 (soldier) statue mounted on this roof with lopsided legs, which you may also **Bu**y from our 販売機 han**bai**ki (vending machines) located near the **Uri**nals in the bathrooms **GROUP:** 続(く) tsuzuku = to continue, # 226; 売(る) uru = to sell, # 425; 読(む) yomu = to read, # 432

Mouth

0426. 口 **PRONUNCIATIONS: ku, kou, kuchi, guchi MEANING:** mouth **EXAMPLES:** 口説く kudoku = to persuade, seduce or make advances; 人口 jinkou = population; 口 kuchi = mouth; 入口 iriguchi = entrance **DESCRIPTION:** a square mouth which resembles a box **CUES:** this square 口 **kuchi** (mouth) drinks **Koo**l-Aid and **Co**la, and it eats **Ku**waiti **Chee**se that I carry in a **Gu**cci handbag **COMPARE:** the katakana character ロ ro; other similar kanji at # **323** and # **2073**

0427. 吸 **PRONUNCIATIONS: su, kyuu MEANING:** to suck **EXAMPLES:** タバコを吸う tabako wo suu = to smoke tobacco; 吸収する kyuushuu suru = to digest **DESCRIPTION:** on the left, 口 kuchi (mouth, # 426), which resembles a box; on the right, a graph of breathing patterns **CUES:** this 口 (mouth) on the left and this graph of breathing patterns on the right remind us of a baby named **Su**e who cannot 吸う **su**u (suck) properly but is very **Cu**te **COMPARE:** similar kanji at # **1131** and # **2073**

0428. 呼 **PRONUNCIATIONS: yo, ko**
MEANINGS: to call out, exhale **EXAMPLES:** 呼ぶ yobu = to call out, to summon; 呼び名 yobina = given name, alias; 呼吸 kokyuu = breathing, respiration **DESCRIPTION:** on the left, 口 kuchi (mouth, # 426), which resembles a box; on the right, a kneeling telephone pole with flames projecting from both sides
CUES: I stood under this kneeling burning telephone pole, opened this 口 (mouth) and 呼んだ **yo**nda (called out) to say that a **Yo**gi was pouring **Co**la on the fire
COMPARE: other similar kanji at # **897** and # **2073**

0429. 告 **PRONUNCIATIONS: koku, tsu**
MEANINGS: to proclaim, inform, or announce
EXAMPLES: 広告 koukoku = advertisement; 報告 houkoku = report; 告げる tsugeru = to inform **DESCRIPTION:** compared to 先(生) sensei (teacher, # 422), this substitutes 口 kuchi (mouth, # 426) for the lopsided legs at the bottom; it retains a person standing on a platform and extending a shield to the left **CUES:** this 口 (mouth) speaks 広告 kou**ko**ku (advertisements), and the person above it holds out this shield to demonstrate that drinking **Co**ke, and wearing the right **Tsu**it (suit), can shield us from unpopularity
GROUP: 先(生) sensei = teacher, # 422; 洗(う) arau = to wash, # 423; (報)告 houkoku = report, # 429; (製)造 seizou = manufacture, # 1108; (残)酷(な) zankoku na = brutal, # 1695

0430. 言 **PRONUNCIATIONS: gen, koto, gon, i MEANINGS:** words, to say **EXAMPLES:** 言語 gengo = language; 言葉 kotoba = words; 伝言 dengon = message; 言う iu = to speak or tell **DESCRIPTION:** at the top, four horizontal lines that represent the four pronunciations of this kanji; at the bottom, 口 kuchi (mouth, # 426)
CUES: Genghis used this 口 (mouth) to 言う **i**u (speak) 言葉 **koto**ba (words) about his favorite instruments, the **Ko**to (Japanese harp) and the **Gon**g, which sound good to his **E**ars **GROUP:** this is a group of one

0431. 信 **PRONUNCIATION: shin**
MEANINGS: to believe, to trust, letter
EXAMPLES: 信じる shinjiru = to believe; 信号 shingou = stoplight; 信念 shinnen = belief; 信徒 shinto = a follower or believer
DESCRIPTION: on the left, a man with a slanted hat; on the right, 言(う) iu (to speak, # 430)
CUE: this man on the left 信じる **shin**jiru (believes) in **Shin**tou, and he tilts his hat back to show his sincerity before he 言 (speaks) about his 信念 **shin**nen (beliefs) **GROUP:** this is a group of one

0432. 読 **PRONUNCIATIONS: doku, do, tou, yo, yomi MEANING:** reading **EXAMPLES:** 読書 dokusho = reading; 読解 dokkai = reading comprehension; 読経 dokyou = sutra chanting; 句読点 kutouten = punctuation marks; 読む yomu = to read; 読売 Yomiuri = name of a newspaper **DESCRIPTION:** compared to 売(る) uru (to sell, # 425), this adds 言(葉) kotoba (words, # 430) on the left; it retains the uranium 士 (soldier) on a roof, which is being sold
CUES: if we want people to 読む **yo**mu (read) our books, we need to 売 (sell) them 言 (words) like this, and we can borrow some good words from a **Do**cument about **Do**es and **To**ads that attend **Yo**ga **Mee**tings led by **Yo**gis **ALSO COMPARE:** other similar kanji at # **425** and # **781**

0433. 話 PRONUNCIATIONS: hana, hanashi, banashi², wa MEANING: to speak EXAMPLES: 話す hanasu = to talk; 話 hanashi = story; 昔話 mukashibanashi = folklore; 会話 kaiwa = conversation DESCRIPTION: compared to (生)活 seikatsu (life, # 260), this substitutes 言(う) iu (to speak, # 430) for the water radical on the left; it retains the 舌 (tongue) CUES: this 舌 (tongue) belongs to **Ha**nnah, and when she 言 (speaks) to **Ha**nnah's **S**heep, who are **Wa**lking around, it 話す **hana**su (talks) ALSO COMPARE: 語る kataru = to talk, # 435; similar kanji at # **1213**

0434. 計 PRONUNCIATIONS: haka, kei MEANINGS: to measure or count EXAMPLES: 計る hakaru = to measure; 時計 tokei = clock, watch; 計画 keikaku = plan DESCRIPTION: on the left, 言(う) iu (to speak, # 430); on the right, 十 juu (ten, # 18) CUES: I 言 (speak) about my 計画 **kei**kaku (plan) to buy a 時計 to**kei** (clock) with these 十 (ten) dollars that I earned in the last **Ha**ck**a**thon, which we held in a **Ca**ve ALSO COMPARE: 許(可) kyoka = permission, # 1141; similar kanji at # **1828**

0435. 語 PRONUNCIATIONS: go, kata, gata², gatari MEANINGS: words, to talk EXAMPLES: 英語 eigo = English; 語る kataru = to talk; 物語る monogataru = to tell or indicate; 物語 monogatari = story DESCRIPTION: on the left, 言(葉) kotoba (words # 430); on the right, 五 go (five, # 179) (identical pronunciation), standing on a box and resembling a golfer staring down a fairway CUES: these 五 (five) **Go**lfers stand on this 口 (box), they stare because they have **Ca**taracts, they know only a little 英語 ei**go** (English), and they mix up 言 (words) like this, saying **Ga**tari**de** instead of **Ga**torade

ALSO COMPARE: 話(す) hanasu = to talk, # 433; other similar kanji at # **179**

0436. 試 PRONUNCIATIONS: tame, shi, kokoro MEANINGS: to test, a trial EXAMPLES: 試す tamesu = to attempt; 試験 shiken = examination; 試みる kokoromiru = to attempt DESCRIPTION: compared to 式 shiki (ceremony, # 249), this adds 言(う) iu (to say, # 430) on the left; it retains the tall woman with a ball over her shoulder, leaning over a shift key CUES: this tall leaning woman with a ball above her shoulder 言 (says) that she prefers **Ta**ll **Me**n, she raises **S**heep and she has a big **Kokoro** (heart), and she 試す **tame**su (tries) to leap over this shift key during a 式 (ceremony) which is a 試験 **shi**ken (test) for her dance class ALSO COMPARE: other similar kanji at # **247** and # **249**

0437. 訳 PRONUNCIATIONS: wake, yaku MEANINGS: reason, translation EXAMPLES: 訳 wake = reason, interpretation; 言い訳 iiwake = excuse; 通訳 tsuuyaku = interpreter, interpretation DESCRIPTION: compared to 駅 eki (station, # 380), this substitutes 言(葉) kotoba (words, # 430) for the 馬 (horse) on the left; it retains the square eye on long legs, which resembles a wakeful eye CUES: the 訳 **wake** (reason) that this 尺 (**Wa**keful eye) is watching these 言 (words) is to check the accuracy of the 通訳 tsuu**yaku** (interpretation) being done for a **Yaku**za (gangster) ALSO COMPARE: other similar kanji at # **1484**

0438. 議 PRONUNCIATION: gi MEANING: to discuss EXAMPLE: 会議 kaigi = meeting DESCRIPTION: on the left, 言(う) iu (to speak, # 430); at the top right, 王 ou (king, # 1077), wearing rabbit ears [this part of the kanji can also be seen as a truncated 羊 hitsuji (sheep, # 1223), missing its tail]; at the lower middle, 手 te (hand, # 23); at the lower right, a halberd (lance and axe)

CUE: I 言 (spoke) at a 会議 kai**gi** (meeting) about the **Gee**se and the truncated 羊 (sheep) that are polluting our garden, and I held this halberd with this 手 (hand) to show that I was serious
ALSO COMPARE: other similar kanji at # **1554**, # **1862** and # **1893**

0439. 説 PRONUNCIATIONS: zei, setsu, zetsu², to   MEANINGS: to explain, opinion
EXAMPLES: 遊説 yuuzei = election campaign; 説明 setsumei = explanation; 小説 shousetsu = novel; 演説 enzetsu = a speech; 説く toku = to explain, persuade, preach   DESCRIPTION: on the left, 言(う) iu (to speak, # 430); on the right, 兄 ani (older brother, # 420), wearing rabbit ears   CUES: this 兄 (older brother), who is wearing these rabbit ears because he is **Z**any, 言 (speaks) and 説明する **setsu**mei suru (explains) about how he **S**et up a **S**uper farm, where he grows **T**omatoes
ALSO COMPARE: other similar kanji at # **708**

0440. 誰 PRONUNCIATION: dare
MEANING: who   EXAMPLE: 誰 dare = who
DESCRIPTION: on the left, 言(う) iu (to speak, # 430); on the right, a net, which can be seen as a man with a slanted hat next to a 主 (master) with an extra pair of arms (see # 203)   CUE: 誰 **dare** (who) **D**ares to 言 (speak) from this net?
COMPARE: other similar kanji at # # **2046**

0441. 調 PRONUNCIATIONS: chou, shira   MEANINGS: to investigate, condition
EXAMPLES: 調子 choushi = condition; 調べる shiraberu = to check
DESCRIPTION: on the left, 言(う) iu (to speak, # 430); on the right, a radical seen in 週 shuu (week, # 346), which reminds us of a 口 (box) under some 土 (soil) inside a tent
CUES: people 言 (say) that a detective has been **Ch**osen to 調べる **shira**beru (check) this box hidden below this 土 (soil) inside this tent to see whether it contains **S**hee**p** or **Ra**bbit food
COMPARE: other similar kanji at # **346**

0442. 研 PRONUNCIATIONS: ken, to
MEANINGS: to hone, to sharpen by grinding
EXAMPLES: 研究 kenkyuu = research; 研ぐ togu = to sharpen, to wash rice   DESCRIPTION: on the left, 石 ishi (stone, # 458); on the right, this resembles a research tower with long toes   CUES: **Ken** is a researcher who does 研究 **ken**kyuu (research) into kidney 石 (stones) like this in this research tower, and this keeps him on his **To**es
COMPARE: other similar kanji at # **573** and # **1775**

Fire
0443. 火 PRONUNCIATIONS: hi, bi², yake, ka   MEANING: fire   EXAMPLES: 火 hi = fire; 花火 hanabi = fireworks; 火曜日 kayoubi = Tuesday; 火傷 yakedo = a burn injury, usually spelled やけど; 火事 kaji = fire
DESCRIPTION: 人 hito (person, # 13) with flames leaping from both sides
CUES: this 人 (person) was surrounded by these flames and feeling the **H**eat from a 火 **hi** (fire), until a **Y**ankee **K**ennedy drove by in a **C**ar and rescued him
ALSO COMPARE: other similar kanji at # **13**; kanji containing 火 at # **1239**

0444. 灰 PRONUNCIATIONS: hai, kai
MEANING: ash   EXAMPLES: 灰 hai = ash; 灰色 haiiro = grey; 石灰岩 sekkaigan = limestone   DESCRIPTION: on the upper left, a one-sided lean-to; inside the lean-to, a high 火 hi (fire, # 443)   CUES: if you light this **H**igh 火 (fire) inside this lean-to, you will generate 灰 **hai** (ash) and make the inside of the lean-to 灰色 **hai**iro (grey), and the **Kai**ser will get mad
ALSO COMPARE: other similar kanji at # **1239**

0445. 秋 **PRONUNCIATIONS: aki, shuu**
MEANING: autumn **EXAMPLES:** 秋 aki = autumn; 晩秋 banshuu = late fall
DESCRIPTION: on the left, 禾 (a grain plant with a ripe head); on the right, 火 hi (fire, # 443)
CUES: Achilles visited us in 秋 **aki** (autumn) to admire this 禾 (ripe grain) and our 火 (fire)-like leaves, and also to show us his new **Sh**oes
ALSO COMPARE: 愁(い) urei = melancholy, # 1785; other similar kanji at # 1239 and # 1797

0446. 焼 **PRONUNCIATIONS: ya, shou, jou²** **MEANING:** to burn **EXAMPLES:** 焼く yaku = to grill, toast, etc.; 焼き鳥 yakitori = grilled skewered chicken; 焼却 shoukyaku = incineration; 芋焼酎 imojouchuu = sweet potato shochu **DESCRIPTION:** on the left, 火 hi (fire, # 443); at the upper right, a triple plant radical (compared to the double plant radical seen at # 43), which resembles three yams on skewers; at the lower right, a base consisting of 一 (one) above lopsided legs **CUES:** using this 火 (fire) on the left, we 焼く yaku (grill) these three **Ya**ms on these skewers above this base with lopsided legs and eat them during movie **Sh**ows
GROUP: 焼(く) yaku = to grill, # 446; 暁 akatsuki = daybreak, # 1855 **ALSO COMPARE:** other similar kanji at # 1239

0447. 赤 **PRONUNCIATIONS: aka, ka, seki** **MEANING:** red **EXAMPLES:** 赤い akai = red; 赤ちゃん akachan = baby; 真っ赤 makka = bright red; 赤道 sekidou = equator
DESCRIPTION: at the top, 十 juu (ten, # 18); at the bottom, a four-legged hen, as seen in 変 hen (strange, # 553), missing its head **CUES:** 十 (ten) headless four-legged hens like this wore 赤い **aka**i (red) jackets and managed to get into the **A**cademy **A**wards in **Ca**lifornia, but a **Se**lfish **Ki**ng sat in front of them at the show **GROUP:** 赤(い) akai = red, # 447; (容)赦 yousha = pardon, # 1901 **ALSO COMPARE:** other similar kanji at # 695

0448. 光 **PRONUNCIATIONS: hika, mitsu, hikari, kou** **MEANING:** light
EXAMPLES: 光る hikaru = to shine, glitter, stand out; 光成 mitsunari = a male name; 光 hikari = light; 日光 nikkou = sunlight
DESCRIPTION: at the top, this is a three-pronged switch, as seen in (本)当 hontou (truth, # 31), but let's call it three streams of fire; at the bottom, a platform on lopsided legs, as seen in 先(生) sensei (teacher, # 422) **CUES:** after the **Hick Karl Meets** his friend the **Hick Carrie**, who is feeling **Co**ld, they light this fire that 光る **hika**ru (shines) on this platform on lopsided legs **ALSO COMPARE:** other similar kanji at # 1855; other kanji containing 光 at # 979

Foot
0449. 足 **PRONUNCIATIONS: ashi, *a*, ta, soku, zoku²** **MEANINGS:** leg, foot, to suffice
EXAMPLES: 足 ashi = leg or foot; 足立 Adachi = a ward in Tokyo; 足りる tariru = to suffice; 不足 fusoku = insufficient; 満足 manzoku = satisfaction
DESCRIPTION: at the bottom, a foot radical, which includes a taser pointing to the right; above the taser, a square that resembles a kneecap **CUES:** I tripped on an **A**shy ashcan and landed on this knee cap on my 足 **ashi** (leg), causing this taser to discharge, and the **A**ccident 足りた **ta**rita (sufficed) to keep me from going to work at the **Ta**x office; I then saw an **U**ber car and used this foot to kick water at it to **So**ak the **U**ber, but my efforts were 不足 fu**soku** (insufficient) **GROUP:** 足 ashi = leg or foot, # 449; 超 chou = super, # 621; 促(進) sokushin = propagation, # 1455

0450. 走 **PRONUNCIATIONS: hashi, sou**
MEANING: to run **EXAMPLES:** 走る hashiru = to run; 脱走 dassou = desertion, escape
DESCRIPTION: at the top, 土 tsuchi (soil, # 59); at the bottom, a foot radical, as seen in 足 ashi (foot, # 449), which includes a taser pointing to the right **CUES:** after smoking **Ha**sh**i**sh in the **So**viet **U**nion, this guy with soil on his feet like this could really 走る **hashi**ru (run) **GROUP:** 走(る) hashiru = to run, # 450; (生)徒 seito = student, # 451; 起(きる) okiru = to get up, # 452; 越(える) koeru = to go across, # 453; 超 chou = super, # 621; 趣(味) shumi = hobby, # 715; 赴(く) omomuku = to go, # 1888

0451. 徒 **PRONUNCIATION: to**
MEANINGS: follower, pupil **EXAMPLES:** 生徒 seito = student; 信徒 shinto = follower, believer **DESCRIPTION:** compared to 走(る) hashiru (to run, # 450), this adds a man with a double hat on the left **CUE:** after he finishes his **To**ast, a 生徒 sei**to** (student) 走 (runs) after his teacher on the left, who lends him one of his two hats, and they go to school
ALSO COMPARE: other similar kanji at # **450**

0452. 起 **PRONUNCIATIONS: o, ki, gi²**
MEANINGS: to get up, to arise **EXAMPLES:** 起こる okoru = to occur, to happen; 起立する kiritsu suru = to stand up; 縁起 engi = omen, luck **DESCRIPTION:** at the lower left, 走(る) hashiru (to run, # 450), which includes a foot at the bottom and a taser; on the right, a 己 (snake) from Ohio, shaped like a backwards "S" **CUES:** if I'm camping in **O**hio and this 己 (snake) appears at the end of this foot, I 起きる **o**kiru (get up), grab my **K**eys and 走 (run) **ALSO COMPARE:** similar kanji at # **450** and # **1078**

0453. 越 **PRONUNCIATIONS: ko, e, koshi, etsu** **MEANINGS:** to cross or go over
EXAMPLES: 引っ越す hikkosu = to move (dwelling); 越える koeru = to go across, to exceed (this can also be spelled 超える koeru, # 621); 越権 ekken = going beyond authority, abuse of confidence; 三越 Mitsukoshi = name of a department store; 超越する chouetsu suru = to stand out or transcend **DESCRIPTION:** at the lower left, 走(る) hashiru (to run, # 450), which includes a taser; in the middle, a hoe (this is more obvious when it is written like this 越); on the right, a halberd (a combination of an axe and a lance), belonging to a Coast Guardsman **CUES:** a **C**oast **G**uardsman has 引っ越した hik**ko**shita (moved his residence), and he 走 (runs) with this hoe and this halberd, since he has to 越える **ko**eru (go across) town in order to **E**mbark with his **Co**-**Sh**ipmates, carrying some **E**tchings from **Su**dan **GROUP:** 越(える) koeru = to exceed, # 453; 以(前に) izen ni = a long time ago, # 601; 真似 mane = imitation, # 824 **ALSO COMPARE:** other similar kanji at # **450** and # **1862**

0454. 題 **PRONUNCIATION: dai**
MEANINGS: title, topic **EXAMPLES:** 話題 wadai = topic; 問題 mondai = problem **DESCRIPTION:** at the bottom, a foot radical, as seen in 足 ashi (foot, # 449), which looks like a boat and includes a taser; on the left end of the boat, a 日 (sun) which resembles a lantern; on the right end of the boat, a boatman who is missing his head, as seen in the radical on the right in 頭 atama (head, # 93) **CUE:** the 話題 wa**dai** (topic) of today's discussion is this headless boatman who will ferry me in this boat by the light of this lantern across the River Styx after I **Di**e; this sounds like a real 問題 mon**dai** (problem) **GROUP:** (問)題 mondai = problem, # 454; 是(非) zehi = by all means, # 1035; 提(出する) teishutsu suru = to hand in, # 1156; 堤 tsutsumi = an embankment, # 1837 **ALSO COMPARE:** other similar kanji at # **1126**

0455. 定 **PRONUNCIATIONS: jou, tei, sada MEANINGS:** to decide, to be fixed **EXAMPLES:** 勘定 kanjou = bill, check, calculation; 予定 yotei = plan; 定年 teinen = retirement age; 定める sadameru = to decide or prescribe **DESCRIPTION:** at the top, a bad haircut; in the middle, a taser weapon pointing to the right; at the bottom, a foot radical as seen in 足 ashi (foot, # 449) **CUES: Jo**an of Arc had a 予定 yo**tei** (plan) to mount this **Ta**ser on this foot and hide from **Sada**m under this bad haircut **COMPARE:** similar kanji at # **913**

Hugging

0456. 左 **PRONUNCIATIONS: sa, hidari MEANING:** left **EXAMPLES:** 左折 sasetsu = left turn; 左手 hidari te = left hand **DESCRIPTION:** on the left, a hugging person named Ringo; on the right, 工 kou (crafted object, # 246), which is a saxophone **CUES:** when I play this 工 (crafted object), which is a **Sa**xophone, I usually hug it like this using this 左 **hidari** (left) arm, but that's difficult now, since I was injured by a **HideA**way bed's **Re**coil **GROUP:** 左 hidari = left, # 456; (補)佐 hosa = aid, # 993; (怠)惰 (な) taida na = lazy, # 2063 **ALSO COMPARE:** other similar kanji at # 457; other kanji containing 工 at # 247

0457. 右 **PRONUNCIATIONS: migi, u, yuu MEANING:** right **EXAMPLES:** 右側 migigawa = right side; 右折 usetsu = right turn; 左右 sayuu = left and right **DESCRIPTION:** on the left, a hugging person; on the right, 口 kuchi (mouth, # 426) **CUES:** I use my 右 **migi** (right) hand to hug food and bring it to this 口 (mouth), but some **Mean Gee**se and an **U**ber strike in the **Yu**kon are making it hard for me to focus on eating **GROUP:** 右 migi = right, # 457; 有(名) yuumei = famous, # 460; 若(い) wakai = young, # 461; 存(在) sonzai = existence, # 462; 怖(い) kowai = afraid, # 463; 希(望) kibou = hope, # 663; 布 nuno = cloth, # 687; (存)在 sonzai = existence, # 1014; 雄 osu = a male, # 1518; 随(分) zuibun = very, # 1670; (承)諾 shoudaku = compliance, # 1945; 匿(名) tokumei = anonymity, # 1962; (真)髄 shinzui = essence, # 1964; (贈)賄 zouwai = bribery, # 1979

0458. 石 **PRONUNCIATIONS: ishi, seki, shaku, se, koku MEANING:** stone **EXAMPLES:** 小石 koishi = pebble; 一石 isseki = one stone; 磁石 jishaku = magnet; 石けん sekken = soap; 石 koku = a unit of rice, approx. 278 liters **DESCRIPTION:** compared to 右 migi (right, # 457), this is missing a vertical line at the top; it resembles a guy with a flat hat leaning over a 口 (box) **CUES:** this guy with a flat hat is leaning over this 口 (box) looking for an 石 **ishi** (stone) that was delivered by an **I**ndonesian **Sh**ip on orders from a **Se**lfish **K**ing to be placed in a **Sh**ack for a **Se**cretary to sit on while she drinks a **Co**ke **ALSO COMPARE:** other similar kanji at # **1775**

0459. 友 **PRONUNCIATIONS: yuu, tomo MEANING:** friend **EXAMPLES:** 友人 yuujin = friend; 友達 tomodachi = friend **DESCRIPTION:** on the left, a hugging person; on the right, 又 mata ("again," # 24), but this resembles a simple table **CUES:** my **Yo**uthful 友達 **tomo**dachi (friend) is hugging this 又 (table) that he made; **Tomo**rrow he will make another **GROUP:** 暖(かい) atatakai = warm, # 38; 友(達) tomodachi = friend, # 459; 髪 kami = hair, # 501; 抜(く) nuku = to extract, # 749; (応)援 ouen = support , # 1177; 緩(い) yurui = lax, # 1330; (愛)媛(県) ehime ken = Ehime Prefecture, # 2084

0460. 有 **PRONUNCIATIONS: a, ari, yuu**
MEANINGS: to exist, to have **EXAMPLES:** 有る aru = to exist (usually written ある); 有難う arigatou = thank you; 有名 yuumei = famous **DESCRIPTION:** on the left, a hugging person; on the right, 月 tsuki (moon, # 148) **CUES:** Arthur, an Aristocrat from the Yukon, symbolically hugs this 有名 yuumei (famous) 月 (moon) which 有る aru (exists), and he says 有難う arigatou (thank you)
ALSO COMPARE: other similar kanji at # **457** and # **2087**

0461. 若 **PRONUNCIATIONS: waka, jaku, nya MEANING:** young **EXAMPLES:** 若い wakai = young; 若年 jakunen = youth, an early age; 般若 hannya = prajna, wisdom
DESCRIPTION: compared to 右 migi (right, # 457), this adds a plant radical at the top **CUES:** when I was 若い wakai (young), I played Whack-A-mole with Jack Nicholson under these plants on the 右 (right) side of our house, and we whacked the moles as we Kneeled in the Yard
ALSO COMPARE: other similar kanji at # **457**

0462. 存 **PRONUNCIATIONS: zon, son**
MEANINGS: to sustain, to humbly know or think **EXAMPLES:** 存じる zonjiru = to humbly know; 存在 sonzai = existence, presence **DESCRIPTION:** on the left, a hugging person, plus an additional vertical line; on the right, 子 ko (child, # 182) **CUES:** when I'm in the Zone, I hug this 子 (child), who plays games that are made by Sony, as I 存じる zonjiru (humbly know)
ALSO COMPARE: other similar kanji at # **457** and # **2078**

0463. 怖 **PRONUNCIATIONS: kowa, fu**
MEANINGS: dreadful, to be frightened
EXAMPLES: 怖い kowai = afraid, scary; 恐怖 kyoufu = fear, horror **DESCRIPTION:** on the left, an erect guy who could be a koala; on the upper right, a hugging person; on the lower right, 巾 (Bo Peep), as seen in 帽(子) boushi (hat, # 243) **CUES:** this guy on the left is a **Ko**ala, and I **Fo**olishly hug this 巾 (Bo Peep) because I'm 怖い kowai (scared), while the koala draws himself up to his full height indignantly
ALSO COMPARE: other similar kanji at # **457**, # **1768** and # **2063**

West
0464. 西 **PRONUNCIATIONS: nishi, *sui, sei, sai, zai*² MEANING:** west
EXAMPLES: 西 nishi = west; 西瓜 suika = watermelon; 西欧 seiou = Western Europe; 関西 Kansai = southwest part of Japan, including Osaka; 東西 touzai = East and West
DESCRIPTION: compared to 四 yon (four, # 6), this adds a handle at the top, which can also be seen as a balcony supported by two pillars
CUES: my Niece has Sheep, and she lives in this house with 四 (four) sides and this high balcony in 西 nishi (west) Sweden, where she feels Safe and can study Science **GROUP:** this is a group of one
ALSO COMPARE: kanji containing 四 (four) with a handle, plus an extra compartment, at # 1480

0465. 酒 **PRONUNCIATIONS: *ki, sake, zake*², *shu, saka, zaka*² MEANING:** alcohol
EXAMPLES: お神酒 omiki = sake offered to the gods; 酒 sake = alcoholic beverage; 冷酒 hiyazake = cold sake, but this is usually pronounced "reishu"; 日本酒 nihonshu = Japanese sake; 洋酒 youshu = foreign liquor; 酒屋 sakaya = liquor store; 居酒屋 izakaya = a bar or pub
DESCRIPTION: on the left, a water radical, suggesting liquid; on the right, 西 nishi (west, # 464) with a basement (this can also be seen as a bucket of sake with a handle) **CUES:** while I was drinking 酒 **sake** made from this water and eating Quiche in this basement in this house, a Salaryman opened a Keg on the 西 (west) side, so I put on my Shoes and went outside to play Sakkaa (soccer)
ALSO COMPARE: other similar kanji at # **1480**

0466. 配 **PRONUNCIATIONS: kuba, hai, pai, bai² MEANINGS:** to distribute, hand out, arrange **EXAMPLES:** 配る kubaru = to deliver, distribute, hand out; 宅配便 takuhaibin = home delivery; 心配する shinpai suru = to worry; 勾配 koubai = a slope **DESCRIPTION:** on the left, 酒 sake (# 465), missing its water radical, which resembles a house; on the right, a 己 (snake) shaped like a backwards "S" **CUES:** a Cool **B**armaid named **H**eidi has brought a **Pi**e to this house containing 酒 (sake), but she sees this 己 (snake) outside, and she 心配する shin**pai** suru (worries) that it may bite **ALSO COMPARE:** other similar kanji at # **1078** and # **1480**

Kangaroo

0467. 汚 **PRONUNCIATIONS: o, yogo, kitana, kega MEANINGS:** dirty, soiled **EXAMPLES:** 汚水 osui = sewage; 汚す yogosu = to soil; 汚い kitanai = dirty; 汚す kegasu = to sully or disgrace; **Note:** both yogosu and kegasu are written 汚す **DESCRIPTION:** on the left, a water radical, suggesting sewage; on the right, a kangaroo from oosutorariya (Australia), with a powerful leg for jumping **CUES:** this kangaroo from **O**osutorariya (Australia) jumps away from this water which is 汚水 **o**sui (sewage), causing me to spill **Y**ogurt made from **G**oat's milk and 汚す **yogo**su (soil) my clothes; the kangaroo also bumps into a **K**itten **A**natomy book and gets it 汚い **kitana**i (dirty), and it spills a **Kega** (keg of) beer **COMPARE:** similar kanji at # **468**

0468. 写 **PRONUNCIATIONS: utsu, sha, ja² MEANING:** to copy **EXAMPLES:** 写す utsusu = to copy; 写真 shashin = photograph; 青写真 aojashin = blueprint **DESCRIPTION:** at the top, a roof; at the bottom, a kangaroo, up to his calves in water, with a powerful leg for jumping **CUES:** this kangaroo flooded the darkroom under this roof while trying to 写す **utsu**su (copy) some 写真 **sha**shin (photos) of people **U**tilizing **S**upermarkets, which he wanted to take back to his **Sh**abby house, and now he's standing in this water **GROUP:** 汚(す) yogosu = to soil, # 467; 写(真) shashin = photograph, # 468; 考(える) kangaeru = to think, # 469; (番)号 bangou = number, # 470; 極めて kiwamete = extremely, # 610; 与(える) ataeru = to give or cause, # 1070; 誇(張) kochou = an exaggeration, # 1635; (技)巧 gikou = technique, # 1727; 顎 ago = a chin, # 1787; (不)朽 fukyuu = eternal, # 2000; 拷(問) goumon = torture, # 2040

0469. 考 **PRONUNCIATIONS: kanga, kou MEANING:** to think thoroughly **EXAMPLES:** 考える kangaeru = to think; 思考 shikou = consideration, thought **DESCRIPTION:** compared to 者 mono (person, # 276), this substitutes a powerful kangaroo leg for 日 (sun) at the bottom; like 者, 考 plays with scissors **CUES:** this **Kanga**roo is this 者 (person) who 考える **kanga**eru (thinks) about how to **Co**pe with the cuts that he gets from these scissors, but he continues to play with them **ALSO COMPARE:** other similar kanji at # **468** and # **1065**

0470. 号 **PRONUNCIATION: gou MEANINGS:** to call in a loud voice, number **EXAMPLES:** 番号 bangou = number; 信号 shingou = traffic light; 六号車 rokugousha = car number six **DESCRIPTION:** at the top, 口 kuchi (mouth, # 426); at the bottom, a kangaroo with a powerful leg for kicking, which resembles a soccer player who can score goals **CUE:** this 口 (mouth) at the top represents a 番号 ban**gou** (number, i.e., the number "0") which this kangaroo wears on his uniform, and he scores **Go**als **COMPARE:** similar kanji at # **468**

Feathers

0471. 弱 **PRONUNCIATIONS: yowa, jaku MEANING:** weak **EXAMPLES:** 弱い yowai = weak; 弱点 jakuten = weak point, weakness **DESCRIPTION:** these two radicals represent feathers; compared to 羽 hane (feather, # 755), they have shafts (at the top) which appear to be twisted and weak and resemble modified versions of the snakes seen in 選(ぶ) erabu (to choose, # 352) **CUES:** a **Y**ogi was **W**andering when he saw **J**ack **N**icholson holding these two feathers with 弱い **yowa**i (weak) shafts **ALSO COMPARE:** other similar kanji at # **1078** and # **1457**

0472. 習 **PRONUNCIATIONS: nara, shuu MEANINGS:** to learn, learning by repeating **EXAMPLES:** 習う narau = to learn; 練習 renshuu = practice; 習字 shuuji = calligraphy practice **DESCRIPTION:** at the top, these two radicals represent feathers, reportedly; at the bottom, 白(い) shiroi (white, # 44) **CUES:** a 白 (white) bird was using these feathers to 習う **nara**u (learn) to fly when a **N**asty **R**ascal threw a **S**hoe at it **ALSO COMPARE:** other similar kanji at # **1457** and # **2014**

Fish Head

0473. 色 **PRONUNCIATIONS: iro, shiki, shoku MEANINGS:** color, amorous **EXAMPLES:** 茶色 cha'iro = brown; 景色 keshiki = view; 血色 kesshoku = complexion **DESCRIPTION:** at the top, a fish head (see # 80); in the middle, a horizontal 日 hi (day, or sun, # 32), but this looks like two eyes; at the bottom, a snake **CUES:** this snake with these two eyes and this fish head has an 色 **iro** (color) like **I**ron; it is sitting up high and has a good 景色 ke**shiki** (view) of a **Shi**ite **K**ing, who lives by the **Sh**ore in **Ku**wait **COMPARE:** other similar kanji at # **87** and # **673**

0474. 勉 **PRONUNCIATION: ben MEANING:** exerting oneself **EXAMPLE:** 勉強 benkyou = study **DESCRIPTION:** on the left, a fish-head guy (see # 80) with glasses and lopsided legs, or tentacles, as seen in 晩 ban (evening, # 35); at the upper right, 力 chikara (force or power, # 107) **CUE:** this fish-head guy with glasses **B**ends this tentacle and kneels, using his 力 (power) of concentration to 勉強する **ben**kyou suru

(study) **ALSO COMPARE:** other similar kanji at # **1140** and # **1846**

0475. 触 **PRONUNCIATIONS: fu, sawa, zawa², shoku MEANINGS:** contact, touch, feel **EXAMPLES:** 触れる fureru = to touch (usually unintentional, including contact with air or electric current); 触る sawaru = to touch (usually intentional, not including contact with air or electric current); (手)触(り) tezawari = touch or feel; 接触する sesshoku suru = to touch or contact **DESCRIPTION:** on the left, 角 kado (corner, # 81), which consists of a fish-head guy (see # 80) with bifocals and straight legs; on the right, 虫 mushi (insect, # 9) **CUES:** this **F**oolish 角 (fish-head guy with bifocals) is sidling up to 触る **sawa**ru (touch) this 虫 (insect) which he **S**aw **W**alking down the road, but he will get **Sh**ocked by its stinger **COMPARE:** other similar kanji at # **618**, # **1032** and # **1754**

Pull

0476. 引 **PRONUNCIATIONS: hi, in, hiki, biki² MEANING:** to pull **EXAMPLES:** 引く hiku = to pull; 引力 inryoku = attraction, gravitational pull, magnetism; 取引 torihiki = business deal; 割引 waribiki = discount **DESCRIPTION:** on the left, 弓 yumi (bow, # 1044), which resembles a twisted tree; on the right, a rope, which can also be seen as a unicorn horn **CUES:** since this **H**ideous tree was twisted, I 引いた **hi**ita (pulled) it down with this rope, but I **I**njured my skin, and now I have a **H**ickey **GROUP:** 引(く) hiku = to pull, # 476; (引っ)張(る) hipparu = to pull, # 477; 強(い) tsuyoi = strong, # 478; 弟 otouto = little brother, # 529; (次)第(に) shidai ni = gradually, # 530; 沸(く) waku = to boil, # 531; 費(用) hiyou = cost, # 656; 弾(く) hiku = to play a piano, # 780; 湾 wan = gulf, # 1016; 弓 yumi = bow, # 1044; (括)弧 kakko = a parenthesis, # 1763; 窮(地) kyuuchi = adversity, # 1805; 弦(楽器) gengakki

= a stringed instrument, # 1860; 弔(う) toumurau = to mourn, # 2053; 弥(生時代) yayoi jidai = the Yayoi era, # 2080 **ALSO COMPARE:** kanji containing backwards "S" snakes at # 1078; other similar kanji at # **985**

0477. 張 **PRONUNCIATIONS: chou, ha, pa, ba²** **MEANINGS:** to stretch, pull or extend **EXAMPLES:** 出張 shucchou = business trip; 張り合う hariau = to compete or contend with; 引っ張る hipparu = to pull; 頑張る ganbaru = to do one's best **DESCRIPTION:** on the left, a twisted 弓 yumi (bow, # 1044), representing something twisted; on the right, 長(い) nagai (long, # 502), or (社)長 shachou (company president, # 502) (identical pronunciation); these include the letters L & Y at the bottom **CUES:** 長 (long) 弓 (twisted) stories are often heard on 出張 shuc**chou** (business trips), where businessmen who are **Ch**osen by their managers sit around the **Ha**rbor, beg each other's **Pa**rdon, and 引っ張る hip**pa**ru (pull) their noses **ALSO COMPARE:** other similar kanji at # **398**, # **476** and # **502**

0478. 強 **PRONUNCIATIONS: tsuyo, zuyo², gou, shi, kyou** **MEANINGS:** strong, to force **EXAMPLES:** 強い tsuyoi = strong; 根強い nezuyoi = firmly rooted, persistent; 強引 gouin = coercive, high-handed; 強いる shiiru = to force; 勉強 benkyou = study **DESCRIPTION:** on the left, a twisted 弓 yumi (bow, # 1044); at the upper right, the katakana character ム mu; at the lower right, 虫 mushi (insect, # 9), but these two radicals on the right, taken together, look like a barbell **CUES:** since I practice archery with this bow and work out with this barbell, I am 強い **tsuyo**i (strong) and can carry **Tsu**itcases (suitcases) of **Yo**gurt made from **Go**at and **Sh**eep milk to sell in my business in **Kyou**to **ALSO COMPARE:** other similar kanji at # **476**, # **1678** and # **1754**

0479. 風 **PRONUNCIATIONS: fuu, puu², fu, pu², kaze, kaza, ka** **MEANINGS:** wind, manner, style **EXAMPLES:** 台風 taifuu = typhoon; 扇風機 senpuuki = an electric fan; 日本風 nihon fuu = Japanese style; 風呂 furo = hot bath; (春)風 shunpu = a spring breeze; 風 kaze = wind; 風向き kazamuki = wind direction; 風邪 kaze = upper respiratory infection **DESCRIPTION:** the continuous line on the left, top and right side of this kanji suggests wind, blowing from left to right; it can also be seen as a two-sided leant-to; under this line of wind, a 虫 mushi (insect, # 9) is wearing a flat hat and seems to be dropping into someone's food **CUES:** when a 台風 tai**fuu** (typhoon) occurs, it creates 風 **kaze** (wind) which may blow these **Fo**olish hat-wearing 虫 (insects) into our **Fo**od or damage the **Ca**zette (cassette) collection from **Ka**zakhstan which we keep in the **Ca**r **GROUP:** 風 kaze = wind, # 479; 凧 tako = kite, # 767; 嵐 arashi = storm, # 1128; (紙)幣 shihei = paper money, # 1411; 網 ami = a net, # 1448; (貢)献 kouken = a contribution, # 1618; 弊(社) heisha = our company, # 2005 **ALSO COMPARE:** similar kanji at # **1754**

Man with a Slanted Hat

0480. 使 **PRONUNCIATIONS: tsuka, shi** **MEANINGS:** to use; servant **EXAMPLES:** 使う tsukau = to use; 使用 shiyou = use, employment **DESCRIPTION:** on the left, a man with a slanted hat; on the right, a servant with a dislocated right hip, wearing ordinary glasses, rather than the bifocals seen in 便(利) benri (convenient, # 481) **CUES:** this man on the left 使う **tsuka**u (uses) this servant on the right, who has a dislocated right hip and wears these ordinary glasses (not bifocals), and the man tilts his hat back to watch when the servant goes to the **Tsu**itcase (suitcase) in the **Ca**r, where there is a fresh **Sh**eet **COMPARE:** other similar kanji at # **1000** and # **1314**

0481. 便 **PRONUNCIATIONS: tayo, ben, bin** **MEANINGS:** service, convenient **EXAMPLES:** 便り tayori = news, letter;

便利 benri = convenient; 郵便 yuubin = mail **DESCRIPTION:** on the left, a tall Yorkshire man with a slanted hat; on the right, a servant named Ben Franklin, with a dislocated right hip; compared to 使う tsukau (to use, # 480), Ben is wearing bifocals, which he invented, and has a flat hat **CUES:** this man on the left is a **T**all **Y**orkshire man who tilts his hat back in order to watch this servant named **Ben** who has this dislocated right hip and wears these bifocals, which are 便利 **ben**ri (convenient) when reading small print in **B**ingo instructions **ALSO COMPARE:** other similar kanji at # **1000** and # **1992**

0482. 作 **PRONUNCIATIONS: tsuku, saku, sa MEANINGS:** to create or make **EXAMPLES:** 作る tsukuru = to make; 作文 sakubun = written composition; 作品 sakuhin = creation, work of art or literature; 作家 sakka = writer; 発作 hossa = attack or fit, e.g., 心臓発作 shinzou hossa = heart attack

DESCRIPTION: compared to 昨(晩) sakuban (last night, # 41) (identical pronunciation), this kanji substitutes a man with a slanted hat for 日 (sun); it retains the serrated axe, which can also be seen as a ladder or stairs **CUES:** this man on the left is tilting his hat back in order to examine the blade on this serrated axe that he carried in his **Ts**uitcase (suitcase) from **Ku**wait to 作る **tsuku**ru (make) a 作品 **saku**hin (creation), which he keeps in a **S**ack whenever he is playing the **Sa**xophone **COMPARE:** other similar kanji at # **41**

0483. 任 **PRONUNCIATIONS: maka, nin MEANINGS:** to take up a burden; responsibility **EXAMPLES:** 任せる makaseru = to entrust; 主任 shunin = foreman **DESCRIPTION:** compared to 住(む) sumu (to reside, # 167), this omits the tiny cap on the right; it retains the man with a slanted hat and the 王 (king), which looks like pieces of macaroni arranged in a pattern **CUES:** this man on the left tilts his hat back to examine this 王 (**Ma**caroni) which he plans to 任せる **maka**seru (entrust) to a 主任 shu**nin** (foreman) who is a **Ni**nja **COMPARE:** 妊婦 ninpu = a pregnant woman, # 1731 (identical pronunciation); other similar kanji at # **2045**

0484. 価 **PRONUNCIATIONS: ka, atai MEANINGS:** value, price **EXAMPLES:** 物価 bukka = price; 価値 kachi = value; 価 atai = value, price **DESCRIPTION:** on the left, a man with a slanted hat; on the right, a carry-on suitcase with its handle extended; note how the radical on the right differs from 西 nishi (west, # 464) **CUES:** this man is tilting his hat back in order to examine the 物価 buk**ka** (price) of this **C**arry-on suitcase that **A T**hai guy wants to buy **GROUP:** this is a group of one

0485. 借 **PRONUNCIATIONS: ka, sha, shaku MEANING:** to borrow **EXAMPLES:** 借りる kariru = to borrow or rent; 借金 shakkin = debt; 借家 shakuya = rented house **DESCRIPTION:** compared to 昔 mukashi (olden days, # 33), which resembles a bank teller's window, this adds a man with a slanted hat on the left **CUES:** in 昔 (the olden days), this man went to this 昔 (bank teller's window), tilted his hat back so that the teller could identify him, 借りた **ka**rita (borrowed) **C**ash and took it to his **Sh**abby **Sh**ack **ALSO COMPARE:** 貸(す) kasu = to lend, # 90; similar kanji at # **33**

0486. 供 **PRONUNCIATIONS: domo, kyou, ku, tomo, sona MEANINGS:** together, both **EXAMPLES:** 子供 kodomo = child; 提供する teikyou suru = to offer, provide, sponsor; 供物 kumotsu = offering; お供する otomo suru = to accompany; 供える sonaeru = to offer at an altar **DESCRIPTION:** on the left, a man with a slanted hat; at the upper right, a plant radical (see # 43) on a platform supported by two slanted lines that may represent a hill **CUES:** this man, who is staying in a **D**opy **M**otel in **Kyo**uto, tilts his hat back in order to watch as 子供 ko**domo** (children) play in these plants above this hill, and he offers them **K**ool-**A**id in exchange for getting **T**omograms, or at least **S**onar exams **GROUP:** 選(挙) senkyo = election, # 352; (子)供 kodomo = child, # 486;

港 minato = port, # 549; 翼 tsubasa = wing # 912; 共(同の) kyoudou no = cooperative, # 969 (identical pronunciation); 異(なる) kotonaru = to differ, # 970; (宮)殿 kyuuden = palace, # 1080; 洪(水) kouzui = flood, # 1119

0487. 化 PRONUNCIATIONS: ke, ba, ka
MEANING: to change EXAMPLES: 化粧 keshou = makeup; 化かす bakasu = to bewitch or enchant; 化学 kagaku = chemistry
DESCRIPTION: compared to 花 hana (flower, # 211), or 花(粉) kafun (pollen, # 211) (identical pronunciation), this kanji omits the plant radical at the top; it retains the man with a slanted hat and the ヒ (hero) who packs flowers into cartons
CUES: this man on the left has studied 化学 **ka**gaku (chemistry), and he tilts his hat back in order to watch this ヒ (hero) mix **Ch**emicals and pack them in **B**ags and **C**artons COMPARE: 科(学) kagaku = science, # 511; other similar kanji at # **1413**

0488. 件 PRONUNCIATION: ken
MEANINGS: case, matter, counter for houses
EXAMPLES: その件 sono ken = the matter being discussed; 事件 jiken = incident; 四件 yonken = four houses DESCRIPTION: on the left, a man with a slanted hat named Ken; on the right, 牛 ushi (cow, # 205) CUES: this man named **Ken** tilts his hat back to investigate a 事件 ji**ken** (incident) at the **Ken**tucky Derby involving this 牛 (cow) belonging to Barbie
ALSO COMPARE: other similar kanji at # **1765**

0489. 夜 PRONUNCIATIONS: yoru, yo, ya MEANING: night EXAMPLES: 夜 yoru = night; 夜中 yonaka = middle of the night; 今夜 konya = tonight DESCRIPTION: at the top, a tire stop, as seen in 対(する) tai suru = to confront, # 674, but this can also be seen as a roof with a chimney; at the lower left, a man with a slanted hat; at the lower right, this can be seen as a dancer, as seen in 各(国) kakkoku (each country, # 1033), with a mark on her cheek
CUES: a **Yo**semite **Roo**ster tripped on this tire stop and scratched this dancer on the cheek one 夜 **yoru** (night), and this man on the left tilted his hat back to examine the wound and advised her to put **Yo**gurt and **Ya**m extract on it GROUP: 夜 yoru = night, # 489; 液(体) ekitai = liquid, # 1241
ALSO COMPARE: other similar kanji at # **1860**

0490. 側 PRONUNCIATIONS: gawa, soba, soku MEANINGS: side, close by
EXAMPLES: 右側 migigawa = right side; 側に soba ni = close to; however, 側 soba is usually written そば, to avoid confusion with gawa; 側面 sokumen = side, aspect
DESCRIPTION: on the left, a man with a slanted hat; in the middle, 貝 kai (shell, or money chest, # 83); on the right, the katakana character リ Ri
CUES: this man on the left tilts his hat back, but it is difficult to see this リ Ri, who is on the opposite 側 **gawa** (side) of this 貝 (money chest), and there is a **Ga**udy **Wa**gon 側に **soba** ni (close by), at which they are both able to buy **Soba** (noodles) **So**aked in broth GROUP: (右)側 migigawa = right side, # 490, (予)測 yosoku = a prediction, # 1031, and (規)則 kisoku = rules, # 1342, all of which can be pronounced "soku"

0491. 宿 PRONUNCIATIONS: shuku, yado, juku MEANING: inn EXAMPLES: 宿題 shukudai = homework; 宿 yado = inn; 新宿 Shinjuku = a ward in Tokyo DESCRIPTION: at the top, a bad haircut; at the lower left, a man with a slanted hat; at the lower right, 百 hyaku (hundred, # 47), which resembles a limousine antenna above 日 hi (sun, # 32) CUES: 百 (one hundred) guys with bad haircuts like this showed up as this man at the lower left tilted his hat back in order to examine his 宿題 **shuku**dai (homework); the guys, who are wearing **Sh**oes from **Ku**wait, are staying at the 宿 **yado** (inn), in the **Ya**rd by the **Do**or, and next to the **Ju**ke**bo**x GROUP: 百 hyaku = hundred, # 47; 宿

yado = inn, # 491; 縮(小) shukushou = a reduction, # 1487 (identical pronunciation) **ALSO COMPARE:** other kanji with limousine antennae at # 522 and # 1126; other similar kanji at # **1487**

0492. 係 PRONUNCIATIONS: kei, kakari, kaka MEANING: person in charge
EXAMPLES: 関係 kankei = relationship; 係員 kakari'in = person in charge; 係り kakari = duty (this can also be spelled 係)
DESCRIPTION: on the left, a man with a slanted hat; on the right, a 糸 (skeet shooter, # 219), with a cape draped across his head **CUES:** this man on the left is a 係員 **kakari** in (person in charge), he tilts his hat back to examine this **Cape** on this 糸 (skeet shooter), and he shows that he **Can Carry** his weight in their 関係 ka**nkei** (relationship) by giving the shooter some **Cacao** beans
ALSO COMPARE: other similar kanji at # **1072**

Lean-to
0493. 店 PRONUNCIATIONS: mise, ten
MEANINGS: shop, store
EXAMPLES: 店 mise = store; 店員 ten'in = store clerk; 喫茶店 kissaten = coffee shop
DESCRIPTION: on the upper left, a lean-to with a chimney; inside the lean-to, a well with a pump handle, which also resembles a taser **CUES:** this is a **Mis**erable 店 **mise** (store) under this lean-to, where people come to buy water pumped from this well by a 店員 **ten**'in (store clerk) who plays **Tenn**is **COMPARE:** 居(間) ima = living room, # 809; other similar kanji at # **1542**

0494. 広 PRONUNCIATIONS: hiro, biro, kou MEANINGS: spacious, wide EXAMPLES:
広い hiroi = wide, spacious; 背広 sebiro = man's suit; 広告 koukoku = advertisement
DESCRIPTION: on the upper left, a lean-to, with a small sign on the top; inside the lean-to, the katakana character ム mu (the sound made by a cow)
CUES: this ム (cow) has a 広い **hiro**i (wide and spacious) lean-to; this sign at the top says that it is intended for **Hero**es who eat a lot of **Bean Ro**lls and

drink **Co**la
COMPARE: other similar kanji at # **1287**

0495. 庭 PRONUNCIATIONS: tei, niwa
MEANING: garden **EXAMPLES:** 庭園 teien = formal Japanese garden; 庭 niwa = garden; 裏庭 uraniwa = back yard
DESCRIPTION: on the upper left, a lean-to with a chimney; inside the lean-to, the radical at the lower left is different from the snail radical seen in many kanji, e.g., 週 shuu (week, # 346); we can call it a "3X snail," since it consists of a 3 intersected at the bottom to form an X **CUES:** this 王 (king) likes to ride on this 3X snail in this lean-to in his 庭 **niwa** (garden), where he is guarded with **T**asers and surrounded by **K**neeling **W**arlords **GROUP:** 庭 niwa = garden, # 495; (法)廷 houtei = a court of law, # 1664 (identical pronunciation) **ALSO COMPARE:** other similar kanji at # **692** and # **2045**

0496. 席 PRONUNCIATIONS: se, seki
MEANING: seat **EXAMPLES:** 寄席 yose = an entertainment hall; 席 seki = seat; 出席 shusseki suru = to attend; 座席 zaseki = the seat of a chair **DESCRIPTION:** on the upper left, a lean-to with a chimney; inside the lean-to, at the top, a bucket with a horizontal line across it; at the bottom, Bo Peep, as seen in 帽(子) boushi (hat, # 243); taken together, these two radicals resemble an infant seat resting on a three-legged stool which belongs to a secretary **CUES:** before feeding the baby, I put him in this infant 席 **seki** (seat) on top of this stool belonging to a **Se**cretary inside this lean-to, but he has a **Seki** (cough) and can't eat
COMPARE: 座(る) suwaru = to sit on a zabuton, # 497; other similar kanji at # **542** and # **1768**

0497. 座 PRONUNCIATIONS: za, suwa
MEANINGS: to sit, seat EXAMPLES:
座布団 zabuton = floor cushion for sitting;
座る suwaru = to sit on a zabuton
DESCRIPTION: on the upper left, a lean-to with a chimney; inside the lean-to, 土 tsuchi (soil, # 59); on each side of 土 (soil), a 人 (person) is sitting
CUES: these two 人 (people) 座る **suwa**ru (sit) on this 土 (soil) in this lean-to, which is a restaurant in **Za**mbia, and they are served **S**oup and **W**ater
ALSO COMPARE: 席 seki = seat, # 496; other similar kanji at # **352**, # **748** and # **1926**

0498. 度 PRONUNCIATIONS: do, tabi, taku MEANINGS: time, degree EXAMPLES:
今度 kondo = this time or next time; 百度 hyakudo = 100 degrees; 転勤の度 tenkin no tabi = transfer's occasion; 支度 shitaku = preparation DESCRIPTION: compared to 席 seki (seat, # 496), this substitutes 又 mata ("again," # 24), which resembles a simple table, for the three-legged stool at the lower right; it retains the lean-to with a chimney and the infant seat, which we can also describe a bucket of food
CUES: 毎度 mai**do** (every time) that **Do**lores prepares this bucket of food in this lean-to, she also feeds it to her **Tab**by cat at this 又 (table), together with **Ta**p water and **Koo**l-Aid
COMPARE: other similar kanji at # **24** and # **542**

0499. 渡 PRONUNCIATIONS: wata, to
MEANINGS: to cross, to hand over EXAMPLES:
渡る wataru = to cross; 渡米 tobei = going to America DESCRIPTION: compared to 度 do (time, # 498), this adds a water radical on the left; it retains the bucket above a table inside a lean-to
CUES: every 度 (time) that we 渡る **wata**ru (cross) this water, we **Wa**lk **Ta**ll and 渡す **wata**su (hand) money to a **To**ll collector
COMPARE: other similar kanji at # **24** and # **542**

0500. 岸 PRONUNCIATIONS: gan, kishi
MEANINGS: beach, shore EXAMPLES: 海岸 kaigan = beach; 岸 kishi = beach, shore
DESCRIPTION: at the top, 山 yama (mountain, # 146); below 山, a one-sided lean-to; inside the lean-to, a telephone pole
CUES: **Gan**dalf visits a 海岸 kai**gan** (beach) under this 山 (mountain), where he has this telephone pole in this lean-to and also **Ke**eps **Sh**eep
COMPARE: similar kanji at # **629** and # **1385**

Hair

0501. 髪 PRONUNCIATIONS: kami, hatsu, patsu², ga MEANING: hair
EXAMPLES: 髪 kami = hair; 白髪 hakuhatsu = white or grey hair; 先発 senpatsu = washing one's hair; 白髪 shiraga = white or grey hair; Note: hakuhatsu and shiraga are both written 白髪
DESCRIPTION: at the upper left, hair flowing to the right; at the middle left, 一 (one) ム (cow), as seen in (部)屋 heya (room, # 63); at the upper right, three lines, which can also be seen as cords, also suggesting hair flowing right; at the bottom, 友(達) tomodachi (friend, # 459)
CUES: this 友 (friend), who is a **Cam**bodian **Im**migrant, owns this 一 (one) ム (cow), and she has these two kinds of 髪 **kami** (hair) flowing right, which she covers with **Ha**ts that she bought in **Ga**za
ALSO COMPARE: other similar kanji at # **459**, # **502**, # **839** and # **1678**

0502. 長 PRONUNCIATIONS: naga, chou MEANINGS: long, chief, principal
EXAMPLES: 長い nagai = long; 社長 shachou = company president DESCRIPTION: at the top, long hair flowing to the right; at the bottom; the letters L & Y which remind us of "Light Years"
CUES: this 社長 sha**chou** (president) with this long hair flowing to the right is Light Years ahead of his peers, and he owns **Naga**ina, a 長い **naga**i (long) cobra who was **Cho**sen to represent her tribe
GROUP: (出)張 shucchou = business trip, # 477

(identical pronunciation); 髪 kami = hair, # 501; 長(い) nagai = long , # 502; (手)帳 techou = pocket notebook, # 1244 (also identical pronunciation); (残)虐(な) zangyaku na = cruel, # 1679 **ALSO COMPARE:** other kanji containing L & Y at # **398**; for kanji with long hair flowing to the *left*, see # 1165

Scorpion

0503. 地 **PRONUNCIATIONS: ji, chi MEANINGS:** ground, soil **EXAMPLES:** 地震 jishin = earthquake; 地下鉄 chikatetsu = subway **DESCRIPTION:** on the left, 土 tsuchi (soil, # 59); on the right, this is reportedly a scorpion, with a long stinging tail **CUES:** this **J**ittery scorpion lives in this 土 (soil) under the 地 **chi** (ground), where it eats **Ch**eese **GROUP:** 地(震) jishin = earthquake, # 503; (乾電)池 kandenchi = battery, # 504 (identical pronunciation); 他(の) hoka no = another, # 505; 施(設) shisetsu = facility, # 1067; (ご)馳(走) gochisou = a delicacy, # 1358 (also identical pronunciation)

0504. 池 **PRONUNCIATIONS: ike, chi MEANING:** pond **EXAMPLES:** 池 ike = pond; 乾電池 kandenchi = battery **DESCRIPTION:** on the left, a water radical (see # 12); on the right, this is reportedly a scorpion, with a long stinging tail **CUES:** this scorpion drank this water from the 池 **ike** (pond) on **Ike**'s (Eisenhower's) farm and ate his **Ch**eese **COMPARE:** similar kanji at # **503**

0505. 他 **PRONUNCIATIONS: hoka, ta MEANING:** others **EXAMPLES:** 他の hoka no = another (undefined) object; 他人 ta'nin = other people, outsiders **DESCRIPTION:** on the left, a man with a slanted hat; on the right, this is reportedly a scorpion, with a long stinging tail **CUES:** ordinary men with flat hats ride in unmarked vehicles, but this 他の **hoka** no (other) man with this slanted hat rides in a **H**opped-up **C**ar marked with scorpion decals like this and hangs out in **Ta**verns, which is why he is considered a 他人 **ta**nin (outsider) **COMPARE:** 外(に) hoka ni = besides, # 163; other similar kanji at # **503**

Skirts

0506. 春 **PRONUNCIATIONS: haru, shun MEANING:** spring **EXAMPLES:** 春 haru = spring; 晩春 banshun = late spring **DESCRIPTION:** at the top, a 人 hito (person, # 13), with the number 三 san (three, # 3) inscribed across it, which reminds us of triplets; at the bottom, 日 hi (sun, # 32) **CUES:** during the first 春 **haru** (spring) when King **Har**old **Ru**led, some 三 (three) 人 (people) combinations (i.e., triplets) were born, but even though they had 日 (sun)-like (i.e., sunny) dispositions, the king **Shun**ned those babies **GROUP:** 春 haru = spring, # 506; (演)奏 ensou = performance, # 757; 棒 bou = stick, # 820; (安)泰 antai = peace, # 1529; 奉(仕) houshi = service, # 1536; 俸(給) houkyuu = a salary, # 2056

0507. 寒 **PRONUNCIATIONS: samu, kan MEANING:** cold atmosphere **EXAMPLES:** 寒い samui = cold atmosphere; 寒気 kanki = a chill; this can also be pronounced "samuke" **DESCRIPTION:** at the top, a bad haircut; under this haircut, a samurai's wife, wearing a corset, with legs spread apart, strattling two icy reflections on the ground; **Note** that this "corset" differs from the "dome" seen in (子)供 kodomo (child, # 486), primarily because it contains three horizontal lines instead of two; in addition, the corset differs from the "bucket" seen in 基(盤) kiban (foundation, # 1198) in that its horizontal lines extend beyond the vertical lines on both sides (like corset laces) and also because it contains three horizontal lines instead of four **CUES:** when it's 寒い **samu**i (cold), this **Sam**urai's wife, who lives in **Kan**sas and sports this bad haircut and this corset, maneuvers around these patches of ice **COMPARE:** other similar kanji at # **234** and # **1227**

East

0508. 東 **PRONUNCIATIONS: higashi, tou** **MEANING:** east **EXAMPLES:** 東 higashi = east; 東京 toukyou = Tokyo **DESCRIPTION:** since 日 hi (sun, # 32) is visible behind this 木 ki (tree, # 118) in the morning, we know that the tree is east of us; this can also be seen as a tree wearing bifocals **CUES:** in a **H**ideous **G**ash on the 東 **higashi** (east) side of this 木 (tree) in 東京 **tou**kyou (Tokyo), there is a family of tree **To**ads that watches this 日 (sun) rise **COMPARE:** other similar kanji at # 1271

0509. 乗 **PRONUNCIATIONS: jou, no** **MEANINGS:** to ride, to get aboard **EXAMPLES:** 乗客 joukyaku = passenger; 乗る noru = to get aboard or ride **DESCRIPTION:** compared to 東 higashi (east, # 508), 乗 has a roof on top, and the bifocals (or sun) behind (or in) the tree have protrusions on both sides, suggesting that this is a streamlined vehicle **CUES: J**oan of Arc is waiting because she wants to be a 乗客 **jou**kyaku (passenger) on this streamlined vehicle in this 木 (tree) with a roof, but when she tries to 乗る **no**ru (board), there is **No** space **ALSO COMPARE:** other similar kanji at # 799

Grain Plants

0510. 私 **PRONUNCIATIONS: watakushi, watashi, shi** **MEANINGS:** I, personal, private **EXAMPLES:** 私 watakushi = I; 私 watashi = I; 私用の shiyou no = private **DESCRIPTION:** on the left, 禾 (a grain plant with a ripe head); on the right, the katakana character ム mu, which is the sound made by a cow **CUES:** 私 **watakushi** (I) feed this 禾 (ripe grain) to my **S**heep and to ム (cows) like this, and I am a **W**ashington **T**ak**ushii** (taxi) driver who uses a lawyer named **W**allace to create **T**ax **Sh**ields **COMPARE:** other similar kanji at # 591 and # 1797

0511. 科 **PRONUNCIATION: ka** **MEANINGS:** section, category **EXAMPLES:** 科学 kagaku = science; 科学者 kagakusha = scientist; 教科書 kyoukasho = textbook; 歯科 shika = dentistry **DESCRIPTION:** on the left, 禾 (a grain plant with a ripe head); on the right, a slanted shelf holding two containers of calcium **CUE:** a 科学者 **ka**gakusha (scientist) extracts **C**alcium from this 禾 (ripe grain) and uses it to fill these two containers on this slanted shelf **COMPARE:** 化(学) kagaku = chemistry, # 487; other similar kanji at # 910 and # 1797

0512. 料 **PRONUNCIATION: ryou** **MEANINGS:** food, fee, provisions **EXAMPLES:** 料理 ryouri = cuisine; 無料 muryou = free of charge; 料金 ryoukin = fee **DESCRIPTION:** compared to 科(学) kagaku (science, # 511), this substitutes 米 kome (uncooked rice, # 326) for the 禾 (scientist with a flat-top haircut) on the left; it retains the shelf holding two containers **CUE:** Pope **L**eo puts this 米 (uncooked rice) into these two containers on this shelf to use in creating 料理 **ryou**ri (cuisine) **ALSO COMPARE:** other similar kanji at # 910 and # 1387

0513. 和 **PRONUNCIATIONS: wa, yawa, nago, o, to, yori** **MEANING:** harmony or Japanese style **EXAMPLES:** 和食 washoku = Japanese food; 温和 onwa = mild, calm, gentle; 和らぐ yawaragu = to soften; 和む nagomu = to be softened, to calm down; 和尚 oshou = Buddhist priest; 大和 yamato = ancient Japan; 日和 hiyori = weather, climatic conditions **DESCRIPTION:** on the left, 禾 (a grain plant with a ripe head); on the right, 口 kuchi (mouth, # 426), which resembles a box **CUES:** when this 禾 (grain plant) gets ripe, we use 口 (mouths) like this to eat 和食 **wa**shoku (Japanese food) served from a **W**agon, experience 平和 hei**wa** (peace), **Y**awn and **W**ash the dishes, but sometimes there are

Nagging Ghosts from Old times, like Tolstoy, and Yogis who have Retired
COMPARE: similar kanji at # 323 and # **1797**

Capital

0514. 京 PRONUNCIATIONS: **kyou, kei**
MEANING: capital EXAMPLES: 京都 kyouto = Kyoto; 東京 toukyou = Tokyo; 京阪 keihan = Kyoto-Osaka DESCRIPTION: at the top, a tire stop, as seen in 対(する) tai suru (to confront, # 674); in the center, a 口 (box) resembling a house; at the bottom, 小(さい) chisaii (small, # 253) which resembles a small hill; taken together, these resemble a house on a small hill, with a tire stop on the roof CUES: a **K**ey that a **Y**ogi gave me fits this 口 (box, or house) on this 小 (small) hill in 京都 **kyou**to (Kyoto), which features a **C**ave under ground and this tire stop on the roof
GROUP: 京(都) kyouto = Kyoto, # 514; 涼(しい) suzushii = cool, # 515; 景(色) keshiki = view, # 516; 影 kage = shadow, # 839; 就(く) tsuku = to obtain a position, # 974; 蹴(る) keru = to kick, # 975; 鯨 kujira = a whale, # 1981 ALSO COMPARE: other similar kanji at # **1474**

0515. 涼 PRONUNCIATIONS: **ryou, suzu** MEANINGS: cool EXAMPLES: 涼風 ryoufuu = a cool breeze; 涼しい suzushii = cool DESCRIPTION: compared to 京(都) kyouto (Kyoto, # 514), this adds a water radical, suggesting rain, on the left; it retains the tire stop above a 口 (box, or house) on a 小 (small) hill in Kyoto CUES: when this rain falls in this 京 (Kyoto), it gets 涼しい **suzu**shii (cool), and Pope **L**eo goes out to buy **S**ouvenirs from the **Z**oo ALSO COMPARE: other similar kanji at # **514** and # **1474**

0516. 景 PRONUNCIATIONS: **ke, kei** MEANINGS: fine view, scene EXAMPLES: 景色 keshiki = view, scenery; 風景 fuukei = view, scenery, landscape DESCRIPTION: compared to 京(都) kyouto (Kyoto, # 514), this adds 日 hi (sun, # 32) at the top; it retains the tire stop above a 口 (box, or house) on a 小 (small) hill in Kyoto CUES: when this 日 (sun) shines above this 京 (Kyoto), the 景色 **ke**shiki (scenery) is lovely, and we drink from a **K**eg and eat **C**ake ALSO COMPARE: other similar kanji at # **514** and # **1474**

Tsutomeru

0517. 勤 PRONUNCIATIONS: **tsuto, kin** MEANINGS: to be employed, to serve EXAMPLES: 勤める tsutomeru = to be employed; 通勤する tsuukin suru = to commute to work; 出勤する shukkin suru = to attend work DESCRIPTION: at the upper left, a plant radical (see # 43); at the lower left, a sincere guy wearing glasses, which can also be seen as two eyes; unlike the sincere guy seen in 理(由) riyuu (reason, # 78), this guy is wearing ordinary glasses, not bifocals, and he has two pairs of arms; on the right, 力 chikara (force, # 107)
CUES: this sincere guy wearing these glasses rides on a **Tsu**ki (moon) **To**boggan to the place where he 勤めている **tsuto**mete iru (is being employed), and he expends this 力 (force) taking care of these plants at a moon **Kin**dergarten
GROUP: 漢(字) kanji = Chinese character, # 197, and 難(しい) muzukashii = difficult, # 198, which are both structured around 大 (big); (通)勤(する) tsuukin suru = to commute, # 517; 謹(慎) kinshin = self-restraint, # 2011 ALSO COMPARE: kanji in which the sincere guy wears *bifocals* rather than glasses and has only one pair of arms, at # 545; other similar kanji at # **1846**

0518. 務 **PRONUNCIATIONS: mu, tsuto**
MEANING: to discharge one's duty
EXAMPLES: 公務員 koumuin = public servant; 事務所 jimusho = office; 務める tsutomeru = to discharge one's duty
DESCRIPTION: this is a portrait of a family who work at an office on the moon: on the left, 矛(盾) mujun (inconsistency, # 1749) (identical pronunciation) which contains the katakana マ ma, reminding us of mother, balanced on an arrow above a nail with her left hip extended; at the upper right, a dancer with a ponytail; at the lower right, 力 chikara (force, # 107) **CUES:** this マ (mother) who balances on this nail with her left hip extended, this dancer, and a guy with this 力 (force) are a family who work at a 事務所 ji**mu**sho (office) on the **Moo**n, to which they ride on **Ts**uki (moon) **To**boggans and then **tsuto**meru 務める (discharge their duties) **COMPARE:** other similar kanji at # **978**, # **1746** and # **1749**

0519. 努 **PRONUNCIATIONS: tsuto, do**
MEANING: to try hard **EXAMPLES:** 努める tsutomeru = to make an effort; 努力 doryoku = effort **DESCRIPTION:** compared to 怒(る) okoru (to get angry, # 319), or (激)怒 gekido (fury, # 319) (identical pronunciation), this kanji substitutes 力 chikara (force, # 107) for 心 (heart) at the bottom; it retains 女 (female) and the 又 (table) where donations were kept **CUES:** this 女 (female) rides in **Ts**uki (moon) **To**boggans and 努める **tsuto**meru (makes an effort) for her job on the moon, where she expends 力 (force) making **Do**ughnuts on this 又 (table) **COMPARE:** other kanji containing 女 on the left at # **2039**; other similar kanji at # **319** and # **1746**

Pleasant

0520. 楽 **PRONUNCIATIONS: ga, gaku, tano, ra, raku, gura** **MEANINGS:** happy, enjoyable, without difficulty **EXAMPLES:** 楽器 gakki = musical instrument; 音楽 ongaku = music; 楽しい tanoshii = pleasant; 楽観 rakkan = optimism; 楽 raku = comfort, pleasure, relief; 神楽 kagura = sacred Shinto music and dance **DESCRIPTION:** at the top, 白(い) shiroi (white, # 44) with rays on the sides, resembling an oven with rays of heat; at the bottom, 木 ki (tree, # 118) **CUES:** this 白 (white) oven is a **Ga**dget which some **Gaku**sei (students) and a **Ta**ll **No**rwegian have mounted on this 木 (tree), and it is 楽しい **tano**shii (pleasant) to stare at when **Ra**bbits, **Ra**ccoons and **G**oofy **Ra**dicals are playing **GROUP:** 楽(しい) tanoshii = pleasant, # 520; 薬 kusuri = medicine, # 521

0521. 薬 **PRONUNCIATIONS: kusuri, gusuri[2], ya, yaku** **MEANINGS:** medicine, pharmaceutical **EXAMPLES:** 薬 kusuri = medicine; 眠り薬 nemurigusuri = sleeping medicine; 薬局 yakkyoku = pharmacy; 薬品 yakuhin = medicine, drug
DESCRIPTION: compared to 楽(しい) tanoshii (pleasant, # 520), this adds a plant radical (see # 43) at the top; it retains the 白 (white) gadget that a tall Norwegian has installed at the top of a 木 (tree) **CUES:** 薬 **kusuri** (medicines), which a doctor will prescribe after a **Cu**rsory exam and which come from **Y**ams and other plants like these, sometimes have 楽 (pleasant) side-effects, such as causing people to **Yak** (talk) too much **ALSO COMPARE:** other similar kanji at # **520**

Dancer

0522. 夏 **PRONUNCIATIONS: natsu, ka, ge** **MEANING:** summer **EXAMPLES:** 夏 natsu = summer; 初夏 shoka = early summer; 夏至 geshi = summer solstice **DESCRIPTION:** at the top, this resembles a limousine antenna; in the middle, 目 me (eye, # 51), which could be the body of the limousine; at the bottom, a dancer with a ponytail **CUES:** in 夏 **natsu** (summer), this dancer with a ponytail wears a **Na**tty **Su**it and is driven in this limousine **Ca**r with this antenna to **Ge**ttysburg

GROUP: (地)面 jimen = the ground, # 282; 夏 natsu = summer, # 522; 優(しい) yasashii = kind, # 528; 端 hashi = edge, # 730; (素)麺 soumen = fine white noodles, # 1228; (忍)耐 nintai = patience, # 1434; 需(要) juyou = a demand, # 1699; 憂(鬱) yuu'utsu = depression, # 1784; 儒(教) jukyou = Confucianism, # 1909 **ALSO COMPARE:** other similar kanji at # **2002**; other kanji with similar antennae at # 491 and # 1126

0523. 愛 **PRONUNCIATIONS:** *e, ai, me, mana,* ito **MEANING:** love **EXAMPLES:** 愛媛県 ehime ken = Ehime Prefecture; 愛情 aijou = love; 愛でる mederu = to love or admire; 愛弟子 manadeshi = favorite student; 愛しい itoshii = lovely, dear, beloved **DESCRIPTION:** at the top, a barbecue grate on a rack; in the middle, 心 kokoro (heart, # 306); at the bottom, a dancer with a ponytail **CUES:** this dancer with a ponytail is an **E**xcellent **I**ce dancer from **M**exico who studies **M**anagement and barbecues **E**els and **T**omatoes on this grate, putting a lot of this 心 (heart) and 愛情 **ai**jou (love) into her cooking **GROUP:** 愛(情) aijou = love, # 523; 優(しい) yasashii = kind, # 528; 悠(々) yuuyuu = quiet, # 985; 慶(事) keiji = an auspicious event, # 1590; 憂(鬱) yuu'utsu = depression, # 1784; 懲(戒) choukai = reprimand, # 1879; 曖(昧な) aimai na = vague, # 1940 **ALSO COMPARE:** other similar kanji at # **1177**

0524. 客 **PRONUNCIATIONS:** *kya, kyaku, kaku* **MEANINGS:** guest, customer **EXAMPLES:** 客観 kyakkan = object (vs. subject); お客 okyaku = honorable guest; 観客 kankyaku = audience; 乗客 joukyaku = passenger; 旅客 ryokaku = passenger, traveler **DESCRIPTION:** at the top, a bad haircut; in the middle, a leaping dancer with a ponytail; at the bottom, a box **CUES:** this dancer with a ponytail, who has this bad haircut, leaps over this box in order to win a **Ki**a from a 客 **kyaku** (customer) who is a **K**ayaker named **K**arl the **K**ool-Aid vendor **GROUP:** (お)客 okyaku = honorable guest, # 524; 額 hitai = forehead, # 791 **COMPARE:** similar kanji at # **1033**

0525. 路 **PRONUNCIATIONS:** *ro, michi, ji* **MEANING:** road **EXAMPLES:** 道路 douro = road; 路子 Michiko = a female given name; 旅路 tabiji = journey **DESCRIPTION:** on the left, a square top on 止(める) tomeru (to stop, # 173), suggesting a hesitant squarehead, as seen in 踊(る) odoru (to dance, # 366); on the right, a dancer with a ponytail leaping over a box, as seen in 客 kyaku (customer, # 524) **CUES:** this 止 (hesitant) squarehead and this dancer with a ponytail who leaps over this box are **Ro**aming on a 道路 dou**ro** (road) in **Mi**chigan, looking for a **J**eep **ALSO COMPARE:** other similar kanji at # **1033** and # **1534**

0526. 落 **PRONUNCIATIONS:** *o, raku* **MEANINGS:** to fall or drop **EXAMPLES:** 落ちる ochiru = to fall; 落とす otosu = to knock down or drop; 落語 rakugo = Japanese comic story telling **DESCRIPTION:** at the top, a plant radical (see # 43), suggesting leaves; on the lower left, a water radical (see # 12), suggesting a flood; on the lower right, a dancer with a ponytail, leaping over a box **CUES:** when this water flowed in from the left, this dancer jumped over this 口 (box) to escape, and her head struck these leaves, causing some **O**ranges and a **R**accoon to 落ちる **o**chiru (fall) from the tree above **GROUP:** 散(歩) sanpo = a walk, # 159; 落(ちる) ochiru = to fall, # 526; 敬(う) uyamau = to respect, # 873; 警(察) keisatsu = the police, # 874; 驚(く) odoroku = to be astonished, # 971 **ALSO COMPARE:** other similar kanji at # **258** and # **1033**

0527. 復 **PRONUNCIATIONS: fuku, puku², fu** **MEANINGS:** again, to repeat **EXAMPLES:** 復習 fukushuu = review; 回復 kaifuku = recovery; 反復 hanpuku = repetition; 復活 fukkatsu = revival, rebirth, restoration **DESCRIPTION:** this is a pleasant scene from Fukuoka: on the left, a man in a double hat, who is a therapist; at the top right, a crutch; at the middle right, 日 hi (sun, # 32); at the bottom right, a dancer with a ponytail (this combination of radicals = CSD = crutch, sun, dancer) **CUES:** in **Fu**koka, this injured dancer works with this therapist with two hats; she uses this crutch, he lends her a hat so that she can sit in this 日 (sun), he gives her good **Foo**d, and she experiences 回復 kai**fuku** (recovery) (CSD = crutch, sun, dancer) **COMPARE:** similar kanji at # **1220**

0528. 優 **PRONUNCIATIONS: yasa, yuu, sugu** **MEANINGS:** actor, excellent, graceful **EXAMPLES:** 優しい yasashii = kind; 優秀 yuushuu = excellent; 優れる sugureru = to excel **DESCRIPTION:** on the left, a man with a slanted hat; at the top right, a radical that looks like 百 hyaku (hundred, # 47) but with one more horizontal line, resembling a limousine with an antenna, resting on a lid; at the middle right, 心 kokoro (heart, # 306); at the bottom right, a youthful dancer with a ponytail **CUES:** this man on the left is 優しい **yasa**shii (kind), he plays a **Y**ankee **S**axophone, he tilts his hat back in order to view this 優秀な **yuu**shuu na (excellent) antenna on his limousine, he acts from this 心 (heart), his girlfriend is this **Yo**uthful dancer with a ponytail, and they will **Soo**n buy a **Goo**se **ALSO COMPARE:** other similar kanji at # **522** and # **523**

Twisted

0529. 弟 **PRONUNCIATIONS: otouto, dai, tei, de** **MEANING:** younger brother **EXAMPLES:** 弟 otouto = younger brother; 兄弟 kyoudai = sibling; 子弟 shitei = younger people; 弟子 deshi = disciple, apprentice **DESCRIPTION:** in the center, 弓 yumi (bow, # 1044), but this resembles a twisted tree, as seen in 引(く) hiku (to pull, # 476); behind this tree, a person wearing rabbit ears, with his left hip extended **CUES:** 弟 **otouto** (younger brother), who wears these rabbit ears and eats only **O**rganic **T**oma**T**oes, which is a strange **D**iet, stands with his left hip extended behind this twisted tree, which he wants to make into a **T**able for a **D**ebutante **COMPARE:** other similar kanji at # **476**, # **1417** and # **1997**

0530. 第 **PRONUNCIATION: dai** **MEANING:** order **EXAMPLES:** 第三課 daisanka = section number three; 次第に shidai ni = gradually; 次第で shidai de = depending on **DESCRIPTION:** at the top, 竹 take (bamboo, # 134), which resembles two clamps; at the bottom, 弟 otouto (younger brother, # 529), which includes a twisted 弓 (bow), without his rabbit ears, who extends his left hip **CUE:** this 弟 (younger brother) has these two 竹 (bamboo) clamps in his hair, indicating that he is 第二 **dai** ni (Number Two) in line at **W**eight **W**atchers; he wants to go on a **D**iet, and he will get to the front of the queue 次第に shi**dai** ni (gradually) **ALSO COMPARE:** other similar kanji at # **476**, # **1417** and # **2074**

0531. 沸 **PRONUNCIATIONS: wa, fu** **MEANINGS:** to seethe, boil **EXAMPLES:** 沸く waku = to boil, intransitive; 沸かす wakasu = to boil, transitive; 沸騰する futtou suru = to boil **DESCRIPTION:** on the left, a water radical; on the right, a twisted 弓 yumi (bow, # 1044) superimposed on two vertical pipes; taken together, these resemble radiator pipes **CUES:** this **W**ater enters these twisted pipes, 沸く **wa**ku (boils) and cooks our **F**ood **COMPARE:** other similar kanji at # **476**

Deep Inside

0532. 奥 **PRONUNCIATIONS: oku, ou** **MEANING:** deep inside **EXAMPLES:** 奥の方 oku no hou = toward the back; 奥さん okusan = someone else's wife; 奥義 ougi = secrets, mysteries **DESCRIPTION:** at the top, a box with a lever on the lid, containing 米 kome (uncooked rice, # 326); at the bottom, a two-legged table **CUES:** this 米 (uncooked rice) is being stored in this **O**ak box on this two-legged table, and an 奥さん **ok**usan (honorable wife) pushes this lever at the top that **O**pens the box **COMPARE:** other similar kanji at # **1360** and # **1387**

0533. 歯 **PRONUNCIATIONS: ha, ba², shi MEANING:** tooth **EXAMPLES:** 歯 ha = tooth; 虫歯 mushiba = decayed tooth; 歯科 shika = dentistry **DESCRIPTION:** at the top, 止 (める) tomeru (to stop, # 173); at the bottom, 米 kome (uncooked rice, # 326), in a box **CUES**: after the **H**arvest, we put this 米 (uncooked rice) in this box and put this 止 (stop) sign at the top to stop **S**heep from chewing it with their 歯 **ha** (teeth) **COMPARE:** (年)齢 nenrei = age, # 989; other similar kanji at # **1360**, # **1387** and # **1929**

Oil Derrick

0534. 歌 **PRONUNCIATIONS: ka, uta MEANINGS:** to sing, a song **EXAMPLES:** 歌手 kashu = singer; 歌う utau = to sing **DESCRIPTION:** on the left, two instances of (許)可 kyoka (permission, # 615), which consists of a simple box (or carton) in a one-sided lean-to and resembles a song sheet hanging from a rack; on the right, 欠(く) kaku (to lack, # 1238), which resembles an oil derrick (see # 399) **CUES:** this 欠 (oil derrick) belongs to a 歌手 **ka**shu (singer) who sings **C**atholic music and reads from a music stand with these two song sheets when she 歌う **uta**u (sings) at an **U**gandan **T**avern **COMPARE:** 唄 uta = a song, # 1870; similar kanji at # **352**, # **536** and # **1176**

0535. 欲 **PRONUNCIATIONS: ho, yo, yoku MEANINGS:** greed, wanting more **EXAMPLES:** 欲しい hoshii = to desire; 欲求 yokkyuu = desire; 欲張り yokubari = greed; 食欲 shokuyoku = appetite **DESCRIPTION:** compared to 浴(室) yokushitsu (bathroom, # 256) (identical pronunciation), this kanji omits the water radical on the left and adds 欠 (く) kaku (to lack, # 1238), which resembles an oil derrick (see # 399), on the right; it retains the bathroom with water vapor rising from it, where one can bathe before eating yogurt and cookies **CUES:** this bathroom with water vapor rising from it and this oil derrick outside are attached to our **H**otel at **Y**osemite, and we tell the waiters in the restaurant that we 欲しい **ho**shii (desire) **Y**ogurt and **C**ookies **COMPARE:** other similar kanji at # **536** and # **660**

0536. 次 **PRONUNCIATIONS: tsugi, shi, tsu, ji MEANING:** next **EXAMPLES:** 次に tsugi ni = next; 次第に shidai ni = gradually; 取り次ぐ toritsugu = to convey or transmit; 次回に jikai ni = next time **DESCRIPTION:** on the left, a water radical; on the right, 欠(く) kaku (to lack, # 1238) which resembles, at the top, a chair that is leaning to the right and, at the bottom, 人 hito (person, # 13) and reminds us of an oil derrick **CUES:** this 欠 (oil derrick) has **T**superior (superior) **G**ears, and we used it to pump this water for our **S**heep, but 次に **tsugi** ni (next) it broke down, and we had to get some spare parts from a **T**suitcase (suitcase) in the **J**eep **GROUP:** 資(金) shikin = capital, # 91 (identical pronunciation); 飲(む) nomu = to drink, # 399; 歌(う) utau = to sing, # 534; 欲(しい) hoshii = to desire, # 535; 次(に) tsugi ni = next, # 536; 吹(く) fuku = to blow, # 537; 羨(ましい) urayamashii = envious, # 662; 姿 sugata = shape, # 763; 茨(城県) ibarakiken = a Japanese prefecture, # 1007; 欠(席) kesseki = absence, # 1238; 炊(く) taku = to cook, # 1239; 盗(む) nusumu = to steal, # 1289; 歓(迎) kangei = welcome, # 1323; 欧(州) oushuu = Europe, # 1334; (詐)欺 sagi = a fraud, # 1859; (柔)軟(な) juunan na = flexible, # 1883

0537. 吹 **PRONUNCIATIONS: fu, sui**
MEANINGS: to blow, to breathe **EXAMPLES:** 吹く fuku = to blow, breathe, whistle; 吹奏楽 suisougaku = music from wind instruments
DESCRIPTION: on the left, 口 kuchi (mouth, # 426) which resembles a box; on the right, 欠(く) kaku (to lack, # 1238), which resembles an oil derrick (see # 399)
CUES: this 欠 (oil derrick) drinks oil as **F**ood and then 吹く **fu**ku (blows) it out through this 口 (mouth) because it's too **S**weet
COMPARE: other similar kanji at # **536** and # **2073**

Platform

0538. 台 **PRONUNCIATIONS: dai, tai**
MEANING: platform **EXAMPLES:** 台 dai = platform; 台所 daidokoro = kitchen; 二台 nidai = two machines, cars etc.; 台風 taifuu = typhoon **DESCRIPTION:** at the top, the katakana character ム mu (the sound made by a cow); at the bottom 口 kuchi (mouth, # 426), but this could be a box or a platform **CUES:** this ム (cow) rests on a 口 (box) that resembles a 台 **d**ai (platform); she is on a **D**iet, and she is **T**ired of it **GROUP:** 台 dai = platform, # 538; 治(す) naosu = to heal, # 539; 始(める) hajimeru = to begin, # 540; 苔 koke = moss, # 957; 怠(慢) taiman = negligent, # 1498, and 胎(児) taiji = a fetus, # 1919, both of which can also be pronounced "tai"

0539. 治 **PRONUNCIATIONS: nao, chi, osa, ji MEANINGS:** to govern, control, cure **EXAMPLES:** 治す naosu = to heal; 治る naoru = to recover from illness; 治安 chian = safety; 治める osameru = to govern or reign; 政治 seiji = politics **DESCRIPTION:** compared to 台 dai (platform, # 538), this adds a water radical on the left; it retains the ム (cow) and the 口 (platform) which can also be seen as a box
CUES: Naomi 治した **nao**shita (cured) this ム (cow) on this 口 (platform) **Ch**eaply by mixing medicine with this water, but **Os**ama bin Laden **J**eered her efforts
ALSO COMPARE: 直(す) naosu = to correct, repair or restore, # 570; 納(める) osameru = to conclude, # 705; 修(める) osameru = to master, # 1049; 収(める) osameru = to conclude, # 1113; other similar kanji at # **538**

0540. 始 **PRONUNCIATIONS: haji, shi**
MEANING: to begin **EXAMPLES:** 始める hajimeru = to begin; 開始する kaishi suru = to begin **DESCRIPTION:** compared to 治(す) naosu (to heal, # 539), this substitutes 女 onna (female, # 235) for the water radical on the left; it retains 台 dai (platform) which can be seen as a ム (cow) on a 口 (box) **CUES:** this 女 (female) leaves her **H**at in her **J**eep and 始める **haji**meru (begins) removing this ム (cow) from this 口 (box) so that she can replace it with a **Sh**eep
ALSO COMPARE: 初(めて) hajimete = for the first time, # 104; other kanji containing 女 on the left at # **2039**; other similar kanji at # **538**

Hanging Bucket

0541. 甘 **PRONUNCIATIONS: ama, kan**
MEANING: sweet **EXAMPLES:** 甘い amai = sweet; 甘味所 kanmidokoro = a cafe featuring Japanese-style sweets **DESCRIPTION:** a bucket hanging from a rod, half-full of liquid
CUES: Amanda bought this half-full bucket of 甘い **ama**i (sweet) molasses and made **C**andy
COMPARE: other similar kanji at # **711**

0542. 世 PRONUNCIATIONS: se, yo, sei
MEANINGS: a world, a generation EXAMPLES: 世界 sekai = the world; 世話をする sewa wo suru = to take care of; 世の中 yo no naka = life, society, world; 世紀 seiki = century
DESCRIPTION: a bucket hanging from a rod supported by a stand CUES: since the 世界 sekai (world) is hanging in this bucket supported by this stand and might fall any Second, people are consulting Yogis to find out how to stay Safe
GROUP: 席 seki = seat, # 496; (今)度 kondo = this time, # 498; 渡(る) wataru = to cross, # 499; 世(界) sekai = the world, # 542; 葉 ha = leaf, # 543; 靴 kutsu = shoe, # 603; 革(靴) kawagutsu = leather shoe, # 1286; 庶(民) shomin = common people, # 1795; 覇(権) haken = hegemony, # 1874; 遮(断) shadan = an interruption, # 1892

0543. 葉 PRONUNCIATIONS: ha, you, ba, ji MEANING: leaf
EXAMPLES: 葉 ha = leaf; 紅葉 kouyou = autumn colors; 言葉 kotoba = word; 紅葉 momiji = Japanese maple, autumn colors; Note: kouyou and momiji are both spelled 紅葉
DESCRIPTION: at the top, a plant radical (see # 43) which reminds us of leaves; in the middle, 世 se (world, # 542) which includes a hanging bucket; at the bottom, a 木 ki (tree, # 118) in Hawaii
CUES: in Hawaii, a Yogi came out of a Bar and saw these 葉 ha (leaves) hanging over this bucket on this 木 (tree) next to his Jeep ALSO COMPARE: other similar kanji at # **542** and # **1352**

Mother Balancing
0544. 予 PRONUNCIATION: yo
MEANINGS: to prepare, preliminary
EXAMPLES: 予定 yotei = plan, schedule; 予約 yoyaku = reservation DESCRIPTION: the katakana マ ma, suggesting a mother, above an arrow balanced on a shaft, resembling a mother balanced on an arrow on top of a nail; Note that this mother doesn't use a stabilizing leg, like the one in 柔(らかい) yawarakai (soft, # 546)
CUE: since this マ (mother) can balance on this arrow on top of this nail without using a stabilizing leg, she will make 予定 yotei (plans) to start Yoga
GROUP: 予(定) yotei = plan, # 544; 野(菜) yasai = vegetable, # 545; 預(金) yokin = bank deposit, # 1259 (identical pronunciation); (順)序 junjo = sequence, # 1483 ALSO COMPARE: kanji with マ (mother) on a nail using a *stabilizing leg* at # 1749

0545. 野 PRONUNCIATIONS: no, ya
MEANINGS: field, outside, outsider
EXAMPLES: 野原 nohara = field; 野菜 yasai = vegetable; 野球 yakyuu = baseball
DESCRIPTION: compared to 予(定) yotei (plan, # 544), this adds 田 (rice paddy, # 68) at the upper left and 土 tsuchi (soil, # 59) at the lower left; together these resemble a sincere guy wearing bifocals, as seen in 黒(い) kuroi (black, #76); this retains the マ (mother) balanced on an arrow above a nail CUES: this sincere guy with these bifocals and this マ (mother), who is balanced on a nail, live in Norway, and they have a 予 (plan) to grow 野菜 yasai (vegetables), including Yams
GROUP: 黒(い) kuroi = black, # 76; 理(由) riyuu = reason, # 78; 野(菜) yasai = vegetable, # 545; 黙(る) damaru = to keep silent, # 836; 裏 ura = rear, # 887; 里 sato = hometown, # 1060; 量 ryou = quantity, # 1061; (児)童 jidou = child, # 1094; 埋(葬) maisou = burial, # 1523; 糧 kate = food, # 1789; 墨 sumi = ink stick, # 1829
ALSO COMPARE: kanji in which the sincere guy wears ordinary glasses rather than bifocals and has two pairs of arms at # 517; other similar kanji at # **544**

0546. 柔 PRONUNCIATIONS: **nyuu, juu, yawa** MEANINGS: tender, gentleness, softness EXAMPLES: 柔和 nyuuwa = gentleness, mildness; 柔道 juudou = judo; 柔らかい yawarakai = soft, tender, limp DESCRIPTION: at the top, 矛(盾) mujun (an inconsistency, # 1749), which resembles a マ (mother) balanced on an arrow above a nail, as seen in 予(定) yotei (plan, # 544), but with a stabilizing leg on the left; at the bottom, 木 ki (tree, # 118) CUES: this マ (mother) from **Nyuu**yooku (New York) practices 柔道 **juu**dou, she balances on this nail with the help of this stablizing leg, she can climb this 木 (tree), although she knows that this activity is **J**uvenile, and she gives her **Yak** **Wa**ter after she descends COMPARE: similar kanji at # 1352 and # **1749**

Snake

0547. 危 PRONUNCIATIONS: **abu, ki, aya** MEANING: danger EXAMPLES: 危ない abunai = dangerous; 危険 kiken = danger; 危うい ayaui = dangerous, risky DESCRIPTION: at the top, an abused fish head (see # 80); under the fish head, a one-sided lean-to; under the lean-to, a snake that is uncoiling CUES: this fish head, who has been **Abu**sed, sits on this lean-to and tries to escape this 危ない **abu**nai (dangerous) uncoiling snake lurking inside, which has already **K**illed an **Aya**tollah GROUP: 危(ない) abunai = dangerous, # 547; 犯(人) hannin = a criminal, # 901; 腕 ude = arm, # 1532; 範(囲) han'i = extent, # 1585; 宛(先) atesaki = a destination, # 1822; 厄(介な) yakkai na = troublesome, # 1863; 怨(念) onnen = a grudge, # 1910 ALSO COMPARE: kanji with backwards "S" snakes at #1078 and # 1861; other similar kanji at # **87**

0548. 包 PRONUNCIATIONS: **hou, bou²**, **tsutsu, zutsumi** MEANING: to wrap EXAMPLES: 包装 housou = wrapping; 出刃包丁 debabouchou = a knife; 包む tsutsumu = to wrap; 小包 kozutsumi = a package sent by mail DESCRIPTION: at the top, a hook, but this can be seen as J-shaped packaging; below, contents shaped like 己 (a backward "S"), which reminds us of a snake CUES: our **Ho**stess will 包む **tsutsu**mu (wrap) this package, which contains this 己 (snake) in addition to **Ts**uits (suits) piled on **Ts**uits, including **Z**oot **Su**its for our **M**eeting COMPARE: other similar kanji at # **1861**

0549. 港 PRONUNCIATIONS: **kou, minato, kon** MEANING: port EXAMPLES: 空港 kuukou = airport; 港 minato = port; 香港 honkon = Hong Kong DESCRIPTION: on the left, a water radical; at the upper right, a modified version of 共(に) tomo ni (together, # 969), but this can also be seen as a broad-based tower; at the lower right, a 己 (snake) shaped like a backwards "S" CUES: at this 港 **minato** (port) in **Co**logne, which is controlled by **M**ighty **NATO**, there is this tower on the upper right that supports cranes used to load ships, and this 己 (snake) on the lower right is swimming in this water and headed for the **Co**ngo COMPARE: other similar kanji at # **486** and # **1078**

0550. 記 PRONUNCIATIONS: **ki, shiru** MEANING: to record EXAMPLES: 記事 kiji = newspaper article; 日記 nikki = diary; 記入 ki'nyuu = entry, filling in forms; 記す shirusu = to record or write DESCRIPTION: on the left, 言(葉) kotoba (words, # 430); on the right, 己 onore (self, # 652), which resembles a snake shaped like a backwards "S" CUES: I read a 記事 **ki**ji (article) containing a lot of 言 (words) about this 己 (snake) that **K**illed a person and the **Sh**eep that escaped to the **R**oof ALSO COMPARE: other similar kanji at # **1078**

Kaeru & Kawaru

0551. 替 PRONUNCIATIONS: **ka, gae, ga**
MEANINGS: to replace, or to exchange money
EXAMPLES: 替える **ka**eru = to replace or exchange money (this can also be spelled 換える, # 554); 両替 ryougae = money exchange; 着替える kigaeru = to change clothes
DESCRIPTION: at the top, two 夫 otto (husbands, # 614) named Carl and Garry Ericson; at the bottom, 日 hi (sun, # 32)
CUES: since **Ca**rl and **Ga**rry Ericson are these two 夫 otto (husbands) who are almost identical, there is no **Ga**p between them as they stand in this 日 (sun), and we can 替える **ka**eru (exchange) one for the other ALSO COMPARE: other similar kanji at # 352 and # 1915

0552. 代 PRONUNCIATIONS: **dai, ka, yo, shiro, tai** MEANINGS: people changing, generations EXAMPLES: 時代 ji**dai** = era; 代わる **ka**waru = to take the place of; 代わりに **ka**wari ni = in place of; 千代田 Chiyoda = a ward in Tokyo; 身代金 minoshirokin = ransom; 永代 eitai = permanence, eternity
DESCRIPTION: on the left, a man with a slanted hat, who is the president; on the right, a tall woman leaning on the president, who has a ball over her right shoulder, and who is the vice president
CUES: this man on the left, who is the president, tilts his hat to examine this face of this tall leaning woman, the vice-president, and he sees that, if he **Di**es, she will start a new 時代 ji**dai** (era) in government; she is **Ca**lculating that she can 代わる **ka**waru (replace him in) his position, and order people to eat more **Yo**gurt and to wear **S**heepskin **R**obes or **Ti**ger pelts COMPARE: other similar kanji at # 249

0553. 変 PRONUNCIATIONS: **hen, ka**
MEANINGS: to change something; strange, extraordinary EXAMPLES: 変な **hen** na = strange; 大変 tai**hen** = terrible; 変える **ka**eru = to change, transitive; 変わる **ka**waru = to change, intransitive DESCRIPTION: at the top, a hen with a head and four legs [Notice how it differs from the Cuban bird seen in (研)究 kenkyuu (research, # 112)]; at the bottom, a dancer with a ponytail CUES: I just saw a 変な **hen** na (strange) sight: this **Hen** with these four legs swooped down over this dancer with a ponytail and tried to 変える **ka**eru (change) her; let's try to **Ca**tch it
COMPARE: other similar kanji at # 695

0554. 換 PRONUNCIATIONS: **ka, kan**
MEANINGS: to replace or exchange
EXAMPLES: 換える **ka**eru = to replace or exchange (this can also be spelled 替える, # 551); 交換する koukan suru = to exchange
DESCRIPTION: on the left, a kneeling guy; at the upper right, a fish head, as seen in 魚 sakana (fish, # 80); at the middle right, 四 yon (four, # 6, which is missing its lower wall; at the lower right, 大(きい) ookii (big, # 188); taken together, these radicals on the right resemble a 大 (big) general with a fish head, who wears two decorations on his chest
CUES: this guy on the left, who is a **Ca**ptain from **Kan**sas, kneels in order to 換える **ka**eru (exchange) this decoration on the right side of this 大 (big) fish-headed general's chest for the one on the left
COMPARE: other similar kanji at # 87 and # 987

0555. 鳥 PRONUNCIATIONS: **to, tori, dori**[2]**, chou** MEANING: bird EXAMPLES: 鳥取県 **tottori** ken = Tottori Prefecture; 小鳥 ko**tori** = small bird; 雄鳥 on**dori** = rooster; 白鳥 haku**chou** = swan DESCRIPTION: this bird has a 白(い) shiroi (white, # 44) tuft on its head, two additional horizontal lines, one of which may represent a feather and, strangely, five toes, which can also be seen as four flames plus a toe
CUES: this 鳥 **tori** (bird) with this 白 (white) tuft on its head, this feather and these five **To**es belongs to a **To**ry who was **Cho**sen to serve in Parliament ALSO COMPARE: other kanji containing four flames without birds at # 611; other kanji containing birds at # 754

0556. 島 **PRONUNCIATIONS: shima, jima², tou MEANING:** island **EXAMPLES:** 島 shima = island; 広島 Hiroshima = a city in Japan; 桜島 Sakurajima = a volcano in southern Kyushu; 半島 hantou = peninsula **DESCRIPTION:** compared to 鳥 tori (bird, # 555), this substitutes 山 yama (mountain, # 146) for four of the bird's toes at the bottom **CUES:** this 鳥 (bird) that lives on this 山 (mountain) on a 島 **shima** (island) near Hiro**Shima** lost its **Toes** to a predator **ALSO COMPARE:** other similar kanji at # **754** and # **2079**

Yak or Sword on a Table

0557. 役 **PRONUNCIATIONS: eki, yaku MEANINGS:** role, service **EXAMPLES:** 兵役 heieki = military service; 役に立つ yaku ni tatsu = to be useful; 区役所 kuyakusho = ward office **DESCRIPTION:** on the left, a man with a double hat; on the right, π (the Greek letter pi, which represents a pious yak here), standing on 又 mata ("again," # 24), but this resembles a simple table **CUES:** this man with two hats received his second hat from **E**dward the **Ki**ng because he 役に立った **yaku** ni tatta (was useful) in taking care of this π (**Yak**) which is standing on this 又 (table) **GROUP:** (区)役(所) kuyakusho = ward office, # 557; 投(げる) nageru = to throw, # 558; 段(々) dandan = gradually, # 559; 没(する) bossuru = to sink, # 806; 殺(す) korosu = to kill, # 838; (一)般(的に) ippanteki ni = usually, # 1050; 設(定する) settei suru = to set up, # 1068; (宮)殿 kyuuden = palace, # 1080; 疫(病) ekibyou = an epidemic, # 1142 (identical pronunciation); 穀(物) kokumotsu = grain, # 1172; (基)盤 kiban = foundation, # 1197; 撃(つ) utsu = to fire a gun, # 1226; 股 momo = a thigh, # 1640; 殴(る) naguru = to beat up, # 1748; 鍛(える) kitaeru = to train, # 1813; 殻 kara = a

shell, # 1904; 搬(送) hansou = transportation, # 1993 **ALSO COMPARE:** kanji containing a tall desk at # 1462

0558. 投 **PRONUNCIATIONS: tou, na MEANING:** to throw **EXAMPLES:** 投資 toushi = investment; 投げる nageru = to throw **DESCRIPTION:** compared to 役に立つ yaku ni tatsu (to be useful, # 557), this substitutes a kneeling guy for the man with a double hat on the left; it retains the π (yak) on a 又 (table) **CUES:** since this guy on the left wants to make **To**ast before taking a **Na**p, he kneels to push this π off this 又 (table) where he keeps his toaster, but he might 投げる **na**geru (throw) the π off instead **COMPARE:** similar kanji at # **557** and # **1389**

0559. 段 **PRONUNCIATION: dan MEANINGS:** step, paragraph, case **EXAMPLES:** 階段 kaidan = stairs; 段々 dandan = gradually; 普段 fudan = usual, every day **DESCRIPTION:** compared to 役に立つ yaku ni tatsu (to be useful, # 557), this substitutes a ladder with four steps, for the man with a double hat; it retains the π (yak) on a 又 (table) **CUE:** a **Dan**cer uses these 階段 kai**dan** (stairs) to climb up and down and give food to this π (yak) on this 又 (table) **COMPARE:** other similar kanji at # **41** and # **557**

0560. 招 **PRONUNCIATIONS: mane, shou MEANING:** to invite **EXAMPLES:** 招く maneku = to invite; 招待 shoutai = invitation **DESCRIPTION:** compared to 召(喚する) shoukan suru (to summon, # 106) (identical pronunciation), this kanji adds a kneeling guy on the left; it retains the 刀 (sword) on a 口 (box), which could be a table **CUES:** this guy on the left wants to write a letter to 招く **mane**ku (invite) a **Man**nequin to a Broadway **Show**, but first he has to kneel in order to remove this 刀 (sword) from this writing 口 (box) **GROUP:** 召(喚する) shoukan suru= to summon, # 106; 招(く) maneku

= to invite, # 560; 超(人的) choujinteki = superhuman, # 621; 紹(介) shoukai = introduction, # 658, and 照(明) shoumei = lighting, # 822, and 昭(和) shouwa = the Showa era, # 1410, all three of which can also be pronounced "shou"; 沼 numa = a swamp, # 1525; (誘)拐 yuukai = an abduction, # 1995, in which 口 (box) is at the top and 刀 (sword) at the bottom

Ri

0561. 別 PRONUNCIATIONS: betsu, waka, be MEANING: to separate EXAMPLES: 別に betsu ni = particularly; 別の betsu no = another (defined) object; 別れる wakareru = to separate; 別居 bekkyo = separation of family members DESCRIPTION: on the left, 口 kuchi (mouth, # 426) above a modified 刀 katana (sword, # 102); let's call this person Betsy; on the right, the katakana character リ Ri, which is sometimes described as a knife
CUES: Betsy with this square head doesn't like this リ Ri with this pointy toe 別に **betsu** ni (particularly), and they 別れる **waka**reru (break up) after リ Ri **W**alks on the **C**at and destroys its **B**ed, causing Betsy to reach for this 刀 (sword) GROUP: 別(に) betsu ni = particularly, # 561; 捌(く) sabaku = to handle, # 1350

0562. 割 PRONUNCIATIONS: sa, wari, wa, katsu MEANINGS: to divide, apportion EXAMPLES: 時間を割く jikan wo saku = to make time for; 割に wari ni = relatively; 割る waru = to break glass and wood, transitive; 割れる wareru = to break, intransitive; 4 割る 2 yon waru ni = 4 divided by 2; 分割する bunkatsu suru = to divide or split DESCRIPTION: at the upper left, a bad haircut; at the middle left, an owl's perch, as seen in 青(い丶) aoi (blue, # 155), but with the shortest rung at the top; at the lower left, a 口 (box), which might be a tomb; on the right, the katakana character リ Ri, which is sometimes described as a knife CUES: this リ Ri plays a **Sa**xophone while this guy with this bad haircut on the left, who is a **Warri**or, carries this owl's perch and **Wa**lks on this 口 (tomb) with his **Ca**ts, trying to 割る **wa**ru (break) the tomb COMPARE: other similar kanji at # 1103, # 1260 and # 1985

0563. 倒 PRONUNCIATIONS: tao, tou, dou MEANINGS: overthrow, fall, collapse, breakdown, become bankrupt EXAMPLES: 倒れる taoreru = to fall, collapse, drop, fall senseless; 倒す taosu = to bring down, knock down, defeat; 倒産 tousan = bankruptcy; 面倒 mendou = annoyance, difficulty, care DESCRIPTION: on the left, a man with a slanted hat; in the center, 一 (one) above the katakana ム mu, which is the sound made by a cow, above 土 tsuchi (soil, # 59); on the right, the katakana character リ Ri
CUES: this man on the left and this リ Ri are using a **T**owel to clean the **T**orso of this 一 (one) ム (cow) which is **D**ozing in this 土 (soil), and both of them feel 面倒 men**dou** (annoyance), but the man tilts his hat in order to inspect their work COMPARE: other similar kanji at # 63 and # 1985

0564. 利 PRONUNCIATIONS: ri, ki MEANINGS: useful, sharp EXAMPLES: 利用する riyou suru = to use; 便利 benri = convenient; 有利 yuuri = advantageous; 利益 rieki = profit; 利く kiku = to be effective (this is usually spelled 効く, # 1139) DESCRIPTION: on the left, 禾 (a grain plant with a ripe head); on the right, the katakana リ Ri (identical pronunciation), which is sometimes described as a knife CUE: this リ Ri 利用する **ri**you suru (uses) this 禾 (ripe grain) to make **Q**uiche COMPARE: other similar kanji at # 1797 and # 1985

0565. 刻 **PRONUNCIATIONS: koku, kiza MEANINGS:** to tick away, to cut into pieces **EXAMPLES:** 遅刻する chikoku suru = to be tardy; 時刻 jikoku = time; 刻む kizamu = to cut, mince, carve **DESCRIPTION:** on the left, this is said to be the skeleton of a wild boar; on the right, the katakana リ Ri, which is sometimes described as a knife **CUES:** after this リ Ri carved up this boar, he stopped to drink a **Co**ke, and to **Ki**d **Za**ch about not helping him, and therefore he will 遅刻する chi**ko**ku suru (be tardy) **COMPARE:** other similar kanji at # **1548** and # **1985**

0566. 帰 **PRONUNCIATIONS: kae, ki MEANINGS:** to go home, to return **EXAMPLES:** 帰る kaeru = to return home; 帰宅 kitaku = a return to one's home **DESCRIPTION:** on the left, the katakana character リ Ri; at the upper right, long hair streaming to the left; at the lower right, 巾 (Bo Peep), as seen in 帽(子) boushi (hat, # 243), under a roof, but this resembles the face of an elephant, with low-hanging ears and a long trunk **CUES:** as this リ Ri watches, a **C**at **E**nters his home, and he will 帰る **kae**ru (return), riding this elephant, with this long hair streaming to the left, to **K**ick the intruder out **COMPARE:** other similar kanji at # **1165**, # **1768** and # **1985**

Vertical Storage

0567. 皿 **PRONUNCIATIONS: sara, zara**[1] **MEANINGS:** plate, dish, saucer **EXAMPLES:** 皿 sara = plate, dish or saucer; 大皿 oozara = large dish **DESCRIPTION:** three rolls of Saran wrap, positioned vertically on a shelf; when used as a radical in some kanji, this can resemble three eyes, as seen in 署(名) shomei (signature, # 1324) **CUE:** I put left-over food on 皿 **sara** (plates) and cover it with **Sar**an wrap taken from these three rolls **COMPARE:** other similar kanji at # **1407**

0568. 冊 **PRONUNCIATIONS: sa, satsu MEANING:** counter for books **EXAMPLE:** 冊子 sasshi = a booklet or pamphlet; 三冊 sansatsu = three books **DESCRIPTION:** a box divided into six compartments for storing satisfying Superman novels **CUES: Sa**dly, only six 冊 **satsu** (volumes) of **Sa**tisfying **Su**perman novels will fit into this bookcase **GROUP:** (三)冊 sansatsu = three books, # 568; 柵 saku = fence, # 899; 編(者) hensha = editor, # 1052; 偏(見) henken = prejudice, # 1757; (普)遍(の) fuhen no = constant, # 1830 **ALSO COMPARE:** other similar kanji at # 813

Shelf Storage

0569. 置 **PRONUNCIATIONS: o, chi MEANINGS:** to place, to leave something **EXAMPLES:** 置く oku = to place something; 位置 ichi = position **DESCRIPTION:** at the top, a thick handle divided into three sections; this can also be seen as three eyes; below this, 直(す) naosu (to correct, # 570), which consists of a thin handle above 目 (eye), which can be seen as a three-drawer shelf cabinet **CUES: O**prah combines this thick handle with this thin handle when she lifts heavy items like **Ch**eese that she stores in this three-drawer cabinet and 置く **o**ku (places) them on shelves like this **GROUP:** 置く oku = to place, # 569; 直(す) naosu (to correct, # 570); 値(段) nedan = price, # 571; 植(える) ueru = to plant, # 1278; (生)殖 seishoku = reproduction, # 1396 **ALSO COMPARE:** other similar kanji at # **1324** and # **1878**

0570. 直 **PRONUNCIATIONS: nao, su, jiki, jika, choku, cho, tada MEANINGS:** straight, direct, to correct **EXAMPLES:** 直す naosu = to correct or repair something; 真っ直ぐ massugu = straight; 正直 shoujiki = honest; 直に jika ni = directly; 直面 chokumen = confrontation; 直行便

chokkoubin = nonstop flight; 直ちに tadachi ni = immediately **DESCRIPTION:** at the top, 十 juu (ten, # 18), which resembles a thin handle; below this, 目 me (eye), which resembles a three-drawer cabinet; at the bottom, a shelf with a back wall, seen from the side **CUES: Na**omi and **Su**perman say that if we use this three-drawer shelf cabinet with this thin handle to store lighter items, like **J**eep **K**eys for our **J**eep **C**ar, and Margaret **Ch**o's **K**ool-Aid packets, we can 直す **nao**su (correct) our storage problems and simplify our **Ch**ores, and we think that they are **Tada**shii (correct) **COMPARE:** 治(す) naosu = to heal, # 539; other similar kanji at # **569** and # **1278**

0571. 値 PRONUNCIATIONS: atai, ne, chi MEANING: value EXAMPLES: 値 atai = value, price; 値段 nedan = price; 価値 kachi = value DESCRIPTION: compared to 直(す) naosu (to repair, #570), this adds a man with a slanted hat on the left; it retains the thin handle on 目 (eye), which can be seen as a three-drawer shelf cabinet CUES: this man on the left, who is **A Th**ai person, tilts his hat back to examine this three-drawer cabinet with a thin handle on this shelf, where we keep lightweight items like **N**ecklaces, and he would like to 直 (repair) the cabinet for a **Ch**eap 値段 **ne**dan (price) ALSO COMPARE: 価 atai = value, price, # 484; other similar kanji at # **569** and # **1278**

0572. 県 PRONUNCIATION: ken MEANING: prefecture EXAMPLES: 県 ken = prefecture; 広島県 hiroshima ken = Hiroshima prefecture DESCRIPTION: 目 me (eye, # 51) on a shelf with three legs; this resembles a three-drawer cabinet on a walking shelf CUE: **Ken** and Barbie like to move around in their 県 **ken** (prefecture), and they keep their maps in this three-drawer cabinet on this three-legged self-propelled shelf GROUP: 県 ken = prefecture, # 572; 懸(念) ke'nen = apprehension, fear, # 1597

Tower

0573. 形 PRONUNCIATIONS: kata, gata², katachi, gyou, kei MEANING: shape EXAMPLES: 形見 katami = keepsake, memento; 髪形 kamigata = hair style; 形 katachi = shape; 人形 ningyou = doll; 形態 keitai = form, shape, system DESCRIPTION: on the left, a tower, which could be part of a catapult and also resembles a welcoming stance; on the right, these three lines look like cords for the catapult CUES: this tower has a symmetrical 形 **katachi** (shape), and it uses these three cords, which can be bought from a **Cata**log, as parts of a machine for **Cata**pulting **Ch**eese, **Gy**oza and **C**ake to prisoners in a jail GROUP: 開く aku = to open, # 413; 研(究) kenkyuu = research, # 442; 形 katachi = shape, # 573; 餅 mochi = rice cake, # 743; 型 kata = form, # 1116 (identical pronunciation); (死)刑 shikei = death penalty, # 1325 (also identical pronunciation); (合)併 gappei = a merger, # 1655; 瓶 bin = a bottle, # 1711; 塀 hei = a fence, # 1850 ALSO COMPARE: other kanji containing towers that can be seen as welcoming stances at # 1924; other similar kanji at # **839**

0574. 飛 PRONUNCIATIONS: to, hi MEANING: to fly EXAMPLES: 飛ぶ tobu = to fly; 飛行機 hikouki = airplane DESCRIPTION: on the left, 升 masu (measuring box, # 2049), which consists of 千 (thousand) and 十 (ten), with a platform on top; taken together, these resemble a tower; on the right, two sets of lips projecting from faces, but these resemble propellers CUES: when these two propellers start spinning like **T**ornados, you will **H**ear a whirring sound, and 升 (one thousand and ten) 飛行機 **hi**kouki (airplanes) will start to 飛ぶ **to**bu (fly) GROUP: this is a group of one ALSO COMPARE: 跳(ぶ) tobu = to jump, # 1084; other similar kanji at # **22**, # **352** and # **1363**

Vertical Lines

0575. 並 **PRONUNCIATIONS: nara, hei, nami, na** **MEANINGS:** to line up; row **EXAMPLES:** 並ぶ narabu = to line up, intransitive; 並列 heiretsu = arrangement, parallel, abreast; 並の nami no = ordinary, usual; 町並み machinami = a townscape **DESCRIPTION:** compared to 普(通) futsuu (ordinarily, # 576), this omits the 日 (sun), or stove, at the bottom and retains the four burners with the antennae, or higher flames, at the top; the result can be seen as various lines on a temple wall in Nara, most of which line up fairly well **CUES:** since there is no 日 (stove body), as seen in 普(通) futsuu (ordinarily, # 576), these are just lines that 並ぶ **nara**bu (line up) on the wall of a temple in **Na**ra, spelling a **Hate**ful message, and the authorities will soon be **Nami**ng the culprit, who must be **Na**sty **GROUP:** 並(ぶ) narabu = to line up, # 575; 普(通) futsuu = ordinarily, # 576; (楽)譜 gakufu = sheet music, # 1848 **ALSO COMPARE:** other similar kanji at # **1300**

0576. 普 **PRONUNCIATION: fu** **MEANINGS:** universal, ordinary **EXAMPLES:** 普通 futsuu = ordinarily **DESCRIPTION:** at the top, 並(ぶ) narabu (to line up, # 575), but this looks like four burners on a stove for cooking food, with the two center burners producing higher flames which resemble antennae at the top; at the bottom, 日 hi (sun, # 32), but this must be the body of the stove **CUE:** this is just a 普通 **fu**tsuu (ordinary) stove, with these four burners and this 日 (stove body), for cooking **F**ood **ALSO COMPARE:** other similar kanji at # **1300** and # **575**

0577. 受 **PRONUNCIATIONS: u, uke, ju** **MEANING:** to receive **EXAMPLES:** 受ける ukeru = to receive, to take or pass an exam or class; 受付 uketsuke = reception; 受験する juken suru = to take an exam **DESCRIPTION:** at the top, a barbecue grate resting on a rack; at the bottom, 又 mata ("again," # 24), which resembles a table **CUES:** when you 受ける **u**keru (take) a cooking exam in **U**ganda or in the **U.K.**, you must cook on this barbecue grate located on this rack on this 又 (table), on which you may also keep a bottle of lemon **Ju**ice for seasoning **ALSO COMPARE:** similar kanji at # **24** and # **1177**

0578. 授 **PRONUNCIATIONS: ju, sazu** **MEANINGS:** to grant or bestow **EXAMPLES:** 授業 jugyou = class instruction; 授ける sazukeru = to give or grant **DESCRIPTION:** compared to 受(ける) ukeru (to take, or pass, an exam or class, # 577), or 受(験する) juken suru (to take a test, # 577) (identical pronunciation), this adds a kneeling guy on the left; it retains the grate above a table **CUES:** this guy on the left is a 教授 kyou**ju** (professor) who drinks **Ju**ice in his 授業 **ju**gyou (class), and he kneels to watch his students 受 (take) an exam about the animals living in the San Diego Zoo **ALSO COMPARE:** similar kanji at # **24**, # **1177** and # **1389**

0579. 両 **PRONUNCIATION: ryou** **MEANINGS:** both, two **EXAMPLES:** 両方 ryouhou = both **DESCRIPTION:** a model of 山 yama (mountain, # 146), with a handle at the top, superimposed on a two-sided lean-to; this can also be seen as a chairlift seat hanging from a support structure **CUE:** 両方 **ryo**hou (both) Pope Leo and his friend rode on this chairlift seat **COMPARE:** other similar kanji at # **1153**

エ & Y

0580. 製 **PRONUNCIATION: sei** **MEANING:** to manufacture **EXAMPLES:** 製品 seihin = finished product; 手製の tesei no = handmade, homemade **DESCRIPTION:** at the top, 牛 ushi (cow, # 205) sits on a revolving chair [this can also be seen as a fusion of 牛 (cow) and (都)市 toshi (city, # 424)], next to リ Ri; at the bottom, 衣(服) ifuku = clothing, # 1042) **CUE:** this 牛 (cow) on a spinning chair and this リ Ri manufacture 製品 **sei**hin (finished products), such as this 衣 (clothing), to be sold at

Safeway stores **ALSO COMPARE:** other similar kanji at # **242**, # **1042**, # **1765** and # **1985**

0581. 袋 PRONUNCIATIONS: *bi, fukuro, bukuro*² MEANINGS: sack, bag, pouch
EXAMPLES: 足袋 tabi = Japanese-style socks; 袋 fukuro = sack, bag; 手袋 tebukuro = gloves; 紙袋 kamibukuro = paper bag
DESCRIPTION: at the top, (時)代 jidai (era, # 552), which includes a man with a slanted hat and a leaning woman with a ball above her shoulder; at the bottom, 衣(服) ifuku (clothing, # 1042)
CUES: this man at the upper left tilts his hat back to examine this leaning woman with a ball above her shoulder, who uses a fancy 袋 **fukuro** (bag) when she carries **B**eer on **F**uku**o**ka **R**oads and tries not to spill it on this 衣 (clothing) **ALSO COMPARE:** other similar kanji at # **249** and # **1042**

0582. 表 PRONUNCIATIONS: *omote, hyou, byou*², *pyou, arawa* MEANINGS: surface, outside, front, to make public
EXAMPLES: 表 omote = surface, front, outside; 表 hyou = a surface, chart or diagram; 裏表紙 urabyoushi = back cover; 発表する happyou suru = to announce, publish, reveal, make a presentation; 表す arawasu = to signify, represent or express
(**Note:** both hyou and omote are spelled 表)
DESCRIPTION: above the line, an owl's perch, as seen in 青(い) aoi (blue, # 155), on the roof of an omote*l* (honorable motel); below the line, the katakana character エ e and the letter Y, which remind us of Eric and Yolanda
CUES: in this **O**mote*l* (honorable motel), there are many 表 **omote** (surfaces), such as the ones in this owl's perch supported by the owners エ (**E**ric) and Y (**Y**olanda), who welcome **H**ealers from **O**regon, guests from **P**yongyang, and **A**rab guests like **W**ali
GROUP: 表 omote = surface, # 582; 猿 saru = monkey, # 1055; (土)俵 dohyou = a sumo ring, # 1492 **ALSO COMPARE:** other similar kanji at # **1103**

Cage
0583. 無 PRONUNCIATIONS: *mu, bu, na* MEANINGS: nothing, to not exist, negation
EXAMPLES: 無理 muri = impossible, unreasonable; 無料 muryou = free of charge; 無駄な muda na = useless, wasteful; 無事 buji = safety, peace, health, good condition; 無くす nakusu = to lose; 無い nai = does not exist, usually written ない **DESCRIPTION:** at the top, a crutch; in the center, a fence with two more horizontal lines and four vertical lines; together, these can be seen as a cage; at the bottom, four flames **CUES:** a **M**ooney says that it's 無理 **mu**ri (impossible) for **B**oozers to escape from this cage above these flames, unless they have a **N**azi friend to open the door
GROUP: 無(理) muri = impossible, # 583; 舞(う) mau = to dance, # 584; (愛)撫 aibu = a caress, # 846 (identical pronunciation)
ALSO COMPARE: other similar kanji at # **611**; kanji that include a *coop* at # 1073 and # 1321

0584. 舞 PRONUNCIATIONS: *ma, bu, mai* MEANING: to dance **EXAMPLES:** 見舞い mimai = visit to a sick person; 舞う mau = to dance; 舞台 butai = stage, setting, scene; 舞 mai = a dance **DESCRIPTION:** at the top, a cage (see # 583); at the lower left, 夕(方) yuugata (evening, # 160); on the lower right, a sitting person, with a knee extending to the left, as seen in 年 nen (year, # 177) **CUES:** **Ma** (Mother) is caught in this cage of illness, so I will お見舞いする omi**mai** suru (pay a visit to a sick person) in the 夕 (evening), sit by her bedside, drink **B**ooze, and listen to **M**ichael **J**ackson music **ALSO COMPARE:** other similar kanji at # **583**, # **801** and # **1808**

Shaky Table

0585. 亡 **PRONUNCIATIONS: na, bou, mou, naki** **MEANINGS:** to pass away, to die **EXAMPLES:** 亡くなる nakunaru = to die; 死亡 shibou = death; 金の亡者 kane no mouja = a money-grubbing person; 亡骸 nakigara = a corpse **DESCRIPTION:** at the top, a tire stop, as seen in 対(する) tai suru (to confront, # 674); at the bottom, an L-shaped structure; taken together, these resemble shaky table with a vase on it **CUES:** we bought this shaky table in **Na**rnia, but if we seat **Bo**no and **Mo**ses at it, it might fall on them, and they might 亡くなる **na**kunaru (die), causing our **Na**sty **Ki**ng to get mad **GROUP:** 忘(れる) wasureru = to forget, # 310; (死)亡 shibou = death, # 585; 忙(しい) isogashii = busy, # 586; (希)望 kibou = hope, # 664; 慌(てる) awateru = to panic, # 710; 荒(い) arai = violent, # 968; 網 ami = a net, # 1448; 妄(想) mousou = a fantasy, # 1961, and 盲(目) moumoku = blindness, # 1980, both of which can also be pronounced "mou"

0586. 忙 **PRONUNCIATIONS: isoga, bou** **MEANING:** busy **EXAMPLES:** 忙しい isogashii = busy; 多忙 tabou = very busy **DESCRIPTION:** compared to 亡(くなる) nakunaru (to die, # 585), this adds an erect man standing on the left; it retains the shaky table **CUES:** this man on the left is an **Iso**lated **Ga**mbler on a **Bo**at, he draws himself up to his full height like this as he tries to stabilize this 亡 (shaky table) without any help just before a card game, and this makes him feel 忙しい **isoga**shii (busy) **ALSO COMPARE:** other similar kanji at # **585** and # **2063**

Fruit

0587. 果 **PRONUNCIATIONS: kuda, ha, ka** **MEANINGS:** fruit, reward **EXAMPLES:** 果物 kudamono = fruit; 果たす hatasu = to accomplish, realize, perform; 結果 kekka = result **DESCRIPTION:** at the top, 田 (rice paddy, # 68), which resembles four fruits available for harvesting; at the bottom, 木 ki (tree, # 118) **CUES:** my **Coo**l **Da**d saw these four 果物 **kuda**mono (fruits) growing on this 木 (tree), so he **Ha**rvested them and **Ca**rved them up **COMPARE:** other similar kanji at # **588**

0588. 課 **PRONUNCIATION: ka** **MEANINGS:** to assign, lesson, section **EXAMPLES:** 課長 kachou = section manager; 第一課 dai ikka = section # 1 **DESCRIPTION:** compared to 果(物) kudamono (fruit, # 587), or (結)果 kekka (result, # 587) (identical pronunciation), this kanji adds 言(う) iu (to say, # 430) on the left; it retains the four fruits at the top of a 木 (tree) **CUE:** when our 課長 **ka**chou (section manager) saw these four fruits at the top of this 木 (tree), he 言 (said) that he wanted to **Ca**rve them up **GROUP:** (結)果 kekka = result, # 587; 課(長) kachou = section manager, # 588; 菓(子) kashi = candy, # 589 (also identical pronunciation); 巣 su = nest, # 972; 裸 hadaka = nudity, # 1615; (語)彙 goi = vocabulary, # 2067

0589. 菓 **PRONUNCIATIONS: ga, ka** **MEANING:** sweets **EXAMPLES:** 和菓子 wagashi = Japanese sweets; お菓子 okashi = pastry, confectionery, candy **DESCRIPTION:** compared to 果(物) kudamono (fruit, # 587), or (結)果 kekka (result, # 587) (identical pronunciation), this kanji adds a plant radical (see # 43) as a cap at the top **CUES:** in our **Ga**rden there is a 果 (fruit)-bearing 木 (tree) like this under a **Ca**p of plants like these, and we **Ca**rve up the fruit to make 菓子 **ka**shi (candy) **ALSO COMPARE:** other similar kanji at # **588** and # **1740**

Kneeling Person

0590. 打 **PRONUNCIATIONS:** u, chi, da
MEANING: to hit **EXAMPLES:** 打つ utsu = to hit or strike; 打ち合わせ uchiawase = a planning meeting; 博打 bakuchi = gambling; 打撃 dageki = shock, impact
DESCRIPTION: on the left, a kneeling guy; on the right, 丁 (目) choume (city block, # 702), which we have described as a nail but which also looks like a dagger
CUES: this guy on the left is an **U**ber gangster who sometimes kneels like this in order to 打つ **u**tsu (strike) his fallen enemies with this **C**heap 丁 (**Da**gger)
COMPARE: other similar kanji at # **702**

0591. 払 **PRONUNCIATIONS:** hara, bara² **MEANINGS:** to pay, to brush away
EXAMPLES: 払う harau = to pay; 支払い shiharai = payment; 着払い chakubarai = cash on delivery **DESCRIPTION:** compared to 私 watashi (I, # 510), this substitutes a kneeling guy for the ripe grain on the left; it retains the ム (cow)
CUE: this guy is kneeling to examine this ム (cow), which is being **Hara**ssed, and he is willing to 払う **hara**u (pay) for it **GROUP:** 私 watashi = I, # 510; 払(う) harau = to pay, # 591; 仏(教) bukkyou = Buddhism, # 678; 雄 osu = a male, # 1518; 勾(配) koubai = a slope, # 2047

0592. 押 **PRONUNCIATIONS:** o, ou, oshi
MEANINGS: to press or push
EXAMPLES: 押す osu = to push; 押収 oushuu = seizure, confiscation; 押入れ oshiire = closet, which can also be written 押し入れ
DESCRIPTION: on the left, a kneeling guy; on the right, 田 (rice paddy, # 68) on a stick, but this looks like a shaky sign
CUES: this **O**ld guy on the left gets onto his knees to 押す **o**su (push) on this shaky sign in **O**hio, causing it to fall onto some **O**ld **S**heep
ALSO COMPARE: other similar kanji at # **1157**

0593. 拝 **PRONUNCIATIONS:** oga, hai
MEANINGS: to worship, to revere, to do something humbly
EXAMPLES: 拝む ogamu = to assume the posture of prayer with hands held together, to revere; 拝見する haiken suru = to humbly read or see
DESCRIPTION: on the left, a kneeling person named Oprah; on the right, a high stalk of flowers; this can also be seen as a telephone pole with a flat top **CUES:** before this person named **O**prah **Ga**mbles, she kneels and 拝む **oga**mu (prays humbly), and since she is holding these flowers **Hi**gh, we can 拝見する **hai**ken suru (humbly see) them **GROUP:** this is a group of one **ALSO COMPARE:** other similar kanji at # **629**

0594. 捨 **PRONUNCIATIONS:** su, sha
MEANING: to throw away
EXAMPLES: 捨てる suteru = to throw away; 四捨五入する shishagonyuu suru = to round to the nearest whole number **DESCRIPTION:** on the left, a kneeling person named Superman; at the top right, a peaked roof on a shabby house; at the middle right, 土 tsuchi (soil, # 59); at the bottom right, 口 kuchi (mouth, # 426), which resembles a box **CUES:** **Su**perman is this person who is crawling toward this **Sh**abby house in order to 捨てる **su**teru (throw away) this 土 (soil) that is defiling this 口 (box)
COMPARE: 拾(う) hirou = to pick up, # 595; other similar kanji at # **745**

0595. 拾 **PRONUNCIATIONS:** hiro, shuu
MEANING: to pick up **EXAMPLE:** 拾う hirou = to pick up; 拾得する shuutoku suru = to acquire or obtain **DESCRIPTION:** on the left, a kneeling person who is a hero; on the right, 合(う) au (to match, # 294), which consists of a roof above a napkin and a 口 (box)
CUES: this guy on the left is a **H**ero who crawls toward this enemy storehouse and 拾う **hiro**u (picks up) this 口 (box) of **S**hoes, which 合 (matches) the needs of our army
COMPARE: 捨(てる) suteru = to throw away, # 594; other similar kanji at # **1251**

0596. 掛 **PRONUNCIATIONS: ka, ga**
MEANINGS: to hang, suspend, or depend
EXAMPLE: 掛ける kakeru = to hang (a picture, etc.), to sit on a chair, to take (time or money), to make a phone call, to multiply, to put on (glasses), to pour or sprinkle, and many other meanings; 心掛ける kokorogakeru = to keep in mind
DESCRIPTION: on the left, a kneeling guy; in the middle, 土 tsuchi (soil, # 59) piled on 土 (soil); on the right, the katakana character ト to, which reminds us of a toboggan on a wall **CUES:** this kneeling guy has a **C**abin where he 掛ける **ka**keru (hangs) this ト (toboggan) as he waits for winter, but when he looks out at the **Ga**rden now, all he sees is this 土 (soil) piled upon 土 (soil)
ALSO COMPARE: similar kanji at # <u>1619</u> and # <u>1826</u>

Everyone
0597. 皆 **PRONUNCIATIONS: kai, mina, minna** **MEANINGS:** all, everyone
EXAMPLES: 皆目 kaimoku = utterly, altogether; 皆 mina = everyone; 皆様 minnasama = very honorable everyone **DESCRIPTION:** at the top, two variations of the katakana ヒ hi, resembling two heroes sitting and facing in the same direction; at the bottom, 白(い) shiroi (white, # 44) **CUES:** 皆 **mina** (everyone), including these two ヒ (heroes), has brought a **K**ite and is sitting on this 白 (white) snowy hill in **Mina**sota (Minnesota), or **Minna**sota, as some spell it
ALSO COMPARE: 階(段) kaidan = stairs, # 598 (identical pronunciation); other similar kanji at # <u>1294</u> and # <u>2014</u>

0598. 階 **PRONUNCIATION: kai**
MEANINGS: story or floor of a building, counter for stories or floors of a building **EXAMPLES:** 階段 kaidan = stairs; 四階 yonkai = the fourth floor **DESCRIPTION:** compared to 皆 mina (everyone, # 597), this adds the Greek letter ß on the left; it retains the two heroes sitting and facing in the same direction on a 白 (white) hill **CUE:** this ß (Greek) guy, who lives on the 三階 san**kai** (third floor) of our building, is bringing a **K**ite to these two seated ヒ (heroes) on a 白 (white) hill
ALSO COMPARE: other similar kanji at # <u>1294</u>, # <u>2014</u> and # <u>2030</u>

Nurse
0599. 喜 **PRONUNCIATIONS: yoroko, ki**
MEANINGS: to feel pleased or happy
EXAMPLES: 喜ぶ yorokobu = to be delighted; 喜劇 kigeki = comedy **DESCRIPTION:** at the top, (兵)士 heishi (soldier, # 66) which resembles a cross worn by a nurse; in the middle, 豆 mame (bean, # 721, but this resembles the nurse herself, wearing a white nurse's cap; at the bottom, a square which is the nurse's white coat; the upper portion of the kanji can also be seen as a 士 (man) above a 口 (box) **CUES:** this nurse 喜ぶ **yoroko**bu (gets delighted) in the **Yoro**pean (European) city of **Co**logne when she gets a **K**ey to the city
GROUP: 喜(ぶ) yorokobu = to be delighted, # 599; 嬉(しい) ureshii = pleased, # 600
ALSO COMPARE: similar kanji at # <u>721</u> and # <u>1453</u>

0600. 嬉 **PRONUNCIATION: ure**
MEANINGS: glad, pleased **EXAMPLE:** 嬉しい ureshii = pleased **DESCRIPTION:** compared to 喜(ぶ) yorokobu (to get delighted, # 599), this adds 女 onna (female, # 235) on the left; it retains the 豆 (nurse wearing a white cap), a cross and a white coat; the upper portion of the kanji can also be seen as a 士 (man) above a 口 (box)
CUE: this 女 (female) 喜 (nurse) is 嬉しい **ure**shii (pleased) about her patient with kidney failure, who is starting to excrete **Ure**a (urea is a major component of urine) **ALSO COMPARE:** other kanji containing 女 on the left at # <u>2039</u>; similar kanji at # <u>599</u>, # <u>721</u> and # <u>1453</u>

Miscellaneous
0601. 以 **PRONUNCIATIONS: mo, i**
MEANINGS: starting point, by means of
EXAMPLES: 前以て maemotte = beforehand,

in advance; 以前に izen ni = a long time ago
DESCRIPTION: on the left, a hoe (this is more obvious when it is written like this 以); in the center, a drop of sweat; on the right, a giraffe
CUES: 以前に **i**zen ni (a long time ago), after digging a trap with this hoe and producing this drop of sweat, **Mo**ses caught this giraffe, and it was **E**asy **GROUP:** 図 zu = drawing, # 281; (前) 以(て) maemotte = beforehand, # 601; 似(ている) nite iru = resembling, # 824 **ALSO COMPARE:** other similar kanji at # **453**

0602. 船 **PRONUNCIATIONS: funa, fune, bune², sen MEANINGS:** ship, boat
EXAMPLES: 船便 funabin = ship mail; 船 fune = ship, boat; 釣り船 tsuribune = fishing boat; 船長 senchou = captain of a ship
DESCRIPTION: on the left, a boat, seen from above, with a pointed prow, and fore and aft compartments, but it is missing a stern in the back; on the right, 八 hachi (eight, # 15), above 口 kuchi (mouth, # 426), which could represent a dock
CUES: this 船 **fune** (boat), which is owned by some **Fo**olish **Na**rcos, is carrying **Fo**od from the **Ne**therlands, and it's wide open at the rear, but there are 八 (eight) **Sen**sible guys on this 口 (dock) who are working on the problem **GROUP:** 船 fune = ship, # 602; 鉛(筆) enpitsu = pencil, # 1092; 沿(革) enkaku = history, # 1414
ALSO COMPARE: other similar kanji at # **1524**

0603. 靴 **PRONUNCIATIONS: kutsu, gutsu² MEANING:** shoe **EXAMPLES:** 靴 kutsu = shoe; 革靴 kawagutsu = leather shoes
DESCRIPTION: on the left, this looks like a needle; unlike the needle in 辛(い) karai (spicy, # 384), it has an open syringe at the top; this radical can also be seen as a hanging bucket at the top, and two eyes above 十 (ten) at the bottom; on the right, 化(学) kagaku (chemistry, # 487), which consists of a man with a slanted hat and a ヒ (hero)
CUE: this man in the center tilts his hat back to examine this ヒ (hero), who is Superman, who is complaining that some 靴 **k**utsu (shoes) he just purchased are too narrow, so that it feels as though open-top needles like this one on the left are **Cu**tting Superman's feet **ALSO COMPARE:** other similar kanji at # **542**, # **1286**, # **1413** and # **1658**

0604. 寄 **PRONUNCIATIONS: ki, yo**
MEANINGS: to be inclined to, to stop by
EXAMPLES: 寄付 kifu = donation; 寄る yoru = to drop in at, to gather, to go closer; 年寄り toshiyori = elderly person
DESCRIPTION: at the top, a bad haircut; below that, 大(きい) ookii (big, # 188); together these two radicals resemble a 大 (big) bird with a bad haircut; at the bottom, a one-sided lean-to containing a box **CUES:** we have **Qui**che and **Y**ogurt in this box in this lean-to, which also contains 寄付 **ki**fu (donations), so if you don't mind this 大 (big) bird with a bad haircut, please 寄る **yo**ru (stop by) **GROUP:** 寄(る) yoru = to drop in, # 604; 奇(妙) kimyou = strange, # 854 (identical pronunciation), which omits the bad haircut; 椅(子) isu = chair, # 855; (長)崎 Nagasaki, # 1081; 騎(手) kishu = jockey, # 1449 (also identical pronunciation); 埼(玉) Saitama = a city near Tokyo, # 1939 **ALSO COMPARE:** other similar kanji at # 1176 and # **1501**

0605. 残 **PRONUNCIATIONS: noko, gori, zan MEANINGS:** to remain, cruel
EXAMPLES: 残る nokoru = to remain; 残す nokosu = to leave behind; 名残 nagori = remnants, traces; 残念 zannen = regrettable; 残業 zangyou = overtime **DESCRIPTION:** on the left, 夕(方) yuugata (evening, # 160) with a cap on it; let's call this a nightcap (an alcoholic drink taken before bedtime); on the right, a halberd (combination lance and axe) with three horizontal lines near the top, suggesting a halberd handle with a triple grip **CUES:** a **No**ble **Co**de allows warriors to drink nightcaps like this and then 残す **noko**su (leave behind) victims of **Gor**y attacks with halberds like this, but this is considered cruel and 残念 **zan**nen (regrettable) behavior in **Zan**zibar

GROUP: 残(る) nokoru = to remain, # 605; (一)銭 issen = 0.01 yen, # 744; 浅(い) asai = shallow, # 1443; (実)践 jissen = implementation, # 1907; 桟(橋) sanbashi = a wharf, # 1977 **ALSO COMPARE:** other similar kanji at # **164**

0606. 球 PRONUNCIATIONS: kyuu, tama MEANINGS: ball, sphere

EXAMPLES: 野球 yakyuu = baseball; 地球 chikyuu = the Earth; 電気の球 denki no tama = lightbulb **DESCRIPTION:** on the left, 王 ou (king, # 1077); at the upper right, the upper portion of 犬 inu (dog, # 190); at the lower right, 水 mizu (water, # 251); together these two radicals on the right may represent a water dog from Cuba **CUES:** this 王 (king) and this 水 (water) 犬 (dog) from **Cuba** are watching a 野球 y**akyuu** (baseball) game while eating **Tam**ales **GROUP:** (地)球 chikyuu = the Earth, # 606; (要)求 youkyuu = demand, # 810 (identical pronunciation); 救(済) kyuusai = help, # 977 (also identical pronunciation) **ALSO COMPARE:** other similar kanji at # **1772**

0607. 寿 PRONUNCIATIONS: su, ju, kotobuki MEANINGS: life, longevity

EXAMPLES: 寿司 sushi = raw fish slices on rice; 寿命 jumyou = lifespan, longevity; 寿 kotobuki = congratulations, felicitations (given at weddings, New Year's, etc.) **DESCRIPTION:** at the top, an owl's perch, as seen in 青(い) aoi (blue, # 155), with an extension of the axis of the owl's perch to the lower left; at the lower right, a sunny guy with some gum on the ground in front of him, as seen in 寸(前) sunzen (on the verge, # 1369) **CUES: Su**perman saw this 寸 (**su**nny guy) sitting in the shade of this elongated owl's perch, and he suggested that they pick up this gum and go get some 寿司 **su**shi with some **J**uice, but the sunny guy was practicing for his **Ko**to (Japanese harp) recital at **Bu**ckingham Palace **GROUP:** 寿(司) sushi = raw fish, # 607;

鋳(型) igata = a mold, # 2010 **ALSO COMPARE:** 看(板) kanban = signboard, # 1164

0608. 司 PRONUNCIATIONS: shi, ji², tsukasado MEANINGS: official, to administer

EXAMPLES: 寿司 sushi = raw fish slices on rice; 司会 shikai = master of ceremonies; 上司 joushi = one's superior (in a company); 健司 kenji = a boy's given name; 司る tsukasadoru = to rule, administer **DESCRIPTION:** compared to 伺(う) ukagau (to visit or ask, # 341), this omits the uber California gambler on the left; it retains the old napkin above the box inside a one-sided lean-to, as seen in 同(じ) onaji (the same, # 339) **CUES:** after my 上司 jou**shi** (superior) removed this napkin from the top of this box inside this lean-to, we found that the box contained **Sh**eep food, in addition to some **T**soup (soup) that **C**asanova left by the **D**oor **ALSO COMPARE:** 可(愛い) kawaii = cute, # 615; other similar kanji at # **341**

Kanji for Volume Two

0609. 至 PRONUNCIATIONS: ita, shi MEANING: to reach an end

EXAMPLES: 至る itaru = to lead to, to reach, to result in; 至急 shikyuu = immediately, urgently; 至難の shinan no = extremely difficult **DESCRIPTION:** compared to 室 shitsu (room, # 62), this omits the bad haircut at the top; it retains 一 (one) ム (cow) resting on 土 tsuchi (soil) **CUES:** on the road that 至る **ita**ru (leads) to some **Ita**lian monuments, I saw a 至難の **shi**nan no (extremely difficult) situation: this 一 (one) ム (cow) had collided with a **Sh**eep and was stuck in this 土 (soil) **COMPARE:** other similar kanji at # **63**

0610. 極 PRONUNCIATIONS: kyoku, goku, kiwa MEANINGS: extreme, to culminate

EXAMPLES: 南極 nankyoku = the antarctic, South Pole; 極力 kyokuryoku = as much as

possible, to the best of one's ability; 至極 shigoku = extremely; 極める kiwameru = to attain or master; 極めて kiwamete = extremely
DESCRIPTION: on the left, 木 ki (tree, # 118); on the right, a kangaroo leg, as seen in 考(える) kangaeru (to think, # 469); to the left of the leg, 口 kuchi (mouth, # 426), which resembles a chair; to the right of the leg, 又 mata (again, # 24), which resembles a folding table; at the bottom, a carpet **CUES:** at the **Kyo**to **Ko**ol-Aid club, on a cold night, this kangaroo sits on this 口 (chair) on this carpet near this 又 (table) next to this 木 (tree) and drinks **Go**ld **Ko**ol-Aid through his 口 (mouth) while pondering 極力 **kyoku**ryoku (as much as possible) how to **K**eep **W**arm, which is 極めて **kiwa**mete (extremely) difficult to do
COMPARE: other similar kanji at # **24** and # **468**

0611. 然 PRONUNCIATIONS: zen, nen
MEANINGS: naturally, yes   **EXAMPLES:** 全然 zenzen = not at all; 自然 shizen = nature; 当然 touzen = justly; 天然 tennen = natural
DESCRIPTION: at the upper left, a three-legged bench with a rocker bottom, as seen in 祭(り) matsuri (festival, # 377); at the upper right, 犬 inu (dog, # 190); at the bottom, four vertical lines suggesting a hot fire   **CUES:** as a **Z**en monk sits on this three-legged bench with a rocker bottom, watching his **N**egative **N**ephew play with this 犬 (dog) near a fire, he looks out at 自然 shi**zen** (Nature) and sees it as 天然 ten**nen** (natural)
GROUP: 点く tsuku = to ignite, # 29; 熱(い) atsui = hot, # 65; 黒(い) kuroi = black, # 76; 魚 sakana = fish, # 80; 無(理) muri = impossible, # 583; 自然 shizen = nature, # 611; 煎(る) iru = to roast, # 650; 漁 ryou = fishing, # 685; 焦(る) aseru = to be impatient, # 750; 照(る) teru = to shine, # 822; 黙(る) damaru = to keep silent, # 836; 撫(でる) naderu = to stroke, # 846; (新)鮮 shinsen = fresh, # 858; 蒸(気) jouki = steam, # 1101; 燃(料) nenryou = fuel, # 1240 (identical pronunciation); 熊 kuma = bear, # 1262; (岩)礁 ganshou = reef, # 1270; 蘇(る) yomigaeru = to revive, # 1279; 煮(る) niru = to boil, # 1377; 熟(す) jukusu = to ripen, # 1427; (猛)烈 mouretsu = fierce, # 1610; 潟 kata = a lagoon, # 1736; 庶(民) shomin = common people, # 1795; 墨 sumi = ink stick, # 1829; 遮(断) shadan = an interruption, # 1892; 窯 kama = an oven, # 1893; 勲(章) kunshou = a medal, # 1938; 薫(製) kunsei = smoked food, # 1951; 鯨 kujira = a whale, # 1981
ALSO COMPARE: other similar kanji at # **377** and # **945**

0612. 到 PRONUNCIATION: tou
MEANING: to arrive   **EXAMPLES:** 到着する touchaku suru = to arrive; 到底 toutei (with negative expressions) = not by any means, not at all
DESCRIPTION: compared to 至(急) shikyuu (immediately, # 609), this adds the katakana リ ri, which includes a prominent toe, on the right; it retains the 一 (one) ム (cow) resting on 土 (soil)   **CUE:** リ **R**i 到着する **tou**chaku suru (arrives) riding on this 一 (one) ム (cow) and 至 (immediately) uses this long **T**oe to clean this 土 (soil) from its hooves   **ALSO COMPARE:** other similar kanji at # **63** and # **1985**

0613. 丈 PRONUNCIATIONS: jou, take
MEANING: length   **EXAMPLES:** 丈夫 joubu = healthy, hearty, strong; 大丈夫 daijoubu = all right; 丈 take = size, height
DESCRIPTION: compared to 大(きい) ookii (big, # 188), this guy's right hip has slipped out of its socket   **CUES:** to impress **Jo**an of Arc, this 大 (big) right-wing guy drinks from a **T**all **Ke**g and then dislocates this right hip; it looks dangerous, but he is 大丈夫 dai**jou**bu (all right)
ALSO COMPARE: 才(能) sainou = talent, # 617; other similar kanji at # **1000**

0614. 夫 **PRONUNCIATIONS:** otto, fuu, fu, bu **MEANINGS:** husband, man **EXAMPLES:** 夫 otto = husband; 夫婦 fuufu = married couple; 工夫 kufuu = ingenuity; 水夫 suifu = sailor; 大丈夫 daijoubu = all right

DESCRIPTION: 人 hito (person, # 13) with the addition of two pairs of arms

CUES: during the **Ott**oman empire, an 夫 **otto** (husband) was often a 人 (person) with two pairs of arms like these who wasted **Foo**d and **Foo**lishly drank lots of **Boo**ze

GROUP: 天 ten (or ama) = sky, # 189; 失(礼) shitsurei = discourtesy, # 206; 夫 otto = husband, # 614; 矢 ya = arrow, # 1045 **ALSO COMPARE:** other similar kanji at # **188** and # **1915**

0615. 可 **PRONUNCIATION:** ka **MEANINGS:** possible, able **EXAMPLES:** 許可 kyoka = permission; 可愛い kawaii = cute (the "w" in kawaii is added for the sake of easy pronunciation); 不可能 fukanou = impossible; 可能 kanou = possible

DESCRIPTION: compared to 何 nani (what, # 338), or (幾)何(学) kikagaku (geometry, # 338) (identical pronunciation), this kanji omits the man with the slanted hat; it retains the carton inside a one-sided lean-to

CUE: this **C**arton inside this lean-to contains some 可愛い **ka**waii (cute) clothing

ALSO COMPARE: (上)司 joushi = one's superior, # 608; (文)句 monku = complaint, # 872; other similar kanji at # **1176**

0616. 能 **PRONUNCIATION:** nou **MEANING:** ability **EXAMPLES:** 能力 nouryoku = ability; 有能 yuunou = able, competent; 性能 seinou = performance, efficiency; 能 nou = Noh, old-style Japanese theater; 不可能 fukanou = impossible

DESCRIPTION: at the upper left, the katakana ム mu, the sound made by a cow; at the lower left, 月 tsuki (moon, # 148); on the right, two stacked katakana ヒ hi's **CUE:** this ム (cow) on this 月 (moon) has the 能力 **nou**ryoku (ability) to ヒ (hear) what we say and to ヒ (heal) our illnesses, but her **No**se is stuffy, and she cannot smell us **GROUP:** 育(てる) sodateru = to raise, # 151; 能(力) nouryoku = ability, # 616; 態(度) taido = attitude, # 960; 熊 kuma = bear, # 1262; 徹(底) tettei = thorough-ness, # 1333; 撤(廃) teppai = abolition, # 1747; 罷(免) himen = dismissal, # 2057 **ALSO COMPARE:** other kanji containing two ヒ's at # **1294**

0617. 才 **PRONUNCIATION:** sai **MEANINGS:** age counter, talent **EXAMPLES:** 九十才 kyuujussai = 90 years old in casual writing; in formal writing, this would be written 九十歳; 才能 sainou = talent; 天才 tensai = genius **DESCRIPTION:** this is a kneeling guy whose left hip has slipped out of its socket **CUE:** this kneeling guy is a left-wing **Sc**ientist whose left hip has slipped out of its socket, and since he is a 天才 ten**sai** (genius), he can put it back by himself **COMPARE:** 丈(夫) joubu = healthy, # 613; other similar kanji at # **1417**

0618. 解 **PRONUNCIATIONS:** kai, to, ge, hodo **MEANINGS:** to undo, to untie, to solve **EXAMPLES:** 理解 rikai = understanding; 解決 kaiketsu = solution; 読解 dokkai = reading comprehension; 解く toku = to solve or undo, transitive; 解ける tokeru = to get untied or solved, intransitive; 解熱 ge'netsu = lowering a fever; 解ける hodokeru = to unravel, to come untied **DESCRIPTION:** on the left, 角 kado (outside corner, # 81), which resembles a fish-head guy (see # 80) with bifocals; at the upper right, 刀 katana (sword, # 102); at the lower right, 牛 ushi (cow, # 205) **CUES:** this 角 (fish-head guy with glasses) is a **Kai**ser who has found that the 解決

kaiketsu (solution) to his financial problems is to sell 刀 (weapons) like this and 牛 (beef) like this, as well as **T**omatoes and **Ge**ckos, and he **H**opes to buy a **D**olphin with the proceeds **GROUP:** 魚 sakana = fish, # 80; 角 kado = outside corner, # 81; 触(れる) fureru = to touch, # 475; (理)解 rikai = understanding, # 618; 漁(業) gyogyou = fishing business, # 685; (新)鮮 shinsen = fresh, # 858; 亀 kame = turtle, # 908; 蘇(る) yomigaeru = to revive, # 1279; (均)衡 kinkou = balance, # 1875; 鯨 kujira = a whale, # 1981 **ALSO COMPARE:** other similar kanji at # **1032**, # **1765** and # **2062**

0619. 確 **PRONUNCIATIONS: kaku, tashi MEANINGS:** certain, firm **EXAMPLES:** 正確 seikaku = precise; 確認 kakunin = confirmation; 確かに tashika ni = for sure, certainly; 確かめる tashikameru = to confirm **DESCRIPTION:** on the left, 石 ishi (stone, # 458); on the upper right, a swooping bird; on the lower right, the net from 進(む) susumu (to advance, # 203), which can be seen as a man with a slanted hat next to a 主 (master) with extra arms **CUES: Ka**rl the **K**ool-**A**id vendor hides behind this 石 (stone) and watches this swooping bird try to attack the **T**alented **Sh**eep that he keeps inside this net, but he thinks that 確かに **tashi**ka ni (certainly) the net will protect them and that his **K**ool-**A**id will provide energy for a counterattack **COMPARE:** other similar kanji at # **698** and # **1775**

0620. 卓 **PRONUNCIATIONS: taku, ta MEANINGS:** table, desk, high **EXAMPLES:** 食卓 shokutaku = dining table; 卓球 takkyuu = pingpong **DESCRIPTION:** this appears to be the California wagon from 朝 asa (morning, # 291), but the wheel at the top is broken [this can also be seen as a taser above 早(い) hayai (early, # 34), or as a taser above 日 (sun) over 十 (ten)]

CUES: sitting at a 食卓 shoku**taku** (dining table) while drinking **Ta**p water and **K**ool-**A**id, **Ta**rzan thinks about how to fix this broken wagon wheel **GROUP:** (食)卓 shokutaku = dining table, # 620;

(哀)悼 aitou = condolence, # 1644 **ALSO COMPARE:** other similar kanji at # **1365**

0621. 超 **PRONUNCIATIONS: chou, ko MEANINGS:** ultra, super, over **EXAMPLES:** 超人的 choujinteki = superhuman; 超満員 chouman'in = overcrowded; 超える koeru = to go across, to exceed (this can also be spelled 越える koeru, # 453) **DESCRIPTION:** on the lower left, 走(る) hashiru (to run, # 450); on the right, 召(喚する) shoukan suru (to summon, # 106), which consists of a 刀 (sword) on a 口 (box) **CUES:** a 走 (runner) who is 超 **chou** (super) fast was **Ch**osen to carry this 刀 (sword) on this 口 (box) in a parade in **Co**lombia **ALSO COMPARE:** similar kanji at # **449**, # **450** and # **560**

0622. 頑 **PRONUNCIATION: gan MEANING:** stubborn **EXAMPLES:** 頑張る ganbaru = to persevere, to do one's best; 頑丈 ganjou = sturdy, strong; 頑固な ganko na = stubborn **DESCRIPTION:** on the left, 元 moto (base, origin, # 421); on the right, 貝 kai (shell, # 83), with a platform on top, where a head could fit, as seen in 頭 atama (head, # 93) **CUE: Ga**ndalf is a 頑固な **gan**ko na (stubborn) wizard who sometimes loses his 頭 (head), but he always 頑張る **gan**baru (does his best), since he operates from this reliable 元 (base) **ALSO COMPARE:** other similar kanji at # **421** and # **1126**

0623. 迷 **PRONUNCIATIONS:** *mai*, mei, mayo **MEANINGS:** to be perplexed or lost **EXAMPLES:** 迷子 maigo = lost person; 迷信 meishin = superstition; 迷惑 meiwaku = trouble, annoyance; 迷う mayou = to lose direction **DESCRIPTION:** 米 kome (uncooked rice, # 326), on a snail **CUES:** **M**ighty **M**ouse helps a **M**ai**d** on this snail which transports **May**onnaise and this 米 (uncooked rice), but he often 迷う **mayo**u (loses direction), becomes a 迷子 **mai**go (lost person) and causes 迷惑 **mei**waku (inconvenience) **GROUP:** 迷(子) maigo = lost person, # 623; 謎 nazo = an enigma, # 1704

0624. 惑 **PRONUNCIATIONS:** *mado*, waku **MEANING:** to confuse **EXAMPLES:** 惑わす madowasu = to delude or seduce; 戸惑う tomadou = to be bewildered; 迷惑 meiwaku = trouble, annoyance; 当惑 touwaku = embarassment, bewilderment **DESCRIPTION:** at the upper right, a halberd (combination lance and axe), forming a one-sided lean-to; at the upper left, 口 kuchi (mouth, # 426), which also resembles a box, with a horizontal line under it, which could represent a window with piece of tape reinforcing the lower frame; at the bottom, 心 kokoro (heart, # 306) **CUES:** when I lived in a **M**ars **D**ome and we fought a **W**ar against the **K**ool-**A**id industry, I had a brave 心 (heart) like this and was assigned to hold this halberd and look out this reinforced 口 (box, or window) for people who might cause us 迷惑 mei**waku** (trouble) **COMPARE:** 感(じる) kanjiru = to feel, # 640, in which there is a two-sided lean-to partly supported by a halberd, and a napkin is *above* 口; other similar kanji at # 1256 and # 1862

0625. 街 **PRONUNCIATIONS:** *kai*, machi, gai **MEANING:** town **EXAMPLES:** 街道 kaidou = highway, path; 街角 machikado = street corner; 街灯 gaitou = street light; 地下街 chikagai = underground shopping mall **DESCRIPTION:** on the left and right 行(く) iku (to go, # 334), suggesting that one is in the middle of going; in the middle of 行, two piles of 土 tsuchi (soil, # 59) **CUES:** when the **Kai**ser is in the middle of 行 (going) around the 街角 **machi**kado (street corner), these two big **M**at**chi**ng piles of 土 (soil) block the way, but the 街灯 **gai**tou (street light) **Gui**des him **GROUP:** 行(く) iku = to go, # 334; 街(道) kaidou = highway, # 625; (手)術 shujutsu = surgery, # 808; 衛(生) eisei = hygiene, # 918; 衝(撃) shougeki = impact, # 1561; (均)衡 kinkou = balance, # 1875; 桁 keta = a beam, # 2025 **ALSO COMPARE:** other similar kanji at # 1619

0626. 灯 **PRONUNCIATION:** tou **MEANINGS:** light, lamp, torch **EXAMPLES:** 街灯 gaitou = street light; 電灯 dentou = electric light; 消灯時間 shoutoujikan = lights out time **DESCRIPTION:** on the left, 火 hi (fire, #443); on the right, 丁(目) choume (city block, # 702), which resembles a nail **CUE:** when I place this 丁 (nail) in this 火 (fire), it glows like a **T**orch (flashlight), but it can't replace a 電灯 den**tou** (electric light) **ALSO COMPARE:** other similar kanji at # 702 and # 1239

0627. 停 **PRONUNCIATION:** tei **MEANINGS:** halt, stopping **EXAMPLES:** バス停 basutei = bus stop; 各駅停車 kakueki-teisha = local train **DESCRIPTION:** on the left, a man with a slanted hat; on the upper right, a tire stop above a 口 (box); on the lower right, 丁(寧) teinei (polite, # 702) (identical pronunciation), which resembles a nail, under a roof **CUE:** this man on the left is a **T**ailor who sits next to this 口 (box) containing thread, which is protected by this tire stop, tilts his hat back in order to see better, and sews with this 丁 (nail) under this roof at a バス停 basu**tei** (bus stop) **ALSO COMPARE:** other similar kanji at # 702 and # 1474

0628. 駄 **PRONUNCIATIONS: ta, da**
MEANING: pack horse
EXAMPLES: 下駄 geta = Japanese clogs; 無駄 muda = useless, wasteful **DESCRIPTION:** on the left, 馬 uma (horse, # 958); on the right, 太(る) futoru (to get fat, # 191)
CUES: Tarzan told his **Da**ughter to exercise this 太 (fat) 馬 (horse), since to do otherwise would be 無駄 m**uda** (useless and wasteful) **ALSO COMPARE:** other similar kanji at # **191** and # **826**

0629. 汗 **PRONUNCIATIONS: ase, kan**
MEANING: sweat
EXAMPLES: 汗をかく ase wo kaku = to sweat; 発汗 hakkan = perspiration
DESCRIPTION: on the left, a water radical, which reminds us of sweat; on the right, a telephone pole
CUES: Asses (donkeys) 汗をかく **ase** wo kaku (sweat) water like this when we make them carry telephone poles like this to **Kan**sas
GROUP: (海)岸 kaigan = beach, # 500; 拝(見する) haiken suru = to humbly read or see, # 593; 汗 ase = sweat, # 629; 刊(行する) kankou suru = to publish, # 990; 幹(部) kanbu = an executive, # 1062; 軒 noki = eaves, # 1146; 干(渉) kanshou = interference, # 1306; 肝(臓) kanzou = the liver, # 1634; **Note** that several of these kanji can be pronounced "kan"

0630. 周 **PRONUNCIATIONS: mawa, shuu MEANINGS:** circumference, surface, lap
EXAMPLES: 周り mawari = surrounding; 周辺 shuuhen = neighborhood, vicinity, circumference; 一周 isshuu = round, tour
DESCRIPTION: compared to 週 shuu (week, # 346) (identical pronunciation), this kanji omits the snail; it retains the 口 (box) containing shoes under some 土 (soil) inside a tent
CUES: some **M**arine **W**arriors live in our 周辺 **shuu**hen (neighborhood); they have **Sh**oes that they hide in this box under this 土 soil in a tent, and they don't need a snail to carry them

ALSO COMPARE: 回(る) mawaru = to rotate, # 4; (お)巡(りさん) omawarisan = policeman, # 778; other similar kanji at # **346**

0631. 差 **PRONUNCIATIONS: sa, za²**
MEANINGS: difference, gap
EXAMPLES: 時差 jisa = time difference; 時差ボケ jisaboke = jet lag; 交差点 kousaten = traffic intersection; 差し上げる sashiageru = to give humbly; 眼差し manazashi = a look or gaze **DESCRIPTION:** compared to 着(く) tsuku (to arrive, # 52), this substitutes the katakana エ e, which reminds us of an egg, for a king's 目 me (eyes); it retains the 王 ou (king, # 1077) wearing rabbit ears [this part of the kanji can also be seen as a truncated 羊 hitsuji (sheep, # 1223), missing its tail] and the long gown
CUE: I 差し上げた **sa**shiageta (humbly gave) our king this エ (egg) to rub in his eyes because he was suffering from 時差ボケ j**i**s**a**boke (jet lag), but the エ was **Salty** **ALSO COMPARE:** other similar kanji at # **247** and # **1893**

0632. 慎 **PRONUNCIATIONS: shin, tsutsushi MEANINGS:** careful, prudent
EXAMPLES: 慎重 shinchou = careful, prudent; 慎む tsutsushimu = to be discreet, to refrain from
DESCRIPTION: compared to 真(実) shinjitsu (truth, # 101) (identical pronunciation), this kanji adds an erect man on the left; it retains the machine with a shiny antenna above a table cabinet, which can also be described as 十 (ten) above 目 (eye) on legs
CUES: the man on the left is a 慎重な **shin**chou na (prudent) **Shin**to priest who draws himself up to his full height like this as he seeks this 真 (truth), and he digs through boxes of **Tsu**its (suits), **Tsu**its and **Sh**eets **ALSO COMPARE:** other similar kanji at # **100**, # **101** and # **2063**

0633. 成 PRONUNCIATIONS: sei, nari, na, jou MEANINGS: to become, to be completed EXAMPLES: 成功 seikou = success; 完成 kansei = completion; 成田 Narita = city and airport near Tokyo; 成り立つ naritatsu = to consist of, to materialize; 成る naru = to consist of; 成仏する joubutsu suru = to enter Nirvana DESCRIPTION: on the left, a truncated 刀 katana (sword, # 102), which we can call a blade; on the right, a halberd (combination axe and lance) CUES: our **Sa**feway store is guarded by a **Na**sty **Ri**ng of **Na**zi guards armed with 刀 (blades) and halberds like this, but **Jo**an of Arc says that it is a 成功 **sei**kou (success) GROUP: 成(功) seikou = success, # 633; 城 shiro = castle, # 1008; 盛(大) seidai = grandiose, # 1018, and 誠(意) seii = sincerity, # 1506, both of which can also be pronounced "sei"

0634. 功 PRONUNCIATION: kou MEANINGS: merit, achievement EXAMPLES: 成功 seikou = success; 功績 kouseki = achievement DESCRIPTION: on the left, 工 kou (crafted object, # 246) (identical pronunciation); on the right, 力 chikara (force, # 107) CUE: if you want to 成功する sei**kou** suru (succeed) in the **Co**al business, you need to use 工 (crafted objects) like this and expend a lot of 力 (force) COMPARE: similar kanji at # 247 and # 1846

0635. 継 PRONUNCIATIONS: tsu, kei MEANINGS: inherit, succeed to EXAMPLES: 継ぐ tsugu = to succeed to, to inherit; 乗り継ぐ noritsugu = to connect to a different flight, train, etc.; 継ぎ目 tsugime = joint, seam; 継承する keishou suru = to succeed to DESCRIPTION: on the left, a 糸 skeet shooter (# 219); on the right, 米 kome (rice, # 326), which is used to make rice tsoup (soup), on a shelf CUES: this 糸 (skeet shooter) is making this 米 (rice) into **Ts**oup (soup) on this shelf in the **C**ave where he lives, but one day he will 継ぐ **tsu**gu (inherit) the title of Chief Skeet Shooter GROUP: 継ぐ tsugu = to inherit, # 635; 断る kotowaru = to refuse, # 704

0636. 単 PRONUNCIATION: tan MEANINGS: simple, only EXAMPLES: 簡単 kantan = easy; 単語 tango = word; 単位 tan'i = credit (school) or unit; 単行本 tankoubon = special book, separate volume DESCRIPTION: at the top, three old boys, as seen in 覚(える) oboeru (to memorize, # 54), but they can be seen as three waves of heat; at the bottom, a 田 (rice paddy, # 68) above 十 juu (ten, # 18), which appears to be spinning CUE: this 田 (rice paddy) was spinning with these three waves of heat emerging from its top, and it was 簡単 kan**tan** (easy) for it to get a **Tan** COMPARE: other similar kanji at # 1625 and # 1694

0637. 余 PRONUNCIATIONS: ama, yo MEANINGS: excess, leftover EXAMPLES: 余り amari = surplus, rest; 余る amaru = to be left over, to remain; 余計 yokei = excessive, all the more; 余分 yobun = surplus, extra DESCRIPTION: compared to 途(中) tochuu (on the way, # 378), this omits the snail; it retains the spinning 丁 (nail) under the stool and below the peaked roof CUES: I was sitting on this stool above this spinning 丁 (nail) under this peaked roof in the **A**mazon, 途 (on the way) to pick up some **Yo**gurt, when I realized that we already had a 余分 **yo**bun (surplus) of milk products GROUP: 途(中) tochuu = on the way, # 378; 余(計) yokei = excessive, # 637; (掃)除 souji = cleaning, # 646; 徐(々に) jojo ni = gradually, # 904; 斜(め) naname = diagonal, # 910; 塗(る) nuru = to paint, # 1041; (自)叙(伝) jijoden = an autobiography, # 2004 ALSO COMPARE: the katakana ホ ho; kanji with a *flying carpet* under a roof with a spinning nail at # 1347

0638. 陣 PRONUNCIATION: jin

MEANINGS: battle array, ranks, camp, position **EXAMPLES:** 陣地 jinchi = encampment, position; 背水の陣 haisui no jin = back to the wall, last stand **DESCRIPTION:** on the left, ß beta from the Greek alphabet; on the right, 車 kuruma (car, # 283) **CUE:** this ß (Greek) guy puts on his **Jean**s, gets in this 車 (car) and drives to his 陣地 **jin**chi (encampment) in Athens **ALSO COMPARE:** other similar kanji at # **2030** and # **2075**

0639. 数 PRONUNCIATIONS: kazo, kazu, zuu, suu

MEANINGS: number, to count **EXAMPLES:** 数える kazoeru = to count; 数 kazu = number; 人数 ninzuu = number of people; 数字 suuji = numeral, figure; 数学 suugaku = mathematics **DESCRIPTION:** on the upper left, 米 kome (rice, # 326); on the lower left, 女 onna (female, # 235); on the right, a dancer with a ponytail **CUES:** this 女 (female), who lives in a **Ca**sino **Zo**ne near a **Ca**lifornia **Zoo**, carries this 米 (rice) to this dancer, who lives at the **Zoo**, and asks her to 数える **kazo**eru (count) the 数 **kazu** (number) of grains in it, since the dancer is **Su**per at 数学 **suu**gaku (mathematics) **COMPARE:** other similar kanji at # **1387**, # **2039** and # **2086**

0640. 感 PRONUNCIATION: kan

MEANING: to feel **EXAMPLES:** 感じる kanjiru = to feel; 感動する kandou suru = to be moved; 感心 kanshin = impressive, admirable; 感じ kanji = impression, perception, feeling **DESCRIPTION:** on the upper left, a one-sided lean-to; under the lean-to, 口 kuchi (mouth, # 426), which also resembles a box, with a line over it representing a napkin; under 口, 心 kokoro (heart, # 306); on the right, a halberd (combination axe and lance) which converts this to a two-sided lean-to **CUE:** in **Kan**sas, when people are locked up in two-sided lean-tos like this, have their 口 (mouths) covered with napkins like this, and are threatened with halberds like this, their 心 (hearts) beat rapidly, and they 感じる **kan**jiru (feel) anger **COMPARE:** (迷)惑 meiwaku (trouble), # 624, in which a piece of tape is *under* 口; other similar kanji at # **915** and # **1620**

0641. 暮 PRONUNCIATIONS: ku, bo, gu

MEANINGS: sunset, end of a year **EXAMPLES:** 暮らし kurashi = living, life; 暮らす kurasu = to make a living; 暮れ kure = year end, nightfall; お歳暮 oseibo = a year-end gift; 日暮れ higure = nightfall, dusk; 一人暮らし hitorigurashi = to live alone **DESCRIPTION:** at the top, a plant radical; below that, 日 hi (sun, # 32); below that, 大(きい) ookii (big, # 188), with a wide base (this combination of radicals = PSB = plants, sun, big); below that, another 日 (sun) **CUES:** this is a tale of two 日 (suns): they both 暮らす **ku**rasu (make a living) by shining light on plants like these, and both of them are 大 (big); the top sun drinks only **Ko**ol-Aid and is **Bo**ring, but the bottom sun is **Go**ofy (PSB = plants, sun, big) **COMPARE:** (応)募 oubo = application, # 1109; 墓(地) bochi = cemetery, # 1275; 慕(情) bojou = longing, # 1959 (identical pronunciations for all three); other similar kanji at # **1353**

0642. 限 PRONUNCIATIONS: gen, kagi
MEANINGS: limit, restrict, best of ability
EXAMPLES: 限界 genkai = limit; 最低限 saiteigen = minimum; 最大限 saidaigen = maximum; 限る kagiru = to be limited to; 限らない kagiranai = not necessarily
DESCRIPTION: on the left, ß beta from the Greek alphabet; on the right, 良(い) yoi (good, # 303), which contains L & Y at its base, without its pointy hat
CUES: this ß (Greek) guy named **Gen**ghis is a 良 (good) hunter who can **C**all **Gee**se, and there is no 限界 **gen**kai (limit) on his activities
ALSO COMPARE: (野)郎 yarou = a guy, # 1343, in which the Greek guy is on the right and hands out roses; other similar kanji at # **805** and # **2030**

0643. 貴 PRONUNCIATIONS: ki, touto
MEANING: precious **EXAMPLES:** 貴重な kichou na = valuable; 貴ぶ toutobu = to value, respect
DESCRIPTION: at the top, 中 naka (inside, # 8), resting on a platform; at the bottom, 貝 kai (shell, or three-drawer money chest, # 83)
CUES: I keep 貴重な **ki**chou na (valuable) things, including my **K**eys and my **T**oasted **T**ortillas, in this three-drawer 貝 (money chest), and the 中 symbol above the chest reminds me that my valuables are 中 (inside) **GROUP:** 貴重な kichou na = valuable, # 643; 遺(産) isan = inheritance, # 1037; 潰(瘍) kaiyou = an ulcer, # 1700

0644. 揃 PRONUNCIATION: soro
MEANINGS: to be complete, to be equal
EXAMPLES: 揃う sorou = to be complete, to be equal, to be the same, to assemble; 揃える soroeru = to arrange, prepare, make uniform
DESCRIPTION: compared to 前 mae (before, # 157), this adds a kneeling guy on the left; it retains 月 (moon) and リ Ri under an upside-down bench
CUE: this guy on the left fell to his knees and expressed **S**orrow when he learned that he had left town 前 (before) the circus came, and he 揃う **soro**u (assembles) with other non-attendees to commiserate **ALSO COMPARE:** other similar kanji at # **157** and # **1236**

0645. 掃 PRONUNCIATIONS: sou, ha
MEANING: to sweep **EXAMPLES:** 掃除する souji suru = to clean; 掃く haku = to sweep; 掃き集める hakiatsumeru = to sweep up together
DESCRIPTION: compared to 帰(る) kaeru (to return home, # 566), this substitutes a kneeling guy for リ Ri on the left; it retains the hair streaming to the left, above Bo Peep, who resembles the face of an elephant, with low-hanging ears and a long trunk
CUES: this guy on the left will 帰 (return home), 掃く **ha**ku (sweep) the house, get on his knees, and use **S**oap to 掃除する **sou**ji suru (clean) the floors in the front **H**all
ALSO COMPARE: other similar kanji at # **1165** and # **1768**

0646. 除 PRONUNCIATIONS: jo, nozo, ji
MEANING: to remove **EXAMPLES:** 削除する sakujo suru = to delete, eliminate; 除く nozoku = to remove; 掃除する souji suru = to clean
DESCRIPTION: compared to 余(計) yokei (excessive, # 637), this adds ß beta from the Greek alphabet on the left; it retains the spinning 丁 (nail) under a stool and a peaked roof
CUES: since this ß (Greek) guy is 余 (excessively) interested in Empress **J**osephine, he drives to see her but ends up parking in the **No Z**one, from which a tow truck 除く **nozo**ku (removes) his **J**eep **ALSO COMPARE:** 覗(く) nozoku = to snoop, # 982; other similar kanji at # **637** and # **2030**

0647. 爪 **PRONUNCIATIONS:** tsuma, tsume **MEANINGS:** nail, claw **EXAMPLES:** 爪楊枝 tsumayouji = toothpick; 爪 tsume = nail, claw; 爪きり tsumekiri = nail cutter **DESCRIPTION:** this resembles a toenail, cut square at the top, with long roots extending toward the bottom (these can also be seen as three long legs) **CUES:** my **Tsu**ma (wife) has long 爪 **tsume** (nails) like this, and she uses them to open **Tsum**e**tai** (cold) cartons of milk **COMPARE:** similar kanji at # **723**

0648. 簡 **PRONUNCIATION:** kan **MEANINGS:** simple and easy **EXAMPLE:** 簡単 kantan = simple and easy **DESCRIPTION:** at the top, 竹 take (bamboo, # 134); at the bottom (時)間 jikan (time, # 411) (identical pronunciation) which depicts a 日 (sun, # 32) between gate posts **CUE:** in **Kan**sas, it's 簡単 **kan**tan (easy) to hang hammocks between 竹 (bamboo) gate posts like these and lie in them for a long 間 (time) under a 日 (sun) like this **COMPARE:** other similar kanji at # **1755** and # **2074**

0649. 涙 **PRONUNCIATION:** namida **MEANINGS:** tear, sympathy **EXAMPLES:** 涙 namida = tears **DESCRIPTION:** compared to 戻(る) modoru (to return, # 75), this adds a water radical on the left; it retains the double-roofed lean-to with snow on top and a 大 (big) modest doorman inside **CUE:** a certain **Na**rco has a **Mi**das touch and plenty of money, but when he 戻 (returns) to see all this water flooding the snow-covered lean-to where his 大 (big) modest doorman stands guard, his 涙 **namida** (tears) will flow **ALSO COMPARE:** similar kanji at # **1134**

0650. 煎 **PRONUNCIATIONS:** sen, i **MEANING:** to boil **EXAMPLES:** 煎じる senjiru = to boil; 煎る iru = to roast or toast **DESCRIPTION:** compared to 前 mae (before, # 157), this adds four flames suggesting a fire at the bottom; it retains 月 (moon) and リ Ri under an upside-down bench **CUES:** when our **Sen**ator came here 前 (before) the election, we 煎じていた **sen**jite ita (were boiling) water over this fire and 煎っていた **i**tte ita (were roasting) **E**els **ALSO COMPARE:** other similar kanji at # **157**, # **611** and # **1236**

0651. 身 **PRONUNCIATIONS:** shin, mi **MEANINGS:** body, flesh **EXAMPLES:** 身長 shinchou = a person's height; 出身 shusshin = birthplace, hometown, alma mater; 身 mi = body, person, e.g., 一人身 hitori mi = one person; 親身に shinmi ni = kindly; 身元 mimoto = identity, lineage **DESCRIPTION:** 自(分) jibun (myself, # 55), resting on a rickety chair, which is bisected and supported by a shiny sword, which can also be seen as an extended left hip **CUES:** when 自 (myself) climbs onto this rickety chair, people from my 出身 shus**shin** (birthplace) try to support me by driving this **Shin**y sword into the ground, so that my 身 **mi** (body) doesn't fall down, and they feed me **Me**als **ALSO COMPARE:** other similar kanji at # **1381** and # **1417**

0652. 己 **PRONUNCIATIONS:** onore, ko **MEANING:** self **EXAMPLES:** 己 onore = self; 利己的な rikoteki na = egostic, self-centered; 利己主義 rikoshugi = egotism, selfishness **DESCRIPTION:** a backwards "S" which resembles a snake **CUES:** this snake was the h**Onore**e at our awards ceremony, but its 己 **onore** (self) got **Co**ld, so it went home **COMPARE:** 乙(女) otome = a maiden, # 1835; similar kanji at # **1078**

0653. 幕 **PRONUNCIATIONS:** maku, baku **MEANINGS:** curtain, drapery **EXAMPLES:** 幕 maku = theater curtain, act of a play; 字幕 jimaku = subtitle; 幕府 bakufu = shogunate administration **DESCRIPTION:** compared to 暮(らす) kurasu (to make a living, # 641), this substitutes 巾 (Bo Peep), as seen in 帽(子) boushi (hat, # 243), for the second 日 (sun) at the bottom; it retains the plant radical, the first 日 (sun) and the extra-wide 大 (big) (this combination of radicals = PSB = plants, sun, big)
CUES: this 日 (sun) makes these plants grow, but it has caused 大 (big) problems for 巾 (Bo Peep), who has **M**ac**u**lar degeneration and spends her days behind closed 幕 **maku** (drapery) enjoying **B**anana **C**ookies (PSB = plants, sun, big)
COMPARE: other similar kanji at # **1353** and # **1768**

0654. 流 **PRONUNCIATIONS:** naga, ru, ha, ryuu **MEANINGS:** a stream, to flow **EXAMPLES:** 流す nagasu = to flush; 流れる nagareru = to flow; 流布 rufu = circulation, dissemination; 流行る hayaru = to become popular or successful (usually spelled はやる); 流行 ryuukou = vogue, fashion; 一流の ichiryuu no = first-rate; 風流な fuuryuu na = refined; 電流 denryuu = electric current **DESCRIPTION:** on the left, a water radical; at the upper right, a ム (cow) wearing a tire stop, as seen in 育(てる) sodateru (to raise, # 151); at the lower right, three legs **CUES:** when this ム (cow) under a tire stop encounters **Naga**ina (a snake from a Kipling story) in a **Ro**om in **Ha**waii, it climbs onto this three-legged stool, empties its **Reu**sable water bottles onto her head, and watches this water 流れる **naga**reru (flow) **ALSO COMPARE:** other similar kanji at # **710** and # **1125**

0655. 韓 **PRONUNCIATION:** kan **MEANING:** Korea **EXAMPLE:** 韓国 kankoku = S. Korea **DESCRIPTION:** on the left, the wagon from 朝 asa (morning, # 291); on the right, 違(う) chigau (to differ, # 355), which contains radicals resembling 五 (five), without its snail **CUE:** in 韓国 **kan**koku (S. Korea), I rode in this wagon which was pulled by a **Kan**garoo, and that was 違 (different) from what I expected **ALSO COMPARE:** other similar kanji at # **1174** and # **1308**

0656. 費 **PRONUNCIATIONS:** tsui, hi, pi² **MEANING:** to spend **EXAMPLES:** 費やす tsuiyasu = to spend time or money; 費用 hiyou = cost; 会費 kaihi = membership fee; 出費 shuppi = expenditures **DESCRIPTION:** at the top, 沸(く) waku (to boil, # 531), which includes a twisted 弓 (bow), without its water radical; at the bottom, 貝 kai (money chest, # 83) **CUES:** in order to make **Tsui**tes (sweets), I 費やす **tsui**yasu (spend) money to buy this 沸 (boiler) for the top of this 貝 (money chest) and **H**eat up the ingredients; therefore my 費用 **hi**you (costs) are high
GROUP: 負(ける) makeru = to lose, # 87; (社)買(う) kau = to buy, # 89; (習)慣 shuukan = customs, # 92; 費(用) hiyou = cost, # 656; 責(任) sekinin = responsibility, # 772; (受)賞(する) jushou suru = to win a prize, # 991; 貧(しい) mazushii = poor, # 1339; 貢(献) kouken = a contribution, # 1617; 貫(く) tsuranuku = to accomplish, # 1621; (探)偵 tantei = a detective, # 1673 **ALSO COMPARE:** kanji with *two* distinct radicals above 貝 can be seen at # 707; other similar kanji at # **476**

0657. 仲 PRONUNCIATIONS: chuu, naka MEANING: relationship EXAMPLES: 仲介 chuukai = mediation; 仲 naka = relationship; 仲良し nakayoshi = close friend DESCRIPTION: on the left, a man with a slanted hat; on the right, 中 naka or chuu (inside, middle, # 8), which helps us with both of these pronunciations and looks like yakitori (grilled chicken on a stick) CUES: this man on the left tilts his hat back to view this 中 (chicken on a stick) that he is Chewing with a 仲良し **naka**yoshi (close friend) who works with him at the National Cathedral GROUP: 中 naka = inside, # 8; 虫 mushi = insect, # 9; 仲 naka = relationship, # 657; (気)遣(う) kizukau = to worry, # 765; 沖(縄) Okinawa, # 1002; 忠(誠) chuusei = loyalty, # 1505; 患(者) kanja = a patient, # 1551; 串 kushi = a skewer, # 2052

0658. 紹 PRONUNCIATION: shou MEANING: to introduce a person to someone EXAMPLES: 紹介 shoukai = introduction; 紹介状 shoukaijou = letter of introduction DESCRIPTION: compared to 招(待) shoutai (invitation, # 560) (identical pronunciation), this kanji substitutes 糸 (skeet shooter, # 219) for the kneeling guy on the left; it retains 刀 (sword) above 口 (mouth), which resembles a box CUE: a Shougun asks this 糸 (skeet shooter) for a 紹介 **shou**kai (introduction) to the skeetshooter's daughter, and he places this 刀 (sword) on this 口 (box) to Show that he is serious about this ALSO COMPARE: 給(料) kyuuryou = salary, # 997; other similar kanji at # **560**

0659. 介 PRONUNCIATION: kai MEANINGS: to mediate, to help EXAMPLES: 紹介 shoukai = introduction; 仲介者 chuukaisha = mediator DESCRIPTION: compared to (世)界 sekai (world, # 69) (identical pronunciation), this kanji omits the 田 (rice paddy); it retains the upwards-pointing arrow CUE: the **Kai**ser plans to serve as a 仲介者 chuu**kai**sha (mediator) in a moon dispute, but first we need to shoot him up into the sky along a trajectory like this ALSO COMPARE: other similar kanji at # **69**

0660. 裕 PRONUNCIATION: yuu MEANINGS: abundant, rich EXAMPLE: 裕福 yuufuku = wealth DESCRIPTION: compared to 浴(室) yokushitsu (bathroom, # 256), this substitutes happy Jimmy Carter with two lips, as seen in 初(めて) hajimete (for the first time, # 104), for the water radical on the left; it retains the bathroom with water vapor rising from it CUE: this happy Jimmy with these two lips acquired 裕福 **yuu**fuku (wealth) and decided to buy this 浴 (bathroom) in the **Yu**kon GROUP: 浴(室) yokushitsu = bathroom, # 256; (内)容 naiyou = content, # 296; 欲(しい) hoshii = desire, # 535; 裕(福) yuufuku = wealth, # 660; 溶(岩) yougan = lava, # 815; 谷 tani = valley, # 1383; (風)俗 fuuzoku = manners, # 1631 ALSO COMPARE: other similar kanji at # **1615**

0661. 福 PRONUNCIATION: fuku MEANINGS: fortune, good luck EXAMPLES: 福 fuku = good luck, fortune; 幸福 koufuku = happiness DESCRIPTION: on the left, the Shah, as seen in (会)社 kaisha (company, # 271); on the upper right, 口 kuchi (mouth, # 426) with a napkin over it; at the lower right, 田(んぼ) tanbo (rice paddy, # 68) CUE: this Shah had the 福 **fuku** (good luck) to find this 田 (rice paddy) in **Fuku**oka, but he doesn't want to talk about it before completing the sale, so he keeps this napkin over this 口 (mouth) COMPARE: similar kanji at # **1160** and # **1185**

0662. 羨 **PRONUNCIATIONS: sen, uraya MEANING:** envy **EXAMPLES:** 羨望 senbou = envy; 羨ましい urayamashii = envious **DESCRIPTION:** at the top, 王 ou (king, # 1077), wearing rabbit ears [this part of the kanji can also be seen as a truncated 羊 hitsuji (sheep, # 1223), missing its tail]; at the bottom, 次 tsugi (next, # 536), which consists of a water radical next to an oil derrick (see # 399) **CUES:** this 王 (king) put on these rabbit ears and gave a **Sen**ator an estate, and 次 (next) the senator found **Ura**nium in the **Ya**rd, which made other politicians feel 羨まし い **uraya**mashii (envious) **ALSO COMPARE:** 茨(城) Ibaraki = a prefecture in Japan, # 1007, which substitutes a plant radical for the 羊 (sheep) at the top; other similar kanji at # **536** and # **1893**

0663. 希 **PRONUNCIATION: ki MEANINGS:** rare, wish **EXAMPLE:** 希望 kibou = hope **DESCRIPTION:** compared to 怖(い) kowai (afraid, # 463), this omits the koala on the left and adds an X at the top; it retains someone hugging 巾 (Bo Peep) **CUE:** I hug my friend 巾 (Bo Peep) in **Ki**ev, while this mysterious X hovers overhead, and we have some 希望 **ki**bou (hope) that the X will turn out to be a good omen **ALSO COMPARE:** other similar kanji at # **457**, # **1768** and # **1953**

0664. 望 **PRONUNCIATIONS: bou, nozo, mou MEANINGS:** to wish, to overlook (a view) **EXAMPLES:** 希望 kibou = hope; 志望 shibou = ambition; 望み nozomi = hope, dream, wish; 所望 shomou = desire, wish, request **DESCRIPTION:** at the upper left, (死)亡 shibou (death, # 585) (identical pronunciation); at the upper right, 月 tsuki (moon, # 148); at the bottom, 王 ou (king, # 1077) **CUES:** this 王 (king) has a 志望 shi**bou** (ambition) to have his **Bo**nes buried on this 月 (moon) after his 亡 (death), but when he summons scientists to his palace to discuss this, they

park in the **No Z**one next to the **Mo**at and get towed **ALSO COMPARE:** other similar kanji at # **585** and # **1876**

0665. 垢 **PRONUNCIATIONS: kou, aka MEANINGS:** dirt, grime **EXAMPLES:** 歯垢 shikou = dental plaque; 垢 aka = dirt **DESCRIPTION:** on the left, 土 tsuchi (soil, # 59); in the middle, an F; on the lower right, 口 kuchi (mouth, # 426) **CUES:** in Co**lo**mbia, I attended an **Aca**demy that was constructed on 土 (soil) like this, and I learned that excessive 垢 **aka** (dirt) on my homework would cause me to get F's like this and that 歯垢 shi**kou** (dental plaque) can be caused by poor 口 (oral) hygiene **COMPARE:** other similar kanji at # **1983**

0666. 離 **PRONUNCIATIONS: hana, ri MEANING:** to separate **EXAMPLES:** 離れる hanareru = to part; 離婚 rikon = divorce; 距離 kyori = distance **DESCRIPTION:** on the left, two stacked cans; the upper can contains an X and the lower one, which is upside-down, contains the katakana ム mu, which protrudes through the top edge; on the right, a net for fishing, which can be seen as a man with a slanted hat next to a 主 (master) with an extra pair of arms (see # 203) **CUES:** **Ha**nnah fishes with this net on a **Ree**f and catches these X's and ム's, which she 離れる **hana**reru (separates) into these two cans **COMPARE:** other similar kanji at # **1678**, # **1953** and # **2046**

0667. 貯 **PRONUNCIATIONS: cho, ta MEANING:** to save money or goods **EXAMPLES:** 貯金 chokin = savings; 貯める tameru = to save (money) **DESCRIPTION:** on the left, 貝 kai (shell, money chest, # 83); on the upper right, a bad haircut; on the lower right, a nail **CUES:** Margaret **Cho**, who has a bad haircut like this one, has a business which uses nails like this to nail **Tar** paper onto roofs, and she 貯める **ta**meru (saves) her 貯金 **cho**kin

(savings) in this 貝 (money chest)
COMPARE: other similar kanji at # **702** and # **2058**

0668. 旦 PRONUNCIATIONS: tan, dan
MEANINGS: dawn, early morning
EXAMPLES: 一旦 ittan = for a moment, once; 旦那 danna = master, husband; 旦那さん dannasan = male customer, master
DESCRIPTION: 日 hi (sun, # 32), with a line under it which could represent a dance floor
CUES: since my 旦那 **dan**na (husband) spends time in this 日 (sun), he has a nice **Tan**, and he likes to **Dan**ce on this floor **GROUP:** 昼 hiru = noon. # 49; 旦(那) danna = master, # 668; 壇 dan = stage, # 679 (identical pronunciation); 得 toku = profit, # 706; 担(当) tantou = charge (duty), # 729 (also identical pronunciation); 垣(根) kakine = hedge, # 777; 量 ryou = quantity, # 1061; 宣(教) senkyou = missionary work, # 1519; (大)胆 daitan = brave, # 1720 (also identical pronunciation); 糧 kate = food, # 1789; 恒(例) kourei = customary, # 1800

0669. 那 PRONUNCIATION: na
MEANING: what? **EXAMPLE:** 旦那 danna = husband **DESCRIPTION:** on the left, 月 tsuki (moon, # 148), but all of the horizontal lines in 月 have been extended to the left; on the right, β beta from the Greek alphabet **CUE:** when my β (Greek) 旦那 dan**na** (husband) visited **Na**rnia, he saw this drawing of the 月 (moon), in which the artist had extended all of the horizontal lines to the left
GROUP: this is a group of one
ALSO COMPARE: other similar kanji at # **1843**

0670. 捕 PRONUNCIATIONS: to, ho, tsuka
MEANINGS: catch, capture, seize
EXAMPLES: 捕る toru = to catch; 捕らえる toraeru = to arrest, capture or understand; 捕虜 horyo = prisoner of war, captive; 捕まえる tsukamaeru = to capture or catch; 捕まる tsukamaru = to be caught
DESCRIPTION: on the left, a kneeling guy; at the upper right, the top part of 犬 inu (dog, # 190) chasing a ball; at the lower right, 用(事) youji (errand, # 364), which resembles a fence
CUES: this guy on the left, who keeps this truncated 犬 (dog) behind this 用 (fence), has a **To**e protruding from a **Ho**le in his sock, but he is kneeling in order to get a leash from the **Tsui**tcase (suitcase) in his **Ca**r, and he will take the 犬 (dog) out to 捕る **to**ru (catch) a burglar
ALSO COMPARE: 補(佐) hosa = aid, # 995 (identical pronunciation); other similar kanji at # **995**

0671. 浮 PRONUNCIATIONS: u, uwa, fu, uki MEANING: to float EXAMPLES:
浮かぶ ukabu = to float, intransitive; 浮く uku = to float, intransitive; 浮気 uwaki = extramarital affair; 浮浪者 furousha = a vagrant; 浮世 ukiyo = floating world, transitory life
DESCRIPTION: on the left, a water radical; at the upper right, a barbecue grate; at the lower right, 子 ko (child, # 182) **CUES:** when an **U**ber car runs into a barbecue grate like this, falls into a river and 浮かぶ **u**kabu (floats) in water like this, even 子 (children) like this say, "**U**ber was **Wa**rned" and "they are hiring **Fo**olish drivers," but other people say, "**U**ber is the **Ke**y to our economy"
GROUP: (牛)乳 gyuunyuu = cow's milk, # 186; 浮く uku = to float, # 671

0672. 未 **PRONUNCIATIONS: ima, mi**
MEANING: yet **EXAMPLES:** 未だに imada ni = even now, still, until this very day; 未来 mirai = future; 未開 mikai = primitive; 未経験 mikeiken = inexperienced
DESCRIPTION: compared to (意)味 imi (meaning, # 245) (identical pronunciation), this kanji omits the 口 (mirror) on the left; it retains the 木 ki (tree, # 118), with two pairs of branches, with the lower branches longer than the upper ones
CUES: an **E**agle at the **M**all 未だに **ima**da ni (even now) perches on the shorter branches at the top of this tree, but in the 未来 **mi**rai (future), it will leave its perch to seek a **M**eal **GROUP:** (週)末 shuumatsu = weekend, # 119, in which the longer pair of branches is at the top; 妹 imouto = little sister, # 244; (意)味 imi = meaning, # 245; 未(来) mirai = future, # 672; 魅(力) miryoku = charm, # 1169; (曖)昧(な) aimai na = ambiguous, # 1941; 抹(殺) massatsu = erasure, # 2017, in which the longer branches are also at the top
ALSO COMPARE: kanji containing a 士 (man) standing on a tree at # 2050

0673. 絶 **PRONUNCIATIONS: ze, zetsu, ta MEANINGS:** to sever, discontinue
EXAMPLES: 絶対に zettai ni = absolutely, by any means; 絶交する zekkou suru = to break off a relationship; 絶望 zetsubou = despair; 絶える taeru = to discontinue or cease
DESCRIPTION: on the left, 糸 skeet shooter (# 219); on the right, 色 iro (color, # 473), which consists of a fish head (see # 80) above a two-eyed snake
CUES: this 糸 (skeet shooter) is a **Z**ealous meditator who 絶対に **ze**ttai ni (absolutely) wants to wear a **Z**en **Ts**uit (suit), but the tsuits they are selling are the wrong 色 (color) and don't fit him because he is too **T**all **GROUP:** 色 iro = color, # 473; 絶(対に) zettai ni = absolutely,

673; 肥(満) himan = overweight = obesity, # 1406; 把(握する) haaku suru = to comprehend, # 1817 **ALSO COMPARE:** other similar kanji at # **87**

0674. 対 **PRONUNCIATIONS: tai, tsui**
MEANINGS: opposing, pair **EXAMPLES:** 絶対に zettai ni = absolutely, by any means; 対して taishite = against, in contrast to, as opposed to, toward; 対する tai suru = to face toward, to confront; 対応する taiou suru = to address a problem; 対決する taiketsu suru = to confront; 対 tsui = pair, e.g., 対の tsui no = in a pair **DESCRIPTION:** on the upper left, a tire stop used in parking lots; on the lower left, an X; on the right, the sunny kneeling guy seen in 寸(前) sunzen (on the verge, # 1369), who has a stick of gum on the ground nearby **CUES:** this sunny kneeling guy, who chews this gum, 対する **tai** suru (opposes) **T**ire stops like this because he thinks they cause **T**ire damage, and he marks them all with **X**'s like this, but a **Ts**u**i**te (sweet) parking lot attendant 対決する **tai**ketsu suru (confronts) him about this practice
ALSO COMPARE: other similar kanji at # **131** and # **259**

0675. 悔 **PRONUNCIATIONS: kai, ku, kuya MEANINGS:** to regret, vexing
EXAMPLES: 後悔 koukai = regret; 悔い kui = regret; 悔やむ kuyamu = to regret, repent; 悔しい kuyashii = vexing, mortifying
DESCRIPTION: compared to 海(外) kaigai (overseas, # 337) (identical pronunciation), this kanji substitutes an erect man for the water radical on the left; it retains 毎 mai (every, # 336)
CUES: this man on the left is a **K**aiser who feels 後悔 kou**kai** (regret) because 毎 (every) day he forgets to bring **K**ool-Aid to his **C**ool **Y**a**k**, and this is 悔しい **kuya**shii (mortifying), but he stands erect and proud like this anyway
ALSO COMPARE: other similar kanji at # **336**, # **2063** and # **2080**

0676. 宗 **PRONUNCIATIONS:** mune, sou, shuu **MEANING:** religious belief **EXAMPLES:** 宗 mune = religion, sect; 宗家 souke = head of family, originator; 宗教 shuukyou = religion **DESCRIPTION:** compared to 祭(り) matsuri (festival, # 377), this substitutes a bad haircut for the decorated peaked roof at the top; it retains the spinning nail and the flying carpet [these can also be seen as 二 (two) above 小 (small)] **CUES:** our 宗教 shuukyou (religion) encourages 祭 (festivals) with spinning 丁 (nails) like this, and it attracts **M**oon **E**xperts with bad haircuts like this who promise to stay **S**ober and wear nice **S**hoes **ALSO COMPARE:** 完(了する) kanryou suru = to finish, # 759, which rests on a 元 (base); other similar kanji at # **1347**

0677. 応 **PRONUNCIATIONS:** kota, ou **MEANING:** to respond willingly **EXAMPLES:** 応える kotaeru = to respond or affect; 応じる oujiru = to respond or comply with; 一応 ichiou = more or less, tentatively, for the time being; 応募 oubo = application, subscription; 応接室 ousetsu shitsu = reception room; 相応 souou = appropriate, suitable **DESCRIPTION:** on the left and top, a lean-to with a small chimney on top; inside the lean-to, 心 kokoro (heart, # 306) **CUES:** my 心 (heart) is in this lean-to with a small chimney in N. Da**K**ota, where I plan to live until I'm **O**ld, or at least 一応 ichi**ou** (for the time being) **GROUP:** 応(える) kotaeru = to respond, # 677; (遠)慮 enryo = reserve, # 1194; 癒(す) iyasu = to heal, # 1293; 慶(事) keiji = an auspicious event, # 1590

0678. 仏 **PRONUNCIATIONS:** butsu, bu, hotoke **MEANING:** Buddha **EXAMPLES:** 仏壇 butsudan = Buddhist altar found in Japanese homes; 仏教 bukkyou = Buddhism; 仏 hotoke = Buddha **DESCRIPTION:** compared to 私 watashi (I, # 510), this substitutes a man with a slanted hat for the ripe grain on the left; it retains the ム (cow) **CUES:** this man on the left tilts his hat back to examine this ム (cow), which he would never eat since he is a 仏教 **bu**kkyou (Buddhism) teacher who wears nice **B**oots, drinks **B**ooze and eats **Hottoke**eki (pancakes) **COMPARE:** 伝(言) dengon = message, # 345; other similar kanji at # **591**

0679. 壇 **PRONUNCIATION:** dan **MEANING:** stage **EXAMPLES:** 壇 dan = stage; 仏壇 butsudan = Buddhist altar found in Japanese homes **DESCRIPTION:** on the left, 土 tsuchi (soil), # 59; on the upper right, a tire stop, as seen in 対(して) tai shite (against, # 673); below that, 回(る) mawaru (to rotate), # 4; below that, 旦(那) danna (husband, # 668) (identical pronunciation) which resembles a 日 (sun) above a dance floor; taken together, the items on the right resemble an older-model TV set with an antenna, resting on a cabinet on a carpet **CUES:** a **Da**ncer sits in this **Da**nk 土 (soil) to watch this TV set with an antenna, on a cabinet above a carpet, which is next to the 仏壇 butsu**dan** (Buddhist altar) in her home **ALSO COMPARE:** other similar kanji at # **4**, # **668** and # **1860**

0680. 反 **PRONUNCIATIONS:** han, so, tan, hon **MEANINGS:** to oppose, to reverse, cloth **EXAMPLES:** 反対 hantai = opposition, the reverse; 反り返る sorikaeru = to bend back or warp; 反物 tanmono = cloth, textile; 謀反 muhon = mutiny, rebellion **DESCRIPTION:** compared to (ご)飯 gohan (cooked rice, # 400) (identical pronunciation), this omits 食 (meal) on the left; it retains the F over an X, which can also be seen as a lean-to containing a 又 (table) **CUES: Han**sel was に反対 ni **han**tai (in opposition to) the witch, and he had a plan to wash her with **S**oap in a **Tan**k in **Hon**duras, but the plan was poor, and Gretel gave it this grade of F and marked it with this X **COMPARE:** 后(妃) kouhi = queen, # 1459; other similar kanji at # **1166**

0681. 香 **PRONUNCIATIONS:** kou, kao, hon, ka **MEANINGS:** incense, smell, perfume **EXAMPLES:** 線香 senkou = incense stick; 香水 kousui = perfume; 香り kaori = fragrance, aroma; 香港 honkon = Hong Kong; 香川県 kagawa ken = Kagawa Prefecture **DESCRIPTION:** at the top, 禾 (a grain plant with a ripe head); at the bottom, 日 hi (sun, # 32) **CUES:** this grain plant with a ripe head in **Co**lombia stands in this 日 (sun), enjoying the 香り **kao**ri (fragrance) of some **Co**ws from **Ho**nduras which are part of a **Ca**rnival **COMPARE:** other similar kanji at # **1797**

0682. 非 **PRONUNCIATION:** hi **MEANINGS:** mistake, negative, wrong **EXAMPLES:** 非常 hijou = emergency, extreme, great; 非難 hinan = criticism, accusation, blame **DESCRIPTION:** reportedly, this represents two wings on opposite sides of a bird; these can also be seen as ladders or stairs **CUE:** this bird is a **H**ero with two wings who can fly in a 非常 **hi**jou (emergency) **COMPARE:** (一)兆 itchou = 1 trillion, # 849; other similar kanji at # **851**

0683. 常 **PRONUNCIATIONS:** jou, tsune **MEANINGS:** constant, always **EXAMPLES:** 非常 hijou = emergency; 非常な hijou na = extreme, great; 通常 tsuujou = usual; 常に tsune ni = always, continually **DESCRIPTION:** at the top, three old boys on a roof, as seen in 覚(える) oboeru (to memorize, # 54); at the bottom, 巾 (Bo Peep), as seen in 帽(子) boushi (hat, # 243), under a big 口 (mouth), who is spinning around looking for Joan of Arc **CUES:** these three old boys on this roof watched this 巾 (Bo Peep) with this big 口 (mouth) as she spun around looking for **J**oan of **A**rc to help with a 非常 hi**jou** (emergency), but Joan's life **Tsoon** (soon) **E**nded **ALSO COMPARE:** similar kanji at # **991** and # **1768**

0684. 営 **PRONUNCIATIONS:** ei, itona **MEANINGS:** to conduct business, barracks **EXAMPLES:** 経営 keiei = management; 営業 eigyou = business; 非営利 hieiri = nonprofit; 営む itonamu = to run a business **DESCRIPTION:** at the top, three old boys on a roof, as seen in 覚(える) oboeru (to memorize, # 54); at the bottom, (風)呂 furo (bath, # 7), which resembles stacked vertebrae **CUES:** honest **A**be used to sit in a 呂 (bath) under this roof where these three old boys stood, and they would invent instruments with **E**erie **Ton**al qualities to sell in their 営業 **ei**gyou (business) **ALSO COMPARE:** other similar kanji at # **991** and # **1079**

0685. 漁 **PRONUNCIATIONS:** ryou, gyo **MEANING:** to fish **EXAMPLES:** 漁 ryou = fishing; 漁師 ryoushi = fisherman; 漁業 gyogyou = fishing business **DESCRIPTION:** compared to 魚 sakana (fish, # 80), this adds a water radical on the left **CUES:** Pope **Leo** looked at this water, saw this 魚 (fish) and decided to start a 漁業 **gyo**gyou (fishing business) to sell fish **Gyo**za **ALSO COMPARE:** other similar kanji at # **611** and # **618**

0686. 団 **PRONUNCIATIONS:** dan, ton **MEANING:** a group of people **EXAMPLES:** 団体 dantai = group of people, an organization; 団結する danketsu suru = to unite or consolidate; 布団 futon = floor cushion, or Japanese bedding **DESCRIPTION:** the sunny kneeling guy seen in 付(く) tsuku (to stick, # 132) is stuck inside a box, with a stick of gum on the ground nearby **CUES:** this sunny kneeling guy wants to **D**ance with **T**ony Blair and the rest of his 団体 **dan**tai (group), but he has gotten 付 (stuck) to this gum that he dropped in this box **ALSO COMPARE:** similar kanji at # **131** and # **1360**

0687. 布 **PRONUNCIATIONS: nuno, fu, bu², pu² MEANINGS:** cloth, to spread **EXAMPLES:** 布 nuno = cloth; 布団 futon = floor cushion, Japanese bedding; 毛布 moufu = blanket; 流布 rufu = circulation, dissemination; 昆布 konbu = kelp; 頒布 hanpu = distribution **DESCRIPTION:** compared to (恐)怖 kyoufu (fear, # 463) (identical pronunciation), this kanji omits the erect koala on the left; it retains the person hugging 巾 (Bo Peep) **CUES:** I'm about to get a **N**ew **No**se from a plastic surgeon, but I don't want to look **Fo**olish, so I plan to hug this friend 巾 (Bo Peep) and keep my face covered with 布 **nuno** (cloth) until the swelling goes down **ALSO COMPARE:** other similar kanji at # **457** and # **1768**

0688. 毛 **PRONUNCIATIONS: mou, ke, ge MEANING:** hair **EXAMPLES:** 毛布 moufu = blanket; 毛 ke = hair, fur, wool; 胸毛 munage = chest hair **DESCRIPTION:** compared to 手 te (hand, # 23), 毛 has a trunk which extends to the right instead of the left; it retains the fingers **CUES: Mo**ses was this right-wing guy, since the base of this 手 (hand) extends to the right, who wore **Ke**ds (a brand of shoes), slept under a 毛布 **mou**fu (blanket) with **Ge**ckos, and had lots of 毛 **ke** (hair) **GROUP:** 毛 ke = hair, # 688; (消)耗(する) shoumou suru = to consume, # 2050 (identical pronunciation)

0689. 巨 **PRONUNCIATION: kyo MEANING:** huge **EXAMPLES:** 巨大 kyodai = huge; 巨人 kyojin = a giant **DESCRIPTION:** this looks like a child's swing set that has been knocked onto its left side **CUE:** a 巨人 **kyo**jin (giant) knocked over this swing set in **Kyo**to **COMPARE:** other similar kanji at # **1246**

0690. 輪 **PRONUNCIATIONS: rin, wa MEANING:** wheel **EXAMPLES:** 車輪 sharin = wheel; 輪 wa = round shape (ring, circle etc.); 内輪 uchiwa = family or inner circle; 指輪 yubiwa = ring **DESCRIPTION:** on the left, 車 kuruma (car, # 283); on the upper right, a peaked roof with a ceiling below; on the lower right, 冊 satsu (counter for books, # 568); taken together, the radicals on the right could represent a library **CUES: Rin**go wanted to go to this 冊 (library), but a 車輪 sha**rin** (wheel) fell off this 車 (car), and he had to **Wa**lk **ALSO COMPARE:** 輸(入する) yu'nyuu suru = to import, # 288; other similar kanji at # **813** and # **1966**

0691. 指 **PRONUNCIATIONS: yubi, shi, sashi, sa, za² MEANING:** finger **EXAMPLES:** 指 yubi = finger; 指定席 shiteiseki = reserved seat; 指図 sashizu = direction, command; 指す sasu = to point; 目指す mezasu = to aim at **DESCRIPTION:** on the left, a kneeling guy; on the right, 旨 (味) umami (a 5th taste category, # 1318), which consists of a ヒ (hero) above 日 hi (sun, # 32) and reminds us of an uber Marine **CUES:** this guy on the left is kneeling to consult with this 旨 (uber Marine) on the right, who controls the **Yu**kon **B**eef industry with one 指 **yubi** (finger); during the day, they kneel and watch their **Sh**eep, but at night they sleep on **Sa**tin **Sh**eets and dream of **Sa**skatchewan **COMPARE:** similar kanji at # **1318**

0692. 廻 **PRONUNCIATION: ne MEANING:** to revolve or turn **EXAMPLE:** 輪廻 rinne = samsara, cycle of death and rebirth **DESCRIPTION:** 回(る) mawaru (to rotate, # 4), riding on a 3x snail (see # 363) **CUES:** I'm stuck in this box traveling on the back of this 3x snail in the **Ne**therlands, 回 (rotating) back and forth and wondering whether my **Ne**xt life can be predicted, according to the doctrine of 輪廻 rin**ne** (samsara)

GROUP: 建(てる) tateru = to build, # 363; 庭 niwa = garden, # 495; (輪)廻 rinne = samsara, # 692; 健(康) kenkou = health, # 811; 延(び る) nobiru = to lengthen, # 842; 誕(生日)

tanjoubi = birthday, # 1122; (法)廷 houtei = a court of law, # 1664; 鍵 kagi = a key, # 1689 **ALSO COMPARE:** 転生 tenshou = reincarnation; 生まれ変わり umarekawari = reincarnation; other similar kanji at # **4**

0693. 興 **PRONUNCIATIONS: kyou, kou, oko MEANINGS:** to raise or start **EXAMPLES:** 興味 kyoumi = interest; 興奮 koufun = excitement; 興す okosu = to revive, to raise up **DESCRIPTION:** in the top center, 同(じ) onaji (the same, # 339), with ladders added on both sides, similar to the one seen in (階)段 kaidan (stairs, # 559); at the bottom, a floor with two legs **CUES:** in **Kyou**to you can find this store which is raised on two legs, with 同 (identical) 段 (stairs) on both sides providing access to the top of the building, where there are **Co**la machines, and since I have a 興味 **kyou**mi (interest) in **O**ld **Co**ats, I buy them there **ALSO COMPARE:** other similar kanji at # **41** and # **1620**

0694. 深 **PRONUNCIATIONS: fuka, buka, shin MEANING:** deep **EXAMPLES:** 深い fukai = deep; 興味深い kyoumibukai = very interesting; 深夜 shinya = dead of night; 深刻 shinkoku = serious **DESCRIPTION:** on the left, a water radical; at the upper right, a platform above lopsided legs; at the bottom right, 木 ki (tree, # 118) **CUES:** a **F**oolish **Ca**shier from **Bu**charest installed this platform with lopsided legs at the top of this 木 (tree) and dove into this water below, but the water was 深い **fuka**i (deep), and a **Shin**to priest had to rescue him
GROUP: 深(い) fukai = deep, # 694; 探(す) sagasu = to search, # 699

0695. 恋 **PRONUNCIATIONS: koi, ren MEANING:** to be in love **EXAMPLES:** 恋 koi = love; 恋人 koibito = lover; 恋しい koishii = longed for, beloved; 恋愛 ren'ai = romantic love **DESCRIPTION:** compared to 変 hen (strange, # 553), this substitutes 心 kokoro (heart, # 306) for the dancer at the bottom; it retains the hen with four legs at the top **CUES:** this four-legged hen is in 恋 **koi** (love) with this 心 (heart), and it's swooping down to give it a **Coin** to help pay the **Rent GROUP:** 変 hen = strange, # 553; 恋 koi = love, # 695; (台)湾 Taiwan, # 1016; 跡 ato = trace, # 1111; (野)蛮 (な) yaban na = barbarous, # 1804 **ALSO COMPARE:** kanji containing soaring Cuban birds at # 112

0696. 職 **PRONUNCIATIONS: shoku, sho MEANINGS:** job, employment **EXAMPLES:** 職業 shokugyou = occupation; 就職する shuushoku suru = to get a job; 職権 shokken = authority **DESCRIPTION:** on the left, 耳 mimi (ear, # 57); in the middle, 音 oto (sound, # 266); on the right, a halberd (combination axe and lance); together these radicals suggest a military musician **CUES:** I listen to 音 (sounds) with this 耳 (ear) while carrying this halberd, and it may **Sho**ck yo**U** to learn that my 職業 **shoku**gyou (occupation) is military musician, but wait until you see my **Sho**w **ALSO COMPARE:** other similar kanji at # **266**, # **753** and # **1713**

0697. 伸 **PRONUNCIATIONS: shin, no MEANINGS:** to expand, stretch, lengthen **EXAMPLES:** 追伸 tsuishin = postscript; 伸ばす nobasu, transitive = to lengthen, stretch, develop, expand; 伸びる nobiru, intransitive = to lengthen, to be postponed (less commonly, this can also be spelled 延びる, # 842) **DESCRIPTION:** compared to 神(道) Shintou (a Japanese religion, # 273) (identical pronunciation), this kanji substitutes a man with a slanted hat for the Shah on the left; it retains 申(す) mousu (to humbly speak, # 10), which resembles a rice paddy on a stick, or lips stitched together **CUES:** this man on the left emerges from a **Shin**to shrine, tilts his hat back, sees that these lips are stitched together, suggesting that **No** one wants to tell him that his ride has gone, and he 申 (humbly says) that he must

伸ばす **no**basu (extend) his visit
ALSO COMPARE: 仲 naka = relationship, # 657; other similar kanji at # **1157**

0698. 勧 PRONUNCIATIONS: kan, susu
MEANINGS: to recommend, advise
EXAMPLES: 勧誘する kan'yuu suru = to invite or urge to join; 勧告 kankoku = recommendation, advice; 勧める susumeru = to advise or recommend **DESCRIPTION:** at the upper left, the upper portion of a Native American chief, as seen in 知(る) shiru (to know, # 323), who is hugging a net (which can be seen as a man with a slanted hat next to a 主 (master) with extra arms, as seen in # 203) on the lower left; **Note:** this chief resembles the swooping bird seen above the net in 確(かめる) tashikameru (to confirm, # 619), but it contains an additional horizontal line, among other differences; on the right, 力 chikara (force, # 107)
CUES: this truncated 矢 (Native American chief) is hugging a net in a zoo, where a wild animal is being kept by 力 (force); the people of **Kan**sas are outraged about this, and the chief 勧める **susu**meru (recommends) that they **Sue** the Superintendent of the zoo
GROUP: 確(かめる) tashikameru = to confirm, # 619; 勧告 kankoku = recommendation, # 698; 観(光) kankou = sightseeing, # 886 (identical pronunciation); 権(威) ken'i = authority, # 916; 歓(迎) kangei = welcome, # 1323 (also identical pronunciation); 鶴 tsuru = a crane, # 1609 **ALSO COMPARE:** other similar kanji at # **1846**

0699. 探 PRONUNCIATIONS: saga, sagu, tan MEANINGS: to search or look for
EXAMPLES: 探す sagasu = to search or look for; 探る saguru = to grope, look for, probe; 探険 tanken = exploration, expedition, # 196 (this can also written 探検 tanken, # 859)
DESCRIPTION: compared to 深(い) fukai (deep, # 694), this substitutes a kneeling guy for the water radical on the left; it retains the platform above lopsided legs and the 木 ki (tree) **CUES:** this guy on the left has **Saga**ciously set up this platform with lopsided legs in this 木 (tree), where he kneels as he uses binoculars to 探す **saga**su (look for) his **Sad Goo**se and where he also works on his **Tan**
ALSO COMPARE: 深(い) fukai = deep, # 694; 採(算) saisan = profit, # 1425; 捜(す) sagasu = to search, # 1520 (usually involving police activity); other similar kanji at # **694**

0700. 改 PRONUNCIATIONS: arata, kai
MEANINGS: to renew, to change **EXAMPLES:** 改める aratameru = to change, correct; 改めて aratamete = again, anew, another time; 改正する kaisei suru = to revise, reform, amend
DESCRIPTION: on the left, 己 onore (self, # 652), which resembles a snake shaped like a backwards "S"; on the right, a dancer with a ponytail **CUES:** the **Ar**ab **Tax** collector on the right, who is a dancer, has gone out to fly her **Ki**te, but 改めて **arata**mete (again) she has encountered this big 己 (snake) on the left
COMPARE: similar kanji at # **1078**

0701. 関 PRONUNCIATIONS: kan, seki, kaka MEANINGS: relating, to connect, checkpoint EXAMPLES: 関係 kankei = relationship; 関する kan suru = to be related to, concerning; 玄関 genkan = front entry; 関所 sekisho = checkpoint; 関わる kakawaru = to be involved
DESCRIPTION: on the top and sides, 門 mon (gate, # 409); inside the gate, an occultist, as seen in 送(る) okuru (to send, # 348)
CUES: this occultist, who wears this hat with two antennae, is thinking of passing through this gate in order to pursue a 関係 **kan**kei (relationship) in **Kan**sas, but she has a **Seki** (cough) and finally decides to **Call a Cab** and return
ALSO COMPARE: other similar kanji at # **348** and # **1755**

0702. 丁 **PRONUNCIATIONS: chou, tei**
MEANING: square block **EXAMPLES:**
丁目 choume = city block, district of a town;
丁寧 teinei = polite, courteous; 丁 tei = counter for guns, tools, leaves or cakes of something
DESCRIPTION: compared to 町(名) choumei (street name, # 70) (identical pronunciation), this kanji omits 田 (paddy) on the left; it retains the nail
CUES: Margaret **Ch**o sold this nail to a 丁寧な **tei**nei na (polite) **T**ailor
GROUP: 町 machi = town, # 70; 歳 sai = age, # 322; 行(く) iku = to go, # 334; 打(つ) utsu = to strike, # 590; (電)灯 dentou = electric light, # 626; (バス)停 basutei = bus stop, # 627; 貯(金) chokin = savings, # 667; 丁 tei = counter for guns, # 702; (丁)寧 teinei = polite, # 703; (登)頂(する) touchou suru = to climb to the summit, # 783; 釘 kugi = nail, # 825; (官)庁 kanchou = government office, # 1444; (料)亭 ryoutei = traditional Japanese restaurant, # 1474; 訂(正) teisei = a correction, # 1950; **Note** that four of these kanji can be pronounced "tei" and two can be pronounced "chou"

0703. 寧 **PRONUNCIATION: nei**
MEANINGS: rather, probably **EXAMPLE:**
丁寧 teinei = polite, courteous **DESCRIPTION:** at the top, a bad haircut; below that, 心 kokoro (heart, # 306); below that, 目 me (eye, # 51) turned horizontally, which could represent three eyes; at the bottom, 丁(目) choume (city block, # 702), which resembles a nail **CUES:** I have a 丁寧 tei**nei** (polite) **N**eighbor with a bad haircut like this one, a good 心 (heart) like this and three eyes like these who tries to live with a small footprint, and therefore he balances his house on this **N**ail
COMPARE: other similar kanji at # **702** and # **1603**

0704. 断 **PRONUNCIATIONS: ta, kotowa, dan** **MEANING:** to cut decisively
EXAMPLES: 断つ tatsu = to cut off, discontinue; 断る kotowaru = to refuse; 中断 chuudan = interruption **DESCRIPTION:** compared to 継(ぐ) tsugu (to inherit, # 635), this omits the skeet shooter on the left and adds a tall pair of pliers on the right; it retains the shelf containing 米 (uncooked rice) **CUES:** this **Ta**ll pair of pliers is blocking access to this shelf full of this 米 (rice) which was intended to be the payment for a koto (Japanese harp), but the **Ko**to is **Wa**rm and covered with **Da**ndruff, and therefore the pliers 断る **kotowa**ru (refuse) to accept it **ALSO COMPARE:** other similar kanji at # **635** and # **892**

0705. 納 **PRONUNCIATIONS: nou, tou, osa, na** **MEANINGS:** accept, deliver, finish
EXAMPLES: 納入 nounyuu = payment of taxes, etc, supply (of goods, etc.), delivery; 出納 suitou = receipts & expenditures; 納める osameru = to pay a bill, to put away (in a closet, etc.), to conclude; this can also be written 収める osameru, # 1113; 納まる osamaru = to be settled or solved; 納得する nattoku suru = to acquiesce, agree
DESCRIPTION: on the left, 糸 skeet shooter (# 219); on the right, 内 uchi (inside, #396), which resembles a 人 (person) emerging from a two-sided lean-to **CUES:** this 糸 (skeet shooter) thinks that he sees either the **No**se or a **To**e of **Osa**ma, who is a **Na**sty man, protruding from 内 (inside) this two-sided lean-to on the right, and he will 納める **osa**meru (conclude) his mission by shooting him with a skeet **ALSO COMPARE:** 治(める) osameru = to govern or reign, # 539; 修(める) osameru = to learn or master, # 1049; other similar kanji at # **397**

0706. 得 **PRONUNCIATIONS: e, u, toku**
MEANING: to gain **EXAMPLES:** 得る eru = to get, earn, understand, receive something; あり得る arieru = it's possible (this can also be pronounced ariuru); なし得る nashieru = to be able to do (this can also be pronounced nashiuru); 得 toku = gain, profit; 得意 tokui = pride, strong

point **DESCRIPTION:** on the left, a man with a double hat; on the upper right, a 日 (sun) above a dance floor, as seen in 旦(那) danna (master, # 668); on the lower right, a 寸 (sunny guy), as seen in 寸(前) sunzen (on the verge, # 1369) **CUES:** this man on the left carries **E**ggs in one of his hats, he thinks that cooking them in this 日 (sun) above this dance floor with this 寸 (sunny guy) is **U**ber and **T**otally **C**ool, and they hope to make a 得 **tok**u (profit) from this activity
COMPARE: other similar kanji at # **131** and # **668**

0707. 賃 **PRONUNCIATION: chin**
MEANINGS: wages, fee, fare **EXAMPLES:** 家賃 yachin = rent; 電車賃 densha chin = train fare **DESCRIPTION:** on the upper left, a man with a slanted hat who is almost falling; on the upper right, 王 ou (king, # 1077); at the bottom, 貝 kai (shell, money chest, # 83) **CUE:** this man on the left tilts his hat back as he gazes at this 王 (king) and demands the 家賃 y**a**chin (rent) for a palace that the king is using, but the king socks him on the **Chin**, and he falls off this money chest
GROUP: 貿(易) boueki = trade, # 85; 質(問) shitsumon = question, # 86; 貸(す) kasu = to lend, # 90; 資(金) shikin = capital, # 91; (家)賃 yachin = rent, # 707; (受)賞(する) jushou suru = to win an award, # 991; (佐)賀(県) sagaken = Saga Prefecture, # 994; 賛(成) sansei = agreement, # 1115; 賢(い) kashikoi = intelligent, # 1290; (硬)貨 kouka = coins, # 1413; 鎖 kusari = a chain, # 1436; (補)償 hoshou = compensation, # 1662; 貪(欲な) don'yoku na = avaricious, # 2034; (来)賓 raihin = a guest, # 2054 **ALSO COMPARE:** kanji with only one distinct radical above 貝 can be seen at # 656; other kanji containing 貝 at # 490, # 772, # 1870, # 1897 and # 2058; other kanji containing 王 (king) at the top at # **1712**

0708. 税 **PRONUNCIATION: zei**
MEANINGS: tax, duty **EXAMPLE:** 税金 zeikin = tax, duty **DESCRIPTION:** compared to (遊)説 yuuzei (election campaign, # 439) (identical pronunciation), this kanji substitutes 禾 (a grain plant with a ripe head) for 言 (to say) on the left; it retains 兄 (older brother) wearing rabbit ears **CUE:** while harvesting this 禾 (ripe grain), 兄 (older brother) put on these rabbit ears and acted **Za**ny, until he realized that he would have to pay 税金 **zei**kin (taxes) on the grain
GROUP: (遊)説 yuuzei = election campaign, # 439; 税(金) zeikin = tax, # 708; 脱(ぐ) nugu = to remove clothes, # 1386; 鋭(い) surudoi = sharp, # 1419; 悦(に入る) etsu ni iru = to be happy, # 1779; (検)閲 ken'etsu = censorship, # 1987 **ALSO COMPARE:** other similar kanji at # **1797**

0709. 氏 **PRONUNCIATIONS: shi, uji**
MEANING: surname **EXAMPLES:** 中村氏 nakamurashi = Mr. Nakamura; 彼氏 kareshi = boyfriend; 氏名 shimei = full name; 氏 uji = clan **DESCRIPTION:** compared to 紙 kami (paper, # 221), or 紙(幣) shihei (paper money, # 221) (identical pronunciation), this kanji omits the skeet shooter on the left; it retains the paper pavilion with a flat roof, which can also be seen as a leaning woman under a lean-to **CUES:** a 氏 **shi** (mister) keeps **S**heep in this 紙 (paper pavilion) and he uses an **U**ber **J**eep to haul them around
ALSO COMPARE: (市)民 shimin = citizen, # 375, which has a *double* roof; other similar kanji at # **1195**

0710. 慌 PRONUNCIATIONS: kou, awa
MEANING: to panic EXAMPLES: 恐慌 kyoukou = a panic; 慌てる awateru = to be confused or panic, to hurry DESCRIPTION: on the left, an erect man; on the upper right, a plant radical; in the upper middle, a shaky table, as seen in 亡(くなる) nakunaru (to die, # 585), which can also be seen as a shaky stool; on the lower right, three lopsided legs CUES: on a **C**old morning, this man on the left was **A**wakened by this guy with three lopsided legs who threw these plants and this shaky stool at him, and first he drew himself up to his full height like this, but then he 慌てた **awa**teta (panicked) GROUP: 流(す) nagasu = to flush, # 654; 慌(てる) awateru = to panic, # 710; 荒(い) arai = violent, # 968; 硫(黄) iou = sulfur, # 2001 ALSO COMPARE: other similar kanji at # **585** and # **2063**

0711. 期 PRONUNCIATIONS: go, ki
MEANINGS: period, to expect EXAMPLES: 末期 matsugo = the hour of death (this can also be pronounced makki); 時期 jiki = time, season; 学期 gakki = semester DESCRIPTION: on the upper left, a bucket as seen in 甘(い) amai (sweet, # 541), but with an additional compartment; on the lower left, a wide skirt as seen in 六 roku (six, # 17); on the right, 月 tsuki (moon, # 148) CUES: when this 月 (moon) is full, it's the 時期 ji**ki** (season) for our **G**oats to play by moonlight, and this woman on the left, who has this bucket with compartments and a wide skirt, makes 甘 (sweet) **Q**uiche from their mi**k** GROUP: 甘(い) amai = sweet, # 541; (時)期 jiki = time, # 711; 箕(面市) Minooshi = a city in Honshu, # 1178; 基(盤) kiban = foundation, # 1198; (国)旗 kokki = national flag, # 1430 (identical pronunciation); (将)棋 shougi = Japanese chess, # 1726; 碁 Go = a Japanese board game, # 1851; (詐)欺 sagi = a fraud, # 1859; 紺(色) kon'iro = navy blue, # 1886

0712. 素 PRONUNCIATIONS: su, *sou, shirou*, so MEANINGS: elementary, principle, uncovered EXAMPLES: 素早い subayai = nimble, speedy; 素麺 soumen (usually spelled そうめん) = fine white noodles; 素人 shirouto = amateur; 要素 youso = component, factor, element; 水素 suiso = hydrogen DESCRIPTION: at the top, an owl's perch, as seen in 青(い) aoi (blue, # 155); at the bottom, 糸 skeet shooter (# 219) CUES: **S**uperman 素早く **su**bayaku (speedily) **S**oared up and dropped this owl's perch onto this 糸 (skeet shooter), but after pulling it off using **S**heepdogs and **R**opes, we **S**old it ALSO COMPARE: other similar kanji at # **1103** and # **1266**

0713. 訪 PRONUNCIATIONS: tazu, otozu, hou MEANING: to visit EXAMPLES: 訪ねる tazuneru = to visit; 訪れる otozureru = to visit or arrive; 訪問する houmon suru = to visit DESCRIPTION: on the left, 言(う) iu (to speak, # 430); on the right, a tall 方 kata (honorable person, # 114), also pronounced 方 hou (direction) (identical pronunciation) CUES: this 方 (honorable person) on the right, who is a **T**all **Z**ookeeper, 言 (speaks) about an **O**toscope that I left at the **Z**oo when he 訪ねる **tazu**neru (visits) my **H**ome ALSO COMPARE: 尋(ねる) tazuneru = to ask, in-quire, search for, # 1512; other similar kanji at # **920**

0714. 加 PRONUNCIATIONS: ka, kuwa
MEANINGS: addition, increase, join, include EXAMPLES: 参加 sanka = participation; 加える kuwaeru = to add or include DESCRIPTION: on the left, 力 chikara (force, # 107), or the katakana 力 ka (identical pronunciation); on the right, 口 kuchi (mouth, # 426), which also resembles a box CUES: a **C**arpenter exerted a lot of 力 (force) to swallow **C**ool **W**ater

through this big 口 (mouth) when he 参加し
た san**ka** shita (cooperated) with some research on
water intoxication **ALSO COMPARE:** other
similar kanji at # **323** and # **1846**

0715. 趣 PRONUNCIATIONS: omomuki, shu

MEANINGS: elegance, grace, charm,
attractive **EXAMPLES:** 趣がある omomuki
ga aru = it's tasteful; 趣味 shumi = hobby, taste
DESCRIPTION: on the lower left, 走(る)
hashiru (to run, # 450); on the upper right, 取(る)
toru (to take, # 58) **CUES:** when I 走 (run) after
alligators and 取 (take) their eggs, I often encounter
Old **M**osquitoes in **M**ucky swamps and lose my
Shoes, but this activity is my 趣味 **shu**mi (hobby)
ALSO COMPARE: 赴(く) omomuku = to go,
1888, which partially helps us to pronounce this;
other similar kanji at # **24**, # **450** and # **1713**

0716. 湖 PRONUNCIATIONS: mizuumi, ko

MEANING: lake **EXAMPLES:** 湖
mizuumi = lake; 湖水 kosui = lake water
DESCRIPTION: on the left, a water radical; in the
middle, 古(い) furui (old, # 392); on the right,
月 tsuki (moon, # 148) **CUES:** this water in a 湖
mizuumi (lake) is connected by a river to the **Mi**zu
(water) in the **U**mi (ocean), and on **C**old nights when
this 月 (moon) is out, I can see reflections of 古
(old) buildings on its surface
ALSO COMPARE: other similar kanji at # **394**

0717. 距 PRONUNCIATION: kyo

MEANING: distance **EXAMPLES:** 距離
kyori = distance, range; 距骨 kyokotsu = talus (the
bone at the top of the foot that supports the tibia)
DESCRIPTION: compared to 巨 kyo (huge,
689) (identical pronunciation), this kanji adds the
止 (hesitant) squarehead seen in 踊(る) odoru (to
dance, # 366); it retains the swing set that a giant
knocked over in Kyoto **CUE:** this 止 (hesitant)
squarehead will carry this swing set to **Kyo**to, which
is a long 距離 **kyo**ri (distance) away

ALSO COMPARE: other similar kanji at # **1246**
and # **1534**

0718. 環 PRONUNCIATION: kan

MEANINGS: circle, round **EXAMPLE:** 環境
kankyou = environment, surroundings
DESCRIPTION: on the left, 王 ou (king, # 1077);
at the upper right, 目 me (eye, # 51) turned
horizontally, which could represent three eyes, above
a platform; at the lower right, a box above a pole
with a handle on the left and two lips on on the right,
which resembles a megaphone, as seen in 遠(い)
tooi (far, # 351) **CUE:** this 王 (king) visited
Kansas, where three eyes like these are common,
and he used this megaphone to address people about
the 環境 **kan**kyou (environment) **GROUP:**
(公)園 kouen = park, # 279; 遠(慮) enryo =
reserve, # 351; 環(境) kankyou = environment,
718; (返)還 henkan = a conversion, # 1587
ALSO COMPARE: other similar kanji at # **1324**
and # **1772**

0719. 境 PRONUNCIATIONS: kyou, sakai, kei

MEANING: boundary **EXAMPLES:**
環境 kankyou = environment, surroundings; 境
sakai = boundary, border; 境内 keidai = the
grounds of a temple **DESCRIPTION:** on the left,
土 tsuchi (soil, # 59); at the upper right, 立(つ)
tatsu (to stand, # 11); at the lower right, 兄 ani (big
brother, # 420), with an additional horizontal line
which represents a scowl; **Note:** this radical on the
lower right is *not* 見(る) miru (# 53), since it only
contains three horizontal lines; it is a 日 (sun) above
lopsided legs
CUES: if you cross this 土 (soil) 境 **sakai**
(boundary) in **Kyou**to, a 兄 (big brother) with a
scowl like this who is 立 (standing) guard may
Sock you in the **E**ye and put you in a **C**age
GROUP: (環)境 kankyou = environment, # 719;
鏡 kagami = mirror, # 1355 **ALSO COMPARE:**
other similar kanji at # **266** and # **1355**

0720. 恵 **PRONUNCIATIONS: e, megu, kei** **MEANINGS:** blessing, grace **EXAMPLES:** 知恵 chie = wisdom, intelligence, idea; 恵む megumu = to bless, show mercy, give money, etc.; 恩恵 onkei = favor, benefit **DESCRIPTION:** at the top, too 十 (ten, # 18); at the bottom, 思(う) omou (to think, # 308) which includes 田 (rice paddy) and 心 (heart) **CUES:** after gathering 十 (ten) **E**ggs, a **M**exican **G**oose and a **Ca**ke for our meal, we 思 (think) that we 恵まれている **megu**marete iru (are being blessed) **GROUP:** 恵(む) megumu = to bless, # 720; 専(門) senmon = specialty, # 1235 **ALSO COMPARE:** kanji containing a rice paddy on a stick at # 1157; kanji containing a rice paddy *above* 十 (ten) at # 1694; other similar kanji at # **308**

0721. 豆 **PRONUNCIATIONS: mame, zu, *zuki*, tou** **MEANING:** bean **EXAMPLES:** 豆 mame = bean; 大豆 daizu = soybean; 小豆 azuki = red bean; 豆腐 toufu = bean curd **DESCRIPTION:** compared to 登(録) touroku (registration, # 297) (identical pronunciation), this kanji omits the bench hats at the top; it retains the TV set under a napkin, resting on two toes supported by a base, which can also be seen as an upside-down bench **CUES:** some **Ma**d **M**en (i.e., those who work on Madison Avenue as advertisers) watch this TV set with a napkin draped across the top, at a **Zo**o with a **Zo**okeeper, supporting it with these **To**es and watching the advertisements that they have created for 豆 **mame** (bean) products **GROUP:** 頭 atama = head, # 93, in which we describe 豆 as a square head on a stand covered by a napkin; 登(録) touroku = registration, # 297; 短(い) mijikai = short, # 324; 喜(ぶ) yorokobu = to be delighted, # 599; 嬉(しい) ureshii = pleased, # 600; 豆 mame = bean, # 721; (奮)闘 funtou = hard struggle, # 728; 樹(木) jumoku = trees, # 1089; 豊(か) yutaka = rich, # 1321; 澄(む) sumu = to become clear, # 1674; (太)鼓 taiko = a drum, # 1776; (天然)痘 tennentou = smallpox, # 2070 (identical pronunciation) **ALSO COMPARE:** other similar kanji at # **2070**

0722. 腐 **PRONUNCIATIONS: kusa, fu** **MEANINGS:** rot, decay, sour **EXAMPLES:** 腐る kusaru = to rot, spoil, be corrupted; 豆腐 toufu = bean curd **DESCRIPTION:** at the upper left, a lean-to, which could be a restaurant, with a chimney; under the roof, 付(く) tsuku (to adhere, # 132); on the ground floor, 肉 niku (meat, # 397) which resembles two 人 (people) emerging from a two-sided lean-to **CUES:** we were eating a **Coo**l **Sa**lad in this restaurant when we noticed that this 肉 (meat) that was 付 (adhering) to this ceiling was beginning to 腐る **kusa**ru (spoil), and we warned the owners about their **F**ood storage practices **COMPARE:** (政)府 seifu = government, # 1004 (identical pronunciation); other similar kanji at # **397** and # **1004**

0723. 孤 **PRONUNCIATION: ko** **MEANINGS:** orphan, alone **EXAMPLES:** 孤独 kodoku = solitude, isolation; 孤児 koji = orphan **DESCRIPTION:** on the left, 子 ko (child, # 182) (identical pronunciation); on the right, 爪 tsume (nail, claw, # 647), with a hammer on the ground just below it **CUES:** this 子 **Ko** (child) lives in 孤独 **ko**doku (isolation) and uses this hammer and his long 爪 (nails) like this to open ears of **Co**rn **GROUP:** 爪 tsume = nail, claw, # 647; 孤(児) koji = orphan, # 723; (括)弧 kakko = a parenthesis, # 1763 (identical pronunciation) **ALSO COMPARE:** other similar kanji at # **2078**

0724. 独 **PRONUNCIATION: doku** **MEANINGS:** alone, single **EXAMPLES:** 孤独 kodoku = solitude, isolation; 独立 dokuritsu = independence; 独身 dokushin = single, unmarried **DESCRIPTION:** on the left, a woman contorting her body, as seen in 猫 neko (cat, # 72); on the right, 虫 mushi (insect, # 9) **CUE:** I saw a

Documentary about this woman who lives in 孤独 ko**doku** (isolation) because she is fond of 虫 (insects) like this and contorts herself for them ALSO COMPARE: other similar kanji at # **948** and # **1754**

0725. 軍 PRONUNCIATION: gun
MEANINGS: military, army EXAMPLES: 軍人 gunjin = soldier; 海軍 kaigun = navy; 陸軍 rikugun = army; 将軍 shougun = Shogun DESCRIPTION: compared to 運 hakobu (to carry, # 354), this omits the snail at the lower left; it retains 車 kuruma (car, # 283), covered with a lid which can function as armor CUE: 軍人 **gun**jin (soldiers) 運 (carry) **Gun**s, and they ride in 車 (cars) covered with armor like this one ALSO COMPARE: other similar kanji at # **1966** and # **2075**

0726. 隊 PRONUNCIATION: tai
MEANINGS: regiment, party, squad EXAMPLES: 軍隊 guntai = army; 兵隊 heitai = soldier DESCRIPTION: on the left, ß beta from the Greek alphabet; on the right, this resembles 家 ie (house, # 405), without the bad haircut, but a pair of rabbit ears that a tiger is wearing are projecting from the top CUE: a ß (Greek) 軍隊 gun**tai** (army) keeps a **T**iger as a pet in this 家 (house), and its ears protrude from the roof ALSO COMPARE: other similar kanji at # **1504**, # **1972** and # **2030**

0727. 奮 PRONUNCIATION: fun
MEANINGS: to muster up strength or be invigorated EXAMPLES: 興奮 koufun = excitement; 奮闘 funtou = hard struggle, strenuous effort DESCRIPTION: at the top, an extra-wide 大(きい) ookii (big, # 188); in the middle, a net, which can be seen as a man with a slanted hat next to a 主 (master) with an extra pair of arms (see # 203); at the bottom, 田 (rice paddy, # 68) CUE: a 大 (big) guy dropped this net into this 田 (rice paddy), causing some 興奮 kou**fun** (excitement), and we had **Fun** trying to fish it out

GROUP: (興)奮 koufun = excitement, # 727; 奪(う) ubau = to rob, # 1568 ALSO COMPARE: other similar kanji at # **220**

0728. 闘 PRONUNCIATIONS: tou, tataka
MEANINGS: fight, war EXAMPLES: 奮闘 funtou = hard struggle, strenuous effort; 闘う tatakau = to fight, make war (usually written 戦う, # 933, which is the more common spelling) DESCRIPTION: on the sides, 門 mon (gate, # 409); inside the gate, on the left, 豆 mame (bean, # 721); on the right, the sunny kneeling guy seen in 寸(前) sunzen (on the verge, # 1369) CUES: these 豆 (beans) in this 門 (gate) 付 (stick) to the **To**es of this 寸 (sunny kneeling guy), and a **T**all **T**axi driver with a **C**ar will go through a 奮闘 fun**tou** (hard struggle) to clean them up ALSO COMPARE: other similar kanji at # **131**, # **721**, # **1755** and # **2070**

0729. 担 PRONUNCIATIONS: nina, tan, katsu
MEANING: to carry (a burden) EXAMPLES: 担う ninau = to carry or bear; 担当 tantou = charge (duty); 担ぐ katsugu = to carry on one's shoulder DESCRIPTION: compared to 旦(那) danna (husband, # 668), or (一)旦 ittan (once, # 668) (identical pronunciation), this kanji adds a kneeling person, who may represent Nancy Pelosi, on the left; it retains the 日 (sun) above a dance floor, where a husband can get a tan CUES: this **K**neeling **Na**ncy on the left has this 旦 (husband), who has a nice **Tan** and 担当す る **tan**tou suru (takes charge of) their **C**ats ALSO COMPARE: other similar kanji at # **668**

0730. 端 PRONUNCIATIONS: **tan, hashi, pashi², pa, bata** MEANINGS: edge, origin EXAMPLES: 万端 ban**tan** = all, everything; 端 **hashi** = end, edge, border; 端くれ **hashi**kure = a scrap or piece, an unimportant person; 片っ端 katap**pashi** = one side, one edge; 半端 han**pa** = insufficient, incomplete, insincere; 道端 michi**bata** = the roadside DESCRIPTION: on the left, 立(つ) tatsu (to stand, # 11); at the upper right, 山 yama (mountain, # 146); at the lower right, the front of a limousine, with a vertically oriented grille and an antenna on the roof CUES: I 立 (stand) below this 山 (mountain) and admire this limousine, which looks as strong as a **Tan**k but is actually patched together with **Hashi** (chopsticks), and I wonder whether 万端 ban**tan** (all) of my friends will be able fit inside of it when we take it to a **Pa**rty at a **Ba**rcelona **Ta**vern ALSO COMPARE: other similar kanji at # **11**, # **522** and # **1385**

0731. 固 PRONUNCIATIONS: **ko, kata** MEANINGS: solid, firm EXAMPLES: 頑固 gan**ko** = stubborn; 固定する **ko**tei suru = to rivet, fix, stabilize; 固体 **ko**tai = solid; 固い **kata**i = hard, firm, upright (this can sometimes be spelled 堅い, # 1246, or 硬い, # 1412); 固める **kata**meru = to harden, solidify, strengthen DESCRIPTION: compared to 個(人) **ko**jin (individual, # 395) (identical pronunciation), this kanji omits the man with a slanted hat; it retains 古 (old) inside a box CUES: I keep an 古 (old) **Co**debook and a **Ca**talogue in this box, which is made of 固体 **ko**tai (solid) plastic ALSO COMPARE: other similar kanji at # **395**

0732. 緊 PRONUNCIATION: **kin** MEANING: tight EXAMPLE: 緊張 **kin**chou = tension DESCRIPTION: at the upper left, 巨 kyo (huge, # 689), which resembles a child's swing set turned on its side, but the swing ropes have been tied on both sides to make the swing inoperable; at the upper right, 又 mata (again, # 24), which resembles a simple table; at the bottom, a 糸 skeet shooter (# 219) CUE: this 糸 (skeet shooter) is trying to juggle this inoperable 巨 (swing set) and this 又 (table) at a **Kin**dergarten, and there is a lot of 緊張 **kin**chou (tension) among the onlooking teachers ALSO COMPARE: other similar kanji at # **24**, # **1246** and # **1266**

0733. 愉 PRONUNCIATION: **yu** MEANINGS: pleasure, happy EXAMPLES: 愉快 **yu**kai = pleasant, cheerful; 不愉快 fu**yu**kai = unpleasant DESCRIPTION: compared to 輸(入する) **yu**'nyuu suru (to import, # 288) (identical pronunciation), this substitues an erect man for the 車 (car) on the left; it retains 前 mae (before), modified to look like a house CUE: this man owned this 愉快 **yu**kai (pleasant) house in the **Yu**kon 前 (before), but the place where he lives now is 不愉快 fu**yu**kai (unpleasant), and he raises himself to his full height to show disapproval GROUP: 輸(入する) **yu**'nyuu suru = to import, # 288; 愉(快) **yu**kai = pleasant, # 733; 癒(す) i**yu**su = to heal, # 1293; 諭す sato**su** = to warn, # 1932 ALSO COMPARE: other similar kanji at # **2063**

0734. 快 PRONUNCIATIONS: **kokoroyo, kai** MEANINGS: pleasant, cheerful EXAMPLES: 快い **kokoroyo**i = pleasant, comfortable; 愉快 yu**kai** = pleasant, cheerful; 全快する zen**kai** suru = to recover completely (from illness) DESCRIPTION: compared to 決(める) kimeru (to arrange, # 180), this substitutes an erect man for the water radical on the left; it retains the tiller on the right, which can also be seen as a single eye on a stand CUES: this man on the left stands tall and proud because he knows that he is training his **Kokoro** (heart) with **Yo**ga, and he is usually 愉快 yu**kai** (cheerful) and often 決 (arranges) to fly **Ki**tes ALSO COMPARE: other similar kanji at # **180**, # **1808** and # **2063**

0735. 札 **PRONUNCIATIONS: fuda, sa, satsu MEANINGS:** paper money, posted note **EXAMPLES:** 値札 nefuda = price tag; 札幌 Sapporo = a city in Hokkaido; 千円札 sen'en satsu = 1,000 yen bill **DESCRIPTION:** on the left, 木 ki (tree, # 118); on the right, L, which resembles a breast, as seen in 乳 nyuu (milk, # 186)
CUES: a **Fo**olish **Da**d needs some 札 **sa**tsu (bank notes), so he pawns his **Sa**xophone while mom nurses their baby at this breast next to this 木 (tree) and reads a **Sat**isfying **Su**perman novel
GROUP: 乳 nyuu = milk, # 186; (お)礼 orei = gratitude, # 275; 札(幌) Sapporo = a city, # 735; 乱(暴) ranbou = violent, # 1020; 孔(子) koushi = Confucius, # 2078

0736. 鳩 **PRONUNCIATION: hato**
MEANINGS: pigeon, dove **EXAMPLES:** 鳩 hato = pigeon, dove **DESCRIPTION:** on the left, 九 kyuu (nine, # 111); on the right, 鳥 tori (bird, # 555) **CUE:** these 九 (nine) 鳥 (birds) are 鳩 **hato** (pigeons), and they eat **Ha**m and **To**ast **ALSO COMPARE:** other similar kanji at # **754** and # **827**

0737. 艦 **PRONUNCIATION: kan**
MEANING: warship **EXAMPLE:** 軍艦 gunkan = warship, battleship **DESCRIPTION:** on the left, a radical seen in fune 船 (boat, # 602) which depicts a boat that is missing its stern; on the upper right, an inoperable swing set lying on its side, as seen in 緊(張) kinchou (tension, # 732), but this can be seen as two cannons, and the horizontal lines to the right can be seen as a crutch and a cannon shell; at the lower right, 皿 sara (dish, # 567)
CUE: this 船 (boat) is equipped with two **Ca**nnons firing these crutches and shells, and it appears to be a 軍艦 gun**kan** (battleship) fighting over this 皿 (dish) **ALSO COMPARE:** other similar kanji at # **1310**, # **1407** and # **1524**

0738. 砲 **PRONUNCIATIONS: hou, pou**
MEANINGS: cannon, gun **EXAMPLES:** 鉄砲 teppou = gun; 大砲 taihou = cannon; 砲火 houka = gunfire **DESCRIPTION:** compared to 包(送) housou (wrapping, # 548) (identical pronunciation), this kanji adds 石 ishi (stone, # 458) on the left; it retains the J-shaped packaging (which can also be seen as a hook) used to wrap a 己 (snake-like object)
CUES: a **Ho**bo in **Po**land 包 (wrapped) this 石 (stone) in cloth and used a 大砲 tai**hou** (cannon) to fire it toward me, so I shot at him with a 鉄砲 tep**pou** (gun) **ALSO COMPARE:** other similar kanji at # **1775** and # **1861**

0739. 現 **PRONUNCIATIONS: gen, arawa MEANINGS:** present, actual **EXAMPLES:** 現実 genjitsu = reality, fact; 現在 genzai = present time; 現金 genkin = cash; 現れる arawareru = to appear or to show up **DESCRIPTION:** on the left, ou 王 (king, # 1077); on the right, 見(る) miru (to watch, # 53) **CUES:** this 王 (king) is named **Gen**ghis, and he tells an **A**rab **W**arrior to 見 (watch) his horse in return for some 現金 **gen**kin (cash) **ALSO COMPARE:** other similar kanji at # **1341** and # **1772**

0740. 漏 **PRONUNCIATIONS: mo, rou**
MEANINGS: leak, escape
EXAMPLES: 漏らす morasu = to let out, to omit; 漏電 rouden = electrical short circuit; 漏水 rousui = water leak **DESCRIPTION:** on the left, a water radical; in the center, a lean-to with a double roof; inside the lean-to, 雨 ame (rain, # 261) **CUES: Mo**ses lived in this lean-to with a double roof, but after this 雨 (rain) penetrated inside and this water accumulated outside, he had to 漏らす **mo**rasu (let out) some water and, when that failed, **Ro**w his boat to safety **ALSO COMPARE:** other similar kanji at # **262** and # **1899**

0741. 根 PRONUNCIATIONS: ne, kon
MEANINGS: root, radical
EXAMPLES: 屋根 yane = roof; 木の根 kinone = tree root; 根拠 konkyo = source or basis (of reasoning, etc.) DESCRIPTION: on the left, a 木 ki (tree, # 118); on the right, 良(い) yoi (good, # 303), which contains L & Y at its base, without its pointy hat
CUES: this 良 (good) 木 (tree) is the 根拠 konkyo (foundation) of the materials that we use to make the 屋根 yane (roofs) that we sell in the Netherlands and the Congo
ALSO COMPARE: other similar kanji at # **805**

0742. 棚 PRONUNCIATIONS: tana, dana MEANINGS: shelf, ledge, rack
EXAMPLES: 棚 tana = shelf; 戸棚 todana = cupboard DESCRIPTION: on the left, 木 ki (wood, # 118); on the right, two 月 tsuki (moons, # 148) CUES: a cowboy in Mon**Tana** who wears a ban**Dana** had a surplus of these 月 (moons), so he used 木 (wood) to build a 棚 **tana** (shelf) on which to store them GROUP: 棚 tana = shelf, # 742; 崩(れる) kuzureru = to collapse, # 973

0743. 餅 PRONUNCIATIONS: mochi, bei MEANING: mochi rice cake EXAMPLES: 餅 mochi = Japanese rice cake; 煎餅 senbei = rice cracker DESCRIPTION: on the left, a simplified version of 食(べる) taberu (to eat, # 398); on the right, a research tower, as seen in 研(究) kenkyuu (research, # 442), wearing rabbit ears CUES: a researcher is celebrating the New Year by putting these rabbit ears on this research tower, and he wants to 食 (eat) **M**ore **Ch**eese with his 餅 **mochi** (Japanese rice cake), so he asks a **B**aker to add some GROUP: 餅 mochi = Japanese rice cake, # 743; (合)併 gappei = a merger, # 1655; 塀 hei = a fence, # 1850
ALSO COMPARE: other similar kanji at # **573** and # **1974**

0744. 銭 PRONUNCIATIONS: sen, zeni
MEANINGS: small change, coins
EXAMPLES: 金銭 kinsen = money; 一銭 issen = 0.01 yen; 小銭 kozeni = coin, small change DESCRIPTION: compared to 残(る) nokoru (to remain, # 605), this substitutes (黄)金 ougon (gold, # 301) for the nightcap on the left; it retains the halberd with a triple grip CUES: our **Sen**ator thought that **Zen** was **E**asy and that one doesn't need 金 (gold) like this and halberds like this to attain enlightenment, so he didn't bring any 金銭 kin**sen** (money) to his first temple visit
ALSO COMPARE: similar kanji at # **605** and # **2010**

0745. 舎 PRONUNCIATIONS: *ka*, sha
MEANING: house EXAMPLES: 田舎 inaka = rural area, hometown; 校舎 kousha = school building DESCRIPTION: compared to 捨(てる) suteru (to throw away, # 594), this omits the kneeling person on the left; it retains 土 (soil) on a 口 (box) under a roof CUES: a **C**arpenter came from the 田舎 ina**ka** (countryside), where he lived in this **Sh**a**bb**y house containing this 土 (soil) and this 口 (box) GROUP: 捨(てる) suteru = to throw away, # 594; (田)舎 inaka = hometown, # 745; 舗(装) hosou = pavement, # 1237

0746. 叫 PRONUNCIATIONS: sake, kyou MEANINGS: shout, exclaim
EXAMPLES: 叫ぶ sakebu = to shout, yell, scream; 絶叫 zekkyou = a scream or shriek
DESCRIPTION: on the left, 口 kuchi (mouth, # 426), which also resembles a box; on the right, this resembles the number 4 CUES: after drinking 4 bottles of **Sake** in **Kyou**to, I opened this 口 (mouth), and a 絶叫 zek**kyou** (scream) emerged GROUP: 叫(ぶ) sakebu = to shout, # 746; 収(入) shuunyuu = income, # 1113; 糾(問) kyuumon = an enquiry, # 2029 ALSO COMPARE: other similar kanji at # **2073**

0747. 血 **PRONUNCIATIONS: ketsu, chi, ji, ke** **MEANING:** blood **EXAMPLES:** 血圧 ketsuatsu = blood pressure; 血 chi = blood; 鼻血 hanaji = a nosebleed; 血管 kekkan = blood vessel **DESCRIPTION:** 皿 sara (dish, # 567), with a line above it; together, these may represent a drop of ketchup being added to a dish of soup **CUES:** when I add this **Ket**chup to the **S**oup in this 皿 (dish), or to my **Chee**rios, I'm careful not to spill it in my **J**eep or on my **Ke**ds (a brand of shoes), and I'm reminded of the 血 **chi** (blood) that was formerly offered to the gods as part of religious rites **ALSO COMPARE:** other similar kanji at # **1407**

0748. 圧 **PRONUNCIATIONS: atsu, a** **MEANINGS:** to press, pressure **EXAMPLES:** 血圧 ketsuatsu = blood pressure; 気圧 kiatsu = atmospheric pressure; 圧力 atsuryoku = pressure; 圧倒的 attouteki = overwhelming **DESCRIPTION:** at the upper left, a one-sided lean-to; at the lower right, 土 tsuchi (soil, # 59) **CUES:** this lean-to **At S**uperman's house was designed by an **A**rchitect, but this 土 (soil) is putting a lot of 圧力 **atsu**ryoku (pressure) on the walls **GROUP:** 座る suwaru = to sit, # 497; 圧(力) atsuryoku = pressure, # 748; 崖 gake = cliff, # 911; (現)在 genzai = nowadays, # 1014; (化)粧 keshou = cosmetics, # 1387; (生)涯 shougai = one's lifetime, # 1682

0749. 抜 **PRONUNCIATIONS: ba, batsu, nu** **MEANINGS:** to extract, pull out, omit **EXAMPLES:** 抜てきする batteki suru = to select; 人気抜群 ninkibatsugun = very popular; 抜く nuku = to extract, omit, outrun, skip, to do something to the end; 抜ける nukeru = to come off, fall out, escape, go through, lack; 抜きに nuki ni = without (omitting) **DESCRIPTION:** compared to 友(達) tomodachi (friend, # 459), this adds a kneeling guy on the left; it retains the friend hugging a 又 (table) **CUES:** this guy on the left is on his knees acting **Bat**ty, and he and this 友 (friend) run around in **Bat S**uits, threatening people with **Noo**ses, so it might be best to 抜く **nu**ku (extract) our citizens from their vicinity **ALSO COMPARE:** other similar kanji at # **459** and # **1389**

0750. 焦 **PRONUNCIATIONS: ase, ko, shou** **MEANINGS:** hurry, impatient, burn, scorch **EXAMPLES:** 焦る aseru = to be in a hurry, be impatient, anxious & eager; 焦げる kogeru = to be scorched or burned; 焦点 shouten = focus, central issue **DESCRIPTION:** at the top, a net, as seen in 集(める) atsumeru = to collect, # 202 and which can be seen as a man with a slanted hat next to a 主 (master) with an extra pair of arms; at the bottom, four vertical lines suggesting fire **CUES:** if **Ass**es (donkeys) in **Co**lombia are put into this net and suspended over this fire as part of a **Sh**ow, you can be sure that they will 焦る **ase**ru (be eager) to escape before they 焦げる **ko**geru (get burned) **ALSO COMPARE:** other similar kanji at # **611** and # **2046**

0751. 鳴 **PRONUNCIATIONS: na, mei** **MEANINGS:** chirp, bark, honk **EXAMPLES:** 鳴る naru = to chime, ring, sound; 鳴く naku = to chirp, bark, cry (animal sounds); 悲鳴 himei = scream, shriek, cry of distress **DESCRIPTION:** on the left, 口 kuchi (mouth, # 426), which also resembles a box; on the right, 鳥 tori (bird, # 555) **CUES:** this 鳥 (bird) serves as a lookout for some **Na**rcos, and it uses this 口 (mouth) to 鳴く **na**ku (chirp) when their **M**ail arrives **ALSO COMPARE:** other similar kanji at # **754** and # **2073**

0752. 組 **PRONUNCIATIONS:** so, ku, kumi, gumi **MEANINGS:** group, to braid **EXAMPLES:** 組織 soshiki = organization; 組む kumu = to assemble, unite, pair, fold (arms or legs), make (a plan); 組 kumi (or gumi) = group, team, school class; 番組 bangumi = TV or radio program **DESCRIPTION:** on the left, a 糸 skeet shooter (# 219); on the right, a solar panel, as seen in 祖(父) sofu (grandfather, # 272) (identical pronunciation) **CUES:** this **So**lar panel will provide electricity to mix the **Koo**l-Aid for a **Coo**l **Mee**ting organized by a 組 **ku**mi (group) of 糸 (skeet shooters) like this, who will shoot **Gum**my snacks into the crowd
GROUP: 助(ける) tasukeru = to help, # 108; 祖(父) sofu = grandfather, # 272; 組(む) kumu = to assemble, # 752; (調)査 chousa = investigation, # 860; 畳 tatami = tatami mat, # 876; 狙(う) nerau = to aim, # 948; 粗(末) somatsu = shabby, # 1326; 阻(害) sogai = an obstruction, # 1838; (便)宜 bengi = convenience, #1903; and 租(税) sozei = taxation, # 2015; **Note** that four of these kanji can be pronounced "so"

0753. 織 **PRONUNCIATIONS:** ori, o, shiki **MEANING:** to weave **EXAMPLES:** 羽織 haori = short jacket worn over kimono; 織る oru = to weave; 組織 soshiki = organization **DESCRIPTION:** compared to 職(業) shokugyou (occupation, # 696), this substitutes 糸 skeet shooter (# 219) for 耳 (ear) on the left; it retains 音 (sound) and the halberd **CUES:** this 糸 (skeet shooter) is shooting at a 組織 so**shiki** (**o**rganization) of **O**riental **O**rthodontists who buy **Sh**eep in **K**iev and work on their teeth with halberds like this, and that is the source of this plaintive 音 (sound)
GROUP: 職(業) shokugyou = occupation, # 696; 織(る) oru = to weave, # 753; (知)識 chishiki = knowledge, # 1335 (identical pronunciation) which

substitutes 言 (to say) on the left **ALSO COMPARE:** other similar kanji at # **266**

0754. 鶏 **PRONUNCIATIONS:** niwatori, kei **MEANING:** chicken **EXAMPLES:** 鶏 niwatori = chicken; 鶏肉 keiniku = chicken meat **DESCRIPTION:** at the upper left, a barbecue grate; at the lower left, 夫 otto (husband, # 614); on the right, 鳥 tori (bird, # 555) **CUES:** in the **Ni**wa (garden), a 鳥 **To**ri (bird) was barbecued by this 夫 (husband) on a grate like this, and it was a 鶏 **niwatori** (chicken) that he kept in a **Ca**ge
GROUP: 鳥 tori = bird, # 555; 島 shima = island, # 556; 鳩 hato = pigeon, # 736; 鳴(る) naru = to ring, # 751; 鶏 niwatori = chicken, # 754; (推)薦 (する) suisen suru = to recommend, # 1030; 為 (に) tame ni = in order to, # 1222; 鶴 tsuru = a crane, # 1609; (虚)偽 kyogi = a lie, # 1622 **ALSO COMPARE:** other similar kanji at # **1177** and # **1915**

0755. 羽 **PRONUNCIATIONS:** hane, ha, wa, u **MEANINGS:** feather, counter for birds & rabbits **EXAMPLES:** 羽 hane = feather, wing; 羽織 haori = short jacket worn over kimono; 一羽 ichiwa = one bird; 羽毛 umou = down, feathers **DESCRIPTION:** two feathers, as seen in the lower half of 弱(い) yowai (weak, # 471) **CUES:** at **Ha**neda airport, I saw these two **hane** 羽 (feathers) in the **Ha**t of a **Wa**rrior who was driving an **U**ber car
ALSO COMPARE: other similar kanji at # **1457**

0756. 演 **PRONUNCIATION:** en **MEANING:** to perform **EXAMPLES:** 演奏 ensou = musical performance; 演じる enjiru = to perform or act **DESCRIPTION:** on the left, a water radical; at the upper right, a bad haircut; in the middle right, a model of a 田 (rice paddy, # 68) connected to a handle; at the lower right, a pair of legs **CUE:** actors with bad haircuts like this 演じる **en**jiru (perform) and **En**tertain us on sets which

include water like this and models of 田 (rice paddies) that are connected to handles like this and attached to legs like these
COMPARE: other similar kanji at # **77** and # **135**

0757. 奏 **PRONUNCIATIONS: kana, sou**
MEANING: to play music **EXAMPLES:** 奏でる kanaderu = to play a stringed instrument; 演奏 ensou = musical performance; 伴奏 bansou = musical accompaniment
DESCRIPTION: compared to 春 haru (spring, # 506), this substitutes 天 ten (sky, # 189) for the 日 (sun) at the bottom; it retains 人 (person) with 三 (three) inscribed across her body
CUES: these 三 (three) 人 (people) gave 演奏 en**sou** (musical performances) under this open 天 (sky) in **Can**ada, featuring **Sou**l music
ALSO COMPARE: other similar kanji at # **506** and # **1811**

0758. 描 **PRONUNCIATIONS: ega, byou, ka** **MEANINGS:** to draw or paint, to depict or describe **EXAMPLES:** 描く egaku = to draw, paint, depict, describe; 描写する byousha suru = to describe; 描く kaku = to draw, paint, depict, describe; **Note:** kaku and egaku are both spelled 描く **DESCRIPTION:** compared to 猫 neko (cat, # 72), this substitutes a kneeling guy for the contorted woman on the left; it retains the 田 (rice paddy) under the plants **CUES:** this guy on the left kneels to make raw eggs into paint next to this 田 (rice paddy) under these plants, and he will 描く **ka**ku (paint) the scene using a technique called **Egg Art** and sell his work to a **B**eerhall **O**wner in **Ca**lifornia **COMPARE:** 書(く) kaku = to write, # 415; other similar kanji at # **1740**

0759. 完 **PRONUNCIATION: kan**
MEANINGS: perfect, completion, end
EXAMPLES: 完了する kanryou suru = to finish; 完成する kansei suru = to complete, accomplish; 完全な kanzen na = perfect, entire
DESCRIPTION: compared to (病)院 byouin (hospital, # 424), this omits the ß (Greek) doctor on the left; it retains the bad haircut and 元 (base)
CUE: in **Kan**sas, a man with a bad haircut like this operates from a strong 元 (base) like this and 完了する **kan**ryou suru (finishes) his projects
COMPARE: 宗(教) shuukyou = religion, # 676, which rests on a *spinning pavilion*; other similar kanji at # **421**

0760. 了 **PRONUNCIATION: ryou**
MEANINGS: to complete, finish **EXAMPLES:** 終了 shuuryou = ending, termination; 完了する kanryou suru = to finish; 了解 ryoukai = agreement, understanding; 了承 ryoushou = acknowledgement, understanding
DESCRIPTION: compared to 子 ko (child, # 182), this kanji lacks arms **CUE:** Pope **Leo** was born without arms, but his 了承 **ryou**shou (understanding) was profound from the beginning
GROUP: 了(承) ryoushou = understanding, # 760; 蒸(気) jouki = vapor, steam, # 1101

0761. 純 **PRONUNCIATION: jun**
MEANING: pure
EXAMPLES: 純粋な junsui na = pure, pure-blooded, genuine; 単純な tanjun na = simple
DESCRIPTION: on the left, a 糸 (skeet shooter, # 219); on the right, 七 nana (seven, # 20) with the letter U superimposed on it; this reminds us of the seven **U**niversal **L**aws
CUE: this 糸 (skeet shooter) is shooting at these 七 (seven) **U**niversal **L**aws because he thinks that they are too 単純 tan**jun** (simple) to ensure survival in a **Jun**gle
COMPARE: other similar kanji at # **1245**

0762. 格 **PRONUNCIATIONS: kou, kaku, ka** **MEANINGS:** status, rank, capacity, character **EXAMPLES:** 格子 koushi = lattice work or grill; 合格する goukaku suru = to pass an exam or be accepted to a school; 性格 seikaku = personality, disposition; 格好 kakkou = form, appearance, suitability (**Note:** the related phrase "kakko ii" = stylish or attractive and is usually written かっこいい or カッコイイ)
DESCRIPTION: compared to (連)絡(する) renraku suru (to contact, # 230), this substitutes 木 ki (tree) for 糸 (skeet shooter) on the left; it retains the dancer jumping over a box
CUES: when this dancer visited a **C**ourthouse, she saw **K**arl the **K**ool-Aid vendor hiding in this 木 (tree), and she expressed her dislike for his 性格 sei**kaku** (personality) by jumping over this box and driving off in her **C**ar
ALSO COMPARE: other similar kanji at # **129** and # **1033**

0763. 姿 **PRONUNCIATIONS: sugata, shi** **MEANINGS:** figure, form **EXAMPLES:** 姿 sugata = figure, shape, condition; 容姿 youshi = appearance, looks; 姿勢 shisei = posture, stance **DESCRIPTION:** at the top, 次 tsugi (next, # 536), which consists of a water radical next to an oil derrick (see # 399); at the bottom, 女 onna (female, # 235)
CUES: this 女 (female) has diabetes and worries about what will happen 次 (next) if her blood sugar gets too low, so she keeps **S**ugar **T**ablets handy, runs with her **S**heep, and maintains a good body 姿 **sugata** (shape)
ALSO COMPARE: other similar kanji at # **536** and # **2086**

0764. 派 **PRONUNCIATIONS: ha, pa** **MEANINGS:** faction, to split, to stand out **EXAMPLES:** 派遣する haken suru = to send (a person), to dispatch; 派手 hade = showy, gaudy, colorful; 立派な rippa na = splendid, impressive **DESCRIPTION:** on the left, a water radical; in the middle, a one-sided lean-to; on the lower right, a radical seen in 旅 tabi (trip, # 116), which appears to be a person stepping out on a journey **CUES:** **P**rince **H**arry has been 派遣された **ha**ken sareta (sent) on a 旅 (trip) by his **Pa** (father), and he is waiting for a boat in this lean-to by this water
ALSO COMPARE: other similar kanji at # **116**

0765. 遣 **PRONUNCIATIONS: ken, tsuka, zuka²** **MEANINGS:** dispatch, send, give, do **EXAMPLES:** 派遣する haken suru = to send (a person), to dispatch; 遣わす tsukawasu = to dispatch; 気遣う kizukau = to care for, worry, pay attention
DESCRIPTION: on the lower left, a snail; at the upper right, 中 naka (inside, # 8) on a platform; at the lower right, a bunk bed being carried on the snail
CUES: Ken 遣わす **tsuka**wasu (dispatches) **B**arbie on a trip aboard this snail, where she will sleep in the bottom bunk and keep her **T**suitcase (suitcase) **C**arry-on above this platform 中 (inside) the top bunk **COMPARE:** 遺(産) isan = inheritance, # 1037; other similar kanji at # **657** and # **880**

0766. 浜 **PRONUNCIATIONS: hama, hin** **MEANINGS:** seacoast, beach **EXAMPLES:** 浜辺 hamabe = beach; 海浜 kaihin = seaside **DESCRIPTION:** on the left, a water radical; on the right, a pair of pliers on a platform with legs, but these resemble a lifeguard's chair on a stand
CUES: a lifeguard bought some **H**am at the **M**all and ate it in this chair near this water at the 海浜 kai**hin** (seaside), but seabird attacks **H**indered his enjoyment of the meal
COMPARE: 兵(隊) heitai = soldier, # 917; other similar kanji at # **892**

0767. 凧 **PRONUNCIATION: tako**
MEANING: kite **EXAMPLE:** 凧 tako = kite **DESCRIPTION:** the continuous line extending from the lower left to the lower right suggests wind, as seen in 風 kaze (wind, # 479); it can also be seen as a two-sided leant-to; under this line stands 巾 (**B**o **P**eep), the spinning lady seen in 帽(子)

boushi (hat, # 243) **CUE:** 巾 (Bo Peep) eats **Ta**cos while she stands under this wind and flies her 凧 **tako** (kite) **ALSO COMPARE:** other similar kanji at # **479** and # **1768**

0768. 揚 **PRONUNCIATIONS: a, you**
MEANINGS: to hoist or to fry in deep fat
EXAMPLES: 揚げる ageru = to hoist, to fly a kite, to fry in deep fat; 抑揚 yokuyou = intonation, inflection **DESCRIPTION:** on the left, a kneeling guy; on the right, a modified version of 易(しい) yasashii (easy, # 402) **CUES:** this guy has to kneel for his **A**gricultural research in **Y**osemite, but his work is 易 (easy), and he often finds time to 揚げる **a**geru (fly) kites
ALSO COMPARE: similar kanji at # **1702**

0769. 壮 **PRONUNCIATION: sou**
MEANINGS: robust, manhood, prosperity
EXAMPLES: 壮大な soudai na = magnificent, imposing; 壮観 soukan = magnificent view
DESCRIPTION: compared to 北 kita (north, # 373), this substitutes 士 shi (man, # 66) for the ヒ (hero) on the right; it retains the bench with two legs, standing on end **CUE:** this 士 (man) sits on this bench admiring a 壮観 **sou**kan (magnificent view) while listening to **Sou**l music **COMPARE:** other similar kanji at # **998** and # **1468**

0770. 脈 **PRONUNCIATION: myaku**
MEANINGS: vein, pulse **EXAMPLES:** 脈 myaku = pulse or vein; 山脈 sanmyaku = mountain range; 動脈 doumyaku = artery
DESCRIPTION: compared to 派(手) hade (showy, gaudy, # 764), this substitutes 月 tsuki (moon, # 148) for the water radical on the left; it retains the person waiting in a one-sided lean-to before stepping out on a journey
CUE: this person is about to step out from this lean-to under the light of this 月 (moon) on a journey to get some **M**iami **K**ool-Aid, and he feels his 脈 **myaku** (veins) throbbing in anticipation
ALSO COMPARE: other similar kanji at # **116**

0771. 美 **PRONUNCIATIONS: utsuku, bi, mi, o** **MEANING:** beautiful **EXAMPLES:** 美しい utsukushii = beautiful; 美術 bijutsu = fine arts; 美人 bijin = beautiful woman; 夏美 Natsumi = a woman's given name; 美味しい oishii = delicious (usually written おいしい) **DESCRIPTION:** at the top, 王 ou (king, # 1077), wearing rabbit ears [this part of the kanji can also be seen as a truncated 羊 hitsuji (sheep, # 1223), missing its tail]; at the bottom, 大 (きい) ookii (big, # 188)
CUES: this 美しい **utsuku**shii (beautiful) truncated 羊 (sheep) rests on a 大 (big) **U**ber **Ts**uitcase (suitcase) full of **K**ool-Aid, and it admires its **B**eauty when it looks into a **M**irror although it is starting to get **O**ld
ALSO COMPARE: other similar kanji at # **1893**

0772. 責 **PRONUNCIATIONS: seki, se**
MEANINGS: liability, to blame
EXAMPLES: 責任 sekinin = responsibility; 責める semeru = to accuse, reproach, torment
DESCRIPTION: at the top, an owl's perch as seen in 青(い) aoi (blue, # 155); at the bottom, 貝 kai (shell, or money chest, # 83) **CUES:** this 貝 (money chest) belongs to a **S**elfish **K**ing who allows an owl to sit on this perch; the owl has **seki**nin 責任 (responsibility) for **S**elling pardons and puts the proceeds in the money chest **GROUP:** 責(任) sekinin = responsibility, # 772, (面)積 menseki = area, # 931, and (成)績 seiseki = achievement, # 1345, all three of which can be pronounced "seki"; (負)債 fusai = debt, # 1571; 漬(ける) tsukeru = to soak, # 1820

0773. 瞬 PRONUNCIATIONS: matata, shun MEANINGS: wink, blink, twinkle EXAMPLES: 瞬く matataku = to blink or twinkle; 瞬く間に matataku ma ni = in an instant; 瞬間 shunkan = moment; 瞬間的に shunkanteki ni = momentarily DESCRIPTION: on the left, 目 me (eye, # 51); at the upper right, a barbecue grate on a rack, as seen in 受(ける) ukeru (to take an exam, etc., # 577); at the lower center, 夕 yuu (evening, # 160); at the lower right, a knee, as seen in 年 nen (year, # 177) CUES: on certain 夕 (evenings) during the 年 (year), this 目 (eye) watches people take exams on knees like this to become **M**aster **T**atami makers and win barbecue grates like this as prizes, and if the eye looks away 瞬間的に **shun**kanteki ni (momentarily), some people may cheat, but if they are caught, they are **Shun**ned ALSO COMPARE: other similar kanji at # **801**, # **1177**, # **1808** and # **2002**

0774. 染 PRONUNCIATIONS: sen, so, ji, shi MEANINGS: dye, color, paint, stain EXAMPLES: 感染 kansen = contagion, infection; 汚染 osen = pollution; 染まる somaru = to be dyed or stained, to be influenced; 馴染む najimu = to adapt or become accustomed to; 染み込む shimikomu = to soak into or penetrate DESCRIPTION: at the upper left, a water radical; at the upper right, 九 kyuu (nine, # 111); at the bottom, 木 ki (tree, # 118) CUES: a **Sen**ator visited **S**omalia in a **J**eep, where he saw some **S**heep, 九 (nine) bodies of water like this and many 木 (trees) like this, but 汚染 o**sen** (pollution) was a problem COMPARE: other similar kanji at # **827** and # **1352**

0775. 胸 PRONUNCIATIONS: kyou, mune, muna MEANING: chest EXAMPLES: 胸中 kyouchuu = heart, mind or intentions; 度胸 dokyou = courage or audacity; 胸 mune = chest; 胸毛 munage = chest hair DESCRIPTION: on the left, 月 tsuki (moon, # 148); on the upper right, the hook seen in 約(束) yakusoku (promise, # 225); under the hook, a box, which resembles the chest of a person, containing an X which may symbolize unknown dreams CUES: when this 月 (moon) shines in **Kyou**to, this hook sometimes snags a person whose 胸 **mune** (chest), represented by this open box, is filled with X's like this, representing dreams of **Moon** Encounters with **Moon** Animals ALSO COMPARE: other similar kanji at # **988**, # **1794** and # **1953**

0776. 駆 PRONUNCIATIONS: ka, ku MEANING: to run EXAMPLES: 駆ける kakeru = to run; 先駆者 senkusha = originator, pioneer DESCRIPTION: compared to 区 ku (ward, # 320) (identical pronunciation), this kanji adds 馬 uma (horse, # 958) on the left CUES: this 馬 (horse) 駆ける **ka**keru (runs) after a **C**ar in this 区 (ward) in **Ku**wait ALSO COMPARE: other similar kanji at # **320**, # **826** and # **1953**

0777. 垣 PRONUNCIATIONS: kaki, *kai* MEANINGS: fence, hedge, wall EXAMPLES: 垣根 kakine = hedge, fence; 垣間見る kaimamiru = to take a peep at, to catch a glimpse of DESCRIPTION: on the left, 土 tsuchi (soil, # 59); on the right, 日 hi (sun, # 32), framed by vertical lines above and below, resembling a window with two panes in a fence CUES: my neighbor put this window in our 垣根 **kaki**ne (fence) so that he could watch me hunt for my **C**ar **K**eys and fly my **K**ite, but I covered it up with this 土 (soil) COMPARE: other similar kanji at # **668**

0778. 巡 PRONUNCIATIONS: jun, megu, *mawa* MEANINGS: patrol, go around, circumference EXAMPLES: 巡査 junsa = patrolman; 巡礼 junrei = Buddhist pilgrimage; 巡る meguru = to go or come around, to surround; お巡りさん omawarisan = a policeman DESCRIPTION: on the lower left, a snail; on the

snail, a chevron as seen on the sleeves of police or military uniforms **CUES:** this snail is wearing this chevron to indicate its status as a **Jun**ior member of the fraternity of **M**en with **Goo**, and as it 巡る **megu**ru (goes around) the neighborhood carrying a grease gun, it behaves like a **M**arine **W**arrior
COMPARE: 回(る) mawaru = to rotate, # 4; 周(り) mawari = surrounding, # 630; other similar kanji at # **1019**

0779. 芝 PRONUNCIATION: *shiba*
MEANINGS: turf, lawn
EXAMPLE: 芝生 shibafu = lawn, turf
DESCRIPTION: at the top, a plant radical which suggests a lawn; at the bottom, a somewhat irregular letter Z which reminds us of zebras
CUE: the **Q**ueen of **Sheba** used to play croquet on a 芝生 **shiba**fu (lawn), represented by this plant radical, with **Z** (**z**ebras) like this watching
COMPARE: other similar kanji at # **1835**

0780. 弾 PRONUNCIATIONS: hi, dan, hazu, tama
MEANINGS: bullet, twang, snap
EXAMPLES: 弾く hiku = to play a piano or guitar; 爆弾 bakudan = bomb; 弾圧する danatsu suru = to oppress or suppress; 弾む hazumu = to become lively, to accelerate; 弾 tama = bullet **DESCRIPTION:** compared to (簡)単 kantan (easy, # 636), this adds the twisted bow seen in 引(く) hiku (to pull, # 476) (identical pronunciation) on the left; it retains the 田 (paddy) spinning with three waves of heat emerging from its top **CUES:** it's 単 (easy) for me to **H**ear the **D**ance music at the **H**awaiian **Z**oo, where people 引 (pull) strings as they 弾く **hi**ku (play) guitars and eat **Tam**ales **ALSO COMPARE:** other similar kanji at # **476**, # **1625** and # **1694**

0781. 詰 PRONUNCIATIONS: tsu, kitsu
MEANINGS: packed, fill, stuff **EXAMPLES:** 詰める tsumeru = to stuff, fill or pack into; 詰まる tsumaru = to be packed, to be blocked; に詰まる ni tsumaru = to be at a loss; 詰問 kitsumon = cross-examination, close questioning
DESCRIPTION: on the left, 言(う) iu (to speak, # 430); at the upper right, 士 shi (man, # 66); at the lower right, 口 kuchi (mouth, # 426), but this could be a tsuitcase (suitcase) or a box **CUES:** this 士 (man) 言 (says) that he has 詰めた **tsu**meta (stuffed) this 口 (**Tsu**itcase) with **K**ittens from **Su**dan, and he is offering them for adoption
GROUP: 読(む) yomu = to read, # 432; 詰(める) tsumeru = to stuff, # 781; (雑)誌 zasshi = magazine, # 786 **ALSO COMPARE:** other similar kanji at # **1453**

0782. 砂 PRONUNCIATIONS: ja, sha, sa, suna
MEANING: sand **EXAMPLES:** 砂利道 jarimichi = gravel path; 土砂降り doshaburi = pouring rain; 砂漠 sabaku = desert; 砂糖 satou = sugar; 砂 suna = sand
DESCRIPTION: on the left, 石 ishi (stone, # 458); on the right, 少(し) sukoshi (a few, # 254); together these suggest a few small stones, or sand **CUES:** a **J**apanese person uses a **Sh**arp tool to turn 少 (a few) 石 (stones) like this into 砂 **suna** (sand) for a **S**alary, but his **S**upervisor **N**ags him endlessly **COMPARE:** other similar kanji at # **1010** and # **1775**

0783. 頂 PRONUNCIATIONS: chou, itadaki, itada
MEANINGS: summit, to receive
EXAMPLES: 登頂する touchou suru = to climb to the summit; 頂 itadaki = peak, summit; 頂く itadaku = to humbly receive (usually written いただく) **DESCRIPTION:** on the left, a nail, as seen in 丁(目) choume (city block, # 702) (identical pronunciation); on the right, 貝 kai (shell, or money chest, # 83), with a platform mounted at the top where a head could fit, as seen in 頭 atama (head, # 93) **CUES:** Margaret **Cho** used this 丁 (nail) to fasten an **I**talian **D**ark **K**imono that she wore when she climbed to an 頂 **itada**ki (summit) to retrieve a 頭 (head) that a friend had lost, and then she performed an **I**talian **D**ance
ALSO COMPARE: other similar kanji at # **702** and # **1126**

0784. 徴 **PRONUNCIATION: chou**
MEANINGS: indications, omen **EXAMPLE:** 特徴 tokuchou = characteristic, special feature **DESCRIPTION:** on the left, a man with two hats; in the upper center, 山 yama (mountain, # 146); in the lower center, 王 ou (king, # 1077); on the right, a dancer with a ponytail **CUE:** this man with two hats will join this 王 (king) on this 山 (mountain), where they will watch this dancer named Margaret Cho, who has 特徴 toku**chou** (special features), and give her one of his hats **GROUP:** (特)徴 tokuchou = characteristic, # 784; 微(妙) bi'myou = subtle, # 1442; 懲(戒) choukai = discipline, # 1879 (identical pronunciation)
ALSO COMPARE: other similar kanji at # **1385** and # **1876**

0785. 雑 **PRONUNCIATIONS: zatsu, zou, za** **MEANINGS:** various, assorted **EXAMPLES:** 複雑な fukuzatsu na = complicated; 雑巾 zoukin = dust cloth, cleaning cloth; 雑誌 zasshi = magazine **DESCRIPTION:** at the upper left, 九 kyuu (nine, # 111); at the lower left, 木 ki (tree, # 118); on the right, a net, which can be seen as a man with a slanted hat next to a 主 (master) with an extra pair of arms (see # 203) **CUES:** 九 (nine) 木 (trees) like this surround this net where **Za**ch's **Ts**uitcase (suitcase) was stored in a 複雑な fuku**zatsu** na (complicated) **Z**one in **Za**mbia **COMPARE:** other similar kanji at # **827**, # **1352** and # **2046**

0786. 誌 **PRONUNCIATION: shi**
MEANINGS: magazine, journal **EXAMPLES:** 雑誌 zasshi = magazine; 週刊誌 shuukanshi = weekly magazine **DESCRIPTION:** compared to 詰(める) tsumeru (to stuff, # 781), this substitutes 心 kokoro (heart, # 306) for the 口 (tsuitcase) on the lower right; it retains 言 (words) and 士 shi (man, # 66) (identical pronunciation)
CUE: this 士 (man) uses 言 (words) well, and he writes articles about 心 (heart) problems in **Sh**eep for a 雑誌 zas**shi** (magazine) **GROUP:** (雑)誌 zasshi = magazine, # 786; 志(望) shibou = ambition, # 1145 (identical pronunciation)

0787. 相 **PRONUNCIATIONS: shou, sou, ai, su, saga** **MEANINGS:** mutual, state, minister **EXAMPLES:** 首相 shushou = prime minister; 相談 soudan = consultation, advice; 相手 aite = opponent or partner; 相撲 sumou = sumo wrestling; 相模原 sagamihara = a city in Kanagawa Prefecture **DESCRIPTION:** on the left, 木 ki (tree, # 118); on the right, 目 me (eye, # 51) **CUES:** I have my 目 (eye) on this 木 (tree) by the **Sh**ore, under which I plan to listen to **Sou**l music and drink **I**ced tea while I 相談する **sou**dan suru (consult) with **Su**perman about the next **Saga** I will write **GROUP:** 箱 hako = box, # 142; 相(談) soudan = consultation, # 787; 想(像) souzou = imagination, # 905 (identical pronunciation); 霜 shimo = frost, # 2032

0788. 炎 **PRONUNCIATIONS: en, honoo**
MEANINGS: inflammation, flare, blaze **EXAMPLES:** 肺炎 haien = pneumonia; 肝炎 kan'en = hepatitis; 火炎 kaen = fire; 炎 honoo = blaze, flame **DESCRIPTION:** at the top, 火 hi (fire, # 443); at the bottom, 火 hi (fire) again **CUES:** an **En**tertainer piled 火 (fire) upon 火 (fire) until a large 火炎 ka**en** (fire) was blazing at my **H**ome in **N**orthern **O**regon
COMPARE: other similar kanji at # **352** and # **1239**

0789. 算 **PRONUNCIATIONS: san, zan, soro** **MEANING:** to count **EXAMPLES:** 計算 keisan = calculation; 算数 sansuu = arithmetic; 暗算 anzan = mental calculation; 算盤 soroban = abacus **DESCRIPTION:** at the top, 竹 take (bamboo, # 134); in the middle, 目 me (eye, # 51); at the bottom, legs with a welcoming stance, as seen in 開(く) aku (to open, # 413) CUES: **Sa**n**ta** Claus holds a 竹 (bamboo) cane over his head when he teaches his 算数 **san**suu (arithmetic) class in **Zan**zibar, and his 目 (eyes) watch the students **Sorro**wfully as he assumes a 開 (welcoming) stance ALSO COMPARE: 鼻 hana = nose, # 795; other similar kanji at # **1924**, # **2002** and # **2074**

0790. 談 PRONUNCIATION: **dan**
MEANING: to talk EXAMPLES: 相談 soudan = consultation; 冗談 joudan = a joke
DESCRIPTION: compared to (火)炎 kaen (fire, # 788), this adds 言(う) iu (to speak, # 430) on the left CUE: a **Dan**cer 言 (spoke) to her neighbors about 炎 (fire) prevention, and their conversation turned into a general 相談 sou**dan** (consultation) ALSO COMPARE: other similar kanji at # **352** and # **1239**

0791. 額 PRONUNCIATIONS: **gaku**, **hitai** MEANINGS: forehead, sum of money, frame EXAMPLES: 金額 kingaku = a sum of money; 額 hitai = forehead DESCRIPTION: compared to 客 kyaku (customer, # 524), this adds 貝 kai (shell, or money chest, # 83), with a platform mounted at the top where a head could fit, as seen in 頭 atama (head, # 93), on the right; it retains the dancer with a bad haircut leaping over a box CUES: this 客 (customer), who is trying to get her 頭 (head) back, offers to exchange a 金額 kin**gaku** (sum of money), a **G**allon of **K**ool-**A**id, and some **H**ebrew **T**iles for it ALSO COMPARE: similar kanji at # **524**, # **1033** and # **1126**

0792. 嘆 PRONUNCIATIONS: **nage, tan**
MEANINGS: sign, lament, moan, grieve
EXAMPLES: 嘆く nageku = to lament, grieve; 感嘆する kantan suru = to admire or be astonished at DESCRIPTION: compared to 漢(字) kanji (# 197), this substitutes 口 kuchi (mouth, # 426), which also resembles a box, for the water radical on the left; it retains the 夫 (husband) wearing glasses and a plant radical on his head CUES: I **Nag** my **Gu**ests to learn 漢 (kanji) like this, but they use 口 (mouths) to 嘆く **nage**ku (lament) the difficulty of the task and would rather work on their **Tan**s ALSO COMPARE: other similar kanji at # **197** and # **2073**

0793. 敗 PRONUNCIATIONS: **hai, pai, yabu** MEANINGS: to lose, to fail EXAMPLES: 敗戦 haisen = a defeat or loss; 失敗する shippai suru = to fail or make a mistake; 敗れる yabureru = to lose or be defeated DESCRIPTION: on the left, 貝 kai (shell or money chest, # 83); on the right, a dancer with a ponytail CUES: this dancer, whose name is **Hei**di, got an idea to mail **Pie**s to foreign countries, but the idea 失敗した ship**pai** shita (failed), and she had to empty this 貝 (money chest) and sell her **Ya**kskin **Boo**ts COMPARE: 破(れる) yabureru = to be torn, # 837; other similar kanji at # **2058**

0794. 喉 PRONUNCIATIONS: **kou, nodo** MEANINGS: throat, voice EXAMPLES: 耳鼻咽喉科 jibiinkouka = ear, nose and throat specialty; 喉 nodo = throat DESCRIPTION: on the left, 口 kuchi (mouth, # 426), which also resembles a box; in the middle, a man with a slanted hat; at the upper right, the katakana ユ yu, which reminds us of the Yukon; at the lower right, a Native American chief, as seen in 知(る) shiru (to know, # 323) CUES: this man in the middle is an ear, nose & throat doctor who takes care of Native American patients like this in ユ (the Yukon) and who knows a lot about the 口 (mouth) and the 喉 (**nodo**) (throat), and he tilts his hat back like this to examine patients, but his bedside manner is **Co**ld, and as a result on some days he earns **No Dough** (money) COMPARE: similar kanji at # **324**, # **996** and # **2073**

0795. 鼻 PRONUNCIATIONS: hana, bi
MEANING: nose EXAMPLES: 鼻 hana = nose; 耳鼻科 jibika = ear, nose & throat specialty
DESCRIPTION: at the top, 自(分) jibun (self, # 55), which has a projection at the top that resembles a nose or possibly a beak; in the middle, 田 (rice paddy, # 68); at the bottom, legs with a welcoming stance, as seen in 開(く) aku (to open, # 413) CUES: this **Ha**waiian **N**anny has this tiny 鼻 **hana** (nose) resembling a **Bea**k on top of her head which expresses her 自 (self), and she welcomes us to this 田 (rice paddy) ALSO COMPARE: 算(数) sansuu = arithmetic, # 789; other similar kanji at # **220**, # **1381** and # **1924**

0796. 邪 PRONUNCIATIONS: ze, ja
MEANINGS: wicked, injustice, wrong
EXAMPLES: 風邪 kaze = upper respiratory infection; 無邪気 mujaki = innocence
DESCRIPTION: on the left, a man wearing a flat-topped helmet with a visor, plus an object protruding from under the visor on the left; on the right, ß beta from the Greek alphabet CUES: the guy on the left is a **Z**esty **J**azz performer from ß (Greece) with this clarinet emerging from under his visor, and he is testing the visor to see if it might prevent 風邪 ka**ze** (upper respiratory infections)
GROUP: (風)邪 kaze = upper respiratory infection, # 796; 牙 kiba = fangs, # 921; (温)雅 onga = graceful, # 922; (発)芽 hatsuga = germination, # 1417; 既(婚) kikon = already married, # 1639; 概(念) gainen = a general idea, # 1647; (憤)慨(する) fungai suru = to be indignant, # 1782 ALSO COMPARE: other similar kanji at # **1417** and # **1843**

0797. 浸 PRONUNCIATIONS: shin, tsu, hita MEANINGS: soak, dip, wet, dunk
EXAMPLES: 浸水する shinsui suru = to be flooded; 浸かる tsukaru = to be soaked in; 浸す hitasu = to soak, dip or drench
DESCRIPTION: on the left, a water radical; on the upper right, long hair flowing to the left; on the lower right, a simple table covered with a cloth CUES: a **Shin**to priest with this long hair flowing to the left saw this water and realized that his shrine had 浸水した **shin**sui shita (flooded), but he was able to save a **Tsu**itcase (suitcase) and a **Hi**ita (heater) by placing them onto this table covered by a cloth COMPARE: other similar kanji at # **24** and # **1165**

0798. 爽 PRONUNCIATION: sou
MEANINGS: refreshing, clear EXAMPLE: 爽快 soukai = refreshing, exhilarating
DESCRIPTION: 大(きい) ookii (big, # 188), with two X's on each side which represent unknown songs CUE: this 大 (big) guy likes to listen to **Sou**l music, and these X's represent four songs that he finds especially 爽快 **sou**kai (refreshing)
COMPARE: other similar kanji at # **352** and # **1953**

0799. 垂 PRONUNCIATIONS: sui, ta
MEANINGS: droop, suspend, hang, slouch
EXAMPLES: 垂直 suichoku = vertical, perpendicular; 垂れる tareru = to hang, droop, dangle, sag, lower DESCRIPTION: this resembles 重(い) omoi (heavy, # 284) which, compared to 車 kuruma (car, # 283), adds hubcaps; this kanji retains the hubcaps at the ends of the axle, but it omits the wheels; it also adds three projections on the right and on the left, which may be wings for streamlining CUES: this streamlined 車 (car) without wheels, which has three projections on the front and on the back, is lying on its side with its hubcaps aligned 垂直に **sui**choku ni (vertically), and it is based on advanced **Sui**dish (Swedish) technology, allowing it to run on these hubcaps and to serve as a **Ta**xi GROUP: 乗(る) noru = to board, # 509; 垂(直) suichoku = vertical, # 799; 睡(眠) suimin = sleep, # 800 (identical pronunciation); (過)剰 kajou = excess, # 1211; 華(やか) hanayaka = dazzling, # 1354; 郵(便局) yuubinkyoku = post office, # 1445; 唾 tsuba = saliva, # 1847

0800. 睡 PRONUNCIATION: sui MEANINGS: drowsy, sleep, die EXAMPLE: 睡眠 suimin = sleep DESCRIPTION: compared to 垂(直) suichoku (vertical, perpendicular, # 799) (identical pronunciation), this kanji adds 目 me (eye, # 51) on the left; it retains the streamlined car on the right CUE: during 睡眠 **sui**min (sleep), I dreamed that these 目 (eyes) saw this streamlined **Sui**dish (Swedish) 車 (car) without wheels lying on its side with its hubcaps aligned 垂 (vertically) ALSO COMPARE: other similar kanji at # <u>799</u> and # <u>2002</u>

0801. 移 PRONUNCIATIONS: utsu, i MEANINGS: to transfer or move EXAMPLES: 移る utsuru = to move (one's lodging), to change or be infected with; 移動する idou suru = to move (an object) DESCRIPTION: on the left, 禾 (a ripe head of grain); on the right, 多(い) ooi (many, # 161) CUES: we **U**tilize **S**uperman to 移動する **i**dou suru (move) 多 (many) stalks of 禾 (grain) like this because it's **E**asy for him GROUP: 夕(方) yuugata = evening, # 160; 多(い) ooi =many, # 161; 外 soto = outside, # 163; 夢 yume = dream, # 165; 隣 tonari = next door, # 329; 舞(う) mau = to dance, # 584; 瞬(間) shunkan = moment, # 773; 移(る) utsuru = to move, # 801; 腕 ude = arm, # 1532; (挨)拶 aisatsu = a greeting, # 1650; (感)銘 kanmei = a deep impression, # 1666; 傑(作) kessaku = a masterpiece, # 1808; 宛(先) atesaki = an address, # 1822; 怨(念) onnen = a grudge, # 1910 ALSO COMPARE: other similar kanji at # <u>352</u> and # <u>1797</u>

0802. 避 PRONUNCIATIONS: sa, hi MEANINGS: to evade, avoid, avert, ward off, shun EXAMPLES: 避ける sakeru = to avoid; 避難 hinan = taking refuge DESCRIPTION: on the lower left, a snail; in the middle, a lean-to with a double roof; inside the lean-to, 口 kuchi (mouth, # 426), which resembles a box; on the right, 辛(い) karai (spicy, # 384), which resembles a needle containing an eye (this combination of radicals = LBN = lean-to, box, needle) CUES: a **Sa**laryman wants to **H**eal this snail and 避ける **sa**keru (avoid) side-effects, and he uses this 辛 (needle) to inject the snail with the medicine in the 口 (box) under this lean-to (LBN = lean-to, box, needle) GROUP: (友)達 tomo-dachi = friend, # 347; 遅(い) osoi = late, # 350; 避(ける) sakeru = to avoid, # 802 ALSO COMPARE: similar kanji at # <u>1214</u>

0803. 暇 PRONUNCIATIONS: hima, ka MEANINGS: spare time, rest, leisure EXAMPLES: 暇 hima = free time; 休暇 kyuuka = vacation, day off DESCRIPTION: on the left, 日 hi (sun, # 32); in the middle, a ladder with a carton at the top; at the upper right, the katana コ ko which reminds us of corn; at the lower right, 又 mata (again, # 24), but this resembles a simple table CUES: this 日 (sun) shines on this ladder in the **Hima**layas, which we climb to place this **Ca**rton of コ (corn) on this 又 (table), when we have 暇 <u>hima</u> (free time) ALSO COMPARE: other similar kanji at # <u>24</u> and # <u>41</u>

0804. 諦 PRONUNCIATION: akira MEANINGS: to abandon, give up EXAMPLE: 諦める akirameru = to give up DESCRIPTION: on the left, 言(う) iu (to say, # 430); on the upper right, 立(つ) tatsu (to stand, # 11), with downward-facing spikes on its base; at the lower right, 巾 (Bo Peep), as seen in 帽(子) boushi (hat, # 243) CUE: people 言 (say) that a cook who 立 (stands) on slippery floors should wear spikes like these on her shoes, but **A**chilles' **R**ack of lamb was ruined because this 巾 (Bo Peep) 諦めた <u>akira</u>meta (gave up) on that advice and switched to ordinary shoes GROUP: 諦(める) akirameru = to give up, # 804; 締(める) shimeru

= to fasten, # 1173; 帝 mikado = the Emperor, # 1538; 傍(ら) katawara = close by, # 1633 **ALSO COMPARE:** other similar kanji at **# 1768**

0805. 浪 PRONUNCIATION: rou
MEANINGS: wandering, waves **EXAMPLES:** 浪費 rouhi = waste, extravagance; 浪人 rounin = wandering samurai without a master, a person waiting for another chance to take a university exam **DESCRIPTION:** on the left, a water radical; on the right, 良(い) yoi (good, # 303), which contains the letters L & Y at the bottom
CUE: a 浪人 **rou**nin (masterless samurai) can find 良 (good) work on this water **Row**ing boats
GROUP: (**Note** that all of these kanji contain 良, # 303, but this is sometimes modified, missing its pointy cap, or with modifications to the "LY" at its base) 銀(行) ginkou = bank, # 302; 良(い) yoi = good, # 303; 娘 musume = daughter, # 316; 食(べる) taberu = to eat, # 398; 限(界) genkai = limit, # 642; (屋)根 yane = roof, # 741; 浪(費) rouhi = waste, # 805; 響(く) hibiku = to resound, # 840; 退(屈) taikutsu = boredom, # 926; (季)節 kisetsu = season, # 1048; 郷(里) kyouri = hometown, # 1059; (新)郎 shinrou = bridegroom, # 1343 (identical pronunciation); 眼(鏡) megane = eyeglasses, # 1423; 即(刻) sokkoku = immediately, # 1502; 爵(位) shaku'i = peerage, # 1603; 廊(下) rouka = corridor, # 1605 (also identical pronunciation); 既(婚) kikon = already married, # 1639; 概(念) gainen = a concept, # 1647; 恨(む) uramu = to bear a grudge, # 1724; (憤)慨(する) fungai suru = to be indignant, # 1782; 痕(跡) konseki = traces, # 1857; 懇(談) kondan = a meeting or talk, # 1869; (開)墾 kaikon = cultivating new land, # 2068 **ALSO COMPARE:** other kanji containing L & Y at # 398 and # 1105

0806. 没 PRONUNCIATIONS: bo, botsu
MEANINGS: drown, sink, hide, fall into, disappear, die **EXAMPLES:** 没頭 bottou = immersing oneself; 没する bossuru = to sink, go down, to set, to pass away, to die, to disappear; 日没 nichibotsu = sunset
DESCRIPTION: compared to 役に立つ yaku ni tatsu (to be useful, # 557), this substitutes a water radical for the man with a double hat on the left; it retains the 冖 (yak) on a 又 (table)
CUES: this 冖 (yak) looks down at this water from his perch on this 又 (table) and **Boa**sts that, if he jumps in, the people in some nearby **Boa**ts will make sure that he doesn't 没する **bo**ssuru suru (sink)
ALSO COMPARE: similar kanji at **# 557**

0807. 悶 PRONUNCIATIONS: moda, mon
MEANINGS: to be in agony, to worry **EXAMPLES:** 悶える modaeru = to be in agony, to worry; 悶々 monmon = worry, agony
DESCRIPTION: on the right and left, 門 mon (gate, # 409) (identical pronunciation); in the center, 心 kokoro (heart, # 306)
CUES: **Mo**ses and his **Da**d have their 心 (hearts) set on this new 門 (gate), but they 悶える **moda**eru (worry) and **Moan** about the expense
ALSO COMPARE: other similar kanji at **# 1755**

0808. 術 PRONUNCIATION: jutsu
MEANINGS: methods, means, trick, skill, technique **EXAMPLES:** 手術 shujutsu = surgery; 美術 bijutsu = visual art
DESCRIPTION: on the left and right, 行(く) iku (to go, # 334), suggesting that one is in the middle of doing something; in the center, a woman wearing a skirt, with something jutting out over her right shoulder **CUE:** this woman in the center is in the middle of 行 (going) out to have 手術 shu**jutsu** (surgery) for this lump that **Juts** out over her right shoulder
GROUP: (手)術 shujutsu = surgery, # 808; (記)述 kijutsu = a written description, # 1328 (identical pronunciation) **ALSO COMPARE:** other similar kanji at **# 625**

0809. 居 **PRONUNCIATIONS:** kyo, i
MEANINGS: to exist or reside **EXAMPLES:** 住居 juukyo = dwelling; 居間 ima = living room **DESCRIPTION:** on the left, a lean-to with a double roof; inside the lean-to, 古(い) furui (old, # 392) **CUES:** I have an 古 (old) 住居 juu**kyo** (residence) in **Kyo**to, which is this lean-to with a double roof, and my life is **E**asy
ALSO COMPARE: 店 mise = store, # 493; other similar kanji at # **394** and # **1899**

0810. 求 **PRONUNCIATIONS:** kyuu, moto **MEANINGS:** to seek, to request **EXAMPLES:** 追求する tsuikyuu suru = to pursue a goal, to chase; 要求 youkyuu = a request or demand; 求む motomu = to seek or demand **DESCRIPTION:** compared to (野)球 yakyuu (baseball, # 606) (identical pronunciation), this kanji omits 王 (king) on the left; it retains the water dog from Cuba with a ball above its right shoulder **CUES:** this 水 (water) 犬 (dog) from **Cu**ba belongs to a 球 (baseball) player who 求む **moto**mu (seeks) a **Mo**torcycle
ALSO COMPARE: other similar kanji at # **606**

0811. 健 **PRONUNCIATIONS:** ken, suko
MEANING: healthy
EXAMPLES: 健康 kenkou = health; 健やか sukoyaka = vigorous, healthy, sound
DESCRIPTION: compared to 建(築) kenchiku (architecture, # 363) (identical pronunciation), this kanji adds a man with a slanted hat on the left; it retains the telephone pole above the 3x snail **CUES:** this man with a slanted hat is named **Ken**, he works as an 建 (architect) with Barbie, and they are **Su**ing **Co**ca Cola over the effects of its beverage on their 健康 **ken**kou (health)
ALSO COMPARE: other similar kanji at # **692**, # **820** and # **877**

0812. 冒 **PRONUNCIATIONS:** oka, bou
MEANINGS: to transfer or move
EXAMPLES: 冒す okasu = to brave or risk, to face or venture; 冒険 bouken = adventure, risk
DESCRIPTION: compared to 帽(子) boushi = hat, # 243 (identical pronunciation), this kanji omits Bo Peep on the left; it retains the 日 (sun) and the 目 (eye) **CUES:** **Occa**sionally, when I go out in my **Bo**at, I use this 目 (eye) to look directly into this 日 (sun), but I know that I am taking a 冒険 **bou**ken (risk) in doing so
ALSO COMPARE: other similar kanji at # **243**

0813. 論 **PRONUNCIATION:** ron
MEANINGS: logic, argument **EXAMPLE:** 口論 kouron = argument, quarrel
DESCRIPTION: on the left, 言(う) iu (to speak, # 430); on the upper right, a peaked roof with a ceiling; on the lower right, 冊 satsu (counter for books, # 568); together, the two radicals on the right suggest a library **CUES:** **Ron**ald Reagan got into a 口論 kou**ron** (argument) at this 冊 (library) and 言 (said) some things that were **Wr**ong
GROUP: (指)輪 yubiwa = ring, # 690; (口)論 kouron = argument, # 813; 倫(理) rinri = ethics, # 1685 **ALSO COMPARE:** other similar kanji at # 568

0814. 氷 **PRONUNCIATIONS:** koori, koo, hyou **MEANING:** ice **EXAMPLES:** 氷 koori = ice; 氷る kooru = to freeze; 氷山 hyouzan = iceberg **DESCRIPTION:** 水 mizu (water, # 251) with one extra line in the upper left corner, suggesting an ice crystal **CUES:** when the Lone Ranger visited **Co**rinth, they served him a drink of this **Co**ld 水 (water) containing one crystal like this that turned out to be 氷 **koori** (ice), and he said "Hi-Yo Silver" **GROUP:** 水 mizu = water, # 251; 小(さい) chiisai = small, # 253; 水)泳 suiei = swimming, # 255; 氷 koori = ice, # 814; 永(久) eikyuu = eternity, # 870; **Note** that in both # 255 and # 870, *two* small lines are added to the upper left corner of 水

0815. 溶 **PRONUNCIATIONS: you, to**
MEANINGS: melt, dissolve, thaw **EXAMPLES:** 溶岩 yougan = lava; 溶ける tokeru = to melt or dissolve, intransitive; 溶かす tokasu = to melt or dissolve, transitive **DESCRIPTION:** compared to (内)容 naiyou (content, # 296) (identical pronunciation), this kanji adds a water radical on the left; it retains the bad haircut and the bathroom at Yosemite with water vapor rising from it **CUES:** after getting this bad haircut, I fled to **Yo**semite, where I used a **T**orch to 溶ける **to**keru (melt) some snow into water like this, before bathing in this bathroom **COMPARE:** other similar kanji at # **296** and # **660**

0816. 岩 **PRONUNCIATIONS: iwa, gan**
MEANING: rock **EXAMPLES:** 岩 iwa = rock; 溶岩 yougan = lava **DESCRIPTION:** at the top, 山 yama (mountain, # 146); at the bottom, 石 ishi (stone, # 458) **CUES:** while fighting in an **Ea**stern **Wa**r, **Ga**ndalf rolled 石 (stones) like this down this 山 (mountain), and the enemy was buried in 岩 **iwa** (rock) **ALSO COMPARE:** similar kanji at # **1385** and # **1775**

0817. 嫌 **PRONUNCIATIONS: gen, iya, kira, ken** **MEANINGS:** to dislike or hate **EXAMPLES:** 機嫌 kigen = mood, feeling; 嫌な iya na = unpleasant, disgusting; 嫌い kirai = to hate; 嫌悪 ken'o = hatred, disgust **DESCRIPTION:** on the left, 女 onna (female, # 235); on the right, this appears to be a 木 ki (tree, # 118) with a trunk that has been split down the middle but which is being held together by a trident piercing it from the right side; there are two extra branches at the top of the tree which can be seen as antennae **CUES:** this 女 (female) on the left is staring at this split 木 (tree) that has been patched together with this trident, and 嫌いです **kira**i desu (she doesn't like it), but her husband **Gen**ghis takes off his **Iya**hon (earphones), grabs a key from his **Key Ra**ck, and goes out to talk to **Ken** and Barbie about the situation **GROUP:** 嫌(い) kirai = to hate, # 817; 謙(虚) kenkyo = modesty, # 965, and 兼用 kenyou = multi-use, # 1401, both of which help us to pronounce this; 鎌 kama = a sickle, # 1667 **ALSO COMPARE:** other kanji with 女 on the left at # **2039**

0818. 匹 **PRONUNCIATIONS: hiki, piki², biki², hi** **MEANINGS:** equal, roll of cloth, counter for small animals **EXAMPLES:** 二匹 nihiki = two small animals or bolts of cloth; 一匹 ippiki = one small animal or bolt of cloth; 三匹 sanbiki = three small animals or bolts of cloth; 匹敵 hitteki suru = to equal or match **DESCRIPTION:** 四 yon (four, # 6), which resembles the floor plan of a house, with a wall missing **CUES:** I kicked a wall out of this house, 四匹 yon**hiki** (four) of my cats escaped, and now I have a **Hi**ckey on my **H**eel **GROUP:** 一匹 ippiki = one small animal, # 818; 勘(定) kanjou = bill, # 1161; 堪(忍) kannin = forgiveness, # 1452; 甚(大) jindai = very great, # 1730 **COMPARE:** other similar kanji at # **320** and # 1161

0819. 泥 **PRONUNCIATIONS: doro, dei**
MEANINGS: mud or mire **EXAMPLES:** 泥棒 dorobou = thief; 泥水 deisui = muddy water, red-light district; 泥酔する deisui suru = to get dead drunk **DESCRIPTION:** on the left, a water radical; on the right, 尼 ama (nun, # 1899), which resembles a lean-to with a double roof that contains the katakana ヒ hi, which reminds us of a heel (a contemptible person) **CUES:** although she is a 尼 (nun), **Do**rothy went on a **Da**te with the Scarecrow under this reinforced lean-to, but he was this ヒ (heel) who threw this water at her and, on top of that, he was a 泥棒 **doro**bou (thief) **COMPARE:** similar kanji at # **1899** and # **2048**

0820. 棒 **PRONUNCIATION:** bou
MEANINGS: club or pole **EXAMPLES:** 棒 bou = a stick or pole; 相棒 aibou = a buddy or partner; 泥棒 dorobou = thief **DESCRIPTION:** on the left, 木 ki (tree, # 118); at the upper right, 人 hito (person, # 13), with the number 三 san (three) inscribed across it, as seen in 春 haru (spring, # 506); at the lower right, a telephone pole **CUE:** these 三 (three) 人 (people) used a **Boat** to bring us a telephone 棒 **bou** (pole) like this made from this 木 (tree) **GROUP:** 建(て る) tateru = to build, # 363; (法)律 houritsu = a law, # 417; 健(康) kenkou = health, # 811; 棒 bou = a stick, # 820; 津(波) tsunami = tidal wave, # 877; 筆 fude = writing brush, # 1091; 奉(仕) houshi = service, # 1536; 鍵 kagi = a key, # 1689; 棒(給) houkyuu = salary, # 2056 **ALSO COMPARE:** other similar kanji at # **506**

0821. 追 **PRONUNCIATIONS:** tsui, o
MEANINGS: to chase, follow, pursue
EXAMPLES: 追求する tsuikyuu suru = to pursue a goal, to chase; 追う ou = to chase; 追いかける oikakeru = to pursue or chase after **DESCRIPTION:** on the lower left, a snail; on the snail, bunk beds for tsuitehearts (sweethearts), with a tiny pillow visible on the top bunk **CUES:** this snail is carrying these **Tsui**teheart (sweetheart) bunk beds to **O**saka and trying to 追いかける **o**ikakeru (chase) a rival snail, but progress is slow
COMPARE: 迫(力) hakuryoku = dynamism, # 1316, in which the snail carries 白 (white); other similar kanji at # **880**

0822. 照 **PRONUNCIATIONS:** te, shou, de **MEANINGS:** to shine or illuminate
EXAMPLES: 照らす terasu = to illuminate or light; 照る teru = to shine; 照れる tereru = to be shy or feel embarrassment; 対照的に taishouteki ni = diametrically opposite; 照明 shoumei = lighting; 日照り hideri = dry weather, drought **DESCRIPTION:** on the left, 日 hi (sun, # 32); at the upper right, katana 刀 (sword, # 102); at the middle right, 口 kuchi (mouth, # 426), but this resembles a television set, or a box; at the bottom, a fire, as seen in 熱 netsu (fever, # 65)
CUES: this 口 (**T**elevision set) displays a **Show** featuring a **D**ebutante who fights with this 刀 (sword), and this 日 (sun) and this fire are being used to 照らす **te**rasu (illuminate) the stage **ALSO COMPARE:** other similar kanji at # **560** and # **611**

0823. 振 **PRONUNCIATIONS:** shin, fu, furi **MEANINGS:** to shake, wave, swing
EXAMPLES: 振動数 shindousuu = frequency; 振る furu = to shake or wave; 振り返る furikaeru = to turn the head, look back, think back; 振り向く furimuku = to turn around; 銀行振込み ginkou furikomi = bank transfer
DESCRIPTION: on the left, a kneeling guy; on the right, the Shinto shrine seen in (地)震 jishin (earthquake, # 265) (identical pronunciation) which is supported by the letter L and the letter Y, and contains a horizontal arrow
CUES: when this guy on the left 振り返った **furi**katta (looked back) at this lean-to and saw these two **Shin**to priests named L and Y **Foo**lishly pointing this arrow at him, he got **Fur**ious, but he fell to his knees in order to become a smaller target
COMPARE: other similar kanji at # **1105**

0824. 似 PRONUNCIATIONS: ni, *ne*, ji
MEANINGS: to resemble or take after
EXAMPLES: 似ている nite iru = resembling; 真似 mane = imitation, mimicry; 類似 ruiji = a resemblance; 類似品 ruijihin = imitation, or similar article   DESCRIPTION: compared to 以 (前) izen (a long time ago, # 601), this adds a man with a slanted hat on the left; it retains the hoe (more obvious when it is written like this 似), the drop of sweat and the giraffe
CUES: this man on the left tilts his hat back to examine this hoe which my **Nie**ce used, while emitting this drop of sweat, to dig a trap for this giraffe, which had a 類似 rui**ji** (resemblance) to one that he caught, but he would ride on the giraffe's **N**eck, while she rode in a **Jee**p   ALSO COMPARE: other similar kanji at # **601** and # **453**

0825. 釘 PRONUNCIATION: kugi
MEANINGS: nail, tack, peg   EXAMPLES: 釘 kugi = nail or peg; 釘付けになる kugizuke ni naru = to be unable to take one's eyes from   DESCRIPTION: on the left, (お)金 okane (money, # 301); on the right, 丁(目) choume (city block, # 702), which resembles a nail
CUE: I paid 金 (money) for 釘 **kugi** (nails) like this to build a shed for my **Cool Gee**se
COMPARE: other similar kanji at # **702** and # **2010**

0826. 騒 PRONUNCIATIONS: sawa, sou
MEANINGS: make noise, disturb, excite
EXAMPLES: 騒ぐ sawagu = to make noise, to make a fuss; 騒々しい souzoushii = noisy
DESCRIPTION: on the left, 馬 uma (horse, # 958); at the upper right, 又 mata ("again," resembling a table, # 24); at the lower right, 虫 mushi (insect, # 9)   CUES: this 馬 (horse) 騒いだ **sawa**ida (made a fuss) when it **Saw** a **W**arlord listening to **Sou**l music at this 又 (table) with this buzzing 虫 (insect) nearby   GROUP: 駅 eki = train station, # 380; 駐(車する) chuusha suru = to park, # 381; (経)験 keiken = experience, # 382; (無)駄 muda = worthless, # 628; 駆(ける) kakeru = to run, # 776; 騒(ぐ) sawagu = to make noise, # 826; 馬 uma = horse, # 958; 驚(く) odoroku = to be surprised, # 971; (ご)馳(走) gochishou = a delicacy, # 1358; 騎(手) kishu = jockey, # 1449; 罵(倒する) batou suru = to abuse, # 1927; (沸)騰(する) futtou suru = to boil, # 1936; (危)篤 kitoku = critical condition, # 1937   ALSO COMPARE: other similar kanji at # **24** and # **1754**

0827. 尻 PRONUNCIATION: shiri
MEANINGS: buttocks, hips   EXAMPLE: お尻 oshiri = buttocks   DESCRIPTION: on the upper left, a lean-to with a double roof; under the lean-to, 九 kyuu (nine, # 111)   CUE: when these 九 (nine) **S**heep **Rea**lized that it was raining, they all sheltered their 尻 **shiri** (buttocks) under this heavy-duty lean-to   GROUP: 九 kyuu = nine, # 111; (研)究 kenkyuu = research, # 112; 鳩 hato = pigeon, # 736; (汚)染 osen = pollution, # 774; 雑(誌) zasshi = magazine, # 785; (お)尻 oshiri = buttocks, # 827; 酔(う) you = to get drunk, # 1476; 枠 waku = a frame, # 1490; (純)粋(な) junsui na = pure # 1778; 軌(道) kidou = an orbit, # 1827; 砕(く) kudaku = to break, # 1845   ALSO COMPARE: other similar kanji at # **1899**

0828. 呆 PRONUNCIATIONS: aki, bo, ho, a   MEANINGS: to be amazed, disgusted or shocked   EXAMPLES: 呆れる akireru = to be disgusted or astonished, usually written あきれる; 呆け boke = fool, usually written ボケ; 阿呆 aho = a fool or silly person, usually written アホ; 呆気にとられる akke ni torareru = to be taken aback, to be dumb-founded
DESCRIPTION: at the top, 口 kuchi (mouth, # 426), which also resembles a box; at the bottom, 木 ki (tree, # 118)   CUES: **A**chilles saw a man

with this big 口 (mouth) **Boa**sting from the top of this 木 (tree), and he 呆れた **aki**reta (got astonished) and went **H**ome to tell his **A**unt **COMPARE:** 吊(るす) tsurusu = to suspend, # 1209; 保(証) hoshou = guarantee, # 1216 (identical pronunciation); other similar kanji at # **1216**

0829. 褒 PRONUNCIATIONS: ho, hou
MEANINGS: to praise or extol
EXAMPLES: 褒める homeru = to praise, admire or speak well of (this can also be spelled 誉める, # 1705); 褒美 houbi = reward
DESCRIPTION: at the top, a tire stop, as seen in 対(する) tai suru (to confront, # 674); at the center left, a man with a slanted hat; at the center right, 呆(れる) akireru (to be astonished, # 828), or (阿)保 aho (a fool, # 828) (identical pronunciation; at the bottom, the katakana エ e and the letter Y **CUES:** this man in the center left tilted his hat back and saw that cars were colliding with **H**otels, as well as the **H**ome of this エ and Y, so he invented this tire stop, and people were 呆 (astonished) and 褒めた **ho**meta (praised) him
ALSO COMPARE: other similar kanji at # **122** and # **1216**

0830. 飼 PRONUNCIATIONS: ka, kai, shi
MEANINGS: to domesticate, raise, keep, feed
EXAMPLES: 飼う kau = to keep a pet or raise livestock; 飼主 kainushi = shepherd, pet owner (also written 飼い主); 飼犬 kaiinu = a pet dog (also written 飼い犬); 飼育 shiiku = breeding, raising, rearing; 飼育員 shiikuin = a caretaker at a zoo or aquarium
DESCRIPTION: on the left, 食(べる) taberu (to eat, # 398); on the right, (寿)司 sushi (# 608) (identical pronunciation), which depicts a box inside a lean-to that contains sheep food but is covered by a napkin
CUES: a 飼主 **kai**nushi (shepherd) in **C**alifornia who is **K**ind removes this napkin from this 口 (box) in this one-sided lean-to and allows his animals to 食 (eat) the **S**heep food found within **ALSO COMPARE:** other similar kanji at # **341** and # **1974**

0831. 康 PRONUNCIATION: kou
MEANINGS: healthy, peaceful **EXAMPLE:** 健康 kenkou = health **DESCRIPTION:** on the upper left, a lean-to with a small chimney; under the lean-to, 水 mizu (water, # 251), with its axis extending up and being pierced by a trident
CUE: after a man was stabbed with this trident, he felt **C**old and crawled into this lean-to to get warm, but he needs 水 (water) like this, since this injury is affecting his 健康 ken**kou** (health)
ALSO COMPARE: other similar kanji at # **1494** and # **1583**

0832. 骨 PRONUNCIATIONS: kotsu, ko, hone
MEANING: bone **EXAMPLES:** 骸骨 gaikotsu = skeleton; 骨折する kossetsu suru = to break a bone; 骨 hone = bone
DESCRIPTION: at the top, the floor plan of a one-room apartment mounted on a base on spikes, with a bathroom in the right lower corner (this can also be seen as a carton slipping inside a box); at the bottom, 月 tsuki (moon, # 148) **CUES:** when I'm in this roof-top apartment on this 月 (moon), I wear several **C**oats, since it's **C**old, and I use a **H**ome **N**etwork to research **hone** 骨 (bone) health, since the moon's low gravity can cause osteoporosis
GROUP: 骨 hone = bone, # 832; 滑(る) suberu = to slip, # 981; 骸(骨) gaikotsu = a skeleton, # 1923; (真)髄 shinzui = essence, # 1964 **ALSO COMPARE:** other similar kanji at # 361

0833. 皮 **PRONUNCIATIONS:** kawa, gawa², hi **MEANING:** skin **EXAMPLES:** 皮 kawa = skin, peel; 毛皮 kegawa = fur; 皮膚 hifu = skin; 皮肉 hiniku = sarcasm, cynicism, irony **DESCRIPTION:** this is Straight Arrow, as seen in 彼 kare (he, # 371), who resembles an arrow intersected by a vertical line, above a 又 (table) that can be seen as springy legs, and who has a long cape that trails down to the floor on the left (this can also be seen as a chimney perforating the top of a lean-to containing a table)
CUES: this Straight Arrow works at a **Ca**r **Wa**sh, he has thin 皮 **kawa** (skin), and he **Hea**rs everything that people say about him **GROUP:** 疲(れる) tsukareru = to get tired, # 370; 彼 kare = he, # 371; 皮 kawa = skin, # 833; 破(る) yaburu = to tear, # 837; (津)波 tsunami = tidal wave, # 878; 披(露宴) hirouen = wedding reception, # 1389 (identical pronunciation); 被(害) higai = damage, # 1447 (also identical pronunciation); (老)婆 rouba = an old woman, # 1688

0834. 隠 **PRONUNCIATIONS:** kaku, in **MEANINGS:** conceal, cover **EXAMPLES:** 隠す kakusu = to hide or cover up; 隠れる kakureru = to conceal oneself or disappear; 隠元豆 ingenmame = green bean, string bean **DESCRIPTION:** on the left, β beta from the Greek alphabet; at the upper right, a barbecue grate; at the middle right, long hair flowing to the left; at the lower right, 心 kokoro (heart, # 306) **CUES: Ka**rl the **Ko**ol-Aid vendor is this β (Greek) guy who was barbecuing on this grate in Athens when this long hair belonging to him caught fire, causing this 心 (heart) to ache, and then he spent time on the **In**ternet and 隠れた **kaku**reta (hid himself) until his hair grew back **COMPARE:** other similar kanji at # 1165, # 1177 and # 2030

0835. 沈 **PRONUNCIATIONS:** shizu, chin **MEANINGS:** sink, submerge, subside, be depressed **EXAMPLES:** 沈める shizumeru = to sink or submerge; 沈む shizumu = to set (sun or moon), to sink, to feel depressed; 沈黙 chinmoku = silence **DESCRIPTION:** on the left, a water radical; at the upper right, a bad haircut; at the lower right, lopsided legs, as seen in 兄 ani (big brother, # 420), with the right leg bent
CUES: this guy with this bad haircut and these lopsided legs was wading in this water with some **Sh**eep at the **Z**oo when one of them struck him on the **Chin,** he injured this right leg, and he 沈めた **shizu**meta (sank) **ALSO COMPARE:** 鎮める shizumeru = to alleviate, # 1722; other similar kanji at # 974

0836. 黙 **PRONUNCIATIONS:** dama, moku **MEANING:** silence **EXAMPLES:** 黙る damaru = to keep silent; 沈黙 chinmoku = silence **DESCRIPTION:** compared to (自)然 shizen (nature, # 611), this substitutes a sincere guy wearing bifocals, as seen in 野(菜) yasai (vegetables, # 545), for the rocker-bottom bench at the upper left; it retains the 犬 (dog) and the fire **CUES:** this sincere guy in **Da**mascus was sitting with this 犬 (dog), and this fire was hot, so he wanted **Mo**re **Ko**ol-Aid, but he 黙った **dama**tta (kept silent) **ALSO COMPARE:** other similar kanji at # 545, # 611 and # 945

0837. 破 **PRONUNCIATIONS:** ha, yabu, pa **MEANINGS:** to break or tear **EXAMPLES:** 読破する dokuha suru = to finish reading a book; 破る yaburu = to break, tear or violate; 破れる yabureru = to be torn, ripped or broken, or to fail; 突破する toppa suru = to break through **DESCRIPTION:** on the left, 石 ishi (stone, # 458); on the right, Straight Arrow, as seen in 皮 kawa (skin, # 833), who stands on springy legs and has a long cape that trails down to the floor (this can also be seen as a chimney perforating the top of a lean-to containing a table)

CUES: this 皮 (Straight Arrow) was in **Ha**waii when he tripped on this 石 (stone), and his **Yak** skin **Boots** 破れた **yabu**reta (tore) apart, so that he couldn't go to a **P**arty   **ALSO COMPARE:** 敗(れる) yabureru = to lose or be defeated, # 793; other similar kanji at # <u>833</u> and # <u>1775</u>

0838. 殺   PRONUNCIATIONS: satsu, sa, koro
MEANINGS: to kill or reduce
EXAMPLES: 殺人 satsujin = murder; 殺到する sattou suru = to rush at or surge; 殺す korosu = to kill
DESCRIPTION: compared to 役に立つ yaku ni tatsu (to be useful, # 557), this substitutes an X, which may represent a drone, and a 木 (tree) for the man with a double hat on the left; it retains the 兀 (yak) on a 又 (table)   **CUES:** I read a **S**atisfying **S**uperman novel about a **S**alaryman who saw this drone fly over this 木 (tree) and 殺す **koro**su (kill) this 兀 (yak) on a 又 (table), after which the man suffered a **C**oronary (heart attack) **COMPARE:** similar kanji at # <u>557</u>, # <u>1352</u> and # <u>1953</u>

0839. 影   PRONUNCIATIONS: ei, kage
MEANINGS: shadow, silhouette, phantom
EXAMPLES: 影響 eikyou = influence, effect; 影 kage = shadow, silhouette
DESCRIPTION: compared to 景(色) keshiki (view, # 516), this adds three cords for a catapult, as seen in 形 katachi (shape, # 573), on the right; it retains the 日 (sun) above the tire stop, the 口 (box, or house) and the 小 (small) hill
CUES: looking at this 景 (view), I saw an **A**pe holding these three cords and using them to cast 影 **kage** (shadows) on a wall, so I **C**alled a **Gue**st to investigate
GROUP: 髪 kami = hair, # 501; 形 katachi = shape, # 573; 影 kage = shadow, # 839; 杉 sugi = cedar tree, # 1154; (必)須 hissu = essential, # 1616; (色)彩 shikisai = color, hue, # 1630; 彫(る) horu = to carve, # 1698; (表)彰 hyoushou = a commendation, # 1807   **ALSO COMPARE:** other similar kanji at # 502, # <u>514</u> and # <u>1474</u>

0840. 響   PRONUNCIATIONS: kyou, hibi
MEANINGS: echo, sound, resound, ring, vibrate   **EXAMPLES:** 影響 eikyou = influence, effect; 響く hibiku = to resound, to be heard far away; 響き hibiki = echo, repercussion, sound
DESCRIPTION: at the upper left, a jagged lightning strike; at the upper middle, 良(い) yoi (good, # 303), which contains L & Y at its base, without its pointy hat; at the upper right, ß beta from the Greek alphabet; at the bottom, 音 oto (sound, # 266)   **CUES:** when this lightning strikes in **Kyou**to, the 影響 ei**kyou** (effect) of this 音 (sound) on my 良 (good) ß (**G**reek) friend is to give him the **Heebee** jeebies, and he's going home to **A**thens   **GROUP:** (影)響 eikyou = influence, # 840; 郷(里) kyouri = hometown, # 1059 (identical pronunciation); 擁(護) yougo = protection, # 1841   **ALSO COMPARE:** other similar kanji at # <u>266</u>, # <u>805</u> and # <u>1843</u>

0841. 添   PRONUNCIATIONS: ten, so, zo²
MEANINGS: annex, accompany, attach, append, garnish   **EXAMPLES:** 添加物 tenkabutsu = an additive (e.g., to food); 添える soeru = to attach to, to garnish a dish, to help or support; 付き添う tsukisou = to accompany, chaperone, take care of; 力添え chikarazoe = assistance, support   **DESCRIPTION:** on the left, a water radical (see # 12); at the upper right, 天 ten (sky, # 189) (identical pronunciation), which reminds us that the sky is like a tent; at the lower right, 小 (さい) chiisai (small, # 253), with a piece of gum lying on the ground to the right   **CUES:** this 天 (sky) is like a **T**ent above a 小 (small) piece of gum, which will interact with this water on the left until it 添える **so**eru (attaches) to a **S**oldier's boot   **ALSO COMPARE:** other similar kanji at # <u>1010</u> and # <u>1811</u>

0842. 延 **PRONUNCIATIONS: en, no, nobe** **MEANINGS:** to extend or postpone **EXAMPLES:** 延期 enki = postponement; 延びる nobiru = to lengthen or be postponed, intransitive (more commonly, this can also be spelled 伸びる, # 697); 延床面積 nobeyuka menseki = total floor area **DESCRIPTION:** at the lower left, a 3X snail, as seen in 建(てる) tateru (to build, # 363), which consists of a 3 intersected at the bottom to form an X; at the upper right, 正(しい) tadashii (correct, # 174) **CUES:** an **E**ngineer who is always 正 (correct) visited **N**orway, and he had to request an 延期 **en**ki (postponement) of his appointments because this 3X snail on which he traveled was so slow, but later he won a **Nobel** prize **ALSO COMPARE:** other similar kanji at # **692** and # **1150**

0843. 餌 **PRONUNCIATIONS: e, esa** **MEANINGS:** animal food, bait **EXAMPLES:** 餌食 ejiki = prey or victim; 餌 esa = animal food or bait **DESCRIPTION:** on the left, a simplified version of 食(べる) taberu (to eat, # 398); on the right, 耳 mimi (ear, # 57) **CUES:** a dog's 耳 (ears) prick up when an **E**xpert dog handler serves it an **E**gg **S**andwich as 餌 **esa** (animal food), and it 食 (eats) the sandwich **ALSO COMPARE:** other similar kanji at # **1713** and # **1974**

0844. 視 **PRONUNCIATION: shi** **MEANINGS:** inspection, regard as, see, look at **EXAMPLES:** 無視 mushi = disregarding, ignoring; 視力 shiryoku = eyesight **DESCRIPTION:** on the left, the **Sh**ah, as seen in (会)社 kaisha (company, # 271); on the right, 見(る) miru (to watch, # 53) **CUE:** this **Sh**ah 見 (watches) his **S**heep, using his good 視力 **shi**ryoku (eyesight) **ALSO COMPARE:** other similar kanji at # **1160** and # **1341**

0845. 肩 **PRONUNCIATIONS: kata, ken** **MEANING:** shoulder **EXAMPLES:** 肩 kata = shoulder; 肩甲骨 kenkoukotsu = shoulder blade or scapula **DESCRIPTION:** on the upper left, a lean-to with a double roof and a cloth on top, but this resembles a shoulder under a shirt, with an arm extending down to the left; on the lower right, 月 tsuki (moon, # 148) **CUES:** there was a **Ca**tastrophe at the **Ken**tucky Derby, and this man with this 月 (moon) tattoo on his chest sustained an injury to this 肩 **ka**ta (shoulder) under this shirt **COMPARE:** similar kanji at # **1134** and # **1991**

0846. 撫 **PRONUNCIATIONS: na, bu** **MEANINGS:** to stroke, pat, smooth down **EXAMPLES:** 撫でる naderu = to rub or stroke; 愛撫 aibu = a caress **DESCRIPTION:** on the left, a kneeling man; on the right, 無(くす) nakusu (to lose, # 583) or 無(事) buji (safety, # 583), both of which help us to pronounce this and consist of a crutch above a fence, or a cage (see # 583), which is above four flames **CUES:** this man on the left was once a **Na**zi and a **Boo**zer, but he 無 (lost) everything that he owned, and now he kneels to 撫でる **na**deru (rub) the heads of stray animals that he meets **ALSO COMPARE:** other similar kanji at # **583** and # **611**

0847. 精 **PRONUNCIATIONS: sei, shou** **MEANINGS:** pure, essence, details, energy, vitality **EXAMPLES:** 精一杯 seiippai = the best of one's ability, with all one's might; 精密な seimitsu na = detailed, precise, thorough; 精神 seishin = mind, soul, spirit; 精神的な seishinteki na = spiritual, mental; 精進料理 shoujin ryouri = vegetarian cuisine, as eaten by Buddhist monks **DESCRIPTION:** compared to 青(い) aoi (blue, # 155), or 青(年) seinen (young man, # 155) (identical pronunciation), this kanji adds 米 kome (uncooked rice, # 326) on the left; it retains the owl's perch on the 月 (moon), where an owl feels safe **CUES:** a **Sai**lor saw this 青 (blue) 米 (rice) at a food **Sh**ow, and the color was so bizarre that it caused him to have 精神的な **sei**shinteki na (mental) problems **ALSO COMPARE:** other similar kanji at # **1112** and # **1387**

0848. 杯 **PRONUNCIATIONS: hai, bai, pai, sakazuki** **MEANINGS:** wine glass, toast **EXAMPLES:** 二杯 nihai = two cups, glasses, spoons or bowls; 三杯 sanbai = three cups; 一杯 ippai = one cup, or full of; 杯をする sakazuki wo suru = to share a cup of sake **DESCRIPTION:** on the left, 木 ki (tree, # 118); on the right, 不 (negation) as seen in 不(便) fuben (inconvenient, # 176) **CUES: Hei**di **Buy**s a **Pie** and goes to play **Sakkaa** (soccer) with a **Zoo Kee**per, but this 木 (tree) in the middle of the field serves to 不 (negate) that idea, so she shares 一杯 ip**pai** (one cup) of sake with him instead **ALSO COMPARE:** other similar kanji at # **172** and # **176**

0849. 兆 **PRONUNCIATIONS: kiza, chou** **MEANINGS:** sign, omen, trillion **EXAMPLES:** 兆し kizashi = sign, omen; 前兆 zenchou = premonition, omen; 一兆円 icchouen = one trillion yen **DESCRIPTION:** two benches stored vertically, with their legs projecting to the sides **CUES:** we were sitting on these two benches, looking at 一兆 ic**chou** (one trillion) stars, and I was getting ready to **Ki**ss **Za**ch when he started talking about Margaret **Cho**, and I took that as a bad 兆し **kiza**shi (omen) **GROUP:** 兆(し) kizashi = sign, # 849; 逃(げる) nigeru = to run away, # 850; 挑(戦する) chousen suru = to challenge, # 1001 (identical pronunciation); 跳(ねる) haneru = to jump, # 1084; 眺(望) choubou = a view, # 1136 (also identical pronunciation); 桃 momo = a peach, # 1728 **ALSO COMPARE:** other similar kanji at # 851

0850. 逃 **PRONUNCIATIONS: ni, tou, noga** **MEANING:** to run away **EXAMPLES:** 逃げる nigeru = to escape or run away; 逃亡 toubou = escape, flight; 逃れる nogareru = to escape; 逃す nogasu = to let go, to allow to escape **DESCRIPTION:** compared to 兆 chou (trillion, # 849), this adds a snail on the lower left **CUES:** my **Nie**ce was on a **To**ll road when she spotted this snail carrying 兆 (a trillion) bacteria that were trying to 逃げる **ni**geru (escape) from a hurricane, and she thought about following them, but her car had **No Ga**s **ALSO COMPARE:** other similar kanji at # **849**

0851. 悲 **PRONUNCIATIONS: hi, kana** **MEANINGS:** sad, sorrow **EXAMPLES:** 悲観する hikan suru = to be pessimistic, feel hopeless; 悲鳴 himei = scream, shriek, cry of distress; 悲しい kanashii = sad **DESCRIPTION:** compared to 非(常) hijou (emergency, # 682) (identical pronunciation), this kanji adds 心 kokoro (heart, # 306) at the bottom; it retains the hero with two wings, which can also be seen as ladders or stairs **CUES:** this 非 (**Hero**) with two wings lives in **Ca**na**d**a, and sometimes his 心 (heart) feels 悲しい **kana**shii (sad) during the long winters **GROUP:** 非(常) hijou = emergency, # 682; 悲(しい) kanashii = sad, # 851; 罪 tsumi = a crime, # 1291; 俳(句) haiku = a poetry style, # 1441; (後)輩 kouhai = junior, # 1607; 排(水) haisui = drainage, # 1623; 扉 tobira = a front door, # 1672 **ALSO COMPARE:** other similar kanji at # 849

0852. 揺 **PRONUNCIATIONS: yu, you** **MEANINGS:** swing, sway, rock, tremble, vibrate **EXAMPLES:** 揺れる yureru = to sway or shake; 動揺 douyou = uneasiness, agitation **DESCRIPTION:** on the left, a kneeling guy; at the upper right, a barbecue grate; at the lower right, a tongue, as seen in 舌 shita (tongue, # 1213), emerging from a 山 yama (mountain, # 146) **CUES:** this guy on the left was barbecuing some **Yu**cca on this grill in **Yo**semite when this 舌 (tongue) emerging from this 山 (mountain) began to talk, startling him so that he 揺れた **yu**reta (shook) and fell to his knees like this **ALSO COMPARE:** (歌)謡(曲) kayoukyoku = a popular song, # **1856** (identical pronunciation); other similar kanji at # **1177** and # **2079**

0853. 器 PRONUNCIATIONS: utsuwa, ki MEANING: container EXAMPLES: 器 utsuwa = container or receptacle, ability; 食器 shokki = tableware; 便器 benki = toilet bowl, urinal DESCRIPTION: at the top, two 口 kuchi (mouths, # 426), which also resemble boxes; in the middle, 大(きい) ookii (big, # 188); at the bottom, two more 口 (mouths, or boxes) CUES: this 大 (big) family has these four 口 (mouths) to feed, and they **U**tilize **S**upermarket **W**alnuts, as well as **Qu**iche, which they store in 器 **utsuwa** (containers)
ALSO COMPARE: other similar kanji at # **1034**

0854. 奇 PRONUNCIATION: ki
MEANINGS: strange, curiosity
EXAMPLES: 奇妙な kimyou na = strange, unique; 好奇心 koukishin = curiosity
DESCRIPTION: compared to 寄(付) kifu (donation, # 604) (identical pronunciation), this kanji omits the bad haircut; it retains 大 (big) above 可 (愛い) kawaii (cute, # 615)
CUE: this reminds us of a 可 (cute) person wearing a **Ki**mono that is too 大 (big) for her, which is a 奇妙な **ki**myou na (strange) sight
ALSO COMPARE: other similar kanji at # **604**

0855. 椅 PRONUNCIATION: i
MEANING: chair EXAMPLE: 椅子 isu = chair DESCRIPTION: on the left, 木 ki (tree, # 118); on the right, 奇(妙) kimyou (strange, # 854), which reminds us of a 可 (cute) person wearing a kimono that is too 大 (big)
CUE: at **E**aster the Pope sat in a 奇 (strange) 椅子 **i**su (chair) made from this 木 (tree)
ALSO COMPARE: other similar kanji at # **604**

0856. 妙 PRONUNCIATIONS: tae, myou
MEANINGS: exquisite, excellent, strange, queer
EXAMPLES: 妙なる taenaru = exquisite; 妙 myou = strange, odd, unique; 奇妙 kimyou = strange; 微妙 bimyou = subtle, delicate, ticklish
DESCRIPTION: on the left, a tall 女 onna (female,# 235); on the right, 少(し) sukoshi (a little, # 254) CUES: this 女 (woman) is a **T**all **E**xpert on cats, but she was 少 (a little) surprised when she heard a **Meow** from a 奇妙な k**imyou** na (strange) animal ALSO COMPARE: other similar kanji at # **1010** and # **2039**

0857. 比 PRONUNCIATIONS: hi, bi², kura MEANING: to compare EXAMPLES: 比較 hikaku = comparison; 対比する taihi suru = to compare, contrast; 恵比寿 Ebisu = a district in Tokyo; 比べる kuraberu = to compare
DESCRIPTION: two variations of the katakana ヒ hi, which remind us of heroes and help us to pronounce this CUES: these two ヒ 's (**H**eroes) both raise **Ku**waiti **Ra**bbits, but they look different, prompting us to 比べる **kura**beru (compare) them COMPARE: similar kanji at # **1294**

0858. 鮮 PRONUNCIATIONS: sen, aza
MEANING: fresh EXAMPLES: 新鮮 shinsen = fresh; 鮮明 senmei = bright, clear, vivid; 鮮やか azayaka = colorful, bright, vivid, impressive, beautiful
DESCRIPTION: on the left, 魚 sakana (fish, # 80); on the right, 羊 hitsuji (sheep, # 1223)
CUES: a **Sen**ator eats this 新鮮な shin**sen** na (fresh) 魚 (fish), while keeping an eye on this 羊 (sheep) to make sure that it doesn't eat his **A**z**a**leas
ALSO COMPARE: similar kanji at # **611**, # **618** and # **1223**

0859. 検 PRONUNCIATION: ken
MEANINGS: to examine or inspect
EXAMPLES: 検査 kensa = investigation, examination; 探検 tanken = exploration, expedition (this can also be written 探険 tanken, # 196)
DESCRIPTION: compared to (危)険 kiken (danger, # 196) (identical pronunciation), this kanji substitutes 木 ki (tree, # 118) for ß (the Greek guy) on the left; it retains the horizontally placed keg stuck under a steep roof inside a 大 (big) washing machine CUE: **Ken** climbs this 木 (tree) in order to 検査する **ken**sa suru (inspect) a keg which is stuck in this 大 (big) washing machine under this steep roof
ALSO COMPARE: similar kanji at # **1432**

0860. 査 PRONUNCIATION: sa
MEANING: to examine closely EXAMPLES: 検査 kensa = investigation, examination; 調査 chousa = investigation, survey, analysis; 巡査 junsa = patrolman DESCRIPTION: at the top, 木 ki (tree, # 118); at the bottom, a solar panel, as seen in 祖(母) sobo (grandmother, # 272)
CUE: after this 木 (tree) was allowed to grow over this solar panel, blocking its sunlight, **Sa**msung conducted a 調査 chou**sa** (investigation)
ALSO COMPARE: other similar kanji at # **752**

0861. 膝 PRONUNCIATION: hiza
MEANINGS: knee, lap EXAMPLE: 膝 hiza = knee, lap DESCRIPTION: on the left, 月 tsuki (moon, # 148); at the upper right, 木 ki (tree, # 118); below that, 人 hito (person, # 13); at the lower right, 水 mizu (water, # 251)
CUE: this 人 (person) squeezed himself between this 木 (tree) and this 水 (water) and then fell onto his 膝 **hiza** (knees) by the light of this 月 (moon), and his wife said, "**He's A** little drunk"
GROUP: 膝 hiza = knee, # 861; 漆(器) shikki = lacquerware, # 1957

ALSO COMPARE: 肘 hiji = an elbow, # 1954; other similar kanji at # **1382** and # **1529**

0862. 我 PRONUNCIATIONS: wa, ware, ga MEANINGS: I, my
EXAMPLES: 我が国 wagakuni = one's country; 我がまま wagamama = selfish, spoiled; 我 ware = self; 我々 wareware = we; 我ら warera = we; 我慢 gaman = patience, endurance, tolerance DESCRIPTION: on the left, 手 te (hand, # 23); on the right, a halberd (combination lance and axe) CUES: this reminds us of General **Wa**shington, who always kept this 手 (hand) on this halberd; he was a **Wa**rrior **Re**bel who had the gift of **Ga**b, and he used to say, "我が国 **wa**gakuni (our country) is going to win"
ALSO COMPARE: similar kanji at # **1554** and # **1862**

0863. 腹 PRONUNCIATIONS: fuku, puku², naka, hara, bara², para²
MEANINGS: abdomen, belly
EXAMPLES: 腹痛 fukutsuu = stomach ache; 空腹 kuufuku = hunger; 満腹 manpuku = full stomach; お腹 onaka = stomach; 腹 hara = stomach, abdomen; 脇腹 wakibara = the flank; 横つ腹 yokoppara = side of the body, the flank
DESCRIPTION: compared to (回)復 kaifuku (recovery, # 527) (identical pronunciation), this kanji substitutes 月 tsuki (moon, # 148) for the man with a double hat; on the right, it retains the crutch at the top, 日 hi (sun) in the middle, and a dancer with a ponytail at the bottom (this combination of radicals = CSD = crutch, sun, dancer)
CUES: this injured sunny dancer from **Fuku**oka has a **Na**sty **Ca**t that **Hara**sses her when this 月 (moon) is full, or when it feels 空腹 kuu**fuku** (hunger) (CSD = crutch, sun, dancer)
ALSO COMPARE: other similar kanji at # **1220**

0864. 寂 **PRONUNCIATIONS: jaku, sabi** **MEANINGS:** loneliness, quietly, mellow **EXAMPLES:** 静寂 seijaku = silence, stillness; 寂しい sabishii = lonely

DESCRIPTION: at the top, a bad haircut; at the lower left, a taser, as seen in (予)定 yotei (plan, # 455) on a platform above a 小 (small) hill; on the lower right, 又 mata (again, # 24), which resembles a simple table **CUES: Jack** Nicholson, who has a bad haircut like this, is seated at this 又 (table), eating **Salty Beans** with only this taser on this 小 (small) hill for company, and he feels 寂しい **sabi**shii (lonely) **COMPARE:** other similar kanji at # **24** and # **1421**

0865. 敷 **PRONUNCIATIONS: shiki, shi** **MEANINGS:** spread, pave, sit **EXAMPLES:** 座敷 zashiki = Japanese-style room with tatami flooring; 屋敷 yashiki = estate, mansion, residence; 敷く shiku = to lay out, spread or enact **DESCRIPTION:** at the upper left, this resembles the top portion of a dog chasing a ball, as seen in 犬 inu (dog, # 190); at the middle left, 田 (rice paddy, # 68); at the lower left, 方 kata (honorable person, # 114), who seems to have the dog and the rice paddy on his mind; on the right, a dancer with a ponytail **CUES:** this 方 (honorable person) on the left has this truncated 犬 (dog) and this 田 (rice paddy) on his mind, but this dancer on the right wants him to explain the use of the **Shift Key** to some **Shi**ites who are waiting in a 座敷 za**shi**ki (Japanese-style room) **GROUP:** 薄(い) usui = pale, # 258; 敷(く) shiku = to lay out, # 865; 博(打) bakuchi = gambling, # 1481; 縛(る) shibaru = to tie, # 1721 (identical pronunciation); (帳)簿 choubo = an account book, # 1788 **ALSO COMPARE:** other similar kanji at # **2016**

0866. 丸 **PRONUNCIATIONS: gan, maru** **MEANINGS:** round, circle, completely, name of a ship **EXAMPLES:** 弾丸 dangan = bullet; 丸い marui = round; 丸 maru = circle **DESCRIPTION:** 九 kyuu (nine, # 111) with a slash drawn through it **CUES: Gan**dalf was **Maroo**ned on a 丸い **maru**i (round) island after pirates slashed his boat 九 (nine) times **ALSO COMPARE:** other similar kanji at # **1737**

0867. 局 **PRONUNCIATION: kyoku** **MEANINGS:** section, circumstances, government agency **EXAMPLES:** 郵便局 yuubinkyoku = post office; 結局 kekkyoku = after all **DESCRIPTION:** on the upper left, a lean-to with a double roof; on the lower right, 可(愛い) kawaii (cute, # 615), which consists of a second lean-to containing a box **CUE:** the **Kyo**to **Koo**l-Aid club is located in this double-roofed lean-to next to the 郵便局 yuubin**kyoku** (post office), and this 可 (cute) person is inside it **ALSO COMPARE:** other similar kanji at # **1176** and # **1899**

0868. 突 **PRONUNCIATIONS: totsu, tsu, to** **MEANINGS:** to thrust or protrude **EXAMPLES:** 突然の totsuzen no = abrupt or sudden; 突き当たり tsukiatari = dead end; 突破する toppa suru = to break through **DESCRIPTION:** compared to 空 sora (sky, # 248), this substitutes 大(きい) ookii (big, # 188) for 工 (crafted object) at the bottom; it retains the soaring bird with two lopsided legs **CUES:** this soaring bird with two lopsided legs appeared 突然に **totsu**zen ni (suddenly), hovered over this 大 (big) guy and offered to **Tote Super**man's **Tsu**itcase (suitcase) to **To**lstoy's house **COMPARE:** other similar kanji at # **112**

0869. 恐 PRONUNCIATIONS: oso, kyou MEANING: to fear EXAMPLES: 恐れ osore = fear; 恐ろしい osoroshii = frightening, terrible; 恐れる osoreru = to fear or be apprehensive; 恐慌 kyoukou = panic DESCRIPTION: at the upper left, the katakana エ e, which stands for eggs; at the upper right, a desk, as seen in 机 tsukue (desk, # 140), with a slash across it; at the bottom, 心 kokoro (heart, # 306) CUES: an Old Soldier was buying エ (eggs) like this in Kyouto when he saw this desk that had been slashed, and he felt 恐 osore (fear) in this 心 (heart) ALSO COMPARE: other similar kanji at # **247** and # **1511**

0870. 永 PRONUNCIATIONS: ei, naga MEANING: long time EXAMPLES: 永遠 eien = eternity; 永眠 eimin = death; 永久 eikyuu = eternity; 永田町 Nagatachou = a district in Tokyo DESCRIPTION: compared to (水)泳 suiei (swimming, # 255) (identical pronunciation), this kanji omits the water radical on the left; it retains 水 (water) with two small lines added above it, which remind us of a hat with two feathers in it CUES: when Honest Abe drank this 水 (water), he would wear a hat with these two feathers in it and tell stories for what seemed like an 永遠 eien (eternity) while Nagaina (a snake) lurked outside ALSO COMPARE: other similar kanji at # **814**

0871. 戸 PRONUNCIATIONS: to, ko, do, be MEANINGS: door, household, counter for houses EXAMPLES: 戸 to = door; 戸締する tojimari suru = to lock the doors and windows; 戸棚 todana = cupboard; 一戸 ikko = one house or household; 井戸 ido = well; 神戸 Koube = a city in Japan DESCRIPTION: a lean-to with a double roof and a layer of snow on top CUES: when Tolstoy returned to this lean-to covered with snow like this on Cold nights, the 戸 to (Door) would always open, and he would go to Bed COMPARE: similar kanji at # **1134**

0872. 句 PRONUNCIATION: ku MEANINGS: phrase, haiku EXAMPLES: 文句 monku = complaint, phrase, words; 俳句 haiku = poem; 句読点 kutouten = punctuation marks DESCRIPTION: compared to 可(愛い) kawaii (cute, # 615), there is an added awning on the upper left, creating a hook with a box in it CUE: our 可 (cute) customer submitted a 文句 monku (complaint) to the effect that this awning we installed didn't keep her house Cool enough GROUP: (文)句 monku = complaint, # 872; 敬(う) uyamau = to respect, # 873; 警(察) keisatsu = the police, # 874; 驚(く) odoroku = to be astonished, # 971; 拘(束) kousoku = a restraint, # 1809

0873. 敬 PRONUNCIATIONS: kei, uyama MEANINGS: to respect or revere EXAMPLES: 敬語 keigo = honorific language; 尊敬する sonkei suru = to respect; 敬う uyamau = to respect or venerate DESCRIPTION: at the upper left, a plant radical; at the lower left, (俳)句 haiku (poem, # 872), but this looks like the mouth of a cave; on the right, a dancer with a ponytail CUES: this dancer, who lives in this Cave in the Ugandan Yama (mountains), wrote a 句 (poem) about these plants around her, which she 敬う uyamau (respects) GROUP: 敬(う) uyamau = to respect, # 873; 警(察) keisatsu = the police, # 874 (identical pronunciation); 驚(く) odoroku = to be astonished, # 971 ALSO COMPARE: other similar kanji at # **526** and # **872**

0874. 警 **PRONUNCIATION: kei**
MEANINGS: admonish, commandment
EXAMPLES: 警察 keisatsu = the police; 警戒する keikai suru = to be cautious or watch out **DESCRIPTION:** compared to (尊)敬 sonkei (respect, # 873) (identical pronunciation), this kanji adds 言(う) iu (to say, # 430) at the bottom; it retains the dancer with a ponytail near the mouth of a cave **CUE:** this dancer with a ponytail 敬 (respects) the 警察 **ke**isatsu (police), and she 言 (says) that they are welcome to attend parties in this **C**ave **ALSO COMPARE:** other similar kanji at # **526**, # **872** and # **873**

0875. 戒 **PRONUNCIATIONS: kai, imashi MEANING:** commandment
EXAMPLES: 警戒する keikai suru = to be cautious or watch out; 戒める imashimeru = to admonish, warn, prohibit, be cautious
DESCRIPTION: compared to (機)械 kikai (machine, # 138) (identical pronunciation), this kanji omits 木 (tree) on the left; it retains the halberd and the handcuffs (which also suggest a welcoming stance) **CUES:** since the **Kai**ser's men carry handcuffs like these and halberds like this, and talk to **I**mages of **Sh**eep, the public should 警戒する ke**ikai** suru (be cautious) **ALSO COMPARE:** other similar kanji at # **1862** and # **1924**

0876. 畳 **PRONUNCIATIONS: tatami, tata, jou MEANINGS:** tatami mat, to fold, counter for tatami mats **EXAMPLES:** 畳 tatami = tatami mat; 畳む tatamu = to fold; 六畳 rokujou = six tatami mats **DESCRIPTION:** at the top, 田 (rice paddy, # 68); in the middle, a tatami mat; at the bottom, a solar panel, as seen in 祖(父) sofu (grandfather, # 272) **CUES:** a **T**all **T**alented **Me**diator came to this 田 (rice paddy), complimented our **Ta**rnished **T**apestries, and asked **Jo**an of Arc to bring this solar panel out from under this 畳 **tatami** mat **ALSO COMPARE:** other similar kanji at # **220** and # **752**

0877. 津 **PRONUNCIATIONS: shin, tsu, zu MEANINGS:** haven, port, harbor, ferry
EXAMPLES: 興味津々 kyoumi shinshin = very interesting; 津波 tsunami = tidal wave; 宮津 Miyazu = a town in Kyoto Prefecture
DESCRIPTION: compared to (法)律 houritsu (law, # 417), this substitutes a water radical for the man with a double hat on the left; it retains the three-fingered trident-like hand grasping a rod (or brush), which perforates two sheets of paper; this rod or brush can also be seen as a telephone pole
CUES: a 津波 **tsu**nami of water like this struck a calligrapher as he was writing messages with this brush on these two sheets of paper at a **Shin**to shrine, causing the brush to perforate them and soaking his **Tsu**it (suit), before going on to strike a **Zoo**
GROUP: 妻 tsuma = wife, # 237; 建(てる) tateru = to build, # 363; 書 kaku = to write, # 415; 事 koto = intangible thing, # 416; (法)律 houritsu = a law, # 417; 健(康) kenkou = health, # 811; 津(波) tsunami = tidal wave, # 877; 筆 fude = writing brush, # 1091; 凄(い) sugoi = great, # 1671; 鍵 kagi = a key, # 1689
ALSO COMPARE: other similar kanji at # **820**

0878. 波 **PRONUNCIATIONS: wa, nami, ha, pa MEANINGS:** waves, billows
EXAMPLES: 阿波踊り Awa'odori = a type of Bon dance; 津波 tsunami = tidal wave; 波止場 hatoba = pier, wharf; 音波 onpa = sound wave **DESCRIPTION:** on the left, a water radical; on the right, 皮 kawa (skin, # 833), also known as Straight Arrow **CUES:** a 津波 tsu**nami** of **W**ater like this struck this 皮 (Straight Arrow), who had just eaten a **N**asty **M**eal with Prince **H**arry and his **Pa** (father)
ALSO COMPARE: 彼 kare = he, # 371; other similar kanji at # **833**

0879. 隙 PRONUNCIATION: suki
MEANINGS: crevice, fissure, discord, opportunity, leisure EXAMPLES: 隙間 sukima = gap, hole; 隙 suki = gap, opening, carelessness, inattentiveness DESCRIPTION: on the left, ß beta from the Greek alphabet; on the right, 日 hi (sun, # 32) above 小(さい) (small, # 253), but these look like an oven spinning on a central rod and surrounded by four offshoots which could be flames CUE: this ß (Greek) person bakes **S**uperior **Qui**che like the kind they make in Athens in this 日 (oven), which rotates on this 小 (rod) and spins out these four flames through 隙間 **suki**ma (gaps) in its sides COMPARE: other similar kanji at # **94** and # **2030**

0880. 官 PRONUNCIATION: kan
MEANINGS: government official, sense EXAMPLES: 警官 keikan = policeman; 仕官 shikan = military officer; 総司令官 soushireikan = commander-in-chief DESCRIPTION: compared to (旅)館 ryokan (Japanese inn, # 305), this kanji omits 食 (eat) on the left; it retains the bunk beds under a bad haircut CUE: a guy from **Kan**sas, who is a 警官 kei**kan** (policeman), retreated to the top of this bunk bed after he got this bad haircut GROUP: (旅)館 ryokan (Japanese inn, # 305) (identical pronunciation), (気)遣(う) kizukau = to care for, # 765; 追(う) ou = to chase, # 821; (警)官 keikan = policeman, # 880; 管(理) kanri = administration, # 1276 (also identical pronunciation); (医)師 ishi = physician, # 1351; (岐)阜 Gifu = a city in Japan, # 1658; 棺 kan = a coffin, # 2012 (also identical pronunciation)

0881. 敵 PRONUNCIATIONS: teki, kataki MEANING: enemy EXAMPLES: 敵 teki = enemy, opponent; 素敵な suteki na = great, wonderful; 敵 kataki = enemy, rival DESCRIPTION: at the upper left, the bell from 音 oto (sound, # 266); at the lower left, compared to 固(体) kotai (solid, # 731), the bottom has fallen out of the box, leaving 古(い) furui (old, # 392) under a two-sided lean-to; on the right, a dancer with a ponytail CUES: this dancer on the right deals with her 敵 **tek**i (enemies), who are **Tech**ies, by hiring an 古 (old) sentry to sit in this lean-to and use this 立 (bell) to make loud sounds, and she will also **C**all a **T**alented **K**ing for help
GROUP: 敵 teki = enemy, # 881, (指)摘 shiteki = pointing out, # 1083, 適(当) tekitou = suitable, # 1280, and 滴 teki = a drop, # 1854, all of which can be pronounced "teki"; 嫡(男) chakunan = an heir, # 2027

0882. 辿 PRONUNCIATION: tado
MEANINGS: to follow (a road) or pursue EXAMPLES: 辿る tadoru = to follow or trace; 辿り着く tadoritsuku = to find one's way to a place at last DESCRIPTION: at the lower left, a snail; at the upper right, 山 yama (mountain, # 146) CUE: a **T**an **D**oe and this snail 辿った **tado**tta (followed) the same path up this 山 (mountain), but the doe arrived at the top first
ALSO COMPARE: other similar kanji at # **1385**

0883. 及 PRONUNCIATIONS: kyuu, oyo
MEANINGS: to reach, in addition EXAMPLES: 普及する fukyuu suru = to become popular or widespread; 及ぶ oyobu = to reach or extend to; 及び oyobi = and, in addition DESCRIPTION: compared to 吸(収する) kyuushuu suru (to digest, # 427) (identical pronunciation), this kanji omits the cute baby's mouth; it retains the graph of its breathing patterns CUES: this graph of a **C**ute baby's breathing patterns 及ぶ **oyo**bu (extends) to occasions when she was fed **O**ld **Yo**gurt
ALSO COMPARE: other similar kanji at # **1131**

0884. 腰 PRONUNCIATIONS: koshi, goshi², you MEANINGS: loins, hip waist EXAMPLES: 腰 koshi = low back, waist, hip; 及び腰 oyobigoshi = a bent back; 腰痛 youtsuu = low back pain DESCRIPTION: compared to (必)要 hitsuyou (necessary, # 238) (identical pronunciation), this kanji adds 月 tsuki (moon, # 148) on the left; it retains the 女 (female) with three eyes who knows necessary things to eat, such as yogurt CUES: this 女 (female) with these three eyes had a **C**obra bite her **S**heepdog on the 腰 **koshi** (waist), and she is wandering under this 月 (moon), searching for some **Y**ogurt which she says is 要 (necessary) for treating the wound ALSO COMPARE: similar kanji at # **1415** and # **2086**

0885. 平 PRONUNCIATIONS: byou, hira, hei, tai MEANINGS: flat, calm EXAMPLES: 平等 byoudou = equality; 平たい hiratai = flat, simple; 平屋 hiraya = one-story house; 平和 heiwa = peace, tranquility; 平気な heiki na = unconcerned, nonchalant; 平らな taira na = flat, level DESCRIPTION: in the center, a telephone pole with a flat top, suggesting a flat or calm surface; on both sides, flames shooting out CUES: a **B**eerhall **O**wner said that a **H**ero **R**an to fight this fire in this flat-topped telephone pole, which was disturbing the 平和 **hei**wa (peace) and creating a **H**aze, but after awhile the hero got **T**ired ALSO COMPARE: other similar kanji at # **1053**

0886. 観 PRONUNCIATIONS: kan, mi MEANING: to look over EXAMPLES: 観光 kankou = sightseeing; 楽観 rakkan = optimism; 花を観る hana wo miru = flower viewing (this can also be written 花を見る) DESCRIPTION: compared to 勧(告) kankoku (recommendation, # 698) (identical pronunciation), this kanji substitutes 見(る) miru (to look, # 53) (also identical pronunciation), for 力 (force) on the right; it retains the truncated 矢 (Native American chief) hugging a net, which can be seen as a man with a slanted hat next to a 主 (master) with an extra pair of arms, as seen in # 203 CUES: this truncated 矢 (Native American chief) made a 勧 (recommendation) that the people of **Kan**sas 見 (look) in the **M**irror and address the problems involving animals in nets like this with 楽観 ra**kkan** (optimism) ALSO COMPARE: other similar kanji at # **698** and # **1341**

0887. 裏 PRONUNCIATIONS: ura, ri MEANINGS: back, reverse EXAMPLES: 裏 ura = back, rear, hidden aspect; 裏切る uragiru = to betray or deceive; 表裏 hyouri = two sides, inside and out DESCRIPTION: at the top, a tire stop, as seen in 対(する) tai suru (to confront, # 674); in the middle, a sincere guy wearing bifocals, as seen in 野(菜) yasai (vegetables, # 545); at the bottom, the katakana エ plus Y CUES: this sincere guy, エ, and Y have a **U**ranium mine, and they've installed this tire stop at the 裏 **ura** (back) of the mine to keep cars from driving in from the **R**ear ALSO COMPARE: other similar kanji at # **545**

0888. 原 PRONUNCIATIONS: gen, hara, bara², wara MEANINGS: field, meadow, original, source EXAMPLES: 原因 gen'in = cause; 野原 nohara = field; 海原 unabara = ocean; 小笠原 Ogasawara = an island group south of Japan DESCRIPTION: at the upper left, a one-sided lean-to; under the lean-to, at the top, 白(い) shiroi (white, # 44); at the bottom, 小(さい) chiisai (small, # 253); these two radicals can be seen as a white oven spinning; they can also be seen as white above small, or sun above small (ignoring the ray above the sun) CUES: **Gen**ghis placed this 小 (small) 白 (white) spinning oven in this lean-to a 野原 no**hara** (field), where no one would **Hara**ss him without a **W**arrant GROUP: 願(う) negau = to wish, # 94; 原(因) gen'in = cause, # 888; (起)源 kigen = origin, # 1267

ALSO COMPARE: other similar kanji at # **94**; kanji that depict *Leo's* oven at # 1069

0889. 畑 **PRONUNCIATIONS: hatake, hata** **MEANING:** agricultural field **EXAMPLES:** 畑 hatake = field for cultivation or field of expertise; 田畑 tahata = field (crops) **DESCRIPTION:** on the left, 火 hi (fire, # 443); on the right, 田 (rice paddy, # 68); these images allude to the practice of periodically burning rice paddies, which was thought to increase nutrients in the soil **CUES:** in **Ha**waii, a **Ta**ll **Ke**nnedy sets this 火 (fire) in this 畑 **hatake** (field) after the harvest, and he pays a **Ha**rbor **Ta**x when he ships his crops **ALSO COMPARE:** other similar kanji at # **220** and # **1239**

0890. 頬 **PRONUNCIATIONS: hoo, hoho** **MEANING:** cheek **EXAMPLES:** 頬 hoo = cheek; 頬張る hoobaru = to stuff one's cheeks or fill one's mouth with food; 頬 hoho = cheek **DESCRIPTION:** on the left, 夫 otto (husband, # 614), a 大 (big) guy with four extra arms, with flames emerging from his sides, as seen in 狭(い) semai (narrow, # 194); on the right, 貝 kai (shell, # 83), with a platform on top, where a head could fit, as seen in 頭 atama (head, # 93) **CUES:** after this 夫 (husband) on the left lost his head from the platform on the right, he was disoriented and walked into these flames; in addition his 頬 **hoo** (cheeks) were stung by **Ho**rnets, and Santa said "**Ho Ho**" when he saw him **ALSO COMPARE:** similar kanji at # **194** and # **1126**

0891. 陽 **PRONUNCIATION: you** **MEANINGS:** sunny, positive **EXAMPLES:** 太陽 taiyou = the sun; 陽性の yousei no = cheerful, positive; 陽気 youki = merry, happy-go-lucky **DESCRIPTION:** compared to 場(所) basho (place, # 403), this substitutes β beta from the Greek alphabet for the 土 (soil) on the left; it retains a modified version of 易(しい) yasashii (easy, # 402) **CUE:** if you live in β (Greece), spend a lot of time in the 太陽 tai**you** (sun) and eat a lot of **Yo**gurt, life seems 易 (easy) **ALSO COMPARE:** other similar kanji at # **1702** and # **2030**

0892. 折 **PRONUNCIATIONS: o, ori, setsu** **MEANINGS:** to break or fold, occasion **EXAMPLES:** 折る oru = to break, transitive; 折れる oreru = to break, intransitive; 折り ori = occasion, opportunity, time; 折り紙 origami = Japanese paper folding; 時折 tokiori = once in awhile; 骨折する kossetsu suru = to break a bone **DESCRIPTION:** compared to 所 tokoro (place, # 391), this substitutes a kneeling person for the P under a roof on the left; it retains the pair of pliers **CUES:** this person kneels in order to pick up this giant pair of pliers, which she uses to hand **O**reo cookies to her customers in the **Ori**ent, after she **Set** up a **Su**per business there, but sometimes the cookies 折れる **o**reru (break) **GROUP:** 質(問) shitsumon = question, # 86; 新(しい) atarashii = new, # 389; 近(い) chikai = close, # 390; 所 tokoro = place, # 391; 断(る) kotowaru = to refuse, # 704; 浜(辺) hamabe = beach, # 766; 折(る) oru = to break, # 892; 兵(隊) heitai = soldier, # 917; 祈(る) inoru = to pray, # 955; 丘 oka = a hill, # 1473; 哲(学) tetsugaku = philosophy, # 1521; 斬(新) zanshin = creative, # 1559; (分)析 bunseki = analysis, # 1606; (巨)匠 kyoshou = a master, # 1653; (山)岳 sangaku = mountains, # 1683; 誓(う) chikau = to vow, # 1780; 暫(定) zantei = tentative, # 1943; 薪 maki = firewood, # 1965; 逝(去) seikyo = death, # 1999; (一)斤 ikkin = one loaf of bread, # 2071

0893. 覆 **PRONUNCIATIONS: oo, fuku, puku², kutsugae** **MEANINGS:** capsize, be ruined, cover, shade, mantle **EXAMPLES:** 覆う oou = to cover, conceal, wrap, disguise; 覆面 fukumen = mask; 転覆する tenpuku suru = to capsize or overturn; 覆す kutsugaesu = to overturn or overthrow **DESCRIPTION:** compared to (回)復 kaifuku (recovery, # 527) (identical pronunciation), this kanji adds three eyes suspended from a platform, as seen in 要(る) iru (to need, # 238); it retains the man with a double hat and CSD = crutch, sun, dancer **CUES:** an Open-minded Old surgeon who uses these three eyes in his work met a guy in Fukuoka who worked for Superman, and the doctor Cut Superman's Guy, 覆った ootta (covered) the wound with a dressing, and achieved 復 (recovery) with the help of this dancer with this crutch sitting in this sun (CSD = crutch, sun, dancer) **ALSO COMPARE:** similar kanji at # 1220 and # 1415

0894. 逆 **PRONUNCIATIONS: saka, gyaku** **MEANINGS:** inverted, reverse, opposite, wicked **EXAMPLES:** 逆らう sakarau = to oppose or disobey; 逆さまの sakasama no = reverse, upside-down, topsy-turvy; 逆説 gyakusetsu = paradox; 逆の gyaku no = contrary, opposite, antithetical **DESCRIPTION:** at the lower left, a snail; on the snail, a ghost floating in the air, with rabbit ears and two arms holding candlesticks, which remind us of Universal laws, as seen in 鈍(い) nibui (dull, # 1245) **CUES:** this ghost, which is wearing rabbit ears and holding candlesticks, floats and plays Sakkaa (soccer), which is a 逆説 gyakusetsu (paradox) since it has no feet, and this snail on which it rides can outrun Geeky Yakuza (gangsters), contrary to known Universal laws **COMPARE:** other similar kanji at # 1245 and # 1997

0895. 鹿 **PRONUNCIATIONS: shika, jika², ka** **MEANING:** deer **EXAMPLES:** 鹿 shika = deer; 小鹿 kojika = fawn; 馬鹿 baka = fool, idiot, usually written バカ **DESCRIPTION:** at the upper left, a lean-to with a chimney; under the lean-to, at the upper right, three eyes suspended from the ceiling; at the lower right, 比(べる) kuraberu (to compare, # 857) **CUES:** these three eyes in this lean-to observe 鹿 shika (deer) and Sheep in California, as they 比 (compare) shelters and Calculate the available space for bedding down **GROUP:** 鹿 shika = deer; # 895; (推)薦(する) suisen suru = to recommend, # 1030; 慶(事) keiji = an auspicious event, # 1590; 麗(しい) uruwashii = lovely, # 1627; 麓 fumoto = the base of a mountain, # 1955 **ALSO COMPARE:** other similar kanji at # 1294

0896. 察 **PRONUNCIATIONS: satsu, sa** **MEANINGS:** to conjecture, perceive, look thoroughly **EXAMPLES:** 警察 keisatsu = police; 観察 kansatsu = observation; 察知する sacchi suru = to perceive **DESCRIPTION:** compared to 祭(り) matsuri (festival, # 377), this adds a bad haircut at the top; it retains the peaked roof with a bench hat on the left, above 二 (two) spinning on 小 (small) **CUES:** a Satisfied Superintendent from the 警察 keisatsu (police) visited this 祭 (festival) where he received this bad haircut, and then he was dissatisfied and a little Sad **ALSO COMPARE:** other similar kanji at # 297 and # 1347

0897. 宇 **PRONUNCIATION: u** **MEANINGS:** roof, space **EXAMPLE:** 宇宙 uchuu = universe, cosmos, space **DESCRIPTION:** at the top, a bad haircut; at the bottom, a kneeling telephone pole **CUE:** in Uganda they place what look like bad haircuts like this over kneeling telephone poles like this to conceal detectors that search the sky for 宇宙人 uchuujin (space aliens) **GROUP:** 呼(ぶ) yobu = to summon, # 428; 宇(宙) uchuu = universe, # 897; (評)判 hyouban = reputation, # 1054; 芋 imo = potato, # 1102; (上)昇 joushou = rising, # 1363; (連)邦 renpou = a federation, # 1593

0898. 宙 PRONUNCIATION: chuu

MEANINGS: space, sky   EXAMPLES: 宇宙 uchuu = universe, cosmos, space; 宙返り chuugaeri = somersault; 宙に浮く chuu ni uku = to float in air

DESCRIPTION: compared to (理)由 riyuu (reason, # 73), which consists of one unit above a rice paddy (or a rice paddy on a stick), this adds a bad haircut at the top
CUE: I put this bad haircut on this unit of rice near this rice paddy to make it less attractive to 宇宙人 uchuujin (space aliens) who might want to **Chew** on it
ALSO COMPARE: other similar kanji at # **942** and # **1157**

0899. 柵 PRONUNCIATION: saku

MEANINGS: fence, stockade   EXAMPLES: 柵 saku = fence; 鉄柵 tessaku = iron fence

DESCRIPTION: on the left, 木 ki (wood, # 118); on the right, 冊 satsu (counter for books, # 568), which reminds us of a bookstore   CUE: when I bought a **Sack** of 冊 (books) like these, I noticed that they had built a 柵 **saku** (fence) around the store, made of 木 (wood) like this
ALSO COMPARE: other similar kanji at # **568**

0900. 汁 PRONUNCIATIONS: juu, shiru, jiru   MEANINGS: soup, liquid, juice

EXAMPLES: 果汁 kajuu = fruit juice; 肉汁 nikujuu = gravy; 汁 shiru = soup; 鼻汁 hanajiru = nasal discharge   DESCRIPTION: on the left, a water radical, which reminds us of juice, which helps us to pronounce this; on the right 十 juu (ten, # 18), which also helps us to pronounce this

CUES: we drank 十 (10) bottles of 果汁 ka**juu** (fruit **J**uice), made from this water, with a **Shi**ite **Ru**ler who parks his **Jee**p under a **R**oof
ALSO COMPARE: similar kanji at # **1828**

0901. 犯 PRONUNCIATIONS: han, oka

MEANINGS: crime, to violate   EXAMPLES: 犯人 hannin = criminal, culprit; 犯す okasu = to violate, to commit (e.g., a crime)
DESCRIPTION: on the left, a woman contorting her body, as seen in 狭(い) semai (narrow, # 194); on the right, an uncoiling snake, as seen in 危(ない) abunai (danger, # 547)   CUES: when **Han**sel walks with Gretel, he **Occa**sionally sees her contorting her body like this to avoid snakes like this one, and he attacks the 犯人 **han**nin (culprits)
ALSO COMPARE: other similar kanji at # **547** and # **948**

0902. 厳 PRONUNCIATIONS: gen, kibi, gon   MEANINGS: strict, stern, rigid

EXAMPLES: 厳格な genkaku na = stern, strict; 厳しい kibishii = stern, rigid, strict; 荘厳な sougon na = solemn   DESCRIPTION: at the top, three old boys, as seen in 覚(える) oboeru (to memorize, # 54), but these resemble three bees on a one-sided lean-to; on the lower left, a diving board, attached to the top of 耳 mimi (ear, # 57); on the lower right, a dancer with a ponytail

CUES: **Gen**ghis, who has big 耳 (ears) like this, lives with this dancer under this lean-to, where he bounces on this diving board, and they **Keep Bees** like these up on the roof, which they frighten with a **Gong**, since they are 厳しい **kibi**shii (strict) with them   COMPARE: similar kanji at # **1340**, # **1625** and # **1713**

0903. 湧 PRONUNCIATION: wa

MEANING: to gush out   EXAMPLE: 湧く waku = to gush out, well up, appear
DESCRIPTION: on the left, a water radical; at the upper right, the katakana マ ma, which reminds us of Ma (mother); at the lower right, 男 otoko (male, # 109)

CUE: this マ (mother) and this 男 (male), who is her son, open a valve, and this **W**ater 湧く **wa**ku (gushes out)
COMPARE: other similar kanji at # **109** and # **1282**

0904. 徐 PRONUNCIATION: jo
MEANINGS: gradually, slowly, deliberately
EXAMPLES: 徐々に jojo ni = gradually, step by step; 徐行する jokou suru = to slow down
DESCRIPTION: compared to (削)除(する) sakujo suru (to delete, # 646) (identical pronunciation), this kanji substitutes a man with two hats for ß, the Greek guy with a 余(計) yokei (excessive, # 637) interest in Empress Josephine; it retains the spinning 丁 (nail) under a stool and a peaked roof CUE: this man with two hats told Empress **Jo**sephine that her spending on hats was 余 (excessive), advised her to 徐行する **jo**kou suru (slow down) her shopping and offered her one of his hats
ALSO COMPARE: similar kanji at # 637

0905. 想 PRONUNCIATIONS: so, sou, omo MEANINGS: to contemplate or think
EXAMPLES: 愛想がいい aiso ga ii = sociable; 想像 souzou = imagination; 想う omou = to imagine or contemplate
DESCRIPTION: compared to 相(談) soudan (consultation, # 787) (identical pronunciation), this kanji adds 心 kokoro (heart, # 306) at the bottom; it retains the 木 (tree) that I had my 目 (eye) on CUES: during the **So**viet era, a **So**ldier with an **O**ld **Mo**torcycle, who had some 想像 **sou**zou (imagination) and this 心 (heart) of courage, had his 目 (eye) on this 木 (tree), and he climbed it to find a way to escape
ALSO COMPARE: other similar kanji at # 787

0906. 象 PRONUNCIATIONS: shou, zou
MEANINGS: elephant, pattern, shape
EXAMPLES: 対象 taishou = an object; 印象 inshou = impression; 象 zou = elephant
DESCRIPTION: at the top, the upper half of 色 iro (color, # 473), which consists of two eyes under a fish head (see # 80); at the bottom, the lower half of 家 ie (house, # 405); taken together, these suggest a colorful house CUES: when you go to see the 象 **zou** (elephant) **Sh**ow, there is a **Z**one that you can visit where you will find 色 (colorful) 家 (houses) like this ALSO COMPARE: other similar kanji at # 87, # 1314 and # 1504

0907. 像 PRONUNCIATION: zou
MEANINGS: image, shape EXAMPLES: 想像 souzou = imagination; 仏像 butsuzou = image or statue of Buddha DESCRIPTION: compared to 象 zou (elephant, # 906) (identical pronunciation), which consists of two eyes under a fish head (see # 80) and above a house radical, this kanji adds a man with a slanted hat on the left
CUE: this man on the left uses his 想像 sou**zou** (imagination) to think of a **Z**one where 象 (elephants) like this can be protected, and he tilts his hat back in order to search for one
ALSO COMPARE: other similar kanji at # 87, # 1314 and # 1504

0908. 亀 PRONUNCIATIONS: kame, game², ki MEANINGS: turtle, tortoise
EXAMPLES: 亀 kame = turtle, tortoise; 海亀 umigame = sea turtle; 亀裂 kiretsu = crack, crevice, fissure DESCRIPTION: at the top, a fish head (see # 80); below that, two 田 (rice paddies, # 68), linked by a long line that terminates in a tail
CUES: this resembles a 亀 **kame** (turtle) that I photographed with my **Ca**mera in **Ki**ev, since it has a head like a fish, a shell that resembles two linked 田 (rice paddies) and a tail ALSO COMPARE: other similar kanji at # 618 and # 1003

0909. 草 PRONUNCIATIONS: kusa, gusa², sou, zou² MEANINGS: grass, plant
EXAMPLES: 草 kusa = grass; 仕草 shigusa gesture, mannerism; 草原 sougen = grasslands, prairie; 草履 zouri = Japanese sandals
DESCRIPTION: at the top, a plant radical, which could represent grass; below that, 早(い) hayai (early, # 34) CUES: some **Co**ol **Sa**xophone players got up 早 (early) and were playing music in this 草 **kusa** (grass) when a **S**oldier joined them
ALSO COMPARE: other similar kanji at # 1365

0910. 斜 PRONUNCIATIONS: **nana, sha**
MEANINGS: diagonal, slanting, oblique
EXAMPLES: 斜めの naname no = diagonal, oblique; 斜面 shamen = slope, slanting surface
DESCRIPTION: on the left, 余(計) yokei (excessive, # 637); on the right, the slanted shelf seen in 料(理) ryouri (cuisine, # 512), holding two cans of food   CUES: when **N**ancy's **N**anny encountered the **Sh**ah, she asked him for these two cans of food from this 斜めの **nana**me no (slanted) shelf, but he said that her request was 余 (excessive)   GROUP: 科(学) kagaku = science, # 511; 料(理) ryouri = cuisine, # 512; 斜(面) shamen = slope, # 910   ALSO COMPARE: other similar kanji at # **637**

0911. 崖 PRONUNCIATIONS: **gake, gai**
MEANINGS: precipice, cliff
EXAMPLES: 崖 gake = precipice, cliff; 断崖 dangai = precipice, cliff   DESCRIPTION: at the top, 山 yama (mountain, # 146) above a one-sided lean-to; under the lean-to, 土 tsuchi (soil, # 59), piled on 土 (soil)   CUES: **Ga**llant **K**en was working as a **G**u**i**de on this 山 (mountain) when he saw this lean-to which was full of 土 (soil) piled on 土 (soil) like this, due to a landslide under a **gake** 崖 (cliff)   ALSO COMPARE: other similar kanji at # **748**, # **1385** and # **1619**

0912. 翼 PRONUNCIATIONS: **tsubasa, yoku**   MEANINGS: wing, plane, flank
EXAMPLES: 翼 tsubasa = wing; 右翼 uyoku = right wing (politics); 左翼 sayoku = left wing (politics)   DESCRIPTION: at the top, 羽 hane (feather, wing, # 755), which reminds us of flying; in the middle, 田 (rice paddy, # 68); at the bottom, 共(に) tomo ni (together, # 969)   CUES: I left this 田 (rice paddy) and 羽 (flew) with my **T**su**i**tcase (suitcase) to **Ba**rcelona's **Sa**ndy beaches, 共 (together) with some friends, where I ate some **Yo**gurt and **C**oo**k**ies, and saw a bird with powerful 翼 tsubasa (wings)   ALSO COMPARE: other similar kanji at # **220**, # **486** and # **1457**

0913. 旋 PRONUNCIATION: **sen**
MEANINGS: rotation, go around   EXAMPLES: 旋回 senkai = rotation, turning   DESCRIPTION: on the left, 方 kata (honorable person, # 114); at the upper right, a crutch; at the lower right, a slightly modified version of the lower portion of (予)定 yotei (plan, # 455), consisting of a taser mounted on a foot   CUE: the 方 (honorable person) on the left is a **Sen**ator who 旋回する **sen**kai suru (turns) to see this crutch and this taser mounted on this foot, suggesting that he needs to work on health care and law enforcement   GROUP: (予)定 yotei = plan, # 455; 旋(回) senkai = rotation, # 913; 疑(問) gimon = doubt, # 978; 凝(る) koru = to grow stiff, # 1680; (基)礎 kiso = a base, # 1716; 錠(剤) jouzai = a pill, # 1914; (破)綻 hatan = failure, # 1949; (花)婿 hanamuko = a bridegroom, # 1960; (模)擬 mogi = imitation, # 2003   ALSO COMPARE: other similar kanji at # **920** and # **2080**

0914. 脅 PRONUNCIATIONS: **odo, kyou, obiya**   MEANINGS: threaten, coerce
EXAMPLES: 脅かす odokasu = to threaten or startle; 脅す odosu = to threaten; 脅威 kyoui = a threat, peril, menace; 脅かす obiyakasu = to menace or threaten; Note: both odokasu and obiyakasu are written 脅かす   DESCRIPTION: at the top, three instances of 力 chikara (force, # 107); at the bottom, 月 tsuki (moon, # 148)   CUES: I looked up to see these three men of 力 (force) dancing on this 月 (moon), and they 脅した **odo**shita (threatened) to send some foul **Od**ors down to us in **Kyou**to, but I just kept on eating **O**ld **B**eans and **Y**ams   GROUP: 脅(す) odosu = to threaten, # 914; 協(力する) kyouryoku suru = to cooperate, # 940 (identical pronunciation); 脇 waki = side or armpit, # 1570   ALSO COMPARE: other similar kanji at # **1991**

0915. 威 PRONUNCIATION: i
MEANINGS: intimidate, dignity, majesty, threaten
EXAMPLES: 権威 ken'i = authority
DESCRIPTION: on the upper left, a one-sided lean-to, supported on the right by a halberd (combination lance and axe), creating a two-sided lean-to; under the lean-to, 女 onna (female, # 235), wearing a flat hat **CUE:** this 女 (woman) with this flat hat enjoys tremendous 権威 ken'**i** (authority), and she finds it **Ea**sy to avoid 脅威 kyou**i** (threats) by hiding in this lean-to, with this big halberd by her side **GROUP:** 歳 sai = age, # 322; 感(じる) kanjiru = to feel, # 640; (権)威 ken'i = authority, # 915; (心)臓 shinzou = the heart, # 951; 減(る) heru = to reduce, # 1148; 茂(る) shigeru = to grow thickly, # 1186; 冷(蔵)庫 reizouko = refrigerator, # 1190; (絶)滅 zetsumetsu = extinction, # 1193; (親)戚 shinseki = a relative, # 1884; (軽)蔑 keibetsu = scorn, # 1983; (遺)憾 ikan = regret, # 2065 **ALSO COMPARE:** other similar kanji at # **2086**

0916. 権 PRONUNCIATIONS: gon, ken
MEANINGS: authority, power, rights
EXAMPLES: 権現 gongen = an incarnation of Buddha, an avatar; 権威 ken'i = authority; 権利 kenri = right, privilege **DESCRIPTION:** on the left, 木 ki (tree, # 118); on the right, a truncated Native American chief hugging a net, as seen in 勧(告) kankoku (recommendation, # 698), which can be seen as a man with a slanted hat next to a 主 (master) with an extra pair of arms **CUES:** this truncated 矢 (Native American chief) named **Gon**zalez used to work at the **Ken**tucky Derby, where he pruned 木 (trees) like this, but now he has 権威 **ken**'i (authority) over a zoo and hugs this net because he cares about the animals in it **ALSO COMPARE:** similar kanji at # **698**

0917. 兵 PRONUNCIATIONS: hei, hyou
MEANINGS: soldier, army, warfare
EXAMPLES: 兵隊 heitai = soldier; 兵庫県 hyougoken = Hyogo prefecture **DESCRIPTION:** compared to 浜(辺) hamabe (beach, # 766), this omits the water radical on the left; it retains the pair of pliers resting on a platform with legs **CUES:** a 兵隊 **hei**tai (soldier), who was using these pliers to create defensive barriers using **Hay**wire, put them on this platform with legs, and the Lone Ranger said "**Hi-yo** Silver" when he saw them **ALSO COMPARE:** similar kanji at # **892**

0918. 衛 PRONUNCIATION: ei
MEANINGS: defense, protection
EXAMPLES: 衛生 eisei = hygiene, sanitation; 衛星 eisei = satellite; 防衛 bouei = defense
DESCRIPTION: on the left and the right, 行(く) iku (to go, # 334), suggesting that one is in the middle of going; in the middle, 違(う) chigau (to differ, # 355), which contains radicals resembling 五 (five), without its snail **CUE:** honest **A**be is in the middle of 行 (going) out to check on the 防衛 bou**ei** (defense) of his capital, and he takes a 違 (different) route every time he goes **ALSO COMPARE:** similar kanji at # **625** and # **1174**

0919. 庫 PRONUNCIATIONS: ko, go
MEANINGS: warehouse, storage **EXAMPLES:** 車庫 shako = garage; 金庫 kinko = a safe; 冷蔵庫 reizouko = refrigerator; 兵庫県 hyougoken = Hyogo prefecture
DESCRIPTION: at the upper left, a lean-to with a chimney, which could be a garage; under the lean-to, 車 kuruma (car, # 283) **CUES:** when it's **Co**ld, I keep this 車 (car) in this 車庫 sha**ko** (garage), except when I take it to the **Go**lf course **ALSO COMPARE:** other similar kanji at # **2075**

0920. 防 PRONUNCIATIONS: fuse, bou
MEANINGS: ward off, defend **EXAMPLES:** 防ぐ fusegu = to prevent or defend; 予防 yobou = prevention **DESCRIPTION:** compared to 訪(ねる) tazuneru (to visit, # 713), this substitutes ß

beta from the Greek alphabet for 言 (to say) on the left; it retains 方 kata (honorable person, # 114), which can be seen as 万 man (ten thousand, # 113) with a feather in its hat, or 万 fused to a tire stop **CUES:** this 方 (honorable person) is a **Fo**od **Se**ller from β (Greece) who **Bo**asts about his record in the 予防 yo**bou** (prevention) of food-borne illness **GROUP:** 方 kata = honorable person, # 114; (家)族 kazoku = family, # 115; 旅(行) ryokou = travel, # 116; 遊(ぶ) asobu = to play, # 360; 訪(ねる) tazuneru = to visit, # 713; 旋(回) senkai = rotation, # 913; (予)防 yobou = prevention, # 920; 施(設) shisetsu = facility, # 1067; (暖)房 danbou = heating, # 1134; 旗 hata = flag, # 1430; (寝)坊 nebou = sleeping in late, # 1576; 傍(ら) katawara = close by, # 1633; 芳(香) houkou = perfume, # 1677; (脂)肪 shibou = fat, # 1849; 妨(害) bougai = an interference, # 1917; 紡(ぐ) tsumugu = to spin (textiles), # 2033; **Note** that five of these kanji can be pronounced "bou" **ALSO COMPARE:** kanji containing 方 with a *dancer* at # 2016; other similar kanji at # **2030**

0921. 牙 **PRONUNCIATIONS: kiba, ge, ga MEANINGS:** fang, tusk **EXAMPLES:** 牙 kiba = fang, tusk; 象牙 zouge = ivory; 牙城 gajou = stronghold **DESCRIPTION:** compared to (風)邪 kaze (upper respiratory infection, # 796), this omits the β (Greek) character on the right; it retains the man wearing a flat-topped helmet with a visor extending to the left and with an extended left hip **CUES:** when the **K**ing of **B**a**g**hdad invited a **Gu**est to his hanging **G**ardens, he wore this helmet with a visor designed to hide his 牙 **ki**b**a** (fangs) **ALSO COMPARE:** similar kanji at # **796** and # **1417**

0922. 雅 **PRONUNCIATIONS: miya, ga MEANINGS:** gracious, elegant, refined **EXAMPLES:** 雅びた miyabita = gracious, elegant, refined; 優雅な yuuga na = elegant; 温雅 onga = graceful, affable **DESCRIPTION:** compared to 牙 kiba (fangs, # 921), or 牙(城) gajou (stronghold, # 921) (identical pronunciation), this kanji adds a net on the right, which can be seen as a man with a slanted hat next to a 主 (master) with an extra pair of arms (see # 203) **CUES:** when I went to **M**eet a **Y**ankee, I noticed a **Ga**mbler in this net, wearing 優雅な yu**uga** na (elegant) robes and sporting these large 牙 (fangs) **ALSO COMPARE:** similar kanji at # **796**, # **1417** and # **2046**

0923. 狩 **PRONUNCIATIONS: ga, kari, ka, shu MEANINGS:** hunt, raid, gather **EXAMPLES:** キノコ狩り kinokogari = mushroom gathering; 石狩 Ishikari = a city in Hokkaido; 狩り kari = hunting, gathering; 狩る karu = to hunt (animals), to gather (mushrooms, etc.); 狩猟 shuryou = hunting **DESCRIPTION:** on the left, a woman contorting her body; on the right, 守(る) mamoru (to protect, # 214) which can be seen as a bad haircut above a sunny guy who has dropped his gum – see # 132 **CUES:** this woman on the left is a **Ga**dfly who contorts her body in order to try to 守 (protect) animals threatened by 狩り **ka**ri (hunting), and she **C**arries a **C**at and **Sh**oos hunters away **ALSO COMPARE:** similar kanji at # **214** and # **948**

0924. 飢 **PRONUNCIATIONS: u, ki MEANINGS:** to starve, to be hungry or thirsty **EXAMPLES:** 飢える ueru = to starve, to be thirsty or hungry; 飢え死に uejini = death from starvation; 飢きん kikin = famine **DESCRIPTION:** on the left, 食(べる) taberu (to eat, # 398); on the right, the tall desk seen in 机 tsukue (desk, # 140) **CUES:** when I 飢えていた **u**ete ita (was starving) in **U**ganda, I found some old **Qui**che in this tall 机 (desk) and 食 (ate) it **ALSO COMPARE:** other similar kanji at # **1462** and # **1974**

0925. 傾 PRONUNCIATIONS: katamu, kei MEANINGS: lean, incline, tilt, sink EXAMPLES: 傾く katamuku = to tilt or incline, to go down; 傾斜する keisha suru = to tilt or slant DESCRIPTION: on the left, a man with a slanted hat; on the right, 頃 koro (approximate time, # 96) which includes a ヒ (hero) next to a headless platform on a money chest, as seen in 頭 atama (head, # 93) CUES: this man on the left, who has a hat that 傾く **katamu**ku (tilts), wants to **Cat**apult this ヒ (hero) to the **Mo**on, but the hero has lost his head, as indicated by this headless platform on the right, and he will retreat to a **Cave** until they find it ALSO COMPARE: other similar kanji at # **1126** and # **1413**

0926. 退 PRONUNCIATIONS: no, shirizo, tai MEANINGS: retreat, withdraw, retire, resign EXAMPLES: 立ち退く tachinoku = to evacuate, vacate; 退く shirizoku = to retreat; 退屈 taikutsu = boredom; 退職 taishoku = retirement, resignation DESCRIPTION: on the lower left, a snail; riding on the snail, 良(い) yoi (good, # 303), which contains L & Y at its base, without its pointy hat CUES: a 良 (good) **N**orwegian rode up on this snail and said that, if **S**heep could **Rea**d the signs of the Zodiac, they might experience less 退屈 **tai**kutsu (boredom), but then a **Ti**ger ate him ALSO COMPARE: other similar kanji at # **805**

0927. 屈 PRONUNCIATIONS: ku, kutsu MEANINGS: to yield, submit, bend EXAMPLES: 屈服する kuppuku suru = to surrender; 退屈 taikutsu = boredom; 理屈 rikutsu = argument, theory, pretext DESCRIPTION: on the upper left, a lean-to with a double roof; under the lean-to, 出(る) dasu (to extract, # 147), which resembles a cooped-up human figure CUES: this 出 (person) under this lean-to with a double roof is **S**uperman and since he's **C**ooped up and suffering from 退屈 tai**kutsu** (boredom), we want to 出 (extract) him, but we must avoid **C**utting **S**uperman in the process GROUP: 出(る) dasu = to extract, # 147; (退)

屈 taikutsu = boredom, # 927; (発)掘 hakkutsu = excavation, # 1402; 堀 hori = a canal, # 1539; 拙(い) tsutanai = clumsy, # 1798; (洞)窟 doukutsu = a cave, # 1920; **Note** that three of these kanji can be pronounced "kutsu" ALSO COMPARE: other similar kanji at # **1899**

0928. 懐 PRONUNCIATIONS: kai, natsu, futokoro MEANINGS: pocket, breast, feelings, heart EXAMPLES: 懐中電灯 kaichuu dentou = flashlight; 懐かしい natsukashii = nostalgic, evocative of times past; 懐 futokoro = bosom, heart; 懐が広い futokoro ga hiroi = is kind-hearted DESCRIPTION: on the left, an erect man; at the upper right, 十 too (ten, # 18), which resembles a cross; below that, 目 me (eye, # 51) turned horizontally, which could represent three eyes; at the lower right, 衣(服) ifuku (clothing, # 1042) CUES: this man on the right is a **Kai**ser with this cross on his crown and these three eyes, and this man on the left, who is wearing this 衣 (clothing) which is a **Nat**ty **Sui**t and holds himself tall and proud, reminds the kaiser of a time when they slept on a **Fut**on in a **Coro**lla, which elicits 懐かしい **natsu**kashii (nostalgic) feelings COMPARE: other similar kanji at # **934**, # **1042** and # **2063**

0929. 群 PRONUNCIATIONS: mu, mura, gun MEANINGS: group, throng, herd EXAMPLES: 群れ mure = herd, crowd, group; 群がる muragaru = to flock or throng; 群集 gunshuu = group of living things, crowd, community; 群衆 gunshuu = group of people, crowd, mob DESCRIPTION: on the left, 君 kimi (you, # 419); on the right, 羊 hitsuji (sheep, # 1223) CUES: I saw 君 (you) in a **M**ovie, painting a **Mur**al of a 群れ **mu**re (herd) of 羊 (sheep) like this, and waving a **Gun** ALSO COMPARE: other similar kanji at # **419** and # **1223**

0930. 衆 **PRONUNCIATION:** shuu
MEANINGS: masses, multitude
EXAMPLE: 群衆 gunshuu = group of people, crowd, mob **DESCRIPTION:** at the top, 血 chi (blood, # 747); at the lower left, two swords; at the lower middle and right, the letters T and Y, which remind us of "thank you"
CUE: when I saw this 血 (blood) and these two swords in a 群衆 gun**shuu** (crowd), I ducked into a **Sh**oe store and said T**Y** (thank you) to the owner **GROUP:** this is a group of one **ALSO COMPARE:** other similar kanji at # **1407**

0931. 積 **PRONUNCIATIONS:** seki, se, tsu **MEANINGS:** volume, acreage, stack
EXAMPLES: 面積 menseki = area; 積極 sekkyoku = positive, progressive; 積もる tsumoru = to pile up (intransitive); 積む tsumu = to heap up, accumulate, load (transitive)
DESCRIPTION: compared to 責(任) sekinin (responsibility, # 772) or 責(める) semeru (to accuse, # 772), both of which help us to pronounce this and feature an owl's perch on top of a money chest, this adds 禾 (a grain plant with a ripe head) on the left **CUES:** a **Se**lfish **K**ing, who 積む **tsu**mu (accumulates) this 禾 (ripe grain) and wants to **Se**ll it, sets up this owl's perch on this 貝 (money chest) overlooking the grain so that an owl can take 責 (responsibility) for **Tsu**pervising (supervising) the sales **ALSO COMPARE:** other similar kanji at # **772** and # **1797**

0932. 射 **PRONUNCIATIONS:** sha, i
MEANING: to shoot **EXAMPLES:** 反射 hansha = reflection; 注射 chuusha = injection; 射る iru = to hit or shoot (an arrow)
DESCRIPTION: on the left, 身 mi (body, person, # 651); on the right, the sunny kneeling guy seen in 寸(前) sunzen (on the verge, # 1369), with a stick of gum on the ground nearby **CUES:** a **Sh**ah tells this kneeling sunny guy on the right to stop chewing gum for a moment and deliver a 注射 chuu**sha** (injection) into the **E**ar of this 身 (body) on the left **COMPARE:** other similar kanji at # **131**, # **1381** and # **1417**

0933. 戦 **PRONUNCIATIONS:** sen, ikusa, tataka **MEANINGS:** war, to fight
EXAMPLES: 戦争 sensou = war; 戦 ikusa = battle; 戦う tatakau = to fight (this can also, less frequently, be written 闘う tatakau, # 728)
DESCRIPTION: on the left, (簡)単 kantan (easy, # 636), which includes three waves of heat at the top that can also be seen as ear cooties; on the right, a halberd (combination lance and axe)
CUES: our **Sen**ator says that it's 単 (easy) to fight a 戦争 **sen**sou (war), if you carry **E**ar **C**ooties like these in a **S**ack to cast on your enemies and if a **T**all **T**axi driver **C**arries this halberd for you **COMPARE:** other similar kanji at # **1625**, # **1694** and # **1862**

0934. 聴 **PRONUNCIATION:** chou
MEANING: to listen **EXAMPLES:** 聴衆 choushuu = audience; 聴解力 choukairyoku = listening comprehension **DESCRIPTION:** on the left, 耳 mimi (ear, # 57); at the top right, 十 too (ten, # 18), which resembles a cross; at the middle right, 目 me (eye, # 51), turned on its side, resembling three eyes; at the lower right, 心 kokoro (heart, # 306) **CUE:** Margaret **Cho** wears this cross on her head and has these three eyes, and she tells her 聴衆 **chou**shuu (audiences) that she has big 耳 (ears) like this and this good 心 (heart)
GROUP: 懐(かしい) natsukashii = nostalgic, # 928; 聴(衆) choushuu = audience, # 934; (道)徳 doutoku = morality, # 1159; 壊(す) kowasu = to break, # 1394 **ALSO COMPARE:** other similar kanji at # **1713**

0935. 競 **PRONUNCIATIONS: kiso, se, kei, kyou** **MEANINGS:** to compete or race, a contest, to sell at auction **EXAMPLES:** 競う kisou = to compete with; 競り seri = auction; 競馬 keiba = horse racing; 競争する kyousou suru = to compete; 競技 kyougi = competition **DESCRIPTION:** two nearly identical figures, each with 立(つ) tatsu (to stand, # 11) at the top and 兄 ani (older brother, # 420) at the bottom, but the 兄 on the left seems to have a broken leg **CUES:** these two 兄 (older brothers) are **K**iller **S**oldiers who 立 (stand) as they ride **S**egways out of **C**aves near **Kyou**to in order to 競争する **kyou**sou suru (compete) **ALSO COMPARE:** other similar kanji at # **269**, # **352**, # **420** and # **1569**

0936. 争 **PRONUNCIATIONS: araso, sou** **MEANINGS:** contend, dispute, argue **EXAMPLES:** 争う arasou = to fight, dispute or compete; 競争する kyousou suru = to compete; 戦争 sensou = war **DESCRIPTION:** compared to 静(か) shizuka (quiet, # 418), this omits 青 (blue) on the left; it retains the monster with a fish head (see # 80) that someone has stabbed with a trident **CUES:** an **A**rab **S**oldier from **S**omalia 争う **araso**u (fights) this fish-headed monster and stabs it with this trident **GROUP:** 静(か) shizuka = quiet, # 418; (戦)争 sensou = war, # 936; (洗)浄 senjou = washing, # 1380

0937. 眩 **PRONUNCIATIONS: kura, mabu** **MEANINGS:** faint, dizzy **EXAMPLES:** 眩む kuramu = to be blinded or dazzled; 眩しい mabushii = dazzling, blinding **DESCRIPTION:** on the left, 目 me (eye, # 51); on the upper right, a tire stop as seen in 対(して) tai shite (against, # 674); on the lower right, the upper half of 糸 (skeet shooter, # 219) **CUES:** this 目 (eye) belongs to a museum **C**ura**t**or who was drinking **Ma**ssachusetts **Boo**ze and didn't see that this tire stop was about to fall on this truncated 糸 (skeet shooter); moreover, a sudden 眩しい **mabu**shii (dazzling) light distracted him **ALSO COMPARE:** other similar kanji at # **1129**, # **1860** and # **2002**

0938. 峰 **PRONUNCIATIONS: hou, pou, mine** **MEANINGS:** summit, peak **EXAMPLES:** 名峰 meihou = famous mountain; 連峰 renpou = mountain range; 峰 mine = mountain peak **DESCRIPTION:** on the left, 山 yama (mountain, # 146); on the upper right, a dancer with a ponytail; on the lower right, a telephone pole **CUES:** this dancer, who is also a **H**ostess, dances on top of this telephone **P**ole next to this 名峰 mei**hou** (famous mountain) in **M**inne**s**ota **GROUP:** (連)峰 renpou = mountain range, # 938; 蜂 hachi = bee, # 1254; 縫(う) nuu = to sew, # 1816 **ALSO COMPARE:** other similar kanji at # **1942**

0939. 富 **PRONUNCIATIONS: fu, to, tomi** **MEANINGS:** wealth, enrich, abundant **EXAMPLES:** 富士山 fujisan = Mt. Fuji; 豊富な houfu na = abundant; 富む tomu = to be rich or prosper; 富 tomi = wealth **DESCRIPTION:** compared to 福 fuku (good luck, # 661), this omits the Shah on the left and adds a bad haircut at the top; it retains 口 (mouth, or box), with a napkin above it, and 田 (rice paddy) **CUES:** this **Foo**lish guy with a bad haircut has 豊富な hou**fu** na (abundant) 田 (rice paddies) like this one and also **T**omato fields, but he has to keep this napkin over this 口 (mouth) to avoid bragging about them, and he has to employ guards with **T**ommy guns to protect his 富 **tomi** (wealth) **ALSO COMPARE:** other similar kanji at # **1185**

0940. 協 PRONUNCIATION: kyou
MEANINGS: to cooperate EXAMPLES: 協力する kyouryoku suru = to cooperate; 協同 kyoudou = cooperation DESCRIPTION: compared to 脅(威) kyoui (threat, # 914) (identical pronunciation), this omits the 月 (moon) at the bottom and adds 十 juu (ten, # 18) on the left; it retains the three instances of 力 (force) CUE: in **Kyou**to, 十 (**ten**) policemen 協力する **kyou**ryoku suru (**cooperate**) with these three men of 力 (**force**) to keep the peace ALSO COMPARE: other similar kanji at # **914** and # **1828**

0941. 襲 PRONUNCIATIONS: oso, shuu MEANING: to attack EXAMPLES: 襲う osou = to attack; 襲撃 shuugeki = an attack DESCRIPTION: on the upper left, 立(つ) tatsu (to stand, # 11) above 月 tsuki (moon, # 148); on the upper right, a complex structure resembling a comb; at the bottom, 衣(服) ifuku (clothing, # 1042)
CUES: an **O**ld **S**oldier once 立 (**s**tood) on this 月 (moon) and used to **Sh**oot at the enemy and 襲う **oso**u (**attack**) them, but now he wears this civilian 衣 (clothing) and combs his hair with this comb GROUP: 襲(う) osou = to attack, # 941; 籠 kago = a basket, # 2074 ALSO COMPARE: other similar kanji at # **1042** and # **1569**

0942. 油 PRONUNCIATIONS: yu, abura
MEANING: oil EXAMPLES: 油断 yudan = negligence, inattentiveness; 石油 sekiyu = petroleum; 油 abura = oil DESCRIPTION: compared to (理)由 riyuu (reason, # 73), which consists of one unit above a rice paddy (or a rice paddy on a stick), this adds a water radical on the left CUES: the 由 (reason) that I have this water plus this 由 (**U**nit of rice) is to provision my **Ab**u Dhabi **Ra**m that lives near an 油 **abura** (**oil**) field
GROUP: (理)由 riyuu = reason, # 73; 届(け る) todokeru = to deliver, # 74; (宇)宙 uchuu = universe, # 898; 油 abura = oil, # 942; 笛 fue = a flute, # 1503; 袖 sode = a sleeve, # 1697; 卑(屈) hikutsu = servile, # 1745; 抽(象) chuushou = an abstraction, # 1760; 軸 jiku = axle, # 1791; (墓)碑 bohi = a gravestone, # 1905
ALSO COMPARE: 脂 abura = fat, # 1180; other similar kanji at # **1157**

0943. 禁 PRONUNCIATION: kin
MEANING: to forbid EXAMPLES: 禁じる kinjiru = to prohibit; 禁物 kinmotsu = a forbidden thing; 禁煙 kin'en = no smoking
DESCRIPTION: at the top, 林 hayashi (grove, # 125) on a platform; at the bottom, a spinning nail under a flying carpet, as seen in 祭(り) matsuri (festival, # 377) [these can also be seen as 二 (two) above 小 (small)] CUE: our **Kin**g 禁じる **kin**jiru (prohibits) spinning of 林 (groves) like these, since it isn't good for the trees
GROUP: 林 hayashi = grove, # 125; 森 mori = a forest, # 127; 禁(じる) kinjiru = to prohibit, # 943; 焚(く) taku = to burn wood, # 1183; (基)礎 kiso = a base, # 1716; 襟 eri = a collar, # 1872; 麓 fumoto = the base of a mountain, # 1955
ALSO COMPARE: tree or trees in lean-to at # 1475; other similar kanji at # **1347**

0944. 吠 PRONUNCIATIONS: ho, bo
MEANINGS: to bark, howl, cry EXAMPLES: 吠える hoeru = to bark, howl, roar, cry; 遠吠え tooboe = howling DESCRIPTION: on the left, 口 kuchi (mouth, # 426), which can also be seen as a box; on the right, 犬 inu (dog, # 190)
CUES: this 犬 (dog) on the right uses this 口 (mouth) to 吠える **ho**eru (**bark**), as he protects his master's **Ho**me and **Bo**at ALSO COMPARE: other similar kanji at # **945** and # **2073**

0945. 伏
PRONUNCIATIONS: fuku, fu, bu **MEANINGS:** prostrated, bend down, bow **EXAMPLES:** 降伏する koufuku suru = to surrender; 伏せる fuseru = to lay an object upside down or face down, to lie down; うつ伏せに utsubuse ni = face down **DESCRIPTION:** on the left, a man with a slanted hat; on the right, 犬 inu (dog, # 190) **CUES:** this man from **Fu**kuoka tilts his hat back to serve as a pillow before he 伏せる **fu**seru (lies down), but first he gives **Fo**od to this 犬 (dog) and drinks some **Bo**oze **GROUP:** 犬 inu = dog, # 190; (全)然 zenzen = not at all, # 611; 黙(る) damaru = to keep silent, # 836; 吠(える) hoeru = to bark, # 944; 伏(せる) fuseru = to lie down, # 945; 嗅(ぐ) kagu = to smell, # 959; 状(態) joutai = condition, # 998; 燃(える) moeru = to burn, # 1240; (監)獄 kangoku = jail, # 1435; (貢)献 kouken = a contribution, # 1618; (野)獣 yajuu = a wild animal, # 1733

0946. 床
PRONUNCIATIONS: yuka, shou, toko **MEANINGS:** floor, bed **EXAMPLES:** 床 yuka = floor; 起床 kishou = rising, getting out of bed; 床 toko = bed, floor; 床屋 tokoya = barbershop **DESCRIPTION:** on the upper left, a lean-to with a chimney; under the lean-to, 木 ki (wood, # 118) **CUES:** a **Y**outhful **C**arpenter works in this lean-to with a chimney, in which he **Sh**ows 木 (wooden) items that he has created, including a 床 **yuk**a (floor) and a **To**y **Co**bra **COMPARE:** other similar kanji at # **1475**

0947. 獲
PRONUNCIATIONS: e, kaku **MEANINGS:** seize, get, find, acquire **EXAMPLES:** 獲物 emono = game (hunting) or catch (fishing); 獲得する kakutoku suru = to win or obtain **DESCRIPTION:** on the left, a woman contorting her body; at the upper right, a plant radical; at the middle right, a net, which can be seen as a man with a slanted hat next to a 主 (master) with an extra pair of arms (see # 203); at the lower right, 又 mata (again, # 24) which resembles a table **CUES:** this woman on the left contorts her body in order to view some **E**ggs stored in this net under these plants on this 又 (table), which she hopes to 獲得する **kaku**toku suru (obtain) from **Ka**rl the **Ko**ol-Aid vendor, who is also in the egg business **GROUP:** 獲(物) emono = game, # 947; (弁)護(し) bengoshi = lawyer, # 1163; (収)穫 shuukaku = harvest, # 1257 (identical pronunciation); (数)隻 suuseki = several ships, # 1895 **ALSO COMPARE:** other similar kanji at # **948**

0948. 狙
PRONUNCIATION: nera **MEANINGS:** aim at, stalk **EXAMPLE:** 狙う nerau = to aim **DESCRIPTION:** on the left, a woman contorting her body; on the right, a solar panel, as seen in 祖(父) sofu (grandfather, # 272) **CUE:** this woman on the left contorts her body as she tries to hide behind this solar panel, since a **N**egative **Ra**scal 狙っている **nera**tte iru (is aiming) at her **GROUP:** 猫 neko = cat, # 72; 狭(い) semai = narrow, # 194; 独 doku = unmarried, # 724; 犯(人) hannin = criminal, # 901; 狩(る) karu = to hunt, # 923; 獲(得する) kakutoku suru = to obtain, # 947; 狙(う) nerau = to aim, # 948; 猛(暑) mousho = fierce heat, # 953; 猿 saru = monkey, # 1055; 猟(師) ryoushi = hunter, # 1397; (監)獄 kangoku = prison, # 1435; 狂(気) kyouki = lunacy, # 1566; 猶(予) yuuyo = a postponement, # 1997 **ALSO COMPARE:** other similar kanji at # **752**

0949. 匂
PRONUNCIATION: nio **MEANINGS:** fragrant, stink, glow, insinuate **EXAMPLES:** 匂う niou = to smell of; 匂い nioi = fragrance, scent; **Note:** niou and nioi can also be written 臭う and 臭い, # 1381 **DESCRIPTION:** on the upper right, a giant hook, as seen in (目)的 mokuteki (purpose, # 45), which reminds us of fish hooks; on the lower left, the katakana ヒ hi, which reminds us of a hero

CUE: on the lower left, this is a **Neo**natologist who is a ヒ (**h**ero) and who likes to fish with hooks like this, but she has a fishy 匂い **nio**i (scent) **ALSO COMPARE:** other similar kanji at # **988** and # **2048**

0950. 闇 PRONUNCIATION: yami
MEANINGS: get dark, gloom, disorder **EXAMPLES:** 闇 yami = darkness; 暗闇 kurayami = darkness **DESCRIPTION:** on the left and right, 門 mon (gate, # 409); in the center, 音 oto (sound, # 266) **CUE:** when I'm out shopping for **Ya**k **M**eat, and the 暗闇 kura**yami** (darkness) increases, my family makes 音 (sounds) in this 門 (gate) to help me find my way home **ALSO COMPARE:** other similar kanji at # **266** and # **1755**

0951. 臟 PRONUNCIATION: zou
MEANINGS: organ, body part **EXAMPLES:** 心臟 shinzou = the heart (organ); 內臟 naizou = internal organ, intestines **DESCRIPTION:** on the left, 月 tsuki (moon, # 148); at the upper right, a plant radical; on the lower right, a two-sided lean-to supported by a halberd (combination axe and lance); under the lean-to, an 臣 (inoperable swing set) lying on its left side, with the swing ropes tied on both sides to make it inoperable **CUE:** my 心臟 shin**zou** (heart) rates can be classified into four different **Z**ones associated with my moods, which can be represented by this 月 (moon) which is volatile, these plants which are soothing, this 臣 (inoperable swing set) which is frustrating, and this halberd which is scary **COMPARE:** (冷)蔵(庫) reizouko = refrigerator, # 1190 (identical pronunciation), in which the moon on the left is missing; other similar kanji at # **915** and # **1246**

0952. 斉 PRONUNCIATION: sei
MEANINGS: adjusted, alike, equal **EXAMPLE:** 一斉に issei ni = all at once, at the same time, all together **DESCRIPTION:** compared to 済(ませる) sumaseru (to end, transitive, # 259), this omits the water radical on the left; it retains 文(化) bunka (culture, # 25), which consists of a tire stop above a crossing (or an X), above a truncated moon **CUE:** this 文 (culture) of worshipping this truncated moon is **S**atanic, and if you cross its adherents, they will attack you 一斉に is**sei** ni (all at once) **ALSO COMPARE:** other similar kanji at # **259** and # **1601**

0953. 猛 PRONUNCIATION: mou
MEANINGS: fierce, rave, become furious, wildness, strength **EXAMPLES:** 猛暑 mousho = fierce heat, heat wave; 猛勉強 moubenkyou = studying extra hard; 猛練習 mourenshuu = hard training; 猛犬 mouken = savage dog **DESCRIPTION:** on the left, a woman contorting her body; on the upper right, 子 ko (child, # 182); on the lower right, 皿 sara (dish, # 567) **CUE:** this woman on the left is contorting her body while anxiously approaching this 子 (child) named **Mo**ses, who is sitting in cold water in this 皿 (dish), trying to cope with a 猛暑 **mou**sho (heat wave) **ALSO COMPARE:** similar kanji at # **948**, # **1407** and # **2078**

0954. 程 PRONUNCIATIONS: hodo, tei
MEANINGS: degree, moderation, a limit **EXAMPLES:** 程 hodo = extent, degree, limits, moderation, approximate time, about so much (usually written ほど); 程度 teido = criterion, standard, extent, degree, amount **DESCRIPTION:** compared to (温)和 onwa (calm, # 513), this adds a 王 ou (king, # 1077) on the lower right; it retains the 禾 (grain plant with a ripe head) and 口 (mouth), which can also be seen as a box **CUES:** this 王 (king) is standing next to this 禾 (ripe grain) on the left, and he says to a servant, "**Hold** the **Do**or while I **Ta**ste this with this 口 (mouth) to determine the 程度 **tei**do (extent) to which it meets my standards" **COMPARE:** other similar kanji at # **323**, # **1797** and # **1876**

0955. 祈 **PRONUNCIATIONS:** ino, ki
MEANINGS: to pray or wish
EXAMPLES: 祈る inoru = to pray; 祈願 kigan = a prayer or supplication **DESCRIPTION:** compared to 所 tokoro (place, # 391), this substitutes the Shah, as seen in (会)社 kaisha (company, # 271), for the P under a roof on the left; it retains the pair of pliers on the right **CUES:** this Shah carries these pliers when he 祈る **ino**ru (prays) for **Inno**cent people in **Ki**ev, since they remind him to be practical in his requests **ALSO COMPARE:** other similar kanji at # **892** and # **1160**

0956. 俺 **PRONUNCIATION:** ore
MEANINGS: I, myself **EXAMPLES:** 俺 ore = I, me; 俺たち oretachi = we, us; 俺ら orera = we, us **DESCRIPTION:** on the left, a man with a slanted hat; at the upper right, an extra-wide 大(きい) ookii (big, # 188); at the lower right, a transformer with a wire emerging from the bottom, as seen in 電(気) denki (electricity, # 263)
CUE: 俺 **ore** (I) am this man on the left, and I tilt my hat back in order to examine this 大 (big) 電 (electric) transformer in **Ore**gon
ALSO COMPARE: other similar kanji at # **1003**

0957. 苔 **PRONUNCIATION:** koke
MEANINGS: moss, lichen **EXAMPLE:** 苔 koke = moss, lichen **DESCRIPTION:** at the top, a plant radical; at the bottom, 台 dai (platform, # 538) which resembles a ム (cow) on a 口 (box)
CUE: after drinking from a **Co**ld **Ke**g, this ム (cow) lay down on this 口 (box) and covered itself with this blanket of 苔 **koke** (moss)
COMPARE: other similar kanji at # **538**

0958. 馬 **PRONUNCIATIONS:** uma, ba, ma **MEANING:** horse **EXAMPLES:** 馬 uma = horse; 馬鹿 baka = stupid person, usually written バカ; 木馬 mokuba = a wooden horse; 競馬 keiba = horse racing; 絵馬 ema = a drawing or painting of a horse **DESCRIPTION:** at the upper right, this resembles the number 5, containing a two-armed telephone pole between its two horizontal arms, with the lowest portion of 5 possibly representing a horse's tail; the four horizontal lines in the resulting radical may represent the horse's mane, flowing to the right; at the lower left, four legs, which can also be seen as four flames
CUES: this 馬 **uma** (horse) with this flowing mane and this long tail belongs to an **U**gandan **Ma**n who works in a **Ba**r at a **Ma**ll
COMPARE: other similar kanji at # **826**

0959. 嗅 **PRONUNCIATIONS:** kyuu, ka
MEANINGS: smell, sniff, scent
EXAMPLES: 嗅覚 kyuukaku = sense of smell; 嗅ぐ kagu = to sniff or smell **DESCRIPTION:** compared to 吠(える) hoeru (to bark, # 944), this adds 自(分) jibun (self, # 155) at the upper right; it retains 口 (mouth), which can also be seen as a box, and 犬 (dog) **CUES:** my 自 (self) is in love with this **Cu**te 犬 (dog) which 嗅ぐ **ka**gu (sniffs) my **Ca**r for bombs and grabs them in this 口 (mouth) **ALSO COMPARE:** other similar kanji at # **945**, # **1381** and # **2073**

0960. 態 **PRONUNCIATION:** tai
MEANINGS: demeanor, appearance of intent or ability **EXAMPLES:** 態度 taido = attitude; 変態 hentai = pervert or perversion, metamorphosis (insect) **DESCRIPTION:** compared to 能(力) nouryoku (ability, # 616), this adds 心 kokoro (heart, # 306) at the bottom; it retains the ム (cow) on the 月 (moon) and the two ヒ 's
CUE: my **Thai** friend has 能 (ability) and a good 心 (heart) like this, as well as a good 態度 **tai**do (attitude)
ALSO COMPARE: 熊 kuma = bear, # 1262; other similar kanji at # **616** and # **1294**

0961. 命 **PRONUNCIATIONS:** inochi, mei, myou **MEANINGS:** life, order
EXAMPLES: 命 inochi = life, most precious possession or person; 命じる meijiru = to

command or appoint; 命令 meirei = a command or order; 寿命 jumyou = life span
DESCRIPTION: at the top, a roof; below the roof, a napkin; on the lower left, kuchi 口 (mouth, # 426), which resembles a box; on the lower right, a wobbly table with an extra-long leg, but this can also be seen as a signature seal, as seen in 印 shirushi (sign, # 1046) **CUES: In**nocent **Ch**ildren live with a **Mai**d in this house with this 口 (box) under this napkin on the left and this wobbly table on the right, and their 命 **inochi** (most precious possession) is a cat that lives in the box and **Meo**ws too much
COMPARE: similar kanji at # **962**, # **1046** and # **1251**

0962. 令 (sometimes written 令)

PRONUNCIATION: rei **MEANINGS:** orders, command, decree **EXAMPLES:** 命令 meirei = a command or order; 号令 gourei = a command or order **DESCRIPTION:** compared to 冷(蔵庫) reizouko (refrigerator, # 299) (identical pronunciation), this kanji omits the water radical on the left; it retains the peaked roof, the napkin and the wobbly table, which also resembles a person who is about to run a race [the **alternative** kanji shown above contains マ ma, which reminds us of Ma (mother), under a drop of rain, below a roof] **CUES:** this person under this roof is about to run a **Ra**ce and is waiting for the 命令 mei**rei** (command) to start [alternatively, this マ ma (mother) has given her landlord a 命令 mei**rei** (command) to fix this **Ra**in leaking from this roof] **GROUP:** 冷(蔵庫) reizouko = refrigerator, # 299; 命(じる) meijiru = to command, # 961, which adds a box on the left; (命)令 meirei = a command, # 962; (年)齢 nenrei = age, # 989 (also identical pronunciation); 領(土) ryoudo = territory, # 1126; 鈴 suzu = a small bell, # 1370; 零 rei = zero, # 1946 **ALSO COMPARE:** other similar kanji at # **1946** (alternative font)

0963. 洞 PRONUNCIATIONS: hora, dou

MEANINGS: den, cave, excavation **EXAMPLES:** 洞穴 horaana = cave, den; 洞窟 doukutsu = cave, grotto; 洞察 dousatsu = insight, discernment **DESCRIPTION:** compared to 同(意) doui (the same opinion, # 339) (identical pronunciation), this kanji adds a water radical on the left, which could represent a stream; it retains the two-sided lean-to containing a cloth that was used to wrap a doughnut, above a box
CUES: I found this two-sided lean-to, containing this cloth above a box next to this stream inside a 洞穴 **hora**ana (cave), but it was a **Ho**me for **Ra**ts that like to feast on **Do**ughnuts
ALSO COMPARE: other similar kanji at # **1620**

0964. 穴 PRONUNCIATION: ana, ketsu

MEANINGS: hole, aperture, cave den **EXAMPLES:** 穴 ana = hole; 洞穴 horaana = cave, den; **Note:** 洞穴 can also be read as douketsu = cave, den **DESCRIPTION:** compared to (研)究 kenkyuu (research, # 112), this omits the 九 (nine) at the bottom; it retains the soaring bird from Cuba, which can also be seen as a bad haircut above 八 hachi (eight, # 15) **CUES:** 八 (eight) students in an **Ana**tomy class have bad haircuts like this, they put **Ke**tchup in their **S**oup, and they are studying the major 穴 **ana** (holes) in a dog's head **GROUP:** this is a group of one **COMPARE:** other similar kanji at # **105**

0965. 謙 PRONUNCIATION: ken

MEANINGS: self-effacing, modest **EXAMPLE:** 謙虚 kenkyo = modesty **DESCRIPTION:** compared to 嫌(悪) ken'o (hatred, # 817) (identical pronunciation), this kanji substitutes 言(う) iu (to speak, # 430) for the 女 (woman) on the left; it retains the split tree trunk on the right, patched together with a trident **CUE:** although **Ken** and Barbie repaired this tree using this trident, they are aware that some people 嫌 (hate) the job they did, and their 謙虚 **ken**kyo (modesty) enables them to 言 (say) that their work wasn't perfect
ALSO COMPARE: other similar kanji at # **817**

0966. 虚 **PRONUNCIATION: kyo**
MEANINGS: void, emptiness, unpreparedness, untruth **EXAMPLE:** 謙虚 kenkyo = modesty **DESCRIPTION:** at the upper left, a one-sided lean-to; at the top, a periscope for observing the outside world; under the roof, 七 shichi (seven, # 20); on the floor, four burners on a stove, as seen in 普 (通) futsuu (ordinarily, # 576) **CUE:** 七 (seven) people who are known for their 謙虚 ken**kyo** (modesty) live in this lean-to, cook on this 普 (ordinary) four-burner stove like the ones they use in **Kyo**to and observe the outside world through this periscope **ALSO COMPARE:** other similar kanji at # **1057** and # **1300**

0967. 嘘 **PRONUNCIATION: uso**
MEANINGS: lie, falsehood **EXAMPLES:** 嘘 uso = lie; 嘘をつく uso wo tsuku = to tell a lie **DESCRIPTION:** compared to (謙)虚 kenkyo (modesty, # 966), this adds 口 kuchi (mouth, # 426), which can also be seen as a box, on the left; it retains the 七 (seven) people in a one-sided lean-to with a periscope who cook on a 普 (ordinary) stove **CUE:** these 七 (seven) people cook on this 普 (ordinary) stove, and one of them used this 口 (mouth) to tell an 嘘 **uso** (lie) when he claimed that they have Uber Solar panels **ALSO COMPARE:** other similar kanji at # **1057**, # **1300** and # **2073**

0968. 荒 **PRONUNCIATIONS: ara, a, kou** **MEANINGS:** laid waste, rough, wild, rude **EXAMPLES:** 荒い arai = violent, rough, rude; 荒らす arasu = to lay waste, damage, devastate; 荒れる areru = to be stormy or rough, to fall into ruin; 荒野 kouya = wilderness, the wild **DESCRIPTION:** compared to 慌(てる) awateru (to panic, # 710), or (恐)慌 kyoukou (a panic, # 710) (identical pronunciation), this kanji omits the erect man on the left; it retains the three-legged man with the plant material, suggesting agriculture, and the shaky table (or stool) **CUES:** this three-legged man named **Ara**fat engages in **A**griculture, as suggested by this plant radical, and he grows **C**orn, but when he invites people to sit on this shaky stool, he is being 荒い **ara**i (rude) **ALSO COMPARE:** other similar kanji at # **585** and # **710**

0969. 共 **PRONUNCIATIONS: tomo, kyou** **MEANING:** together **EXAMPLES:** 共に tomo ni = together; 共同の kyoudou no = cooperative, communal; 共感 kyoukan = sympathy; 共通の kyoutsuu no = common, mutual **DESCRIPTION:** compared to (子)供 kodomo (child, # 486), this omits the man with a slanted hat on the left; it retains the plant radical on a platform above a hill in Kyouto **CUES:** these plants on this hill are 共に **tomo** ni (together), and they are located outside of a **Tomo**graphy center in **Kyou**to **ALSO COMPARE:** other similar kanji at # **486**

0970. 異 **PRONUNCIATIONS: koto, i** **MEANINGS:** uncommon, strangeness **EXAMPLES:** 異なる kotonaru = to differ; 驚異 kyoui = miracle, marvel; 異議 igi = objection **DESCRIPTION:** compared to 翼 tsubasa (feather, # 912), this omits the feathers at the top; it retains the 田 (rice paddy) above 共(に) tomo ni (together, # 969) **CUES:** I attended a **K**oto (Japanese harp) concert on **E**aster at this 田 (rice paddy), 共 (together) with some friends, and I found that it 異なった **koto**natta (differed) from the one I attended last year **ALSO COMPARE:** other similar kanji at # **220** and # **486**

0971. 驚 **PRONUNCIATIONS: kyou, odoro** **MEANINGS:** to wonder, be surprised, amazed, frightened **EXAMPLES:** 驚異 kyoui = miracle, marvel; 驚く odoroku = to be astonished **DESCRIPTION:** at the top, 敬(う) uyamau (to respect, # 873); at the bottom, 馬 uma (horse, # 958) **CUES:** I 敬 (respect) 馬 (horses) like this that I see in **Kyou**to, but I 驚く **odoroku** (get astonished) at the **O**dorous drinks served at the riding academies there **COMPARE:** 警(察)

keisatsu = police, # 874; other similar kanji at # **526**, # **826**, # **872** and # **873**

0972. 巣 PRONUNCIATIONS: sou, su
MEANING: nest **EXAMPLES:** 卵巣 ransou = ovary; 精巣 seisou = testicle; 巣 su = nest, animal habitat, cobweb, honeycomb, den
DESCRIPTION: compared to 果(物) kudamono (fruit, # 587), which includes 木 ki (tree, # 118), this adds three old boys at the top, as seen in 覚(える) oboeru (to memorize, # 54)
CUES: a **S**oldier asked **S**uperman to check on these three old boys who were making a 巣 **su** (nest) at the top of this 果 (fruit) 木 (tree) **ALSO COMPARE:** other similar kanji at # **588** and # **1625**

0973. 崩 PRONUNCIATIONS: kuzu, hou
MEANINGS: crumble, demolish, die
EXAMPLES: 崩れる kuzureru = to collapse, be destroyed; 崩壊 houkai = collapse, crumbling, decay **DESCRIPTION:** at the top, 山 yama (mountain, # 146); at the bottom, two 月 tsuki (moons, # 148) **CUES:** I'm **C**ooped up in a **Z**oo on this 山 (mountain), and this is my **H**ome, but if these two 月 (moons) drift apart, the mountain and the zoo will 崩れる **kuzu**reru (collapse)
ALSO COMPARE: 棚 tana = shelf, # 742; other similar kanji at # **742**, # **1385** and # **2087**

0974. 就 PRONUNCIATIONS: shuu, tsu
MEANINGS: to take up a job, to be completed
EXAMPLES: 就職する shuushoku suru = to find employment; 就く tsuku = to set out, obtain a position **DESCRIPTION:** on the left, 京(都) kyouto (Kyoto, # 514), which consists of a tire stop above a 口 (box, or house) on a 小 (small) hill in Kyoto; on the right, a modified 犬 inu (dog, # 190), with lopsided legs, as seen in 兄 ani (big brother, # 420), but the right leg is bent **CUES:** I went to this 京 (Kyoto) in order to 就職する **shuu**shoku suru (find employment) and to buy a

Shoe to put on this 犬 (dog)'s bent right leg, and I brought the footwear home in a **Tsu**itcase (suitcase)
GROUP: 沈(黙) chinmoku = silence, # 835; 就(く) tsuku = to set out, # 974; 蹴(る) keru = to kick, # 975; 虎 tora = tiger, # 1057; 既(婚) kikon = already married, # 1639; 概(念) gainen = a general idea, # 1647; (容)貌 youbou = features, # 1687; 稽(古) keiko = training, # 1715; 枕 makura = a pillow, # 1770; (憤)慨(する) fungai suru = to be indignant, # 1782 **ALSO COMPARE:** other similar kanji at # **514** and # **1474**

0975. 蹴 PRONUNCIATION: ke
MEANING: to kick **EXAMPLES:** 蹴る keru = to kick; 蹴飛ばす ketobasu = to kick away, to refuse curtly **DESCRIPTION:** compared to 就(職) shuushoku (employment, # 974), this adds the 止 (hesitant) squarehead seen in 踊(る) odoru (to dance, # 366) on the left; it retains 京 (Kyoto) and the 犬 (dog) with a bent leg
CUE: this 止 (hesitant) squarehead, who wears **K**e**d**s (a brand of shoes), 蹴る **ke**ru (kicks) balls in this 京 (Kyoto), and this disabled 犬 (dog) chases them **ALSO COMPARE:** other similar kanji at # **514**, # **974**, # **1474** and # **1534**

0976. 黄 PRONUNCIATIONS: ou, kou, ki
MEANING: yellow **EXAMPLES:** 卵黄 ran'ou = egg yolk; 黄金 ougon = gold; 黄砂 kousa = yellow dust from the Yellow River region; 黄色 kiiro = yellow; 黄身 kimi = egg yolk
DESCRIPTION: compared to 横(断する) oudan suru (to cross, # 135) (identical pronunciation), this kanji omits the 木 (tree) on the left; it retains the model of a rice paddy with a handle, under a plant radical
CUES: this model of a rice paddy with a handle and plants on top, which is symmetrical like the Y in **Y**ellow, 横 (crossed) the **O**cean on a **C**oal ship and can be accessed with a 黄色 **ki**iro (yellow) **K**ey **COMPARE:** other similar kanji at # **77**, # **135** and # **1740**

0977. 救 **PRONUNCIATIONS: suku, kyuu** **MEANINGS:** salvation, help, rescue, reclaim **EXAMPLES:** 救う sukuu = to rescue; 救い sukui = help, hope; 救急車 kyuukyuusha = ambulance; 救済 kyuusai = help, rescue, relief **DESCRIPTION:** on the left, (要)求 youkyuu (a request or command, # 810) (identical pronunciation), which we have described as a water dog from Cuba; on the right, a dancer with a ponytail **CUES:** this dancer on the right gets energy from **S**uperior **K**ool-Aid and uses this 水 (water) 犬 (dog) from **Cu**ba to help her 救う **suku**u (rescue) drowning people **ALSO COMPARE:** similar kanji at # **606**

0978. 疑 **PRONUNCIATIONS: utaga, gi** **MEANING:** to doubt **EXAMPLES:** 疑う utagau = to doubt or suspect; 疑問 gimon = a question or doubt; 疑惑 giwaku = a suspicion or doubt **DESCRIPTION:** at the upper left, the katakana ヒ hi, which reminds us of a hero; at the lower left, a Native American chief, as seen in 知(る) shiru (to know, # 323); at the upper right, the katakana マ ma, which reminds us of Ma (Mother); at the lower right, a taser mounted on 足 ashi (foot, # 449), as seen in (予)定 yotei (plan, # 455) **CUES:** this ヒ (**h**ero), this マ **M**a (Mother), and this Native American chief are a family traveling in an **U**ber **T**axi to **G**amble, and they plan to hunt **Ge**ese with this taser that they have mounted on Ma's 足 (foot), which some people 疑う **utaga**u (doubt) is a good idea **GROUP:** (事)務(所) jimusho = office, # 518; 疑(問) gimon = doubt, # 978; 凝(る) koru = to grow stiff, # 1680; (模)擬 mogi = imitation, # 2003 **ALSO COMPARE:** other similar kanji at # **324**, # **913** and # **2048**

0979. 輝 **PRONUNCIATIONS: ki, kagaya** **MEANINGS:** radiance, shine, sparkle, gleam **EXAMPLES:** 光輝 kouki = brightness, splendor; 輝く kagayaku = to shine, glitter, sparkle **DESCRIPTION:** on the left, 光 hikari (light, # 448); on the right, 軍(人) gunjin (soldier, # 725) **CUES:** this 光 (light) on the left 輝く **kagaya**ku (shines), and it is being used in a signal lamp in **Ki**ev by this 軍 (soldier) to **C**all a **G**allant **Y**achtsman **GROUP:** 光 hikari = light, # 448; (光)輝 kouki = brightness, # 979; (札)幌 Sapporo, a city on Hokkaido Island, # 2082 **ALSO COMPARE:** other similar kanji at # **2075**

0980. 肌 **PRONUNCIATION: hada** **MEANINGS:** texture, skin, body, grain **EXAMPLES:** 肌 hada = skin, personality; 肌着 hadagi = underwear; 木肌 kihada = bark of a tree **DESCRIPTION:** on the left, 月 tsuki (moon, # 148); on the right, a tall desk, as seen in 机 tsukue (desk, # 140) **CUE:** my **Ha**waiian **Da**ughter hides under this 机 (desk) during the day and only exposes her 肌 **hada** (skin) to the sky when this 月 (moon) shines **ALSO COMPARE:** similar kanji at # **1462**

0981. 滑 **PRONUNCIATIONS: sube, name, katsu** **MEANINGS:** slippery, slide, slip, flunk **EXAMPLES:** 滑る suberu = to slide or slip, to fail an exam; 滑りやすい suberiyasui = slippery; 滑らかな nameraka na = smooth, mellow (usually written なめらかな); 円滑 enkatsu = smooth, harmonious **DESCRIPTION:** compared to 骨 hone (bone, # 832), which depicts a roof-top apartment on the 月 (moon), this adds a water radical on the left **CUES:** I rest my 骨 (bones) in this roof-top apartment, which I can afford thanks to my job as a **Sub**-editor, and I have a **N**anny from **Me**xico who takes care of my **C**ats, but this water is leaking, and our floors are 滑りやすい **sube**riyasui (slippery) **ALSO COMPARE:** other similar kanji at # **832**

0982. 覗 PRONUNCIATION: nozo
MEANINGS: peek, peep, come in sight
EXAMPLES: 覗く nozoku = to snoop, often spelled のぞく; 覗き込む nozokikomu = to peer into DESCRIPTION: on the left, (寿)司 sushi (# 608), which depicts a napkin above a box in a one-sided lean-to; on the right, 見(る) miru (to see, # 53) CUE: when I wanted to 見 (see) what was under the napkin on this box in this lean-to, I parked in a **No Zo**ne and ran over to 覗く **nozo**ku (snoop)
COMPARE: 除(く) nozoku = to remove, # 646; other similar kanji at # **341** and # **1341**

0983. 井 PRONUNCIATIONS: jou, i, *ino*
MEANINGS: well, community
EXAMPLES: 天井 tenjou = ceiling; 井戸 ido = water well; 井上 Inoue = a family name
DESCRIPTION: the pound sign (#)
CUES: **Jo**an of Arc decided to try to lose some # (pounds) like this on **Ea**ster, so she walked down to an 井戸 **i**do (well) with some **Inno**cent kids
COMPARE: other similar kanji at # **1202**

0984. 桜 PRONUNCIATIONS: sakura, zakura² MEANING: cherry EXAMPLES: 桜の花 sakura no hana = cherry blossoms; 夜桜見物 yozakura kenbutsu = going out to look at cherry blossoms in the evening DESCRIPTION: on the left, 木 ki (tree, # 118); at the upper right, three old boys, as seen in 覚(える) oboeru (to memorize, # 54), but these can also be seen as flowers; at the lower right, 女 onna (female, # 235)
CUE: when this 女 (female) said that these three 桜 **sakura** (cherry) flowers were blooming on this 木 (tree), a **Sa**laryman turned off his **Kuu**ra**a** (cooler, or air conditioner) and went out to see them
COMPARE: 櫻 sakura = cherry, # 2086; other similar kanji at # **1625** and # **2086**

0985. 悠 PRONUNCIATION: yuu
MEANINGS: permanence, long time, leisure
EXAMPLES: 悠々 yuuyuu = quiet, calm, leisurely; 悠長 yuuchou = leisurely, slow, deliberate, easy-going; 悠久の yuukyuu no = eternal DESCRIPTION: at the upper left, a man with a slanted hat facing a vertical line, which is the horn of a unicorn; at the upper right, a dancer with a ponytail; at the bottom, 心 kokoro (heart, # 306)
CUE: this man with a slanted hat on the left and this dancer on the right have good 心 (hearts) like this, but they keep this **U**nicorn horn between them, for the sake of keeping things 悠 **yuu**yuu (quiet or calm) GROUP: 引(く) hiku = to pull, # 476; 悠(々) yuuyuu = quiet, # 985; (気)候 kikou = climate, # 996; 旧(年) kyuunen = last year, # 1017; 修(理) shuuri = repairs, # 1049, which substitutes a rocker-bottom shoe for 心 (heart); (孤)児 koji = orphan, # 1093 ALSO COMPARE: other similar kanji at # **523**

0986. 抱 PRONUNCIATIONS: bou, hou, da, ida, kaka MEANINGS: embrace, hug, hold in arms EXAMPLES: 辛抱 shinbou = endurance, patience; 抱擁する houyou suru = to embrace; 抱く daku = to embrace, hold or hug; 抱きしめる dakishimeru = to hug someone tightly; 抱く idaku = to embrace, hold or entertain (an idea); 抱える kakaeru = to hold or carry under or in the arms, to have (e.g., problems with debt), to employ or hire; Note: daku and idaku are both spelled 抱く DESCRIPTION: compared to (大)砲 taihou (cannon, # 738) (identical pronunciation), this kanji substitutes a kneeling guy for 石 (stone) on the left; it retains 包 (to wrap), which resembles a hook containing a snake
CUES: this kneeling guy 包 (wraps) a **Bo**wling ball with three **Ho**les as a present for his **Da**ughter, who loves **E**astern **Da**nce, and then he 抱く **da**ku (embraces) her and **Ca**lls a **Ca**b
ALSO COMPARE: other similar kanji at # **1861**

0987. 融 **PRONUNCIATION: yuu**
MEANINGS: dissolve, melt **EXAMPLES:**
金融 kin'yuu = finance, loaning money; 融合 yuugou = fusion, adhesion, blending
DESCRIPTION: at the top left, 口 kuchi (mouth, # 426), with a napkin above it; at the lower left, 四 yon (four, # 6), which is the floor plan of a house, with a missing wall at the bottom and the letter T inside, which reminds us of Tarantulas; on the right, 虫 mushi (insect, # 9) **CUE:** on the lower left, this is the floor plan of a house in the **Yu**kon, with a wall missing at the bottom, which promotes a sense of 融合 **yuu**gou (fusion) between the inside of the house and the outside but allows 虫 (insects) like this Tarantula to get in, so that the occupants need to keep napkins like this over 口 mouths like this to avoid screaming when they see them **GROUP:** 換(える) kaeru = to replace, # 554; 融(合) yuugou = fusion, # 987; 商(品) shouhin = commodity, # 1217; (間)隔 kankaku = an interim, # 1729; 喚(く) wameku = to yell, # 1885
ALSO COMPARE: other similar kanji at # **1729** and # **1754**

0988. 均 **PRONUNCIATION: kin**
MEANINGS: level, average
EXAMPLE: 平均 heikin = average, mean
DESCRIPTION: on the left, tsuchi 土 (soil, # 59); on the right, a hook; inside the hook, two lines representing nearly horizontal plants which are not very healthy **CUE:** at our **Kin**dergarten, we plow this 土 (soil) with this hook and grow plants like these, but our results are only 平均 hei**kin** (average) **GROUP:** (目)的 mokuteki = purpose, # 45; (予)約 yoyaku = reservation, # 225; 胸 mune = chest, # 775; 匂(う) niou = to smell of, # 949; (平)均 heikin = average, # 988; (中)旬 chuujun = around the middle of a month, # 1304; 釣(る) tsuru = to fish, # 1547; 菊 kiku = chrysanthemum, # 1611; 潟 kata = a lagoon, # 1736; 陶(器) touki = pottery, # 1741; 濁(る) nigoru = to be muddy, # 1831; (媒)酌 baishaku = matchmaking, # 1958; 勾(配) koubai = an incline, # 2047

0989. 齢 (sometimes written 齡)
PRONUNCIATION: rei MEANING: age
EXAMPLE: 年齢 nenrei = age
DESCRIPTION: on the left, 歯 ha (tooth, # 533); on the right, (命)令 meirei (command, # 962) (identical pronunciation), which looks like a person under a roof and a napkin who is preparing to run a race (the **alternative** kanji shown above also contains a peaked roof on the right, above a drop of rain and マ ma) **CUE:** during the **Ra**ce of life, our 年齢 nen**rei** (age) increases, and we develop problems with 歯 (teeth) like this, but we also get to give more 令 (orders) to younger people

[**alternatively**, マ ma (mother)'s 年齡 nen**rei** (age) has increased, and she has problems with 歯 (teeth) like this, which hurt when it **Ra**ins and when drops like this penetrate this roof]
ALSO COMPARE: similar kanji at # **962**, # **1387**, # **1929** and # **1946** (alternative font)

0990. 刊 **PRONUNCIATION: kan**
MEANING: to publish **EXAMPLES:** 朝刊 choukan = morning paper; 週刊誌 shuukanshi = weekly magazine; 刊行する kankou suru = to publish **DESCRIPTION:** compared to (発)汗 hakkan (perspiration, # 629) (identical pronunciation), this kanji omits the water radical on the left and adds the katakana リ ri on the right; it retains the telephone pole being carried to Kansas **CUE:** in **Kan**sas, リ Ri has an office next to this telephone pole, where he 刊行する **kan**kou suru (publishes) books
COMPARE: other similar kanji at # **629** and # **1985**

0991. 賞 **PRONUNCIATION: shou**
MEANINGS: prize, reward, praise **EXAMPLES:** 受賞する jushou suru = to win an award or prize; 入賞する nyuushou suru = to win an award or prize **DESCRIPTION:** compared to 員 in (member, # 88), this adds three old boys on a roof,

as seen in 覚(える) oboeru (to memorize, # 54) **CUE:** these three old boys on a roof, who are 員 (members) of a club, 覚 (memorize) scripts for **Show**s and 入賞する nyuu**shou** suru (win prizes) **GROUP:** 覚(える) oboeru = to memorize, # 54; (食)堂 shokudou = dining hall, # 64; 学(校) gakkou = school, # 184; (非)常 hijou = emergency, # 683; (経)営 keiei = management, # 684; (入)賞(する) nyuushou suru = to win an award, # 991; (苦)労 kurou = hardship, # 1075; 栄(養) eiyou = nutrition, # 1263; (政)党 seitou = political party, # 1399; (補)償 hoshou = compensation, # 1662; 誉(れ) homare = honor, # 1705; (車)掌 shashou = a train conductor, # 1717; 蛍(光灯) keikoutou = a fluorescent light, # 2023; **Note** that three of these kanji can be pronounced "shou" **ALSO COMPARE:** kanji with a three-pronged switch on *lopsided legs* at # 979; other kanji with a three-pronged switch and *no roof* at # 1625; other similar kanji at # **88** and # **707**

0992. 躍 PRONUNCIATION: yaku
MEANINGS: leap, dance, skip **EXAMPLES:** 躍進 yakushin = progress; 活躍する katsuyaku suru = to be active **DESCRIPTION:** compared to 曜 you (day of the week, # 200), this substitutes a 止 (hesitant) squarehead with a square top, as seen in 踊(る) odoru (to dance, # 366), for 日 (sun) on the left; it retains the feathers and the net, which can be seen as a man with a slanted hat next to a 主 (master) with an extra pair of arms (see # 203) **CUE:** this 止 (hesitant) squarehead fights against the **Yaku**za (gangsters), and he 活躍する katsu**yaku** suru (is active) every 曜 (day of the week) **ALSO COMPARE:** other similar kanji at # **200** and # **1534**

0993. 佐 PRONUNCIATION: sa
MEANINGS: assistant, help **EXAMPLES:** 佐賀県 saga ken = Saga Prefecture; 大佐 taisa = colonel; 補佐 hosa = aid, help **DESCRIPTION:** on the left, a man with a slanted hat; on the right, 左 hidari (left, # 456), or 左(翼) sayoku (left-wing politics, # 456) (identical pronunciation) **CUE:** this man on the left had some **S**agging on the 左 (left) side of his face, so he tilted his hat to show a plastic surgeon, who was able to offer 補佐 ho**sa** (help) **COMPARE:** other similar kanji at # **456**

0994. 賀 PRONUNCIATION: ga
MEANINGS: congratulations, joy **EXAMPLES:** 祝賀会 shukugakai = celebration; 佐賀県 saga ken = Saga Prefecture; 年賀状 nengajou = New Year's card **DESCRIPTION:** at the upper left, 力 chikara (force, # 102); at the upper right, 口 kuchi (mouth, # 426); at the bottom, 貝 kai (shell, or money chest, # 83) **CUE:** a **G**ambler uses this 力 (force) to protect the money in this 貝 (money chest) which he spends on 祝賀会 shuku**ga**kai (celebrations) where he puts food in this 口 (mouth) **ALSO COMPARE:** similar kanji at # **88**, # **707** and # **1846**

0995. 補 PRONUNCIATIONS: ho, ogina
MEANINGS: supplement, supply **EXAMPLES:** 補佐 hosa = aid, help; 補給する hokyuu suru = to supply or supplement; 候補 kouho = candidate; 補う oginau = to supplement or compensate for **DESCRIPTION:** compared to 捕(虜) horyo (captive, # 670) (identical pronunciation), this kanji substitutes happy Jimmy Carter with two lips, as seen in 初(めて) hajimete (for the first time, # 104), for the kneeling guy on the left; it retains the upper part of 犬 (dog) juggling a ball and the 用 (fence) (see # 364) **CUES:** this happy Jimmy with two lips is a 候補 kou**ho** (candidate), and he keeps this truncated 犬 (dog) behind this 用 (fence) at his **H**ome to impress the voters, while some of **O**prah's **G**eese take a **N**ap **GROUP:** 捕(虜) horyo = captive, # 670; 補(佐) hosa = aid, # 995; 舗(装) hosou = pave-

ment, # 1237; 浦(田) urata = a family name, # 1552; 哺(乳) ho'nyuu = lactation, # 2066; **Note** that three of these kanji can be pronounced "ho" **ALSO COMPARE:** other similar kanji at # **1615**

0996. 候 PRONUNCIATION: kou
MEANINGS: climate, season, weather
EXAMPLES: 気候 kikou = climate; 天候 tenkou = weather; 候補 kouho = candidate
DESCRIPTION: compared to (耳鼻咽)喉(科) jibiinkouka (ENT specialty, # 794) (identical pronunciation), this kanji omits 口 (mouth) on the left and adds a unicorn horn in the left hand of the Native American chief, which it retains together with the katakana ユ yu, which reminds us of the Yukon **CUE:** this man on the left slants his hat back to examine this unicorn horn and tells this Native American chief that he should move to ユ (the Yukon), where he can use the horn and work as a prison guard, but the chief says that the 気候 ki**kou** (climate) up there is too **C**old
GROUP: 喉 nodo = throat, # 794; (気)候 kikou = climate, # 996 **ALSO COMPARE:** other similar kanji at # **324** and # **985** and # 1207

0997. 給 PRONUNCIATION: kyuu
MEANINGS: salary, wage, gift, bestow on
EXAMPLES: 給料 kyuuryou = salary; 補給する hokyuu suru = to supply or supplement **DESCRIPTION:** compared to 絵(本) ehon (picture book, # 223), this substitutes 合(う) au (to match, # 294) for 会 (meeting) on the right; it retains 糸 (skeet shooter) on the left **CUE:** this 糸 (skeet shooter) 合 (matched) up with a produce company and now earns a high 給料 **kyuu**ryou (salary) shooting **C**ucumbers **ALSO COMPARE:** 紹(介) shoukai = introduction, # 658; other similar kanji at # **1251**

0998. 状 PRONUNCIATION: jou
MEANINGS: condition, letter **EXAMPLES:** 状態 joutai = condition, circumstances, state; 紹介状 shoukaijou = letter of introduction **DESCRIPTION:** compared to 壮(大) soudai (magnificent, # 769), this substitutes 犬 inu (dog, # 190) for the 士 (man) on the right; it retains the two-legged bench standing on end **CUE: J**oan of Arc thought that the 状態 **jou**tai (circumstances) were right to bring this 犬 (dog) to a park, and she sat on this bench while the dog ran around **GROUP:** 寝(る) neru = to sleep, # 372; 北 kita = north, # 373; 将(来) shourai = the future, # 374; 壮(大) soudai = magnificent, # 769; 状(態) joutai = condition, # 998; (服)装 fukusou = dress style, # 1043; (別)荘 bessou = summer house, # 1468; 奨(励) shourei = encouragement, # 1906 **ALSO COMPARE:** other similar kanji at # **945**

0999. 録 PRONUNCIATION: roku
MEANING: to record **EXAMPLES:** 記録 kiroku = a record; 録音 rokuon = a sound recording; 登録 touroku = registration, enrollment
DESCRIPTION: compared to 緑 midori (green, # 227), this substitutes 金 kane (money, # 301) for the skeet shooter on the left; it retains the green flag, which can also be seen as hair streaming left, on a platform, floating in 水 (water) **CUE:** if you pay this 緑 (green) 金 (money) to a **R**obotic **K**ool-Aid dispenser, it will mix some Kool-Aid for you, and it will also make a 記録 ki**roku** (record) of the transaction **GROUP:** 緑 midori = green, # 227; (登)録 touroku = registration, # 999; 剥(奪する) hakudatsu suru = to deprive of, # 1567 **ALSO COMPARE:** other kanji with hair streaming left at # 1165; other similar kanji at # **2010**

1000. 更 PRONUNCIATIONS: kou, sara
MEANINGS: again, further, night watch
EXAMPLES: 変更 henkou = a change or alteration; 更新 koushin = renewal; 更に sara ni = again, furthermore **DESCRIPTION:** compared to 便(利) benri (convenient, # 481), this omits the man with a slanted hat on the left; it retains the radical that resembles Benjamin Franklin, who has a

dislocated right hip and wears bifocals **CUES:** this Benjamin Franklin, who invented these bifocals and has this dislocated right hip, made a 変更 hen**kou** (change) in his kitchen, stipulating that leftover food should be kept **C**old and covered with **S**aran wrap **GROUP:** (大)使 taishi = ambassador, # 480; 便(利) benri = convenient, # 481; 丈 take = height, # 613; (変)更 henkou = a change, # 1000; (歴)史 rekishi = history, # 1314; 硬(貨) kouka = coins, # 1412, and 梗(塞) kousoku = a stoppage, # 1992, both of which can also be pronounced "kou" **ALSO COMPARE:** other similar kanji at # **1992**

1001. 挑 **PRONUNCIATIONS: chou, ido**
MEANINGS: challenge, contend for, to pressure someone for sex, to woo
EXAMPLES: 挑戦する chousen suru = to challenge; 挑む idomu = to challenge
DESCRIPTION: compared to 兆 chou (trillion, # 849) (identical pronunciation), this kanji adds a kneeling man on the left **CUES:** this kneeling guy has to clean the floor and do a 兆 (trillion) other **C**hores that 挑む **ido**mu (challenge) him, but he has to wait until his **E**agle is **D**ozing
ALSO COMPARE: similar kanji at # **849**

1002. 沖 **PRONUNCIATION: oki**
MEANINGS: open sea, off the coast, rise high into sky **EXAMPLES:** 沖 oki = open sea, off the coast; 沖縄 Okinawa **DESCRIPTION:** on the left, a water radical; on the right, 中 chuu (inside, # 8) **CUE:** an **O**ld **K**ing who lived in 沖縄 **Oki**nawa used to get 中 (inside) this water **ALSO COMPARE:** other similar kanji at # **657**

1003. 縄 **PRONUNCIATIONS: nawa, jou**
MEANINGS: straw rope, cord
EXAMPLES: 縄 nawa = rope; 沖縄 Okinawa; 縄文時代 joumon jidai = the Jomon period (14,000 - 300 BC) **DESCRIPTION:** on the left, 糸 ito (skeet shooter, # 219); on the right, two 田 (rice paddies, # 68), linked by a rope **CUES:** this skeet shooter fires at these 田 (rice paddies) that are joined by this 縄 **nawa** (rope) that **N**arco **W**arlords made from straw, and **J**oan of Arc is impressed **GROUP:** 電(気) denki = electricity, # 263; 亀 kame = turtle, # 908; 俺 ore = I, # 956; 縄 nawa = rope, # 1003; 奄(美大島) Amami Ooshima = an island south of Kyushu, # 1095; 滝 taki = waterfall, # 1179; (恐)竜 kyouryuu = a dinosaur, # 1569

1004. 府 **PRONUNCIATION: fu**
MEANINGS: borough, government office, urban prefecture, storehouse **EXAMPLES:** 都道府県 todoufuken = administrative division of Japan; 政府 seifu = government; 京都府 kyoutofu = Kyouto prefecture **DESCRIPTION:** compared to (豆)腐 toufu (bean curd, # 722) (identical pronunciation), this kanji omits 肉 (meat) at the lower right; it retains 付 (to adhere) under a lean-to with a chimney **CUE:** our 政府 sei**fu** (government) stores **F**ood under lean-tos like this, but the food tends to 付 (adhere) together when it rains **GROUP:** 付(く) tsuku = to adhere, # 132; (切)符 kippu = ticket, # 133; 腐(る) kusaru = to rot, # 722; (政)府 seifu = government, # 1004

1005. 阪 **PRONUNCIATIONS: saka, han**
MEANINGS: slope, heights **EXAMPLES:** 大阪 oosaka = Osaka, large hill; 阪神 hanshin = Osaka and Kobe **DESCRIPTION:** compared to 反(対) hantai (opposition, # 680) (identical pronunciation), this kanji adds ß from the Greek alphabet; it retains the F and the X, which suggest opposition or rejection **CUES:** when a ß (Greek) team played **S**ak**ka**a (soccer) in 大阪 oo**saka** (Osaka), **Han**sel was in 反 (opposition, i.e., on the opposing team) **ALSO COMPARE:** other similar kanji at # **1166** and # **2030**

1006. 奈 PRONUNCIATION: na

MEANING: Nara **EXAMPLES:** 奈良 Nara = ancient capital of Japan; 神奈川県 Kanagawa ken = a prefecture in Japan **DESCRIPTION:** compared to 宗(教) shuukyou (religion, # 676), this substitutes an extra-wide 大(きい) ookii (big, # 188) for the bad haircut at the top; it retains the spinning nail under a flying carpet [these can also be seen as 二 (two) above 小 (small)] **CUE:** in 奈良 **Na**ra, a 大 (big) **Na**zi who is 宗 (religious) rides on flying carpets above spinning nails like this **ALSO COMPARE:** similar kanji at # **1347**

1007. 茨 PRONUNCIATION: ibara

MEANINGS: briar, thorn **EXAMPLE:** 茨城県 Ibaraki ken = Ibaraki prefecture **DESCRIPTION:** at the top, a plant radical; at the bottom, 次 tsugi (next, # 536), which consists of a water radical next to an oil derrick (see # 399) **CUE:** at E**a**ster, B**ara**ch Obama bought these plants, and 次 (next) he took them to 茨城県 **ibara**ki ken (Ibaraki Prefecture) **ALSO COMPARE:** 羨(ましい) urayamashii = envious, # 662, which substitutes 羊 (sheep) for the the plant radical at the top; other similar kanji at # **258** and # **536**

1008. 城 PRONUNCIATIONS: ki, gi², shiro, jou

MEANING: castle **EXAMPLES:** 茨城県 ibaraki ken = Ibaraki prefecture; 宮城県 miyagi ken = Miyagi Prefecture; 城 shiro = castle; 荒城 koujou = ruined castle; 名城 meijou = famous castle **DESCRIPTION:** compared to 成(功) seikou (success, # 633), this adds 土 tsuchi (soil, # 59) on the left; it retains a 刀 (blade) and a halberd **CUES:** after I had 成 (success), I decided to build a 城 **shiro** (castle) in **Ki**ev, guarded by 刀 (blades) and halberds like this, on this patch of 土 (soil) where **S**heep used to **R**oam, in order to impress **Jo**an of Arc **ALSO COMPARE:** other similar kanji at # **633**

1009. 挟 PRONUNCIATION: hasa

MEANINGS: pinch, between **EXAMPLES:** 挟む hasamu = to hold or place between, to pinch; 挟まる hasamaru = to get between, to get caught in **DESCRIPTION:** compared to 狭(い) semai (narrow, # 194), this substitutes a kneeling guy for the contorted lady on the left; it retains the 夫 (husband) with flames shooting out from both sides **CUE:** this guy kneels to try to help this 夫 (husband), a **H**andsome **Sa**laryman who 挟まった **hasa**matta (got caught between) two walls of flame **ALSO COMPARE:** 鋏 hasami = scissors, not included in this catalogue but usually written はさみ; other similar kanji at # **194**

1010. 省 PRONUNCIATIONS: shou, habu, sei

MEANINGS: focus, conserve, government ministry **EXAMPLES:** 省略 shouryaku = abbreviation, omission; 省く habuku = to omit, to cut down (cost); 反省 hansei = scrutiny, self-scrutiny, regret **DESCRIPTION:** at the top, 少(し) sukoshi (a little, # 254), which seems to be pushing down on 目 me (eye, # 51) **CUES:** a **Shou**gun drank 少 (a little) **Ha**waiian **Boo**ze and felt that it was pushing down on this 目 (eye), causing him to worry about his **S**a**f**ety, so he did some 反省 han**sei** (self-scrutiny) and decided to 省く **habu**ku (cut down) on his drinking **GROUP:** 小(さい) chiisai = small, # 253; 少(し) sukoshi = a little, # 254; 歩(く) aruku = to walk, # 408; 砂 suna = sand, # 782; 添(える) soeru = to support, # 841; 妙 myou = strange, # 856; (反)省 hansei = scrutiny, # 1010; (対)称 taishou = symmetry, # 1123; 秒 byou = a second (time), # 1137; 頻(繁) hinpan = frequent, # 1265; (干)渉 kanshou = interference, # 1307; (紙)幣 shihei = paper money, # 1411; (ご無)沙(汰) gobusata = a long silence, # 1612; 劣(る) otoru =

to be inferior, # 1746; 弊(社) heisha = our company, # 2005; 抄(本) shouhon = an excerpt, # 2043; (来)賓 raihin = a guest, # 2054; 弥(生時代) yayoi jidai = the Yayoi era, # 2080 **ALSO COMPARE:** other similar kanji at # **2002**

1011. 携 PRONUNCIATIONS: **tazusa, kei** MEANINGS: portable, carry in hand EXAMPLES: 携わる tazusawaru = to engage (in); 携える tazusaeru = to carry with; 携帯する keitai suru = to carry; 携帯電話 keitai denwa = cellular phone; 提携する teikei suru = to form a partnership or cooperate DESCRIPTION: on the left, a kneeling guy; at the upper right, a net, which can be seen as a man with a slanted hat next to a 主 (master) with an extra pair of arms (see # 203); at the lower right, a graph similar to the one seen in 及(ぶ) oyobu (to reach, # 883) but missing the horizontal slash CUES: this guy on the left is a **T**all **Z**o**o**keeper from **Sa**pporo, and he is so tall that he has to **k**neel to show us this graph that he 携帯する **kei**tai suru (carries) depicting **e**scape attempts by animals from this net and from **C**ages at the zoo **COMPARE:** other similar kanji at # **1131** and # **2046**

1012. 帯 PRONUNCIATIONS: **obi, tai** MEANINGS: belt, sash, to carry on the body EXAMPLES: 帯 obi = a kimono sash; 携帯電話 keitai denwa = cellular phone; 所帯 shotai = household, family DESCRIPTION: at the top, 山 yama (mountain, # 146), with a horizontal line drawn through it which resembles cloud cover; at the bottom, 巾 Bo Peep, as seen in 帽(子) boushi (hat, # 243), covered by a roof CUES: **O**prah drank **B**eer with this 巾 (Bo Peep) while standing under this roof below this cloud-covered 山 (mountain) in **T**ha**i**land, and afterwards her 帯 **obi** (sash) no longer reached around her GROUP: (所)帯 shotai = household, # 1012; (渋)滞 juutai = congestion, # 1013 (identical pronunciation); (破)棄(する) haki suru = to abolish, # 1624 **ALSO COMPARE:** other similar kanji at # **1768**

1013. 滞 PRONUNCIATIONS: **tai, todokoo** MEANINGS: stagnate, be delayed or overdue EXAMPLES: 滞在する taizai suru = to stay (at a hotel, etc.); 渋滞 juutai = congestion (e.g., traffic), delay, stagnation; 滞る todokooru = to stagnate, be delayed or be overdue DESCRIPTION: compared to (携)帯(電話) keitai denwa (cellular phone, # 1012) (identical pronunciation), this kanji adds a water radical on the left; it retains 巾 (Bo Peep) below a roof under a cloud-covered 山 (mountain) in Thailand CUE: in **T**h**ai**land, I 滞在した **tai**zai shita (stayed) at a hot springs inn and, when I heard that a **T**ornado had blown the **D**oor off a **C**ourthouse, I accidentally dropped this 帯 (phone) into this water **ALSO COMPARE:** other similar kanji at # **1012** and # **1768**

1014. 在 PRONUNCIATIONS: **zai, a** MEANINGS: exist, outskirts, located in EXAMPLES: 滞在する taizai suru = to stay (at a hotel, etc.); 現在 genzai = nowadays, present time; 在る aru = to exist, usually written ある (compare 有る aru = to exist, # 460) DESCRIPTION: compared to 存(じる) zonjiru (to humbly know, # 462), this substitutes 土 tsuchi (soil, # 59) for 子 (child); it retains the hugging person above a vertical line, which can be seen as a one-side lean-to CUES: this person hugging this 土 (soil) may be expressing the **Z**eitgeist (spirit of the **A**ge) of certain people at the 現在 gen**zai** (present time), who are embracing **A**griculture **COMPARE:** 圧(倒的) attouteki = overwhelming, # 748 (identical pronunciation); other similar kanji at # **457** and # **748**

1015. 陸 PRONUNCIATION: riku
MEANING: land EXAMPLES: 大陸 tairiku = continent, mainland (China); 離陸する ririku suru = to take off (flight); 陸軍 rikugun = army DESCRIPTION: on the left, ß beta from the Greek alphabet; at the upper right, 土 tsuchi (soil, # 59), with a pair of lopsided legs; at the lower right, 土 (soil) again CUE: this ß (Greek) guy lives on an island where 土 (soil) like this walks on more 土 (soil), and he will have to swim to the 大陸 tai**riku** (mainland) in order to get some **Real Kool-Aid** ALSO COMPARE: other similar kanji at # **1989** and # **2030**

1016. 湾 PRONUNCIATION: wan
MEANINGS: gulf, bay, inlet EXAMPLES: 湾 wan = gulf, bay; 台湾 taiwan = Taiwan DESCRIPTION: on the left, a water radical; at the upper right, a four-legged hen, as seen in 変 hen (strange, # 553); at the lower right, a twisted 弓 yumi (bow, # 1044) CUE: when I visited 台湾 Tai**wan** and **W**andered over to this water, I saw this four-legged hen flying over this 弓 (bow) COMPARE: other similar kanji at # **476** and # **695**

1017. 旧 PRONUNCIATION: kyuu
MEANINGS: old times, former EXAMPLES: 旧正月 kyuu shougatsu = lunar New Year, or Chinese New Year; 旧年 kyuunen = last year DESCRIPTION: on the left, a vertical line which resembles a 1 but can also be seen as a unicorn horn; on the right, 日 hi (day, # 32) CUE: the # 1 日 (day) of the year is 旧正月 **kyuu** shougatsu (lunar New Year), and it's a good time to eat a **C**ucumber salad GROUP: 旧(年) kyuunen = last year, # 1017; (孤)児 koji = orphan, # 1093; 稲 ine = rice plant, # 1229; (欠)陥 kekkan = a defect, # 1660 ALSO COMPARE: other similar kanji at # **985**

1018. 盛 PRONUNCIATIONS: mo, saka, jou, sei MEANINGS: to thrive, prosperous EXAMPLES: 盛る moru = to fill or pile up; 盛ん sakan = active, enthusiastic, energetic, thriving; 繁盛 hanjou = success or prosperity (in business); 全盛 zensei = culmination, heyday, peak; 盛大 seidai = grandiose, pompous, thriving, successful DESCRIPTION: compared to 成(功) seikou (success, # 633) (identical pronunciation), this adds 皿 sara (dish, # 567) at the bottom; it retains a 刀 (blade) supported by a halberd CUES: **Mo**ses was a **Sakkaa** (soccer) player, but now he and **Jo**an of Arc are having a lot of 成 (success) like this with a factory that makes 皿 (dishes) like this and 盛んだ **saka**n da (is thriving), selling its products at **Sa**feway stores ALSO COMPARE: other similar kanji at # **633**, # **1407** and # 1862

1019. 災 PRONUNCIATIONS: sai, wazawa MEANINGS: serious trouble, calamity EXAMPLES: 震災 shinsai = great earthquake; 火災 kasai = fire; 災難 sainan = misfortune, disaster; 災い wazawai = calamity, disaster DESCRIPTION: at the top, a chevron like those sewn onto uniforms, as seen in 巡(る) meguru (to go around, # 778); at the bottom, 火 hi (fire, # 443) CUES: this chevron is a **S**ign that a 災難 **sai**nan (disaster) is likely, since it suggests that **W**acky **Z**ambian **W**arriors are 巡 (going around) in uniforms decorated with chevrons like this and starting 火 (fires) like this GROUP: 巡(る) meguru = to go around, # 778; (火)災 kasai = fire, # 1019; (挨)拶 aisatsu = a greeting, # 1650; (比)喩 hiyu = a simile, # 2021 ALSO COMPARE: other similar kanji at # **1239**

1020. 乱 PRONUNCIATIONS: mida, ran
MEANING: to be out of order
EXAMPLES: 乱れる midareru = to become chaotic or windblown (hair); 乱暴 ranbou = violent, disorderly DESCRIPTION: on the left, 舌 shita (tongue, # 1213); on the right, L, which resembles a breast, as seen in 乳 nyuu (milk, # 186) CUES: during a Meal with Darwin, when we discussed the evolution of 乳 (breast) feeding, he stuck this 舌 (tongue) out at us, became 乱暴 ran**bou** (violent) and **Ran**sacked the place ALSO COMPARE: similar kanji at # **735** and # **1213**

1021. 暴 PRONUNCIATIONS: bou, aba, baku MEANINGS: to expose, violent
EXAMPLES: 乱暴な ranbou na = violent or disorderly; 暴れる abareru = to become violent; 暴露 bakuro = exposure or revelation
DESCRIPTION: at the top, 日 hi (sun, # 32); below that, a modified 共 tomo (together, # 969); at the bottom, 水 mizu (water, # 251) CUES: when **B**oys are **A**bandoned, they go to **B**ars to get **K**ool-**A**id and then sit 共 (together) in this 水 (water) under this 日 (sun) and threaten to become 乱暴 ran**bou** (violent). GROUP: (乱)暴(な) ranbou na = violent, # 1021; 爆(弾) bakudan = bomb, # 1022 (identical pronunciation)
ALSO COMPARE: other similar kanji at # **1529**

1022. 爆 PRONUNCIATION: baku
MEANINGS: bomb, burst open, pop, split
EXAMPLES: 爆弾 bakudan = bomb; 原爆 genbaku = atomic bomb
DESCRIPTION: compared to (乱)暴 ranbou (violent, # 1021), or 暴(露) bakuro (exposure, # 1021) (identical pronunciation), this kanji adds 火 hi (fire, # 443) on the left; it retains the 日 (sun) under which boys sit 共 (together) in 水 (water) after going to bars to get Kool-Aid
CUE: I was sitting in a **B**ar drinking **K**ool-**A**id when a 暴 (violent) person set off a 爆弾 **baku**dan (bomb) and started this 火 (fire)
ALSO COMPARE: other similar kanji at # **1021** and # **1239**

1023. 縁 PRONUNCIATION: en
MEANINGS: chance, fate, destiny EXAMPLES: 縁起 engi = omen, sign of luck, origin, causation
DESCRIPTION: compared to 緑 midori (green, # 227), this substitutes a radical seen in 家 ie (house, # 405) for 水 (water) at the lower right; it retains the 糸 (skeet shooter) and the green flag, which can also be seen as hair streaming left
CUE: this 糸 (skeet shooter) shoots at this 緑 (green) flag flying from this 家 (house), which he thinks is a good 縁起 **en**gi (omen), suggesting that **En**tertainers are inside ALSO COMPARE: other similar kanji at # **1165** and # **1504**

1024. 怪 PRONUNCIATIONS: aya, ke, kai MEANINGS: suspicious, mystery, apparition
EXAMPLES: 怪しい ayashii = suspicious, doubtful; 怪我 kega = serious injury, often written けが; 怪物 kaibutsu = monster
DESCRIPTION: compared to 経(験) keiken (experience, # 224), this substitutes an erect man for the skeet shooter on the left; it retains the dog groomer's 又 (table) on 土 (soil) CUES: this man on the left is an **Aya**tollah who is 怪しい **aya**shii (doubtful) whether this dog grooming business is suitable for his dog, and he draws himself up to his full height when he sees that this 又 (table) holds a **K**eg of beer, the room is full of this 土 (soil), and the owner is out flying **K**ites
ALSO COMPARE: other similar kanji at # **1894** and # **2063**

1025. 松 **PRONUNCIATIONS: matsu, shou MEANING:** pine tree **EXAMPLES:** 松 matsu = pine tree; 松竹梅 shouchikubai = pine, bamboo and plum, a symbol of good luck **DESCRIPTION:** compared to 公(園) kouen (public park, # 16), this adds 木 ki (tree, # 118) on the left; it retains the 八 (eight) ム (cows) with thick coats **CUES:** this 木 (tree) is a 松 **matsu** (pine tree), and people sit under it on **Mats, Show** off their legs and watch these 八 (eight) ム (cows) **ALSO COMPARE:** other similar kanji at # **1546**

1026. 江 **PRONUNCIATIONS: e, kou MEANINGS:** creek, inlet, bay **EXAMPLES:** 江戸 edo = old name for Tokyo; 長江 choukou = Yangtze River in China **DESCRIPTION:** on the left, a water radical; on the right, 工 kou (crafted object, # 246) (identical pronunciation) **CUES:** Excellent craftsmen carved 工 (crafted objects) like this from **C**oral, found in water like this, during the 江戸 **e**do (ancient Tokyo) period **ALSO COMPARE:** similar kanji at # **247**

1027. 講 **PRONUNCIATION: kou MEANING:** to lecture **EXAMPLE:** 講義 kougi = lecture **DESCRIPTION:** compared to (結)構 kekkou (fine, # 141) (identical pronunciation), this kanji substitutes 言(う) iu (to speak, # 430) for 木 (wood) on the left; it retains the courthouse with a 井 (well) and a 再 (model of a rice paddy with a handle) in the lobby **CUE:** when a woman 言 (spoke) and gave a 講義 **kou**gi (lecture) in this **C**ourthouse with this 井 (well) and this 再 (rice paddy model with a handle), her explanations seemed 構 (fine) to me **ALSO COMPARE:** other similar kanji at # **1032** and # **1825**

1028. 義 **PRONUNCIATION: gi MEANINGS:** justice, morality **EXAMPLES:** 義理 giri = moral debt, limited duty; 義務 gimu = unlimited duty to the emperor, ancestors, etc.

講義 kougi = lecture **DESCRIPTION:** compared to (会)議 kaigi (meeting, # 438) (identical pronunciation), this kanji omits 言 (to speak); it retains the 王 (king) wearing rabbit ears [this part of the kanji can also be seen as a truncated 羊 hitsuji (sheep, # 1223), missing its tail], the 手 (hand), and the halberd **CUE:** I attended a 講義 kou**gi** (lecture) about people who grasp halberds like this with 手 (hands) like this to attack **Ge**ese and truncated 羊 (sheep) like this **ALSO COMPARE:** other similar kanji at # **1554**, # **1862** and # **1893**

1029. 推 **PRONUNCIATIONS: sui, o MEANINGS:** to push forward, recommend, guess **EXAMPLES:** 推薦する suisen suru = to recommend; 推す osu = to recommend or endorse **DESCRIPTION:** compared to 誰 dare (who, # 440), this substitutes a kneeling guy for 言 (to speak) on the left; it retains the net on the right, which can be seen as a man with a slanted hat next to a 主 (master) with an extra pair of arms (see # 203) **CUES:** this guy on the left is **Sw**edish, and he kneels in front of this net in which I am confined and 推薦する **sui**sen suru (recommends) that my jailer **O**pen it **COMPARE:** similar kanji at # **2046**

1030. 薦 **PRONUNCIATIONS: susu, sen MEANINGS:** recommend, advise **EXAMPLES:** 薦める susumeru = to advise (this is usually written 勧める susumeru, # 698); 推薦する suisen suru = to recommend **DESCRIPTION:** at the top, a plant radical; below that, a lean-to with a chimney; suspended from the ceiling of the lean-to, three eyes; below the eyes, the lower half of 鳥 tori (bird, # 555) **CUES:** the three eyes in this lean-to saw the lower half of this 鳥 (bird), which was eating these plants, and **S**oon called **S**uperman, who 推薦した sui**sen** shita (recommended) that the **Sen**ate pass a law to protect the bird **COMPARE:** other similar kanji at # **754** and # **895**

1031. 測

PRONUNCIATIONS: haka, soku **MEANINGS:** fathom, plan, scheme, measure **EXAMPLES:** 測る hakaru = to measure or gauge (usually written 計る hakaru, # 434); 推測 suisoku = an assumption or guess; 予測 yosoku = a prediction or supposition **DESCRIPTION:** compared to 側(面) sokumen (side, # 490) (identical pronun-ciation), this kanji substitutes a water radical for the man with a slanted hat on the left; it retains the 貝 (money chest) and リ Ri **CUES:** リ Ri made a 推測 sui**soku** (assumption) that the man with a slanted hat was still standing on the opposite 側 (side) of this 貝 (money chest), but the man had left to attend a **Hacka**thon, and that allowed this water to pour in, so that the 貝 (chest) and リ Ri got **Soaked** **ALSO COMPARE:** other similar kanji at # **490**

1032. 再

PRONUNCIATIONS: sai, futata, *sa* **MEANING:** again **EXAMPLES:** 再会する saikai suru = to meet again; 再開する saikai suru = to reopen or resume; 再三 saisan = many times, again and again; 再び futatabi = again; 再来年 sarainen = the year after next **DESCRIPTION:** a model of a 田 (rice paddy) with a vertical handle standing on the legs of 円 (yen), as seen in 構う kamau (to mind, # 141) **CUES:** a Scientist made this model of a rice paddy with a handle and strong legs and was hoping to get some 円 (yen) for it, but a woman who was eating **F**ood on a **Ta**tami mat wouldn't buy it, even though he asked her 再び **futata**bi (again), and he felt **S**ad **GROUP:** 角 kado = outside corner, # 81; 構(う) kamau = to mind, # 141; 触(れる) fureru = to touch, # 475; (理)解 rikai = understanding, # 618; 講(義) kougi = lecture, # 1027; 再(三) saisan = many times, # 1032; 購(入する) kounyuu suru = to purchase, # 1269; (排水)溝 haisuikou = drainage, # 1825 **ALSO COMPARE:** other similar kanji at # **77**

1033. 各

PRONUNCIATIONS: kaku, *ka* **MEANINGS:** each one, individual **EXAMPLES:** 各自の kakuji no = each, one's own; 各駅 kakueki = each station; 各国 kakkoku = each country **DESCRIPTION:** compared to 性格 seikaku (personality, # 762), or 格(好) kakkou (appearance, # 762), both of which help us to pronounce this, this kanji omits the 木 (tree) on the left; it retains the dancer who jumps over a box to escape Karl the Kool-Aid vendor **CUES:** after this dancer jumps over this box, she breaks up with **Kar**l the **Koo**l-Aid vendor, and they drive away in 各自の **kaku**ji no (their own) **C**ars **GROUP:** (連)絡(する) renraku suru = to contact, # 230; 客 kyaku = guest, # 524; (道)路 douro = road, # 525; 落(ちる) ochiru = to fall, # 526; (性)格 seikaku = personality, # 762; (金)額 kingaku = a sum of money, # 791; 各(駅) kakueki = each station, # 1033; 略 ryaku = an omission, # 1272; 露 tsuyu = dew, # 1390; (内)閣 naikaku = the Cabinet, # 1409; 啓(発) keihatsu = inspiration, # 1744; 酪(農) rakunou = dairy farming, # 2069; **Note** that four of these kanji can be pronounced "kaku" or "gaku"

1034. 繰

PRONUNCIATION: ku **MEANINGS:** winding, spin, refer to **EXAMPLES:** 繰り返す kurikaesu = to repeat, to do something over again **DESCRIPTION:** on the left, 糸 skeet shooter (# 219); at the upper right, 品(物) shinamono (merchandise, # 5); at the lower right, 木 ki (tree, # 118) **CUE:** this 糸 (skeet shooter) sees this 品 (merchandise), which is three packages of **Ko**ol-Aid, stuck at the top of this 木 (tree), tries to shoot it down and then 繰り返す **ku**rikaesu (does it again) **GROUP:** 品(物) shinamono = merchandise, # 5; (食)器 shokki = tableware, # 853; 繰(り返す) kurikaesu = to repeat, # 1034; 操(作) sousa = operation (machine), # 1192; 臨(時) rinji =

temporary, # 1515; 顎 ago = a chin, # 1787; 喪(失) soushitsu = a loss, # 1828; (乾)燥 kansou = dryness, # 1930; (海)藻 kaisou = seaweed, # 2008; 癌 gan = cancer, # 2079 **ALSO COMPARE:** other similar kanji at # <u>1216</u>

1035. 是 PRONUNCIATIONS: ze, kore
MEANINGS: just so, this **EXAMPLES:** 是非とも zehitomo = by all means; 是認 zenin = approval; 是等 korera = these (usually written これら); 是程 kore hodo = so much, this much (usually written これほど)
DESCRIPTION: compared to (予)定 yotei (plan, # 455), this substitutes 日 hi (sun, # 32) for the bad haircut at the top; it retains the foot radical with a taser mounted on it
CUES: a **Ze**alous policeman who has this taser mounted on this foot sits in this 日 (sun) and says that 是非とも **ze**hitomo (by all means) he will use this taser **Co**rrectly
ALSO COMPARE: other similar kanji at # <u>454</u>

1036. 認 PRONUNCIATIONS: nin, mito
MEANING: to recognize **EXAMPLES:** 是認 zenin = approval; 確認 kakunin = confirmation; 認める mitomeru = to recognize, admit or allow
DESCRIPTION: on the left, 言(う) iu (to speak, # 430); at the upper right, 刀 katana (sword, # 102), with a slash across it; at the lower right, 心 kokoro (heart, # 306) **CUES:** when a **Ni**nja goes to **M**eet **To**lstoy to get 是認 ze**nin** (approval) for an undercover project, he 言 (speaks) from this 心 (heart) and shows Tolstoy this 刀 (sword), which was slashed during one of his missions
ALSO COMPARE: other similar kanji at # <u>1488</u>

1037. 遺 PRONUNCIATIONS: i, yui
MEANINGS: bequeathe, leave behind, reserve
EXAMPLES: 遺産 isan = inheritance, legacy, heritage; 遺言 yuigon = will, deathbed instructions **DESCRIPTION:** compared to 貴(重) kichou (valuable, # 643), this adds a snail at the lower left; it retains 中 (inside) resting on a platform above 貝 (money chest) **CUES:** my father keeps only dried **E**els 中 (inside) this 貝 (money chest), which will be his 遺産 **i**san (legacy) to me, together with a **Yu**kon **E**agle and this snail, none of which is very 貴 (valuable)
ALSO COMPARE: other similar kanji at # <u>643</u>

1038. 総 PRONUNCIATION: sou
MEANINGS: all, whole **EXAMPLES:** 総じて soujite = in general, on the whole; 総理大臣 souridaijin = prime minister; 総会 soukai = general meeting **DESCRIPTION:** on the left, 糸 (skeet shooter, # 219); at the upper right, 公 kou (public, # 16), which reminds us of 八 (eight) ム (cows); at the lower right, 心 kokoro (heart, # 306)
CUE: this 糸 (skeet shooter) is shooting at these 八 (eight) ム (cows), but he has this good 心 (heart) 総じて **sou**jite (in general) and is employed as a **So**ldier
ALSO COMPARE: other similar kanji at # <u>1546</u>

1039. 臣 PRONUNCIATIONS: shin, jin
MEANINGS: subject, minister
EXAMPLES: 臣民 shinmin = royal subject; 総理大臣 souridaijin = prime minister
DESCRIPTION: compared to 巨(大) kyodai (huge, # 689), the ropes of this child's swing set turned on its side have been tied to make the swing inoperable
CUES: a **Shin**to priest, who is a 臣民 **shin**min (royal subject), put on his **Jean**s before turning this swing set on its side and tying these swing ropes in order to prevent harm to children
COMPARE: other similar kanji at # <u>1246</u>

1040. 姫 PRONUNCIATION: hime
MEANING: princess **EXAMPLE:** 姫 hime = princess **DESCRIPTION:** on the left, 女 (female, # 235); on the right, 臣(民) shinmin (royal subject, # 1039), which resembles an inoperable

swing set on its side   CUE: the emperor's daughter is a 女 (female) and a 姫 **hime** (princess) who is attracted to **He-M**en, but she is too young to use this swing set safely, so it has been made inoperable   ALSO COMPARE: 媛 hime = princess, # 2084; other kanji containing 女 on the left at # **2039**; other similar kanji at # **1246**

1041. 塗 PRONUNCIATIONS: to, nu

MEANINGS: paint, plaster, smear, coating   EXAMPLES: 塗装 tosou = a coat of paint; 塗る nuru = to paint, plaster, spread, smear; 塗り替える nurikaeru = to repaint, rewrite   DESCRIPTION: at the upper left, a water radical; at the upper right, 余(り) amari (surplus, # 637), which resembles a spinning 丁 (nail) under a stool and a peaked roof; at the lower right, 土 tsuchi (soil, # 59)   CUES: I have this 余 (spinning nail structure) that I use for 余 (surplus) **T**omatoes, and it's sitting on this pile of 土 (soil) and exposed to this water, but I want to 塗る **nu**ru (paint) the top so that it will look **N**ew   ALSO COMPARE: other similar kanji at # **637**

1042. 衣 PRONUNCIATIONS: e, i, *kata, koromo*

MEANINGS: clothes, garment, dressing   EXAMPLES: 衣紋 emon = clothing; 衣服 ifuku = clothing; 衣類 irui = clothing; 浴衣 yukata = informal summer kimono; 衣 koromo = coating or breading (food), clothes   DESCRIPTION: at the top, a tire stop as seen in 対(して) tai shite (against, # 674); at the bottom, 工 and Y   CUES: 工 and Y stand near this tire stop and make **E**xciting **E**aster 衣服 **i**fuku (clothing) to sell from **Cat**alogues, and they use their **Co**rolla's **Mo**tor for warmth   GROUP: 製(品) seihin = finished product, # 580; 袋 fukuro = bag, # 581; 懐(かしい) natsukashii = nostalgic, # 928; 襲(う) osou = to attack, # 941; 衣(服) ifuku = clothing. # 1042; 装(置) souchi = equipment, # 1043; 壊(す) kowasu = to break,

1394; 裁(判) saiban = trial, # 1450; (分)裂 bunretsu = division, # 1465; 依(頼) irai = a request, # 1557; (老)衰 rousui = senility, # 1753

1043. 装 PRONUNCIATIONS: sou, yoso, shou

MEANINGS: to wear or equip   EXAMPLES: 服装 fukusou = outfit, dress style, attire; 装置 souchi = equipment, device; 装備 soubi = equipment; 装う yosou = to serve or dish up; 衣装 ishou = clothing, costume   DESCRIPTION: compared to 壮(大) soudai (magnificent, # 769) (identical pronunciation), this kanji adds 衣(服) ifuku (clothing, # 1042) at the bottom; it retains the 士 (man) sitting on a bench and listening to soul music   CUES: this 士 (man) likes **Sou**l music, and he can **Yo**del when he's **So**ber; he leans this bench up against a wall in order to clear a space for a **S**how and examines this 衣 (clothing) which will be his 服装 fuku**sou** (outfit) during the performance   COMPARE: other similar kanji at # **998**, # **1042** and # **1468**

1044. 弓 PRONUNCIATIONS: yumi, kyuu

MEANING: bow   EXAMPLES: 弓 yumi = bow; 弓矢 yumiya = bow and arrow; 弓道 kyuudou = archery   DESCRIPTION: this is the twisted bow seen in 引(く) hiku (to pull, # 476)   CUES: **I** 引 (pulled) the string on this 弓 **yumi** (bow) at a **Yo**uth **Mee**ting when I visited **Cu**ba   COMPARE: other similar kanji at # **476**

1045. 矢 PRONUNCIATION: ya

MEANING: arrow   EXAMPLES: 矢 ya = arrow; 矢印 yajirushi = arrow (on a map or sign); 弓矢 yumiya = bow and arrow   DESCRIPTION: this is a Native American chief, as seen in 知(る) shiru (to know, # 323); compared to 失(敗する) shippai suru (to fail, # 206), this kanji omits the head of the 牛 (cow, # 205)   CUE: this Native American chief guards his **Ya**rd with 弓矢 yumi**ya** (bows and arrows)   ALSO COMPARE: other similar kanji at # **324** and # **614**

1046. 印 **PRONUNCIATIONS: shirushi, jirushi², in** **MEANINGS:** sign, seal, symbol **EXAMPLES:** 印 shirushi = sign, symbol, indication; 矢印 yajirushi = arrow (on a map or sign); 印鑑 inkan = signature seal; 印象的 inshouteki = impressive **DESCRIPTION:** on the left, a ladder, as seen in (階)段 kaidan (stairs, # 559); on the right, this radical reportedly represents a signature seal used to stamp documents; the seal is located at the lower tip of the vertical line on the left, and the rest is a handle **CUES:** a **Shi**ite is **Rush**ing up this ladder to get some **In**k for this seal, which he'll use to add a 印 **shi**rushi (symbol) to his document **GROUP:** 卵 tamago = egg, # 28; 迎(える) mukaeru = to greet/welcome, # 358; 命 inochi = life, # 961; 印 shirushi = sign, # 1046; (季)節 kisetsu = season, # 1048; 卸 oroshi = wholesale, # 1218; (制)御 seigyo = control, # 1440; 即(刻) sokkoku = immediately, # 1502; 柳 yanagi = willow, # 1535; (信)仰 shinkou = belief, # 1549; (返)却(する) henkyaku suru = to return something borrowed, # 1562; 脚(本) kyakuhon = a script, # 1563; 抑(える) osaeru = to suppress, # 1584 **ALSO COMPARE:** other similar kanji at # **41**

1047. 季 **PRONUNCIATION: ki** **MEANINGS:** season, a quarter of a year **EXAMPLES:** 季節 kisetsu = season; 四季 shiki = the four seasons **DESCRIPTION:** at the top, 禾 (a grain plant with a ripe head); at the bottom, 子 ko (child, # 182) **CUE:** the **K**ey to remembering the 季節 **ki**setsu (seasons), is to associate this 禾 (ripe grain) with autumn and this 子 (child) with spring **COMPARE:** other similar kanji at # **1797** and # **2078**

1048. 節 **PRONUNCIATIONS: setsu, sechi, fushi** **MEANINGS:** section, holiday, occasion, joint, tune **EXAMPLES:** 季節 kisetsu = season; 関節 kansetsu = joint (e.g., knee); 節約する setsuyaku suru = to economize; お節料理 osechi ryouri = food served during the New Year's holidays; 節 fushi = knot (wood), joint (body), melody **DESCRIPTION:** at the top, 竹 take (bamboo, # 134); at the lower left, a modified version of 良(い) yoi (good, # 303), missing projections on the top and at the lower right corner; at the lower right, this is the "seal" radical seen in 印 shirushi (sign, # 1046) **CUES:** we **Set** up a **Super** farm during the spring 季節 ki**setsu** (season) in order to grow 竹 (bamboo) like this to make 良 (good) seals like this one, and we also **Sell Chee**se so that we can buy **F**ood for our **Sh**eep **ALSO COMPARE:** other similar kanji at # **805**, # **1046** and # **2074**

1049. 修 **PRONUNCIATIONS: osa, shuu, shu** **MEANINGS:** to learn or master **EXAMPLES:** 修める osameru = to learn or master; 修理 shuuri = repairs; 修行 shugyou = training, apprenticeship **DESCRIPTION:** compared to 悠(々) yuuyuu (calm, # 985), this omits the 心 (heart) on the bottom and adds a rocker-bottom shoe, similar to the one seen in 参(る) mairu (to humbly come or go, # 406), at the lower right; it retains the man with a slanted hat, the unicorn horn and the dancer **CUES:** this guy on the left is **Osa**ma bin Laden, who is tilting his hat back to show his face to this dancer with this 参 (rocker-bottom) **Sh**oe, whom he wants to recruit for 修行 **shu**gyou (training), but the dancer always keeps this unicorn horn between them and is prepared to **Shoot** him **ALSO COMPARE:** 治(める) osameru = to govern or reign, # 539; 納(める) osameru = to put away or conclude, # 705; 収(める) osameru = to put away or conclude, # 1113; other similar kanji at # **406** and # **985**

1050. 般 **PRONUNCIATIONS: han, pan** **MEANINGS:** carrier, carry, all **EXAMPLES:** 般若 hannya = prajna, wisdom, insight into the nature of reality (Buddhism); 一般的に ippanteki ni = commonly, generally, usually

DESCRIPTION: compared to 役に立つ yaku ni tatsu (to be useful, # 557), this substitutes a boat, as seen in 船 fune (boat, # 602), for the man with a double hat on the left; it retains the 兀 (yak) on a 又 (table) CUES: Hansel 一般的に ip**pan**teki ni (usually) keeps a **Pan**da on the top of this 又 (table) in this 舟 (boat), but sometimes he keeps 兀 (yaks) like this on it as well ALSO COMPARE: other similar kanji at # **557** and # **1524**

1051. 壁 PRONUNCIATIONS: kabe, heki, peki MEANINGS: wall, fence EXAMPLES: 壁 kabe = wall; 壁画 hekiga = mural painting; 絶壁 zeppeki = cliff DESCRIPTION: compared to 避(ける) sakeru (to avoid, # 802), this omits the snail at the lower left and adds 土 tsuchi (soil, # 59) at the bottom; it retains the lean-to with a double roof, the 口 (box), and the 辛 (needle) (this combination of radicals = LBN = lean-to, box, needle) CUES: I **C**alled **B**en Franklin and asked him to **H**elp the **K**ing by inventing a 壁 **kabe** (wall) for the castle, since birds are **P**ecking the old one, and he came up with this defensive design using this lean-to with a double roof, 口 (boxes) and 辛 (needles) like these, plus 土 (soil) like this (LBN = lean-to, box, needle) ALSO COMPARE: similar kanji at # **1214**

1052. 編 PRONUNCIATIONS: hen, pen, a MEANINGS: to arrange, edit or knit EXAMPLES: 編集 henshuu = editing; 編者 hensha = editor; 短編 tanpen = short story or film; 編む amu = to knit DESCRIPTION: on the left, 糸 (skeet shooter, # 219); at the upper right, a lean-to with a double roof, covered with a layer of snow; at the lower right, 冊 satsu (counter for books, # 568) CUES: this 糸 (skeet shooter) is shooting at this snow-covered double-roofed lean-to because he disapproves of the 編者 **hen**sha (editor) inside, who is working on this 冊 (book) about **Hen**s that use **Pen**s to make **A**rt ALSO COMPARE: similar kanji at # **568** and # **1134**

1053. 評 PRONUNCIATION: hyou MEANING: to comment EXAMPLES: 評判 hyouban = reputation, popularity, rumor; 評価 hyouka = assessment, evaluation; 不評 fu'hyou = bad reputation or review, unpopularity; 定評 teihyou = reputation, notoriety DESCRIPTION: compared to 平(和) heiwa (peace, tranquility, # 885), this adds 言(う) iu (to speak, # 430) on the left; it retains the telephone pole with a flat top that is on fire CUE: the Lone Ranger has a good 評判 **hyou**ban (reputation) in these parts, and when he heard that this telephone pole was on fire, he stopped by to 言 (say) "Hi-Yo Silver" GROUP: 平(和) heiwa = peace, # 885; 評(判) hyouban = reputation, # 1053; 坪 tsubo = 3.3 square meters, # 1824 COMPARE: other similar kanji at # 629

1054. 判 (sometimes written 判) PRONUNCIATIONS: han, ban, pan MEANING: to judge EXAMPLES: 判断する handan suru = to judge; 評判 hyouban = reputation, popularity, rumor; 審判 shinpan = referee DESCRIPTION: compared to 半 han (half, # 331) (identical pronunciation), which can be seen as a telephone pole on fire, this kanji adds the katakana リ ri on the right; this can sometimes be written with a *leaning* (or kneeling) pole as 判 CUES: **Han**sel says that, when he went to a **Ban**quet, he only received 半 (half) a serving of **Pan** (bread), and he 判断した **han**dan shita (judged) that this guy リ **R**i was responsible [alternatively, **Han**sel went to a **Ban**quet, where he was eating **Pan** (bread) with this guy リ **R**i and he 判断した **han**dan shita (judged) that this leaning telephone was about to fall on them] GROUP: 半 han = half, # 331, (評)判 hyouban = reputation, # 1054, (同)伴(する) douhan suru

= to accompany, # 1599, and (湖)畔 kohan = lake shore, # 1988, all of which can be pronounced "han" or "ban" **ALSO COMPARE:** other similar kanji at # **897** and # **1985**

1055. 猿 PRONUNCIATIONS: saru, zaru², en MEANING: monkey
EXAMPLES: 猿 saru = monkey; 日本猿 nihonzaru = Japanese macaque; 類人猿 ruijin'en = ape **DESCRIPTION:** on the left, a person contorting her body, as seen in 狭(い) semai (narrow, # 194); at the upper right, 土 (soil) above a box, as seen in 遠(慮) enryo (reserve, # 351) (identical pronunciation); on the lower right, エ and Y **CUES:** this woman is contorting herself to support **Saru**man's scheme to train 猿 **saru** (monkeys) to work as **E**ntertainers in Middle Earth, taking them out of this 土 (soil) where they live, keeping them in boxes like this, and giving them names that start with エ and Y, like Eric and Yolanda **ALSO COMPARE:** other similar kanji at # **351**, # **582** and # **948**

1056. 芸 PRONUNCIATION: gei
MEANINGS: art, skill; artistic skill or technique **EXAMPLES:** 芸 gei = art or craft, animal trick; 芸術 geijutsu = art; 芸術館 geijutsukan = art museum; 芸者 geisha = female entertainer **DESCRIPTION:** at the top, a plant radical; in the middle, 二 ni (two, # 2); at the bottom, the katakana ム mu, which is the sound made by a cow **CUE:** I'm playing a computer **G**ame in which I teach these 二 (two) ム (cows) to perform 芸 **gei** (tricks) with plants like this **GROUP:** 絵(本) ehon = picture book, # 223; 雲 kumo = cloud, # 264; (自)転(車) jitensha = bicycle, # 285; 会(社) kaisha = company, # 293; 伝(える) tsutaeru = to convey, # 345; 芸 gei = craft, # 1056; 陰(謀) inbou = a plot, # 1543; 魂 tamashii = a soul, # 1636; 曇(る) kumoru = to become cloudy, # 1911

1057. 虎 PRONUNCIATION: tora
MEANING: tiger **EXAMPLE:** 虎 tora = tiger **DESCRIPTION:** compared to (謙)虚 kenkyo (modesty, # 966), this substitutes two lopsided legs, as seen in 見(る) miru (to look, # 53), for the four burners on a stove; it retains the 七 (seven) people living in a one-sided lean-to and observing the world through a periscope **CUE:** 七 (seven) people who live in this lean-to and observe the outside world through this periscope are holding **Tol**stoy for **Ran**som, and they sometimes dangle these lopsided legs out through a window to entice passing 虎 **tora** (tigers) **GROUP:** (謙)虚 kenkyo = modesty, # 966; 嘘 uso = a lie, # 967; 虎 tora = tiger, # 1057; 劇 geki = a play, # 1058; (捕)虜 horyo = captive, # 1107; (遠)慮 enryo = reserve, # 1194; (残)虐(な) zangyaku na = cruel, # 1679; 戯(れる) tawamureru = to play, # 1756; (皮)膚 hifu = skin, # 1777 **ALSO COMPARE:** kanji containing a *chimney* passing through a roof at # 1494; other similar kanji at # **974**

1058. 劇 PRONUNCIATION: geki
MEANINGS: a drama, intensely **EXAMPLES:** 劇 geki = a play; 劇場 gekijou = a theater; 歌劇 kageki = opera **DESCRIPTION:** at the upper left, a one-sided lean-to; at the top, a periscope for observing the outside world; under the roof, 七 shichi (seven, # 20); on the floor, a radical seen in 豚 buta (pig, # 1504); on the right, the katakana リ Ri **CUE:** this guy リ Ri has a **Gu**est **Key** for this lean-to in which 七 (seven) people observe the world through this periscope, keep this 豚 (pig) and enjoy going to the 劇場 **geki**jou (theater) **ALSO COMPARE:** similar kanji at # **1057**, # **1504** and # **1985**

1059. 郷 PRONUNCIATIONS: sato, kyou, gou MEANINGS: hometown, village
EXAMPLES: 故郷 furusato = hometown, often written ふるさと, or ふる里, # 1060;

故郷 can also be pronounced kokyou, with the same meaning; 郷里 kyouri = hometown; 水郷 suigou = riverside or lakeside location
DESCRIPTION: compared to (影)響 eikyou = influence, # 840 (identical pronunciation), this kanji omits 音 (sound) at the bottom; it retains the jagged lightning strike, a modified 良 (good) without its pointy hat and ß beta from the Greek alphabet
CUES: after my 良 (good) ß (Greek) friend saw this lightning hit a **S**atellite **T**ower in **Kyou**to, which is my 郷里 **kyou**ri (hometown), he was afraid to play **G**olf and went back to Athens   **ALSO COMPARE:** 里 sato = village, # 1060; other similar kanji at # **805**, # **840** and # **1843**

1060. 里 PRONUNCIATIONS: sato, zato², ri
MEANINGS: village, ri (approx 4 km)
EXAMPLES: 里 sato = hometown, village; ふる里 furusato = hometown, often written ふるさと or 故郷, # 1059; 人里 hitozato = human habitation; 郷里 kyouri = hometown
DESCRIPTION: compared to 理(由) riyuu (reason, # 78) (identical pronunciation), this kanji omits 王 (king) on the left; it retains the sincere guy wearing bifocals   **CUES:** this sincere guy admires a **S**atellite **T**ower that is covered in **C**hristmas **W**reaths, located in a 里 **sato** (village)
ALSO COMPARE: 郷 sato = village, # 1059; other similar kanji at # **545**

1061. 量 PRONUNCIATIONS: ryou, haka
MEANINGS: mass, amount
EXAMPLES: 量 ryou = quantity; 大量 tairyou = large amount; 量る hakaru = to weigh
DESCRIPTION: at the top, 日 hi (sun, # 32); in the middle, a rug; at the bottom, 里 sato (hometown, # 1060), which reminds us of a sincere guy wearing bifocals   **CUES:** Pope **L**eo, who is this sincere guy wearing these bifocals, **H**arvests **C**arnations, and when he has 大量 tai**ryou** (a large amount), he arranges them on this rug in this 日 (sun)   **ALSO COMPARE:** other similar kanji at # **545** and # **668**

1062. 幹 PRONUNCIATIONS: miki, kan
MEANINGS: trunk of a tree, main
EXAMPLES: 幹 miki = tree trunk; 幹部 kanbu = an executive; 新幹線 shinkansen = bullet train
DESCRIPTION: on the left, the wagon seen in 朝 asa (morning, # 291); on the right, a telephone pole sheltered by a peaked roof
CUES: Mickey Mouse lives in this Disney wagon in **Kan**sas next to this sheltered telephone pole made from a 幹 **miki** (tree trunk)
ALSO COMPARE: 韓(国) kankoku = S. Korea, # 655 (identical pronunciation); other similar kanji at # **629**, # **1308** and # **1382**

1063. 央 PRONUNCIATION: ou
MEANINGS: center, middle   **EXAMPLE:** 中央 chuu'ou = center, middle   **DESCRIPTION:** this is a movie screen, as seen in 映(画) eiga (movie, # 36); it can also be seen as two eyes on a stand
CUE: I like to watch movies starring **O**prah on this 映 (movie) screen, and I sit in the 中央 chuu**ou** (middle) of the theater   **ALSO COMPARE:** other similar kanji at # **43** and # **1314**

1064. 請 PRONUNCIATIONS: sei, ko
MEANINGS: solicit, invite, ask
EXAMPLES: 請求 seikyuu = demand, request; 申請する shinsei suru = to apply for or request; 請う kou = to beg or ask; 請い求める koimotomeru = to beg or request   **DESCRIPTION:** compared to 精(神) seishin (spirit, # 847) (identical pronunciation), this kanji substitutes 言 (う) iu (to speak, # 430) for 米 (uncooked rice) on the left; it retains 青 (blue)   **CUES:** a **S**ailor 言 (speaks) about his love for skies that are 青 (blue) like this, and he 請求する **sei**kyuu suru (demands) an end to air pollution caused by **C**oal   **ALSO COMPARE:** similar kanji at # **1112**

1065. 老 PRONUNCIATIONS: o, rou, fu
MEANING: old EXAMPLES: 老いる o'iru = to grow old; 老人 roujin = elderly person; 老ける fukeru = to age or lose one's youthful appearance DESCRIPTION: compared to 者 mono (person, # 276), this substitutes the katakana ヒ hi, which reminds us of hearing loss, for the 日 (sun) at the bottom CUES: this Old 者 (person) is a 老人 **rou**jin (elderly person) who has ヒ (hearing loss) and employs **Ro**bots to prepare her **Fo**od GROUP: 考(える) kangaeru = to think, # 469; 老(人) roujin = elderly person, # 1065; 拷問 goumon = torture, # 2040
ALSO COMPARE: other similar kanji at # 2048

1066. 祉 PRONUNCIATION: shi
MEANINGS: welfare, happiness EXAMPLE: 福祉 fukushi = welfare DESCRIPTION: on the left, the Shah, as seen in (会)社 kaisha (company, # 271); on the right, 止(める) tomeru (to stop, # 173) CUE: this Shah tries to 止 (stop) **Sh**eep rustling in order to ensure the 福祉 fuku**shi** (welfare) of his wool business ALSO COMPARE: similar kanji at # 1160 and # 1929

1067. 施 PRONUNCIATIONS: se, hodoko, shi MEANINGS: give alms, apply bandages or first aid EXAMPLES: お布施 ofuse = alms or offerings (e.g., given to monks); 施す hodokosu = to donate, perform, give time; 施設 shisetsu = facility, institution, equipment DESCRIPTION: compared to 旅(行) ryokou (travel, # 116), this substitutes a scorpion, as seen in 池 ike (pond, # 504), for the traveling person on the lower right; it retains the 方 (honorable person) and the crutch CUES: this 方 (honorable person) uses this crutch and has to use a **Se**gway to get around, but she can **H**old the **D**oor for a **Co**-worker while he carries a **Sh**eep that has been stung by this scorpion into a treatment 施設 **shi**setsu (facility)

ALSO COMPARE: other similar kanji at # 503, # 920 and # 2080

1068. 設 PRONUNCIATIONS: mou, setsu, se MEANINGS: to set up EXAMPLES: 設ける moukeru = to set up; 設備 setsubi = equipment, facility; 設計 sekkei = design or plan; 設定する settei suru = to set up
DESCRIPTION: compared to 役に立つ yaku ni tatsu (to be useful, # 557), this substitutes 言(う) iu (to speak, # 430) for the man with a double hat on the left; it retains the 几 (yak) on a 又 (table) CUES: **Mo**ses 言 (said) that he will **Se**t up a **Su**per 設備 **setsu**bi (facility) where he will **Se**ll 几 (yaks) like the one on this 又 (table)
ALSO COMPARE: similar kanji at # 557

1069. 療 PRONUNCIATION: ryou
MEANINGS: heal, cure EXAMPLE: 治療 chiryou = medical treatment
DESCRIPTION: at the upper left, a vertical bed as seen in 病(気) byouki (illness, # 369), with legs pointing to the left and a headboard at the top; just below the headboard, a wide 大(きい) ookii (big, # 188) with props under its arms; at the lower right, a 日 (sun, or oven) spinning on 小(さい) chiisai (small, # 253) which resembles a rod
CUE: Pope Leo is a 大 (big) man, and when he's 病 (sick), he lies in this bed with his arms propped up like this and undergoes chi**ryou** 治療 (medical treatment), consisting of heat therapy that is produced by this spinning 日 (oven)
GROUP: (治)療 chiryou = medical treatment, # 1069; 寮 ryou = a dormitory, # 1501, (官)僚 kanryou = a bureaucrat, # 1592, and (明)瞭な meiryou na = obvious, # 2002, all of which can be pronounced "ryou" ALSO COMPARE: other similar kanji at # 94 and # 369

1070. 与 PRONUNCIATIONS: ata, yo
MEANINGS: bestow, participate in, give, provide EXAMPLES: 与える ataeru = to give, award,

cause; 賞与 shouyo = reward, bonus
DESCRIPTION: compared to 写(真) shashin (photograph, # 468), this omits the roof at the top; it retains a kangaroo up to its calves in liquid, which might be yogurt **CUES:** after this kangaroo got **A**tta**c**ked, it jumped into this pool of **Yo**gurt, so let's 与える **ata**eru (give) it credit for quick thinking **ALSO COMPARE:** other similar kanji at # **468**

1071. 州 **PRONUNCIATIONS: su, shuu**
MEANINGS: sandbank, large area, state (in the U.S.) **EXAMPLES:** 三角州 sankakusu = a delta; 本州 honshuu = Honshu island
DESCRIPTION: compared to 川 kawa (river, # 250), this adds three handles, suggesting three toboggans lined up **CUES: Su**perman lost a **Sh**oe when he rode these three toboggans in 本州 Hon**shuu** **GROUP:** 本州 honshuu = Honshu island, # 1071; (報)酬 houshuu = a reward, # 1902 (identical pronunciation) **ALSO COMPARE:** other similar kanji at # **352** and # **1090**

1072. 孫 **PRONUNCIATIONS: son, mago**
MEANINGS: grandchild, offspring **EXAMPLES:** 子孫 shison = descendant; 孫 mago = grandchild; 孫娘 magomusume = granddaughter
DESCRIPTION: compared to (関)係 kankei (relationship, # 492), this substitutes 子 ko (child, # 182) for the man with a slanted hat on the left; it retains the 糸 (skeet shooter) with a cape over his head **CUES:** this 子 (child) is the 孫 **mago** (grandchild) of this 糸 (skeet shooter), with whom he has a good 係 (relationship), and the skeet shooter waves this cape and sings a **So**ng when the child scores a **M**agnificent **G**oal **GROUP:** (関)係 kankei = relationship, # 492; 孫 mago = grandchild, # 1072; 系(統) keitou = system, # 1393; 懸(賞) kenshou = a prize, # 1597; (謙)遜 kenson = modesty, # 2044 (identical pronunciation) **ALSO COMPARE:** other similar kanji at # **2078**

1073. 遭 **PRONUNCIATIONS: sou, a**
MEANINGS: encounter, meet, association **EXAMPLES:** 遭難 sounan = accident, disaster; 遭う au = to be involved (in an accident, etc.), to get caught in **DESCRIPTION:** on the lower left, a snail; riding on the snail, at the top, 曲 kyoku (tunes, # 82), which resembles a coop, with a horizontal line drawn through its wires, representing a short circuit; at the bottom, 日 hi (sun, # 32)
CUES: this snail uses this 日 (sun) for **S**olar power to listen to these 曲 (tunes) as it travels, but a switch in its sound system tends to get this short circuit, and sometimes it 遭う **a**u (gets involved) in **A**ccidents **GROUP:** 遭(難) sounan = accident, # 1073, (軍)曹 gunsou = a sergeant, # 1598 and (水)槽 suisou = a water tank, # 1986, all of which can be pronounced "sou"
ALSO COMPARE: kanji that contain a coop with **un**crossed wires at # 1321; kanji with a *cage* at # 583

1074. 昏 **PRONUNCIATION: kon**
MEANINGS: dark, evening **EXAMPLE:** 昏睡 konsui = coma, stupor **DESCRIPTION:** compared to (結)婚 kekkon (marriage, # 240) (identical pronunciation), this kanji omits 女 (female) on the left; it retains 氏 (mister), which we have described as a paper pavilion, and the Congolese 日 (sun)
CUE: this 氏 (mister) from the **Co**ngo stood in this 日 (sun) too long and fell into a 昏睡 **kon**sui (stupor) **ALSO COMPARE:** similar kanji at # **1195**

1075. 労 **PRONUNCIATION: rou**
MEANINGS: labor, reward for, toil, trouble **EXAMPLE:** 苦労 kurou = hardship
DESCRIPTION: compared to 覚(える) oboeru (to memorize, # 54), this substitutes 力 chikara (power, # 107) for 見 (to look) at the bottom; it retains the three old boys on a roof
CUE: these three old boys go through a lot of 苦労 ku**rou** (hardship) as they train 力 (powerful) **R**obots on this roof **ALSO COMPARE:** similar kanji at # **991** and # **1746**

1076. 叶 PRONUNCIATION: kana
MEANINGS: grant, answer EXAMPLES: 叶える kanaeru = to grant or answer a request, to meet requirements; 叶う kanau = to come true or be fulfilled (referring to a wish or dream) DESCRIPTION: compared to (時)計 tokei (clock, # 434), this substitutes 口 kuchi (mouth, # 426), which also resembles a box, for 言 (to say) on the left; it retains 十 (ten) CUE: I had to open this 口 (mouth) 十 (ten) times and beg before they 叶えた **kana**eta (granted) me **Cana**dian citizenship ALSO COMPARE: other similar kanji at # **1828** and # **2073**

1077. 王 PRONUNCIATION: ou
MEANINGS: king, rule, jade EXAMPLES: 王様 ousama = king; 女王 jo'ou = queen; 王子 ouji = prince DESCRIPTION: compared to 主(人) shujin (master, # 166), this is missing its tiny cap CUE: when an **O**ld 主 (master) met the 王様 **ou**sama (king), he removed his tiny cap GROUP: 主(人) shujin = husband, # 166; 玉 tama = ball, # 169; 全部 zenbu = all, # 300; 王(子) ouji = prince, # 1077 ALSO COMPARE: other similar kanji at # **1712**, # **1772** and # **2045**

1078. 妃 PRONUNCIATION: hi
MEANINGS: queen, princess
EXAMPLE: 王妃 ouhi = queen
DESCRIPTION: on the left, 女 onna (female, # 235); on the right, 己 onore (self, # 652), which is a backwards "S" and resembles a snake CUE: this 女 (female), who is an 王妃 ou**hi** (queen), **H**ears this 己 (snake) in her bedroom GROUP: 選(ぶ) erabu = to choose, # 352; 起(きる) okiru = to get up, # 452; (心)配(する) shinpai suru = to worry, # 466; 弱(い) yowai = weak, # 471; 港 minato = port, # 549; 記(事) kiji = newspaper article, # 550; 己 onore = self, # 652;

改(める) aratameru = to change, # 700; (王)妃 ouhi = queen, # 1078; 巻(き込む) makikomu = to get entangled in, # 1309; (世)紀 seiki = century, # 1464; (首都)圏 shutoken = the capital city, # 1681; (一周)忌 isshuuki = first anniversary of a death, # 1922; (左)遷 sasen = a demotion, # 1952; 溺(れる) oboreru = to drown, # 1978 ALSO COMPARE: kanji with uncoiling snakes at # 547; other kanji with backwards "S" snakes as part of *packaging* at # 1861; kanji containing bows at # 476; other kanji containing 女 on the left at # **2039**

1079. 宮 PRONUNCIATIONS: guu, kyuu, miya MEANINGS: palace, prince EXAMPLES: 神宮 jinguu = high-status Shinto shrine, e.g., 平安神宮 Heian Jinguu, a shrine in Kyoto; 宮殿 kyuuden = palace; 子宮 shikyuu = uterus; お宮参り omiyamairi = shrine visit DESCRIPTION: compared to 営(業) eigyou (business, # 684), this substitutes a bad haircut for the three old boys on a roof; it retains 呂 (bath) which resembles stacked vertebrae CUES: a **G**oofy **Cu**ban dictator with a bad haircut like this built a 宮殿 **kyuu**den (palace) with this 呂 (bath), where he planned to **M**eet **Y**ankees GROUP: (風)呂 furo = bath, # 7; 営(業) eigyou= business, # 684; 宮(殿) kyuuden = palace, # 1079; (僧)侶 souryo = a monk, # 1982

1080. 殿 PRONUNCIATIONS: den, tono
MEANINGS: lord, hall, mansion, temple
EXAMPLES: 宮殿 kyuuden = palace; 殿様 tonosama = daimyo, feudal lord DESCRIPTION: on the upper left, a lean-to with a double roof; under the lean-to, 共(に) tomo ni (together, # 969); on the right, π (the Greek letter pi, or a pious yak), standing on 又 mata ("again," # 24), which resembles a simple table CUES: a **Den**tist plans to enlarge this lean-to with a double roof until it's a 宮殿 kyuu**den** (palace) where she can live 共 (together) with this π (yak) on this 又 (table), and

she says that this is all **Totally Normal**
ALSO COMPARE: other similar kanji at # **486**, # **557** and # **1899**

1081. 崎 PRONUNCIATION: saki, zaki²
MEANINGS: cape, promontory   **EXAMPLES:** 川崎 Kawasaki = a city in Japan; 長崎 Nagasaki = a city in Japan; 宮崎県 miyazaki ken = Miyazaki Prefecture   **DESCRIPTION:** on the left, 山 yama (mountain, # 146); on the right, 奇 (妙) kimyou (strange, # 854), which reminds us of the 奇 (strange) sight of a 可 (cute) person wearing a kimono that is too 大 (big)   **CUE:** I ate some **S**alty **Qui**che on this 山 (mountain) overlooking 長崎 Naga**saki**, and then I felt 奇 (strange)   **ALSO COMPARE:** other similar kanji at # **604** and # **1942**

1082. 批 PRONUNCIATION: hi
MEANING: to disparage   **EXAMPLES:** 批判 hihan = criticism; 批評 hihyou = review, remark, criticism   **DESCRIPTION:** compared to (対)比(する) taihi suru (to compare, # 857) (identical pronunciation), this kanji adds a kneeling guy on the left; it retains the two ヒ (heroes)
CUE: this guy on the left kneels to examine and 比 (compare) these two ヒ (**H**eroes), and he directs 批判 **hi**han (criticism) at the one he finds lacking
ALSO COMPARE: other similar kanji at # **1294**

1083. 摘 PRONUNCIATIONS: teki, tsu
MEANINGS: pinch, pick, pluck, clip   **EXAMPLES:** 指摘 shiteki = pointing out, identification; 摘む tsumu = to pick tea, cotton, etc.   **DESCRIPTION:** compared to 敵 teki (enemy, # 881) (identical pronunciation), this kanji adds a kneeling person on the left and omits the dancer on the right; it retains the 立 (bell) used by an 古 (old) sentry in a two-sided lean-to to make loud 音 (sounds), intended to frighten techies
CUES: this person on the left is a **Techie** who is kneeling, even though it might damage his **Ts**uit (suit), in order to 指摘する shi**teki** suru (point out) that this 古 (old) sentry in this two-sided lean-to is using this 立 (bell) to make loud sounds
ALSO COMPARE: 積(む) tsumu = to heap up, # 931; other similar kanji at # **881**

1084. 跳 PRONUNCIATIONS: ha, to
MEANINGS: hop, leap up, spring   **EXAMPLES:** 跳ねる haneru = to jump or hop, to splash; 跳ぶ tobu = to jump or leap; 跳び箱 tobibako = a vaulting box   **DESCRIPTION:** compared to 兆 chou (trillion, # 849), this kanji adds the 止 (hesitant) squarehead seen in 踊(る) odoru (to dance, # 366) on the left
CUES: this 止 (hesitant) squarehead has 踊 (danced) with a 兆 (trillion) partners, including Prince **H**arry and **T**olstoy, but he only knows how to 跳ねる **ha**neru (hop)
ALSO COMPARE: 飛(ぶ) tobu = to fly, # 574; other similar kanji at # **849** and # **1534**

1085. 症 PRONUNCIATION: shou
MEANINGS: symptoms, illness   **EXAMPLES:** 症状 shoujou = symptoms, condition of a patient; 感染症 kansenshou = infectious disease   **DESCRIPTION:** at the upper left, a vertical bed as seen in 病(気) byouki (illness, # 369), with legs pointing to the left and a headboard at the top; below the headboard, 正(直) shoujiki (honest, # 174) (identical pronunciation)   **CUE:** if you are in this 病 (sick) bed, the 正 (honest) thing to do is to **Show** a doctor a list of your 症状 **shou**jou (symptoms)
ALSO COMPARE: other similar kanji at # **369** and # **1150**

1086. 版 PRONUNCIATIONS: han, pan²
MEANINGS: printing block, edition
EXAMPLES: 版画 hanga = woodblock print; 出版 shuppan = publication DESCRIPTION: compared to 反(対) hantai (opposition, # 680) (identical pronunciation), this kanji adds (破)片 hahen (fragment, # 181), which resembles a person kneeling and holding a tray with something on it, on the left; it retains the F over an X
CUE: **Han**sel is kneeling on the left, showing Gretel a 版画 **han**ga (woodblock print) on this tray, but she gives it this F and marks it with this X ALSO COMPARE: similar kanji at # 181 and # 1166

1087. 翻 PRONUNCIATION: hon
MEANINGS: flip, turn over, flutter, change (mind)
EXAMPLE: 翻訳 hon'yaku = translation
DESCRIPTION: on the left, 番 ban (number, # 328); on the right, 羽 hane (feather, # 755)
CUE: a guy from **Hon**duras wrote a book saying that these 羽 (feathers) from his country are 番 (number) one, and he 翻訳した **hon**'yaku shita (translated) his book into English
ALSO COMPARE: other similar kanji at # 220, # 1368 and # 1457

1088. 著 PRONUNCIATIONS: cho, arawa, ichijiru MEANINGS: to write, conspicuous, remarkable EXAMPLES: 著者 chosha = a writer; 著名 chomei = famous; 著す arawasu = to write or publish; 著しい ichijirushii = remarkable, conspicuous
DESCRIPTION: at the top, a plant radical which could represent poison ivy; at the bottom, 者 mono (person, # 276), which can be seen as a pair of scissors separating 土 (soil) and 日 (sun)
CUES: Margaret **Cho** is this 者 (person) who is the 著者 **cho**sha (writer) of a book which she was scheduled to discuss on TV, but her pants came into contact with this poison ivy plant and, although her **Ar**ab friend **Wa**shed them, the **I**tchy **J**eans **R**uined her TV appearance GROUP: (一)緒(に) issho ni = together, # 232; 者 mono = person, # 276; 都

(市) toshi = city, # 277; 暑(い) atsui = hot atmosphere, # 278; 著(者) chosha = a writer, # 1088; 箸 hashi = chopsticks, # 1144; 諸(問題) shomondai = various problems, # 1315, 署(名) shomei = signature, # 1324; 煮(る) niru = to cook, # 1377; 賭(ける) kakeru = to bet, # 1761

1089. 樹 PRONUNCIATIONS: ju, ki
MEANINGS: tree, to establish
EXAMPLES: 樹木 jumoku = trees; 直樹 naoki = a man's given name
DESCRIPTION: on the far left and the far right, 村 mura (village, # 131), which consists of a 木 (tree) and a 寸 (sunny guy); inserted into this village are 士 shi (man, # 66) at the top and a modified version of 豆 mame (bean, # 721) at the bottom; the upper central portion can also be seen as a 士 (man) above a 口 (box)
CUES: this 士 (man) stands under this (tree) and makes **J**uice and **Q**uiche with 豆 (beans) like this, and he has inserted himself into this 村 (village) that contains 樹木 **ju**moku (trees)
ALSO COMPARE: other similar kanji at # 131, # 721 and # 1453

1090. 訓 PRONUNCIATION: kun
MEANINGS: lesson, Japanese (as opposed to Chinese) reading of kanji EXAMPLES: 訓練 kunren = training; 教訓 kyoukun = moral, teaching, lesson DESCRIPTION: on the left, 言(う) iu (to speak, # 430); on the right, 川 kawa (river, # 250) CUE: a **Kun**g fu master 言 (speaks) about the 訓練 **kun**ren (training) that he received when he worked on this 川 (river)
GROUP: 川 kawa = river, # 250; (本)州 honshuu = Honshu island, # 1071; 訓(練) kunren = training. # 1090; 順(番) junban = one's turn, # 1348

1091. 筆 **PRONUNCIATIONS: fude, hitsu, pitsu², hi** **MEANING:** writing brush **EXAMPLES:** 筆 fude = writing brush; 毛筆 mouhitsu = writing (painting) brush; 鉛筆 enpitsu = pencil; 筆者 hissha = writer **DESCRIPTION:** at the top, 竹 take (bamboo, # 134); at the bottom, a vertical line with a three-fingered hand grasping it near the top, resembling the brush seen in 書(く) kaku (to write, # 415), with two sheets of paper below it; this brush can also be seen as a telephone pole **CUES:** a **F**oolish **D**ebutante grasps this 竹 (bamboo) handle at the top of a 筆 **fude** (brush), **H**its yo**U** with it and bruises your **H**eel **ALSO COMPARE:** other similar kanji at # **820**, # **877** and # **2074**

1092. 鉛 **PRONUNCIATIONS: namari, en** **MEANING:** lead (the element) **EXAMPLES:** 鉛 namari = lead; 鉛筆 enpitsu = lead pencil **DESCRIPTION:** compared to 船 fune (boat, # 602), this substitutes 金 kane (money, # 301) for the leaky boat on the left; it retains 八 hachi (eight, # 15) above 口 kuchi (mouth, # 426), which reminds us of eight guys working on a dock **CUES:** a **Na**rco named **Ma**rio uses this 金 (money) to buy 鉛 **namari** (lead) for the bullets that he uses to **En**force discipline on the 八 (eight) guys who are working on this 口 (dock) **ALSO COMPARE:** other similar kanji at # **602** and # **2010**

1093. 児 **PRONUNCIATIONS: ni, ji, go** **MEANING:** very young child **EXAMPLES:** 小児科 shounika = pediatrics; 児童 jidou = child; 孤児 koji = orphan; 鹿児島 Kagoshima = a city in Kyushu **DESCRIPTION:** compared to 旧(正月) kyuushougatsu (lunar New Year, # 1017), this adds a pair of lopsided legs at the bottom, with a deformed knee on the right; it retains the vertical line, which may represent a rod (or could also be seen as a unicorn horn), plus 日 (day) **CUES:** this guy with this deformed right **K**nee holds up this rod on 旧 (lunar New Year) to salute a 児童 **ji**dou (child) who can drive a **J**eep on the **G**olf course **COMPARE:** other similar kanji at # **985** and # **1017**

1094. 童 **PRONUNCIATION:** *dou* **MEANING:** child **EXAMPLES:** 児童 jidou = child; 童話 douwa = fairy tale **DESCRIPTION:** at the top, 立(つ) tatsu (to stand, # 11); at the bottom, 里 sato (village or hometown, # 1060), which resembles a sincere guy wearing bifocals **CUE:** this sincere guy wearing bifocals, who is a 児童 ji**dou** (child), 立 (stands) as he eats a **Dou**ghnut **ALSO COMPARE:** similar kanji at # **545** and # **1840**

1095. 奄 **PRONUNCIATION:** *ama* **MEANINGS:** cover, obstruct **EXAMPLE:** 奄美大島 Amami Ooshima = an island between Kyushu and Okinawa **DESCRIPTION:** compared to 俺 ore (I, # 956), this omits the man with a slanted hat; it retains the wide 大 (big) and the transformer with a wire seen in 電 (electricity) **CUE:** an **Am**ateur engineer built this 大 (big) 電 (electric transformer) on 奄美大島 **Ama**mi Ooshima (an island) **COMPARE:** other similar kanji at # **1003**

1096. 底 **PRONUNCIATIONS: soko, zoko², tei** **MEANING:** bottom **EXAMPLES:** 底 soko = bottom; 靴底 kutsuzoko = shoe sole; 海底 kaitei = bottom of the sea **DESCRIPTION:** at the upper left, a lean-to with a chimney; inside the lean-to, 氏 shi (mister, # 709) which we have described as a paper pavilion in 紙 kami (paper, # 221), but this pavilion is taped to a rock **CUES:** after he **S**old his **C**oal, this 氏 (mister) hit 底 **soko** (bottom), and now he lives in this paper pavilion **T**aped to a rock inside this lean-to with a chimney **ALSO COMPARE:** other similar kanji at # **1195**

1097. 径 PRONUNCIATION: kei
MEANING: narrow straight path **EXAMPLES:** 直径 chokkei = diameter; 半径 hankei = radius
DESCRIPTION: compared to 経(験) keiken (experience, # 224) (identical pronunciation), this kanji substitutes a man with a double hat for the skeet shooter on the left; it retains the 又 (dog groomer's table) above 土 (soil)
CUE: this man on the left keeps dogs in **C**ages, where he also stores his extra hats, above this 又 (dog groomer's table) on this 土 (soil), and the cages have narrow 直径 chok**kei** (diameters)
ALSO COMPARE: other similar kanji at # **1894**

1098. 種 PRONUNCIATIONS: tane, shu
MEANINGS: seed, kind **EXAMPLES:** 種 tane = seed; 種類 shurui = variety, type; 人種 jinshu = race of people; 一種の isshu no = a kind of, a type of **DESCRIPTION:** on the left, 禾 (a grain plant with a ripe head); on the right, 重(い) omoi (heavy, # 284) **CUES:** in order to grow 重 (heavy) 禾 (ripe grain) like this, I store 種 **tane** (seeds) in **Tan** Eggshells and **Sh**oot them over my fields
COMPARE: other similar kanji at # **284** and # **1797**

1099. 酎 PRONUNCIATION: chuu
MEANING: sake **EXAMPLE:** 焼酎 shouchuu = a Japanese spirit distilled from sweet potatoes, rice, etc. **DESCRIPTION:** on the left, compared to 酒 sake (# 465), this omits the water radical (this can also be seen as a bucket of sake with a handle); on the right, it adds 寸(前) sunzen (on the verge, # 1369), which resembles a kneeling sunny guy who has dropped his gum on the ground
CUE: this kneeling sunny guy on the right was drinking 酒 (sake) while **Ch**ewing this gum, but after he drank 焼酎 shou**chuu** (Japanese liquor) as well, he dropped the gum on the ground **ALSO COMPARE:** other similar kanji at # **131** and # **1480**

1100. 沢 PRONUNCIATIONS: sawa, zawa², taku
MEANING: swamp **EXAMPLES:** 沢村 Sawamura = a family name; 金沢 Kanazawa = a city in Honshu; 光沢 koutaku = luster; 沢山 takusan = many or much (usually written たくさん) **DESCRIPTION:** on the left, a water radical; on the right, the wakeful eye seen in 訳 wake (reason, # 437) **CUES:** this 尺 (wakeful eye) **Saw** this **Wa**ter, and it reminded him of the 沢山 **taku**san (many) 訳 (reasons) that he likes to use **Tap** water to make **Ko**ol-Aid
ALSO COMPARE: (状)況 joukyou = circumstances, # 1249; other similar kanji at # **1484**

1101. 蒸 PRONUNCIATIONS: jou, mu
MEANING: steam **EXAMPLES:** 蒸気 jouki = vapor, steam; 蒸発 jouhatsu = evaporation; 蒸す musu = to steam, to be hot and humid; 蒸し暑い mushiatsui = hot and humid
DESCRIPTION: in the top row, a plant radical; in the middle row, on the left, the katakana フ fu, which reminds us of food; in the center, a child without arms, as seen in 了(承) ryoushou (understanding, # 760); on the right, the letter Y which reminds us of Yams; at the bottom, a fire; over-all, this resembles a pyramid
CUES: when **Jo**an of Arc was in the **Mo**od to eat these Y (yams) growing on these plants, she asked this 了 (child without arms) to help her 蒸す **mu**su (steam) them over this fire and arrange them in a pyramidal shape like this, after which she ate them as フ (food) **GROUP:** 蒸(す) musu = to steam, # 1101; 基(盤) kiban = foundation, # 1198; 為(に) tame ni = in order to, # 1222; 承(知) shouchi = consent, # 1344; (選)挙 senkyo = election, # 1362; (利)益 rieki = profit, # 1407; 偽(物) nisemono = a counterfeit, # 1622 **ALSO COMPARE:** other similar kanji at # **611** and # **760**

1102. 芋 PRONUNCIATION: imo

MEANING: potato **EXAMPLES:** 芋 imo = potato; じゃが芋 jagaimo = Irish potato (usually written ジャガイモ)

DESCRIPTION: at the top, a plant radical; at the bottom, a kneeling telephone pole, as seen in 宇(宙) uchuu (universe, # 897)

CUE: when I was eating 芋 **imo** (potatoes) and saw these plants sprouting from the top of this kneeling telephone pole, I experienced positive **Emo**tions **ALSO COMPARE:** other similar kanji at # **897**

1103. 麦 PRONUNCIATIONS: baku, ba, mugi MEANING: barley plant

EXAMPLES: 麦芽 bakuga = malt; 蕎麦屋 sobaya = a soba restaurant, usually spelled そば屋; 麦 mugi = barley, wheat; 小麦 komugi = wheat; 小麦粉 komugiko = wheat flour

DESCRIPTION: compared to 表 omote (surface, # 582), this substitutes a dancer with a ponytail for エ and Y at the bottom; it retains the owl's perch at the top **CUES:** this dancer is a **Ba**rmaid who drinks **Ko**ol-Aid, as well as beer made from 麦 **mugi** (barley), and when she carries this owl's perch into our **Ba**r, we have to **M**ove our **Ge**ar

GROUP: 喫(煙) kitsuen = smoking, # 192; 割(る) waru = to break glass, # 562; 表 omote = surface, # 582; 素(晴らしい) subarashii = wonderful, # 712; (小)麦 komugi = wheat, # 1103; (清)潔 seiketsu = clean, # 1212; (素)麺 soumen = fine white noodles, # 1228; (損)害 songai = harm, # 1260; 毒(物) dokubutsu = poison, # 1349; 俵 tawara = a straw bag, # 1492; 契(約) keiyaku = a contract, # 1602

1104. 粉 PRONUNCIATIONS: kona, ko, fun MEANING: flour EXAMPLES: 粉 kona = flour, powder; 小麦粉 komugiko = wheat flour; 花粉 kafun = pollen DESCRIPTION: on the left, 米 kome (rice, # 326); on the right, 分(か る) wakaru (to understand, # 105)

CUES: **Co**nan O'Brien 分 (understands) that this 米 (rice) can be made into 粉 **ko**na (flour), but he spills it onto his **Co**at while trying to be **Fun**ny **ALSO COMPARE:** other similar kanji at # **1387** and # **2076**

1105. 農 PRONUNCIATION: nou

MEANINGS: agricultural, farming **EXAMPLES:** 農業 nougyou = agriculture; 農家 nouka = farmer, farmhouse; 農夫 noufu = farmer

DESCRIPTION: compared to (地)震 jishin (earthquake, # 265), this substitutes 曲 kyoku (song, # 82), which resembles a coop, for 雨 (rain) at the top; it retains the one-sided lean-to containing L and Y, who are supporting an arrow **CUE:** L and Y are 農家 **nou**ka (farmers) who work in this lean-to, and they sing 曲 (songs) as they use arrows like this to scratch **No**tes about their crops in the dirt

GROUP: (地)震 jishin = earthquake, # 265; 振(る) furu = to shake or wave, # 823; 農(家) nouka = farmer, # 1105; 濃(い) koi = dark, # 1106; 唇 kuchibiru = the lips, # 1565; (妊)娠 ninshin = pregnancy, # 1732; (屈)辱 kutsujoku = humiliation, # 1799 **ALSO COMPARE:** other similar kanji at # **1321**

1106. 濃 PRONUNCIATIONS: ko, nou

MEANINGS: dark, strong **EXAMPLES:** 濃い koi = dark, thick, strong, dense; 濃度 noudo = concentration **DESCRIPTION:** compared to 農(家) nouka (farmer, # 1105) (identical pronunciation), this kanji adds a water radical on the left; it retains the 曲 (songs), which resemble a coop,, the lean-to and the arrow that L and Y use to take notes **CUES:** after this 農 (farmer) added this water to his **Co**rn field, L and Y used this arrow to scratch a **No**te in the dirt, stating that the field had become 濃い **ko**i (dark) **ALSO COMPARE:** other similar kanji at # **1105** and # **1321**

1107. 虜 PRONUNCIATIONS: toriko, ryo MEANINGS: captive, barbarian EXAMPLES: 虜 toriko = captive, prisoner; 捕虜 horyo = prisoner of war, captive DESCRIPTION: at the upper left, a one-sided lean-to; at the top, a periscope for observing the outside world; under the roof, 七 shichi (seven, # 20); on the floor, 男 otoko (male, # 109) CUES: the 七 (seven) **To**ry **C**orporals who live in this lean-to with this periscope have captured this 男 (male) 虜 **toriko** (prisoner of war) named Pope **Leo** ALSO COMPARE: similar kanji at # 109 and # 1057

1108. 造 PRONUNCIATIONS: tsuku, zou MEANING: to create EXAMPLES: 造り tsukuri = structure (usually written 作り, # 482); 造り酒屋 tsukurizakaya = a sake brewery; 造る tsukuru = to create or make (usually written 作る); 製造 seizou = manufacture, production; 改造 kaizou = remodeling DESCRIPTION: compared to (報)告 houkoku (report, # 429), this adds a snail at the lower left; it retains the person holding out a shield to the left, plus 口 (mouth) CUES: this person with this big 口 (mouth), is traveling on this snail with a **Tsu**itcase (suitcase) from **Ku**wait and holding out this shield as he heads to the Canal **Z**one, where he plans to 製造する sei**zou** suru (manufacture) shields like this one ALSO COMPARE: other similar kanji at # 429

1109. 募 PRONUNCIATIONS: tsuno, bo MEANINGS: recruit, campaign, gather (contributions), grow violent EXAMPLES: 募る tsunoru = to advertise, recruit, intensify; 応募 oubo = application, subscription DESCRIPTION: compared to (お歳)暮 oseibo (year-end gift, # 641) (identical pronunciation), this kanji substitutes 力 chikara (force, # 107) for the 日 (sun) at the bottom; it retains the plant radical at the top, the 日 (sun) in the middle, and the wide 大 (big) below that (this combination of radicals = PSB = plants, sun, big) CUES: this is a poster designed to 募る **tsuno**ru (recruit) **Ts**uperior (superior) **N**orwegians for a **B**oat trip to a land where these plants are 大 (big), this 日 (sun) shines abundant light, and this 力 (force) is strong (PSB = plants, sun, big) ALSO COMPARE: other similar kanji at # 1353 and # 1746

1110. 催 PRONUNCIATIONS: moyoo, sai MEANINGS: sponsor, hold (a meeting or dinner) EXAMPLES: 催す moyoosu = to hold an event; 催し moyooshi = an event or meeting; 開催する kaisai suru = to hold a meeting or open an exhibition DESCRIPTION: on the left, a man with a slanted hat; at the upper right, 山 yama (mountain, # 146); at the lower right, a net, which can be seen as a man with a slanted hat next to a 主 (master) with an extra pair of arms (see # 203), suggesting a zoo CUES: this man on the left tilts his hat back to examine this 山 (mountain) where he will 催す **moyoo**su (hold) a convention of zookeepers, and he will ask a **Mo**tormouth **Yo**gi to **O**pen the ceremonies and demonstrate this **S**cientifically designed net COMPARE: similar kanji at # 1385 and # 2046

1111. 跡 PRONUNCIATIONS: seki, ato MEANINGS: tracks, mark, impression EXAMPLES: 奇跡 kiseki = miracle, wonder, marvel; 跡 ato = trace, track, ruin DESCRIPTION: on the left, a square head on 止(める) tomeru (to stop, # 173) which suggests a hesitant squarehead, as seen in 踊(る) odoru (to dance, # 366); on the right, the four-legged hen seen in 変 hen (strange, # 553) CUES: this 止 (hesitant) squarehead on the left is a **S**elfish **K**ing who has been developing an **At**omic bomb with help from this four-legged hen, which has 跡 **ato** (traces) of radiation on its feathers ALSO COMPARE: other similar kanji at # 695 and # 1534

1112. 清 PRONUNCIATIONS: sei, kiyo

MEANINGS: pure, clean **EXAMPLES:** 清掃 seisou = cleaning; 清算 seisan = adjustment (financial); 清い kiyoi = clear, pure; 清らか kiyoraka = clean, pure, chaste; 清める kiyomeru = to purify or cleanse; 清水 kiyomizu = spring water, pure water **DESCRIPTION:** compared to 青(い) aoi (blue, # 155), or 青(年) seinen (young man, # 155) (identical pronunciation), this kanji adds a water radical on the left; it retains the owl's perch above a 月 (moon) **CUES:** this 清い **kiyo**i (pure) water on the left is **S**afe to drink, it comes in a bottle that is 青 (blue) like this, and we will use it to make the **K**ing's **Y**ogurt **GROUP:** 晴(天) seiten = fair weather, # 37; 青(年) seinen = young man, # 155; (愛)情 aijou = love, # 156; (安)静 ansei = rest, # 418; 精(神) seishin = mind, # 847; 請(求) seikyuu = demand, # 1064; 清(掃) seisou = cleaning, # 1112; Note that six of these kanji can be pronounced "sei" **ALSO COMPARE:** other kanji containing owl's perches at # 772 and # 1103

1113. 収 PRONUNCIATIONS: osa, shuu

MEANINGS: to collect or store **EXAMPLES:** 収める osameru = to put away in a closet, conclude, pay a bill (this can also be written 納める, # 705); 回収する kaishuu suru = to recover, recall, collect (bills or garbage); 収入 shuunyuu = income **DESCRIPTION:** on the left, this resembles the number 4; on the right, 又 mata (again, # 24), which looks like a simple table **CUES:** since his 収入 **shuu**nyuu (income) was high, **Osa**ma had 4 又 (tables) like this where he 収めた **osa**meta (put away) his **Sh**oes **ALSO COMPARE:** 治(める) osameru = to govern, # 539; 叫(ぶ) sakebu = to shout, # 746; 修(める) osameru = to learn or master, # 1049; other similar kanji at # 24 and # 746

1114. 拭 PRONUNCIATIONS: nugu, fu

MEANINGS: to wipe, mop, swab **EXAMPLES:** 拭う nuguu = to wipe; 拭く fuku = to wipe or mop **DESCRIPTION:** compared to 式 shiki (ceremony, # 249), which features a woman leaning over a crafted object, this adds a kneeling guy on the left **CUES:** a **N**eutered **Goo**se scattered **F**ood on the floor just before this 式 (ceremony), and this guy on the left had to get down on his knees to 拭く **fu**ku (wipe) it up **ALSO COMPARE:** other similar kanji at # 247 and # 249

1115. 賛 PRONUNCIATION: san

MEANINGS: to assist or praise **EXAMPLES:** 賛成 sansei = agreement; 絶賛する zessan suru = to praise highly **DESCRIPTION:** compared to 替(える) kaeru (to exchange money, # 551), this substitutes 貝 kai (money chest # 83) for the 日 (sun) at the bottom; it retains the two 夫 (husbands) at the top **CUE:** these two 夫 (husbands) 賛成する **san**sei suru (agree) to use the money from this 貝 (money chest) to buy **S**andwiches **ALSO COMPARE:** other similar kanji at # 352, # 707 and # 1915

1116. 型 PRONUNCIATIONS: kata, gata[2], kei

MEANINGS: mold, pattern **EXAMPLES:** 型 kata = form (e.g., dance), posture, style; 髪型 kamigata = hair style (this can also be written 髪形); 典型的 tenkeiteki = typical **DESCRIPTION:** at the upper left, a tower which is part of a catapult, as seen in 形(見) katami (memento, # 573), or 形(態) keitai (form, # 573), both of which help us to pronounce this; at the upper right, the katakana リ ri; at the bottom, 土 tsuchi (soil, # 59) **CUES:** this リ **R**i uses a **C**atapult which is attached to this tower on the upper left to send **C**ake to prisoners who are being held in this 土 (soil), and he always insists on using proper 型 **kata** (form) when doing so **ALSO COMPARE:** other similar kanji at # 573 and # 1985

1117. 典 PRONUNCIATION: ten

MEANINGS: law, code **EXAMPLES:** 百科事典 hyakkajiten = encyclopedia; 典型的な tenkeiteki na = typical; 古典 koten = classical work, classic **DESCRIPTION:** 曲 kyoku (tune, # 82), which resembles a coop, on a two-legged table **CUE:** we keep CD's of 古典の koten no (classical) 曲 (tunes) like this, which resemble a coop, on this two-legged table and listen to them while we play Tennis **COMPARE:** other similar kanji at # **1321**

1118. 侍 PRONUNCIATION: samurai

MEANINGS: samurai, waiter, to serve
EXAMPLE: 侍 samurai = Japanese warrior
DESCRIPTION: compared to 寺 tera (temple, # 213), this adds a man with a slanted hat on the left **CUE:** this man on the left tilts his hat back to gaze at this 寺 (temple), where he has come to pray because he is **S**ad that a **M**oonie took his **R**ice and gave it to a 侍 **samurai** (Japanese warrior) **COMPARE:** other similar kanji at # **215**

1119. 洪 PRONUNCIATION: kou

MEANINGS: deluge, flood **EXAMPLE:** 洪水 kouzui = flood **DESCRIPTION:** compared to 共(に) tomo ni (together, # 969), this adds a water radical, which suggests a flood, on the left; it retains the plants balanced on a hill
CUE: due to this water from a 洪水 **kou**zui (flood) at a **Cou**rthouse, we had to climb up onto this hill 共 (together) and find shelter in these plants **ALSO COMPARE:** other similar kanji at # **486**

1120. 遇 PRONUNCIATION: guu

MEANINGS: treat, entertain, encounter (e.g., an accident) **EXAMPLES:** 遭遇する souguu suru = to encounter; 待遇 taiguu = treatment (of customer), salary and benefits **DESCRIPTION:** compared to 隅 sumi (inside corner, # 79), this omits ß on the left and adds a snail; it retains the roots of a 田 (rice paddy) growing more vigorously on the right side of its pot **CUE:** a **G**oose 遭遇 sou**guu** shita (encountered) this 田 (rice paddy) with asymmetrical roots in this pot that was riding on this snail, and it ate the snail
GROUP: 隅 sumi = inside corner, # 79; (待)遇 taiguu = treatment, # 1120; 偶(然) guuzen = coincidence, # 1288 (identical pronunciation); (金)属 kinzoku = metal, # 1296; 嘱(託) shokutaku = commission, # 1366; 愚(痴) guchi = complaint, # 1580

1121. 妓 PRONUNCIATION: ko

MEANINGS: singing girl, geisha **EXAMPLES:** 舞妓 maiko = an apprentice geisha, a dancing girl; 芸妓 geiko = 芸者 geisha **DESCRIPTION:** on the left, 女 onna (female, # 235); on the right, 支(社) shisha (branch office, # 26), which contains a 十 (man) standing on a sheet on a 又 (table) **CUE:** this 女 (female) who is drinking **Co**la at this 支 (branch office) is a 舞妓 mai**ko** (apprentice geisha) **GROUP:** 支(社) shisha = branch office, # 26; 枝 eda = branch, # 128; (舞)妓 maiko = an apprentice geisha, # 1121; 技(術) gijutsu = technology, # 1133; (歌舞)伎 kabuki = Japanese drama, # 1356; (分)岐(点) bunkiten = a crossroads, # 1657; (太)鼓 taiko = a drum, # 1776; (下)肢 kashi = a leg, # 1900
ALSO COMPARE: other kanji containing 女 on the left at # **2039**

1122. 誕 PRONUNCIATION: tan

MEANING: to be born **EXAMPLES:** 誕生する tanjou suru = to be born; 誕生日 tanjoubi = birthday **DESCRIPTION:** compared to 延(期) enki (postponement, # 842), this adds 言(う) iu (to speak, # 430) on the left; it retains the engineer who is always 正 (correct) and travels on this 3x snail **CUE:** this 延 [engineer who is always 正 (correct)] 言 (spoke) and had a **Tan**trum after we forgot his 誕生日 **tan**joubi (birthday) and made him ride on this slow 3x snail **ALSO COMPARE:** other similar kanji at # **692** and # **1150**

1123. 称 PRONUNCIATION: shou
MEANINGS: name, title, admire, fame
EXAMPLES: 対称 taishou = symmetry; 対称的な taishouteki na = symmetrical; 通称 tsuushou = a nickname or alias
DESCRIPTION: on the left, 禾 (a grain plant with a ripe head); on the right, a crutch above 小(さい) chiisai (small, # 253) suggesting a handicapped guy who is small **CUE:** this guy on the right, who is 小 (small) and carries this crutch and who has the 通称 tsuu**shou** (nickname) of **Sh**orty, is celebrating the harvest of 禾 (ripe grain) **COMPARE:** other similar kanji at # **1010**, # **1797** and # **2080**

1124. 列 PRONUNCIATIONS: retsu, re
MEANINGS: line, row **EXAMPLES:** 列 retsu = line; 配列 hairetsu = arrangement, disposition; 列車 ressha = train **DESCRIPTION:** on the left, 夕 yuu (evening, # 160), wearing a flat hat; let's call this a nightcap (an alcoholic drink taken before bedtime); on the right, the katakana リ ri **CUES:** after this リ Ri put on a **Re**tro **S**uit and stood in 列 **retsu** (line) at a **Re**staurant, he drank this nightcap **GROUP:** 列 retsu = line, # 1124; 例 rei = example, # 1317; 裂(ける) sakeru = to split, # 1465; (猛)烈 mouretsu = fierce, # 1610 **ALSO COMPARE:** other similar kanji at # **164**

1125. 統 PRONUNCIATION: tou
MEANINGS: to unify, ruling **EXAMPLES:** 統計 toukei = statistics; 大統領 daitouryou = president of a country **DESCRIPTION:** on the left, 糸 skeet shooter (# 219); at the upper right, a ム (cow) under a tire stop, as seen in 育(てる) sodateru (to raise, # 151); at the lower right, a pair of lopsided legs **CUE:** our 大統領 dai**tou**ryou (president) saw this 糸 (skeet shooter) shooting **To**ads at this ム (cow) under this tire stop which was standing on these lopsided legs **GROUP:** 育(てる) sodateru = to raise, # 151; 流(す) nagasu = to flush, # 654; 統(計) toukei = statis-tics, # 1125; 徹(底) tettei = thoroughness, # 1333; 充(実) juujitsu = perfection, # 1478; (拳)銃 kenjuu = a handgun, # 1555; (破)棄(する) haki suru = to abolish, # 1624; 撤(廃) teppai = abolition, # 1747; 硫(黄) iou = sulfur, # 2001 **ALSO COMPARE:** other similar kanji at # **1990**

1126. 領 (sometimes written 領)
PRONUNCIATION: ryou **MEANINGS:** head, chief, domain **EXAMPLES:** 領土 ryoudo = territory; 領収書 ryoushuusho = receipt; 大統領 daitouryou = president of a country
DESCRIPTION: compared to (命)令 meirei (command, # 962), which resembles a house containing a wobbly table under a napkin, this adds 貝 kai (shell, money chest, # 83) with a platform at the top where a head could fit, as seen in 頭 atama (head, # 93); this radical on the right can also be seen as a limousine antenna above a money chest [the **alternative** kanji shown above contains, on the left side, a peaked roof above a drop of rain and マ ma (mother)] **CUE:** Pope **Leo** is missing his 頭 (head), and he is living in this 令 (house with a wobbly table) while he waits for the 大統領 daitou**ryou** (president) to find it [alternatively, Pope Leo's マ ma (mother) is living under this peaked roof and this rain, waiting for the 大統領 daitou**ryou** (president) to find Leo's head]
GROUP: 頭 atama = head, # 93; 願(う) negau = to beg, # 94; 顔 kao = face, # 95; 頃 koro = approximate time, # 96; (書)類 shorui = documents, # 97; 頼(む) tanomu = to request, # 98; (問)題 mondai = problem, # 454; 頑(張る) ganbaru = to do one's best, # 622; (登)頂(する) touchou suru = to climb to a summit, # 783; (金)額 kingaku = a sum of money, # 791; 頬 hoo =

cheek, # 890; 傾(く) katamuku = to tilt, # 925; 領(土) ryoudo = territory, # 1126; (整)頓 seiton = orderliness, # 1248; 預(かる) azukaru = to take care of, # 1259; 頻(繁) hinpan = frequent, # 1265; 順(番) junban = one's turn, # 1348; 瀬(戸際) setogiwa = brink, # 1550; (要)項 youkou = outline, # 1573; (必)須(の) hissu no = essential, # 1616; 顧(問) komon = an advisor, # 1648; 顕(著) kencho = conspicuous, # 1725; 顎 ago = a chin, # 1787; 煩(う) wazurau = to worry about, # 2007; 頒(布) hanpu = distribution, # 2076 **ALSO COMPARE:** other kanji with a limousine antenna above eye at # 522; kanji with a limousine antenna above sun at # 491; other similar kanji at # **962** and # **1946** (alternative font)

1127. 慢 PRONUNCIATION: man
MEANINGS: ridicule, laziness **EXAMPLES:** 自慢 jiman = pride, boast; 我慢 gaman = patience, endurance **DESCRIPTION:** on the left, an erect man; at the upper right, 日 hi (sun, # 32); at the middle right, 目 me (eye, # 51), turned on its side, resembling three eyes; at the lower right, 又 mata ("again," # 24), which resembles a simple table **CUES:** this guy on the left stands proudly near this 又 (table) in **Ma**nhattan and 自慢する ji**man** suru (boasts) about these three 目 (eyes) which are never bothered by this 日 (sun) **GROUP:** (自)慢 jiman = pride, # 1127; 漫(画) manga = cartoon, # 1319 (identical pronunciations) **ALSO COMPARE:** other similar kanji at # **2063**

1128. 嵐 PRONUNCIATION: arashi
MEANINGS: storm, tempest **EXAMPLE:** 嵐 arashi = storm **DESCRIPTION:** at the top, 山 yama (mountain, # 146); at the bottom, 風 kaze (wind, # 479), which resembles an insect wearing a flat hat inside a two-sided lean-to **CUE:** an **Ar**ab who is a **Shi**ite visited this 山 (mountain), and was caught in an 嵐 **arashi** (storm) with strong 風 (winds) like this **ALSO COMPARE:** similar kanji at # **479**, # **1385** and # **1754**

1129. 幻 PRONUNCIATIONS: gen, maboroshi
MEANINGS: apparition, vision, dream **EXAMPLES:** 幻想 gensou = fantasy, illusion; 幻覚 genkaku = hallucination; 幻 maboroshi = illusion, vision **DESCRIPTION:** on the left, a 糸 (skeet shooter, # 219) without its legs, consisting of two flexed elbows; on the right, the katakana フ fu, which looks like an oar **CUES: Gen**ghis saw this truncated 糸 (skeet shooter) holding this フ (oar), and he thought it was a **Ma**riner using a **Bo**at to **Ro**w **Sh**eep across a lake, but this turned out to be a 幻想 **gen**sou (illusion) **GROUP:** 眩(しい) mabushii = dazzling, # 937; 幻(想) gensou = fantasy, # 1129; 玄(関) genkan = entranceway, # 1252; 幼(い) osanai = childish, # 1400; 率 ritsu = percentage, # 1408; 畜(生) chikushou = a beast, # 1773; (貯)蓄 chochiku = savings, # 1774; 弦(楽器) gengakki = a stringed instrument, # 1860; **Note:** three of these kanji can be pronounced "gen" **ALSO COMPARE:** kanji containing *two* truncated skeet shooters at # 1908

1130. 坂 PRONUNCIATIONS: saka, zaka²
MEANINGS: slope, incline **EXAMPLES:** 坂 saka = slope, hill; 下り坂 kudarizaka = downward slope **DESCRIPTION:** compared to (大)阪 oosaka (Osaka, # 1005) (identical pronunciation), this kanji substitutes 土 tsuchi (soil, # 59) for ß (Greek) on the left; it retains the F over an X **CUE:** we don't mind playing **Sakk**aa (soccer) on this 土 (soil), but you get this F and this X for making us play on a steep 坂 **saka** (slope) **COMPARE:** other similar kanji at # **1166**

1131. 級 PRONUNCIATION: kyuu

MEANINGS: order, class **EXAMPLES:** 高級 koukyuu = high class or quality; 同級生 doukyuusei = classmate; 等級 toukyuu = grade, ranking **DESCRIPTION:** compared to 吸(収する) kyuushuu suru (to digest, # 427) (identical pronunciation), this kanji substitutes 糸 (skeet shooter, # 219) for 口 (mouth) on the left; it retains the graph of breathing patterns on the right **CUE:** this 糸 (skeet shooter) is examining these breathing patterns of a **C**ute baby, which it thinks will grow up to be a 高級な kou**kyu**u na (high class) person who shoots skeets **GROUP:** 吸(収する) kyuushuu suru = to digest, # 427; (普)及(する) fukyuu suru = to become popular, # 883 (also identical pronunciation); 携(帯電話) keitai denwa = cellular phone, # 1011; (高)級 koukyuu = high class, # 1131; 透(明) toumei = transparency, # 1253; 誘(う) sasou = to invite, # 1405; (優)秀 yuushuu = outstanding, # 1517; 扱(う) atsukau = to deal with, # 1577

1132. 等 PRONUNCIATIONS: tou, dou, ra, hito, nado

MEANINGS: equal, equivalent, etcetera **EXAMPLES:** 上等 joutou = excellent, very good; 二等 nitou = second class or place; 平等 byoudou = equal; これ等 korera = these (usually written これら); 等しい hitoshii = same, equal; 等々 nadonado = etcetera **DESCRIPTION:** at the top, 竹 take (bamboo, # 134); at the bottom, 寺 tera (temple, # 213) **CUES:** these two 竹 (bamboo) clamps at the top of this 寺 (temple) indicate that it has earned a ranking of 二等 n**itou** (2nd place) for the bamboo toys it sells, including small statues of **To**ads, **Do**es, **R**abbits and **Hi**to (people), but it also sells **N**asty **Do**ughnuts, and overall it is about 等しい hitoshii (equal) to other temples **ALSO COMPARE:** other similar kanji at # **215** and # **2074**

1133. 技 PRONUNCIATIONS: gi, waza

MEANINGS: skill, work, deed **EXAMPLES:** 技術 gijutsu = technology, technique, skill; 競技 kyougi = competition; 技 waza = skill, technique **DESCRIPTION:** compared to 支(社) shisha (branch office, # 26), this adds a kneeling guy on the left; it retains the 十 (man) standing on a 又 (table) **CUES:** this **Ge**ek (an unfashionable or eccentric person) went down onto his knees at this 支 (branch office) after a **W**atercooler got **Z**apped by a power surge, since we had asked him to fix it, knowing that he has 技術 **gi**jutsu (skill) in repairing things **ALSO COMPARE:** other similar kanji at # **128**, # **1121** and # **1389**

1134. 房 PRONUNCIATIONS: bou, fusa

MEANINGS: bunch, house, room **EXAMPLES:** 暖房 danbou = heating, heater; 冷房 reibou = air conditioning; 女房 nyoubou = one's wife; 房 fusa = a bunch, cluster, tassel **DESCRIPTION:** at the upper left, 戸 to (door, # 871), which depicts a lean-to with a double roof and a layer of snow on top; inside the lean-to, 方 kata (honorable person, # 114) **CUES:** in winter, this 方 (honorable person) lives a **B**oring life in this lean-to with this double roof and this layer of snow on top, which is heated by a single 暖房 dan**bou** (heater), and his only **F**ood is **S**ardines **GROUP:** 戻(る) modoru = to return, # 75; 所 tokoro = place, # 391; 涙 namida = tears, # 649; 肩 kata = shoulder, # 845; 戸 to = door, # 871; 編(者) hensha = editor, # 1052; (暖)房 danbou = heater, # 1134; 雇(う) yatou = to employ, # 1398; 顧(問) komon = an adviser, # 1648; 扉 tobira = a front door, # 1672; 啓(発) keihatsu = education, # 1744; 偏(見) henken = prejudice, # 1757; 炉 ro = a fireplace, # 1758; (普)遍(の) fuhen no = eternal, # 1830; 扇(子) sensu = a folding fan, # 1833 **ALSO COMPARE:** kanji containing a double-roof lean-to without snow at # 1899; other similar kanji at # **920**

1135. 粒 **PRONUNCIATIONS: tsubu, ryuu MEANINGS:** a grain or drop **EXAMPLES:** 粒 tsubu = grains, drops, counter for tiny particles; 雨粒 amatsubu = raindrop; 粒子 ryuushi = a particle or grain **DESCRIPTION:** on the left, 米 kome (uncooked rice, # 326); on the right, 立(つ) tatsu (to stand, # 11) **CUES:** I was 立 (standing) around looking at 粒 **tsubu** (grains) of this 米 (rice) that had fallen onto my **Ts**upervisor's (supervisor's) **Boo**ts, and I realized that I could sweep them up and **Reu**se them **ALSO COMPARE:** other similar kanji at # **11** and # **1387**

1136. 眺 **PRONUNCIATIONS: naga, chou MEANINGS:** watch, look at, see **EXAMPLES:** 眺める nagameru = to gaze or look at; 眺め nagame = a view; 眺望 choubou = a view **DESCRIPTION:** compared to 兆 chou (trillion, # 849) (identical pronunciation), this adds 目 me (eye, # 51) on the left **CUES:** this is the 目 (eye) of **Naga**ina (a snake from a Kipling story), which she uses to survey the 眺め **naga**me (view) in front of her, as she imagines that there are **Chou** 兆 (a trillion) mice out there and that her primary **Cho**re is to catch them **ALSO COMPARE:** similar kanji at # **849** and # **2002**

1137. 秒 **PRONUNCIATION: byou MEANINGS:** tiny, second **EXAMPLES:** 一秒 ichibyou = a second (1/60 minute); 秒針 byoushin = the second hand on a clock **DESCRIPTION:** on the left, 禾 (a grain plant with a ripe head); on the right, 少(し) sukoshi (a little, # 254) **CUE:** a **B**ee **O**wner has only 少 (a little) of this 禾 (ripe grain), but he enjoys seeing one or more of his bees fly through it every 秒 **byou** (second) **COMPARE:** other similar kanji at # **1010** and # **1797**

1138. 針 **PRONUNCIATIONS: hari, shin MEANING:** needle **EXAMPLES:** 針 hari = needle; 方針 houshin = a policy, principle or direction; 秒針 byoushin = the second hand on a clock **DESCRIPTION:** on the left, (お)金 okane (money, # 301); on the right, 十 too (ten, # 18) **CUES:** Prince **Har**ry paid this 金 (money) to a **Shin**to priest for 十 (ten) 針 **hari** (needles) **ALSO COMPARE:** similar kanji at # **1828** and # **2010**

1139. 効 **PRONUNCIATIONS: ki, kou MEANING:** having an effect **EXAMPLES:** 効く kiku = to be effective; 効果 kouka = an effect **DESCRIPTION:** compared to 交(通) koutsuu (traffic, # 144) (identical pronunciation), this kanji adds 力 chikara (force, # 107) on the right; it retains 六 roku (six, # 17) roads above an X (intersection) in Korea, which can also be seen as a tire stop above 父 chichi (father, # 143) **CUES:** the threat of 力 (force) like this is the **K**ey to 交 (traffic) code enforcement in **Ko**rea, and it 良く効く yoku **ki**ku (has a good effect) **GROUP:** (学)校 gakkou = school, # 130; 交(通) koutsuu = traffic, # 144; 郊(外) kougai = a suburb, # 145; 効(果) kouka = an effect, # 1139; (比)較 hikaku = a comparison, # 1632; 絞(殺) kousatsu = strangulation, # 1739; **Note** that five of these kanji can be pronounced "kou" **ALSO COMPARE:** other similar kanji at # **1846**

1140. 免 **PRONUNCIATIONS: men, manuga MEANINGS:** excuse, dismissal **EXAMPLES:** 免許 menkyo = a license; 免除 menjo = an exemption; 免状 menjou = a diploma or license; 免疫 men'eki = immunity; 免れる manugareru = to be exempted from, to avoid **DESCRIPTION:** compared to 晩 ban (evening, # 35), this omits the 日 (sun) on the left side; it retains the fish-head guy (see # 80) with glasses and lopsided legs **CUES:** this fish-head guy with glasses knows that success is all **Men**tal and that he has to stand on these two lopsided legs, and he will **Man**age a **New Ga**s station after getting his 免状 **men**jou (diploma)　**GROUP:** (今)晩 konban = this evening, # 35; 勉(強) benkyou = study, # 474; 免(許) menkyo = a license, # 1140; 逸(話) itsuwa = an anecdote, # 1706　**ALSO COMPARE:** other similar kanji at # **1314**

1141. 許　PRONUNCIATIONS: yuru, kyo
MEANINGS: permit, approve　**EXAMPLES:** 許す yurusu = to forgive, accept, permit; 免許 menkyo = a license; 許可 kyoka = permission, approval　**DESCRIPTION:** on the left, 言(う) iu (to speak, # 430); on the right, 午 go (noon, # 207)　**CUES: You Ru**ined the class at **Kyo**to University when you 言 (said) that everyone had 許可 **kyo**ka (permission) to show up at 午 (noon)　**ALSO COMPARE:** (時)計 tokei = clock, # 434; other similar kanji at # **207** and # **1658**

1142. 疫　PRONUNCIATION: eki
MEANING: epidemic　**EXAMPLES:** 疫病 ekibyou = a plague or epidemic; 免疫 men'eki = immunity　**DESCRIPTION:** on the upper left, a sick bed with a headboard, as seen in 病(気) byouki (sick, # 369); in the bed, π (the Greek letter pi, also known as a pious yak) on 又 mata ("again," # 24), which resembles a simple table　**CUE:** this π (yak) on this 又 (table) was 病 (sick) in this sick bed during an 疫病 **eki**byou (epidemic), but it was healed by **E**dward the **K**ing　**ALSO COMPARE:** similar kanji at # **369** and # **557**

1143. 樋　PRONUNCIATIONS: toi, hi, doi
MEANINGS: water pipe, gutter　**EXAMPLES:** 樋 toi = a gutter; 樋口 Higuchi = a family name; 雨樋 amadoi = a rain gutter　**DESCRIPTION:** on the left, 木 ki (wood, # 118); on the right, 通(る) tooru (pass through, # 365), which resembles a マ (mammoth) on a 用 (fence, # 364) on a snail　**CUES:** this snail 通 (passes through) a 木 (wood) 雨樋 ama**doi** (gutter) and carries this **Toy** マ (mammoth) on a 用 (fence), but it can't **Hear** us because it has **Doi**lies stuffed into its ears　**GROUP:** 通(り) toori = street, # 365; 踊(る) odoru = to dance, # 366; 痛(い) itai = painful, # 368; 樋 toi = a gutter, # 1143

1144. 箸　PRONUNCIATIONS: hashi, bashi[2]
MEANING: chopsticks　**EXAMPLES:** 箸 hashi = chopsticks; 割り箸 waribashi = splittable (disposable) chopsticks　**DESCRIPTION:** compared to 著(者) chosha (writer, # 1088), this substitutes 竹 take (bamboo, # 134) for the plant radical at the top; it retains 者 (person), with a knife under its right shoulder　**CUE:** this 者 (person) carrying a knife under his right shoulder uses 竹 (bamboo) 箸 **hashi** (chopsticks) to **H**arm **S**heep　**ALSO COMPARE:** other similar kanji at # **1088** and # **2074**

1145. 志　PRONUNCIATIONS: kokoroza, kokorozashi, shi
MEANINGS: will, aspiration　**EXAMPLES:** 志す kokorozasu = to intend or aspire to; 志 kokorozashi = ambition, wish, goal; 志望 shibou = ambition, wish, goal　**DESCRIPTION:** compared to (雑)誌 zasshi (magazine, # 786) (identical pronunciation), this kanji omits 言 (to say) on the left; it retains the 士 shi (man) (also identical pronunciation) who writes about heart problems in sheep, and the 心 kokoro (heart) (also a similar pronunciation)　**CUES:** this 士 (man) has this 心 **Kokoro** (heart) set on **Za**mbia, and in particular he has this **Kokoro** set on **Za**mbian **S**heep, since his 志望 **shi**bou (ambition) is to help **S**heep with heart problems　**ALSO COMPARE:** other similar kanji at # **786**

1146. 軒 PRONUNCIATIONS: ken, noki

MEANINGS: flats, eaves, counter for houses
EXAMPLES: 一軒 ikken = one house; 軒 noki = eaves **DESCRIPTION:** on the left, 車 kuruma (car, # 283); on the right, a telephone pole **CUES:** Ken and Barbie parked this 車 (car) next to this telephone pole while they were visiting 一軒 ikken (one house), but they had **No Key**
ALSO COMPARE: other similar kanji at # **629** and # **1966**

1147. 激 PRONUNCIATIONS: hage, geki

MEANINGS: intense, agitated, violent
EXAMPLES: 激しい hageshii = fierce, tempestuous, crowded (traffic), frequent (change); 激減 gekigen = sharp decrease; 過激 kageki = aggressive, radical; 激戦 gekisen = fierce competition or battle **DESCRIPTION:** on the left, a water radical; at the upper middle, 白(い) shiroi (white, # 44); at the lower middle, 方 kata (honorable person, # 114); on the right, a dancer with a ponytail **CUES:** when we lived in a 白 (white) house by this water, we had a 過激 ka**geki** (aggressive) **Ha**waiian **Gue**st who was a dancer like this and whom we thought was an 方 (honorable person), but she stole our **Gue**st **K**ey
ALSO COMPARE: other similar kanji at # **2014** and # **2016**

1148. 減 PRONUNCIATIONS: gen, he

MEANING: to reduce **EXAMPLES:** 激減 gekigen = sharp decrease; 減少 genshou = a decrease; 加減する kagen suru = to moderate, downgrade; 減る heru = to reduce, lose (weight)
DESCRIPTION: compared to 感(じる) kanjiru (to feel, # 640), this adds a water radical on the left, and it omits 心 (heart) from the bottom; it retains the lean-to, the 口 (mouth, or box) with a napkin over it, and the halberd on the right **CUES:** **Gen**ghis went through **He**ll when he lived in this two-sided lean-to near this water which he could not drink due to this napkin covering this 口 (mouth), and where he was guarded by this halberd, causing him to 減る **he**ru (lose) weight **ALSO COMPARE:** other similar kanji at # **915** and # **1620**

1149. 処 PRONUNCIATIONS: dokoro, sho

MEANING: deal with **EXAMPLES:** お食事処 oshokujidokoro = restaurant (Japanese style); 処理する shori suru = to deal with, handle, eliminate; 対処する taisho suru = to deal with; 処分 shobun = disposal, expulsion, punishment **DESCRIPTION:** on the left, a dancer with a ponytail and a long right leg; on the dancer's right leg, a tall desk, as seen in 机 tsukue (desk, # 140 **CUES:** a **D**oorman's **Coro**lla hit this desk, causing it to land on this dancer's right leg, but he 処理した **sho**ri shita (dealt with) the situation and later attended her **Sho**w
ALSO COMPARE: similar kanji at # **1462**

1150. 証 PRONUNCIATIONS: shou, aka, akashi

MEANINGS: to certify, proof
EXAMPLES: 証明 shoumei = proof, identification; 証す akasu = to prove or verify; 証 akashi = proof, certificate **DESCRIPTION:** compared to 正(直) shoujiki (honest, # 174) (identical pronunciation), or 正(しい) tadashii (correct, # 174), this kanji adds 言(う) iu (to speak, # 430) on the left **CUES:** it's 正 (correct) to 言 (say) that we should **Sho**w 証明 **shou**mei (identification) before we start our **Aca**demic studies at the **Aca**demy of **Sheep** Farming
GROUP: 正(直) shoujiki = honest, # 174; 政(治) seiji = politics, # 175; 延(期) enki = postponement, # 842; 症(状) shoujou = symptom, # 1085 (also identical pronunciation); 誕(生日) tanjoubi = birthday, # 1122; 証(明) shoumei = proof, # 1150; (制)御 seigyo = control, # 1440; (遠)征 ensei = an expedition, # 1641

1151. 拠 PRONUNCIATIONS: ko, kyo

MEANINGS: foothold, based on **EXAMPLES:** 証拠 shouko = evidence, proof, testimony; 拠点 kyoten = position, location, base, point;

根拠 konkyo = basis or foundation (of a belief, etc.) **DESCRIPTION:** compared to 処(理する) shori suru (to deal with, # 1149), this adds a kneeling guy on the left; it retains the 机 (desk) resting on the right leg of a dancer with a ponytail **CUES:** this kneeling guy crawled from **Ko**be to **Kyo**to to give 証拠 shou**ko** (testimony) to support this dancer whose leg had been injured by this 机 (desk) **ALSO COMPARE:** similar kanji at # **1462**

1152. 唱 PRONUNCIATIONS: shou, tona
MEANINGS: to recite or sing energetically **EXAMPLES:** 合唱 gasshou = chorus, singing in a chorus; 唱える tonaeru = to advocate or recite **DESCRIPTION:** on the left, 口 kuchi (mouth, # 426), which also resembles a box; on the right, two 日 hi (suns, # 32) **CUES:** a 合唱 gas**shou** (chorus) of singers opened 口 (mouths) like this to sing for a **Sho**w on a planet with two 日 (suns) like these, and their **Ton**al quality was excellent **GROUP:** (合)唱 gasshou = chorus, # 1152; 晶 shou = crystal, # 1231 (identical pronunciation) **COMPARE:** other similar kanji at # **352** and # **2073**

1153. 満 PRONUNCIATIONS: mi, man
MEANINGS: full, to be filled **EXAMPLES:** 満ちる michiru = to become full; 満腹 manpuku = full stomach; 満足 manzoku = satisfaction; 不満 fuman = dissatisfaction **DESCRIPTION:** on the left, a water radical; at the upper right, a plant radical; at the lower right, 両(方) ryouhou (both, # 579), which can be seen as a model of a mountain with a handle, superimposed on a lean-to, or as a mountain below a tongue; this can also be seen as a chairlift seat hanging from a support structure **CUES:** since I consumed 両 (both) this water and this plant material at a **Me**al in **Man**hattan, I had 満腹 **man**puku (a full stomach) **GROUP:** 両(方) ryouhou = both, # 579; 満(足) manzoku = satisfaction, # 1153 **ALSO COMPARE:** other similar kanji at # **258**

1154. 杉 PRONUNCIATION: sugi
MEANING: Japanese cedar tree **EXAMPLE:** 杉 sugi = Japanese cedar tree **DESCRIPTION:** on the left, 木 ki (tree, # 118); on the right, three cords **CUE:** this 木 (tree), which is a 杉 **sugi** (Japanese cedar tree), has these three cords attached to it, which we use to tie up Superman's **Ge**ese **ALSO COMPARE:** other similar kanji at # **839**

1155. 制 PRONUNCIATION: sei
MEANINGS: to put in order, to control **EXAMPLES:** 制度 seido = system or regime; 制服 seifuku = a uniform **DESCRIPTION:** compared to 製(品) seihin (finished product, # 580) (identical pronunciation), this omits the tire stop supported by エ and Y; it retains ushi 牛 (cow, # 205), sitting on a revolving chair [this can also be seen as a fusion of 牛 (cow) and (都)市 toshi (city, # 424)], and the katakana リ ri **CUE:** this 牛 (cow) on a spinning chair and リ **Ri** work for **Sa**feway, where they have set up 制度 **sei**do (systems) to control the workers **ALSO COMPARE:** other similar kanji at # **242**, # **1765** and # **1985**

1156. 提 PRONUNCIATION: tei
MEANINGS: to carry, hold hands, commander **EXAMPLES:** 提出する teishutsu suru = to hand in or submit; 前提 zentei = premise, prerequisite **DESCRIPTION:** compared to 是(非) zehi (by all means, # 1035), this adds a kneeling guy on the left; it retains the policeman with a taser mounted on his foot, as seen in (予)定 yotei (plan, # 455) (identical pronunciation), sitting in the 日 (sun) **CUE:** this guy kneels in order to advise this policeman sitting in this 日 (sun) that the use of this **Ta**ser mounted on this foot is unethical and that he should 提出する **tei**shutsu suru (hand in) his resignation **ALSO COMPARE:** other similar kanji at # **454**

1157. 甲 PRONUNCIATION: kou

MEANINGS: armor, high (voice), first class
EXAMPLES: 甲羅 koura = shell

DESCRIPTION: compared to 押(す) osu (to push, # 592), this omits the kneeling guy on the left; it retains the shaky sign on a pole and reminds us of a rice paddy on a stick **CUE:** I can **C**ope with stress by grabbing this shaky sign and using it to break 甲羅 **kou**ra (shells) **GROUP:** 申(す) mousu = to humbly speak, # 10; (理)由 riyuu = reason, # 73; 届(ける) todokeru = to deliver, # 74; 神 kami = god, # 273; 押(す) osu = to push, # 592; 伸(ばす) nobasu = to lengthen, # 697; (宇)宙 uchuu = universe, # 898; 油 abura = oil, # 942; 甲(羅) koura = shell, # 1157; 笛 fue = a flute, # 1503; 捜(す) sagasu = to look for, # 1520; 袖 sode = a sleeve, # 1697; 抽(象) chuushou = an abstraction, # 1760; 挿(入する) sounyuu suru = to insert, # 1769; 軸 jiku = axle, # 1791; 紳(士) shinshi = a gentleman, # 1821; 岬 misaki = a cape, # 1942 **ALSO COMPARE:** kanji containing a rice paddy above 十 (ten) at # 1694, below 十 (ten) at # 720

1158. 羅 PRONUNCIATION: ra

MEANINGS: to carry, thin silk **EXAMPLE:** 甲羅 koura = shell **DESCRIPTION:** at the top, 目 me (eye, # 51), turned on its side, resembling three eyes; at the lower left, 糸 skeet shooter (# 219); at the lower right, a net, which can be seen as a man with a slanted hat next to a 主 (master) with an extra pair of arms (see # 203) **CUE:** these three eyes observe this 糸 (skeet shooter), who is a **Ra**scal, shooting at the 甲羅 kou**ra** (shell) of a turtle that is being held in this net **GROUP:** (甲)羅 koura = shell, # 1158; 維(持) iji = maintenance, # 1556 **ALSO COMPARE:** other similar kanji at # **1324**

1159. 徳 PRONUNCIATION: toku

MEANING: virtue **EXAMPLES:** 美徳 bitoku = virtue **DESCRIPTION:** compared to 聴(衆) choushuu (audience, # 934), this substitutes a man with two hats for (ear) on the left; it retains the woman named Margaret Cho, with this cross [which can also be seen as 十 juu (ten, # 18)] on her head, these three eyes and this good 心 (heart) **CUE:** this man with two hats thinks that this woman, who resembles 聴 (Margaret Cho) without her 耳 (ears), is a paragon of 美徳 bi**toku** (virtue) and that she is **T**otally **Co**ol, and he will offer her one of his hats
ALSO COMPARE: other similar kanji at # **934**

1160. 祥 PRONUNCIATION: shou

MEANINGS: happiness, good fortune
EXAMPLES: 発祥 hasshou = origin

DESCRIPTION: compared to 洋(服) youfuku (Western clothes, # 330), this substitutes the Shah, as seen in (会)社 kaisha (company, # 271), for the water radical on the left; it retains the 羊 (sheep) **CUE:** this Shah traces the 発祥 has**shou** (origin) of his wool business to a **Show** about 羊 (sheep) like this that he watched in his youth **GROUP:** (会)社 kaisha = company, # 271; 祖(先) sosen = ancestor, # 272; 神 kami = god, # 273; 祝(う) iwau = to celebrate, # 274; (お)礼 orei = gratitude, # 275; 福 fuku = good luck, # 661; 視(力) shiryoku = eyesight, # 844; 祈(る) inoru = to pray, # 955; (福)祉 fukushi = welfare, # 1066; (発)祥 hasshou = origin, # 1160; 禅(宗) zenshuu = Zen Buddhism, # 1694; (戦)禍 senka = war damages, # 2042 **ALSO COMPARE:** other similar kanji at # **1223**

1161. 勘 PRONUNCIATION: kan

MEANINGS: intuition, perception **EXAMPLES:** 勘弁 kanben = pardon, forgiveness; 勘違い kanchigai = misunderstanding, wrong guess; 勘定 kanjou = bill, check, calculation **DESCRIPTION:**

at the upper left, a bucket with three compartments; at the lower left, 匹 hiki (counter for small animals, # 818), which can also be seen as 四 yon (four, # 6), or the floor plan of a house, with a missing right wall; on the right, 力 chikara (force, # 107) **CUE:** my lunch was served in this bucket with three compartments carried by this 匹 (small animal), which is known in **Kan**sas for exerting a lot of 力 (force) like this, and I was happy until I saw the 勘定 **kan**jou (check) **GROUP:** 勘(定) kanjou = bill, # 1161; 堪(忍) kannin = forgiveness, # 1452 (identical pronunciation); 甚(大) jindai = very great, # 1730 **ALSO COMPARE:** other similar kanji at # **818** and # **1846**

1162. 弁 PRONUNCIATIONS: ben, bira

MEANINGS: speech, flower, petal, valve **EXAMPLES:** 弁護士 bengoshi = lawyer; 弁当 bentou = box lunch; 弁 ben = dialect, e.g., 名古屋弁 nagoyaben = Nagoya dialect; 弁解 benkai = excuse, justification; 花弁 hanabira = a flower petal **DESCRIPTION:** at the top, the katakana ム mu, which is the sound made by a cow; at the bottom, legs with a welcoming stance as seen in 葬(式) soushiki (funeral, # 1273), but these can also be seen as a tower **CUES:** this ム (cow) is working at the top of this tower, but it isn't happy with the **Ben**efits the job provides and plans to contact its 弁護士 **ben**goshi (lawyer) and look for a position on a **Be**autiful **R**anch **ALSO COMPARE:** other similar kanji at # **1678** and # **1924**

1163. 護 PRONUNCIATION: go

MEANING: to protect **EXAMPLES:** 弁護士 bengoshi = lawyer; 看護婦 kangofu = female nurse **DESCRIPTION:** compared to 獲(得す る) kakutoku suru (to obtain, # 947), this substitutes 言(う) iu (to speak, # 430) for the contorted woman on the left; it retains the plant radical, the net, which can be seen as a man with a slanted hat next to a 主 (master) with an extra pair of arms (see # 203), and the 又 (table) **CUE:** a 看護婦 kan**go**fu (nurse) heard a **Gho**st 言 (speak) from this net on this 又 (table) under these hanging plants **COMPARE:** similar kanji at # **947**

1164. 看 PRONUNCIATION: kan

MEANINGS: watch over, see **EXAMPLES:** 看板 kanban = signboard; 看護婦 kangofu = female nurse **DESCRIPTION:** at the top, 三 san (three, # 3) superimposed on the katakana ノ no; at the bottom 目 me (eye, # 51) **CUE:** 三 (three) ノ (no)-nonsense people with good 目 (eyes) like this went to **Kan**sas to train as 看護婦 **kan**gofu (nurses) **GROUP:** this is a group of one **ALSO COMPARE:** 寿(司) sushi = sushi, # 607; other similar kanji at # **2002**

1165. 婦 PRONUNCIATIONS: fu, pu²

MEANING: woman **EXAMPLES:** 婦人 fujin = woman; 主婦 shufu = housewife; 夫婦 fuufu = married couple; 看護婦 kangofu = female nurse; 新婦 shinpu = a bride **DESCRIPTION:** compared to 帰(る) kaeru (to return, # 566), this substitutes 女 onna (female, # 235) for リ Ri on the left; it retains the long hair streaming left and Bo Peep, who resembles the face of an elephant, with low-hanging ears and a long trunk **CUE:** when this 婦人 **fu**jin (woman) with this long hair 帰 (returns), she will give **Fo**od to this elephant **GROUP:** (本)当 hontou = truth, # 31; 緑 midori = green, # 227; 雪 yuki = snow, # 262; 急(ぐ) isogu = to hurry, # 312; 寝(る) neru = to sleep, # 372; 帰(る) kaeru = to return, # 566; 掃(除) souji = cleaning, # 645; 浸(す) hitasu = to soak, # 797; 隠(す) kakusu = to hide, # 834; 縁(起) engi = omen, # 1023; 婦(人) fujin = woman, # 1165; 尋(ねる) tazuneru = to inquire, # 1512; 侵(す) okasu = to invade, # 1591; 穏(やか な) odayaka na = calm, # 1703 **ALSO COMPARE:** other kanji containing 女 on the left at # **2039**; other similar kanji at # **1768**; other kanji with hair streaming left at # 999; kanji with hair streaming to the *right* at # 502

1166. 板 PRONUNCIATIONS: **ban, ita, pan** MEANINGS: plank, board, plate EXAMPLES: 看板 kanban = signboard; 板 ita = wooden board, metal plate; 鉄板焼き teppanyaki = food grilled on an iron griddle DESCRIPTION: compared to (出)版 shuppan (publication, # 1086) (identical pronunciation), this kanji substitutes 木 ki (tree, # 118) for the kneeling person holding a tray on the left; it retains the F over an X, which can also be seen as 又 mata (again, # 24), which resembles a simple table, under a one-sided lean-to CUES: I cut down this **Ban**ana 木 (tree) to make an 板 **ita** (wooden board) to cut Italian **Pan** (bread) on, but my teacher graded my work with this F and marked it with this X GROUP: 返(す) kaesu = to return something, # 356; (ご)飯 gohan = meal, # 400; 反(対) hantai = opposition, # 680; (大)阪 oosaka = Osaka, # 1005; (出)版 shuppan = publication, # 1086; 坂 saka = slope, # 1130; 板 ita = wooden board, # 1166; 販(売) hanbai = sales, # 1199; 仮(定) katei = supposition, # 1456

1167. 盆 PRONUNCIATION: **bon** MEANINGS: basin, lantern festival, tray EXAMPLES: お盆 Obon = a Buddhist festival devoted to ancestor worship; 盆踊り bonodori = a dance performed at Obon DESCRIPTION: at the top, 分(かる) wakaru (to understand, #105); at the bottom, 皿 sara (dish, # 567) CUE: I bought this 皿 (dish) at お盆 O**bon** (a Buddhist festival), and as a **Bon**us the seller helped me to 分 (understand) how it was made COMPARE: other similar kanji at # **1407** and # **2076**

1168. 鬼 PRONUNCIATIONS: **oni, ki** MEANINGS: ghost, devil EXAMPLES: 鬼 oni = devil, cruel person; 殺人鬼 satsujinki = killer, cutthroat DESCRIPTION: at the top, 田 (rice paddy, # 68) with one unit of rice above it, but this resembles a person wearing bifocals and a pointy hat; at the bottom, two lopsided tentacles, as seen in 勉(強) benkyou (study, # 474); above the tentacle on the right, the katakana ム mu, which is the sound made by a cow CUES: this 鬼 **oni** (devil) wears this pointy hat and these bifocals, stands on these lopsided tentacles, and is **Own**ing this ム (cow) which he plans to **K**eep ALSO COMPARE: other similar kanji at # **1169** and # **1678**

1169. 魅 PRONUNCIATION: **mi** MEANINGS: charm, fascination, glamour EXAMPLES: 魅力 miryoku = attractiveness, charm; 魅力的 miryokuteki = fascinating, charming DESCRIPTION: on the left, 鬼 oni (devil, # 1168); on the right, 未(来) mirai (future, # 672) (identical pronunciation) CUE: this 鬼 (devil) is looking into this 未 (future) to try to determine what his next **M**eal will be, a question that he finds 魅力的 **mi**ryokuteki (fascinating) GROUP: 鬼 oni = devil, # 1168; 魅(力) miryoku = charm, # 1169; (悪)魔 akuma = demon, # 1332; 魂 tamashii = a soul, # 1636; 塊 katamari = a lump, # 1738; 醜(い) minikui = ugly, # 1882 ALSO COMPARE: other similar kanji at # **672** and # **1678**

1170. 倉 PRONUNCIATIONS: **sou, kura** MEANINGS: storage, warehouse EXAMPLES: 倉庫 souko = warehouse; 穀倉 kokusou = granary; 倉 kura = storehouse (this can also be written 蔵, # 1190) DESCRIPTION: at the top, a peaked roof, with a ceiling; below that, a lean-to with a triple roof; below that, 口 kuchi (mouth, # 426), which resembles a kuuraa (cooler, or air conditioner) CUES: since **S**oldiers value 口 **Kuura**as (coolers) like this highly, they store them in secure 倉庫 **sou**ko (warehouses) like this, with several layers of roofing above them GROUP: 倉(庫) souko = warehouse, # 1170; 創(造) souzou = creation, # 1171 (identical pronunciation) ALSO COMPARE: other similar kanji at #**321**

1171. 創 PRONUNCIATION: sou

MEANINGS: to start, create, hurt
EXAMPLES: 創造 souzou = creation; 創立する souritsu suru = to establish; 創設する sousetsu suru = to found, establish; 独創性 dokusousei = originality, creativity
DESCRIPTION: compared to 倉(庫) souko (warehouse, # 1170) (identical pronunciation), this kanji adds the katakana リ ri on the right; the structure on the left can be seen as a lean-to containing a 口 (box) under both a triple roof and a second, peaked, roof and ceiling **CUE:** this guy リ Ri is a **So**ldier who helped to 創立する **sou**ritsu suru (establish) this army 倉 (warehouse) containing this 口 (box) **ALSO COMPARE:** other similar kanji at # **321**, # **1170** and # **1985**

1172. 穀 PRONUNCIATION: koku

MEANING: grain **EXAMPLES:** 穀倉 kokusou = granary; 穀物 kokumotsu = grain, cereal
DESCRIPTION: at the upper left, 士 shi (man, # 66); at the middle left, a roof; at the lower left, 禾 (a grain plant with a ripe head); at the upper right, π (the Greek letter pi, also known as a pious yak); at the lower right, 又 (a simple table) **CUE:** this 士 (man) stands high on this roof and drinks **Co**ke as he surveys this 禾 (grain plant with a ripe head), and he wonders how much of the 穀物 **ko**kumotsu (grain) will be eaten by this π (yak) on this 又 (table) **COMPARE:** similar kanji at # **557**, # **1468** and # **1797**

1173. 締 PRONUNCIATIONS: shimari, ji, shi

MEANINGS: tighten, tie, shut, lock, fasten
EXAMPLES: 取締役 torishimariyaku = a representative director (a director chosen by a board to represent it); 戸締まり tojimari = door fastening; 締める shimeru = to fasten (seatbelt), tie (necktie), strangle, tighten (transitive); 締まる shimaru = to tighten (intransitive); 締め切り shimekiri = closing, deadline **DESCRIPTION:** compared to 諦(める) akirameru (to give up, # 804), this substitutes 糸 (skeet shooter, # 219) for 言 (to say) on the left; it retains 立 (to stand) and 巾 (Bo Peep), who stands on slippery floors wearing these spikes on her shoes
CUES: this 巾 (Bo Peep) on the lower right, who 立 (stands) on slippery floors wearing these spikes on her shoes, and this 糸 (skeet shooter) fell in love, and **She Marri**ed him, but sometimes she slides around in spite of her spikes, so he went out to his **Jee**p and got a harness made out of a **Shee**t to 締める **shi**meru (fasten) her to the ceiling
ALSO COMPARE: other similar kanji at # **804** and # **1768**

1174. 偉 PRONUNCIATIONS: i, era

MEANINGS: admirable, greatness, famous
EXAMPLES: 偉人 ijin = an exceptional person; 偉大 idai = great, grand; 偉い erai = great, excellent, eminent, distinguished
DESCRIPTION: compared to 違(反) ihan (violation, # 355) (identical pronunciation), this kanji substitutes a man with a slanted hat for the snail; it retains the two feet resembling 五 (five) facing in opposite directions and separated by a box **CUES:** this man on the left is tilting his hat back to examine this guy with feet like these facing in opposite directions, realizing that the guy's life wasn't **Ea**sy during an **Era** when people had to walk everywhere and that he was an 偉人 **i**jin (exceptional person) **GROUP:** 違(反) ihan = violation, # 355; 韓(国) kankoku = South Korea, # 655; 衛(生) eisei = sanitation, # 918; 偉(大) idai = great, # 1174; 緯(度) ido = latitude, # 1810
ALSO COMPARE: other kanji containing 五 at # **179**

1175. 載 PRONUNCIATIONS: no, sai
MEANINGS: to publish in, load with
EXAMPLES: 載る noru = to be printed or placed on; 載せる noseru = to put on top of, to publish; 記載 kisai = record, listing, entry
DESCRIPTION: at the upper left, 土 tsuchi (soil, # 59); at the lower left, 車 kuruma (car, # 283); on the right, a halberd (combination axe and lance)
CUES: a **N**orwegian who is a **S**cientist is guarding this 車 (car) with this halberd, but he notices this 土 (soil) on the car and checks his 記載 ki**sai** (records) to determine when it was last washed
COMPARE: similar kanji at # 1862 and # 1966

1176. 阿 PRONUNCIATION: a
MEANINGS: to flatter, fawn upon **EXAMPLES:** 阿波踊り Awa Odori = a dance festival held in Tokushima City during Obon; 阿呆 aho = a fool or silly person, usually written アホ
DESCRIPTION: compared to 可(愛い) kawaii (cute, # 615), which resembles a simple box (or carton) in a one-sided lean-to, this adds ß beta from the Greek alphabet on the left **CUE:** this ß (Greek) **A**rtist looked 可 (cute) when she danced in the 阿波踊り **a**wa'odori (an Obon dance festival)
GROUP: 何 nani = what, # 338; 荷(物) nimotsu = luggage, # 342; 歌(う) utau = to sing, # 534; 可(愛い) kawaii = cute, # 615; (結)局 kekkyoku = after all, # 867; 阿(波踊り) Awa Odori = a dance festival, # 1176; (運)河 unga = canal, # 1182; (砂)糖 satou = sugar, # 1494; 唐(突) toutotsu = sudden, # 1600; 苛(立つ) iradatsu = to get irritated, # 1792
ALSO COMPARE: other similar kanji at # 604 and # 2030

1177. 援 PRONUNCIATION: en
MEANINGS: aid, help, cheering
EXAMPLES: 応援 ouen = support; 援助 enjo = assistance, support; 救援 kyuuen = rescue; 声援 seien = support, cheering
DESCRIPTION: compared to 暖(かい) atatakai (warm, # 38), this substitutes a kneeling guy for 日 (sun) on the left; it retains the barbecue grate and 友 (friend) **CUE:** when this guy on the left is kneeling to put food on this grate, the house gets 暖 (warm), but the kneeling guy gets 応援 ou**en** (support) and **En**couragement from this 友 (friend)
GROUP: 暖(かい) atatakai = warm, # 38; 将(来) shourai = the future, # 374; 愛 ai = love, # 523; 受(ける) ukeru = to receive, # 577; 授(業) jugyou = class, # 578; 鶏 niwatori = chicken, # 754; 瞬(間) shunkan = moment, # 773; 隠(す) kakusu = to hide, # 834; 揺(れる) yureru = to sway, # 852; (応)援 ouen = support, # 1177; 稲 ine = rice plant, # 1229; 緩(い) yurui = loose, # 1330; 渓(谷) keikoku = valley, # 1384; 爵(位) shaku'i = peerage, # 1603; 穏(やかな) odayaka na = calm, # 1703; 謡 utai = Noh chanting, # 1856; 淫(らな) midara na = indecent, # 1877; 奨(励) shourei = encouragement, # 1906; 妥(協) dakyou = a compromise, # 1916; 曖(昧な) aimai na = ambiguous, # 1940; (愛)媛(県) ehime ken = Ehime Prefecture, # 2084 **ALSO COMPARE:** other similar kanji at # 459 and # 1389

1178. 箕 PRONUNCIATION: mi
MEANING: winnowing **EXAMPLE:** 箕面市 Minooshi = a city north of Osaka **DESCRIPTION:** at the top, 竹 take (bamboo, # 134); at the bottom, a woman with a wide skirt and a bucket with several compartments, as seen in (時)期 jiki (time, # 711) **CUE:** I had a **M**eal in 箕面市 **Mi**nooshi with

this woman with this wide skirt and this bucket with several compartments, and we ate these 竹 (bamboo) shoots **ALSO COMPARE:** similar kanji at # **711** and # **2074**

1179. 滝 PRONUNCIATION: taki

MEANINGS: waterfall, rapids **EXAMPLE:** 滝 taki = waterfall, cascade **DESCRIPTION:** on the left, a water radical; at the upper right, 立 (つ) tatsu (to stand, # 11); at the lower right, a transformer with a wire protruding from it, as seen in 電(気) denki (electricity, # 263) **CUE:** we were 立 (standing) and **Tal**king about a scheme to make 電 (electricity) like this using hydropower from this water that flows over a 滝 **tak**i (waterfall) **ALSO COMPARE:** other similar kanji at # **1003** and # **1569**

1180. 脂 PRONUNCIATIONS: shi, abura

MEANINGS: fat, grease, tallow, lard **EXAMPLES:** 脂肪 shibou = fat; 脂 abura = fat **DESCRIPTION:** compared to 指 yubi (finger, # 691), or 指(定席) shiteiseki (reserved seats, # 691) (identical pronunciation), this kanji substitutes 月 tsuki (moon, # 148) for the kneeling guy on the left; it retains the 旨 (uber Marine) **CUES:** this 旨 (uber Marine) works under this 月 (moon) caring for his **Sh**eep, including **Abu** Dhabi **Ra**ms, and they have a high 脂 **abura** (fat) content **ALSO COMPARE:** 油 abura = oil, # 942; other similar kanji at # **1318**

1181. 悩 PRONUNCIATIONS: naya, nou

MEANINGS: trouble, worry, in pain, distress **EXAMPLES:** 悩む nayamu = to be troubled or worried; 悩み nayami = distress, worry; 苦悩 kunou = agony, anguish **DESCRIPTION:** on the left, an erect man; at the upper right, three old boys, as seen in 覚(える) oboeru (to memorize, # 54), but these resemble buzzing bees; at the lower right, an open box with an X inside, which represents an unknown number of bees inside a hive **CUES:** when this man on the left took a **Nap** in the **Ya**rd, these three buzzing bees, out of the X (unknown number) in this hive, stung him on the Nose, causing him to jump up to his full height like this and experience 悩み **naya**mi (distress) **GROUP:** 悩(み) nayami = distress, # 1181; 脳 nou = brain, # 1461 **ALSO COMPARE:** other similar kanji at # **1794** and # **2063**

1182. 河 PRONUNCIATIONS: ka, ga, kawa

MEANING: large river **EXAMPLES:** 河口 kakou = mouth of a river; 運河 unga = canal; 河 kawa = river (usually written 川, # 250) **DESCRIPTION:** compared to 可(愛い) kawaii (cute, # 615) (identical pronunciation), this kanji adds a water radical on the left; it retains the carton (or box) inside a one-sided lean-to **CUES:** I took this **C**arton of cleaning supplies to my **Ga**rage, which is this one-sided lean-to, and I used this water from a 河 **kawa** (river) to do a **Ca**r **Wa**sh **ALSO COMPARE:** other similar kanji at # **1176**

1183. 焚 PRONUNCIATION: ta

MEANINGS: burn, build a fire, cook **EXAMPLES:** 焚き火 takibi = bonfire; 焚く taku = to burn (wood) **DESCRIPTION:** at the top, 林 hayashi (grove, # 125); at the bottom, 火(事) kaji (fire, # 443) **CUE:** **Ta**rzan started this 火 (fire) in this 林 (grove) in order to make a 焚き火 **ta**kibi (bonfire) **ALSO COMPARE:** other similar kanji at # **943** and # **1239**

1184. 梨 PRONUNCIATION: nashi

MEANING: pear tree **EXAMPLE:** 梨 nashi = pear tree, or a pear **DESCRIPTION:** at the upper left, 禾 (a grain plant with a ripe head); at the upper right, the katakana リ ri; at the bottom, 木 ki (tree, # 118) **CUE:** リ **Ri** climbed into this 木 (tree) belonging to his enemy, saw that its 梨 **nashi** (pears) were 禾 (ripe), and started **Gnash**ing his teeth in anger **COMPARE:** other similar kanji at # **1352**, # **1797** and # **1985**

1185. 幅 PRONUNCIATION: haba
MEANINGS: hanging scroll, width
EXAMPLE: 幅 haba = width
DESCRIPTION: compared to 福 fuku (good luck, # 661), this substitutes 巾 (Bo Peep), as seen in 帽(子) boushi (hat, # 243), for the Shah on the left; it retains 口 kuchi (mouth, # 426) with a napkin over it, suggesting that this person is being inhibited from talking, plus 田 (rice paddy, # 68)
CUE: this 巾 (Bo Peep) is a **Ha**waiian **Ba**rber with this napkin over this 口 (mouth) which prevents her from complaining about the 幅 **haba** (width) of this 田 (rice paddy) next to her shop GROUP: 福 fuku = good luck, # 661; 富(士山) fujisan = Mt. Fuji, # 939; 幅 haba = width, # 1185; 副(産物) fukusanbutsu = a byproduct, # 1206
ALSO COMPARE: other similar kanji at # **1768**

1186. 茂 PRONUNCIATION: shige
MEANINGS: to grow thickly, be rampant
EXAMPLE: 茂る shigeru = to grow thickly; this is the more common spelling, compared to 繁る shigeru, # 1266 DESCRIPTION: at the top, a plant radical; at the bottom, a two-sided lean-to supported by a halberd (combination lance and axe)
CUE: the **Sh**eep at **G**ettysburg feed on these plants which 茂る **shige**ru (grow thickly), and then they sleep in lean-tos supported by halberds like this
COMPARE: similar kanji at # **915**

1187. 秘 PRONUNCIATIONS: pi, hi
MEANING: to keep secret EXAMPLES: 神秘 shinpi = a mystery; 秘密 himitsu = a secret; 秘書 hisho = a secretary DESCRIPTION: compared to 必(死に) hisshi ni (desperately, # 307) (identical pronunciation), or 必(要) hitsuyou (necessary, # 307), this kanji adds 禾 (a grain plant with a ripe head) on the left
CUES: our 秘書 **hi**sho (secretary) **P**eeks out the window and, seeing this 禾 (ripe grain), realizes that it's 必 (necessary) to take off her **H**eels and trample it to separate the wheat from the chaff
ALSO COMPARE: other similar kanji at # **1297** and # **1797**

1188. 密 PRONUNCIATIONS: mitsu, mi, hiso MEANINGS: secrecy, density, carefulness
EXAMPLES: 秘密 himitsu = a secret; 綿密 menmitsu = detailed, meticulous; 密会 mikkai = secret meeting; 密かに hisoka ni = secretly, behind the scenes
DESCRIPTION: at the top, a bad haircut; in the middle, 必(要) hitsuyou (necessary, # 307); at the bottom, 山 yama (mountain, # 146)
CUES: it's 必 (necessary) that you **M**eet **Su**perman on this 山 (mountain), sympathize with this bad haircut, share his **M**eals, and **H**ear his **S**ordid 秘密 hi**mitsu** (secrets) GROUP: (秘)密 himitsu = a secret, # 1188; (蜂)蜜 hachimitsu = honey, # 1255 ALSO COMPARE: other similar kanji at # **1297** and # **2079**

1189. 綿 PRONUNCIATIONS: wata, men MEANING: cotton EXAMPLES: 綿 wata = cotton; 綿 men = cotton; 木綿 momen = cotton; 綿密 menmitsu = detailed, meticulous
DESCRIPTION: compared to 線 sen (line, # 228), this substitutes 巾 (Bo Peep), as seen in 帽(子) boushi (hat, # 243), for 水 (water) at the lower right; it retains 糸 ito (thread or skeet shooter) and 白 (white) CUES: this 巾 (Bo Peep) **W**alks **T**all, and all of the **M**en admire her outfit made from this 白 (white) 綿 **men** (cotton) 糸 (thread)
ALSO COMPARE: other similar kanji at # **1768** and # **2014**

1190. 蔵 PRONUNCIATIONS: zou, kura
MEANINGS: vault, treasure, storage
EXAMPLES: 冷蔵庫 reizouko = refrigerator; 蔵書 zousho = a book collection or library; 蔵 kura = a storehouse (this can also be written 倉, # 1170) DESCRIPTION: compared to (心)臓

shinzou (heart, # 951) (identical pronunciation), this omits the 月 (moon) on the left; it retains the plant radical, the two-sided lean-to supported by a halberd, and the 臣 (inoperable swing set), which are associated with different heart rate zones
CUES: my heart rate is classified into three **Z**ones represented by these soothing plants, this frustrating 臣 (disabled swing set) and this scary halberd supporting this lean-to, and sometimes I move it into a fourth zone by taking a beer from the 冷蔵庫 rei**zou**ko (refrigerator) and turning on the **Kuu**raa (air conditioner)
ALSO COMPARE: other similar kanji at # **915** and # **1246**

1191. 胴 PRONUNCIATION: dou
MEANINGS: trunk, torso
EXAMPLE: 胴体 doutai = body, torso
DESCRIPTION: compared to 同(情) doujou (sympathy, # 339) (identical pronunciation), this kanji adds 月 tsuki (moon, # 148) on the left; it retains the old napkin that had been used to wrap a doughnut, above a box inside a two-sided lean-to
CUE: when this 月 (moon) is full, I somehow feel 同 (sympathy) for hungry people, and so I eat **Dough**nuts like the one that was previously wrapped in this napkin, and that's why my 胴体 **dou**tai (torso) is so large
ALSO COMPARE: other similar kanji at # **1620**

1192. 操 PRONUNCIATIONS: ayatsu, sou
MEANINGS: to operate, fidelity
EXAMPLES: 操る ayatsuru = to control, manipulate, handle; 操作 sousa = operation (of a machine); 体操 taisou = gymnastics, exercise
DESCRIPTION: compared to 繰(り返す) kurikaesu (to repeat, # 1034), this substitutes a kneeling guy for 糸 (skeet shooter) on the left; it retains the three packages of Kool-Aid stuck in a tree
CUES: an **Aya**tollah **Tsu**ed (sued) the skeet shooter who was 繰 (repeatedly) unable to dislodge these Kool-Aid 品 (packages) from this 木 (tree) and then told this guy on the left, who is a **S**oldier, to kneel in order to 操作する **sou**sa suru (operate) a machine to do the job

ALSO COMPARE: other similar kanji at # **1034** and # **1216**

1193. 滅 PRONUNCIATIONS: metsu, me, horo MEANINGS: destroy, ruin, overthrow, perish EXAMPLES: 絶滅 zetsumetsu = extinction; 破滅 hametsu = devastation, ruin; 不滅の fumetsu no = immortal, eternal; 滅入る meiru = to feel depressed; 滅ぼす horobosu = to ruin or destroy
DESCRIPTION: compared to 減(る) heru (to reduce weight, # 1148), this substitutes 火 hi (fire, # 443), which is covered by a napkin, for 口 (mouth), also covered by a napkin; it retains the water radical on the left and the two-sided lean-to supported by a halberd CUES: when I **Met Super**man in this lean-to in **Me**xico, he told me that, according to his **Horo**scope, we were threatened with 絶滅 zetsu**metsu** (extinction) from a combination of this water, this napkin-covered 火 (fire) and halberds like this one
ALSO COMPARE: other similar kanji at # **915** and # **1239**

1194. 慮 PRONUNCIATION: ryo
MEANINGS: prudence, thought, concern
EXAMPLES: 配慮 hairyo = consideration, concern; 考慮 kouryo = consideration; 遠慮 enryo = hesitation, reserve, restraint, modesty
DESCRIPTION: compared to (捕)虜 horyo (captive, # 1107) (identical pronunciation), this kanji substitutes 思(う) omou (to think/feel, # 308) for the 男 (male) prisoner named Leo; it retains the one-sided lean-to containing 七 (seven) Tory corporals with a periscope at the top
CUE: when Pope **Leo** revisited the 七 (seven) jailers in this lean-to with this periscope at the top, he 思 (thought) that they should give more 配慮 hai**ryo** (consideration) to the welfare of their 虜 (captives) ALSO COMPARE: similar kanji at # **308**, # **677** and # **1057**

1195. 抵 PRONUNCIATION: tei

MEANINGS: resist, reach, touch **EXAMPLES:** 抵抗 teikou = resistance, opposition; 抵当 teitou = mortgage **DESCRIPTION:** compared to (最)低 saitei (the worst, # 222) (identical pronunciation), this kanji substitutes a kneeling guy for the guy with a slanted hat; it retains the shi 氏 (mister, # 709) which we have described as a 紙 (paper) pavilion, and which can also be seen as a leaning woman under a one-sided lean-to, taped to a flat rock **CUE:** this guy is kneeling in order to move this 紙 (paper) pavilion, but the **T**ape that was used to attach it to this flat rock produces too much 抵抗 **tei**kou (resistance)

GROUP: 紙 kami = paper, # 221; (最)低 saitei = the worst, # 222; (結)婚 kekkon = marriage, # 240; (彼)氏 kareshi = boyfriend, # 709; 昏(睡) konsui = coma, # 1074; (海)底 kaitei = the bottom of the sea, # 1096; 抵(抗) teikou = resistance, # 1195; 邸(宅) teitaku = mansion, # 1422; Note that four of these kanji can be pronounced "tei" **ALSO COMPARE:** other similar kanji at # 249 and # 376

1196. 抗 PRONUNCIATION: kou

MEANINGS: confront, resist, defy, oppose **EXAMPLES:** 抵抗 teikou = resistance, opposition; 抗議 kougi = protest; 反抗 hankou = rebellion, defiance, resistance; 対抗する taikou suru = to oppose or fight **DESCRIPTION:** on the left, a kneeling guy; at the upper right, a tire stop, as seen in 対(して) taishite (against, # 674); at the lower right, a tall desk, as seen in 机 tsukue (desk, # 140) **CUE:** this guy doesn't like this tire stop which was installed on this desk at a **C**ourthouse, and he kneels to ask for its removal before organizing a 抗議 **kou**gi (protest) against it **ALSO COMPARE:** similar kanji at # 1462 and # 1860

1197. 盤 PRONUNCIATION: ban

MEANINGS: tray, shallow bowl **EXAMPLES:** 吸盤 kyuuban = suction cup, sucker; 基盤 kiban = foundation, basis **DESCRIPTION:** compared to (一)般(的に) ippanteki ni (usually, # 1050), this adds 皿 sara (bowl, # 567) at the bottom; it retains the boat radical found in 船 fune (boat, # 602), a 兀 (pious yak) and a 又 (table) **CUE:** **Ban**anas are shipped on this 舟 (boat), and I mash them in this 皿 (bowl) before eating them with this 兀 (yak) at this 又 (table), since they are the 基盤 ki**ban** (foundation) of our diet **COMPARE:** other similar kanji at # 557, # 1407 and # 1524

1198. 基 PRONUNCIATIONS: moto, ki

MEANINGS: foundation, base **EXAMPLES:** 基ずく motozuku = to be based on; に基づいて ni motozuite = based on, according to; 基準 kijun = criterion, standard; 基盤 kiban = foundation, basis; 基金 kikin = fund; 基地 kichi = base **DESCRIPTION:** at the top, a bucket with three compartments above a wide skirt, but this could be a drone; at the bottom, 土 tsuchi (soil, # 59), but this resembles a propeller on a motor **CUES:** this drone is powered by this **M**otor at the bottom, and our surveillance around **K**iev will 基ずく **moto**zuku (be based on) it **ALSO COMPARE:** 塞(ぐ) fusagu = to obstruct, # 1227, which contains a corset instead of a bucket and also adds a bad haircut; other similar kanji at # 711 and # 1101

1199. 販 PRONUNCIATION: han

MEANINGS: marketing, sell, trade **EXAMPLES:** 販売 hanbai = sales, marketing; 自働販売機 jidouhanbaiki = vending machine **DESCRIPTION:** compared to 反(対) hantai (opposition, # 680) (identical pronunciation), this kanji adds 貝 kai (shell, or a three-drawer money chest, # 83) on the left; it retains the F over an X **CUE: Han**sel wanted a career in 販売 **han**bai (marketing) so that he could fill up this 貝 (money chest), but he got this F on his final exam, and Gretel also marked it with this X **COMPARE:** similar kanji at # 1166 and # 2058

1200. 綱 **PRONUNCIATIONS: tsuna, zuna²** **MEANINGS:** rope, cord, cable
EXAMPLES: 綱 tsuna = a rope, cord, cable; 綱引き tsunahiki = tug of war; 命綱 inochizuna = lifeline **DESCRIPTION:** on the left, 糸 (skeet shooter, # 219); on the right, 岡 oka (hill, # 1528), which resembles a two-sided lean-to containing a model of a 山 (mountain), with a handle and two antennae above it (the radical inside the lean-to can also be seen as a chairlift seat hanging from two frayed cables)
CUE: this 糸 (skeet shooter) was shooting at this 岡 (hill), which resembles a two-sided lean-to containing this chairlift seat hanging from two frayed 綱 **tsuna** (cables), when a **Tsuna**mi swept him away **GROUP:** 綱 tsuna = a rope, # 1200; (鉄)鋼 tekkou = steel, # 1472; 岡 oka = hill, # 1528; 剛(健) gouken = vigor, # 1663

1201. 雰 **PRONUNCIATIONS: fun,** *fu*
MEANING: atmosphere
EXAMPLE: 雰囲気 fu'inki (a colloquial way of saying fun'iki) = atmosphere, ambience, mood
DESCRIPTION: at the top, 雨 ame (rain, # 261); at the bottom, 分 fun (minute, # 105) (identical pronunciation)
CUES: this 雨 (rain) is going to fall any 分 (minute) now, but we are having **Fun,** and the rain won't spoil the 雰囲気 **fu**'inki (ambience) of our party, where already some **Foo**ls are staring at me
COMPARE: other similar kanji at # **262** and # **2076**

1202. 囲 **PRONUNCIATIONS: kako, i,** *in*
MEANINGS: surround, enclosure
EXAMPLES: 囲む kakomu = to surround or circle; 周囲 shuu'i = surroundings; 雰囲気 fu'inki (a colloquial way of saying fun'iki) = atmosphere, ambience, mood
DESCRIPTION: a fence surrounding 井(戸) ido (water well, # 983) (identical pronunciation)
CUES: a **C**arpentry **C**orporation built this fence to 囲む **kako**mu (surround) this 井 (well), and now it's **E**asy to keep **I**ntruders out

GROUP: 井(戸) ido = water well, # 983; 囲 (む) kakomu = to surround, # 1202; 耕(す) tagayasu = to plow, # 1312; 井 donburi = a porcelain bowl, # 1984 **ALSO COMPARE:** other similar kanji at # **1360**

1203. 飾 **PRONUNCIATIONS: shika, kaza, shoku** **MEANINGS:** decorate, ornament
EXAMPLES: 葛飾 katsushika = a ward in Tokyo; 飾る kazaru = to decorate; 装飾 soushoku = decoration
DESCRIPTION: on the left, 食(事) shokuji (meal, # 398) (identical pronunciation); on the right side, 巾 (Bo Peep), as seen in 帽(子) boushi (hat, # 243), balancing a crutch on her head
CUES: this 巾 (Bo Peep), who uses this crutch, lives in **Chica**go but just got back from **Kaza**khstan, and if you invite her to a 食 (meal) like this she will **Shock** yo**U** by offering to 飾る **kaza**ru (decorate) your house **ALSO COMPARE:** other similar kanji at # **1768**, # **1974** and # **2080**

1204. 詣 **PRONUNCIATIONS: mou, moude, kei** **MEANING:** visit a temple
EXAMPLES: 詣でる mouderu = to make a pilgrimage or visit a temple; 詣で moude = a temple or shrine visit; 初詣 hatsumoude = first shrine visit of the year (this can also be written 初詣で); 造詣 zoukei = knowledge, mastery
DESCRIPTION: compared to 指 yubi (finger, # 691), this substitutes 言(う) iu (to speak, # 430) for the kneeling guy on the left; it retains the 旨 (uber Marine) **CUES:** this 旨 (uber Marine) is thinking about **Mo**wing the lawn, but he puts his 指 (finger) in the air and 言 (says), "This isn't a **Mow Day**. Let's do a 詣で **mou**de (temple visit) instead and then get some **C**a**k**e."
ALSO COMPARE: other similar kanji at # **1318**

1205. 寛 PRONUNCIATION: kan

MEANINGS: tolerance, leniency, be at ease, generosity **EXAMPLES:** 寛大 kandai = understanding, lenient, tolerant, generous, broad-minded; 寛容 kanyou = tolerance, open-mindedness, forbearance, generosity **DESCRIPTION:** at the top, a bad haircut; under the haircut, a plant radical; at the bottom, 見(る) miru (to look, # 53) **CUE:** this guy came to **Kan**sas to 見 (look) around, but this bad haircut and these plants on his head affect his 見 (vision), so please be 寛大 **kan**dai (tolerant) **ALSO COMPARE:** other similar kanji at # **1341**

1206. 副 PRONUNCIATION: fuku

MEANINGS: duplicate, copy, deputy **EXAMPLES:** 副作用 fukusayou = a side-effect; 副産物 fukusanbutsu = a byproduct; 副住職 fukujuushoku = vice-priest **DESCRIPTION:** compared to 福 fuku (good luck, # 661) (identical pronunciation), this omits the Shah on the left and adds リ ri on the right; it retains the 口 (mouth), with a napkin over it, and the 田 (rice paddy) **CUE:** リ Ri might buy this 田 (rice paddy) in **Fuku**oka, but he has put this napkin over his 口 (mouth), since he's not allowed to talk about it yet, and a 副産物 **fuku**sanbutsu (byproduct) of his silence is that he seems to be sulking **ALSO COMPARE:** similar kanji at # **1185** and **1985**

1207. 互 PRONUNCIATIONS: go, taga

MEANINGS: mutually, reciprocally, together **EXAMPLES:** 相互 sougo = each other, one another, mutuality; 互い tagai = each other, one another; 互いに tagai ni = with each other, mutually, reciprocally **DESCRIPTION:** this resembles two katakana ユ yu characters, one upside down and the other right side up, touching in the center, which remind us of youths; this also resembles 五 go (five, # 179) (identical pronunciation) **CUES:** these two ユ (youths) have discovered a **Go**ld mine in the Philippines, and they speak **Taga**log 互いに **taga**i ni (with each other) **GROUP:** 互(い) tagai = each other, # 1207; 剥(ぐ) hagu = to strip, # 1567; (語)彙 goi = vocabulary, # 2067 **ALSO COMPARE:** other similar kanji at # **179** and # **996**

1208. 尊 PRONUNCIATIONS: son, touto

MEANINGS: to revere or respect **EXAMPLES:** 尊重する sonchou suru = to respect or value; 尊敬する sonkei suru = to respect; 尊い toutoi = sacred, important, valuable **DESCRIPTION:** at the top, 酒 sake (# 465), without its water radical on the left (this can also be seen as a bucket of sake with a handle) and with two rabbit ears added at the top; at the bottom, 寸(前) sunzen (on the verge, # 1369), which depicts a kneeling sunny guy who has dropped his gum **CUES:** this 寸 (kneeling sunny guy) has dropped his gum, he's drinking this modified 酒 (sake, to which he's added these rabbit ears), he works for **Son**y, he eats **To**asted **To**rtillas and he 尊敬する **son**kei suru (respects) everyone **ALSO COMPARE:** other similar kanji at # **131**, # **1480** and # **1997**

Kanji for Volume Three

1209. 吊 PRONUNCIATION: tsu

MEANINGS: suspend, hang, wear (sword) **EXAMPLE:** 吊るす tsurusu = to suspend or hang up **DESCRIPTION:** compared to (非)常 hijou (emergency, # 683), this omits the hat with three antennae; it retains 巾 (Bo Peep) with a big 口 (mouth) **CUE:** this 巾 (Bo Peep), who has this big 口 (mouth), spins around looking for her **Tsu**it (suit) which someone has 吊るした **tsu**rushita (hung) from a tree **ALSO COMPARE:** 呆れる akireru = to be astonished, # 828; other similar kanji at # **1768**

1210. 菌 **PRONUNCIATION:** kin
MEANINGS: germ, fungus, bacteria
EXAMPLE: 細菌 saikin = bacterium, germ
DESCRIPTION: at the top, a plant radical; at the bottom, 禾 (a grain plant with a ripe head) in a box
CUE: some **Kin**dergarten students left this 禾 (ripe grain plant) in this closed box and covered it with this plant material, but it was soon consumed by 細菌 sai**kin** (bacteria) **COMPARE:** other similar kanji at # **1360** and # **2055**

1211. 剰 **PRONUNCIATION:** jou
MEANINGS: surplus, besides **EXAMPLE:** 過剰 kajou = excess, surplus **DESCRIPTION:** compared to 乗(車する) jousha suru (to board a train, # 509) (identical pronunciation), this kanji adds the katakana リ ri on the right; it retains the streamlined vehicle in a tree **CUE:** whenever **Jo**an of Arc and this リ **Ri** have 過剰 ka**jou** (a surplus) of time, they like to 乗 (board trains) **ALSO COMPARE:** other similar kanji at # **799** and # **1985**

1212. 潔 **PRONUNCIATIONS:** isagiyo, ketsu, ke **MEANINGS:** undefiled, pure, clean
EXAMPLES: 潔い isagiyoi = unhesitating, manly, wholehearted, sportsmanlike; 清潔 seiketsu = clean; 潔白 keppaku = innocence
DESCRIPTION: on the left, a water radical; at the upper middle, an owl's perch, as seen in 青(い) aoi (blue, # 155); at the upper right, 刀 katana (sword, # 102); at the lower right, 糸 (skeet shooter), # 219) **CUES:** when she was watching this 糸 (skeet shooter) juggle this owl's perch and this sword, Queen **I**sabella liked to eat **Ge**ese with **Yo**gurt sauce, and she would put **Ket**chup in her **Soup** and drink this 清潔な sei**ketsu** na (clean) water from a **Ke**ttle **COMPARE:** other similar kanji at # **1103**, # **1266** and # **2062**

1213. 舌 **PRONUNCIATIONS:** shita, zetsu
MEANINGS: tongue, reed **EXAMPLES:** 舌 shita = tongue; 弁舌 benzetsu = eloquence, persuasiveness **DESCRIPTION:** a 口 (mouth) with a tongue emerging from it; compared to 古(い) furui (old , # 392), this adds a slanted cap at the top **CUES:** when I eat **Shi**ite **Ta**ffy, I have to stick out this 舌 **shita** (tongue) because the taffy sticks to it, and sometimes it gets onto my **Zen Tsu**it (suit) **GROUP:** (生)活 seikatsu = livelihood, # 260; 辞(書) jisho = dictionary, # 387; 話(す) hanasu = to speak, # 433; 乱(暴) ranbou = violent, # 1020; 舌 shita = tongue, # 1213; (休)憩 kyuukei = a rest, # 1477; 括(弧) kakko = a parenthesis, # 1762 **ALSO COMPARE:** kanji with a tongue emerging from a *mountain* at # 1856

1214. 辟 **PRONUNCIATION:** heki
MEANINGS: false, punish, crime, law
EXAMPLE: 辟易する hekieki suru = to feel overwhelmed, to get tired of **DESCRIPTION:** compared to 壁(画) hekiga (mural painting, # 1051) (identical pronunciation), this kanji removes 土 (soil) from the bottom; it retains the lean-to with a double roof, the 口 (box), and the 辛 (needle) (this combination of radicals = LBN = lean-to, box, needle) **CUE:** a **H**ealthy **Ki**ng injected some medicine from this 口 (box) under this lean-to using this 辛 (needle), and he 辟易した **hek**ieki shita (was overwhelmed) (LBN = lean-to, box, needle) **GROUP:** 避(ける) sakeru = to avoid, # 802; 壁(画) hekiga = mural painting, # 1051; 辟(易する) hekieki suru = to get tired of, # 1214; (悪)癖 akuheki = bad habit, # 1215 (also identical pronunciation); (完)璧(な) kanpeki na = perfect, # 1933

1215. 癖 **PRONUNCIATIONS: heki, peki, kuse, guse²** **MEANINGS:** mannerism, trait **EXAMPLES:** 悪癖 akuheki = bad habit; 潔癖な keppeki na = fastidious, particular, loving cleanliness; 癖 kuse = habit, e.g., 癖がつく kuse ga tsuku = to acquire a habit; 悪癖 waruguse = a bad habit **DESCRIPTION:** on the upper left, a sick bed, as seen in 病(気) byouki (illness, # 369); inside the bed, 辟(易する) hekieki suru (to feel overwhelmed, # 1214) (identical pronunciation) which combines lean-to, box and needle (LBN) **CUES:** a **H**ealthy **K**ing picked up some 悪癖 aku**heki** (bad habits), such as **P**ecking trees, from a **K**ool-Aid **S**eller, and then he began to feel 辟 (overwhelmed) before ending up in this sick bed (LBN = lean-to, box, needle) **ALSO COMPARE:** similar kanji at # **369** and # **1214**

1216. 保 **PRONUNCIATIONS: tamo, ho** **MEANINGS:** protect, guarantee, preserve **EXAMPLES:** 保つ tamotsu = to keep or maintain; 保証 hoshou = guarantee, assurance **DESCRIPTION:** compared to 呆(れる) akireru (to get astonished, # 828), this adds a man with a slanted hat on the left; it retains the big 口 (mouth), which can also be seen as a box, which Achilles saw boasting from a 木 (tree) **CUES:** this man gets 呆 (astonished) when he sees this big 口 (mouth) boasting from the top of this 木 (tree), and he jumps onto his **T**acky **M**otorcycle to ride **H**ome, but the bike doesn't work because he doesn't 保つ **tamo**tsu (maintain) it, so he tilts his hat back to inspect it **GROUP:** 呆(れる) akireru = to get astonished, # 828; 褒(める) homeru = to praise, # 829; 繰(り返す) kurikaesu = to repeat, # 1034; 操(作) sousa = operation (machine), # 1192; 保(証) hoshou = guarantee, # 1216; (担)架 tanka = a stretcher, # 1790; (乾)燥 kansou = dryness, # 1930; (海)藻 kaisou = seaweed, # 2008 **ALSO COMPARE:** other similar kanji at # **122**

1217. 商 (sometimes written 商) **PRONUNCIATIONS: akina, shou** **MEANINGS:** selling, merchant **EXAMPLES:** 商う akinau = to trade in or sell; 商い akinai = trade, business; 商品 shouhin = commodity, merchandise **DESCRIPTION:** at the top, the upper portion of 立(つ) tatsu (to stand, # 11), which resembles a bell; at the bottom, 四 yon (four, # 6), which resembles the floor plan of a house, missing its lower wall; inside the house, 口 kuchi (mouth, # 426), but this could represent a bed **CUES: A**chilles was taking a **N**ap in this 口 (bed) inside this three-walled 四 (house) when someone rang this 立 (bell) and tried to **S**how him some 商品 **shou**hin (merchandise) **ALSO COMPARE:** other similar kanji at # **987** and # **1569**

1218. 卸 **PRONUNCIATIONS: oro, oroshi** **MEANING:** wholesale **EXAMPLES:** 卸す orosu = to sell wholesale; 卸 oroshi = wholesale **DESCRIPTION:** at the upper left, the upper portion of 矢 ya (arrow, # 1045) which we have described as a Native American chief wearing a war bonnet; at the lower left, 正(しい) tadashii (correct, # 174); on the right, the seal seen in 印(鑑) inkan (signature seal, # 1046) **CUES:** this 矢 (Native American chief), who is always 正 (correct), put on an **O**ld **R**obe and walked along an **O**ceanside **R**oad with his **S**heepdog to a store where he bought this 印 (seal) for an 卸 **oroshi** (wholesale) price **ALSO COMPARE:** (制)御 seigyo = control, # **1440**; other similar kanji at # **1046**

1219. 築 **PRONUNCIATIONS: chiku, kizu, tsuki** **MEANINGS:** fabricate, construct **EXAMPLES:** 建築 kenchiku = architecture; 築く kizuku = to establish, build; 築地 tsukiji = reclaimed land, a district in Tokyo **DESCRIPTION:** at the top, 竹(林) chikurin

(bamboo grove, # 134) (identical pronunciation); in the middle, the katakana エ e and a desk with a slash across it, both of which are seen in 恐(れ) osore (fear, # 869); at the bottom, 木 moku (wood, # 118) **CUES:** a 建築家 ken**chiku**ka (architect) wants to 築く **kizu**ku (build) a structure from this 竹 (bamboo) and 木 (wood), but he's 恐 (afraid) of criticism, he drinks **C**heap **Ko**ol-Aid, and he left his **K**eys at the **Z**oo, including his **Ts**uitcase (suitcase) **K**eys
ALSO COMPARE: other similar kanji at # **247**, # **1352**, # **1511** and # **2074**

1220. 履 PRONUNCIATIONS: ha, ri
MEANINGS: footgear, put on (the feet)
EXAMPLES: 履く haku = to put on or wear lower body clothing or shoes; 草履 zouri = Japanese sandals **DESCRIPTION:** compared to (回)復 kaifuku (recovery, # 527), this adds a lean-to with a double roof at the upper left; it retains the therapist with a double hat, plus CSD = crutch, sun, dancer **CUES:** this lean-to with a double roof near the **H**arbor is a shoe store where this injured sunny dancer is pursuing 復 (recovery), and one **Rea**son she is making progress is that they are having her 履く h**a**ku (wear) orthopedic shoes (CSD = crutch, sun, dancer) **GROUP:** (回)復 kaifuku = recovery, # 527; (お)腹 onaka = stomach, # 863; 覆(う) oou = to cover, # 893; 履(く) haku = to put on shoes, # 1220; 複(雑) fukuzatsu = complicated, # 1281 **ALSO COMPARE:** other similar kanji at # **1899**

1221. 廃 PRONUNCIATIONS: suta, hai, pai
MEANINGS: abolish, abandon, obsolete
EXAMPLES: 廃れる sutareru = to become obsolete, to decline; 廃駅 haieki = abandoned station; 撤廃 teppai = abolition
DESCRIPTION: compared to (出)発 shuppatsu (departure, # 298), this adds a lean-to with a small chimney on the upper left; it retains the happy yodeler with lopsided legs, bench hats and a hole in his sock **CUES: Su**perman and **Ta**rzan were **Hi**ding in this lean-to near a 廃駅 **hai**eki (abandoned station) prior to their 発 (departure) and eating **Pie**s
GROUP: (出)発 shuppatsu = departure, # 298; 廃(れる) sutareru = to decline, # 1221
ALSO COMPARE: other similar kanji at # **297**

1222. 為 PRONUNCIATIONS: tame, i
MEANINGS: do, for, because **EXAMPLES:** 為に tame ni = in order to; 行為 koui = deed, action **DESCRIPTION:** protruding from the top, a pair of feathers, but these can also be seen as antennae; in the middle, a pyramid containing terraces, but this resembles the body of a bird; at the bottom, the five toes seen at the bottom of 鳥 tori (bird, # 555) **CUES:** this 鳥 (bird) lives above a **Ta**vern in Mexico, and it finds it **E**asy to do good 行為 ko**ui** (deeds), since it has these two feathers and these five toes, and it can arrange its body in a pyramidal shape like this **COMPARE:** other similar kanji at # **754**, # **1101** and # **1997**

1223. 羊 PRONUNCIATIONS: you, hitsuji
MEANING: sheep **EXAMPLES:** 羊毛 youmou = wool; 羊 hitsuji = sheep
DESCRIPTION: compared to 洋(服) youfuku (Western clothes, # 330) (identical pronunciation), this kanji omits the water radical on the left; it retains the sheep with a head, two horns, two ears which can also be seen as antennae, a body with four legs, and a tail; this can also be seen as an upside-down bench above a telephone pole **CUES:** when I'm trying to milk this 羊 **hitsuji** (sheep) for my **Y**ogurt business, it wags its tail and often **Hits** my **U**ber **Je**ep
GROUP: 洋(服) youfuku = Western clothes, # 330 (identical pronunciation); 遅(い) osoi = late, # 350; (新)鮮 shinsen = fresh, # 858; 群(れ) mure = herd, # 929; (発)祥 hasshou = origin, # 1160; 羊 hitsuji = sheep, # 1223; (改)善 kaizen = improvement, # 1336; 詳(しい) kuwashii = detailed, # 1579; (一)膳 ichizen = one bowl, # 1690; (修)繕 shuuzen = a repair, # 2037

1224. 逮 PRONUNCIATION: tai
MEANINGS: arrest, apprehension, capture
EXAMPLE: 逮捕 taiho = arrest, apprehension, capture **DESCRIPTION:** compared to (健)康 kenkou (health, # 831), this omits the lean-to with a chimney at the upper left and adds a snail on the lower left; it retains the trident that is piercing the upper portion of the axis of 水 (water) **CUE:** the man who has been stabbed with this trident is Tired and therefore has to ride on this snail, and he wants some 水 (water) like this, in addition to the 逮捕 **tai**ho (apprehension) of the responsible person **ALSO COMPARE:** similar kanji at # **1583**

1225. 柱 PRONUNCIATIONS: chuu, hashira
MEANINGS: pillar, post, cylinder
EXAMPLES: 電柱 denchuu = telephone pole or electricity pole; 柱 hashira = pillar, post, column **DESCRIPTION:** compared to 注(意) chuui (caution, # 168) (identical pronunciation), this kanji substitutes 木 ki (wood, # 118) for the water radical on the left; it retains 主 (master) **CUES:** this 主 (master) stands next to a 電柱 den**chuu** (telephone pole) made from this 木 (wood) and **Ch**ews gum as he smokes **Hashi**sh with his **R**adical friends **ALSO COMPARE:** similar kanji at # **166**

1226. 撃 PRONUNCIATIONS: geki, u
MEANINGS: beat, attack, defeat **EXAMPLES:** 突撃 totsugeki = assault, charge, attack; 撃つ utsu = to fire a gun **DESCRIPTION:** at the upper left, 車 kuruma (car, # 283); at the upper right, π (the Greek letter pi, also known as a pious yak) on 又 mata (a simple table, # 24); at the bottom, 手 te (hand, # 23) **CUES:** this 手 (hand) committed a 突撃 totsu**geki** (assault) on this π (pious yak) on this table and stole its **Gu**est **K**ey for this **U**ber 車 (car) **COMPARE:** other similar kanji at # **557**, # **1554** and # **1966**

1227. 塞 PRONUNCIATIONS: fusa, sai, soku
MEANINGS: close, block, obstruct
EXAMPLES: 塞ぐ fusagu = to stop up, close, obstruct, take up space; 要塞 yousai = fortress, fortification; 心筋梗塞 shinkinkousoku = heart attack **DESCRIPTION:** compared to 寒(い) samui (cold, # 507), which resembles a woman with a bad haircut wearing a corset, this substitutes 土 tsuchi (soil, # 59) for the children under the woman's skirt; **Note** that this "corset" differs from the "dome" seen in (子)供 kodomo (child, # 486), primarily because it contains three horizontal lines instead of two; in addition, the corset differs from the "bucket" seen in 基(盤) kiban (foundation, # 1198) in that its horizontal lines extend beyond the vertical lines on both sides (like corset laces) and also because it contains three horizontal lines instead of four **CUES:** a **F**oolish **Sa**laryman approached this woman with a bad haircut wearing a corset and asked about the **S**izes of the children hiding under her skirt, since this 土 (soil) 塞いだ **fusa**ida (obstructed) his view, but she got mad and **So**aked him with a pot of coffee
GROUP: 寒(い) samui = cold, # 507; 塞(ぐ) fusagu = to stop up, # 1227

1228. 麺 PRONUNCIATION: men
MEANINGS: noodles, wheat flour **EXAMPLE:** 素麺 soumen = fine white noodles
DESCRIPTION: on the left, 麦 mugi (barley or wheat, # 1103), which resembles a dancer carrying an owl's perch; on the right, (地)面 jimen (the surface of the earth, # 282) (identical pronunciation), which resembles a limousine with an antenna **CUE:** the **Men** driving this limousine with an antenna parked it on the leg of this dancer carrying this owl's perch, but she felt better after eating some 素麺 sou**men** (fine white noodles) **ALSO COMPARE:** other similar kanji at # **522** and # **1103**

1229. 稲 PRONUNCIATIONS: ine, ina, se
MEANING: rice plant **EXAMPLES:** 稲 ine = rice plant; お稲荷さん o'inarisan = the god of harvests and wealth; 早稲田 Waseda = a university in Shinjuku **DESCRIPTION:** on the left side, 禾 (a grain plant with a ripe head); at the upper right, a barbecue grate; at the lower right, 旧(正月) kyuu shougatsu (lunar New Year, # 1017)

CUES: when our 稲 **ine** (rice plants) get 禾 (ripe) like this, we grill them on barbecue grates like this one, which is an **In**expensive way although possibly **In**appropriate way to **C**elebrate 旧 (lunar New Year)   ALSO COMPARE: other similar kanji at # **1017**, # **1177** and # **1797**

1230. 郡   PRONUNCIATION: gun

MEANINGS: county, district   EXAMPLES: 郡 gun = county or district; 郡部 gunbu = rural districts   DESCRIPTION: compared to 群(衆) gunshuu (a group of people, # 929) (identical pronunciation), this kanji substitutes ß beta from the Greek alphabet for 羊 (sheep) on the right; it retains 君 (you)   CUE: 君 (you) told this ß (Greek) guy that he should buy a **G**un if he plans to live in this 郡 **gun** (county)   ALSO COMPARE: other similar kanji at # **419** and # **1843**

1231. 晶   PRONUNCIATION: shou

MEANINGS: crystal, crystallization   EXAMPLES: 晶 shou = crystal; 水晶 suishou = crystal   DESCRIPTION: compared to (合)唱 gasshou (chorus, # 1152) (identical pronunciation), this kanji omits the 口 (mouth) on the left and adds a 日 (sun) at the bottom; it retains the two existing 日 hi (suns)   CUE: these three 日 (suns) are evenly arranged like the atoms in a 水晶 sui**shou** (crystal), and they put on quite a **Sh**ow   ALSO COMPARE: similar kanji at # **352** and # **1152**

1232. 銅   PRONUNCIATION: dou

MEANING: copper   EXAMPLE: 銅 dou = copper   DESCRIPTION: compared to 同(情) doujou (sympathy, # 339) (identical pronunciation), or 同(じ) onaji (the same, # 339), this adds (お)金 okane (money, # 301) on the left   CUE: I paid this 金 (money) for a 銅 **dou** (copper) **D**oor knob which is 同 (the same) as the one you have   ALSO COMPARE: other similar kanji at # **1620** and # **2010**

1233. 栽   PRONUNCIATION: sai

MEANINGS: plantation, planting   EXAMPLES: 栽培 saibai = cultivation; 盆栽 bonsai = miniature potted plant   DESCRIPTION: at the upper left, 土 tsuchi (soil, # 59); at the lower left, 木 ki (tree, # 118); on the right, a halberd (combination lance and axe)   CUE: after a **S**cientist buys a 盆栽 bon**sai** (potted plant), she uses this halberd to dig up this 土 (soil) near this 木 (tree) in order to add it to the pot   ALSO COMPARE: similar kanji at # **1352** and # **1862**

1234. 培   PRONUNCIATIONS: bai, tsuchika

MEANINGS: cultivate, foster   EXAMPLES: 栽培 saibai = cultivation; 培う tsuchikau = to nourish, cultivate   DESCRIPTION: compared to 倍(増する) baizou suru (to double, # 269) (identical pronunciation), this kanji substitutes 土 tsuchi (soil, # 59) (a similar pronunciation), for the man with a slanted hat on the left; it retains the 立 (bell) on a 口 (box)   CUES: after someone **B**uys this 立 (bell) on a 口 (box) that I'm selling, I'll use the money to start a 栽培 sai**bai** (cultivation) business, which will use this 土 **T**suchi (soil) for growing **C**abbages   ALSO COMPARE: other similar kanji at # **269**

1235. 専   PRONUNCIATIONS: sen, moppa

MEANINGS: specialty, exclusive   EXAMPLES: 専門 senmon = specialty; 専ら moppara = exclusively, chiefly   DESCRIPTION: compared to 恵む megumu (to bless, # 720), this substitutes 寸(前) sunzen (on the verge, # 1369), which depicts a kneeling sunny guy who has dropped his gum, for 心 (heart) at the bottom; it retains 十 (ten) above the 田 (rice paddy)   CUES: a **Sen**ator with a 専門 **sen**mon (specialty) in transportation went to this 田 (rice paddy) with 十 (ten) of his **M**otorcycle **P**als and met this 寸 (kneeling sunny guy who had dropped his gum)   ALSO COMPARE: similar kanji at # **720** and # **1721**

1236. 磁 PRONUNCIATION: ji
MEANINGS: magnet, porcelain EXAMPLE: 磁石 jishaku = magnet DESCRIPTION: on the left, 石 ishi (stone, # 458); at the upper right, an upside-down bench; at the lower right, these resemble the upper halves of two 糸 (skeet shooters, # 219), each consisting of two flexed elbows CUE: these two truncated 糸 (skeet shooters) were carrying this upside-down bench to their **Jee**p when they tripped on this 石 (stone) and discovered that it was a 磁石 **ji**shaku (magnet)
GROUP: 前 mae = before, # 157; 揃(う) sorou = to be complete, # 644; 煎(じる) senjiru = to boil, # 650; 磁石 jishaku = magnet, # 1236; (改)善 kaizen = improvement, # 1336; (利)益 rieki = profit, # 1407; 慈(善) jizen = charity, # 1451; (一)膳 ichizen = one bowl, # 1690; 滋(養) jiyou = nourishment, # 1908; (修)繕 shuuzen = a repair, # 2037; Note that three of these kanji can be pronounced "ji" ALSO COMPARE: other similar kanji at # **1775** and # **1908**

1237. 舗 PRONUNCIATIONS: po, ho
MEANINGS: shop, store EXAMPLES: 店舗 tenpo = shop, store; 舗装 hosou = pavement
DESCRIPTION: compared to 補(佐) hosa (aid, # 995) (identical pronunciation), this kanji substitutes (田)舎 inaka (hometown, # 745), which resembles a shabby house containing 土 (soil) and a 口 (box), for happy Jimmy on the left; it retains the upper portion of 犬 (dog) above 用 (fence) (see # 364) CUES: although our town contains many 舎 (shabby houses) containing 土 (soil) and 口 (boxes) like this, we use **P**olice, truncated 犬 (dogs) like this and 用 (fences) like this to protect our **H**omes and 店舗 ten**po** (stores)
ALSO COMPARE: other kanji with the upper portion of 犬 (dog) on a 用 (fence) at # **995**; kanji containing マ (mammoth) on 用 (fence) at # 1143; other similar kanji at # **745**

1238. 欠 PRONUNCIATIONS: ka, ke, ketsu, ga MEANINGS: lack, gap, fail
EXAMPLES: 欠く kaku = to lack; 欠ける kakeru = to lack, to be chipped; 欠席 kesseki = absence; 不可欠 fukaketsu = indispensable; 身欠き migaki = the process of removing poison from fugu fish DESCRIPTION: at the top, an h-shaped chair that is leaning to the right and, at the bottom, 人 hito (person, # 13); taken together, these resemble an oil derrick
CUES: this oil derrick belongs to a **Ca**tholic who wears **Ke**ds (a brand of shoes), puts **Ke**tchup in his Soup and owns a **Ga**s station, but now people are concerned about his 欠席 **ke**sseki (absence)
ALSO COMPARE: 次(に) tsugi ni = next, # 536; other similar kanji at # **13** and # **536**

1239. 炊 PRONUNCIATIONS: ta, sui
MEANINGS: cook, boil EXAMPLES: 炊く taku = to cook (rice, etc.); 雑炊 zousui = rice gruel with fish, vegetables, etc.
DESCRIPTION: on the left, 火(事) kaji (fire, # 443); on the right, 欠(席) kesseki (absence, # 1238), which resembles an oil derrick
CUES: when **T**arzan visited **Swe**den, he tried to 炊く **ta**ku (cook) some rice next to this 欠 (oil derrick) and accidentally started this 火 (fire)
GROUP: 火(事) kaji = fire, # 443; 灰 hai = ash, # 444; 秋 aki = autumn, # 445; 焼(く) yaku = to grill, # 446; (街)灯 gaitou = street light, # 626; (肺)炎 haien = pneumonia, # 788; (相)談 soudan = consultation, # 790; 畑 hatake = field, # 889; (火)災 kasai = fire, # 1019; 爆(弾) bakudan = bomb, # 1022; 焚(く) taku = to burn, # 1183; (絶)滅 zetsumetsu = extinction, # 1193; 炊(く) taku = to cook, # 1239; 燃(える) moeru = to burn, # 1240; 炭 sumi = charcoal, # 1385; 煙 kemuri = smoke, # 1415; 淡(い) awai = faint, # 1654; 炉 ro = a fireplace, # 1758; (郷)愁 kyoushuu = nostalgia, # 1785; (乾)燥 kansou

= dryness, # 1930; 煩(う) wazurau = to worry about, # 2007 **ALSO COMPARE:** other similar kanji at # **536**

1240. 燃 PRONUNCIATIONS: nen, mo

MEANINGS: burn, blaze, glow **EXAMPLES:** 燃料 nenryou = fuel; 燃える moeru = to burn, intransitive; 燃やす moyasu = to burn, transitive **DESCRIPTION:** compared to (天)然 tennen (natural, # 611) (identical pronunciation), this kanji adds 火(事) kaji (fire, # 443) on the left; it retains the rocker bottom bench and another fire near which a negative nephew plays with a 犬 (dog) **CUES:** I have a **N**egative **N**ephew who sits on this rocker bottom bench with this 犬 (dog) and **M**oses, and they watch 火 (fires) like this one on the left and this other fire with four tongues of flame at the bottom 燃える **mo**eru (burn) because they say they are 然 (natural) **ALSO COMPARE:** other similar kanji at # **377**, # **611**, # **945** and # **1239**

1241. 液 PRONUNCIATION: eki

MEANINGS: fluid, liquid, juice **EXAMPLES:** 液体 ekitai = liquid; 血液 ketsueki = blood **DESCRIPTION:** compared to 夜 yoru (night, # 489), this adds a water radical on the left; it retains the man with a slanted hat eating yogurt near a dancer with a mark on her cheek, which can also be seen as a yoke, under a roof at night **CUE:** when I visited an **E**ki (station) during this 夜 (night), I saw 液体 **eki**tai (liquid) on the floor, but it was only this water **ALSO COMPARE:** other similar kanji at # **489** and # **1860**

1242. 診 PRONUNCIATIONS: shin, mi

MEANINGS: checkup, seeing, diagnose **EXAMPLES:** 診察 shinsatsu = medical examination; 診断 shindan = diagnosis; 診てもらう mite morau = to consult a doctor **DESCRIPTION:** on the left, 言(う) iu (to speak, # 430); on the right, a rocker-bottom shoe, resembling the one seen in 参(る) mairu (to humbly go, # 406) **CUES:** a **Shin**to priest 参 (humbly goes) for a 診察 **shin**satsu (medical examination), and the doctor 言 (speaks) to suggest that he look in the **Mi**rror to see how he looks in this rocker-bottom shoe **ALSO COMPARE:** other similar kanji at # **406** and # **1382**

1243. 几 PRONUNCIATION: ki

MEANING: table **EXAMPLES:** 几帳面 kichoumen = scrupulous, meticulous **DESCRIPTION:** this is a desk, as seen in 机 tsukue (desk, # 140); it can be seen as a taller version of the pious yak seen in 役(に立つ) yaku ni tatsu (to be useful, # 557) **CUE:** I am 几帳面 **ki**choumen (scrupulous) about storing my **K**eys in this 机 (desk) **ALSO COMPARE:** similar kanji at # **1462**

1244. 帳 PRONUNCIATION: chou

MEANINGS: notebook, album **EXAMPLES:** 手帳 techou = pocket notebook; 几帳面 kichoumen = scrupulous, meticulous **DESCRIPTION:** compared to 長(時間) choujiikan (a long time, # 502) (identical pronunciation), this adds 巾 (Bo Peep), as seen in 帽(子) boushi (hat, # 243) on the left **CUE:** this 巾 (Bo Peep) bought a 手帳 te**chou** (pocket notebook) for Margaret **Cho** a 長 (long) time ago **ALSO COMPARE:** other similar kanji at # **398**, # **502** and # **1768**

1245. 鈍 PRONUNCIATIONS: nibu, don
MEANINGS: dull, blunt, slow, foolish
EXAMPLES: 鈍い nibui = dull, dim-witted; 鈍感な donkan na = insensitive
DESCRIPTION: compared to (単)純 tanjun (simple, # 761), this substitutes 金 kane (money, # 301) for the 糸 (skeet shooter) on the left; it retains 七 nana (seven) with the letter U superimposed on it, which reminds us of the seven Universal Laws of the jungle
CUES: if you think that spending this 金 (money) on **K**nee-high **B**oots and a **D**onkey before your trip can substitute for knowledge of these 七 (seven) Universal Laws, you are 鈍い **nibu**i (dim-witted)
GROUP: (単)純 tanjun = simple, # 761; 逆(の) gyaku no = contrary, # 894; 鈍(い) nibui = dull, # 1245; (整)頓 seiton = orderliness, # 1248; (駐)屯 chuuton = stationing (troops), # 2028
ALSO COMPARE: other similar kanji at # **2010**

1246. 堅 PRONUNCIATIONS: ken, kata
MEANINGS: strict, hard, tough, reliable
EXAMPLES: 中堅 chuuken = mainstay, nucleus, main body, center field (baseball); 堅い katai = hard, solid, strong, obstinate (this can also be spelled 固い, # 731 [the most common spelling], or 硬い, # 1412); 堅苦しい katakurushii = overly formal, stiff, rigid
DESCRIPTION: compared to 緊(張) kinchou (tension, # 732), this substitutes 土 tsuchi (soil, # 59) for 糸 (skeet shooter) at the bottom; it retains the inoperable swing set and the table
CUES: since this inoperable swing set and table are 堅い **kata**i (strong), **Ken** and **B**arbie **Ca**tapulted them onto this pile of 土 (soil), and they sustained no damage
GROUP: 巨(大) kyodai = huge, # 689; 距(離) kyori = distance, # 717; 緊(張) kinchou = tension, # 732; (心)臓 shinzou = the heart, # 951; 臣(民) shinmin = royal subject, # 1039; 姫 hime = princess, # 1040; (冷)蔵(庫) reizouko = refrigerator, # 1190; (中)堅 chuuken = nucleus, # 1246; 賢(い) kashikoi = intelligent, # 1290; 臨(時) rinji = temporary, # 1515; 拒(否) kyohi = rejection, # 1646; 腎(臓) jinzou = kidneys, # 1991
ALSO COMPARE: other similar kanji at # **1894**

1247. 整 PRONUNCIATIONS: sei, totono
MEANINGS: be ready or prepared
EXAMPLES: 整理する seiri suru = to arrange, put in order; 整う totonou = to be ready or in order; 整える totonoeru = to put in order, prepare
DESCRIPTION: at the upper left, (約)束 yakusoku (promise, # 99); at the upper right, a dancer with a ponytail; at the bottom, 正(しい) tadashii (correct, # 174)
CUES: this dancer made this 束 (promise) to help **T**olstoy 整う **totono**u (be ready) for winter, which was the 正 (correct) thing to do, since she **S**aved **T**olstoy's **T**oes and **N**ose from frostbite
ALSO COMPARE: other similar kanji at # **175** and # **1806**

1248. 頓 PRONUNCIATION: ton
MEANINGS: suddenly, immediately, in a hurry
EXAMPLE: 整頓 seiton = orderliness
DESCRIPTION: on the left, 七 nana (seven) intersecting the letter U, which reminds us of the seven Universal Laws of the jungle, as seen in (単)純 tanjun (simple, # 761); on the right, 貝 kai (money chest, # 83) with a platform mounted on top, where a head could fit, as seen in 頭 atama (head, # 93)
CUE: **T**ony Blair pursued 整頓 sei**ton** (orderliness) and followed these 七 (seven) Universal Laws, but he still lost his 頭 (head), as suggested by this headless platform
ALSO COMPARE: other similar kanji at # **1126** and # **1245**

1249. 況 PRONUNCIATION: kyou
MEANINGS: condition, situation
EXAMPLES: 盛況 seikyou = success, prosperity; 状況 joukyou = circumstance, state

DESCRIPTION: compared to 兄 ani (older brother, # 420), or 兄(弟) kyoudai (siblings, # 420) (identical pronunciation), this kanji adds a water radical on the left
CUE: my 兄 (older brother) sells this water in **Kyou**to and has achieved 盛況 sei**kyou** (success) ALSO COMPARE: (光)沢 koutaku = luster, # 1100; other similar kanji at # **420**

1250. 層 PRONUNCIATION: sou

MEANINGS: stratum, social class, layer, story
EXAMPLES: 高層 kousou = multi-storied, high-rise; 断層 dansou = fault, discrepancy, gap
DESCRIPTION: compared to (倍)増(する) baizou suru (to double, # 61), this omits 土 (soil) on the left and adds a lean-to with a double roof at the upper left; it retains the 田 (rice paddy) above a 日 hi (sun), with two units of rice at the top
CUE: this double roof on this lean-to above this 田 (rice paddy) that produces these two units of rice could support a 高層 kou**sou** (multi-storied) structure, including **So**lar panels that use the light from this 日 (sun) ALSO COMPARE: other similar kanji at # **61** and # **1899**

1251. 塔 PRONUNCIATION: tou

MEANINGS: pagoda, tower EXAMPLE: 塔 tou = pagoda, tower DESCRIPTION: on the left, 土 tsuchi (soil, # 59); at the upper right, a plant radical; at the lower right, 合(う) au (to match, # 294), which resembles a house with a ceiling and a peaked roof CUE: some **To**ads live in this house with a ceiling and a peaked roof which resembles a small 塔 **tou** (tower), and they are sheltered by these plants and this 土 (soil), which 合 (match) their needs GROUP: (具)合 guai = condition, # 294; 答(える) kotaeru = to reply, # 295; 拾(う) hirou = to pick up, # 595; (田)舎 inaka = hometown, # 745; 命 inochi = life, # 961; 給(料) kyuuryou = salary, # 997; 塔 tou = pagoda, # 1251; 搭(乗) toujou = boarding, # 1931; (比)喩 hiyu = a simile, # 2021

1252. 玄 PRONUNCIATIONS: kurou, gen

MEANINGS: mysterious, occult, profound
EXAMPLE: 玄人 kurouto = expert, professional; 玄関 genkan = entranceway DESCRIPTION: compared to 眩(しい) mabushii (dazzling, # 937), this omits the 目 (eye) on the left; it retains the truncated skeet shooter under a tire stop
CUES: while walking on a **Ku**waiti **Roa**d, I saw this truncated 糸 (skeet shooter) carry this tire stop into the 玄関 **gen**kan (entranceway) of a house belonging to **Gen**ghis ALSO COMPARE: other similar kanji at # **1129** and # **1860**

1253. 透 PRONUNCIATIONS: su, tou

MEANINGS: transparent, permeate
EXAMPLES: 透き通った sukitootta = transparent, clear; 透明 toumei = transparent, clean DESCRIPTION: at the lower left, a snail; on the snail, at the top, 禾 (a grain plant with a ripe head); below that, a graph, similar to the one seen in 吸(う) suu (to suck, # 427) (identical pronunciation), which reminds us of a cute baby named **Su**e
CUES: this snail is carrying this 禾 (ripe grain), plus a baby named **Su**e, to **To**ronto, but it's slow, and this graph makes it 透き通った **su**kitootta (clear) that the baby is having breathing problems and may not survive the trip ALSO COMPARE: other similar kanji at # **1131** and # **2055**

1254. 蜂 PRONUNCIATION: hachi

MEANINGS: bee, wasp, hornet EXAMPLES: 蜂 hachi = bee; 蜂蜜 hachimitsu = honey
DESCRIPTION: compared to 峰 mine (mountain peak, # 938), this substitutes 虫 mushi (insect, # 9) for 山 (mountain) on the left; it retains the dancer with a ponytail and the telephone pole in Minnesota
CUE: when this dancer climbed this telephone pole to inspect this 虫 (insect), she saw some 蜂 **hachi** (bees) that were just **Hatch**ing ALSO COMPARE: other similar kanji at # **938** and # **1754**

1255. 蜜 **PRONUNCIATION: mitsu**
MEANINGS: honey, nectar **EXAMPLE:** 蜂蜜 hachimitsu = honey **DESCRIPTION:** compared to (秘)密 himitsu (a secret, # 1188) (identical pronunciation), this kanji substitutes 虫 mushi (insect, # 9) for 山 (mountain) at the bottom; it retains the bad haircut and 必 (necessary) **CUE:** a bee is an 虫 (insect) like this that is busy making 蜂蜜 hachi**mitsu** (honey) and, as a result, it's 必 (necessary) for it to skip trips to the barber, so when it **M**eets yo**U**, don't be surprised to see a bad haircut like this **ALSO COMPARE:** other similar kanji at # **1188**, # **1297** and # **1754**

1256. 域 **PRONUNCIATION: iki**
MEANINGS: range, limits, region, stage, level **EXAMPLE:** 地域 chiiki = region, area **DESCRIPTION:** compared to (迷)惑 meiwaku (annoyance, # 624), this adds 土 tsuchi (soil, # 59) on the left and removes 心 (heart) from the bottom; it retains the window with the lower frame reinforced by tape and the halberd on the right **CUE:** an **E**astern **K**ing set up a fortress with this reinforced box (or window) on this pile of 土 (soil) in a certain 地域 chi**iki** (region), and it's guarded by halberds like this **GROUP:** (迷)惑 meiwaku = trouble, # 624; (地)域 chiiki = region, # 1256 **ALSO COMPARE:** other similar kanji at # **1862**

1257. 穫 **PRONUNCIATION: kaku**
MEANINGS: harvest, reap **EXAMPLE:** 収穫 shuukaku = harvest, crop **DESCRIPTION:** compared to 獲(得する) kakutoku suru (to obtain, # 947) (identical pronunciation), this substitutes 禾 (a grain plant with a ripe head) for the contorted woman on the left; it retains the plant guarding a net, which can be seen as a man with a slanted hat next to a 主 (master) with an extra pair of arms (see # 203), on a 又 (table) **CUE:** after the 収穫 shuu**kaku** (harvest), **K**arl the **K**ool-Aid vendor, who is also in the storage business, stores this 禾 (ripe grain) in this net on this 又 (table), under these plants **ALSO COMPARE:** other similar kanji at # **947** and # **1797**

1258. 損 **PRONUNCIATIONS: son, soko, sokona** **MEANINGS:** damage, loss, disadvantage **EXAMPLES:** 損害 songai = harm, loss; 損なう sokonau (also spelled 損う) = to injure, mar or spoil or (if used as a suffix) to fail to do something **DESCRIPTION:** compared to (社)員 shain (company employee, # 88), this adds a kneeling guy on the left **CUES:** this guy on the left is kneeling to beg this **Son**y 員 (employee) to identify a **S**oviet **C**oder who **S**old **C**odes to the Nazis, causing 損害 **son**gai (harm) **ALSO COMPARE:** other similar kanji at # **88**

1259. 預 **PRONUNCIATIONS: azu, yo**
MEANINGS: deposit, custody, leave to **EXAMPLES:** 預かる azukaru = to keep, be in charge of, take care of; 預金 yokin = bank deposit **DESCRIPTION:** on the left, 予(定) yotei (plan, # 544) (identical pronunciation), which depicts a マ (mother) balancing on a nail before a yoga class; on the right, 貝 kai (money chest, # 83) with a platform at the top where a head could fit, as seen in 頭 atama (head, # 93) **CUES:** after she lost her 頭 (head), this マ (mother) was still able to balance on this nail, but she was living off her 預金 **yo**kin (bank deposits) and feeling **Az**ul (blue, in Spanish) until she started a **Y**oga class **ALSO COMPARE:** other similar kanji at # **544** and # **1126**

1260. 害 **PRONUNCIATION: gai**
MEANINGS: harm, injury **EXAMPLES:** 被害 higai = damage, loss; 損害 songai = harm, loss **DESCRIPTION:** compared to 割(る) waru (to break, # 562), this omits the warrior リ Ri on the right; it retains the bad haircut, the owl's perch, and the 口 (box) **CUES:** we hired a man with a bad haircut like this to install this owl's perch on this 口 (box), but he didn't install the **G**uy wires properly,

and it sustained 被害 hi**gai** (damage) when the wind blew   **GROUP:** 割(る) **waru** = to break, # 562; (被害) **higai** = damage, # 1260; 憲(法) **kenpou** = a constitution, # 1438; (管)轄 **kankatsu** = jurisdiction, # 1966   **ALSO COMPARE:** other similar kanji at # **1103**

1261. 導   **PRONUNCIATIONS: dou,**
michibi   **MEANINGS:** guidance, leading, usher
EXAMPLES: 指導 **shidou** = guidance, coaching; 導く **michibiku** = to guide, direct, lead
DESCRIPTION: at the top, 道(路) **douro** (road, # 349) or 道 **michi** (street, # 349), both of which help us to pronounce this; at the bottom, 寸(法) **sunpou** (measurement, # 1369), which resembles a kneeling sunny guy who is about to pick up some gum   **CUES:** when I was looking for my **D**ormitory on this 道 (street) in **Michi**gan that leads to a **B**ea**ch**, I saw this 寸 (kneeling sunny guy picking up some gum) and asked him for 指導 shi**dou** (guidance)   **ALSO COMPARE:** other similar kanji at # **131** and # **349**

1262. 熊   **PRONUNCIATION: kuma**
MEANING: bear   **EXAMPLE:** 熊 **kuma** = bear
DESCRIPTION: compared to 態(度) **taido** (attitude, # 960), this substitutes a hot fire for 心 (heart) at the bottom; it retains 能(力) **nouryoku** (ability, # 616), which depicts a ム (cow) on the 月 (moon) and two ヒ (heroes)   **CUE:** a 熊 **kuma** (bear) is at a **Ku**waiti **Ma**ll trying to escape from this fire, and this ム (cow) on this 月 (moon) plus these two ヒ (heroes) will try to help it
ALSO COMPARE: other similar kanji at # **611**, # **616** and # **1194**

1263. 栄   **PRONUNCIATIONS: ei, ba,**
saka, ha   **MEANINGS:** flourish, prosperity, honor
EXAMPLES: 栄養 **eiyou** = nutrition; 繁栄 **han'ei** = prosperity; 見栄え **mibae** = pretensions, ostentation, appearance; 栄える **sakaeru** = to prosper or thrive; 栄える **haeru** = to look attractive (this is usually spelled 映える, # 36)
DESCRIPTION: compared to 覚(える) **oboeru** (to memorize, # 54), this substitutes 木 **ki** (tree, # 118) for 見 (to look) at the bottom; it retains the three old boys on a platform   **CUES:** these three old boys have set up this platform at the top of this 木 (tree), from which they can watch **A**pes kick **B**alls as they play **Sakka**a (soccer) near the **H**arbor, and they 栄えている **saka**ete iru (are thriving)
ALSO COMPARE: similar kanji at # **991** and # **1352**

1264. 養   **PRONUNCIATIONS: you,**
yashina   **MEANINGS:** foster, develop, nurture
EXAMPLES: 栄養 **eiyou** = nutrition; 養う **yashinau** = to feed, nourish, support, cultivate
DESCRIPTION: at the top, a truncated 羊 **hitsuji** (sheep, # 1223), or 羊(毛) **youmou** (wool, # 1223) (identical pronunciation), missing its tail [this can also be seen as 王 **ou** (king, # 1077), wearing rabbit ears]; at the bottom, 食(べる) **taberu** (to eat, # 398)   **CUES:** I 養っている **yashina**tte iru (am supporting) this abbreviated 羊 (sheep) that produces milk for making **Y**ogurt, and it 食 (eats) well, but some of the **Y**ankee **Sh**eep are **N**asty to it   **ALSO COMPARE:** other similar kanji at # **398**, # **1893** and # **1974**

1265. 頻   **PRONUNCIATION: hin**
MEANINGS: repeatedly, recur   **EXAMPLE:** 頻繁 **hinpan** = frequent, incessant
DESCRIPTION: on the left, 歩(く) **aruku** (to walk, # 408); on the right, 貝 **kai** (money chest, # 83) with a platform at the top where a head could fit, as seen in 頭 **atama** (head, # 93)   **CUE:** a **H**indu man takes 頻繁 **hin**pan (frequent) 歩 (walks) to check this platform in order to see whether or not his 頭 (head) has reappeared
ALSO COMPARE: similar kanji at # **1010**, # **1126** and # **1929**

1266. 繁
PRONUNCIATIONS: han, pan, shige **MEANINGS:** luxuriant, overgrown, frequency, complexity **EXAMPLES:** 繁栄 han'ei = prosperity; 頻繁 hinpan = frequent, incessant; 繁る shigeru = to grow luxuriantly (茂る shigeru, # 1186, is the more common spelling) **DESCRIPTION:** at the upper left, 每 mai (every, # 336); at the upper right, a dancer with a ponytail; at the bottom, 糸 (skeet shooter, # 219) **CUES:** this 糸 (skeet shooter) juggles this dancer 毎 (every) day for **Han**sel, who enjoys 繁栄 **han**'ei (prosperity) and owns a **Pan**da and some **She**ep at **Ge**ttysburg **GROUP:** 素(晴らしい) subarashii = wonderful, # 712; 緊(張) kinchou = tension, # 732; (清)潔 seiketsu = clean, # 1212; (頻)繁 hinpan = frequent, # 1266; 索(引) sakuin = index, # 1361; 紫 murasaki = purple, # 1665; 累(積) ruiseki = an accumulation, # 2006 **ALSO COMPARE:** other similar kanji at # **336** and # **2080**

1267. 源
PRONUNCIATIONS: gen, minamoto **MEANINGS:** source, origin **EXAMPLES:** 資源 shigen = resources; 起源 kigen = origin; 源 minamoto = origin, source **DESCRIPTION:** compared to 原(因) gen'in (cause, # 888) (identical pronunciation), this kanji adds a water radical on the left; it retains the 小 (small) 白 (white) spinning oven in a one-sided lean-to; this can also be seen as a sun above small (ignoring the ray above the sun) **CUES: Gen**ghis placed this 小 (small) 白 (white) spinning oven in this lean-to where he also kept his **Mina**sota (Minnesota) **Mot**orcycle, but the lean-to leaked this water, and that was the 源 **minamoto** (origin) of some of his problems **ALSO COMPARE:** other similar kanji at # **94** and # **888**

1268. 噴
PRONUNCIATION: fun **MEANINGS:** erupt, spout, emit **EXAMPLES:** 噴水 funsui = a water fountain; 噴火 funka = a volcanic eruption **DESCRIPTION:** on the left, 口 kuchi (mouth, # 426), which can also be seen as a box; at the upper right, a triple plant radical, which can also be seen as bushes; at the lower right, 貝 kai (money chest, # 83) **CUE:** this 口 (mouth) of a 噴水 **fun**sui (water fountain) is watering these bushes, and it's **Fun**ny that this 貝 (money chest) is also getting wet **GROUP:** 焼(く) yaku = to grill, # 446; 噴(水) funsui = a water fountain, # 1268; 憤(慨する) fungai suru = to be indignant, # 1781; 暁 akatsuki = daybreak, # 1855; (古)墳 kofun = an ancient tomb, # 1897 **ALSO COMPARE:** other similar kanji at # **1897** and # **2073**

1269. 購
PRONUNCIATION: kou **MEANINGS:** subscription, buy **EXAMPLE:** 購入する kounyuu suru = to purchase **DESCRIPTION:** compared to (結)構 kekkou (fine, # 141) (identical pronunciation), this kanji substitutes 貝 kai (money chest, # 83) for the 木 (wood) on the left; it retains the courthouse with a 井 (well) and a 再 (model of a rice paddy with a handle) in the lobby **CUES:** I took money from this 貝 (money chest) to a store near this **Cou**rthouse with this 井 (well) and this 再 (model of a rice paddy with a handle) and used it to 購入する **kou**nyuu suru (buy) some items **ALSO COMPARE:** other similar kanji at # **1032**, # **1825** and # **2058**

1270. 礁
PRONUNCIATION: shou **MEANINGS:** reef, sunken rock **EXAMPLE:** 岩礁 ganshou = reef **DESCRIPTION:** on the left, 石 seki (stone, # 458); on the right, 焦(点) shouten (focus, # 750) (identical pronunciation), which resembles a net that can be seen as a man with a slanted hat next to a master with an extra pair of arms (see # 203), suspended above a fire **CUE:** while exiting this net suspended over this fire, I tripped on this 石 (stone) and hurt my **Sho**ulder on a 岩礁 gan**shou** (reef) **ALSO COMPARE:** other similar kanji at # **611**, # **1775** and # **2046**

1271. 棟 **PRONUNCIATIONS: tou, mune**
MEANINGS: ridgepole, ridge, a counter for large buildings **EXAMPLES:** 病棟 byoutou = hospital ward; 別棟 betsumune = separate building, outbuilding **DESCRIPTION:** on the left, 木 ki (tree, # 118); on the right, 東(洋) touyou (the east, # 508) (identical pronunciation), which can be seen as a tree wearing bifocals **CUES:** I saw some **To**ads from the 東 (east) in this 木 (tree) outside a 病棟 byou**tou** (hospital ward), but the **Moon E**xpert whom I told wasn't interested **GROUP:** 練(習) renshuu = practice, # 229; 東 higashi = east, # 508; (病)棟 byoutou = hospital ward, # 1271; 欄 ran = column, # 1470; 凍(る) kooru = to freeze, # 1707; 陳(述) chinjutsu = a statement, # 1742; (鍛)錬(する) tanren suru = to train, # 1814; 蘭 ran = an orchid, # 2088
ALSO COMPARE: other similar kanji at # **128**

1272. 略 **PRONUNCIATION: ryaku**
MEANINGS: abbreviation, omission
EXAMPLES: 略 ryaku = an abbreviation or omission; 前略 zenryaku = a salutation in a letter indicating that the writer is dispensing with formalities; 省略 shouryaku = abbreviation, omission **DESCRIPTION:** on the left, 田 (rice paddy, # 68); on the right, 各(駅) kakueki (each station, # 1033), which features a dancer jumping over a box **CUE:** this dancer left this 田 (rice paddy) and jumped over this 口 (box), intending to dance from **Ri**yadh to **Ku**wait, but she 省略した shou**ryaku** shita (omitted) her lunch when she packed her bag **ALSO COMPARE:** other similar kanji at # **220** and # **1033**

1273. 葬 **PRONUNCIATIONS: houmu, sou MEANINGS:** internment, bury, shelve
EXAMPLES: 葬る houmuru = to bury or suppress; 葬式 soushiki = funeral
DESCRIPTION: at the top, a plant radical; in the middle, 死(ぬ) shinu (to die, # 164); at the bottom, legs with a welcoming or open stance, as seen in 開(ける) akeru (to open, # 413), which resemble the letter H and remind us of Homer **CUES:** when this H (**Ho**mer) went to the **Mo**on, the rocket exploded and he 死 (died), so that they had to 葬る **houmu**ru (bury) him under these plants, but the angels 開 (welcomed) his **Sou**l to Heaven **ALSO COMPARE:** other similar kanji at # **164**, # **1924** and # **2048**

1274. 壷 (sometimes written 壺)
PRONUNCIATION: tsubo MEANINGS: jar, pot **EXAMPLES:** 壷 tsubo = jar, pot, urn (usually spelled つぼ); 骨壷 kotsutsubo = funerary urn **DESCRIPTION:** at the top, 士 shi (man, # 66); at the bottom, 亜 (the Red Cross logo), as seen in 悪(い) warui (bad, # 313), with modifications to the edges of the upper platform; this logo can also be seen as five jars of air strapped together in a frame to form a flotation device **CUE:** this 士 (man) took his **Tsu**itcase (suitcase) onto a **Bo**at supported by five 壷 **tsubo** (jars) of air strapped together in a frame like this, and he had to be rescued by this 亜 (Red Cross) **ALSO COMPARE:** other similar kanji at # **313**, # **1415** and # **1468**

1275. 墓 **PRONUNCIATIONS: bo, haka**
MEANINGS: grave, tomb **EXAMPLES:** 墓地 bochi = cemetery, graveyard, churchyard; 墓 haka = gravestone, graveyard, tomb
DESCRIPTION: compared to (お歳)暮 oseibo (year-end gift, # 641) (identical pronunciation), this kanji retains the upper sun which is 大 (big) and shines on plants like these (this combination of radicals = PSB = plants, sun, big); it substitutes 土 tsuchi (soil, # 59) for the second 日 (sun) at the bottom **CUES:** this 日 (sun) is 大 (big), it shines light on these plants, and it's **Bo**ring, but it sponsors **Hacka**thons that are held in this 土 (dirt) in 墓地 **bo**chi (graveyards) (PSB = plants, sun, big)
ALSO COMPARE: other similar kanji at # **1353**

1276. 管 PRONUNCIATIONS: kuda, kan
MEANINGS: tube, pipe, wind instrument
EXAMPLES: 管 kuda = tube, pipe; 管理 kanri = supervision, administration, management
DESCRIPTION: compared to (警)官 keikan (policeman, # 880) (identical pronunciation), this kanji adds 竹 take (bamboo, # 134) at the top; it retains the bad haircut which caused the Canadian policeman to retreat to this bunk bed
CUES: this 官 (policeman) is a **C**ool **Da**d who makes **C**andles using 竹 (bamboo) 管 **kuda** (pipes) as molds
ALSO COMPARE: other similar kanji at # **880** and # **2074**

1277. 鉢 PRONUNCIATIONS: hachi, bachi² MEANINGS: bowl, pot EXAMPLES: 鉢 hachi = bowl, flower pot; 植木鉢 uekibachi = a flower pot DESCRIPTION: on the left, (お)金 okane (money, # 301); on the right, 本 hon (book, # 123)
CUES: since this 本 (book) recommends 鉢 **hachi** (flower pots), I paid 金 (money) for one, but my hen is **Hatch**ing eggs in it
ALSO COMPARE: other similar kanji at # **123** and # **2010**

1278. 植 PRONUNCIATIONS: u, ue, shoku MEANING: to plant EXAMPLES: 田植え taue = rice planting; 植える ueru = to plant, grow, raise; 植木 ueki = a garden plant or tree, a potted plant; 植物 shokubutsu = plant, vegetation DESCRIPTION: compared to 直(す) naosu (to repair or correct, # 570), this adds 木 ki (tree, # 118) on the left; it retains the 目 (eye), which can be seen as a three-drawer cabinet, with a thin handle, on a shelf, used by Naomi to correct her storage problems CUES: an **U**gandan **Ue**itaa (waiter) planted this 木 (tree), but he had to 直 (repair) it a few times, so it was a **Shock** when it became a nice 植物 **shoku**butsu (plant)
GROUP: 直(す) naosu = to correct, # 570; 値(段) nedan = price, 571; 植(える) ueru = to plant, # 1278; (生)殖 seishoku = reproduction, # 1396 ALSO COMPARE: other similar kanji at # **569**

1279. 蘇 PRONUNCIATIONS: yomigae, so MEANINGS: to be resuscitated or revived
EXAMPLES: 蘇る yomigaeru = to revive or rise from the dead; 阿蘇山 asozan = Mt. Aso (in Kyushu) DESCRIPTION: at the top, a plant radical; on the lower left, 魚 sakana (fish, # 80); on the lower right, 禾 (a grain plant with a ripe head) CUES: a **Yo**gi **M**eets a **Ga**bby **E**xpert on sorcery, and they sit on a **So**fa and make a potion from these plants, this fish and this 禾 (ripe grain) in order to make people 蘇る **yomigae**ru (rise from the dead)
COMPARE: other similar kanji at # **611**, # **618** and # **2055**

1280. 適 PRONUNCIATION: teki
MEANINGS: suitable, qualified, capable
EXAMPLE: 適当 tekitou = appropriate, suitable, reasonable DESCRIPTION: compared to 敵 teki (opponent, # 881) (identical pronunciation), this kanji adds a snail at the lower left and omits the dancer on the right; it retains the 立 (bell) used by an 古 (old) sentry in a two-sided lean-to [Note: compared to 週 shuu (week, # 346), this adds the upper portion of a 立 (bell) at the top]
CUE: this 古 (old) sentry in this two-sided lean-to thinks that using this 立 (bell) to make noise while riding on this snail is a 適当 **teki**tou (suitable) means of scaring away **Techie**s, even though the snail is rather slow
ALSO COMPARE: other similar kanji at # **881**

1281. 複 PRONUNCIATION: fuku
MEANINGS: duplicate, double, compound
EXAMPLE: 複雑 fukuzatsu = complicated, difficult **DESCRIPTION:** compared to (回)復 kaifuku (recovery, # 527) (identical pronunciation), this kanji substitutes happy Jimmy Carter with two lips, as seen in 初(めて) hajimete (for the first time, # 104), for the man with a double hat on the left; it retains the crutch, the sun, and the injured dancer (this combination of radicals = CSD = crutch, sun, dancer), recovering in Fukuoka
CUE: this happy Jimmy Carter with two lips went to **Fuku**oka to try to help this injured dancer, but the situation there was 複雑 **fuku**zatsu (complicated) (CSD = crutch, sun, dancer)
ALSO COMPARE: other similar kanji at # **1220** and # **1615**

1282. 勇 PRONUNCIATIONS: isa, yuu
MEANINGS: courage, cheer **EXAMPLES:** 勇ましい isamashii = courageous, invigorating; 勇気 yuuki = courage **DESCRIPTION:** compared to 湧(く) waku = to gush out, # 903, this omits the water radical on the left; it retains 男 (male) and マ (mother) **CUES:** this マ (mother), who was Queen **Isa**bella, had this 男 (male) son with 勇気 **yuu**ki (courage) who explored the **Yu**kon **GROUP:** 湧(く) waku = to gush out, # 903; 勇(気) yuuki = courage, # 1282; 承(知) shouchi = consent, # 1344; 疎(い) utoi = ignorant, # 1806 **ALSO COMPARE:** other similar kanji at # **109**

1283. 謝 PRONUNCIATIONS: ayama, sha
MEANINGS: apologize, thank, refuse
EXAMPLES: 謝る ayamaru = to apologize; 感謝 kansha = gratitude **DESCRIPTION:** compared to (注)射 chuusha (injection, # 932) (identical pronunciation), this kanji adds 言(う) iu (to speak, # 430) on the left; it retains 身 (body) next to a kneeling sunny guy and a stick of gum **CUES:** when the **Aya**tollah was reading a **Ma**gazine, the **Sha**h 言 (said) that he hoped that this kneeling sunny guy would stop chewing this gum and 射 (inject) something painful into the Ayatollah's 身 (body), but later he had to 謝る **ayama**ru (apologize) **ALSO COMPARE:** 誤(る) ayamaru = to make a mistake, # 1285; other similar kanji at # **131**, # **1381** and # **1417**

1284. 刺 PRONUNCIATIONS: toge, shi, sa, *sashi*
MEANINGS: thorn, pierce, stab, sting
EXAMPLES: 刺 toge = thorn (usually spelled とげ); 刺激 shigeki = stimulation; 名刺 meishi = business card; 刺す sasu = to stab, sting or bite (insect); 刺身 sashimi = sliced raw fish or seafood **DESCRIPTION:** on the left, (都)市 toshi (city, # 242) (identical pronunciation), grafted onto the lower half of 木 ki (tree, # 118); on the right, the katakana リ, which is sometimes described as a knife
CUES: I went to this miniature 市 (city) up in this 木 (tree) **T**ogether with this リ Ri, to get some 刺激 **shi**geki (stimulation) and also to buy a **Sh**ield and some **Sa**lt for our **Sa**d **Sh**eep
GROUP: 刺(す) sasu = to stab, # 1284; (政)策 seisaku = a policy, # 1479 **ALSO COMPARE:** other similar kanji at # **1985**

1285. 誤 PRONUNCIATIONS: ayama, go
MEANINGS: mistake, do wrong, mislead
EXAMPLES: 誤る ayamaru = to make a mistake; 誤解 gokai = misunderstanding
DESCRIPTION: on the left, 言(う) iu (to say, # 430); on the right, this resembles a pitcher standing on a mound, who is about to throw a square ball to the right **CUES:** when the **Aya**tollah was reading a **Ma**gazine, he thought about baseball pitchers like this one and 言 (said) that they often 誤(った) **ayama**tta (made mistakes) due to **Go**phers infesting their mounds **COMPARE:** 謝(る) ayamaru = to apologize, # 1283; other similar kanji at # **1686**

1286. 革 **PRONUNCIATIONS: kaku, kawa** **MEANINGS:** leather, skin, hide **EXAMPLES:** 改革する kaikaku suru = to reform; 革靴 kawagutsu = leather shoe **DESCRIPTION:** compared to 靴 kutsu (shoe, # 603), this omits the man with a slanted hat and the ヒ (hero) on the right; it retains the open-top syringe above a needle; this can also be seen as a hanging bucket at the top, and two eyes above 十 (ten) at the bottom **CUES: Kar**l the **Kool**-Aid vendor arrives at a **Car Wa**sh, fills this syringe/needle with water, and squirts it on his car while protecting his 革靴 **kawa**gutsu (leather shoes) **GROUP:** 靴 kutsu = shoe, # 603; 革(靴) kawagutsu = leather shoe, # 1286; 覇(権) haken = hegemony, # 1874 **ALSO COMPARE:** other similar kanji at # **542** and # **1658**

1287. 拡 **PRONUNCIATION: kaku** **MEANINGS:** broaden, extend, enlarge **EXAMPLE:** 拡大 kakudai = magnification, enlargement **DESCRIPTION:** compared to 広(い) hiroi (spacious, # 494), this adds a kneeling guy on the left; it retains the lean-to with a sign at the top and a ム (cow) inside **CUE: Kar**l the **Kool**-Aid vendor kneels next to this lean-to and plans to evict this ム (cow) living inside, after which he will arrange for a 拡大 **kaku**dai (enlargement) of this space so that he can store more Kool-Aid in it **GROUP:** 広(い) hiroi = spacious, # 494; 拡(大) kakudai = enlargement, # 1287; 鉱(山) kouzan = mine, # 1327

1288. 偶 **PRONUNCIATION: guu** **MEANINGS:** accidentally, even number, couple **EXAMPLES:** 偶然 guuzen = coincidence; 偶数 guusuu = even number **DESCRIPTION:** compared to (遭)遇(する) souguu suru (to encounter, # 1120) (identical pronunciation), this kanji omits the snail and adds a man with a slanted hat on the left; it retains the roots of a 田 (rice paddy) growing more vigorously on the right side of its pot **CUE:** this man on the left tilts his hat back to examine these roots that are growing more vigorously on the right side of the pot below this 田 (rice paddy), which he thinks is more than a 偶然 **guu**zen (coincidence), since a **Goo**se has been digging into the pot **ALSO COMPARE** other similar kanji at # **1120**

1289. 盗 **PRONUNCIATIONS: nusu, tou** **MEANINGS:** steal, rob **EXAMPLES:** 盗む nusumu = to steal; 強盗 goutou = a burglar, robber **DESCRIPTION:** at the top, 次 tsugi (next, # 536), which consists of a water radical next to an oil derrick (see # 399); at the bottom, 皿 sara (dish, # 567) **CUES:** a 強盗 gou**tou** (burglar) took so many 皿 (dishes) like this from his neighbors that he was able to buy a **New Suit**, and 次 (next) he plans to 盗む **nusu**mu (steal) their **T**oasters **ALSO COMPARE:** other similar kanji at # **536** and # **1407**

1290. 賢 **PRONUNCIATIONS: ken, kashiko** **MEANINGS:** intelligent, wise, clever **EXAMPLES:** 賢明 kenmei = wise; 賢い kashikoi = intelligent **DESCRIPTION:** compared to (中)堅 chuuken = mainstay, # 1246 (identical pronunciation), this kanji substitutes 貝 kai (shell or money chest, # 83) for the 土 (soil) at the bottom; it retains the 臣 (inoperable swing set) lying on its side next to a 又 (simple table) **CUES: K**en and Barbie are 賢い **kashiko**i (intelligent), and after **Cash**ing in their **Co**al stocks and selling this 臣 (inoperable swing set) and this 又 (table), they keep all of their proceeds in this 貝 (money chest) **ALSO COMPARE:** other similar kanji at # **24**, # **707** and # **1246**

1291. 罪 **PRONUNCIATIONS: tsumi, zai**
MEANINGS: guilt, sin, crime, offense
EXAMPLES: 罪 tsumi = crime; 罪悪 zaiaku = crime, sin, vice; 犯罪 hanzai = crime
DESCRIPTION: compared to 非(常) hijou (emergency, # 682), this adds 目 me (eye, # 51) turned on its side, which resembles three eyes, at the top; it retains the hero with wings **CUES:** these three eyes observe many 非 (emergencies) and also 罪 **tsumi** (crimes), such as people filling their **Tsu**itcases (suitcases) with **M**eat and walking out of stores without paying, and these seem to reflect the **Zei**tgeist (spirit of the age) **ALSO COMPARE:** similar kanji at # 851 and # 1324

1292. 宝 **PRONUNCIATIONS: takara, hou** **MEANINGS:** treasure, wealth, valuables
EXAMPLES: 宝 takara = treasure; 宝石 houseki = jewel, precious
DESCRIPTION: at the top, a bad haircut; at the bottom, 玉 tama = ball or jewel, # 169, which resembles a ball next to a 王 (king)
CUES: Tarzan's **C**aravans carry 宝 **takara** (treasure) consisting of 玉 (jewels) like this, and they are pulled by **H**orses with bad haircuts like this **ALSO COMPARE:** other similar kanji at # 170

1293. 癒 **PRONUNCIATIONS: yu, iya**
MEANINGS: healing, cure, quench (thirst)
EXAMPLES: 癒着 yuchaku = adhesion, union; 癒す iyasu = to heal, cure, quench (thirst)
DESCRIPTION: compared to 輸(入する) yu'nyuu suru (to import, # 288) (identical pronunciation), this kanji omits 車 kuruma (car, # 283) on the left, it adds a sick bed as seen in 病(気) byouki (illness, # 369) at the upper left, and it adds 心 kokoro (heart, # 306) at the bottom; it retains the house in the Yukon which I owned 前 (before)
CUES: I lie in this sick bed suffering from 心 (heart) disease, but I focus on this house with a peaked roof in the **Yu**kon which I owned 前 (before), and I listen to good music with **Iya**hon (earphones), which will help to 癒す **iya**su (heal) me **ALSO COMPARE:** other similar kanji at # 369, # 677 and # 733

1294. 混 **PRONUNCIATIONS: ma, kon, ko** **MEANINGS:** mix, blend, confuse
EXAMPLES: 混ぜる mazeru = to mix (this can also be spelled 交ぜる mazeru, # 144); 混乱 konran = confusion, chaos; 混雑 konzatsu = crowdedness, congestion; 混同 kondou = confusion, mix-up; 混む komu = to get crowded (often spelled 込む, # 357) **DESCRIPTION:** on the left, a water radical, which reminds us of a waterfall; at the upper right, 日 hi (sun, # 32); at the lower right, 比(較) hikaku (comparison, # 857), which consists of two ヒ (heroes)
CUES: these two ヒ (heroes) lost their **M**aps, and in the 混乱 **kon**ran (**C**onfusion) that followed, they marched in this 日 (sun) until they arrived at this waterfall in **Co**lombia **GROUP:** 皆 mina = everyone, # 597; 階(段) kaidan = stairs, # 598; 能(力) nouryoku = ability, # 616; 比(較) hikaku = comparison, # 857; 鹿 shika = deer, # 895; 態(度) taido = attitude, # 960; 批(判) hihan = criticism, # 1082; 熊 kuma = bear, # 1262; 混(乱) konran = confusion, # 1294; 陛(下) heika = the Emperor, # 1460; 麗(しい) uruwashii = beautiful, # 1627; 昆(虫) konchuu = an insect, # 1866; (山)麓 sanroku = the base of a mountain, # 1955; 罷(免) himen = dismissal, # 2057; 楷(書) kaisho = square style of calligraphy, # 2077
ALSO COMPARE: kanji containing *one* ヒ at # 2048

1295. 航 PRONUNCIATION: kou

MEANINGS: navigate, sail, cruise **EXAMPLES:** 航海 koukai = sailing, voyage; 航空 koukuu = aviation, flying; 航空便 koukuubin = air mail **DESCRIPTION:** compared to (抵)抗 teikou (opposition, # 1196) (identical pronunciation), this kanji substitutes the boat radical seen in 船 fune (boat, 602) for the kneeling guy on the left; it retains the tire stop on a desk in a courthouse **CUE:** I bought this tire stop and this 机 (desk) for a Courthouse and put them onto this 船 (boat) for a long 航海 koukai (voyage) **ALSO COMPARE:** other similar kanji at # 1462, # 1524 and # 1860

1296. 属 PRONUNCIATION: zoku

MEANINGS: belong, affiliated, genus **EXAMPLES:** 金属 kinzoku = metal; 属性 zokusei = attribute; 所属する shozoku suru = to belong to **DESCRIPTION:** on the upper left, a lean-to with a double roof; inside the lean-to, 虫 mushi (insect, # 9), wearing a spiffy hat and standing behind a two-legged table; the lower portion of this radical also resembles a pot with asymmetrical roots, as seen in (待)遇 taiguu (treatment, # 1120) **CUE:** Zooey's Kool-Aid is kept cold on this two-legged table in this double-roofed lean-to which has certain 属性 zokusei (attributes), including an infestation with 虫 (insects) wearing spiffy hats like this, and a potted plant with asymmetrical roots like these **COMPARE:** other similar kanji at # 1120, # 1754 and # 1899

1297. 泌 PRONUNCIATIONS: hi, pitsu

MEANINGS: ooze, flow, secrete **EXAMPLES:** 泌尿 hi'nyou = urination; 分泌 bunpitsu = secretion **DESCRIPTION:** compared to 必(死に) hisshi ni (desperately, # 307) (identical pronunciation), or 必(要) hitsuyou (necessary, # 307), this kanji adds a water radical on the left; it retains the 心 kokoro (heart, # 306) with a slash across it **CUES:** it's 必 (necessary) for Peter Pan and St. Peter to Hear each other, but this water on the left separates them, and the two Petes experience a 分泌 bunpitsu (secretion) of stress hormones as they strain to listen **GROUP:** 必(死に) hisshi ni = desperately, # 307; 秘(密) himitsu = a secret, # 1187; (秘)密 himitsu = a secret, # 1188; (蜂)蜜 hachimitsu = honey, # 1255; (分)泌 bunpitsu = secretion, # 1297

1298. 尿 PRONUNCIATION: nyou

MEANING: urine **EXAMPLE:** 尿 nyou = urine **DESCRIPTION:** on the upper left, a lean-to with a double roof; under the lean-to, 水 mizu (water, # 251) **CUE:** this heavy-duty lean-to belongs to some Neo-Nazis, and it's full of 水 (water) and 尿 nyou (urine), since they use it as a toilet **ALSO COMPARE:** other similar kanji at # 1529 and # 1899

1299. 梅 PRONUNCIATIONS: ume, bai, tsu

MEANING: plum **EXAMPLES:** 梅 ume = plum; 梅雨 baiu = rainy season (June and early July), a less common pronunciation, or 梅雨 tsuyu = rainy season, a *more* common pronunciation **DESCRIPTION:** on the left, 木 ki (tree, # 118); on the right, 毎 mai (every, # 336) **CUES:** 毎 (every) 木 (tree) in a certain orchard bears 梅 ume (plums), and Ugandan Medical personnel who work nearby Buy the fruit and carry it home in their Tsuitcases (suitcases) **ALSO COMPARE:** other similar kanji at # 336 and # 2080

1300. 湿 PRONUNCIATIONS: shi, shitsu, shime

MEANINGS: damp, wet, moist **EXAMPLES:** 湿気 shikke = dampness, humidity; 湿度 shitsudo = humidity level; 湿る shimeru = to get damp; 湿す shimesu = to wet or moisten **DESCRIPTION:** on the left, a water radical; at the upper right, 日 hi (sun, # 32); at the lower right, the four burners seen in 普(通) futsuu (ordinarily, # 576) **CUES:** a Shiite tried to use this 日 (sun) and these four 普 (burners) to dry his Sheets, but since this water had caused too much 湿気 shikke (dampness), the **Sh**ee**t**s got **M**essed up **GROUP:** 並(ぶ) narabu = to line up, # 575; 普(通) futsuu = ordinarily, # 576; (謙)虚 kenkyo = modesty, # 966; 嘘 uso = lie, # 967; 湿(す) shimesu = to wet, # 1300; 霊 rei = soul, # 1575; 顕(著) kencho = conspicuous, # 1725; 戯(れる) tawamureru = to play, # 1756; 繊(維) sen'i = fiber, # 1815; (楽)譜 gakufu = sheet music, # 1848

1301. 詩 PRONUNCIATION: shi

MEANINGS: poem, poetry **EXAMPLES:** 詩 shi = poem; 詩人 shijin = poet **DESCRIPTION:** on the left, 言(う) iu (to speak, # 430); on the right, 寺 tera (temple, # 213) **CUE:** a **Sh**iite who is a 詩人 **sh**ijin (poet) 言 (spoke) at this 寺 (temple) **ALSO COMPARE:** 諸(問題) shomondai = various problems, # 1315; (検)討 kentou = an investigation, # 1493; other similar kanji at # **215**

1302. 株 PRONUNCIATION: kabu

MEANINGS: stock, shares, counter for small plants **EXAMPLE:** 株 kabu = stock, stump, a counter for small plants **DESCRIPTION:** on the left, 木 ki (tree, # 118); on the right, an 牛 ushi (cow, # 205), merged with a second 木 (tree) **CUE:** if I can get this 牛 (cow) to come down from this 木 (tree) on the right, I plan to sell both of these trees and use the proceeds to buy 株 **kabu** (stocks) in a **Ca**boose company **COMPARE:** similar kanji at # 128 and # **1675**

1303. 標 PRONUNCIATION: hyou

MEANINGS: signpost, seal, symbol, target **EXAMPLE:** 目標 mokuhyou = aim, goal **DESCRIPTION:** on the left, 木 ki (tree, # 118); at the upper right, three eyes suspended from a platform, as seen in (必)要 hitsuyou (necessary, # 238); at the lower right, a spinning nail under a flying carpet, as seen in 宗(教) shuukyou (religion, # 676) [these can also be seen as 二 (two) above 小 (small)] **CUE:** a **Hea**ler from **O**regon with three eyes like these, who uses his third eye for 宗 (religious) insights, climbed this 木 (tree) with the 目標 moku**hyo**u (aim) of observing this spinning nail under this flying carpet **ALSO COMPARE:** other similar kanji at # **1347** and # **1415**

1304. 旬 PRONUNCIATIONS: jun, shun

MEANING: season (for specific products) **EXAMPLES:** 中旬 chuujun = around the middle of a month; 旬の魚 shun no sakana = fish in season **DESCRIPTION:** on the upper right, a giant hook, as seen in (目)的 mokuteki (purpose, # 45), which reminds us of fish hooks; on the lower left, 日 hi (sun, # 32) **CUES:** it was 中旬 chuu**jun** (the middle of the month) when my father saw me looking through the eye of this fish hook at this 日 (sun), and he said, "**Jun**ior, you will ruin your vision doing that, and then you may be **Shun**ned by your peers" **ALSO COMPARE:** similar kanji at # **988**

1305. 券 PRONUNCIATION: ken

MEANINGS: sword, knife **EXAMPLES:** 券 ken = ticket; 券売機 kenbaiki = ticket machine **DESCRIPTION:** compared to (優)勝 yuushou (victory, # 149), this omits the 月 (moon) on the left, and it substitutes 刀 katana (sword, # 102) for 力 (force) at the bottom; it retains the bonfire at the top, which consists of 二 (two) inscribed on 人 (person), plus flames at the top **CUE:** this bonfire in **Ken**ya celebrates a 勝 (victory) which was achieved with this 刀 (sword), but a 券 **ken** (ticket) is needed in order to attend the celebration **GROUP:** (優)勝 yuushou = victory, # 149; 券 ken = ticket, # 1305; 巻(き込む) makikomu = to get involved, # 1309; (葛)藤 kattou = conflict, # 1530; 拳銃 kenjuu = a handgun, # 1554; (首都)圏 shutoken = the capital city, # 1681; (沸)

騰(する) futtou suru = to boil, # 1936; **Note** that three of these kanji can be pronounced "ken" **ALSO COMPARE:** 狭い semai = narrow, # 194, where the flames appear *between* the arms of the person, rather than above them; other similar kanji at # **2062**

1306. 干 **PRONUNCIATIONS: kan, ho, bo, hi MEANINGS:** dry, parch **EXAMPLES:** 干渉 kanshou = interference, intervention; 干す hosu = to dry; 梅干し umeboshi = pickled Japanese plum; 潮干狩り shiohigari = shell gathering, clamming **DESCRIPTION:** compared to (発)汗 hakkan (perspiration, # 629) (identical pronunciation), this omits the water radical on the left; it retains the telephone pole **CUES:** in **Kan**sas, telephone poles like this surround my **H**ome and **B**oat, **H**ear my conversations and enable 干渉 **kan**shou (interference) in my private life **ALSO COMPARE:** 千 sen = 1,000, # 22; other similar kanji at # **629**

1307. 渉 **PRONUNCIATION: shou MEANINGS:** ford, ferry, port **EXAMPLES:** 干渉 kanshou = interference, intervention; 交渉 koushou = negotiation, bargaining, contact **DESCRIPTION:** compared to 歩(く) aruku (to walk, # 408), this adds a water radical on the left **CUE:** as I 歩 (walk) in this water along the **S**hore, I feel 干渉 kan**shou** (interference) from the waves **COMPARE:** other similar kanji at # **1010** and # **1929**

1308. 潮 **PRONUNCIATIONS: chou, shio MEANINGS:** tide, salt water, opportunity **EXAMPLES:** 満潮 manchou = high tide; 引き潮 hikishio = low tide; 潮干狩り shiohigari = shell gathering, clamming **DESCRIPTION:** compared to 朝 asa (morning, # 291), or 朝(食) choushoku (breakfast, # 291) (identical pronunciation), this kanji adds a water radical on the left; it retains the California wagon and the 月 (moon) **CUES:** I was **Ch**osen to observe this water, which contains a lot of **Shio** (salt), at 満

潮 man**chou** (high tide) during this 朝 (morning) **GROUP:** 乾(く) kawaku = to get dry, # 290; 朝 asa = morning, # 291; 韓(国) kankoku = S. Korea, # 655; 幹(部) kanbu = an executive, # 1062; (満)潮 manchou = high tide, # 1308; 嘲(笑) choushou = ridicule, # 1971 (also identical pronunciation)

1309. 巻 **PRONUNCIATIONS: ma, maki, kan MEANINGS:** scroll, coil, book **EXAMPLES:** 巻き込む makikomu = to get involved or entangled in; 鉄火巻 tekka maki = raw tuna sushi wrapped in seaweed; 一巻 ikkan = one volume (book) **DESCRIPTION:** compared to 券 ken (ticket, # 1305), this substitutes 己 honore (self, # 652), which resembles a snake shaped like a backwards "S," for the 刀 (sword) at the bottom; it retains the bonfire at the top **CUES:** when this 己 (snake) crawled up to this bonfire to try to 巻き込む **mak**ikomu (get involved), we hit it with **M**agazines and rolled-up **Mack**intoshes (raincoats) and also threw **C**andles at it **ALSO COMPARE:** other similar kanji at # **1078** and # **1305**

1310. 鑑 **PRONUNCIATION: kan MEANINGS:** specimen, learn from **EXAMPLES:** 鑑賞 kanshou = appreciation (e.g., of art), listening (to music); 印鑑 inkan = a stamp or seal **DESCRIPTION:** compared to (軍)艦 gunkan (battleship, # 737) (identical pronunciation), this kanji substitutes 金 kane (money, # 301) for the 舟 (boat) on the left; it retains the two cannons firing crutches and shells over a 皿 (dish) **CUE:** it takes 金 (money) to keep these **C**annons firing over this dish, and I 鑑賞する **kan**shou suru (appreciate) the spectacle that they create **GROUP:** (軍)艦 gunkan = battleship, # 737; 監(督) kantoku = director, # 1420; (展)覧(会) tenrankai = an exhibition, # 1514; 臨(時) rinji = temporary, # 1515; 藍 ai = indigo, # 1812; **Note**

that three of these kanji can be pronounced "kan" **ALSO COMPARE:** other similar kanji at # **1407** and # **2010**

1311. 笠 PRONUNCIATIONS: kasa, gasa² MEANINGS: bamboo hat, one's influence

EXAMPLES: 笠 kasa = a bamboo hat, a lamp shade; 雨笠 amagasa = a rain hat

DESCRIPTION: at the top, 竹 take (bamboo, # 134); at the bottom, 立(つ) tatsu (to stand, # 11)

CUES: Casanova is 立 (standing) under this 竹 (bamboo), wearing a 笠 **kasa** (bamboo hat) to keep the leaves out of his hair

ALSO COMPARE: 傘 kasa = umbrella, # 1743; other similar kanji at # **11** and # **2074**

1312. 耕 PRONUNCIATIONS: tagaya, kou MEANINGS: till, plow, cultivate

EXAMPLES: 耕す tagayasu = to plow or cultivate; 耕作 kousaku = cultivation (of land)

DESCRIPTION: on the left, 土 shi (man, # 66) standing on 木 (tree); on the right, 井(戸) ido (well, # 983)

CUES: this 土 (man) standing on this 木 (tree) is a **Taga**log farmer watching his **Ya**rd, where he will 耕す **tagaya**su (plow) a field of **C**orn that will be watered by this 井 (well)

ALSO COMPARE: other similar kanji at # **1202** and # **2050**

1313. 歴 PRONUNCIATION: reki

MEANINGS: curriculum, continuation, passage of time **EXAMPLES:** 歴史 rekishi = history; 学歴 gakureki = academic background

DESCRIPTION: on the upper left, a one-sided lean-to; inside the lean-to, at the top, 林 hayashi (grove, # 125); at the bottom, 止(める) tomeru (to stop, # 173) **CUE:** according to 歴 **reki**shi (history), the practice of hanging 林 (groves) of trees from the tops of lean-tos like this was 止 (stopped) because it was **Wreck**ing the lean-tos

ALSO COMPARE: similar kanji at # **1475** and # **1929**

1314. 史 PRONUNCIATION: shi

MEANINGS: history, chronicle **EXAMPLES:** 歴史 rekishi = history **DESCRIPTION:** compared to 丈(夫) joubu (healthy, # 613), this substitutes a pair of glasses for the arms of the right-wing guy, who has a dislocated right hip **CUE:** this right-wing guy with a dislocated hip put on these glasses in order to read a 歴史 rek**i**shi (history) of **Shee**p farming **GROUP:** (今)晩 konban = this evening, # 35; 映(画) eiga = movie, # 36; (千)円 sen'en = 1,000 yen, # 39; 声 koe = voice, # 40; 英(雄) eiyuu = hero, # 43; 事 koto = intangible thing, # 416; 使(う) tsukau = to use, # 480; 象 zou = elephant, # 906; (想)像 souzou = imagination, # 907; (中)央 chuu'ou = center, # 1063; 免(許) menkyo = a license, # 1140; (歴)史 rekishi = history, # 1314; 眉(毛) mayuge = an eyebrow, # 1645; 逸(話) itsuwa = an anecdote, # 1706

ALSO COMPARE: other similar kanji at # **1000**

1315. 諸 PRONUNCIATIONS: moro, sho

MEANINGS: various, many, together

EXAMPLES: 諸々 moromoro = various things; 諸問題 shomondai = various problems

DESCRIPTION: compared to (一)緒(に) issho ni (together, # 232) (identical pronunciation), this kanji substitutes 言(う) iu (to speak, # 430) for the skeet shooter on the left; it retains 者 mono (person, # 276) on the right, which includes a pair of scissors **CUES:** this 者 (person) in **Mo**rocco **Sho**ws us these scissors and 言 (speaks) about the 諸問題 **sho**mondai (various problems) that they cause

ALSO COMPARE: 詩 shi = poem, # 1301; other similar kanji at # **1088**

1316. 迫 PRONUNCIATIONS: sema, haku MEANINGS: urge, force, imminent EXAMPLES: 迫る semaru = to draw near or urge; 迫力 hakuryoku = dynamism, power DESCRIPTION: compared to 白(髪) hakuhatsu (white hair, # 44) (identical pronunciation), this kanji adds a snail at the lower left CUES: a guy is **S**elling **Ma**rine products, including this 白 (white) snail, at the **H**arbor in **Ku**wait, and he demonstrates a lot of 迫力 **haku**ryoku (dynamism) ALSO COMPARE: 追(う) ou = to chase, # 821, in which the snail carries bunk beds; other similar kanji at # **2014**

1317. 例 PRONUNCIATIONS: tato, rei MEANINGS: example, custom, precedent EXAMPLES: 例えば taoeba = for example; 例 rei = example DESCRIPTION: compared to 列 retsu (line, # 1124), this adds a man with a slanted hat on the left CUES: this man on the left is tilting his hat back to examine his **Ta**ttoos, which he says are a 例 **rei** (example) of fine art, while standing in 列 (line) before a **R**ace ALSO COMPARE: other similar kanji at # **164** and # **1124**

1318. 旨 PRONUNCIATIONS: uma, shi MEANINGS: delicious, purport, will EXAMPLES: 旨味 umami = a 5th taste category recognized in Japan (apart from sweet, sour, salty, and bitter); 要旨 youshi = the gist or main idea DESCRIPTION: compared to 指 yubi (finger, # 691), or 指(定席) shiteiseki (reserved seat, # 691) (identical pronunciation), this kanji omits the kneeling guy on the left; it retains the ヒ (hero) and the 日 (sun) CUES: this ヒ (hero) is an **U**ber **Ma**rine who spends time in this 日 (sun), and his 要旨 you**shi** (main idea) is that he must **Sh**ield his country from danger GROUP: 指 yubi = finger, # 691; 脂 abura = fat, # 1180; 詣(で) moude = temple visit, # 1204; (要)旨 youshi = the gist, # 1318; 稽(古) keiko = rehearsal, # 1715

1319. 漫 PRONUNCIATION: man MEANINGS: cartoon, involuntarily, corrupt EXAMPLE: 漫画 manga = cartoon (usually spelled マンガ) DESCRIPTION: compared to (自)慢 jiman (pride, # 1127) (identical pronunciation), this substitutes a water radical for the erect man on the left; it retains the 日 (sun), the three eyes and the 又 (table) CUES: this water poured onto this 又 (table) in **Man**hattan, where a guy with these three eyes that are never bothered by this 日 (sun) was drawing some 漫画 **man**ga (cartoons) ALSO COMPARE: other similar kanji at # **1127**

1320. 詞 PRONUNCIATION: shi MEANINGS: part of speech, words, poetry EXAMPLES: 名詞 meishi = a noun; 動詞 doushi = a verb DESCRIPTION: on the left, 言(葉) kotoba (word, # 430); on the right, (上)司 joushi (one's superior, # 608) (identical pronunciation), which depicts a box that contains sheep food, under a napkin inside a lean-to CUE: this box under this napkin inside this lean-to contains **Sh**eep food, and the 言 (word) "sheep" is a 名詞 mei**shi** (noun) ALSO COMPARE: other similar kanji at # **341** and # 1620

1321. 豊 PRONUNCIATIONS: yuta, hou MEANINGS: bountiful, excellent, rich EXAMPLES: 豊か yutaka = rich; 豊富 houfu = abundant DESCRIPTION: at the top, 曲(が る) magaru (to turn, # 82), which resembles a coop; at the bottom, 豆 mame (bean, # 721) CUES: a woman in **U**tah invented a machine to 曲 (turn) these 豆 (beans) while she baked them in her **H**ome, she fed the beans to some birds that she kept in a coop like this, and she became 豊か **yuta**ka (rich) GROUP: 曲(がる) magaru = to turn, # 82; 農(業) nougyou = agriculture, # 1105; 濃(度) noudo = concentration, # 1106; (古)典

koten = a classic, # 1117; 豊(か) yutaka = rich, # 1321   **ALSO COMPARE:** other similar kanji at # **721** and # **2070**; kanji that include a coop with crossed wires at # 1073; kanji that include a *cage* at # 583

1322. 穣   **PRONUNCIATION:** jou
MEANINGS: good crops, prosperity
EXAMPLES: 豊穣 houjou = good harvest; 五穀豊穣 gokoku houjou = a bumper crop
DESCRIPTION: on the left, 禾 (a grain plant with a ripe head); at the upper right, 六 roku (six, # 17); at the middle right, 井(戸) ido (well, # 983), or (天)井 tenjou (ceiling, # 983) (identical pronunciation); at the lower right, 衣(服) ifuku (clothing, # 1042), without its pointy hat   **CUE: Joan** of Arc saw this 禾 (ripe grain), which had been watered by 六 (six) 井 (wells) like this, and she anticipated a (豊)穣 hou**jou** (good harvest), after which she planned to buy some 衣 (clothes) like this   **GROUP:** (豊)穣 houjou = good harvest, # 1322; (お)嬢(さん) ojousan = a young girl, # 1659; 譲(歩) jouho = a concession, # 1669, (土)壌 dojou = soil, # 1898, and 醸(造) jouzou = brewing, # 1996; **Note** that all of these kanji can be pronounced "jou"   **ALSO COMPARE:** other similar kanji at # **1797**

1323. 歓   **PRONUNCIATION:** kan
MEANINGS: delight, joy
EXAMPLES: 歓迎 kangei = welcome; 歓声 kansei = cheer, shout of joy
DESCRIPTION: compared to 勧(告) kankoku (recommendation, # 698) (identical pronunciation), this kanji substitutes 欠(く) kaku (to lack, # 1238), which resembles an oil derrick, for 力 (force) on the right; it retains the Native American chief hugging a net, which can be seen as a man with a slanted hat next to a 主 (master) with an extra pair of arms, at a zoo in Kansas   **CUE:** when the people of **Kan**sas saw that this Native American chief had struck this 欠 (oil) near this net, they reacted with

歓声 **kan**sei (cheers)   **ALSO COMPARE:** other similar kanji at # **536** and # **698**

1324. 署   **PRONUNCIATION:** sho
MEANINGS: signature, government office
EXAMPLES: 署名 shomei = signature; 警察署 keisatsusho = police station
DESCRIPTION: compared to 諸(問題) shomondai (various problems, # 1315) (identical pronunciation), this kanji omits 言 (to say) on the left and adds three eyes at the top; it retains 者 (person)   **CUE:** this 者 (person) **Sho**ws us these three eyes, which make him useful at the 警察署 keisatsu**sho** (police station)
GROUP: 買(う) kau = to buy, # 89; 置(く) oku = to place, # 569; 環(境) kankyou = environment, # 718; (甲)羅 koura = shell, # 1158; 罪 tsumi = crime, # 1291; 署(名) shomei = signature, # 1324; (返)還 henkan = a restoration, # 1587; 罰(金) bakkin = a penalty, # 1691; 濁(る) nigoru = to be muddy, # 1831; 罵(倒す る) batou suru = to abuse, # 1927; 罷(免) himen = dismissal, # 2057   **ALSO COMPARE:** other similar kanji at # **1088**

1325. 刑   **PRONUNCIATION:** kei
MEANINGS: punish, penalty, sentence
EXAMPLES: 刑務所 keimusho = prison; 死刑 shikei = death penalty   **DESCRIPTION:** compared to 型 kata (form, # 1116), or (典)型 (的) tenkeiteki (typical, # 1116) (identical pronunciation), this kanji omits 土 (soil) at the bottom; it retains the tower and the katakana リ ri   **CUE:** when this Ri went to 刑務所 **kei**musho (prison), he stayed in this tower, where he was kept in a **C**age   **ALSO COMPARE:** other similar kanji at # **573** and # **1985**

1326. 粗 PRONUNCIATIONS: so, ara
MEANINGS: coarse, rough, rugged
EXAMPLES: 粗末 somatsu = cheap, poor, shabby; 粗い arai = coarse, rugged
DESCRIPTION: compared to 祖(父) sofu (grandfather, # 272) (identical pronunciation), this substitutes 米 kome (uncooked rice, # 326) for the Shah on the left; it retains the solar panel
CUES: as he subsisted on this 米 (uncooked rice) next to this Solar panel, **Ara**fat found his life 粗末 **so**matsu (shabby)   ALSO COMPARE: other similar kanji at # **752** and # **1387**

1327. 鉱 PRONUNCIATION: kou
MEANINGS: mineral, ore   EXAMPLES: 鉱山 kouzan = mine; 鉱物 koubutsu = mineral
DESCRIPTION: on the left, (お)金 okane (money, # 301); on the right, 広(い) hiroi (spacious, # 494) which consists of a ム (cow) in a lean-to   CUE: I paid this 金 (money) for this ム (cow) in this lean-to and will use it to haul **Co**al out of my 鉱山 **kou**zan (mine)   ALSO COMPARE: other similar kanji at # **1287** and # **2010**

1328. 述 PRONUNCIATIONS: jutsu, no
MEANINGS: mention, speak, relate
EXAMPLES: 記述 kijutsu = a written description; 述べる noberu = to tell or state
DESCRIPTION: at the lower left, a snail; at the upper right, 十 juu (ten, # 18), surrounded by three lines, but this resembles a woman wearing a skirt, with a ball above her right shoulder, which may represent something jutting out, as seen in (手)術 shujutsu (surgery, # 808) (identical pronunciation)
CUES: this woman with a tumor that **Jut**s out over her right shoulder 述べる **no**beru (tells) us that she is traveling on this snail to **No**rway for 術 (surgery)   COMPARE: similar kanji at # **808** and # **1828**

1329. 否 PRONUNCIATIONS: hi, ina, pi
MEANINGS: negate, refuse, deny   EXAMPLES: 否定 hitei = rejection, denial; か否か ka'inaka = whether or not; 賛否 sanpi = yes and no, for and against; 安否 anpi = safety   DESCRIPTION: at the top, 不 fu (negation, # 176); at the bottom, 口 kuchi (mouth, # 426), which resembles the back of an upright piano   CUES: when I **H**ear someone saying **In**appropriate things from behind this 口 (**Pi**ano), I 不 (negate) them by issuing a 否定 **hi**tei (rejection)   ALSO COMPARE: other similar kanji at # **172** and # **176**

1330. 緩 PRONUNCIATIONS: kan, yuru
MEANINGS: slacken, loosen, relax   EXAMPLES: 緩和 kanwa = relief, alleviation, relaxation; 緩い yurui = lax, loose, slow   DESCRIPTION: compared to 暖(かい) atatakai (warm atmosphere, # 38), this substitutes 糸 (skeet shooter, # 219) for the 日 (sun) on the left; it retains the barbecue grate above 友 (friend)   CUES: when this 糸 (skeet shooter) felt 暖 (warm), he noticed this 友 (friend) melting **Ca**ndy on this barbecue grate, fired some skeets at him, said "You're **Ru**ining it!" and accused me of being too 緩い **yuru**i (lax) with the guy   ALSO COMPARE: other similar kanji at # **459** and # **1177**

1331. 撮 PRONUNCIATIONS: satsu, to
MEANINGS: snapshot, take pictures
EXAMPLES: 撮影 satsuei = filming, photographing; 撮る toru = to take (a photo)
DESCRIPTION: compared to 最(高) saikou (the best, # 42), this adds a kneeling guy on the left; it retains a 日 (sun) above 取(る) toru (to take, # 58) (identical pronunciation)
CUES: this guy on the left is my **Sat**isfied Supervisor, and he is kneeling to 撮る **to**ru (take) the 最 (best) picture of my **To**rtoise
ALSO COMPARE: other similar kanji at # **1389** and # **1713**

1332. 魔 PRONUNCIATION: ma
MEANINGS: witch, demon, evil spirit
EXAMPLES: 悪魔 akuma = devil, evil spirit; 魔法 mahou = magic, witchcraft; 魔女 majo = witch   DESCRIPTION: compared to 歴(史) rekishi (history, # 1313), this substitutes 鬼 oni (demon, # 1168) for 止 (to stop) at the bottom; it retains 林 hayashi (grove, # 125) inside a lean-to with a chimney   CUE: this 鬼 (demon) asked a 魔女 **ma**jo (witch) to use 魔法 **ma**hou (**Ma**gic) to hang this 林 (grove) inside this lean-to
ALSO COMPARE: other similar kanji at # **1169**, # **1475** and # **1678**

1333. 徹 PRONUNCIATIONS: tetsu, te
MEANINGS: penetrate, clear, pierce, sit up (all night)   EXAMPLES: 徹夜 tetsuya = all night; 徹底 tettei = thoroughness, completeness
DESCRIPTION: on the left, a man with a double hat; in the middle, 育(つ) sodatsu (to be raised, # 151), which includes a ム (cow) under a tire stop and above a moon; on the right, a dancer with a ponytail   CUES: this dancer was 育 (raised) by this man with two hats to work in his **Te**tracycline factory in **Su**dan, and when her work showed 徹底 **te**ttei (thoroughness), he rewarded her with **Te**ddy bears and gave her one of his hats
ALSO COMPARE: 撤(廃) teppai = abolition, # 1747 (identical pronunciation); other similar kanji at # **616** and **1125**

1334. 欧 PRONUNCIATION: ou
MEANING: Europe   EXAMPLES: 欧州 oushuu = Europe   DESCRIPTION: on the left, 区(役所) kuyakusho (ward office, # 320); on the right, 欠(く) kaku (to lack, # 1238), which resembles an oil derrick   CUE: I visited this 区 (ward office), where I saw a poster of this 欠 (oil derrick) in the **O**cean in 欧州 **ou**shuu (Europe)
ALSO COMPARE: other similar kanji at # **320**, # **536** and # **1953**

1335. 識 PRONUNCIATION: shiki
MEANINGS: discriminating, know, write
EXAMPLE: 知識 chishiki = knowledge
DESCRIPTION: compared to (組)織 soshiki (organization, # 753) (identical pronunciation), this substitutes 言(う) iu (to speak, # 430) for the skeet shooter on the left; it retains 音 oto (sound, # 266) in the middle and a halberd on the right
CUE: I have 知識 chi**shiki** (knowledge) about **Sh**eep in **Ki**ev which 言 (speak) 音 (sounds) like this when their teeth are subjected to halberds like this   ALSO COMPARE: other similar kanji at # **266** and # **753**

1336. 善 PRONUNCIATIONS: zen, yo
MEANINGS: virtuous, goodness
EXAMPLES: 改善 kaizen = improvement; 善人 zennin = good people; 善し悪し yoshiashi = good or bad, right or wrong (this can also be spelled 良し悪し yoshiashi)
DESCRIPTION: at the top, 羊 hitsuji (sheep, # 1223); at the bottom, an upside-down bench above a 口 (box)   CUES: a **Zen** monk told me that 善人 **zen**nin (good people) do not make 羊 (sheep) like this stand on upside-down benches above 口 (boxes) like this, but that it's OK to eat **Yo**gurt made from their milk   ALSO COMPARE: other similar kanji at # **1223** and # **1236**

1337. 唯 PRONUNCIATION: yui
MEANINGS: solely, merely, simply   EXAMPLE: 唯一 yui'itsu = only, sole, unique
DESCRIPTION: compared to 誰 dare (who, # 440), this substitutes 口 kuchi (mouth, # 426), which can also be seen as a box, for 言 (to speak) on the left; it retains the net on the right, which can be seen as a man with a slanted hat next to a 主 (master) with an extra pair of arms (see # 203)
CUE: a **Yu**kon **E**agle is the 唯一 **yui**'itsu (only) bird in this net, and it uses this 口 (mouth) to shriek at us   COMPARE: other similar kanji at # **2046** and # **2073**

1338. 励 PRONUNCIATIONS: hage, rei

MEANINGS: encourage, be diligent, inspire **EXAMPLES:** 励ます hagemasu = to cheer or encourage (there is no plain speech equivalent); 励む hagemu = to be diligent or make an effort (there is no "masu" form); 激励 gekirei = encouragement **DESCRIPTION:** on the left, a one-sided lean-to; under the lean-to, 万 man (10,000, # 113); on the right, 力 chikara (force, # 107)

CUES: a **Ha**waiian **Gue**st rented this lean-to for 万 (10,000) yen, and she's resting in it to build up this 力 (force) so that she can 励む **hage**mu (make an effort) in an upcoming **R**ace **ALSO COMPARE:** other similar kanji at # **113** and # **1846**

1339. 貧 PRONUNCIATIONS: mazu, bin, hin

MEANINGS: poverty, poor **EXAMPLES:** 貧しい mazushii = poor; 貧乏 binbou = poverty, poor person; 貧困 hinkon = poverty **DESCRIPTION:** compared to (お)盆 obon (a Buddhist festival, # 1167), this substitutes 貝 kai (shell, or money chest, # 83) for 皿 (dish) at the bottom; it retains 分 (to understand) at the top **CUES:** I am 貧しい **mazu**shii (poor), and I 分 (understand) that this 貝 (money chest) doesn't contain enough money to buy the **M**ap of the **Z**oo and the **B**eans that I promised to get for my **H**indu friends **ALSO COMPARE:** other similar kanji at # **656** and # **2076**

1340. 乏 PRONUNCIATIONS: bou, tobo

MEANINGS: destitution, scarce, limited **EXAMPLES:** 貧乏 binbou = poverty, poor person; 乏しい toboshii = scarce **DESCRIPTION:** compared to 芝(生) shibafu (lawn, # 779), this substitutes a tiny diving board for the plant radical at the top; it retains the somewhat irregular Z, which reminds us of Zero **CUES:** I own this tiny diving **B**oard which I've attached to my **T**oy **B**oat, but otherwise I have **Z** (zero) money and suffer from 貧乏 bin**bou** (poverty) **GROUP:** 厳(しい) kibishii = strict, # 902; (貧)乏 binbou = poverty, # 1340; (勇)敢(な) yuukan na = brave, # 1852 **ALSO COMPARE:** other similar kanji at # **1835**

1341. 規 PRONUNCIATION: ki

MEANINGS: standard, measure **EXAMPLE:** 規則 kisoku = rules, regulations **DESCRIPTION:** on the left, 夫 otto (husband, # 614); on the right, 見(る) miru (to look, # 53) **CUE:** when I wear my **Ki**mono, this 夫 (husband) always 見 (looks) to make sure that I'm following the 規則 **ki**soku (regulations) regarding the wearing of formal clothes **GROUP:** 見(る) miru = to look, # 53; 覚(える) oboeru = to memorize, # 54; 親 oya = parent. # 383; 現(金) genkin = cash, # 739; 視(力) shiryoku = eyesight, # 844; 観(光) kankou = sightseeing, # 886; 覗(く) nozoku = to snoop, # 982; 寛(容) kanyou = tolerance, # 1205; 規(則) kisoku = rules, # 1341; (展)覧(会) tenrankai = an exhibition, # 1514 **ALSO COMPARE:** other similar kanji at # **1915**

1342. 則 PRONUNCIATION: soku

MEANINGS: rule, follow, based on **EXAMPLES:** 規則 kisoku = rules, regulations; 原則 gensoku = a general rule **DESCRIPTION:** compared to (予)測 yosoku (prediction, # 1031) (identical pronunciation), this kanji omits the water radical on the left; it retains 貝 kai (shell, or money chest, # 83) and the katakana リ ri **CUE:** this リ **R**i follows all 規則 ki**soku** (rules) when he **S**oaks in hot springs, and he pays the fees from this 貝 (money chest) **ALSO COMPARE:** other similar kanji at # **490** and # **2058**

1343. 郎 PRONUNCIATION: rou

MEANING: son **EXAMPLES:** 野郎 yarou = a guy or rascal; 新郎 shinrou = bridegroom **DESCRIPTION:** on the left, a modified 良(い) yoi (good, # 303), with an altered Y at the lower right; on the right, ß beta from the Greek alphabet **CUE:** this ß (Greek) 野郎 ya**rou** (guy) is a 良 (good) person who gives me **R**oses **COMPARE:** 限(界) genkai = limit, # 642, in which ß (Greek) is on the left; other similar kanji at # **805** and # **1843**

1344. 承 PRONUNCIATIONS:

uketamawa, shou MEANINGS: receive, take over, comply with **EXAMPLES:** 承る uketamawaru = to hear, to be told, to undertake, to take (a message or reservation), to comply; 承知 shouchi = acceptance, consent, understanding; 承認 shounin = approval, recognition, sanction **DESCRIPTION:** at the top, a modified katakana マ ma, which reminds us of ma (mother); on the left, the katakana フ fu, which reminds us of food; in the center, 手 te (hand, # 23); on the right, the letter Y, which reminds us of yams; over-all, this has the shape of a pyramid **CUES:** an **U**ber **Ke**nyan who ran a **Ta**xing **Ma**rathon in **Wa**shington tells this マ (mother) about it, she **Sho**ws her 承認 **shou**nin (approval), and then she uses this 手 (hand) to arrange this フ (food), including Y (yams), into a pyramidal shape like this **ALSO COMPARE:** 蒸(す) musu = to steam, # 1101; other similar kanji at # **1101**, # **1282** and # **1554**

1345. 績 PRONUNCIATION: seki

MEANING: exploits **EXAMPLES:** 成績 seiseki = achievement, school grades; 業績 gyouseki = accomplishments, results, performance (business); 功績 kouseki = achievement; 実績 jisseki = accomplishment, achievement **DESCRIPTION:** compared to 責(任) sekinin (responsibility, # 772) (identical pronunciation), which resembles an owl's perch above a 貝 (money chest) owned by a selfish king, this adds 糸 (skeet shooter, # 219) on the left **CUE:** a **Se**lfish **Ki**ng told this 糸 (skeet shooter) to shoot at this owl's perch above this 貝 (money chest), and their main 功績 kou**seki** (achievement)

so far has been to scare the owls **COMPARE:** other similar kanji at # **772**

1346. 展 PRONUNCIATION: ten

MEANINGS: unfold, expand **EXAMPLES:** 発展 hatten = development, prosperity; 展開 tenkai = development **DESCRIPTION:** at the upper left, a lean-to with a double roof; under the lean-to, a plant radical (see # 43) on a platform supported by L and Y **CUE:** L and Y live in this double-roofed lean-to with these house plants, but they are planning a big 展開 **ten**kai (development) on their property which will include a **Te**nnis court **COMPARE:** similar kanji at # **398** and # **1899**

1347. 示 PRONUNCIATIONS: shime, shi, ji

MEANINGS: show, indicate, display **EXAMPLES:** 示す shimesu = to show or point out; 図示 zushi = illustration; 展示 tenji = display, exhibition **DESCRIPTION:** this is 丁 tei (a counter for tools, # 702), which resembles a nail, with projections on the sides that suggest spinning, plus a flying carpet above it; compared to 宗(教) shuukyou (religion, # 676), it omits the bad haircut; this can also be seen as 二 (two) above 小 (small) **CUES:** in this basic spinning 丁 (nail) structure under a flying carpet, which is a center for our 宗 (religion), we create **Sh**eep **Me**dicine for our **Sh**eep, and if you come outside, I can 示す **shime**su (show) you our **J**eep **GROUP:** 祭(り) matsuri = festival, # 377; (国)際 kokusai = international, # 379; 宗(教) shuukyou = religion, # 676; (警)察 keisatsu = police, # 896; 禁(じる) kinjiru = to prohibit, # 943; 奈(良) Nara, # 1006; (目)標 mokuhyou = aim, # 1303; 示(す) shimesu = to show, # 1347; (摩)擦 masatsu = friction, # 1429; 票 hyou = a vote, # 1510; (書)斎 shosai = a home library, # 1560; (奴)隷 dorei = a slave, # 1583; 崇(拝) suuhai = worship, # 1656; 漂(白剤) hyouhakuzai = bleach, # 1693; (中)尉 chuui = a first lieutenant, # 1751; 慰(める) nagusameru = to console, # 1752; 襟 eri = a collar,

1872 ALSO COMPARE: the katakana ホ ho; kanji with a *stool* above a spinning nail structure at # 637

1348. 順 PRONUNCIATION: jun
MEANINGS: obey, order, turn
EXAMPLES: 順番 junban = one's turn, order; 順調 junchou = smooth, no problem
DESCRIPTION: on the left, 川 kawa (river, # 250); on the right, 貝 kai (money chest, # 83) with a platform at the top where a head could fit, as seen in 頭 atama (head, # 93) **CUE:** I was waiting for my 順番 **jun**ban (turn) to cross this 川 (river) in the **Jun**gle when I realized that a fellow traveler's head was missing from this platform **ALSO COMPARE:** 訓(練) kunren = training, # **1090**; other similar kanji at # **1126**

1349. 毒 PRONUNCIATION: doku
MEANINGS: poison, germ **EXAMPLES:** 気の毒 ki no doku = pitiful; 毒物 dokubutsu = poison
DESCRIPTION: compared to 毎(日) mainichi (every day, # 336), this substitutes an owl's perch, as seen in 青(い) aoi (blue, # 155), for the crutch at the top; it retains the modified rice paddy
CUE: 毎 (every) day I climb onto this owl's perch and check it for 毒物 **doku**butsu (poison) as part of a **Doc**umentary that I'm filming **ALSO COMPARE:** similar kanji at # **336** and # **1103**

1350. 捌 PRONUNCIATION: saba
MEANINGS: to handle or deal with
EXAMPLE: 捌く sabaku = to handle or process, to prepare (meat or fish) for cooking, to sell out (stock) **DESCRIPTION:** compared to 別(れる) wakareru (to separate, # 561), this adds a kneeling guy on the left; it retains Betsy, with a square head, and リ Ri **CUE:** this guy on the left is kneeling in order to get down to eye level with this Betsy and this リ Ri, who are 別 (separated), trying to persuade them to take **Sab**baticals together in order to learn how to 捌く **sab**aku (prepare) fish for cooking **ALSO COMPARE:** other similar kanji at # **561** and # **1985**

1351. 師 PRONUNCIATION: shi
MEANINGS: expert, teacher, master
EXAMPLES: 教師 kyoushi = teacher (classroom); 医師 ishi = physician **DESCRIPTION:** on the left, a bunk bed with a tiny pillow visible on the top bunk, as seen in 追(う) ou (to chase, # 821); on the right, 巾 (Bo Peep), as seen in 帽(子) boushi (hat, # 243), wearing a flat hat
CUE: when this 巾 (Bo Peep) consulted her 医師 **ishi** (physician), he advised her to wear this flat hat and rest in the top bunk of this bunk bed, while using only this tiny pillow and covering herself with a single **Sh**eet **ALSO COMPARE:** other similar kanji at # **880** and # **1768**

1352. 条 PRONUNCIATION: jou
MEANINGS: article, clause, item, stripe
EXAMPLES: 条件 jouken = condition, requirement **DESCRIPTION:** at the top, a dancer with a ponytail; at the bottom 木 ki (tree, # 118)
CUE: **Jo**an of Arc was this dancer, and she jumped over 木 (trees) on the 条件 **jou**ken (condition) that her audience would give money to her cause
GROUP: 集(まる) atsumaru = to congregate, # 202; 葉 ha = leaf, # 543; 柔(らかい) yawarakai = soft, # 546; (汚)染 osen = pollution, # 774; 雑誌 zasshi = magazine, # 785; 殺(す) korosu = to kill, # 838; 梨 nashi = pear, # 1184; (建)築 kenchiku = architecture, # 1219; 栽(培) saibai = cultivation, # 1233; 栄(養) eiyou = nutrition, # 1263; 条(件) jouken = condition, # 1352; (破)棄(する) haki suru = to abolish, # 1624
ALSO COMPARE: other similar kanji at # **129**

1353. 模 PRONUNCIATIONS: mo, bo, *mi*
MEANINGS: imitation, copy, mock
EXAMPLES: 模様 moyou = design, pattern; 大規模 daikibo = large-scale; 相模原 sagamihara = a city in Kanagawa Prefecture
DESCRIPTION: on the left, 木 ki (tree, # 118); at the upper right, a plant radical which reminds us of

grass; at the middle right, 日 hi (sun, # 32); at the lower right, 大(きい) ookii (big, # 188) (this combination of radicals = PSB = plants, sun, big) **CUES:** a 大 (big) man is **Mo**wing this grass, represented by this plant radical, under this 木 (tree) in this 日 (sun), but he finds the job **Bo**ring and would rather be working on his 模様 **mo**you (designs) for **M**irrors (PSB = plants, sun, big) **GROUP:** 暮(らす) kurasu = to make a living, # 641; 幕 maku = theater curtain, # 653; (応)募 oubo = application, # 1109; 墓(地) bochi = cemetery, # 1275; 模(様) moyou = design, # 1353; (砂)漠 sabaku = a desert, # 1614; 膜 maku = a membrane, # 1759; 慕(情) bojou = longing, # 1959 **ALSO COMPARE:** other similar kanji at # 33

1354. 華 PRONUNCIATIONS: hana, ke, ka, ge
MEANINGS: splendor, flower, shine **EXAMPLES:** 華やか hanayaka = dazzling, gorgeous; 法華経 hokekyou = the Lotus Sutra; 中華料理 chuuka ryouri = Chinese cuisine; 万華鏡 mangekyou = kaleidoscope **DESCRIPTION:** at the top, a plant radical; in the middle, a streamlined vehicle, as seen in 乗(る) noru (to board, # 509); at the bottom, a spinning base, as seen in 早(い) hayai (early, # 34) **CUES:** this streamlined vehicle on this spinning base is covered with these plants, and it stops to allow a **Ha**waiian **Na**nny to 乗 (board) with a 華やかな **hana**yaka na (gorgeous) **K**ettle of **Ca**shews for her **Gu**ests **ALSO COMPARE:** other similar kanji at # **799** and # **1658**

1355. 鏡 PRONUNCIATIONS: kagami, kyou, gane
MEANINGS: mirror, barrel head, round rice cake offering **EXAMPLES:** 鏡 kagami = mirror; 望遠鏡 bouenkyou = telescope; 眼鏡 megane = eyeglasses (this can also be pronounced gankyou = eyeglasses) **DESCRIPTION:** compared to (環)境 kankyou (environment, # 719) (identical pronunciation), this kanji substitutes 金 kane (money, # 301) for 土 (soil) on the left; it retains 立 (to stand) and 兄 (big brother) with an additional horizontal line that resembles a scowl [this radical at the lower right is *not* 見(る) (to see), since it only contains three horizontal lines; it is a 日 (sun) above lopsided legs] **CUES:** when a **Ca**rpenter was **Gam**ing in **Kyou**to, he used a 鏡 **kagami** (mirror) to watch this 兄 (big brother) with a scowl 立 (standing) behind him, who made sure that this 金 (money) that he won was donated to a **Ga**rden in the **Ne**therlands **GROUP:** (環)境 kankyou = environment, # 719; 鏡 kagami = mirror, # 1355; (容)貌 youbou = features, # 1687 **ALSO COMPARE:** 鐘 kane = a bell, # 1840; other similar kanji at # **266**, # **719** and # **2010**

1356. 伎 PRONUNCIATION: ki
MEANINGS: deed, skill **EXAMPLE:** 歌舞伎 kabuki = traditional Japanese drama **DESCRIPTION:** compared to 支(店) shiten (branch store, # 26), this adds a man with a slanted hat on the left **CUE:** this man on the left went to a 支 (branch store), tilted his hat back to examine their **Ki**monos, bought one and wore it to a 歌舞伎 kabu**ki** (traditional Japanese drama) performance **ALSO COMPARE:** similar kanji at # **1121**

1357. 豪 PRONUNCIATION: gou
MEANINGS: overpowering, great, excelling **EXAMPLES:** 豪華 gouka = wonderful, gorgeous; 富豪 fugou = a person of great wealth **DESCRIPTION:** at the top, the upper portion of 高(い) takai (expensive, # 19; at the bottom, 家 ie (house, # 405), without its chimney **CUE:** a 富豪 fu**gou** (person of great wealth) bought this 高 (expensive) 家 (house) and paid for it with **Go**ld **ALSO COMPARE:** other similar kanji at # **1474** and # **1504**

1358. 馳 PRONUNCIATION: chi
MEANINGS: run, gallop, sail, win (fame)
EXAMPLE: ご馳走 gochisou = a delicacy
DESCRIPTION: compared to 地(下鉄) chikatetsu (subway, # 503) (identical pronunciation), this kanji substitutes 馬 uma (horse, # 958) for the 土 (soil) on the left; it retains the scorpion that eats cheese CUE: this 馬 (horse) and this scorpion both eat **Ch**eese, and they say ご馳走様でした go**chi**sou sama deshita (it was a feast) when they are finished ALSO COMPARE: other similar kanji at # **503** and # **826**

1359. 粘 PRONUNCIATIONS: nen, neba
MEANINGS: sticky, glutinous, greasy
EXAMPLES: 粘土 nendo = clay; 粘る nebaru = to get sticky DESCRIPTION: compared to 店 mise (store, # 493), this adds 米 kome (uncooked rice, # 326) on the left; it retains the 占 (well with a pump handle) CUES: when my **N**egative **N**ephew and his **N**egative **B**arber get hungry, they add water from this 占 (well with a pump handle) to this 米 (uncooked rice) and cook it, and the rice 粘る **neba**ru (gets sticky) ALSO COMPARE: other similar kanji at # **1387** and # **1542**

1360. 因 PRONUNCIATION: in
MEANINGS: cause, factor EXAMPLES: 原因 gen'in = cause; 要因 youin = factor
DESCRIPTION: 大(きい) ookii (big, # 188) inside a box CUE: the 原因 gen'**in** (cause) of this 大 (big) guy's **In**sanity is the fact that he's stuck in this box GROUP: 回(る) mawaru = to turn, # 4; 四 yon = four, # 6; 国 kuni = country, # 170; (公)園 kouen = park, # 279; 困(る) komaru = to be inconvenienced, # 280; 図(書館) toshokan = library, # 281; 奥(さん) okusan = wife, # 532; 歯 ha = tooth, # 533; 団(体) dantai = group, # 686; 囲(む) kakomu = to surround, # 1202; (細)菌 saikin = bacterium, # 1210; (原)因 gen'in = cause, # 1360; 恩 on = obligation, # 1388; (首都)圏 shutoken = the capital city, # 1681; 囚(人) shuujin = a prisoner, # 1926; (耳鼻)咽(喉科) jibiinkouka = otorhinolaryngology, # 1967, and (婚)姻 kon'in = marriage, # 2039, both of which can also be pronounced "in"

1361. 索 PRONUNCIATION: saku
MEANINGS: cord, rope EXAMPLES: 検索 kensaku = looking up or retrieval (e.g., words or data); 索引 sakuin = index
DESCRIPTION: compared to 素(早い) subayai (speedy, # 712), this substitutes 十 juu (ten, # 18), fastened to a roof, for the owl's perch at the top, it retains the 糸 (skeet shooter) at the bottom CUE: this 糸 (skeet shooter) had to feed these 十 (ten) guests on this roof, so he 検索した ken**saku** shita (looked up) a retailer on the internet and ordered some **S**alty **C**oo**k**ies
ALSO COMPARE: other similar kanji at # **1266** and # **1828**

1362. 挙 PRONUNCIATIONS: kyo, age
MEANINGS: plan, project, behavior
EXAMPLES: 選挙 senkyo = election; 挙句 ageku = a negative outcome DESCRIPTION: at the top, three old boys standing on a platform, as seen in 覚(える) oboeru (to memorize, # 54); the platform is supported by slanted walls; at the bottom, 手 te (hand, # 23) CUES: these three old boys got up on this platform to ask for votes during a 選挙 sen**kyo** (election) in **Kyo**to, and they waved 手 (hands) like this one, but an **A**rgumentative **Gu**est contradicted them ALSO COMPARE: similar kanji at # **1101**, # **1554** and # **1625**

1363. 昇 **PRONUNCIATIONS: shou, nobo**
MEANING: rise up **EXAMPLES:** 上昇 joushou = rising, ascending, climbing; 昇進 shoushin = promotion (rising in rank); 昇る noboru = to rise (used for sunrise and moonrise)
DESCRIPTION: at the top, 日 hi (sun, # 32); at the lower left, 千 sen (one thousand, # 22); at the lower right, 十 too (ten, # 18) **CUES:** 千十 (1,010) people watched this 日 (sun) 昇る **nobo**ru (rise), and it was quite a **Show**, but **No Boys** were present **GROUP:** 飛(ぶ) tobu = to fly, # 574; (上)昇 joushou = rising, # 1363; (一)升 isshou = 1.8 liters, # 2049 (identical pronunciation) **ALSO COMPARE:** other similar kanji at # **22**, # **897** and # **1658**

1364. 委 **PRONUNCIATIONS: yuda, i**
MEANINGS: committee, entrust to **EXAMPLES:** 委ねる yudaneru = to entrust; 委員会 iinkai = committee **DESCRIPTION:** compared to 季(節) kisetsu (season, # 1047), this substitutes 女 onna (female, # 235) for 子 (child) at the bottom; it retains the 禾 (stalk of ripe grain) **CUES:** I have 委ねた **yuda**neta (entrusted) this 禾 (ripe grain) to this 女 (female), who is my **Y**outhful **D**aughter, who finds it **E**asy to carry, since she is youthful **ALSO COMPARE:** other similar kanji at # **1797** and # **2086**

1365. 章 **PRONUNCIATION: shou**
MEANINGS: badge, chapter, composition
EXAMPLES: 章 shou = chapter; 文章 bunshou = sentence, composition, writing
DESCRIPTION: at the top, 立(つ) tatsu (to stand, # 11); at the bottom, 早(い) hayai (early, # 34) **CUE:** I wrote a 文章 bun**shou** (composition) arguing that one should 立 (stand) 早 (early) when the national anthem begins, to **Show** support for the country **GROUP:** 早(い) hayai = early, # 34; (食)卓 shokutaku = dining table, # 620; 草 kusa = grass, # 909; 章 shou = chapter, # 1365; 障(害) shougai = an obstacle, # 1495; (哀)悼 aitou = condolences, # 1644; (表)彰 hyoushou = public acknowledgment, # 1807; **Note** that three of these kanji can be pronounced "shou" **ALSO COMPARE:** other similar kanji at # **266**

1366. 嘱 **PRONUNCIATION: shoku**
MEANINGS: entrust, request, send a message
EXAMPLE: 嘱託 shokutaku = commission, entrusting, a temporary employee
DESCRIPTION: compared to (金)属 kinzoku (metal, # 1296), this adds 口 kuchi (mouth, # 426), which can also be seen as a box, on the left; it retains 虫 (insect) wearing a spiffy hat and standing behind a two-legged table where Zooey keeps her Kool-Aid, inside a lean-to with a double roof
CUE: this 虫 (insect) with a spiffy hat standing behind this table in this double-roofed lean-to has a 嘱託 **shoku**taku (commission) to **Show Kool**-Aid samples, and it uses this 口 (mouth) to try to sell them **ALSO COMPARE:** other similar kanji at # **1120**, # **1754**, # **1899** and # **2073**

1367. 託 **PRONUNCIATION: taku**
MEANINGS: consign, entrusting with
EXAMPLES: 託する taku suru = to entrust; 信託 shintaku = a trust (finance)
DESCRIPTION: compared to (お)宅 otaku (home, # 21) (identical pronunciation), this kanji omits the roof that resembles a bad haircut and adds 言(う) iu (to speak, # 430) on the left; it retains the 七 (seven) tall people who were cooped up under that roof while wearing slanted hats
CUE: 七 (seven) **T**all people who were **C**ooped up under a roof while wearing slanted hats like this have been released, and now people 言 (say) that we can 託する **taku** suru (entrust) them with important responsibilities
COMPARE: other similar kanji at # **21**

1368. 審 **PRONUNCIATION: shin**
MEANINGS: hearing, judge, trial **EXAMPLES:** 審査 shinsa = hearing, examination; 審議 shingi = discussion, scrutiny **DESCRIPTION:** compared to 番 ban (turn, # 328), this adds a bad haircut at the top **CUE:** when it's my 番 (turn) to get a bad haircut like this, I have a 審議 **shin**gi (discussion) with the barber and then say a **Shin**to prayer **GROUP:** 番(号) bangou = number, # 328; 翻(訳) hon'yaku = translation, # 1087; 審(議) shingi = discussion, # 1368; (解)釈 kaishaku = an explanation, # 1516; 藩(士) hanshi = warrior, # 1537 **ALSO COMPARE:** other similar kanji at # **220**

1369. 寸 **PRONUNCIATION: sun**
MEANINGS: measurement, inch **EXAMPLES:** 寸前 sunzen = just before, on the verge; 寸法 sunpou = measurement or size **DESCRIPTION:** this is the radical seen on the right in 付(く) tsuku (to adhere, # 132), depicting a kneeling sunny guy who has dropped a piece of gum on the ground **CUE:** this is a kneeling **Sun**ny guy who is 寸前 **sun**zen (on the verge) of picking up his gum **ALSO COMPARE:** other similar kanji at # **131**

1370. 鈴 (sometimes written 鈴)
PRONUNCIATIONS: suzu, rin **MEANINGS:** small bell, buzzer **EXAMPLES:** 鈴 suzu = a small bell; 風鈴 fuurin = wind chime **DESCRIPTION:** on the left, 金 kane (money, # 301); on the right, (命)令 meirei (command, # 962), which looks like a person under a roof and a napkin who is about to run a race [the **alternative** kanji above contains a peaked roof on the right, above a drop of rain and マ ma (mother)] **CUES:** this person on the right is about to run a race, and he's spent this 金 (money) to buy a 鈴 **suzu** (small bell), which was sold as a **Souv**enir at the **Zoo** and which he will **Ring** as he runs [**alternatively**, this マ ma (mother) is trying to stay out of this rain that penetrates this roof, but she plans to go out and use this 金 (money) to buy a 鈴 **suzu** (small bell), which is sold as a **Souv**enir at the **Zoo**, so that she can **Ring** it on special occasions] **ALSO COMPARE:** other similar kanji at # **962**, # **1946** (alternative font) and # **2010**

1371. 遂 **PRONUNCIATIONS: sui, to**
MEANINGS: accomplish, attain **EXAMPLES:** 未遂 misui = a failed attempt; 遂げる togeru = to accomplish **DESCRIPTION:** compared to (軍)隊 guntai (army, # 726), this omits the ß Greek) army on the left and adds a snail at the lower left; it retains the rabbit ears that a tiger is wearing, protruding from the top of a 家 (house) **CUES:** this snail is carrying this pet with rabbit ears in this 家 (house) to **Swe**den, where it will 遂げる **to**geru (accomplish) the task of riding on a **To**rtoise **ALSO COMPARE:** other similar kanji at # **1504** and # **1972**

1372. 握 **PRONUNCIATIONS: nigi, aku**
MEANINGS: grip, hold **EXAMPLES:** 握る nigiru = to grasp or hold tight; 握手 akushu = handshake **DESCRIPTION:** compared to (部)屋 heya (room, # 63), this adds a kneeling geek on the left **CUES:** this **K**neeling **G**eek (an unfashionable or eccentric person) is 握ってい る **nigi**tte iru (holding on) to this wall while peering into this 屋 (room) where **Acu**puncture treatments are given **ALSO COMPARE:** other similar kanji at # **63** and # **1899**

1373. 酢 **PRONUNCIATIONS: su, zu**
MEANINGS: vinegar, sour, acid **EXAMPLE:** 酢 su = vinegar; 米酢 komezu = rice vinegar **DESCRIPTION:** on the left, compared to 酒 sake (alcoholic beverage, # 465), this omits the water radical on the left (this can also be seen as a bucket of sake with a handle); on the right, a serrated axe, which can also be seen as a ladder or stairs, as seen in 作(る) tsukuru (to make, # 482) **CUES:** I used this serrated axe to open this 酒 (sake) and then poured some of it, plus a little 酢 **su** (vinegar), into my **Sou**p made from

Zucchini ALSO COMPARE: other similar kanji at # **41** and # **1480**

1374. 鍋 PRONUNCIATION: nabe

MEANINGS: pot, pan, kettle EXAMPLE: 鍋 nabe = pot, pan DESCRIPTION: compared to 過(ぎる) sugiru (to exceed, # 361), this omits the snail on the lower left and adds 金 kane (money, # 301) on the left; it retains the two boxes, with a slipping carton in the upper box CUE: after a **Na**rco **Be**t that he could 過 (exceed) ten pounds of weight loss, he won this 金 (money) and bought himself a 鍋 **nabe** (pot) ALSO COMPARE: other similar kanji at # **361** and # **2010**

1375. 撲 PRONUNCIATIONS: boku, mou

MEANINGS: slap, strike, hit EXAMPLES: 打撲傷 dabokushou = a bruise; 相撲 sumou = sumo wrestling DESCRIPTION: compared to 僕 boku (I, # 333) (identical pronunciation), this substitutes a kneeling guy for the man with a slanted hat on the left; it retains the 夫 (husband) with an extra pair of arms and a Christmas-tree top CUES: this guy on the left is a **Bo**ny **Ko**ol-Aid salesman who is kneeling next to this 夫 (husband) with an extra pair of arms and a Christmas-tree top, and the kneeling guy kicked a **Mo**le and got some 打撲傷 da**boku**shou (bruises) on his feet, which is why he's kneeling ALSO COMPARE: other similar kanji at # **332** and # **333**

1376. 傷 PRONUNCIATIONS: kizu, do, shou

MEANINGS: wound, hurt, scar, gash EXAMPLES: 傷 kizu = scar, wound, injury, defect; 火傷 yakedo = a burn injury, usually spelled やけど; 負傷 fushou = injury, wound DESCRIPTION: on the left, a man with a slanted hat; at the upper right, a crutch; at the lower right, a modified version of 易(しい) yasashii (easy, # 402) CUES: when this man on the left was **Ki**cked at the **Zoo**, he took a **Do**se of aspirin, carried this crutch, tilted his hat back to **Sho**w us the 傷 **kizu** (injury) on his face, and said that he would heal 易 (easily) COMPARE: other similar kanji at # **1702** and # **2080**

1377. 煮 PRONUNCIATION: ni

MEANINGS: boil, cook EXAMPLE: 煮る niru = to boil or cook DESCRIPTION: compared to 者 sha (person, # 276), this adds a fire, as seen in 熱(い) atsui (hot object, # 65), at the bottom CUE: my **Ni**ece is this 者 (person) who 煮る **ni**ru (cooks) with this hot fire ALSO COMPARE: similar kanji at # **611** and # **1088**

1378. 材 PRONUNCIATION: zai

MEANINGS: lumber, wood, talent EXAMPLES: 材木 zaimoku = timber; 材料 zairyou = material, ingredient; 素材 sozai = material, ingredient DESCRIPTION: on the left, 木 ki (wood, # 118); on the right, compared to 才(能) sainou (talent, # 617), this left-wing scientist's hip has come back into its socket CUE: this left-wing guy on the right traveled to **Zai**re (former name of the Congo) to get 材木 **zai**moku (timber) for his 木 (wooden) building projects ALSO COMPARE: 財(産) zaisan = assets, # 1437 (identical pronunciation); other similar kanji at # **128** and # **1417**

1379. 飽 PRONUNCIATIONS: hou, a

MEANINGS: tired of, bored EXAMPLES: 飽和状態 houwa joutai = saturation; 飽きる akiru = to get tired of DESCRIPTION: compared to (大)砲 taihou (cannon, # 738) (identical pronunciation), this kanji substitutes 食(べ物) tabemono (food, # 398) for 石 (stone) on the left; it retains the object wrapped in cloth, which reminds us of a hobo's bundle and can also be seen as a hook containing a snake CUES: when **Ho**bos in **A**frica 飽きる **a**kiru (get tired of) their 食 (food), they wrap it up in 包 (bundles) like this and save it for later ALSO COMPARE: other similar kanji at # **1861** and # **1974**

1380. 浄 PRONUNCIATION: jou
MEANINGS: clean, purify, exorcise
EXAMPLE: 洗浄 senjou = washing, laundering
DESCRIPTION: compared to (戦)争 sensou (war, # 936), this adds a water radical on the left; it retains the monster with a fish head (see # 80) that has been stabbed with a trident
CUE: when **Jo**an of Arc was doing her 洗浄 sen**jou** (laundering), this injured monster with a fish head appeared in this water
ALSO COMPARE: 静(脈) joumyaku = vein, # 418 (identical pronunciation); other similar kanji at # **936**

1381. 臭 PRONUNCIATIONS: kusa, nio, shuu
MEANINGS: odor, stink, suspicious looking
EXAMPLES: 臭い kusai = smelly, stinking, suspicious; 臭う niou = to smell of; 悪臭 akushuu = a bad smell; **Note:** niou and nioi can also be written 匂う and 匂い, # 949
DESCRIPTION: at the top, 自(分) jibun (oneself, # 55), which consists of a ray above 目 me (eye, # 51); at the bottom, 大(きい) ookii (big, # 188) **CUES:** I 自 (myself) am a 大 (big) guy, a **C**ool **Sa**xophone player and a **Ne**onatologist, but sometimes my **Sh**oes have 悪臭 aku**shuu** (a bad smell) **GROUP:** 自(分) jibun = oneself, # 55; 息 iki = breath, # 315; 身 mi = body, # 651; 鼻 hana = nose, # 795; (反)射 hansha = reflection, # 932; 嗅(ぐ) kagu = to sniff, # 959; (感)謝 kansha = gratitude, # 1283; 臭(い) kusai = smelly, # 1381; (休)憩 kyuukei = a rest, # 1477; 窮(地) kyuuchi = plight, # 1805

1382. 企 PRONUNCIATIONS: ki, kuwada
MEANINGS: scheme, design, attempt, plan
EXAMPLES: 企画 kikaku = project, plan; 企てる kuwadateru = to attempt or plot
DESCRIPTION: at the top, a peaked roof; at the bottom, 止(める) tomeru (to stop, # 173)
CUES: I 止 (stopped) under this peaked roof, and my 企画 **ki**kaku (plan) was to eat some **Qui**che and give **C**ool **W**ater to my **D**aughter
GROUP: 茶 cha = tea, # 212; 絵(画) kaiga = painting, # 223; 会(社) kaisha = company, # 293; 全(部) zenbu = all, # 300; 珍(しい) mezurashii = unusual, # 407; 膝 hiza = knee, # 861; 幹 miki = tree trunk, # 1062; 診(断) shindan = diagnosis, # 1242; 企(画) kikaku = project, # 1382; 傘 kasa = an umbrella, # 1743; 漆(器) shikki = lacquerware, # 1957; (比)喩 hiyu = a simile, # 2021
ALSO COMPARE: other similar kanji at # **1929**

1383. 谷 PRONUNCIATIONS: ya, tani, koku, gaya
MEANING: valley **EXAMPLES:** 渋谷 Shibuya = a ward in Tokyo; 谷 tani = valley; 渓谷 keikoku = valley, canyon; 世田谷 Setagaya = a special ward in Tokyo
DESCRIPTION: compared to 浴(室) yokushitsu (bathroom, # 256), this omits the water radical on the left; it retains the house with water vapor rising from it, which can also be seen as a tanning booth
CUES: when a **Ya**nkee was **Tan**ing himself inside this booth in a 谷 **tani** (valley), he began to sweat these vapors of water, and then he drank a **Co**ke and fed **Ga**rlic to his **Ya**k
ALSO COMPARE: other similar kanji at # **660**

1384. 渓 PRONUNCIATION: kei
MEANINGS: mountain stream, valley
EXAMPLES: 渓谷 keikoku = valley, canyon
DESCRIPTION: on the left, a water radical; at the upper right, a barbecue grate; at the lower right, 夫 otto (husband, # 614) **CUE:** this water is flooding this barbecue grate that my 夫 (husband) set up in a **C**ave in a 渓谷 **kei**koku (canyon)
ALSO COMPARE: other similar kanji at # **1177** and # **1915**

1385. 炭 PRONUNCIATIONS: tan, sumi
MEANINGS: charcoal, coal **EXAMPLES:** 石炭 sekitan = coal; 炭 sumi = charcoal
DESCRIPTION: compared to 灰(色) haiiro

(grey, # 444), this adds 山 yama (mountain, # 146) at the top **CUES:** when I climbed this 山 (mountain) to get a **Tan**, I saw something 灰 (grey) in the rocks which might be 石炭 seki**tan** (coal), but you will have to **Sue Me** to make me to tell you where it was **GROUP:** 山 yama = mountain, # 146; (海)岸 kaigan = beach, # 500; 端 hashi = edge, # 730; (特)徴 tokuchou = characteristic, # 784; (溶)岩 yougan = lava, # 816; 辿(る) tadoru = to follow, # 882; 崖 gake = cliff, # 911; 崩(れる) kuzureru = to collapse, # 973; 催(す) moyoosu = to hold an event, # 1110; 嵐 arashi = a storm, # 1128; 炭 sumi = charcoal, # 1385; 微(妙) bi'myou = subtle, # 1442; 崇(拝) suuhai = adoration, # 1656; 懲(戒) choukai = reprimand # 1879 **ALSO COMPARE:** other similar kanji at # **1239**

1386. 脱 PRONUNCIATIONS: nu, da, datsu
MEANINGS: undress, removing, escape from, get rid of **EXAMPLES:** 脱ぐ nugu = to remove clothing; 脱出 dasshutsu = flight or escape; 脱毛 datsumou = hair loss
DESCRIPTION: compared to 説(明) setsumei (explanation, # 439), this substitutes 月 tsuki (moon, # 148) for 言 (to say) on the left; it retains 兄 (older brother) wearing rabbit ears
CUES: 兄 (older brother) was standing under this 月 (moon), straining to read the **N**ewspaper, which informed him that his **Da**ughter had 脱出した **da**sshutsu shita (escaped) from the **Datsu**n where kidnappers were holding her, and he put on these rabbit ears and cheered
ALSO COMPARE: other similar kanji at # **708**

1387. 粧 PRONUNCIATION: shou
MEANINGS: cosmetics, adorn (one's person)
EXAMPLE: 化粧 keshou = cosmetics, make-up
DESCRIPTION: on the left, 米 kome (uncooked rice, # 326); on the right, 圧(力) atsuryoku = pressure, # 748, which contains 土 (soil) inside a lean-to
CUE: they were selling this 米 (uncooked rice) at a food **Sh**ow in this lean-to and, even though the venue was full of this 土 (soil), I put on some 化粧 ke**shou** (makeup) and went **GROUP:** (書)類 shorui = docu-ments, # 97; 米 kome = uncooked rice, # 326; 来(る) kuru = to come, # 327; 隣 tonari = next door, # 329; 料(理) ryouri = cuisine, # 512; 奥(さん) okusan = someone else's wife, # 532; 歯 ha = tooth, # 533; 数 kazu = number, # 639; 精(神) seishin = mind, # 847; (年)齢 nenrei = age, # 989; 粉 kona = flour, # 1104; 粒 tsubu = drops, # 1135; 粗(末) somatsu = shabby, # 1326; 粘(土) nendo = clay, # 1359; (化)粧 keshou = cosmetics, # 1387; (砂)糖 satou = sugar, # 1494; 菊 kiku = chrysanthemum, # 1611; (純)粋(な) junsui na = pure, # 1778; 糧 kate = food, # 1789; (摩天)楼 matenrou = a skyscraper, # 1819; (自)粛 jishuku = self-restraint, # 1925
ALSO COMPARE: other similar kanji at # **748**

1388. 恩 PRONUNCIATION: on
MEANINGS: grace, kindness, mercy, blessing
EXAMPLES: 恩 on = indebtedness, obligation, gratitude; 恩返し ongaeshi = returning a favor; 恩恵 onkei = a favor or benefit
DESCRIPTION: at the top, (原)因 gen'in (cause, # 1360), which shows a 大 (big) guy stuck in a box, resulting in insanity; at the bottom, 心 kokoro (heart, # 306) **CUE:** this 大 (big) guy in this box is the **O**wner of this 心 (heart), and he needs us to do him an 恩恵 **on**kei (favor) and get him some medicine for it
ALSO COMPARE: similar kanji at # **1360**

1389. 披 PRONUNCIATION: hi
MEANINGS: expose, open, excellent, rich
EXAMPLE: 披露 hirou = an announcement or demonstration; 披露宴 hirouen = wedding reception DESCRIPTION: compared to 皮 kawa (skin, # 833), also known as Straight Arrow, or 皮(肉) hiniku (sarcasm, # 833) (identical pronunciation), this adds a kneeling guy on the left
CUE: this guy on the left is kneeling to whisper to this 皮 (Straight Arrow), who wants to **H**ear what happened at the 披露宴 **hi**rouen (wedding reception)
GROUP: 投げる nageru = to throw, # 558; 授(業) jugyou = class, # 578; 抜(く) nuku = to extract, # 749; 技(術) gijutsu = technology, # 1133; (応)援 ouen = support, # 1177; 撮(影) satsuei = filming, # 1331; 披(露) hirou = an announcement, # 1389; 捜(査) sousa = a police investigation, # 1520; 搬(送) hansou = transportation, # 1993 ALSO COMPARE: other kanji featuring Straight Arrow at # 833

1390. 露 PRONUNCIATIONS: ro, rou, tsuyu MEANINGS: dew, tears, expose
EXAMPLES: 暴露 bakuro = exposure or revelation; 披露宴 hirouen = wedding reception; 露 tsuyu = dew
DESCRIPTION: compared to (道)路 douro (road, # 525) (identical pronunciation), this kanji adds 雨 ame (rain, # 261) at the top
CUES: I was **R**olling to a 披露宴 h**irou**en (wedding reception) on this 路 (**R**oad), carrying a **Tsu**itcase (suitcase) of **Yu**cca roots as gifts, when this 雨 (rain) started falling ALSO COMPARE: other similar kanji at # 262, # 1033 and # 1534

1391. 宴 PRONUNCIATION: en
MEANINGS: banquet, feast, party EXAMPLE: 宴会 enkai = party or banquet DESCRIPTION: at the top, a bad haircut; in the middle, 日 hi (sun, # 32); at the bottom, 女 onna (female, # 235)

CUE: a 女 (female) **E**ntertainer with this bad haircut and a 日 (sunny) personality performed at our 宴会 **en**kai (banquet)
ALSO COMPARE: other similar kanji at # 120 and # 2086

1392. 刷 PRONUNCIATIONS: satsu, su
MEANINGS: printing, print EXAMPLES: 印刷 insatsu = printing; 刷る suru = to print
DESCRIPTION: at the upper left, a lean-to with a double roof; inside the lean-to, 巾 (Bo Peep), as seen in 帽(子) boushi (hat, # 243); on the right, the katakana リ ri CUES: リ **R**i came to see this 巾 (Bo Peep) at this reinforced lean-to to request an 印刷 in**sat**su (printing) of her **Sat**isfying **Su**perman novel, and Bo Peep **Su**pervised the work
ALSO COMPARE: other similar kanji at # 1768, # 1899 and # 1985

1393. 系 PRONUNCIATION: kei
MEANINGS: lineage, system EXAMPLES: 系統 keitou = system; 家系 kakei = lineage, geneology DESCRIPTION: compared to (関)係 kankei (relationship, # 492) (identical pronunciation), this kanji omits the man with a slanted hat; it retains the skeet shooter, with a cape over his head CUE: this 糸 (skeet shooter) waves this **C**ape over his head and talks about his 家系 ka**kei** (lineage) ALSO COMPARE: other similar kanji at # 1072

1394. 壊 PRONUNCIATIONS: kai, kowa
MEANINGS: demolition, break, destroy
EXAMPLES: 破壊 hakai = destruction; 壊す kowasu = to break or destroy DESCRIPTION: compared to 懐(中電灯) kaichuu dentou (flashlight, # 928) (identical pronunciation), this kanji substitutes 土 tsuchi (soil, # 59) for the erect man on the left; it retains the Kaiser with the cross [which can also be seen as 十 juu (ten, # 18)] in his crown, three eyes and nice 衣 (clothing)
CUES: this **Kai**ser wearing this cross in his crown, and with these three eyes, keeps a **Koa**la outside in

this 土 (soil), lest it 壊す **kowa**su (destroy) this nice 衣 (clothing) **ALSO COMPARE:** other similar kanji at # **934** and # **1042**

1395. 攻 **PRONUNCIATIONS: se, kou**
MEANINGS: aggression, attack **EXAMPLES:** 攻める semeru = to attack or invade; 攻撃 kougeki = attack, criticism; 専攻 senkou = major subject, specialty **DESCRIPTION:** on the left, 工 kou (crafted object, # 246) (identical pronunciation); on the right, a dancer with a ponytail **CUES:** this dancer is a **S**ecretary who uses 工 (crafted objects) in her work at a **C**oal mine but attracts 攻撃 **kou**geki (criticism) for dancing at work **COMPARE:** other similar kanji at # **247**

1396. 殖 **PRONUNCIATION: shoku**
MEANINGS: augment, multiply, raise
EXAMPLES: 繁殖 hanshoku = proliferation, breeding, propaganda; 生殖 seishoku = reproduction, procreation **DESCRIPTION:** compared to 列 retsu (line, # 1124), this substitutes 直(す) naosu (to repair, # 570), which resembles 目 me (eye, # 51), which can be seen as a box, with a thin handle, on a shelf, for リ ri on the right; it retains 夕 (evening) wearing a flat hat, which can be seen as a nightcap **CUE:** I want to attempt some sort of 生殖 sei**shoku** (procreation), so I hope it won't **Shock** yo**U** if I try to 直 (repair) my relationship with my wife by giving her this nightcap **ALSO COMPARE:** other similar kanji at # **164**, # **569** and # **1278**

1397. 猟 **PRONUNCIATION: ryou**
MEANINGS: game-hunting, shooting
EXAMPLES: 狩猟 shuryou = hunting; 猟師 ryoushi = hunter **DESCRIPTION:** on the left, a woman contorting herself, as seen in 猫 neko (cat, # 72); on the right, three old boys, as seen in 覚(える) oboeru (to memorize, # 54), standing on a modified version of 用(事) youji (errand, # 364), which resembles a Japanese fence **CUE:** Pope **L**eo is one of these three old boys who (狩)猟(して いる) shu**ryou** shite iru (are hunting) while standing on this 用 (fence), as this contorted woman expresses disapproval **ALSO COMPARE:** similar kanji at # **367**, # **948** and # **1625**

1398. 雇 **PRONUNCIATIONS: yato, ko**
MEANINGS: employ, hire **EXAMPLES:** 雇う yatou = to employ or hire; 解雇 kaiko = discharge, dismissal **DESCRIPTION:** at the upper left, 戸 to (door, # 871), which resembles a lean-to with a double roof and a layer of snow on top; inside the lean-to, a net, as seen in 誰 dare (who, # 440), which can be seen as a man with a slanted hat next to a 主 (master) with an extra pair of arms (see # 203)
CUES: when **Y**ankees grow **T**obacco, they 雇う **yato**u (hire) workers and let them sleep inside this net in this lean-to with this layer of snow on top, but the workers say that the lean-to is too **C**old **ALSO COMPARE:** similar kanji at # **1134** and # **2046**

1399. 党 **PRONUNCIATION: tou**
MEANINGS: party, faction, clique **EXAMPLE:** 政党 seitou = political party **DESCRIPTION:** at the top, three old boys on a roof, as seen in 覚(える) oboeru (to memorize, # 54); at the bottom, 兄 ani (big brother, # 420)
CUE: these three old boys belong to a 政党 sei**tou** (political party) headed by **T**olstoy, whom they regard as a 兄 (big brother)
ALSO COMPARE: similar kanji at # **420** and # **991**

1400. 幼 PRONUNCIATIONS: osana, you
MEANINGS: infancy, childhood EXAMPLES: 幼い osanai = childish, very young; 幼児 youji = young child DESCRIPTION: on the left, the upper portion of 糸 (skeet shooter, # 219), consisting of two flexed elbows; on the right, 力 chikara (force, # 107) CUES: this truncated 糸 (skeet shooter) is a 幼児 **you**ji (young child) who lives in an **O**ld **San**atarium, and he has a lot of 力 (force) like this in his lungs, so they are teaching him to **Yo**del ALSO COMPARE: other similar kanji at # **1129** and # **1846**

1401. 兼 PRONUNCIATIONS: ga, ken, ka
MEANINGS: concurrently, and
EXAMPLES: 気兼ね kigane = hesitation, reserve; 兼用 ken'you = multi-use; 兼ねる kaneru = to serve multiple purposes at the same time, to be unable to do (when used as a suffix), e.g., 待ち兼ねる machikaneru = to wait eagerly for (literally, to be unable to wait)
DESCRIPTION: compared to 嫌(悪) ken'o (hatred, # 817) (identical pronunciation), this kanji omits the female radical on the left; it retains the 木 (tree) split down the middle and held together by a trident
CUES: this tree in the **Ga**rden has been split in half, and it can 兼ねる **ka**neru (serve multiple purposes) for **Ken** and Barbie, who have repaired it with this trident and **C**arved their initials on it
ALSO COMPARE: other similar kanji at # **817**

1402. 掘 PRONUNCIATIONS: ho, kutsu, bori MEANINGS: dig, excavate
EXAMPLES: 掘る horu = to dig; 発掘 hakkutsu = excavation, discovery; 山谷掘 Sanyabori = a park in Tokyo
DESCRIPTION: compared to (退)屈 taikutsu (boredom, # 927) (identical pronunciation), this kanji adds a kneeling guy on the left; it retains the cooped-up Superman under a lean-to with a double roof
CUES: since Superman is trapped under this lean-to with a double roof, this guy kneels to 掘る **ho**ru (dig) a **H**ole under this wall, and he will try not to **C**ut Superman, even though this will make the work more 屈 (**B**oring)
ALSO COMPARE: other similar kanji at # **927** and # **1899**

1403. 択 PRONUNCIATION: taku
MEANINGS: choose, select, prefer
EXAMPLE: 選択 sentaku = selection, choice
DESCRIPTION: compared to (光)沢 koutaku (luster, # 1100) (identical pronunciation), this substitutes a kneeling guy for the water radical on the left; it retains the 尺 (wakeful eye)
CUE: this guy on the left is kneeling to pick up some bottles of **T**ap water and **K**ool-Aid, which are his first 選択 sen**taku** (selection) for drinks, in order to give them to this 尺 (wakeful eye)
ALSO COMPARE: other similar kanji at # **1484**

1404. 蚕 PRONUNCIATIONS: san, kaiko
MEANING: silkworm EXAMPLES: 養蚕業 yousangyou = the sericulture (silkworm) industry; 蚕 kaiko = a silkworm DESCRIPTION: at the top, 天 ten (sky, # 189), with a wide base; at the bottom, 虫 mushi (insect, # 9) CUES: this 虫 (insect) under this 天 (sky) in **San** Francisco is a 蚕 **kaiko** (silkworm) being raised by one of the **Kai**ser's **Co**rporations ALSO COMPARE: other similar kanji at # **1754** and # **1811**

1405. 誘 PRONUNCIATIONS: yuu, saso
MEANINGS: tempt, invite, seduce
EXAMPLES: 誘惑 yuuwaku = seduction, temptation; 誘う sasou = to invite, entice, encite
DESCRIPTION: compared to 透(明) toumei (transparency, # 1253), this omits the snail at the lower left and adds 言(う) iu (to say, # 430) on the left; it retains 禾 (the grain plant with a ripe head) and the graph CUES: I 言 (**s**aid) to a **You**th that I would 誘う **saso**u (invite) him to help with the harvest of this 禾 (ripe grain) and, in return, I would play a **S**axophone **S**olo and make a graph like this showing how much grain we harvested
ALSO COMPARE: other similar kanji at # **1131** and # **2055**

1406. 肥

PRONUNCIATIONS: hi, ko
MEANINGS: fertilizer, get fat, pamper
EXAMPLES: 肥満 himan = overweight, obesity; 肥える koeru = to put on weight, to become fertile
DESCRIPTION: on the left, 月 tsuki (moon, # 148); on the right, a radical seen in 色 iro (color, # 473), which resembles a cobra with two eyes
CUES: since I **H**ear this **␣Co**bra with two eyes slithering around under this 月 (moon), I can't go outside, and I'm 肥えている **ko**ete iru (putting on weight)
ALSO COMPARE: other similar kanji at # **673**

1407. 益

PRONUNCIATIONS: masu, eki
MEANINGS: benefit, profit, advantage
EXAMPLES: 益々 masumasu = increasingly (usually spelled ますます); 利益 rieki = profit, advantage, interests
DESCRIPTION: at the top, a woman with antennae, welcoming arms and a wide skirt (this can also be seen as an upside-down bench above a skirt); at the bottom, 皿 sara (bowl, # 567) which can resemble three eyes when used as a radical in some kanji
CUES: this woman with antennae, welcoming arms and a wide skirt has prepared this 皿 (bowl) of **M**ango **S**oup for **E**dward the **K**ing, and she hopes to make 利益 r**i**eki (profit) as a result
GROUP: 塩 shio = salt, # 60; 温(かい) atatakai = warm (object), # 257; 皿 sara = plate or dish, # 567; (軍)艦 gunkan = battleship, # 737; 血 chi = blood, # 747; (群)衆 gunshuu = a crowd, # 930; 猛(犬) mouken = savage dog, # 953; 盛(ん) sakan = active, # 1018; (お)盆 Obon = a Buddhist festival, # 1167; (基)盤 kiban = foundation, # 1197; 盗(む) nusumu = to steal, # 1289; 鑑(賞) kanshou = appreciation, # 1310; (利)益 rieki = profit, # 1407; 監(督) kantoku = director, # 1420, (同)盟 doumei = an alliance, # 1513; 蓋 futa = a cover, # 1793; 藍 ai = indigo, # 1812
ALSO COMPARE: other similar kanji at # **1101**, # **1236** and # **1997**

1408. 率

PRONUNCIATIONS: ritsu, so, sotsu, hiki
MEANINGS: ratio, rate, proportion
EXAMPLES: 率 ritsu = percentage, proportion, rate; 率直 socchoku = frank, candid, straightforward; 軽率 keisotsu = thoughtless, hasty; 率いる hikiiru = to lead
DESCRIPTION: at the top, a tire stop; in the center, a truncated skeet shooter, consisting of two flexed elbows, as seen in 幻(想) gensou (fantasy, # 1129), flanked by slanted lines; at the bottom, 十 juu (ten); taken together, these resemble a scouring brush, with a handle at the top and another handle at the bottom
CUES: at the **R**itz hotel, a chief cleaner 率いる **hiki**iru (leads) his colleagues in using two-handled scouring brushes like this to clean **So**fas before guests like **So**tted **Su**perman arrive wearing **H**ideous **K**imonos
ALSO COMPARE: 卒(業) sotsugyou = graduation, # **27** (identical pronunciation); other similar kanji at # **1129**, # **1658** and # **1860**

1409. 閣

PRONUNCIATION: kaku
MEANINGS: tower, palace
EXAMPLE: 内閣 naikaku = the Cabinet
DESCRIPTION: compared to 各(自の) kakuji no (one's own, # 1033) (identical pronunciation), which resembles a dancer with a ponytail leaping over a box as she escapes from **K**arl the **K**ool-Aid vendor, this adds 門 mon (gate, # 409) on the right and left
CUE: after **K**arl the **K**ool-Aid vendor was appointed to the 内閣 nai**kaku** (Cabinet), he looked through this gate and saw this dancer leaping away from him
ALSO COMPARE: other similar kanji at # **1033** and # **1755**

1410. 昭 PRONUNCIATION: shou
MEANINGS: shining, bright
EXAMPLE: 昭和 shouwa = the Showa era (1926-1989) **DESCRIPTION:** compared to 紹(介) shoukai (introduction, # 658) (identical pronunciation), this substitutes 日 hi (sun) for the skeet shooter on the left; it retains the Shougun's 刀 (sword) on a 口 (box) **CUES:** during 昭和 **shou**wa (the Showa era), this 日 (sun) shines brightly on this **Shou**gun's 刀 (sword) on this 口 (box) **ALSO COMPARE:** similar kanji at # **560**

1411. 幣 PRONUNCIATION: hei
MEANINGS: cash, gift **EXAMPLE:** 紙幣 shihei = paper money, bank note **DESCRIPTION:** at the upper left, this is a three-pronged switch above a two-sided lean-to containing a modified 小(さい) chiisai (small, # 253); at the upper right, a dancer with a ponytail; at the bottom, 巾 (Bo Peep), as seen on the left in 帽(子) boushi (hat, # 243) **CUE:** this 巾 (Bo Peep) and this dancer share this 小 (small) lean-to with this three-pronged switch on top where they keep their 紙幣 shi**hei** (paper money), and they **H**ate each other **ALSO COMPARE:** 弊(社) heisha = our company, # 2005 (identical pronunciation); other similar kanji at # **479**, # **1010**, # **1625** and # **1768**

1412. 硬 PRONUNCIATIONS: kata, kou
MEANINGS: stiff, hard **EXAMPLES:** 硬い katai = hard, solid, tough (this can also be spelled 固い katai, # 731, or 堅い katai, # 1246); 硬貨 kouka = coins **DESCRIPTION:** on the left, 石 seki = stone, # 458; on the right, (変)更 henkou = a change, # 1000 (identical pronunciation), which resembles Benjamin Franklin, who has a dislocated right hip and wears bifocals **CUES:** this Benjamin Franklin, who has this dislocated right hip, put on these bifocals to examine this 石 (stone), and although he had **C**ataracts, he was able to determine that it was 硬い **kata**i (hard) and **C**old **ALSO COMPARE:** other similar kanji at # **1000**, # **1775** and # **1992**

1413. 貨 PRONUNCIATION: ka
MEANINGS: freight, goods, property
EXAMPLES: 硬貨 kouka = coins; 通貨 tsuuka = currency; 貨物 kamotsu = freight
DESCRIPTION: compared to 貸(す) kasu (to lend, # 90) (identical pronunciation), this kanji substitutes the katakana ヒ hi, which reminds us of a hero, for the bending woman on the upper right; it retains the man with a slanted hat who is almost falling from the top of a 貝 (money chest)
CUE: this ヒ (hero) jumped up and **C**aught this man with a slanted hat before he could fall, and he will be rewarded with some 硬貨 kou**ka** (coins) from this 貝 (money chest) **GROUP:** 花 hana = flower, # 211; 化(学) kagaku = chemistry, # 487; 靴 kutsu = shoe, # 603; 傾(く) katamuku = to tilt, # 925; (硬)貨 kouka = coins, # 1413 **ALSO COMPARE:** other similar kanji at # **707**

1414. 沿 PRONUNCIATIONS: zo, en, so
MEANINGS: follow along, run along
EXAMPLES: 川沿い kawazoi = along the river; 沿革 enkaku = history, development; 沿う sou = to run along, to follow a plan; 期待に沿う kitai ni sou = to meet expectations; に沿って ni sotte = in accordance with, along, parallel to
DESCRIPTION: compared to 船 fune (boat, # 602), this substitutes a water radical for the boat radical on the left; it retains the 八 (eight) guys working on a 口 (dock) **CUES:** these 八 (eight) guys, who are working on this 口 (dock) in the Canal **Z**one, **En**counter this wave of water, and it **So**bers them up, but they have an 沿革 **en**kaku (history) of similar experiences
ALSO COMPARE: 浴(びる) abiru = to bathe, # 256; other similar kanji at # **602**

1415. 煙 PRONUNCIATIONS: **kemu, kemuri, en** MEANING: smoke
EXAMPLES: 煙たい kemutai = smoky; 煙 kemuri = smoke; 喫煙 kitsuen = smoking
DESCRIPTION: on the left, 火 hi (fire, # 443); at the upper right, three eyes hanging from a platform, as seen in (必)要 hitsuyou (necessary, # 238), which reminds us of a Canadian mermaid with three eyes who knows necessary things; at the lower right, 土 tsuchi (soil, # 59) CUES: this 火 (fire) caused 煙 **kemu**ri (smoke) and this 土 (soil) to get onto my house, but this mermaid with three eyes who knows 要 (necessary) things told me to call **Kelly-Moo**re (a paint company), I used **Kelly-Moo**re paint to **R**efresh the paint job, and now I can **En**tertain guests again GROUP: (必)要 hitsuyou = necessary, # 238; 悪(い) warui = bad, # 313; 腰 koshi = low back, # 884; 覆(う) oou = to cover, # 893; 壷 tsubo = jar, # 1274; (目)標 mokuhyou = aim, # 1303; 煙 kemuri = smoke, # 1415; 票 hyou = a vote, # 1510; 亜(鉛) aen = zinc, # 1589; 漂(白剤) hyouhakuzai = bleach, # 1693; 覇(権) haken = hegemony, # 1874; (左)遷 sasen = a demotion, # 1952 ALSO COMPARE: other similar kanji at # **1239**

1416. 往 PRONUNCIATION: **ou**
MEANINGS: going, past, future EXAMPLES: 往来 ourai = traffic; 往復 oufuku = round trip
DESCRIPTION: compared to 住(む) sumu (to reside, # 167), this substitutes a man with a two hats for the man with a slanted hat on the left; it retains the 主 (master) on the right, who wears a tiny cap
CUE: when this 主 (master) makes an 往復 **ou**fuku (round trip) to the **O**cean, this man with two hats is ready with an extra hat in case the master's cap blows away
ALSO COMPARE: other similar kanji at # **166**

1417. 芽 PRONUNCIATIONS: **ga, me**
MEANINGS: bud, sprout, germ EXAMPLES: 発芽 hatsuga = germination, budding, sprouting; 芽生え mebae = budding, awakening
DESCRIPTION: compared to 牙 kiba (fangs, # 921), or 牙(城) gajou (stronghold, # 921) (identical pronunciation), this kanji adds a plant radical at the top; it retains the king of Baghdad wearing a helmet with a visor, with an extended left hip, inside his hanging gardens CUES: the king of Baghdad puts on this helmet and visor and goes out to his hanging **Ga**rdens to check these plants from **Me**xico which are undergoing 芽生え **me**bae (budding), but the visor blocks his vision
GROUP: 閉(める) shimeru = to close, # 414; 弟 otouto = younger brother, # 529; (次)第(に) shidai ni = gradually, # 530; 才(能) sainou = talent, # 617; 身 mi = body, # 651; (風)邪 kaze = upper respiratory infection, # 796; 牙 kiba = fangs, # 921; (温)雅 onga = graceful, # 922; (注)射 chuusha = injection, # 932; (感)謝 kansha = gratitude, # 1283; 材(料) zairyou = material, # 1378; (発)芽 hatsuga = germination, # 1417; 財(布) saifu = a wallet, # 1437; 既(婚) kikon = already married, # 1639; 概(念) gainen = a general idea, # 1647; (憤)慨(する) fungai suru = to be indignant, # 1782; 窮(地) kyuuchi = plight, adversity, # 1805 ALSO COMPARE: other kanji with an extended left hip at # **796**

1418. 武 PRONUNCIATIONS: **bu, mu**
MEANINGS: warrior, military, arms
EXAMPLES: 武器 buki = weapon, arms; 影武者 kagemusha = a double (an impersonator), also the name of a Japanese movie, the title of which was translated as "Shadow Warrior"
DESCRIPTION: at the upper left, a horizontal line which resembles a spear; at the lower left, 止(める) tomeru (to stop, # 173); on the right, a leaning woman with a ball above her shoulder, as seen in 式 shiki (ceremony, # 249) CUES: this leaning woman with a ball above her shoulder is juggling this spear above her left arm, but she is a **Bu**ddhist who doesn't like to use 武器 **bu**ki (weapons), so she wants to 止 (stop) and watch a **M**ovie instead ALSO COMPARE: other similar kanji at # **249** and # **1929**

1419. 鋭 PRONUNCIATIONS: surudo, ei
MEANINGS: pointed, edge, sharp EXAMPLES: 鋭い surudoi = acute, sharp, insightful, keen; 精鋭 sei'ei = elite DESCRIPTION: on the left, 金 kane (money, # 301); on the right, 兄 ani (big brother, # 420) wearing rabbit ears
CUES: this 兄 (big brother), who needs this 金 (money), has a nose that is a **S**uperior version of **Rudo**lph's, with a 鋭い **surudo**i (keen) sense of smell plus an ability to light the way, and after he learned that honest **Ab**e will pay him to serve as a pathfinder, he put on rabbit ears to celebrate ALSO COMPARE: other similar kanji at # **708** and # **2010**

1420. 監 PRONUNCIATION: kan
MEANINGS: oversee, rule, administrator
EXAMPLES: 監禁 kankin = incarceration, confinement; 監督 kantoku = director, superintendent, manager DESCRIPTION: compared to (軍)艦 gunkan (battleship, # 737) (identical pronunciation), this kanji omits the boat radical on the left side; it retains the two cannons firing crutches and shells over a 皿 (dish) CUE: people who use **Can**nons like these to fire crutches and shells over 皿 (dishes) like this are subject to 監禁 **kan**kin (incarceration) ALSO COMPARE: other similar kanji at # **1310** and # **1407**

1421. 督 PRONUNCIATION: toku
MEANINGS: coach, command, supervise
EXAMPLES: 監督 kantoku = director, manager DESCRIPTION: at the upper left, a taser on a 小 (small) hill, as seen in 寂(しい) sabishii (sad, # 864); at the upper right, 又 mata (again, # 24), but this resembles a simple table; at the bottom, 目 me (eye, # 51) CUE: when I was a 監督 kan**toku** (director), I sat at this 又 (table), filmed tasers on 小 (small) hills like this and relied on this 目 (eye) to find **T**otally **C**ool sequences GROUP: 寂 (しい) sabishii = sad, # 864; (監)督 kantoku = director, # 1421; 淑(女) shukujo = a lady, # 1684;

(親)戚 shinseki = a relative, # 1884 ALSO COMPARE: other similar kanji at # **24** and # **2002**

1422. 邸 PRONUNCIATION: tei
MEANINGS: residence, mansion EXAMPLE: 邸宅 teitaku = mansion, residence
DESCRIPTION: compared to (最)低 saitei (the worst, # 222) (identical pronunciation), this kanji omits the man with a slanted hat on the left and adds ß beta from the Greek alphabet on the right; it retains the 氏 shi (mister) which we have also described as a 紙 (paper) pavilion, taped to a flat rock CUE: this ß (Greek) guy is building a 邸宅 **tei**taku (mansion) in Athens, but in the meantime he is living in this paper pavilion that has been **T**aped to this flat rock ALSO COMPARE: other similar kanji at # **1195** and # **1843**

1423. 眼 PRONUNCIATIONS: gan, *mana*, me MEANING: eyeball EXAMPLES: 眼科 ganka = ophthalmology; 眼差し manazashi = a look, gaze; 眼鏡 megane = eyeglasses (Note: this can also be pronounced gankyou = eyeglasses)
DESCRIPTION: on the left, 目 me (eyes, # 51) (identical pronunciation); on the right, 良(い) yoi (good, # 303), with L & Y at its base, but without its pointy hat CUES: since **Gan**dalf has 良 (good) 目 (eyes) like this, he is the **Mana**ger of the New York **Me**ts, but he still wears 眼鏡 **me**gane (eyeglasses) ALSO COMPARE: other similar kanji at # **243**, # **805** and # **2002**

1424. 揮 PRONUNCIATION: ki
MEANINGS: brandish, swing, shake
EXAMPLES: 指揮 shiki = conducting, direction, command; 指揮者 shikisha = a conductor or commander DESCRIPTION: compared to 軍(人) gunjin (soldier, # 725), this adds a kneeling guy on the left; it retains the 車 (car) with armor above it CUE: this guy is kneeling in order to offer some **Qui**che to this 軍 (soldier) who is his 指揮者 shi**ki**sha (commander)
ALSO COMPARE: other similar kanji at # **2075**

1425. 採 PRONUNCIATIONS: to, sai
MEANINGS: pick, take, fetch EXAMPLES: 採る toru = to hire, adopt, collect or pick up; 採算 saisan = profit, surplus; 採用 saiyou = adoption, acceptance, employment; 採点 saiten = grading, marking DESCRIPTION: compared to 野)菜 yasai (vegetables, # 121) (identical pronunciation), this kanji omits the plant radical at the top and adds a kneeling guy on the left; it retains the barbecue grate above 木 (wood, or tree) CUES: during the Vietnam war, this guy on the left knelt to avoid a **To**rnado in **Sai**gon that blew barbecue grates like this into 木 (trees) like this, and later he pulled them down again, earning a 採算 **sai**san (profit) ALSO COMPARE: 探(す) sagasu = to search, # 699; other similar kanji at # **1935**

1426. 筋 PRONUNCIATIONS: suji, kin
MEANINGS: muscle, tendon, fiber EXAMPLES: 筋 suji = streak (line), fiber, muscle, tendon, story line, logic, lineage; 筋肉 kinniku = muscle DESCRIPTION: at the top, 竹 take (bamboo, # 134); at the lower left, 月 tsuki (moon, # 148); at the lower right, 力 chikara (force, # 107) CUES: since I have **Su**perior **Ge**nes, my 筋肉 **kin**niku (muscles) are strong like this 竹 (bamboo), and when the **Ki**ng ordered me to defend his base on this 月 (moon), I used them to exert a lot of 力 (force) like this ALSO COMPARE: other similar kanji at # **1746**, # **1991** and # **2074**

1427. 熟 PRONUNCIATIONS: juku, u
MEANINGS: mellow, ripen, mature, acquire skill EXAMPLES: 熟す jukusu = to ripen or mature; 成熟 seijuku = maturity, ripeness; 熟れる ureru = to ripen DESCRIPTION: compared to 熱(い) atsui (hot objects, # 65), this substitutes a tire stop [as seen in 対(して) taishite = against, # 674], 口 (mouth, # 426), which resembles a jukebox, and 子 ko (child, # 182) for the 土 (soil) walking on 土 (soil) in the upper left; it retains 九 kyuu (nine, # 11) with a slash across it, as well as a hot fire at the bottom CUES: this 子 (child) has this 口 (**Ju**kebox), which he slashed 九 (nine) times, and he cooks on this **U**ber fire and plays with this tire stop all day, but we are waiting for him to 熟す **juku**su (mature) GROUP: 熟(す) jukusu = to ripen, # 1427; 塾 juku = cram school, # 1737 (identical pronunciation); 享(受する) kyouju suru = to enjoy, # 1842; (輪)郭 rinkaku = an outline, # 1843 ALSO COMPARE: other similar kanji at # **611** and # **1737**

1428. 摩 PRONUNCIATION: ma
MEANINGS: chafe, rub, polish, grind, scrape EXAMPLE: 摩擦 masatsu = friction, rubbing DESCRIPTION: compared to 歴(史) rekishi (history, # 1313), this substitutes 手 te (hand, # 23) for 止 (to stop); it retains the 林 (grove) inside a lean-to with a chimney CUES: my **Ma**ster hung this 林 (grove) of trees from the top of this lean-to, and he uses this 手 (hand) to rub them, since they like 摩擦 **ma**satsu (friction) ALSO COMPARE: similar kanji at # **1475** and # **1554**

1429. 擦 **PRONUNCIATIONS: satsu, kosu, su** **MEANINGS:** grate, rub, scratch, scrape **EXAMPLES:** 摩擦 masatsu = friction, rubbing; 擦る kosuru = to rub or scrub; 擦れる sureru = to rub against, wear down, become jaded; 擦りむく surimuku = to abrade or scrape; 擦り切れる surikireru = to wear out **DESCRIPTION:** compared to (警)察 keisatsu (police, # 896) (identical pronunciation), this kanji adds a kneeling guy on the left; it retains the bad haircut on top of a peaked roof with a bench hat on the left, above 二 (two) spinning on 小 (small) **CUES:** the guy on the right with this bad haircut is a **Sat**isfied **Su**perintendent at the 察 (police) department who is having some 摩擦 ma**satsu** (friction) with this **Co-Su**perintendent on the left, who has to kneel after the superintendent stepped on his foot, and they are **Su**ing each other **ALSO COMPARE:** other similar kanji at # **297** and # **1347**

1430. 旗 **PRONUNCIATIONS: ki, hata** **MEANINGS:** national flag, banner, standard **EXAMPLES:** 国旗 kokki = national flag; 旗 hata = banner, flag **DESCRIPTION:** on the left, 方 kata (honorable person, # 114); at the upper right, a horizontal crutch; at the lower right, a bucket above a wide skirt, as seen in (時)期 jiki (season, # 711) (identical pronunciation), which reminds us of a woman with a bucket with several compartments and a wide skirt **CUES:** this woman on the right with this wide skirt makes **Qui**che in this bucket at a **Ha**waiian **Ta**vern for this 方 (honorable person) on the left, and she holds this crutch up like a 旗 **hata** (flag) when the food is ready **ALSO COMPARE:** other similar kanji at # **711**, # **920** and # **2080**

1431. 汽 **PRONUNCIATION: ki** **MEANINGS:** vapor, steam **EXAMPLE:** 汽車 kisha = a train with a steam locomotive **DESCRIPTION:** compared to 気(持ち) kimochi (feeling, # 321) (identical pronunciation), this kanji omits the X at the bottom and adds a water radical on the left, suggesting steam; it retains the lean-to with a triple roof **CUE:** after I received a **K**ey to a 汽車 **ki**sha (a train with a steam locomotive), I tried to park it under this lean-to with a triple roof, but it crashed, causing this water to leak **COMPARE:** other similar kanji at # **321**

1432. 剣 **PRONUNCIATIONS: ken, tsurugi** **MEANINGS:** sabre, sword, blade **EXAMPLES:** 真剣 shinken = earnest, sincere; 剣道 kendou = Japanese fencing with bamboo swords; 剣 tsurugi = a sword **DESCRIPTION:** compared to (危)険 kiken (danger, # 196) (identical pronunciation), this kanji omits ß on the left and adds the katakana リ ri, which is sometimes described as a knife, on the right; it retains the horizontally placed keg stuck in a 大 (big) washing machine, which can also be seen as two eyes on a person with a flat cap, under a roof **CUES:** after **Ken** and リ **Ri** finish working on this stuck-keg problem, they will get a **Tsui**tcase (suitcase) from their **R**oom with their **Gea**r and go to the 剣道 **ken**dou (Japanese fencing) club **GROUP:** (危)険 kiken = danger, # 196; (試)験 shiken = examination, # 382, 検(査) kensa = investigation, # 859; 剣(道) kendou = Japanese fencing, # 1432; 倹(約) ken'yaku = thrift, # 2064; **Note** that all of these kanji can be pronounced "ken" **ALSO COMPARE:** other similar kanji at # **1985**

1433. 忍 **PRONUNCIATIONS: shino, nin** **MEANINGS:** endure, conceal, spy, sneak **EXAMPLES:** 忍ぶ shinobu = to endure, to conceal oneself; 忍者 ninja = a spy or secret agent; 忍耐 nintai = patience **DESCRIPTION:** compared to (確)認 kakunin (confirmation, # 1036) (identical pronunciation), this kanji omits 言 (to say) on the left; it retains 刀 katana (sword, # 102), with a slash across its handle, above 心 kokoro (heart, # 306) **CUES:** when a 忍者 **nin**ja had his mission sabotaged by a **S**heep from **No**rway and this sword got slashed, he felt like a **Nin**ny, and this 心 (heart) started to ache **ALSO COMPARE:** other similar kanji at # **1488**

1434. 耐 PRONUNCIATIONS: **tai, ta**
MEANINGS: proof, enduring EXAMPLES:
忍耐 nin**tai** = patience; 耐久力 **ta**ikyuuryoku
= durability; 耐久性 **ta**ikyuusei = durability;
耐える **ta**eru = to endure or resist
DESCRIPTION: at the upper left, a limousine antenna, as seen in 面(白い) omoshiroi (interesting, # 282); at the lower left, this is a modified book shelf, as seen in 冊 satsu (counter for books, # 568); on the right, a kneeling sunny guy next to a piece of gum, as seen in 寸(前) sunzen (on the verge, # 1369) CUES: this 寸 (kneeling sunny guy) attaches this limousine antenna to this 冊 (book shelf) with this gum because he is **T**ired of poor reception at the **Ta**vern he frequents, but it takes 忍耐 nin**tai** (patience) to make the new system work
ALSO COMPARE: other similar kanji at # **131** and # **522**

1435. 獄 PRONUNCIATION: **goku**
MEANINGS: prison, jail EXAMPLES: 地獄 ji**goku** = hell; 監獄 kan**goku** = jail, prison
DESCRIPTION: on the left, a woman contorting her body, as seen in 猫 neko (cat, # 72); in the middle, 言(う) iu (to speak, # 430); on the right, 犬 inu (dog, # 190)
CUE: 地獄 ji**goku** (hell) might consist of being trapped between this 猫 (cat) and this 犬 (dog), while having to listen to someone 言 (speak) commercials for **G**old **Ko**ol-Aid for eternity
ALSO COMPARE: similar kanji at # **945** and # **948**

1436. 鎖 PRONUNCIATIONS: **sa, kusari**
MEANINGS: chain, irons, connection
EXAMPLES: 閉鎖 heisa = closing, shutdown; 鎖 kusari = a chain DESCRIPTION: on the left, 金 kane (money, # 301); at the upper right, three old boys, as seen in 覚(える) oboeru (to memorize, # 54), but these resemble a three-pronged switch; at the lower right, 貝 kai (money chest, # 83) CUES: this 貝 (money chest), where I deposit my **Sa**lary, has this three-pronged switch at the top which I turn whenever I need to get 金 (money) like this in order to buy **Co**ol **Sa**ri**s** to wear with my 鎖 **kusari** (chains)
ALSO COMPARE: other similar kanji at # **707**, # **1625** and # **2010**

1437. 財 PRONUNCIATIONS: **sai, zai**
MEANINGS: property, wealth, assets
EXAMPLES: 財布 **sai**fu = a wallet or purse; 財産 **zai**san = assets, fortune, property
DESCRIPTION: compared to (素)材 so**zai** (ingredient, # 1378) (identical pronunciation), this kanji substitutes 貝 kai (shell, or money chest, # 83) for 木 (tree) on the left; it retains the left-wing scientist who has put his left hip back into its socket CUES: this guy on the right is a left-wing **S**cientist who will travel to **Zai**re (the former name of the Congo) after he gets some money from this 貝 (money chest) and puts it into his 財布 **sai**fu (wallet) ALSO COMPARE: other similar kanji at # **1417** and # **2058**

1438. 憲 PRONUNCIATION: **ken**
MEANINGS: constitution, law
EXAMPLE: 憲法 **ken**pou = a constitution
DESCRIPTION: on the top level, a bad haircut; on the second level, an owl's perch as seen in 青(い) aoi (blue, # 155), but the shortest rung on the perch is at the top rather than in the middle; on the third level, 目 me (eye, # 51), turned horizontally, resembling three eyes; on the bottom level, 心 kokoro (heart, # 306) CUE: after **Ken** received this bad haircut, he felt pain in this 心 (heart), but he climbed this owl's perch and read the 憲法 **ken**pou (constitution) with these three eyes, to see if he could sue his barber
COMPARE: other similar kanji at # **1260** and # **1603**

1439. 絹 **PRONUNCIATION: kinu**
MEANING: silk **EXAMPLE:** 絹 kinu = silk
DESCRIPTION: on the left, 糸 ito (thread, # 219); at the upper right, 口 kuchi (mouth, # 426); at the lower right, 月 tsuki (moon, # 148)
CUE: my **Ki**mono looks **N**ew, and I try to keep it that way, holding this 糸 (thread) made of 絹 **kinu** (silk), in this 口 (mouth) while I use it to make repairs under this 月 (moon)
COMPARE: other similar kanji at # **2087**

1440. 御 **PRONUNCIATIONS: go, gyo, o, on** **MEANINGS:** honorable, manipulate
EXAMPLES: 御連絡 gorenraku = honorable contact or communication (this can also be spelled ご連絡); 制御 seigyo = control, governing, checking; 御中元 ochuugen = an honorable mid-summer gift (this can also be spelled お中元); 満員御礼 man'in onrei = a banner of thanks for a full house (seen at concerts, tournaments, etc.)
DESCRIPTION: compared to 卸 oroshi (wholesale, # 1218), this adds a man with a double hat on the left; it retains the upper portion of a Native American chief, 正 (correct) and a signature seal
CUES: this man on the left will buy a **G**oat for a 卸 (wholesale) price and, once he has 制御 sei**gyo** (control) of it, he will feed it **G**yoza, **O**ranges and **O**nions, in addition to one of his hats
GROUP: 卸 oroshi = wholesale, # 1218; (制)御 seigyo = control, # 1440 **ALSO COMPARE:** other similar kanji at # **1046** and # **1150**

1441. 俳 **PRONUNCIATION: hai**
MEANINGS: haiku, actor **EXAMPLES:** 俳優 haiyuu = actor, actress; 俳句 haiku = a style of Japanese poetry, or a poem written in this style
DESCRIPTION: compared to 非(常) hijou (emergency, # 682), this adds a man with a slanted hat on the left; it retains the hero with two wings
CUE: this man is tilting his hat to show his face to this winged 非 (hero) and asking for help to **Hi**de from some crooks, and he plans to write a 俳句 **hai**ku (poem) about this **ALSO COMPARE:** similar kanji at # **851**

1442. 微 **PRONUNCIATIONS: hoho, bi, kasu** **MEANINGS:** delicate, minute, insignificance
EXAMPLES: 微笑め hohoemu = to smile; 微熱 binetsu = a slight fever; 微妙 bi'myou = subtle, delicate; 微か kasuka = faint or vague (usually written かすか)
DESCRIPTION: compared to (特)徴 tokuchou (characteristic, # 784), this substitutes π (the Greek letter pi, also known as a pious yak) for the 王 (king) in the lower center; it retains the man with two hats, a 山 (mountain) and the dancer with a ponytail, who is beautiful
CUES: this man with two hats keeps this π (pious yak) under this 山 (mountain), which is a **H**ome to **H**ornets, and he has a relationship with this **B**eautiful dancer, about which he is rather 微か **kasu**ka (vague), apart from saying that he will give her a hat, plus some **C**arrot **S**oup
ALSO COMPARE: other similar kanji at # **784** and # **1385**

1443. 浅 **PRONUNCIATIONS: sen, asa**
MEANINGS: shallow, superficial, light (sleep), pale, short (time), early, young
EXAMPLES: 浅見 senken = a shallow view or superficial idea; 浅い asai = shallow, superficial, frivolous, wretched, shameful
DESCRIPTION: compared to (金)銭 kinsen (money, # 744) (identical pronunciation), this kanji substitutes a water radical for 金 (money) on the left; it retains the halberd that our senator thought he didn't need to attain enlightenment
CUES: our **Sen**ator used this halberd to **A**ssault a colleague who was swimming in this water, but this only created an 浅い **asa**i (superficial) wound
ALSO COMPARE: other similar kanji at # **605**

1444. 庁 PRONUNCIATION: chou
MEANING: government office
EXAMPLE: 官庁 kanchou = government office
DESCRIPTION: at the upper left, a lean-to with a chimney; inside the lean-to, 丁 (目) choume (city block, # 702) (identical pronunciation), which resembles a nail   **CUE:** Margaret **Cho** stores 丁 (nails) like this in this lean-to and uses them for building 官庁 kan**chou** (government offices)
ALSO COMPARE: other similar kanji at # **702**

1445. 郵 PRONUNCIATION: yuu
MEANINGS: mail, stagecoach stop
EXAMPLES: 郵便局 yuubinkyoku = the post office; 郵政 yuusei = the postal system
DESCRIPTION: compared to 垂(直) suichoku (vertical, # 799), this adds ß beta from the Greek alphabet on the right; it retains the streamlined Swedish 車 (car) that runs on hubcabs   **CUE:** our 郵政 **yuu**sei (postal system) uses 垂 (streamlined Swedish cars) like this to carry packages to ß (Greece) and the **Yu**kon   **ALSO COMPARE:** other similar kanji at # **799** and # **1843**

1446. 接 PRONUNCIATIONS: se, setsu
MEANINGS: touch, contact, adjoin, piece together
EXAMPLES: 接する sessuru = to border on, adjoin or encounter; 直接 chokusetsu = directly
DESCRIPTION: on the left, a kneeling guy; at the upper right, 立(つ) tatsu (to stand, # 11), which resembles a bell; at the lower right, 女 onna (female, # 235)   **CUES:** this guy on the left kneels to try to **Se**ll this 立 (bell) 直接 choku**setsu** (directly) to this 女 (female) customer after he **Set** up a **Super** store   **ALSO COMPARE:** other similar kanji at # **1569** and # **2086**

1447. 被 PRONUNCIATIONS: kabu, hi
MEANINGS: incur, cover, wear, be exposed (film)
EXAMPLES: 被る kaburu = to wear on the head (this is usually written かぶる); 被害 higai = damage or loss   **DESCRIPTION:** compared to 披(露) hirou (announcement, # 1389) (identical pronunciation), this substitutes Happy Jimmy Carter with two lips, as seen in 初(めて) hajimete (for the first time, # 104), for the kneeling guy on the left; it retains 皮 kawa (skin, # 833) on the right, which is sometimes known as Straight Arrow   **CUES:** this Happy Jimmy with two lips and this Straight Arrow want to buy a **Ca**b**oo**se and turn it into a medical clinic where they can try to **He**al some of the 被害 **hi**gai (damage) caused by train wrecks   **ALSO COMPARE:** other similar kanji at # **833** and # **1615**

1448. 網 PRONUNCIATIONS: ami, mou
MEANINGS: netting, network   **EXAMPLES:** 網 ami = a net; データ網 deeta mou = a data network   **DESCRIPTION:** on the left, 糸 ito (thread, # 219); on the right, a two-sided lean-to, as seen in 同(じ) onaji (the same, # 339); inside the lean-to, two antennae above a T, which reminds us of Tiberius; at the bottom, a shaky table as seen in 亡(くなる) nakunaru (to die, # 585)
CUES: Emperor Tiberius, represented by this T, is wearing these two antennae and sitting on this 亡 (shaky table) inside this two-sided lean-to, using this 糸 (thread) to make an 網 **ami** (net) with his **Ami**gos (friends, in Spanish), to keep people from falling into the **M**oat outside his castle
ALSO COMPARE: other similar kanji at # **479**, # **585** and # **1997**

1449. 騎 PRONUNCIATION: ki
MEANINGS: equestrian, riding horses
EXAMPLE: 騎手 kishu = a jockey
DESCRIPTION: on the left, 馬 uma (horse, # 958); on the right, 奇(妙) kimyou (strange, # 854) (identical pronunciation), which reminds us of a 可 (cute) person wearing a kimono that's too 大 (big)   **CUE:** a 奇 (strange) person wearing a Kimono that's too 大 (big) is a 騎手 **ki**shu (jockey) who rides this 馬 (horse)   **ALSO COMPARE:** similar kanji at # **604** and at # **826**

1450. 裁 PRONUNCIATIONS: sai, ta

MEANINGS: tailor, judge, decision **EXAMPLES:** 裁判 saiban = trial or judgment; 裁判官 saibankan = a judge; 裁つ tatsu = to cut (cloth) **DESCRIPTION:** compared to 栽(培) saibai (cultivation, # 1233) (identical pronunciation), this kanji substitutes 衣(服) ifuku (clothing, # 1042) for the 木 (tree) at the lower left; it retains 土 (soil) and a halberd **CUES:** this reminds us of **P**sychological **T**actics used by prosecutors during 裁判 **sai**ban (trials), such as throwing this 土 (soil) onto this 衣 (clothing) belonging to defendants and threatening them with halberds like this **COMPARE:** similar kanji at # **1042** and # **1862**

1451. 慈 PRONUNCIATIONS: ji, itsuku

MEANING: mercy **EXAMPLES:** 慈善 jizen = charity; 慈しむ itsukushimu = to love or be affectionate, to cherish, to pity **DESCRIPTION:** compared to 磁(石) jishaku (magnet, # 1236) (identical pronunciation), this kanji omits 石 (stone) on the left and adds 心 kokoro (heart, # 306) at the bottom; it retains the two truncated 糸 (skeet shooters), each consisting of two flexed elbows, carrying an upside-down bench, who discovered a magnet and were hailed as geniuses **CUES:** these two truncated 糸 (skeetshooters), who have big 心 (hearts) like this, carry this two-legged bench to their **J**eep to take to a 慈善 **ji**zen (charity) event, where one of them **E**ats **C**ookies and the other eats vegetables **ALSO COMPARE:** other similar kanji at # **1236** and # **1908**

1452. 堪 PRONUNCIATIONS: ta, kan, tan

MEANINGS: withstand, endure, support, resist **EXAMPLES:** 堪える taeru = to endure or resist (this is usually spelled 耐える, # 1434); 堪忍 kannin = forgiveness, patient endurance; 堪能 tannou = skillful (a na adjective), or enjoyment/satisfaction (a noun) **DESCRIPTION:** compared to 勘(定) kanjou (a bill, # 1161) (identical pronunciation), this kanji omits 力 (force) on the right and adds 土 tsuchi (soil, # 59) on the left; it retains the bucket with three compartments in which lunch was served in Kansas, and the 匹 (counter for small animals) **CUES:** **T**arzan visited **Kan**sas, saw this 匹 (small animal) carrying this bucket, and had a **Tan**trum when he saw that it was full of this 土 (soil), but later he asked for 堪忍 **kan**nin (forgiveness) **ALSO COMPARE:** other similar kanji at # **1161**

1453. 吉 PRONUNCIATIONS: kichi, yoshi, kitsu

MEANINGS: good luck, joy **EXAMPLES:** 吉 kichi = good fortune; 吉野 Yoshino = an old province of Japan; 不吉 fukitsu = ill omen, unlucky, ominous **DESCRIPTION:** compared to 詰(問) kitsumon (cross-examination, # 781) (identical pronunciation), this kanji omits 言 (to speak) on the left; it retains the 士 (man) above a 口 (tsuitcase) which contains kittens from Sudan **CUES:** this 士 (man), wearing **Kit**schy clothes made from the wool of **Yo**semite **Sh**eep, stands on this 口 (tsuitcase) containing **Kit**tens from **Su**dan and offers to sell them, claiming that they will bring 吉 **kichi** (good fortune) **GROUP:** 結(果) kekka = result, # 231; 喜(ぶ) yorokobu = to be delighted, # 599; 嬉(しい) ureshii = pleased, # 600; 詰(問) kitsumon = cross examination, # 781; 樹(木) jumoku = trees, # 1089; 吉 kichi = good fortune, # 1453

1454. 渋 PRONUNCIATIONS: juu, shibu

MEANING: astringent **EXAMPLES:** 渋滞 juutai = gridlock (traffic); 渋る shiburu = to hesitate or be reluctant **DESCRIPTION:** on the left, a water radical, which reminds us of juice; at the upper right, 止(める) tomeru (to stop, # 173); at the lower right, a segmented X **CUES:** I 止 (stop) and 渋る **shibu**ru (hesitate) before drinking **J**uice made from this water, since I may spill it on my **Shi**ite **B**oots, and I mark such suggestions with segmented X's like this **GROUP:** 渋(る) shiburu

= to hesitate, # 1454; 摂(取) sesshu = absorption, # 1713; 塁 rui = a base (baseball), # 1853   **ALSO COMPARE:** other similar kanji at # **1929**

1455. 促 PRONUNCIATIONS: soku, unaga MEANINGS: stimulate, urge
EXAMPLES: 促進 sokushin = propagation, promotion; 促す unagasu = to urge
DESCRIPTION: compared to 足 ashi (foot, # 449), or (不)足 fusoku (insufficient, # 449) (identical pronunciation), this kanji adds a man with a slanted hat on the left
CUES: this man on the left tilts his hat back in order to see a faucet that he will turn on with this 足 (foot), **S**oaking his **U**nappreciated **G**arden, which he 促す **unaga**su (urges) us to enjoy
ALSO COMPARE: other similar kanji at # **449**

1456. 仮 PRONUNCIATIONS: kari, ka, ke, ga MEANINGS: temporary, interim
EXAMPLES: 仮に kari ni = if; 仮定 katei = supposition, hypothesis, conjecture; 仮病 kebyou = a feigned illness; 平仮名 hiragana
DESCRIPTION: compared to 反(対) hantai (opposition, # 680), this adds a man with a slanted hat; it retains the F and the X
CUES: this man on the left tilts his hat back to examine my 反 (opposition) to the 仮定 **ka**tei (supposition) that if you **C**arry a **C**at in a **K**ettle into a **G**arden full of dogs, it will be calm
ALSO COMPARE: similar kanji at # **1166**

1457. 翌 PRONUNCIATION: yoku
MEANINGS: the following, next
EXAMPLE: 翌日 yokujitsu = the next day
DESCRIPTION: compared to (左)翼 sayoku (left-wing politics, # 912) (identical pronunciation), this kanji substitutes 立(つ) tatsu (to stand, # 11) for the 田 (rice paddy) and the plants balanced on a hill at the bottom; it retains 羽 (feather) at the top
CUE: one day I was 立 (standing) in a cloud of these 羽 (feathers), but 翌日 **yoku**jitsu (the next day) I was at home eating **Y**ogurt and **C**ookies

GROUP: 弱(い) yowai = weak, # 471; 習(う) narau = to learn, # 472; 羽 hane = feather, # 755; 翼 tsubasa = wing, # 912; 翻(訳) hon'yaku = translation, # 1087; 翌(日) yokujitsu = the next day, # 1457; 扇(子) sensu = a folding fan, # 1833; 溺(れる) oboreru = to drown, # 1978
ALSO COMPARE: other similar kanji at # **11** and # **352**

1458. 皇 PRONUNCIATIONS: ou, nou, kou MEANING: emperor
EXAMPLES: 皇子 ouji = an imperial prince; 天皇 tennou = the Emperor of Japan; 皇居 koukyo = the Imperial Palace
DESCRIPTION: at the top, 白 shiro (white, # 44); at the bottom, 王(様) ousama (king, # 1077) (identical pronunciation)
CUES: this 王 (king) is **O**ld, he wears garments that are 白 (white) like this, he has a good **N**ose, he proclaims himself 天皇 ten**nou** (Emperor of Japan), and he holds **C**ourt in the capital
ALSO COMPARE: other similar kanji at # **1876** and # **2014**

1459. 后 PRONUNCIATIONS: gou, kou
MEANINGS: empress, queen
EXAMPLES: 皇后 kougou = an empress; 后妃 kouhi = a queen
DESCRIPTION: compared to 垢 aka (dirt, 665), or (歯)垢 shikou (dental plaque, # 665) (identical pronunciation), this kanji omits the 土 (soil) on the left; it retains the F, which reminds us of Failure, above 口 (mouth)
CUES: a 后妃 **kou**hi (queen) paid **G**old to a dentist who came to **C**ourt to repair problems in this 口 (mouth), but the work was a **F**ailure and received this F
ALSO COMPARE: other similar kanji at # **1983**

1460. 陛 PRONUNCIATION: hei
MEANING: highness EXAMPLE: 陛下 heika = the Emperor, Your Majesty DESCRIPTION: on the left, β beta from the Greek alphabet; at the upper right, 比(べる) kuraberu (to compare, # 857, which reminds us of two heroes); at the lower right, 土 tsuchi (soil, # 59) CUE: this β (Greek) guy Hates to see these two 比 (heroes) living in this 土 (soil), and he asks the 陛下 heika (Emperor) to help them ALSO COMPARE: other similar kanji at # **1294** and # **2030**

1461. 脳 PRONUNCIATION: nou
MEANINGS: brain, memory
EXAMPLES: 脳 nou = the brain; 頭脳 zunou = brains, head; 首脳 shunou = leader, top executive
DESCRIPTION: compared to (苦)悩 kunou (agony, # 1181) (identical pronunciation), this kanji substitutes 月 tsuki (moon, # 148) for the erect man on the left; it retains the three lines above the open box with an X inside, which represent a bee hive containing an unknown number of bees
CUE: while my 脳 **nou** (brain) was thinking about how to fly to this 月 (moon), these three bees, out of the X (unknown number) living in this hive, stung my Nose ALSO COMPARE: other similar kanji at # **1181** and # **1794**

1462. 冗 PRONUNCIATION: jou
MEANINGS: superfluous; uselessness
EXAMPLE: 冗談 joudan = a joke, humor
DESCRIPTION: at the top, an asymmetrical roof; at the bottom, a tall desk, as seen in 机 tsukue (desk, # 140) CUE: **Jo**an of Arc put this asymmetrical roof over this 机 (desk), and she must have a sense of 冗談 **jou**dan (humor), since the desk was already inside a house
GROUP: 机 tsukue = desk, # 140; 飢(える) ueru = to starve, # 924; 肌 hada = skin, # 980; 処 (理する) shori suru = to deal with, # 1149; (証) 拠 shouko = evidence, # 1151; (反)抗 hankou = rebellion, # 1196; 几(帳面) kichoumen = scrupulous, # 1243; 航(空) koukuu = aviation, # 1295; 冗(談) joudan = a joke, # 1462
ALSO COMPARE: kanji containing 几, which can be seen as a shorter desk, at # 557; kanji with slashed desks at # 1511

1463. 致 PRONUNCIATIONS: ita, chi
MEANINGS: do, forward EXAMPLES: 致す itasu = to do honorably; 一致 icchi = agreement, coincidence, conformity, cooperation; 致命傷 chimeishou = a fatal mistake or injury
DESCRIPTION: compared to 至(る) itaru (to lead to, # 609) (identical pronunciation), this kanji adds a dancer with a ponytail on the right; it retains 一 (one) 厶 (cow) resting on 土 (soil) on a road leading to some Italian ruins
CUES: when this dancer saw this 一 (one) 厶 (cow) stuck in this 土 (soil) on a road leading to some **It**alian monuments, she got some milk from it for making **Ch**eese, which she 致した **ita**shita (did honorably)
ALSO COMPARE: other similar kanji at # **63**

1464. 紀 PRONUNCIATION: ki
MEANINGS: chronicle, history, geologic period
EXAMPLES: 世紀 seiki = century; 紀元 kigen = era, A.D.; 紀元前 kigenzen = B.C.
DESCRIPTION: compared to 記(事) kiji (newspaper article, # 550) (identical pronunciation), this kanji substitutes 糸 (skeet shooter, # 219) for 言 (to say) on the left; it retains the 己 (snake) that killed Jimmy Carter
CUE: during the last 世紀 sei**ki** (century), this 糸 (skeet shooter) fired skeets and **K**illed this 己 (snake)
ALSO COMPARE: similar kanji at # **1078**

1465. 裂 PRONUNCIATIONS: retsu, sa
MEANINGS: split, rend, tear
EXAMPLES: 分裂 bunretsu = division, separation; 裂ける sakeru = to split or tear, intransitive; 裂く saku = to split or rip, transitive;

引き裂く hikisaku = to tear off or separate
DESCRIPTION: at the top, 列 retsu (line, # 1124) (identical pronunciation); at the bottom, 衣(服) ifuku (clothing, # 1042)
CUES: when I was standing in a 列 (line) like this, the **Re**tro **Sui**t that I use as this 衣 (clothing) **Sa**gged in the back, and it 裂けた **sa**keta (split)
ALSO COMPARE: other similar kanji at # **164**, # **1042** and # **1124**

1466. 掲 PRONUNCIATIONS: kaka, kei
MEANINGS: put up, display, publish
EXAMPLES: 掲げる kakageru = to put up (e.g., a flag); 掲示 keiji = a written notice or announcement; 掲載する keisai suru = to publish or print
DESCRIPTION: on the left, a kneeling guy; at the upper right, 日 hi (sun, # 32), but this could be a cabinet with two drawers; at the lower right, 匂(い) nioi = fragrance, # 949   **CUES:** this guy on the left is a **Ca**lifornia **Ca**rpenter who is kneeling to read a 掲示 **kei**ji (written notice) on the 日 (two-drawer cabinet) at the upper right, which has this nice 匂 (fragrance) because it's full of **Ca**ke
GROUP: 掲(載する) keisai suru = to publish, # 1466; 渇(く) kawaku = to be thirsty, # 1928; 喝(采) kassai = applause, # 1934; 褐(色) kasshoku = dark brown, # 2059   **ALSO COMPARE:** other similar kanji at # **2048**

1467. 稿 PRONUNCIATION: kou
MEANINGS: draft, copy, manuscript
EXAMPLES: 投稿 toukou = a post or written contribution (e.g., to a journal); 草稿 soukou = a draft or manuscript   **DESCRIPTION:** compared to 高(い) takai (tall, # 19), or 高(校) koukou (high school, # 19) (identical pronunciation), this kanji adds 禾 (a grain plant with a ripe head) on the left; it retains the tall courthouse, which contains a box without a napkin inside a two-sided lean-to
CUE: I wrote a 投稿 tou**kou** (written contribution) about the beauty of this 高 (tall) Courthouse standing next to this ripe grain
GROUP: 高(い) takai = tall, # 19; 橋 hashi = bridge, # 139; 向(く) muku = to face toward, # 340; (草)稿 soukou = a draft, # 1467; (高)尚 (な) koushou na = noble, # 1629; 矯(正) kyousei = a correction, # 2061   **ALSO COMPARE:** other similar kanji at # **19**, # **1474** and # **1797**

1468. 荘 PRONUNCIATION: sou
MEANINGS: villa, inn, cottage
EXAMPLE: 別荘 bessou = a summer house, villa or cottage   **DESCRIPTION:** compared to 壮(大) soudai (magnificent, # 769) (identical pronunciation), this adds a plant radical at the top; it retains the 士 (man) sitting on a bench listening to soul music   **CUE:** this 士 (man) sits on this bench at his 別荘 bes**sou** (summer house) and listens to **Sou**l music, while enjoying these hanging plants
GROUP: 声 koe = voice, # 40; (紳)士 shinshi = gentleman, # 66; 仕(事) shigoto = work, # 67; 壮(大な) soudai na = magnificent, # 769; 装(置) souchi = equipment, # 1043; 穀(物) kokumotsu = grain, # 1172; 壷 tsubo = jar, # 1274; (別)荘 bessou = a summer house, # 1468; (奴)隷 dorei = a slave, # 1583; (太)鼓 taiko = a drum, # 1776; 殻 kara = a shell, # 1904; 壱 ichi = one, # 2048   **ALSO COMPARE:** other similar kanji at # **998**

1469. 牧 PRONUNCIATION: boku
MEANINGS: breed, care for, feed, pasture
EXAMPLES: 牧師 bokushi = a pastor or minister; 牧場 bokujou = stock farm, ranch, pasture   **DESCRIPTION:** compared to 特(別) tokubetsu (special, # 218), this substitutes a dancer with a ponytail for 寺 (temple) on the right; it retains 牛 (cow)   **CUE:** this dancer thinks that this 牛 (cow) which lives on her 牧場 **boku**jou (ranch) is **B**oring but **C**ool
ALSO COMPARE: other similar kanji at # **1765**

1470. 欄 PRONUNCIATION: ran
MEANINGS: column, blank, space
EXAMPLE: 欄 ran = column (newspaper)
DESCRIPTION: on the left, 木 ki (tree, # 118); on the right, 門 mon (gate, # 409); inside the gate, 東 higashi (east, # 508), which can be seen as a tree wearing bifocals
CUE: when I write my newspaper 欄 **ran** (columns), I sit near this 木 (tree) on my **Ran**ch and look 東 (east) through this 門 (gate)
ALSO COMPARE: other similar kanji at # **1271** and # **1755**

1471. 孝 PRONUNCIATION: kou
MEANINGS: child, sign of the rat
EXAMPLES: 孝行 koukou = filial piety; 親孝行 oyakoukou = filial piety
DESCRIPTION: compared to 考(える) kangaeru (to think, # 469), or (思)考 shikou (thought, # 469) (identical pronunciation), this kanji substitutes 子 ko (child, # 182) for the kangaroo's leg at the bottom; it retains the 土 (soil) and the scisssors
CUE: this 子 (child) has to **Co**pe with the consequences of playing with these scissors, but at least she displays 親孝行 oya**kou**kou (filial piety)
GROUP: 教(える) oshieru = to teach, # 187; 孝(行) koukou = filial piety, # 1471; 酵(素) kouso = an enzyme, # 1836

1472. 鋼 PRONUNCIATION: kou
MEANING: steel EXAMPLES: 鉄鋼 tekkou = steel; 鋼鉄 koutetsu = steel; 製鋼業 seikougyou = steel industry DESCRIPTION: compared to 綱 tsuna (cable, # 1200), this substitutes (お)金 okane (money, # 301) for 糸 (skeet shooter) on the left; it retains the 岡 (hill), which rsembles a model of a mountain with a handle and antennae, inside a two-sided lean-to (this radical inside the lean-to can also be seen as a chairlift seat hanging from two frayed cables)

CUE: I paid this 金 (money) for this 岡 (hill) which contains a mine, where I use 鉄鋼 tek**kou** (steel) cables to pull **Co**al out of the ground
ALSO COMPARE: other similar kanji at # **1200** and # **2010**

1473. 丘 PRONUNCIATIONS: oka, kyuu
MEANINGS: hill, knoll EXAMPLES: 丘 oka = a hill; 砂丘 sakyuu = a sand dune
DESCRIPTION: compared to 兵(隊) heitai (soldier, # 917), this omits the legs at the bottom; it retains the pair of pliers set up on a platform by a soldier CUES: Occasionally people in **Cu**ba put pliers on platforms like this on 丘 **oka** (hills) to make them more visible ALSO COMPARE: 近(い) chikai = close, # 390; 岡 oka = a hill, # 1528; other similar kanji at # **892**

1474. 亭 PRONUNCIATION: tei
MEANINGS: pavilion, restaurant, music hall
EXAMPLES: 亭主 teishu = husband, owner; 料亭 ryoutei = a traditional Japanese restaurant
DESCRIPTION: compared to (バス)停 basutei (bus stop, # 627) (identical pronunciation), this kanji omits the man with a slanted hat on the left; it retains a tire stop above a 口 (box) on a roof above a 丁 (nail) CUE: my 亭主 **tei**shu (husband), who is a **Tai**lor, sews with this 丁 (nail) under this roof, near this 口 (box) of thread that is protected by this tire stop GROUP: 高(い) takai = high, # 19; 京(都) kyouto = Kyoto, # 514; 涼(しい) suzushii = cool, # 515; 景(色) keshiki = view, # 516; (バス)停 basutei = bus stop, # 627; 影 kage = shadow, # 839; 就(職する) shuushoku suru = to find employment, # 974; 蹴(る) keru = to kick, # 975; 豪(華) gouka = wonderful, # 1357; (草)稿 soukou = a draft, # 1467; 亭(主) teishu = husband, # 1474; 哀(れ) aware = pity, # 1643; 鯨 kujira = a whale, # 1981 ALSO COMPARE: other similar kanji at # **702**

1475. 麻 PRONUNCIATIONS: ma, asa
MEANINGS: hemp, flax **EXAMPLES:**
麻薬 mayaku = a narcotic; 麻酔 masui = anesthesia; 麻 asa = hemp, linen
DESCRIPTION: compared to 摩(擦) masatsu (friction, # 1428) (identical pronunciation), this kanji omits the 手 (hand) at the bottom; it retains the lean-to with a chimney, containing a 林 hayashi (grove, # 125) which is massaged by a master
CUES: my **Ma**ster must have been on 麻薬 **ma**yaku (narcotics) when he planted this 林 (grove) under this lean-to, and later he **A**ssaulted me
GROUP: 磨(く) migaku = to brush, # 126; 床 yuka = floor, # 946; 歴(史) rekishi = history, # 1313; (悪)魔 akuma = devil, # 1332 (also identical pronunciation); 摩(擦) masatsu = friction, # 1428; 麻 asa = hemp, # 1475; 暦 koyomi = a calendar, # 1801 **ALSO COMPARE:** other kanji with multiple trees at # 943

1476. 酔 PRONUNCIATIONS: yo, sui
MEANINGS: drunk, feel sick
EXAMPLES: 酔う you = to get drunk; 酔っ払う yopparau = to get drunk; 麻酔 masui = anesthesia **DESCRIPTION:** on the left, 酒 sake (alcoholic beverage, # 465), without its water radical (this can also be seen as a bucket of sake with a handle); at the upper right, 九 kyuu (nine, # 111); at the lower right, 十 juu (ten, # 18) **CUES:** a **Y**ogi drank 九十 kyuujuu (ninety) cups of this 酒 (sake) in **Sw**eden and 酔っ払った **yo**paratta (got drunk) **ALSO COMPARE:** other similar kanji at # **827**, # **1480**, and # **1658**

1477. 憩 PRONUNCIATIONS: kei, iko
MEANINGS: rest, relax, repose
EXAMPLES: 休憩 kyuukei = a rest or break; 憩い ikoi = rest **DESCRIPTION:** at the upper left, 舌 shita (tongue, # 1213); at the upper right, 自(分) jibun (myself, # 55); at the bottom, 心 kokoro (heart, # 306)
CUES: speaking from this 心 (heart) belonging to 自 (myself), I want to stick this 舌 (tongue) out at the material world, move to a **C**ave, take a 休憩 kyuu**kei** (break) and live **E**conomically **ALSO COMPARE:** similar kanji at # **1213** and # **1381**

1478. 充 PRONUNCIATION: juu
MEANINGS: allot, fill **EXAMPLES:** 充実 juujitsu = fullness, completion, perfection; 充電する juuden suru = to charge (a battery) **DESCRIPTION:** compared to (大)統(領) daitoryou (president, # 1125), this omits the 糸 (skeet shooter) on the left; it retains the ム (cow) under a tire stop on lopsided legs
CUE: this ム (cow) under a tire stop on lopsided legs has a lot of **Ju**ice (energy), and it aspires to 充実 **juu**jitsu (perfection)
ALSO COMPARE: other similar kanji at # **1125** and # **1990**

1479. 策 PRONUNCIATION: saku
MEANINGS: scheme, plan, means **EXAMPLES:** 策 saku = a plan, scheme or device; 政策 seisaku = a policy; 対策 taisaku = measures (actions), strategy **DESCRIPTION:** compared to 刺 toge (thorn, # 1284), this adds 竹 take (bamboo, # 134) at the top and omits 刂 ri on the right; it retains, 市 (city) grafted onto the lower half of 木 (tree)
CUE: I had a 策 **saku** (plan) to airdrop some **S**alty **C**ookies to this minature 市 (city) up in this 木 (tree), but it's shielded by this 竹 (bamboo) roof
ALSO COMPARE: other similar kanji at # **1284** and # **2074**

1480. 酸 PRONUNCIATIONS: su, san
MEANINGS: acid, bitterness, sour
EXAMPLES: 酸っぱい suppai = sour; 酸素 sanso = oxygen; 酸性 sansei = acidity
DESCRIPTION: on the left, 酒 sake (alcoholic beverage, # 465), without its water radical [this can also be seen as a bucket of sake with a handle, or a 四 (four) with a handle and an extra compartment]; at the upper right, the katakana ム mu, which is the sound made by a cow, resting on lopsided legs; at the lower right, a dancer with a ponytail CUES: this ム (cow) on lopsided legs and this dancer tried this 酒 (sake), but the taste was too 酸っぱい **su**ppai (sour), and the cow gave its portion to **S**uperman while the dancer gave hers to **San**ta Claus GROUP: 酒 sake = alcoholic beverage, # 465; (心)配 shinpai = worry, # 466; (焼)酎 shouchuu = a Japanese liquor, # 1099; 尊(敬する) sonkei suru = to respect, # 1208; 酢 su = vinegar, # 1373 (identical pronunciation); 酔(う) you = to get drunk, # 1476; 酸(素) sanso = oxygen, # 1480; (残)酷(な) zankoku na = brutal, # 1695; 酵(素) kouso = an enzyme, # 1836; 醜(い) minikui = ugly, # 1882; (報)酬 houshuu = a reward, # 1902; (覚)醒 kakusei = waking up, # 1918; (媒)酌 baishaku = matchmaking, # 1958; 醸(造) jouzou = brewing, # 1996; 猶(予) yuuyo = a postponement, # 1997; 酪(農) rakunou = dairy farming, # 2069 ALSO COMPARE: other similar kanji at # **1990**

1481. 博 PRONUNCIATIONS: haku, baku², paku², haka MEANINGS: Dr., Ph.D., wide knowledge, gamble EXAMPLES: 博物館 hakubutsukan = a museum (other than art); 博打 bakuchi = gambling; 万博 banpaku = a world fair; 博士 hakase = a doctoral degree holder
DESCRIPTION: compared to 薄(情) hakujou (cruel, # 258) (identical pronunciation), this kanji substitutes 十 juu (ten, # 18) for the water radical on the left, and it omits the plant radical at the top; it retains the upper portion of 犬 (dog), the 田 (rice paddy) and the 寸 (kneeling sunny guy who has dropped his gum) CUES: 十 (ten) hackers, including this 寸 (kneeling sunny guy who is a 博士 **haka**se (doctoral holder), play with this truncated 犬 (dog) in this 田 (rice paddy) and, since they think that **H**awaii is **C**ool, they go there for a **Hacka**thon ALSO COMPARE: other similar kanji at # **865**, # **1721** and # **1828**

1482. 秩 PRONUNCIATIONS: chitsu, chichi MEANINGS: regularity, salary, order
EXAMPLES: 秩序 chitsujo = order; 無秩序 muchitsujo = chaos, disorder; 秩父 Chichibu = a city in Saitama Prefecture
DESCRIPTION: on the left, 禾 (a grain plant with a ripe head); on the right, 失(う) ushinau (to lose, # 206), which is a fusion of 牛 (cow) and 大 (big) CUES: after this 禾 (grain) becomes ripe, this 大 (big) 牛 (cow) **Chea**ts by eating more than its share, and then I have to eat mainly **Chea**p **Chee**se, which contributes to a sense of 無秩序 mu**chitsu**jo (disorder) ALSO COMPARE: other similar kanji at # **304** and # **1797**

1483. 序 PRONUNCIATION: jo
MEANINGS: preface, beginning
EXAMPLES: 順序 junjo = order, sequence; 序文 jobun = a preface or introduction
DESCRIPTION: compared to 予(定) yotei (plan, # 544), this adds a lean-to with a chimney at the upper left; it retains the マ (mother) balanced on a nail who makes plans to attend a yoga class
CUE: this マ (mother) balanced on this nail in this lean-to with this chimney is Empress **J**osephine, and she explains her strange activities in the 序文 **jo**bun (introduction) to her book about Napoleon ALSO COMPARE: other similar kanji at # **544**

1484. 尺 **PRONUNCIATIONS:** jaku, shaku **MEANINGS:** Japanese foot, measure, scale, rule **EXAMPLES:** 巻き尺 makijaku = a tape measure; 尺度 shakudo = criterion, measure; 尺八 shakuhachi = a Japanese bamboo flute **DESCRIPTION:** we have referred to this as a wakeful eye in 訳 wake (reason, # 437), but it can also be seen as a shack with a double roof and a diagonal support beam **CUES: Jack** Nicholson lives in this 尺 (**Shack**, also known as a wakeful eye) with this double roof, which meets the 尺 **shaku**do (criteria) for earthquake safety now that he has added this diagonal support beam **GROUP:** 昼 hiru = noon,# 49; 駅 eki = station, # 380; 訳 wake = reason, # 437; (光)沢 koutaku = lustre, # 1100; (選)択 sentaku = selection, # 1403; 尺 (度) shakudo = criterion, # 1484; 尽(きる) tsukiru = to be used up, # 1507; (解)釈 kaishaku = an explanation, # 1516 (identical pronunciation)

1485. 従 **PRONUNCIATIONS:** shitaga, juu **MEANINGS:** accompany, obey, follow **EXAMPLES:** 従う shitagau = to obey or follow; 従事する juuji suru = to work or engage in (a profession); 服従 fukujuu = obedience, submission **DESCRIPTION:** compared to (生)徒 seito (student, # 451), this substitutes a V for 十 (ten) at the top right, making this radical resemble the upper portion of 羊 hitsuji (sheep, # 1223); the structures at the upper right can also be seen as antennae or as an upside-down bench; this retains the man with a double hat on the left, and the 足 (foot) radical at the lower right, which includes a taser **CUES:** this man on the left is troubled by this truncated 羊 (sheep) standing on this 足 (foot), and the **Sheep Tag**s **A**long when he goes out to buy **J**uice and doesn't 従う **shitaga**u (obey) when he tells it to go home, even when he offers it one of his two hats **GROUP:** 従(う) shitagau = to obey, # 1485; 縦 tate = length, # 1486

1486. 縦 **PRONUNCIATIONS:** tate, juu **MEANINGS:** vertical, length, height, self-indulgent **EXAMPLES:** 縦 tate = length or height; 縦の線 tate no sen = a vertical line; 操縦 soujuu = management, handling, operation; **DESCRIPTION:** compared to (服)従 fukujuu (obedience, # 1485) (identical pronunciation), this kanji adds 糸 (skeet shooter, # 219) on the left; it retains the head of a 羊 (sheep), with what could be considered antennae, or also an upside-down bench, standing on the foot of a man with a double hat, which is attached to a taser **CUES:** since the shoe of this man in the center with two hats is getting **T**attered, as a result of this truncated 羊 (sheep) standing on it while he is trying to buy some **J**uice, this 糸 (skeet shooter) tries to help by firing over the hats of the man, but the skeet shooter's 操縦 sou**juu** (handling) of this situation may be wrong **ALSO COMPARE:** other similar kanji at # **1485**

1487. 縮 **PRONUNCIATIONS:** shuku, chiji **MEANINGS:** shrink, contract, reduce **EXAMPLES:** 縮小 shukushou = a reduction or cutback; 恐縮する kyoushuku suru = to feel grateful or embarrassed; 縮む chijimu = to shrink or become short, to cringe **DESCRIPTION:** compared to 宿(題) shukudai (homework, # 491) (identical pronunciation), this kanji adds 糸 (skeet shooter,# 219) on the left; it retains the man with a slanted hat and 百 (a hundred) guys wearing shoes from Kuwait, all of whom have bad haircuts **CUES:** this 糸 (skeet shooter) is **Shooting Kool**-Aid at these 百 (100) guys with bad haircuts like this to get their attention, since they have **Cheap Jeans**, which he wants to buy if they will 縮小する **shuku**shou suru (reduce) their prices; meanwhile, this man in the center tilts his hat back to watch **GROUP:** 宿 yado = inn, # 491; 縮(小) shukushou = a reduction, # 1487 **ALSO COMPARE:** other similar kanji at # **491**

1488. 刃 PRONUNCIATIONS: **ha, ba**
MEANINGS: blade, sword, edge   EXAMPLES: 刃 ha = a blade; 刃物 hamono = a knife or cutting tool; 出刃包丁 debabouchou = a knife or pointed carver   DESCRIPTION: 刀 katana (sword, # 102), with a slash across its handle, as seen in 忍(者) ninja (spy, # 1433)   CUES: when Prince **Ha**rry brings this 刀 (sword) into a **Ba**r, people notice this slash across the handle, which resulted from a 刃物 **ha**mono (knife) attack   GROUP: (確)認 kakunin = confirmation, # 1036; 忍(者) ninja = spy, # 1433; 刃 ha = a blade, # 1488

1489. 塚 PRONUNCIATIONS: **tsuka, zuka²**   MEANINGS: hillock, mound   EXAMPLES: 塚 tsuka = a mound; 塚穴 tsukaana = a grave; モグラ塚 mogurazuka = a mound created by a mole   DESCRIPTION: on the left, 土 tsuchi (soil, # 59); on the right, 家 ie (house, # 405), without its chimney   CUES: a **Tsu**itcase (suitcase) of **Ca**bbages was found in a 塚穴 **tsuka**ana (grave) under this 土 (soil) next to this 家 (house) without a chimney   ALSO COMPARE: other similar kanji at # **1504**

1490. 枠 PRONUNCIATION: **waku**
MEANING: frame   EXAMPLES: 枠 waku = a frame, framework, limit; 枠組 wakugumi = a frame or framework   DESCRIPTION: compared to 酔(う) you (to get drunk, # 1476), this substitutes 木 moku (wood, # 118) for the abbreviated 酒 (sake) on the left; it retains the 九 (nine) and the 十 (ten)   CUE: during the **Wa**r against the **Ku**ol-Aid industry, we used this 木 (wood) to build 枠 **waku** (frames) around 九十 (ninety) gunports, from which we fired on the enemy   ALSO COMPARE: other similar kanji at # **827** and # **1658**

1491. 含 PRONUNCIATIONS: **gan, fuku**
MEANINGS: include, understand   EXAMPLES: 含有 gan'yuu = content; 含む fukumu = to contain or include   DESCRIPTION: at the top, 今 ima (now, # 292), which contains a 7 under a ceiling under a peaked roof; at the bottom, 口 kuchi (mouth, # 426)   CUES: 今 (now) **Gan**dalf is using this 口 (mouth) in **Fuku**oka to eat some food, and he will 含む **fuku**mu (include) some local specialties [Hint: the 口 in 含(む) fukumu is *under* 今 (now), suggesting that Gandalf is under time pressure to include local specialties in Fukuoka; in contrast, the 口 in 吟(味) ginmi, # 1873, is *beside* or *independent of* 今 (now), suggesting that there is *no* time pressure to check brands of gin]   GROUP: 今 ima = now, # 292; (残)念 zannen = too bad, # 314; 含(む) fukumu = to contain, # 1491; 陰 kage = shade, # 1543; 琴 koto = a Japanese harp, # 1712; 吟(味する) ginmi suru = to check, # 1873; 捻(挫) nenza = a sprain, # 1975; 貪(欲な) don'yoku na = greedy, # 2034

1492. 俵 PRONUNCIATIONS: **tawara, dawara², hyou, pyou²**   MEANINGS: bag, bale, sack, counter for bags   EXAMPLES: 俵 tawara = a straw bag; 米俵 komedawara = a bag of rice; 土俵 dohyou = a sumo ring; 一俵 ippyou = one straw bag   DESCRIPTION: compared to 表(面) hyoumen (surface, # 582) (identical pronunciation), this kanji adds a man with a slanted hat on the left; it retains the owl's perch on the roof of the honorable motel where healers from Oregon stay   CUES: after this man on the left learned that a **Ta**x **Warra**nt had been filed against him, he decided to disguise this 表 (surface) of his skin, so he tilted his hat back to show his sincerity to a **H**ealer from **O**regon, who agreed to remove some tattoos in exchange for a 俵 **tawara** (straw bag)   ALSO COMPARE: similar kanji at # **582** and # **1103**

1493. 討 PRONUNCIATIONS: **tou**, u
MEANINGS: chastise, attack, defeat
EXAMPLES: 検討 ken**tou** = examination, investigation, consideration; 討論 **tou**ron = a debate or discussion; 討つ utsu = to shoot at, attack, defeat, destroy; 敵を討つ kataki wo utsu = to revenge DESCRIPTION: on the left, 言(う) iu (to say, # 430); on the right, 寸(前) sunzen (on the verge, # 1369), which depicts a kneeling sunny guy with a long toe and a stick of gum on the ground nearby CUES: this 寸 (kneeling sunny guy) 言 (says) that this gum is sticking to this **To**e, and he wants a 検討 ken**tou** (investigation) by the **U**gandan authorities
ALSO COMPARE: 詩 shi = a poem, # 1301; other similar kanji at # **131**

1494. 糖 PRONUNCIATION: **tou**
MEANING: sugar EXAMPLES: 砂糖 sa**tou** = sugar; 糖尿病 **tou**nyoubyou = diabetes
DESCRIPTION: on the left, 米 kome (uncooked rice, # 326); on the right, a lean-to with a chimney that passes downward through the roof of the lean-to, but this chimney has been perforated by a trident; on the lower right, 口 kuchi (mouth, # 426), but this could be a toaster CUE: since someone has stabbed this chimney with this trident, I can't cook this 米 (rice), so I'll have to use this 口 (toaster) to make **To**ast to eat with 砂糖 sa**tou** (sugar) instead
GROUP: (健)康 kenkou = health, # 831; (砂)糖 satou = sugar, # 1494; 唐(突) toutotsu = sudden, # 1600 (identical pronunciation); (自)粛 jishuku = self-restraint, # 1925; (凡)庸 bonyou = mediocre, # 2035 ALSO COMPARE: kanji containing a *periscope* passing through a roof at # 1057; other similar kanji at # **1176** and # **1387**

1495. 障 PRONUNCIATIONS: **shou**, sawa, zawa² MEANINGS: hinder, hurt, harm
EXAMPLES: 障害 **shou**gai = an obstacle; 故障 ko**shou** = a breakdown or malfunction; 障る **sawa**ru = to harm or annoy; 障り **sawa**ri = a hindrance, obstacle or harm; 目障り meza**wa**ri = an eyesore or an unpleasant sight
DESCRIPTION: compared to (文)章 bunshou (a sentence, # 1365) (identical pronunciation), this adds ß beta from the Greek alphabet on the left; it retains 立 (to stand) and 早 (early) CUES: this ß (Greek) guy came to our **Sh**ow in Athens, and when he 立 (st**oo**d) up 早 (early), he **Sa**w **Wa**ter on the stage, which would have been a 障り **sawa**ri (hindrance) to our performance
ALSO COMPARE: (表)彰 hyou**shou** = public acknowledgment, # 1807; other similar kanji at # **266**, # **1365**, # **1569** and # **2030**

1496. 仁 PRONUNCIATIONS: **jin**, *nin*, ni
MEANINGS: humanity, benevolence, virtue
EXAMPLES: 仁徳 **jin**toku = benevolence or goodness; 仁徳天皇 Nintoku Tennou = Emperor Nintoku, a legendary emperor from the 5th century A.D.; 仁王 niou = two fierce guardians of Buddha whose statues stand at the entrance of many Buddhist temples
DESCRIPTION: on the left, a man with a slanted hat; on the right, 二 ni (two, # 2) (identical pronunciation) CUES: this man on the left tilts his hat back to examine his 二 (two) pairs of **Jean**s; he's going to give one to a **Nin**ja with bad **Kn**ees out of 仁徳 **jin**toku (benevolence) GROUP: 二 ni = two, # 2; 仁(徳) jintoku = benevolence, # 1496
ALSO COMPARE: the hiragana に ni (also identical pronunciation)

1497. 腸 PRONUNCIATION: chou

MEANINGS: intestines, guts, bowels
EXAMPLES: 腸 chou = intestine, bowel; 大腸 daichou = the large intestine
DESCRIPTION: compared to (太)陽 taiyou (the sun, # 891), this substitutes 月 tsuki (moon, # 148) for ß (Greece) on the left; it retains a modified version of 易 (easy), which depicts streamers under a 日 (sun), suggesting things that are easy
CUE: when I went to this 月 (moon), I took Chocolate, since it's 易 (easy) for my 腸 **chou** (intestines) to digest **ALSO COMPARE:** similar kanji at # **154** and # **1702**

1498. 怠 PRONUNCIATIONS: nama, tai, okota

MEANINGS: neglect, laziness
EXAMPLES: 怠ける namakeru = to be lazy; 怠慢 taiman = negligent; 怠る okotaru = to be lazy, to overlook or neglect
DESCRIPTION: compared to 台(風) taifuu (typhoon, # 538) (identical pronunciation), this kanji adds 心 kokoro (heart, # 306) at the bottom; it retains the tired ム (cow) on a 口 (box)
CUES: Joe **Nama**th has this good 心 (heart), and when he saw this **T**ired ム (cow) stuck on this 口 (box), he threw an **O**ld **C**oat over it and **T**ackled it, but later he 怠った **okota**tta (neglected) it
ALSO COMPARE: other similar kanji at # **538**

1499. 姓 PRONUNCIATIONS: sei, shou

MEANING: surname **EXAMPLES:** 姓 sei = a family name or surname; 姓名 seimei = a full name; 百姓 hyakushou = a farmer
DESCRIPTION: on the left, 女 onna (female, # 235); on the right, (先)生 sensei (teacher, # 208), or (一)生 isshou (a lifetime, # 208), both of which help us to pronounce this, or 生(きる) ikiru (to live, # 208) **CUES:** this 女 (female) is a **S**ailor who 生 (lives) near the **S**hore, but I've forgotten her 姓名 **sei**mei (full name)
ALSO COMPARE: other kanji containing 女 on the left at # **2039**; other similar kanji at # **1918**

1500. 聖 PRONUNCIATION: sei

MEANINGS: holy, saint, master, priest
EXAMPLES: 聖人 seijin = a saint; 神聖 shinsei = holy or sacred; 聖書 seisho = the Bible
DESCRIPTION: at the upper left, 耳 mimi (ear, # 57); at the upper right, 口 kuchi (mouth, # 426); at the bottom, 王 ou (king, # 1077)
CUE: this 王 (king) has big 耳 (ears) like this and a big 口 (mouth) like this, which suggest that he is a **S**aint and a 神聖 shin**sei** (holy) man
ALSO COMPARE: other similar kanji at # **323**, # **1713** and # **1876**

1501. 寮 PRONUNCIATION: ryou

MEANINGS: dormitory, hostel
EXAMPLE: 寮 ryou = a dormitory
DESCRIPTION: compared to (治)療 chiryou (medical treatment, # 1069) (identical pronunciation), this kanji omits the sick bed at the upper left and adds a bad haircut at the top; it retains the slightly modified 大 (big) and the 日 (sun, or oven) spinning on 小 (small) **CUE:** Pope **L**eo is a 大 (big) man who got this bad haircut when he lived in a 寮 **ryou** (dormitory), where they had this spinning 日 (oven) **GROUP:** 寄(付) kifu = donation, # 604; 寮 ryou = a dormitory, # 1501
ALSO COMPARE: other similar kanji at # **94** and # **1069**

1502. 即 PRONUNCIATIONS: so, soku

MEANINGS: instant, namely, as is **EXAMPLES:** 即刻 sokkoku = immediately; 即日 sokujitsu = the same day; 即座に sokuza ni = immediately
DESCRIPTION: on the left, a modifed version of 良(い) yoi (good, # 303); on the right, a seal, as seen in 印(鑑) inkan (signature seal, # 1046)
CUES: when a **S**oldier saw this 良 (good) 印

(seal), he picked it up 即刻 **so**kkoku (immediately) and **So**aked it in ink **ALSO COMPARE:** other similar kanji at # **805** and # **1046**

1503. 笛 **PRONUNCIATIONS: teki, fue, bue MEANINGS:** flute, clarinet, whistle **EXAMPLES:** 汽笛 kiteki = a steam whistle; 笛 fue = a flute or whistle; 口笛 kuchibue = whistling **DESCRIPTION:** at the top, 竹 take (bamboo, # 134); at the bottom, (理)由 riyuu (reason, # 73) which reminds us of one unit of rice above a paddy, or of a rice paddy on a stick **CUES:** my **Te**chie friend is a **Foo**d **Ex**pert and a **Boo**ze **Ex**pert, and the 由 (reason) she traded this 由 (unit of rice) for this 竹 (bamboo) is so that she could make a 笛 **fue** (flute) **ALSO COMPARE:** other similar kanji at # **942**, # **1157** and # **2074**

1504. 豚 **PRONUNCIATIONS: ton, buta MEANINGS:** pork, pig **EXAMPLES:** 豚カツ tonkatsu = pork cutlet; 豚 buta = a pig or a despicable person **DESCRIPTION:** on the left, 月 tsuki (moon, # 148); on the right, 家 ie (house, # 405), without its bad haircut **CUES:** when this 月 (moon) was shining, I went to this modified 家 (house) where 豚 **buta** (pigs) are kept, stuck my **Ton**gue out at them and then went to drink **Boo**ze at a **Ta**vern **GROUP:** 家 ie = house, # 405; (軍)隊 guntai = army, # 726; 象 zou = elephant, # 906; (想)像 souzou = imagination, # 907; 縁(起) engi = omen, # 1023; 劇 geki = a play, # 1058; 豪(華) gouka = wonderful, # 1357; 遂(げる) togeru = to accomplish, # 1371; 塚 tsuka = a mound, # 1489; 豚 buta = a pig, # 1504; 嫁 yome = a bride, # 1527; 稼(ぐ) kasegu = to earn, # 1668; (駆)逐 kuchiku = expulsion, # 1970; 墜(落) tsuiraku = a plane crash, # 1972 **ALSO COMPARE:** kanji resembling 易(しい) yasashii at # 402

1505. 忠 **PRONUNCIATION: chuu MEANINGS:** loyalty, fidelity **EXAMPLES:** 忠告 chuukoku = advice or admonition; 忠誠 chuusei = loyalty, allegiance **DESCRIPTION:** at the top, 中 chuu (inside, # 8) (identical pronunciation); at the bottom, 心 kokoro (heart, # 306) **CUE:** if you look 中 (inside) this 心 (heart), you will see the 忠誠 **chuu**sei (loyalty) that led me to **Choo**se you as my friend **ALSO COMPARE:** other similar kanji at # **657**

1506. 誠 **PRONUNCIATIONS: sei, makoto MEANINGS:** sincerity, truth **EXAMPLES:** 誠意 seii = sincerity; 誠に makoto ni = really, truly **DESCRIPTION:** compared to 成(功) seikou (success, # 633) (identical pronunciation), this kanji adds 言(う) iu (to speak, # 430) on the left **CUES: Sa**feway stores enjoy 成 (success) like this because their employees exhibit 誠意 **sei**i (sincerity) when they 言 (speak), as they did while selling us **Ma**'s (**Mo**ther's) **Ko**to (Japanese harp) **ALSO COMPARE:** 真(に) makoto ni = really, truly, # 101 (both spellings are commonly used); other similar kanji at # **633**

1507. 尽 **PRONUNCIATIONS: jin, tsu MEANINGS:** exhaust, use up, deplete **EXAMPLES:** 理不尽 rifujin = unfair or absurd; 尽くす tsukusu = to use up, to exert oneself; 尽きる tsukiru = to be used up **DESCRIPTION:** we have referred to the outer framework of this kanji as a wakeful eye in 訳 wake (reason, # 437), and as a shack in 尺(度) shakudo (measure, # 1484); this character adds two lines representing two kinds of clothing **CUES:** when I lived in this 尺 (shack, also known as a wakeful eye), I only had two changes of clothes, my **Jean**s and my **Tsu**it (suit), represented by these two lines, a situation which I thought was 理不尽 rifu**jin** (absurd) **ALSO COMPARE:** other similar kanji at # **234** and # **1484**

1508. 肺 PRONUNCIATION: hai

MEANING: lungs EXAMPLES: 肺 hai = a lung; 肺炎 haien = pneumonia DESCRIPTION: on the left, 月 tsuki (moon, # 148); on the right, (都)市 toshi (city, # 242) CUE: when the man in this 月 (moon) is looking for me, I **Hi**de in this 市 (city), but its air is bad for my 肺 **hai** (lungs) ALSO COMPARE: other similar kanji at # 242

1509. 班 PRONUNCIATION: han

MEANINGS: squad, unit, group EXAMPLE: 班長 hanchou = a squad or group leader DESCRIPTION: on the left, and again on the right, 王 ou (king, # 1077); in the middle, 刂 ri CUE: this 刂 Ri is talking with these two 王 (kings) who think that he may be **Han**dsome enough to be named a 班長 **han**chou (squad leader) ALSO COMPARE: other similar kanji at # <u>1772</u>, # <u>1985</u> and # <u>2045</u>

1510. 票 PRONUNCIATIONS: hyou, pyou

MEANINGS: ballot, label, ticket, sign EXAMPLES: 票 hyou = a vote; 投票 touhyou = voting, vote; 伝票 denpyou = a receipt, bill or slip DESCRIPTION: compared to (目)標 mokuhyou (goal, # 1303) (identical pronunciation), this omits the 木 (tree) on the left; it retains the three eyes suspended from a platform, which belong to a healer from Oregon who uses his third eye for 宗 (religious) insights, and the spinning nail under a flying carpet [these can also be seen as 二 (two) above 小 (small)] CUES: a **He**aler from **O**regon with these three eyes, who uses his third eye for 宗 (religious) insights, is standing on this spinning nail structure, trying to get 票 **hyou** (votes) with the 標 (goal) of becoming President, after which he plans to conduct diplomacy with **Pyong**yang ALSO COMPARE: other similar kanji at # <u>1347</u> and # <u>1415</u>

1511. 凡 PRONUNCIATIONS: oyo, bon

MEANING: mediocre EXAMPLES: 凡そ oyoso = an estimate or outline, approximately; 平凡 heibon = commonplace, mediocre, ordinary; 非凡 hibon = unusual, outstanding DESCRIPTION: this is a tall desk, as seen in 机 tsukue (desk, # 140), but it appears to have been slashed CUES: I spilled some **O**ld **Yo**gurt on this tall 机 (desk), and someone used a **Bon**e to put this slash on it, and now it is only 平凡 hei**bon** (mediocre) GROUP: 恐(れ) osore = fear, # 869; (建)築 kenchiku = architecture, # 1219; (平)凡 heibon = commonplace, # 1511; 帆(走) hansou = sailing, # 1768 ALSO COMPARE: kanji containing tall desks *without* slashes at # 1462

1512. 尋 PRONUNCIATIONS: tazu, jin

MEANINGS: inquire, fathom, look for EXAMPLES: 尋ねる tazuneru = to ask, inquire or look for; 尋問する jinmon = interrogation DESCRIPTION: at the top, long hair flowing to the left, as seen in 寝(る) neru (to sleep, # 372); at the middle left, the katakana エ e, which reminds us of eggs; at the middle right, 口 kuchi (mouth) which resembles a box; at the bottom, 寸(前) sunzen (on the verge, # 1369), which depicts a kneeling sunny guy on the verge of picking up some gum CUES: this 寸 (kneeling sunny guy) is picking up these エ (eggs) to put in this 口 (box) to carry to **T**arzan at the **Z**oo, who has this long hair, and he will 尋ねる **tazu**neru (inquire) whether Tarzan needs some **Jean**s ALSO COMPARE: 訪(ねる) tazuneru = to visit, # 713; similar kanji at # <u>131</u>, # <u>247</u> and # <u>1165</u>

1513. 盟 PRONUNCIATION: mei

MEANINGS: alliance, oath EXAMPLES: 同盟 doumei = an alliance, league or union; 国際連盟 kokusairenmei = the League of Nations DESCRIPTION: compared to (鮮)明 senmei (bright, vivid, clear, # 154) (identical pronunciation), this adds 皿 sara (dish, # 567) at the bottom; it retains the 日 (sun) and the 月 (moon), which are bright

CUE: our **May**or drank a 明 (bright) liquid from this 皿 (dish) as a toast to seal a political 同盟 dou**mei** (alliance) **ALSO COMPARE:** other similar kanji at # **154** and # **1407**

1514. 覧 PRONUNCIATION: ran
MEANINGS: perusal, see
EXAMPLES: 展覧会 tenrankai = an exhibition; ご覧になる goran ni naru = to honorably see, look or watch **DESCRIPTION:** compared to 監(督) kantoku (director, # 1420), this substitutes 見(る) miru (to see, # 53) for the dish at the bottom; it retains two cannons firing a crutch and a cannon shell **CUE:** if you want to 見 (see) these two cannons fire crutches and shells like these, come to our **Ran**ch for a 展覧会 ten**ran**kai (exhibition) **ALSO COMPARE:** other similar kanji at # **1310** and # **1341**

1515. 臨 PRONUNCIATIONS: nozo, rin
MEANINGS: look to, meet, confront, call on
EXAMPLES: 臨む nozomu = to attend or look out upon; 臨時 rinji = temporary, extraordinary, emergency
DESCRIPTION: on the left, 臣(民) shinmin (royal subject, # 1039), which resembles an inoperable swing set; at the upper right, a crutch; at the lower right, 品(物) shinamono (merchandise, # 5) **CUES:** when I 臨む **nozo**mu (look out upon) the poor-quality 品 (merchandise) in my store, such as this 臣 (inoperable swing set) and this crutch, I feel a desire to travel to **N**orthern **Z**ones in search of better stock, such as wedding **R**ings **ALSO COMPARE:** other similar kanji at # **1034**, # **1246** and # **2080**

1516. 釈 PRONUNCIATION: shaku
MEANING: explanation
EXAMPLES: 解釈 kaishaku = an explanation or interpretation; 釈放 shakuhou = release, liberation, or acquittal **DESCRIPTION:** compared to 尺(八) shakuhachi (Japanese flute, # 1484) (identical pronunciation), this kanji adds 米 kome (rice, # 326) on the left, with a slash over it, as seen in 番 ban (turn, # 328), which reminds us of someone's turn; it retains the shack, also known as a wakeful eye **CUE:** if you want a 解釈 kai**shaku** (explanation), the reason that I'm staying in this 尺 (**Shack**, also known as a wakeful eye) is that it's my 番 (turn) **ALSO COMPARE:** other similar kanji at # **1368** and # **1484**

1517. 秀 PRONUNCIATIONS: shuu, hii
MEANINGS: excel, excellence, surpass
EXAMPLES: 優秀 yuushuu = outstanding, prominent; 秀才 shuusai = an outstanding student or an able person; 秀でる hiideru = to excel or surpass **DESCRIPTION:** compared to 誘(う) sasou (to invite, # 1405), this omits 言 (to say); it retains 禾 (a grain plant with a ripe head) and a graph, which seems to demonstrate a decline on the right **CUES:** this graph shows that your policy of **Shoo**ing away the animals that have been eating this 禾 (ripe grain) has been a 優秀 yuu**shuu** (outstanding) success, and we **H**ear that it's **E**asy to implement **ALSO COMPARE:** other similar kanji at # **1131** and # **1797**

1518. 雄 PRONUNCIATIONS: *on*, osu, yuu
MEANINGS: masculine, male, hero, leader
EXAMPLES: 雄鳥 ondori = a rooster; 雄 osu = a male (animal); 英雄 eiyuu = a hero; 雄弁 yuuben = eloquent **DESCRIPTION:** on the left, a hugging person, as seen in 友(達) tomodachi (friend, # 459); in the middle, the katakana ム mu, which is the sound made by cows; on the right, a net, which can be seen as a man with a slanted hat next to a 主 (master) with an extra pair of arms (see # 203) **CUES:** this person who is hugging this 雄 **osu** (male) ム (cow, i.e., bull) is the **O**nly one who went to **Osu**torariya (Australia) to release it from this net, and he brought it home to the **Yu**kon **COMPARE:** 雌 mesu = a female (animal), # 2031; other similar kanji at # **457**, # **591** and # **2046**

1519. 宣 PRONUNCIATION: sen
MEANINGS: proclaim, say, announce
EXAMPLES: 宣伝 senden = advertising, publicity; 宣告 senkoku = a sentence or judgment
DESCRIPTION: at the top, a bad haircut; at the bottom, a window with two panes above a floor in a fence, as seen in 垣(根) kakine (fence, # 777)
CUE: this bad haircut belongs to a **Sen**ator who is standing behind this window in this prison 垣 (fence), after he received a 宣告 **sen**koku (sentence) for taking bribes
ALSO COMPARE: other similar kanji at # **668**

1520. 捜 PRONUNCIATIONS: sou, saga
MEANINGS: search for, locate **EXAMPLES:** 捜索する sousaku suru = to investigate or search; 捜す sagasu = to look for or search, usually referring to police activities
DESCRIPTION: on the left, a kneeling guy; at the upper right, 申(す) mousu (to humbly speak, # 10), which resembles a rice paddy on a stick; at the lower right, 又 mata (again, # 24), but this resembles a simple table **CUES:** this guy on the left is a **S**oldier who 申 (says humbly) that he has a **Saga** to tell, and he kneels to help the police 捜索する **sou**saku suru (search) for evidence under this 又 (table) **ALSO COMPARE:** 探(す) sagasu = to look for or search, # 699, usually used for activities not involving the police; other similar kanji at # **1157** and # **1389**

1521. 哲 PRONUNCIATION: tetsu
MEANINGS: philosophy, clear
EXAMPLE: 哲学 tetsugaku = philosophy
DESCRIPTION: compared to 折(る) oru (to break, # 892), this adds 口 kuchi (mouth, # 426), which resembles a simple box, at the bottom; it retains the kneeling guy and the pair of pliers **CUE:** this guy on the left kneels to take these pliers from this 口 (box) at the **Tet**racycle factory in **Su**dan where he works, but his mind is always focused on 哲学 **tetsu**gaku (philosophy)
ALSO COMPARE: other similar kanji at # **892**

1522. 僧 PRONUNCIATION: sou, zou
MEANINGS: Buddhist priest, monk **EXAMPLE:** 僧 sou = a monk or priest; 小僧 kozou = a novice priest, a boy **DESCRIPTION:** compared to (倍)増(する) baizou suru (to double, # 61) (identical pronunciation), this kanji substitutes a man with a slanted hat for 土 (soil) on the left; it retains the 田 (rice paddy) above a 日 (sun) in an agricultural zone with two units of rice at the top **CUES:** this man on the left is a 僧 **sou** (monk) with a pure **S**oul who lives in an agricultural **Z**one, and he tilts his hat back to examine this 田 (rice paddy) in this 日 (sun), which produces these two units of rice
ALSO COMPARE: other similar kanji at # **61**

1523. 埋 PRONUNCIATIONS: u, mai
MEANINGS: bury, be filled up, embedded
EXAMPLES: 埋もれる umoreru = to be buried in; 埋葬 maisou = burial
DESCRIPTION: compared to 理(由) riyuu (reason, # 78), this substitutes 土 tsuchi (soil, # 59) for 王 (king) on the left; it retains 里 sato (hometown, # 1060), which resembles a sincere guy wearing bifocals
CUES: this 里 (sincere guy) wearing bifocals is **U**ber, and he digs in this 土 (soil) in a **M**ine, as he prepares for the 埋葬 **mai**sou (burial) of a fellow miner **ALSO COMPARE:** similar kanji at # **545**

1524. 舟 PRONUNCIATIONS: fune, bune², shuu MEANINGS: boat, ship
EXAMPLES: 舟 fune = a ship or boat; 小舟 kobune = a small boat; 舟航 shuukou = sailing, navigation **DESCRIPTION:** compared to 船 fune (boat, # 602) (identical pronunciation), this omits the 八 (eight) guys working on a 口 (dock) on the right; it retains the boat with a missing stern **CUES:** this 舟 **fune** (boat) is carrying **F**ood from the **N**etherlands and **Sh**oes, but some of the cargo is falling out through this missing stern
GROUP: 船 fune = boat, # 602; (軍)艦 gunkan = battleship, # 737; (一)般(的) ippanteki =

commonly, # 1050; (基)盤 kiban = foundation, # 1197; 航(空) koukuu = aviation, # 1295; 舟 fune = a ship, # 1524; 丹(念) tannen = precise, # 1588; 搬(送) hansou = transportation, # 1993; 舶(来の) hakurai no = imported, # 2014

1525. 沼 PRONUNCIATION: numa
MEANINGS: marsh, lake, bog, swamp, pond
EXAMPLES: 沼 numa = a swamp; 泥沼 doronuma = a marsh, bog or swamp
DESCRIPTION: compared to 招(く) shoutai (invitation, # 560), this substitutes a water radical for the kneeling guy on the left; it retains a 刀 (sword) on a 口 (box)
CUE: I bought a **N**ew **Ma**chine to pump this water from a 沼 **numa** (swamp), and I guard it with this 刀 (sword) that I keep on this 口 (box)
ALSO COMPARE: similar kanji at # **560**

1526. 悟 PRONUNCIATIONS: go, sato
MEANINGS: perceive, discern, realize
EXAMPLES: 覚悟 kakugo = preparedness, readiness; 悟る satoru = to realize, fathom, become enlightened **DESCRIPTION:** compared to (英)語 eigo (English, # 435) (identical pronunciation), this kanji substitutes an erect man for 言 (to say) on the left; it retains 五 go (five, # 179) (also identical pronunciation), which resembles a golfer staring down a fairway, and 口 (mouth), which resembles a box **CUES:** this man on the left raises himself to his full height as he tries to see over this **G**olfer on the right, who gets up on this 口 (box) and stares down the fairway at a **S**atellite **T**ower, and they both 悟る **sato**ru (realize) how technology is changing the world **ALSO COMPARE:** other similar kanji at # **179** and # **2063**

1527. 嫁 PRONUNCIATIONS: totsu, yome
MEANINGS: marry into, bride
EXAMPLES: 嫁ぐ totsugu = to get married (used for women); 嫁 yome = a bride, or one's daughter-in-law; 花嫁 hanayome = a bride; 嫁入り yome'iri = marriage
DESCRIPTION: on the left, 女 onna (female, # 235); on the right, 家 ie (house, # 405)
CUES: this 女 (female) just became a 嫁 **yome** (bride), and she **Tot**es her **Sui**tcases into this 家 (house) hurriedly, since her frozen **Y**ogurt is **M**elting
ALSO COMPARE: other kanji containing 女 on the left at # **2039**; other similar kanji at # **1504**

1528. 岡 PRONUNCIATION: oka
MEANINGS: mount, hill, knoll
EXAMPLES: 岡 oka = a hill; 福岡 Fukuoka = a city on Kyushu Island **DESCRIPTION:** compared to 綱 tsuna (rope, # 1200), this omits 糸 (skeet shooter) on the left; it retains the model of a mountain with a handle and antennae (this radical inside the lean-to can also be seen as a chairlift seat hanging from two frayed cables) **CUE:** we **Oc**casionally put chairlift seats with frayed cables in two-sided lean-to's like this on an 岡 **oka** (hill) near our home **ALSO COMPARE:** 丘 oka = hill, # 1473; other similar kanji at # **1200**

Kanji for Volume Four
1529. 泰 PRONUNCIATION: tai
MEANINGS: peaceful, calm **EXAMPLE:** 安泰 antai = peace **DESCRIPTION:** compared to 春 haru (spring, # 506), this substitutes 水 mizu (water, # 251) for the 日 (sun) at the bottom; it retains 人 hito with the number 三 san inscribed across it **CUE:** 三 (three) 人 (people) like this swam in this **Thai** 水 (water) and enjoyed 安泰 an**tai** (peace) **GROUP:** 様(子) yousu = condition, # 136; 緑 midori = green, # 227; 線 sen = line, # 228; 泉 izumi = fountain, # 252; 膝 hiza = knee, # 861; (乱)暴(な) ranbou na = violent, # 1021; 尿 nyou = urine, # 1298; (安)泰 antai = peace,

1529; (葛)藤 kattou = conflict, # 1530; 漆 urushi = lacquer, # 1957 **ALSO COMPARE:** other similar kanji at # **506**

1530. 藤 PRONUNCIATIONS: tou, dou, fuji MEANING: wisteria **EXAMPLES:** 葛藤 kattou = conflict, friction; 工藤 kudou = a family name; 藤 fuji = wisteria, usually spelled ふじ **DESCRIPTION:** at the top, a plant radical; at the lower left, 月 tsuki (moon, # 148); at the middle right, this resembles a bonfire, as seen in 勝(つ) katsu (to win, # 149); at the lower right, 水 (water, # 251) **CUES:** the people who attended this bonfire under this 月 (moon) made **To**ast, fried **Dou**ghnuts, filled bottles with this 水 (water), gathered these edible plants, and then loaded all the **Food** into a **Jee**p to take to needy people in order to try to reduce 葛藤 kat**tou** (conflict) **ALSO COMPARE:** 勝(つ) katsu = to win, # 149; other similar kanji at # **1305** and # **1529** and # **2087**

1531. 葛 PRONUNCIATIONS: kuzu, katsu, ka MEANING: arrowroot **EXAMPLES:** 葛 kuzu (known as kudzu in English) = arrowroot, used to make a starchy food additive; 葛飾 katsushika = a ward in Tokyo; 葛藤 kattou = conflict, friction **DESCRIPTION:** at the top, a plant radical above 日 hi (sun, # 32); at the lower left, a man with a slanted hat; at the lower right, a one-sided lean-to containing a 人 (person) sitting on a rug **CUES:** at the **Ku**waiti **Z**oo, this 日 (sun) shines brightly on these plants, and this 人 (person) sitting on this rug in this lean-to talks to this man with a slanted hat, who is a zookeeper, about how to control the big **Ca**ts that are causing 葛藤 **ka**ttou (conflict) with the **Ca**ttle **ALSO COMPARE:** other similar kanji at # **33** and # **1926**

1532. 腕 PRONUNCIATIONS: ude, wan MEANINGS: arm, ability **EXAMPLES:** 腕 ude = arm; 腕白 wanpaku = naughty **DESCRIPTION:** on the left, 月 tsuki (moon, # 148); at the upper right, a bad haircut; at the lower middle, 夕 yuu (evening, # 160); at the lower right, an uncoiling snake, as seen in 危(ない) abunai (dangerous, # 901) **CUES:** my **U**gandan **D**entist has this bad haircut, and he **Wan**ders under this 月 (moon) during the 夕 (evenings) and wraps snakes like this around his 腕 **ude** (arms) **ALSO COMPARE:** other similar kanji at # **547** and # **801**

1533. 柄 PRONUNCIATIONS: gara, hei, e MEANINGS: design, pattern, handle **EXAMPLES:** 人柄 hitogara = personality; 横柄 ouhei = arrogant; 取り柄 torie = merit **DESCRIPTION:** on the left, 木 ki (tree, # 118); on the right, 内 uchi (inside, # 396), which resembles a 人 (person) emerging from a two-sided lean-to, wearing a flat hat **CUES:** my 人柄 hito**gara** (personality) makes me sit 内 (inside) my **Ga**rage in the shade of this 木 (tree), wearing this flat hat and **Ha**zing people that walk by, which I find **E**xciting
ALSO COMPARE: other similar kanji at # **397**

1534. 踏 PRONUNCIATIONS: fu, tou MEANINGS: step, trample, carry through, appraise, evade payment **EXAMPLES:** 踏む fumu = to step on; 雑踏 zattou = crowd, congestion **DESCRIPTION:** on the left, a square top on 止(める) tomeru (to stop, # 173), as seen in 踊(る) odoru (to dance, # 366), suggesting a hesitant squarehead; at the upper right, 水 mizu (water, # 251); at the lower right, 日 hi (sun, # 32) **CUES:** when this 止 (hesitant) squarehead 踊 (dances) in this 日 (sun), he sweats this 水 (water) and sometimes **Foo**lishly 踏む **fu**mu (steps) on his partner's **To**es **GROUP:** 踊(る) odoru = to dance, # 366; (道)路 douro = road, # 525; 距(離) kyori = distance, # 717; 蹴(る) keru = to kick, # 975; (活)躍(する) katsuyaku suru = to be active, # 992; 跳(ぶ) tobu = to jump, # 1084; 跡 ato = trace, # 1111; (暴)露 bakuro = exposure, # 1390; 踏(む) fumu = to step on, # 1534; (実)践 jissen = implementation, # 1907

1535. 柳 PRONUNCIATIONS: yanagi, ryuu MEANINGS: willow EXAMPLES: 柳 yanagi = willow; 川柳 senryuu = a satiric poem **DESCRIPTION:** on the left, 木 ki (tree), # 118); on the right, a modified version of the two Moonies who call out to donors in 迎(える) mukaeru (to greet/welcome, # 358); the radical on the right resembles a signature seal, as seen in 印 shirushi (sign, # 1046) **CUES:** when we stopped to rest under a 柳 yanagi (willow) 木 (tree) like this, my **Ya**ks were **Nag**ging me for water, and these two Moonies offered us some from their **Reu**sable bottles **GROUP:** 卵 tamago = egg, # 28; 迎(える) mukaeru = to greet/welcome, # 358; 柳 yanagi = willow, # 1535; (信)仰 shinkou = belief, # 1549; 抑(える) osaeru = to suppress, # 1584 **ALSO COMPARE:** other similar kanji at # **1046**

1536. 奉 PRONUNCIATIONS: bu, hou MEANINGS: observance, dedicate EXAMPLES: 奉行 bugyou = a Samurai magistrate; 奉仕 houshi = service **DESCRIPTION:** compared to 棒 bou (stick, # 820), this omits the 木 (tree) on the left; it retains the 人 (person) inscribed with the number 三 (three) above a telephone pole **CUES:** these 三 (three) 人 (people) have a simple **B**uddhist **H**ome on this telephone pole, from which they provide 奉仕 **hou**shi (service) to the public **ALSO COMPARE:** other similar kanji at # **506** and # **820**

1537. 藩 PRONUNCIATION: han MEANINGS: clan, enclosure EXAMPLE: 藩士 hanshi = a feudal retainer or warrior **DESCRIPTION:** compared to 番 ban (a turn, # 328), this adds a water radical on the left and a plant radical at the top; it retains the 米 (uncooked rice), with a slash over it, above a 田 (rice paddy) in Bangladesh **CUE:** some **H**andsome 藩士 **han**shi (feudal warriors) ate these plants and drank this water because it was their 番 (turn) **ALSO COMPARE:** other similar kanji at # **220**, # **258** and # **1368**

1538. 帝 PRONUNCIATIONS: mikado, tei MEANING: Emperor of Japan EXAMPLES: 帝 mikado = the Emperor; 帝国 teikoku = empire **DESCRIPTION:** compared to 諦める akirameru (to give up, # 804), this omits 言 on the left; it retains 立(つ) tatsu (to stand, # 11), with downward-facing spikes on its base, and 巾 (Bo Peep), as seen in boushi 帽(子) (hat, # 243) **CUES:** this 巾 (Bo Peep) could barely walk after she attached these spikes to her shoes, but she 立 (stood) and went to meet the 帝 **mikado** (Emperor of Japan), and when she looked into the **M**irror on her **C**ar **D**oor, she saw that she had good **T**aste **ALSO COMPARE:** other similar kanji at # **804** and # **1768**

1539. 堀 PRONUNCIATIONS: hori, bori MEANINGS: ditch, canal EXAMPLE: 堀 hori = a canal or moat; 土佐堀川 tosaborigawa = a river in Osaka **DESCRIPTION:** compared to 掘(る) horu (to dig, # 1402), or (山谷)掘 sanyabori (a park in Tokyo, # 1402) (identical pronunciation), this kanji substitutes 土 tsuchi (soil, # 59) for the kneeling guy on the left; it retains the cooped-up Superman under a lean-to with a double roof **CUES:** when I visited a 堀 **hori** (canal), I saw this 土 (soil) which Superman had left next to this lean-to after he dug himself out, and it seemed to me that this was **H**oly soil – although somewhat **B**oring **ALSO COMPARE:** other similar kanji at # **927** and # **1899**

1540. 憶 PRONUNCIATION: oku
MEANINGS: recollection, think EXAMPLE: 記憶する kioku suru = to remember
DESCRIPTION: compared to 億 oku (100 million, # 318) (identical pronunciation), this substitutes an erect man on the left for the man with a slanted hat; on the right, it retains 意(味) imi (meaning, # 317), which includes a bell at the top CUE: this man 記憶する ki**oku** suru (remembers) that this bell can play **O**ld **Ko**ol-Aid jingles that are full of 意 (meaning), and his erect posture suggests that he is proud to know quite a few of them ALSO COMPARE: other similar kanji at # **266** and # **2063**

1541. 儀 PRONUNCIATION: gi
MEANINGS: ceremony, a case
EXAMPLE: 礼儀 reigi = civility, etiquette
DESCRIPTION: compared to (会)議 kaigi (meeting, # 438) (identical pronunciation), this kanji substitutes a man with a slanted hat for 言 (to speak) on the left; it retains the 王 (king) wearing rabbit ears [this part of the kanji can also be seen as a truncated 羊 hitsuji (sheep, # 1223), missing its tail], the 手 (hand), and the halberd CUE: this man on the left goes to 議 (meetings) to discuss **Ge**ese, tilts his hat back to demonstrate his sincerity and always behaves with 礼儀 rei**gi** (civility) ALSO COMPARE: other similar kanji at # **1554**, # **1862** and # **1893**

1542. 占 PRONUNCIATIONS: sen, urana, shi MEANING: fortune-telling
EXAMPLES: 独占 dokusen = a monopoly; 占い uranai = fortune telling; 占める shimeru = to occupy DESCRIPTION: compared 店 mise (store, # 493), this omits the lean-to at the upper left; it retains the well with a pump handle; this can also be seen as a taser on a box CUES: when a **Sen**ator visited a **Ura**nium mine in Na**r**nia, she saw this well with a pump handle outside and used it to give water to some **Sh**eep which 占めた **shi**meta (occupied) a pasture nearby GROUP: 点(く) tsuku = to

ignite, # 29; 店 mise = store, # 493; 粘(土) nendo = clay, # 1359; 占(い) uranai = fortune telling, # 1542; 貼(る) haru = to paste, # 1766

1543. 陰 PRONUNCIATIONS: kage, in
MEANINGS: shade, shadow EXAMPLES: 陰 kage = shade, gloominess; 陰謀 inbou = a plot or conspiracy DESCRIPTION: on the left, β beta from the Greek alphabet; at the upper right, 今 ima (now, # 292), which contains a 7 under a ceiling under a peaked roof; at the lower right, 二 (two) ム (cows), as seen in 伝(える) tsutaeru (to convey, # 345)
CUES: this β (Greek) guy on the left is 今 (now) Calling a **Gue**st to show him these 二 (two) ム (cows) that he is keeping **In**doors in the 陰 **kage** (shade) ALSO COMPARE: other similar kanji at # **1056**, # **1491** and # **2030**

1544. 謀 PRONUNCIATIONS: mu, bou, haka MEANINGS: conspire, scheme, deceive
EXAMPLES: 謀反 muhon = a mutiny or rebellion; 陰謀 inbou = a plot or conspiracy; 謀る hakaru = to plot or attempt
DESCRIPTION: on the left, 言(う) iu (to speak, # 430); at the upper right, 甘(い) amai (sweet, # 541) which consists of a bucket hanging from a rod; at the lower right, 木 ki (tree, # 118)
CUES: some **Moo**nies were 言 (speaking) and **Boa**sting at a **Hacka**thon about some weapons they were hiding in this 甘 (bucket) up in this 木 (tree) which they planned to use for a 謀反 **mu**hon (rebellion) GROUP: 謀(る) hakaru = to plot, # 1544; 某(日) boujitsu = a certain day, # 1887; 媒(介) baikai = a medium, # 1889

1545. 訴 PRONUNCIATIONS: utta, so
MEANINGS: accusation, sue EXAMPLES: 訴える uttaeru = to sue, appeal or complain of;

訴訟 soshou = a lawsuit **DESCRIPTION:** on the left, 言(う) iu (to speak, # 430); on the right, a pair of pliers, as seen in 所 tokoro (place, # 391), with a slash across the handle
CUES: an Ugandan Taxi driver 言 (says) that a Soldier slashed these pliers, and he is filing a 訴訟 soshou (lawsuit) about this
ALSO COMPARE: other similar kanji at # **2060**

1546. 訟 PRONUNCIATION: shou
MEANINGS: sue, accuse
EXAMPLE: 訴訟 soshou = a lawsuit
DESCRIPTION: compared to 松 matsu (pine tree, # 1025), or 松(竹梅) shouchikubai (pine, bamboo and plum, # 1025) (identical pronunciation), this kanji substitutes 言(う) iu (to speak, # 430) for 木 (tree) on the left; it retains the hachi 八 (eight, # 15) ム (cows) which people watch while showing off their legs **CUES:** a Shougun 言 (said) that that he would buy these 八 (eight) ム (cows), but he reneged on the deal, and now he's facing a 訴訟 soshou (lawsuit)
GROUP: 公(園) kouen = park, # 16; 松 matsu = pine tree, # 1025; 総(じて) soujite = in general, # 1038; (訴)訟 soshou = a lawsuit, # 1546

1547. 釣 PRONUNCIATION: tsu
MEANING: fishing **EXAMPLE:** 釣る tsuru = to fish, to lure in **DESCRIPTION:** on the left, (お)金 okane (money, # 301); on the right, a hook containing a drop of water, as seen in 約(束) yakusoku (promise, # 225) **CUE:** I used this 金 (money) to buy this hook in order to 釣る tsuru (fish), but it got caught on my fishing Tsuit (suit), and I shed this tear **ALSO COMPARE:** other similar kanji at # **988** and # **2010**

1548. 核 PRONUNCIATION: kaku
MEANINGS: nucleus, core, kernel **EXAMPLE:** 核心 kakushin = core, center, central issue, kernel **DESCRIPTION:** compared to (遅)刻 chikoku (lateness, # 565), this omits リ Ri on the right and adds 木 ki (tree, # 118) on the left; it retains the skeleton of a wild boar
CUE: when Karl the Kool-Aid vendor encountered this skeleton of a boar that died after drinking Kool-Aid and then climbing this 木 (tree), he realized that Kool-Aid consumption was the 核心 kakushin (central issue) behind its death
GROUP: (遅)刻 chikoku = lateness, # 565; 核(心) kakushin = core, # 1548; 骸(骨) gaikotsu = a skeleton, # 1923; 該(当) gaitou = correspondence, # 1969

1549. 仰 PRONUNCIATIONS: kou, ao, gyou **MEANINGS:** face up, respect
EXAMPLES: 信仰 shinkou = belief, religion; 仰ぐ aogu = to look up; 仰天する gyouten suru = to be astounded **DESCRIPTION:** compared to 迎(える) mukaeru (to greet, # 358), this omits the snail at the lower left and adds a man with a slanted hat on the left; it retains the two standing Moonies on the right; the radical on the right resembles a signature seal, as seen in 印 shirushi (sign, # 1046) **CUES:** this man on the left tilts his hat back to examine these two Moonies, and he realizes that they work in a Coal mine near the Arctic Ocean, so he buys them some Gyoza, and they 仰天する gyouten suru (get astonished)
ALSO COMPARE: other similar kanji at # **1046** and # **1535**

1550. 瀬 PRONUNCIATION: se
MEANINGS: current, shallows **EXAMPLE:** 瀬戸際 setogiwa = brink, critical moment
DESCRIPTION: on the left, a water radical; in the middle, (約)束 yakusoku (promise, # 99); on the right, 貝 kai (shell, money chest, # 83) with a platform at the top where a head could fit, as seen in 頭 atama (head, # 93) **CUE:** I made a 束 (promise) to a Secretary that I would try to retrieve her 頭 (head) from this water, but at the 瀬戸際 setogiwa (critical moment), I lost my nerve
ALSO COMPARE: other similar kanji at # **1126** and # **1806**

1551. 患
PRONUNCIATIONS: wazura, kan **MEANINGS:** afflicted, disease **EXAMPLES:** 患う wazurau = to suffer from illness; 患者 kanja = a patient **DESCRIPTION:** at the top, compared to 中 naka (inside, # 8), which we described as yakitori (grilled chicken on a stick), this includes an extra piece of chicken; at the bottom, 心 kokoro (heart, # 306) **CUES:** a **Wa**lrus from the **Zoo** was **R**abid, and it ate too much **Ca**ndy and 中 (yakitori) with extra chicken like this, which were bad for this 心 (heart) so that it 患った **wazura**tta (suffered from illnesses) **ALSO COMPARE:** other similar kanji at # **657**

1552. 浦
PRONUNCIATION: ura **MEANINGS:** bay, creek, beach **EXAMPLE:** 浦田 urata = a family name **DESCRIPTION:** compared to 捕(る) toru (to catch, # 670), this substitutes a water radical for the kneeling guy on the left; it retains the top part of 犬 (dog) chasing a ball above 用 (errand), which resembles a fence (see # 364) **CUE:** this water influx forced this truncated dog to exit a **U**ranium mine belonging to 浦田さん **Ura**ta-san and to climb up on this fence **ALSO COMPARE:** other similar kanji at # **995**

1553. 執
PRONUNCIATIONS: shuu, shitsu, shi, to **MEANINGS:** tenacious, grab, take to heart **EXAMPLES:** 執着 shuuchaku = attachment, persistence; 固執する koshitsu suru = to be persistent; 執行する shikkou suru = to carry out or execute; 執り行う toriokonau = to hold a ceremony **DESCRIPTION:** on the left, 幸(せ) shiawase (happiness, # 385), which resembles a needle with a syringe and a handle; on the right, 丸 maru (circle, # 866), which is a 九 (nine) that has been slashed **CUES:** after I was slashed 九 (nine) times with this 幸 (needle), I reassessed my 執着 **shuu**chaku (attachment) to my possessions, including my **Sh**oes, my **Sh**eets, my **Sh**eep, and my **T**ortoise **ALSO COMPARE:** other similar kanji at # **383**, # **1737** and # **1803**

1554. 拳
PRONUNCIATIONS: kobushi, gen, ken **MEANING:** fist **EXAMPLES:** 拳 kobushi = a fist; 拳固 genko = a fist, usually spelled げんこ; 拳銃 kenjuu = a handgun **DESCRIPTION:** at the top, a bonfire, as seen in 勝(つ) katsu (to win, # 149); at the bottom, 手 te (hand, # 23), which consists of fingers on a trunk **CUES:** this 手 (hand) is closed into a 拳 **ko**bushi (fist) because it's holding the reins of a **Co**lt with a **Bushy** tail which is trying to get away from this bonfire; the colt's owner is **Gen**ghis, and he plans to enter it in the **Ken**tucky Derby **GROUP:** 手 te = hand, # 23; (会)議 kaigi = meeting, # 438; 我 ware = self, # 862; 義(務) gimu = unlimited duty, # 1028; 撃(つ) utsu = to fire a gun, # 1226; 承(知) shouchi = acceptance, # 1344; (選)挙 senkyo = election, # 1362; 摩(擦) masatsu = friction, # 1428; (礼)儀 reigi = civility, # 1541; 拳(銃) kenjuu = a handgun, # 1554; 掌 tenohira = the palm of the hand, # 1717; 犠(牲) gisei = a victim, # 1764; 餓(死) gashi = starvation, # 1974 **ALSO COMPARE:** other similar kanji at # **1305**

1555. 銃
PRONUNCIATION: juu **MEANINGS:** gun **EXAMPLE:** 拳銃 kenjuu = a handgun **DESCRIPTION:** on the left, (お)金 okane (money, # 301); on the right, 充(実) juujitsu = perfection, # 1478 (identical pronunciation), which depicts a ム (cow) under a tire stop on lopsided legs that has a lot of juice (energy) **CUE:** this ム (cow) under a tire stop on lopsided legs paid this 金 (money) for a 拳銃 ken**juu** (handgun), and the cow has a lot of **Ju**ice (energy) **ALSO COMPARE:** other similar kanji at # **1125**, # **1990** and # **2010**

1556. 維 PRONUNCIATION: i
MEANINGS: fiber, tie, rope
EXAMPLE: 維持 iji = maintenance
DESCRIPTION: compared to (甲)羅 koura (shell, # 1158), this omits the three eyes at the top; it retains the rascally skeet shooter and the net, which can be seen as a man with a slanted hat next to a 主 (master) with an extra pair of arms (see # 203)
CUE: it's **Ea**sy for this 糸 (skeet shooter) to keep his skeets in this net, where he can inspect them to see if they need 維持 **i**ji (maintenance) **ALSO COMPARE:** other similar kanji at # **1158**

1557. 依 PRONUNCIATIONS: i, yo
MEANINGS: reliant, depend on **EXAMPLES:** 依頼 irai = a request or commission; 依る yoru = to depend on, usually written よる
DESCRIPTION: compared to 衣(服) ifuku (clothing, # 1042) (identical pronunciation), this kanji adds a man with a slanted hat on the left; it retains エ and Y standing near a tire stop, making Easter clothing **CUES:** this man tilts his hat so that we can see his face and makes an 依頼 **i**rai (request) that we allow him to wear this 衣 (clothing) to an **E**aster service at **Y**osemite **ALSO COMPARE:** other similar kanji at # **1042**

1558. 吐 PRONUNCIATIONS: to, ha
MEANINGS: spit, vomit, belch
EXAMPLES: 吐息 toiki = a sigh; 吐く haku = to vomit, exhale or spit
DESCRIPTION: on the left, 口 kuchi (mouth, # 426), which resembles a box; on the right, 土 tsuchi (earth, # 59)
CUES: I grow **T**omatoes in this 土 (earth) in **Ha**waii and then eat them with this 口 (mouth), but sometimes I 吐く **ha**ku (vomit) later
ALSO COMPARE: other similar kanji at # **2073**

1559. 斬 PRONUNCIATION: zan
MEANINGS: beheading, murder
EXAMPLE: 斬新 zanshin = creative, original
DESCRIPTION: on the left, 車 kuruma (car, # 283); on the right, a pair of pliers, as seen in 折(る) oru (to break, # 892)
CUE: I use these pliers, which are based on a 斬新な **zan**shin na (original) design, to work on this 車 (car) in **Zan**zibar **ALSO COMPARE:** other similar kanji at # **892** and # **1966**

1560. 斎 PRONUNCIATION: sai
MEANINGS: purification, worship **EXAMPLE:** 書斎 shosai = a library (home) or study
DESCRIPTION: at the top, 文(化) bunka (culture, # 25), which consists of a tire stop above a crossing (or an X); below that, walls projecting down on both sides to form a container; in the center of this container, a modified version of 示(す) shimesu (to show, # 1347), which resembles a spinning nail under a flying carpet [these can also be seen as 二 (two) above 小 (small)] **CUE:** a **S**cientist known for her 文 (culture) is spinning nails under flying carpets like this in containers like this in her 書斎 sho**sai** (home library) **ALSO COMPARE:** (救)済 kyuusai = rescue, # 259 (identical pronunciation); other similar kanji at # **259** and # **1347**

1561. 衝 PRONUNCIATION: shou
MEANINGS: collide, pierce, stab
EXAMPLE: 衝撃 shougeki = impact, shock
DESCRIPTION: on the left and the right, 行(く) iku (to go, # 334), suggesting that one is in the middle of going; in the center, 重(い) omoi (heavy, # 284) **CUE:** when I was in the middle of 行 (going) along the **Sho**re, a wave carried a 重 (heavy) object that struck me and had a considerable 衝撃 **shou**geki (impact) **ALSO COMPARE:** other similar kanji at # **284** and # **625**

1562. 却 PRONUNCIATION: kyaku
MEANINGS: instead, on the contrary
EXAMPLE: 返却する henkyaku suru = to return something borrowed DESCRIPTION: compared to 去(る) saru (to leave, # 343), this adds the seal seen in 印(鑑) inkan (signature seal, # 1046) on the right; it retains the samurai's ム (cow) covered with 土 (soil) CUE: since I needed to borrow this 印 (signature seal), I 去 (left) my island home in a **Kayak** to get it, and later I 返却 した hen**kyaku** shita (returned) it ALSO COMPARE: other similar kanji at # **343** and # **1046**

1563. 脚 PRONUNCIATION: kyaku
MEANINGS: skids, leg EXAMPLE: 脚本 kyakuhon = a script or screenplay
DESCRIPTION: compared to (返)却(する) henkyaku suru (to return something borrowed, # 1562) (identical pronunciation), this adds 月 tsuki (moon, # 148) on the left; it retains 去 (to leave) and the 印 (signature seal)
CUE: I wrote a 脚本 **kyaku**hon (script) about the time I 去 (left) my island home in a **Kayak** to borrow this 印 (signature seal) and didn't return it until this 月 (moon) was shining ALSO COMPARE: other similar kanji at # **343** and # **1046**

1564. 仙 PRONUNCIATION: sen
MEANINGS: hermit, wizard EXAMPLE: 仙台 Sendai = a city on northern Honshu Island
DESCRIPTION: compared to 山 yama (mountain, # 146), this adds a man with a slanted hat on the left CUE: this man on the left tilting his hat back is a **Sen**ator who is admiring this 山 (mountain) near 仙台 **Sen**dai (a Japanese city)
ALSO COMPARE: other similar kanji at # **2079**

1565. 唇 PRONUNCIATION: kuchibiru
MEANINGS: lips EXAMPLE: 唇 kuchibiru = the lips DESCRIPTION: compared to 振(る) furu (to shake, # 823), this omits the kneeling guy on the left and adds 口 kuchi (mouth, # 426) (similar pronunciation), at the bottom; it retains the one-sided lean-to containing an arrow supported by the letter L and the letter Y
CUE: I was playing with this arrow supported by L and Y inside this lean-to and using this 口 **Kuchi** (mouth) to drink **Biiru** (beer) when I accidentally cut my 唇 **kuchibiru** (lip)
ALSO COMPARE: other similar kanji at # **1105**

1566. 狂 PRONUNCIATIONS: kyou, kuru MEANINGS: madness, insanity
EXAMPLES: 狂気 kyouki = lunacy, madness; 気が狂う ki ga kuruu = to go crazy
DESCRIPTION: on the left, a woman contorting her body, as seen in 犯(人) hannin (criminal, # 901); on the right, 王 ou (king, # 1077)
CUES: when this woman on the left approached this 王 (king) in **Kyou**to and contorted her body while offering him a **Kuwaiti Rooster**, people said that she was affected by 狂気 **kyou**ki (lunacy) ALSO COMPARE: other similar kanji at # **948** and # **2045**

1567. 剥 (sometimes written 剝)
PRONUNCIATIONS: haku, mu, ha
MEANINGS: come off, fade, peel EXAMPLES: 剥奪する hakudatsu suru = to deprive of; 剥く muku = to peel, usually written むく; 剥げる hageru = to come off or peel off, usually written はげる; 剥がす hagasu = to strip (the skin) from something, to reveal, usually written はがす; 剥ぐ hagu = to strip (the skin) from something, to reveal DESCRIPTION: compared to 緑 midori (green, # 227), this omits the skeet shooter on the left and adds the katakana リ ri, which is sometimes described as a knife, on the right; it retains the green flag, which can also be seen as hair streaming left, on a platform floating in 水 (water) [the **alternative** kanji above contains tagai

互い (one another, # 1207) at the upper left, without its flat hat, which reminds us of two ユ (youths) who speak Tagalog; it retains the 水 (water) and リ ri] **CUES:** when this リ Ri visited the **H**arbor in **K**u**w**ait, he saw this platform carrying this 緑 (green) flag floating in this 水 (water), and he 剥がした **ha**gashita (revealed) that he was planning to become a **Moo**nie after the **H**arvest [alternatively, when this リ Ri visited the **H**arbor in **K**u**w**ait and saw these two 互 (youths), who were missing their flat hat, floating in this 水 (water), he 剥がした **ha**gashita (revealed) to them that he would become a **Moo**nie after the **H**arvest] ALSO COMPARE: other similar kanji at # **999**, # **1207** and # **1985**

1568. 奪 **PRONUNCIATIONS: uba, datsu**
MEANINGS: rob, plunder, usurp
EXAMPLES: 奪う ubau = to rob, to fascinate; 収奪 shuudatsu = plundering, exploitation
DESCRIPTION: compared to (興)奮 koufun (excitement, # 727), this substitutes 寸(前) sunzen (on the verge, # 1369), which depicts a kneeling sunny guy on the verge of picking up some gum, for 田 (rice paddy) at the bottom; it retains an extra-wide 大 (big) above a net, which can be seen as a man with a slanted hat next to a 主 (master) with an extra pair of arms (see # 203) **CUES:** a 大 (big) guy dropped this net onto this 寸 (kneeling sunny guy), who was in an **U**ber **B**ar at the time, trying to pick up this gum, and the big guy wanted to 奪う **uba**u (rob) him, but the sunny guy escaped and drove away in a **Datsu**n ALSO COMPARE: other similar kanji at # **131** and # **727**

1569. 竜 **PRONUNCIATIONS: ryuu, tatsu**
MEANINGS: imperial, dragon **EXAMPLES:** 恐竜 kyouryuu = a dinosaur; 竜 tatsu = a dragon
DESCRIPTION: compared to 滝 taki (waterfall, # 1179), this omits the water radical on the left; it retains 立(つ) tatsu (to stand) (similar pronunciation), and the 電 (electric) transformer with a wire emerging from it **CUES:** since I wanted to see a 竜 **tatsu** (dragon) that came to town, I **Re**used this 電 (electric) transformer as a platform to 立 (stand) on, but it exploded, and I ended up with a **T**attered **S**uit **GROUP:** 顔 kao = face, # 95; 産(業) sangyou = industry, # 210; 競(技) kyougi = competition, # 935; 襲(撃) shuugeki = an attack, # 941; 滝 taki = waterfall, # 1179; 商(品) shouhin = merchandise, # 1217; (面)接 mensetsu = inter-view, # 1446; 障(る) sawaru = to harm, # 1495; 竜 tatsu = a dragon, # 1569 ALSO COMPARE: other similar kanji at # **1003**

1570. 脇 **PRONUNCIATION: waki**
MEANINGS: armpit, side
EXAMPLE: 脇 waki = side or armpit
DESCRIPTION: compared to 協(力) kyouryoku (cooperation, # 940), this substitutes tsuki 月 (moon, # 148) for 十 (ten) on the left; it retains the three men of 力 (force) on the right
CUE: these three men of 力 (force) are **W**alking by my 脇 **waki** (side) under this 月 (moon), since I'm not allowed to be out alone after dark ALSO COMPARE: other similar kanji at # **914**

1571. 債 **PRONUNCIATION: sai**
MEANINGS: debt, liabilities **EXAMPLES:** 債務 saimu = debt; 負債 fusai = debt
DESCRIPTION: compared to 責(任) sekinin (responsibility, # 772), this adds a man with a slanted hat on the left; it retains the owl's perch on the 貝 (money chest) which belongs to a selfish king **CUE:** this man on the left is a **S**cientist who keeps his hat tilted back in order to investigate an owl selling pardons from this owl's perch, since this 貝 (money chest) is still empty and the king's 負債 fu**sai** (debt) remains high
ALSO COMPARE: other similar kanji at # **772**

1572. 伯 PRONUNCIATIONS: o, haku

MEANINGS: chief, uncle **EXAMPLES:** 伯母さん obasan = an aunt or middle-aged woman; 伯父さん ojisan = an uncle; 伯仲 hakuchuu = fierce competition, well-matched

DESCRIPTION: compared to 白(い) shiroi (white, # 44), or 白(米) hakumai (white rice, # 44) (identical pronunciation), this kanji adds a man with a slanted hat on the left

CUES: this man on the left is an 伯父さん ojisan (uncle) who is **O**ld and wears clothes that are 白 (white) like this, and he tilts his hat back to enjoy the view when he visits the **H**arbor in **K**uwait

ALSO COMPARE: other similar kanji at # **2014**

1573. 項 PRONUNCIATION: kou

MEANINGS: paragraph, clause **EXAMPLE:** 要項 youkou = outline, main point

DESCRIPTION: compared to 頃 koro (approximate time, # 96), this substitutes 工 kou (crafted object, # 246) (identical pronunciation), which resembles an I-beam seen in coal mines, for the ヒ (hero) on the left; it retains the headless guy who needs a coroner

CUE: a **C**oal miner was writing an 要項 you**kou** (outline) for a book when he collided with this 工 (I-beam) and lost his 頭 (head)

ALSO COMPARE: other similar kanji at # **247** and # **1126**

1574. 幽 PRONUNCIATION: yuu

MEANINGS: seclude, confine, dark, profound
EXAMPLES: 幽閉する yuuhei suru = to confine **DESCRIPTION:** the outside structure is 山 yama (mountain, # 146), but this resembles two prison cells; inside the cells, the upper halves of two 糸 (skeet shooters, # 219), each consisting of two flexed elbows **CUE:** these two 糸 (skeet shooters) were 幽閉した **yuu**hei shita (confined) in these prison cells on this 山 (mountain) in the **Y**ukon
ALSO COMPARE: other similar kanji at # **1908** and # **2079**

1575. 霊 PRONUNCIATION: rei

MEANINGS: spirits, soul **EXAMPLE:** 霊 rei = soul or ghost **DESCRIPTION:** at the top, 雨 ame (rain, # 261); in the middle, 二 ni (two); at the bottom, four burners on a stove, as seen in 普(通) futsuu (ordinarily, # 576) **CUE:** this 雨 (**R**ain) fell 二 (two) times, extinguishing the burners on this stove, but we thought that 霊 **rei** (ghosts) might have been responsible
ALSO COMPARE: other similar kanji at # **262** and # **1300**

1576. 坊 PRONUNCIATIONS: bo, bou

MEANINGS: boy, priest
EXAMPLES: 坊っちゃん bocchan = another person's son, a boy (often spelled 坊ちゃん); 寝坊 nebou = sleeping in late

DESCRIPTION: compared to (予)防 yobou (prevention, # 920) (identical pronunciation), this kanji substitutes 土 tsuchi (soil, # 59) for ß on the left; it retains the 方 kata (honorable person, # 114) who boasts

CUES: this 方 (honorable person) used to live in this 土 (soil), but now he **Bo**asts that he owns a **Bo**at and can 寝坊 ne**bou** (sleep in late) every day
GROUP: (寝)坊 nebou = sleeping in late, # 1576; 傲(慢な) gouman na = insolent, # 2013 **ALSO COMPARE:** other similar kanji at # **920**

1577. 扱 PRONUNCIATION: atsukau

MEANINGS: handle, treat, take care of
EXAMPLE: 扱う atsukau = to deal with or deal in, to take care of **DESCRIPTION:** compared to 及(ぶ) oyobu (to reach, # 883), this adds a kneeling guy on the left; it retains the graph of a baby's breathing patterns
CUE: this guy on the left kneels like this in order to **A**ttach a **S**uperior **C**atheter to the breathing tube of a sick baby that he 扱う **atsuka**u (takes care of), and then this graph of her breathing patterns improves
ALSO COMPARE: other similar kanji at # **1131**

1578. 如 **PRONUNCIATIONS:** jo, goto, ika **MEANINGS:** like, such as **EXAMPLES:** 如才ない josainai = clever, shrewd; 如し gotoshi = like, as if, the same as; 如何 ikaga = how? (deferential; usually spelled いかが)
DESCRIPTION: on the left, 女(性) josei (woman, # 235) (identical pronunciation); on the right, 口 kuchi (mouth, # 426), which can be seen as a box
CUES: Empress **Jo**sephine was this 如才ない **jo**sainai (shrewd) 女 (woman) who put **Go**lden **To**matoes and **Ea**ster **Ca**ndy in this 口 (mouth)
ALSO COMPARE: other kanji containing 女 on the left at # 2039; other similar kanji at # 323

1579. 詳 **PRONUNCIATIONS:** shou, kuwa **MEANING:** detailed **EXAMPLE:** 詳細 shousai = details; 詳しい kuwashii = detailed, fully explained **DESCRIPTION:** compared to (発)祥 hasshou (origin, # 1160) (identical pronunciation), this kanji substitutes 言(う) iu (to speak, # 430) for the Shah on the left; it retains 羊 (sheep) on the right **CUES:** I 言 (spoke) after seeing a **Sh**ow of 羊 (sheep) like this in **Ku**wait, and I gave a 詳しい **kuwa**shii (detailed) description of the events
ALSO COMPARE: other similar kanji at # 1223

1580. 愚 **PRONUNCIATIONS:** gu, oro
MEANINGS: folly, absurdity **EXAMPLE:** 愚痴 guchi = a complaint; 愚かな oroka na = foolish **DESCRIPTION:** compared to (待)遇 taiguu (treatment, # 1120), this omits the snail at the lower left and adds 心 kokoro (heart, # 306) at the bottom; it retains the roots of a 田 (rice paddy) growing more vigorously on the right side of a pot, since a goose has been digging on the opposite side **CUES:** this 心 (heart) was troubled by a **Go**ose that was digging in this pot, and it expressed a 愚痴 **gu**chi (complaint) to the **O**ld **Ro**gue who owned the bird
ALSO COMPARE: other similar kanji at # 1120

1581. 痴 **PRONUNCIATION:** chi
MEANINGS: stupid, foolish **EXAMPLES:** 愚痴 guchi = a complaint; 痴漢 chikan = a sexual pervert **DESCRIPTION:** compared to 知(識) chishiki (knowledge, # 323) (identical pronunciation), this kanji adds a sick bed, as seen in 病(気) byouki (illness, # 369), at the upper left; it retains the Native American chief and the 口 (mouth) **CUE:** this Native American chief is stuck in this sick bed, this 口 (mouth) is full of **Che**ese, and his 愚痴 gu**chi** (complaint) is that he 知 (knows) more than his doctor **ALSO COMPARE:** other similar kanji at # 323, # 324 and # 369

1582. 奴 **PRONUNCIATIONS:** yatsu, do
MEANINGS: guy, slave **EXAMPLES:** 奴 yatsu = he, she, a guy, that person, a fellow (slang; usually spelled やつ); 奴隷 dorei = a slave
DESCRIPTION: compared to 努(力) doryoku (effort, # 519) (identical pronunciation), this omits 力 (force) at the bottom; it retains 女 (female) and the 又 (table) **CUES:** this 女 (female), who is a **Y**acht club **Su**pervisor, works like a 奴隷 **do**rei (slave) during the day, and then she makes **Do**ughnuts at this 又 (table) at night
ALSO COMPARE: other kanji containing 女 on the left at # 2039; other similar kanji at # 24

1583. 隷 PRONUNCIATION: rei
MEANINGS: slave, servant, prisoner
EXAMPLE: 奴隷 dorei = a slave
DESCRIPTION: at the upper left, 士 shi (man, # 66); at the lower left, 示(す) shimesu (to show, # 1347), which depicts a spinning nail under a flying carpet [these can also be seen as 二 (two) above 小 (small)]; on the right, a trident piercing the upper axis of 水 (water), as seen in (健)康 kenkou (health, # 831)   CUE: this 士 (man) on this 示 (spinning nail structure) feels **Ra**ge as he views this trident that has stabbed a person in this 水 (water), but he is just a 奴隷 do**rei** (slave) and must remain silent
GROUP: (健)康 kenkou = health, # 831; 逮(捕) taiho = arrest, # 1224; (奴)隷 dorei = a slave, # 1583   ALSO COMPARE: other similar kanji at # **1347** and # **1468**

1584. 抑 PRONUNCIATIONS: osa, yoku
MEANINGS: repress, push   EXAMPLES:
抑える osaeru = to suppress or control;
抑制する yokusei suru = to control or curb
DESCRIPTION: compared to (信)仰 shinkou (belief, # 1549), this substitutes a kneeling guy for the man with a slanted hat on the left; it retains the two standing Moonies who work in a coal mine; the radical on the right resembles a signature seal, as seen in 印 shirushi (sign, # 1046)
CUES: when **Osa**ma set out to 抑える **osa**eru (control) these two Moonies, he began by kneeling like this and offering them **Yo**gurt and **C**ookies   ALSO COMPARE: other similar kanji at # **1046** and # **1535**

1585. 範 PRONUNCIATION: han
MEANINGS: pattern, example, model
EXAMPLE: 範囲 han'i = extent, area, range
DESCRIPTION: at the top, 竹 take (bamboo, # 134); at the lower left, 車 kuruma (car, # 283); at the lower right, a radical seen in 犯(人) hannin (criminal, # 901) (identical pronunciation), which resembles an uncoiling snake attacked by Hansel

CUE: **Han**sel drives this 車 (car) throughout a large 範囲 **han**'i (range), and he carries a 竹 (bamboo) stick in case he encounters snakes like this   ALSO COMPARE: other similar kanji at # **547**, # **1966** and # **2074**

1586. 潜 PRONUNCIATIONS: mogu, sen
MEANINGS: submerge, conceal   EXAMPLES:
潜る moguru = to dive or hide; 潜水 sensui = diving   DESCRIPTION: compared to 替(える) kaeru (to exchange money, # 551), this adds a water radical on the left; it retains the two 夫 (husbands) standing in the 日 (sun)   CUES: these two 夫 (husbands) are **Mogu**ls in the swimming pool industry who became **Sen**ators, and they are standing in this 日 (sun) prior to 潜水 **sen**sui (diving) into this water   ALSO COMPARE: other similar kanji at # **352** and # **1915**

1587. 還 PRONUNCIATION: kan
MEANINGS: send back, return   EXAMPLE:
返還 henkan = a return or restoration
DESCRIPTION: compared to 環(境) kankyou (environment, # 718) (identical pronunciation), this kanji omits the 王 (king) on the left and adds a snail at the lower left; it retains the three eyes on a platform above a box on a pole, with a handle on the left and two lips on the right, which resembles a toy megaphone
CUE: a person in **Kan**sas, where three eyes like these are common, is moving slowly on this snail as he examines the environment, while using this megaphone to promote the 返還 hen**kan** (restoration) of forest lands   ALSO COMPARE: other similar kanji at # **718** and # **1324**

1588. 丹 PRONUNCIATION: tan
MEANINGS: red, sincerity   EXAMPLE:
丹念 tannen = precise, meticulous
DESCRIPTION: compared to 舟 fune (ship, # 1524), this omits the prow at the top and the cargo in its aft compartment at the bottom
CUE: this 舟 (ship) is a **Tan**ker that has lost its prow and half of its cargo, but the crew is 丹念 **tan**nen (meticulous) and will repair it soon   ALSO COMPARE: other similar kanji at # **1524**

1589. 亜 PRONUNCIATION: a
MEANINGS: Asian, rank next
EXAMPLE: 亜鉛 aen = zinc
DESCRIPTION: this is the Red Cross logo sandwiched between two platforms, as seen in 悪(い) warui (bad, # 313)
CUE: this Red Cross logo is seen outside a clinic in Africa, where they are using 亜鉛 **a**en (zinc) ointment to help treat wounds
ALSO COMPARE: other similar kanji at # **313** and # **1415**

1590. 慶 PRONUNCIATIONS: kei, yoroko
MEANINGS: jubilation, congratulate
EXAMPLE: 慶事 keiji = an auspicious (prosperous or fortunate) event; 慶ぶ yorokobu = to be delighted (usually written 喜ぶ, # 599)
DESCRIPTION: on the upper left, a lean-to with a chimney; inside the lean-to, at the top, three eyes resting on a platform; below that, 心 kokoro (heart, # 306); at the bottom, a dancer with a ponytail
CUES: these three eyes in this lean-to are watching this dancer with a ponytail, whose 心 (heart) is enjoying a 慶事 **kei**ji (auspicious event) which she celebrates with a **C**ake in the **Yoro**pean (European) city of **Co**logne
ALSO COMPARE: other similar kanji at # **523**, # **677** and # **895**

1591. 侵 PRONUNCIATIONS: shin, oka
MEANINGS: invade, trespass, violate
EXAMPLES: 侵入 shinnyuu = an invasion; 侵す okasu = to invade
DESCRIPTION: compared to 浸(水する) shinsui suru (to be flooded, # 797) (identical pronunciation), this substitutes a man with a slanted hat for the water radical on the left; it retains the long hair flowing to the left, above a 又 (simple table) covered with cloth
CUES: this man on the left, who is a **Shin**to priest with this long hair flowing to the left, **Occa**sionally tilts his hat back to examine his hair before standing at this 又 (table) covered with this cloth and telling us about his faith, but he is careful not to 侵す **oka**su (invade) the privacy of our religious lives
COMPARE: other similar kanji at # **24** and # **1165**

1592. 僚 PRONUNCIATION: ryou
MEANINGS: colleague, companion
EXAMPLE: 官僚 kanryou = a government official or bureaucrat
DESCRIPTION: compared to 寮 ryou (dormitory, # 1501) (identical pronunciation), this omits the bad haircut at the top and adds a man with a slanted hat on the left; it retains the slightly modified 大 (big) and the 日 (oven) spinning on 小 (small)
CUE: this man on the left is a 官僚 kan**ryou** (bureaucrat) who tilts his hat back to examine Pope **Leo**, who is this 大 (big) man who has moved out of this 寮 (dormitory) and repaired his bad haircut but who still bakes bread in this spinning 日 (oven)
ALSO COMPARE: similar kanji at # **94** and # **1069**

1593. 邦 PRONUNCIATIONS: pou, hou
MEANING: home country
EXAMPLES: 連邦 renpou = a federation; ソビエト連邦 sobieto renpou = the Soviet Union; 邦楽 hougaku = traditional Japanese music
DESCRIPTION: on the left, a leaning (or kneeling) telephone pole with three crosspieces; on the right, β beta from the Greek alphabet
CUES: this β (Greek) guy, who was living in the ソビエト連邦 sobieto ren**pou** (Soviet Union), called the **P**olice because this leaning telephone **P**ole was about to fall onto his **H**ome
COMPARE: similar kanji at # **897** and # **1843**

1594. 隆 PRONUNCIATION: ryuu
MEANINGS: hump, prosperity
EXAMPLES: 興隆 kouryuu = rise, prosperity; 興隆する kouryuu suru = to prosper
DESCRIPTION: compared to 降(る) furu (to rain, # 178), this substitutes 生(きる) ikiru (to live, # 208) for the sitting figure at the lower right; it retains β (Greek) and the dancer
CUE: this β (Greek) guy and this dancer have been **Re**united, and they hope to 生 (live) long lives and 興隆する kou**ryuu** suru (prosper)
ALSO COMPARE: other similar kanji at # **1918** and # **2030**

1595. 胞
PRONUNCIATIONS: bou, hou
MEANINGS: placenta, sac, sheath **EXAMPLES:** 細胞 saibou = a cell (biology); 胞子 houshi = a spore **DESCRIPTION:** on the left, 月 tsuki (moon, # 148); on the right, 包(装) housou (wrapping, # 548) (identical pronunciation) and depicts a 己 (snake) shaped like a backwards "S," being wrapped by a hostess
CUES: when we went out in a **Boat** under this 月 (moon), our **Hostess** 包 (wrapped) herself in a blanket, but she said that her 細胞 sai**bou** (cells) still felt chilly
ALSO COMPARE: other similar kanji at # **1861**

1596. 双
PRONUNCIATION: futa
MEANINGS: pair, counter for pairs
EXAMPLE: 双子 futago = twins
DESCRIPTION: these are two variations of 又 mata (again, #24), which resembles a simple table, but the table on the left has a damaged leg
CUE: some 双子 **futa**go (twins) tried to put these two 又 (tables) into a **Fu**ll **Ta**xi, but they wouldn't fit, and one of the legs got damaged
ALSO COMPARE: other similar kanji at # **24**

1597. 懸
PRONUNCIATIONS: ken, ke
MEANINGS: suspend, install, consults
EXAMPLES: 懸賞 kenshou = an award or prize; 懸念 ke'nen = apprehension, fear;
DESCRIPTION: at the upper left, 県 ken (prefecture, # 572) (identical pronunciation), which consists of 目 (eye) that can be seen as a three-drawer cabinet, on a shelf with three legs which Ken uses to hold maps; at the upper right, a skeet shooter wearing a cape, as seen in (関)係 kankei (relationship, # 492); at the bottom, 心 kokoro (heart, # 306) **CUES: Ken** and Barbie received a 懸賞 **ken**shou (prize), which was a **Ke**g of beer, for inventing this three-legged self-propelled cabinet, and this 糸 (skeet shooter) demonstrated his warm 心 (heart) by cheering and waving this cape
ALSO COMPARE: other similar kanji at # **572** and # **1072**

1598. 曹
PRONUNCIATION: sou
MEANINGS: cadet, friend **EXAMPLE:** 軍曹 gunsou = a sergeant; 重曹 juusou = baking soda
DESCRIPTION: compared to 遭(難) sounan (accident, # 1073) (identical pronunciation), this omits the snail at the lower left; it retains the 曲 (tunes), which resemble a coop with wires, above a 日 (sun) being used for solar power in a sound system affected by a short circuit **CUE:** a 軍曹 gun**sou** (sergeant) likes to use 日 (**So**lar) power to listen to 曲 (tunes) like this, but now his sound system is being affected by this short circuit
ALSO COMPARE: other similar kanji at # **1073**

1599. 伴
PRONUNCIATIONS: han, ban, tomona **MEANINGS:** accompany, companion
EXAMPLES: 同伴する douhan suru = to go together, to accompany; 伴奏 bansou = musical accompaniment; 伴う tomonau = to take with, to be accompanied by **DESCRIPTION:** compared to 半(分) hanbun (half, # 331) (identical pronunciation), which can be seen as a telephone pole on fire, this adds a man with a slanted hat on the left
CUES: this man tilted this hat back, and we could see from his face that he was only 半 (half)-hearted about his plan to 同伴する dou**han** suru (accompany) **Han**sel to a **Ban**quet after **Tomo**rrow's **Na**p
ALSO COMPARE: other similar kanji at # **1054**

1600. 唐
PRONUNCIATIONS: tou, kara
MEANINGS: T'ang, China **EXAMPLES:** 唐突 toutotsu = sudden, abrupt; 唐揚げ karaage = deep-fried food, usually spelled カラアゲ **DESCRIPTION:** compared to (砂)糖 satou (sugar, # 1494) (identical pronunciation), this omits 米 (uncooked rice) on the left; it retains the lean-to with a chimney perforated by a trident, with a box below which might represent a toaster
CUES: after a 唐突 **tou**totsu (sudden) event in which this chimney above this 口 (toaster) was perforated by this trident, I could only cook **Toast**,

and it tested my **Cha**rac**ter** ALSO COMPARE: other similar kanji at # **1176** and # **1494**

1601. 剤 PRONUNCIATION: zai

MEANINGS: dose, medicine
EXAMPLE: 洗剤 senzai = detergent
DESCRIPTION: compared to (経)済 keizai (economy, # 259) (identical pronunciation), this kanji omits the water radical on the left and adds the katakana リ ri on the right; it retains the 文 (culture), which consists of a tire stop above a crossing (or X), and is associated with a scientist and the truncated moon that she is studying in Zaire
CUE: a person known for her 文 (culture) studies this truncated moon in **Za**ire (former name of the Congo), and this friend リ **Ri** sometimes sends her 洗剤 sen**zai** (detergent) GROUP: (経)済 keizai = economy, # 259; (一)斉(に) issei ni = all together, # 952; 洗剤 senzai = detergent, # 1601 ALSO COMPARE: other similar kanji at # **259** and # **1985**

1602. 契 PRONUNCIATIONS: chigi, kei

MEANINGS: pledge, promise EXAMPLES: 契る chigiru = to vow or pledge; 契約 keiyaku = a contract DESCRIPTION: compared to 喫(煙) kitsuen (smoking, # 192), this omits the 口 (mouth) on the left; it retains the owl's perch, the 刀 (sword) and 大 (big) CUES: this 大 (big) guy signed a 契約 **kei**yaku (contract) in which he agreed to juggle this owl's perch and this 刀 (sword) in exchange for a **Ch**ea**p Gui**tar and some **Ca**ke ALSO COMPARE: other similar kanji at # **1103** and # **2062**

1603. 爵 PRONUNCIATION: shaku

MEANINGS: baron, peerage, court rank
EXAMPLE: 爵位 shaku'i = peerage, court rank
DESCRIPTION: at the top, a barbecue grate; below that, three eyes; at the lower left, 良(い) yoi (good, # 303), without its pointy hat; at the lower right, 寸(前) sunzen (on the verge, # 1369), which resembles a kneeling sunny guy who is on the verge of picking up some gum CUE: this kneeling sunny guy owns this barbecue grate, has these three eyes and is a 良 (good) person, but he lives in a **Sha**ck, has to pick up this gum in order to rechew it, and can only dream of being admitted to the 爵位 **shaku**'i (peerage) GROUP: 夢 yume = dream, # 165; (丁)寧 teinei = polite, # 703; 憲(法) kenpou = a constitution, # 1438; 爵(位) shaku'i = court rank, # 1603; (軽)蔑 keibetsu = scorn, # 1983 ALSO COMPARE: other similar kanji at # **131**, # **805** and # **1177**

1604. 籍 PRONUNCIATION: seki

MEANINGS: enroll, membership EXAMPLE: 国籍 kokuseki = nationality DESCRIPTION: at the top, 竹 take (bamboo, # 134); on the lower left, 士 shi (man, # 66) standing on 木 (tree); on the lower right, 昔 mukashi (olden times, # 33), or 昔(日) sekijitsu (old times, # 33) (identical pronunciation)
CUE: in the 昔 (olden times), this 士 (man), who was a **Se**lfish **K**ing and who was proud of his 国籍 koku**seki** (nationality), stood on this 木 (tree) and surveyed these 竹 (bamboo) groves
ALSO COMPARE: other similar kanji at # **33**, # **2050** and # **2074**

1605. 廊 PRONUNCIATION: rou

MEANINGS: corridor, hallway
EXAMPLE: 廊下 rouka = corridor or hallway
DESCRIPTION: compared to (野)郎 yarou (a guy, # 1343) (identical pronunciation), this kanji adds a lean-to with a chimney at the upper left; it retains a modified 良 (good) and the ß (Greek) guy who gives me roses
CUE: this ß (Greek) 郎 (guy) is 良 (good), and he decorated the 廊下 **rou**ka (corridor) inside this lean-to with **Ro**ses ALSO COMPARE: other similar kanji at # **805** and # **1843**

1606. 析 PRONUNCIATION: seki

MEANINGS: analyze **EXAMPLE:** 分析 bunseki = analysis **DESCRIPTION:** compared to 所 tokoro (place, # 391), this substitutes 木 ki (wood, # 118) for the P under a roof on the left; it retains the pair of pliers on the right **CUE:** our **S**elfish **Ki**ng ordered us to perform a 分析 bun**seki** (analysis) of the savings we could achieve by making pliers like this out of 木 (wood) like this **ALSO COMPARE:** other similar kanji at # **892**

1607. 輩 PRONUNCIATIONS: pai, hai

MEANINGS: comrade, companion
EXAMPLES: 先輩 senpai = a senior, elder, predecessor; 後輩 kouhai = a junior (in age or rank), a subordinate **DESCRIPTION:** compared to 俳(句) haiku (a style of poem, # 1441) (identical pronunciation), this kanji omits the man with a slanted hat on the left and adds 車 kuruma (car, # 283) at the bottom; it retains the hero that the man wanted to hide **CUES:** this 非 (hero with two wings) has this 車 (car) which he has filled with **Pi**es, and he is trying to **H**ide them from his 後輩 kou**hai** (subordinates) **ALSO COMPARE:** other similar kanji at # **851**, # **1966** and # **2075**

1608. 敏 PRONUNCIATION: bin

MEANINGS: cleverness, agile, alert
EXAMPLE: 敏感な binkan na = sensitive, delicate **DESCRIPTION:** on the left, 毎 mai (every, # 336); on the right, a dancer with a ponytail **CUE:** this dancer with a ponytail eats **B**ea**n**s 毎 (every) day, since she has a 敏感な **bin**kan na (sensitive) stomach
ALSO COMPARE: other similar kanji at # **336** and # **2080**

1609. 鶴 PRONUNCIATION: tsuru, zuru²

MEANING: crane **EXAMPLE:** 鶴 tsuru = a crane; 折り鶴 orizuru = a folded paper crane
DESCRIPTION: compared to 確(かめる) tashikameru (to confirm, # 619), this omits 石 (stone) on the left and adds 鳥 tori (bird, # 555) on the right; it retains another bird swooping above a net, which can be seen as a man with a slanted hat next to a 主 (master) with an extra pair of arms **CUE:** I used this net to capture this swooping bird on the left, and I plan to keep it with this other 鳥 (bird) on the right, which is a 鶴 **tsuru** (crane), in a **Tsu**itcase (suitcase) in my **R**oom **ALSO COMPARE:** other similar kanji at # **698** and # **754**

1610. 烈 PRONUNCIATION: retsu

MEANINGS: ardent, violent, extreme
EXAMPLE: 猛烈 mouretsu = fierce, fervent
DESCRIPTION: compared to 列 retsu (line, # 1124) (identical pronunciation), this adds a fire at the bottom; it retains リ Ri standing in line at a restaurant, before drinking a nightcap
CUE: this リ **R**i preaches a 猛烈 mou**retsu** (fervent) religion while wearing a **Re**tro **Su**it, and his followers stand in this 列 (line) in order to hear his warnings about this fire from Hell
ALSO COMPARE: other similar kanji at # **164**, # **611** and # **1124**

1611. 菊 PRONUNCIATION: kiku

MEANING: chrysanthemum **EXAMPLE:** 菊 kiku = chrysanthemum **DESCRIPTION:** at the top, a plant radical; below that, a hook; inside the hook, 米 kome (uncooked rice, # 326), which resembles petals in a chrysanthemum flower
CUE: the **K**ing of **Ku**wait grows 菊 **kiku** (chrysan-themums), whose white petals are made of plant material like this and resemble 米 (uncooked rice) like this, and he surrounds them with hooks like this to discourage theft **ALSO COMPARE:** other similar kanji at # **988** and # **1387**

1612. 沙 PRONUNCIATION: sa

MEANING: sand **EXAMPLE:** ご無沙汰 gobusata = a long silence, not contacting for a while
DESCRIPTION: compared to 砂(漠) sabaku (desert, # 782) (identical pronunciation), this kanji substitutes a water radical for 石 (stone) on the left; it retains 少(し) sukoshi (a little, # 254) on the

right **CUE:** I had to clean my **Sa**xophone after 少 (a little) of this water got into it, and that's why I was guilty of ご無沙汰 gobu**sa**ta (not contacting you for a while)
ALSO COMPARE: other similar kanji at # **1010**

1613. 汰 PRONUNCIATION: ta
MEANING: select
EXAMPLE: ご無沙汰 gobusata = a long silence, not contacting for a while
DESCRIPTION: compared to 太(る) futoru (to get fat, # 191), or 太(郎) Tarou (a boy's given name, # 191) (identical pronunciation), this kanji adds a water radical on the left; it retains 大 (big) with a ball near its left leg, reminding us of a big person who worries about tar in his cigarettes
CUE: this 太 (fat) person has been worried about this rising water at his **Ta**vern, and that's why he's guilty of ご無沙汰 gobus**ata** (not contacting us for a while)
ALSO COMPARE: other similar kanji at # **191**

1614. 漠 PRONUNCIATION: baku
MEANINGS: vague, obscure, desert
EXAMPLES: 砂漠 sabaku = a desert; 漠然 bakuzen = obscure, vague **DESCRIPTION:** compared to 模(様) moyou (design, # 1353), this substitutes a water radical for 木 (tree) on the left; it retains the plant radical, 日 (sun) and 大 (big) (this combination of radicals = PSB = plants, sun, big)
CUE: this 大 (big) guy walks in this 日 (sun) in a 砂漠 sa**baku** (desert), chewing on plants like this and wishing he had brought more water like this, until he finally arrives at a **B**ar selling **K**ool-Aid (PSB = plants, sun, big)
ALSO COMPARE: other similar kanji at # **1353**

1615. 裸 PRONUNCIATIONS: hadaka, ra
MEANINGS: naked, uncovered **EXAMPLES:** 裸 hadaka = nudity; 裸体 ratai = naked
DESCRIPTION: on the left, happy Jimmy Carter, as seem in 初(めて) hajimete (for the first time, # 104), who has two lips; on the right, 果(物) kudamono (fruit, # 587) **CUES:** when this happy Jimmy with two lips saw a **H**awaiian **D**ancer who was **C**arving this 果 (fruit), he saw that she was 裸体 **ra**tai (naked) and asked a **R**abbi to accompany him **GROUP:** 初(めて) hajimete = for the first time, # 104; 裕(福) yuufuku = wealth, # 660; 補(佐) hosa = help, # 995; 複(雑) fukuzatsu = complicated, # 1281; 被(害) higai = damage, # 1447; 裸 hadaka = nudity, # 1615; 袖 sode = a sleeve, # 1697; 裾 suso = a hem, # 1796; 襟 eri = a collar, # 1872; 褐(色) kasshoku = dark brown, # 2059 **ALSO COMPARE:** other similar kanji at # **588**

1616. 須 PRONUNCIATION: su
MEANINGS: ought, necessary
EXAMPLES: 必須の hissu no = essential, imperative, necessary
DESCRIPTION: compared to 頭 atama (head, # 93), this substitutes three spare cords for a catapult, as seen in 形 katachi (shape, # 573), for the 豆 (beans) on the left; it retains the platform with a missing head
CUE: since I lost my 頭 (head), I can no longer speak, and my family put me into a nursing home, where I find that these three cords are 必須 his**su** (essential) for summoning a **Su**pervisor when I feel neglected **ALSO COMPARE:** other similar kanji at # **839** and # **1126**

1617. 貢 PRONUNCIATION: kou
MEANINGS: tribute, support, finance
EXAMPLE: 貢献 kouken = a contribution
DESCRIPTION: at the top, 工 kou (crafted object, # 246) (identical pronunciation); at the bottom, 貝 kai (shell, or money chest, # 83) **CUE:** this 工 (crafted object) on top of this 貝 (money chest) will be our 貢献 **kou**ken (contribution) to the new **Co**al mine **ALSO COMPARE:** other similar kanji at # **247** and # **656**

1618. 献 PRONUNCIATIONS: ken, kon
MEANINGS: offering, present EXAMPLES: 貢献 kouken = a contribution; 献立 kondate = a menu, bill of fare, program DESCRIPTION: on the left, 南 minami (south, # 388), which includes 十 juu (ten, # 18) at the top and a compass needle inside a 2-sided lean-to; on the right, (番)犬 banken (watchdog, # 190) (identical pronunciation) CUES: **Ken** and Barbie traveled 南 (south) to the **Con**go with this 犬 (dog) to try to make a 貢献 kou**ken** (contribution) to the fight against poverty ALSO COMPARE: other similar kanji at # **479**, # **945** and # **1828**

1619. 封 PRONUNCIATIONS: hou, fuu
MEANINGS: seal, closing EXAMPLES: 封建時代 houken jidai = the feudal period; 封筒 fuutou = an envelope DESCRIPTION: on the left 土 (soil) piled upon 土 (soil), as seen in 崖 gake (cliff, # 911); on the right, 寸(前) sunzen (on the verge, # 1369), which resembles a kneeling sunny guy who is on the verge of picking up his gum CUES: this 寸 (kneeling sunny guy) was **Ho**meless and his **Fo**od was often covered in 土 (soil) piled on 土 (soil) like this, but then some good news arrived in a 封筒 **fuu**tou (envelope) GROUP: 掛(ける) kakeru = to hang, # 596; 街(角) machikado = street corner, # 625; 崖 gake = cliff, # 911; 封(筒) fuutou = an envelope, # 1619; 佳(作) kasaku = honorable mention, # 1642; (生)涯 shougai = one's lifetime, # 1682 ALSO COMPARE: kanji in which soil *walks* on soil at # 1989; other similar kanji at # **131**

1620. 筒 PRONUNCIATIONS: tsutsu, tou
MEANINGS: cylinder, tube
EXAMPLES: 筒 tsutsu = a cylinder; 円筒 entou = a cylinder DESCRIPTION: compared to 同(じ) onaji (the same, # 339), this adds 竹 take (bamboo, # 134) at the top; it retains the two-sided lean-to containing the old napkin above a box CUES: I have a 筒 **tsutsu** (cylinder) made from 竹 (bamboo) like this, on which I hang big **Tsu**its (suits) and small **Tsu**its, and it has 同 (the same) diameter as my big **To**e GROUP: 同(じ) onaji = the same, # 339; 感(じる) kanjiru = to feel, # 640; 興(味) kyoumi = interest, # 693; 洞(穴) horaana = cave, # 963; 減(る) heru = to reduce, # 1148; 胴(体) doutai = torso, # 1191; 銅 dou = copper, # 1232; 筒 tsutsu = a cylinder, # 1620; (遺)憾 ikan = regret, # 2065 ALSO COMPARE: other similar kanji at # **2074**

1621. 貫 PRONUNCIATIONS: tsuranu, kan MEANINGS: pierce, penetrate
EXAMPLES: 貫く tsuranuku = to penetrate, to accomplish, to carry out; 一貫 ikkan = consistency, coherence, integration
DESCRIPTION: compared to (習)慣 shuukan (customs, # 92) (identical pronunciation), this kanji omits the erect man on the left; it retains the string of coins above 貝 (money chest), tilted to the right CUES: when **Tsu**perman (Superman) visits our **Ran**ch with **New**s, I always go to this 貝 (money chest) and get him a coin from this string at the top to buy himself some **Can**dy, since I believe in 一貫 ik**kan** (consistency)
ALSO COMPARE: 貴(重) kichou = precious, # 643; other similar kanji at # **135**, # **336** and # **656**

1622. 偽 PRONUNCIATIONS: nise, itsuwa, gi MEANINGS: lie, pretend, forgery
EXAMPLES: 偽物 nisemono = a counterfeit or fake; 偽る itsuwaru = to lie, deceive or pretend; 虚偽 kyogi = a deception DESCRIPTION: compared to 為(に) tame ni (in order to, # 1222), this adds a man with a slanted hat on the left; it retains the bird with two feathers at the top and five toes, arranged in a pyramidal shape CUES: this man on the left tilts his hat back to examine this pyramid-shaped bird with two feathers and five toes which my **Ni**ece is **Se**lling, and he determines that its feathers are 偽物 **nise**mono (counterfeit), but she says that it **E**ats **Wa**ffles and is friendly with **Gee**se

ALSO COMPARE: other similar kanji at # **754**, # **1101** and # **1997**

1623. 排 PRONUNCIATION: hai
MEANINGS: exclude, expel
EXAMPLE: 排水 haisui = drainage
DESCRIPTION: compared to 俳(句) haiku (poem, # 1441) (identical pronunciation), this kanji substitutes a kneeling guy for the man with a slanted hat on the left; it retains the 非 (hero) with two wings who needs a place to hide
CUE: this kneeling guy is crawling into a 排水 **hai**sui (drainage) pipe where he wants to **H**ide with the help of this 非 (hero)
ALSO COMPARE: other similar kanji at # **851**

1624. 棄 PRONUNCIATIONS: ki, su
MEANINGS: abandon, discard **EXAMPLES:** 破棄する haki suru = to abolish or cancel; 棄てる suteru = to throw away or abandon (this is usually spelled 捨てる, # 594)
DESCRIPTION: at the top, a ム (cow) under a tire stop, as seen in 育(てる) sodateru (to raise, # 151); in the middle, a mountain under cloud cover, as seen in 帯 obi (sash, # 1012); at the bottom, 木 ki (tree, # 118)
CUES: this ム (cow) under a tire stop was 棄てた **su**teta (abandoned) in **K**iev and ended up living up in this 木 (tree) under this cloud-covered 山 (mountain) until it was rescued by **S**uperman
COMPARE: similar kanji at # **1012**, # **1125** and # **1352**

1625. 肖 PRONUNCIATION: shou
MEANING: resemblance **EXAMPLE:** 肖像画 shouzouga = a portrait **DESCRIPTION:** compared to 消(化) shouka (digestion, # 158) (identical pronunciation), this kanji omits the water radical on the left; it retains the 月 (moon) with the three-pronged switch (not on a roof) that affects events in Kiev, where there are good shows **CUE:** an astronaut went to this 月 (moon) to use this three-pronged switch to control the lights for a **Show**, and she had her 肖像画 **shou**zouga (portrait) painted

GROUP: (本)当 hontou = truth, # 31; 消(す) kesu = to erase, # 158; 学(校) gakkou = school, # 184; (簡)単 kantan = easy, # 636; 弾 tama = bullet, # 780; 厳(しい) kibishii = strict, # 902; 戦(争) sensou = war, # 933; 巣 su = nest, # 972; 桜 sakura = cherry, # 984; (選)挙 senkyo = election, # 1362; (狩)猟 shuryou = hunting, # 1397; (紙)幣 shihei = paper money, # 1411; 鎖 kusari = a chain, # 1436; 肖(像画) shouzouga = a portrait, # 1625; 削(減) sakugen = a reduction, # 1626; (高)尚(な) koushou na = noble, # 1629; 禅(宗) zenshuu = Zen, # 1694; (名)誉 meiyo = honor, # 1705; (野)獣 yajuu = a wild animal, # 1733; (今)宵 koyoi = this evening, # 1994; 弊(社) heisha = our company, # 2005 ALSO COMPARE: kanji with a three-pronged switch on *lopsided legs* at # 979; kanji with three *old boys* on a *roof* at # 991; other similar kanji at # **1991**

1626. 削 PRONUNCIATIONS: so, kezu, saku
MEANINGS: plane, sharpen, pare
EXAMPLES: 削ぐ sogu = to shave off, slice, diminish or spoil; 削る kezuru = to shave, sharpen or cut down; 削減 sakugen = a curtailment or reduction **DESCRIPTION:** compared to 肖(像画) shouzouga (a portrait, # 1625), this adds the katakana リ ri on the right, which is sometimes described as a knife and reminds us of shaving; it retains the three-pronged switch on the 月 (moon)
CUES: this リ **R**i dreams of traveling to this 月 (moon) to turn this three-pronged switch, but he's only a **S**oldier who 削る **kezu**ru (shaves) every day, wears **K**eds (a shoe brand) to the **Z**oo when he's off-duty and eats **S**alty **C**ookies
ALSO COMPARE: other similar kanji at # **1625**, # **1985** and # **1991**

1627. 麗 PRONUNCIATION: uruwa

MEANING: lovely EXAMPLE: 麗しい uruwashii = beautiful, charming DESCRIPTION: compared to 鹿 shika (deer, # 895), which reminds us of a deer with three eyes 比 (comparing) lean-tos containing sheep in California, this kanji adds two inverted containers containing antlers at the top, each with a cloth above it CUE: this 麗しい **uruwa**shii (lovely) 鹿 (deer), with its antlers concealed by these two containers and their cloth coverings, must be careful when drinking **Uru**gua-yan **Wa**ter, lest its antler covers fall off COMPARE: other similar kanji at # **352**, **895** and # **1294**

1628. 幾 PRONUNCIATIONS: iku, ki

MEANINGS: how many or much EXAMPLES: 幾分 ikubun = somewhat, somehow, to some extent; 幾何学 kikagaku = geometry

DESCRIPTION: compared to 機(械) kikai (machine, # 137) (identical pronunciation), this kanji omits 木 (wood) on the left; it retains the two truncated 糸 (skeet shooters), each consisting of two flexed elbows, riding on a platform supported by 人 hito (person, # 13) and a halberd

CUES: these two truncated 糸 (skeet shooters) ride on this platform supported by this 人 (person) and this halberd to 幾何学 **ki**kagaku (geometry) class, and they are separated by this halberd, since one of them suffers from **E**ar **C**ooties and they are not allowed to **K**iss ALSO COMPARE: other similar kanji at # **1862**, # **1908** and # **1926**

1629. 尚 PRONUNCIATIONS: nao, shou

MEANINGS: esteem, furthermore, still

EXAMPLES: 尚 nao = further, in addition, still; 高尚な koushou na = noble, high-brow, refined

DESCRIPTION: compared to 向(く) muku (to face toward, # 340), this adds two more lines above the box, reminding us of the three old boys seen in 覚(える) oboeru (to memorize, # 54), but these can be see as three beams of light, or as a three-pronged switch CUES: when **Na**omi met the Shougun, who was a 高尚な kou**shou** na (noble) person, she 向 (faced) him and saw these three beams of light rise from his head ALSO COMPARE: other similar kanji at # **1467** and # **1625**

1630. 彩 PRONUNCIATION: sai

MEANINGS: coloring, paint, makeup

EXAMPLE: 色彩 shikisai = color, hue

DESCRIPTION: compared to 採(算) saisan (surplus, # 1425) (identical pronunciation), which reminds us of a 木 (tree) in Saigon with a barbecue grate at the top, this kanji omits the kneeling guy on the left and adds three cords on the right CUE: this 木 (tree) with a barbecue grate at the top is located in **Sai**gon, where people are using these three cords of different 色彩 shiki**sai** (colors) to pull the grate down ALSO COMPARE: other similar kanji at # **839** and # **1935**

1631. 俗 PRONUNCIATION: zoku

MEANINGS: vulgar, customs, manners

EXAMPLE: 風俗 fuuzoku = manners or customs

DESCRIPTION: compared to 浴(室) yokushitsu (bathroom, # 256), this substitutes a man with a slanted hat for the water radical on the left; it retains the tanning booth with water vapor rising from the roof, where people eat yogurt and cookies

CUE: this man approaches this 浴 (bathroom) and tilts his hat back to examine **Zo**oey's **K**ool-Aid, which he buys there according to his usual 風俗 fuu**zoku** (custom) ALSO COMPARE: other similar kanji at # **660**

1632. 較 PRONUNCIATION: kaku

MEANINGS: contrast, compare EXAMPLE: 比較 hikaku = a comparison DESCRIPTION: compared to 交(通) koutsuu (traffic, # 144), this adds 車 kuruma (car, # 283) CUE: **Ka**rl the Kool-Aid vendor drives this 車 (car) in this 交 (traffic) while making 比較 hi**kaku** (comparisons) between himself and other drivers ALSO COMPARE: similar kanji at # **1139** and # **1966**

1633. 傍 PRONUNCIATIONS: katawa, bou MEANINGS: bystander, side, nearby EXAMPLES: 傍ら katawara = close by, beside, in addition to, besides; 傍観する boukan suru = to be an onlooker DESCRIPTION: on the left, a man with a slanted hat; at the upper right, 立 tatsu (to stand, # 11) with downward-facing spikes on its base, as seen in 諦(める) akirameru (to give up, # 804); at the lower right, 方 kata (honorable person, # 114) CUES: this man on the left tilted his hat back to examine a Catalogue of Watches, but this 方 (honorable person) nearby finds it Boring and feels that the man is rather too 傍ら katawara (close by), but since she 立 (stands) with these spikes on her shoes, it's hard for her to escape ALSO COMPARE: other similar kanji at # 804 and # 920

1634. 肝 PRONUNCIATIONS: kan, kimo MEANINGS: liver, pluck, nerve EXAMPLES: 肝臓 kanzou = the liver; 肝 kimo = liver, courage DESCRIPTION: on the left, 月 tsuki (moon, # 148); on the right, 干(渉) kanshou (interference, # 1306) (identical pronunciation), which resembles a telephone pole CUES: when I visited Kansas, I stood under this 月 (moon) next to this telephone pole, clutching my Kimono to stay warm, while I worried about my 肝臓 kanzou (liver) ALSO COMPARE: other similar kanji at # 629

1635. 誇 PRONUNCIATIONS: hoko, ko MEANINGS: boast, pride EXAMPLES: 誇る hokoru = to take pride in; 誇張 kochou = an exaggeration DESCRIPTION: on the left, 言(う) iu (to tell, # 430); at the upper right, 大(きい) ookii (big, # 188); at the lower right, the leg of a kangaroo, as seen in 考(える) kangaeru (to think, # 469), with a horizontal line above it, representing a corridor CUES: this 考 (kangaroo) 言 (tells) us how 大 (big) its Home's Corridors like this are, but a nearby Cobra says that this is a 誇張 kochou (exaggeration) ALSO COMPARE: other similar kanji at # 468

1636. 魂 PRONUNCIATIONS: kon, tamashii MEANINGS: soul, spirit EXAMPLES: 霊魂 reikon = a soul or spirit; 魂 tamashii = a soul or spirit DESCRIPTION: compared to the 鬼 oni (devil, # 1168) which is owning this ム (cow) above its right tentacle, this adds another 二 (two) ム (cows), as seen in (自)転(車) jitensha (bicycle, # 285), on the left CUES: this 鬼 (devil) in the Congo has these 二 (two) ム (cows) on the left, in addition to the other one above its right tentacle, and it gives Tamales to Shiites and lends them these three cows to gain their confidence before stealing their 魂 tamashii (souls) ALSO COMPARE: other similar kanji at # 1056, # 1169 and # 1678

1637. 控 PRONUNCIATIONS: kou, hika MEANINGS: detain, deduct, complain EXAMPLES: 控除 koujo = a deduction or subtraction; 控える hikaeru = to refrain from, to take notes, to be imminent (an event), to be in waiting DESCRIPTION: compared to 空 sora (sky, # 248), which depicts a soaring bird from Cuba above 工 kou (crafted object, # 246) (identical pronunciation), this kanji adds a kneeling guy on the left CUES: this guy on the left kneels to look at this bird which is landing on this 工 (crafted object) outside a Courthouse, and although he Hears a Camera clicking, he is so absorbed that he 控える hikaeru (refrains from) from turning around ALSO COMPARE: other similar kanji at # 112 and # 247

1638. 紛 PRONUNCIATIONS: magi, fun
MEANINGS: distract, be mistaken for
EXAMPLES: 紛らわしい magirawashii = confusing or misleading; 紛争 funsou = a dispute or fight **DESCRIPTION:** on the left, a 糸 (skeet shooter, # 219); on the right, 分(かる) wakaru (to understand, # 105), or 分 fun (minute, # 105) (identical pronunciation)
CUES: this 糸 (skeet shooter) 分 (understands) that, while shooting at **M**agnificent **Gee**se is **Fun**, it is 紛らわしい **magi**rawashii (confusing) to beginners
ALSO COMPARE: other similar kanji at # **2076**

1639. 既 PRONUNCIATIONS: sude, ki
MEANINGS: previously, already, long ago
EXAMPLES: 既に sude ni = already, usually spelled すでに; 既婚 kikon = already married **DESCRIPTION:** on the left, a modified 良(い) yoi (good, # 303), without its pointy hat; on the right, a modified version of 牙 kiba (fang, # 921), with a bent right leg **CUES:** **S**uperman's **D**entist is 良 (good) at filing down teeth, but this 牙 (fang) has 既に **sude** ni (already) grown back, and is affecting Superman's **K**isses **ALSO COMPARE:** other similar kanji at # **796**, # **805**, # **974** and # **1417**

1640. 股 PRONUNCIATIONS: mata, momo, ko
MEANINGS: thigh, crotch, yarn
EXAMPLES: 股 mata = a thigh or groin; 股 momo = a thigh; 股関節 kokansetsu = the hip joint **DESCRIPTION:** compared to 役に立つ yaku ni tatsu (to be useful, # 557), this substitutes tsuki 月 (moon, # 148) for the man with a double hat on the left; it retains the 几 (yak) on a 又 (table) **CUES:** a **M**atador gets up early on **M**ost **M**ornings when it's **C**old, to feed this 几 (yak) on this 又 (table) by the light of this 月 (moon), and he exercises his 股 **momo** (thighs) as he does so
ALSO COMPARE: other similar kanji at # **557**

1641. 征 PRONUNCIATION: sei
MEANINGS: subjugate, collect taxes
EXAMPLE: 遠征 ensei = an expedition **DESCRIPTION:** on the left, a man with two hats; on the right, seikaku 正(確) (accurate, # 174) (identical pronunciation), or 正(しい) tadashii (correct, # 174) **CUE:** this man on the left, who is always 正 (correct), is about to leave on an 遠征 en**sei** (expedition), and he wants to be **S**afe, so he brought this extra hat
ALSO COMPARE: other similar kanji at # **1150**

1642. 佳 PRONUNCIATION: ka
MEANINGS: excellent, beautiful
EXAMPLE: 佳作 kasaku = a good piece of work, honorable mention
DESCRIPTION: on the left, a man with a slanted hat; on the right, 土 (soil) piled upon 土 (soil), as seen in 掛(ける) kakeru (to hang, # 596) (identical pronunciation), which reminds us of 土 (soil) piled upon 土 (soil)
CUES: this man on the left slants his hat back to look at this 土 (soil) piled upon 土 (soil), where he plans to build a **C**abin, and later he enters the structure into a contest, where he receives a 佳作 **ka**saku (honorable mention)
ALSO COMPARE: other similar kanji at # **1619**

1643. 哀 PRONUNCIATIONS: ai, awa
MEANINGS: pathetic, grief, sympathize
EXAMPLES: 哀悼 aitou = condolences; 哀れ aware = pity, misery; 哀れな aware na = pitiable, miserable **DESCRIPTION:** compared to 京(都) Kyouto (# 514), this substitutes エ and Y for the 小 (small) axis; it retains the tire stop and 口 (mouth), which can also be seen as a box **CUES:** when I slipped on some **I**ce, this tire stop hit me in this 口 (mouth), and now I **Aw**ait medical treatment, but this エ and Y are supporting me in my 哀れ **awa**re (misery)
ALSO COMPARE: other similar kanji at # **1474**

1644. 悼 PRONUNCIATION: tou
MEANINGS: lament, grieve over EXAMPLE: 哀悼 aitou = condolences DESCRIPTION: compared to (食)卓 shokutaku (dining table, # 620), this adds an erect man on the left CUE: this guy on the left stubbed his **To**e on this 卓 (dining table) and, as he awaits our 哀悼 ai**tou** (condolences), he indignantly draws himself up to his full height
ALSO COMPARE: other similar kanji at # **620**, # **1365** and # **2063**

1645. 眉 PRONUNCIATION: mayu
MEANING: eyebrow
EXAMPLE: 眉毛 mayuge = an eyebrow
DESCRIPTION: on the upper left, a mask with openings for two eyes, as seen in 声 koe (voice, # 40); on the lower right, 目 me (eye, # 51)
CUE: I **Ma**rried a **You**th with no 眉毛 **mayu**ge (eyebrows), but he wears this mask with two eye holes that shows only his 目 (eyes), so that no one will notice ALSO COMPARE: other similar kanji at # **1314** and # **2002**

1646. 拒 PRONUNCIATIONS: kyo, koba
MEANINGS: reject, decline EXAMPLES: 拒否 kyohi = rejection, refusal; 拒む kobamu = to refuse or reject DESCRIPTION: compared to 巨(大) kyodai (huge, # 689) (identical pronunciation), which resembles a swing set in Kyoto turned on its side, this adds a kneeling guy on the left CUES: this guy is kneeling to try to pick up this fallen swing set in **Kyo**to, and he asks a **C**orpulent **B**arber for help, but the barber 拒む **koba**mu (refuses)
ALSO COMPARE: other similar kanji at # **1246**

1647. 概 PRONUNCIATION: gai
MEANINGS: outline, condition, generally
EXAMPLE: 概念 gainen = a concept or general idea DESCRIPTION: compared to 既(に) sude ni (already, # 1639), this adds 木 ki (tree, # 118) on the left; it retains a modified 良 (good), without its pointy hat, and a modified version of 牙 (fang), including a bent right leg CUE: although this is a 良 (good) 牙 (fang), our **Gui**delines include the 概念 **gai**nen (general idea) that one should not use one's teeth to cut down 木 (trees) like this
ALSO COMPARE: other similar kanji at # **796**, # **805**, # **974** and # **1417**

1648. 顧 PRONUNCIATIONS: ko, kaeri
MEANINGS: advisor, consultant
EXAMPLES: 顧問 komon = an advisor or counselor; 顧みる kaerimiru = to look back on
DESCRIPTION: compared to (解)雇 kaiko (dismissal, # 1398) (identical pronunciation), this kanji adds a platform with a missing head, as seen in 頭 atama (head, # 93), on the right; it retains the net, which can be seen as a man with a slanted hat next to a 主 (master) with an extra pair of arms (see # 203), inside a cold double-roofed lean-to with a layer of snow on top CUES: since I lost my 頭 (head), I've been sleeping in this net in this **C**old snow-covered lean-to, but I'm going to get someone to **C**all **E**ric, who is my 顧問 **ko**mon (advisor), and ask him for a blanket ALSO COMPARE: other similar kanji at # **1126**, # **1134** and # **2046**

1649. 挨 PRONUNCIATION: ai
MEANING: push open EXAMPLE: 挨拶 aisatsu = a greeting or salutation; this is usually spelled あいさつ DESCRIPTION: on the left, a kneeling guy; at the upper right, the katakana ム mu, which is the sound made by a cow; at the lower right, 矢 ya (arrow, # 1045), which resembles a Native American chief
CUE: this guy on the left slipped on some **I**ce cream made from milk produced by this ム (cow) and hurt his foot, so that now he has to crawl, but he speaks a friendly 挨拶 **ai**satsu (greeting) to this 矢 (Native American chief) ALSO COMPARE: other similar kanji at # **324** and # **1678**

1650. 拶 PRONUNCIATION: satsu
MEANING: be imminent
EXAMPLE: 挨拶 aisatsu = a greeting or salutation; this is usually spelled あいさつ
DESCRIPTION: on the left, a kneeling guy; at the upper right, a chevron, as seen in 巡(る) meguru (to go around, # 778), which reminds us of the military; at the lower right, 夕(方) yuugata (evening, # 160) CUE: this guy on the left is a **Sa**tisfied **S**upervisor of a shoe store who kneels in his store by day but wears this chevron in the 夕 (evenings), when he gives his neighbors 挨拶 ai**satsu** (greetings) like a military man ALSO COMPARE: other similar kanji at # **801** and # **1019**

1651. 憎 PRONUNCIATIONS: niku, zou
MEANINGS: hate, detest EXAMPLES: 憎む nikumu = to hate or detest; 愛憎 aizou = simultaneous love and hate DESCRIPTION: compared to (倍)増(する) baizou suru (to double, # 61) (identical pronunciation), this kanji substitutes an erect man for the man with a slanted hat on the left; it retains the 田 (rice paddy) above a 日 (sun) in an agricultural zone that produces two units of rice CUES: this guy on the left forces my **Ni**ece in **Ku**wait to work under this 日 (sun) in this 田 (rice paddy) that produces these two units of rice in an agricultural **Z**one, and she 憎む **niku**mu (detests) him because he's so tall and rigid ALSO COMPARE: other similar kanji at # **61** and # **2063**

1652. 賊 PRONUNCIATION: zoku
MEANINGS: bandit, brigand EXAMPLE: 盗賊 touzoku = a robber or burglar
DESCRIPTION: on the left, 貝 kai (shell, or money chest, # 83); in the middle, 十 too (ten, # 18); on the right, a halberd (combination lance and axe) CUE: 十 (ten) 盗賊 tou**zoku** (burglars) armed with halberds like this broke into this 貝 (money chest) and stole **Z**ooey's **Ko**ol-Aid
ALSO COMPARE: other similar kanji at # **1658**, # **1862** and # **2058**

1653. 匠 PRONUNCIATIONS: shou, takumi MEANINGS: artisan, workman
EXAMPLE: 巨匠 kyoshou = a master or a preeminent person; 匠 takumi = an artisan, craftsman or carpenter DESCRIPTION: compared to 丘 oka (hill, # 1473), this adds a one-sided lean-to at the upper left CUES: a 匠 **takumi** (artisan) piled up dirt to build this small 丘 (hill) inside this lean-to, and he uses it in **Show**s where he sells his work, mostly **Ta**cky **Ku**waiti **Mi**rrors ALSO COMPARE: other similar kanji at # **320** and # **892**

1654. 淡 PRONUNCIATIONS: awa, tan
MEANINGS: thin, faint, fleeting
EXAMPLE: 淡い awai = thin, faint, pale, fleeting; 冷淡な reitan na = cool, indifferent
DESCRIPTION: compared to 炎 honoo (blaze, # 788), this adds a water radical on the left; it retains 火 (fire) piled on 火 (fire)
CUES: when I **Awa**kened and found myself caught between this water and this 炎 (blaze), I had an 淡い **awa**i (faint) hope that I might be able to escape by driving off in my **Tan**k
ALSO COMPARE: other similar kanji at # **352** and # **1239**

1655. 併 PRONUNCIATIONS: hei, pei
MEANINGS: join, unite, collective EXAMPLES: 併用する heiyou suru = to use simultaneously; 合併 gappei = a merger, combination or union
DESCRIPTION: compared to 餅 mochi (rice cake, # 743), this substitutes a man with a slanted hat for 食 (to eat) on the left; it retains the research tower decorated with rabbit ears
CUES: this man on the left tilts his hat in order to observe this tower that a researcher has decorated with rabbit ears, but he **Ha**tes to see this when he is unable to do the same thing with his building, and he asks if they can 併用する **hei**you suru [use (the ears) simultaneously], for which he is willing to **Pay**
ALSO COMPARE: other similar kanji at # **573** and # **743**

1656. 崇 PRONUNCIATIONS: aga, suu
MEANINGS: adore, respect, worship
EXAMPLES: 崇める agameru = to worship or adore; 崇拝 suuhai = adoration, worship
DESCRIPTION: at the top, 山 yama (mountain, # 146); at the bottom, 宗(教) shuukyou (religion, # 676) **CUES:** in this 宗 (religion), we have to climb this 山 (mountain) **Ag**ain and again in order to 崇める **aga**meru (worship), but if we sell **Sou**venirs, we get extra credit   **ALSO COMPARE:** other similar kanji at # **1347** and # **1385**

1657. 岐 PRONUNCIATIONS: ki, gi
MEANINGS: branch off, fork in road
EXAMPLES: 分岐点 bunkiten = a crossroads, juncture, watershed; 岐阜 Gifu = a prefecture and city in Japan   **DESCRIPTION:** on the left, 山 yama (mountain, # 146); on the right, 支(社) shisha (branch office, # 26), which resembles a 士 (man) standing on a 又 (table)
CUES: this 士 (man) went to a 支 (branch office) in 岐(阜) **Gi**fu, bought a **Ki**mono and wore it to this 山 (mountain) in order to watch some **Gee**se   **ALSO COMPARE:** other similar kanji at # **1121** and # **1942**

1658. 阜 PRONUNCIATION: fu
MEANINGS: hill, mound   **EXAMPLE:** 岐阜 Gifu = a prefecture and city in Japan
DESCRIPTION: at the top, a bunk bed with a pillow on the top bunk, as seen in (教)師 kyoushi (teacher, # 1351); at the bottom, too 十 (ten, # 18), but this could be an axis for a spinning bunkbed
CUE: when I moved to 岐阜 Gi**fu**, I bought this bunkbed with a pillow on the top bunk, and I **Fo**olishly spin it on this axis   **GROUP:** 卒(業) sotsugyou = graduation, # 27; 準(備) junbi = preparation, # 204; 午(後) gogo = in the afternoon, # 207; 茶 cha = tea, # 212; 靴 kutsu = shoe, # 603; 許(可) kyoka = permission, # 1141; 革(靴) kawagutsu = leather shoe, # 1286; 華(やか) hanayaka = gorgeous, # 1354; (上)昇 joushou = rising, # 1363; 率 ritsu = percentage, # 1408; 酔(う) you = to get drunk, # 1476; 枠 waku = a frame, # 1490; (盗)賊 touzoku = a burglar, # 1652; (岐)阜 Gifu = a prefecture, # 1658; 傘 kasa = an umbrella, # 1743; 卑(し い) iyashii = despicable, # 1745; (純)粋 junsui = pure, # 1778; 砕(く) kudaku = to break, # 1845; 奔(放) honpou = unrestrained, # 1864; (墓)碑 bohi = a gravestone, # 1905; 迅(速な) jinsoku na = fast, # 1968   **ALSO COMPARE:** other similar kanji at # **880**

1659. 嬢 PRONUNCIATION: jou
MEANINGS: girl, miss, daughter
EXAMPLE: お嬢さん ojousan = a young girl, someone else's daughter   **DESCRIPTION:** compared to (豊)穣 houjou (good harvest, # 1322) (identical pronunciation), this kanji substitutes 女 onna (female, # 235) for the ripe grain on the left; it retains 六 (six), 井 (well) and some 衣 (clothing) for Joan of Arc
CUE: when **Jo**an of Arc, who was 女 (female), was an お嬢さん o**jou**san (young girl), her family owned 六 (six) 井 (wells) like this, and they could buy her nice 衣 (clothes) like this
ALSO COMPARE: other kanji containing 女 on the left at # **2039**; other similar kanji at # **1322**

1660. 陥 PRONUNCIATIONS: kan, ochii
MEANINGS: collapse, fall into
EXAMPLES: 欠陥 kekkan = a flaw or defect; 陥る ochiiru = to fall into, to be trapped in
DESCRIPTION: on the left, ß beta from the Greek alphabet; at the upper right, a fish head, as seen in 魚 sakana (fish, # 80), but this can also be seen as an h-shaped chair leaning to the right; at the lower right, 旧(正月) kyuu shougatsu (lunar new year, # 1017), which reminds us of the # 1 日 (day) of the year CUES: on this # 1 日 (day) of the year, this ß (Greek) guy lit some **Ca**ndles and fed some **O**ld **Chee**se to his **E**agles, but when he sat down in this h-shaped chair, it had a 欠陥 kek**kan** (defect) that made it lean to the right like this
ALSO COMPARE: other similar kanji at # **87**, # **1017** and # **2030**

1661. 賠 PRONUNCIATION: bai
MEANINGS: compensation, indemnity
EXAMPLE: 賠償 baishou = compensation, reparation DESCRIPTION: compared to 倍(増する) baizou suru (to double, # 269) (identical pronunciation), this kanji substitutes 貝 kai (shell, money chest, # 83) for the man with a slanted hat on the left; it retains the bell on a box
CUE: I'm going to take some 賠償 **bai**shou (compensation) out of this 貝 (money chest) and use it to **B**uy this 立 (bell) on a 口 (box) ALSO COMPARE: other similar kanji at # **269** and # **2058**

1662. 償 PRONUNCIATION: tsuguna, shou MEANINGS: reparation, make up for
EXAMPLES: 償う tsugunau = to compensate; 補償 hoshou = compensation
DESCRIPTION: compared to (受)賞(する) jushou suru (to win a prize, # 991) (identical pronunciation), this kanji adds a man with a slanted hat on the left; it retains the three old boys on a roof getting ready for a show CUES: these three old boys, who are 員 (members) of a cast, are interrupted by this man on the left, whose **Ts**uitcase (suitcase) was taken by a **Goo**se from **N**arnia, which has a role in their **Sh**ow, and he tilts his hat back like this to show his face and requests 補償 ho**shou** (compensation) ALSO COMPARE: other similar kanji at # **88**, # **707** and # **991**

1663. 剛 PRONUNCIATION: gou
MEANINGS: sturdy, strength
EXAMPLE: 剛健 gouken = vigor, health, sturdiness DESCRIPTION: compared to 岡 oka (hill, # 1528), this adds the katakana リ Ri on the right; it retains the model of a mountain with a handle and antennae, inside a lean-to (this radical inside the lean-to can also be seen as a chairlift seat hanging from two frayed cables)
CUE: this リ Ri ran up this 岡 (hill) to play **G**olf at the top, demonstrating his 剛健 **gou**ken (vigor) ALSO COMPARE: other similar kanji at # **1200** and # **1985**

1664. 廷 PRONUNCIATION: tei
MEANINGS: courts, government office
EXAMPLE: 法廷 houtei = a court of law
DESCRIPTION: compared to 庭(園) teien (formal Japanese garden, # 495) (identical pronunciation), this omits the lean-to with a chimney at the upper left; it retains the 王 (king) riding on a 3x snail, who is guarded with tasers CUE: when this 王 (king) rides on this 3x snail on his way to his 法廷 hou**tei** (court of law), he is guarded with **T**asers ALSO COMPARE: other similar kanji at # **692** and # **2045**

1665. 紫 PRONUNCIATIONS: shi, murasaki MEANINGS: purple, violet
EXAMPLES: 紫外線 shigaisen = ultraviolet rays; 紫 murasaki = purple DESCRIPTION: at the upper left, 止(める) tomeru (to stop, # 173), which reminds us of a stop sign; at the upper right, the katakana ヒ hi, which reminds us of a hero; at the bottom, 糸 (skeet shooter, # 219)
CUES: this 糸 (skeet shooter), who was busy juggling this 止 (stop sign) and this ヒ (hero), forgot to feed his **Sh**eep, not to mention work on a **Mur**al for a **S**arcastic **K**ing, and his face turned 紫

murasaki (purple) ALSO COMPARE: other similar kanji at # <u>1266</u>, # <u>1929</u> and # <u>2048</u>

1666. 銘 PRONUNCIATION: mei

MEANINGS: inscription, signature (of artisan)
EXAMPLE: 感銘 kanmei = a deep impression
DESCRIPTION: compared to (有)名 yuumei (famous, # 162) (identical pronunciation), this kanji adds 金 kane (money, # 301) on the left; it retains the card that Napoleon's maid hung from a 夕 (half moon)
CUE: the fact that a **Ma**id hung this card from this 夕 (half moon) and became 名 (famous) made a 感銘 kan**mei** (deep impression) on me, and I gave her this 金 (money) ALSO COMPARE: other similar kanji at # <u>801</u> and # <u>2010</u>

1667. 鎌 PRONUNCIATION: kama

MEANINGS: sickle, scythe, trick
EXAMPLE: 鎌 kama = a sickle or scythe
DESCRIPTION: compared to 兼(用) ken'you (multi-use, # 1401), this adds 金 kane (money, # 301) on the left; it retains the 木 (tree) split down the middle and held together with a trident supplied by Ken and Barbie CUE: this split 木 (tree) was damaged by a 鎌 **kama** (sickle) and then partially repaired, but since I recently received this 金 (money), I plan to **Ca**ll a **Ma**ster arborist who can fix it properly ALSO COMPARE: other similar kanji at # <u>817</u> and # <u>2010</u>

1668. 稼 PRONUNCIATIONS: ka, kase

MEANINGS: earnings, work
EXAMPLES: 稼業 kagyou = trade, business, occupation; 稼ぐ kasegu = to earn (money)
DESCRIPTION: compared to 家 ie (house, # 405), or 家(族) kazoku (family, # 405) (identical pronunciation), which depicts a cabin, this kanji adds 禾 (a grain plant with a ripe head) on the left
CUES: I own this 家 (house), which is a **Ca**bin, and this 禾 (ripe grain) growing next to it is one ingredient in the **Ca**sseroles that I sell in my 稼

業 **ka**gyou (business) ALSO COMPARE: other similar kanji at # <u>1504</u> and # <u>1797</u>

1669. 譲 PRONUNCIATIONS: jou, yuzu

MEANINGS: transfer, hand over
EXAMPLES: 譲歩 jouho = concession, compromise; 譲る yuzuru = to give way, hand over, sell, bequeath DESCRIPTION: compared to (お)嬢(さん) ojousan (young girl, # 1659) (identical pronunciation), this kanji substitutes 言 (う) iu (to say, # 430) for 女 (female) on the left; it retains 六 (six), 井 (well) and some 衣 (clothing) for Joan of Arc
CUES: since **Jo**an of Arc had these 六 (six) 井 (wells), she was able to buy nice 衣 (clothes) like this, and when a **Yo**uthful **Zo**okeeper 言 (said) that he needed water for his animals, she would 譲る **yuzu**ru (sell) him some
ALSO COMPARE: other similar kanji at # <u>1322</u>

1670. 随 PRONUNCIATION: zui

MEANINGS: follow, obey, abide by
EXAMPLE: 随分 zuibun = very
DESCRIPTION: on the left, β beta from the Greek alphabet; in the middle, a snail; on the snail, 有(名) yuumei (famous, # 460), which resembles a person from the Yukon symbolically hugging a famous 月 (moon) to show gratitude
CUE: when this β (Greek) guy saw this person symbolically hugging this famous 月 (moon) while riding on this snail, he thought that he would prefer to hug a **Zo**oming **E**agle like the ones they have in Athens, since their speed is 随分 **zui**bun (very) impressive ALSO COMPARE: other similar kanji at # <u>457</u>, # <u>2030</u> and # <u>2087</u>

1671. 凄 PRONUNCIATIONS: susa, sugo
MEANINGS: uncanny, weird, threatening
EXAMPLES: 凄まじい susamajii = amazing, horrible, usually written すさまじい; 凄い sugoi = great, wonderful, terrific, terrible, usually written すごい
DESCRIPTION: compared to 妻 tsuma (wife, # 237), this adds a water radical on the left; it retains the 女 (female) with a cross and a comb in her hair
CUES: I want to rescue this 妻 (wife) from this water because she makes **S**uperior **S**alads, she plays **S**uperior **G**olf, and she is 凄い **sugo**i (terrific)
ALSO COMPARE: other similar kanji at # **877** and # **2086**

1672. 扉 PRONUNCIATION: tobira
MEANINGS: front door, title page
EXAMPLE: 扉 tobira = a front door, a title page
DESCRIPTION: compared to 戸 to (door, # 871), this adds 非(常) hijou (emergency, # 682), which reminds us of a hero with two wings, at the lower right; it retains the lean-to with a double roof and a layer of snow on top
CUE: when this 非 (hero) came out of the 扉 **tobira** (front door) of this snow-covered lean-to, he encountered a **T**ortoise and a **B**eaming **R**abbit, and he could guess which one had won their race
ALSO COMPARE: other similar kanji at # **851** and # **1134**

1673. 偵 PRONUNCIATION: tei
MEANING: spy **EXAMPLE:** 探偵 tantei = a detective **DESCRIPTION:** on the left, a man with a slanted hat; at the upper right, a modified taser, as seen in (予)定 yotei (plan, # 455) (identical pronunciation); at the lower right, 貝 kai (shell, or money chest, # 83)
CUE: this man on the left is a 探偵 tan**tei** (detective) who tilts his hat back to examine this **Ta**ser on this 貝 (money chest), which he uses to protect his money
GROUP: 上 ue = up, # 171; (探)偵 tantei = a detective, # 1673 **ALSO COMPARE:** other similar kanji at # **656**

1674. 澄 PRONUNCIATION: su
MEANINGS: lucidity, clear, clarify
EXAMPLE: 澄む sumu = to become clear or transparent **DESCRIPTION:** compared to 登(る) noboru (to climb, # 297) this adds a water radical, which reminds us of rain, on the left; it retains the peaked roof with bench hats, above 豆 (beans) **CUE:** when Superman 登 (climbed) a mountain, he encountered water like this in the form of rain, but then the weather 澄んだ **su**nda (cleared) **ALSO COMPARE:** other similar kanji at # **297**, # **721** and # **2070**

1675. 殊 PRONUNCIATIONS: shu, koto
MEANINGS: particularly, especially
EXAMPLES: 特殊な tokushu na = unique, peculiar, special; 殊に koto ni = especially, moreover, what is more, usually spelled ことに
DESCRIPTION: compared to 列 retsu (line, # 1124), this substitutes a 牛 (cow) in a 木 (tree), as seen in 株 kabu (stock, # 1302), for リ Ri on the right; it retains 夕 (evening), wearing a flat hat (a nightcap)
CUES: when I was drinking this nightcap, this 牛 (cow) came down from this 木 (tree) and stepped on my **Sh**oe, and then I got **C**old **T**oes, which was a 特殊な toku**shu** na (peculiar) experience
GROUP: 株 kabu = stock, # 1302; (特)殊(な) tokushu na = unique, # 1675; 朱(印) shuin = a red seal, # 1692 (identical pronunciation); 珠 tama = jewel, # 1772 **ALSO COMPARE:** kanji that combine 牛 (cow) with 大 (big) at # 304; other similar kanji at # **164**

1676. 紋 PRONUNCIATION: mon
MEANINGS: family crest, figures
EXAMPLE: 指紋 shimon = a fingerprint
DESCRIPTION: compared to 文(句) monku (complaint, # 25) (identical pronunciation), this kanji adds 糸 (skeet shooter, # 219) on the left; it retains 文(化) bunka (culture) on the right

CUE: this 糸 (skeet shooter) is a thief, and he has some 文 (culture) like this, in the sense that he steals **Mon**et paintings, but he sometimes leaves his 指紋 shi**mon** (fingerprints) behind
ALSO COMPARE: other similar kanji at # **259**

1677. 芳 PRONUNCIATIONS: **kanba, hou** MEANINGS: perfume, balmy, flavorable, fragrant EXAMPLES: 芳しい **kanba**shii = fragrant; 芳香 **hou**kou = perfume or fragrance
DESCRIPTION: compared to 方 kata (honorable person, #114), or 方(法) houhou (method, #114) (identical pronunciation), this kanji adds a plant radical at the top
CUES: a **Kan**sas **B**arber goes to **H**otels to cut the hair of 方 (honorable people) like this and then adds plant material like this to their scalps, which he douses with 芳香 **hou**kou (perfume)
ALSO COMPARE: other similar kanji at # **920**

1678. 惨 PRONUNCIATIONS: **san, zan², miji** MEANINGS: wretched, disaster, cruelty
EXAMPLES: 悲惨な hi**san** na = woeful, pitiable, miserable; 無惨な mu**zan** na = heartless, tragic (this is usually spelled 無残な); 惨めな **miji**me na = miserable
DESCRIPTION: compared to 参(加) sanka (participation, # 406) (identical pronunciation), this kanji adds an erect man on the left; it retains the ム (cow) traveling to San Francisco on a rocker-bottom shoe CUES: when this ム (cow) was traveling to **San** Francisco on this rocker-bottom shoe, it encountered a **M**iniature **J**eep driven by this man on the left who, when he makes himself erect like this, is too tall to drive it properly, and then things got 惨め **miji**me (miserable) GROUP: 窓 mado = window, # 311; 参(る) mairu = to humbly go, # 406; 強(い) tsuyoi = strong, # 478; 髪 kami = hair, # 501; 離(婚) rikon = divorce, # 666; 弁(当) bentou = box lunch, # 1162; 鬼 oni = devil, # 1168; 魅(力) miryoku = charm, # 1169; (悪)魔 akuma = devil, # 1332; 魂 tamashii = a soul, # 1636; 挨(拶) aisatsu = a greeting, # 1649; 惨(めな) **miji**me na = miserable, # 1678; (血)塊 kekkai = blood clot, # 1738; 醜(い) minikui = ugly, # 1882 ALSO COMPARE: other similar kanji at # **406** and # **2063**

1679. 虐 PRONUNCIATIONS: **gyaku, shiita** MEANINGS: tyranize, oppress
EXAMPLES: 残虐な zan**gyaku** na = cruel, inhuman; 虐げる **shiita**geru = to persecute or oppress DESCRIPTION: compared to (謙)虚 kenkyo (modesty, # 966), this substitutes long hair streaming to the right, as seen in 長(い) nagai (long), # 502, for the four-burner stove at the bottom; it retains the one-sided lean-to with 七 (seven) people who use a periscope to observe the outside world CUES: 七 (seven) **G**eeky **Y**akuzas with this hair streaming to the right live in this lean-to, and they have some **S**heep from **I**taly which they watch through this periscope and 虐げる **shiita**geru (oppress) ALSO COMPARE: other similar kanji at # **502** and # **1057**

1680. 凝 PRONUNCIATION: **gyou, ko** MEANINGS: congeal, freeze, be absorbed in EXAMPLES: 凝縮 **gyou**shuku = condensation; 凝る **ko**ru = to grow stiff (muscles), to be absorbed in or obsessed with DESCRIPTION: compared to 疑(う) utagau (to doubt, # 978), this adds a water radical on the left; it retains the ヒ (hero), the 矢 (Native American chief) and the マ Ma, a family who traveled to Utah wearing gaudy jewelry, carrying a taser mounted on a 足 (foot) CUES: this ヒ (hero), this 矢 (Native American chief) and this マ Ma are a family who want to make **G**yoza, and they 凝る **ko**ru (are absorbed) in asking whether they should use **C**orn cooked in this water over a fire that was lit with this taser mounted on this foot ALSO COMPARE: other similar kanji at # **324**, # **913**, # **978** and # **2048**

1681. 圏 **PRONUNCIATION:** ken
MEANINGS: circle, radius, range **EXAMPLE:** 首都圏 shutoken = the capital city, often Tokyo, typically denoting the portion within a 50-km radius around the center **DESCRIPTION:** compared to 巻(き込む) makikomu (to get involved in, # 1309), this adds a box on the perimeter; it retains the 己 (snake) below a bonfire, which consists of 二 (two) inscribed on 人 (person), plus flames **CUE:** when **Ken** and Barbie encountered this 己 (snake) near this bonfire in 首都圏 shuto**ken** (the capital city), they built this fence around the snake and the fire **ALSO COMPARE:** 券 ken = ticket, # 1305 (identical pronunciation); other similar kanji at # **1078**, # **1305** and # **1360**

1682. 涯 **PRONUNCIATION:** gai
MEANINGS: horizon, shore **EXAMPLE:** 生涯 shougai = one's lifetime or career **DESCRIPTION:** compared to (断)崖 dangai = cliff, # 911 (identical pronunciation), this kanji omits 山 (mountain) at the top and adds a water radical on the left, it retains the one-sided lean-to full of 土 (soil) piled upon 土 (soil) that was discovered by a guide **CUE:** during my 生涯 shou**gai** (career) as a mountain **G**u**i**de, I saw this water trigger a landslide that filled this lean-to with this 土 (soil) piled upon 土 (soil) **ALSO COMPARE:** other similar kanji at # **748** and # **1619**

1683. 岳 **PRONUNCIATIONS:** gaku, dake
MEANINGS: point, mountain
EXAMPLES: 山岳 sangaku = mountains; 北岳 Kitadake = the name of a mountain in Japan **DESCRIPTION:** at the top, 丘 oka (hill, # 1473), which resembles a pair of pliers on a platform, something that is occasionally seen on hills in Cuba; at the bottom, 山 yama (mountain, # 146) **CUES:** after Darwin and I had climbed this 丘 (hill) and this 山 (mountain), I drank a **Ga**llon of **K**ool-Aid from **D**arwin's **K**ettle while looking at the 山岳 san**gaku** (mountains) around me

ALSO COMPARE: other similar kanji at # **892** and # **2079**

1684. 淑 **PRONUNCIATION:** shuku
MEANINGS: graceful, gentle, pure
EXAMPLE: 淑女 shukujo = a lady
DESCRIPTION: compared to (監)督 kantoku (director, # 1421), this omits 目 (eye) at the bottom and adds a water radical on the left; it retains the taser on a 小 (small) hill and 又 mata (a simple table) **CUE:** when a 淑女 **shuku**jo (lady) saw that this water was rising, she put her **Sh**oes from **Ku**wait on this 又 (table) to save them, but she wasn't able to rescue this taser on this 小 (small hill) **ALSO COMPARE:** other similar kanji at # **24** and # **1421**

1685. 倫 **PRONUNCIATION:** rin
MEANINGS: ethics, companion **EXAMPLE:** 倫理 rinri = ethics **DESCRIPTION:** compared to (車)輪 sharin (wheel, # 690) (identical pronunciation), this kanji substitutes a man with a slanted hat for the 車 (car) on the left; it retains the library visited by Ringo on the right **CUE:** this man on the left is **Rin**go, and he visits this library on the right in order to read books on 倫 **rin**ri (ethics), tilting his hat to expose his face and show his sincerity
ALSO COMPARE: other similar kanji at # **813**

1686. 呉 **PRONUNCIATION:** go
MEANINGS: give, do something for **EXAMPLE:** 呉服 gofuku = cloth (for Japanese clothes), textile
DESCRIPTION: compared to 誤(解) gokai (misunderstanding, # 1285) (identical pronunciation), this kanji omits 言 (to say) on the left; it retains the pitcher on a gopher-infested mound, throwing a square ball
CUE: this pitcher is wearing a uniform made from good 呉服 **go**fuku (cloth), but he is worried about the **G**ophers infesting this mound
GROUP: 誤(解) gokai = misunderstanding, # 1285; 呉(服) gofuku = cloth, # 1686; 娯(楽) goraku = diversion, # 2019; **Note** that all of these kanji can be pronounced "go"

1687. 貌 PRONUNCIATION: bou
MEANINGS: form, appearance, countenance
EXAMPLE: 容貌 youbou = face, features, looks
DESCRIPTION: at the upper left, a mouth with two teeth; at the lower left, the katakana ヲ wo, which reminds us of a wolf; on the right, 白(い) shiroi (white, # 44), with two lopsided legs; if we ignore the ray above 日 (sun), it can be seen as a sun above lopsided legs **CUE:** a guy wearing a 白 (white) outfit like this is walking around on these two lopsided legs **Bo**asting about his 容貌 you**bou** (looks), especially when compared to this ugly ヲ (wolf) with these two teeth in this mouth
ALSO COMPARE: other similar kanji at # 974, # 1355, # 2014 and # 2068

1688. 婆 PRONUNCIATION: ba
MEANINGS: old woman, grandma
EXAMPLE: 老婆 rouba = an old woman
DESCRIPTION: at the top, 波 nami (wave, # 878), which consists of a water radical and 皮 (Straight Arrow, # 833), who has just eaten a nasty meal; at the bottom, 女 onna (female, # 235)
CUE: this 女 (female), who was a 老婆 rou**ba** (old woman), rescued this 皮 (Straight Arrow) from this water, and they went to a **Ba**r **ALSO COMPARE:** other similar kanji at # 833 and # 2086

1689. 鍵 PRONUNCIATION: kagi
MEANING: key **EXAMPLE:** 鍵 kagi = a key, or a clue **DESCRIPTION:** on the left, (お)金 okane (money, # 301); on the right, 建(物) tatemono (a building, # 363), which includes a telephone pole, riding on a snail **CUE:** I paid this 金 (money) for this 建 (building), where I keep **Ca**lifornia **Ge**ese, and of course I have a 鍵 **kagi** (key) to it **ALSO COMPARE:** other similar kanji at # 692, # 820, # 877 and # 2010

1690. 膳 PRONUNCIATION: zen
MEANINGS: small low table, tray **EXAMPLE:** 一膳 ichizen = one bowl (of cooked rice) **DESCRIPTION:** compared to 善(人) zennin (good people, # 1336) (identical pronunciation), this kanji adds 月 tsuki (moon, # 148) on the left; it retains the 羊 (sheep) standing on an upside-down bench above a 口 (box) **CUE:** a **Zen** monk, who likes to eat when this 月 (moon) is shining, saw this 羊 (sheep) standing on this upside-down bench above this 口 (box) and joined it while he ate 一膳 ichi**zen** (a bowl) of cooked rice
ALSO COMPARE: other similar kanji at # 1223 and # 1236

1691. 罰 PRONUNCIATIONS: ba, batsu, bachi
MEANINGS: penalty, punishment
EXAMPLES: 罰金 bakkin = a penalty or fine; 罰する bassuru = to punish or penalize; 罰 batsu = discipline, penalty; 罰当たりな bachiatari na (or no) = spiteful, sinful, cursed
DESCRIPTION: at the top, 目 me (eye, # 51) turned horizontally, which could represent three eyes; at the lower left, 言(う) iu (to tell, # 430); at the lower right, the katakana リ ri
CUES: a woman with these three eyes observed this リ Ri as he visited a **B**ar wearing a **B**at **Su**it and stole a **B**ag of **Ch**eese, and she 言 (told) the owner, so Ri will have to pay a 罰金 **ba**kkin (penalty)
ALSO COMPARE: other similar kanji at # 1324 and # 1985

1692. 朱 PRONUNCIATION: shu
MEANINGS: scarlet, red **EXAMPLE:** 朱印 shuin = a red seal (calligraphy)
DESCRIPTION: compared to (特)殊(な) tokushu na (unique, # 1675) (identical pronunciation), this kanji omits 夕 (evening) wearing a flat hat on the left; it retains the 牛 (cow) up in a 木 (tree) **CUE:** when I was practicing calligraphy, this 牛 (cow) came down from this 木 (tree) and stepped on my **Sh**oe, so I applied my 朱印 **shu**in (red seal) and left
ALSO COMPARE: other similar kanji at # 1675

1693. 漂 PRONUNCIATIONS: hyou, tadayo
MEANINGS: drift, float EXAMPLES: 漂白剤 hyouhakuzai = bleach; 漂う tadayou = to drift DESCRIPTION: compared to 票 hyou (a vote, # 1510) (identical pronunciation), this kanji adds a water radical on the left; it retains the healer from Oregon with three eyes, who uses his third eye for 宗 (religious) insights, standing on a spinning nail structure [this can also be seen as 二 (two) above 小 (small)] CUES: when this wave of water hit this three-eyed **He**aler from **O**regon, who uses his third eye for 宗 (religious) insights, he was on this spinning nail structure, and he 漂った **tadayo**tta (drifted) out to sea, but my **T**all **Da**ughter held onto a **Yo**gi and was saved ALSO COMPARE: other similar kanji at # **1347** and # **1415**

1694. 禅 PRONUNCIATION: zen
MEANINGS: Zen, silent meditation EXAMPLE: 禅宗 zenshuu = Zen Buddhism DESCRIPTION: compared to (簡)単 kantan (easy, # 636), this adds the Shah, as seen in (会)社 kaisha (company, # 271), on the left; it retains a spinning 田 (rice paddy) above 十 (ten), with three old boys on top, as seen in 覚(える) oboeru (to memorize, # 54) CUE: a **Z**en monk told this Shah that 禅宗 **zen**shuu (Zen Buddhism) is 単 (easy) GROUP: (簡)単 kantan = easy, # 636; 弾 tama = bullet, # 780; 戦(争) sensou = war, # 933; 禅(宗) zenshuu = Zen, # 1694 ALSO COMPARE: kanji containing a rice paddy on a stick at # 1157; kanji containing a rice paddy *below* ten at # 720; other similar kanji at # **1160** and # **1625**

1695. 酷 PRONUNCIATION: koku
MEANINGS: cruel, severe, unjust EXAMPLE: 残酷な zankoku na = brutal, atrocious DESCRIPTION: compared to (報)告 houkoku (report, # 429) (identical pronunciation), this kanji adds 酒 sake (alcoholic beverage, # 465), without its water radical, on the left (this can also be seen as a bucket of sake with a handle); it retains the person holding out a shield to demonstrate that drinking Coke can shield us from unpopularity, standing above a 口 (mouth) CUE: if you suffer from 残酷な zan**koku** na (brutal) treatment at the hands of the world, this 口 (mouth) tells us that drinking **Co**ke and this 酒 (alcohol) can shield you to some degree, as shown by the person holding a shield at the upper right ALSO COMPARE: other similar kanji at # **429** and # **1480**

1696. 霧 PRONUNCIATIONS: kiri, mu
MEANINGS: fog, mist EXAMPLES: 霧 kiri = fog or mist; 濃霧 noumu = heavy fog DESCRIPTION: compared to (事)務(所) jimusho (office, # 518) (identical pronunciation), this kanji adds 雨 ame (rain, # 261) at the top; it retains the four workers at an office on the moon: マ Ma, a barbed nail representing a guy with a barbed wit, a dancer with a ponytail, and a guy with 力 (force) CUES: these four people in an 務 (office) were looking for a **Ki**tty when they were surprised to see this 雨 (rain) fall, followed by some 霧 **kiri** (fog), since they were on the **M**oon ALSO COMPARE: other similar kanji at # **262**, # **1746** and # **1749**

1697. 袖 PRONUNCIATION: sode
MEANINGS: sleeve, wing (building), extension EXAMPLE: 袖 sode = a sleeve DESCRIPTION: on the left, happy Jimmy Carter with two lips, as seen in 初(めて) hajimete (for the first time, # 104); on the right, (理)由 riyuu (reason, # 73), which resembles a unit of rice above a 田 (rice paddy), or a rice paddy on a stick CUE: this happy Jimmy with two lips found this unit of rice above this 田 (rice paddy), **So**ld it to a **De**ntist and put the money he received in his 袖 **sode** (sleeve) ALSO COMPARE: other similar kanji at # **942**, # **1157** and # **1615**

1698. 彫 PRONUNCIATIONS: chou, ho
MEANINGS: carve, engrave, chisel
EXAMPLES: 彫刻 choukoku = a sculpture or carving; 彫る horu = to engrave, carve or chisel
DESCRIPTION: compared to 調(子) choushi (condition, # 441) (identical pronunciation), this kanji omits 言 (to say) on the left and adds three spare cords for a catapult, as seen in 形 katachi (shape, # 573), on the right; it retains the box hidden under 土 (dirt) in a tent, which reminds us of the detective who was chosen to check the box
CUES: when a sculptor was **Cho**sen to 彫る **horu** (carve) a likeness of a **Ho**rse, he used the tools that he kept in this 口 (box) under this 土 (dirt) in this tent and used these three cords to hold the animal while he worked ALSO COMPARE: other similar kanji at # **346** and # **839**

1699. 需 PRONUNCIATION: ju
MEANINGS: demand, request, need
EXAMPLES: 必需品 hitsujuhin = a necessary or essential item; 需要 juyou = a demand or request DESCRIPTION: at the top, 雨 ame (rain, # 261); at the bottom, a limousine antenna mounted on a book shelf, as seen in (忍)耐 nintai (patience, # 1434) CUE: when this 雨 (rain) is falling and you can't get good reception for your TV using this limousine antenna, another 必需品 hitsu**ju**hin (essential item) for your satisfaction is **Ju**ice, which you can make from rain water ALSO COMPARE: other similar kanji at # **262** and # **522**

1700. 潰 PRONUNCIATIONS: kai, tsubu
MEANINGS: crush, smash EXAMPLES: 潰瘍 kaiyou = an ulcer; 潰れる tsubureru = to be smashed or go bankrupt, usually spelled つぶれる DESCRIPTION: compared to 貴(重) kichou (valuable, # 643), this adds a water radical on the left; it retains 中 (inside) on a platform above 貝 kai (money chest) (identical pronunciation)
CUES: a **Kai**ser had a 貴 (valuable) **Tsui**tcase (suitcase) of **Boo**ze bottles which he tried to put 中 (inside) this 貝 (money chest), but this water made the floor slippery and some bottles were **tsubu**reta 潰れた (smashed)
COMPARE: other similar kanji at # **643**

1701. 腫 PRONUNCIATIONS: ha, shu
MEANINGS: tumor, swelling
EXAMPLES: 腫れる hareru = to swell up; 腫瘍 shuyou = a tumor
DESCRIPTION: compared to 種(類) shurui (variety, # 1098) (identical pronunciation), this kanji substitutes 月 tsuki (moon, # 148) for the 禾 (ripe grain) on the left; it retains 重 (heavy)
CUES: as I walked under this 月 (moon), I felt something **H**ard in my **S**hoe, and my heart was 重 (heavy) when I discovered that I had a 腫瘍 **shu**you (tumor) on my foot
ALSO COMPARE: other similar kanji at # **284**

1702. 瘍 PRONUNCIATION: you
MEANINGS: boil, carbuncle EXAMPLE: 潰瘍 kaiyou = an ulcer DESCRIPTION: compared to (太)陽 taiyou (sun, # 891) (identical pronunciation), this kanji omits ß (Greece) on the left and adds a sick bed, as seen in 病(気) byouki (sick, # 369), at the upper left; it retains a modified version of 易(しい) yasashii (easy, # 402)
CUE: a 潰瘍 kai**you** (ulcer) is 易 (easy) to treat if you stay in this sick bed and eat lots of **Yo**gurt GROUP: 易(しい) yasashii = easy, # 402; 場(所) basho = place, # 403; 湯 yu = hot water, # 404; 揚(げる) ageru = to deep fry, # 768; (太)陽 taiyou = sun, # 891; 傷 kizu = injury, # 1376; 腸 chou = intestine, # 1497; (潰)瘍 kaiyou = an ulcer, # 1702 ALSO COMPARE: other similar kanji at # **369**

1703. 穏

PRONUNCIATIONS: oda, on
MEANINGS: calm, quiet, moderation
EXAMPLES: 穏やかな odayaka na = calm, peaceful; 平穏な heion na = peaceful, calm
DESCRIPTION: compared to 隠(す) kakusu (to hide, # 834), this substitutes 禾 (a ripe head of grain) for the ß (Greek) guy on the left; it retains the barbecue grate, the long hair flowing to the left, and 心 (heart) **CUES:** my **O**lder **D**aughter, who has this long hair flowing to the left, cooks this 禾 (ripe grain) on this grate that she **O**wns, since she's older, and she feels 穏やか **oda**yaka (peaceful) in this 心 (heart)
ALSO COMPARE: other similar kanji at # **1165**, # **1177** and # **1797**

1704. 謎

PRONUNCIATION: nazo
MEANINGS: riddle, puzzle, enigma **EXAMPLE:** 謎 nazo = an enigma, puzzle or riddle
DESCRIPTION: compared to 迷(う) mayou (to lose direction, # 623), this adds 言(う) iu (to say, # 430) on the left; it retains the 米 (uncooked rice) on a snail that also carries mayonnaise
CUE: this snail 言 (says) that when it carried this cargo of 米 (uncooked rice) into a **N**arco **Z**one, it encountered a 謎 **nazo** (puzzle) that it couldn't solve
COMPARE: other similar kanji at # **623**

1705. 誉

PRONUNCIATIONS: homa, ho, yo **MEANINGS:** praise, honor, glory
EXAMPLES: 誉れ homare = honor or distinction; 誉める homeru = to praise, admire or speak well of (this can also be spelled 褒める, # 829); 名誉 meiyo = honor or glory
DESCRIPTION: compared to (選)挙 senkyo (election, # 1362), this subsitutes 言(う) iu (to speak, # 430) for 手 (hand) at the bottom; it retains the three old boys in Kyoto standing on a platform supported by slanted walls
CUES: **Ho**mer got **M**arried in this **H**otel with slanted walls in **Y**osemite, where he 言 (spoke) his vows while these three old boys on this platform 誉めた **ho**meta (praised) him
ALSO COMPARE: other similar kanji at # **1625**

1706. 逸

PRONUNCIATIONS: so, itsu
MEANINGS: deviate, diverge, elude
EXAMPLES: 逸らす sorasu = to dodge, to turn away; 逸話 itsuwa = an anecdote
DESCRIPTION: compared to 免(許) menkyo (a license, # 1140), this adds a snail at the lower left; it retains the fish-head guy (see # 80) with glasses on lopsided legs, who knows that success is all mental
CUES: this fish-head guy with glasses on lopsided legs uses this snail as a **S**ofa and **E**ats snacks while it 逸らす **so**rasu (dodges) work
ALSO COMPARE: other similar kanji at # **1140** and # **1314**

1707. 凍

PRONUNCIATIONS: koo, kogo, tou **MEANINGS:** frozen, congeal, refrigerate
EXAMPLES: 凍る kooru = to freeze; 凍える kogoeru = to be chilled or frozen; 冷凍する reitou suru = to freeze **DESCRIPTION:** compared to 東 higashi (east, # 508), this adds a water radical on the left; it retains the tree wearing bifocals
CUES: when an icy wind blows from the 東 (east), it gets **C**old, this water 凍る **koo**ru (freezes) and even **C**ozy **G**ophers get icy **T**oes
ALSO COMPARE: other similar kanji at # **1271**

1708. 惜

PRONUNCIATION: o
MEANINGS: pity, be sparing of, regret
EXAMPLE: 惜しい oshii = unfortunate, regrettable, precious, almost but not quite, too good
DESCRIPTION: compared to 昔 mukashi (olden times, # 33), this adds an erect man on the left
CUES: in the 昔 (olden times), this man on the left said that it was 惜しい **o**shii (unfortunate) to get **O**ld but that at least he could still stand straight and tall like this **ALSO COMPARE:** other similar kanji at # **33** and # **2063**

1709. 措 PRONUNCIATION: so
MEANINGS: keep, put, behavior EXAMPLE: 措置 sochi = an action DESCRIPTION: compared to 借(りる) kariru (to borrow, # 485), this substitutes a kneeling guy for the man with a slanted hat on the left; it retains 昔 (olden times) CUE: in the 昔 (olden times), this **So**ldier on the left went into 措置 **so**chi (action) and sustained foot injuries, forcing him to crawl like this ALSO COMPARE: other similar kanji at # **33**

1710. 瓦 PRONUNCIATIONS: kawara, ga MEANINGS: tile, gram EXAMPLES: 瓦 kawara = a roof tile; 瓦解 gakai = collapse, downfall DESCRIPTION: compared to 五 go (five, # 179), this substitutes a snake, partially enveloping a smaller snake, for the knee on the right, suggesting a family of snakes; it retains the two horizontal lines connected by a vertical line on the left CUES: my **Ca**r has a **Wa**rranty, but after it ran out of **Ga**s next to a house, it was struck by a 瓦 **ka**wara (roof tile) that was dislodged by this family of 五 (five) snakes, and the insurance company wouldn't pay ALSO COMPARE: other similar kanji at # **179**

1711. 瓶 PRONUNCIATIONS: kame, bin
MEANINGS: flower pot, bottle, jar, urn
EXAMPLES: 瓶 kame = an earthenware jar; 瓶 bin = a bottle, jar or decanter DESCRIPTION: compared to 瓦 kawara (roof tile, # 1710), this adds a research tower with rabbit ears on the left, as seen in 餅 mochi (rice cake, # 743); it retains the family of 五 (five) snakes that damaged a car with a warranty CUES: when a researcher was studying vegetables in this research tower that he had decorated with rabbit ears for a New Year's celebration, a **Ca**mel was frightened by this 瓦 (family of five snakes) and broke the 瓶 **bin** (jar) in which the researcher was keeping his **Be**ans ALSO COMPARE: other similar kanji at # **179**, # **573** and # **1997**

1712. 琴 PRONUNCIATION: koto
MEANINGS: harp, koto EXAMPLE: 琴 koto = a Japanese harp DESCRIPTION: at the top, two 王 ou (kings, # 1077); at the bottom, 今 ima (now, # 292), which contains a 7 under a ceiling under a peaked roof CUE: 今 (now) these two 王 (kings) have **Co**ld **To**es, after sitting through a concert of 琴 **koto** (Japanese harp) music
GROUP: (家)賃 yachin = rent, # 707; 王(様) ousama = king, # 1077; 琴 koto = a Japanese harp, # 1712; (翻)弄(する) honrou suru = to trifle with, # 1924 ALSO COMPARE: other similar kanji at # **352** and # **1491**

1713. 摂 PRONUNCIATION: se
MEANINGS: vicarious, surrogate, in addition to EXAMPLES: 摂取 sesshu = intake, absorption, assimilation; 摂氏 sesshi = degrees Celsius DESCRIPTION: on the left, a kneeling guy; at the upper right, 耳 mimi (ear, # 57); at the lower right, a segmented X, as seen in 渋(滞) juutai (gridlock, # 1454) CUE: this guy on the left, who is kneeling to snoop around, is **Se**lfish and has big 耳 (ears) like this, and he recently heard about plans for the 摂取 **se**sshu (assimilation) of poor people into society, which he marks with segmented X's like this, to show disapproval GROUP: 最(近) saikin = recently, # 42; 耳 mimi = ear, # 57; 取(る) toru = to take, # 58; 恥 haji = shame, # 309; 聞(く) kiku = to hear, # 412; 職(業) shokugyou = occupation, # 696; 趣(味) shumi = hobby, # 715; 餌 esa = animal food, # 843; 厳(しい) kibishii = strict, # 902; 聴(衆) choushuu = audience, # 934; 撮(影) satsuei = filming, # 1331; 聖(人) seijin = a saint, # 1500; 摂(取) sesshu = intake, # 1713; (勇)敢(な) yuukan na = brave, # 1852 ALSO COMPARE: other similar kanji at # **1454**

1714. 拍 PRONUNCIATIONS: hyou, byou², haku MEANINGS: clap, beat (music) EXAMPLES: 拍子 hyoushi = musical time or rhythm; 三拍子 sanbyoushi = triple time (music); 拍手 hakushu = applause DESCRIPTION: compared to 白(髪) hakuhatsu (white hair, # 44) (identical pronunciation), this kanji adds a kneeling guy on the left CUES: this guy on the left, who is a **Hea**ler from Oregon, kneeled to kiss the ground when he arrrived at the **Ha**rbor in **Ku**wait wearing 白 (white) robes, and he was greeted with 拍手 **haku**shu (applause) ALSO COMPARE: other similar kanji at # **2014**

1715. 稽 PRONUNCIATION: kei MEANINGS: think, consider, quarrel EXAMPLE: 稽古 keiko = rehearsal, practice, training DESCRIPTION: on the left, 禾 (a grain plant with a ripe head); at the upper right, an unusual radical that may represent an athlete with lopsided legs, with a ball above his right shoulder; at the lower right, 旨(味) umami (a 5th taste category, # 1318), which depicts a ヒ (hero) in the 日 (sun), who is an uber Marine CUE: after this athlete with this ball and these lopsided legs and this 旨 (uber Marine) 稽古する **kei**ko suru (practice), they reward themselves with **Ca**ke made from this 禾 (ripe grain) ALSO COMPARE: other similar kanji at # **974**, # **1318** and # **1797**

1716. 礎 PRONUNCIATION: so MEANINGS: cornerstone, foundation stone EXAMPLES: 基礎 kiso = a foundation, base or basis DESCRIPTION: on the left, 石 ishi (stone, # 458); at the upper right, 林 hayashi (grove, # 125); at the lower right, a taser mounted on a foot, as seen in (予)定 yotei (plan # 455) CUE: we are using 石 (stones) like this to build the 基礎 ki**so** (foundation) for a factory under this 林 (grove), which will produce 定 (foot-mounted tasers) like this for **So**ldiers ALSO COMPARE: other similar kanji at # **913**, # **943** and # **1775**

1717. 掌 PRONUNCIATIONS: shou, tenohira MEANINGS: manipulate, rule, administer EXAMPLES: 車掌 shashou = a bus or train conductor; 掌 tenohira = the palm of the hand DESCRIPTION: compared to (受)賞(する) jushou suru (to win a prize, # 991) (identical pronunciation), this kanji substitutes 手 te (hand, # 23) for the money chest at the bottom; it retains three old boys on a roof preparing for a show and 口 (mouth), which resembles a square and may represent the flat part of a hand CUES: as these three old boys prepare for a **Sh**ow on this roof, one of them exposes the 掌 **tenohira** (palm) of this 手 (hand) to their audience, but their **Ten**or has run off with a **Hi**deous **Ra**bbit ALSO COMPARE: other similar kanji at # **991** and # **1554**

1718. 克 PRONUNCIATION: koku MEANINGS: overcome, kindly, skillfully EXAMPLE: 克明な kokumei na = detailed, minute DESCRIPTION: this is a fusion of 古(い) furui (old, # 392) and 兄 ani (big brother, # 420) CUE: since this 兄 (big brother) is 古 (old), he tends to engage in 克明な **koku**mei na (detailed) discussions about **Co**ke, a drink that was popular when he was young ALSO COMPARE: other similar kanji at # **394** and # **420**

1719. 据 PRONUNCIATION: su MEANINGS: set, lay a foundation, install EXAMPLE: 据える sueru = to place or set up DESCRIPTION: compared to (住)居 juukyo (dwelling, # 809), this adds a kneeling guy on the left; it retains 古 (old) inside a lean-to with a double roof in Kyoto CUE: this guy on the left 据えた **su**eta (set up) this 居 (dwelling) as a café where 古 (old) people can eat lunch, and now he is kneeling to look through a window and see how they like their **Sou**p ALSO COMPARE: other similar kanji at # **394** and # **1899**

1720. 胆 PRONUNCIATION: tan
MEANINGS: gallbladder, pluck
EXAMPLE: 大胆 daitan = bold or brave
DESCRIPTION: compared to (一)旦 ittan (for a moment, # 668) (identical pronunciation), or 旦(那) danna (husband), this kanji adds 月 tsuki (moon, # 148) on the left; it retains the 日 (sun) that is tanning a man who dances on a floor
CUE: this 旦 (husband) dances on this floor under this 日 (sun) and has a **Tan**, but he is 大胆 dai**tan** (brave) enough to dance under this 月 (moon) at night too
ALSO COMPARE: other similar kanji at # **668**

1721. 縛 PRONUNCIATIONS: baku, shiba
MEANINGS: truss, arrest, tie, bind
EXAMPLES: 束縛 sokubaku = a restraint, restriction or confinement; 縛る shibaru = to tie or bind **DESCRIPTION:** compared to 博(打) bakuchi (gambling, # 1481) (identical pronunciation), this kanji substitutes 糸 (skeet shooter, # 219) for 十 (ten) on the left; it retains the top part of a 犬 (dog) chasing a ball above a 田 (rice paddy) and 寸 (the kneeling sunny guy who has dropped his gum, # 215) **CUES:** this 糸 (skeet shooter) was shooting balls for this truncated 犬 (dog) at this 田 (rice paddy), and this 寸 (kneeling sunny guy) came along, but when they started eating **Ba**nana **Coo**kies, the Queen of **Sheba** told them that there were 束縛 soku**baku** (restrictions) against snacking **GROUP:** 薄(い) usui = pale, # 258; 専(門) senmon = specialty, # 1235; 博(打) bakuchi = gambling, # 1481; 縛(る) shibaru = to tie, # 1721; (帳)簿 choubo = an account book, # 1788 **ALSO COMPARE:** other similar kanji at # **865**

1722. 鎮 PRONUNCIATION: shizu, chin
MEANINGS: tranquilize **EXAMPLES:** 鎮める shizumeru = to alleviate or suppress, to calm; 鎮火する chinka suru = to put out a fire
DESCRIPTION: on the left, 金 kane (money, # 301); on the right, 真(実) shinjitsu (truth, # 101), which resembles a table cabinet with a machine above it that includes a shiny antenna [this can also be described as 十 (ten) above 目 (eye) on legs] **CUES:** after a **Sh**eep at the **Z**oo bumped into me and injured my **Chin**, I told the 真 (truth), and the zoo paid me this 金 (money), which I hope will 鎮める **shizu**meru (alleviate) my stress
ALSO COMPARE: 沈める shizumeru = to sink, # 835, or 沈(黙) chinmoku = silence, # 835, both of which are pronounced like this kanji although they don't resemble it; other similar kanji at # **100**, # **101** and # **2010**

1723. 雷 PRONUNCIATIONS: kaminari, rai
MEANINGS: thunder, lightning bolt
EXAMPLES: 雷 kaminari = thunder or lightning; 雷鳴 raimei = thunder **DESCRIPTION:** compared to 電(気) denki (electricity, # 263), this omits the wire at the bottom; it retains the 雨 (rain) and the 田 (rice paddy) **CUES:** when some **Commie**s (communists) from **Na**rita were harvesting **Ri**ce from this 田 (paddy), they heard 雷 **kaminari** (thunder), and then this 雨 (rain) began to fall **ALSO COMPARE:** other similar kanji at # **220** and # **262**

1724. 恨 PRONUNCIATIONS: ura, kon
MEANINGS: regret, resentment, malice
EXAMPLE: 恨む uramu = to bear a grudge; 痛恨 tsuukon = contrition, regretful, bitter
DESCRIPTION: on the left, an erect man; on the right, 良(い) yoi (good), including L & Y at its base, without its pointy hat **CUES:** this man had a 良 (good) **U**ranium mine in the **Con**go, but he lost his title to it, and now he maintains this rigid posture since he 恨む **ura**mu (bears a grudge) **ALSO COMPARE:** other similar kanji at # **805** and # **2063**

1725. 顕 **PRONUNCIATION: aki, ken**
MEANINGS: appear, existing **EXAMPLE:** 顕らか akiraka = obvious, clear (this is usually spelled 明らか, # 154); 顕著な kencho na = conspicuous, remarkable **DESCRIPTION:** compared to 湿(る) shimeru (to get damp, # 1300), this omits the water radical on the left and, on the right, it adds a 貝 (money chest) with a platform at the top where a head could fit, as seen in 頭 atama (head, # 93); it retains the 日 (sun) and the four burners **CUES:** an African King from Kenya lost a head from this platform on the right, but later he found it sitting in this 日 (sun) on this four-burner stove, where it was rather 顕著 kencho (conspicuous) **ALSO COMPARE:** other similar kanji at # **1126** and # **1300**

1726. 棋 **PRONUNCIATION: ki, gi**
MEANING: chess piece **EXAMPLE:** 棋士 kishi = a shougi or go player; 将棋 shougi = Japanese chess **DESCRIPTION:** compared to (時)期 jiki (season, # 711) (identical pronunciation), this kanji omits 月 (moon) on the right and adds 木 ki (tree, # 118) on the left; it retains the woman with a bucket with several compartments and a wide skirt, who makes quiche
CUES: as we played 将棋 shougi (Japanese chess) a waitress with this wide skirt and this bucket with several compartments served us Quiche, while some Geese that were watching from this 木 (tree) ate the leftovers
ALSO COMPARE: other similar kanji at # **711**

1727. 巧 **PRONUNCIATIONS: taku, kou**
MEANINGS: adroit, skilled, ingenuity
EXAMPLES: 巧みな takumi na = skillful; 技巧 gikou = technique, skill **DESCRIPTION:** on the left, 工(場) koujou (factory, # 246) (identical pronunciation), which represents a crafted object; on the right, a kangaroo, as seen in (番)号 bangou (number, # 470) **CUES:** when Tarzan visited Kuwait, he found this 工 (crafted object) outside a Courthouse and wielded it with 技巧 gikou (skill) to control this kangaroo **ALSO COMPARE:** other similar kanji at # **247** and # **468**

1728. 桃 **PRONUNCIATIONS: tou, momo** **MEANING:** peach tree **EXAMPLE:** 桃花 touka = a peach blossom; 桃 momo = a peach **DESCRIPTION:** compared to 兆 chou (trillion, # 849), this kanji adds 木 ki (tree, # 118) on the left **CUES:** after a Tornado destroyed 兆 (a trillion) 木 (trees) like this, Most Motorists didn't drive out to check the damage, but some asked if the affected trees were 桃 **momo** (peach) trees **ALSO COMPARE:** other similar kanji at # **849**

1729. 隔 **PRONUNCIATIONS: kaku, heda** **MEANINGS:** isolate, distance, separate
EXAMPLES: 間隔 kankaku = an interim, interval, pause or space; 隔たる hedataru = to be distant **DESCRIPTION:** compared to 融(合) yuugou (fusion, # 987), this omits 虫 (insect) on the right and adds ß beta from the Greek alphabet on the left; it retains the 口 (mouth) with a napkin over it and the floor plan of a house, with a missing wall at the bottom and the letter T inside, which reminds us of Tarantulas **CUES:** when Karl the Kool-Aid vendor was selling Kool-Aid in ß (Greece), he encountered this napkin-covered 口 (mouth) which screamed about these T (tarantulas) that perform Hellish Dances in this house with a missing wall, and he tried to put some 間隔 kan**kaku** (space) between it and himself **GROUP:** 融(合) yuugou = fusion, # 987; (間)隔 kankaku = a pause, # 1729
ALSO COMPARE: other similar kanji at # **987** and # **2030**

1730. 甚 PRONUNCIATION: jin
MEANINGS: tremendous, exceedingly
EXAMPLE: 甚大 jindai = very great, enormous, serious **DESCRIPTION:** compared to 勘(弁) kanben (pardon, # 1161), this omits 力 (force) on the right; it retains the 匹 (small animal) carrying a bucket with three compartments
CUE: a **Gen**ius told me that 匹 (small animals) like this can carry 甚大 **jin**dai (enormous) buckets like this if you feed them vitamins
ALSO COMPARE: other similar kanji at # **1161**

1731. 妊 PRONUNCIATION: nin
MEANING: pregnancy **EXAMPLE:** 妊婦 ninpu = a pregnant woman **DESCRIPTION:** compared to (主)任 shunin = foreman, # 483 (identical pronunciation), this kanji substitutes 女 onna (female, # 235) for the man with a slanted hat on the left; it retains the 壬 (king) on the right
CUE: when this 壬 (king) asked this 女 (female) who was responsible for her 妊娠 **nin**shin (pregnancy), she named a certain **Nin**ja
ALSO COMPARE: other kanji containing 女 on the left at # **2039**; other similar kanji at **2045**

1732. 娠 PRONUNCIATION: shin
MEANING: with child, pregnancy
EXAMPLE: 妊娠 ninshin = pregnancy
DESCRIPTION: compared to 振(る) furu (to shake, # 823), or 振(動数) shindousuu (frequency, # 823) (identical pronunciation), this kanji substitutes 女 onna (female, # 235) for the kneeling guy on the left; it retains the Shinto shrine which contains a horizontal arrow and is supported by the letter L and the letter Y
CUE: this 女 (female) gets help from this L and Y, who are supporting this **Shin**to shrine, during her 妊娠 nin**shin** (pregnancy), and they provide this arrow for her protection
ALSO COMPARE: other kanji containing 女 on the left at # **2039**; other similar kanji at # **1105**

1733. 獣 PRONUNCIATIONS: kemono, juu
MEANINGS: animal, beast **EXAMPLES:** 獣 kemono = an animal 野獣 yajuu = a wild animal; **DESCRIPTION:** at the upper left, three old boys, as seen in 覚(える) oboeru (to memorize, # 54), standing over 田(んぼ) tanbo (rice paddy, # 68); at the lower left, a napkin above a 口 (box); on the right, 犬 inu (dog, # 190)
CUES: these three old boys have brought this 犬 (dog) to this 田 (rice paddy), where they've spread this napkin on this 口 (box) and are drinking beer, but they think that drinking from a **K**eg is **Mono**tonous and want to drink **J**uice; in addition, they want to see some 野獣 ya**juu** (wild animals)
ALSO COMPARE: other similar kanji at # **220**, # **945**, # **1625** and # **2070**

1734. 疾 PRONUNCIATION: shi
MEANING: rapidly **EXAMPLE:** 内臓疾患 naizou shikkan = internal disease **DESCRIPTION:** compared to 知(る) shiru (to know, # 323) (identical pronunciation), this kanji omits the 口 (mouth) on the right and adds a sick bed, as seen in 病(気) byouki (illness, # 369), at the upper left; it retains 矢 ya (arrow, # 1045), which resembles a Native American chief **CUE:** this 矢 (Native American chief) has 内臓疾患 naizou **shi**kkan (internal disease), and he lies in this sick bed with his **Sh**eepdog **ALSO COMPARE:** other similar kanji at # **324** and # **369**

1735. 臼 PRONUNCIATION: usu
MEANING: mortar **EXAMPLE:** 臼 usu = a mortar, i.e., a receptacle in which ingredients are crushed **DESCRIPTION:** two side-by-side ladders **CUE:** when we need to climb to the second floor of our house to use the 臼 **usu** (mortar) there, **Us**ually we don't have to wait, since we have these two side-by-side ladders
COMPARE: other similar kanji at # **41**

1736. 潟 PRONUNCIATIONS: kata, gata²

MEANING: lagoon **EXAMPLES:** 潟 kata = a lagoon; 新潟 Niigata = a city on Honshu Island
DESCRIPTION: on the left, a water radical; on the upper right, 臼 usu (a mortar, # 1735), which resembles two side-by-side ladders; at the lower right, a hook, as seen in 釣(る) tsuru (to fish, # 1547), containing four pieces of bait which can also be seen as four flames
CUE: when we were fishing using this hook and these four pieces of bait, our 潟 **kata** (lagoon) suddenly overflowed with this water, but we avoided a **Ca**tastrophe by climbing out on these two side-by-side ladders   **ALSO COMPARE:** other similar kanji at # **41**, # **611** and # **988**

1737. 塾 PRONUNCIATION: juku

MEANINGS: cram school, private school
EXAMPLE: 塾 juku = cram school, private school
DESCRIPTION: compared to 熟(す) jukusu (to ripen, # 1427) (identical pronunciation), this kanji substitutes 土 tsuchi (soil, # 59) for the hot fire at the bottom; it retains the tire stop, the 口 (jukebox), the 子 (child), and the 九 (nine, #111) with a slash across it   **CUE:** this 子 (child) with this tire stop and this 口 (**Ju**kebox), which he slashed 九 (nine) times, attends a 塾 **juku** (cram school) located on this pile of 土 (soil)
GROUP: 熱(い) atsui = hot (objects), # 65; (大)勢 oozei = many people, # 110; 丸 maru = circle, # 866; 熟(す) jukusu = to ripen, # 1427; 執(着) shuuchaku = attachment, # 1553; 塾 juku = cram school, # 1737   **ALSO COMPARE:** other similar kanji at # **1427**

1738. 塊 PRONUNCIATIONS: kai, katamari

MEANINGS: clod, lump, clot, mass
EXAMPLES: 血塊 kekkai = a clot of blood; 塊 katamari = a lump or mass (this can also be spelled 固まり, # 731)   **DESCRIPTION:** compared to 鬼 oni (demon, # 1168), this adds 土 tsuchi (soil, # 59) on the left   **CUES:** when this 鬼 (demon) went out to fly his **Ki**te, he kicked a big 塊 **katamari** (lump) of this 土 (soil) into a pond, which was a **Ca**tastrophe for the **Mar**ine life there   **COMPARE:** similar kanji at # **1169** and # **1678**

1739. 絞 PRONUNCIATIONS: shi, shibo, kou

MEANINGS: strangle, constrict, wring
EXAMPLES: 絞める shimeru = to strangle or constrict; 絞る shiboru = to wring, squeeze or narrow down (this can also be spelled 搾る, # 2038); 絞殺 kousatsu = strangulation
DESCRIPTION: compared to 交(通) koutsuu (traffic, # 144) (identical pronunciation), this adds a 糸 (skeet shooter, # 219) on the left; it retains a 六 (six) above an intersection outside a courthouse which can also be seen as a tire stop above 父 chichi (father, # 143)
CUES: this 糸 (skeet shooter) 絞めた **shi**meta (strangled) 六 (six) **Sh**eep and then shot the **Sh**eep **Bo**nes into this intersection outside a **Cou**rthouse   **ALSO COMPARE:** other similar kanji at # **1139**

1740. 苗 PRONUNCIATION: nae

MEANINGS: seedling, sapling, shoot
EXAMPLE: 苗 nae = a seedling
DESCRIPTION: at the top, a plant radical; at the bottom, 田(んぼ) tanbo (rice paddy, # 68)
CUE: I'm trying to grow plants like these from 苗 **nae** (seedlings) in this 田 (paddy), but the only thing that has sprouted so far is a **Na**sty **E**ggplant
GROUP: 猫 neko = cat, # 72; 横 yoko = side, # 135; 薄(い) usui = thin, # 258; 菓(子) kashi = candy, # 589; 描(く) kaku = to draw, # 758; 黄(色) kiiro = yellow, # 976; 苗 nae = a seedling, # 1740

1741. 陶 PRONUNCIATION: tou

MEANINGS: pottery, porcelain
EXAMPLE: 陶器 touki = chinaware, pottery
DESCRIPTION: on the left, ß beta from the Greek

alphabet; on the right, a hook; inside the hook, 午 go (noon, # 207) merged with 山 yama (mountain, # 146) **CUE:** this ß (Greek) guy was going to use this hook in a fishing contest and win some 陶器 **tou**ki (pottery), but he encountered **Tol**stoy on this Russian 山 (mountain) at 午 (noon), and he missed the contest
ALSO COMPARE: other similar kanji at # **207**, # **988**, # **1832**, # **2030** and # **2079**

1742. 陳 **PRONUNCIATION: chin**
MEANINGS: exhibit, state, explain
EXAMPLE: 陳述 **chin**jutsu = a statement, an oral report **DESCRIPTION:** compared to 陣(地) jinchi (encampment, # 638), this substitutes 東 higashi (east, # 508), which can be seen as a tree wearing bifocals, for the 車 (car) on the right; it retains ß beta from the Greek alphabet
CUE: after he hurt his **Chin**, this ß (Greek) guy made a 陳述 **chin**jutsu (statement) to the effect that he would travel 東 (east) to Athens for treatment **ALSO COMPARE:** other similar kanji at # **1271** and # **2030**

1743. 傘 **PRONUNCIATION: kasa**
MEANING: umbrella **EXAMPLE:** 傘 kasa = an umbrella **DESCRIPTION:** at the top, a pointed roof that reminds us of an umbrella; under the roof, 十 too (ten), which resembles the umbrella's central shaft and is connected to a platform occupied by four 人 (people) **CUE:** these four 人 (people), who live in **Casa**blanca, sit together on this platform under this 傘 **kasa** (umbrella) when it rains
COMPARE: 笠 kasa = a bamboo hat, # 1311; other similar kanji at # **352**, # **1382**, # **1658** and # **1926**

1744. 啓 **PRONUNCIATION: kei**
MEANINGS: disclose, open, say **EXAMPLE:** 啓発 **kei**hatsu = education, edification, inspiration, public awareness **DESCRIPTION:** at the upper left, 戸 to (door, # 871); on the right, a dancer with a ponytail jumping over a box, as seen in 各 kaku (each, # 1033), but this box can also be seen as the mouth of a cave **CUE:** this dancer with a ponytail is exiting this 戸 (door) and jumping over this 口 (mouth) of a **Cave**, where she plans to study undisturbed and seek 啓発 **kei**hatsu (edification)
ALSO COMPARE: other similar kanji at # **1033** and # **1134**

1745. 卑 **PRONUNCIATIONS: iya, hi**
MEANINGS: lowly, vile, vulgar
EXAMPLES: 卑しい **iya**shii = despicable, mean; 卑屈な hikutsu na = servile, subservient
DESCRIPTION: at the top, a modified (理)由 riyuu (reason, # 73), which can be seen as a 田 (rice paddy) with a unit of rice above it; at the bottom, 十 too (ten) with an earphone above its left shoulder **CUES:** 十 (ten) guys who carry **Iya**hon (earphones) like this above their left shoulders listen to 卑しい **iya**shii (despicable) music, which is the 由 (reason) they are losing their **H**earing **ALSO COMPARE:** other similar kanji at # **942** and # **1658**

1746. 劣 **PRONUNCIATIONS: oto, retsu**
MEANINGS: inferiority, to be worse
EXAMPLES: 劣る **oto**ru = to be inferior, to fall behind; 卑劣な hiretsu na = mean, contemptible, vicious **DESCRIPTION:** at the top, 少(し) sukoshi (a little, # 254); at the bottom, 力 chikara (force, # 107) **CUES:** during the **Otto**man era, workers who exerted 少 (little) 力 (force) like this and wore **Retro Su**its were said to 劣る **oto**ru (be inferior) to their co-workers **GROUP:** 男 otoko = male # 109; (大)勢 oozei = many people, # 110; 勝(つ) katsu = to win, # 149; 務(める) tsutomeru = to discharge one's duty, # 518; 努(力) doryoku = effort, # 519; (苦)労 kurou = hardship, # 1075; (応)募 oubo = application, # 1109; 筋(肉) kinniku = muscle, # 1426; 霧 kiri = fog, # 1696; 劣る otoru = to be inferior, # 1746 **ALSO COMPARE:** other similar kanji at # **1010**

1747. 撤 PRONUNCIATION: te

MEANINGS: remove, withdraw, exclude
EXAMPLES: 撤退 tettai = evacuation, withdrawal, retreat; 撤廃 teppai = abolition
DESCRIPTION: compared to 徹(底) tettei (thoroughness, # 1333) (identical pronunciation), this substitutes a kneeling guy for the man with a double hat on the left; it retains the dancer with a ponytail who was 育 (raised) to expect teddy bears as rewards **CUE:** this guy on the left kneels to examine the 育 (upbringing) of this dancer with a ponytail and to give her a **Te**ddy bear, since he needs her cooperation as he works toward the 撤廃 **te**ppai (abolition) of child labor **ALSO COMPARE:** other similar kanji at # **616** and # **1125**

1748. 殴 PRONUNCIATION: nagu

MEANINGS: assault, hit, beat, thrash
EXAMPLE: 殴る naguru = to beat up, punch or slap **DESCRIPTION:** compared to 役に立つ yaku ni tatsu (to be useful, # 557), this substitutes 区 ku (ward or section, # 320) for the man with a double hat on the left; it retains the 几 (yak) on a 又 (table) **CUE:** when I went to this 区 (ward) office to help this 几 (yak) who was stuck on this 又 (table), a **Na**sty **Goo**n 殴った **nagu**tta (punched) me **ALSO COMPARE:** other similar kanji at # **320**, # **557** and # **1953**

1749. 矛 PRONUNCIATION: mu

MEANINGS: halberd, arms, spear
EXAMPLE: 矛盾 mujun = an inconsistency or contradiction **DESCRIPTION:** compared to 予(定) yotei (plan, # 544), this adds an extended hip on the left; it retains the マ (mother) balanced on a nail **CUE:** this マ (mother) says that she can balance on this nail, but since this stabilizing leg on the left prevents her from **Mo**ving, she isn't really balancing, and her statement contains a 矛 **mu**jun (inconsistency) **GROUP:** (事)務(所) jimusho = office, # 518 (identical pronunciation); 柔(道) juudou = judo, # 546; 霧 kiri = fog,

1696; 矛(盾) mujun = an inconsistency, # 1749 **ALSO COMPARE:** other kanji with an extended left hip at # 1417; マ (mother) on a nail *without* a stabilizing leg at # 544

1750. 盾 PRONUNCIATIONS: jun, tate

MEANINGS: shield, pretext
EXAMPLE: 矛盾 mujun = an inconsistency or contradiction; 盾 tate = a shield
DESCRIPTION: compared to 直(す) naosu (to correct, # 570), this omits the shelf at the lower left and adds a one-sided lean-to at the upper left; it retains 目 me (eye, # 51) attached to a thin handle, which reminds us of a three-drawer cabinet with a handle **CUES:** storing **Ju**nk like **Ta**cky **Te**ddy bears in this three-drawer cabinet with this thin handle inside this lean-to is a 矛盾 mu**jun** (contradiction) of your promise to stop hoarding **ALSO COMPARE:** other similar kanji at # **1878**

1751. 尉 PRONUNCIATION: i

MEANINGS: military officer, rank, old man
EXAMPLE: 中尉 chuui = a first lieutenant
DESCRIPTION: on the upper left, a lean-to with a double roof; inside the lean-to, 示(す) shimesu (to show, # 1347), which is a basic spinning nail under a flying carpet [these can also be seen as 二 (two) above 小 (small)]; on the right, 寸(前) sunzen (on the verge, # 1369), which resembles a kneeling sunny guy on the verge of picking up his gum **CUE:** this kneeling sunny guy with this gum finds it **E**asy to keep this 丁 (nail) spinning under this carpet inside this lean-to with a double roof, and he is a 中尉 chu**ui** (first lieutenant) **ALSO COMPARE:** 慰(安) ian = consolation, # **1752** (identical pronunciation); other similar kanji at # **1347** and # **1899**

1752. 慰 PRONUNCIATIONS: nagusa, i

MEANINGS: consolation, comfort
EXAMPLES: 慰める nagusameru = to console or divert; 慰安 ian = consolation, comfort, recreation **DESCRIPTION:** compared to (中)尉 chuui (a first lieutenant, # 1751) (identical

pronunciation), this kanji adds 心 kokoro (heart, # 306) at the bottom; it retains the 寸 (kneeling sunny guy with gum, # 1369) who owns a spinning 丁 (nail) under a flying carpet [these can also be seen as 二 (two) above 小 (small)] inside a lean-to with a double roof **CUES:** after a **N**asty **G**oose **S**at on this sunny guy's gum, he retreated to this double-roofed lean-to, where he found it **Ea**sy to spin this nail, and a friend with a big 心 (heart) like this 慰めた **nagusa**meta (consoled) him **GROUP:** (中)尉 chuui = a first lieutenant, # 1751; 慰(安) ian = consolation, # 1752 **ALSO COMPARE:** other similar kanji at # <u>1347</u> and # <u>1899</u>

1753. 衰 PRONUNCIATIONS: otoro, sui
MEANINGS: decline, wane, weaken
EXAMPLES: 衰える otoroeru = to become infirm, to decline; 老衰 rousui = senility
DESCRIPTION: at the top, a tire stop, as seen in 対(する) tai suru (to confront, # 674); in the middle, 日 hi (day, # 32), with its horizontal line extended, suggesting an extended day; at the bottom, the katakana character エ e and the letter Y
CUES: エ and Y were having an extended 日 (day) like this as they traveled along an **O**ld **T**oll **R**oad in **S**we**d**en, and they drove over this tire stop, possibly due to their 老衰 rou**sui** (senility)
ALSO COMPARE: other similar kanji at # <u>1042</u>

1754. 蛇 PRONUNCIATIONS: hebi, ja, da
MEANING: snake **EXAMPLES:** 蛇 hebi = a snake; 蛇口 jaguchi = a water faucet; 長蛇 chouda = a long snake, a long line (of people, etc.)
DESCRIPTION: on the left, 虫 mushi (insect, # 9), which could represent a bee; at the upper right, a bad haircut; at the lower right, the katakana ヒ hi, which reminds us of a hero **CUES:** this ヒ (hero) with this bad haircut rescued this 虫 (**H**ealthy **B**ee) that was stuck in some **J**am before it got eaten by a 蛇 **hebi** (snake) with a **D**arting tongue **GROUP:** 虫 mushi = insect, # 9; 触(れる) fureru = to touch, # 475; 強(い) tsuyoi = strong, # 478; (台)

風 taifuu = typhoon, # 479; (孤)独 kodoku = solitude, # 724; 騒(ぐ) sawagu = to make noise, # 826; 融(合) yuugou = fusion, # 987; 嵐 arashi = storm, # 1128; 蜂 hachi = a bee, # 1254; (蜂)蜜 hachimitsu = honey, # 1255; (金)属 kinzoku = metal, # 1296; 嘱(託) shokutaku = commission, # 1366; 蚕 kaiko = a silkworm, # 1404; 蛇 hebi = a snake, # 1754; (野)蛮(な) yaban na = barbarous, # 1804; 濁(る) nigoru = to be cloudy, # 1831; 蚊 ka = a mosquito, # 2009; 虹 niji = a rainbow, # 2018; 蛍(光灯) keikoutou = a fluorescent light, # 2023 **ALSO COMPARE:** other similar kanji at # <u>2048</u>

1755. 潤 PRONUNCIATIONS: uru, uruo, jun
MEANINGS: wet, be watered, profit by
EXAMPLES: 潤む urumu = to moisten, to be blurred; 潤う uruou = to become moist, to profit; 利潤 rijun = profit **DESCRIPTION:** on the left, a water radical; on the right, 門 mon (gate, # 409); inside the gate, 王 ou (king, # 1077)
CUES: this 王 (king) plans to divert this water through this 門 (gate) in **U**ruguay in order to irrigate some **U**ruguayan **O**ats in the **J**ungle, and he hopes to make a 利潤 ri**jun** (profit)
GROUP: 門 mon = gate, # 409; 問(題) mondai = a problem, # 410; 間(違える) machigaeru = to make a mistake, # 411; 聞(く) kiku = to hear, # 412; 開(ける) akeru = to open, # 413; 閉(める) shimeru = to close, # 414; 簡単 kantan = easy, # 648; 関(係) kankei = relationship, # 701; (奮)闘 funtou = hard struggle, # 728; 悶々 monmon = worry, # 807; 闇 yami = darkness, # 950; (内)閣 naikaku = the Cabinet, # 1409; 欄 ran = column (newspaper), # 1470; (利)潤 rijun = profit, # 1755; (財)閥 zaibatsu = a financial combine, # 1823; 閑(静) kansei = quiet,

1913; (検)閲 ken'etsu = censorship, # 1987; 蘭 ran = an orchid, # 2088 **ALSO COMPARE:** other similar kanji at # **1876**

1756. 戯 PRONUNCIATIONS: tawamu, gi
MEANINGS: frolic, play, sport **EXAMPLES:** 戯れる tawamureru = to play, to be amused (with something); 戯曲 gikyoku = a drama or play **DESCRIPTION:** compared to (謙)虚 kenkyo (modesty, # 966), this adds a halberd (combination axe and lance) on the right; it retains the 七 (seven) people who live in a one-sided lean-to in Kyoto, cook on a four-burner stove and observe the world through a periscope **CUES:** this tall halberd belongs to a **T**all **W**arrior who has **M**oved into this lean-to with 七 (seven) people because they cook **Ge**ese on this four-burner stove, and he 戯れる **tawamu**reru (is amused) by looking through this periscope **ALSO COMPARE:** other similar kanji at # **1057**, # **1300** and # **1862**

1757. 偏 PRONUNCIATION: katayo, hen
MEANINGS: biased **EXAMPLE:** 偏る katayoru = to lean to one side, to be partial to; 偏見 henken = prejudice or bigotry **DESCRIPTION:** compared to 編(者) hensha (editor, # 1052) (identical pronunciation), this kanji substitutes a man with a slanted hat for the 糸 (skeet shooter) on the left; it retains the lean-to with a double roof, which contains 冊 (a counter for books) and is covered with snow and where an editor is working on a book about hens **CUES:** after suffering a **Ca**tastrophe in **Y**osemite, which was caused by a **Hen** and knocked his hat off balance, this man on the left retired to this snow-covered lean-to and wrote 冊 (books) like this, which were full of 偏見 **hen**ken (prejudice) **ALSO COMPARE:** other similar kanji at # **568** and # **1134**

1758. 炉 PRONUNCIATION: ro
MEANINGS: hearth, furnace, kiln, reactor **EXAMPLE:** 炉 ro = a fireplace or furnace **DESCRIPTION:** on the left, 火 hi (fire, # 443); on the right, 戸 to (door, # 871) **CUE:** before **R**oasting chestnuts, I open this 戸 (door) to a 炉 **ro** (fireplace) and light this 火 (fire) **ALSO COMPARE:** other similar kanji at # **1134** and # **1239**

1759. 膜 PRONUNCIATION: maku
MEANING: membrane **EXAMPLE:** 膜 maku = a membrane or film **DESCRIPTION:** compared to 模(様) moyou (design, # 1353), this substitutes 月 tsuki (moon, # 148) for 木 (tree) on the left; it retains the plant radical, the 日 (sun) and the 大 (big) man mowing the grass (this combination of radicals = PSB = plants, sun, big) **CUE:** this 大 (big) man standing under this 日 (sun) mowed this grass before eating some **M**agic **C**ookies that only work when this 月 (moon) is full and stimulate his 膜 **maku** membranes (PSB = plants, sun, big) **ALSO COMPARE:** other similar kanji at # **1353**

1760. 抽 PRONUNCIATION: chuu
MEANING: extract **EXAMPLE:** 抽象 chuushou = an abstraction **DESCRIPTION:** compared to 袖 sode (sleeve, # 1697), this substitutes a kneeling guy for happy Jimmy on the left; it retains the 由 (unit of rice on a paddy); it can also be seen as a rice paddy on a stick **CUE:** this guy got onto his knees in order to **Ch**ew this unit of rice near this rice paddy, but he soon realized that the unit was only a 抽象 **chuu**shou (abstraction) **ALSO COMPARE:** other similar kanji at # **942** and # **1157**

1761. 賭 PRONUNCIATIONS: to, ka
MEANINGS: gamble, wager, bet **EXAMPLES:** 賭博 tobaku = gambling; 賭ける kakeru = to bet or gamble; 賭け事 kakegoto = gambling **DESCRIPTION:** on the left, 貝 kai (shell, or money chest, # 83); on the right, a 者 mono (person, # 276) carrying a knife under his right shoulder **CUES:** this 者 (person) carrying a knife under his right shoulder spent some of the funds in this money chest on **To**bacco and the rest on

賭博 **to**baku (gambling) with **C**ards
ALSO COMPARE: other similar kanji at # **1088** and # **2058**

1762. 括 PRONUNCIATIONS: katsu, ka, kuku
MEANINGS: fasten, tie up, constrict
EXAMPLES: 総括する soukatsu suru = to generalize or summarize; 括弧 kakko = a parenthesis or bracket; 括る kukuru = to bind or bundle **DESCRIPTION:** compared to (生)活 seikatsu (livelihood, # 260) (identical pronunciation), this kanji substitutes a kneeling guy for the water radical on the left; it retains the 舌 (tongue) seen in cats **CUES:** this guy on the left is examining tongues like this in his **C**ats that live in **C**alifornia, but the cats, to 総括する sou**katsu** suru (generalize), think he is **C**uckoo (crazy) because he's ruining his pants by kneeling like this
ALSO COMPARE: other similar kanji at # **1213**

1763. 弧 PRONUNCIATION: ko
MEANINGS: arc, arch, bow
EXAMPLE: 括弧 kakko = a parenthesis or bracket **DESCRIPTION:** compared to 孤(児) koji (orphan, # 723) (identical pronunciation), this kanji substitutes a twisted 弓 yumi (bow, # 1044) for 子 (child) on the left; it retains the long 爪 (nails) and the hammer **CUE:** I once used 弓 (bows) like this to shoot at ripe **C**orn stalks, and I used 爪 (nails) like this and hammers like this to open the ears of corn, but that was during a 括弧 ka**kko** (parenthesis) in my life **ALSO COMPARE:** other similar kanji at # **476** and # **723**

1764. 犠 PRONUNCIATION: gi
MEANING: sacrifice
EXAMPLE: 犠牲 gisei = a victim, a sacrifice
DESCRIPTION: compared to (講)義 kougi (a lecture, # 1028) (identical pronunciation), which consists of a 王 (king) wearing rabbit ears [this part of the kanji can also be seen as a truncated 羊 hitsuji (sheep, # 1223), missing its tail], above a 手 (hand) and a halberd, this kanji adds 牛 ushi (cow, # 205) on the left
CUE: I listened to a 義 (lecture) about 牛 (cows) like this and **Ge**ese, which are often the 犠牲 **gi**sei (victims) of hungry humans **ALSO COMPARE:** other similar kanji at # **1554**, # **1765**, # **1862** and # **1893**

1765. 牲 PRONUNCIATION: sei
MEANINGS: animal sacrifice, offering
EXAMPLE: 犠牲 gisei = a victim, a sacrifice
DESCRIPTION: on the left, 牛 ushi (a cow, # 205); on the right, 生 sei (a living thing or person, # 208) (identical pronunciation), which also resembles a 牛 (cow), standing on a platform
CUE: this 牛 (cow) on the left is now a 生 (living thing), but it will become a 犠牲 gi**sei** (victim) when it is sacrificed to **S**ave the life of a sick child
GROUP: 牛 ushi = a cow, # 205; 特(に) toku ni = especially, # 218; 物 mono = tangible thing, # 401; (事)件 jiken = incident, # 488; 製(品) seihin = product, # 580; (理)解 rikai = understanding, # 618; 制(服) seifuku = uniform, # 1155; 牧(師) bokushi = a pastor, # 1469; 犠(牲) gisei = a victim, # 1764; (犠)牲 gisei = a victim, # 1765 **ALSO COMPARE:** other similar kanji at # **1918**

1766. 貼 PRONUNCIATION: ha
MEANINGS: stick, paste, apply
EXAMPLE: 貼る haru = to paste, stick or attach (**Note:** this can also be spelled 張る haru, # 477) **DESCRIPTION:** compared to 粘(土) nendo (clay, # 1359), this substitutes 貝 kai (shell, or money chest, # 83) for the 米 (uncooked rice) on the left; it retains the 占 (well with a pump handle)
CUES: using some funds from this 貝 (money chest), I installed this new pump handle on this well near the **Ha**rbor and 貼った **ha**tta (pasted) up a notice asking people to use it carefully
ALSO COMPARE: 占 dokusen = a monopoly, # 1542; other similar kanji at # **1542** and # **2058**

1767. 拉 PRONUNCIATIONS: **hishi, ra**
MEANINGS: kidnap, crush
EXAMPLES: 拉ぐ hishigu = to crush; 拉致 rachi = kidnapping, taking captive
DESCRIPTION: on the left, a kneeling guy; on the right, 立(つ) tatsu (to stand, # 11), which resembles a bell
CUES: this guy is kneeling to examine this 立 (bell) that is attached to a **H**imalayan **S**heep, which he intends to 拉致する **ra**chi suru (kidnap) and introduce to his **R**am
ALSO COMPARE: other similar kanji at # **11**

1768. 帆 PRONUNCIATIONS: **ho, han, pan** MEANING: sail EXAMPLES: 帆 ho = a sail; 帆走 hansou = sailing; 出帆 shuppan = sailing, departure DESCRIPTION: compared to (平)凡 heibon (mediocre, # 1511), this adds 巾 (Bo Peep), as seen in 帽(子) boushi (hat, # 243), on the left; it retains the tall desk that has been slashed with a bone CUES: this 巾 (**B**o **P**eep) found this 凡 (desk with a slash on it) in a **H**otel, where it had been slashed when it was **H**andled by a **Pan**da before its 出帆 shup**pan** (departure)
GROUP: 帽(子) boushi = hat, # 243; 怖(い) kowai = afraid, # 463; 席 seki = seat, # 496; 帰(る) kaeru = to return home, # 566; 掃(除する) souji suru = to clean, # 645; 幕 maku = theater curtain, # 653; 希(望) kibou = hope, # 663; (非)常 hijou = emergency, # 683; 布 nuno = cloth, # 687; 凧 tako = kite, # 767; 諦(める) akirameru = to give up, # 804; (携)帯(電話) keitai denwa = cellular phone, # 1012; (渋)滞 juutai = congestion, # 1013; 婦(人) fujin = a woman, # 1165; 締(める) shimeru = to fasten, # 1173; 幅 haba = width, # 1185; 綿 men = cotton, # 1189; 飾(る) kazaru = to decorate, # 1203; 吊(るす) tsurusu = to suspend, # 1209; (手)帳 techou = pocket notebook, # 1244; (医)師 ishi = physician, # 1351; (印)刷 insatsu = printing, # 1392; (紙)幣 shihei = paper money, # 1411; 帝 mikado = the Emperor, # 1538; 帆 ho = a sail, # 1768; 錦 nishiki = brocade, # 1880; (雑)巾 zoukin = a dust cloth, # 1921; (札)幌 Sapporo = a city on Hokkaido Island, # 2082 ALSO COMPARE: other kanji containing Bo Peep at # 242; other similar kanji at # **1511**

1769. 挿 PRONUNCIATIONS: **sashi, sou**
MEANINGS: insert, put in EXAMPLES: 挿絵 sashie = an illustration; 挿入する sounyuu suru = to insert DESCRIPTION: on the left, a kneeling guy; at the upper right, 千 sen (1,000, # 22), fused with, at the lower right, 申(す) mousu (to humbly speak, # 10), which can be seen as a rice paddy on a stick CUES: this guy on the left 申 (humbly says) that he has 千 (1,000) **S**atisfied **S**heep in **S**omalia, and he gets down on his knees to show us 挿絵 **sashi**e (illustrations) of them ALSO COMPARE: other similar kanji at # **22** and # **1157**

1770. 枕 PRONUNCIATION: **makura**
MEANING: pillow EXAMPLE: 枕 makura = a pillow DESCRIPTION: compared to 沈(黙) chinmoku (silence, # 835), this substitutes 木 ki (tree, # 118) for the water radical on the left; it retains the bad haircut above a pair of lopsided legs CUE: this guy with this bad haircut and these lopsided legs injured this right leg, and he asked a **M**agical **K**uwaiti **R**abbit to come down from this 木 (tree) and bring him a 枕 **makura** (pillow) on which to elevate it
ALSO COMPARE: other similar kanji at # **128** and # **974**

1771. 錯 PRONUNCIATIONS: saku, sa
MEANINGS: confused, mix, be in disorder
EXAMPLE: 倒錯 tousaku = perversion; 錯覚 sakkaku = an illusion or misunderstanding
DESCRIPTION: on the left, 金 kane (money, # 301); on the right, 昔 mukashi (olden times, # 33)
CUES: in 昔 (olden times) people with 金 (money) like this sometimes fell into 倒錯 tou**saku** (perversion) and overdosed on **S**alty **C**ookies and **S**alami **ALSO COMPARE:** other similar kanji at # **33** and # **2010**

1772. 珠 PRONUNCIATIONS: tama, ju
MEANINGS: pearl, gem, jewel **EXAMPLES:** 珠 tama = jewel, bead, drop; 真珠 shinju = a pearl
DESCRIPTION: compared to 株 kabu (stock, # 1302), this substitutes 王 ou (king, # 1077) for 木 (tree) on the left; it retains a 牛 (cow) in a 木 (tree) **CUES:** this 王 (king) was startled by this 牛 (cow) up in this 木 (tree), and he dropped a **Tama**le and a 珠 **tama** (**J**ewel)
GROUP: 理(由) riyuu = reason, # 78; 珍(しい) mezurashii = unusual, # 407; (野)球 yakyuu = baseball, # 606; 環(境) kankyou = environment, # 718; 現(金) genkin = cash, # 739; 王(様) ousama = king, # 1077; 班(長) hanchou = a squad leader, # 1509; 珠 tama = jewel, # 1772
ALSO COMPARE: kanji with 王 (king) at the *top* at # 1712; kanji with 王 (king) on the *right* at # 2045; kanji with 王 (king) at the *bottom* at # 1876; other similar kanji at # **1675**

1773. 畜 PRONUNCIATION: chiku
MEANINGS: livestock, domestic animals
EXAMPLE: 畜生 chikushou = a beast or brute, a repulsive person, damn it! (interjection)
DESCRIPTION: compared to 玄(関) genkan (entranceway, # 1252), this adds 田(んぼ) tanbo (rice field, # 68) at the bottom; it retains the truncated 糸 (skeet shooter), consisting of two flexed elbows, carrying a tire stop into the house of Genghis **CUE:** this truncated 糸 (skeet shooter) has placed this tire stop next to this 田 (rice paddy) to prevent us from driving in to buy the **C**heap **C**ookies sold there, and we think he is a 畜生 **chiku**shou (brute)
ALSO COMPARE: (貯)蓄 chochiku = savings, # 1774 (identical pronunciation); other similar kanji at # **220**, # **1129** and # **1860**

1774. 蓄 PRONUNCIATIONS: takuwa, chiku
MEANINGS: amass, keeping a concubine
EXAMPLES: 蓄える takuwaeru = to store or save; 貯蓄 chochiku = savings
DESCRIPTION: compared to 畜(生) chikushou (a brute, # 1773) (identical pronunciation), this kanji adds a plant radical at the top; it retains the tire stop, the truncated 糸 (skeet shooter) consisting of two flexed elbows, and the 田 (rice paddy) where cheap cookies are sold **CUES:** this truncated 糸 (skeet shooter) sees these plants rising above a **T**all **Ku**waiti **Wa**ll as he uses this tire stop to prevent people from eating **C**heap **C**ookies near this 田 (rice paddy), and he's planning to sell the tire stop and 蓄える **takuwa**eru (save) the proceeds
ALSO COMPARE: other similar kanji at # **220**, # **1129** and # **1860**

1775. 拓 PRONUNCIATION: taku
MEANINGS: clear (land), break up (land), open
EXAMPLE: 開拓する kaitaku suru = to develop (wilderness), to open up (new markets, etc.)
DESCRIPTION: compared to 石 ishi (stone, # 458), this adds a kneeling guy on the left; it retains the guy with a flat hat leaning over a box
CUE: this guy on the left is kneeling in order to try to remove all 石 (stones) like this from his land in order to 開拓する kai**taku** suru (develop) it, but then he will have to pay more **T**axes in **Ku**wait
GROUP: 磨(く) migaku = to brush, # 126; 研(究) kenkyuu = research, # 442; 石 ishi = stone, # 458; 確(認) kakunin = confirmation, # 619; (鉄)砲 teppou = gun, # 738; 砂 suna = sand,

782; 岩 iwa = rock, # 816; 破(る) yaburu = to break, # 837; 磁(石) jishaku = magnet, # 1236; (岩)礁 ganshou = reef, # 1270; 硬(い) katai = hard, # 1412; (基)礎 kiso = a foundation, # 1716; (開)拓(する) kaitaku suru = to develop, # 1775; 砕(く) kudaku = to break, # 1845; 碁 Go = a Japanese board game, # 1851; (嫉)妬 shitto = jealousy, # 1891; (墓)碑 bohi = a gravestone, # 1905; 硫(黄) iou = sulfur, # 2001

1776. 鼓 PRONUNCIATION: ko, tsuzumi
MEANINGS: drum, beat, rouse, muster
EXAMPLE: 太鼓 taiko = a drum; 小鼓 kotsuzumi = a hand drum (spelled kotsudumi in electronic dictionaries) **DESCRIPTION:** at the upper left, 士 shi (man, warrior, # 66); at the lower left, the lower portion of 豆(腐) toufu (bean curd, # 721), which resembles a TV set supported by toes; on the right, 支(える) sasaeru (to support, # 26), which resembles a 士 (man) standing on a 又 (table) **CUES:** these two 士 (men) are standing on this TV set and on this 又 (table) trying to escape a Cobra that they found in their 太鼓 tai**ko** (drum), and a video of their encounter would be **Tsu**itable (suitable) for **Zoom**ing **ALSO COMPARE:** other similar kanji at # **721**, # **1121** and # **1468**

1777. 膚 PRONUNCIATION: fu
MEANINGS: skin, body, grain, texture
EXAMPLE: 皮膚 hifu = skin
DESCRIPTION: compared to 虎 tora (tiger, # 1057), this substitutes 胃 i (stomach, # 153), which contains a 田 (rice paddy) and a 月 (moon) seen from Iraq, for the two lopsided legs at the bottom; it retains the one-sided lean-to containing 七 (seven) people, who were holding Tolstoy for ransom, using a periscope to observe the outside world **CUE:** the 七 (seven) people who live in this lean-to observe the outside world via this periscope, put **F**ood into 胃 (stomachs) like this, and choose nutrients that are healthy for their 皮膚 hi**fu** (skin)

ALSO COMPARE: other similar kanji at # **220** and # **1057** and # **1991**

1778. 粋 PRONUNCIATIONS: sui, iki
MEANINGS: chic, style, cream **EXAMPLES:** 純粋な junsui na (or no) = pure, pure-blooded, genuine; 小粋 ko'iki = stylish, conceited
DESCRIPTION: compared to (麻)酔 masui (anesthesia, # 1476) (identical pronunciation), this kanji substitutes 米 kome (uncooked rice, # 326) for the radical seen in 酒 (alcoholic beverage) on the left; it retains 九十 kyuujuu (ninety) on the right **CUES:** After I went to **Swe**den and ate 九十 (90) bowls of rice made from this 米 (uncooked rice), I felt 純粋な jun**sui** na (pure) joy, but later I felt **Ick**y **ALSO COMPARE:** other similar kanji at # **827**, # **1387** and # **1658**

1779. 悦 PRONUNCIATION: etsu
MEANINGS: ecstasy, joy, rapture
EXAMPLE: 悦に入る etsu ni iru = to be gratified or happy **DESCRIPTION:** compared to 税(金) zeikin (tax, 708), this substitutes an erect guy for the 禾 (grain plant with a ripe head) on the left; it retains the zany 兄 (big brother) wearing rabbit ears **CUE:** when this guy on the left saw that this 兄 (big brother) had received **Et**chings from **Su**dan, and that big brother 悦に入った **etsu** ni itta (was happy) and had put on these rabbit ears to celebrate, the guy drew himself up to his full height to express his irritation
ALSO COMPARE: other similar kanji at # **708** and # **2063**

1780. 誓 PRONUNCIATIONS: sei, chika
MEANINGS: vow, swear, pledge **EXAMPLES:** 宣誓 sensei = an oath or vow; 誓う chikau = to vow, pledge or swear; 誓い chikai = a vow
DESCRIPTION: compared to 哲(学) tetsugaku (philosophy, # 1521), this substitutes 言(う) iu (to speak, # 430) for the 口 (box) at the bottom; it retains the kneeling guy and the pair of pliers from a tetracycline factory in Sudan

CUES: this guy on the upper left is a **Sa**int, and he kneels to pray before picking up pliers like this for his practical work and also 言 (speaks) a 宣誓 sen**sei** (vow) to drive only **C**heap **C**ars **ALSO COMPARE:** other similar kanji at # **892**

1781. 憤 PRONUNCIATIONS: ikidoo, fun, pun
MEANINGS: aroused, resent, anger
EXAMPLES: 憤る ikidooru = to resent or get indignant; 憤慨する fungai suru = to be indignant; 鬱憤 uppun = anger, frustration (usually written うっぷん)
DESCRIPTION: compared to 噴(火) funsui (water fountain, # 1268) (identical pronunciation), this kanji substitutes an erect guy for the fountain's 口 (mouth) on the left; it retains the triple plant radical, which can also be seen as bushes, and the 貝 (money chest)
CUES: when this guy on the left discovered that an **I**cky **D**oorman had left this 貝 (money chest) under these bushes, he didn't think it was **Fun**ny, and he 憤りました **ikidoo**rimashita (got indignant), rose to his full height like this and **Pun**ished the man **ALSO COMPARE:** other similar kanji at # **1268**, # **1897** and # **2063**

1782. 慨 PRONUNCIATION: gai
MEANINGS: rue, be sad, sigh, lament
EXAMPLE: 憤慨する fungai suru = to be indignant **DESCRIPTION:** compared to 概(念) gainen (concept, # 1647) (identical pronunciation), this kanji substitutes an erect man for 木 (tree) on the left; it retains a modified 良 (good), without its pointy hat, and a modified version of 牙 (fangs), with a bent right leg **CUE:** this man on the left has 良 (**g**ood) 牙 (fangs) like this, but he has to follow **Gui**delines about when to display them, which makes him draw himself up to his full height like this and 憤慨する fun**gai** suru (get indignant) **ALSO COMPARE:** other similar kanji at # **796**, # **805**, # **974**, # **1417** and # **2063**

1783. 鬱 PRONUNCIATIONS: utsu, u
MEANINGS: gloom, depression, melancholy
EXAMPLES: 鬱病 utsubyou = depression; 鬱憤 uppun = anger, frustration (usually written うっぷん) **DESCRIPTION:** at the top, two 木 ki (trees, # 118) flanking 午 go (noon, # 207), which is fused with 山 yama (mountain, # 146); these structures are resting on a lid; at the center left, a bucket containing the skeleton of a six-legged animal; at the lower left, the katakana ヒ hi; at the lower right, three cords, or perhaps a rocker bottom shoe; taken together, the lower portion resembles an American flag (with stars in the upper left corner and stripes below that and to the right) **CUES:** when my **U**ber **Tsu**pervisor (supervisor) saw that our **U**ber country's flag was being compressed under this 山 (mountain) fused with 午 (noon) and flanked by these two 木 (trees), she began to suffer from 鬱病 **utsu**byou (depression) **COMPARE:** other kanji containing three cords at # **406**; other kanji containing 午 at # **207** and # **1832**; other kanji containing ヒ at # **2048**

1784. 憂 PRONUNCIATIONS: yuu, u, ure
MEANINGS: melancholy, grieve, lament
EXAMPLES: 憂鬱 yuu'utsu = depression, melancholy; 憂さ晴らし usabarashi = a diversion or distraction; 憂い urei = melancholy, sorrow, anxiety (this can also be spelled 愁い, # 1785) **DESCRIPTION:** compared to 優(秀) yuushuu (excellent, # 528) (identical pronunciation), this kanji omits the man with a slanted hat on the left; it retains the limousine with an antenna resting on a lid, the 心 (heart), and the youthful dancer with a ponytail
CUES: this **You**thful dancer with a ponytail, seen at the bottom, lives in **U**ganda, owns an **U**gandan **Re**staurant, and rides around in this limousine with this antenna, but her 心 (heart) is affected by 憂鬱 **yuu**'utsu (depression) **ALSO COMPARE:** other similar kanji at # **522**, # **523** and # **2002**

1785. 愁 PRONUNCIATIONS: ure, shuu
MEANINGS: distress, grieve, lament, be anxious
EXAMPLES: 愁い urei = melancholy, sorrow, anxiety (this can also be spelled 憂い, # 1784); 郷愁 kyoushuu = nostalgia, homesickness
DESCRIPTION: compared to 秋 aki (autumn, # 445), this adds 心 kokoro (heart, # 306) at the bottom; it retains the 禾 (ripe grain) admired by Achilles, and 火 (fire) CUES: during this 秋 (autumn), customers stopped coming to my **U**gandan **R**estaurant, and my **Sh**oes wore out, and this 心 (heart) experienced 愁い **ure**i (sorrow)
ALSO COMPARE: other similar kanji at # **1239** and # **1797**

1786. 冠 PRONUNCIATIONS: kanmuri, kan MEANINGS: crown, best, peerless
EXAMPLES: 冠 kanmuri = a crown; 王冠 oukan = a royal crown   DESCRIPTION: at the top, a wide lid which reminds us of a crown; at the lower left, 元 moto (base, # 421); on the right, 寸(前) sunzen (on the verge, # 1369), which reminds us of a kneeling sunny guy picking up some gum
CUES: a **Can**cer-survivor named **Mur**iel wanted to wear this wide lid as a 王冠 ou**kan** (royal crown), and she had this wide 元 (base) of support, including this 寸 (kneeling sunny guy), until she got **Can**celled   ALSO COMPARE: other similar kanji at # **131** and # **421**

1787. 顎 PRONUNCIATIONS: ago, gaku
MEANINGS: jaw, chin, gill EXAMPLES: 顎 ago = a chin or jaw, usually written あご; 顎関節 gakukansetsu = the jaw (temporomandibular) joint DESCRIPTION: on the upper left, two 口 (boxes) above a piece of cloth; on the lower left, a kangaroo, as seen in (番)号 bangou (number, # 470); on the right, an empty platform above a 貝 (money chest) where a head could fit, as seen in 頭 atama (head, # 93)   CUES: this kangaroo lost its 頭 (head) from this platform, and it's in **Ag**ony, but it traded a **G**allon of **Ko**ol-Aid for these two 口 (boxes) on this piece of cloth, one of which may contain its 顎 **ago** (chin)
ALSO COMPARE: (金)額 kingaku = a sum of money, # 791 (identical pronunciation); other similar kanji at # **468**, # **1034** and # **1126**

1788. 簿 PRONUNCIATION: bo
MEANINGS: register, record book
EXAMPLE: 帳簿 choubo = an account book
DESCRIPTION: compared to 薄(い) usui (pale, # 258), this substitutes 竹 take (bamboo, # 134) for the plant radical at the top; it retains the water radical on the left, the upper part of the 犬 (dog) above the 田 (rice paddy), and the 寸 (kneeling sunny guy who has dropped his gum) CUE: this 寸 (kneeling sunny guy) was working on his 帳簿 chou**bo** (account books), but he was surrounded by water like this and 竹 (bamboo) walls like this, and he felt **Bo**red, so he took this truncated 犬 (dog) out to this 田 (rice paddy)   ALSO COMPARE: other similar kanji at # **865**, # **1721** and # **2074**

1789. 糧 PRONUNCIATIONS: ryou, kate
MEANINGS: quantity, weight, amount, measure
EXAMPLES: 食糧 shokuryou = food, usually spelled 食料, # 512; 糧 kate = food
DESCRIPTION: compared to 量 ryou (quantity, # 1061) (identical pronunciation), this kanji adds 米 kome (uncooked rice, # 326) on the left; it retains the sincere guy named Pope Leo wearing bifocals and standing below a 日 (sun) and a rug CUES: this sincere guy wearing bifocals is Pope **Le**o and, since this 米 (uncooked rice) is infested with **Cat**erpillars, he's picking them out of his 糧 **kate** (food) on this rug in this 日 (sun)   ALSO COMPARE: other similar kanji at # **545**, # **668** and # **1387**

1790. 架 PRONUNCIATION: ka
MEANINGS: erect, frame, construct
EXAMPLES: 担架 tanka = a stretcher; 架か

る kakaru = to span **DESCRIPTION:** compared to (参)加 sanka (participation, # 714) (identical pronunciation), this kanji adds 木 ki (tree, # 118) at the bottom; it retains the 力 (force) exerted by a carpenter via his 口 (mouth), which can also be seen as a box **CUE:** a **C**arpenter exerted a lot of 力 (force) to climb this 木 (tree) and speak with this 口 (mouth), but later they had to carry him away on a 担架 tan**ka** (stretcher)
ALSO COMPARE: other similar kanji at # **1216** and # **1846**

1791. 軸 PRONUNCIATION: jiku

MEANINGS: axis, pivot **EXAMPLE:** 軸 jiku = axle, axis, center **DESCRIPTION:** compared to 袖 sode (sleeve, # 1697), this substitutes 車 kuruma (car, # 283) for happy Jimmy on the left; it retains the 由 (unit of rice above a rice paddy); this can also be seen as a rice paddy on a stick **CUE:** this 車 (car), which is a **J**eep from **Ku**wait, was hauling this 由 (unit of rice) when its 軸 **jiku** (axle) broke **ALSO COMPARE:** other similar kanji at # **942**, # **1157** and # **1966**

1792. 苛 PRONUNCIATIONS: ka, iji, ira

MEANINGS: torment, scold, chastise **EXAMPLES:** 苛酷 kakoku = severity, rigor, cruelty (nouns), or harsh (a na adjective) (this can also be spelled 過酷, # 361); 苛める ijimeru = to bully or abuse, usually written いじめる; 苛立つ iradatsu = to get irritated, to fret **DESCRIPTION:** compared to 荷物 nimotsu (luggage, # 342) or (出)荷(する) shukka suru (to ship, # 342) (identical pronunciation), this kanji omits the man with a slanted hat on the left; it retains the plant radical and the carton inside a one-sided lean-to **CUES:** the **C**arton in this lean-to contains my **E**astern **J**eans from **I**ran, which are made from plants like this, and I 苛立った **ira**datta (got irritated) when its shipment was delayed
ALSO COMPARE: 荷(物) nimotsu = luggage, # 342; other similar kanji at # **1176**

1793. 蓋 PRONUNCIATIONS: gai, futa

MEANINGS: cover, lid, flap **EXAMPLES:** 頭蓋骨 zugaikotsu = a skull; 蓋 futa = a cover, bottle cap or lid **DESCRIPTION:** at the top, a plant radical, which reminds us of a branch; in the middle, 去(る) saru (to leave, # 343), which reminds us of a samurai's ム (cow) covered in 土 (soil); at the bottom, 皿 sara (dish, # 567)
CUES: our **Gui**delines for cleaning 土 (soiled) ム (cows) like this state that one should remove the 蓋 **futa** (cover) from this 皿 (dish) of water, pour the water over the cow, and scrub it with branches like this, but that seems like **Fo**olish **T**alk **ALSO COMPARE:** other similar kanji at # **343** and # **1407**

1794. 凶 PRONUNCIATION: kyou

MEANINGS: villain, evil, bad luck, disaster **EXAMPLE:** 凶悪 kyouaku = brutal, inhuman **DESCRIPTION:** this is an X in a hive, as seen in 悩(み) nayami (worry, # 1181), where it represents an unknown number of bees **CUE:** in **Kyou**to, I saw this open box containing X (an unknown number) of bees which were 凶悪 **kyou**aku (brutal) in attacking nearby people **GROUP:** (映)画 eiga = movie, # 77; 胸 mune = chest, # 775; 悩(み) nayami = worry, # 1181; 脳 nou = the brain, # 1461; 凶(悪) kyouaku = brutal, # 1794 **ALSO COMPARE:** other similar kanji at # **1953**

1795. 庶 PRONUNCIATION: sho

MEANINGS: commoner, all, bastard **EXAMPLE:** 庶民 shomin = common people, the masses **DESCRIPTION:** at the upper left, a lean-to with a chimney; inside the lean-to, a bucket with a single compartment, as seen in 世(界) sekai (world, # 542), above a hot fire, as seen in 熱(い) atsui (hot, # 65) **CUE:** this lean-to with this chimney, where some 庶民 **sho**min (common people) live, is located near the **Sho**re, and it contains this bucket of food cooking over this fire **ALSO COMPARE:** other similar kanji at # **542** and # **611**

1796. 裾 PRONUNCIATION: suso
MEANINGS: cuff, hem, foot of mountain
EXAMPLE: 裾 suso = a hem or cuff, the foot of a mountain   DESCRIPTION: compared to (住)居 juukyo (dwelling, # 809), this adds happy Jimmy Carter with two lips, as seen in 初(めて) hajimete (for the first time, # 104), on the left; it retains 古 (old) inside a lean-to with a double roof   CUE: this happy Jimmy with two lips sits on a Superior Sofa in this 居 (dwelling) and mends the 裾 suso (hem) of his pants
ALSO COMPARE: other similar kanji at # **394**, # **1615** and # **1899**

1797. 稚 PRONUNCIATION: chi
MEANINGS: immature, young
EXAMPLE: 幼稚園 youchien = kindergarten
DESCRIPTION: compared to 誰 dare (who, # 440), this substitutes 禾 (a grain plant with a ripe head) for 言 (to speak) on the left; it retains the net on the right, which can be seen as a man with a slanted hat next to a 主 (master) with an extra pair of arms (see # 203)   CUE: I gather this 禾 (ripe grain) in this net in order to pay for my Children to attend 幼稚園 you**chi**en (kindergarten)
GROUP: 秋 aki = autumn, # 445; 私 watakushi = I, # 510; 科(学) kagaku = science, # 511; 和(食) washoku = Japanese food, # 513; (便)利 benri = convenient, # 564; 香(り) kaori = fragrance, # 681; 税(金) zeikin = tax, # 708; 移(る) utsuru = to move, # 801; 積(む) tsumu = accumulate, # 931; 程(度) teido = criterion, # 954; 季(節) kisetsu = season, # 1047; 種 tane = seed, # 1098; (対)称 taishou = symmetry, # 1123; 秒 byou = a second, # 1137; 穀(物) kokumotsu = grain, # 1172; 梨 nashi = a pear, # 1184; 秘(密) himitsu = a secret, # 1187; 稲 ine = rice plant, # 1229; (収)穫 shuukaku = harvest, # 1257; (豊)穣 houjou = good harvest, # 1322; 委(ねる)

yudaneru = to entrust, # 1364; (投)稿 toukou = a written contribution, # 1467; 秩(序) chitsujo = order, # 1482; (優)秀 yuushuu = outstanding, # 1517; 稼(ぐ) kasegu = to earn, # 1668; 穏(やかな) odayaka na = calm, # 1703; 稽古 keiko = rehearsal, # 1715; 愁(い) urei = melancholy, # 1785; (幼)稚(園) youchien = kindergarten, # 1797; 租(税) sozei = taxation, # 2015; 萎(縮する) ishuku suru = to flinch, # 2022
ALSO COMPARE: other similar kanji at # **2046**

1798. 拙 PRONUNCIATIONS: tsutana, setsu   MEANINGS: bungling, clumsy, unskillful
EXAMPLES: 拙い tsutanai = clumsy, unskillful; 稚拙 chisetsu = unskilled, childish, crude
DESCRIPTION: on the left, a kneeling guy; on the right, 出(す) dasu (to put out, # 147)
CUES: this guy is kneeling to 出 (put out) a Tsuitcase (suitcase) of Tangy Apples, but he Sets it on Superman's foot, since he's 拙い **tsutana**i (clumsy)
ALSO COMPARE: other similar kanji at # **927**

1799. 辱 PRONUNCIATIONS: joku, hazukashi   MEANINGS: embarrass, humiliate, shame   EXAMPLES: 屈辱 kutsujoku = humiliation, disgrace; 辱める hazukashimeru = to humiliate, dishonor or rape
DESCRIPTION: compared to 唇 kuchibiru (the lips, # 1565), this substitutes 寸(前) sunzen (on the verge, # 1369), which reminds us of a kneeling kneeling sunny guy on the verge of picking up his gum, for 口 (mouth) at the bottom; it retains the one-sided lean-to containing an arrow, supported by the letter L and the letter Y   CUES: this 寸 (kneeling sunny guy) told a Joke, saying that Prince Harry's Zoo is Cashing in on body parts, but L and Y didn't find it funny and came out of this lean-to to threaten him with this arrow, and he experienced 屈辱 kutsu**joku** (humiliation)   ALSO COMPARE: other similar kanji at # **131** and # **1105**

1800. 恒 PRONUNCIATION: kou
MEANINGS: constancy, always EXAMPLE: 恒例 kourei = customary DESCRIPTION: compared to 垣(根) kakine (fence, # 777), this substitutes an erect guy for 土 (soil) on the left; it retains the window with two panes CUE: this guy is standing next to this window with two panes, watching the activity in the Courthouse next door, as is 恒例 **kou**rei (customary) for him, and he stands up straight like this to get a better view ALSO COMPARE: other similar kanji at # **668** and # **2063**

1801. 暦 PRONUNCIATIONS: koyomi, reki MEANINGS: calendar, almanac EXAMPLES: 暦 koyomi = a calendar; 西暦 seireki = A.D., the Christian era DESCRIPTION: compared to 歴(史) rekishi (history, # 1313) (identical pronunciation), this kanji substitutes 日 hi (sun, # 32) for 止 (stop) at the bottom; it retains the 林 (grove) that is wrecking a one-sided lean-to CUES: the practice of hanging 林 (groves) like this from the tops of lean-tos provides shade from this 日 (sun), and it creates spaces for Coyotes to Meet, but it was canceled during 西暦sei**reki** (the Christian era) because it was **W**recking the lean-tos ALSO COMPARE: other similar kanji at # **1475**

1802. 峠 PRONUNCIATION: touge
MEANINGS: mountain peak or pass, climax, crest EXAMPLE: 峠 touge = a mountain pass or peak, a crucial point DESCRIPTION: on the left, 山 yama (mountain, # 146); at the upper right, 上 ue (up, # 171); at the lower right, 下 shita (down, # 172) CUES: we climbed 上 (up) to the 峠 **touge** (peak) of this 山 (mountain), and then we walked 下 (down) **T**ogether ALSO COMPARE: other similar kanji at # **172** and # **1942**

1803. 宰 PRONUNCIATION: sai
MEANINGS: superintend, manager, rule EXAMPLE: 主宰 shusai = supervision, chairmanship DESCRIPTION: compared to 辛(い) karai (spicy, # 384), which consists of 立 (a bell) above 十 (ten) and resembles a syringe and a needle with an eye, this adds a bad haircut at the top CUES: if you cover this 辛 (needle) with this bad haircut, it is less **P**sychologically threatening, which is why we are using this image as part of our 主宰 shu**sai** (supervision) of vaccination outreach programs GROUP: (人)達 hitotachi = people, # 347; 辛(い) karai = spicy, # 384; 幸(せ) shiawase = happiness, # 385; 報(告) houkoku = report, # 386; 辞(める) yameru = to resign, # 387; (固)執(する) koshitsu suru = to be persistent, # 1553; (主)宰 shusai = sponsorship, # 1803
ALSO COMPARE: other similar kanji at # **383**

1804. 蛮 PRONUNCIATION: ban
MEANING: barbarian EXAMPLE: 野蛮な yaban na = barbarous, uncivilized DESCRIPTION: compared to 変 hen (strange, # 553), this substitutes 虫 mushi (insect, # 9) for the dancer with a ponytail at the bottom; it retains the swooping hen with four legs CUE: this four-legged hen ate this 虫 (insect), but later the hen was served at a 野蛮な ya**ban** na (barbarous) **B**anquet ALSO COMPARE: other similar kanji at # **695** and # **1754**

1805. 窮 PRONUNCIATION: kyuu
MEANINGS: destitute, perplexed, suffer, cornered EXAMPLE: 窮地 kyuuchi = plight, adversity, dilemma DESCRIPTION: at the top, a soaring Cuban bird with two lopsided legs, as seen in (研)究 kenkyuu (research, # 112) (identical pronunciation); at the lower left, 身 mi (body, # 651); at the lower right, 弓 yumi (bow, # 1044), or 弓(道) kyuudou (archery, # 1044) (also identical pronunciation) CUE: when this 身 (body) was threatened by this **Cu**ban soaring bird with two lopsided legs, I faced 窮地 **kyuu**chi (adversity),

but I used this **Cuban** 弓 (bow) to drive the bird away **ALSO COMPARE:** other similar kanji at #**112**, #**476**, #**1381** and #**1417**

1806. 疎 PRONUNCIATIONS: uto, so, oroso
MEANINGS: sparse, negligent, know a little of **EXAMPLES:** 疎い utoi = ignorant, estranged from; 空疎な kuuso na = insubstantial, vain, futile; 疎か orosoka = neglect, negligence, not to mention **DESCRIPTION:** at the upper left, a modified katakana マ ma, which reminds us of **Ma** (mother); at the lower left, 止(める) tomeru (to stop, # 173); on the right, (約)束 yakusoku (promise, # 99), which can be seen as incorporating two eyes **CUES:** this マ (mother) is a **U**topian and a **So**cialist who wears an **O**ld **Ro**be from **So**malia, and she made this 束 (promise) to try to 止 (stop) war, but her efforts were 空疎 kuu**so** (futile) **GROUP:** 頼(む) tanomu = to request, # 98; (約)束 yakusoku = appointment, # 99; 速(達) sokutatsu = express mail, # 359; 整(理する) seiri suru = to arrange, # 1247; 瀬(戸際) setogiwa = brink, # 1550; 疎(い) utoi = ignorant, # 1806 **ALSO COMPARE:** other similar kanji at #**1282** and #**1929**

1807. 彰 PRONUNCIATION: shou
MEANINGS: patent, clear **EXAMPLE:** 表彰 hyoushou = public acknowledgment, commendation **DESCRIPTION:** compared to (文)章 bunshou (sentence, # 1365) (identical pronunciation), this kanji adds three cords for a catapult, as seen in 形 katachi (shape, # 573), on the right; it retains 立 (to stand) above 早 (early) **CUE:** when I 立 (stood) up 早 (early) and **Sho**wed my teacher these three catapult cords that I had made, I received a 表彰 hyou**shou** (commendation) **ALSO COMPARE:** 障(害) shougai = an obstacle, # 1495 (also identical pronunciation); other similar kanji at #**266**, #**839** and #**1365**

1808. 傑 PRONUNCIATIONS: ketsu, ke
MEANINGS: gentleness, excell, surpass, actor **EXAMPLES:** 豪傑 gouketsu = a hero or great man; 傑作 kessaku = a masterpiece **DESCRIPTION:** on the left, a man with a slanted hat; at the upper center, 夕(方) yuugata (evening, # 160), which resembles a half moon; at the upper right, a knee, as seen in 年 nen (year, # 177); at the lower right, 木 ki (tree, # 118) **CUES:** this man on the left tilts his hat back to examine this 夕 (half moon), this knee and this 木 (tree) before painting them into a 傑作 **ke**ssaku (masterpiece), after which he puts **Ket**chup in his **S**oup and drinks a **Keg** of beer **GROUP:** 年 nen = year, # 177; 降(りる) oriru = to get off a train, # 178; 決(める) kimeru = to decide, # 180; 隣 tonari = next door, # 329; 舞(う) mau = to dance, # 584; 快(い) kokoroyoi = pleasant, # 734; 瞬(間) shunkan = moment, # 773; 傑(作) kessaku = a masterpiece, # 1808 **ALSO COMPARE:** other similar kanji at #**122** and #**801**

1809. 拘 PRONUNCIATIONS: kaka, kou
MEANINGS: arrest, seize, adhere to **EXAMPLES:** 拘わらず kakawarazu = regardless, in spite of, nevertheless (usually spelled かかわらず); 拘束 kousoku = a restraint or restriction **DESCRIPTION:** compared to monku (文)句 (complaint, # 872), this adds a kneeling guy on the left; it retains 可(愛い) kawaii (cute, # 615), with an awning added at the top; this radical on the right can also be seen as a hook with a box in it **CUES:** this guy is a **Ca**lifornia **Ca**rpenter who is kneeling to install this awning, which will act as a 拘束 **kou**soku (restriction) on sunlight, for a 可 (cute) customer, and he works for a **Co**rporation **ALSO COMPARE:** other similar kanji at #**872**

1810. 緯 PRONUNCIATION: i
MEANINGS: woof, latitude, left and right **EXAMPLE:** 緯度 ido = latitude **DESCRIPTION:** compared to 偉(大) idai (grand, # 1174) (identical pronunciation), this kanji

substitutes 糸 (skeet shooter, # 219) for the man with a slanted hat on the left; it retains the two feet, which resemble 五 (five), facing in opposite directions and separated by a 口 (box)
CUE: this 糸 (skeet shooter) is shooting at this guy with two feet facing in opposite directions to encourage him to hurry, since they must walk at a high 緯度 **i**do (latitude) to get to their **I**gloo
ALSO COMPARE: other similar kanji at # **1174**

1811. 妖 PRONUNCIATION: you
MEANINGS: attractive, bewitching, calamity
EXAMPLE: 妖怪 youkai = a ghost or phantom
DESCRIPTION: on the left, 女 onna (female, # 235); on the right, 天 ten (sky, # 189)
CUE: when this 女 (female) visited **Y**osemite, she looked up into this 天 (sky) and saw a 妖怪 **you**kai (ghost) **GROUP:** 天 ten = sky, # 189; 咲 (く) saku = to blossom, # 193; 笑(う) warau = to laugh, # 199; (演)奏 ensou = musical performance, # 757; 添(える) soeru = to attach to, # 841; 蚕 kaiko = a silkworm, # 1404; 妖(怪) youkai = a ghost, # 1811 **ALSO COMPARE:** other kanji containing 女 on the left at # **2039**

1812. 藍 PRONUNCIATION: ai
MEANING: indigo **EXAMPLE:** 藍 ai = indigo
DESCRIPTION: compared to 監(督) kantoku (director, # 1420), this adds a plant radical at the top; it retains the two cannons firing crutches and shells over a 皿 (dish) **CUE:** these plants are used to make an 藍 **ai** (indigo) dye for the **I**ce cream in this 皿 (dish), and pirates who want to eat it are firing these cannons over it **ALSO COMPARE:** other similar kanji at # **1310** and # **1407**

1813. 鍛 PRONUNCIATIONS: tan, kita
MEANINGS: forge, discipline, train
EXAMPLES: 鍛錬する tanren suru = to train; 鍛える kitaeru = to train or strengthen oneself

DESCRIPTION: compared to (階)段 kaidan (stairs, # 559), this adds 金 kane (money, # 301) on the left; it retains the ladder with four steps climbed by a dancer in order to give food to π (a pious yak) standing on a 又 (table) **CUES:** the dancer who climbs these 段 (stairs) to pay this 金 (money) in exchange for **Tan**go lessons from this π (pious yak) on this 又 (table) would like to 鍛える **kita**eru (train) more, but the yak just **K**eeps **T**alking
ALSO COMPARE: other similar kanji at # **41**, # **557** and # **2010**

1814. 錬 PRONUNCIATION: ren
MEANING: refine **EXAMPLE:** 鍛錬する tanren suru = to train **DESCRIPTION:** compared to 練(習する) renshuu suru (to practice, # 229) (identical pronunciation), this kanji substitutes 金 kane (money, # 301) for the 糸 (skeet shooter) on the left; it retains 東 (east), where a rent collector lives, on the right, which can also be seen as a tree wearing bifocals
CUE: I pay this 金 (money) for a **R**ental apartment in the 東 (east), where I 鍛錬する tan**ren** suru (train) for the Olympics **ALSO COMPARE:** other similar kanji at # **1271** and # **2010**

1815. 繊 PRONUNCIATION: sen
MEANINGS: slender, fine, thin kimono
EXAMPLE: 繊維 sen'i = fiber
DESCRIPTION: on the left, 糸 (skeet shooter, # 219); at the upper center, 土 tsuchi (soil, # 59); at the lower center, four burners on a stove, as seen in (謙)虚 kenkyo (modesty, # 966); on the right, a halberd (combination axe and lance) **CUE:** a **Sen**ator told this 糸 (skeet shooter) to use 繊維 **sen**'i (fiber) cloth to clean this 土 (soil) from this four-burner stove and this halberd
ALSO COMPARE: other similar kanji at # **1300** and # **1862**

1816. 縫 PRONUNCIATIONS: hou, nu
MEANINGS: sew, stitch, embroider
EXAMPLES: 裁縫 saihou = sewing; 縫う nuu = to sew DESCRIPTION: on the left, 糸 (skeet shooter, # 219); at the upper right, a dancer with a ponytail, who is a hostess, standing on a telephone pole, as seen in (名)峰 meihou (famous mountain, # 938) (identical pronunciation); below the telephone pole, a snail CUES: this 糸 (skeet shooter) is shooting at this dancer on this telephone pole, who is a **H**ostess and who has promised to 縫う **nu**u (sew) him a coat, and he wants her to turn around and tell him any **N**ews about the project, which is moving at the pace of this snail
ALSO COMPARE: other similar kanji at # **938**

1817. 把 PRONUNCIATIONS: ha, wa, pa
MEANINGS: grasp, counter for bundles
EXAMPLES: 把握する ha'aku suru = to comprehend or understand; 一把 ichiwa = a bundle or bunch; 大雑把 oozappa = rough or sketchy DESCRIPTION: compared to 肥(える) koeru (to put on weight, # 1406), this substitutes a kneeling guy for 月 (moon) on the left; it retains the snake with two eyes CUES: this guy on the left is kneeling to tell this snake with two eyes not to **H**arm the **W**alrus on the **Pa**tio, but it doesn't 把握する **ha**'aku suru (understand)
ALSO COMPARE: other similar kanji at # **673**

1818. 峡 PRONUNCIATION: kyou
MEANINGS: gorge, ravine EXAMPLE: 峡谷 kyoukoku = a canyon or ravine
DESCRIPTION: compared to 狭(い) semai (narrow, # 194), or 狭(小) kyoushou (cramped, # 194) (identical pronunciation), this kanji substitutes 山 yama (mountain, # 146) for the person contorting her body on the left; it retains the 夫 (husband) surrounded by flames
CUE: this 夫 (husband) visited this 山 (mountain) near **Kyou**to, but he got caught in this fire in a 峡谷 **kyou**koku (canyon) ALSO COMPARE: other similar kanji at # **194** and # **1942**

1819. 楼 PRONUNCIATION: rou
MEANINGS: watchtower, lookout, high building
EXAMPLE: 摩天楼 matenrou = a skyscraper
DESCRIPTION: compared to 数(える) kazoeru (to count, # 639), this omits the dancer on the right and adds 木 ki (tree, # 118) on the left; it retains the 女 (female), who lives in a casino zone and carries 米 (rice) CUE: this 女 (female) struggles to carry this 米 (rice) from this 木 (tree) to her 摩天楼 maten**rou** (skyscraper) and wishes she had a **R**obot to do it for her ALSO COMPARE: other similar kanji at # **1387** and # **2086**

1820. 漬 PRONUNCIATION: tsu
MEANINGS: pickling, soak EXAMPLE: 漬ける tsukeru = to soak or marinade
DESCRIPTION: compared to 責(任) sekinin (responsibility, # 772), this adds a water radical on the left; it retains the owl's perch above a 貝 (money chest) belonging to a selfish king
CUE: this water came in and 漬けた **tsu**keta (soaked) a **Ts**uit (suit) that I had hung on this owl's perch above this 貝 (money chest)
ALSO COMPARE: other similar kanji at # **772**

1821. 紳 PRONUNCIATION: shin
MEANINGS: sire, good belt, gentleman
EXAMPLE: 紳士 shinshi = a gentleman
DESCRIPTION: on the left, 糸 (skeet shooter, # 219); on the right, 申(す) mousu (to humbly say, # 10), which resembles two lips stitched together and can be seen as a rice paddy on a stick
CUE: when this 糸 (skeet shooter) fired roof **Shin**gles at me, I 申 (humbly said) "no thank you," since I'm a 紳士 **shin**shi (gentleman)
ALSO COMPARE: other similar kanji at # **1157**

1822. 宛 PRONUNCIATIONS: a, ate
MEANINGS: address, just like, fortunately
EXAMPLES: 宛てる ateru = to address (mail); 宛先 atesaki = an address or destination

DESCRIPTION: compared to 腕 ude (arm, # 1532), this omits the 月 (moon) on the left; it retains the bad haircut belonging to an Ugandan dentist, the 夕 (evening) and the uncoiling snake CUES: an African mail carrier with this bad haircut made an Attempt to deliver a package to an 宛先 atesaki (address) one 夕 (evening), until she saw this snake ALSO COMPARE: other similar kanji at # 547 and # 801

1823. 閥 PRONUNCIATION: batsu
MEANINGS: clique, faction, lineage, clan
EXAMPLE: 財閥 zaibatsu = a financial combine or business conglomerate DESCRIPTION: on the left and right, 門 mon (gate, # 409); inside the gate, on the left, a man with a slanted hat and, on the right, a single-grip halberd (combination axe and lance) CUE: this man with a slanted hat stands inside this 門 (gate) while holding this single-grip halberd and guarding a compound controlled by a 財閥 zaibatsu (financial combine), and he wears a Bat Suit to frighten intruders away
ALSO COMPARE: other similar kanji at # 1755 and # 1862

1824. 坪 PRONUNCIATION: tsubo
MEANINGS: two-mat area
EXAMPLES: 坪 tsubo = a unit of area comprising 3.3 square meters, or 2 tatami mats
DESCRIPTION: on the left, 土 tsuchi (soil, # 59); on the right, 平(和) heiwa (peace, # 885), which resembles a telephone pole with a flat top and flames shooting out from the sides, creating a haze CUE: when we attended the Tsuper (Super) Bowl, we saw this burning telephone pole, and we threw this 土 (soil) on it, but then we went to our assigned area consisting of 一坪 hitotsubo (3.3 square meters) ALSO COMPARE: other similar kanji at # 1053

1825. 溝 PRONUNCIATIONS: mizo, kou, dobu MEANINGS: gutter, ditch, sewer, drain
EXAMPLES: 溝 mizo = a ditch, groove or gap; 排水溝 haisuikou = drainage, gutter, ditch; 溝水 dobumizu = ditch water

DESCRIPTION: compared to (結)構 kekkou (fine, # 141) (identical pronunciation), this kanji substitutes a water radical for the 木 (tree) on the left; it retains the courthouse with a 井 (well) and a 再 (model of a rice paddy with a handle) in the lobby CUES: we were standing in the Meeting Zone outside this Courthouse with this 井 (well) and this 再 (model of a rice paddy with a handle) when this water from this 井 (well) poured through a 溝 mizo (ditch) and woke up a Dozing Bookkeeper
GROUP: (結)構 kekkou = fine, # 141; 講(義) kougi = lecture, # 1027; 購(入する) kounyuu suru = to purchase, # 1269; (排水)溝 haisuikou = drainage, # 1825; Note that all of these kanji can be pronounced "kou" ALSO COMPARE: other similar kanji at # 1032

1826. 朴 PRONUNCIATION: boku
MEANINGS: crude, simple, plain, docile
EXAMPLE: 素朴な soboku na = simple, naïve, unpretentious DESCRIPTION: on the left, 木 ki (tree, # 118); on the right, the katakana ト to, which reminds us of toes CUE: a Bony Kool-Aid salesman lives a 素朴な soboku na (unpretentious) life under this 木 (tree), often inspecting this bony ト (toe) GROUP: 外 soto = outside, # 163; 掛(ける) kakeru = to hang, # 596; (素)朴(な) soboku na = simple, # 1826; 赴(く) omomuku = to go or tend toward, # 1888; 訃(報) fuhou = an obituary, # 2072

1827. 軌 PRONUNCIATION: ki
MEANINGS: rut, wheel, track
EXAMPLE: 軌道 kidou = an orbit
DESCRIPTION: on the left, 車 kuruma (car, # 283); on the right, 九 kyuu (nine, # 111)
CUE: these 九 (nine) 車 (cars) were launched into 軌道 kidou (orbit) from a site in Kiev
ALSO COMPARE: other similar kanji at # 827 and # 1966

1828. 喪 **PRONUNCIATIONS: mo, sou**
MEANINGS: miss, mourning **EXAMPLES:**
喪服 mofuku = mourning dress; 喪失 soushitsu
= a loss **DESCRIPTION:** at the top, 十 juu (ten,
18), flanked by two 口 (boxes); at the bottom, a
platform supported by L and Y
CUES: this L and this Y are carrying these two 口
(boxes) containing the ashes of 十 (ten) **Mo**les
whose **Sou**ls have gone to Heaven, and they regret
their 喪失 **sou**shitsu (loss) **GROUP:** 十 juu =
ten, # 18; 南 minami = south, # 388; (時)計
tokei = clock, # 434; 汁 shiru = soup, # 900; 協
(同) kyoudou = cooperation, # 940; 叶(う)
kanau = to come true, # 1076; 針 hari = needle,
# 1138; 述(べる) noberu = to tell , # 1328; (検)
索 kensaku = retrieval, # 1361; 博(打) bakuchi =
gambling, # 1481; (貢)献 kouken = a contribution, # 1618; 喪(失) soushitsu = a loss, # 1828;
勃(発) boppatsu = an outbreak, # 1846; (一)升
isshou = 1.8 liters, # 2049
ALSO COMPARE: other similar kanji at # **398** and
1034

1829. 墨 **PRONUNCIATIONS: boku,**
sumi MEANINGS: black ink, ink stick
EXAMPLES: 墨汁 bokujuu = India (black) ink;
墨 sumi = ink stick, black ink
DESCRIPTION: at the top, 黒(い) kuroi (black,
76); at the bottom, 土 tsuchi (soil, # 59)
CUES: a **Bo**at from **Ku**wait carries this 黒 (black)
土 (soil) to make 墨汁 **boku**juu (India ink), and
its captain will **Sue Me** if I reveal his secret **ALSO**
COMPARE: other similar kanji at # **545** and # **611**

1830. 遍 **PRONUNCIATIONS: hen, pen**
MEANINGS: everywhere, widely, generally
EXAMPLES: 普遍の fuhen no = constant,
unchanging, eternal; 一遍 ippen = one time, once
DESCRIPTION: compared to 編(者) hensha
(editor, # 1052), or (短)編 tanpen (short story,
1052), both of which help us to pronounce this,
this kanji omits the skeet shooter on the left and adds
a snail at the lower left; it retains 冊 (a counter for
books) inside a 戸 (snow-covered double-roofed
lean-to), where an editor works on books about hens
that use pens to make art
CUES: this snail has to transport an 編 (editor) as
he edits 冊 (books) about **Hen**s that use **Pen**s, and
it's a 普遍の fu**hen** no (constant) struggle
ALSO COMPARE: other similar kanji at # **568** and
1134

1831. 濁 **PRONUNCIATIONS: nigo, daku**
MEANINGS: uncleanness, wrong, impurity
EXAMPLES: 濁る nigoru = to be muddy, cloudy
or unclear; 濁流 dakuryuu = a muddy stream
DESCRIPTION: on the left, a water radical; at the
upper right, three eyes; at the lower right, a hook
containing 虫 mushi (worm, # 9) **CUES:** a
Nea**r**sighted **Gho**st with these three eyes baited this
hook with this 虫 (worm) while standing on a **Da**m
in **Ku**wait, but this water 濁った **nigo**tta (was
muddy), and the fish couldn't see the bait
ALSO COMPARE: other similar kanji at # **988**,
1324 and # **1754**

1832. 缶 **PRONUNCIATION: kan**
MEANINGS: tin can, container, jar
EXAMPLE: 缶 kan = a tin can, jar or container
DESCRIPTION: 午 go (noon, # 207) merged with
山 yama (mountain, # 146) **CUE:** a **Kan**garoo
drank a 缶 **kan** (can) of milk on this 山
(mountain) at 午 (noon) **GROUP:** 陶(器) touki
= chinaware, # 1741; 鬱(病) utsubyou =
depression, # 1783; 缶 kan = a tin can, # 1832
ALSO COMPARE: other similar kanji at # **207** and
2079

1833. 扇 **PRONUNCIATIONS: sen, ougi**
MEANINGS: fan, folding fan **EXAMPLES:**
扇子 sensu = a folding fan; 扇 ougi = a folding
fan **DESCRIPTION:** compared to 戸 to (door,

871), this adds 羽 hane (feather, # 755) at the lower right; it retains the lean-to with a layer of snow on top **CUES:** a **Sen**ator keeps some **O**ld **Gee**se in this 戸 (snow-covered lean-to) and, since they are old, he plucks these 羽 (feathers) from them in order to produce 扇子 **sen**su (folding fans) **ALSO COMPARE:** other similar kanji at # **1134** and # **1457**

1834. 枯 PRONUNCIATIONS: ka, ko
MEANINGS: wither, die, dry up
EXAMPLES: 枯れる kareru = to wither; 枯木 koboku = a dead tree
DESCRIPTION: compared to 古(代) kodai (ancient times, # 392) (identical pronunciation), or 古(い) furui (old, # 392), this kanji adds 木 ki (tree, # 118) on the left; it retains 古(い) furui (old), which resembles a tomb where a coach was buried **CUES:** I erected this **Ca**tholic 古 (tomb) with a cross on it for my **Co**ach under this 古 (old) 木 (tree), but later the tree 枯れた **ka**reta (dried up) **ALSO COMPARE:** other similar kanji at # **128** and # **394**

1835. 乙 PRONUNCIATIONS: otsu, oto
MEANINGS: the latter, duplicate, second, strange
EXAMPLES: 乙 otsu = the second, the latter; 乙女 otome = a maiden **DESCRIPTION:** this resembles the letter Z, which reminds us of Zebras **CUES:** this 乙 (zebra) eats **O**ats and **O**ld **T**omatoes, and it belongs to an 乙女 **oto**me (maiden) **GROUP:** 乾(く) kawaku = to get dry, # 290; 芝(生) shibafu = lawn, # 779; (貧)乏 binbou = poverty, # 1340; 乙(女) otome = a maiden, # 1835; 乞(食) kojiki = a beggar, # 1839

1836. 酵 PRONUNCIATION: kou
MEANING: fermentation **EXAMPLE:** 酵素 kouso = an enzyme **DESCRIPTION:** compared to 孝(行) koukou (filial piety, # 1471) (identical pronunciation), this kanji adds 酒 sake (alcoholic beverage, # 465), without its water radical, on the left (this can also be seen as a bucket of sake with a handle); it retains the 子 (child) who copes with the consequences of playing with scissors
CUE: this 子 (child) **C**opes with the effects of playing with scissors, and she has developed a 酵素 **kou**so (enzyme) to ferment grain and make 酒 (alcohol) like this **ALSO COMPARE:** other similar kanji at # **1471** and # **1480**

1837. 堤 PRONUNCIATIONS: tei, tsutsumi
MEANINGS: dike, bank, embankment
EXAMPLES: 堤防 teibou = an embankment or dike; 堤 tsutsumi = an embankment or dike
DESCRIPTION: compared to 提(出する) teitshutsu suru (to submit, # 1156) (identical pronunciation), this kanji substitutes 土 tsuchi (soil, # 59) for the kneeling guy on the left; it retains the 日 (sun) shining on a foot with a taser mounted on it **CUES:** this 日 (sun) shines down on this foot with a **Ta**ser mounted on it, which is guarding a 堤 **tsutsumi** (embankment) made of 土 (soil), on which we have placed **Tsu**itcases (suitcases) and **Tsu**itcases of **M**eat **ALSO COMPARE:** other similar kanji at # **454**

1838. 阻 PRONUNCIATIONS: haba, so
MEANINGS: prevent, obstruct, separate from
EXAMPLES: 阻む habamu = to block or stop; 阻害 sogai = an obstruction or inhibition
DESCRIPTION: compared to 祖(父) sofu (grandfather, # 272) (identical pronunciation), this kanji substitutes ß beta from the Greek alphabet for the Shah on the left; it retains the solar panel on the right
CUES: when this ß (Greek) guy was playing **H**ard**B**all, he saw this **S**olar panel as a 阻害 **so**gai (obstruction) and said that they have better ones in Athens, where they play softball
ALSO COMPARE: other similar kanji at # **752** and # **2030**

1839. 乞 PRONUNCIATION: ko
MEANINGS: beg, invite, ask
EXAMPLE: 乞食 kojiki = a beggar, or begging
DESCRIPTION: compared to 乙(女) otome (a maiden, # 1835), this adds a crutch at the top; it retains the letter Z, which reminds us of zebras that eat organic tomatoes
CUE: a Cold-hearted man used to beat this 乙 (zebra) with this crutch, but then he lost everything and became a 乞食 **ko**jiki (beggar)
ALSO COMPARE: other similar kanji at # **1835** and # **2080**

1840. 鐘 PRONUNCIATIONS: shou, kane
MEANINGS: bell, gong, chimes
EXAMPLES: 鐘楼 shourou = a bell tower; 鐘 kane = a bell, gong or chimes
DESCRIPTION: compared to (児)童 jidou (child, # 1094), this adds 金 kane (money, # 301) (identical pronunciation), on the left **CUES:** this 童 (child) is at the **Sh**ore selling **Kan**sas Eggs in exchange for this 金 **Kane** (money) until a 鐘 **kane** (bell) rings to tell him to go home
GROUP: (児)童 jidou = child, # 1094; 鐘 kane = a bell, # 1840; 瞳 hitomi = a pupil, # 1865; 憧 (れる) akogareru = to admire, # 1956 **ALSO COMPARE:** other similar kanji at # **2010**

1841. 擁 PRONUNCIATION: you
MEANINGS: hug, embrace, protect, lead
EXAMPLES: 擁護 yougo = protection; 抱擁する houyou suru = to embrace or hug
DESCRIPTION: on the left, a kneeling guy; at the upper right, a tire stop; at the lower center, a jagged lightning strike, as seen in (故)郷 furusato (hometown, # 1059); at the lower right, a net, which can be seen as a man with a slanted hat next to a 主 (master) with an extra pair of arms (see # 203)
CUE: this guy on the left kneels to examine this net under this tire stop in **Yo**semite, where he planned to sleep, but he realizes that the stop provides little 擁護 **you**go (protection) from lightning strikes like this **ALSO COMPARE:** other similar kanji at # **840**, # **1860** and # **2046**

1842. 享 PRONUNCIATION: kyou
MEANINGS: receive, undergo, take, catch
EXAMPLE: 享受する kyouju suru = to enjoy
DESCRIPTION: compared to 熟(す) jukusu (to ripen, # 1427), this omits the slashed 丸 (nine) at the upper right and the fire at the bottom; it retains the tire stop, the 口 (mouth) and the 子 (child)
CUE: this 子 (child) 享受した **kyou**ju shita (enjoyed) playing with this tire stop in **Kyou**to until he tripped, and it struck him in this 口 (mouth)
COMPARE: other similar kanji at # **1427**

1843. 郭 PRONUNCIATION: kaku
MEANINGS: enclosure, fortification
EXAMPLE: 輪郭 rinkaku = an outline, contour or summary
DESCRIPTION: compared to 享(受する) kyouju suru (to enjoy, # 1842), this adds ß beta from the Greek alphabet on the right; it retains the 子 (child) playing with a tire stop who gets hit in the 口 (mouth) **CUE:** **Ka**rl the **Ko**ol-Aid vendor is this ß (Greek guy), and he tells his customers the 輪郭 rin**kaku** (outline) of a story about this 子 (child) who played with this tire stop until it struck him in this 口 (mouth)
GROUP: 郊(外) kougai = suburbs, # 145; 部(屋) heya = room, # 267; 都(市) toshi = city, # 277; (旦)那 danna = husband, # 669; (風)邪 kaze = upper respiratory infection, # 796; (影)響 eikyou = influence, # 840; (故)郷 furusato = hometown, # 1059; 郡 gun = county, # 1230; (新)郎 shinrou = bridegroom, # 1343; 邸(宅) teitaku = mansion, # 1422; 郵(政) yuusei = the postal system, # 1445; (連)邦 renpou = a federation, # 1593; 廊(下) rouka = corridor, # 1605; (輪)郭 rinkaku = an outline, # 1843
ALSO COMPARE: kanji with ß on the *left* at # 2030; other similar kanji at # **1427**

1844. 呪 PRONUNCIATION: noro

MEANINGS: spell, curse, charm, malediction

EXAMPLES: 呪い noroi = a curse

DESCRIPTION: on the left, 口 kuchi (mouth, #426), which can also be seen as a box; on the right, 兄 ani (big brother, #420)

CUE: when this 兄 (big brother) was driving on a bad **Nor**wegian **Ro**ad, 呪い **noro**i (curses) came out of this 口 (mouth) **ALSO COMPARE:** other similar kanji at #**420** and #**2073**

1845. 砕 PRONUNCIATIONS: kuda, sai

MEANINGS: smash, break, crush

EXAMPLES: 砕く kudaku = to break or smash; 砕石 saiseki = rubble, broken stone

DESCRIPTION: compared to 酔(う) you (to get drunk, #1476), this substitutes 石 seki (stone, #458) for the modified 酒 (alcoholic beverage) on the left; it retains 九 kyuu (nine, #111) and 十 juu (ten, #18)

CUES: my **C**ool **D**ad is a **S**cientist, and when he was experimenting on this 石 (stone), he 砕いた **kuda**ita (smashed) it into 九十 (ninety) pieces **ALSO COMPARE:** other similar kanji at #**827**, #**1658** and #**1775**

1846. 勃 PRONUNCIATION: bo

MEANINGS: suddenness, rise **EXAMPLE:** 勃発 boppatsu = an outbreak or sudden occurrence

DESCRIPTION: on the upper left, juu 十 (ten) above a roof; at the lower left, 子 ko (child, #182); on the right, 力 chikara (energy or force, #107)

CUES: this 子 (child) threw 十 (ten) **Bo**ws onto this roof after he had a 勃発 **bo**ppatsu (outbreak) of 力 (energy) **GROUP:** 力 chikara = force, #107; 助(ける) tasukeru = to help, #108; 動(く) ugoku = to move, #286; 働(く) hataraku = to labor, #287; 勉(強) benkyou = study, #474; 勤(める) tsutomeru = to be employed, #517;

(成)功 seikou = success, #634; 勧(告) kankoku = recommendation, #698; (参)加 sanka = participation, #714; (年)賀(状) nengajou = New Year's card, #994; 効(果) kouka = an effect, #1139; 勘(弁) kanben = pardon, #1161; 励(む) hagemu = to be diligent, #1338; 幼(い) osanai = childish, #1400; (担)架 tanka = a stretcher, #1790; 勃(発) boppatsu = an outbreak, #1846; 勲(章) kunshou = a medal, #1938 **ALSO COMPARE:** other similar kanji at #**1828** and #**2078**

1847. 唾 PRONUNCIATIONS: tsuba, da

MEANINGS: saliva, sputum **EXAMPLES:** 唾 tsuba = saliva; 唾液 daeki = saliva

DESCRIPTION: compared to 垂(直) suichoku (vertical, #799), this adds 口 kuchi (mouth, #426), which can also be seen as a box, on the left; it retains the streamlined Swedish car that runs on hubcaps

CUES: when I rented this 垂 (streamlined Swedish car), I put my **Tsu**itcase (suitcase) in the **Ba**ck and then, since this 口 (mouth) was **Da**mp, I spat some 唾 **tsuba** (saliva) out the window **ALSO COMPARE:** other similar kanji at #**799** and #**2073**

1848. 譜 PRONUNCIATION: fu

MEANINGS: musical score, music, note, genealogy

EXAMPLE: 楽譜 gakufu = sheet music

DESCRIPTION: compared to 普(通) futsuu (ordinarily, #576) (identical pronunciation), this kanji adds 言(う) iu (to say, #430) on the left; it retains the stove with four burners used for cooking food, with flames at the top that can also be seen as antennae **CUE:** since you 言 (said) that you have this 普 (stove), will you cook some **F**ood for me, in exchange for some 楽譜 gaku**fu** (sheet music)? **ALSO COMPARE:** other similar kanji at #**575** and #**1300**

1849. 肪 PRONUNCIATION: bou
MEANINGS: obese, fat
EXAMPLE: 脂肪 shibou = fat
DESCRIPTION: compared to (予)防 yobou (prevention, # 920) (identical pronunciation), this kanji substitutes 月 tsuki (moon, # 148) for ß on the left; it retains the 方 (honorable person) who boasts **CUES:** this 方 (honorable person) **B**oasts about the nice view of this 月 (moon) from his house, and he carries some 脂肪 shi**bou** (fat) on his body
ALSO COMPARE: other similar kanji at # **920**

1850. 塀 PRONUNCIATIONS: bei, hei
MEANINGS: fence, wall **EXAMPLES:** 石塀 ishibei = a stone wall; 塀 hei = a fence or wall
DESCRIPTION: compared to 併(用する) heiyou suru (to use simultaneously, # 1655) (identical pronunciation), this kanji substitutes 土 tsuchi (soil, # 59) for the man with a slanted hat on the left, and it adds a lean-to with a double roof; it retains the research tower, wearing rabbit ears **CUES:** a researcher put these rabbit ears on this research tower to celebrate a **B**aby that he keeps in this lean-to with a double roof, but he **H**ates to see this 土 (soil) sliding toward the dwelling, so he is building a 塀 **hei** (wall) to protect the child
ALSO COMPARE: other similar kanji at # **573**, # **743** and # **1899**

1851. 碁 PRONUNCIATION: go
MEANING: a Japanese board game played with stones **EXAMPLE:** 碁 go = a Japanese board game **DESCRIPTION:** at the top, a woman with a bucket with several compartments and a wide skirt, as seen in (将)棋 shougi (Japanese chess, # 1726); at the bottom, 石 ishi (stone, # 458) **CUE:** when we play 碁 **go** (a Japanese board game) with 石 (stones) like this, this waitress with a wide skirt and this bucket with compartments brings us drinks, and I pay her in **G**old **ALSO COMPARE:** other similar kanji at # **711** and # **1775**

1852. 敢 PRONUNCIATIONS: kan, a
MEANING: daring **EXAMPLES:** 勇敢な yuukan na = brave; 敢えて aete = daring to do something, venturing, usually spelled あえて
DESCRIPTION: on the left, 耳 mimi (ear, # 57), with a diving board at the top; on the right, a dancer with a ponytail **CUES:** this dancer with a ponytail went from **Kan**sas to **A**frica to jump off this diving board and, although she was 勇敢 yuu**kan** (brave), she landed on this 耳 (ear)
ALSO COMPARE: (貧)乏 binbou = poverty, # **1340**; other similar kanji at # **1713**

1853. 塁 PRONUNCIATION: rui
MEANINGS: bases, fort, rampart, wall
EXAMPLE: 塁 rui = a base (baseball)
DESCRIPTION: at the top, 田(んぼ) tanbo (rice paddy, # 68); in the middle, a segmented X; at the bottom, 土 tsuchi (soil, # 59)
CUE: King **L**ou**i**s drew X's like this in the 土 (soil) of this 田 (rice paddy) and used them for baseball 塁 **rui** (bases)
ALSO COMPARE: other similar kanji at # **220** and # **1454**

1854. 滴 PRONUNCIATIONS: shitata, teki
MEANINGS: drip, drop **EXAMPLES:** 滴る shitataru = to drip; 滴 teki = a drop
DESCRIPTION: compared to (指)摘 shiteki (pointing out, # 1083) (identical pronunciation), this kanji substitutes a water radical for the kneeling guy on the left; it retains the 立 (bell) used by an 古 (old) sentry in a two-sided lean-to to frighten techies **CUES:** after a **Sh**i**it**e **T**alked **T**arzan into using this water on the left to harrass their enemies, who were **T**echies, this 古 (old) sentry in this two-sided lean-to noticed that some 滴 **teki** (drops) had fallen onto this 立 (bell)
ALSO COMPARE: other similar kanji at # **881**

1855. 暁 **PRONUNCIATION: akatsuki**
MEANINGS: daybreak, dawn, in the event
EXAMPLES: 暁 akatsuki = daybreak, beginning, ending **DESCRIPTION:** compared to 焼(き鳥) yakitori (skewered chicken, # 446), this substitutes 日 hi (sun, # 32) for 火 (fire) on the left; it retains the triple plant radical at the upper right, which resembles yams on skewers, grilled on a platform standing on lopsided legs **CUE:** when I attended the **Aca**demy of **Tsuki** (moon) Studies, I used to eat yams on skewers like these, grilled on a platform with lopsided legs like these, while watching this 日 (sun) come up at 暁 **akatsuki** (daybreak)
GROUP: 先(生) sensei = teacher, # 422; 洗(う) arau = to wash, # 423; 焼(く) yaku = to grill, # **446**; 光 hikari = light, # 448; 暁 akatsuki = daybreak, # 1855 **ALSO COMPARE:** other similar kanji at # **1268**

1856. 謡 **PRONUNCIATIONS: you, utai, uta MEANING:** Noh chanting **EXAMPLES:** 歌謡曲 kayoukyoku = a popular song; 謡 utai = Noh chanting (this can also be spelled 謡い) **DESCRIPTION:** compared to (動)揺 douyou (uneasiness, # 852) (identical pronunciation), this kanji substitutes 言(う) iu (to say, # 430) for the kneeling guy on the left; it retains the barbecue grate above a tongue emerging from a mountain in Yosemite **CUES:** this tongue emerging from this mountain under this barbecue grate in **Yo**semite 言 (says) that it used to sing 歌謡曲 ka**you**kyoku (popular songs) with an **U**gandan **T**iger in an **U**gandan **Ta**vern **GROUP:** 揺(れる) yureru = to sway, # 852; (歌)謡(曲) kayoukyoku = a popular song, # 1856 **ALSO COMPARE:** other kanji with tongues at # 1213; kanji with *noon* merged with a mountain at # 1832; 謡う utau = to sing, # 534; other similar kanji at # **1177** and # **2079**

1857. 痕 **PRONUNCIATIONS: ato, kon**
MEANINGS: mark, footprint **EXAMPLES:** 傷痕 kizuato = a scar (this can also be spelled 傷跡, #1111, or 傷あと); 痕跡 konseki = traces, vestiges **DESCRIPTION:** at the upper left, a sick bed, as seen in 病(気) byouki (illness, # 369; inside the bed, 良(い) yoi (good, # 303), which includes L & Y at its base, without its pointy hat **CUES:** after I was injured by an **At**omic bomb, I got 良 (good) medical care as I lay in this sick bed in the **Con**go, but I was left with some 傷痕 **kizu**ato (scars) **ALSO COMPARE:** other similar kanji at # **369** and # **805**

1858. 詐 **PRONUNCIATION: sa**
MEANINGS: lie, deceive, pretend
EXAMPLES: 詐欺 sagi = a fraud or hoax
DESCRIPTION: compared to 作(家) sakka (writer, # 482) (identical pronunciation), this kanji substitutes 言(う) iu (to say, # 430) for the man with a slanted hat on the left; it retains the serrated axe, which can also be seen as a ladder or stairs **CUE:** someone 言 (said) that he would trade a **Sa**xophone for this serrated axe, but his offer was a 詐欺 **sa**gi (hoax) **ALSO COMPARE:** other similar kanji at # **41**

1859. 欺 **PRONUNCIATIONS: azamu, gi**
MEANINGS: deceive, cheat, delude
EXAMPLES: 欺く azamuku = to deceive or trick; 詐欺 sagi = a fraud or hoax
DESCRIPTION: compared to (時)期 jiki (season, # 711), this substitutes 欠(く) kaku (to lack, # 1238), which resembles an oil derrick, for 月 (moon) on the right; it retains the woman with a wide skirt and a bucket with several compartments, who makes quiche **CUES:** this woman with a wide skirt and a bucket with several compartments tried to sell this 欠 (oil derrick) to get money for her project to plant **Az**aleas with some **Moo**nies, but the **Ge**ars in the oil derrick were defective, and she was accused of 詐欺 **sa**gi (fraud) **ALSO COMPARE:** other similar kanji at # **536** and # **711**

1860. 弦 PRONUNCIATION: gen
MEANINGS: bowstring, chord, hypotenuse
EXAMPLE: 弦楽器 gengakki = a stringed instrument **DESCRIPTION:** compared to 玄(関) genkan (entranceway, # 1252) (identical pronunciation), this kanji adds a twisted 弓 yumi (bow, # 1044) on the left; it retains the truncated 糸 (skeet shooter), consisting of two flexed elbows, carrying a tire stop into the house of Genghis **CUE:** after this truncated 糸 (skeet shooter) delivered this tire stop to **Gen**ghis, he was rewarded with this 弓 (bow) and a 弦楽器 **gen**gakki (stringed instrument)
GROUP: 六 roku = six, # 17; 卒(業) sotsugyou = graduation, # 27; 来(る) kuru = to come, # 327; 夜 yoru = night, # 489; 壇 dan = stage, # 679; 眩(しい) mabushii = dazzling, # 937; (反)抗 hankou = rebellion, # 1196; 液(体) ekitai = liquid, # 1241; 玄(関) genkan = entranceway, # 1252; 航(空) koukuu = aviation, # 1295; 率 ritsu = percentage, # 1408; 畜(生) chikushou = a beast, # 1773; (貯)蓄 chochiku = savings, # 1774; 擁(護) yougo = protection, # 1841; 弦(楽器) gengakki = a stringed instrument, # 1860 **ALSO COMPARE:** other similar kanji at # **476** and # **1129**

1861. 泡 PRONUNCIATIONS: hou, pou, awa
MEANINGS: bubbles, foam, suds, froth
EXAMPLES: 気泡 kihou = an air bubble; 発泡酒 happoushu = sparkling wine, low-malt beer; 泡 awa = bubbles, foam **DESCRIPTION:** compared to 包(装) housou (wrapping, # 548) (identical pronunciation), this kanji adds a water radical on the left; it retains the J-shaped packaging wrapped by a hostess around contents that are shaped like 己 (a backward "S"); this can also be seen as a hook containing a snake **CUES:** our **H**ostess from **P**oland was **Aw**akened by this water which soaked this J-shaped packaging and its 己 (contents) and formed lots of 泡 **aw**a (bubbles)
GROUP: 包(装) housou = wrapping, # 548; (鉄)砲 teppou = gun, # 738; (辛)抱 shinbou = patience, # 986; 飽(きる) akiru = to tire of, # 1379; (細)胞 saibou = a cell, # 1595; 泡 awa = bubbles, # 1861 **ALSO COMPARE:** kanji with *uncoiling* snakes at # 547; other kanji with backwards "S" snakes at # 1078

1862. 伐 PRONUNCIATIONS: ba, batsu
MEANINGS: fell, strike, attack, punish
EXAMPLE: 伐採 bassai = logging; 伐木 batsuboku = logging **DESCRIPTION:** compared to (財)閥 zaibatsu (financial combine, # 1823) (identical pronunciation), this kanji omits the 門 (gate) on the perimeter; it retains the man with a slanted hat and the single-grip halberd
CUES: this man on the left is a **Ba**rber who wears a **Bat Sui**t and is tilting his hat back in order to examine the blade on this halberd, which he uses to cut hair and for 伐採 **ba**ssai (logging)
GROUP: 機(械) kikai = machine, # 137; (機)械 kikai = machine, # 138; (会)議 kaigi = meeting, # 438; 越(える) koeru = to go across, # 453; (迷)惑 meiwaku = trouble, # 624; 我 ware = self, # 862; 戒(める) imashimeru = to admonish, # 875; 戦(争) sensou = war, # 933; 義(理) giri = moral debt, # 1028; 載(せる) noseru = to publish, # 1175; 栽(培) saibai = cultivation, # 1233; (地)域 chiiki = region, # 1256; 裁(判) saiban = trial, # 1450; (礼)儀 reigi = civility, # 1541; 幾(何学) kikagaku = geometry, # 1628; (盗)賊 touzoku = a robber, # 1652; 戯(曲) gikyoku = a drama, # 1756; 犠(牲) gisei = a victim, # 1764; 繊(維) sen'i = fiber, # 1815; (財)閥 zaibatsu = a financial combine, # 1823; 伐(採) bassai = logging, # 1862; 餓(死) gashi = starvation, # 1974; (便)箋 binsen = writing paper, # 2051
ALSO COMPARE: other kanji with single-grip halberds at # 633, # 753 and # 915; kanji with *triple-grip* halberds at # 605

1863. 厄 PRONUNCIATIONS: ya, yaku
MEANINGS: unlucky, misfortune, disaster
EXAMPLES: 厄介な yakkai na = troublesome, awkward; 厄 yaku = misfortune, disaster
DESCRIPTION: compared to 危(ない) abunai (dangerous, # 547), this omits the abused fish head at the top; it retains the one-sided lean-to containing an uncoiling snake CUES: when a **Ya**nkee found this snake in this lean-to where he keeps his **Ya**k, it was a 厄介な **ya**kkai na (troublesome) situation
ALSO COMPARE: other similar kanji at # **547**

1864. 奔 PRONUNCIATION: hon
MEANINGS: run, bustle EXAMPLE: 奔放な honpou na = unrestrained, free, wild
DESCRIPTION: at the top, 大(きい) ookii (big, # 188); in the middle, 十 juu (ten, # 18); at the bottom, some legs with a welcoming stance, as seen in 葬(る) houmuru (to bury, # 1273), which resemble the letter H and remind us of Honduras CUE: a 大 (big) man who lives in **H**onduras, which is spelled with an "H" like this, stands like this and welcomes 十 (ten) friends who want to live a 奔放な **hon**pou na (wild) life
ALSO COMPARE: other similar kanji at # **1658** and # **1924**

1865. 瞳 PRONUNCIATION: hitomi
MEANING: pupil EXAMPLE: 瞳 hitomi = a pupil (eye) DESCRIPTION: compared to 鐘 kane (bell, # 1840), this substitutes 目 me (eye, # 51) for 金 (money) on the left; it retains the 童 (child) CUE: I saw this 童 (child), and **He** **T**old **M**e that these glasses help him to adapt to changes in the lens near the 瞳 **hitomi** (pupil) of this 目 (eye)
ALSO COMPARE: other similar kanji at # **1840** and # **2002**

1866. 昆 PRONUNCIATION: kon
MEANINGS: descendants, older brother, insect
EXAMPLE: 昆虫 konchuu = an insect
DESCRIPTION: compared to 混(乱) konran (confusion, # 1294) (identical pronunciation), this kanji omits the water radical on the left; it retains the two 比 (heroes) who were affected by confusion, and the 日 hi (sun) CUE: these two 比 (heroes) are standing under this 日 (sun), where they are being bitten by 昆虫 **kon**chuu (insects), and they feel **Con**fusion as to which repellants to use
ALSO COMPARE: other similar kanji at # **1294**

1867. 脊 PRONUNCIATION: seki
MEANINGS: stature, height EXAMPLE: 脊椎 sekitsui = the spine DESCRIPTION: at the top, 人 hito (person, # 13), with flames shooting out from both sides; at the bottom, 月 tsuki (moon, # 148) CUE: after this 人 (person) bruised the 脊椎 **seki**tsui (spine) of a **Se**lfish **Ki**ng, he was sent to this 月 (moon) and set on fire like this
ALSO COMPARE: other similar kanji at # **352**, # **1926** and # **1991**

1868. 椎 PRONUNCIATION: tsui
MEANINGS: oak, mallet
EXAMPLE: 脊椎 sekitsui = the spine
DESCRIPTION: compared to 誰 dare (who, # 440), this substitutes 木 ki (tree, # 118) for 言 (to speak) on the left; it retains the net, which can be seen as a man with a slanted hat next to a 主 (master) with an extra pair of arms (see # 203)
CUE: when I climbed this 木 (tree) to get some **Tsui**te (sweet) apples to put into this net, I fell and hurt my 脊椎 seki**tsui** (spine)
ALSO COMPARE: other similar kanji at # **2046**

1869. 懇 PRONUNCIATION: kon
MEANINGS: sociable, kind, cordial
EXAMPLE: 懇談 kondan = a meeting or talk
DESCRIPTION: at the upper left, an ugly ヲ (wolf) with two teeth, as seen in (容)貌 youbou (features, # 1687); at the upper right, 良(い) yoi (good, # 303), with L & Y at its base, but without its pointy hat; at the bottom, 心 kokoro (heart, # 306)
CUE: I had a 良 (good) 懇談 **kon**dan (meeting) with my doctor to talk about this 心 (heart), but this ugly ヲ (wolf) with these two teeth was watching us, and that made it hard for us to Co**n**centrate
ALSO COMPARE: other similar kanji at # **805** and # **2068**

1870. 唄 PRONUNCIATION: uta
MEANING: songs with samisen
EXAMPLE: 長唄 naga'uta = a long epic song
DESCRIPTION: on the left, 口 kuchi (mouth, # 426), which can also be seen as a box; on the right, 貝 kai (shell or money chest, # 83)
CUE: I went to an Ugandan Tavern to sing a 長唄 naga'**uta** (long epic song) using this 口 (mouth), and afterwards I got paid from this 貝 (money chest) GROUP: 貝 kai = shell or money chest, # 83; (長)唄 naga'uta = a long epic song, # 1870; 櫻 sakura = cherry, # 2086 ALSO COMPARE: other similar kanji at # **2073**

1871. 渦 PRONUNCIATIONS: ka, uzu
MEANINGS: whirlpool, eddy, vortex
EXAMPLES: 戦渦 senka = the turmoil of war; 渦巻き uzumaki = a whirlpool, spiral or coil
DESCRIPTION: compared to 過(去) kako (past, # 361) (identical pronunciation), or 過(ぎる) sugiru (to exceed, # 361), this kanji omits the snail at the lower left and adds a water radical on the left; it retains the two cartons, one of which is slipping, inside of boxes
CUES: after this water level 過 (exceeded) expectations, these two boxes containing Cartons fell into this water at an U**b**er **Z**oo and were swallowed up in an 渦巻き **uzu**maki (whirlpool)
ALSO COMPARE: other similar kanji at # **361**

1872. 襟 PRONUNCIATION: eri
MEANINGS: collar, neck, lapel
EXAMPLES: 襟 eri = a collar or lapel
DESCRIPTION: compared to 禁(じる) kinjiru (to prohibit, # 943), this kanji adds happy Jimmy with two lips, as seen in 初(めて) hajimete (for the first time, # 104), on the left; it retains the spinning nail under a flying carpet [these can also be seen as 二 (two) above 小 (small)] below a 林 (grove), the excessive spinning of which was prohibited by our king CUE: when this happy Jimmy with two lips saw Eric Clapton spinning this 林 (grove) on this 丁 (nail) under a flying carpet, he grabbed him by the 襟 **eri** (collar) and said "that is 禁 (prohibited)" ALSO COMPARE: other similar kanji at # **943**, # **1347** and # **1615**

1873. 吟 PRONUNCIATION: gin
MEANINGS: versify, singing, recital
EXAMPLE: 吟味する ginmi suru = to check in detail, to examine DESCRIPTION: on the left, 口 kuchi (mouth, # 426), which can also be seen as a box; on the right, 今 ima (now, # 292), which contains a 7 under a ceiling under a peaked roof
CUE: 今 (now) this 口 (mouth) wants to drink some **Gin**, but first its owner will 吟味 **gin**mi suru (check in detail) the brands that are available
COMPARE: 含(む) fukumu = to include, # 1491, which reminds us that Gandalf will include local specialties in the food he eats in Fukuoka [Hint: the 口 in 含(む) fukumu is *under* 今 (now), suggesting that Gandalf is under time pressure to include local food in Fukuoka, whereas the 口 in 吟(味) ginmi is *beside* or *independent of* 今 (now), suggesting that there is no time pressure to check brands of gin]
ALSO COMPARE: other similar kanji at # **1491** and # **2073**

1874. 覇 PRONUNCIATION: ha

MEANINGS: hegemony, supremacy, leadership
EXAMPLE: 覇権 haken = hegemony
DESCRIPTION: at the top, three eyes hanging from a platform, as seen in (必)要 hitsuyou (necessary, # 238); on the lower left, 革 kawa (leather, # 1286), which resembles an open-top syringe above a needle (this radical can also be seen as a hanging bucket at the top, with two eyes above 十 (ten) at the bottom); at the lower right, 月 tsuki (moon, # 148) **CUE:** these three eyes belong to a tyrant who uses needles and syringes like this to **H**arm people by injecting drugs into them by the light of this 月 (moon) in order to maintain 覇権 **ha**ken (hegemony) over the country
ALSO COMPARE: other similar kanji at # **542**, # **1286**, # **1415** and # **2087**

1875. 衡 PRONUNCIATION: kou

MEANINGS: equilibrium, measuring rod, scale
EXAMPLE: 均衡 kinkou = balance or equilibrium **DESCRIPTION:** on the left and the right, 行(く) iku (to go, # 334); in the upper center, the upper portion of 魚 sakana (fish, # 80); at the lower center, 大(きい) ookii (big, # 188); together, these two radicals in the center resemble a big fish-headed guy **CUE:** when this 大 (big) fish-headed guy 行 (goes) to **C**ourt, he takes a middle path like this, striking a 均衡 kin**kou** (balance) between the rights of those who live in water and those who live on land
ALSO COMPARE: other similar kanji at # **618** and # **625**

1876. 呈 PRONUNCIATION: tei

MEANINGS: display, offer, present, exhibit
EXAMPLE: 贈呈する zoutei suru = to donate or present a gift **DESCRIPTION:** compared to 程(度) teido (criterion, # 954) (identical pronunciation), this kanji omits the grain plant with a ripe head on the left; it retains the 王 (king) and the 口 (mouth) he uses for tasting **CUE:** this 王 (king) opened this 口 (mouth) and **T**asted a cake that one of his subjects 贈呈した zou**tei** shita (donated) **GROUP:** (希)望 kibou = hope, # 664; (特)徴 tokuchou = characteristic, # 784; 程 hodo = extent, # 954; (天)皇 tennou = the Emperor of Japan, # 1458; 聖(書) seisho = the Bible, # 1500; (利)潤 rijun = profit, # 1755; (贈)呈(する) zoutei suru = to donate, # 1876; 淫(らな) midara na = indecent, obscene, # 1877
ALSO COMPARE: kanji with 王 (king) at the *top* at # 1712; kanji with 王 on the *left* at # 1772

1877. 淫 PRONUNCIATION: mida

MEANINGS: lewdness, licentiousness
EXAMPLE: 淫らな midara na = indecent, obscene **DESCRIPTION:** on the left, a water radical; at the upper right, a barbecue grate; at the lower right, 王 ou (king, # 1077)
CUE: Midas was this 王 (king) who owned this barbecue grate and played 淫らな **mida**ra na (indecent) games in this water
ALSO COMPARE: other similar kanji at # **1177**, # **1876** and # **2045**

1878. 循 PRONUNCIATION: jun

MEANINGS: sequential, fellow **EXAMPLE:** 循環 junkan = circulation, circular movement
DESCRIPTION: compared to (矛)盾 mujun (an inconsistency, # 1750) (identical pronunciation), this kanji adds a man with two hats on the left; it retains the one-sided lean-to containing 目 (eye) attached to a thin handle which, taken together, resemble a three-drawer cabinet that contains junk **CUE:** this man with two hats keeps **Jun**k in this three-drawer cabinet with a thin handle inside this lean-to, but he plans to put some of the items back into 循環 **jun**kan (circulation) to make room for his extra hat **GROUP:** (矛)盾 mujun = an inconsistency, # 1750; 循(環) junkan = circulation, # 1878

1879. 懲 PRONUNCIATIONS: chou, ko
MEANINGS: penal, punish, discipline
EXAMPLES: 懲戒 choukai = reprimand, discipline; 懲りる koriru = to learn a lesson or get sick of, usually written こりる
DESCRIPTION: compared to (特)徴 tokuchou (characteristic, # 784) (identical pronunciation), this kanji adds 心 kokoro (heart, # 306) at the bottom; it retains the man with a double hat and the 王 (king) watching a dancer named Margaret Cho on a 山 (mountain) CUES: this 王 (king) told this man with a double hat to climb this 山 (mountain) in order to spy on this dancer named Margaret Cho, who has this Cold 心 (heart), or else face 懲戒 choukai (discipline) ALSO COMPARE: other similar kanji at # 523, # 784 and # 1385

1880. 錦 PRONUNCIATION: nishiki
MEANINGS: brocade, fine dress, honors
EXAMPLE: 錦 nishiki = brocade, fine dress
DESCRIPTION: compared to 綿 men (cotton, # 1189), this substitutes 金 kane (money, # 301) for 糸 (thread) on the left; it retains 白 (white) above 巾 (Bo Peep) CUE: this 巾 (Bo Peep) used this 金 (money) to buy a 白 (white) 錦 nishiki (brocade) dress before Kneeling in front of a Shiite King ALSO COMPARE: other similar kanji at # 1768, # 2010 and # 2014

1881. 箇 PRONUNCIATION: ka
MEANING: counters for things
EXAMPLE: 箇所 kasho = a place or point
DESCRIPTION: compared to 固(体) kotai (solid, # 731), this adds 竹 take (bamboo, # 134) at the top; it retains 古 (old) inside a 口 (box) CUE: there is a 箇所 kasho (place) in California, which I have marked with this 竹 (bamboo), where I have buried this 口 (box) of 古 (old) things ALSO COMPARE: other similar kanji at # 395 and # 2074

1882. 醜 PRONUNCIATIONS: miniku, shuu
MEANINGS: ugly, unclean, shame, bad looking EXAMPLES: 醜い minikui = ugly; 醜聞 shuubun = a scandal DESCRIPTION: on the left, 酒 sake (alcoholic beverage, # 465), without its water radical (this can also be seen as a bucket of sake with a handle); on the right, 鬼 oni (devil, # 1168) CUES: after this 鬼 (devil) drank up this 酒 (alcoholic beverage), he started eating Miniature Cookies and Shooting guns, which caused a 醜聞 shuubun (scandal) ALSO COMPARE: other similar kanji at # 1169, # 1480 and # 1678

1883. 軟 PRONUNCIATION: nan
MEANING: soft EXAMPLE: 柔軟な juunan na = flexible DESCRIPTION: on the left, 車 kuruma (car, # 283); on the right, 欠(く) kaku (to lack, # 1238), which resembles an oil derrick CUE: our Nanny's 車 (car) runs on gas derived from oil pumped by this 欠 (oil derrick), but it is 柔軟 juunan (flexible) and can also run on electricity ALSO COMPARE: other similar kanji at # 536 and # 1966

1884. 戚 PRONUNCIATION: seki
MEANING: grieve
EXAMPLE: 親戚 shinseki = a relative
DESCRIPTION: at the top, a two-sided lean-to supported on the right by a halberd (combination axe and lance); inside the lean-to, a taser on a 小 (small) hill, as seen in 寂(しい) sabishii (sad, # 864) CUE: this taser on this 小 (small) hill and this halberd that supports this lean-to have been set up to protect a Selfish King and his 親戚 shinseki (relatives)
ALSO COMPARE: other similar kanji at # 915 and # 1421

1885. 喚 PRONUNCIATIONS: kan, wame
MEANINGS: yell, cry, scream
EXAMPLES: 召喚する shoukan suru = to

summon; 喚く wameku = to yell or shriek

DESCRIPTION: compared to (交)換(する) koukan suru (to exchange, # 554) (identical pronunciation), this kanji substitutes 口 kuchi (mouth, # 426) for the kneeling guy on the left; it retains the 大 (big) general with a fish head (see # 80) and two decorations on his chest

CUES: this 大 (big) fish-headed general with two decorations on his chest, who is from **Kan**sas, opened this 口 (mouth) to 喚く **wame**ku (yell) about his **W**ar **M**emories
ALSO COMPARE: other similar kanji at # **87**, # **987** and # **2073**

1886. 紺 PRONUNCIATION: kon

MEANINGS: dark blue, navy

EXAMPLE: 紺色 kon'iro = navy blue

DESCRIPTION: on the left, 糸 (skeet shooter, # 219); on the right, 甘(い) amai (sweet, # 541), which resembles a half-full bucket

CUE: this 糸 (skeet shooter) took this half-full bucket of 紺色 **kon**iro (navy blue) paint and shot it at the walls of his **Con**dominium
ALSO COMPARE: other similar kanji at # **711**

1887. 某 PRONUNCIATIONS: nanigashi, bou

MEANINGS: so-and-so, one, that person

EXAMPLES: 某 nanigashi = so-and-so, one, that person; 某日 boujitsu = a certain day

DESCRIPTION: compared to (陰)謀 inbou (a plot, # 1544) (identical pronunciation), this kanji omits 言 (to say) on the left; it retains the bucket in a 木 (tree) containing weapons that someone was boasting about

CUES: I keep some knives in this bucket in this 木 (tree), since our **Nan**ny was **Gash**ing herself with them, but I bring them out on 某日 **bou**jitsu (certain days) to **Bo**ast about them
ALSO COMPARE: other similar kanji at # **1544**

1888. 赴 PRONUNCIATIONS: omomu, fu

MEANINGS: proceed, tend, get, become

EXAMPLES: 赴く omomuku = to go or tend toward; 赴任 funin = one's post or place of appointment

DESCRIPTION: compared to 趣 omomuki (charm, # 715), which partially helps us to pronounce this, this kanji substitutes the katakana ト to, which reminds us of toes, for 取 (to take) at the upper right; it retains 走 (to run) at the lower left **CUES:** I 赴く **omomu**ku (tend to) 走 (run) around getting stung by **O**ld **M**osquitoes on the **M**oor, which is **Fo**olish, since I often hurt my ト (toes) **ALSO COMPARE:** other similar kanji at # **450** and # **1826**

1889. 媒 PRONUNCIATION: bai

MEANINGS: mediator, go-between

EXAMPLE: 媒介 baikai = a carrier, medium or agent; mediation **DESCRIPTION:** compared to 某(日) boujitsu (a certain day, # 1887), this adds 女 onna (female, # 235) on the left; it retains the bucket of knives in a 木 (tree), about which I boast

CUE: this 女 (female) wants to **Buy** this bucket of knives in this 木 (tree), and she is looking for a 媒介 **bai**kai (agent) to help her with the transaction **ALSO COMPARE:** other kanji containing 女 on the left at # **2039**; other similar kanji at # **1544**

1890. 嫉 PRONUNCIATION: shi

MEANINGS: jealous, envy **EXAMPLE:** 嫉妬 shitto = jealousy **DESCRIPTION:** compared to 疾(患) shikkan (a disease, # 1734) (identical pronunciation), this kanji adds 女 onna (female, # 235) on the left; it retains the 矢 (Native American chief) lying in a sick bed and covered by a sheet **CUE:** this 矢 (Native American chief), who is lying in this sick bed with his **Shee**pdog, feels 嫉妬 **shi**tto (jealousy) when he sees this 女 (female) who is healthy **ALSO COMPARE:** other kanji containing 女 on the left at # **2039**; other similar kanji at # **324** and # **369**

1891. 妬 PRONUNCIATIONS: **to, neta**
MEANINGS: jealous, envy EXAMPLES: 嫉妬 shitto = jealousy; 妬む netamu = to be jealous, to envy, usually written ねたむ DESCRIPTION: on the left, 女 onna (female, # 235); on the right, 石 ishi (a stone, # 458) CUES: when this 女 (female) stubbed her **T**oe on this 石 (stone) and dropped a **N**et of **A**pples, my brother ate one, and I felt 嫉妬 shi**tto** (jealousy)

ALSO COMPARE: other kanji containing 女 on the left at # **2039**; other similar kanji at # **1775**

1892. 遮 PRONUNCIATIONS: **saegi, sha**
MEANINGS: intercept, interrupt, obstruct
EXAMPLES: 遮る saegiru = to block or interrupt; 遮断 shadan = an interruption
DESCRIPTION: compared to 庶(民) shomin (common people, # 1795), this adds a snail at the lower left; it retains the bucket of food being cooked over a fire inside a lean-to with a chimney, near the shore CUES: during a 遮断 **sha**dan (interruption) in his career, a **S**ad **E**ntertainer with a **G**uitar lived in this lean-to with a chimney while it was being transported by this snail, cooked in this pot over this fire and performed for the **Shah**, who was fond of snails ALSO COMPARE: other similar kanji at # **542** and # **611**

1893. 窯 PRONUNCIATION: **kama, gama**
MEANINGS: kiln, oven, furnace EXAMPLES: 窯 kama = an oven, furnace or kiln; 炭窯 sumigama = a charcoal kiln DESCRIPTION: at the top, a soaring bird, as seen in (研)究 kenkyuu (research, # 112); in the middle, 王 ou (king, # 1077), wearing rabbit ears [this part of the kanji can also be seen as a truncated 羊 hitsuji (sheep, # 1223), missing its tail]; at the bottom, a fire, as seen in 熱(い) atsui (hot objects, # 65)
CUES: Karl Ma**r**x built a 窯 **kama** (oven) in which he baked soaring birds and truncated 羊 (sheep) like these over fires like this, after sterilizing them with **G**amma rays GROUP: 着(る) kiru = to wear

clothes, # 52; 様(子) yousu = condition, # 136; (会)議 kaigi = meeting, # 438; 差(し上げる) sashiageru = to give humbly, # 631; 羨(ましい) urayamashii = envious, # 662; 美(しい) utsukushii = beautiful, # 771; 義(理) giri = moral debt, # 1028; (栄)養 eiyou = nutrition, # 1264; (礼)儀 reigi = civility, # 1541; 犠(牲) gisei = a victim, # 1764; 窯 kama = an oven, # 1893 ALSO COMPARE: other similar kanji at # **112** and # **611**

1894. 茎 PRONUNCIATIONS: **kuki, guki², kei** MEANINGS: stalk, stem
EXAMPLES: 茎 kuki = a stalk or stem; 歯茎 haguki = the gums (mouth); 陰茎 inkei = a penis DESCRIPTION: at the top, a plant radical; in the middle, 又 mata (again, # 24), which resembles a simple table; at the bottom, 土 tsuchi (soil, # 59)
CUES: I keep my **C**ookies and **C**ake on this 又 (table), where they are shaded by the 茎 **kuki** (stalks) of this plant above and protected from this 土 (soil) below GROUP: 経(験) keiken = experience, # 224 (identical pronunciation); 軽(い) karui = light, # 289; 怪(しい) ayashii = suspicious, # 1024; (半)径 hankei = radius, # 1097 (also identical pronunciation); 堅(い) katai = hard, # 1246; 茎 kuki = a stalk, # 1894

1895. 隻 PRONUNCIATION: **seki**
MEANINGS: one of a pair, counter for ships
EXAMPLE: 数隻の船 suuseki no fune = several boats DESCRIPTION: compared to (看)護(婦) kangofu (nurse, # 1163), this omits 言 (to speak) on the left and the plant radical at the top; it retains the net, which can be seen as a man with a slanted hat next to a 主 (master) with an extra pair of arms (see # 203), on the 又 (table)
CUE: a **S**elfish **K**ing stores fishing nets like this on 又 (tables) like this on 数隻の船 suu**seki** no fune (several boats) that he owns ALSO COMPARE: other similar kanji at # **947**

1896. 釜 PRONUNCIATION: kama
MEANINGS: kettle, cauldron, iron pot
EXAMPLE: 釜 kama = a pot in which rice is cooked DESCRIPTION: at the top, 父 chichi (father, # 143); at the bottom, this can be seen as the lower portion of 金 kane (money, # 301), without its peaked roof CUE: Karl Marx was this 父 (father) who spent this modified 金 (money) to buy a 釜 **kama** (pot for cooking rice)
ALSO COMPARE: other similar kanji at # **143** and # **2010**

1897. 墳 PRONUNCIATION: fun
MEANINGS: tomb, mound EXAMPLE: 古墳 kofun = an ancient tomb or burial mound
DESCRIPTION: compared to 噴(水) funsui (water fountain, # 1268) (identical pronunciation), this kanji substitutes 土 tsuchi (soil, # 59) for the 口 (mouth) on the left; it retains the triple plant radical, which can also be seen as bushes, and the 貝 (money chest) that got wet in a way that we thought was funny
CUE: we found a 古墳 ko**fun** (ancient tomb) containing a 貝 (money chest) like this and some **Fun**ny carvings, which were located under this 土 (soil) and these bushes
GROUP: 噴(水) funsui = water fountain, # 1268; 憤(る) ikidooru = to resent, # 1781; (古)墳 kofun = an ancient tomb, # 1897
ALSO COMPARE: other similar kanji at # **1268**

1898. 壌 PRONUNCIATION: jou
MEANINGS: lot, earth, soil EXAMPLE: 土壌 dojou = soil, breeding ground DESCRIPTION: compared to (豊)穣 houjou (good harvest, # 1322) (identical pronunciation), this kanji substitutes 土 tsuchi (soil) for the 禾 (ripe grain plant) on the left; it retains the 六 (six) 井 (wells) plus some 衣 (clothing) for Joan of Arc
CUE: **Jo**an of Arc grew up on a farm with 六 (six) 井 (wells) like this, which was a 土壌 do**jou** (breeding ground) for animals and where this 衣 (clothing) often got covered in this 土 (soil)
ALSO COMPARE: other similar kanji at # **1322**

1899. 尼 PRONUNCIATIONS: ni, ama
MEANINGS: nun EXAMPLES: 尼僧 nisou = a nun or priestess; 尼 ama = a nun
DESCRIPTION: compared to 泥(棒) dorobou (thief, # 819), this omits the water radical on the left; it retains the lean-to with a double roof and the katakana character ヒ hi, which could represent a hero CUES: my **Ni**ece is this ヒ (hero) who lived in this lean-to with a double roof in the **Am**azon and decided to become a 尼 **ama** (nun) and serve the poor GROUP: 昼 hiru = noon, # 49; (部)屋 heya = room, # 63; 届(ける) todokeru = to deliver, # 74; 遅(い) osoi = late, # 350; (市)民 shimin = citizen, # 375; 眠(る) nemuru = to sleep, # 376; 漏(水) rousui = water leak, # 740; (住)居 juukyo = dwelling, # 809; 泥(棒) dorobou = thief, # 819; (お)尻 oshiri = buttocks, # 827; (結)局 kekkyoku = after all, # 867; (理)屈 rikutsu = argument, # 927; (宮)殿 kyuuden = palace, # 1080; 履(く) haku = to wear shoes, # 1220; (断)層 dansou = discrepancy, # 1250; (金)属 kinzoku = metal, # 1296; 尿 nyou = urine, # 1298; (発)展 hatten = development, # 1346; 嘱(託) shokutaku = commission, # 1366; 握(る) nigiru = to grasp, # 1372; (印)刷 insatsu = printing, # 1392; 掘(る) horu = to dig, # 1402; 堀 hori = a canal, # 1539; 据(える) sueru = to set up, # 1719; (中)尉 chuui = a first lieutenant, # 1751; 慰(める) nagusameru = to console, # 1752; 裾 suso = a hem, # 1796; 塀 hei = a fence, # 1850; 尼 ama = a nun, # 1899; (洞)窟 doukutsu = a cave, # 1920 ALSO COMPARE: other kanji containing a lean-to with a double roof at # 1484; kanji containing snow above a double-roof

lean-to at # 1134; other kanji containing ヒ at # **2048**

1900. 肢 PRONUNCIATION: shi
MEANINGS: limb, arms and legs **EXAMPLE:** 下肢 kashi = a leg **DESCRIPTION:** compared to 支(社) shisha (branch office, # 26) (identical pronunciation), this kanji adds 月 tsuki (moon, # 148) on the left; it retains the 士 (man) standing on a 又 (table) covered by a sheet **CUE:** this 士 (man) put a **Sh**eet over this 又 (table) and climbed on it in order to admire this 月 (moon), but the sheet slipped, and he broke his 下肢 ka**shi** (leg) **ALSO COMPARE:** other similar kanji at # **1121**

1901. 赦 PRONUNCIATION: sha
MEANINGS: pardon, forgiveness **EXAMPLE:** 容赦 yousha = pardon, forgiveness **DESCRIPTION:** compared to 赤(い) akai (red, # 447), which consists of 土 (soil) above four legs, this adds a dancer with a ponytail on the right **CUE:** this dancer with a ponytail broke a dish, and then she had a face that was 赤 (red) like this, but the **Sh**ah granted her 容赦 you**sha** (forgiveness) **ALSO COMPARE:** other similar kanji at # **447**

1902. 酬 PRONUNCIATION: shuu
MEANINGS: repay, reward, retribution **EXAMPLES:** 報酬 houshuu = a reward or remuneration **DESCRIPTION:** compared to (本)州 honshuu (Honshu Island, # 1071) (identical pronunciation), this kanji adds 酒 sake (alcoholic beverage, # 465), without its water radical, on the left (this can also be seen as a bucket of sake with a handle); it retains the three toboggans lined up in a chute **CUE:** after drinking some of this 酒 (alcohol), a guy rode these three toboggans down a **Ch**ute and received a 報酬 hou**shuu** (reward) **ALSO COMPARE:** other similar kanji at # **1071** and # **1480**

1903. 宜 PRONUNCIATION: gi, yoro
MEANINGS: best regards, good **EXAMPLES:** 便宜 bengi = convenience, assistance; 宜しい yoroshii = good, usually written よろしい **DESCRIPTION:** compared to (調)査 chousa (investigation, # 860), this substitutes a bad haircut for the 木 (tree) at the top; it retains the solar panel **CUE:** a **G**eek (unfashionable or eccentric person) from **Yo**rope (Europe) put this bad haircut on top of this solar panel for 便宜 ben**gi** (convenience), and also due to his poor fashion sense **ALSO COMPARE:** other similar kanji at # **752**

1904. 殻 PRONUNCIATION: kara
MEANINGS: husk, nut, shell **EXAMPLE:** 殻 kara = a shell or crust **DESCRIPTION:** compared to 穀(物) kokumotsu (grain, # 1172), this substitutes π (the Greek letter pi, which we have described as a pious yak), for 禾 (the grain plant with a ripe head) at the lower left; it retains, at the upper left, 士 (man) standing high on a roof and, on the right, another π, standing on a 又 (table) **CUE:** this 士 (man) stands high on this roof eating nuts and throwing the 殻 **kara** (shells) onto these two π (yaks), including the one on this 又 (table), but that's just his **Cara**cter **ALSO COMPARE:** other similar kanji at # **557** and # **1468**

1905. 碑 PRONUNCIATION: hi
MEANINGS: tombstone, monument **EXAMPLE:** 墓碑 bohi = a gravestone or tombstone **DESCRIPTION:** compared to 卑(屈) hikutsu (servile, # 1745) (identical pronunciation), this kanji adds 石 ishi (stone, # 458) on the left; it retains 由 (reason), and the 十 (ten) guys with earphones above their left shoulders who are at risk for hearing loss **CUE:** 十 (ten) guys carried earphones like this above their left shoulders which was the 由 (reason) they developed 石 (stones) like this in their ears and lost their

Hearing, and when they died, their graves were marked with 墓碑 bo**hi** (gravestones)
ALSO COMPARE: other similar kanji at # **942**, # **1658** and # **1775**

1906. 奨 PRONUNCIATION: shou

MEANINGS: exhort, urge, encourage
EXAMPLE: 奨励 **shou**rei = encouragement or promotion **DESCRIPTION:** compared to 将(来) shourai (the future, # 374) (identical pronunciation), this kanji adds 大(きい) ookii (big, # 188) at the bottom; it retains the vertical bench at the upper left and the barbecue grate, plus the 寸 (kneeling sunny guy who has dropped his gum), who wants to show us life as it will be in the future, at the upper right **CUE:** this 寸 (kneeling sunny guy) at the middle right wants to **Sh**ow us life as it will be for workers in the 将 (future), when they will have barbecue grates and benches like this, and he gets 奨励 **shou**rei (encouragement) from the support of this 大 (big) guy
ALSO COMPARE: other similar kanji at # **131**, # **998** and # **1177**

1907. 践 PRONUNCIATION: sen

MEANINGS: tread, step on, practice
EXAMPLE: 実践 ji**ssen** = implementation, practice **DESCRIPTION:** compared to (金)銭 kinsen (money, # 744) (identical pronunciation), this kanji substitutes a 止 (hesitant) squarehead, as seen in (道)路 douro (road, # 525), for 金 (gold) on the left; it retains the triple-grip halberd which a senator thought he wouldn't need to attain enlightenment **CUE:** our **Sen**ator is this 止 (hesitant) squarehead on the left, but he voted for the 実践 ji**ssen** (implementation) of a law that would allow all citizens to use triple-grip halberds like this for self-defense ALSO COMPARE: other similar kanji at # **605** and # **1534**

1908. 滋 PRONUNCIATIONS: ji, shi

MEANINGS: nourishing, be luxuriant
EXAMPLES: 滋養 **ji**you = nourishment, nutrition; 滋賀県 **shi**ga ken = Shiga Prefecture
DESCRIPTION: compared to 磁(石) jishaku (magnet, # 1236) (identical pronunciation), this kanji substitutes a water radical, which reminds us of a flood, for 石 (stone) on the left; it retains the two truncated 糸 (skeet shooters), each consisting of two flexed elbows, who were carrying an upside-down bench to their Jeep and discovered a magnet **CUES:** these two truncated 糸 (skeet shooters) are carrying this upside-down bench to their **J**eep, which they will drive away from this flood which has damaged their **Sh**eep food, and now they are worried about the 滋養 **ji**you (nutrition) of their herd
GROUP: 機(械) kikai = machine, # 137; 磁(石) jishaku = magnet, # 1236; 慈(善) jizen = charity, # 1451 (also identical pronunciation); 幽(閉する) yuuhei suru = to confine, # 1574; 幾(何学) kikagaku = geometry, # 1628; 滋(養) jiyou = nutrition, # 1908 ALSO COMPARE: kanji containing *one* truncated skeet shooter at # 1129; other similar kanji at # **1236**

1909. 儒 PRONUNCIATION: ju

MEANING: Confucian
EXAMPLE: 儒教 **ju**kyou = Confucianism
DESCRIPTION: compared to 需(要) juyou (a demand, # 1699) (identical pronunciation), this kanji adds a man with a slanted hat on the left; it retains 雨 (rain) above a limousine antenna mounted on a book shelf, which reminds us that, if rain is affecting our TV reception, we can drink juice **CUE:** this man on the left finds that this 雨 (rain) affects the reception of this TV limousine antenna, but he lives in harmony with nature in accordance with 儒教 **ju**kyou (Confucianism), so he tilts his hat back to examine the situation and decides to make **J**uice, which he can make from rain water, instead of watching television
ALSO COMPARE: other similar kanji at # **262** and # **522**

1910. 怨 PRONUNCIATION: on
MEANINGS: grudge, show resentment
EXAMPLES: 怨念 onnen = a grudge, malice, hatred DESCRIPTION: compared to 宛(先) atesaki (an address, # 1822); this omits the bad haircut at the top and adds 心 kokoro (heart, # 306) at the bottom; it retains 夕 (evening) and the uncoiling snake CUE: this pet snake went out in the 夕 (evening) with this 心 (heart) full of 怨 **on**nen (hatred) and attacked its **Ow**ner ALSO COMPARE: other similar kanji at # **547** and # **801**

1911. 曇 PRONUNCIATION: kumo
MEANINGS: cloudy weather, cloud up
EXAMPLE: 曇る kumoru = to become cloudy, to be in a gloomy mood DESCRIPTION: compared to 雲 kumo (cloud, # 264) (identical pronunciation), this kanji adds 日 hi (sun, # 32) at the top; it retains the 二 (two) ム (cows) belonging to Governor Cuomo, under some 雨 (rain) CUE: when Governor **Cu**omo saw this 日 (sun) peaking above this 雲 (cloud), he hoped that it would 曇る **kumo**ru (become cloudy) again ALSO COMPARE: other similar kanji at # **262** and # **1056**

1912. 刈 PRONUNCIATION: ka
MEANINGS: reap, cut, clip, trim, prune
EXAMPLE: 刈る karu = to reap or mow, to cut hair DESCRIPTION: on the left, an X, which suggests negation; on the right, the katakana リ Ri, which is sometimes described as a knife
CUES: this リ Ri felt this X (negation) after a barber 刈る **ka**ru (cut) the hair of his **Ca**t and did a poor job
COMPARE: similar kanji at # **1953** and # **1985**

1913. 閑 PRONUNCIATION: kan
MEANING: leisure EXAMPLE: 閑静な kansei na = quiet (neighborhood) DESCRIPTION: on the left and right, 門 mon (gate, # 409); inside the gate, 木 ki (tree, # 118) CUE: a certain town in **Kan**sas is so 閑静 **kan**sei (quiet) that this 木 (tree) has grown up inside this 門 (gate)
ALSO COMPARE: other similar kanji at # **1755**

1914. 錠 PRONUNCIATION: jou
MEANINGS: lock, fetters, shackles
EXAMPLES: 錠剤 jouzai = a tablet or pill; 錠前 joumae = a lock DESCRIPTION: compared to (勘)定 kanjou (a bill, # 455) (identical pronunciation), this kanji adds 金 kane (money, # 301) on the left; it retains the bad haircut above a taser mounted on a foot, which was used by Joan of Arc CUE: **Jo**an of Arc installed this taser under this bad haircut and on this foot before robbing people of 金 (money) like this in order to buy some 錠剤 **jou**zai (pills) for her mother
ALSO COMPARE: other similar kanji at # **913** and # **2010**

1915. 扶 PRONUNCIATION: fu
MEANINGS: aid, help, assist
EXAMPLE: 扶養 fuyou = support, raising (of children) DESCRIPTION: compared to 夫 otto (husband, # 614), or (水)夫 suifu (sailor, # 614) (identical pronunciation), this kanji adds a kneeling guy on the left; it retains the 人 (person) with two pairs of arms who foolishly ran around
CUE: this guy on the left kneels to plead with this 夫 (husband), saying "You are **Fo**olish to refuse to pay child 扶養 **fu**you (support)"
GROUP: 替(える) kaeru = to replace, # 551; 夫 otto = husband, # 614; 鶏 niwatori = chicken, # 754; 贊(成) sansei = agreement, # 1115; 規(則) kisoku = rules, # 1341; 渓(谷) keikoku = valley, # 1384; 潜(水) sensui = diving, # 1586; 扶(養) fuyou = support, # 1915

1916. 妥 PRONUNCIATION: da
MEANINGS: gentle, peace, depravity
EXAMPLE: 妥協 dakyou = a compromise
DESCRIPTION: at the top, a barbecue grate; at the bottom, 女 onna (female, # 235)

CUE: my **Da**ughter, who is this 女 (female), is carrying this barbecue grate which I bought her as a 妥協 **da**kyou (compromise), since she wanted a stove **ALSO COMPARE:** other similar kanji at # **1177** and # **2086**

1917. 妨 PRONUNCIATIONS: **sama**ta, **bou** MEANINGS: disturb, prevent, hamper, obstruct **EXAMPLES:** 妨げる **sama**tageru = to hinder or obstruct; 妨害 **bou**gai = an interference, disturbance, intrusion or obstacle **DESCRIPTION:** compared to (予)防 yobou (prevention, # 920) (identical pronunciation), this kanji substitutes 女 onna (female, # 235) for ß (Greek) on the left; it retains 方 (honorable person) **CUES:** this 女 (female) tried to be a **G**ood **Sama**ritan by **T**alking to this 方 (honorable person), but he was **B**oring and 妨げた **sama**tageta (obstructed) her work **ALSO COMPARE:** other kanji containing 女 on the left at # **2039**; other similar kanji at # **920**

1918. 醒 PRONUNCIATION: **sei**
MEANINGS: awake, be disillusioned, sober up **EXAMPLE:** 覚醒 kaku**sei** = waking up, disillusionment **DESCRIPTION:** compared to 星 hoshi (star, # 48), or 星(座) seiza (constellation, # 48) (identical pronunciation), this kanji adds 酒 sake (alcoholic beverage, # 465), without its water radical, on the left (this can also be seen as a bucket of sake with a handle); it retains 日 (sun) and 生 (to live, # 208) [or (先)生 sensei (teacher, # 208) (also identical pronunciation)] **CUE:** a **Sai**lor who was watching 星 (stars) like this and drinking this 酒 (sake) experienced a 覚醒 kaku**sei** (waking up) **GROUP:** 星(座) seiza = constellation, # 48; (人)生 jinsei = human life, # 208; 性 sei = gender, # 209; 産(業) sangyou = industry, # 210; 姓(名) seimei = a full name, # 1499; (興)隆 kouryuu = prosperity, 1594; (犠)牲 gisei = a victim, # 1765; (覚)醒 kakusei = waking up, # 1918; Note that six of these kanji can be pronounced "sei" **ALSO COMPARE:** other similar kanji at # **1480**

1919. 胎 PRONUNCIATION: **tai**
MEANINGS: womb, uterus **EXAMPLE:** 胎児 **tai**ji = a fetus **DESCRIPTION:** compared to 台(風) taifuu (typhoon, # 538) (identical pronunciation), this kanji adds 月 tsuki (moon, # 148) on the left; it retains the tired 厶 (cow) on a box **CUE:** this 厶 (cow) lies on this 口 (box) under this 月 (moon), waiting for a 胎児 **tai**ji (fetus) to be born, and it's **Ti**red **ALSO COMPARE:** other similar kanji at # **538**

1920. 窟 PRONUNCIATION: **kutsu**
MEANING: cavern **EXAMPLE:** 洞窟 dou**kutsu** = a cave or grotto **DESCRIPTION:** compared to (理)屈 rikutsu (argument, # 927) (identical pronunciation), this kanji adds a soaring Cuban bird with two lopsided legs, as seen in (研)究 kenkyuu (research, # 112), at the top; it retains the cooped-up Superman, whom we must avoid cutting, under a double-roofed lean-to **CUE:** this soaring **Cu**ban bird with two lopsided legs landed on this double-roofed lean-to in a 洞窟 dou**kutsu** (cave) where Superman was cooped up and **Cut** Superman with its talons **ALSO COMPARE:** other similar kanji at # **112**, # **927** and # **1899**

1921. 巾 PRONUNCIATION: **kin**
MEANINGS: towel, hanging scroll, turban **EXAMPLE:** 雑巾 zou**kin** = a dust cloth or cleaning cloth **DESCRIPTION:** this is Bo Peep, as seen in 帽(子) boushi (hat, # 243), who resembles a spinning lady with wide hips **CUE:** when this Bo Peep was in **Kin**dergarten, she learned to clean her classroom with a 雑巾 zou**kin** (dust cloth) **ALSO COMPARE:** other similar kanji at # **1768**

1922. 忌 PRONUNCIATION: ki
MEANINGS: mourning, abhor, death anniversary
EXAMPLE: 一周忌 isshuuki = the first anniversary of a death DESCRIPTION: compared to 記(事) kiji (newspaper article, # 550) (identical pronunciation), this kanji omits 言 (to say) on the left and adds 心 kokoro (heart, # 306) at the bottom; it retains the 己 (snake shaped like a backwards "S") that killed Jimmy Carter
CUE: after this 己 (snake) **K**illed a person, my 心 (heart) was sad, and I visited the grave on the 一周忌 isshuu**ki** (first anniversary of the death)
ALSO COMPARE: other similar kanji at # **1078**

1923. 骸 PRONUNCIATIONS: gai, *gara*
MEANINGS: bone, body, corpse
EXAMPLES: 骸骨 gaikotsu = a skeleton; 亡骸 nakigara = a corpse DESCRIPTION: compared to 骨 hone (bone, # 832), this adds the skeleton of a boar, as seen in 刻(む) kizamu (to cut, # 565), on the right; it retains the floor plan of an apartment, on a base, above a 月 (moon)
CUES: I work as a **Gui**de for hunters, and when I came across a 骸骨 **gai**kotsu (skeleton) of a boar like this, I brought it back to this roof-top apartment on this 月 (moon), and later I stored it downstairs in the **Gara**ge ALSO COMPARE: other similar kanji at # **832** and # **1548**

1924. 弄 PRONUNCIATION: rou
MEANINGS: play with, tamper, trifle with
EXAMPLE: 翻弄する honrou suru = to play with or trifle with, to toss about (a ship)
DESCRIPTION: at the top, 王 ou (king, # 1077); at the bottom, legs with a welcoming or open stance, as seen in 葬(る) houmuru (to bury, # 1273), which resemble the letter H and remind us of Homer
CUE: when this 王 (king) was traveling down a **R**oad, he encountered this H (person with a welcoming stance), and the king 翻弄した hon**rou** shita (trifled with) him
GROUP: (機)械 kikai = machine, # 138;

算(数) sansuu = arithmetic, # 789; 鼻 hana = nose, # 795; 戒(める) imashimeru = to admonish, # 875; 弁(護士) bengoshi = lawyer, # 1162; 葬(式) soushiki = funeral, # 1273; 奔(放) honpou = unrestrained, # 1864; (翻)弄(する) honrou suru = to trifle with, # 1924; 弊(社) heisha = our company, # 2005 ALSO COMPARE: other kanji with towers that can be seen as welcoming stances at # 573; other similar kanji at # **1712**

1925. 粛 PRONUNCIATION: shuku
MEANINGS: solemn, quietly, softly
EXAMPLE: 自粛 jishuku = self-restraint, self-discipline DESCRIPTION: at the top, a trident perforating a vertical rod, as seen in (法)律 houritsu (law, # 417), which can be seen as a chimney; at the bottom, a two-sided container which could be a house, containing 米 kome (uncooked rice, # 326) CUE: when someone used this trident to stab the chimney of this house, I exercised 自粛 ji**shuku** (self-restraint) and took a moment to put on my **Sh**oes from **Ku**wait before running away with this 米 (uncooked rice) ALSO COMPARE: other similar kanji at # **1387** and # **1494**

1926. 囚 PRONUNCIATION: shuu
MEANINGS: captured, criminal, arrest, catch
EXAMPLES: 囚人 shuujin = a prisoner
DESCRIPTION: compared to (原)因 gen'in (cause, # 1360), this substitutes 人 hito (person, # 13) for 大 (big) inside the 口 box
CUE: this 人 (person) is hiding in this 口 (box) because he thinks that the police want to **Sh**oot him, or at least make him a 囚人 **shuu**jin (prisoner)
GROUP: 人 hito = person, # 13; 卒(業) sotsugyou = graduation, # 27; 機(械) kikai = machine, # 137; 座(る) suwaru = to sit, # 497; 葛 kuzu = arrowroot, # 1531; 幾(何学) kikagaku = geometry, # 1628; 傘 kasa = an umbrella, # 1743; 脊(椎) sekitsui = the spine, # 1867; 挫(折) zasetsu = a failure, # 1976;

囚(人) shuujin = a prisoner, # 1926 **ALSO COMPARE:** other similar kanji at # **1360**

1927. 罵 PRONUNCIATIONS: nonoshi, ba MEANINGS: abuse, insult EXAMPLE:
罵る nonoshiru = to revile, abuse or swear at, usually written ののしる; 罵倒する batou suru = to abuse or yell at **DESCRIPTION:** compared to 馬 uma (horse, # 958), or 馬(鹿) baka (a stupid person, # 958) (identical pronunciation), this kanji adds three eyes at the top **CUES:** although the person who owns these three eyes has special visual powers, he takes **No No**tice of **S**heep farmers when he rides this 馬 (horse), thinking that they are **Ba**d and, if he's forced to acknowledge them, he 罵倒する **ba**tou suru (abuses) them **ALSO COMPARE:** other similar kanji at # **826** and # **1324**

1928. 渇 PRONUNCIATION: kawa
MEANINGS: thirst, dry up, parch
EXAMPLE: 渇く kawaku = to be thirsty, usually used in the form 喉が渇く nodo ga kawaku (literally, "the throat gets thirsty")
DESCRIPTION: compared to 掲(げる) kakageru (to put up, # 1466), this substitutes a water radical for the kneeling guy on the left; it retains 日 (sun), which resembles a two-drawer cabinet, above 匂(い) nioi (fragrance, # 949), suggesting a cabinet full of fragrant cake built by a carpenter **CUE:** after building this 日 (two-drawer cabinet) to hold 匂 (fragrant) cake, a **C**arpenter drank this **W**ater because 喉が渇いた nodo ga **kawa**ita (he got thirsty)
ALSO COMPARE: 乾く kawaku = to get dry, # 290; other similar kanji at # **1466** and # **2048**

1929. 肯 PRONUNCIATION: kou
MEANINGS: agreement, consent, comply with
EXAMPLES: 肯定する koutei suru = to affirm, answer positively or admit
DESCRIPTION: at the top, 止(める) tomeru (to stop, # 173); this can be seen as containing a taser, as seen in 点(く) tsuku (to ignite, # 29); at the bottom, 月 tsuki (moon, # 148) **CUE:** this 止 (stop) sign on this 月 (moon) is telling **C**orporations to stop ruining the climate here on Earth, and they should 肯定する **kou**tei suru (answer affirmatively) **GROUP:** 止(める) tomeru = to stop, # 173; 歳 sai = age, # 322; 歩(く) aruku = to walk, # 408; 歯 ha = tooth, # 533; (年)齢 nenrei = age, # 989; (福)祉 fukushi = welfare, # 1066; 頻(繁) hinpan = frequent, # 1265; (干)渉 kanshou = interference, # 1307; 歴(史) rekishi = history, # 1313; 企(画) kikaku = project, # 1382; 武(器) buki = weapon, # 1418; 渋(滞) juutai = gridlock, 1454; 紫 murasaki = purple, # 1665; 疎(か) orosoka = neglect, # 1806; 肯(定する) koutei suru = to affirm, # 1929; 雌 mesu = a female, # 2031; (月)賦 geppu = a monthly installment, # 2058 **ALSO COMPARE:** other similar kanji at # **2087**

1930. 燥 PRONUNCIATION: sou
MEANINGS: parch, dry up
EXAMPLE: 乾燥 kansou = dryness
DESCRIPTION: compared to 操(作) sousa (operation of a machine, # 1192) (identical pronunciation), this kanji substitutes 火 hi (fire, # 443) for the kneeling guy on the left; it retains the 品 (three packages of Kool-Aid) stuck in a 木 (tree), which a soldier is trying to dislodge **CUE:** as a **So**ldier works to dislodge these 品 (three packages of Kool-Aid) from this 木 (tree), he feels the 乾燥 kan**sou** (dryness) caused by this nearby 火 (fire) **ALSO COMPARE:** other similar kanji at # **1034**, # **1216** and # **1239**

1931. 搭 PRONUNCIATION: tou
MEANINGS: board, load (a vehicle), ride
EXAMPLE: 搭乗 toujou = boarding (a ship or plane) **DESCRIPTION:** compared to 塔 tou (tower, # 1251) (identical pronunciation), this kanji substitutes a kneeling guy for 土 (soil) on the left; it retains 合(う) au (to match, # 294), resembling a house with a ceiling and a peaked roof, where some toads live, plus some sheltering plants above **CUES:** this guy is kneeling as he removes the **Toads** from this house with a ceiling and a peaked roof, which is sheltered by plants that 合 (match) their needs, before he 搭乗する **tou**jou suru (boards) a ship taking them to their new home **ALSO COMPARE:** other similar kanji at # **1251**

1932. 諭 PRONUNCIATIONS: sato, satoshi
MEANINGS: rebuke, admonish, warn
EXAMPLE: 諭す satosu = to warn or advise; 諭 is one of several ways to write the common Japanese given name "Satoshi" (used for males)
DESCRIPTION: compared to 輸(入する) yu'nyuu suru (to import, # 288), this substitutes 言(う) iu (to speak, # 430) for 車 (car) on the left; it retains the house to which I moved, after living in another one 前 (before)
CUE: in this house where I lived 前 (before), I often 言 (spoke) to my children to 諭す **sato**su (warn) them against climbing **S**atellite **T**owers and feeding **S**alt to **T**olstoy's **S**heep **ALSO COMPARE:** other similar kanji at # **733**

1933. 璧 PRONUNCIATION: peki
MEANINGS: sphere, ball **EXAMPLE:** 完璧 な kanpeki na = perfect, complete, flawless
DESCRIPTION: compared to 壁 kabe (wall, # 1051), or (絶)壁 zeppeki (cliff, # 1051) (identical pronunciation), this kanji substitutes 玉 tama (ball, # 169) for 土 (soil) at the bottom; it retains the lean-to with a double roof, the 口 (box) and the 辛 (needle) (LBN = lean-to, box, needle) which are components of a castle wall that is being built to replace one that was damaged by pecking **CUE:** this lean-to, this 口 (box) and this 辛 (needle) are needed to replace a castle 壁 (wall), which was 完璧 kan**peki** (perfect) until it was damaged by **P**ecking and by this 玉 (ball) that the children were throwing against it (LBN = lean-to, box, needle) **ALSO COMPARE:** other similar kanji at # **170** and # **1214**

1934. 喝 PRONUNCIATIONS: ka, katsu
MEANINGS: hoarse, scold **EXAMPLES:** 喝采 kassai = applause; 恐喝 kyoukatsu = blackmail or extortion **DESCRIPTION:** compared to 掲(げる) kakageru (to put up, # 1466), this substitutes 口 kuchi (mouth, # 426), which can also be seen as a box, for the kneeling guy on the left; it retains the 日 (two-drawer cabinet) full of 匂 (fragrant) cake which was built by a carpenter
CUES: this 日 (two-drawer cabinet), which a **C**arpenter built, is full of 匂 (fragrant) sweets, and he tasted them with this 口 (mouth) before breaking into 喝采 **ka**ssai (applause), which startled his **C**ats **ALSO COMPARE:** other similar kanji at # **1466**, # **2048** and # **2073**

1935. 采 PRONUNCIATION: sai
MEANINGS: dice, form, take, coloring
EXAMPLE: 風采 fuusai = personal appearance or presence **DESCRIPTION:** compared to 採(算) saisan (surplus, # 1425) (identical pronunciation), this kanji omits the kneeling guy on the left; it retains the 木 (tree) in Saigon with a barbecue grate at the top
CUE: the guy who installed this barbecue grate at the top of this 木 (tree) in **S**aigon has a bizarre 風采 fuu**sai** (personal appearance) **GROUP:** (野)菜 yasai = vegetable, # 121; 採(算) saisan = surplus, # 1425; (色)彩 shikisai = color, # 1630; (風)采 fuusai = personal appearance, # 1935

1936. 騰 PRONUNCIATION: tou
MEANINGS: inflation, advancing, going
EXAMPLE: 沸騰する futtou suru = to boil
DESCRIPTION: compared to (優)勝 yuushou (victory, # 149), this substitutes 馬 uma (horse, # 958) for 力 (force) at the lower right; it retains the 月 (moon) on the left and the bonfire at the upper right, which consists of 二 (two) inscribed on 人 (person), plus flames CUE: under the light of this 月 (moon), **To**lstoy rode this 馬 (horse) up to this bonfire, placed a pot of water and waited for it to fut**tou** suru 沸騰する (boil) ALSO COMPARE: other similar kanji at # **826** and # **1305**

1937. 篤 PRONUNCIATION: toku
MEANINGS: fervent, kind, serious, deliberate
EXAMPLE: 危篤 kitoku = critical condition (health) DESCRIPTION: at the top, 竹 take (bamboo, # 134); at the bottom, 馬 uma (horse, # 958) CUE: riding a 馬 (horse) like this into a thicket of 竹 (bamboo) like this seems **T**otally **C**ool, but sometimes people who do so end up in 危篤 ki**toku** (critical condition) ALSO COMPARE: other similar kanji at # **826** and # **2074**

1938. 勲 PRONUNCIATION: kun
MEANINGS: meritorious deed, merit
EXAMPLE: 勲章 kunshou = a medal or decoration DESCRIPTION: compared to 動(く) ugoku (to move, # 286), this adds a fire, as seen in 熱(い) atsui (hot objects, # 65), at the bottom; it retains 重 (heavy) and 力 (force)
CUE: a **Kun**g fu master 動 (moved) a 重 (heavy) victim away from this fire using 力 (force) like this, and he received a 勲章 **kun**shou (medal)
ALSO COMPARE: other similar kanji at # **284**, # **611** and # **1846**

1939. 埼 PRONUNCIATION: sai
MEANINGS: cape, spit, promontory
EXAMPLE: 埼玉 Saitama = a city just north of Tokyo DESCRIPTION: compared to (川)崎 Kawasaki (# 1081), this substitutes 土 tsuchi (soil, # 59) for 山 (mountain) on the left; it retains 奇(妙) kimyou (strange, # 854) on the right, which reminds us of a 可 (cute) person wearing a kimono that is too 大 (big)
CUE: a Psychiatrist in 埼玉 **Sai**tama rolled in this 土 (soil) and acted 奇 (strange)
ALSO COMPARE: other similar kanji at # **604**

1940. 曖 PRONUNCIATION: ai
MEANINGS: dark, not clear EXAMPLE: 曖昧な aimai na = ambiguous, vague, unsure
DESCRIPTION: compared to 愛(情) aijou (love, # 523) (identical pronunciation), this kanji adds 日 hi (sun, # 32) on the left; it retains the barbecue grate on a rack, 心 (heart) and the ice dancer with a ponytail CUE: this dancer with a ponytail is an **I**ce dancer with this big 心 (heart) who barbecues on this grate, but she is 曖昧 **ai**mai (unsure) whether this 日 (sun) might cause the ice in her rink to melt
ALSO COMPARE: 暖(かい) atatakai = warm, # 38, which substitutes 友 (friend) for 心 (heart) and the ice dancer at the lower right; other similar kanji at # **523** and # **1177**

1941. 昧 PRONUNCIATION: mai

MEANINGS: dark, foolish **EXAMPLE:** 曖昧 な aimai na = ambiguous, vague, unsure **DESCRIPTION:** compared to 未(来) mirai (future, # 672), this adds 日 hi (sun, # 32) on the left; it retains the 未 (tree with two pairs of branches, with the longer branch at the bottom) **CUE:** as he stood in this 日 (sun) while pondering this 未 (future), Michael Jackson felt an 曖昧 ai**mai** (vague) unease **ALSO COMPARE:** 味 aji = taste. # 245; other similar kanji at # **672**

1942. 岬 PRONUNCIATION: misaki

MEANINGS: headland, cape, promontory **EXAMPLE:** 岬 misaki = a cape or promontory **DESCRIPTION:** on the left, 山 yama (mountain, # 146); on the right, 甲(羅) koura (shell, # 1157), which resembles a shaky sign used to break coconuts and can be seen as a rice paddy on a stick **CUE:** after injuring his ankle, a **Mi**serable **A**chi**l**les got a job standing by a road leading to this 山 (mountain), holding this 甲 (shaky sign) with directions to a nearby 岬 **misaki** (cape) **GROUP:** 山 yama = mountain, # 146; 峰 mine = mountain peak, # 938; (長)崎 Nagasaki, # 1081, in which 崎 saki means a cape or promontory; 岐 (阜) Gifu = a city in Japan, # 1657; 峠 touge = a mountain pass, # 1802; 峡(谷) kyoukoku = a canyon, # 1818; 岬 misaki = a cape, # 1942 **ALSO COMPARE:** other similar kanji at # **1157**

1943. 暫 PRONUNCIATIONS: shibara, zan

MEANINGS: temporarily, awhile, moment, long time **EXAMPLES:** 暫く shibaraku = for awhile, for a short time, for a long time, usually written しばらく; 暫定 zantei = tentative, temporary **DESCRIPTION:** compared to 斬(新) zanshin (original, # 1559) (identical pronunciation), this kanji adds 日 hi (sun, # 32) at the bottom; it retains the 車 (car) and the pair of pliers in Zanzibar **CUES:** the Queen of **Sheba Ra**n a business under this 日 (sun) in **Zan**zibar 暫く **shibara**ku (for awhile), and she repaired 車 (cars) like this using pliers like these **ALSO COMPARE:** other similar kanji at # **892** and # **1966**

1944. 詮 PRONUNCIATION: sen

MEANINGS: discussion, methods called for, selection, result **EXAMPLES:** 詮索 sensaku = an inquiry into; 所詮 shosen = after all **DESCRIPTION:** compared to 全(部) zenbu (everything, # 300), this adds 言(う) iu (to speak, # 430) on the left, plus a small horizontal line at the top which may represent a flag flying in the wind; it retains the 王 (king) sitting in a Zen temple with a peaked roof **CUE:** this 王 (king) demands to 言 (speak) to a **Sen**ator, whom he wants to conduct a 詮索 **sen**saku (inquiry) into the practice of flying flags like this from Zen temples like this **ALSO COMPARE:** 栓 sen = a cork, # 2026 (identical pronunciation); similar kanji at # **2026**

1945. 諾 PRONUNCIATION: daku

MEANINGS: consent, assent, agreement **EXAMPLE:** 承諾 shoudaku = compliance, approval **DESCRIPTION:** compared to 若(い) wakai (young, # 461), this adds 言(う) iu (to talk, # 430) on the left; it retains the plants on the 右 (right) side of a house where I used to play whack-a-mole **CUE:** my **Da**ughter who lives in **Ku**wait is too 若 (young) to 言 (talk), but she expresses her (承)諾 shou**daku** (approval) of certain toys **ALSO COMPARE:** other similar kanji at # **457**

1946. 零 (sometimes written 零)

PRONUNCIATION: rei **MEANINGS:** zero, cypher, nothing **EXAMPLE:** 零 rei = zero, often written ゼロ **DESCRIPTION:** compared to (命)令 meirei (a command, # 962) (identical pronunciation), this kanji adds 雨 ame (rain, # 261) at the top; it retains the person under a roof and a napkin who is about to run a race [the **alternative** kanji shown above depicts (rain) above a peaked roof, under which we find another drop of rain above マ Ma (mother)] **CUES:** this person under this roof is about to run a **Ra**ce, but with this 雨 (**Rain**) about to fall, the race may be cancelled, and the payback for his training may amount to 零 **rei** (zero) [**alternatively**, this マ **Ma** (mother) is sheltering from this 雨 (**Rain**) under this peaked roof, but this water drop has gotten through, and her chances of staying dry appear to be 零 **rei** (zero)]

GROUP (alternative font): 冷(たい) tsumetai = cold object, # 299; (命)令 meirei = a command, # 962; (年)齢 nenrei = age, # 989; 領(土) ryoudo = territory, # 1126; 鈴 suzu = a small bell, # 1370; 零 rei = zero, # 1946   **ALSO COMPARE:** other similar kanji at # **262** and # **962**

1947. 柿 PRONUNCIATION: kaki
MEANINGS: persimmon, shingle
EXAMPLE: 柿 kaki = a persimmon
DESCRIPTION: on the left, 木 ki (tree, # 118); on the right, (都)市 toshi (city, # 242)
CUE: when I went to this 市 (city) and saw this 木 (tree) loaded with 柿 **kaki** (persimmons), I dropped my **C**ar **K**eys   **ALSO COMPARE:** other similar kanji at # **128** and # **242**

1948. 芯 PRONUNCIATION: shin
MEANINGS: wick, marrow, stuffing
EXAMPLE: 芯 shin = a wick or core
DESCRIPTION: compared to 心 kokoro (heart, # 306), or 心(配) shinpai (worry, # 306) (identical pronunciation), this kanji adds a plant radical at the top that resembles a wick, tied at both ends
CUE: a **Shin**to priest with this good 心 (heart) used this plant material to make 芯 **shin** (wicks) for his candles   **GROUP:** this is a group of one

1949. 綻 PRONUNCIATIONS: hokoro, tan
MEANINGS: to be ripped, unravel, begin to open   **EXAMPLES:** 綻びる hokorobiru = to be torn or tear apart, to begin to bloom (flower); 破綻 hatan = failure, bankruptcy   **DESCRIPTION:** compared to (予)定 yotei (plan, # 455), this adds ito 糸 (skeet shooter, # 219) on the left; it retains the bad haircut above a taser mounted on a foot   **CUES:** after **Ho**mer had a **Co**ronary (heart attack) and couldn't fight, he asked this 糸 (skeet shooter) for help, but when the shooter fired at a **Tan**k using this foot-mounted taser under this bad haircut, the assault was a 破綻 ha**tan** (failure)
ALSO COMPARE: other similar kanji at # **913**

1950. 訂 PRONUNCIATION: tei
MEANINGS: revise, correct, decide
EXAMPLE: 訂正 teisei = a correction
DESCRIPTION: compared to 丁(寧) teinei (polite, # 702) (identical pronunciation), this kanji adds 言(う) iu (to say, # 430) on the left; it retains the nail which I resold to a tailor
CUE: a **T**ailor who was sewing with this 丁 (nail) 言 (said) that he needed to make a 訂正 **tei**sei (correction) to his work
ALSO COMPARE: other similar kanji at # **702**

1951. 薫 PRONUNCIATIONS: kun, kao
MEANINGS: fragrant, to be scented
EXAMPLE: 薫製 kunsei = smoked food; 薫り kaori = fragrance, scent, smell, aroma (this is often spelled 香り, # 681)

DESCRIPTION: compared to 勲(章) kunshou (medal, # 1938) (identical pronunciation), this kanji omits 力 (force) on the right and adds a plant radical at the top; it retains 重 (heavy) and the hot fire, which remind us of a heavy victim who was 動 (moved) away from a fire by a kung fu master
CUES: after a **Kun**g fu master rescued a 重 (heavy) **C**ow from this hot fire, he was rewarded with some 薫製 **kun**sei (smoked food), and the cow ate these plants   **ALSO COMPARE:** other similar kanji at # **284** and # **611**

1952. 遷 PRONUNCIATION: sen
MEANINGS: transition, move, change
EXAMPLE: 左遷 sasen = a demotion
DESCRIPTION: at the lower left, a snail; riding on the snail, at the top, three eyes hanging from a platform; in the middle, a wide 大 (きい) ookii (big, # 188); below that, 己 onore (self, # 652), which resembles a snake shaped like a backwards "S" **CUE:** a guy with these three eyes, which are very **Sen**sitive, owns this 大 (big) pet 己 (snake) and this snail, and he got a 左遷 sa**sen** (demotion) for bringing them to work
ALSO COMPARE: other similar kanji at # **1078** and # **1415**

1953. 枢 PRONUNCIATION: suu
MEANINGS: hinge, pivot, door
EXAMPLE: 中枢 chuusuu = center, the most important person or thing **DESCRIPTION:** compared to 区(役所) kuyakusho (a ward office, # 320), this adds 木 ki (tree, # 118) on the left; it retains the storefront with an X in it
CUE: this 木 (tree) was about to fall on this 区 (ward office), but **Su**perman caught it just in time, and the 中枢 chuu**suu** (most important thing) is that no one got hurt **GROUP:** 図 zu = drawing, # 281; 区(役所) kuyakusho = a ward office, # 320; (天)気 tenki = weather, # 321; 希(望) kibou = hope, # 663; 離(れる) hanareru = to part, # 666; 胸 mune = chest, # 775; 駆(ける) kakeru = to run, # 776; 爽(快) soukai = refreshing, # 798; 殺(す) korosu = to kill, # 838; 欧(州) oushuu = Europe, # 1334; 殴(る) naguru = to beat up, # 1748; 凶(悪) kyouaku = brutal, # 1794; 刈(る) karu = to reap, # 1912; (中)枢 chuusuu = center, # 1953 **ALSO COMPARE:** other kanji containing boxes that are open on the right at # **320**

1954. 肘 PRONUNCIATION: hiji
MEANINGS: elbow, arm **EXAMPLE:** 肘 hiji = an elbow, usually written ひじ **DESCRIPTION:** on the left, 月 tsuki (moon, # 148); on the right, 寸(前) sunzen (on the verge, # 1369), which resembles a kneeling sunny guy who has dropped his gum in Singapore, where gum littering is illegal **CUE:** after this kneeling sunny guy in Singapore drops this piece of gum under this 月 (moon), he **H**ears a **J**eep coming, which he thinks might be a police car, so he drops down onto his 肘 **hiji** (elbows) **ALSO COMPARE:** 膝 hiza = a knee, # 861; other similar kanji at # **131**

1955. 麓 PRONUNCIATIONS: fumoto, roku MEANINGS: foot of a mountain
EXAMPLES: 麓 fumoto = the base of a mountain, usually spelled ふもと; 山麓 sanroku = the base of a mountain **DESCRIPTION:** compared to 鹿 shika (deer, # 895), this adds 林 hayashi (grove, # 125) at the top; it retains the deer with three eyes that 比 (compares) lean-tos with chimneys occupied by sheep in California **CUES:** when this 鹿 (deer) was walking through this 林 (grove) at the 麓 **fumoto** (base of a mountain), a **Fo**olish **Mo**torcyclist collided with a **R**obotic **K**ool-Aid dispenser **ALSO COMPARE:** other similar kanji at # **895**, # **943** and # **1294**

1956. 憧 PRONUNCIATION: akoga
MEANINGS: yearn after, long for, aspire to
EXAMPLE: 憧れる akogareru = to admire or long for **DESCRIPTION:** compared to 鐘 kane (a bell, # 1840), this substitutes an erect guy for 金 (money) on the left; it retains the 童 (child)
CUE: this guy on the left stands erect and proud after he discovered how to plant 立 (**A**corns) like this in his **G**arden, and this 童 (child) 憧れる **akoga**reru (admires) this discovery **ALSO COMPARE:** other kanji containing 立 at the top at # 1569; other similar kanji at # **1840** and # **2063**

1957. 漆 PRONUNCIATIONS: **urushi, shi**
MEANINGS: lacquer, varnish, seven
EXAMPLES: 漆 urushi = lacquer, lacquerware; 漆器 shikki = lacquerware DESCRIPTION: compared to 膝 hiza (knee, # 861), this substitutes a water radical for the 月 (moon) on the left; it retains the 人 (person) between 木 (tree) and a second 水 (water) CUES: this 人 (person) squeezed himself between this 木 (tree) and this 水 (water) with his **U**ruguayan **Shee**pdog, and he used a 漆器 **shi**kki (lacquerware) container to gather some of this additional water on the left for his **Shee**p ALSO COMPARE: other similar kanji at # **861**, # **1382** and # **1529**

1958. 酌 PRONUNCIATION: **shaku**
MEANINGS: serving sake EXAMPLE: 媒酌 baishaku = matchmaking DESCRIPTION: on the left, 酒 sake (alcoholic beverage, # 465), without its water radical (this can also be seen as a bucket of sake with a handle); on the right, a giant hook containing a drop of water, as seen in 約(束) yakusoku (promise, # 225) CUE: when we visited a **Sh**ack for some 媒酌 bai**shaku** (matchmaking), we saw this 酒 (alcoholic beverage) and this giant hook, both of which the matchmaker was using to get clients, who sometimes shed tears like this ALSO COMPARE: other similar kanji at # **988** and # **1480**

1959. 慕 PRONUNCIATIONS: **bo, shita**
MEANINGS: pining, yearn for, love dearly
EXAMPLES: 慕情 bojou = longing, yearning; 慕う shitau = to adore or yearn for
DESCRIPTION: compared to (お歳)暮 oseibo (year-end gift, # 641) (identical pronunciation), this kanji substitutes, at the bottom, 小(さい) chiisai (small, # 253), plus a piece of gum lying on the ground, for the goofy 日 (sun); it retains the plant radical, the boring 日 (sun) at the top and the wide 大 (big) (this combination of radicals = PSB = plants, sun, big) CUES: this 日 (sun) which shines light on these plants is 大 (big) and **B**oring, and it wants to call a **Shi**ite **Ta**xi, but this 小 (small) piece of gum at its front door make it hesitate, since it doesn't want gum on its shoes ALSO COMPARE: other similar kanji at # **1353**

1960. 婿 PRONUNCIATION: **muko**
MEANINGS: bridegroom, son-in-law
EXAMPLE: 花婿 hanamuko = a bridegroom
DESCRIPTION: on the left, 女 onna (female, # 235); at the upper right, a taser mounted on a foot, as seen in (予)定 yotei (plan, # 455); at the lower right, 月 tsuki (moon, # 148) CUE: this 女 (female) stands under this 月 (**M**oon) in **Ko**rea, dreaming of her 花婿 hana**muko** (bridegroom), who is in the army and wears this 定 (taser mounted on a foot) ALSO COMPARE: other kanji containing 女 on the left at # **2039**; other similar kanji at # **913** and # **2087**

1961. 妄 PRONUNCIATION: **mou**
MEANINGS: delusion, reckless, unnecessarily
EXAMPLE: 妄想 mousou = a fantasy or delusion
DESCRIPTION: compared to 亡(くなる) nakunaru (to die, # 585), or 亡(者) mouja (a money-grubbing person, # 585) (identical pronunciation), this kanji adds 女 onna (female, # 235) at the bottom; it retains the shaky table with a vase on it, where we might seat Moses
CUE: this 女 (female) carrying this 亡 (shaky table) has the 妄想 **mou**sou (fantasy) that she will deliver it to **Mo**ses, who will use it to display the Ten Commandments ALSO COMPARE: other similar kanji at # **585** and # **2086**

1962. 匿 **PRONUNCIATIONS: kakuma, toku** **MEANINGS:** hide, shelter, shield **EXAMPLES:** 匿う kakumau = to shelter, shield or hide; 匿名 tokumei = anonymity **DESCRIPTION:** a building open on one side, as seen in 区 ku (a ward, # 320); inside the building, 若(い) wakai (young, # 461) **CUES:** when **K**arl the **K**ool-Aid vendor's **Ma** (mother) was 若 (young) like this, she thought it was **T**otally **C**ool to 匿う **kakuma**u (hide) in this open-sided building **ALSO COMPARE:** other similar kanji at # **320** and # **457**

1963. 侮 **PRONUNCIATIONS: bu, anado** **MEANINGS:** scorn, despise, contempt **EXAMPLES:** 侮辱 bujoku = insult, contempt, disrespect; 侮る anadoru = to look down on, despise or make light of **DESCRIPTION:** compared to 毎 mai = every, # 336, this adds a man with a slanted hat on the left; it retains Michael Jackson's crutch above the 田 (rice paddy) with several extended lines **CUES:** 毎 (every) day, this man on the left drinks **Boo**ze, tilts his hat back to look at this crutch belonging to a person who works in this 田 (rice paddy), and invents 侮辱 **bu**joku (insults) involving **Ana**logies to a **Do**ughnut, directed at her body shape **ALSO COMPARE:** other similar kanji at # **336** and # **2080**

1964. 髄 **PRONUNCIATION: zui** **MEANINGS:** marrow, pith **EXAMPLES:** 髄 zui = marrow, pith; 真髄 shinzui = essence or gist **DESCRIPTION:** compared to 随(分) zuibun (very, # 1670) (identical pronunciation), this kanji substitutes 骨 hone (bone, # 832) for ß on the left; it retains 有 (famous), which reminds us of a person who is symbolically hugging a famous 月 (moon), while riding on a snail **CUE:** this person at the upper right is hugging a 月 (moon), and the 真髄 shin**zui** (gist) of his conversation today was that, if he weren't afraid that he might break some 骨 (bones) like this, he would prefer to get off this snail and hug a **Z**ooming **E**agle instead

ALSO COMPARE: other similar kanji at # **457**, # **832** and # **2087**

1965. 薪 **PRONUNCIATION: maki** **MEANINGS:** fuel, firewood, kindling **EXAMPLE:** 薪 maki = firewood, usually spelled まき **DESCRIPTION:** compared to 新(し い) atarashii (new, # 389), this adds a plant radical at the top; it retains the 立 (bell) at the upper left, which can be seen as a syringe containing an eye, and the 木 (tree) at the bottom left, which can be seen as a needle, plus the pair of pliers on the right **CUE:** I keep this needle and syringe, and this pair of pliers, with my 新 (new) **Mac**intosh computer under these plants, where I also keep my 薪 **maki** (firewood) **ALSO COMPARE:** other similar kanji at # **383**, # **389** and # **892**

1966. 轄 **PRONUNCIATION: katsu** **MEANINGS:** control, wedge **EXAMPLE:** 管轄 kankatsu = jurisdiction or control **DESCRIPTION:** compared to 害 gai (harm, # 1260), this adds 車 kuruma (car, # 283) on the left; it retains the guy with a bad haircut installing an owl's perch on a 口 (box) using guy-wires **CUE:** since 車 (cars) like this sometimes cause 害 (harm) to **C**ats, people should maintain 管轄 kan**katsu** (control) over their pets **GROUP:** 車 kuruma = car, # 283; 転(ぶ) korobu = to fall, # 285; 輸(入する) yu'nyuu suru = to import, # 288; 軽(い) karui = light, # 289; (車)輪 sharin = wheel, # 690; 軍(人) gunjin = soldier, # 725; 軒 noki = eaves, # 1146; 載(る) noru = to be printed, # 1175; 撃(つ) utsu = to fire a gun, # 1226; 斬(新) zanshin = creative, # 1559; 範(囲) han'i = extent, # 1585; (先)輩 senpai = a senior, # 1607; (比)較 hikaku = a comparison, # 1632; 軸 jiku = axle, # 1791; 軌(道) kidou = an orbit, # 1827; (柔)軟(な) juunan na = flexible, # 1883; 暫(定) zantei =

tentative, # 1943; (管)轄 kankatsu = jurisdiction, # 1966 **ALSO COMPARE:** other similar kanji at # **1260**

1967. 咽 PRONUNCIATION: in
MEANINGS: choked, smothered, stuffy
EXAMPLE: 耳鼻咽喉科 jibiinkouka = otorhinolaryngology **DESCRIPTION:** compared to (原)因 gen'in (cause, # 1360) (identical pronunciation), this kanji adds 口 kuchi (mouth, # 426), which can also be seen as a box, on the left; it retains the 大 (big) guy who is stuck in a 口 (box) and has become insane **CUES:** this 大 (big) guy stuck in this 口 (box) may be **In**sane, but he's having problems with this 口 (mouth), and he wants to see a doctor specializing in 耳鼻咽喉科 jib**iin**kouka (otorhinolaryngology)
ALSO COMPARE: other similar kanji at # **1360** and # **2073**

1968. 迅 PRONUNCIATION: jin
MEANINGS: swift, fast
EXAMPLE: 迅速な jinsoku na = fast, prompt
DESCRIPTION: at the lower left, a snail; at the upper right, a one-sided lean-to containing the number 十 (ten) **CUE:** as I was sitting in this lean-to, this snail crawled across my **Jean**s in 十 (ten) seconds, which was 迅速 **jin**soku (fast) for a snail
ALSO COMPARE: other similar kanji at # **1658**

1969. 該 PRONUNCIATION: gai
MEANINGS: above-stated, the said, that specific
EXAMPLES: 該当 gaitou = application, correspondence; 該当する gaitou suru = to correspond, apply or fall under
DESCRIPTION: compared to 骸(骨) gaikotsu (skeleton, # 1923) (identical pronunciation), this kanji substitutes 言(う) iu (to say, # 430) for 骨 (bone) on the left; it retains the skeleton of a boar, for which a guide is responsible, on the right
CUE: the **Gui**de who disposed of this boar skeleton 言 (says) that doing so 該当した **gai**tou shita

(corresponded) to his responsibilities
ALSO COMPARE: other similar kanji at # **1548**

1970. 逐 PRONUNCIATION: chiku
MEANINGS: pursue, drive away, chase
EXAMPLES: 逐次 chikuji = one by one, sequentially, successively; 駆逐 kuchiku = expulsion
DESCRIPTION: compared to 豚 buta (pig, # 1504), this omits the 月 (moon) on the left and adds a snail on the lower left; it retains the 家 (house) without its bad haircut
CUE: since this 豚 (pig) riding on this snail drinks **Cheap Kool**-Aid, it is subject to 駆逐 ku**chiku** (expulsion) from the snail's back
ALSO COMPARE: other similar kanji at # **1504**

1971. 嘲 PRONUNCIATIONS: chou, azake
MEANINGS: ridicule, insult
EXAMPLES: 嘲笑 choushou = ridicule; 嘲る azakeru = to ridicule, mock or scoff
DESCRIPTION: compared to 朝 asa (morning, # 291), or 朝(食) choushoku (breakfast, # 291) (identical pronunciation), this kanji adds 口 kuchi (mouth, # 426), which can also be seen as a box, on the left; it retains the 月 (moon) next to a California wagon, where I'm feeling sad that I was chosen
CUES: I've been **Cho**sen to get up in the 朝 (morning) to water the **Aza**leas with a **K**ettle, and my friend uses this 口 (mouth) to 嘲る **azake**ru (ridicule) me for being assigned this thankless task
ALSO COMPARE: other similar kanji at # **1308** and # **2073**

1972. 墜 PRONUNCIATION: tsui

MEANINGS: crash, fall down EXAMPLES: 墜落 tsuiraku = a plane crash or a fall; 墜落する tsuiraku suru = to fall or crash DESCRIPTION: compared to (軍)隊 guntai (army, # 726), this adds 土 tsuchi (soil, # 59) at the bottom; it retains the ß (Greek) army that keeps a pet tiger with what appear to be rabbit ears in a 家 (house) CUE: a ß (Greek) 隊 (army) took this pet wearing rabbit ears out of this 家 (house), gave it some **Tsui**tes (sweets) to keep it calm and put it on a plane, but unfortunately the plane 墜落した **tsui**raku shita (crashed) into this 土 (soil) GROUP: (軍)隊 guntai = army, # 726; 遂(げる) togeru = to accomplish, # 1371; 墜(落) tsuiraku = a plane crash, # 1972 ALSO COMPARE: other similar kanji at # **1504** and # **2030**

1973. 臆 PRONUNCIATION: oku

MEANINGS: timidity, heart, mind, cowardice EXAMPLES: 臆病な okubyou na = timid DESCRIPTION: compared to 億 oku (100 million, # 318) (identical pronunciation), this kanji substitutes 月 tsuki (moon, # 148) for the man with the slanted hat on the left; it retains 意(味) imi (meaning, # 317) CUE: I'm too 臆病 **oku**byou (timid) to walk alone under this 月 (moon) and, to boost my courage, I sing 億 (100 million) **O**ld **K**ool-Aid jingles, which are full of this 意 (meaning) for me ALSO COMPARE: other similar kanji at # **266**

1974. 餓 PRONUNCIATION: ga

MEANINGS: starve, hungry, thirst EXAMPLES: 餓死 gashi = starvation; 餓死する gashi suru = to die of starvation DESCRIPTION: compared to 我(慢) gaman (patience, # 862) (identical pronunciation), this kanji adds 食(べる) taberu (to eat, # 398) on the left; it retains 我 ware (self, # 862) CUE: my 我 (self) tries to 食 (eat), but food makes me **Ga**g, and I am afraid that I may 餓死する **ga**shi suru (die of starvation) GROUP: (旅)館 ryokan = Japanese inn, # 305; 食(べる) taberu = to eat, # 398; 飲(む) nomu = to drink, # 399; (ご)飯 gohan = meal, cooked rice, # 400; 餅 mochi = Japanese rice cake, # 743; 飼(う) kau = to keep a pet, # 830; 餌 esa = animal food, # 843; 飢(える) ueru = to starve, # 924; 飾(る) kazaru = to decorate, # 1203; (栄)養 eiyou = nutrition, # 1264; 飽(きる) akiru = to get tired of, # 1379; 餓(死) gashi = starvation, # 1974 ALSO COMPARE: other similar kanji at # **1554** and # **1862**

1975. 捻 PRONUNCIATION: nen

MEANINGS: twirl, twist, play with EXAMPLE: 捻挫 nenza = a sprain DESCRIPTION: compared to (残)念 zannen (too bad, # 314) (identical pronunciation), this kanji adds a kneeling guy on the left; it retains 今 (now), which contains a 7 under a ceiling under a peaked roof, and 心 (heart), reminding us of something that is happening now in my negative nephew's heart CUE: this guy on the left is kneeling due to a 捻挫 **nen**za (sprain) in his ankle, and 今 (now) his condition is sparking compassion in this 心 (heart) belonging to my **N**egative **N**ephew ALSO COMPARE: other similar kanji at # **1491**

1976. 挫 PRONUNCIATIONS: za, kuji

MEANINGS: crush, break, sprain, discourage EXAMPLES: 挫折 zasetsu = a failure or setback; 挫ける kujikeru = to lose heart or be discouraged DESCRIPTION: compared to 座(る) suwaru (to sit, # 497), or 座(布団) zabuton (floor cushion, # 497) (identical pronunciation), this kanji omits the lean-to with a chimney at the upper left and adds a kneeling guy on the left; it retains the two 人 (people) sitting on 土 (soil) CUES: this guy on the left kneeled to beg these two

人 (people) 座 (sitting) on this 土 (soil) in Zambia to sell him their Kuwaiti Jeep, but the negotiations were a 挫折 zasetsu (failure) **ALSO COMPARE:** other similar kanji at # **352** and # **1926**

1977. 桟 PRONUNCIATION: san
MEANINGS: scaffold, frame
EXAMPLE: 桟橋 sanbashi = a wharf, bridge, jetty or pier **DESCRIPTION:** on the left, 木 ki (wood, # 118); on the right, a halberd (combination axe and lance), with three horizontal lines near the top, suggesting a handle with a triple grip
CUE: **San**ta Claus used this halberd to cut this 木 (wood) in order to make a 桟橋 **san**bashi (wharf) at the North Pole **ALSO COMPARE:** other similar kanji at # **128** and # **605**

1978. 溺 PRONUNCIATIONS: obo, deki
MEANINGS: drown, indulge
EXAMPLES: 溺れる oboreru = to drown or to indulge in, usually spelled おぼれる; 溺愛する dekiai suru = to dote on or indulge
DESCRIPTION: compared to 弱(い) yowai (weak, # 471), this adds a water radical on the left; it retains the two feathers, with weak shafts at the top that can also be seen as backwards-S snakes
CUES: some **O**ld **B**oys decided to honor a **D**ead **K**ing by making a boat out of these 弱 (weak) feathers and sailing it in this water to a memorial service, but they 溺れた **obo**reta (drowned) **ALSO COMPARE:** other similar kanji at # **1078** and # **1457**

1979. 賄 PRONUNCIATION: wai
MEANINGS: bribery, corruption, graft
EXAMPLE: 贈賄 zouwai = bribery
DESCRIPTION: compared to 有(名) yuumei (famous, # 460), this adds 貝 kai (shell, or money chest, # 83) on the left; it retains the aristocrat from the Yukon symbolically hugging a 月 (moon)
CUE: this aristocrat hugging this 月 (moon) keeps his proceeds from 贈賄 zou**wai** (bribery in this 貝 (money chest), until he takes them out to show

his **W**ife **ALSO COMPARE:** other similar kanji at # **457**, # **2058** and # **2087**

1980. 盲 PRONUNCIATION: mou
MEANINGS: blind, blind man, ignoramus
EXAMPLE: 盲目 moumoku = blindness
DESCRIPTION: at the top, 亡(くなる) nakunaru (to die, # 585), or 亡(者) mouja (a money-grubbing person, # 585) (identical pronunciation), which resembles a shaky table; at the bottom, 目 me (eye, # 51) **CUE:** **Mo**ses suffered from 盲目 **mou**moku (blindness) after the retinal cells in his 目 (eyes) 亡 (died), and we used to seat him at this 亡 (shaky table) **ALSO COMPARE:** other similar kanji at # **585** and # **2002**

1981. 鯨 PRONUNCIATIONS: gei, kujira
MEANING: whale **EXAMPLES:** 捕鯨 hogei = whaling; 鯨 kujira = a whale, usually spelled くじら **DESCRIPTION:** on the left, 魚 sakana (fish, # 80); on the right, 京(都) kyouto (Kyoto, # 514), which resembles a tire stop over a 口 (box, or house) on a 小 (small) hill in Kyoto
CUES: when I ordered this 魚 (fish) in 京 (Kyoto), we were served 鯨 **ku**jira (whale) meat, and I **Ga**ped at the waiter, while my **Ku**waiti friend **Jee**red **At** me **ALSO COMPARE:** other similar kanji at # **514**, # **611**, # **618** and # **1474**

1982. 侶 PRONUNCIATION: ryo
MEANINGS: companion, follower
EXAMPLES: 僧侶 souryo = a monk or priest;
DESCRIPTION: compared to (風)呂 furo (a bath, # 7), this adds a man with a slanted hat on the left; it retains the two stacked vertebrae
CUE: this man on the left is a former 僧侶 sou**ryo** (priest) whose name is Pope **Leo**, and he tilts his hat back to examine this 呂 (bath)
ALSO COMPARE: other similar kanji at # **1079**

1983. 蔑 PRONUNCIATIONS: sagesu, betsu
MEANINGS: ignore, despise, neglect, ridicule
EXAMPLES: 蔑む sagesumu = to look down on, to scorn or despise; 軽蔑 keibetsu = scorn, disdain
DESCRIPTION: at the top, three eyes under a plant radical, as seen in 夢 yume (dream, # 165); at the lower left, the letter F; at the lower right, a halberd (combination axe and lance)
CUES: **Sa**ssy **Ge**nghis **Su**ed his school and waved this halberd around after he received this F in a class that required him to identify plants like this, even though he has three eyes like this, and he **Bets** that he will get better marks at another school, even though he has 軽蔑 kei**betsu** (disdain) for homework
GROUP: 垢 aka = dirt, # 665; 后(妃) kouhi = queen, # 1459; (軽)蔑 keibetsu = scorn, # 1983
ALSO COMPARE: other similar kanji at # **915** and # **1603**

1984. 丼 PRONUNCIATIONS: don, donburi
MEANINGS: bowl, bowl of food
EXAMPLES: 親子丼 oyakodon = chicken and egg on rice in a bowl; 丼 donburi = a porcelain bowl for noodles etc.
DESCRIPTION: compared to 井(戸) ido (well, # 983), this adds an extra mark in the center, which could represent a bowl
CUES: when **Don** Quixote visited this 井 (well) near the place where Sancho's **Don**key was **Bur**ied, he saw this object floating in the center, which turned out to be a 丼 **donburi** (porcelain bowl)
ALSO COMPARE: other similar kanji at # **1202**

1985. 剖 PRONUNCIATION: bou
MEANINGS: divide
EXAMPLE: 解剖 kaibou = anatomy, autopsy, dissection
DESCRIPTION: compared to 部(屋) heya (room, # 267), this substitutes the katakana リ ri, which is sometimes described as a knife, for ß on the right; it retains the bell on a 口 (box)
CUE: this リ **Ri** rings this bell on this 口 (box) whenever he gets **Bo**red while doing 解剖 kai**bou** (autopsies) at a hospital
GROUP: 割(る) waru = to break, # 562; 倒(れる) taoreru = to collapse, # 563; (便)利 benri = convenient, # 564; (時)刻 jikoku = time, # 565; 帰(る) kaeru = to return, # 566; 製(品) seihin = product, # 580; 到(着する) touchaku suru = to arrive, # 612; 刊(行する) kankou suru = to publish, # 990; 判(断する) handan suru = to judge, # 1054; 劇 geki = a play, # 1058; 型 kata = form, # 1116; 制(度) seido = system, # 1155; 創(造) souzou = creation, # 1171; 梨 nashi = pear, # 1184; 副(産物) fukusanbutsu = a byproduct, # 1206; (過)剰 kajou = excess, # 1211; 刺(す) sasu = to stab, # 1284; 刑(務所) keimusho = prison, # 1325; 捌(く) sabaku = to handle, # 1350; (印)刷 insatsu = printing, # 1392; 剣 tsurugi = a sword, # 1432; 班(長) hanchou = a squad leader, # 1509; 剥(く) muku = to peel, # 1567; (洗)剤 senzai = detergent, # 1601; 削(ぐ) sogu = to slice, # 1626; 剛(健) gouken = vigor, # 1663; 罰(金) bakkin = a penalty, # 1691; 刈(る) karu = to reap, # 1912; (解)剖 kaibou = anatomy, # 1985; (下)痢 geri = diarrhea, # 2055
ALSO COMPARE: other similar kanji at # **269**

1986. 槽 PRONUNCIATION: sou
MEANINGS: vat, tub, tank
EXAMPLE: 水槽 suisou = a water tank
DESCRIPTION: compared to (重)曹 juusou (baking soda, # 1598) (identical pronunciation), this kanji adds 木 ki (wood, # 118) on the left; it retains the 曲 (tunes), which resemble a coop with wires and can be interrupted by a short circuit, and the 日 (sun) providing solar power
CUE: I used this 木 (wood) to make a 水槽 sui**sou** (water tank), in which I sit while listening to 曲 (tunes) like this powered by **So**lar power from this 日 (sun), but my music is sometimes interrupted by this short circuit
ALSO COMPARE: other similar kanji at # **1073**

1987. 閲 PRONUNCIATION: etsu
MEANINGS: review, inspection, revision
EXAMPLES: 検閲 ken'etsu = censorship, inspection; 閲覧 etsuran = inspection, reading, browsing (e.g., the web) DESCRIPTION: compared to 悦(に入る) etsu ni iru (to be happy, # 1779) (identical pronunciation), this kanji omits the erect guy on the left and adds 門 mon (gate, # 409) on both sides; it retains 兄 (big brother) wearing rabbit ears to celebrate receiving etchings from Sudan CUE: this 兄 (big brother) stood in this 門 (gate) and put on these rabbit ears to celebrate after getting Etchings from Sudan, but he had to submit them to his father for 検閲 ken'**etsu** (inspection) ALSO COMPARE: other similar kanji at # **708** and # **1755**

1988. 畔 PRONUNCIATION: han
MEANINGS: paddy ridge, levee
EXAMPLE: 湖畔 kohan = a lake shore or lakeside DESCRIPTION: compared to 半(分) hanbun (half, # 331) (identical pronunciation), which can be seen as a telephone pole on fire, this kanji adds 田(んぼ) tanbo (rice paddy, # 68) on the left CUE: when **Han**sel visits this 田 (rice paddy), he eats 半 (half) of his lunch and saves the other half for his trip to the 湖畔 ko**han** (lake shore) nearby ALSO COMPARE: other similar kanji at # **220** and # **1054**

1989. 睦 PRONUNCIATIONS: mutsu, boku MEANINGS: intimate, friendly, harmonious
EXAMPLES: 睦まじい mutsumajii = harmonious, happy, affectionate; 親睦 shinboku = friendship DESCRIPTION: compared to 陸(軍) rikugun (army, # 1015), this substitutes 目 me (eye, # 51) for ß (Greek) on the left; it retains 土 (soil) on lopsided legs walking on more 土 (soil)
CUES: this 目 (eye) watches some **Mutts** (dogs), which were **Bo**rn in **Ku**wait, playing on this 土 (soil) that is walking on 土 (soil), and enjoying their 親睦 shin**boku** (friendship) GROUP: 熱(い) atsui = hot object, # 65; (大)勢 oozei = many people, # 110; 陸(軍) rikugun = army, # 1015; (親)睦 shinboku = friendship, # 1989
ALSO COMPARE: kanji in which soil is piled directly on soil at # 1619; other similar kanji at # **2002**

1990. 唆 PRONUNCIATION: sa
MEANINGS: tempt, seduce, investigate, promote
EXAMPLE: 示唆 shisa = an implication or suggestion DESCRIPTION: compared to 酸(っぱい) suppai (sour, # 1480), this substitutes 口 kuchi (mouth, # 426), which can also be seen as a box, for the modified 酒 (alcoholic beverage) on the left; it retains the ム (cow) on lopsided legs above a dancer with a ponytail
CUE: this ム (cow) on lopsided legs used this 口 (mouth) to make a 示唆 shi**sa** (suggestion) that this dancer bring it some **S**alt GROUP: (大)統(領) daitouryou = president, # 1125; 充(実) juujitsu = perfection, # 1478; 酸(っぱい) suppai = sour, # 1480; (拳)銃 kenjuu = a handgun, # 1555; (示)唆 shisa = an implication, # 1990
ALSO COMPARE: other similar kanji at # **2073**

1991. 腎 PRONUNCIATION: jin
MEANINGS: kidney EXAMPLE: 腎臓 jinzou = a kidney DESCRIPTION: compared to 緊(張) kinchou (tension, # 732), this substitutes 月 tsuki (moon, # 148) for the 糸 (skeet shooter) at the bottom; it retains (総理大)臣 souridaijin (prime minister, # 1039) (identical pronunciation), which resembles an 臣 (inoperable swing set), and a 又 (table) CUE: a **Gen**ius succeeded in shooting this 臣 (inoperable swing set) and this 又 (table) to this 月 (moon), but later he died of 腎臓 **jin**zou (kidney) disease
GROUP: 背 se = height, # 152; 消(す) kesu = to erase, # 158; 肩 kata = shoulder, # 845; 脅(す)

odosu = to threaten, # 914; 筋 suji = streak, # 1426; 肖(像画) shouzouga = a portrait, # 1625; 削(減) sakugen = a reduction, # 1626; (皮)膚 hifu = skin, # 1777; 脊(椎) sekitsui = the spine, # 1867; 腎(臓) jinzou = a kidney, # 1991; (今)宵 koyoi = this evening, # 1994; (比)喩 hiyu = a simile, # 2021; 罷(免) himen = dismissal, # 2057; (怠)惰(な) taida na = lazy, # 2063 **ALSO COMPARE**: other similar kanji at # **24** and # **1246**

1992. 梗 PRONUNCIATION: kou
MEANINGS: for the most part, close up
EXAMPLE: 梗塞 kousoku = a stoppage, tightness or block, an infarction
DESCRIPTION: compared to (変)更 henkou (a change, # 1000) (identical pronunciation), this kanji adds 木 ki (tree, # 118) on the left; it retains 更 (Benjamin Franklin), who has a dislocated right hip, wears bifocals and likes his leftover food kept cold **CUE**: this 更 (Benjamin Franklin), who has this dislocated right hip and wears these bifocals, relies on this 木 (tree) plus air-conditioning to keep his home **C**old during the summer, as advised by his doctor after his myocardial 梗塞 **kou**soku (infarction) **GROUP**: 便(利) benri = convenient, # 481; (変)更 henkou = a change, # 1000; 硬(貨) kouka = coins, # 1412; 梗(塞) kousoku = an infarction, # 1992; **Note** that three of these kanji can be pronounced "kou" **ALSO COMPARE**: other kanji which could be described as containing bifocals at # 1157; other similar kanji at # **1000**

1993. 搬 PRONUNCIATIONS: han, pan
MEANINGS: conveyor, carry, transport
EXAMPLES: 搬送 hansou = transportation, conveyance, delivery; 運搬 unpan = carriage, transport **DESCRIPTION**: compared to (一)般(的に) ippanteki ni (commonly, # 1050) (identical pronunciation), this kanji adds a kneeling guy on the left; it retains the 舟 (boat) and the 兀 (yak) on a 又 (table), where Hansel also keeps a Panda **CUES**: **Han**sel is this guy kneeling next to this 舟 (boat), begging the captain to provide 搬送 **han**sou (transportation) for both this 兀 (yak) on this 又 (table) and a **Pan**da **ALSO COMPARE**: other similar kanji at # **557**, # **1389** and # **1524**

1994. 宵 PRONUNCIATION: yoi
MEANINGS: wee hours, evening, early night
EXAMPLE: 今宵 koyoi = this evening
DESCRIPTION: compared to 肖(像画) shouzouga (a portrait, # 1625), this adds a bad haircut at the top; it retains the three-pronged switch above a 月 (moon) **CUE**: a **Yo**gi from India waited until 今宵 ko**yoi** (this evening) to drop this bad haircut onto this three-pronged switch above this 月 (moon), causing it to malfunction
ALSO COMPARE: other similar kanji at # **1625** and # **1991**

1995. 拐 PRONUNCIATION: kai
MEANINGS: kidnap, falsify **EXAMPLE**: 誘拐 yuukai = an abduction **DESCRIPTION**: on the left, a kneeling guy; at the upper right, kuchi 口 (mouth, # 426), which resembles a box; at the lower right, 刀 katana (sword, # 102) **CUE**: this guy is kneeling in order to remove this 刀 (sword) from under this 口 (box), and he plans to use it to 誘拐する yuu**kai** suru (abduct) the **Kai**ser **ALSO COMPARE**: similar kanji at # 560, in which 刀 (sword) is depicted *above* 口 (mouth, or box), instead of below it; other similar kanji at # **560**

1996. 醸 PRONUNCIATIONS: jou, kamo
MEANING: brew **EXAMPLES**: 醸造 jouzou = brewing, distilling; 醸しだす kamoshidasu = to engender, to bring about, to cause, to give rise to
DESCRIPTION: compared to (豊)穣 houjou (good harvest, # 1322) (identical pronunciation), on the left, this kanji substitutes 酒 sake (alcoholic beverage, # 465), without its water radical, for 禾 (ripe grain) (this can also be seen as a bucket of sake with a handle); it retains 六 (six) 井 (wells) and

some 衣 (clothing) belonging to Joan of Arc
CUES: **Jo**an of Arc had these 六 (**six**) 井 (**wells**), and sometimes she would use their water to 醸造する **jou**zou suru (brew) some 酒 (sake) like this, and then put on this 衣 (clothing) and **C**all **Mo**ses to come over for a drink
ALSO COMPARE: other similar kanji at # **1322** and # **1480**

1997. 猶 PRONUNCIATION: yuu
MEANINGS: furthermore, still, yet
EXAMPLE: 猶予 yuuyo = a postponement or reprieve **DESCRIPTION:** on the left, a woman contorting her body, as seen in 猫 neko (cat, # 72); on the right, 酒 sake (# 465), without its water radical (this can also be seen as a bucket of sake with a handle) and with rabbit ears added at the top, as seen in 尊(敬する) sonkei suru (to respect, # 1208) **CUE:** this woman who is contorting her body has added these rabbit ears to her 酒 (sake), as she prepares to celebrate the 猶予 **yuu**yo (postponement) of her move to the **Yu**kon
GROUP: 弟 otouto = little brother, # 529; 逆(説) gyakusetsu = paradox, # 894; 尊(敬する) sonkei suru = to respect, # 1208; (行)為 koui = deed, # 1222; (利)益 rieki = profit, # 1407; 網 ami = a net, # 1448; 偽(物) nisemono = a counterfeit, # 1622; 瓶 bin = a bottle, # 1711; 猶(予) yuuyo = a postponement, # 1997
ALSO COMPARE: other similar kanji at # **948** and # **1480**

1998. 畏 PRONUNCIATION: i
MEANINGS: fear, majestic, graciously
EXAMPLE: 畏敬 ikei = awe and respect, reverence **DESCRIPTION:** at the top, 田(んぼ) tanbo (rice paddy, # 68); at the bottom, L and Y, supporting a platform
CUE: it's **E**asy for L and Y to support this platform holding this miniature 田 (rice paddy), and they are doing it to show their 畏敬 **i**kei (reverence) for the god of harvests **ALSO COMPARE:** other similar kanji at # **220** and # **398**

1999. 逝 PRONUNCIATION: sei
MEANINGS: departed, die
EXAMPLE: 逝去 seikyo = death
DESCRIPTION: compared to 誓(い) chikai (a vow, # 1780), this substitutes a snail at the lower left for 言 (speak) at the bottom; it retains the kneeling guy and the pair of pliers
CUE: this guy in the middle is a **Sai**nt who kneels in prayer as he carries these pliers, to remind him of his 誓 (vow) to complete his practical tasks before his 逝去 **sei**kyo (death), but he seems unlikely to finish them given his dependence on this slow snail
ALSO COMPARE: other similar kanji at # **892**

2000. 朽 PRONUNCIATIONS: kyuu, ku
MEANINGS: decay, rot, remain in seclusion
EXAMPLES: 不朽の fukyuu no = eternal, immortal; 朽ちる kuchiru = to rot or decay
DESCRIPTION: on the left, 木 ki (tree, # 118); on the right, a kangaroo, as seen in (番)号 bangou (number, # 470) **CUES:** this kangaroo carried this 木 (tree) from **Cu**ba to **Ku**wait, but the tree 朽ちた **ku**chita (rotted) along the way
ALSO COMPARE: other similar kanji at # **468**

2001. 硫 PRONUNCIATIONS: i, ryuu
MEANING: sulfur **EXAMPLES:** 硫黄 iou = sulfur; 硫酸塩 ryuusanen = sulfate
DESCRIPTION: compared to 流(行) ryuukou (fashion, # 654) (identical pronunciation), this kanji substitutes 石 ishi (stone, # 458) for the water radical on the left; it retains the ム (cow) under a tire stop that climbs onto a three-legged stool and pours water from reusable bottles **CUES:** this ム (cow) under a tire stop sitting on this three-legged stool sees this 石 (stone) made of 硫黄 **i**ou (sulfur), which it has been using as a footrest, but it thinks that it would be **E**asy to **Reu**se it as medicine
ALSO COMPARE: other similar kanji at # **710**, # **1125** and # **1775**

2002. 瞭 PRONUNCIATION: ryou

MEANING: clear   EXAMPLE: 明瞭な meiryou na = obvious, clear

DESCRIPTION: compared to (官)僚 kanryou (bureaucrat, # 1592) (identical pronunciation), this kanji substitutes 目 me (eye, # 51) for the man with a slanted hat on the left; it retains the slightly modified 大 (big) 日 (sun, or oven) spinning on 小 (small)   CUE: this 目 (eye) examines Pope Leo, who is this 大 (big) man with this spinning 日 (oven), and it's 明瞭 mei**ryou** (obvious) that the oven needs to be cleaned   GROUP: 着(る) kiru = to wear, # 52; 貝 kai = shell, # 83; 帽(子) boushi = hat, # 243; 面(倒) mendou = annoyance, # 282; 道 michi = street, # 349; 眠(る) nemuru = to sleep, # 376; 夏 natsu = summer, # 522; 瞬(間) shunkan = a moment, # 773; (計)算 keisan = calculation, # 789; 睡(眠) suimin = sleep, # 800; 眩(しい) mabushii = dazzling, # 937; (反)省 hansei = scrutiny, # 1010; 眺(め) nagame = a view, # 1136; 看(板) kanban = signboard, # 1164; (監)督 kantoku = director, # 1421; 眼(鏡) megane = eyeglasses, # 1423; 眉(毛) mayuge = an eyebrow, # 1645; 憂(鬱) yuu'utsu = depression, # 1784; 瞳 hitomi = a pupil, # 1865; 盲(目) moumoku = blindness, # 1980; (親)睦 shinboku = friendship, # 1989; (明)瞭(な) meiryou na = obvious, # 2002   ALSO COMPARE: other similar kanji at # **94**, # **243** and # **1069**

2003. 擬 PRONUNCIATION: gi

MEANINGS: mimic, imitate   EXAMPLE: 模擬 mogi = imitation, mock   DESCRIPTION: compared to 疑(問) gimon (doubt, # 978) (identical pronunciation), this kanji adds a kneeling guy on the left; it retains the ヒ (hero), his マ Ma and the Native American chief, a family who plan to hunt geese with this taser mounted on Ma's 足 (foot)   CUES: this guy on the left watches this family consisting of this ヒ (hero), this マ Ma and this Native American chief hunting **Ge**ese with this taser, and he kneels to examine the weapon more closely and decides that it looks like a 模擬 mo**gi** (imitation)   ALSO COMPARE: other similar kanji at # **324**, # **913**, # **978** and # **2048**

2004. 叙 PRONUNCIATION: jo

MEANINGS: confer, narrate, describe   EXAMPLE: 自叙伝 jijoden = an autobiography   DESCRIPTION: compared to (削)除(する) sakujo suru (to delete, # 646) (identical pronunciation), this kanji omits ß (Greek) on the left and adds 又 mata (again, # 24), which resembles a simple table, on the right; it retains 余(計) yokei (excessive, # 637) which consists of a spinning 丁 (nail) structure with a stool under its peaked roof, the home of Empress Josephine   CUE: when Empress **Jo**sephine was ready to write her 自叙伝 ji**jo**den (autobiography) she had to step out of this spinning structure, which was making her 余 (excessively) dizzy, and sit down at this 又 (table)   ALSO COMPARE: similar kanji at # **24** and # **637**

2005. 弊 PRONUNCIATION: hei

MEANINGS: collapse, crumble   EXAMPLES: 疲弊 hihei = exhaustion, impoverishment, ruin; 弊社 heisha = our company   DESCRIPTION: compared to (紙)幣 shihei (paper money, # 1411) (identical pronunciation), which reminds us of people who hate each other, this kanji substitutes the letter H, as seen in 葬(る) houmuru (to bury, # 1273), which reminds us of Homer (and also resembles a welcoming stance), for the 巾 (Bo Peep) at the bottom; it retains the three-pronged switch above a two-sided lean-to containing a modified 小 (small) at the upper left, and a dancer with a ponytail at the upper right   CUE: this H (Homer) embodies a welcoming stance, but since he has to carry this two-sided lean-to with this switch plus this dancer with a ponytail, he **Ha**tes his job and is suffering from 疲弊 hi**hei** (exhaustion)   ALSO COMPARE: other similar kanji at # **479**, # **1010**, # **1625** and # **1924**

2006. 累 PRONUNCIATION: rui

MEANING: accumulate **EXAMPLE:** 累積 ruiseki = an accumulation **DESCRIPTION:** at the top, 田(んぼ) tanbo (rice paddy, # 68); at the bottom, a 糸 (skeet shooter, # 219), who appears to be juggling **CUE:** this 糸 (skeet shooter) in **Lou**isiana has to juggle this 田 (rice paddy), plus a 累積 **rui**seki (accumulation) of problems **GROUP:** 細い hosoi = thin, # 220; 累(積) ruiseki = an accumulation, # 2006 **ALSO COMPARE:** other similar kanji at # 220 and # 1266

2007. 煩 PRONUNCIATIONS: bon, wazura

MEANINGS: trouble, worry, noisy **EXAMPLES:** 煩悩 bonnou = worldly desire; 煩う wazurau = to worry about, to have trouble doing; 煩わしい wazurawashii = complicated, troublesome **DESCRIPTION:** on the left, 火 hi (fire, # 443); on the right, 貝 kai (shell, money chest, # 83) with a platform mounted on top where a head could fit, as seen in 頭 atama (head, # 93) **CUES:** when I see this 火 (fire) approach this 貝 (money chest) with this headless platform on top, I 煩う **wazura**u (worry) about the **Bon**us that I keep in the chest's drawers, but since my head is absent from this platform, it's in no danger, and my **W**acky **Z**oo **R**abbits will just run away **ALSO COMPARE:** other similar kanji at # 1126 and # 1239

2008. 藻 PRONUNCIATION: sou, mo

MEANINGS: seaweed, duckweed **EXAMPLES:** 海藻 kaisou = seaweed; 藻 mo = algae, seaweed **DESCRIPTION:** compared to 操(作) sousa (operation of a machine, # 1192) (identical pronunciation), this kanji substitutes a water radical for the kneeling guy on the left, and it adds a plant radical at the top; it retains the 品 (three packages of Kool-Aid) which a soldier tried to dislodge from a 木 (tree) **CUES:** when a **S**oldier saw that these 品 (three packages of Kool-Aid) in this 木 (tree) were getting **M**oldy from exposure to this water, he used this plant, which is 海藻 kai**sou** (seaweed), to knock them down **ALSO COMPARE:** other similar kanji at # 258, # 1034 and # 1216

2009. 蚊 PRONUNCIATION: ka

MEANING: mosquito **EXAMPLE:** 蚊 ka = a mosquito **DESCRIPTION:** on the left, 虫 mushi (insect, # 9); on the right, 文(化) bunka (culture, # 25) **CUE:** this 虫 (insect), which is a 蚊 **ka** (mosquito), has no 文 (culture), and therefore it can't learn how to get into a closed **C**ar **ALSO COMPARE:** other similar kanji at # 259 and # 1754

2010. 鋳 PRONUNCIATIONS: i, chuu

MEANINGS: casting, mint **EXAMPLES:** 鋳型 igata = a mold or cast; 鋳造 chuuzou = casting or minting **DESCRIPTION:** on the left, 金 kane (money, # 301); on the right, 寿(司) sushi (raw fish, # 607), which consists of an owl's perch with a long axis leaning over a 寸 (sunny guy) encountered by Superman, who wanted to get some sushi **CUES:** this 寸 (sunny guy) under this elongated owl's perch has this 金 (money) for 寿 (sushi) but, since it's **E**aster, he will instead **Choo**se pudding chilled in a bunny 鋳型 **i**gata (mold) **GROUP:** 金 kane = money, # 301; 銀(行) ginkou = bank, # 302; 鉄 tetsu = iron, # 304; (小)銭 kozeni = small change, # 744; 釘 kugi = nail, # 825; (記)録 kiroku = a record, # 999; 鉛(筆) enpitsu = pencil, # 1092; 針 hari = needle, # 1138; 銅 dou = copper, # 1232; 鈍(い) nibui = dull, # 1245; 鉢 hachi = bowl, # 1277; (印)鑑 inkan = a stamp, # 1310; 鉱(山) kouzan = mine, # 1327; 鏡 kagami = mirror, # 1355; 鈴 suzu = a small bell, # 1370; 鍋 nabe = pot, # 1374; 鋭(い) surudoi = acute, # 1419; 鎖 kusari = a chain, # 1436; (鉄)鋼 tekkou = steel, # 1472; 釣(る) tsuru = to fish, # 1547; (拳)銃 kenjuu = a handgun, # 1555; (感)銘 kanmei = a deep impression, # 1666; 鎌 kama = a sickle, # 1667; 鍵 kagi = a key, # 1689; 鎮(める) shizumeru = to alleviate, # 1722; (倒)錯 tousaku = perversion, # 1771; 鍛(錬する) tanren suru = to train, # 1813; (鍛)錬(する) tanren suru = to train, # 1814; 鐘 kane = a bell, # 1840; 錦 nishiki = brocade, # 1880; 釜 kama = a pot, # 1896; 錠(剤) jouzai = a tablet, # 1914; 鋳(造) chuuzou = casting, # 2010   **ALSO COMPARE:** other similar kanji at # **607**

2011. 謹 PRONUNCIATION: kin
MEANINGS: discreet, reverently, humbly
EXAMPLES: 謹慎 kinshin = penitence, discipline, house arrest, self-restraint; 不謹慎な fukinshin na = indiscreet   **DESCRIPTION:** compared to (出)勤(する) shukkin suru (to attend work, # 517) (identical pronunciation), this kanji adds 言(う) iu (to speak, # 430) on the left, and it omits 力 (force) on the right; it retains the plant radical above a sincere guy wearing ordinary glasses [not bifocals, as seen in 里 sato (hometown, # 1060)], who takes care of these plants at a kindergarten   **CUE:** this sincere guy on the right, who wears these ordinary glasses, takes care of these plants at a **K**indergarten, where he 言 (speaks) with 謹慎 **kin**shin (self-restraint)
ALSO COMPARE: other similar kanji at # **517**

2012. 棺 PRONUNCIATION: kan
MEANINGS: coffin, casket   **EXAMPLE:** 棺 kan = a coffin   **DESCRIPTION:** compared to (警)官 keikan (policeman, # 880) (identical pronunciation), this kanji adds 木 ki (wood, # 118) on the left; it retains the bad haircut and the bunk bed in Kansas   **CUE:** in **Kan**sas, people with bad haircuts like this sometimes sleep in bunkbeds like this and, if they die, their 棺 **kan** (coffins) are often constructed from 木 (wood) like this
ALSO COMPARE: other similar kanji at # **880**

2013. 傲 PRONUNCIATION: gou
MEANING: be proud   **EXAMPLE:** 傲慢な gouman na = insolent, arrogant
DESCRIPTION: on the left, a man with a slanted hat; at the upper center, 土 tsuchi (soil, # 59); at the lower center, 方 kata (honorable person, # 114); on the right, a dancer with a ponytail
CUE: this man on the left tilts his hat back to examine this 土 (soil) in which this 方 (honorable person) is digging, trying to find a **G**opher, but this 傲慢な **gou**man na (arrogant) dancer walks away
ALSO COMPARE: 模倣 mohou = imitation, # 2016, which omits the 土 (soil); other similar kanji at # **1576** and # **2016**

2014. 舶 PRONUNCIATION: haku
MEANINGS: liner, ship   **EXAMPLE:** 舶来の hakurai no = imported   **DESCRIPTION:** compared to 白(髪) hakuhatsu (white hair, # 44) (identical pronunciation), this kanji adds 舟 fune (ship, # 1524) on the left   **CUE:** we saw this 白 (white) 舟 (ship) in the **H**arbor in **Ku**wait and learned that it was carrying 舶来の **haku**rai no (imported) goods   **GROUP:** 白 shiro = white, # 44; (目)的 mokuteki = purpose, # 45; (二)泊 nihaku = a two-night stay, # 46; 習(う) narau = to learn, # 472; 皆 mina = everyone, # 597; 階(段) kaidan = stairs, # 598; 激(しい) hageshii = fierce, # 1147; 綿 men = cotton, # 1189; 迫(力) hakuryoku = dynamism, # 1316; (天)皇 tennou = the Emperor, # 1458; 伯仲 hakuchuu = fierce competition, # 1572; (容)貌 youbou = looks, # 1687; 拍(手) hakushu = applause, # 1714; 錦 nishiki = brocade, # 1880; 舶(来の) hakurai no = imported, # 2014; 楷(書) kaisho = block script, # 2077; Note that five of these kanji can be pronounced "haku"   **ALSO COMPARE:** other similar kanji at # **1524**

2015. 租 PRONUNCIATION: so
MEANINGS: tariff, crop tax, borrowing
EXAMPLE: 租税 sozei = taxation
DESCRIPTION: compared to 祖(先) sosen (ancestor, # 272) (identical pronunciation), this kanji substitutes 禾 (a grain plant with a ripe head) for the Shah on the left; it retains the tomb that resembles a solar panel on the right
CUE: this 禾 (ripe grain) and this **S**olar panel are both subject to 租税 **so**zei (taxation) **ALSO COMPARE:** other similar kanji at # **752** and # **1797**

2016. 倣 PRONUNCIATION: hou
MEANINGS: emulate, imitate
EXAMPLE: 模倣 mohou = imitation
DESCRIPTION: compared to 放(送) housou (broadcasting, # 117) (identical pronunciation), this kanji adds a man with a slanted hat on the left; it retains the 方 kata (honorable person) named Hopeful Hannah and the dancer with a ponytail
CUES: this man on the left tilts his hat back in order to watch this 方 (honorable person), who is **H**opeful, and this dancer, since he is trying to create a 模倣 mo**hou** (imitation) of their routine
GROUP: 放(送) housou = broadcasting, # 117; 敷(く) shiku = spread, # 865; 激(減) gekigen = sharp decrease, # 1147; 傲(慢な) gouman na = insolent, # 2013; (模)倣 mohou = imitation, # 2016 **ALSO COMPARE:** other kanji containing 方 at # 920

2017. 抹 PRONUNCIATION: ma
MEANINGS: rub, paint, erase
EXAMPLES: 抹殺 massatsu = erasure, denial, ignoring (an opinion); 抹茶 maccha = powdered green tea for ceremonies
DESCRIPTION: compared to 末(期) makki (hour of death, # 119) (identical pronunciation), this kanji adds a kneeling guy on the left; it retains the magic 木 (tree) with an extra pair of branches, which are longer at the top
CUE: this guy on the left is kneeling in order to worship this 末 (tree with two pairs of branches which are longer at the top), since it's **M**agic and is capable of arranging his 抹殺 **ma**ssatsu (erasure) if he doesn't
ALSO COMPARE: other similar kanji at # **128** and # **672**

2018. 虹 PRONUNCIATION: niji
MEANING: rainbow **EXAMPLE:** 虹 niji = a rainbow **DESCRIPTION:** on the left, 虫 mushi (insect, # 9); on the right, 工(場) koujou (factory, # 246), which represents a crafted object needed to operate a Jeep, such as a key **CUE:** when I **N**eeded my **J**eep to drive out and look for 虹 **nij**i (rainbows), this 虫 (insect) was attached to this 工 (crafted object) which is my windshield wiper
ALSO COMPARE: other similar kanji at # **247** and # **1754**

2019. 娯 PRONUNCIATION: go
MEANINGS: recreation, pleasure
EXAMPLE: 娯楽 goraku = diversion, recreation, entertainment **DESCRIPTION:** compared to (服)呉 gofuku (cloth, # 1686) (identical pronunciation), this kanji adds 女 onna (female, # 235) on the left; it retains the pitcher on a gopher-infested mound **CUE:** this 呉 (pitcher on a **G**opher-infested mound) is trying to throw this square ball, but this 女 (female) wants him to try some other 娯楽 **go**raku (entertainment)
ALSO COMPARE: other kanji containing 女 on the left at # **2039**; other similar kanji at # **1686**

2020. 腺 PRONUNCIATION: sen

MEANING: gland **EXAMPLE:** 腺 sen = a gland; 甲状腺 koujousen = the thyroid gland **DESCRIPTION:** compared to (温)泉 onsen (hot spring, # 252) (identical pronunciation), this kanji adds 月 tsuki (moon, # 148) on the left; it retains Senator 白 Shiro [white, # 44, which consists of 日 (sun) under a ray] and 水 (water) **CUE:** this Senator 白 (White), who has overactive 腺 sen (glands) that are influenced by this 月 (moon), is rafting in this 水 (water) **ALSO COMPARE:** other similar kanji at # **228**

2021. 喩 PRONUNCIATION: yu

MEANING: metaphor **EXAMPLE:** 比喩 hiyu = a simile or metaphor **DESCRIPTION:** on the left, 口 kuchi (mouth, # 426), which can also be seen as a box; at the upper right, 入(る) hairu (to enter, # 14), which resembles the roof of a house with snow blowing off the top; below that, a horizontal line which may represent a ceiling; at the lower center, a modified 月 tsuki (moon, # 148); at the lower right, an abbreviated chevron, as seen in 巡(査) junsa (patrolman, # 778) **CUES:** we live in this house in the Yukon and use 口 (mouths) like this to express 比喩 hi**yu** (similes) comparing 月 (moons) like this to chevrons like this **ALSO COMPARE:** other similar kanji at # **14**, # **1019**, # **1382**, # **1991** and # **2073**

2022. 萎 PRONUNCIATIONS: i, na

MEANINGS: wither, droop, lame **EXAMPLES:** 萎縮 ishuku = withering, atrophy, contraction; 萎える naeru = to lose strength, to become weak, to wither or droop **DESCRIPTION:** compared to 委(員会) iinkai (a committee, # 1364) (identical pronunciation), this kanji adds a plant radical at the top; it retains the 女 (female) carrying some 禾 (ripe grain) which she finds it easy to carry **CUES:** this 女 (female) was carrying this 禾 (ripe grain) which was Easy until someone added these additional plants at the top, causing her to stumble and take a Nasty fall, and now her muscles are affected by 萎縮 ishuku (withering) **ALSO COMPARE:** other similar kanji at # **1797** and # **2086**

2023. 蛍 PRONUNCIATIONS: kei, hotaru

MEANINGS: lightning bug, firefly **EXAMPLES:** 蛍光灯 keikoutou = a fluorescent light; 蛍 hotaru = a firefly, often written ホタル **DESCRIPTION:** compared to 覚(える) oboeru (to memorize, # 54), this substitutes 虫 mushi (insect, # 9) for 見 (to look) at the bottom; it retains the three old boys on a roof **CUES:** these three old boys on a roof saw Santa fly into a Cave full of 蛍 hotaru (fireflies), which are 虫 (insects) like this, and then they watched him fly Home to Talk to Rudolph about better lighting for his sleigh **ALSO COMPARE:** other similar kanji at # **991** and # **1754**

2024. 窒 PRONUNCIATION: chi

MEANINGS: plug up, obstruct **EXAMPLE:** 窒素 chisso = nitrogen **DESCRIPTION:** compared to 至(る) itaru (to lead to, # 609), this adds a soaring Cuban bird, as seen in (研)究 kenkyuu (research, # 112), at the top; it retains the 一 (one) ム (cow) stuck in some 土 (soil) **CUE:** this soaring bird flies over this 一 (one) ム (cow) that is stuck in this 土 (soil) and offers it some Cheese, and they are both breathing mostly 窒素 **chi**sso (nitrogen) **ALSO COMPARE:** other similar kanji at # **63** and # **112**

2025. 桁 PRONUNCIATION: keta

MEANINGS: beam, girder, column (accounting) **EXAMPLE:** 桁 keta = a beam, girder, unit or numerical column (accounting) **DESCRIPTION:** on the left, 木 ki (tree, # 118); on the right, 行(く) iku (to go, # 334) **CUE:** I will 行 (go) to get a 木 (tree) like this to make a 桁 keta (beam) for Kennedy's Tavern **ALSO COMPARE:** other similar kanji at # **625**

2026. 栓 PRONUNCIATION: sen
MEANINGS: plug, bolt, cork, stopper
EXAMPLE: 栓 sen = a bottle cap, cork or stopper
DESCRIPTION: compared to 全(て) subete (all, # 300), this kanji adds 木 ki (tree, # 118) on the left; it retains the 王 (king) in a Zen temple with a peaked roof CUE: a **Sen**ator wants to cut 全 (all) of the 木 (trees) in a forest to make 栓 **sen** (corks)
GROUP: 全(部) zenbu = everything, # 300; 詮(索) sensaku = an inquiry into, # 1944 (identical pronunciation); 栓 sen = a bottle cap, # 2026

2027. 嫡 PRONUNCIATION: chaku
MEANINGS: legitimate wife, direct descendant (non-bastard) EXAMPLE: 嫡男 chakunan = an heir or oldest son DESCRIPTION: compared to (指)摘 shiteki (pointing out, # 1083), this substitutes 女 onna (female, # 235) for the kneeling techie on the left; it retains the 立 (bell) used by an 古 (old) sentry in a two-sided lean-to to make loud 音 (sounds) CUE: when this 女 (female) met this 古 (old) sentry who was ringing this 立 (bell) from this two-sided lean-to, he told her that he was the 嫡男 **chaku**nan (heir) to a fortune and would buy her a **Cha**ndelier from **Ku**wait
ALSO COMPARE: other kanji containing 女 on the left at # **2039**; other similar kanji at # **881**

2028. 屯 PRONUNCIATION: ton
MEANINGS: barracks, police station, camp
EXAMPLE: 駐屯 chuuton = stationing (troops), occupancy DESCRIPTION: compared to (整)頓 seiton (orderliness, # 1248) (identical pronunciation), this kanji omits the headless platform on a money chest on the right; it retains the number 七 (seven) with the letter U superimposed on it, reminding us of the seven Universal Laws followed by Tony Blair
CUE: **Ton**y Blair was following the 七 (seven) Universal Laws when he decided to 駐屯する

chuu**ton** suru (station) soldiers in Iraq
ALSO COMPARE: other similar kanji at # **1245**

2029. 糾 PRONUNCIATION: kyuu
MEANINGS: twist, investigate, verify, ask
EXAMPLE: 糾問 kyuumon = an enquiry
DESCRIPTION: compared to 叫(ぶ) sakebu (to shout, # 746), this substitutes 糸 (skeet shooter, # 219) for the 口 (mouth) on the left; it retains the number 4 CUE: this 糸 (skeet shooter) visited **Cu**ba 4 times for skeet-shooting contests, violating sanctions, and he is the subject of an 糾問 **kyuu**mon (enquiry)
ALSO COMPARE: other similar kanji at # **746**

2030. 陪 PRONUNCIATION: bai
MEANINGS: follow, accompany, attend on
EXAMPLE: 陪審 baishin = a jury
DESCRIPTION: compared to 倍(増する) baizou suru (to double, # 269) (identical pronunciation), this kanji substitutes ß beta from the Greek alphabet for the man with a slanted hat on the left; it retains the bell on a box which the man wanted to buy; Note: this is a reverse image of 部(屋) heya (room, # 267), in which a right-wing ß (Greek) person named Helen is on the *right*
CUE: this left-wing ß (Greek) guy tried to **Buy** this bell on this box with a fake credit card, and now a 陪審 **bai**shin (jury) will determine his fate
GROUP: 隅 sumi = inside corner, # 79; 降(る) furu = to rain, # 178; (危)険 kiken = danger, # 196; 隣 tonari = next door, # 329; (国)際 kokusai = international, # 379; (病)院 byouin = hospital, # 424; 階(段) kaidan = stairs, # 598; 陣(地) jinchi = encampment, # 638; 限(界) genkai = limit, # 642; (掃)除(する) souji suru = to clean, # 646; (軍)隊 guntai = army, # 726; 隠(す) kakusu = to hide, # 834; 隙 suki = gap, # 879; (太)陽 taiyou = the sun, # 891; (予)防 yobou = prevention, # 920; (大)阪 oosaka = Osaka, # 1005; 陸(軍) rikugun = army, # 1015;

阿(呆) aho = a fool, # 1176; 陛(下) heika = the Emperor, # 1460; (故)障 koshou = a breakdown, # 1495; 陰 kage = shade, # 1543; (興)隆 kouryuu = prosperity, # 1594; (欠)陥 kekkan = a flaw, # 1660; 随(分) zuibun = very, # 1670; (間)隔 kankaku = an interim, # 1729; 陶(器) touki = chinaware, # 1741; 陳(述) chinjutsu = a statement, # 1742; 阻(害) sogai = an obstruction, # 1838; 墜(落) tsuiraku = a plane crash, # 1972; 陪(審) baishin = a jury, # 2030
ALSO COMPARE: kanji with ß on the *right* at # 1843; other similar kanji at # **269**

2031. 雌 PRONUNCIATION: mesu
MEANINGS: feminine, female
EXAMPLE: 雌 mesu = a female (animal)
DESCRIPTION: on the left, 止(める) tomeru (to stop, # 173); in the center, the katakana ヒ hi, which reminds us of a hero; on the right, a net, which can be seen as a man with a slanted hat next to a 主 (master) with an extra pair of arms (see # 203)
CUE: this ヒ (hero) is a **M**edical **S**upervisor who 止 (stopped) a 雌 **mes**u (female) cat from getting trapped in this net   ALSO COMPARE: 雄 osu = a male (animal), # 1518; other similar kanji at # **1929**, # **2046** and # **2048**

2032. 霜 PRONUNCIATION: shimo
MEANING: frost   EXAMPLE: 霜 shimo = frost
DESCRIPTION: compared to 相(談) soudan (advice, # 787), this adds 雨 ame (rain, # 261) at the top; it retains the 木 (tree) that I have my 目 (eye) on, under which I plan to listen to soul music
CUE: I had my 目 (eye) on this 木 (tree), and after this 雨 (rain) turned to 霜 **shim**o (frost) and my **S**heep started **Mo**aning from the cold, I gathered the flock under it   ALSO COMPARE: other similar kanji at # **262** and # **787**

2033. 紡 PRONUNCIATIONS: tsumu, bou
MEANING: spinning   EXAMPLES: 紡ぐ tsumugu = to spin (textiles); 紡績 bouseki = spinning (textiles)   DESCRIPTION: compared to (予)防 yobou (prevention, # 920) (identical pronunciation), this kanji substitutes 糸 ito (skeet shooter, # 219) for ß (Greek) on the left; it retains 方 (honorable person)
CUES: this 糸 (skeet shooter) wears humble **Ts**uits (suits) made by **Moo**nies, and he fires irritably at this 方 (honorable person) who is **Bo**asting about wearing suits made from the 紡績 **bou**seki (spinning) of the finest cloth
ALSO COMPARE: other similar kanji at # **920**

2034. 貪 PRONUNCIATION: don
MEANINGS: covet, indulge in   EXAMPLE: 貪欲な don'yoku na = avaricious, greedy
DESCRIPTION: at the top, 今 ima (now, # 292), which contains a 7 under a ceiling under a peaked roof; at the bottom, 貝 kai (shell, money chest, # 83)   CUE: I asked the 貪欲な **don**'yoku na (greedy) person who keeps money in this 貝 (money chest) to **Don**ate 今 (now), but he refused
ALSO COMPARE: other similar kanji at # **707** and # **1491**

2035. 庸 PRONUNCIATION: you
MEANINGS: commonplace, ordinary, employment
EXAMPLE: 凡庸 bon'you = mediocre, commonplace   DESCRIPTION: compared to (健)康 kenkou (health, # 831), this substitutes 用(事) youji (errand, # 364) (identical pronunciation), which resembles a Japanese fence, for 求 (demand) at the lower right; it retains the lean-to with a chimney containing a man who has been stabbed with a trident   CUE: after this chimney inside this lean-to was stabbed with this trident, I was figuratively on this 用 (fence) about what to do and finally just ate some **Y**ogurt, but later I was told that my decision was 凡庸 bon'**you** (mediocre)
COMPARE: other similar kanji at # **367** and # **1494**

2036. 韻 PRONUNCIATION: in
MEANINGS: rhyme, elegance, tone
EXAMPLES: 韻文 inbun = verse or poetry; 余韻 yoin = a reverberation, a lingering memory
DESCRIPTION: compared to 音 oto (sound, # 266), or (母)音 boin (vowel, # 266) (identical pronunciation), this kanji adds 員 in (group member, # 88) (also identical pronunciation), which reminds us of an insider, on the right CUES: this 員 (Insider) write some 韻文 **in**bun (poetry) about 音 (sounds) like this ALSO COMPARE: other similar kanji at # **88** and # **266**

2037. 繕 PRONUNCIATIONS: zen, tsukuro MEANINGS: darning, repair, mend
EXAMPLES: 修繕 shuuzen = a repair; 繕う tsukurou = to mend or repair
DESCRIPTION: compared to (改)善 kaizen (improvement, # 1336) (identical pronunciation), this kanji adds 糸 (skeet shooter, # 219) on the left; it retains the 羊 (sheep) standing on an upside-down bench above a 口 (box) CUES: this 糸 (skeet shooter) fired at this 羊 (sheep) standing on this upside-down bench above this 口 (box) and tore its coat, but a **Z**en monk who was walking with his **Ts**uitcase (suitcase) on a **Ku**waiti **R**oad 繕った **tsukuro**tta (repaired) the wound
ALSO COMPARE: other similar kanji at # **1223** and # **1236**

2038. 搾 PRONUNCIATIONS: shibo, saku MEANING: squeeze EXAMPLES: 搾る shiboru = to wring, squeeze or narrow down (this is usually spelled 絞る, # 1739); 搾取 sakushu = exploitation DESCRIPTION: on the left, a kneeling guy; at the upper right, a soaring Cuban bird, as seen in (研)究 kenkyuu (research, # 112); at the lower right, a serrated axe, as seen in 作(品) sakuhin (a work of literature, # 482) (identical pronunciation), which fits in a sack and which can also be seen as a ladder or stairs
CUES: after a **Sh**eep was **B**orn, this soaring bird attacked it, and this guy on the left kneeled in order to defend the baby, using this serrated axe which he had in a **Sack,** but then he was accused of 搾取 **saku**shu (exploitation) of wildlife ALSO COMPARE: other similar kanji at # **41** and # **112**

2039. 姻 PRONUNCIATION: in
MEANINGS: matrimony, marry
EXAMPLE: 婚姻 kon'in = marriage
DESCRIPTION: compared to (原)因 gen'in (cause, # 1360) (identical pronunciation), this kanji adds 女 onna (female, # 235) on the left; it retains the 大 (big) guy with insanity resulting from his being stuck in this box
CUE: this 女 (female) is considering 婚姻 kon'**in** (marriage) to this 大 (big) guy stuck in this box, even though he suffers from **In**sanity
GROUP: 女 onna = female, # 235; 安(い) yasui = cheap , # 236; 妻 tsuma = wife, # 237; 要(る) iru = to need, # 238; 好(き) suki = liking, # 239; (結)婚 kekkon = marriage, # 240; 姉 ane = older sister, # 241; 妹 imouto = younger sister, # 244; 娘 musume = daughter, # 316; 怒(る) okoru = to get angry, # 319; 努(力) doryoku = effort, # 519; 始(める) hajimeru = to begin, # 540; 嬉(しい) ureshii = pleased, # 600; 数 kazu = number, # 639; 嫌(い) kirai = hating, # 817; 妙 myou = strange, # 856; 姫 hime = princess, # 1040; (王)妃 ouhi = queen, # 1078; (舞)妓 maiko = dancing girl, # 1121; 婦(人) fujin = woman, # 1165; 姓 sei = a surname, # 1499; 嫁 yome = bride, # 1527; 如(才ない) josainai = clever, # 1578; 奴(隷) dorei = slave, # 1582; (お)嬢(さん) ojousan = young girl, # 1659; 妊(婦) ninpu = pregnant woman, # 1731; (妊)娠 ninshin = pregnancy, # 1732; 妖(怪) youkai = ghost, # 1811; 媒(介) baikai = a medium, # 1889; 嫉(妬) shitto = jealousy, # 1890; 妬(む) netamu = to be jealous, # 1891; 妨(げる) samatageru = to

obstruct, # 1917; (花)婿 hanamuko = bridegroom, # 1960; 娯(楽) goraku = diversion, # 2019; 嫡(男) chakunan = heir, # 2027; (婚)姻 kon'in = marriage, # 2039; (愛)媛(県) ehime ken = Ehime Prefecture, # 2084   ALSO COMPARE: other similar kanji at # **1360**

2040. 拷 PRONUNCIATION: gou

MEANINGS: torture, beat   **EXAMPLE:** 拷問 goumon = torture   **DESCRIPTION:** compared to 考(える) kangaeru (to think, # 469), this adds a kneeling guy on the left; it retains the kangaroo who is a 者 (person) that plays with scissors

CUE: this guy on the left 考 (thinks) that if he kneels and offers **G**old, this kangaroo might stop subjecting itself to the 拷問 **gou**mon (torture) that often results from playing with scissors like these   ALSO COMPARE: other similar kanji at # **468** and # **1065**

2041. 堆 PRONUNCIATION: tai

MEANING: piled high   **EXAMPLE:** 堆積物 taisekibutsu = sediment, deposit   **DESCRIPTION:** compared to 誰 dare (who, # 440), this substitutes 土 tsuchi (soil, # 59) for 言 (to speak) on the left; it retains the net on the right, which can be seen as a man with a slanted hat next to a 主 (master) with an extra pair of arms (see # 203)   **CUE:** this net contains a **T**iger which is covered in 堆積物 **tai**sekibutsu (deposits) of 土 (soil) like this   ALSO COMPARE: other similar kanji at # **2046**

2042. 禍 PRONUNCIATION: ka

MEANINGS: calamity, misfortune, evil, curse
EXAMPLE: 戦禍 senka = the ravages of war, war damages (this can also be spelled 戦火, # 443, which implies fire damage from war)
DESCRIPTION: compared to (戦)渦 senka (the turmoil of war, # 1871) (identical pronunciation), this kanji substitutes the Shah, as seen in (会)社 kaisha (company, # 271), for the water radical on the left; it retains the two cartons, one of which is slipping, inside boxes, as seen in 過(ぎる) sugiru (to exceed, # 361)   **CUE:** after 戦禍 sen**ka** (war damages) 過 (exceeded) expectations, this Shah saw that the **Ca**rton in this upper box had been dislodged   ALSO COMPARE: other similar kanji at # **361** and # **1160**

2043. 抄 PRONUNCIATION: shou

MEANINGS: extract, selection, summary, copy
EXAMPLES: 抄本 shouhon = an excerpt, abstract or abbreviated transcript; 戸籍抄本 kosekishouhon = an official copy of a family registry extract   **DESCRIPTION:** compared to 少(々) shoushou (a little, # 254) (identical pronunciation), or 少(ない) sukunai (few, scarce, # 254), this kanji adds a kneeling guy on the left; it retains ノ (no) below 小 (small)
CUE: since I'm **Sh**ort, this guy on the left is kneeling to allow me to see a book 抄本 **shou**hon (excerpt) that he's holding, which contains only 少 (a few) pages
ALSO COMPARE: other similar kanji at # **1010**

2044. 遜 PRONUNCIATION: son

MEANINGS: humble, modest
EXAMPLES: 謙遜 kenson = modesty; 謙遜な kenson na = humble, modest
DESCRIPTION: compared to 孫 mago (grandchild, # 1072), or (子)孫 shison (descendant, # 1072) (identical pronunciation), this kanji adds a snail at the lower left; it retains the 子 (child) and the 糸 (skeet shooter) with a cape over its head, who sings songs   **CUE:** this 子 (child) rides on this snail as he sings **S**ongs, and this 糸 (skeet shooter) covers his head with this cape due to 謙遜 ken**son** (modesty)   ALSO COMPARE: other similar kanji at # **1072** and # **2078**

2045. 旺 PRONUNCIATION: ou

MEANINGS: flourishing, successful, vigorous
EXAMPLE: 旺盛な ousei na = flourishing, active, high   **DESCRIPTION:** compared to 王 ou (king, # 1077) (identical pronunciation), this kanji

adds 日 hi (sun, # 32) on the left **CUE:** since this 王 (king) is **O**ld, he can't stand in this 日 (sun) for very long, but his kingdom is 旺盛 **ou**sei (flourishing) **GROUP:** (主)任 shunin = foreman, # 483; 庭 niwa = garden, # 495; 王 ou = king, # 1077; 班(長) hanchou = a squad leader, # 1509; 狂(気) kyouki = lunacy, # 1566; (法)廷 houtei = a court of law, # 1664; 妊(婦) ninpu = a pregnant woman, # 1731; 淫(らな) midara na = indecent, # 1877; 旺(盛な) ousei na = flourishing, # 2045

2046. 准 PRONUNCIATION: jun
MEANINGS: quasi-, semi-, associate
EXAMPLE: 批准 hijun = ratification
DESCRIPTION: compared to 準(備) junbi (preparation, # 204) (identical pronunciation), this kanji omits 十 (ten) at the bottom; it retains the water radical and the net used for jungle fishing, which can be seen as a man with a slanted hat next to a 主 (master) with an extra pair of arms (see # 203) **CUE:** we expect 批准 hi**jun** (ratification) of an agreement allowing the use of nets like this in water like this for **J**ungle fishing **GROUP:** 難(しい) muzukashii = difficult, # 198; 集(まる) atsumaru = to congregate, # 202; 進む susumu = to advance, # 203; 準(備) junbi = preparation, # 204; 誰 dare = who, # 440; 離(れる) hanareru = to part, # 666; 焦(点) shouten = focus, # 750; 雑(誌) zasshi = magazine, # 785; (温)雅 onga = graceful, # 922; 携(帯電話) keitai denwa = cellular phone, # 1011; 推(す) osu = to recommend, # 1029; 催(す) moyoosu = to hold an event, # 1110; (岩)礁 ganshou = reef, # 1270; 唯(一) yuiitsu = unique, # 1337; 雇(う) yatou = to employ, # 1398; (英)雄 eiyuu = a hero, # 1518; 顧(問) komon = an advisor, # 1648; (幼)稚(園) youchien = kindergarten, # 1797; 擁(護) yougo = protection, # 1841; (脊)椎 sekitsui = the spine, # 1868; 雌 mesu = a female (animal), # 2031; 堆(積物) taisekibutsu = sediment, # 2041; (批)准 hijun = ratification, # 2046

2047. 勾 PRONUNCIATION: kou
MEANINGS: be bent, slope, capture
EXAMPLES: 勾配 koubai = a slope or incline
DESCRIPTION: compared to 匂(う) niou (to smell of, # 949), this substitutes the katakana ム mu, which reminds us of cows, for the ヒ (hero) in the middle; it retains the hook that a neonatologist uses for fishing **CUE:** when this ム (**c**ow) gets **C**old, it walks into this giant fish hook for shelter, but then it emerges and climbs the 勾配 **kou**bai (slope) that takes it home **ALSO COMPARE:** other similar kanji at # **591** and # **988**

2048. 壱 PRONUNCIATION: ichi
MEANING: one **EXAMPLES:** 壱 ichi = one, usually written 一; 壱万円 ichiman'en = 10,000 yen, usually written 一万円
DESCRIPTION: at the top, (紳)士 shinshi (gentleman, # 66), standing on a platform; at the bottom, the katakana ヒ hi, which reminds us of a hero **CUE:** there is 壱 **ichi** (one) 士 (man) standing above this platform and 壱 **ichi** (one) ヒ (hero) standing below it, and even though they have had no contact, they are both feeling **It**chy **GROUP:** 頃 koro = approximate time, # 96; 背 sei = height, # 152; 死(ぬ) shinu = to die, # 164; 北 kita = north, # 373; 泥(棒) dorobou = thief, # 819; 匂(い) nioi = fragrance, # 949; 疑(う) utagau = to doubt, # 978; 老(人) roujin = elderly person, # 1065; 葬(式) soushiki = funeral, # 1273; 掲(示) keiji = a written notice, # 1466; 紫 murasaki = purple, # 1665; 凝(る) koru = to grow stiff, # 1680; 蛇 hebi = a snake, # 1754; 鬱(病)

utsubyou = depression, # 1783; 尼 ama = a nun, # 1899; 渇(く) kawaku = to be thirsty, # 1928; 喝(采) kassai = applause, # 1934; (模)擬 mogi = imitation, # 2003; 雌 mesu = a female, # 2031; 壱 ichi = one, # 2048; 褐(色) kasshoku = dark brown, # 2059; 叱(責) shisseki = a reprimand, # 2073 **ALSO COMPARE:** kanji containing two ヒ's at # 1294; other similar kanji at # **1468**

2049. 升 PRONUNCIATIONS: masu, shou
MEANINGS: measuring box, 1.8 liters
EXAMPLES: 升 masu = a small square measuring box, sometimes used for sake; 一升 isshou = an old liquid measurement unit equaling 1.8 liters
DESCRIPTION: compared to (上)昇 joushou (rising, # 1363) (identical pronunciation), this kanji omits 日 (sun) at the top; it retains the 千 (thousand) and 十 (ten) people who watched a show
CUES: there are 千十 (1,010) ways to make **Ma**ngo **Sou**p, and I will **Show** you how to make 一升 is**shou** (1.8 liters) of it **ALSO COMPARE:** other similar kanji at # **22**, # **1363** and # **1828**

2050. 耗 PRONUNCIATION: mou
MEANING: decrease **EXAMPLE:** 消耗する shoumou suru = to consume, use up or deplete
DESCRIPTION: compared to 毛(布) moufu (blanket, # 688) (identical pronunciation), this kanji adds 士 shi (man, # 66) standing on 木 (tree) on the left; it retains the reversed 手 (hand) of a right-wing guy named Moses **CUE:** this 士 shi (man) standing on this 木 (tree) is **Mo**ses, who is surveying the forest, and he will use this 毛 (reversed hand) to cut down many 木 (trees) and 消耗する shou**mou** suru (deplete) their supply
GROUP: 耕(す) tagayasu = to plow, # 1312; (国)籍 kokuseki = nationality, # 1604; (消)耗(する) shoumou suru = to consume, # 2050
ALSO COMPARE: kanji depicting trees with two pairs of branches at # 672; other similar kanji at # **688**

2051. 箋 PRONUNCIATION: sen
MEANINGS: paper, label, letter, composition
EXAMPLE: 便箋 binsen = writing paper, stationery **DESCRIPTION:** at the top, 竹 take (bamboo, # 134); in the middle, a halberd (combination axe and lance), at the bottom, another halberd
CUE: a **Sen**ator uses these two halberds to chop this 竹 (bamboo) into pulp in order to make 便箋 bin**sen** (writing paper)
ALSO COMPARE: other similar kanji at # **352**, # **1862** and # **2074**

2052. 串 PRONUNCIATION: kushi
MEANINGS: shish kebab, spit, skewer
EXAMPLE: 串 kushi = a skewer
DESCRIPTION: compared to 患(者) kanja (a patient, # 1551), this omits the 心 (heart) at the bottom; it retains the 中 (yakitori) with an extra piece of chicken
CUE: I have a **Cush**y job that involves using a 串 **kushi** (skewer) to pierce pieces of food like this
ALSO COMPARE: other similar kanji at # **657**

2053. 弔 PRONUNCIATIONS: tomura, chou
MEANINGS: condolences, mourning, funeral **EXAMPLES:** 弔う tomurau = to mourn, to hold a funeral; 弔辞 chouji = a message of condolence or a memorial address
DESCRIPTION: compared to a twisted 弓 yumi (bow, # 1044), this adds a pole in the center
CUES: after a great archer died, **To**lstoy painted a **Mur**al of this 弓 (bow) hanging from a pole, and Margaret **Cho** delivered the 弔辞 **chou**ji (memorial address)
ALSO COMPARE: other similar kanji at # **476**

2054. 賓 PRONUNCIATION: hin
MEANINGS: V.I.P., guest
EXAMPLE: 来賓 raihin = a guest or visitor
DESCRIPTION: compared to 貧(困) hinkon (poverty, # 1339) (identical pronunciation), this kanji substitutes a bad haircut, a horizontal carpet and 少 (し) sukoshi (a little, # 254) for 分 (understand) at the top; it retains the 貝 (money chest) **CUE:** I had just gotten this bad haircut, and all that I had in the world were this small carpet and 少 (a little) money in this 貝 (money chest), but my **H**indu friend greeted me as an honored 来賓 rai**hin** (guest)
ALSO COMPARE: other similar kanji at # **707** and # **1010**

2055. 痢 PRONUNCIATION: ri
MEANING: diarrhea **EXAMPLE:** 下痢 geri = diarrhea **DESCRIPTION:** compared to 利(用する) riyou suru (to use, # 564) (identical pronunciation), this kanji adds a sick bed, as seen in 病(気) byouki (illness, # 369), at the upper left; it retains the 禾 (grain plant with a ripe head), and the katakana リ ri (also identical pronunciation)
CUES: after eating this 禾 (ripe grain), this リ **R**i entered this sick bed, and the **Rea**son was 下痢 ge**ri** (diarrhea) **GROUP:** (細)菌 saikin = bacterium, # 1210; 透(明) toumei = transparent, # 1253; 蘇(る) yomigaeru = to revive, # 1279; 誘(う) sasou = to invite, # 1405; (下)痢 geri = diarrhea, # 2055 **ALSO COMPARE:** other similar kanji at # **369** and # **1985**

2056. 俸 PRONUNCIATIONS: pou, hou
MEANINGS: stipend, salary
EXAMPLES: 年俸 nenpou = an annual salary; 俸給 houkyuu = a salary **DESCRIPTION:** compared to 奉(仕) houshi (service, # 1536) (identical pronunciation), this adds a man with a slanted hat on the left; it retains the 三 (three) 人 (people) who have their home on this telephone pole **CUES:** this man on the left raises his hat to be **P**olite as he meets these 三 (three) 人 (people), and he wants to join their **H**ome on this telephone pole and share his 俸給 **hou**kyuu (salary) with them
ALSO COMPARE: 棒 bou = a stick, # 820; other similar kanji at # **506** and # **820**

2057. 罷 PRONUNCIATION: hi
MEANINGS: quit, stop, leave, withdraw
EXAMPLES: 罷免 himen = dismissal, discharge; 罷免する himen suru = to dismiss (from a job)
DESCRIPTION: compared to 能(力) nouryoku (ability, # 616), this adds 目 me (eye, # 51), turned sideways, which resembles three eyes, at the top; it retains the ム (cow) with a stuffy nose on a 月 (moon) and the two ヒ hi's, which remind us of heroes **CUES:** these three eyes are shielding this ム (cow) on this 月 (moon) and these two ヒ (heroes) from the **H**eat of the sun, while at the same time spying on them to see if they deserve 罷免 **hi**men (dismissal)
ALSO COMPARE: other similar kanji at # **616**, # **1294**, # **1324** and # **1991**

2058. 賦 PRONUNCIATION: pu
MEANINGS: levy, tribute, installment, poem
EXAMPLE: 月賦 geppu = a monthly installment or payment **DESCRIPTION:** compared to 武(器) buki (weapon, # 1418), this adds 貝 kai (money chest, # 83) on the left; it retains the leaning Buddhist woman with a ball above her shoulder, the horizontal line resembling a spear, and 止 (stop)
CUE: although this leaning woman with a ball above her shoulder is **P**oor, she's been taking money from this 貝 (money chest) to make 月賦 gep**pu** (monthly payments) for this spear, but now she wants to 止 (stop) paying
GROUP: 貝 kai = money chest, # 83; 贈(る) okuru = to give a present, # 84; 貯(金) chokin = savings, # 667; 敗(れる) yabureru = to lose, # 793; 販(売) hanbai = sales, # 1199; 購(入する) kounyuu suru = to purchase, # 1269; (規)則 kisoku = rules, # 1342; 財(布) saifu = a wallet,

1437; (盗)賊 touzoku = a robber, # 1652; 賠(償) baishou = compensation, # 1661; 賭(ける) kakeru = to bet, # 1761; 貼(る) haru = to paste, # 1766; (贈)賄 zouwai = bribery, # 1979; (月)賦 geppu = a monthly payment, # 2058
ALSO COMPARE: other similar kanji at # **249** and # **1929**

2059. 褐 PRONUNCIATION: ka
MEANINGS: brown, woolen kimono
EXAMPLE: 褐色 kasshoku = dark brown
DESCRIPTION: compared to 喝(采) kassai (applause, # 1934) (identical pronunciation), this kanji substitutes happy Jimmy with two lips, as seen in 初(めて) hajimete (for the first time, # 104), for 口 (mouth) on the left; it retains 日 hi (sun, # 32), which resembles a two-drawer cabinet, and 匂 (fragrance), suggesting a cabinet full of fragrant sweets
CUES: this happy Jimmy with two lips, who is a **Ca**rpenter, built this 褐色 **ka**sshoku (dark brown) 日 (two-drawer cabinet) full of 匂 (fragrant) sweets   **ALSO COMPARE:** other similar kanji at # **1466**, # **1615** and # **2048**

2060. 斥 PRONUNCIATION: seki
MEANINGS: reject, recede, withdraw, repel
EXAMPLES: 排斥 haiseki = exclusion, boycott, shut-out; 排斥する haiseki suru = to expel, boycott or shut out   **DESCRIPTION:** compared to 訴(訟) soshou (lawsuit, # 1545), this omits 言 (to say) on the left; it retains the pair of pliers with a slash on its handle
CUE: when a **Se**lfish **Ki**ng saw that a servant had slashed the handle of this pair of pliers, he 排斥した hai**seki** shita (expelled) the guy
GROUP: 訴(訟) soshou = lawsuit, # 1545; (排)斥 haiseki = exclusion, # 2060
ALSO COMPARE: kanji containing pliers *without* slashes at # 892

2061. 矯 PRONUNCIATION: kyou
MEANINGS: rectify, straighten, reform, cure
EXAMPLES: 矯正 kyousei = a correction; 矯正する kyousei suru = to correct
DESCRIPTION: compared to 橋 hashi (bridge, # 139), or (歩道)橋 hodoukyou (pedestrian bridge, # 139) (identical pronunciation), this kanji substitutes a Native American chief, as seen in 知(る) shiru (to know, # 323), for 木 (wood) on the left; it retains the right portion of a 橋 (bridge) in Kyouto, which is capped by a 天 (sky, # 189)
CUE: when this Native American chief visited **Kyou**to, he saw this 橋 (bridge) under this 天 (sky) and suggested some 矯正 **kyou**sei (corrections) to it   **ALSO COMPARE:** other similar kanji at # **139**, # **324** and # **1467**

2062. 窃 PRONUNCIATION: se
MEANINGS: stealth, steal, secret
EXAMPLE: 窃盗 settou = theft
DESCRIPTION: compared to 切(る) kiru (to cut, # 103), this adds a soaring bird, as seen in (研)究 kenkyuu (research, # 112), at the top; it retains 七 (seven, # 20) and 刀 (sword, # 102)
CUE: after this soaring bird completes the 窃盗 **se**ttou (theft) of these 七 (seven) 刀 (swords), it plans to **Se**ll them
GROUP: 刀 katana = sword, # 102; 切(る) kiru = to cut, # 103; (最)初 saisho = the beginning, # 104; 分 fun = minute, # 105; 喫(煙) kitsuen = smoking, # 192; 辺 hen = area, # 362; (理)解 rikai = understanding, # 618; (清)潔 seiketsu = clean, # 1212; 券 ken = ticket, # 1305; 契(約) keiyaku = a contract, # 1602; 窃(盗) settou = theft, # 2062   **ALSO COMPARE:** other similar kanji at # **20** and # **112**

2063. 惰 PRONUNCIATION: da
MEANINGS: laziness, idleness, sloth
EXAMPLE: 怠惰な taida na = lazy
DESCRIPTION: on the left, an erect man; at the

upper right, 左 hidari (left, # 456); at the lower right, 月 tsuki (moon, # 148)
CUES: this man on the left, whose name is **Darwin**, is tall and proud like this, but he drives on the 左 (left) side of the road when he's on this 月 (moon), and he's 怠惰 tai**da** (lazy)
GROUP: (習)慣 shuukan = customs, # 92; (愛)情 aijou = love, # 156; 性 sei = gender, # 209; 怖(い) kowai = afraid, # 463; 忙(しい) isogashii = busy, # 586; 慎(重) shinchou = careful, # 632; (後)悔 koukai = regret, # 675; 慌(てる) awateru = to panic, # 710; 愉(快) yukai = pleasant, # 733; (愉)快 yukai = pleasant, # 734; 懐(かしい) natsukashii = nostalgic, # 928; 怪(しい) ayashii = suspicious, # 1024; (自)慢 jiman = pride, # 1127; 悩(み) nayami = distress, # 1181; 悟(る) satoru = to realize, # 1526; (記)憶(する) kioku suru = to remember, # 1540; 哀悼 aitou = condolences, # 1644; 憎(む) nikumu = to hate, # 1651; 惨(めな) mijime na = miserable, # 1678; 惜(しい) oshii = unfortunate, # 1708; 恨(む) uramu = to bear a grudge, # 1724; 悦(に入る) etsu ni iru = to be happy, # 1779; 憤(慨する) fungai suru = to be indignant, # 1781; (憤)慨(する) fungai suru = to be indignant, # 1782; 恒(例) kourei = customary, # 1800; 憧(れる) akogareru = to admire, # 1956; (怠)惰(な) taida na = lazy, # 2063; (遺)憾 ikan = regret, # 2065
ALSO COMPARE: other similar kanji at # **456** and # **1991**

2064. 倹 PRONUNCIATION: ken
MEANINGS: frugal, economy, thrifty
EXAMPLES: 倹約 ken'yaku = thrift
DESCRIPTION: compared to (危)険 kiken (danger, # 196) (identical pronunciation), this kanji substitutes a man with a slanted hat for the ß (Greek) guy named Ken on the left; it retains the horizontal keg with a handle stuck in a 大 (big) washing machine
CUE: **Ken** asked this man on the left to tilt his hat back in order to examine this horizontal keg that is stuck in this washing machine, but he didn't offer the guy any compensation, since Ken is known for his 倹約 **ken**'yaku (thrift)
ALSO COMPARE: other similar kanji at # **1432**

2065. 憾 PRONUNCIATION: kan
MEANINGS: remorse, regret, be sorry
EXAMPLES: 遺憾 ikan = regret (noun); 遺憾な ikan na = regrettable, unsatisfactory
DESCRIPTION: compared to 感(じる) kanjiru (to feel, # 640) (identical pronunciation), this kanji adds an erect man on the left; it retains the two-sided lean-to in Kansas where people have their 口 (mouths) covered with napkins, are threatened with halberds and feel their 心 (hearts) beat rapidly
CUE: when this man saw this lean-to in **Kan**sas where people have their 口 (mouths) covered with napkins, are threatened with halberds and feel their 心 (hearts) beat rapidly, he drew himself up to his full height like this and felt 遺憾 i**kan** (regret) that he could not help them
ALSO COMPARE: other similar kanji at # **915**, # **1620** and # **2063**

2066. 哺 PRONUNCIATION: ho
MEANINGS: nurse, suckle
EXAMPLE: 哺乳 honyuu = lactation, suckling
DESCRIPTION: compared to 捕(虜) horyo (captive, # 670) (identical pronunciation), this kanji substitutes 口 kuchi (mouth, # 426), which can also be seen as a box, for the kneeling guy with a hole in his sock; it retains the 犬 (dog) behind the 用 (fence) (see # 364) CUES: this truncated 犬 (dog) is a puppy that has a **H**ome in a **H**ole behind this 用 (fence), and it uses this 口 (mouth) to take advantage of 哺乳 **ho**nyuu (lactation) in its mother
ALSO COMPARE: other similar kanji at # **995** and # **2073**

2067. 彙 PRONUNCIATION: i

MEANING: same kind **EXAMPLE:** 語彙 goi = vocabulary **DESCRIPTION:** at the top, 互(い) tagai (one another, # 1207), without its flat hat, which reminds us of two ユ (youths), one upside down and the other right side up, who speak Tagalog; in the center, a platform; at the bottom, 果(物) kudamono (fruit, # 587), which reminds us of four fruits growing on a 木 (tree) **CUE:** when these two ユ (youths) climbed onto this platform on this 木 (tree) to get this 果 (fruit), an **E**agle interrupted them, and they directed some angry 語彙 go**i** (vocabulary) at the bird **ALSO COMPARE:** other similar kanji at # **588**, # 996 and # **1207**

2068. 墾 PRONUNCIATION: kon

MEANINGS: ground-breaking, open up farmland **EXAMPLE:** 開墾 kaikon = cultivating new land **DESCRIPTION:** compared to 懇(談) kondan (meeting, # 1869) (identical pronunciation), this kanji substitutes 土 tsuchi (soil, # 59) for 心 (heart) at the bottom; it retains the ugly ヨ (wolf) with two teeth that makes it hard to concentrate, and 良 (good), with L & Y at its base, but without its flat hat **CUE:** when I was looking at this 良 (good) 土 (soil), this ugly ヨ (wolf) with these two teeth made it difficult for me to **Con**centrate, but I decided to 開墾する kai**kon** suru (cultivate) the land anyway **GROUP:** (容)貌 youbou = features, looks, # 1687; 懇(談) kondan = meeting, # 1869; (開)墾 kaikon = cultivating new land, # 2068 **ALSO COMPARE:** other similar kanji at # **805**

2069. 酪 PRONUNCIATION: raku

MEANINGS: dairy products, whey **EXAMPLE:** 酪農 rakunou = dairy farming **DESCRIPTION:** compared to (連)絡(する) renraku suru (to contact, # 230) (identical pronunciation), which resembles a dancer escaping a skeet shooter by jumping over a box, this kanji substitutes 酒 sake (alcoholic beverage, # 465), without its water radical (which can also be seen as a bucket of sake with a handle), for the 糸 (skeet shooter) on the left **CUE:** when this dancer saw that a **R**accoon had been drinking this 酒 (sake), she jumped over this box to escape it and went on to a career in 酪農 **raku**nou (dairy farming) **ALSO COMPARE:** other similar kanji at # **1033** and # **1480**

2070. 痘 PRONUNCIATION: tou

MEANINGS: pox, smallpox **EXAMPLE:** 天然痘 tennentou = smallpox **DESCRIPTION:** compared to 豆(腐) toufu (bean curd, # 721) (identical pronunciation), this kanji adds a sick bed at the upper left, as seen in 病(気) byouki (illness, # 369); it retains the 口 (box, or TV set) covered with a napkin and supported by toes **CUE:** when I had 天然痘 tennen**tou** (smallpox), I spent time in this sick bed, eating 豆 (beans) like this and watching this 豆 (TV set supported by these **To**es) **GROUP:** 頭 atama = head, # 93; 登(録) touroku = registration, # 297 (also identical pronunciation); 短(い) mijikai = short, # 324; 豆 mame = bean, # 721; (奮)闘 funtou = hard struggle, # 728 (also identical pronunciation); 融(合) yuugou = fusion, # 927; 豊(か) yutaka = rich, # 1321; 澄(む) sumu = to become clear, # 1674; 獣 kemono = an animal, # 1733; (天然)痘 tennentou = smallpox, # 2070 **ALSO COMPARE:** other similar kanji at # **369** and # **721**

2071. 斤 PRONUNCIATION: kin

MEANINGS: axe, counter for loaves of bread **EXAMPLE:** 一斤 ikkin = one loaf of bread **DESCRIPTION:** compared to 近(所) kinjo (neighborhood, # 390) (identical pronunciation), this kanji omits the snail; it retains the pair of pliers being used near a kindergarten **CUE:** after I took this pair of pliers to a **K**indergarten to do some repair work, they gave me 一斤 ik**kin** (a loaf of bread) **ALSO COMPARE:** other similar kanji at # **892**

2072. 訃 PRONUNCIATION: fu

MEANING: obituary **EXAMPLE:** 訃報 fuhou = an obituary, news of a person's death

DESCRIPTION: on the left, 言 (う) iu (to say, # 430); on the right, the katakana ト to, which reminds us of toes **CUE:** a 訃報 **fu**hou (obituary) 言 (said) that a man died after **Foo**lishly exposing a ト (toe) like this to an alligator

ALSO COMPARE: other similar kanji at # **1826**

2073. 叱 PRONUNCIATIONS: shi, shika

MEANINGS: scold, reprove **EXAMPLES:** 叱責 shisseki = a reprimand or rebuke; 叱る shikaru = to scold, usually written しかる

DESCRIPTION: on the left, 口 kuchi (mouth, # 426), which can also be seen as a box; on the right, the katakana ヒ hi, which reminds us of a hero **CUES:** this ヒ (hero) used this 口 (mouth) to 叱る **shi**karu (scold) his **Shee**pdog for running away to **Chica**go

GROUP: 喫(煙) kitsuen = smoking, # 192; 咲(く) saku = to blossom, # 193; 味 aji = taste, # 245; 口 kuchi = mouth, # 426; 吸(う) suu = to suck, # 427; 呼(ぶ) yobu = to call out, to summon, # 428; 吹(く) fuku = to blow, # 537; 叫(ぶ) sakebu = to shout, # 746; 鳴(く) naku = to chirp, # 751; 嘆(く) nageku = to lament, # 792; 喉 nodo = throat, # 794; 吠(える) hoeru = to bark, # 944; 嗅(ぐ) kagu = to smell, # 959; 嘘 uso = lie, # 967; 叶(う) kanau = to come true, # 1076; (合)唱 gasshou = chorus, # 1152; 噴(水) funsui = water fountain, # 1268; 唯(一) yui'itsu = only, # 1337; 嘱(託) shokutaku = commission, # 1366; 吐(く) haku = to vomit, # 1558; 呪(い) noroi = a curse, # 1844; 唾 tsuba = saliva, # 1847; (長)唄 naga'uta = a long epic song, # 1870; 吟(味する) ginmi suru = to check in detail, # 1873; 喚(く) wameku = to yell, # 1885; 喝(采) kassai = applause, # 1934; (耳鼻)咽(喉科) jibiinkouka = otorhinolaryngology, # 1967; 嘲(笑) choushou = ridicule, # 1971; (示)唆 shisa = an implication, # 1990; (比)喩 hiyu = a simile, # 2021; 哺(乳) honyuu = lactation, # 2066; 叱(責) shisseki = a reprimand, # 2073 **ALSO COMPARE:** kanji with 口 (mouth or box) on the *right* side at # 323; other similar kanji at # **2048**

2074. 籠 PRONUNCIATIONS: kago, ko

MEANINGS: basket, devote or seclude oneself **EXAMPLES:** 籠 kago = a basket or birdcage, usually written かご; 籠もる komoru = to seclude oneself, to be confined in, usually written こもる

DESCRIPTION: compared to 襲 (う) osou (to attack, # 941), this kanji adds 竹 take (bamboo, # 134) at the top and omits 衣 (clothing) at the bottom; it retains the 月 (moon) where an old soldier once 立 (stood), and the complex comb **CUES:** the old soldier who used to 立 (stand) on this 月 (moon), and who uses this comb, has a 籠 **kago** (basket) made from this 竹 (bamboo), in which he carries **CarGo**, including **Co**rn

GROUP: (切)符 kippu = ticket, # 133; 竹 take = bamboo, # 134; 箱 hako = box, # 142; 笑(う) warau = to laugh, # 199; 答(える) kotaeru = to reply, # 295; (次)第(で) shidai de = depending on, # 530; 簡(単) kantan = easy, # 648; (計)算 keisan = calculation, # 789; (季)節 kisetsu = season, # 1048; 筆 fude = writing brush, # 1091; (平)等 byoudou = equal, # 1132; 箸 hashi = chopsticks, # 1144; 箕(面市) Minooshi = a city north of Osaka, # 1178; (建)築 kenchiku = architecture, # 1219; 管 kuda = tube, # 1276; 笠 kasa = straw hat, # 1311; 筋(肉) kinniku = muscle,

1426; (政)策 seisaku = a policy, # 1479; 笛 fue = a flute, # 1503; 範(囲) han'i = extent, # 1585; (国)籍 kokuseki = nationality, # 1604; 筒 tsutsu = a cylinder, # 1620; (帳)簿 choubo = an account book, # 1788; 箇(所) kasho = a place, # 1881; (危)篤 kitoku = critical condition, # 1937; (便)箋 binsen = writing paper, # 2051; 籠 kago = a basket, # 2074   ALSO COMPARE: other similar kanji at # **941**

2075. 蓮 PRONUNCIATIONS: ren, hasu
MEANING: lotus   **EXAMPLES:** 蓮根 renkon = lotus root; 蓮 hasu = lotus
DESCRIPTION: compared to 連(絡) renraku (contact, # 353) (identical pronunciation), this kanji adds a plant radical at the top; it retains the rental car being carried by a snail
CUES: after this **Ren**tal 車 (car) broke down, and before it was carried away by this snail, I took my **Ha**waiian **Sou**venirs and this plant material, which was 蓮根 **ren**kon (lotus root), out of the trunk
GROUP: 車 kuruma = car, # 283; 連(絡する) renraku suru = to contact, # 353; 運(ぶ) hakobu = to carry, # 354; 陣(地) jinchi = encampment, # 638; 軍(人) gunjin = soldier, # 725; (車)庫 shako = garage, # 919; 輝(く) kagayaku = to shine, # 979; (指)揮 shiki = conducting, # 1424; (先)輩 senpai = a senior, # 1607; 蓮 hasu = lotus, # 2075

2076. 頒 PRONUNCIATION: han
MEANINGS: distribute, disseminate, partition
EXAMPLE: 頒布 hanpu = distribution
DESCRIPTION: on the left, 分(かる) wakaru (to understand, # 105); on the right, a platform where a head could fit, above a 貝 (money chest), as seen in 頭 atama (head, # 93)   **CUE: Han**sel 分 (understands) that his head is missing from this platform on the right, but he believes that it will be returned during a 頒布 **han**pu (distribution) of lost items   **GROUP:** 分(かる) wakaru = to under-

stand, # 105; 粉 kona = flour, # 1104; (お)盆 Obon = a Buddhist festival, # 1167; 雰(囲気) fu'inki = atmosphere, # 1201; 貧(しい) mazushii = poor, # 1339; 紛(らわしい) magirawashii = confusing, # 1638; 頒(布) hanpu = distribution, # 2076   ALSO COMPARE: other similar kanji at # **1126**

2077. 楷 PRONUNCIATION: kai
MEANINGS: square character style, correctness
EXAMPLE: 楷書 kaisho = block or standard style of printed typeface, square script (calligraphy)
DESCRIPTION: compared to 皆 mina (everyone, # 597), or 皆(目) kaimoku (utterly, # 597) (identical pronunciation), this kanji adds 木 ki (wood, # 118) on the left; it retains the two ヒ (heroes) sitting on a 白 (white) hill in Minasota (Minnesota) and carrying kites   **CUE:** these two ヒ (heroes) are sitting on this 白 (white) hill and using this 木 (wood) to make **Ki**tes, on which they write 楷書 **kai**sho (square-style) calligraphy
ALSO COMPARE: other similar kanji at # **1294** and # **2014**

2078. 孔 PRONUNCIATION: kou
MEANINGS: cavity, hole   **EXAMPLE:** 孔子 koushi = Confucius   **DESCRIPTION:** on the left, 子 ko (child, # 182); on the right, L, which resembles a breast, as seen in 乳 nyuu (milk, # 186)   **CUE:** when 孔子 **kou**shi (Confucius) was a 子 (child) like this, he would sometimes feel **Co**ld and snuggle next to this mother's breast
GROUP: 子 ko = child, # 182; (漢)字 kanji = kanji, # 183; 学(校) gakkou = school, # 184; 厚(い) atsui = thick, # 185; 好(きです) suki desu = I like it, # 239; 遊(ぶ) asobu = to play, # 360; 存(在) sonzai = existence, # 462; 孤(児) koji = orphan, # 723; 猛(暑) mousho = heat wave, # 953; 季(節) kisetsu = season, # 1047; 孫 mago =

grandchild, # 1072; 勃(発) boppatsu = an outbreak, # 1846; (謙)遜 kenson = modesty, # 2044; 孔(子) koushi = Confucius, # 2078 **ALSO COMPARE:** other similar kanji at # **735**

2079. 癌 PRONUNCIATION: gan
MEANINGS: cancer, cancerous evil
EXAMPLE: 癌 gan = cancer, usually written がん **DESCRIPTION:** at the upper left, a sick bed, as seen in 病(気) byouki (illness, # 369); inside the bed, at the top, 品(物) shinamono (merchandise, # 5); at the bottom, 山 yama (mountain, # 146) **CUE:** when I was in this sick bed with 癌 **gan** (cancer), my family visited Gandalf on this 山 (mountain) in order to get this healing 品 (merchandise) to treat me **GROUP:** 山 yama = mountain, # 146; 島 shima = island, # 556; (動)揺 douyou = uneasiness, # 852; (秘)密 himitsu = a secret, # 1188; 綱 tsuna = a rope, # 1200; (鉄)鋼 tekkou = steel, # 1472; 岡 oka = hill, # 1528; 仙(台) Sendai = a city in Japan, # 1564; 幽(閉する) yuuhei suru = to confine, # 1574; 剛(健) gouken = vigor, # 1663; (山)岳 sangaku = mountains, # 1683; 陶(器) touki = chinaware, # 1741; 缶 kan = a tin can, # 1832; (歌)謡(曲) kayoukyoku = a popular song, # 1856; 癌 gan = cancer, # 2079
ALSO COMPARE: other similar kanji at # **369** and # **1034**

2080. 弥 PRONUNCIATION: ya
MEANINGS: all the more, increasingly
EXAMPLE: 弥生時代 yayoi jidai = the Yayoi era (300 BC – 300 AD) **DESCRIPTION:** compared to (対)称 taishou (symmetry, # 1123), this substitutes a twisted 弓 yumi (bow, # 1044) for the 禾 (grain plant with a ripe head) on the left; it retains the 小 (small) guy named Shorty, who carries a crutch **CUE:** this 小 (small) guy, who carried this crutch during the 弥生時代 **ya**yoi jidai (Yayoi era), also carried this 弓 (bow) to protect his **Ya**rd **GROUP:** 塩 shio = salt, # 60; (家)族 kazoku = family, # 115; 旅 tabi = trip, # 116; 年 nen = year, # 177; 午(後) gogo = in the afternoon, # 207; 乾(く) kawaku = to get dry, # 290; 毎 = every, # 336; 海 umi = ocean, # 337; 遊(ぶ) asobu = to play, # 360; (後)悔 koukai = regret, # 675; 旋(回) senkai = rotation, # 913; 施(設) shisetsu = facility, # 1067; (対)称 taishou = symmetry, # 1123; 飾(る) kazaru = to decorate, # 1203; (頻)繁 hinpan = frequent, # 1266; 梅 ume = plum, # 1299; 傷 kizu = scar, # 1376; 旗 hata = flag, # 1430; 臨(時) rinji = temporary, # 1515; 敏(感な) binkan na = sensitive, # 1608; 乞(食) kojiki = a beggar, # 1839; 侮(辱) bujoku = insult, # 1963; 弥(生時代) yayoi jidai = the Yayoi era, # 2080 **ALSO COMPARE:** other similar kanji at # **476** and # **1010**

2081. 伊 PRONUNCIATION: i
MEANING: Italy, that one **EXAMPLES:** 伊勢崎 isesaki = a city in Gunma Prefecture; 伊勢神宮 ise jinguu = the Ise Grand Shrine in Ise (Mia Prefecture) **DESCRIPTION:** compared to 君 kimi (you, # 419), this adds a man with a slanted hat on the left and omits the 口 (mouth) at the lower right; it retains Kimmy, the guy who has been stabbed in the face with a trident **CUE:** this man tilts his hat back examine this 君 (Kimmy), whose **E**ar was damaged when he was stabbed with this trident, in 伊勢崎 **i**sesaki (a city)
ALSO COMPARE: other similar kanji at # **419**

2082. 幌 PRONUNCIATION: poro
MEANINGS: canopy, awning, hood, curtain
EXAMPLE: 札幌 sapporo = Sapporo, a city in Hokkaido **DESCRIPTION:** on the left, 巾 (Bo Peep), a spinning lady with wide hips, as seen in 帽(子) boushi (hat, # 243), but this can also be seen as a police robot with long arms; at the upper right, 日 hi (sun, 32); at the lower right, 光 hikari (light, # 448) **CUE:** this 巾 (Bo Peep) bought a **P**olice **R**obot that looked just like her and took it to 札幌 sap**poro** (Sapporo), where it stood in this 日 (sun) to receive this 光 (light), since it was solar-powered **ALSO COMPARE:** other similar kanji at # **979** and # **1768**

2083. 堺 PRONUNCIATION: sakai
MEANING: world **EXAMPLE:** 堺 sakai = Sakai, a city in Osaka Prefecture **DESCRIPTION:** compared to (世)界 sekai (the world, # 69), this kanji adds 土 tsuchi (soil, # 59) on the left; it retains the 田 (square kite) with 介 (an arrow pointing up) **CUE:** when I was flying this 田 (kite) 介 (up) into the sky at 堺 **S**a**kai** (a city in Osaka Prefecture), I crashed it into this 土 (dirt), and its owner **S**ocked me in the **E**ye **ALSO COMPARE:** other similar kanji at # **69** and # **220**

2084. 媛 PRONUNCIATION: hime
MEANINGS: beautiful woman, princess
EXAMPLE: 愛媛県 ehime ken = Ehime Prefecture on Shikoku Island **DESCRIPTION:** compared to 暖(かい) atatakai (warm atmosphere, # 38), this kanji substitutes 女 onna (female, # 235) for 日 (sun) on the left; it retains the barbecue grate and the 友 (friend) **CUE:** when this 女 (female) visited 愛媛県 e**hime** ken (Ehime Prefecture), she felt 暖 (warm), and she noticed that some **He-M**en, who were 友 (friends) were barbecuing on this grate
ALSO COMPARE: 姫 hime = princess, # 1040; other kanji containing 女 on the left at # **2039**; other similar kanji at # **459** and # **1177**

2085. 栃 PRONUNCIATION: tochi
MEANING: horse chestnut
EXAMPLE: 栃木県 tochigi ken = Tochigi Prefecture on Honshu Island **DESCRIPTION:** compared to 励(む) hagemu (to be diligent, # 1338), this adds 木 ki (tree, # 118) on the left and omits 力 (force) on the right; it retains the one-sided lean-to containing 万 (10,000) and occupied by a Hawaiian guest **CUE:** in this lean-to near this 木 (tree) in 栃木県 **tochi**gi ken (Tochigi Prefecture), 万 (10,000) **T**omatoes are **C**heap to buy
ALSO COMPARE: other similar kanji at # **113**

2086. 櫻 PRONUNCIATION: sakura
MEANING: cherry **EXAMPLE:** 櫻 sakura = cherry, used in proper nouns **DESCRIPTION:** on the left, 木 ki (tree, # 118); at the upper right, two 貝 kai (money chests, # 83); at the lower right, 女 onna (female, # 235) **CUE:** this 女 (female) sells 櫻 **sakura** (cherries) from this 木 (tree) and fills these two 貝 (money chests) with the proceeds, and a **S**alaryman turns off his **Kuura**a (air conditioner) before going outside to see them
GROUP: 妻 tsuma = wife, # 237; (必)要 hitsuyou = necessity, # 238; 数 kazu = number, # 639; 姿 sugata = shape, # 763; 腰 koshi = waist, # 884; (権)威 ken'i = authority, # 915; 桜 sakura = cherry, # 984; 委(ねる) yudaneru = to entrust, # 1364; 宴(会) enkai = banquet, # 1391; (面)接 mensetsu = interview, # 1446; 凄(い) sugoi = great, # 1671; (老)婆 rouba = an old woman, # 1688; (摩天)楼 matenrou = a skyscraper, # 1819; 妥(協) dakyou = a compromise, # 1916; 妄(想) mousou = a fantasy, # 1961; 萎(縮する) ishuku suru = to flinch, # 2022; 櫻 sakura =

cherry, # 2086 **ALSO COMPARE:** other similar kanji at # **352** and # **1870**

2087. 萌 PRONUNCIATIONS: moe, mo
MEANINGS: sprout, bud **EXAMPLES:** 萌 moe = feelings of affection directed at certain anime and manga characters; 萌える moeru = to sprout or bud **DESCRIPTION:** compared to 明(るい) akarui (bright, # 154), this adds a plant radical at the top; it retains the 日 (sun) and the 月 (moon) **CUES:** since these plants at the top need More Energy in order to 萌える **mo**eru (sprout), I expose them to 明 (bright) light, and when they get too big, I **M**ow them **GROUP:** 胃 i = stomach, # 153; 散(歩) sanpo = a walk, # 159; 有(名) yuumei = famous, # 460; 崩(れる) kuzureru = to collapse, # 973; 絹 kinu = silk, # 1439; (葛)藤 kattou = conflict, # 1530; 随(分) zuibun = very, # 1670; 覇(権) haken = hegemony, # 1874; 肯(定する) koutei suru = to affirm, # 1929; (花)婿 hanamuko = a bridegroom, # 1960; 髄 zui = marrow, # 1964; (贈)賄 zouwai = bribery, # 1979; 萌(える) moeru = to sprout, # 2087
ALSO COMPARE: other similar kanji at # **154**

2088. 蘭 PRONUNCIATION: ran
MEANINGS: orchid, Holland **EXAMPLE:** 蘭 ran = an orchid, sometimes used as a proper noun **DESCRIPTION:** compared to 欄 ran (newspaper column, # 1470) (identical pronunciation), this kanji omits the 木 (tree) on the left and adds a plant radical at the top; it retains the 門 (gate) at my ranch, facing 東 (east); the structure inside the gate can also be seen as a tree wearing bifocals **CUE:** if you look 東 (east) through this 門 (gate) on my **Ran**ch, you can see 蘭 **ran** (orchid) plants like these **ALSO COMPARE:** other similar kanji at # **1271** and # **1755**

Hiragana Review

わ wa	ら ra	や ya	ま ma	は ha	な na	た ta	さ sa	か ka	あ a
	り ri		み mi	ひ hi	に ni	ち chi	し shi	き ki	い i
を wo	る ru	ゆ yu	む mu	ふ fu	ぬ nu	つ tsu	す su	く ku	う u
	れ re		め me	へ he	ね ne	て te	せ se	け ke	え e
ん n	ろ ro	よ yo	も mo	ほ ho	の no	と to	そ so	こ ko	お o

Katakana Review

ワ wa	ラ ra	ヤ ya	マ ma	ハ ha	ナ na	タ ta	サ sa	カ ka	ア a
	リ ri		ミ mi	ヒ hi	ニ ni	チ chi	シ shi	キ ki	イ i
ヲ wo	ル ru	ユ yu	ム mu	フ fu	ヌ nu	ツ tsu	ス su	ク ku	ウ u
	レ re		メ me	ヘ he	ネ ne	テ te	セ se	ケ ke	エ e
ン n	ロ ro	ヨ yo	モ mo	ホ ho	ノ no	ト to	ソ so	コ ko	オ o

Kanji Table

This table is provided so that you may use Kanji ID to practice looking up individual characters. Please see "How to Use Kanji ID" on page xi.

0001 一	0002 二	0003 三	0004 回	0005 品	0006 四	0007 呂	0008 中	0009 虫	0010 申
0011 立	0012 泣	0013 人	0014 入	0015 八	0016 公	0017 六	0018 十	0019 高	0020 七
0021 宅	0022 千	0023 手	0024 又	0025 文	0026 支	0027 卒	0028 卵	0029 点	0030 久
0031 当	0032 日	0033 昔	0034 早	0035 晩	0036 映	0037 晴	0038 暖	0039 円	0040 声
0041 昨	0042 最	0043 英	0044 白	0045 的	0046 泊	0047 百	0048 星	0049 昼	0050 母
0051 目	0052 着	0053 見	0054 覚	0055 自	0056 首	0057 耳	0058 取	0059 土	0060 塩
0061 増	0062 室	0063 屋	0064 堂	0065 熱	0066 士	0067 仕	0068 田	0069 界	0070 町
0071 留	0072 猫	0073 由	0074 届	0075 戻	0076 黒	0077 画	0078 理	0079 隅	0080 魚
0081 角	0082 曲	0083 貝	0084 贈	0085 貿	0086 質	0087 負	0088 員	0089 買	0090 貸
0091 資	0092 慣	0093 頭	0094 願	0095 顔	0096 頃	0097 類	0098 頼	0099 束	0100 具
0101 真	0102 刀	0103 切	0104 初	0105 分	0106 召	0107 力	0108 助	0109 男	0110 勢
0111 九	0112 究	0113 万	0114 方	0115 族	0116 旅	0117 放	0118 木	0119 末	0120 案
0121 菜	0122 休	0123 本	0124 体	0125 林	0126 磨	0127 森	0128 枝	0129 枚	0130 校
0131 村	0132 付	0133 符	0134 竹	0135 横	0136 様	0137 機	0138 械	0139 橋	0140 机
0141 構	0142 箱	0143 父	0144 交	0145 郊	0146 山	0147 出	0148 月	0149 勝	0150 服

0151	0152	0153	0154	0155	0156	0157	0158	0159	0160
育	背	胃	明	青	情	前	消	散	夕
0161	0162	0163	0164	0165	0166	0167	0168	0169	0170
多	名	外	死	夢	主	住	注	玉	国
0171	0172	0173	0174	0175	0176	0177	0178	0179	0180
上	下	止	正	政	不	年	降	五	決
0181	0182	0183	0184	0185	0186	0187	0188	0189	0190
片	子	字	学	厚	乳	教	大	天	犬
0191	0192	0193	0194	0195	0196	0197	0198	0199	0200
太	喫	咲	狭	実	険	漢	難	笑	曜
0201	0202	0203	0204	0205	0206	0207	0208	0209	0210
濯	集	進	準	牛	失	午	生	性	産
0211	0212	0213	0214	0215	0216	0217	0218	0219	0220
花	茶	寺	守	時	持	待	特	糸	細
0221	0222	0223	0224	0225	0226	0227	0228	0229	0230
紙	低	絵	経	約	続	緑	線	練	絡
0231	0232	0233	0234	0235	0236	0237	0238	0239	0240
結	緒	終	冬	女	安	妻	要	好	婚
0241	0242	0243	0244	0245	0246	0247	0248	0249	0250
姉	市	帽	妹	味	工	紅	空	式	川
0251	0252	0253	0254	0255	0256	0257	0258	0259	0260
水	泉	小	少	泳	浴	温	薄	済	活
0261	0262	0263	0264	0265	0266	0267	0268	0269	0270
雨	雪	電	雲	震	音	部	暗	倍	位
0271	0272	0273	0274	0275	0276	0277	0278	0279	0280
社	祖	神	祝	礼	者	都	暑	園	困
0281	0282	0283	0284	0285	0286	0287	0288	0289	0290
図	面	車	重	転	動	働	輸	軽	乾
0291	0292	0293	0294	0295	0296	0297	0298	0299	0300
朝	今	会	合	答	容	登	発	冷	全
0301	0302	0303	0304	0305	0306	0307	0308	0309	0310
金	銀	良	鉄	館	心	必	思	恥	忘
0311	0312	0313	0314	0315	0316	0317	0318	0319	0320
窓	急	悪	念	息	娘	意	億	怒	区
0321	0322	0323	0324	0325	0326	0327	0328	0329	0330
気	歳	知	短	医	米	来	番	隣	洋

0331 半	0332 業	0333 僕	0334 行	0335 後	0336 毎	0337 海	0338 何	0339 同	0340 向
0341 伺	0342 荷	0343 去	0344 法	0345 伝	0346 週	0347 達	0348 送	0349 道	0350 遅
0351 遠	0352 選	0353 連	0354 運	0355 違	0356 返	0357 込	0358 迎	0359 速	0360 遊
0361 過	0362 辺	0363 建	0364 用	0365 通	0366 踊	0367 備	0368 痛	0369 病	0370 疲
0371 彼	0372 寝	0373 北	0374 将	0375 民	0376 眠	0377 祭	0378 途	0379 際	0380 駅
0381 駐	0382 験	0383 親	0384 辛	0385 幸	0386 報	0387 辞	0388 南	0389 新	0390 近
0391 所	0392 古	0393 苦	0394 故	0395 個	0396 内	0397 肉	0398 食	0399 飲	0400 飯
0401 物	0402 易	0403 場	0404 湯	0405 家	0406 参	0407 珍	0408 歩	0409 門	0410 問
0411 間	0412 聞	0413 開	0414 閉	0415 書	0416 事	0417 律	0418 静	0419 君	0420 兄
0421 元	0422 先	0423 洗	0424 院	0425 売	0426 口	0427 吸	0428 呼	0429 告	0430 言
0431 信	0432 読	0433 話	0434 計	0435 語	0436 試	0437 訳	0438 議	0439 説	0440 誰
0441 調	0442 研	0443 火	0444 灰	0445 秋	0446 焼	0447 赤	0448 光	0449 足	0450 走
0451 徒	0452 起	0453 越	0454 題	0455 定	0456 左	0457 右	0458 石	0459 友	0460 有
0461 若	0462 存	0463 怖	0464 西	0465 酒	0466 配	0467 汚	0468 写	0469 考	0470 号
0471 弱	0472 習	0473 色	0474 勉	0475 触	0476 引	0477 張	0478 強	0479 風	0480 使
0481 便	0482 作	0483 任	0484 価	0485 借	0486 供	0487 化	0488 件	0489 夜	0490 側
0491 宿	0492 係	0493 店	0494 広	0495 庭	0496 席	0497 座	0498 度	0499 渡	0500 岸
0501 髪	0502 長	0503 地	0504 池	0505 他	0506 春	0507 寒	0508 東	0509 乗	0510 私

0511 科	0512 料	0513 和	0514 京	0515 涼	0516 景	0517 勤	0518 務	0519 努	0520 楽
0521 薬	0522 夏	0523 愛	0524 客	0525 路	0526 落	0527 復	0528 優	0529 弟	0530 第
0531 沸	0532 奥	0533 歯	0534 歌	0535 欲	0536 次	0537 吹	0538 台	0539 治	0540 始
0541 甘	0542 世	0543 葉	0544 予	0545 野	0546 柔	0547 危	0548 包	0549 港	0550 記
0551 替	0552 代	0553 変	0554 換	0555 鳥	0556 島	0557 役	0558 投	0559 段	0560 招
0561 別	0562 割	0563 倒	0564 利	0565 刻	0566 帰	0567 皿	0568 冊	0569 置	0570 直
0571 値	0572 県	0573 形	0574 飛	0575 並	0576 普	0577 受	0578 授	0579 両	0580 製
0581 袋	0582 表	0583 無	0584 舞	0585 亡	0586 忙	0587 果	0588 課	0589 菓	0590 打
0591 払	0592 押	0593 拝	0594 捨	0595 拾	0596 掛	0597 皆	0598 階	0599 喜	0600 嬉
0601 以	0602 船	0603 靴	0604 寄	0605 残	0606 球	0607 寿	0608 司	0609 至	0610 極
0611 然	0612 到	0613 丈	0614 夫	0615 可	0616 能	0617 才	0618 解	0619 確	0620 卓
0621 超	0622 頑	0623 迷	0624 惑	0625 街	0626 灯	0627 停	0628 駄	0629 汗	0630 周
0631 差	0632 慎	0633 成	0634 功	0635 継	0636 単	0637 余	0638 陣	0639 数	0640 感
0641 暮	0642 限	0643 貴	0644 揃	0645 掃	0646 除	0647 爪	0648 簡	0649 涙	0650 煎
0651 身	0652 己	0653 幕	0654 流	0655 韓	0656 費	0657 仲	0658 紹	0659 介	0660 裕
0661 福	0662 羨	0663 希	0664 望	0665 垢	0666 離	0667 貯	0668 旦	0669 那	0670 捕
0671 浮	0672 未	0673 絶	0674 対	0675 悔	0676 宗	0677 応	0678 仏	0679 壇	0680 反
0681 香	0682 非	0683 常	0684 営	0685 漁	0686 団	0687 布	0688 毛	0689 巨	0690 輪

0691	0692	0693	0694	0695	0696	0697	0698	0699	0700
指	廻	興	深	恋	職	伸	勧	探	改
0701	0702	0703	0704	0705	0706	0707	0708	0709	0710
関	丁	寧	断	納	得	賃	税	氏	慌
0711	0712	0713	0714	0715	0716	0717	0718	0719	0720
期	素	訪	加	趣	湖	距	環	境	恵
0721	0722	0723	0724	0725	0726	0727	0728	0729	0730
豆	腐	孤	独	軍	隊	奮	闘	担	端
0731	0732	0733	0734	0735	0736	0737	0738	0739	0740
固	緊	愉	快	札	鳩	艦	砲	現	漏
0741	0742	0743	0744	0745	0746	0747	0748	0749	0750
根	棚	餅	銭	舎	叫	血	圧	抜	焦
0751	0752	0753	0754	0755	0756	0757	0758	0759	0760
鳴	組	織	鶏	羽	演	奏	描	完	了
0761	0762	0763	0764	0765	0766	0767	0768	0769	0770
純	格	姿	派	遣	浜	凧	揚	壮	脈
0771	0772	0773	0774	0775	0776	0777	0778	0779	0780
美	責	瞬	染	胸	駆	垣	巡	芝	弾
0781	0782	0783	0784	0785	0786	0787	0788	0789	0790
詰	砂	頂	徴	雑	誌	相	炎	算	談
0791	0792	0793	0794	0795	0796	0797	0798	0799	0800
額	嘆	敗	喉	鼻	邪	浸	爽	垂	睡
0801	0802	0803	0804	0805	0806	0807	0808	0809	0810
移	避	暇	諦	浪	没	悶	術	居	求
0811	0812	0813	0814	0815	0816	0817	0818	0819	0820
健	冒	論	氷	溶	岩	嫌	匹	泥	棒
0821	0822	0823	0824	0825	0826	0827	0828	0829	0830
追	照	振	似	釘	騒	尻	呆	褒	飼
0831	0832	0833	0834	0835	0836	0837	0838	0839	0840
康	骨	皮	隠	沈	黙	破	殺	影	響
0841	0842	0843	0844	0845	0846	0847	0848	0849	0850
添	延	餌	視	肩	撫	精	杯	兆	逃
0851	0852	0853	0854	0855	0856	0857	0858	0859	0860
悲	揺	器	奇	椅	妙	比	鮮	検	査
0861	0862	0863	0864	0865	0866	0867	0868	0869	0870
膝	我	腹	寂	敷	丸	局	突	恐	永

0871 戸	0872 句	0873 敬	0874 警	0875 戒	0876 畳	0877 津	0878 波	0879 隙	0880 官
0881 敵	0882 迅	0883 及	0884 腰	0885 平	0886 観	0887 裏	0888 原	0889 畑	0890 頬
0891 陽	0892 折	0893 覆	0894 逆	0895 鹿	0896 察	0897 宇	0898 宙	0899 柵	0900 汁
0901 犯	0902 厳	0903 湧	0904 徐	0905 想	0906 象	0907 像	0908 亀	0909 草	0910 斜
0911 崖	0912 翼	0913 旋	0914 脅	0915 威	0916 権	0917 兵	0918 衛	0919 庫	0920 防
0921 牙	0922 雅	0923 狩	0924 飢	0925 傾	0926 退	0927 屈	0928 懐	0929 群	0930 衆
0931 積	0932 射	0933 戦	0934 聴	0935 競	0936 争	0937 眩	0938 峰	0939 富	0940 協
0941 襲	0942 油	0943 禁	0944 吠	0945 伏	0946 床	0947 獲	0948 狙	0949 匂	0950 闇
0951 臓	0952 斉	0953 猛	0954 程	0955 祈	0956 俺	0957 苔	0958 馬	0959 嗅	0960 態
0961 命	0962 令	0963 洞	0964 穴	0965 謙	0966 虚	0967 嘘	0968 荒	0969 共	0970 異
0971 驚	0972 巣	0973 崩	0974 就	0975 蹴	0976 黄	0977 救	0978 疑	0979 輝	0980 肌
0981 滑	0982 覗	0983 井	0984 桜	0985 悠	0986 抱	0987 融	0988 均	0989 齢	0990 刊
0991 賞	0992 躍	0993 佐	0994 賀	0995 補	0996 候	0997 給	0998 状	0999 録	1000 更
1001 挑	1002 沖	1003 縄	1004 府	1005 阪	1006 奈	1007 茨	1008 城	1009 挟	1010 省
1011 携	1012 帯	1013 滞	1014 在	1015 陸	1016 湾	1017 旧	1018 盛	1019 災	1020 乱
1021 暴	1022 爆	1023 縁	1024 怪	1025 松	1026 江	1027 講	1028 義	1029 推	1030 薦
1031 測	1032 再	1033 各	1034 繰	1035 是	1036 認	1037 遺	1038 総	1039 臣	1040 姫
1041 塗	1042 衣	1043 装	1044 弓	1045 矢	1046 印	1047 季	1048 節	1049 修	1050 般

1051 壁	1052 編	1053 評	1054 判	1055 猿	1056 芸	1057 虎	1058 劇	1059 郷	1060 里
1061 量	1062 幹	1063 央	1064 請	1065 老	1066 祉	1067 施	1068 設	1069 療	1070 与
1071 州	1072 孫	1073 遭	1074 昏	1075 労	1076 叶	1077 王	1078 妃	1079 宮	1080 殿
1081 崎	1082 批	1083 摘	1084 跳	1085 症	1086 版	1087 翻	1088 著	1089 樹	1090 訓
1091 筆	1092 鉛	1093 児	1094 童	1095 奄	1096 底	1097 径	1098 種	1099 酎	1100 沢
1101 蒸	1102 芋	1103 麦	1104 粉	1105 農	1106 濃	1107 虜	1108 造	1109 募	1110 催
1111 跡	1112 清	1113 収	1114 拭	1115 贅	1116 型	1117 典	1118 侍	1119 洪	1120 遇
1121 妓	1122 誕	1123 称	1124 列	1125 統	1126 領	1127 慢	1128 嵐	1129 幻	1130 坂
1131 級	1132 等	1133 技	1134 房	1135 粒	1136 眺	1137 秒	1138 針	1139 効	1140 免
1141 許	1142 疫	1143 樋	1144 箸	1145 志	1146 軒	1147 激	1148 減	1149 処	1150 証
1151 拠	1152 唱	1153 満	1154 杉	1155 制	1156 提	1157 甲	1158 羅	1159 徳	1160 祥
1161 勘	1162 弁	1163 護	1164 看	1165 婦	1166 板	1167 盆	1168 鬼	1169 魅	1170 倉
1171 創	1172 穀	1173 締	1174 偉	1175 載	1176 阿	1177 援	1178 箕	1179 滝	1180 脂
1181 悩	1182 河	1183 焚	1184 梨	1185 幅	1186 茂	1187 秘	1188 密	1189 綿	1190 蔵
1191 胴	1192 操	1193 滅	1194 慮	1195 抵	1196 抗	1197 盤	1198 基	1199 販	1200 綱
1201 雰	1202 囲	1203 飾	1204 詣	1205 寛	1206 副	1207 互	1208 尊	1209 吊	1210 菌
1211 剰	1212 潔	1213 舌	1214 辟	1215 癖	1216 保	1217 商	1218 卸	1219 築	1220 履
1221 廃	1222 為	1223 羊	1224 逮	1225 柱	1226 撃	1227 塞	1228 麺	1229 稲	1230 郡

1231 晶	1232 銅	1233 栽	1234 培	1235 専	1236 磁	1237 舗	1238 欠	1239 炊	1240 燃
1241 液	1242 診	1243 几	1244 帳	1245 鈍	1246 堅	1247 整	1248 頓	1249 況	1250 層
1251 塔	1252 玄	1253 透	1254 蜂	1255 蜜	1256 域	1257 穫	1258 損	1259 預	1260 害
1261 導	1262 熊	1263 栄	1264 養	1265 頻	1266 繁	1267 源	1268 噴	1269 購	1270 礁
1271 棟	1272 略	1273 葬	1274 壷	1275 墓	1276 管	1277 鉢	1278 植	1279 蘇	1280 適
1281 複	1282 勇	1283 謝	1284 刺	1285 誤	1286 革	1287 拡	1288 偶	1289 盗	1290 賢
1291 罪	1292 宝	1293 癒	1294 混	1295 航	1296 属	1297 泌	1298 尿	1299 梅	1300 湿
1301 詩	1302 株	1303 標	1304 旬	1305 券	1306 干	1307 渉	1308 潮	1309 巻	1310 鑑
1311 笠	1312 耕	1313 歴	1314 史	1315 諸	1316 迫	1317 例	1318 旨	1319 漫	1320 詞
1321 豊	1322 穣	1323 歓	1324 署	1325 刑	1326 粗	1327 鉱	1328 述	1329 否	1330 緩
1331 撮	1332 魔	1333 徹	1334 欧	1335 識	1336 善	1337 唯	1338 励	1339 貧	1340 乏
1341 規	1342 則	1343 郎	1344 承	1345 績	1346 展	1347 示	1348 順	1349 毒	1350 捌
1351 師	1352 条	1353 模	1354 華	1355 鏡	1356 伎	1357 豪	1358 馳	1359 粘	1360 因
1361 索	1362 挙	1363 昇	1364 委	1365 章	1366 嘱	1367 託	1368 審	1369 寸	1370 鈴
1371 遂	1372 握	1373 酢	1374 鍋	1375 撲	1376 傷	1377 煮	1378 材	1379 飽	1380 浄
1381 臭	1382 企	1383 谷	1384 渓	1385 炭	1386 脱	1387 粧	1388 恩	1389 披	1390 露
1391 宴	1392 刷	1393 系	1394 壌	1395 攻	1396 殖	1397 猟	1398 雇	1399 党	1400 幼
1401 兼	1402 掘	1403 択	1404 蚕	1405 誘	1406 肥	1407 益	1408 率	1409 閣	1410 昭

1411 幣	1412 硬	1413 貨	1414 沿	1415 煙	1416 往	1417 芽	1418 武	1419 鋭	1420 監
1421 督	1422 邸	1423 眼	1424 揮	1425 採	1426 筋	1427 熟	1428 摩	1429 擦	1430 旗
1431 汽	1432 剣	1433 忍	1434 耐	1435 獄	1436 鎖	1437 財	1438 憲	1439 絹	1440 御
1441 俳	1442 微	1443 浅	1444 庁	1445 郵	1446 接	1447 被	1448 網	1449 騎	1450 裁
1451 慈	1452 堪	1453 吉	1454 渋	1455 促	1456 仮	1457 翌	1458 皇	1459 后	1460 陛
1461 脳	1462 冗	1463 致	1464 紀	1465 裂	1466 掲	1467 稿	1468 荘	1469 牧	1470 欄
1471 孝	1472 鋼	1473 丘	1474 亭	1475 麻	1476 酔	1477 憩	1478 充	1479 策	1480 酸
1481 博	1482 秩	1483 序	1484 尺	1485 従	1486 縦	1487 縮	1488 刃	1489 塚	1490 枠
1491 含	1492 俵	1493 討	1494 糖	1495 障	1496 仁	1497 腸	1498 怠	1499 姓	1500 聖
1501 寮	1502 即	1503 笛	1504 豚	1505 忠	1506 誠	1507 尽	1508 肺	1509 班	1510 票
1511 凡	1512 尋	1513 盟	1514 覧	1515 臨	1516 釈	1517 秀	1518 雄	1519 宣	1520 捜
1521 哲	1522 僧	1523 埋	1524 舟	1525 沼	1526 悟	1527 嫁	1528 岡	1529 泰	1530 藤
1531 葛	1532 腕	1533 柄	1534 踏	1535 柳	1536 奉	1537 藩	1538 帝	1539 堀	1540 憶
1541 儀	1542 占	1543 陰	1544 謀	1545 訴	1546 訟	1547 釣	1548 核	1549 仰	1550 瀬
1551 患	1552 浦	1553 執	1554 拳	1555 銃	1556 維	1557 依	1558 吐	1559 斬	1560 斎
1561 衝	1562 却	1563 脚	1564 仙	1565 唇	1566 狂	1567 剥	1568 奪	1569 竜	1570 脇
1571 債	1572 伯	1573 項	1574 幽	1575 霊	1576 坊	1577 扱	1578 如	1579 詳	1580 愚
1581 痴	1582 奴	1583 隷	1584 抑	1585 範	1586 潜	1587 還	1588 丹	1589 亜	1590 慶

1591	1592	1593	1594	1595	1596	1597	1598	1599	1600
侵	僚	邦	隆	胞	双	懸	曹	伴	唐
1601	1602	1603	1604	1605	1606	1607	1608	1609	1610
剤	契	爵	籍	廊	析	輩	敏	鶴	烈
1611	1612	1613	1614	1615	1616	1617	1618	1619	1620
菊	沙	汰	漠	裸	須	貢	献	封	筒
1621	1622	1623	1624	1625	1626	1627	1628	1629	1630
貫	偽	排	棄	肖	削	麗	幾	尚	彩
1631	1632	1633	1634	1635	1636	1637	1638	1639	1640
俗	較	傍	肝	誇	魂	控	紛	既	股
1641	1642	1643	1644	1645	1646	1647	1648	1649	1650
征	佳	哀	悼	眉	拒	概	顧	挨	拶
1651	1652	1653	1654	1655	1656	1657	1658	1659	1660
憎	賊	匠	淡	併	崇	岐	阜	嬢	陥
1661	1662	1663	1664	1665	1666	1667	1668	1669	1670
賠	償	剛	廷	紫	銘	鎌	稼	譲	随
1671	1672	1673	1674	1675	1676	1677	1678	1679	1680
凄	扉	偵	澄	殊	紋	芳	惨	虐	凝
1681	1682	1683	1684	1685	1686	1687	1688	1689	1690
圏	涯	岳	淑	倫	呉	貌	婆	鍵	膳
1691	1692	1693	1694	1695	1696	1697	1698	1699	1700
罰	朱	漂	禅	酷	霧	袖	彫	需	潰
1701	1702	1703	1704	1705	1706	1707	1708	1709	1710
腫	瘍	穏	謎	誉	逸	凍	惜	措	瓦
1711	1712	1713	1714	1715	1716	1717	1718	1719	1720
瓶	琴	摂	拍	稽	礎	掌	克	据	胆
1721	1722	1723	1724	1725	1726	1727	1728	1729	1730
縛	鎮	雷	恨	顕	棋	巧	桃	隔	甚
1731	1732	1733	1734	1735	1736	1737	1738	1739	1740
妊	娠	獣	疾	臼	潟	塾	塊	絞	苗
1741	1742	1743	1744	1745	1746	1747	1748	1749	1750
陶	陳	傘	啓	卑	劣	撤	殴	矛	盾
1751	1752	1753	1754	1755	1756	1757	1758	1759	1760
尉	慰	衰	蛇	潤	戯	偏	炉	膜	抽
1761	1762	1763	1764	1765	1766	1767	1768	1769	1770
賭	括	弧	犠	牲	貼	拉	帆	挿	枕

1771 錯	1772 珠	1773 畜	1774 蓄	1775 拓	1776 鼓	1777 膚	1778 粋	1779 悦	1780 誓
1781 憤	1782 慨	1783 鬱	1784 憂	1785 愁	1786 冠	1787 顎	1788 簿	1789 糧	1790 架
1791 軸	1792 苛	1793 蓋	1794 凶	1795 庶	1796 裾	1797 稚	1798 拙	1799 辱	1800 恒
1801 暦	1802 峠	1803 宰	1804 蛮	1805 窮	1806 疎	1807 彰	1808 傑	1809 拘	1810 緯
1811 妖	1812 藍	1813 鍛	1814 錬	1815 繊	1816 縫	1817 把	1818 峡	1819 楼	1820 漬
1821 紳	1822 宛	1823 閥	1824 坪	1825 溝	1826 朴	1827 軌	1828 喪	1829 墨	1830 遍
1831 濁	1832 缶	1833 扇	1834 枯	1835 乙	1836 酵	1837 堤	1838 阻	1839 乞	1840 鐘
1841 擁	1842 享	1843 郭	1844 呪	1845 砕	1846 勃	1847 唾	1848 譜	1849 肪	1850 塀
1851 碁	1852 敢	1853 塁	1854 滴	1855 暁	1856 謡	1857 痕	1858 詐	1859 欺	1860 弦
1861 泡	1862 伐	1863 厄	1864 奔	1865 瞳	1866 昆	1867 脊	1868 椎	1869 懇	1870 唄
1871 渦	1872 襟	1873 吟	1874 覇	1875 衡	1876 呈	1877 淫	1878 循	1879 懲	1880 錦
1881 箇	1882 醜	1883 軟	1884 戚	1885 喚	1886 紺	1887 某	1888 赴	1889 媒	1890 嫉
1891 妬	1892 遮	1893 窯	1894 茎	1895 隻	1896 釜	1897 墳	1898 壌	1899 尼	1900 肢
1901 赦	1902 酬	1903 宜	1904 殻	1905 碑	1906 奨	1907 践	1908 滋	1909 儒	1910 怨
1911 曇	1912 刈	1913 閑	1914 錠	1915 扶	1916 妥	1917 妨	1918 醒	1919 胎	1920 窟
1921 巾	1922 忌	1923 骸	1924 弄	1925 粛	1926 囚	1927 罵	1928 渇	1929 肯	1930 燥
1931 搭	1932 諭	1933 璧	1934 喝	1935 采	1936 騰	1937 篤	1938 勲	1939 埼	1940 曖
1941 昧	1942 岬	1943 暫	1944 詮	1945 諾	1946 零	1947 柿	1948 芯	1949 綻	1950 訂

1951 薫	1952 遷	1953 枢	1954 肘	1955 麓	1956 憧	1957 漆	1958 酌	1959 慕	1960 婿
1961 妄	1962 匿	1963 侮	1964 髄	1965 薪	1966 轄	1967 咽	1968 迅	1969 該	1970 逐
1971 嘲	1972 墜	1973 臆	1974 餓	1975 捻	1976 挫	1977 桟	1978 溺	1979 賄	1980 盲
1981 鯨	1982 侶	1983 蔑	1984 丼	1985 剖	1986 槽	1987 閲	1988 畔	1989 睦	1990 唆
1991 腎	1992 梗	1993 搬	1994 宵	1995 拐	1996 醸	1997 猶	1998 畏	1999 逝	2000 朽
2001 硫	2002 瞭	2003 擬	2004 叙	2005 弊	2006 累	2007 煩	2008 藻	2009 蚊	2010 鋳
2011 謹	2012 棺	2013 傲	2014 舶	2015 租	2016 倣	2017 抹	2018 虹	2019 娯	2020 腺
2021 喩	2022 萎	2023 蛍	2024 窒	2025 桁	2026 栓	2027 嫡	2028 屯	2029 糾	2030 陪
2031 雌	2032 霜	2033 紡	2034 貪	2035 庸	2036 韻	2037 繕	2038 搾	2039 姻	2040 拷
2041 堆	2042 禍	2043 抄	2044 遜	2045 旺	2046 准	2047 勾	2048 壱	2049 升	2050 耗
2051 箋	2052 串	2053 弔	2054 賓	2055 痢	2056 俸	2057 罷	2058 賦	2059 褐	2060 斥
2061 矯	2062 窃	2063 惰	2064 倹	2065 憾	2066 哺	2067 彙	2068 墾	2069 酪	2070 痘
2071 斤	2072 訃	2073 叱	2074 籠	2075 蓮	2076 頒	2077 楷	2078 孔	2079 癌	2080 弥
2081 伊	2082 幌	2083 堺	2084 媛	2085 栃	2086 櫻	2087 萌	2088 蘭		

Kanji Group Index

0001 – One and similar kanji 一
0004 – Kite, concentric boxes 回
0006 – Four (floor plan) (group of one) 四
0011 – Bell (to stand) on floor (tire stop as part of bell) 立
0013 – Person (hito) & similar kanji 人
0014 – Enter or insert 入
0019 – Tall (takai), other 高
0020 – Seven, other 七
0021 – Seven wearing hat 宅
0022 – Thousand 千
0024 – Mata table, other 又
0027 – Sotted Superman (brush w/ 2 handles) 卒
0030 – Faceless dancer (group of one) 久
0032 – Sun (day) (group of one) 日
0033 – Plants above sun, other 昔
0039 – Yen (en) (group of one) 円
0041 – Ladder (stairs, axe), other 昨
0043 – Movie screen 英
0050 – Breasts (mother) (group of one) 母
0051 – Eye & similar kanji 目
0059 – Soil (group of one) 土

0061 – Rice paddy above sun, w/ two units (or antennae or rabbit ears), agricultural zone 増
0062 – Bad haircut above cow (mu) (group of one) 室
0063 – Cow (mu) below one & above soil 至
0064 – Box above soil (group of one) 堂
0067 – Slanted hat w/ man (soldier) (group of one) 仕
0069 – Up arrow (peaked roof) 界
0071 – Backpack & sword 留
0077 – Rice paddy model w/ handle, w/out well 画
0087 – Fish head (h chair leaning to right), other 負
0088 – Member (box above money chest) 員
0094 – Small below sun 願
0100 – Eye above table, other 具
0101 – Ten above eye on table 真
0102 – Blade (sword) & similar kanji (nine) 刀
0105 – Eight, other 分
0109 – Rice paddy above force (male) 男
0112 – Cuban bird 究
0113 – Ten thousand, other 万
0116 – Travel (trip, person stepping out) 旅

0118 – Tree & similar kanji 木
0120 – Bad haircut above female 案
0122 – Slanted hat w/ tree 休
0123 – Tree w/ open book 本
0128 – Branch of tree lining up 枝
0129 – Tree w/ dancer 杁
0131 – Sunny guy, other 村
0135 – Rice paddy above slanted legs 横
0139 – Bridge (sky above boxes) 橋
0143 – X (crossing) under eyebrows 父
0148 – Moon (group of one) 月
0150 – Dressing room (table under clothes hook) 服
0154 – Sun & moon 明
0157 – Moon & Ri under bench 前
0162 – Half moon above box 名
0164 – Evening (half moon), capped (nightcap) 死
0166 – Master (king under cap) 主
0170 – Jewel (ball next to king) 国
0172 – Up & down 上下
0173 – Stop & similar kanji (taser) 止

Group Index

0175 – Dancer w/ correct 政
0176 – Negation (fu) 不
0179 – Five (knee), other 五
0180 – Tiller (one eye above stand) 決
0181 – Kneeling w/ tray 片
0187 – Child w/ dancer (group of one) 教
0188 – Big & similar kanji 大
0191 – Fat 太
0194 – Husband (person w/ 2 pairs of arms) on fire 狭
0197 – Husband wearing glasses (two eyes, Chinese) 漢
0200 – Feathers above net 曜
0205 – Cow & similar kanji 牛
0207 – Noon (crutch above ten) 午
0214 – Protect (sunny guy under bad haircut) 守
0215 – Temple (soil above sunny guy), other 時
0219 – Skeet shooter (thread, two elbows above three legs) (group of one) 糸
0220 – Rice paddy, other 細
0227 – Skeet shooter w/ water 緑
0228 – White above water 線

0230 – Skeet shooter, including truncated, w/ dancer 絡
0233 – Dancer w/ ice 終
0234 – Winter (ice, other) 冬
0240 – Pavilion above sun (marriage) 婚
0242 – City (Bo Peep under a tire stop), other 市
0243 – Eye plus sun 帽
0247 – Crafted object (I-beam), other 紅
0249 – Leaning woman w/ ball (ceremony; single-grip halberd minus left hip) 式
0253 – Small & similar kanji 小
0258 – Water plus plant radicals 薄
0259 – Tire stop above X, culture 済
0262 – Rain 雪
0266 – Bell above sun (sound) 音
0269 – Bell above box 倍
0284 – Heavy (car w/ hubcaps) 重
0296 – Bad haircut above peaked roof 容
0297 – Bench hats 登
0304 – Big fused w/ cow 鉄
0306 – Heart (group of one) 心
0308 – Rice paddy above heart 思
0313 – Red Cross 悪
0319 – Female w/ table 怒

0320 – Box, open to right, other 区
0321 – Triple roof on lean-to 気
0323 – Box on right 知
0324 – Native American chief, other 短
0332 – Christmas tree (tree or husband under lights; eye, one, below lights) 業
0333 – Husband (person w/ 2 pairs of arms) w/ a 3rd pair 僕
0336 – Rice paddy w/ extended lines (mai) 毎
0341 – Box w/ napkin in 1-sided lean-to 伺
0343 – Soil above mu (cow) 去
0346 – Soil above box in 2-sided lean-to 週
0347 – Soil above sheep (group of one) 達
0348 – Oklahoma's uber Ruth (antennae above sky) 送
0349 – Antennae above neck (michi, path; neck above eye) 道
0351 – Soil above box 遠
0352 – Multiple duplicate radicals, other 選
0361 – Carton slipping, other 過
0367 – Fence, other (telephone pole inside 2-sided lean-to) 備
0369 – Sick bed 病
0376 – Leaning woman, double roof w/out snow 眠

Group Index

0377 – Three-legged bench (rocker bottom) 祭
0383 – Bell as eye of needle, other 親
0384 – Needles, four basic types 辛
0388 – South (compass needle in 2-sided lean-to) 南
0389 – Bell above tree 新
0394 – Old (ten above box, other) 故
0395 – Old in closed box (ten above box in box) 個
0397 – Person emerging from 2-sided lean-to 肉
0398 – L&Y, other 食
0401 – Streamers w/out sun (easy) (group of one) 物
0406 – Rocker bottom shoe [three cords under other object(s)] 参
0419 – Trident perforating face (kimi, you) 君
0420 – Big brother (lopsided legs under box), other 兄
0421 – Two above lopsided legs (base) 元
0423 – Lopsided legs below shield 洗
0425 – Man above roof w/ lopsided legs 売
0429 – Shield, other 告
0430 – Words, other (say, speak, talk) (group of one) 言
0431 – Words w/ slanted hat (group of one) 信
0446 – Triple plant radical above base above lopsided legs 焼

0447 – Red (4 legs under soil) 赤
0449 – Foot below box 足
0450 – Foot below soil 走
0453 – Hoe 越
0454 – Foot below sun 題
0456 – Left (crafted object, hugged) 左
0457 – Hugging, other 右
0459 – Hugged table (friend) 友
0464 – Four w/ handle (west) (group of one) 西
0468 – Kangaroo 写
0476 – Bow (twisted) 引
0479 – Lean-to, two-sided, other 風
0484 – Carry-on suitcase, handle (group of one) 価
0486 – Kyouto dome (together, plants above dome), other 供
0489 – Yoke (dancer w/ mark on cheek) 夜
0490 – Money chest plus Ri 側
0491 – Hundred (sun below limousine antenna) 宿
0495 – King above snail 庭
0502 – Hair to the right 長
0503 – Scorpion 他
0506 – Spring (three superimposed on person, other) 春
0514 – Small below box 京
0517 – Sincere guy w/ glasses (2 eyes) 勤

0520 – White (oven) above tree 楽
0522 – Limousine antenna, other 夏
0523 – Dancer w/ heart 愛
0524 – Bad haircut above dancer 客
0526 – Dancer w/ plants 落
0536 – Oil derrick (h-shaped chair leaning above person) 次
0538 – Mu (cow) above box 台
0542 – Hanging bucket 世
0544 – Ma マ above nail w/out stabilizing leg 予
0545 – Rice paddy above soil (sincere guy w/ bifocals, other) 野
0547 – Snake, uncoiling 危
0557 – Yak above table 役
0560 – Sword above or below box 招
0561 – Betsy w/ a square head (box above sword w/ Ri) 別
0568 – Books, other 冊
0569 – Eye above shelf w/o legs 置
0572 – Shelf above three straight legs (eye above shelf w/ legs) 県
0573 – Catapult tower (welcoming stance) 形
0574 – Propellers (lips, fly) (group of one) 飛
0575 – Antennae above stove burners 並

Group Index

0582 – E (エ) & Y, other 表
0583 – Cage (negation) (crutch above fence) 無
0585 – Shaky table (tire stop above L) 亡
0588 – Rice paddy above tree (fruit) 課
0591 – Mu (cow) on floor 払
0593 – Kneeling guy w/ high stalk of flowers (telephone pole w/ flat top) (group of one) 拝
0599 – Nurse (man above beans) 喜
0601 – Giraffe 以
0602 – Eight above box 船
0604 – 1-sided lean-to containing box w/out napkin, w/ big 奇
0605 – Halberd, triple grip 残
0606 – Cuban water dog (dog's head above water) 球
0607 – Owl's perch above sunny guy 寿
0611 – Fire (4 flames, other) 然
0614 – Husband, sky & similar kanji 夫
0616 – Mu (cow) above moon 能
0618 – Fish head (h chair leaning to right) above rice paddy 解
0620 – Dining table (sun above ten under taser; California wagon w/ broken wheel) 卓

0623 – Uncooked rice above snail 迷
0625 – "Go" (iku) (hammer & nail w/ double hat) 街
0629 – Telephone pole, flat top, other 汗
0633 – Success (blade & halberd) 成
0635 – Uncooked rice above shelf 継
0637 – Stool above spinning nail under peaked roof 余
0643 – Money chest under inside (naka) 貴
0656 – Money chest below one item, otheer 費
0657 – Inside, other (box or chicken on stick, yakitori) 仲
0660 – Bathroom (peaked roof) w/ vapor rising 裕
0668 – Sun above platform (dance floor) 旦
0669 – Moon w/ extended lines 那
0671 – Child under grate 浮
0672 – Tree w/ two pairs of branches 未
0673 – Two eyes on snake 絶
0677 – Heart in lean-to 応
0688 – Fur, hair (fingers right) 毛
0692 – 3x snail 廻
0694 – Roof above lopsided legs, above tree 深
0695 – Four-legged hen (bird) 変

0698 – Hugging net 勧
0702 – Nail, other 丁
0707 – Money chest w/ two+ items on top 賃
0708 – Big brother (box above lopsided legs) & rabbit ears (antennae) 税
0710 – Three lopsided legs 慌
0711 – Bucket, other 期
0718 – Megaphone, two lips 環
0719 – Big brother w/ scowl on lopsided legs 境
0720 – Ten above rice paddy 恵
0721 – TV above toes (beans, upside-down bench) 豆
0723 – Nails (claws) 孤
0727 – Big above net 奮
0733 – Peaked roof above moon & Ri 愉
0735 – Breast (L) 札
0742 – Two moons 棚
0743 – Tower under antennae 餅
0745 – Shack (box under soil under peaked roof) 舎
0746 – Four (4) 叫
0748 – Soil in lean-to 圧
0752 – Solar panel 組
0753 – Bell w/ halberd (leaning woman w/ ball, plus left hip) 織
0754 – Bird, other (four flames); most entries include white 鶏

Group Index

0760 – Child without arms 了

0772 – Money chest below owl's perch 責

0781 – Man & words 詰

0784 – Dancer near mountain 徴

0786 – Man (soldier) above heart 誌

0787 – Tree plus eye 相

0796 – Helmet w/ visor (one eye) 邪

0799 – Streamlined car w/ hubcaps 垂

0801 – Half moon (evening), other 移

0802 – Needle on snail 避

0804 – Bell above spikes 諦

0805 – L&Y (good) 浪

0808 – Jutting lump (ball above right shoulder, other) 術

0813 – Library (peaked roof) 論

0814 – Water (ice) & similar kanji 氷

0817 – Trident perforating (mending) split tree, w/ antennae 嫌

0818 – Floor plan (four) w/ missing right wall 匹

0820 – Telephone pole, other 棒

0826 – Horse (telephone pole inside 5, four flames) 騒

0827 – Nine, other 尻

0832 – Apartment above moon (bone, carton slipping) 骨

0833 – Straight Arrow (skin, arrow above table; chimney above table) 皮

0839 – Three cords, other 影

0840 – Lightning 響

0849 – Trillion (two vertical benches) 兆

0851 – Hero w/ 2 wings (ladders, stairs) 悲

0861 – Tree above peaked roof 膝

0865 – Rice paddy under dog's head 敷

0872 – Box in hook, other 句

0873 – Dancer w/ cave (box in hook) 敬

0877 – Trident perforating, other 津

0880 – Bunk beds 官

0881 – 2-sided lean-to w/ box under ten (old) & under bell 敵

0888 – White above small 原

0892 – Pliers, other 折

0895 – Three eyes in lean-to 鹿

0897 – Kneeling (or leaning) telephone pole, flat or pointed tops 宇

0910 – Slanted shelf 斜

0913 – Foot, other 旋

0914 – Three men of force 脅

0915 – Halberd (leaning woman w/ ball, plus left hip) supporting lean-to 威

0920 – Honorable person, other (ten thousand w/ feather in cap, tire stop on ten thousand) 防

0927 – Cooped-up Superman (mountains stacked, leave) 屈

0930 – TY (thank you) (group of one) 衆

0934 – Three eyes under ten 聴

0936 – Perforated fish-head (h chair leaning to right) monster w/ trident 争

0938 – Hostess (dancer) above telephone pole 峰

0941 – Comb w/ bell above moon 襲

0942 – Rice paddy under one unit, other 油

0943 – Trees in group (grove, forest), other 禁

0945 – Dog, other (ball above right shoulder) 伏

0947 – Net above table 獲

0948 – Contorted woman 狙

0962 – Wobbly table below napkin & peaked roof 令

0964 – Bad haircut above eight (group of one) 穴

0974 – Lopsided legs, other 就

0978 – Family w/ マ Ma 疑

0979 – Light (3-pronged switch above lopsided legs) 輝

0985 – Unicorn horn (isolated vertical line) 悠

0987 – Four (floor plan) w/ missing lower wall 融

Group Index

0988 – Hook, other 均
0991 – Three old boys (3-pronged switch) on distinct roof 覚
0995 – Dog's head above fence 補
0996 – Yu ユ, other 候
0998 – Vertical bench 状
0999 – Water under hair to the left (green flag) 録
1000 – Right hip 更
1003 – Rope w/ rice paddy or paddies (transformer) 縄
1004 – Sunny guy w/ man w/ slanted hat 府
1010 – Little (small), other 省
1012 – Cloud above (Thai) mountain 帯
1017 – Number-one day 旧
1019 – Chevron 災
1021 – Water plus together, under sun 暴
1032 – Rice paddy above straight legs 再
1033 – Dancer above box 各
1034 – Merchandise (articles, boxes, packages) 繰
1042 – E (工) & Y below tire stop (clothing) 衣
1046 – Calligraphy seal 印
1053 – Flat-top telephone pole on fire 評
1054 – Half (telephone pole on fire) 判
1056 – Two (二) above cow (mu) 芸

1057 – Lean-to containing periscope & seven 虎
1065 – Scissors, other 老
1069 – Leo's oven, below big and above small 療
1071 – Chute (toboggans) 州
1072 – Skeet shooter below cape 孫
1073 – Coop w/ 6 sections and crossed wires 遭
1077 – King & similar kanji 王
1078 – Snake (backwards "S"), other 妃
1079 – Bath (stacked vertebrae, spine) 宮
1088 – Person (mono), sun below scissors 著
1090 – River 訓
1101 – Pyramid (triangle) 蒸
1103 – Owl's perch above object(s), other 麦
1105 – L & Y supporting an arrow 農
1112 – Owl's perch above moon 清
1120 – Asymmetrical roots 遇
1121 – Man (soldier) above table (sheet) 妓
1124 – Ri w/ capped evening (nightcap) (retsu) 列
1125 – Mu (cow) under tire stop 統
1126 – Missing head platform (limousine antenna above money chest) 領
1127 – Three eyes above table 慢
1129 – Skeet shooter, truncated, other 幻

1131 – Breathing graph 級
1134 – Lean-to w/ double roof, w/ snow 房
1139 – Crossing (X) under six (tire stop above father) 効
1140 – Fish-head (chair leaning to right) guy w/ glasses above lopsided legs 免
1143 – Ma (mammoth) above fence (telephone pole inside 2-sided lean-to) 樋
1150 – Correct (cap above stop), other 証
1152 – Multiple suns 唱
1153 – Model of mountain w/ handle, superimposed on a lean-to (or a mountain below a forked tongue, or chair-lift seat, normal) 満
1157 – Rice paddy on stick 甲
1158 – Skeet shooter w/ net 羅
1160 – Shah 祥
1161 – Four (floor plan) w/ missing right wall (box open to right, small animal) w/ bucket 勘
1164 – Three superimposed on no (group of one) 看
1165 – Hair to the left, other 婦
1166 – F over X (lean-to containing table) 板
1169 – Devil (demon, lopsided tentacle, rice paddy under one unit) 魅
1170 – Warehouse (peaked roof above triple roof) 倉

Group Index

1174 – Reversed feet (five reversed, different) 偉
1176 – 1-sided lean-to containing box *w/out* napkin, *w/out* big 阿
1177 – Barbecue grate, other 援
1181 – Nose stung by bees (X in bee hive, three old boys) 悩
1185 – Box w/ napkin above rice paddy 幅
1188 – Bad haircut above slashed heart 密
1195 – Woman leaning, single roof (pavilion) 抵
1200 – Lean-to, 2-sided, containing model of mountain w/ handle & antennae (or cable seat, frayed cable) 綱
1202 – Well, other 囲
1207 – Tagalog youths (コ) 互
1213 – Forked tongue (box under tongue), other 舌
1214 – Lean-to, box & needle 辟
1216 – Box(es) above tree 保
1220 – CSD (crutch, sun, dancer) 履
1221 – Lopsided legs below bench hats 廃
1223 – Sheep (antennae, upside-down bench above telephone pole), other 羊
1227 – Corset under bad haircut 塞
1236 – Upside-down bench, other 磁
1239 – Fire, other 炊
1245 – Seven universal laws 純

1246 – Swing set, other 堅
1251 – Napkin above box under peaked roof 塔
1256 – Window w/ lower frame reinforced 域
1260 – Owl's perch below bad haircut 害
1266 – Skeet shooter below other object(s) 緊
1268 – Triple plant radical, other 噴
1271 – East (sun behind tree; tree wearing bifocals) 棟
1278 – Ten above eye 植
1282 – Ma マ, other 勇
1284 – City merged w/ tree 刺
1286 – Needle w/ open syringe (two eyes above ten) 革
1287 – Mu (cow) in lean-to 拡
1294 – Two heroes 混
1297 – Slashed heart 泌
1300 – Stove burners 湿
1305 – Bonfire (two pairs of arms on person, plus flames) 券
1308 – California wagon (morning) 潮
1310 – Cannons (swing set) firing crutch 鑑
1314 – Two eyes, other 史
1318 – Hero above sun 旨
1321 – Songs (6-section coop w/ 2 *un*crossed wires) 豊
1322 – E (エ) & Y (clothes) w/ six & well 穣

1324 – Three eyes at top 署
1340 – Diving board 乏
1341 – Look/see (eye above lopsided legs) 規
1347 – Spinning nail under flying carpet (two above small) 示
1352 – Tree below object(s), other 条
1353 – PSB (plants above sun & big) 模
1355 – Sun above lopsided legs 鏡
1360 – Box, closed, other 因
1363 – One thousand ten 昇
1365 – Sun above ten (early) 章
1368 – Slashed uncooked rice 審
1381 – Self (ray above eye) 臭
1382 – Peaked roof, other 企
1385 – Mountain at top 炭
1387 – Uncooked rice, other 粧
1389 – Kneeling guy near table 技
1407 – Bowl or dish, three eyes (bowl) 益
1413 – Slanted hat w/ hero 貨
1415 – Three eyes hanging from platform 煙
1417 – Left hip, other 芽
1421 – Taser above spinning nail (small below taser on platform) 督
1427 – Child w/ tire stop & jukebox 熟

1432 – Keg stuck in washing machine w/ handle (peaked roof above person w/ 2 eyes & flat cap) 劍
1440 – Head of Native American chief above correct 御
1453 – Man (soldier) above box 吉
1454 – X, segmented 渋
1457 – Feathers, other 翌
1462 – Desk, other 冗
1466 – Sun above hook 揭
1467 – Box w/out napkin in 2-sided lean-to 稿
1468 – Man (soldier), other 莊
1471 – Child under soil & scissors 孝
1474 – Tire stop above box, other 亭
1475 – Tree(s) or grove in lean-to 麻
1480 – Sake bucket w/ handle, four w/ handle + extra compartment 酸
1484 – Wakeful eye/shack (lean-to w/ double roof w/out snow) 尺
1485 – Antennae above foot radical 從
1487 – Bad haircut above hundred 縮
1488 – Slashed sword 刃
1491 – Now (seven below ceiling under peaked roof) 含
1494 – Chimney, trident perforating 糖
1496 – Two 仁
1501 – Bad haircut above big 寮
1504 – Pig (house) 豚

1511 – Slashed desk 凡
1524 – Boat 舟
1529 – Water below item(s) 泰
1534 – Hesitant square-head (box above stop) 踏
1535 – Moonies (eggs) 柳
1542 – Well w/ handle (taser above box) 占
1544 – Bucket above tree 謀
1546 – Eight above cow (mu) 訟
1548 – Boar skeleton (tire stop) 核
1554 – Hand (fingers left) 拳
1569 – Bell above object(s), other 竜
1576 – Soil w/ honorable person 坊
1583 – Trident piercing upper axis of water 隷
1601 – Truncated moon 剤
1603 – Three eyes, other 爵
1615 – Happy Jimmy (two lips) 裸
1619 – Soil above soil, other 封
1620 – Box w/ napkin in 2-sided lean-to, w/ or w/out halberd support 筒
1625 – Three-pronged switch (old boys), not on distinct roof, other 肖
1658 – Ten below object(s), other 阜
1673 – Taser, other 偵
1675 – Cow merged w/ tree 殊

1678 – Mu (cow), other 惨
1686 – Pitcher (square ball) 呉
1694 – Rice paddy above ten 禅
1702 – Sun above streamers (easy) 瘍
1712 – King on top 琴
1713 – Ear 摂
1721 – Rice paddy above sunny guy 縛
1729 – Tarantula below box w/ napkin 隔
1737 – Nine, slashed 塾
1740 – Fluffy cat (plants above rice paddy) 苗
1746 – Force below other object(s) 劣
1749 – Ma マ above nail w/ stabilizing leg (left hip) 矛
1752 – Sunny guy plus double-roof lean-to w/out snow 慰
1754 – Insect 蛇
1755 – Gate 潤
1765 – Cow, other 牲
1768 – Bo Peep, other 帆
1772 – King on left 珠
1775 – Stone (leaning guy w/ flat hat) 拓
1794 – Open-top box 凶
1797 – Ripe grain on left 稚
1803 – Bell above ten (axis) 宰
1806 – Tree wearing glasses (bundle, two eyes on tree) 疎
1808 – Knee, other 傑
1811 – Sky (big below horizontal line, other 妖

Group Index

- 1825 – Model of rice paddy w/ handle w/ well 溝
- 1826 – Toe 朴
- 1828 – Ten (juu), other 喪
- 1832 – Noon merged w/ mountain 缶
- 1835 – Z 乙
- 1840 – Sincere guy w/ bifocals below bell 鐘
- 1843 – ß Beta on the right 郭
- 1846 – Force, other 勃
- 1855 – One (base, platform) above lopsided legs, other 曉
- 1856 – Mountain w/ forked tongue emerging 謠
- 1860 – Tire stop, other 弦
- 1861 – Wrapping (backwards "S" snake inside a hook) 泡
- 1862 – Halberd, single grip, other 伐
- 1870 – Money chest on right 唄
- 1876 – King under item(s), other 呈
- 1878 – Ten above eye in lean-to 循
- 1893 – King wearing rabbit ears (antennae), truncated sheep (no tail) 窯
- 1894 – Table above soil 莖
- 1897 – Money chest below plants 墳
- 1899 – Lean-to w/ double roof w/o snow 尼
- 1908 – Skeet shooter, truncated, double 滋

- 1915 – Husband (person w/ 2 pairs of arms), other 扶
- 1918 – Life (live) 醒
- 1924 – Welcoming (open) stance, other 弄
- 1926 – Person (hito), other 囚
- 1929 – Stop, other (taser) 肯
- 1935 – Barbecue grate in tree 采
- 1942 – Mountain on left 岬
- 1946 – Peaked roof above マ ma (alternative font) 零
- 1948 – Heart under plants (group of one) 芯
- 1953 – X, other 枢
- 1966 – Car on the left 轄
- 1972 – House w/ rabbit ears 墜
- 1974 – Eat (peaked roof) 餓
- 1983 – F, other 蔑
- 1985 – Ri, other 剖
- 1989 – Soil walking on soil 睦
- 1990 – Mu (cow) above two lopsided legs 唆
- 1991 – Moon below multiple items 腎
- 1992 – Rice paddy forming bifocals, other 梗
- 1997 – Antennae (rabbit ears), other 猶
- 2002 – Eye, other 瞭
- 2006 – Rice paddy w/ skeet shooter 累
- 2010 – Money (gold, peaked roof) 鋳

- 2014 – White (sun under ray), other 舶
- 2016 – Hopeful Hannah (dancer w/ honorable person) 倣
- 2026 – Everything (king under peaked roof) 栓
- 2030 – Beta (ß) on left 陪
- 2039 – Female on left 婚
- 2045 – King on right 旺
- 2046 – Net (slanted hat w/ master w/ extra pair of arms), other 准
- 2048 – Hero (or heel), other 壱
- 2050 – Man standing on tree 耗
- 2055 – Ripe grain, other 痢
- 2058 – Money chest on left 賦
- 2060 – Slashed pliers 斥
- 2062 – Sword, other 窃
- 2063 – Erect man 情
- 2068 – Wolf ヲ 墾
- 2070 – Box w/ napkin 痘
- 2073 – Box on left 叱
- 2074 – Bamboo (2 crutches above vertical lines) 籠
- 2075 – Car, other 蓮
- 2076 – Understand (minute) 頒
- 2078 – Child, other (ma above thin body w/ arms) 孔
- 2079 – Mountain on floor 癌
- 2080 – Crutch, other 弥
- 2086 – Female below item(s), other 櫻
- 2087 –Moon below single item, other 萌

Kanji Trait Index

Above & below 上下 – 0172
Again 又 – see table
Alcohol (sake bucket w/ handle) 酘 – 1480
Antenna (limo) above money chest 領 – 1126
Antenna (limo) above sun (hundred) 宿 – 0491
Antenna (limo), other 夏 – 0522
Antennae above big brother 税 – 0708
Antennae above foot radical 從 – 1485
Antennae above house 墜 – 1972
Antennae above king 窯 – 1893
Antennae above model of mountain 綱 – 1200
Antennae above rice paddy 増 – 0061
Antennae above six-section rice paddy (two-pronged switch) 豊 – see songs
Antennae above split tree 嫌 – 0817
Antennae above sky (Uber Ruth) 送 – 0348
Antennae above stove burners 並 – 0575
Antennae above tower 餅 – 0743
Antennae as part of sheep 羊 – see sheep
Antennae on platform above neck 道 – 0349
Antennae, other 猶 – 1997
Apartment above moon (bone, carton slipping) 骨 – 0832

Arrow above L & Y (L&Y) 農 – 1105
Arrow above table (Straight Arrow) 皮 – 0833
Arrow up 界 – 0069
Articles 緑 – 1034
Asymmetrical legs or tentacles – see lopsided
Asymmetrical roots 遇 – 1120
Axe (stairs, ladder), other 昨 – 0041
Backpack & sword 留 – 0071
Backwards feet 偉 – 1174
Backwards S snake in wrapping (or hook) 泡 – 1861
Backwards S snake, other 妃 – 1078
Bad haircut above big 寮 – 1501
Bad haircut above corset 塞 – 1227
Bad haircut above cow (mu) (group of one) 室 – 0062
Bad haircut above dancer 客 – 0524
Bad haircut above eight (group of one) 穴 – 0964
Bad haircut above female 案 – 0120
Bad haircut above hundred 縮 – 1487
Bad haircut above owl's perch 害 – 1260
Bad haircut above peaked roof 容 – 0296
Bad haircut above slashed heart 密 – 1188
Bad haircut above sunny guy 守 – 0214
Ball above right shoulder, dog 伏 – 0945

Ball above right shoulder, other 術 – 0808
Ball next to king (jewel) 国 – 0170
Bamboo (2 crutches above vertical lines) 籠 – 2074
Barbecue grate 采 – see grate
Base (lopsided legs below one) 暁 – 1855
Base (lopsided legs below roof), above tree 深 – 0694
Base (lopsided legs below two) 元 – 0421
Bath (stacked vertebrae) 宮 – 1079
Bathroom w/ vapors rising 裕 – 0660
Beans below man (soldier) (nurse) 喜 – 0599
Beans (TV above toes), other 豆 – 0721
Bed, sick 病 – 0369
Beds, bunk 官 – 0880
Bees 悩 – 1181
Bell above box 倍 – 0269
Bell above (on) floor 立 – 0011
Bell above moon w/ comb 襲 – 0941
Bell above sincere guy w/ bifocals 鐘 – 1840
Bell above spikes 諦 – 0804
Bell above sun (sound) 音 – 0266
Bell above ten 宰 – 1803
Bell above tree 新 – 0389
Bell above two-sided lean-to containing old 敵 – 0881
Bell above object(s), other 竜 – 1569

Trait Index

Bell as eye of needle, on snail 避 – 0802
Bell as eye of needle, w/ lean-to & box 辟 – 1214
Bell as eye of needle, other 親 – 0383
Bell w/ halberd 織 – 0753
Bench hats above lopsided legs 廃 – 1221
Bench hats, other 登 – 0297
Bench, rocker bottom, three-legged 祭 – 0377
Bench, upside-down – see upside-down bench
Bench, vertical 状 – 0998
Bench, vertical, two 兆 – 0849
Beta (ß) on the left 陪 – 2030
Beta (ß) on the right 郭 – 1843
Betsy w/ square head (box above sword w/ Ri) 別 – 0561
Bifocals on sincere guy below bell 鐘 – 1840
Bifocals on sincere guy, other 野 – 0545
Bifocals on tree 棟 – 1271
Bifocals, other 梗 – 1992
Big 大
 Big & similar kanji 大 – 0188
 Big above lean-to w/ box w/out napkin 寄 – 0604
 Big above net 奮 – 0727
 Big below bad haircut 寮 – 1501
 Big below horizontal line (sky), other 妖 – 1811
 Big below plants & sun (PSB) 模 – 1353
 Big merged w/ cow 鉄 – 0304
Big brother
 Big brother w/ rabbit ears 税 – 0708
 Big brother w/ scowl 境 – 0719
 Big brother, other 兄 – 0420
Bird (hen w/ 4 legs) 変 – 0695
Bird, Cuban 究 – 0112
Bird, other 鶏 – 0754
Blade & halberd 成 – 0633
Blade kanji 刀 – 0102
Bo Peep below tire stop (city), other 市 – 0242
Bo Peep, other 帆 – 1768
Boar skeleton (tire stop) 核 – 1548
Boat 舟 – 1524
Bone (apartment above moon, carton slipping) 骨 – 0832
Bonfire (two arms on person, plus flames) 券 – 1305
Book 本 – 0123
Books below peaked roof (library) 論 – 0813
Books, other 冊 – 0568
Bow (twisted) 引 – 0476
Bowl 益 – 1407
Box, concentric 回 – 0004
Box in hook w/ dancer (cave) 敬 – 0873
Box in hook, other 句 – 0872
Box above
 Box above foot 足 – 0449
 Box above soil (group of one) 堂 – 0064
 Box above money chest (member) 員 – 0088
 Box above small 京 – 0514
 Box above stop (hesitant squarehead) 踏 – 1534
 Box above lopsided legs (big brother) w/ rabbit ears 税 – 0708
 Box above legs (big brother), other 兄 – 0420
 Box above sword (Betsy w/ square head) w/ Ri 別 – 0561
 Box(es) above tree 保 – 1216
 Box above upside-down bench 豆 – 0721
Box below
 Box below bell 倍 – 0269
 Box below dancer 各 – 1033
 Box below eight 船 – 0602
 Box below half moon 名 – 0162
 Box below man (soldier) 吉 – 1453
 Box below mu (cow) 台 – 0538
 Box below napkin 司 – see box with napkin
 Box(es) below sky (bridge) 橋 – 0139
 Box below soil in 2-sided lean-to 週 – 0346
 Box below soil below peaked roof 舎 – 0745
 Box below soil, other 遠 – 0351
 Box below or above sword 招 – 0560
 Box below taser (well w/ handle) 占 – 1542
 Box below ten in box 個 – 0395

Box below ten (old) in 2-sided lean-to below bell 敵 – 0881
Box below ten, other 故 – 0394
Box below tire stop w/ child 熟 – 1427
Box below tire stop, other 亭 – 1474
Box below tongue 舌 – 1213
Box(es), concentric 回 – 0004

Box on
  Box on left 叱 – 2073
  Box on right 知 – 0323
  Box on stick 仲 – see inside

Box with contents
  Box, closed, containing old 個 – 0395
  Box, closed, other 因 – 1360
  Box, open bottom – see lean-to, 2-sided
  Box, open top 凶 – 1794
  Box, open to right plus bucket 勘 – 1161
  Box, open to right, other 区 – 0320

Box with napkin
  Box w/ napkin, above rice paddy 幅 – 1185
  Box w/ napkin, above tarantula 隔 – 1729
  Box w/ napkin in 1-sided lean-to 伺 – 0341
  Box w/ napkin in 2-sided lean-to 筒 – 1620
  Box w/ napkin below peaked roof 塔 – 1251
  Box w/ napkin, other 痘 – 2070

Box without napkin, in lean-to
  Box w/out napkin in 1-sided lean-to, *with* big 寄 – 0604
  Box w/out napkin in 1-sided lean-to, *w/out* big 阿 – 1176
  Box w/out napkin in 2-sided lean-to 稿 – 1467

Box (window) w/ lower frame reinforced 域 – 1256
Box w/ lean-to & needle 辟 – 1214
Box w/ slipping carton above moon 骨 – 0832
Box w/ slipping carton, other 過 – 0361
Boxes, other (merchandise, packages, articles) 繰 – 1034
Branch of tree lining up 枝 – 0128
Breast 札 – 0735
Breasts 母 (group of one) – 0050
Breathing graph 級 – 1131
Bridge 橋 – 0139
Brush w/ 2 handles 卒 – 0027
Bucket above tree 謀 – 1544
Bucket, hanging 世 – 0542
Bucket of sake w/ handle 酸 – 1480
Bucket plus small animal 勘 – 1161
Bucket, other 期 – 0711
Bundle (tree w/ glasses) 疎 – 1806
Bunk beds 官 – 0880
Burners for stove 湿 – 1300
Cable, frayed 綱 – 1200
Cable, normal 満 – 1153
Cage (negation) (crutch above fence) 無 – 0583
California wagon, intact 潮 – 1308

California wagon w/ broken wheel 卓 – 0620
Calligraphy seal 印 – 1046
Cannons (swing set) firing crutch 鑑 – 1310
Cap above evening (half moon) (nightcap) w/ Ri 列 – 1124
Cap above evening (half moon) (nightcap), other 死 – 0164
Cap above stop (correct, other) 証 – 1150
Cap above tree 禾 – see ripe grain
Cape above skeet shooter 孫 – 1072
Car on left 轄 – 1966
Car w/ hubcaps 重 – 0284
Car, streamlined, w/ hubcaps 垂 – 0799
Car, other 蓮 – 2075
Carpet, flying, above spinning nail 示 – 1347
Carry-on suitcase (group of one) 価 – 0484
Carton slipping above moon 骨 – 0832
Carton slipping, other 過 – 0361
Cat, fluffy 苗 – 1740
Catapult tower 形 – 0573
Cave (box in hook) w/ dancer 敬 – 0873
Center 仲 – see inside
Ceremony 式 – 0249
Chair (h) leaning to right above person (oil derrick) 次 – 0536
Chair (h) leaning to right, other 負 – see fish head
Chairlift seat, frayed cable 綱 – 1200
Chairlift seat, normal 満 – 1153

Cheek w/ mark 夜 – 0489
Chevron 災 – 1019
Chicken on stick 仲 – see inside
Chief, Native American, head above correct 御 – 1440
Chief, Native American, other 短 – 0324
Child below grate 浮 – 0671
Child below soil & scissors 孝 – 1471
Child w/ dancer (group of one) 教 – 0187
Child w/ tire stop & jukebox 熟 – 1427
Child without arms 了 – 0760
Child, other 孔 – 2078
Chimney above table (Straight Arrow, skin) 皮 – 0833
Chimney, perforated 糖 – 1494
Chinese husband wearing glasses 漢 – 0197
Christmas tree (lights) 業 – 0332
Chute 州 – 1071
Chuu 仲 – see inside
City (Bo Peep below tire stop) in tree 刺 – 1284
City (Bo Peep below tire stop), other 市 – 0242
Claws (nails) 孤 – 0723
Closed box – see box w/ contents, box, closed
Clothes hook 服 – 0150
Clothing 衣 – see tire stop above E (エ) & Y
Cloud above mountain 帯 – 1012
Comb w/ bell above moon 襲 – 0941
Compartments in bucket 期 – 0711

Concentric boxes 回 – 0004
Contorted woman 狙 – 0948
Coop w/ 6 sections & 2 wires, w/ short circuit 遭 – 1073
Coop w/ 6 sections & 2 *un*crossed wires 豊 – 1321
Cooped-up Superman 屈 – 0927
Cords, three – see three cords
Correct below head of Native American chief 御 – 1440
Correct w/ dancer 政 – 0175
Correct, other 証 – 1150
Corset below bad haircut 塞 – 1227
Cow & similar kanji 牛 – 0205
Cow merged w/ big 鉄 – 0304
Cow merged w/ tree 殊 – 1675
Cow, other 牲 – 1765
Cow (mu) 台 – see mu (cow)
Crafted object, hugged (left) 左 – 0456
Crafted object, other 紅 – 0247
Crossing 父 – see X
Crutch above dancer & sun (CSD) 履 – 1220
Crutch above fence (cage) (negation) 無 – 0583
Crutch above sun & dancer (CSD) 履 – 1220
Crutch above ten (noon) 午 – 0207
Crutch above X 冬 – see dancer
Crutch fired by swing set cannons 鑑 – 1310

Crutches, two, above vertical lines (bamboo) 籠 – 2074
Crutch, other 弥 – 2080
CSD (crutch above sun & dancer) 履 – 1220
Cuban bird 究 – 0112
Cuban water dog 球 – 0606
Culture 済 – 0259
Dance floor 旦 – 0668
Dancer above box 各 – 1033
Dancer above pole 峰 – 0938
Dancer above tree 条 – 0129
Dancer below bad haircut 客 – 0524
Dancer, faceless (group of one) 久 – 0030
Dancer near mountain 徴 – 0784
Dancer w/ cave (box in hook) 敬 – 0873
Dancer w/ child (group of one) 教 – 0187
Dancer w/ correct 政 – 0175
Dancer w/ heart 愛 – 0523
Dancer w/ honorable person 倣 – 2016
Dancer w/ ice 終 – 0233
Dancer w/ mark on cheek 夜 – 0489
Dancer w/ plants 落 – 0526
Dancer w/ skeet shooter (including truncated) 絡 – 0230
Dancer w/ sun + crutch (CSD) 履 – 1220
Dancer w/ tree 枚 – 0129
Day # 1 旧 – 1017
Day, other (sun) (group of one) 日 – 0032
Demon 魅 – 1169
Derrick 次 – 0536

Trait Index

Desk, slashed 凡 – 1511
Desk, other 冗 – 1462
Devil (lopsided tentacle) 魅 – 1169
Different 偉 – 1174
Dining table 卓 – 0620
Dirt 土 – see soil
Dish 益 – 1407
Diving board 乏 – 1340
Dog's head above fence 補 – 0995
Dog's head above rice paddy 敷 – 0865
Dog's head above water 球 – 0606
Dog, other 伏 – 0945
Dome below plants 供 – see together
Double hat w/ nail & hammer 街 – 0625
Double radicals 選 – see multiple identical radicals
Double roof lean-to 屈 – see lean-to w/ 2+ roofs
Down (fu) 不 – 0176
Down & up 上下 – 0172
Dressing room 服 – 0150
Duplicate radicals 選 – see multiple identical radicals
E&Y (エ E & Y) below tire stop 衣 – 1042
E&Y (エ E & Y), w/ six & well 穣 – 1322
E&Y (エ E & Y), other 表 – 0582
Ear 摂 – 1713
Early 章 – 1365
East (sun behind tree) 棟 – 1271
Easy (streamers) 瘍 – 1702
Eat (peaked roof) 餓 – 1974

Eggs (Moonies) 柳 – 1535
Eight above box 船 – 0602
Eight above cow (mu) 訟 – 1546
Eight below bad haircut (group of one) 穴 – 0964
Eight, other 分 – 0105
Elbows, two, above three legs 糸 – see skeet shooter
En (group of one) 円 – 0039
Enter or insert 入 – 0014
Erect man 情 – 2063
Evening (half moon) above box 名 – 0162
Evening, capped (nightcap), w/ Ri 列 – 1124
Evening, capped (nightcap), other 死 – 0164
Evening (half moon), other 移 – 0801
Everything (king below peaked roof) 栓 – 2026
Eye 目
  Eye & similar kanji 目 – 0051
  Eye above shelf w/ three straight legs 県 – 0572
  Eye above shelf w/out legs 置 – 0569
  Eye above lopsided legs (look/see) 規 – 1341
  Eye above table & below ten 真 – 0101
  Eye above table, other 具 – 0100
  Eye below neck (michi, path) 道 – 0349
  Eye below ray (self) 臭 – 1381
  Eye below ten & above table 真 – 0101

Eye below ten in lean-to 循 – 1878
Eye below ten, other 植 – 1278
Eye w/ sun 帽 – 0243
Eye w/ tree 相 – 0787
Eye, other 瞭 – 2002
Eye, one, above stand (tiller) 決 – 0180
Eye, one, below lights 業 – 0332
Eye, one, in helmet w/ visor 邪 – 0796
Eye, one, in needle – see needle containing bell (eye)
Eyes, two 免 – see two eyes
F over X 板 – 1166
F, other 莪 – 1983
Faceless dancer (group of one) 久 – 0030
Family w/ マ Ma 疑 – 0978
Fat 太 – 0191
Father (X below eyebrows) below tire stop 効 – 1139
Father (X below eyebrows), other 父 – 0143
Feathers above net 曜 – 0200
Feathers, other 翌 – 1457
Feet, reversed 偉 – 1174
Female below bad haircut 案 – 0120
Female below item(s), other 櫻 – 2086
Female on left 婚 – 2039
Female w/ table 怒 – 0319
Fence below crutch (cage) 無 – 0583
Fence below dog's head 補 – 0995
Fence below ma (マ) (mammoth) 樋 – 1143
Fence, other 備 – 0367

Fingers left (hand) 拳 – 1554
Fingers right (fur, hair) 毛 – 0688
Fire (4 flames) 然 – see four flames
Fire (bonfire) (two pairs of arms on person, plus flames at top) 券 – 1305
Fire on husband (two pairs of arms on person, plus flames in middle) 狭 – 0194
Fire in flat-top telephone pole 評 – 1053
Fire in pointed-top telephone pole (half) 判 – 1054
Fire, other 炊 – 1239
Fish head (leaning h chair)
   Fish head above rice paddy 解 – 0618
   Fish head guy w/ glasses above lopsided legs 免 – 1140
   Fish head monster w/ trident 争 – 0936
   Fish head, other 負 – 0087
Five 五, reversed 偉 – 1174
Five 五 (knee), other 五 – 0179
Five (5) surrounding telephone pole (horse) 騒 – 0826
Flames 然 – see four flames
Flat-top telephone pole on fire 評 – 1053
Flat-top telephone pole, other 汗 – 0629
Floor plan – see four (四)
Fluffy cat 苗 – 1740
Fly (propellers, lips) (group of one) 飛 – 0574

Flying carpet above spinning nail 示 – 1347
Foot below antennae 従 – 1485
Foot below box 足 – 0449
Foot below soil 走 – 0450
Foot below sun 題 – 0454
Foot, other 旋 – 0913
Force below rice paddy 男 – 0109
Force below other object(s) 劣 – 1746
Force x 3 脅 – 0914
Force, other 勃 – 1846
Forest 禁 – 0943
Forked tongue emerging from mountain 満 謡 – 1153, 1856
Forked tongue, other 舌 – 1213
Four (四) (floor plan) (group of one) 四 – 0006
Four (四) w/ handle (group of one) 西 – 0464
Four (四) w/ handle & extra compartment 酸 – 1480
Four (四) w/ missing lower wall 融 – 0987
Four (四) w/ missing right wall plus bucket 勘 – 1161
Four (四) w/ missing right wall, other 匹 – 0818
Four (4) 叫 – 0746
Four basic needle types 辛 – 0384
Four flames below bird 鶏 – 0754
Four flames below horse 騒 – 0826
Four flames, other 然 – 0611

Four legs below soil (red) 赤 – 0447
Four-legged hen 変 – 0695
Friend (hugging table) 友 – 0459
Fruit (rice paddy above tree) 課 – 0588
Fu (negation) 不 – 0176
Fur (hair) 毛 – 0688
Fusion of city & tree 刺 – 1284
Fusion of cow & big 鉄 – 0304
Fusion of cow & tree 殊 – 1675
Fusion of noon & mountain 缶 – 1832
Gate 潤 – 1755
Gentleman 士 – see man (soldier)
Giraffe 以 – 0601
Glasses on husband 漢 – 0197
Glasses on sincere guy 勤 – 0517
Glasses on tree 疎 – 1806
Go 街 – 0625
Gold (money) 鋳 – 2010
Good (L & Y) (L&Y) 浪 – 0805
Grain, ripe, on left 稚 – 1797
Grain, ripe, other 痢 – 2055
Graph, breathing 級 – 1131
Grate in tree 采 – 1935
Grate above child 浮 – 0671
Grate, other 援 – 1177
Greek ß – see beta
Green flag above water 録 – 0999
Grove or tree in lean-to 麻 – 1475
Grove, other 禁 – 0943

Trait Index

h chair – see fish head 免; also, oil derrick 次
Hair (fur) 毛 – 0688
Hair to the left above water 録 – 0999
Hair to the left, other 婦 – 1165
Hair to the right 長 – 0502
Halberd, single grip, & bell 織 – 0753
Halberd, single grip, supporting lean-to, w/ blade 成 – 0633
Halberd, single grip, supporting lean-to, other 威 – 0915
Halberd, single grip, other 伐 – 1862
Halberd, single grip, minus left hip (woman leaning w/ ball) 式 – 0249
Halberd, triple grip 残 – 0605
Half (telephone pole on fire) 判 – 1054
Half moon 名 – see evening; see also truncated moon 剤
Hammer w/ nail 街 – 0625
Hand (fingers left) 拳 – 1554
Handle above carry-on suitcase (group of one) 価 – 0484
Handle above eye in lean-to 循 – 1878
Handle above four (group of one) 西 – 0464
Handle above mountain model 綱 – 1200
Handle above sake bucket 酸 – 1480
Handle above well (taser on box) 占 – 1542
Hanging bucket 世 – 0542
Hannah, hopeful (dancer w/ honorable person) 做 – 2016

Happy Jimmy (two lips) 裸 – 1615
Hat above seven 宅 – 0021
Hat, slanted – see slanted hat
Hats, bench 登 – 0297
Head of dog – see dog's head
Head of fish – see fish head
Head of Native American chief above correct 御 – 1440
Headless platform 領 – 1126
Heart (group of one) 心 – 0306
Heart below man (soldier) 誌 – 0786
Heart below plants (group of one) 芯 – 1948
Heart below rice paddy 思 – 0308
Heart in lean-to 応 – 0677
Heart, slashed 泌 – see slashed heart
Heart w/ dancer 愛 – 0523
Heavy 重 – 0284
Heel ヒ – see hero
Helmet w/ visor (one eye) 邪 – 0796
Hen w/ 4 legs 変 – 0695
Hero (ヒ) above sun 旨 – 1318
Hero (ヒ) w/ slanted hat 貨 – 1413
Hero (ヒ) (or heel), other 壱 – 2048
Heroes (ヒ), two 混 – 1294
Hero (非) w/ 2 wings 悲 – 0851
Hesitant squarehead (box above stop) 踏 – 1534
Hi ヒ – see hero or heroes

High stalk of flowers w/ kneeling guy (group of one) 拝 – 0593
Hip – see left hip, right hip
Hoe 越 – 0453
Honorable person w/ dancer 傲 – 2016
Honorable person w/ soil 坊 – 1576
Honorable person, other 防 – 0920
Hook containing box (cave) w/ dancer 敬 – 0873
Hook containing box, other 句 – 0872
Hook containing snake 泡 – 1861
Hook for clothes above table 服 – 0150
Hook below sun 掲 – 1466
Hook, other 均 – 0988
Hopeful Hannah (dancer w/ honorable person) 傲 – 2016
Horse 騒 – 0826
Hostess above pole 峰 – 0938
House (pig) 家 – 1504
House w/ rabbit ears 墜 – 1972
Hubcaps on car, standard 重 – 0284
Hubcaps on car, streamlined 垂 – 0799
Hugging crafted object 左 – 0456
Hugging table (friend) 友 – 0459
Hugging net 勧 – 0698
Hugging, other 右 – 0457
Hundred (sun below limo antenna) below bad haircut 縮 – 1487
Hundred (sun below limo antenna), other 宿 – 0491

Husband (person w/ 2 pairs of arms) & similar kanji 夫 – 0614
Husband (person w/ 2 pairs of arms) below lights 僕 – 0332
Husband (person w/ 2 pairs of arms) on fire 狭 – 0194
Husband (person w/ 2 pairs of arms) plus a 3rd pair 僕 – 0333
Husband (person w/ 2 pairs of arms) wearing glasses 漢 – 0197
Husband (person w/ 2 pairs of arms), other 扶 – 1915
Ice w/ dancer 終 – 0233
Ice, other 冬 – 0234
Iku 街 – 0625
I-beam (crafted object), other 紅 – 0247
Ice & similar kanji 氷 – 0814
Identical repeated radicals 選 – see multiple identical radicals
Insect 蛇 – 1754
Insert or enter 入 – 0014
Inside (naka) above money chest 貴 – 0643
Inside (naka), other (box on stick, yakitori) 仲 – 0657
Jewel (ball next to king) 国 – 0170
Jimmy Carter (two lips) 裸 – 1615
Journey 旅 – 0116
Jukebox w/ tire stop & child 熟 – 1427
Jump (propellers, lips) (group of one) 飛 – 0574
Jutting lump 術 – 0808
Juu 十 – see ten
Kangaroo 写 – 0468

Kata 方 – see honorable person
Keg stuck in washing machine w/ handle 剣 – 1432
Kimi (you) 君 – 0419
King & similar kanji 王 – 1077
King above snail 庭 – 0495
King below cap (master) 主 – 0166
King below peaked roof (everything) 栓 – 2026
King below rabbit ears 窒 – 1893
King below item(s), other 呈 – 1876
King next to ball (jewel) 国 – 0170
King on left 珠 – 1772
King on right 旺 – 2045
King on top 琴 – 1712
Kite 回 – 0004
Knee (five) 五 – 0179
Knee, other 傑 – 1808
Kneeling guy near table 技 – 1389
Kneeling guy w/ high stalk of flowers (group of one) 拝 – 0593
Kneeling sunny guy 寸 – see sunny guy
Kneeling or leaning telephone pole 宇 – 0897
Kneeling w/ tray 片 – 0181
Knife (ri) 利 – see ri
Kyouto dome 供 – see together
L&Y below arrow 農 – 1105
L&Y (L & Y) (good) 浪 – 0805
L&Y, other 食 – 0398

L below tire stop 亡 – 0585
L (breast) 札 – 0735
Ladder (hero w/ 2 wings) 悲 – 0851
Ladder (axe, stairs), other 昨 – 0041
Leaning chair (h) above person (oil derrick) 次 – 0536
Leaning chair (h), other 負 – see fish head
Leaning guy w/ flat hat (stone) 拓 – 1775
Leaning or kneeling telephone pole 宇 – 0897
Leaning woman w/ ball + left hip 伐 – see halberd, single grip
Leaning woman w/ ball, other 式 – 0249
Leaning woman, double roof 眠 – 0376
Leaning woman, single roof (pavilion) 抵 – 1195
Lean-to, 1-sided, single roof, containing box
Lean-to, 1 sided, w/ box w/ napkin 伺 – 0341
Lean-to, 1 sided, w/ box w/out napkin, w/ big 寄 – 0604
Lean-to, 1 sided, w/ box w/out napkin & w/out big 阿 – 1176
Lean-to, 1-sided, single roof, other
Lean-to containing eye w/ handle 循 – 1878
Lean-to containing heart 応 – 0677
Lean-to containing mu (cow) 拡 – 1287
Lean-to containing periscope & seven 虎 – 1057
Lean-to containing soil 圧 – 0748
Lean-to containing table 板 – 1166

Lean-to containing three eyes 鹿 – 0895
Lean-to containing tree(s) 麻 – 1475
Lean-to, 2-sided, single roof
Lean-to, 2-sided, below bell, containing old 敵 – 0881
Lean-to, 2-sided, containing telephone pole w/ 2 arms (i.e., fence) 備 – see fence
Lean-to, 2-sided, w/ halberd support, w/ blade 成 – 0633
Lean-to, 2 sided, w/ or w/out halberd support, w/ box & w/ napkin 筒 – 1620
Lean-to, 2 sided, w/ box w/out napkin 稿 – 1467
Lean-to, 2-sided, w/ halberd support, other 威 – 0915
Lean-to, 2-sided, containing model of mountain w/ handle & antennae 綱 – 1200
Lean-to, 2-sided, superimposed on model of mountain w/ handle 満 – 1153
Lean-to, 2-sided, w/ compass needle (south) 南 – 0388
Lean-to, 2-sided, w/ person emerging 肉 – 0397
Lean-to, 2-sided, w/ soil above box 週 – 0346
Lean-to, 2-sided, other 風 – 0479
Lean-to w/ 2+ roofs
Lean-to w/ double roof, w/ snow 房 – 1134
Lean-to w/ double roof, w/o snow, & w/ box & needle 辟 – 1214
Lean-to w/ double roof, w/out snow & w/ sunny guy 慰 – 1752

Lean-to w/ double roof, w/out snow & w/ support on right (shack) 尺 – 1484
Lean-to w/ double roof, w/out snow & w/ woman leaning 眠 – 0376
Lean-to w/ double roof, w/out snow, other 尼 – 1899
Lean-to w/ triple roof 気 – 0321
Leave 屈 – 0927
Left (hugging crafted object) 左 – 0456
Left hip on halberd 伐 – see halberd
Left hip w/ マ (mother) 矛 – 1749
Left hip, other 芽 – 1417
Legs, slanted, below rice paddy 横 – 0135
Legs, straight, below rice paddy 再 – 1032
Legs, lopsided 兄 – see lopsided legs
Leo's oven, below big & above small 療 – 1069
Li – see ri
Library (peaked roof above books) 論 – 0813
Life 醒 – 1918
Light 輝 – 0979
Lights above tree or husband 業 – 0332
Lightning 響 – 0840
Limousine antenna 夏 – see antenna (limo)
Lining up 枝 – 0128
Lips, four (propellers) (group of one) 飛 – 0574
Lips, two (happy Jimmy) 裸 – 1615
Lips, two (megaphone) 環 – 0718
Little 小 – see small

Live 醒 – 1918
Look/see (eye above lopsided legs) 規 – 1341
Lopsided legs below
Lopsided legs below base & triple plants 焼 – 0446
Lopsided legs below bench hats 廃 – 1221
Lopsided legs below box (big brother) w/ rabbit ears 税 – 0708
Lopsided legs below box (big brother) w/ scowl 境 – 0719
Lopsided legs below box (big brother), other 兄 – 0420
Lopsided legs below eye (look/see) 規 – 1341
Lopsided legs below fish-head guy w/ glasses 免 – 1140
Lopsided legs below mu (cow) 銑 – 1990
Lopsided legs below one, other 暁 – 1855
Lopsided legs below roof, above tree 深 – 0694
Lopsided legs below roof supporting man (soldier) 売 – 0425
Lopsided legs below shield 洗 – 0423
Lopsided legs below sun 鏡 – 1355
Lopsided legs below three-pronged switch 輝 – 0979
Lopsided legs below two 元 – 0421
Lopsided legs, three 慌 – 0710
Lopsided legs, other 就 – 0974
Lopsided tentacle (devil) 魅 – 1169
Lump jutting 術 – 0808

Trait Index

Ma マ above fence (mammoth) 樋 – 1143
Ma マ above nail w/ stabilizing leg (extended left hip) 矛 – 1749
Ma マ above nail, w/out stabilizing leg 予 – 0544
Ma マ above thin body w/ arms (child, other) 孔 – 2078
Ma マ below peaked roof (alternative font) 零 – 1946
Ma マ w/ family 疑 – 0978
Ma マ, other 勇 – 1282
Mai (rice paddy w/ extended lines) 每 – 0336
Male 男 – 0109
Mammoth (マ ma) above fence 樋 – 1143
Man (soldier) above beans (nurse) 喜 – 0599
Man (soldier) above box 吉 – 1453
Man (soldier) above heart 誌 – 0786
Man (soldier) above roof w/ lopsided legs 売 – 0425
Man (soldier) above table 妓 – 1121
Man (soldier) & words 詰 – 0781
Man (soldier) next to man w/ slanted hat (group of one) 仕 – 0067
Man (soldier) standing on tree 耗 – 2050
Man (soldier), other 荘 – 1468
Man, erect 情 – 2063
Man w/ a slanted hat 休 – see slanted hat

Mark on cheek 夜 – 0489
Marriage (pavilion above sun) 婚 – 0240
Master w/ extra pair of arms, w/ slanted hat 准 – see net
Master (king below cap), other 主 – 0166
Megaphone (two lips) 環 – 0718
Member 員 – 0088
Merchandise (packages, boxes, articles) 繰 – 1034
Merger – see fusion
Michi (neck, path) 道 – 0349
Middle 仲 – see inside
Minute 頒 – 2076
Missing head platform 領 – 1126
Model of mountain w/ handle, superimposed on lean-to 満 – 1153
Model of mountain w/ handle & antennae, in lean-to 綱 – 1200
Model of rice paddy w/ handle, w/ well 溝 – 1825
Model of rice paddy w/ handle, w/out well 画 – 0077
Mom – see ma マ
Money (gold) 鋳 – 2010
Money chest below
 Money chest below box (member) 員 – 0088
 Money chest below limousine antenna 領 – 1126
 Money chest below naka (inside) 貴 – 0643
 Money chest below owl's perch 責 – 0772
 Money chest below plants 墳 – 1897
 Money chest below platform 領 – 1126

Money chest below one item, other 費 – 0656
Money chest below two+ items 賃 – 0707
Money chest on left 賦 – 2058
Money chest on right 唄 – 1870
Money chest plus Ri 側 – 0490
Mono (person, sun below scissors) 著 – 1088
Moon (group of one) 月 – 0148
Moon, half 移 – see evening; see also moon, truncated
Moon & Ri below bench 前 – 0157
Moon & Ri below peaked roof 愉 – 0733
Moon & sun 明 – 0154
Moon, truncated 剤 – 1601
Moon below
 Moon below apartment (bone, carton slipping) 骨 – 0832
 Moon below bell w/ comb 襲 – 0941
 Moon below mu (cow) 能 – 0616
 Moon below owl's perch 清 – 1112
 Moon below single item, other 萌 – 2087
 Moon below multiple items 腎 – 1991
Moon w/ extended lines 那 – 0669
Moons, two 棚 – 0742
Moonies (eggs) 柳 – 1535
Morning 潮 – 1308
Mother (group of one) 母 – 0050
Mother マ – see ma マ
Mountain at top 炭 – 1385
Mountain below cloud 帯 – 1012

Mountain below forked tongue 満 謡 – 1153, 1856
Mountain merged w/ noon 缶 – 1832
Mountain model 綱 – see model of mountain
Mountain near dancer 徴 – 0784
Mountain on floor 癌 – 2079
Mountain on left 岬 – 1942
Mountains stacked 屈 – 0927
Mouth 口 – see box
Movie screen 英 – 0043
Mu (cow) above box 台 – 0538
Mu (cow) above moon 能 – 0616
Mu (cow) above soil & below one 至 – 0063
Mu (cow) above two lopsided legs 唆 – 1990
Mu (cow) below
  Mu (cow) below bad haircut (group of one) 室 – 0062
  Mu (cow) below eight 訟 – 1546
  Mu (cow) below one & above soil 至 – 0063
  Mu (cow) below soil 去 – 0343
  Mu (cow) below tire stop 統 – 1125
  Mu (cow) below two (二) 芸 – 1056
Mu (cow) in lean-to 拡 – 1287
Mu (cow) on floor 払 – 0591
Mu (cow), other 惨 – 1678
Multiple identical radicals (MIR)
  MIR, boxes 繰 – 1034

MIR, three cords – see three cords
MIR, feathers 翌 – 1457
MIR, force 脅 – 0914
MIR, heroes 混 – 1294
MIR, ice 冬 – 0234
MIR, moons 棚 – 0742
MIR, soil, walking 睦 – 1989
MIR, soil, other 封 – 1619
MIR, suns 唱 – 1152
MIR, trees, in lean-to 麻 – 1475
MIR, trees, other 森 – 0943
MIR, truncated skeet shooters 滋 – 1908
MIR, other 選 – 0352
Nail & hammer w/ double hat 街 – 0625
Nail below マ (mother) w/ stabilizing leg (extended left hip) 矛 – 1749
Nail below マ (mother) w/out stabilizing leg 予 – 0544
Nail, spinning 示 – see spinning nail
Nail, other 丁 – 0702
Nails (claws) 孤 – 0723
Naka 仲 – see inside
Napkin 司 – see box with napkin and box without napkin
Native American chief 矢 – see chief, Native American
Necessary 必 – see slashed heart
Neck above eye (michi, path) 道 – 0349
Needle containing bell (eye), four basic types 辛 – 0384
Needle containing bell (eye), on snail 避 – 0802

Needle containing bell (eye), w/ lean-to & box 辟 – 1214
Needle containing bell (eye), other 親 – 0383
Needle, compass, in 2-sided lean-to (south) 南 – 0388
Needle w/ open syringe (two eyes above ten) 革 – 1286
Negation (cage) 無 – 0583
Negation (fu) 不 – 0176
Net above table 獲 – 0947
Net below big 奮 – 0727
Net below feathers 曜 – 0200
Net, hugging 勧 – 0698
Net w/ skeet shooter 羅 – 1158
Net, other 准 – 2046
Nightcap (half moon w/ cap), w/ Ri 列 – 1124
Nightcap (half moon w/ cap), w/out Ri 死 – 0164
Nine & similar kanji 九 – 0102
Nine, slashed 塾 – 1737
Nine, other 尻 – 0827
No ノ superimposed on three (group of one) 看 – 1164
Noon (crutch above ten) 午 – 0207
Noon merged w/ mountain 缶 – 1832
Nose stung by bees 悩 – 1181
Now 含 – 1491
Number-one day 旧 – 1017
Nurse (man above beans) 喜 – 0599
Object, crafted – see crafted object
Oil derrick 次 – 0536

Oklahoma's uber Ruth 送 – 0348
Old in box 個 – 0395
Old in 2-sided lean-to below bell 敵 – 0881
Old under slanted cap 舌 – see forked tongue
Old, other 故 – 0394
Old boys, switch (not on distinct roof) 肖 – 1625
Old boys on distinct roof, other 覚 – 0991
One and similar kanji 一 – 0001
One above cow (mu) 至 – 0063
One above lopsided legs 暁 – 1855
One eye above stand (tiller) 決 – 0180
One eye in helmet w/ visor 邪 – 0796
One eye in needle – see needle containing bell (eye)
One thousand & ten 昇 – 1363
One unit above rice paddy (devil) 魅 – 1169
One unit above rice paddy, other 油 – 0942
Open book below tree 本 – 0123
Open-top box 凶 – 1794
Open (welcoming) stance 弄 – 1924
Oven, Leo's 療 – 1069
Oven (white) above tree 楽 – 0520
Owl's perch 責 above money chest – 0772
Owl's perch above moon 清 – 1112
Owl's perch above sunny guy 寿 – 0607
Owl's perch above object(s), other 麦 – 1103

Owl's perch below bad haircut 害 – 1260
Packages 繰 – 1034
Paddy 田 – see rice paddy
Paper pavilion 氏 – see pavilion
Pavilion above sun (marriage) 婚 – 0240
Pavilion, other 抵 – 1195
Peaked roof above
  Peaked roof above books (library) 論 – 0813
  Peaked roof above box w/ napkin 塔 – 1251
  Peaked roof above king (everything) 栓 – 2026
  Peaked roof above マ ma (alternative font) 零 – 1946
  Peaked roof above moon & Ri 愉 – 0733
  Peaked roof above soil above box 舎 – 0745
  Peaked roof above spinning nail w/ stool 余 – 0637
  Peaked roof above stuck keg in washing machine w/ handle 劍 – 1432
  Peaked roof above triple roof (warehouse) 倉 – 1170
  Peaked roof (& napkin) above wobbly table 令 – 0962
Peaked roof (arrow) 界 – 0069
Peaked roof below bad haircut 容 – 0296
Peaked roof below tree 膝 – 0861
Peaked roof below vapors 裕 – 0660
Peaked roof (eat) 餓 – 1974
Peaked roof (money, gold) 鑄 – 2010

Peaked roof (now) 含 – 1491
Peaked roof, other 企 – 1382
People (hito) 人 – see person (hito)
Perforating 君 – see trident perforating
Periscope & seven in lean-to 虎 – 1057
Person, honorable, w/ dancer 傲 – 2016
Person, honorable, other 防 – 0920
Person stepping out 旅 – 0116
Person (hito) & similar kanji 人 – 0013
Person (hito) below leaning chair (h) (oil derrick) 次 – 0536
Person (hito) emerging from 2-sided lean-to 肉 – 0397
Person (hito) superimposed on three (spring) 春 – 0506
Person (hito) w/ 2 eyes & flat cap below peaked roof 劍 – 1432
Person (hito) w/ 2 pairs of arms plus flames (bonfire) 券 – 1305
Person (hito) w/ 2 pairs of arms (husband), plus flames 狭 – 0194
Person (hito) w/ 2 pairs of arms (husband), other 扶 – 1915
Person (hito), other 囚 – 1926
Person (mono) (scissors above sun) 著 – 1088
Pig (house) 豚 – 1504
Pitcher 呉 – 1686
Plants above dome, other 供 – 0486
Plants above heart (group of one) 芯 – 1948

Trait Index

Plants above money chest 墳 – 1897
Plants above peaked roof 茶 – 0212
Plants above rice paddy 苗 – 1740
Plants above sun & big (PSB) 模 – 1353
Plants above sun, other 昔 – 0033
Plants (triple) above base above lopsided legs 燒 – 0446
Plants w/ dancer 落 – 0526
Plants w/ water radicals 薄 – 0258
Platform consisting of one above lopsided legs, other 曉 – 1855
Platform consisting of roof above lopsided legs, above tree 深 – 0694
Platform for missing head 領 – 1126
Pliers, slashed 斥 – 2060
Pliers, other 折 – 0892
Pole – 汗 see telephone pole
Pound symbol 囲 – 1202
Propellers (lips) (group of one) 飛 – 0574
Protect 守 – 0214
PSB (Plants above sun & big) 模 – 1353
Pyramid 蒸 – 1101
Rabbit ears 送 – see antennae
Rain 雪 – 0262
Ray above eye (self) 臭 – 1381
Ray above sun (white), other 舶 – 2014
Red (four legs below soil) 赤 – 0447
Red Cross 悪 – 0313
Reinforced lower frame on window 域 – 1256

Repeated radicals 選 – see multiple identical radicals
Retsu (Ri w/ capped evening) (nightcap) 列 – 1124
Reversed feet 偉 – 1174
Ri & moon below bench 前 – 0157
Ri & moon below peaked roof 愉 – 0733
Ri plus money chest 側 – 0490
Ri w/ box above sword (Betsy w/ square head) 別 – 0561
Ri w/ capped evening (nightcap) (retsu) 列 – 1124
Ri, other 剖 – 1985
Rice paddy above
 Rice paddy above force 男 – 0109
 Rice paddy above heart 思 – 0308
 Rice paddy above soil 野 – see sincere guy w/ bifocals
 Rice paddy above slanted legs 横 – 0135
 Rice paddy above straight legs 再 – 1032
 Rice paddy above sun 増 – 0061
 Rice paddy above sunny guy 縛 – 1721
 Rice paddy above ten 禅 – 1694
 Rice paddy above tree (fruit) 課 – 0588
Rice paddy below
 Rice paddy below box w/ napkin 幅 – 1185
 Rice paddy below dog's head 敷 – 0865
 Rice paddy below fish head 解 – 0618

Rice paddy below handle 再 – see model of rice paddy
Rice paddy below one unit (devil) 魅 – 1169
Rice paddy below one unit, other 油 – 0942
Rice paddy below two units 増 – 0061
Rice paddy below plants 苗 – 1740
Rice paddy below rabbit ears (antennae) 増 – 0061
Rice paddy below ten 恵 – 0720
Rice paddy forming bifocals, other 梗 – 1992
Rice paddy model 再 – see model of rice paddy
Rice paddy on stick 甲 – 1157
Rice paddy w/ 6 sections 豊 – see songs
Rice paddy w/ extended lines (mai) 毎 – 0336
Rice paddy w/ rope 縄 – 1003
Rice paddy w/ skeet shooter 累 – 2006
Rice paddy, other 細 – 0220
Rice, uncooked 米 – see uncooked rice
Right hip 更 – 1000
Right (hugging) 右 – 0457
Ripe grain on left 稚 – 1797
Ripe grain, other 痢 – 2055
River 訓 – 1090
Rocker-bottom bench 祭 – 0377
Rocker bottom [three cords below other object(s)] 参 – 0406

Trait Index

Roof above lopsided legs, above tree 深 – 0694
Roof above lopsided legs, supporting man (soldier) 売 – 0425
Roof, peaked 企 – see peaked roof
Room – see floor plan
Roots, asymmetrical 遇 – 1120
Rope w/ rice paddy or paddies 縄 – 1003
S snake, backwards, in wrapping (or hook) 泡 – 1861
S snake, backwards, other 妃 – 1078
Sake bucket w/ handle 酸 – 1480
Say 信 – see words
Scissors above sun (person, mono) 著 – 1088
Scissors between soil & child 孝 – 1471
Scissors, other 老 – 1065
Scorpion 他 – 0503
Scowl on big brother 境 – 0719
Screen, movie 英 – 0043
Seal 印 – 1046
See/look (eye above lopsided legs) 規 – 1341
Segmented X 渋 – 1454
Self (eye below ray) 臭 – 1381
Seven in lean-to w/ periscope 虎 – 1057
Seven below ceiling below peaked roof (now) 含 – 1491
Seven universal laws 純 – 1245
Seven wearing hat 宅 – 0021
Seven, other 七 – 0020
Shack 舎 – 0745

Shack/wakeful eye 尺 – 1484
Shah 祥 – 1160
Shaky table 亡 – 0585
Sheep below soil (group of one) 達 – 0347
Sheep, truncated (no tail) 窯 – 1893
Sheep, other 羊 – 1223
Sheet 妓 – 1121
Shelf above three straight legs 県 – 0572
Shelf below uncooked rice 継 – 0635
Shelf, slanted 斜 – 0910
Shelf w/out legs below eye 置 – 0569
Shield above lopsided legs 洗 – 0423
Shield, other 告 – 0429
Short circuit on coop w/ 6 sections & wires 遭 – 1073
Sick bed 病 – 0369
Sincere guy w/ bifocals below bell 鐘 – 1840
Sincere guy w/ bifocals, other 野 – 0545
Sincere guy w/ glasses 勤 – 0517
Single eye above stand (tiller) 決 – 0180
Single grip halberd 伐 – see halberd, single grip
Six above X 効 – 1139
Six above well & clothes 穣 – 1322
Six-section rice paddy 豊 – see songs
Skeet shooter (thread) (group of one) 糸 – 0219
Skeet shooter below cape 孫 – 1072
Skeet shooter below other object(s) 緊 – 1266
Skeet shooter (including truncated) w/ dancer 絡 – 0230

Skeet shooter w/ net 羅 – 1158
Skeet shooter w/ rice paddy 累 – 2006
Skeet shooter w/ water 緑 – 0227
Skeet shooter, truncated, single 幻 – 1129
Skeet shooters, truncated, double 滋 – 1908
Skeleton of boar (tire stop) 核 – 1548
Skewer 仲 – see inside
Skin (table below arrow, Straight Arrow) 皮 – 0833
Sky & similar kanji 夫 – 0614
Sky above boxes (bridge) 橋 – 0139
Sky below antennae (Uber Ruth) 送 – 0348
Sky, other 妖 – 1811
Slanted hat w/ hero 貨 – 1413
Slanted hat w/ man (soldier) (group of one) 仕 – 0067
Slanted hat w/ master w/ extra pair of arms 准 – see net
Slanted hat w/ sunny guy 府 – 1004
Slanted hat w/ tree 休 – 0122
Slanted hat w/ words (group of one) 信 – 0431
Slanted legs below rice paddy 横 – 0135
Slanted shelf 斜 – 0910
Slashed desk 凡 – 1511
Slashed heart under bad haircut 密 – 1188
Slashed heart, general 泌 – 1297
Slashed nine 塾 – 1737
Slashed pliers 斥 – 2060
Slashed sword 刃 – 1488

Slashed uncooked rice 審 – 1368
Slipping carton above moon 骨 – 0832
Slipping carton, other 過 – 0361
Small & similar kanji 小 – 0253
Small animal plus bucket 勘 – 1161
Small below box 京 – 0514
Small below sun 願 – 0094
Small below sun and big, Leo's oven 療 – 1069
Small below taser on platform 督 – 1421
Small below truncated skeet shooter (i.e., skeet shooter in alternative font 糸) – see skeet shooter
Small below two 示 – 1347
Small below white 原 – 0888
Small, other 省 – 1010
Snail below king 庭 – 0495
Snail below needle 避 – 0802
Snail below uncooked rice 迷 – 0623
Snail, 3x 廻 – 0692
Snake, backwards S, in wrapping (or hook) 泡 – 1861
Snake, backwards S, other 妃 – 1078
Snake, uncoiling 危 – 0547
Snake w/ two eyes 絶 – 0673
Snow above lean-to w/ double roof 房 – 1134
Soil (group of one) 土 – 0059
Soil above

Soil above box below peaked roof 舎 – 0745
Soil above box in 2-sided lean-to 週 – 0346
Soil above box, other 遠 – 0351
Soil above child & scissors 孝 – 1471
Soil above foot 走 – 0450
Soil above four legs (red) 赤 – 0447
Soil above mu (cow) 去 – 0343
Soil above sheep (group of one) 達 – 0347
Soil above soil, walking 睦 – 1989
Soil above soil, other 封 – 1619
Soil above sunny guy (temple) 時 – 0215
Soil below
Soil below box (group of one) 堂 – 0064
Soil below mu (cow) 至 – 0063
Soil below rice paddy 野 – see sincere guy w/ bifocals
Soil below table 茎 – 1894
Soil in lean-to 圧 – 0748
Soil w/ honorable person 坊 – 1576
Solar panel 組 – 0752
Soldier 士 – see man (soldier)
Songs w/ short circuit (coop w/ 6 sections w/ crossed wires) 遭 – 1073
Songs w/o short circuit (coop w/ 6 sections & *un*crossed wires) 豊 – 1321
Sotted Superman 卒 – 0027

Sound (bell above sun) 音 – 0266
South 南 – 0388
Speak 信 – see words
Spikes below bell 諦 – 0804
Spine 宮 – 1079
Spinning nail below flying carpet 示 – 1347
Spinning nail below peaked roof w/ stool 余 – 0637
Spinning nail below short vertical line [a version of the 木 ki radical resembling the lower part of 示] – see tree
Spinning nail below taser 督 – 1421
Spinning on ten 早 – see ten as axis
Spring (three superimposed on person, above sun) 春 – 0506
Square ball 呉 – 1686
Squarehead, hesitant (box above stop) 踏 – 1534
Square-headed Betsy (box above sword w/ Ri) 別 – 0561
Stacked mountains 屈 – 0927
Stacked vertebrae 宮 – 1079
Stairs (hero w/ 2 wings) 悲 – 0851
Stairs (axe, ladder), other 昨 – 0041
Stalk of flowers w/ kneeling guy (group of one) 拝 – 0593
Stand (verb) 立 – see bell
Stepping out 旅 – 0116
Stick penetrating box or chicken 仲 – see inside
Stick penetrating rice paddy 甲 – 1157

Stone (leaning guy w/ flat hat) 拓 – 1775
Stool below peaked roof & above spinning nail 余 – 0637
Stop & similar kanji 止 – 0173
Stop below box (hesitant squarehead) 踏 – 1534
Stop below cap (correct, other) 証 – 1150
Stop, other 肯 – 1929
Stove burners under antennae 並 – 0575
Stove burners, other 湿 – 1300
Straight Arrow (skin, arrow above table) 皮 – 0833
Straight legs below rice paddy 再 – 1032
Streamers below sun 瘍 – 1702
Streamers w/out sun (easy) (group of one) 物 – 0401
Streamlined car (vehicle) w/ hubcaps 垂 – 0799
Stuck keg in washing machine w/ handle (peaked roof) 剣 – 1432
Sturdy legs – see lopsided
Success 成 – 0633
Suitcase, carry-on (group of one) 価 – 0484
Sun (day) (group of one) 日 – 0032
Sun & eye 冒 – 0243
Sun & moon 明 – 0154
Sun above
 Sun above dancer + crutch (CSD) 履 – 1220
 Sun above foot 題 – 0454
 Sun above hook 掲 – 1466
 Sun above platform (dance floor) 旦 – 0668
 Sun above small 願 – 0094
 Sun above streamers 瘍 – 1702
 Sun above lopsided legs 鏡 – 1355
 Sun above ten, below taser 卓 – 0620
 Sun above ten, other 章 – 1365
 Sun above together (dome below plants) plus water 暴 – 1021
 Sun behind tree 棟 – 1271
Sun below
 Sun below bell 音 – 0266
 Sun below hero 旨 – 1318
 Sun below limousine antenna (hundred) 宿 – 0491
 Sun below pavilion 婚 – 0240
 Sun below plants & above big (PSB) 模 – 1353
 Sun below plants, other 昔 – 0033
 Sun below ray (white), other 舶 – 2014
 Sun below rice paddy 増 – 0061
 Sun below scissors, person (mono) 著 – 1088
Sun, multiple 唱 – 1152
Sunny guy below bad haircut 守 – 0214
Sunny guy below owl's perch 寿 – 0607
Sunny guy below rice paddy 縛 – 1721
Sunny guy below soil (temple) 時 – 0215
Sunny guy plus double-roof lean-to 慰 – 1752
Sunny guy w/ man w/ slanted hat 府 – 1004
Sunny guy, other 村 – 0131
Superman, cooped up 屈 – 0927
Swing set as cannons firing crutch 鑑 – 1310
Swing set, other 堅 – 1246
Switch w/ 3 prongs (old boys) on a distinct roof 覚 – 0991
Switch w/ 3 prongs (not on distinct roof), other 肖 – 1625
Sword & similar kanji 刀 – 0102
Sword above or below box 招 – 0560
Sword & backpack 留 – 0071
Sword, slashed 刃 – 1488
Sword, other 窃 – 2062
T (tarantula) 隔 – 1729
Table, dining 卓 – 0620
Table, mata 又
 Table above soil 茎 – 1894
 Table below arrow (or below chimney) (Straight Arrow, skin) 皮 – 0833
 Table below clothes hook 服 – 0150
 Table below lean-to 板 – 1166
 Table below man (soldier) 妓 – 1121
 Table below net 獲 – 0947
 Table below three eyes 慢 – 1127
 Table below yak 役 – 0557
 Table, hugged 友 – 0459
 Table w/ female 怒 – 0319

Trait Index

Table w/ kneeling guy 技 – 1389
Table, other 又 – 0024
Table below eye & ten 真 – 0101
Table below eye, other 具 – 0100
Table, shaky 亡 – 0585
Table, wobbly, below napkin & peaked roof 令 – 0962
Tagalog ユ (youths) 互 – 1207
Talk 信 – see words
Tall (takai) 高 – 0019
Tarantula below box w/ napkin 隔 – 1729
Taser above box (well w/ handle) 占 – 1542
Taser above foot – see foot
Taser above platform above small 督 – 1421
Taser above sun 卓 – 0620
Taser as part of stop 止, 肯 – 0173, 1929
Taser, other 偵 – 1673
Telephone pole, flat top
  Telephone pole, flat top, on fire 評 – 1053
  Telephone pole, flat top, under antennae – see sheep
  Telephone pole, flat top, other 汗 – 0629
  Telephone pole, kneeling, flat top or pointed 宇 – 0897
Telephone pole, pointed
  Telephone pole below dancer (hostess) 峰 – 0938
  Telephone pole inside 2-sided lean-to 備 – see fence
  Telephone pole inside 5 (horse) 騒 – 0826

  Telephone pole on fire (half) 判 – 1054
  Telephone pole below upside-down bench (sheep), other 羊 – see sheep
  Telephone pole other 棒 – 0820
Television above toes (bean) 豆 – 0721
Temple (soil above sunny guy) 時 – 0215
Ten above
  Ten above box (old) in box 個 – 0395
  Ten above box (old) in 2-sided lean-to 敵 – 0881
  Ten above box (old), other 故 – 0394
  Ten above eye above table 真 – 0101
  Ten above eye in lean-to 循 – 1878
  Ten above eye, other 植 – 1278
  Ten above rice paddy 恵 – 0720
  Ten above three eyes 聴 – 0934
Ten below
  Ten below bell 宰 – 1803
  Ten below crutch (noon) 午 – 0207
  Ten below rice paddy 禅 – 1694
  Ten below sun, below taser 卓 – 0620
  Ten below sun, other 章 – 1365
  Ten below two eyes 革 – 1286
  Ten below object(s), other 阜 – 1658
Ten, other 喪 – 1828
Ten thousand w/ feather in cap (honorable person) 防 – 0920
Ten thousand, other 万 – 0113

Thai mountain 帯 – 1012
Thank you (TY) (group of one) 衆 – 0930
Thousand 千 – 0022
Thousand & ten 昇 – 1363
Thread 糸 – see skeet shooter
Three bees 悩 – 1181
Three cords below other object(s) (rocker-bottom shoe) 参 – 0406
Three cords, other 影 – 0839
Three eyes
  Three eyes above table 慢 – 1127
  Three eyes at top 署 – 1324
  Three eyes below ten 聴 – 0934
  Three eyes (bowl) 益 – 1407
  Three eyes hanging from platform 煙 – 1415
  Three eyes in lean-to 鹿 – 0895
  Three eyes, other 爵 – 1603
Three legs
  Three legs below two elbows 糸 – see skeet shooter
  Three legs on rocker-bottom bench 祭 – 0377
  Three lopsided legs 慌 – 0710
  Three straight legs below shelf 県 – 0572
  Three straight legs, other (nails) 孤 – 0723
Three men of force 脅 – 0914
Three old boys, not on roof, w/ bee hive & X 悩 – 1181
Three old boys, not on distinct roof, other 肖 – 1625

Three old boys on distinct roof – see three-pronged switch
Three pairs of arms on husband 僕 – 0333
Three plant radicals – see triple plant radical
Three-pronged switch (three old boys) on distinct roof 覚 – 0991
Three-pronged switch, not on distinct roof, above lopsided legs 輝 – 0979
Three-pronged switch, not on distinct roof, other 肖 – 1625
Three superimposed on ノ no (group of one) 看 – 1164
Three superimposed on person 春 – 0506
Three switches – see three-pronged switch
Three roofs on lean-to 気 – 0321
Three x snail 廻 – 0692
Tiller 決 – 0180
Tire stop above
  Tire stop above Bo Peep (city) 市 – 0242
  Tire stop above boar skeleton 核 – 1548
  Tire stop above box & child 熟 – 1427
  Tire stop above box, other 亭 – 1474
  Tire stop above E (エ) & Y (clothing) & below six and well 穣 – 1322
  Tire stop above E (エ) & Y (clothing), other 衣 – 1042
  Tire stop above father 効 – 1139
  Tire stop above mu (cow) 統 – 1125
  Tire stop above L 亡 – 0585

Tire stop above X 済 – 0259
Tire stop as part of bell 立 – 0011
Tire stop fused to ten thousand (honorable person) 防 – 0920
Tire stop, other 弦 – 1860
Toboggans 州 – 1071
Toe 朴 – 1826
Together (dome below plants) between sun & water 暴 – 1021
Together (dome below plants), other 供 – 0486
Tongue, forked, emerging from mountain 謡 – 1856
Tongue, forked, other 舌 – 1213
Tower for catapult 形 – 0573
Tower under antennae 餅 – 0743
Transformer 縄 – 1003
Travel 旅 – 0116
Tray, kneeling 片 – 0181
Tree & similar kanji 木 – 0118
Tree above peaked roof 膝 – 0861
Tree below
  Tree below barbecue grate 采 – 1935
  Tree below bell 新 – 0389
  Tree below box(es) 保 – 1216
  Tree below bucket 謀 – 1544
  Tree below cap 禾 – see ripe grain
  Tree below dancer 条 – 0129
  Tree below lights 業 – 0332
  Tree below rice paddy (fruit) 課 – 0588

Tree below roof w/ lopsided legs 深 – 0694
Tree below white (oven), 楽 – 0520
Tree below object(s), other 条 – 1352
Tree merged w/ city 刺 – 1284
Tree merged w/ cow 殊 – 1675
Tree plus eye 相 – 0787
Tree split, w/ antennae 嫌 – 0817
Tree superimposed on sun 東 – see tree wearing bifocals
Tree wearing bifocals 棟 – 1271
Tree wearing glasses (bundle) 疎 – 1806
Tree w/ dancer 枚 – 0129
Tree w/ man standing on it 耗 – 2050
Tree w/ open book 本 – 0123
Tree w/ slanted hat 休 – 0122
Tree w/ two pairs of branches 未 – 0672
Tree(s) in lean-to 麻 – 1475
Trees in group, other 森 – 0943
Triangle 蒸 – 1101
Trident perforating chimney 糖 – 1494
Trident perforating face 君 – 0419
Trident perforating fish-head monster 争 – 0936
Trident perforating (mending) split tree, w/ antennae 嫌 – 0817
Trident perforating upper axis of water 隶 – 1583

Trident perforating, other 津 – 0877
Trillion 兆 – 0849
Trip 旅 – 0116
Triple grip halberd 残 – 0605
Triple plant radical on base above lopsided legs 焼 – 0446
Triple plant radical, other 噴 – 1268
Triple roof on lean-to 気 – 0321
Truncated moon 剤 – 1601
Truncated sheep (no tail) 窯 – 1893
Truncated skeet shooter, double 滋 – 1908
Truncated skeet shooter, single 幻 – 1129
Tune 豊 – see songs
TV above toes (bean) 豆 – 0721
Twisted (bow) 引 – 0476
Two (二) above cow (mu) 芸 – 1056
Two (二) above small 示 – 1347
Two (二) above lopsided legs 元 – 0421
Two (二), other 仁 – 1496
Two crutches above vertical lines (bamboo) 籠 – 2074
Two elbows above three legs – see skeet shooter
Two eyes
  Two eyes above ten 革 – 1286
  Two eyes on fish-head guy w/ lopsided legs 免 – 1140
  Two eyes on husband 漢 – 0197
  Two eyes on person (hito) w/ flat cap below peaked roof 剣 – 1432
  Two eyes on sincere guy 勤 – 0517
  Two eyes on snake 絶 – 0673
  Two eyes on tree 疎 – 1806
  Two eyes, other 史 – 1314
Two-handled brush 卒 – 0027
Two heroes 皆 – see multiple identical radicals, heroes
Two identical radicals 羽 – see multiple identical radicals
Two lips (happy Jimmy) 裸 – 1615
Two lips (megaphone) 環 – 0718
Two moons 棚 – see multiple identical radicals, moons
Two pairs of arms on person plus flames (bonfire) 券 – 1305
Two pairs of arms on person (husband), other 扶 – 1915
Two pairs of arms on person (husband), plus flames 狭 – 0194
Two pairs of branches on tree 未 – 0672
Two-pronged switch 豊 – see songs
Two units above rice paddy 増 – 0061
Songs w/ short circuit (coop w/ 6 sections w/ crossed wires) 遭 – 1073
Songs w/out short circuit (coop w/ 6 sections & *un*crossed wires) 豊 – 1321
TY (thank you) (group of one) 衆 – 0930
Uber Ruth 送 – 0348
Uncoiling snake 危 – 0547
Uncooked rice above shelf 継 – 0635
Uncooked rice above snail 迷 – 0623
Uncooked rice, slashed 審 – 1368
Uncooked rice, other 粧 – 1387
Understand 頒 – 2076
Unequal or uneven legs or tentacles – see lopsided
Unicorn horn 悠 – 0985
Unit, one, above rice paddy (devil) 魅 – 1169
Unit, one, above rice paddy, other 油 – 0942
Units, two above rice paddy 増 – 0061
Universal laws 純 – 1245
Up & down 上下 – 0172
Up arrow 界 – 0069
Upside-down bench above telephone pole (sheep), other 羊 – see sheep
Upside-down bench below box 豆 – 0721
Upside-down bench, other 磁 – 1236; also, see antennae
Vapors above peaked roof 裕 – 0660
Vehicle – see car
Vertebrae, stacked 宮 – 1079
Vertical bench 状 – 0998
Vertical benches, two 兆 – 0849
Vertical line, isolated (unicorn horn) 悠 – 0985
Visor on helmet (one eye) 邪 – 0796
Volumes – see books
Wagon, California 朝 – see California wagon
Wakeful eye/shack 尺 – 1484

Trait Index

Warehouse (peaked roof above triple roof) 倉 – 1170
Washing machine w/ handle w/ stuck keg 劍 – 1432
Water & similar kanji 氷 – 0814
Water axis pierced by trident 隸 – 1583
Water below hair to the left 錄 – 0999
Water below together (dome below plants) in sun 暴 – 1021
Water below trident 隸 – 1583
Water below white 線 – 0228
Water below item(s), other 泰 – 1529
Water dog, Cuban (water below dog's head) 球 – 0606
Water w/ skeet shooter 緑 – 0227
Water radical w/ plant radicals 薄 – 0258
Welcoming (open) stance, tower 形 – 0573
Welcoming (open) stance, other 弄 – 1924
Well below six & above clothes 穢 – 1322
Well w/ handle (taser on box) 占 – 1542
Well w/ model of rice paddy w/ handle 溝 – 1825

Well, other 囲 – 1202
West (group of one) 西 – 0464
White above bird (most entries) 鶏 – 0754
White above small 原 – 0888
White above water 線 – 0228
White (oven) above tree 楽 – 0520
White, other 舶 – 2014
Window reinforced 域 – 1256
Winged hero 悲 – 0851
Winter (ice) 冬 – 0234
Wires w/ short circuit on coop w/ 6 sections 遭 – 1073
Wires w/out short circuit on coop w/ 6 sections 豊 – 1321
Wobbly table & napkin below peaked roof 令 – 0962
Wolf ヲ 墾 – 2068
Woman, contorted 狙 – 0948
Woman leaning, double roof 眠 – 0376
Woman leaning, single roof (pavilion) 抵 – 1195
Woman leaning w/ ball 式 – 0249
Woman leaning w/ ball, plus left hip 伐 – see halberd, single-grip

Words & man (soldier) 詰 – 0781
Words w/ slanted hat (group of one) 信 – 0431
Words, other (say, speak, talk) (group of one) 言 – 0430
Wrapping (or hook) containing snake 泡 – 1861
X below crutch 冬 – see dancer
X below eyebrows 父 – 0143
X below six 効 – 1139
X below tire stop 済 – 0259
X in bee hive 悩 – 1181
X, segmented 渋 – 1454
X, other 枢 – 1953
Yak above table 役 – 0557
Yakitori (naka, inside) on stick 仲 – see inside
Yen (group of one) 円 – 0039
Yoke 夜 – 0489
You (kimi) 君 – 0419
Yu ユ (Tagalog) 互 – 1207
Yu ユ, other 候 – 0996
Z 乙 – 1835
Zone, agricultural 増 – 0061

Rendaku

Rendaku is a phenomenon that can affect the pronunciations of kanji in compound words, when kanji appear in the middle or at the end of a word. Kanji pronunciations that contain the consonants in the following table can change as shown below.

ch → j (e.g., chi → ji)	k → g (e.g., koto → goto)
f → b (e.g., fun → bun)	s → z (e.g., sushi → zushi)
f → p (e.g., fuku → puku)	sh → j (e.g., sha → ja)
h → b (e.g., hito → bito)	t → d (e.g., toki → doki)
h → p (e.g., hai → pai)	ts → z (e.g., tsukai → zukai)

If you cannot find a kanji pronunciation that you are seeking in the Pronunciation Index starting on page 455, it may have been affected by rendaku. If so, you may be able to use the table above to help find it.

In the Kanji Catalogue, we are unable to provide retrieval cues for all of the alternative pronunciations associated with the rendaku phenomenon. For this reason, you will sometimes see a kanji pronunciation without an accompanying cue in the Catalogue. For example, 人 hito, reference # 13, can also be pronounced "bito," but only a retrieval cue for "hito" is provided. [The cue is "Hiro**Hito** was a 人 **hito** (person)..."] In this reference, and in some other kanji references, we use a superscripted "2" to identify pronunciations like bito[2], for which no retrieval cues are provided. The footnote to which this superscript refers appears only on page 3.

In some words, two Japanese kanji are repeated, one after the other, and the second kanji is replaced by the repetition symbol 々. If this repetition occurs with kanji pronunciations that are affected by rendaku, the second kanji may be pronounced differently from the first one, in accordance with the rules of rendaku. For example, 木々 kigi = many trees, 人々 hitobito = people, 口々 kuchiguchi = every mouth, 久々 hisabisa = a long time ago, 日々 hibi = every day, 国々 kuniguni = countries, 時々 tokidoki = sometimes, 様々 samazama = various and 花々 hanabana = flowers.

For some words containing the repetition symbol 々, like 少々 shoushou (a little) and 次々 tsugitsugi (one after the other), the rules of rendaku are not applied, and both kanji are pronounced in the same way. Words like 色々 iroiro (various), which don't contain any of the consonants listed in the table above, are obviously not affected by rendaku.

Kanji Pronunciation Index

Some kanji pronunciations are non-standard, i.e., they are neither "on'yomi" (Chinese readings) nor "kun'yomi" (Japanese readings) nor "nanori" (readings associated primarily with Japanese names), and they only appear in a single word. We call these pronunciations **exceptional** because they are unique exceptions to the standard ways in which the kanji are pronounced, and we mark them with **italics** in the Kanji Catalogue and in the Index.

For example, consider the word 海女 *ama* (female pearl diver), which we italicize in romaji in the Kanji Catalogue and the Index. The **italics** tell us that the "a" pronunciation is exceptional, meaning that when "a" is used as a pronunciation for 海, it is neither on'yomi nor kun'yomi nor nanori, and it is used in only one word. The same thing is true for the "ma" pronunciation in this word.

Japanese people use kanji combinations for some words without breaking the words into separate pronunciations for each kanji. In spite of that, we have chosen to break such words into separate pronunciations whenever it seemed practical to do so, so that students would be able to look them up easily.

For example, 足袋 *tabi* (Japanese socks) is recognized as a single word by Japanese people, not as a combination of two kanji with different pronunciations that can be combined. The same thing is true for 今日 *kyou* (today), 一日 *tsuitachi* (the first of the month), 昨日 *kinou* (yesterday), 大人 *otona* (adult), and so forth. The pronunciations that we assign to the individual kanji in these words are only intended to help people who are looking up pronunciations in this book, and they have no other significance.

There are two words used in this book that contain kanji with exceptional pronunciations which cannot be practically divided into separate sounds for each kanji: *obaasan* お祖母さん (grandmother) and お祖父さん *ojiisan* (grandfather). These two pronunciations, "*baa* 祖母" and "*jii* 祖父," are the only ones listed in this Index as **combinations** of kanji.

Finally, please note that sometimes **stem forms** of verbs, i.e., pre-masu forms, are used as pronunciations for kanji. For example, hanashi, derived from 話します hanashimasu (to speak), is a possible pronunciation of 話. Also, 読 yomi, derived from 読みます yomimasu (to read), is a possible pronunciation of 読. In this Index, we include a number of pronunciations based on stem forms, but there are may be others that we omit.

A 当 – 31	Ai 曖 – 1940	Ara 荒 – 968
A 明 – 154	Aida 間 – 411	Ara 粗 – 1326
A 上 – 171	Aji 味 – 245	Arashi 嵐 – 1128
A 空 – 248	Aka 明 – 154	Araso 争 – 936
A 小 – 253	Aka 赤 – 447	Arata 改 – 700
A 浴 – 256	Aka 垢 – 665	Arawa 表 – 582
A 会 – 293	*Aka* 証 – 1150	Arawa 現 – 739
A 合 – 294	Akashi 証 – 1150	Arawa 著 – 1088
A 悪 – 313	Akatsuki 暁 – 1855	Ari 有 – 460
A 海 – 337	Ake 明 – 154	Aru 歩 – 408
A 開 – 413	Aki 明 – 154	Asa 朝 – 291
A 足 – 449	Aki 秋 – 445	Asa 浅 – 1443
A 有 – 460	Aki 呆 – 828	Asa 麻 – 1475
A 圧 – 748	Aki 顕 – 1725	Ase 汗 – 629
A 揚 – 768	Akina 商 – 1217	Ase 焦 – 750
A 呆 – 828	Akira 諦 – 804	*Ashi* 明 – 154
A 荒 – 968	Akoga 憧 – 1956	Ashi 足 – 449
A 在 – 1014	Aku 悪 – 313	Aso 遊 – 360
A 編 – 1052	Aku 握 – 1372	*Ata* 当 – 31
A 遭 – 1073	Ama 天 – 189	Ata 辺 – 362
A 阿 – 1176	Ama 雨 – 261	Ata 与 – 1070
A 飽 – 1379	Ama 甘 – 541	Atai 価 – 484
A 亜 – 1589	Ama 余 – 637	Atai 値 – 571
A 宛 – 1822	*Ama* 奄 – 1095	Atama 頭 – 93
A 敢 – 1852	Ama 尼 – 1899	Atara 新 – 389
Aba 暴 – 1021	Ame 雨 – 261	Atata 暖 – 38
Abu 危 – 547	Ami 網 – 1448	Atata 温 – 257
Abura 油 – 942	An 案 – 120	Ate 宛 – 1822
Abura 脂 – 1180	An 安 – 236	Ato 後 – 335
Aga 崇 – 1656	An 暗 – 268	Ato 跡 – 1111
Age 挙 – 1362	Ana 穴 – 964	Ato 痕 – 1857
Ago 顎 – 1787	Anado 侮 – 1963	Atsu 熱 – 65
Ai 合 – 294	Ane 姉 – 241	Atsu 厚 – 185
Ai 愛 – 523	Ani 兄 – 420	Atsu 集 – 202
Ai 相 – 787	Ao 青 – 155	Atsu 暑 – 278
Ai 哀 – 1643	Ao 仰 – 1549	Atsu 圧 – 748
Ai 挨 – 1649	Ara 新 – 389	Atsuka 扱 – 1577
Ai 藍 – 1812	Ara 洗 – 423	Awa 慌 – 710

Awa 哀 – 1643	Bai 杯 – 848	Be 別 – 561
Awa 淡 – 1654	Bai 培 – 1234	*Be* 戸 – 871
Awa 泡 – 1861	Bai 梅 – 1299	Bei 米 – 326
Aya 危 – 547	Bai 賠 – 1661	Bei 餅 – 743
Aya 怪 – 1024	Bai 媒 – 1889	Bei 塀 – 1850
Ayama 過 – 361	Bai 陪 – 2030	Ben 勉 – 474
Ayama 謝 – 1283	Bako 箱 – 142	Ben 便 – 481
Ayama 誤 – 1285	Baku 幕 – 653	Ben 弁 – 1162
Ayatsu 操 – 1192	Baku 暴 – 1021	Beni 紅 – 247
Ayu 歩 – 408	Baku 爆 – 1022	Betsu 別 – 561
Aza 鮮 – 858	Baku 麦 – 1103	Betsu 蔑 – 1983
Azake 嘲 – 1971	Baku 博 – 1481	Bi 日 – 32
Azu 預 – 1259	Baku 漠 – 1614	Bi 備 – 367
Azumu 欺 – 1859	Baku 縛 – 1721	Bi 火 – 443
Ba 晴 – 37	Ban 晩 – 35	*Bi* 袋 – 581
Ba 母 – 50	Ban 万 – 113	Bi 美 – 771
Ba 生 – 208	Ban 番 – 328	Bi 鼻 – 795
Ba 場 – 403	Ban 判 – 1054	Bi 比 – 857
Ba 張 – 477	Ban 板 – 1166	Bi 微 – 1442
Ba 化 – 487	Ban 盤 – 1197	Biki 引 – 476
Ba 菌 – 533	Ban 伴 – 1599	Biki 匹 – 818
Ba 葉 – 543	Ban 蛮 – 1804	Bin 便 – 481
Ba 抜 – 749	Bana 花 – 211	Bin 貧 – 1339
Ba 馬 – 958	Banashi 話 – 433	Bin 敏 – 1608
Ba 麦 – 1103	Bara 払 – 591	Bin 瓶 – 1711
Ba 栄 – 1263	Bara 腹 – 863	Bira 弁 – 1162
Ba 刃 – 1488	Bara 原 – 888	Biro 広 – 494
Ba 婆 – 1688	Bashi 橋 – 139	Bito 人 – 13
Ba 罰 – 1691	Bashi 箸 – 1144	Bo 母 – 50
Ba 伐 – 1862	Bata 端 – 730	Bo 暮 – 641
Ba 罵 – 1927	Batsu 抜 – 749	Bo 没 – 806
Baa 祖母 – 272	Batsu 罰 – 1691	Bo 呆 – 828
Bachi 鉢 – 1277	Batsu 閥 – 1823	Bo 吠 – 944
Bachi 罰 – 1691	Batsu 伐 – 1862	Bo 募 – 1109
Bai 買 – 89	Baya 早 – 34	Bo 墓 – 1275
Bai 倍 – 269	Bayashi 林 – 125	Bo 干 – 1306
Bai 売 – 425	Be 部 – 267	Bo 模 – 1353
Bai 配 – 466	Be 辺 – 362	Bo 坊 – 1576

Bo 簿 – 1788	Bou 貌 – 1687	Byou 表 – 582
Bo 勃 – 1846	Bou 肪 – 1849	Byou 描 – 758
Bo 慕 – 1959	Bou 某 – 1887	Byou 平 – 885
Boku 目 – 51	Bou 妨 – 1917	Byou 秒 – 1137
Boku 木 – 118	Bou 剖 – 1985	Byou 拍 – 1714
Boku 僕 – 333	Bou 紡 – 2033	Cha 茶 – 212
Boku 北 – 373	Bu 分 – 105	Chaku 着 – 52
Boku 撲 – 1375	Bu 父 – 143	Chaku 嫡 – 2027
Boku 牧 – 1469	Bu 不 – 176	Chi 千 – 22
Boku 朴 – 1826	Bu 降 – 178	*Chi* 刀 – 102
Boku 墨 – 1829	Bu 部 – 267	Chi 散 – 159
Boku 睦 – 1989	Bu 物 – 401	Chi 乳 – 186
Bon 本 – 123	Bu 無 – 583	Chi 歳 – 322
Bon 盆 – 1167	Bu 舞 – 584	Chi 知 – 323
Bon 凡 – 1511	Bu 夫 – 614	Chi 遅 – 350
Bon 煩 – 2007	Bu 仏 – 678	Chi 地 – 503
Bori 掘 – 1402	Bu 布 – 687	Chi 池 – 504
Bori 堀 – 1539	Bu 撫 – 846	Chi 治 – 539
Boso 細 – 220	Bu 伏 – 945	Chi 置 – 569
Botsu 没 – 806	Bu 武 – 1418	Chi 値 – 571
Bou 貿 – 85	Bu 奉 – 1536	*Chi* 打 – 590
Bou 帽 – 243	Bu 侮 – 1963	Chi 血 – 747
Bou 忘 – 310	Bue 笛 – 1503	Chi 馳 – 1358
Bou 包 – 548	Buka 深 – 694	Chi 致 – 1463
Bou 亡 – 585	*Buki* 雪 – 262	Chi 痴 – 1581
Bou 忙 – 586	Bukuro 袋 – 581	Chi 稚 – 1797
Bou 望 – 664	Bumi 文 – 25	Chi 窒 – 2024
Bou 冒 – 812	Bun 文 – 25	Chichi 父 – 143
Bou 棒 – 820	Bun 分 – 105	Chichi 乳 – 186
Bou 防 – 920	Bun 聞 – 412	Chichi 秩 – 1482
Bou 抱 – 986	Bune 船 – 602	Chiga 違 – 355
Bou 暴 – 1021	Bune 舟 – 1524	Chigi 契 – 1602
Bou 房 – 1134	Buta 豚 – 1504	Chii 小 – 253
Bou 乏 – 1340	Buto 太 – 191	Chiji 縮 – 1487
Bou 謀 – 1544	Butsu 物 – 401	Chika 近 – 390
Bou 坊 – 1576	Butsu 仏 – 678	Chika 誓 – 1780
Bou 胞 – 1595	Byaku 百 – 47	Chikara 力 – 107
Bou 傍 – 1633	Byou 病 – 369	Chiku 竹 – 134

Chiku 築 – 1219	Chuu 中 – 8	Dama 黙 – 836
Chiku 畜 – 1773	Chuu 虫 – 9	Dan 暖 – 38
Chiku 蓄 – 1774	Chuu 昼 – 49	Dan 男 – 109
Chiku 逐 – 1970	Chuu 注 – 168	Dan 段 – 559
Chin 珍 – 407	Chuu 駐 – 381	Dan 旦 – 668
Chin 賃 – 707	Chuu 仲 – 657	Dan 壇 – 679
Chin 沈 – 835	Chuu 宙 – 898	Dan 団 – 686
Chin 鎮 – 1722	Chuu 酎 – 1099	Dan 断 – 704
Chin 陳 – 1742	Chuu 柱 – 1225	Dan 弾 – 780
Chitsu 秩 – 1482	Chuu 忠 – 1505	Dan 談 – 790
Cho 緒 – 232	Chuu 抽 – 1760	Dana 棚 – 742
Cho 直 – 570	Chuu 鋳 – 2010	Dare 誰 – 440
Cho 貯 – 667	Da 立 – 11	Date 立 – 11
Cho 著 – 1088	Da 田 – 68	Date 館 – 305
Choku 直 – 570	Da 出 – 147	Datsu 脱 – 1386
Chou 町 – 70	Da 建 – 363	Datsu 奪 – 1568
Chou 重 – 284	Da 打 – 590	Dawara 俵 – 1492
Chou 朝 – 291	Da 駄 – 628	De 手 – 23
Chou 調 – 441	Da 抱 – 986	De 出 – 147
Chou 張 – 477	Da 脱 – 1386	De 鉄 – 304
Chou 長 – 502	Da 蛇 – 1754	De 弟 – 529
Chou 鳥 – 555	Da 唾 – 1847	De 照 – 822
Chou 超 – 621	Da 妥 – 1916	Dei 泥 – 819
Chou 丁 – 702	Da 惰 – 2063	Deki 溺 – 1978
Chou 頂 – 783	*Dachi* 立 – 11	Den 田 – 68
Chou 徴 – 784	Dachi 達 – 347	Den 電 – 263
Chou 兆 – 849	Dai 大 – 188	Den 伝 – 345
Chou 聴 – 934	Dai 内 – 396	Den 殿 – 1080
Chou 挑 – 1001	Dai 題 – 454	Dera 寺 – 213
Chou 眺 – 1136	Dai 弟 – 529	Do 取 – 58
Chou 帳 – 1244	Dai 第 – 530	Do 土 – 59
Chou 潮 – 1308	Dai 台 – 538	Do 止 – 173
Chou 庁 – 1444	Dai 代 – 552	Do 怒 – 319
Chou 腸 – 1497	Daka 高 – 19	Do 読 – 432
Chou 彫 – 1698	Dake 岳 – 1683	Do 度 – 498
Chou 懲 – 1879	Daku 濁 – 1831	Do 努 – 519
Chou 嘲 – 1971	Daku 諾 – 1945	Do 戸 – 871
Chou 弔 – 2053	Dama 玉 – 169	*Do* 傷 – 1376

Do 奴 – 1582	E 恵 – 720	Era 偉 – 1174
Dobu 溝 – 1825	E 餌 – 843	Eri 襟 – 1872
Doi 樋 – 1143	E 獲 – 947	Esa 餌 – 843
Doki 時 – 215	*E* 衣 – 1042	Etsu 越 – 453
Dokoro 所 – 391	E 江 – 1026	Etsu 悦 – 1779
Dokoro 処 – 1149	E 柄 – 1533	Etsu 閲 – 1987
Doku 読 – 432	Eda 枝 – 128	Fu 増 – 61
Doku 独 – 724	Ega 描 – 758	Fu 負 – 87
Doku 毒 – 1349	Ei 映 – 36	Fu 付 – 132
Domo 供 – 486	Ei 英 – 43	Fu 符 – 133
Don 鈍 – 1245	Ei 泳 – 255	Fu 父 – 143
Don 丼 – 1984	Ei 営 – 684	Fu 不 – 176
Don 貪 – 2034	Ei 影 – 839	Fu 降 – 178
Donburi 丼 – 1984	Ei 永 – 870	*Fu* 生 – 208
Doo 遠 – 351	Ei 衛 – 918	Fu 怖 – 463
Doo 通 – 365	Ei 栄 – 1263	Fu 触 – 475
Dori 鳥 – 555	Ei 鋭 – 1419	Fu 風 – 479
Doro 泥 – 819	Eki 駅 – 380	Fu 復 – 527
Dou 堂 – 64	Eki 易 – 402	Fu 沸 – 531
Dou 動 – 286	Eki 役 – 557	Fu 吹 – 537
Dou 働 – 287	Eki 疫 – 1142	Fu 普 – 576
Dou 同 – 339	Eki 液 – 1241	Fu 夫 – 614
Dou 道 – 349	Eki 益 – 1407	Fu 浮 – 671
Dou 倒 – 563	En 円 – 39	Fu 布 – 687
Dou 洞 – 963	En 塩 – 60	Fu 腐 – 722
Dou 童 – 1094	En 園 – 279	Fu 振 – 823
Dou 等 – 1132	En 遠 – 351	Fu 富 – 939
Dou 胴 – 1191	En 演 – 756	Fu 伏 – 945
Dou 銅 – 1232	En 炎 – 788	Fu 府 – 1004
Dou 導 – 1261	En 延 – 842	Fu 老 – 1065
Dou 藤 – 1530	En 縁 – 1023	Fu 拭 – 1114
E 笑 – 199	En 猿 – 1055	Fu 婦 – 1165
E 絵 – 223	En 鉛 – 1092	*Fu* 雰 – 1201
E 重 – 284	En 援 – 1177	Fu 踏 – 1534
E 会 – 293	En 宴 – 1391	Fu 阜 – 1658
E 越 – 453	En 沿 – 1414	Fu 膚 – 1777
E 愛 – 523	En 煙 – 1415	Fu 譜 – 1848
E 得 – 706	Era 選 – 352	Fu 赴 – 1888

Fu 扶 – 1915	Futa 双 – 1596	Gai 概 – 1647
Fu 訃 – 2072	Futa 蓋 – 1793	Gai 涯 – 1682
Fuda 札 – 735	Futata 再 – 1032	Gai 慨 – 1782
Fude 筆 – 1091	Futo 太 – 191	Gai 蓋 – 1793
Fue 笛 – 1503	Futokoro 懐 – 928	Gai 骸 – 1923
Fuji 藤 – 1530	*Futsu* 二 – 2	Gai 該 – 1969
Fuka 深 – 694	Fuu 風 – 479	Gake 崖 – 911
Fuku 服 – 150	Fuu 夫 – 614	Gaku 学 – 184
Fuku 復 – 527	Fuu 封 – 1619	Gaku 楽 – 520
Fuku 福 – 661	Fuyu 冬 – 234	Gaku 額 – 791
Fuku 腹 – 863	Ga 画 – 77	Gaku 岳 – 1683
Fuku 覆 – 893	Ga 学 – 184	Gaku 顎 – 1787
Fuku 伏 – 945	Ga 合 – 294	Gama 構 – 141
Fuku 副 – 1206	Ga 何 – 338	Gama 窯 – 1893
Fuku 複 – 1281	*Ga* 髪 – 501	Game 亀 – 908
Fuku 含 – 1491	*Ga* 楽 – 520	Gami 紙 – 221
Fukuro 袋 – 581	Ga 替 – 551	Gami 神 – 273
Fumoto 麓 – 1955	Ga 菓 – 589	Gan 願 – 94
Fun 分 – 105	Ga 掛 – 596	Gan 顔 – 95
Fun 奮 – 727	Ga 我 – 862	Gan 元 – 421
Fun 粉 – 1104	Ga 牙 – 921	Gan 岸 – 500
Fun 霧 – 1201	Ga 雅 – 922	Gan 頑 – 622
Fun 噴 – 1268	Ga 狩 – 923	Gan 岩 – 816
Fun 紛 – 1638	Ga 賀 – 994	Gan 丸 – 866
Fun 憤 – 1781	Ga 河 – 1182	Gan 眼 – 1423
Fun 墳 – 1897	Ga 欠 – 1238	Gan 含 – 1491
Funa 船 – 602	Ga 兼 – 1401	Gan 癌 – 2079
Fune 船 – 602	Ga 芽 – 1417	*Gane* 鏡 – 1355
Fune 舟 – 1524	Ga 仮 – 1456	Gao 顔 – 95
Furi 振 – 823	Ga 瓦 – 1710	Gara 柄 – 1533
Furu 震 – 265	Ga 餓 – 1974	*Gara* 骸 – 1923
Furu 古 – 392	Gae 返 – 356	Garu 軽 – 289
Furu 故 – 394	Gae 替 – 551	Gasa 笠 – 1311
Fusa 房 – 1134	Gai 外 – 163	Gata 方 – 114
Fusa 塞 – 1227	Gai 会 – 293	Gata 難 – 198
Fuse 防 – 920	Gai 街 – 625	Gata 語 – 435
Fushi 節 – 1048	Gai 崖 – 911	Gata 形 – 573
Futa 二 – 2	Gai 害 – 1260	Gata 型 – 1116

Gata 潟 – 1736	Getsu 月 – 148	Go 悟 – 1526
Gatari 語 – 435	Gi 着 – 52	Go 呉 – 1686
Gato 難 – 198	Gi 切 – 103	Go 碁 – 1851
Gatsu 月 – 148	Gi 木 – 118	Go 娯 – 2019
Gawa 川 – 250	Gi 気 – 321	Goe 声 – 40
Gawa 側 – 490	Gi 聞 – 412	*Goko* 心 – 306
Gawa 皮 – 833	Gi 議 – 438	Goku 国 – 170
Gaya 谷 – 1383	Gi 起 – 452	Goku 極 – 610
Ge 月 – 148	Gi 疑 – 978	Goku 獄 – 1435
Ge 外 – 163	*Gi* 城 – 1008	Gome 米 – 326
Ge 下 – 172	Gi 義 – 1028	Gon 金 – 301
Ge 気 – 321	Gi 技 – 1133	Gon 言 – 430
Ge 家 – 405	Gi 儀 – 1541	Gon 厳 – 902
Ge 夏 – 522	Gi 偽 – 1622	Gon 権 – 916
Ge 解 – 618	Gi 岐 – 1657	*Gori* 残 – 605
Ge 毛 – 688	Gi 棋 – 1726	Goro 頃 – 96
Ge 牙 – 921	Gi 戯 – 1756	Goshi 腰 – 884
Ge 華 – 1354	Gi 犠 – 1764	Goto 毎 – 336
Gei 迎 – 358	Gi 欺 – 1859	Goto 事 – 416
Gei 芸 – 1056	Gi 宜 – 1903	Goto 如 – 1578
Gei 鯨 – 1981	Gi 擬 – 2003	Gou 合 – 294
Geki 劇 – 1058	Gin 金 – 301	Gou 業 – 332
Geki 激 – 1147	Gin 銀 – 302	Gou 号 – 470
Geki 撃 – 1226	Gin 吟 – 1873	Gou 強 – 478
Gen 間 – 411	Giwa 際 – 379	Gou 郷 – 1059
Gen 元 – 421	Go 五 – 179	Gou 豪 – 1357
Gen 言 – 430	Go 子 – 182	Gou 后 – 1459
Gen 限 – 642	Go 午 – 207	Gou 剛 – 1663
Gen 現 – 739	Go 後 – 335	Gou 傲 – 2013
Gen 嫌 – 817	Go 古 – 392	Gou 拷 – 2040
Gen 原 – 888	Go 語 – 435	Gu 具 – 100
Gen 厳 – 902	Go 期 – 711	Gu 暮 – 641
Gen 幻 – 1129	Go 庫 – 919	Gu 愚 – 1580
Gen 減 – 1148	Go 児 – 1093	Guchi 口 – 426
Gen 玄 – 1252	Go 護 – 1163	Guki 茎 – 1894
Gen 源 – 1267	Go 互 – 1207	Gumi 組 – 752
Gen 拳 – 1554	Go 誤 – 1285	Gumo 雲 – 264
Gen 弦 – 1860	Go 御 – 1440	Gun 軍 – 725

Gun 群 – 929	*Ha* 流 – 654	Hai 輩 – 1607
Gun 郡 – 1230	Ha 羽 – 755	Hai 排 – 1623
Gura 楽 – 520	Ha 派 – 764	Haji 初 – 104
Gurai 位 – 270	Ha 破 – 837	Haji 恥 – 309
Guro 黒 – 76	Ha 波 – 878	Haji 始 – 540
Guru 苦 – 393	Ha 跳 – 1084	Haka 図 – 281
Gusa 草 – 909	Ha 履 – 1220	Haka 計 – 434
Guse 癖 – 1215	Ha 栄 – 1263	Haka 測 – 1031
Gusuri 薬 – 521	Ha 刃 – 1488	Haka 量 – 1061
Gutsu 靴 – 603	Ha 吐 – 1558	Haka 墓 – 1275
Guu 宮 – 1079	Ha 剥 – 1567	Haka 博 – 1481
Guu 遇 – 1120	Ha 剝 – 1567	Haka 謀 – 1544
Guu 偶 – 1288	Ha 腫 – 1701	Hako 箱 – 142
Gyaku 逆 – 894	Ha 貼 – 1766	Hako 運 – 354
Gyaku 虐 – 1679	Ha 把 – 1817	Haku 白 – 44
Gyo 魚 – 80	Ha 覇 – 1874	Haku 泊 – 46
Gyo 漁 – 685	Haba 幅 – 1185	Haku 薄 – 258
Gyo 御 – 1440	Haba 阻 – 1838	Haku 迫 – 1316
Gyoku 曲 – 82	Habu 省 – 1010	Haku 博 – 1481
Gyoku 玉 – 169	Hachi 八 – 15	Haku 剥 – 1567
Gyou 業 – 332	Hachi 蜂 – 1254	Haku 剝 – 1567
Gyou 行 – 334	Hachi 鉢 – 1277	Haku 伯 – 1572
Gyou 形 – 573	Hada 肌 – 980	Haku 拍 – 1714
Gyou 仰 – 1549	Hadaka 裸 – 1615	Haku 舶 – 2014
Gyou 凝 – 1680	Hage 激 – 1147	Hama 浜 – 766
Gyuu 牛 – 205	Hage 励 – 1338	Han 半 – 331
Ha 二 – 2	Haguku 育 – 151	Han 飯 – 400
Ha 八 – 15	Haha 母 – 50	Han 反 – 680
Ha 映 – 36	Hai 入 – 14	Han 犯 – 901
Ha 晴 – 37	Hai 背 – 152	Han 阪 – 1005
Ha 生 – 208	Hai 灰 – 444	Han 般 – 1050
Ha 発 – 298	Hai 配 – 466	Han 判 – 1054
Ha 恥 – 309	Hai 拝 – 593	Han 版 – 1086
Ha 張 – 477	Hai 敗 – 793	Han 販 – 1199
Ha 歯 – 533	Hai 杯 – 848	Han 繁 – 1266
Ha 葉 – 543	Hai 廃 – 1221	Han 班 – 1509
Ha 果 – 587	Hai 俳 – 1441	Han 藩 – 1537
Ha 掃 – 645	Hai 肺 – 1508	Han 範 – 1585

Han 伴 – 1599	Hayashi 林 – 125	Hi 非 – 682
Han 帆 – 1768	Hazu 外 – 163	Hi 弾 – 780
Han 畔 – 1988	Hazu 弾 – 780	Hi 避 – 802
Han 搬 – 1993	Hazukashi 辱 – 1799	Hi 匹 – 818
Han 頒 – 2076	*He* 下 – 172	Hi 皮 – 833
Hana 放 – 117	He 経 – 224	Hi 悲 – 851
Hana 花 – 211	He 部 – 267	Hi 比 – 857
Hana 話 – 433	He 減 – 1148	Hi 妃 – 1078
Hana 離 – 666	Hebi 蛇 – 1754	Hi 批 – 1082
Hana 鼻 – 795	Heda 隔 – 1729	Hi 筆 – 1091
Hana 華 – 1354	Hei 閉 – 414	Hi 樋 – 1143
Hanashi 話 – 433	Hei 並 – 575	Hi 秘 – 1187
Hane 羽 – 755	Hei 平 – 885	Hi 泌 – 1297
Har 晴 – 37	Hei 兵 – 917	Hi 干 – 1306
Hara 払 – 591	Hei 幣 – 1411	Hi 否 – 1329
Hara 腹 – 863	Hei 陛 – 1460	Hi 披 – 1389
Hara 原 – 888	Hei 柄 – 1533	Hi 肥 – 1406
Hari 針 – 1138	Hei 併 – 1655	Hi 被 – 1447
Haru 春 – 506	Hei 塀 – 1850	Hi 卑 – 1745
Hasa 挟 – 1009	Hei 弊 – 2005	Hi 碑 – 1905
Hashi 橋 – 139	Heki 壁 – 1051	Hi 罷 – 2057
Hashi 走 – 450	Heki 辟 – 1214	Hibi 響 – 840
Hashi 端 – 730	Heki 癖 – 1215	Hidari 左 – 456
Hashi 箸 – 1144	Hen 片 – 181	Higashi 東 – 508
Hashira 柱 – 1225	Hen 返 – 356	Hii 秀 – 1517
Hasu 蓮 – 2075	Hen 辺 – 362	Hiji 肘 – 1954
Hata 機 – 137	Hen 変 – 553	Hika 光 – 448
Hata 畑 – 889	Hen 編 – 1052	Hika 控 – 1637
Hata 旗 – 1430	Hen 偏 – 1757	Hikari 光 – 448
Hatake 畑 – 889	Hen 遍 – 1830	Hiki 引 – 476
Hatara 働 – 287	Hi 日 – 32	Hiki 匹 – 818
Hato 鳩 – 736	Hi 冷 – 299	Hiki 率 – 1408
Hatsu 初 – 104	Hi 必 – 307	Hiku 低 – 222
Hatsu 発 – 298	Hi 疲 – 370	Hima 暇 – 803
Hatsu 髪 – 501	Hi 火 – 443	Hime 姫 – 1040
Hatsu 鉢 – 1277	Hi 引 – 476	Hime 媛 – 2084
Haya 早 – 34	Hi 飛 – 574	Hin 品 – 5
Haya 速 – 359	Hi 費 – 656	Hin 浜 – 766

Hin 頻 – 1265	Ho 哺 – 2066	Hou 宝 – 1292
Hin 貧 – 1339	*Hodo* 解 – 618	Hou 豊 – 1321
Hin 賓 – 2054	Hodo 程 – 954	Hou 飽 – 1379
Hira 開 – 413	Hodoko 施 – 1067	Hou 奉 – 1536
Hira 平 – 885	Hoho 頬 – 890	Hou 邦 – 1593
Hiro 広 – 494	*Hoho* 微 – 1442	Hou 胞 – 1595
Hiro 拾 – 595	Hoka 外 – 163	Hou 封 – 1619
Hiru 昼 – 49	Hoka 他 – 505	Hou 芳 – 1677
Hisa 久 – 30	Hoko 誇 – 1635	Hou 縫 – 1816
Hishi 拉 – 1767	Hokoro 綻 – 1949	Hou 泡 – 1861
Hiso 密 – 1188	Hoku 北 – 373	Hou 倣 – 2016
Hita 浸 – 797	Homa 誉 – 1705	Hou 俸 – 2056
Hitai 額 – 791	Hon 本 – 123	Houmu 葬 – 1273
Hito 一 – 1	Hon 反 – 680	*Hya* 百 – 47
Hito 人 – 13	*Hon* 香 – 681	Hyaku 百 – 47
Hito 等 – 1132	Hon 翻 – 1087	Hyou 表 – 582
Hitomi 瞳 – 1865	Hon 奔 – 1864	Hyou 氷 – 814
Hitsu 必 – 307	Hone 骨 – 832	Hyou 兵 – 917
Hitsu 筆 – 1091	Honoo 炎 – 788	Hyou 評 – 1053
Hitsuji 羊 – 1223	Hoo 頬 – 890	Hyou 標 – 1303
Hiza 膝 – 861	Hora 洞 – 963	Hyou 俵 – 1492
Ho 発 – 298	Hori 堀 – 1539	Hyou 票 – 1510
Ho 法 – 344	Horo 滅 – 1193	Hyou 漂 – 1693
Ho 北 – 373	Hoshi 星 – 48	Hyou 拍 – 1714
Ho 歩 – 408	Hoso 細 – 220	I 入 – 14
Ho 欲 – 535	Hotaru 蛍 – 2023	I 胃 – 153
Ho 捕 – 670	Hotoke 仏 – 678	I 生 – 208
Ho 呆 – 828	Hou 方 – 114	I 要 – 238
Ho 褒 – 829	Hou 放 – 117	*I* 味 – 245
Ho 吠 – 944	Hou 法 – 344	I 位 – 270
Ho 補 – 995	Hou 報 – 386	I 良 – 303
Ho 保 – 1216	Hou 包 – 548	I 息 – 315
Ho 舗 – 1237	Hou 訪 – 713	I 意 – 317
Ho 干 – 1306	Hou 砲 – 738	I 医 – 325
Ho 掘 – 1402	Hou 褒 – 829	I 行 – 334
Ho 彫 – 1698	Hou 峰 – 938	I 違 – 355
Ho 誉 – 1705	Hou 崩 – 973	I 易 – 402
Ho 帆 – 1768	Hou 抱 – 986	I 言 – 430

I 以 – 601	Iki 息 – 315	Isa 勇 – 1282
I 煎 – 650	Iki 域 – 1256	Isagiyo 潔 – 1212
I 移 – 801	Iki 粋 – 1778	Ishi 石 – 458
I 居 – 809	Ikidoo 憤 – 1781	Iso 急 – 312
I 椅 – 855	Ikio 勢 – 110	Isoga 忙 – 586
I 威 – 915	Iko 憩 – 1477	*Ita* 分 – 105
I 射 – 932	Iku 育 – 151	Ita 痛 – 368
I 異 – 970	Iku 幾 – 1628	Ita 至 – 609
I 井 – 983	Ikusa 戦 – 933	Ita 板 – 1166
I 遺 – 1037	Ima 今 – 292	Ita 致 – 1463
I 衣 – 1042	Ima 未 – 672	Itada 頂 – 783
I 偉 – 1174	Imashi 戒 – 875	Itadaki 頂 – 783
I 囲 – 1202	Imo 芋 – 1102	Ito 糸 – 219
I 為 – 1222	Imouto 妹 – 244	Ito 愛 – 523
I 委 – 1364	In 員 – 88	Itona 営 – 684
I 維 – 1556	In 音 – 266	Itsu 一 – 1
I 依 – 1557	In 飲 – 399	Itsu 五 – 179
I 尉 – 1751	In 院 – 424	Itsu 逸 – 1706
I 慰 – 1752	In 引 – 476	Itsuku 慈 – 1451
I 緯 – 1810	In 隠 – 834	Itsuwa 偽 – 1622
I 畏 – 1998	In 印 – 1046	Iwa 祝 – 274
I 硫 – 2001	*In* 囲 – 1202	Iwa 岩 – 816
I 鋳 – 2010	In 因 – 1360	Iya 嫌 – 817
I 萎 – 2022	In 陰 – 1543	Iya 癒 – 1293
I 彙 – 2067	In 咽 – 1967	Iya 卑 – 1745
I 伊 – 2081	In 韻 – 2036	Izumi 泉 – 252
Ibara 茨 – 1007	In 姻 – 2039	Ja 社 – 271
Ichi 一 – 1	*Ina* 田 – 68	Ja 者 – 276
Ichi 市 – 242	Ina 居 – 1229	Ja 写 – 468
Ichi 壱 – 2048	Ina 否 – 1329	Ja 砂 – 782
Ichijiru 著 – 1088	Ine 稲 – 1229	Ja 邪 – 796
Ida 抱 – 986	Ino 祈 – 955	Ja 蛇 – 1754
Ido 挑 – 1001	*Ino* 井 – 983	Jaku 昔 – 33
Ie 家 – 405	Inochi 命 – 961	Jaku 若 – 461
Iji 苛 – 1792	Inu 犬 – 190	Jaku 弱 – 471
Ika 怒 – 319	Ira 苛 – 1792	Jaku 寂 – 864
Ika 如 – 1578	Iri 入 – 14	Jaku 尺 – 1484
Ike 池 – 504	Iro 色 – 473	Ji 十 – 18

Ji 自 – 55	Jiki 直 – 570	Jou 常 – 683
Ji 耳 – 57	Jiku 軸 – 1791	Jou 畳 – 876
Ji 士 – 66	Jima 島 – 556	Jou 井 – 983
Ji 仕 – 67	Jin 人 – 13	Jou 状 – 998
Ji 枝 – 128	Jin 進 – 203	Jou 縄 – 1003
Ji 父 – 143	Jin 神 – 273	Jou 城 – 1008
Ji 死 – 164	Jin 心 – 306	Jou 盛 – 1018
Ji 子 – 182	Jin 陣 – 638	Jou 蒸 – 1101
Ji 字 – 183	Jin 臣 – 1039	Jou 剰 – 1211
Ji 実 – 195	Jin 仁 – 1496	Jou 穣 – 1322
Ji 寺 – 213	Jin 尽 – 1507	Jou 条 – 1352
Ji 時 – 215	Jin 尋 – 1512	Jou 浄 – 1380
Ji 持 – 216	Jin 甚 – 1730	Jou 冗 – 1462
Ji 面 – 282	Jin 迅 – 1968	Jou 嬢 – 1659
Ji 知 – 323	Jin 腎 – 1991	Jou 譲 – 1669
Ji 辞 – 387	Jiru 汁 – 900	Jou 壌 – 1898
Ji 事 – 416	Jirushi 印 – 1046	Jou 錠 – 1914
Ji 地 – 503	Jitsu 日 – 32	Jou 醸 – 1996
Ji 路 – 525	Jitsu 実 – 195	Ju 十 – 18
Ji 次 – 536	Jo 助 – 108	Ju 受 – 577
Ji 治 – 539	Jo 女 – 235	Ju 授 – 578
Ji 葉 – 543	Jo 所 – 391	Ju 寿 – 607
Ji 司 – 608	Jo 除 – 646	Ju 樹 – 1089
Ji 除 – 646	Jo 徐 – 904	Ju 需 – 1699
Ji 血 – 747	Jo 序 – 1483	Ju 珠 – 1772
Ji 染 – 774	Jo 如 – 1578	Ju 儒 – 1909
Ji 似 – 824	Jo 叙 – 2004	
Ji 児 – 1093	Joku 辱 – 1799	Juku 宿 – 491
Ji 締 – 1173	Jou 情 – 156	Juku 熟 – 1427
Ji 磁 – 1236	Jou 上 – 171	Juku 塾 – 1737
Ji 示 – 1347	Jou 生 – 208	Jun 準 – 204
Ji 慈 – 1451	Jou 場 – 403	Jun 純 – 761
Ji 滋 – 1908	Jou 静 – 418	Jun 巡 – 778
Jii 祖父 – 272	Jou 焼 – 446	Jun 旬 – 1304
Jika 近 – 390	Jou 定 – 455	Jun 順 – 1348
Jika 直 – 570	Jou 乗 – 509	Jun 盾 – 1750
Jika 鹿 – 895	Jou 丈 – 613	Jun 潤 – 1755
Jiki 食 – 398	Jou 成 – 633	Jun 循 – 1878
		Jun 准 – 2046

Jutsu 術 – 808	Ka 替 – 551	Ka 喝 – 1934
Jutsu 述 – 1328	Ka 代 – 552	Ka 蚊 – 2009
Juu 中 – 8	Ka 変 – 553	Ka 禍 – 2042
Juu 十 – 18	Ka 換 – 554	Ka 褐 – 2059
Juu 住 – 167	Ka 果 – 587	*Kaa* 母 – 50
Juu 重 – 284	Ka 課 – 588	Kabe 壁 – 1051
Juu 柔 – 546	Ka 菓 – 589	Kabu 株 – 1302
Juu 汁 – 900	Ka 掛 – 596	Kabu 被 – 1447
Juu 渋 – 1454	Ka 可 – 615	Kado 角 – 81
Juu 充 – 1478	Ka 香 – 681	Kado 門 – 409
Juu 従 – 1485	Ka 加 – 714	Kae 返 – 356
Juu 縦 – 1486	*Ka* 舎 – 745	Kae 帰 – 566
Juu 銃 – 1555	Ka 描 – 758	Kaeri 顧 – 1648
Juu 獣 – 1733	Ka 格 – 762	Kagami 鏡 – 1355
K 今 – 292	Ka 駆 – 776	Kagaya 輝 – 979
Ka 日 – 32	Ka 暇 – 803	Kage 影 – 839
Ka 買 – 89	Ka 飼 – 830	Kage 陰 – 1543
Ka 貸 – 90	Ka 鹿 – 895	Kagi 限 – 642
Ka 交 – 144	Ka 狩 – 923	Kagi 鍵 – 1689
Ka 勝 – 149	Ka 嗅 – 959	Kago 籠 – 2074
Ka 下 – 172	*Ka* 各 – 1033	Kai 回 – 4
Ka 花 – 211	Ka 河 – 1182	Kai 界 – 69
Ka 活 – 260	Ka 欠 – 1238	Kai 貝 – 83
Ka 神 – 273	Ka 華 – 1354	Kai 買 – 89
Ka 何 – 338	Ka 兼 – 1401	Kai 械 – 138
Ka 荷 – 342	Ka 貨 – 1413	Kai 絵 – 223
Ka 過 – 361	Ka 仮 – 1456	Kai 会 – 293
Ka 家 – 405	Ka 葛 – 1531	Kai 海 – 337
Ka 書 – 415	Ka 佳 – 1642	Kai 開 – 413
Ka 火 – 443	Ka 稼 – 1668	Kai 灰 – 444
Ka 赤 – 447	Ka 賭 – 1761	Kai 皆 – 597
Ka 風 – 479	Ka 括 – 1762	Kai 階 – 598
Ka 価 – 484	Ka 架 – 1790	Kai 解 – 618
Ka 借 – 485	Ka 苛 – 1792	Kai 街 – 625
Ka 化 – 487	Ka 枯 – 1834	Kai 介 – 659
Ka 科 – 511	Ka 渦 – 1871	Kai 悔 – 675
Ka 夏 – 522	Ka 箇 – 1881	Kai 改 – 700
Ka 歌 – 534	Ka 刈 – 1912	Kai 快 – 734

Kai 垣 – 777	Kakuma 匿 – 1962	Kan 管 – 1276
Kai 飼 – 830	Kama 構 – 141	Kan 干 – 1306
Kai 戒 – 875	Kama 鎌 – 1667	Kan 巻 – 1309
Kai 懐 – 928	Kama 窯 – 1893	Kan 鑑 – 1310
Kai 怪 – 1024	Kama 釜 – 1896	Kan 歓 – 1323
Kai 壊 – 1394	Kame 亀 – 908	Kan 緩 – 1330
Kai 潰 – 1700	Kame 瓶 – 1711	Kan 監 – 1420
Kai 塊 – 1738	Kami 上 – 171	Kan 堪 – 1452
Kai 拐 – 1995	Kami 紙 – 221	Kan 患 – 1551
Kai 楷 – 2077	Kami 神 – 273	Kan 還 – 1587
Kaiko 蚕 – 1404	*Kami* 将 – 374	Kan 貫 – 1621
Kaka 係 – 492	Kami 髪 – 501	Kan 肝 – 1634
Kaka 関 – 701	Kaminari 雷 – 1723	Kan 陥 – 1660
Kaka 抱 – 986	Kamo 醸 – 1996	Kan 冠 – 1786
Kaka 揭 – 1466	Kan 慣 – 92	Kan 缶 – 1832
Kaka 拘 – 1809	Kan 漢 – 197	Kan 敢 – 1852
Kakari 係 – 492	Kan 乾 – 290	Kan 喚 – 1885
Kaki 垣 – 777	Kan 館 – 305	Kan 閑 – 1913
Kaki 柿 – 1947	Kan 間 – 411	Kan 棺 – 2012
Kako 囲 – 1202	Kan 寒 – 507	Kan 憾 – 2065
Kaku 覚 – 54	Kan 甘 – 541	Kana 金 – 301
Kaku 画 – 77	Kan 換 – 554	Kana 奏 – 757
Kaku 角 – 81	Kan 汗 – 629	Kana 悲 – 851
Kaku 客 – 524	Kan 感 – 640	Kana 叶 – 1076
Kaku 確 – 619	Kan 簡 – 648	Kanba 芳 – 1677
Kaku 格 – 762	Kan 韓 – 655	Kaname 要 – 238
Kaku 隠 – 834	Kan 勧 – 698	Kanara 必 – 307
Kaku 獲 – 947	Kan 関 – 701	Kane 金 – 301
Kaku 各 – 1033	Kan 環 – 718	Kane 鐘 – 1840
Kaku 穫 – 1257	Kan 艦 – 737	Kanga 考 – 469
Kaku 革 – 1286	Kan 完 – 759	Kanmuri 冠 – 1786
Kaku 拡 – 1287	Kan 官 – 880	Kano 彼 – 371
Kaku 閣 – 1409	Kan 観 – 886	Kao 顔 – 95
Kaku 核 – 1548	Kan 刊 – 990	Kao 香 – 681
Kaku 較 – 1632	Kan 幹 – 1062	Kao 薫 – 1951
Kaku 隔 – 1729	Kan 勘 – 1161	Kara 絡 – 230
Kaku 括 – 1762	Kan 看 – 1164	Kara 空 – 248
Kaku 郭 – 1843	Kan 寛 – 1205	Kara 辛 – 384

Kara 唐 – 1600	Katsu 葛 – 1531	Kei 計 – 434
Kara 殻 – 1904	Katsu 括 – 1762	Kei 係 – 492
Karada 体 – 124	Katsu 喝 – 1934	Kei 京 – 514
Kare 彼 – 371	Katsu 轄 – 1966	Kei 景 – 516
Kari 狩 – 923	Kawa 川 – 250	Kei 形 – 573
Kari 仮 – 1456	Kawa 乾 – 290	Kei 継 – 635
Karo 軽 – 289	Kawa 皮 – 833	Kei 境 – 719
Karu 軽 – 289	Kawa 河 – 1182	Kei 恵 – 720
Kasa 重 – 284	Kawa 革 – 1286	Kei 鶏 – 754
Kasa 笠 – 1311	Kawa 渇 – 1928	Kei 敬 – 873
Kasa 傘 – 1743	Kawara 瓦 – 1710	Kei 警 – 874
Kase 稼 – 1668	Kayo 通 – 365	Kei 傾 – 925
Kashiko 賢 – 1290	Kaza 風 – 479	Kei 競 – 935
Kashira 頭 – 93	Kaza 飾 – 1203	Kei 携 – 1011
Kasu 微 – 1442	Kaze 風 – 479	Kei 径 – 1097
Kata 方 – 114	Kazo 数 – 639	Kei 型 – 1116
Kata 片 – 181	Kazu 数 – 639	Kei 詣 – 1204
Kata 語 – 435	Ke 消 – 158	Kei 刑 – 1325
Kata 形 – 573	Ke 決 – 180	Kei 渓 – 1384
Kata 固 – 731	Ke 結 – 231	Kei 系 – 1393
Kata 肩 – 845	*Ke* 今 – 292	Kei 掲 – 1466
Kata 衣 – 1042	Ke 気 – 321	Kei 憩 – 1477
Kata 型 – 1116	Ke 家 – 405	Kei 慶 – 1590
Kata 堅 – 1246	Ke 化 – 487	Kei 契 – 1602
Kata 硬 – 1412	*Ke* 景 – 516	Kei 稽 – 1715
Kata 潟 – 1736	Ke 毛 – 688	Kei 啓 – 1744
Katachi 形 – 573	Ke 血 – 747	Kei 茎 – 1894
Katamari 塊 – 1738	Ke 蹴 – 975	Kei 蛍 – 2023
Kataki 敵 – 881	Ke 怪 – 1024	Kemono 獣 – 1733
Katamu 傾 – 925	Ke 潔 – 1212	Kemu 煙 – 1415
Katana 刀 – 102	Ke 欠 – 1238	Kemuri 煙 – 1415
Katawa 傍 – 1633	Ke 華 – 1354	Ken 見 – 53
Katayo 偏 – 1757	Ke 仮 – 1456	Ken 犬 – 190
Kate 糧 – 1789	Ke 懸 – 1597	Ken 険 – 196
Katsu 活 – 260	Ke 傑 – 1808	Ken 建 – 363
Katsu 割 – 562	Kega 汚 – 467	Ken 験 – 382
Katsu 担 – 729	Kei 経 – 224	Ken 間 – 411
Katsu 滑 – 981	Kei 軽 – 289	Ken 研 – 442
	Kei 兄 – 420	

Ken 件 – 488	Ki 消 – 158	Ki 騎 – 1449
Ken 県 – 572	Ki 決 – 180	Ki 紀 – 1464
Ken 遣 – 765	Ki 喫 – 192	Ki 棄 – 1624
Ken 健 – 811	Ki 生 – 208	Ki 幾 – 1628
Ken 嫌 – 817	Ki 気 – 321	Ki 既 – 1639
Ken 肩 – 845	Ki 来 – 327	Ki 岐 – 1657
Ken 検 – 859	Ki 聞 – 412	Ki 棋 – 1726
Ken 権 – 916	Ki 起 – 452	Ki 軌 – 1827
Ken 謙 – 965	*Ki* 酒 – 465	Ki 忌 – 1922
Ken 軒 – 1146	Ki 危 – 547	Kiba 牙 – 921
Ken 堅 – 1246	Ki 記 – 550	Kibi 厳 – 902
Ken 賢 – 1290	Ki 利 – 564	Kichi 吉 – 1453
Ken 券 – 1305	Ki 帰 – 566	Kiku 菊 – 1611
Ken 兼 – 1401	Ki 喜 – 599	Kimi 君 – 419
Ken 剣 – 1432	Ki 寄 – 604	Kimo 肝 – 1634
Ken 憲 – 1438	Ki 貴 – 643	Kin 金 – 301
Ken 拳 – 1554	Ki 希 – 663	Kin 近 – 390
Ken 懸 – 1597	Ki 期 – 711	Kin 勤 – 517
Ken 献 – 1618	Ki 器 – 853	Kin 緊 – 732
Ken 圏 – 1681	Ki 奇 – 854	Kin 禁 – 943
Ken 顕 – 1725	Ki 亀 – 908	Kin 均 – 988
Ken 倹 – 2064	Ki 飢 – 924	Kin 菌 – 1210
Keta 桁 – 2025	Ki 祈 – 955	Kin 筋 – 1426
Ketsu 決 – 180	Ki 黄 – 976	Kin 巾 – 1921
Ketsu 結 – 231	Ki 輝 – 979	Kin 謹 – 2011
Ketsu 血 – 747	*Ki* 城 – 1008	Kin 斤 – 2071
Ketsu 穴 – 964	Ki 季 – 1047	Kinu 絹 – 1439
Ketsu 潔 – 1212	Ki 樹 – 1089	Kira 嫌 – 817
Ketsu 欠 – 1238	Ki 効 – 1139	Kiri 霧 – 1696
Ketsu 傑 – 1808	Ki 鬼 – 1168	Kishi 岸 – 500
Kewa 険 – 196	Ki 基 – 1198	Kiso 競 – 935
Kezu 削 – 1626	Ki 几 – 1243	Kita 北 – 373
Ki 昨 – 41	Ki 規 – 1341	Kita 鍛 – 1813
Ki 着 – 52	Ki 伎 – 1356	Kitana 汚 – 467
Ki 切 – 103	Ki 企 – 1382	Kitsu 喫 – 192
Ki 木 – 118	Ki 揮 – 1424	Kitsu 詰 – 781
Ki 機 – 137	Ki 旗 – 1430	Kitsu 吉 – 1453
Ki 机 – 140	Ki 汽 – 1431	Kiwa 際 – 379

Kiwa 極 – 610	Ko 顧 – 1648	Kon 建 – 363
Kiyo 清 – 1112	Ko 凝 – 1680	*Kon* 港 – 549
Kiza 刻 – 565	Ko 弧 – 1763	Kon 根 – 741
Kiza 兆 – 849	Ko 鼓 – 1776	Kon 昏 – 1074
Kizu 築 – 1219	Ko 枯 – 1834	Kon 混 – 1294
Kizu 傷 – 1376	Ko 乞 – 1839	Kon 献 – 1618
Ko 木 – 118	Ko 懲 – 1879	Kon 魂 – 1636
Ko 国 – 170	Ko 籠 – 2074	Kon 恨 – 1724
Ko 子 – 182	Koba 拒 – 1646	Kon 痕 – 1857
Ko 小 – 253	Kobushi 拳 – 1554	Kon 昆 – 1866
Ko 今 – 292	Koe 声 – 40	Kon 懇 – 1869
Ko 来 – 327	Kogo 凍 – 1707	Kon 紺 – 1886
Ko 去 – 343	Koi 恋 – 695	Kon 墾 – 2068
Ko 込 – 357	Koke 苔 – 957	Kona 粉 – 1104
Ko 古 – 392	*Koko* 心 – 306	Kono 好 – 239
Ko 故 – 394	Kokono 九 – 111	Koo 氷 – 814
Ko 個 – 395	Kokoro 心 – 306	Koo 凍 – 1707
Ko 呼 – 428	Kokoro 試 – 436	Koori 氷 – 814
Ko 越 – 453	Kokoroyo 快 – 734	Kore 是 – 1035
Ko 超 – 621	Kokoroza 志 –1145	Koro 頃 – 96
Ko 己 – 652	Kokorozashi 志 – 1145	Koro 転 – 285
Ko 湖 – 716	Koku 黒 – 76	Koro 殺 – 838
Ko 孤 – 723	Koku 国 – 170	Koromo 衣 – 1042
Ko 固 – 731	Koku 告 – 429	Koshi 越 – 453
Ko 焦 – 750	Koku 石 – 458	Koshi 腰 – 884
Ko 骨 – 832	Koku 刻 – 565	Kosu 擦 – 1429
Ko 戸 – 871	Koku 穀 – 1172	Kota 答 – 295
Ko 庫 – 919	Koku 谷 – 1383	Kota 応 – 677
Ko 請 – 1064	Koku 酷 – 1695	Koto 事 – 416
Ko 粉 – 1104	Koku 克 – 1718	Koto 言 – 430
Ko 濃 – 1106	Koma 細 – 220	Koto 異 – 970
Ko 妓 – 1121	Koma 困 – 280	Koto 殊 – 1675
Ko 拠 – 1151	Kome 米 – 326	Koto 琴 – 1712
Ko 混 – 1294	Komi 込 – 357	Kotobuki 寿 – 607
Ko 雇 – 1398	Kon 婚 – 240	Kotowa 断 – 704
Ko 肥 – 1406	Kon 困 – 280	Kotsu 骨 – 832
Ko 誇 – 1635	Kon 今 – 292	Kou 公 – 16
Ko 股 – 1640	Kon 金 – 301	Kou 高 – 19

Kou 校 – 130	Kou 航 – 1295	Ku 暮 – 641
Kou 構 – 141	Kou 耕 – 1312	Ku 悔 – 675
Kou 交 – 144	Kou 鉱 – 1327	Ku 組 – 752
Kou 郊 – 145	Kou 攻 – 1395	Ku 駆 – 776
Kou 降 – 178	Kou 硬 – 1412	Ku 句 – 872
Kou 厚 – 185	Kou 皇 – 1458	Ku 屈 – 927
Kou 好 – 239	Kou 后 – 1459	Ku 繰 – 1034
Kou 工 – 246	Kou 稿 – 1467	Ku 朽 – 2000
Kou 紅 – 247	Kou 孝 – 1471	Kuba 配 – 466
Kou 神 – 273	Kou 鋼 – 1472	Kubi 首 – 56
Kou 行 – 334	Kou 仰 – 1549	Kuchi 口 – 426
Kou 後 – 335	Kou 項 – 1573	Kuchibiru 唇 – 1565
Kou 向 – 340	Kou 貢 – 1617	Kuda 下 – 172
Kou 幸 – 385	Kou 控 – 1637	*Kuda* 果 – 587
Kou 口 – 426	Kou 巧 – 1727	Kuda 管 – 1276
Kou 光 – 448	Kou 絞 – 1739	Kuda 砕 – 1845
Kou 考 – 469	Kou 恒 – 1800	*Kue* 方 – 114
Kou 広 – 494	Kou 拘 – 1809	Kugi 釘 – 825
Kou 港 – 549	Kou 溝 – 1825	Kuji 挫 – 1976
Kou 功 – 634	Kou 酵 – 1836	Kujira 鯨 – 1981
Kou 垢 – 665	Kou 衡 – 1875	Kuki 茎 – 1894
Kou 香 – 681	Kou 肯 – 1929	Kuma 熊 – 1262
Kou 興 – 693	Kou 梗 – 1992	Kumi 組 – 752
Kou 慌 – 710	Kou 勾 – 2047	Kumo 雲 – 264
Kou 格 – 762	Kou 孔 – 2078	Kumo 曇 – 1911
Kou 喉 – 794	Kowa 怖 – 463	Kun 君 – 419
Kou 康 – 831	Kowa 壊 – 1394	Kun 訓 – 1090
Kou 荒 – 968	Ku 公 – 16	Kun 勲 – 1938
Kou 黄 – 976	Ku 久 – 30	Kun 薫 – 1951
Kou 侯 – 996	Ku 九 – 111	Kuni 国 – 170
Kou 更 – 1000	Ku 工 – 246	Kura 暗 – 268
Kou 江 – 1026	Ku 区 – 320	Kura 比 – 857
Kou 講 – 1027	*Ku* 気 – 321	Kura 眩 – 937
Kou 洪 – 1119	Ku 来 – 327	Kura 倉 – 1170
Kou 効 – 1139	Ku 苦 – 393	Kura 蔵 – 1190
Kou 甲 – 1157	Ku 食 – 398	Kurai 位 – 270
Kou 抗 – 1196	Ku 口 – 426	Kuro 黒 – 76
Kou 購 – 1269	Ku 供 – 486	*Kurou* 玄 – 1252

Kuru 苦 – 393	Kyou 橋 – 139	Kyuu 及 – 883
Kuru 狂 – 1566	Kyou 教 – 187	Kyuu 嗅 – 959
Kuruma 車 – 283	Kyou 狭 – 194	Kyuu 救 – 977
Kusa 腐 – 722	Kyou 経 – 224	Kyuu 給 – 997
Kusa 草 – 909	Kyou 今 – 292	Kyuu 旧 – 1017
Kusa 臭 – 1381	Kyou 兄 – 420	Kyuu 弓 – 1044
Kusari 鎖 – 1436	Kyou 強 – 478	Kyuu 宮 – 1079
Kuse 癖 – 1215	Kyou 供 – 486	Kyuu 級 – 1131
Kushi 串 – 2052	Kyou 京 – 514	Kyuu 丘 – 1473
Kusuri 薬 – 521	Kyou 興 – 693	Kyuu 窮 – 1805
Kutsu 靴 – 603	Kyou 境 – 719	Kyuu 朽 – 2000
Kutsu 屈 – 927	Kyou 叫 – 746	Kyuu 糾 – 2029
Kutsu 掘 – 1402	Kyou 胸 – 775	*Ma* 手 – 23
Kutsu 窟 – 1920	Kyou 響 – 840	Ma 増 – 61
Kutsugae 覆 – 893	Kyou 恐 – 869	Ma 曲 – 82
Kuu 空 – 248	Kyou 脅 – 914	Ma 負 – 87
Kuwa 加 – 714	Kyou 競 – 935	Ma 真 – 101
Kuwa 詳 – 1579	Kyou 協 – 940	Ma 末 – 119
Kuwada 企 – 1382	Kyou 共 – 969	Ma 磨 – 126
Kuya 悔 – 675	Kyou 驚 – 971	Ma 交 – 144
Kuzu 崩 – 973	Kyou 郷 – 1059	Ma 待 – 217
Kuzu 葛 – 1531	Kyou 況 – 1249	*Ma* 女 – 235
Kya 客 – 524	Kyou 鏡 – 1355	Ma 間 – 411
Kyaku 客 – 524	Kyou 狂 – 1566	Ma 先 – 422
Kyaku 却 – 1562	Kyou 凶 – 1794	Ma 舞 – 584
Kyaku 脚 – 1563	Kyou 峡 – 1818	Ma 馬 – 958
Kyo 去 – 343	Kyou 享 – 1842	Ma 混 – 1294
Kyo 巨 – 689	Kyou 矯 – 2061	Ma 巻 – 1309
Kyo 距 – 717	Koyomi 暦 – 1801	Ma 魔 – 1332
Kyo 居 – 809	Kyuu 泣 – 12	Ma 摩 – 1428
Kyo 虚 – 966	Kyuu 久 – 30	Ma 麻 – 1475
Kyo 許 – 1141	Kyuu 九 – 111	Ma 抹 – 2017
Kyo 拠 – 1151	Kyuu 究 – 112	Maboroshi 幻 - 1129
Kyo 挙 – 1362	Kyuu 休 – 122	Mabu 眩 – 937
Kyo 拒 – 1646	Kyuu 急 – 312	Machi 町 – 70
Kyoku 曲 – 82	Kyuu 吸 – 427	Machi 街 – 625
Kyoku 極 – 610	Kyuu 球 – 606	Mado 窓 – 311
Kyoku 局 – 867	Kyuu 求 – 810	Mado 惑 – 624

Mae 前 – 157	Masu 升 – 2049	Metsu 滅 – 1193
Magi 紛 – 1638	Mata 又 – 24	Mezura 珍 – 407
Mago 孫 – 1072	Mata 股 – 1640	Mi 三 – 3
Mai 枚 – 129	Matata 瞬 – 773	Mi 見 – 53
Mai 妹 – 244	Mato 的 – 45	Mi 土 – 59
Mai 米 – 326	Matsu 末 – 119	Mi 実 – 195
Mai 毎 – 336	Matsu 祭 – 377	Mi 味 – 245
Mai 参 – 406	Matsu 松 – 1025	Mi 神 – 273
Mai 舞 – 584	Matsuri 祭 – 377	Mi 身 – 651
Mai 迷 – 623	Matta 全 – 300	Mi 未 – 672
Mai 埋 – 1523	Mawa 回 – 4	Mi 美 – 771
Mai 昧 – 1941	Mawa 周 – 630	Mi 観 – 886
Maji 交 – 144	*Mawa* 巡 – 778	Mi 満 – 1153
Maka 任 – 483	Mayo 迷 – 623	Mi 魅 – 1169
Maki 巻 – 1309	Mayu 眉 – 1645	Mi 箕 – 1178
Maki 薪 – 1965	Mazu 貧 – 1339	Mi 密 – 1188
Makoto 真 – 101	Me 目 – 51	Mi 診 – 1242
Makoto 誠 – 1506	Me 召 – 106	*Mi* 模 – 1353
Maku 幕 – 653	Me 女 – 235	Michi 道 – 349
Maku 膜 – 1759	*Me* 愛 – 523	Michi 路 – 525
Makura 枕 – 1770	Me 滅 – 1193	Michibi 導 – 1261
Mame 豆 – 721	Me 芽 – 1417	Mida 乱 – 1020
Mamo 守 – 214	Me 眼 – 1423	Mida 淫 – 1877
Man 万 – 113	Megu 恵 – 720	Midori 緑 – 227
Man 慢 – 1127	Megu 巡 – 778	Miga 磨 – 126
Man 満 – 1153	Mei 明 – 154	Migi 右 – 457
Man 漫 – 1319	Mei 名 – 162	Miji 惨 – 1678
Mana 学 – 184	Mei 迷 – 623	Mijika 短 – 324
Mana 愛 – 523	Mei 鳴 – 751	Mikado 帝 – 1538
Mana 眼 – 1423	Mei 命 – 961	Miki 幹 – 1062
Mane 招 – 560	Mei 盟 – 1513	Mimi 耳 – 57
Manuga 免 – 1140	Mei 銘 – 1666	Min 明 – 154
Maro 円 – 39	Men 面 – 282	Min 民 – 375
Maru 円 – 39	Men 免 – 1140	Min 眠 – 376
Maru 丸 – 866	Men 綿 – 1189	Mina 皆 – 597
Masa 勝 – 149	Men 麺 – 1228	Minami 南 – 388
Masa 正 – 174	Meshi 飯 – 400	Minamoto 源 – 1267
Masu 益 – 1407	Mesu 雌 – 2031	Minato 港 – 549

Mine 峰 – 938	Moku 黙 – 836	Mu 夢 – 165
Miniku 醜 – 1882	*Momi* 紅 – 247	Mu 向 – 340
Minna 皆 – 597	Momo 股 – 1640	Mu 務 – 518
Mino 実 – 195	Momo 桃 – 1728	Mu 無 – 583
Misaki 岬 – 1942	Mon 文 – 25	Mu 群 – 929
Mise 店 – 493	Mon 門 – 409	Mu 蒸 – 1101
Mito 認 – 1036	Mon 問 – 410	Mu 武 – 1418
Mitsu 三 – 3	Mon 悶 – 807	Mu 謀 – 1544
Mitsu 光 – 448	Mon 紋 – 1676	Mu 剥 – 1567
Mitsu 密 – 1188	Mono 者 – 276	Mu 剝 – 1567
Mitsu 蜜 – 1255	Mono 物 – 401	Mu 霧 – 1696
Miya 雅 – 922	Moppa 専 – 1235	Mu 矛 – 1749
Miya 宮 – 1079	Mori 森 – 127	Mugi 麦 – 1103
Miyako 都 – 277	Mori 守 – 214	Mui 六 – 17
Mizo 溝 – 1825	Moro 諸 – 1315	Muka 迎 – 358
Mizu 水 – 251	Moto 本 – 123	Mukashi 昔 – 33
Mizuka 自 – 55	Moto 下 – 172	Muko 婿 – 1960
Mizuumi 湖 – 716	Moto 元 – 421	Muku 報 – 386
Mo 文 – 25	Moto 求 – 810	Muna 空 – 248
Mo 最 – 42	Moto 基 – 1198	Muna 胸 – 775
Mo 木 – 118	Motsu 物 – 401	Mune 宗 – 676
Mo 持 – 216	Motto 最 – 42	Mune 胸 – 775
Mo 以 – 601	Mou 申 – 10	Mune 棟 – 1271
Mo 漏 – 740	Mou 亡 – 585	Mura 村 – 131
Mo 盛 – 1018	Mou 望 – 664	Mura 群 – 929
Mo 燃 – 1240	Mou 毛 – 688	Murasaki 紫 – 1665
Mo 模 – 1353	Mou 猛 – 953	Muro 室 – 62
Mo 喪 – 1828	Mou 設 – 1068	Mushi 虫 – 9
Mo 藻 – 2008	Mou 詣 – 1204	Musu 結 – 231
Mo 萌 – 2087	*Mou* 撲 – 1375	*Musu* 息 – 315
Mochi 用 – 364	Mou 網 – 1448	Musume 娘 – 316
Mochi 餅 – 743	Mou 妄 – 1961	Mutsu 睦 – 1989
Moda 悶 – 807	Mou 盲 – 1980	Muzuka 難 – 198
Modo 戻 – 75	Mou 耗 – 2050	Myaku 脈 – 770
Moe 萌 – 2087	Moude 詣 – 1204	Myou 明 – 154
Mogu 潜 – 1586	Moushi 申 – 10	Myou 名 – 162
Moku 目 – 51	Moyoo 催 – 1110	Myou 妙 – 856
Moku 木 – 118	Mu 六 – 17	Myou 命 – 961

Na 泣 – 12	Name 滑 – 981	Nega 願 – 94
Na 人 – 13	Nami 並 – 575	Nei 寧 – 703
Na 慣 – 92	Nami 波 – 878	Neko 猫 – 72
Na 菜 – 121	Namida 涙 – 649	Nemu 眠 – 376
Na 名 – 162	Nan 男 – 109	Nen 年 – 177
Na 生 – 208	Nan 難 – 198	Nen 念 – 314
Na 投 – 558	Nan 何 – 338	Nen 然 – 611
Na 並 – 575	Nan 南 – 388	Nen 燃 – 1240
Na 無 – 583	Nan 軟 – 1883	Nen 粘 – 1359
Na 亡 – 585	Nana 七 – 20	Nen 捻 – 1975
Na 成 – 633	Nana 斜 – 910	Nera 狙 – 948
Na 那 – 669	Nani 何 – 338	Neta 妬 – 1891
Na 納 – 705	Nanigashi 某 – 1887	Netsu 熱 – 65
Na 鳴 – 751	Nano 七 – 20	Ni 二 – 2
Na 撫 – 846	Nao 治 – 539	Ni 日 – 32
Na 奈 – 1006	Nao 直 – 570	Ni 荷 – 342
Na 萎 – 2022	Nao 尚 – 1629	Ni 似 – 824
Nabe 辺 – 362	Nara 習 – 472	Ni 逃 – 850
Nabe 鍋 – 1374	Nara 並 – 575	Ni 児 – 1093
Nado 等 – 1132	Nari 成 – 633	Ni 煮 – 1377
Nae 苗 – 1740	Nasa 情 – 156	Ni 仁 – 1496
Naga 長 – 502	Nashi 梨 – 1184	Ni 尼 – 1899
Naga 流 – 654	*Nata* 向 – 340	Nibu 鈍 – 1245
Naga 永 – 870	Natsu 夏 – 522	Nichi 日 – 32
Naga 眺 – 1136	Natsu 懐 – 928	Niga 苦 – 393
Nage 嘆 – 792	Nawa 縄 – 1003	Nigi 握 – 1372
Nago 和 – 513	Naya 悩 – 1181	Nigo 濁 – 1831
Nagu 殴 – 1748	Nazo 謎 – 1704	Nii 新 – 389
Nagusa 慰 – 1752	Ne 熱 – 65	*Nii* 兄 – 420
Nai 内 – 396	Ne 練 – 229	Niji 虹 – 2018
Naka 中 – 8	Ne 音 – 266	Niku 難 – 198
Naka 半 – 331	Ne 寝 – 372	Niku 肉 – 397
Naka 仲 – 657	Ne 値 – 571	Niku 憎 – 1651
Naka 腹 – 863	Ne 廻 – 692	Nin 人 – 13
Naki 亡 – 585	Ne 根 – 741	Nin 任 – 483
Nama 生 – 208	*Ne* 似 – 824	Nin 認 – 1036
Nama 怠 – 1498	Neba 粘 – 1359	Nin 忍 – 1433
Namari 鉛 – 1092	*Nee* 姉 – 241	Nin 仁 – 1496

Nin 妊 – 1731	Nozo 望 – 664	O 美 – 771
Nina 担 – 729	Nozo 覗 – 982	O 追 – 821
Nio 匂 – 949	Nozo 臨 – 1515	O 折 – 892
Nio 臭 – 1381	Nu 抜 – 749	O 推 – 1029
Nise 偽 – 1622	Nu 塗 – 1041	O 老 – 1065
Nishi 西 – 464	Nu 脱 – 1386	O 御 – 1440
Nishiki 錦 – 1880	Nu 縫 – 1816	O 伯 – 1572
Niwa 庭 – 495	Nugu 拭 – 1114	O 惜 – 1708
Niwatori 鶏 – 754	Nuku 温 – 257	Obi 帯 – 1012
No 飲 – 399	Numa 沼 – 1525	Obiya 脅 – 914
No 乗 – 509	Nuno 布 – 687	Obo 覚 – 54
No 野 – 545	Nushi 主 – 166	Obo 溺 – 1978
No 伸 – 697	Nusu 盗 – 1289	Ochii 陥 – 1660
No 延 – 842	Nya 若 – 461	Oda 穏 – 1703
No 退 – 926	Nyou 女 – 235	Odo 踊 – 366
No 載 – 1175	Nyou 尿 – 1298	Odo 脅 – 914
No 述 – 1328	Nyuu 入 – 14	Odoro 驚 – 971
Nobe 延 – 842	Nyuu 乳 – 186	Oga 拝 – 593
Nobo 上 – 171	Nyuu 柔 – 546	Ogina 補 – 995
Nobo 登 – 297	O 一 – 1	Oka 冒 – 812
Nobo 昇 – 1363	O 百 – 47	Oka 犯 – 901
Nochi 後 – 335	O 負 – 87	Oka 丘 – 1473
Nodo 喉 – 794	O 男 – 109	Oka 岡 – 1528
Noga 逃 – 850	O 下 – 172	Oka 侵 – 1591
Noki 軒 – 1146	O 降 – 178	Oki 沖 – 1002
Noko 残 – 605	O 生 – 208	Oko 怒 – 319
Nonoshi 罵 – 1927	O 緒 – 232	Oko 興 – 693
Noo 面 – 282	O 終 – 233	Okona 行 – 334
Noro 呪 – 1844	O 女 – 235	Okota 怠 – 1498
Nou 日 – 32	O 小 – 253	Oku 屋 – 63
Nou 能 – 616	O 悪 – 313	Oku 贈 – 84
Nou 納 – 705	O 起 – 452	Oku 億 – 318
Nou 農 – 1105	O 汚 – 467	Oku 送 – 348
Nou 濃 – 1106	O 和 – 513	Oku 遅 – 350
Nou 悩 – 1181	O 落 – 526	Oku 奥 – 532
Nou 皇 – 1458	O 置 – 569	Oku 憶 – 1540
Nou 脳 – 1461	O 押 – 592	Oku 臆 – 1973
Nozo 除 – 646	O 織 – 753	Omo 母 – 50

Omo 主 – 166	Oshi 押 – 592	Pa 把 – 1817
Omo 面 – 282	Oso 教 – 187	Pai 配 – 466
Omo 重 – 284	Oso 遅 – 350	Pai 敗 – 793
Omo 思 – 308	Oso 恐 – 869	Pai 杯 – 848
Omo 想 – 905	Oso 襲 – 941	Pai 廃 – 1221
Omomu 赴 – 1888	Osu 雄 – 1518	Pai 輩 – 1607
Omomuki 趣 - 715	*Oto* 大 – 188	Paku 白 – 44
Omote 表 – 582	Oto 音 – 266	Paku 泊 – 46
On 温 – 257	Oto 劣 – 1746	Paku 博 – 1481
On 音 – 266	Oto 乙 – 1835	Pan 飯 – 400
On 恩 – 1388	Otoko 男 – 109	Pan 般 – 1050
On 御 – 1440	Otoro 衰 – 1753	Pan 判 – 1054
On 雄 – 1518	Otouto 弟 – 529	Pan 版 – 1086
On 穏 – 1703	Otozu 訪 – 713	Pan 板 – 1166
On 怨 – 1910	Otsu 乙 – 1835	Pan 繁 – 1266
Ona 同 – 339	Otto 夫 – 614	Pan 帆 – 1768
Oni 鬼 – 1168	Ou 横 – 135	Pan 搬 – 1993
Onna 女 – 235	Ou 奥 – 532	Pana 放 – 117
Ono 自 – 55	Ou 押 – 592	Para 腹 – 863
Onore 己 – 652	Ou 応 – 677	Pashi 端 – 730
Oo 多 – 161	Ou 黄 – 976	Patsu 発 – 298
Oo 大 – 188	Ou 央 – 1063	Patsu 髪 – 501
Oo 覆 – 893	Ou 王 – 1077	Pei 併 – 1655
Ooyake 公 – 16	Ou 欧 – 1334	Peki 壁 – 1051
Ore 俺 – 956	Ou 往 – 1416	Peki 癖 – 1215
Ori 織 – 753	Ou 皇 – 1458	Peki 璧 – 1933
Ori 折 – 892	Ou 旺 – 2045	Pen 片 – 181
Oro 卸 – 1218	Ougi 扇 – 1833	Pen 編 – 1052
Oro 愚 – 1580	Owa 終 – 233	Pen 遍 – 1830
Oroshi 卸 – 1218	Oya 親 – 383	Pi 費 – 656
Oroso 疎 – 1806	Oyo 泳 – 255	Pi 秘 – 1187
Osa 治 – 539	Oyo 及 – 883	Pi 否 – 1329
Osa 納 – 705	Oyo 凡 – 1511	Piki 匹 – 818
Osa 修 – 1049	Pa 張 – 477	Pin 品 – 5
Osa 収 – 1113	Pa 端 – 730	Piru 昼 – 49
Osa 抑 – 1584	Pa 派 – 764	Pitsu 筆 – 1091
Osana 幼 – 1400	Pa 破 – 837	Pitsu 泌 – 1297
Oshi 教 – 187	Pa 波 – 878	Po 歩 – 408

Po 舗 – 1237	Raku 落 – 526	Ri 痢 – 2055
Pon 本 – 123	Raku 酪 – 2069	Richi 律 – 417
Poro 幌 – 2082	Ran 卵 – 28	Riki 力 – 107
Pou 方 – 114	Ran 乱 – 1020	Riku 陸 – 1015
Pou 放 – 117	Ran 欄 – 1470	Rin 林 – 125
Pou 法 – 344	Ran 覧 – 1514	Rin 隣 – 329
Pou 砲 – 738	Ran 蘭 – 2088	Rin 輪 – 690
Pou 峰 – 938	Re 列 – 1124	Rin 鈴 – 1370
Pou 邦 – 1593	Rei 礼 – 275	Rin 臨 – 1515
Pou 泡 – 1861	Rei 冷 – 299	Rin 倫 – 1685
Pou 俸 – 2056	Rei 令 – 962	Ritsu 立 – 11
Pu 付 – 132	Rei 令 – 962	Ritsu 律 – 417
Pu 符 – 133	Rei 齢 – 989	Ritsu 率 – 1408
Pu 風 – 479	Rei 例 – 1317	Ro 呂 – 7
Pu 婦 – 1165	Rei 励 – 1338	Ro 六 – 17
Pu 賦 – 2058	Rei 霊 – 1575	Ro 路 – 525
Puku 服 – 150	Rei 隷 – 1583	Ro 露 – 1390
Puku 復 – 527	Rei 零 – 1946	Ro 炉 – 1758
Puku 腹 – 863	Reki 歴 – 1313	Roku 六 – 17
Puku 覆 – 893	Reki 暦 – 1801	Roku 録 – 999
Pun 分 – 105	Ren 練 – 229	Roku 麓 – 1955
Pun 憤 – 1781	Ren 連 – 353	Ron 論 – 813
Puu 風 – 479	Ren 恋 – 695	Rou 漏 – 740
Pyaku 百 – 47	Ren 錬 – 1814	Rou 浪 – 805
Pyou 表 – 582	Ren 蓮 – 2075	Rou 老 – 1065
Pyou 俵 – 1492	Retsu 列 – 1124	Rou 労 – 1075
Pyou 票 – 1510	Retsu 裂 – 1465	Rou 郎 – 1343
Ra 良 – 303	Retsu 烈 – 1610	Rou 露 – 1390
Ra 楽 – 520	Retsu 劣 – 1746	Rou 廊 – 1605
Ra 等 – 1132	Ri 立 – 11	Rou 楼 – 1819
Ra 羅 – 1158	Ri 人 – 13	Rou 弄 – 1924
Ra 裸 – 1615	Ri 理 – 78	Ru 留 – 71
Ra 拉 – 1767	*Ri* 荷 – 342	Ru 流 – 654
Rai 頼 – 98	Ri 利 – 564	Rui 類 – 97
Rai 来 – 327	Ri 離 – 666	Rui 塁 – 1853
Rai 雷 – 1723	Ri 裏 – 887	Rui 累 – 2006
Raku 絡 – 230	Ri 里 – 1060	Ryaku 略 – 1272
Raku 楽 – 520	Ri 履 – 1220	Ryo 旅 – 116

Ryo 虜 – 1107	Sa 割 – 562	Sai 際 – 379
Ryo 慮 – 1194	Sa 冊 – 568	Sai 西 – 464
Ryo 侶 – 1982	Sa 差 – 631	Sai 才 – 617
Ryoku 力 – 107	Sa 指 – 691	Sai 災 – 1019
Ryoku 緑 – 227	Sa 札 – 735	Sai 再 – 1032
Ryou 良 – 303	Sa 砂 – 782	Sai 催 – 1110
Ryou 料 – 512	Sa 避 – 802	Sai 載 – 1175
Ryou 涼 – 515	Sa 殺 – 838	Sai 塞 – 1227
Ryou 両 – 579	Sa 査 – 860	Sai 栽 – 1233
Ryou 漁 – 685	Sa 察 – 896	Sai 採 – 1425
Ryou 了 – 760	Sa 佐 – 993	Sai 財 – 1437
Ryou 量 – 1061	*Sa* 再 – 1032	Sai 裁 – 1450
Ryou 療 – 1069	Sa 刺 – 1284	Sai 斎 – 1560
Ryou 領 – 1126	Sa 鎖 – 1436	Sai 債 – 1571
Ryou 猟 – 1397	Sa 裂 – 1465	Sai 彩 – 1630
Ryou 寮 – 1501	Sa 沙 – 1612	Sai 宰 – 1803
Ryou 僚 – 1592	Sa 錯 – 1771	Sai 砕 – 1845
Ryou 糧 – 1789	Sa 詐 – 1858	Sai 采 – 1935
Ryou 瞭 – 2002	Sa 唆 – 1990	Sai 埼 – 1939
Ryuu 立 – 11	Saba 捌 – 1350	Saiwa 幸 – 385
Ryuu 留 – 71	Sabi 寂 – 864	Saka 酒 – 465
Ryuu 流 – 654	Sachi 幸 – 385	Saka 逆 – 894
Ryuu 粒 – 1135	Sada 定 – 455	Saka 阪 – 1005
Ryuu 柳 – 1535	Saegi 遮 – 1892	Saka 盛 – 1018
Ryuu 竜 – 1569	Saga 性 – 209	Saka 坂 – 1130
Ryuu 隆 – 1594	Saga 探 – 699	Saka 栄 – 1263
Ryuu 硫 – 2001	*Saga* 相 – 787	Sakai 境 – 719
Sa 早 – 34	Saga 捜 – 1520	Sakai 堺 – 2083
Sa 覚 – 54	Sagesu 蔑 – 1983	Sakana 魚 – 80
Sa 下 – 172	Sagu 探 – 699	Sakazuki 杯 – 848
Sa 咲 – 193	Sai 最 – 42	Sake 酒 – 465
Sa 茶 – 212	Sai 切 – 103	Sake 叫 – 746
Sa 朝 – 291	Sai 菜 – 121	Saki 先 – 422
Sa 冷 – 299	Sai 細 – 220	Saki 崎 – 1081
Sa 後 – 335	Sai 妻 – 237	Saku 昨 – 41
Sa 去 – 343	Sai 済 – 259	Saku 作 – 482
Sa 左 – 456	Sai 歳 – 322	Saku 柵 – 899
Sa 作 – 482	Sai 祭 – 377	Saku 索 – 1361

Saku 策 – 1479	Satsu 殺 – 838	Sei 生 – 208
Saku 削 – 1626	Satsu 察 – 896	Sei 性 – 209
Saku 錯 – 1771	Satsu 撮 – 1331	Sei 歳 – 322
Saku 搾 – 2038	Satsu 刷 – 1392	Sei 静 – 418
Sakura 桜 – 984	Satsu 擦 – 1429	Sei 西 – 464
Sakura 櫻 – 2086	Satsu 拶 – 1650	Sei 世 – 542
Sama 様 – 136	Sawa 触 – 475	Sei 製 – 580
Samata 妨 – 1917	Sawa 騒 – 826	Sei 成 – 633
Same 雨 – 261	Sawa 沢 – 1100	Sei 精 – 847
Samu 寒 – 507	Sawa 障 – 1495	Sei 斉 – 952
Samurai 侍 – 1118	Sazu 授 – 578	Sei 省 – 1010
San 三 – 3	*Se* 士 – 66	Sei 盛 – 1018
San 山 – 146	*Se* 勢 – 110	Sei 請 – 1064
San 散 – 159	Se 背 – 152	Sei 清 – 1112
San 産 – 210	Se 石 – 458	Sei 制 – 1155
San 参 – 406	*Se* 席 – 496	Sei 整 – 1247
San 算 – 789	Se 世 – 542	Sei 姓 – 1499
San 賛 – 1115	Se 責 – 772	Sei 聖 – 1500
San 蚕 – 1404	Se 積 – 931	Sei 誠 – 1506
San 酸 – 1480	Se 競 – 935	Sei 征 – 1641
San 惨 – 1678	Se 施 – 1067	Sei 牲 – 1765
San 桟 – 1977	Se 設 – 1068	Sei 誓 – 1780
Sao 青 – 155	*Se* 稲 – 1229	Sei 醒 – 1918
Sara 皿 – 567	Se 攻 – 1395	Sei 逝 – 1999
Sara 更 – 1000	Se 接 – 1446	Seki 昔 – 33
Saru 猿 – 1055	Se 瀬 – 1550	Seki 赤 – 447
Sasa 支 – 26	Se 摂 – 1713	Seki 石 – 458
Sashi 指 – 691	Se 窃 – 2062	Seki 席 – 496
Sashi 刺 – 1284	Seba 狭 – 194	Seki 関 – 701
Sashi 挿 – 1769	Sechi 節 – 1048	Seki 責 – 772
Saso 誘 – 1405	Sei 晴 – 37	Seki 積 – 931
Sato 郷 – 1059	Sei 声 – 40	Seki 跡 – 1111
Sato 里 – 1060	Sei 星 – 48	Seki 績 – 1345
Sato 悟 – 1526	Sei 勢 – 110	Seki 籍 – 1604
Sato 諭 – 1932	Sei 背 – 152	Seki 析 – 1606
Satoshi 諭 – 1932	Sei 青 – 155	Seki 脊 – 1867
Satsu 冊 – 568	Sei 正 – 174	Seki 戚 – 1884
Satsu 札 – 735	Sei 政 – 175	Seki 隻 – 1895

Seki 斥 – 2060	Setsu 設 – 1068	Shi 思 – 308
Sema 狭 – 194	Setsu 接 – 1446	Shi 知 – 323
Sema 迫 – 1316	Setsu 拙 – 1798	Shi 閉 – 414
Sen 千 – 22	*Sha* 三 – 3	Shi 試 – 436
Sen 線 – 228	Sha 社 – 271	Shi 強 – 478
Sen 川 – 250	Sha 者 – 276	Shi 使 – 480
Sen 泉 – 252	Sha 車 – 283	Shi 私 – 510
Sen 選 – 352	Sha 写 – 468	Shi 歯 – 533
Sen 先 – 422	Sha 借 – 485	Shi 次 – 536
Sen 洗 – 423	Sha 捨 – 594	Shi 始 – 540
Sen 船 – 602	Sha 舎 – 745	Shi 司 – 608
Sen 煎 – 650	Sha 砂 – 782	Shi 至 – 609
Sen 羨 – 662	Sha 斜 – 910	Shi 指 – 691
Sen 銭 – 744	Sha 射 – 932	Shi 氏 – 709
Sen 染 – 774	Sha 謝 – 1283	Shi 姿 – 763
Sen 鮮 – 858	Sha 遮 – 1892	Shi 染 – 774
Sen 旋 – 913	Sha 赦 – 1901	Shi 誌 – 786
Sen 戦 – 933	Shaku 石 – 458	Shi 飼 – 830
Sen 薦 – 1030	Shaku 借 – 485	Shi 視 – 844
Sen 専 – 1235	Shaku 尺 – 1484	Shi 敷 – 865
Sen 浅 – 1443	Shaku 釈 – 1516	Shi 祉 – 1066
Sen 宣 – 1519	Shaku 爵 – 1603	Shi 施 – 1067
Sen 占 – 1542	Shaku 酌 – 1958	Shi 志 – 1145
Sen 仙 – 1564	Shi 四 – 6	Shi 締 – 1173
Sen 潜 – 1586	Shi 支 – 26	Shi 脂 – 1180
Sen 繊 – 1815	Shi 自 – 55	Shi 刺 – 1284
Sen 扇 – 1833	Shi 室 – 62	Shi 湿 – 1300
Sen 践 – 1907	Shi 士 – 66	Shi 詩 – 1301
Sen 詮 – 1944	Shi 仕 – 67	Shi 史 – 1314
Sen 遷 – 1952	Shi 資 – 91	Shi 旨 – 1318
Sen 腺 – 2020	Shi 死 – 164	Shi 詞 – 1320
Sen 栓 – 2026	Shi 止 – 173	Shi 示 – 1347
Sen 箋 – 2051	Shi 子 – 182	Shi 師 – 1351
Setsu 切 – 103	Shi 失 – 206	Shi 占 – 1542
Setsu 雪 – 262	Shi 糸 – 219	Shi 執 – 1553
Setsu 説 – 439	Shi 紙 – 221	Shi 紫 – 1665
Setsu 折 – 892	Shi 姉 – 241	Shi 疾 – 1734
Setsu 節 – 1048	Shi 市 – 242	Shi 絞 – 1739

Shi 嫉 – 1890	Shin 心 – 306	Shita 舌 – 1213
Shi 肢 – 1900	Shin 寝 – 372	Shita 慕 – 1959
Shi 滋 – 1908	Shin 親 – 383	Shitaga 従 – 1485
Shi 漆 – 1957	Shin 辛 – 384	Shitata 滴 – 1854
Shi 叱 – 2073	Shin 新 – 389	Shitsu 室 – 62
Shiawa 幸 – 385	Shin 信 – 431	Shitsu 質 – 86
Shiba 芝 – 779	Shin 慎 – 632	Shitsu 失 – 206
Shiba 縛 – 1721	Shin 身 – 651	Shitsu 湿 – 1300
Shibara 暫 – 1943	Shin 深 – 694	Shitsu 執 – 1553
Shibo 絞 – 1739	Shin 伸 – 697	Shizu 静 – 418
Shibo 搾 – 2038	Shin 浸 – 797	Shizu 沈 – 835
Shibu 渋 – 1454	Shin 振 – 823	Shizu 鎮 – 1722
Shichi 七 – 20	Shin 津 – 877	Sho 初 – 104
Shichi 質 – 86	Shin 臣 – 1039	Sho 緒 – 232
Shige 茂 – 1186	Shin 針 – 1138	Sho 暑 – 278
Shige 繁 – 1266	Shin 診 – 1242	Sho 所 – 391
Shiita 虐 – 1679	Shin 審 – 1368	Sho 食 – 398
Shika 鹿 – 895	Shin 侵 – 1591	Sho 書 – 415
Shika 飾 – 1203	Shin 娠 – 1732	Sho 職 – 696
Shika 叱 – 2073	Shin 紳 – 1821	Sho 処 – 1149
Shiki 式 – 249	Shin 芯 – 1948	Sho 諸 – 1315
Shiki 色 – 473	Shina 品 – 5	Sho 署 – 1324
Shiki 織 – 753	Shino 忍 – 1433	Sho 庶 – 1795
Shiki 敷 – 865	Shio 塩 – 60	Shoku 食 – 398
Shiki 識 – 1335	Shio 潮 – 1308	Shoku 色 – 473
Shima 島 – 556	Shira 白 – 44	Shoku 触 – 475
Shimari 締 – 1173	Shira 調 – 441	Shoku 職 – 696
Shime 湿 – 1300	Shiri 尻 – 827	Shoku 飾 – 1203
Shime 示 – 1347	Shirizo 退 – 926	Shoku 植 – 1278
Shimo 下 – 172	Shiro 白 – 44	Shoku 嘱 – 1366
Shimo 霜 – 2032	Shiro 代 – 552	Shoku 殖 – 1396
Shimobe 僕 – 333	Shiro 城 – 1008	Shou 召 – 106
Shin 申 – 10	*Shirou* 素 – 712	Shou 勝 – 149
Shin 真 – 101	Shiru 記 – 550	Shou 消 – 158
Shin 森 – 127	Shiru 汁 – 900	Shou 正 – 174
Shin 進 – 203	Shirushi 印 – 1046	Shou 笑 – 199
Shin 震 – 265	Shita 下 – 172	Shou 生 – 208
Shin 神 – 273	Shita 親 – 383	Shou 性 – 209

Shou 小 – 253	Shou 匠 – 1653	Shuu 周 – 630
Shou 少 – 254	Shou 償 – 1662	Shuu 宗 – 676
Shou 将 – 374	Shou 掌 – 1717	Shuu 衆 – 930
Shou 焼 – 446	Shou 彰 – 1807	Shuu 襲 – 941
Shou 招 – 560	Shou 鐘 – 1840	Shuu 就 – 974
Shou 紹 – 658	Shou 奨 – 1906	Shuu 修 – 1049
Shou 焦 – 750	Shou 抄 – 2043	Shuu 州 – 1071
Shou 相 – 787	Shou 升 – 2049	Shuu 収 – 1113
Shou 照 – 822	Shu 手 – 23	Shuu 臭 – 1381
Shou 精 – 847	Shu 首 – 56	Shuu 秀 – 1517
Shou 象 – 906	Shu 取 – 58	Shuu 舟 – 1524
Shou 床 – 946	Shu 出 – 147	Shuu 執 – 1553
Shou 賞 – 991	Shu 主 – 166	Shuu 愁 – 1785
Shou 省 – 1010	Shu 守 – 214	Shuu 醜 – 1882
Shou 松 – 1025	Shu 酒 – 465	Shuu 酬 – 1902
Shou 装 – 1043	Shu 趣 – 715	Shuu 囚 – 1926
Shou 症 – 1085	Shu 狩 – 923	So 卒 – 27
Shou 称 – 1123	Shu 修 – 1049	So 祖 – 272
Shou 証 – 1150	Shu 種 – 1098	So 反 – 680
Shou 唱 – 1152	Shu 殊 – 1675	So 素 – 712
Shou 祥 – 1160	Shu 朱 – 1692	So 組 – 752
Shou 商 – 1217	Shu 腫 – 1701	So 染 – 774
Shou 晶 – 1231	Shuku 祝 – 274	So 添 – 841
Shou 礁 – 1270	Shuku 宿 – 491	So 想 – 905
Shou 渉 – 1307	Shuku 縮 – 1487	So 蘇 – 1279
Shou 承 – 1344	Shuku 淑 – 1684	So 粗 – 1326
Shou 昇 – 1363	Shuku 粛 – 1925	So 率 – 1408
Shou 章 – 1365	Shun 春 – 506	So 沿 – 1414
Shou 傷 – 1376	Shun 瞬 – 773	So 即 – 1502
Shou 粧 – 1387	Shun 旬 – 1304	So 訴 – 1545
Shou 昭 – 1410	Shutsu 出 – 147	So 削 – 1626
Shou 障 – 1495	Shuu 集 – 202	So 逸 – 1706
Shou 姓 – 1499	Shuu 終 – 233	So 措 – 1709
Shou 訟 – 1546	Shuu 祝 – 274	So 礎 – 1716
Shou 衝 – 1561	Shuu 週 – 346	So 疎 – 1806
Shou 詳 – 1579	Shuu 秋 – 445	So 阻 – 1838
Shou 肖 – 1625	Shuu 習 – 472	So 租 – 2015
Shou 尚 – 1629	Shuu 拾 – 595	Soba 側 – 490

Soda 育 – 151	Sou 素 – 712	Su 捨 – 594
Sode 袖 – 1697	Sou 奏 – 757	Su 寿 – 607
Soko 底 – 1096	Sou 壮 – 769	Su 素 – 712
Soko 損 – 1258	Sou 相 – 787	*Su* 相 – 787
Sokona 損 – 1258	Sou 爽 – 798	Su 巣 – 972
Soku 束 – 99	Sou 騒 – 826	Su 州 – 1071
Soku 息 – 315	Sou 想 – 905	Su 透 – 1253
Soku 速 – 359	Sou 草 – 909	Su 酢 – 1373
Soku 足 – 449	Sou 争 – 936	Su 刷 – 1392
Soku 側 – 490	Sou 巣 – 972	Su 擦 – 1429
Soku 測 – 1031	Sou 総 – 1038	Su 酸 – 1480
Soku 塞 – 1227	Sou 装 – 1043	Su 須 – 1616
Soku 則 – 1342	Sou 遭 – 1073	Su 棄 – 1624
Soku 促 – 1455	Sou 倉 – 1170	Su 澄 – 1674
Soku 即 – 1502	Sou 創 – 1171	Su 据 – 1719
Somu 背 – 152	Sou 操 – 1192	Sube 全 – 300
Son 村 – 131	Sou 層 – 1250	Sube 滑 – 981
Son 存 – 462	Sou 葬 – 1273	Sude 既 – 1639
Son 孫 – 1072	Sou 荘 – 1468	Sue 末 – 119
Son 尊 – 1208	Sou 捜 – 1520	Sugata 姿 – 763
Son 損 – 1258	Sou 僧 – 1522	Sugi 杉 – 1154
Son 遜 – 2044	Sou 曹 – 1598	*Sugo* 過 – 361
Sona 備 – 367	Sou 挿 – 1769	Sugo 凄 – 1671
Sona 供 – 486	Sou 喪 – 1828	Sugu 優 – 528
Sono 園 – 279	Sou 燥 – 1930	Sui 出 – 147
Sora 空 – 248	Sou 槽 – 1986	Sui 水 – 251
Soro 揃 – 644	Sou 藻 – 2008	*Sui* 西 – 464
Soro 算 – 789	*Su* 日 – 32	Sui 吹 – 537
Soso 注 – 168	Su 磨 – 126	Sui 垂 – 799
Soto 外 – 163	Su 住 – 167	Sui 睡 – 800
Sotsu 卒 – 27	Su 子 – 182	Sui 推 – 1029
Sotsu 率 – 1408	Su 守 – 214	Sui 炊 – 1239
Sou 早 – 34	Su 好 – 239	Sui 遂 – 1371
Sou 窓 – 311	Su 空 – 248	Sui 酔 – 1476
Sou 送 – 348	Su 済 – 259	Sui 衰 – 1753
Sou 走 – 450	Su 過 – 361	Sui 粋 – 1778
Sou 掃 – 645	Su 吸 – 427	Suji 筋 – 1426
Sou 宗 – 676	Su 直 – 570	Suke 助 – 108

Suki 隙 – 879	Ta 他 – 505	Tai 態 – 960
Suko 少 – 254	Ta 卓 – 620	Tai 帯 – 1012
Suko 健 – 811	Ta 駄 – 628	Tai 滞 – 1013
Suku 少 – 254	Ta 貯 – 667	Tai 逮 – 1224
Suku 救 – 977	Ta 絶 – 673	Tai 耐 – 1434
Sumi 隅 – 79	Ta 断 – 704	Tai 怠 – 1498
Sumi 速 – 359	Ta 垂 – 799	Tai 泰 – 1529
Sumi 炭 – 1385	Ta 焚 – 1183	Tai 胎 – 1919
Sumi 墨 – 1829	Ta 炊 – 1239	Tai 堆 – 2041
Sun 寸 – 1369	Ta 耐 – 1434	Taka 高 – 19
Suna 砂 – 782	Ta 裁 – 1450	Takara 宝 – 1292
Surudo 鋭 – 1419	Ta 堪 – 1452	Take 竹 – 134
Susa 凄 – 1671	Ta 汰 – 1613	Take 丈 – 613
Suso 裾 – 1796	Taba 束 – 99	Taki 滝 – 1179
Susu 進 – 203	Tabi 旅 – 116	Tako 凧 – 767
Susu 勧 – 698	Tabi 度 – 498	Taku 宅 – 21
Susu 薦 – 1030	*Tachi* 立 – 11	Taku 濯 – 201
Susumu 進 – 203	*Tachi* 日 – 32	Taku 度 – 498
Suta 廃 – 1221	Tachi 達 – 347	Taku 卓 – 620
Suu 数 – 639	Tada 正 – 174	Taku 沢 – 1100
Suu 崇 – 1656	Tada 直 – 570	Taku 託 – 1367
Suu 枢 – 1953	Tadayo 漂 – 1693	Taku 択 – 1403
Suwa 座 – 497	Tado 辿 – 882	Taku 巧 – 1727
Suzu 涼 – 515	Tae 妙 – 856	Taku 拓 – 1775
Suzu 鈴 – 1370	*Taga* 違 – 355	Takumi 匠 – 1653
Ta 立 – 11	Taga 互 – 1207	Takuwa 蓄 – 1774
Ta 十 – 18	Tagaya 耕 – 1312	Tama 玉 – 169
Ta 手 – 23	Tai 貸 – 90	Tama 球 – 606
Ta 点 – 29	Tai 体 – 124	Tama 弾 – 780
Ta 日 – 32	Tai 大 – 188	Tama 珠 – 1772
Ta 田 – 68	Tai 太 – 191	Tamago 卵 – 28
Ta 多 – 161	Tai 待 – 217	Tamashii 魂 – 1636
Ta 太 – 191	Tai 台 – 538	Tame 試 – 436
Ta 経 – 224	Tai 代 – 552	Tame 為 – 1222
Ta 達 – 347	Tai 対 – 674	Tami 民 – 375
Ta 建 – 363	Tai 隊 – 726	Tamo 保 – 1216
Ta 食 – 398	Tai 平 – 885	Tan 短 – 324
Ta 足 – 449	Tai 退 – 926	Tan 単 – 636

Tan 旦 – 668	Tazusa 携 – 1011	Ten 典 – 1117
Tan 反 – 680	Tchou 張 – 477	Ten 展 – 1346
Tan 探 – 699	Te 手 – 23	Tenohira 掌 – 1717
Tan 担 – 729	*Te* 日 – 32	Tera 寺 – 213
Tan 端 – 730	Te 鉄 – 304	Tetsu 鉄 – 304
Tan 嘆 – 792	Te 照 – 822	Tetsu 徹 – 1333
Tan 誕 – 1122	Te 徹 – 1333	Tetsu 哲 – 1521
Tan 炭 – 1385	Te 撤 – 1747	To 人 – 13
Tan 堪 – 1452	Tei 体 – 124	To 泊 – 46
Tan 丹 – 1588	Tei 低 – 222	To 取 – 58
Tan 淡 – 1654	Tei 定 – 455	To 土 – 59
Tan 胆 – 1720	Tei 庭 – 495	To 留 – 71
Tan 鍛 – 1813	Tei 弟 – 529	To 止 – 173
Tan 綻 – 1949	Tei 停 – 627	*To* 時 – 215
Tana 棚 – 742	Tei 丁 – 702	To 特 – 218
Tane 種 – 1098	Tei 程 – 954	To 都 – 277
Tani 谷 – 1383	Tei 底 – 1096	To 図 – 281
Tano 頼 – 98	Tei 提 – 1156	To 登 – 297
Tano 楽 – 520	Tei 抵 – 1195	To 途 – 378
Tao 倒 – 563	Tei 邸 – 1422	To 問 – 410
Tashi 確 – 619	Tei 亭 – 1474	To 閉 – 414
Tasu 助 – 108	Tei 帝 – 1538	To 説 – 439
Tata 畳 – 876	Tei 廷 – 1664	To 研 – 442
Tataka 闘 – 728	Tei 偵 – 1673	To 徒 – 451
Tataka 戦 – 933	Tei 堤 – 1837	*To* 作 – 482
Tatami 畳 – 876	Tei 呈 – 1876	To 渡 – 499
Tate 建 – 363	Tei 訂 – 1950	*To* 和 – 513
Tate 縦 – 1486	Teki 的 – 45	To 鳥 – 555
Tate 盾 – 1750	Teki 敵 – 881	To 飛 – 574
Tato 例 – 1317	Teki 摘 – 1083	To 解 – 618
Tatsu 達 – 347	Teki 適 – 1280	To 捕 – 670
Tatsu 竜 – 1569	Teki 笛 – 1503	To 溶 – 815
Tawamu 戯 – 1756	Teki 滴 – 1854	To 突 – 868
Tawara 俵 – 1492	Ten 点 – 29	To 戸 – 871
Tayo 頼 – 98	Ten 天 – 189	To 富 – 939
Tayo 便 – 481	Ten 転 – 285	To 塗 – 1041
Tazu 訪 – 713	Ten 店 – 493	To 跳 – 1084
Tazu 尋 – 1512	Ten 添 – 841	To 撮 – 1331

To 遂 – 1371	Too 十 – 18	Tou 討 – 1493
To 採 – 1425	Too 遠 – 351	Tou 糖 – 1494
To 執 – 1553	Too 通 – 365	Tou 藤 – 1530
To 吐 – 1558	Tora 虎 – 1057	Tou 踏 – 1534
To 賭 – 1761	Tori 取 – 58	Tou 唐 – 1600
To 妬 – 1891	Tori 鳥 – 555	Tou 筒 – 1620
Tobira 扉 – 1672	Toriko 虜 – 1107	Tou 悼 – 1644
Tobo 乏 – 1340	Toshi 年 – 177	Tou 凍 – 1707
Tochi 栃 – 2085	Totono 整 – 1247	Tou 桃 – 1728
Todo 留 – 71	Totsu 突 – 868	Tou 陶 – 1741
Todo 届 – 74	Totsu 嫁 – 1527	Tou 搭 – 1931
Todoke 届 – 74	Tou 当 – 31	Tou 騰 – 1936
Toge 刺 – 1284	Tou 頭 – 93	Tou 痘 – 2070
Toi 日 – 32	Tou 刀 – 102	Touge 峠 – 1802
Toi 樋 – 1143	*Tou* 父 – 143	Touto 貴 – 643
Toki 時 – 215	Tou 冬 – 234	Touto 尊 – 1208
Toko 床 – 946	Tou 答 – 295	*Tozo* 卒 – 27
Tokoro 所 – 391	Tou 登 – 297	*Tsu* 十 – 18
Toku 特 – 218	Tou 道 – 349	Tsu 点 – 29
Toku 得 – 706	Tou 湯 – 404	Tsu 着 – 52
Toku 徳 – 1159	Tou 読 – 432	Tsu 付 – 132
Toku 督 – 1421	Tou 東 – 508	Tsu 都 – 277
Toku 篤 – 1937	Tou 島 – 556	Tsu 連 – 353
Toku 匿 – 1962	Tou 投 – 558	Tsu 告 – 429
Tomi 富 – 939	Tou 倒 – 563	Tsu 次 – 536
Tomo 友 – 459	Tou 到 – 612	Tsu 継 – 635
Tomo 供 – 486	Tou 灯 – 626	Tsu 詰 – 781
Tomo 共 – 969	Tou 納 – 705	Tsu 浸 – 797
Tomona 伴 – 1599	Tou 豆 – 721	Tsu 突 – 868
Tomura 弔 – 2053	Tou 闘 – 728	Tsu 津 – 877
Ton 問 – 410	Tou 逃 – 850	Tsu 積 – 931
Ton 団 – 686	Tou 統 – 1125	Tsu 就 – 974
Ton 頓 – 1248	Tou 等 – 1132	Tsu 摘 – 1083
Ton 豚 – 1504	Tou 塔 – 1251	Tsu 吊 – 1209
Ton 屯 – 2028	Tou 透 – 1253	*Tsu* 梅 – 1299
Tona 唱 – 1152	Tou 棟 – 1271	Tsu 尽 – 1507
Tonari 隣 – 329	Tou 盗 – 1289	Tsu 釣 – 1547
Tono 殿 – 1080	Tou 党 – 1399	Tsu 潰 – 1820

Tsuba 唾 – 1847
Tsubasa 翼 – 912
Tsubo 壺 – 1274
Tsubo 壼 – 1274
Tsubo 坪 – 1824
Tsubu 粒 – 1135
Tsubu 潰 – 1700
Tsuchi 土 – 59
Tsuchika 培 – 1234
Tsuda 伝 – 345
Tsudo 集 – 202
Tsugi 次 – 536
Tsuguna 償 – 1662
Tsui 一 – 1
Tsui 費 – 656
Tsui 対 – 674
Tsui 追 – 821
Tsui 椎 – 1868
Tsui 墜 – 1972
Tsuka 支 – 26
Tsuka 仕 – 67
Tsuka 束 – 99
Tsuka 疲 – 370
Tsuka 使 – 480
Tsuka 捕 – 670
Tsuka 遣 – 765
Tsuka 塚 – 1489
Tsukasado 司 - 608
Tsuke 付 – 132
Tsuki 月 – 148
Tsuki 築 – 1219
Tsuku 作 – 482
Tsuku 造 – 1108
Tsukue 机 – 140
Tsukuro 繕 – 2037
Tsuma 妻 – 237
Tsuma 爪 – 647
Tsume 冷 – 299

Tsume 爪 – 647
Tsumi 罪 – 1291
Tsumu 紡 – 2033
Tsuna 綱 – 1200
Tsune 常 – 683
Tsuno 角 – 81
Tsuno 募 – 1109
Tsura 面 – 282
Tsura 連 – 353
Tsura 辛 – 384
Tsuranu 貫 – 1621
Tsuru 鶴 – 1609
Tsurugi 剣 – 1432
Tsuta 伝 – 345
Tsutana 拙 – 1798
Tsuto 勤 – 517
Tsuto 務 – 518
Tsuto 努 – 519
Tsutsu 包 – 548
Tsutsu 筒 – 1620
Tsutsumi 堤 – 1837
Tsutsushi 慎 – 632
Tsuu 通 – 365
Tsuu 痛 – 368
Tsuyo 強 – 478
Tsuyu 露 – 1390
Tsuzu 続 – 226
Tsuzumi 鼓 – 1776
U 上 – 171
U 乳 – 186
U 失 – 206
U 生 – 208
U 産 – 210
U 雨 – 261
U 売 – 425
U 右 – 457
U 受 – 577
U 打 – 590

U 浮 – 671
U 得 – 706
U 羽 – 755
U 宇 – 897
U 飢 – 924
U 撃 – 1226
U 植 – 1278
U 熟 – 1427
U 討 – 1493
U 埋 – 1523
U 鬱 – 1783
U 憂 – 1784
Uba 奪 – 1568
Ubu 産 – 210
Uchi 内 – 396
Uchi 家 – 405
Ude 腕 – 1532
Ue 上 – 171
Ue 植 – 1278
Ugo 動 – 286
Uji 氏 – 709
Ukaga 伺 – 341
Uke 受 – 577
Uketamawa 承 – 1344
Uki 浮 – 671
Uma 馬 – 958
Uma 旨 – 1318
Ume 梅 – 1299
Umi 海 – 337
Un 雲 – 264
Un 運 – 354
Una 海 – 337
Unaga 促 – 1455
Uo 魚 – 80
Ura 裏 – 887
Ura 浦 – 1552
Ura 恨 – 1724
Urana 占 – 1542

Uraya 湊 – 662	Wa 羽 – 755	Ya 夜 – 489
Ure 嬉 – 600	Wa 我 – 862	Ya 薬 – 521
Ure 憂 – 1784	*Wa* 波 – 878	Ya 野 – 545
Ure 愁 – 1785	Wa 湧 – 903	Ya 矢 – 1045
Uri 売 – 425	Wa 把 – 1817	*Ya* 谷 – 1383
Uru 潤 – 1755	Wai 賄 – 1979	Ya 厄 – 1863
Uruo 潤 – 1755	Waka 若 – 461	Ya 弥 – 2080
Urushi 漆 – 1957	Waka 別 – 561	Yabu 敗 – 793
Uruwa 麗 – 1627	Wake 訳 – 437	Yabu 破 – 837
Ushi 牛 – 205	Waki 脇 – 1570	Yado 宿 – 491
Ushi 後 – 335	Waku 惑 – 624	*Yage* 産 – 210
Ushina 失 – 206	Waku 枠 – 1490	Yakata 館 – 305
Uso 嘘 – 967	Wame 喚 – 1885	*Yake* 火 – 443
Usu 薄 – 258	Wan 湾 – 1016	Yaku 約 – 225
Usu 臼 – 1735	Wan 腕 – 1532	Yaku 訳 – 437
Uta 歌 – 534	Wara 笑 – 199	Yaku 薬 – 521
Uta 謡 – 1856	*Wara* 原 – 888	Yaku 役 – 557
Uta 唄 – 1870	Ware 我 – 862	Yaku 躍 – 992
Utaga 疑 – 978	Wari 割 – 562	Yaku 厄 – 1863
Uto 疎 – 1806	Waru 悪 – 313	Yama 山 – 146
Utsu 映 – 36	Wasu 忘 – 310	*Yama* 大 – 188
Utsu 写 – 468	Wata 渡 – 499	Yamai 病 – 369
Utsu 移 – 801	Wata 綿 – 1189	Yanagai 柳 – 1535
Utsu 鬱 – 1783	Watakushi 私 – 510	Yami 闇 – 950
Utsuku 美 – 771	Watashi 私 – 510	Yasa 易 – 402
Utsuwa 器 – 853	Waza 業 – 332	Yasa 優 – 528
Utta 訴 – 1545	Waza 技 – 1133	Yashina 養 – 1264
Uwa 上 – 171	Wazawa 災 - 1019	Yashiro 社 – 271
Uwa 浮 – 671	Wazura 患 – 1551	Yasu 休 – 122
Uyama 敬 – 873	Wazura 煩 – 2007	Yasu 安 – 236
Uzu 渦 – 1871	Ya 八 – 15	Yato 雇 – 1398
Wa 早 – 34	Ya 屋 – 63	Yatsu 奴 – 1582
Wa 分 – 105	Ya 止 – 173	Yawa 和 – 513
Wa 話 – 433	*Ya* 行 – 334	Yawa 柔 – 546
Wa 和 – 513	Ya 病 – 369	Yo 四 – 6
Wa 沸 – 531	Ya 辞 – 387	Yo 良 – 303
Wa 割 – 562	Ya 家 – 405	Yo 呼 – 428
Wa 輪 – 690	Ya 焼 – 446	Yo 読 – 432

Yo 夜 – 489	You 要 – 238	Yuka 床 – 946
Yo 欲 – 535	You 容 – 296	Yuki 雪 – 262
Yo 世 – 542	You 洋 – 330	Yume 夢 – 165
Yo 予 – 544	You 用 – 364	Yumi 弓 – 1044
Yo 代 – 552	You 踊 – 366	Yuru 許 – 1141
Yo 寄 – 604	You 葉 – 543	Yuru 緩 – 1330
Yo 余 – 637	You 揚 – 768	Yuta 豊 – 1321
Yo 与 – 1070	You 溶 – 815	Yuu 由 – 73
Yo 預 – 1259	You 揺 – 852	Yuu 夕 – 160
Yo 善 – 1336	You 腰 – 884	Yuu 遊 – 360
Yo 酔 – 1476	You 陽 – 891	Yuu 右 – 457
Yo 依 – 1557	You 羊 – 1223	Yuu 友 – 459
Yo 誉 – 1705	You 養 – 1264	Yuu 有 – 460
Yogo 汚 – 467	You 幼 – 1400	Yuu 優 – 528
Yoi 生 – 208	You 瘍 – 1702	Yuu 裕 – 660
Yoi 宵 – 1994	You 妖 – 1811	Yuu 悠 – 985
Yoko 横 – 135	You 擁 – 1841	Yuu 融 – 987
Yoku 浴 – 256	You 謡 – 1856	Yuu 勇 – 1282
Yoku 欲 – 535	You 庸 – 2035	Yuu 誘 – 1405
Yoku 翼 – 912	Yowa 弱 – 471	Yuu 郵 – 1445
Yoku 翌 – 1457	Yu 由 – 73	Yuu 雄 – 1518
Yoku 抑 – 1584	Yu 結 – 231	Yuu 幽 – 1574
Yome 嫁 – 1527	*Yu* 浴 – 256	Yuu 憂 – 1784
Yomi 読 – 432	*Yu* 雨 – 261	Yuu 猶 – 1997
Yomigae 蘇 – 1279	Yu 輸 – 288	Yuzu 譲 – 1669
Yon 四 – 6	Yu 行 – 334	Za 覚 – 54
Yone 米 – 326	Yu 湯 – 404	Za 咲 – 193
Yori 和 – 513	Yu 愉 – 733	Za 座 – 497
Yoro 宜 – 1903	Yu 揺 – 852	Za 差 – 631
Yoroko 喜 – 599	Yu 油 – 942	Za 指 – 691
Yoroko 慶 – 1590	Yu 癒 – 1293	Za 雑 – 785
Yoru 夜 – 489	Yu 喩 – 2021	Za 挫 – 1976
Yoshi 吉 – 1453	Yubi 指 – 691	Zai 済 – 259
Yoso 装 – 1043	Yuda 委 – 1364	Zai 歳 – 322
You 八 – 15	Yue 故 – 394	Zai 西 – 464
You 日 – 32	Yui 由 – 73	Zai 在 – 1014
You 様 – 136	Yui 遺 – 1037	Zai 罪 – 1291
You 曜 – 200	Yui 唯 – 1337	Zai 材 – 1378

Zai 財 – 1437	Zen 前 – 157	Zou 草 – 909
Zai 剤 – 1601	Zen 全 – 300	Zou 臓 – 951
Zaka 酒 – 465	Zen 然 – 611	Zou 造 – 1108
Zaka 坂 – 1130	Zen 善 – 1336	Zou 蔵 – 1190
Zakana 魚 – 80	Zen 膳 – 1690	Zou 僧 – 1522
Zake 酒 – 465	Zen 禅 – 1694	Zou 憎 – 1651
Zaki 崎 – 1081	Zen 繕 – 2037	Zu 手 – 23
Zakura 桜 – 984	Zeni 銭 – 744	Zu 頭 – 93
Zama 覚 – 54	Zetsu 説 – 439	Zu 付 – 132
Zan 山 –146	Zetsu 絶 – 673	Zu 主 – 166
Zan 残 – 605	Zetsu 舌 – 1213	Zu 好 – 239
Zan 算 – 789	Zo 祖 – 272	Zu 図 – 281
Zan 斬 – 1559	Zo 添 – 841	*Zu* 途 – 378
Zan 惨 – 1678	Zo 沿 – 1414	Zu 豆 – 721
Zan 暫 – 1943	Zoko 底 – 1096	Zu 津 – 877
Zara 皿 – 567	Zoku 族 – 115	Zu 酢 – 1373
Zaru 猿 – 1055	Zoku 続 – 226	Zui 水 – 251
Zato 里 – 1060	Zoku 足 – 449	Zui 随 – 1670
Zatsu 雑 – 785	Zoku 属 – 1296	Zui 髄 – 1964
Zawa 触 – 475	Zoku 俗 – 1631	Zuka 遣 – 765
Zawa 沢 – 1100	Zoku 賊 – 1652	Zuka 塚 – 1489
Zawa 障 – 1495	Zon 存 – 462	*Zuki* 豆 – 721
Ze 絶 – 673	Zono 園 – 279	Zuma 妻 – 237
Ze 邪 – 796	Zora 空 – 248	Zuna 綱 – 1200
Ze 是 – 1035	Zou 増 – 61	*Zutsumi* 包 – 548
Zei 勢 – 110	Zou 贈 – 84	Zuu 数 – 639
Zei 説 – 439	Zou 雑 – 785	Zuyo 強 – 478
Zei 税 – 708	Zou 象 – 906	
Zen 千 – 22	Zou 像 – 907	

Books in the *Learn to Read in Japanese* Series

1. *Learn to Read in Japanese,* Volume I. Published in 2016, it teaches 608 target kanji and includes a kanji catalogue, plus 4,200 reading practice sentences.
2. *Learn to Read in Japanese,* Volume II. Published in 2018, it teaches 600 additional target kanji, with an expanded kanji catalogue. It includes 2,900 vocabulary terms and 1,660 sentences for reading practice. It also suggests extensive supplemental reading material.
3. *Learn to Read in Japanese,* Volume III. Published in 2020, it teaches 320 more target kanji, with an expanded kanji catalogue. It includes 2,100 vocabulary terms and 912 sentences for reading practice. It also suggests extensive supplemental reading material.
4. *Learn to Read in Japanese,* Volume IV. Published in 2022, it teaches 560 more target kanji. Due to space limitations, it does not include a kanji catalogue, which is published separately (see Item # 5, below). It includes 3,800 vocabulary terms and 1,623 sentences for reading practice.
5. *Core Kanji, a Catalogue of 2,088 Essential Kanji.* Published in 2022 and expanded in 2024, it includes memorable kanji descriptions, retrieval cues for kanji readings and comparisons among similar characters, as well as an index to 4,300 kanji pronunciations. It also contains tools that can be used for identifying kanji, a technique known as Kanji ID.
6. *Learn to Read in Japanese, a Glossary.* Published in 2020 and expanded in 2022, it lists more than 9,700 Japanese vocabulary terms, with definitions, mnemonics and comparisons among terms.
7. *Kanji Memorization Drills,* Version One. Published in 2025, it contains drills for learning to recognize and pronounce 608 kanji. A supplement to *Learn to Read in Japanese,* Volume I.
8. *Kanji Memorization Drills,* Version Two. Published in 2025, it contains drills for learning to recognize and pronounce 1,208 kanji. A supplement to *Learn to Read in Japanese,* Volume II.
9. *Kanji Memorization Drills,* Version Three. Published in 2025, it contains drills for learning to recognize and pronounce 1,528 kanji. A supplement to *Learn to Read in Japanese,* Volume III.
10. *Kanji Memorization Drills,* Version Four. Published in 2025, it contains drills for learning to recognize and pronounce 2,088 kanji. A supplement to *Learn to Read in Japanese,* Volume IV.

www.ingramcontent.com/pod-product-compliance
Lightning Source LLC
Chambersburg PA
CBHW070520010526
44118CB00012B/1034